THE SONATA

SINCE

BEETHOVEN

The Third and Final Volume of
A History of the Sonata Idea

By WILLIAM S. NEWMAN

SECOND EDITION

The Norton Library
W · W · NORTON & COMPANY · INC ·
NEW YORK

To Claire
who has seen through all these
volumes with me

ISBN 0 393 00624 7

PRINTED IN THE UNITED STATES OF AMERICA

3 4 5 6 7 8 9 0

Preface

As with its two predecessors, this third and final volume in *A History of the Sonata Idea* has benefitted substantially from the expert help of colleagues, librarians, and research assistants, far and near. Especially during the past thirty months of final writing, it has benefitted from uncommonly generous responses to unconscionably urgent requests for particular advices, materials, and aids. When such help can be identified with specific discussions in the text, I have acknowledged it in footnotes. But I have also wanted to acknowledge that and other help collectively, in this Preface.

For critical readings and evaluations of entire sections and chapters, I am grateful to Professor Roger Hannay at The University of North Carolina at Chapel Hill (with regard to 20th-c. dilemmas, ssB I), to Professor Martin Chusid at New York University (Schubert, ssB VII), to Professor Edward A. Lippmann at Columbia University (Schumann, ssB VIII), to Professor Eric Werner at Tel Aviv University in Ramat Aviv, Israel (Mendelssohn, ssB VIII), to Professor Karl Geiringer at the University of California in Santa Barbara (Brahms, ssB IX), to Mr. Edward Waters at The Library of Congress (Liszt, ssB X), to Professor Nicholas Temperley at the University of Illinois in Urbana (19th-c. England, ssB XIV), and to Professors Erna F. Novikova and Aleksandr Dmitrievich Alekseev of Moscow (19th-c. Russia, ssB XVIII).

For more specific advices and/or making valued materials available, I am likewise grateful to Dr. Birgitte Moyer of Menlo Park, Calif. (Reicha, Czerny, and A. B. Marx on "sonata form," ssB II), Professor Rey M. Longyear at the University of Kentucky (German literary references, ssB II), Dr. Harry Bergholz at The University of North Carolina at Chapel Hill (Strindberg's *Spöksonaten*, ssB II), Mrs. Alice (William J.) Mitchell of New York City (Czerny, ssB VII), Dr. Ingeborg Heussner of Marburg, West Germany (Moscheles, ssB VII), Dr. Marc-André Souchay of Hannover-Kleefeld, West Germany (Schubert, ssB VII), Mr. Arthur Hedley of London (Liszt and Chopin, ssB X and

XII), Miss Friedelind Wagner of Bayreuth (Wagner, SSB X), Dr. Rita Benton at the State University of Iowa in Iowa City (Wagner and Pleyel, SSB X), the late Mr. Arthur Loesser of Cleveland (Wagner and Hallé, SSB X), Mr. Clarence Adler of New York City (Godowsky, SSB XI), Dr. Stephen Young at Meredith College in Raleigh (Karg-Elert, SSB XI), Professor Alexander Ringer at the University of Illinois in Urbana (Gernsheim, SSB XI, and constructive evaluations throughout SSB), Professor Ronald E. Booth, Jr., at The University of North Carolina at Charlotte (Heller, SSB XII), Mr. Joseph Bloch at the Juilliard School of Music and Mr. Raymond Lewenthal of New York City (Alkan, SSB XII), Professors Aloys Fleischman at University College in Cork and Brian Boydell at the University of Dublin (Irish sons., SSB XV), Professor Ingmar Bengtsson of Uppsala (Swedish sons., SSB XV), Professor Howard Allen Craw at Loma Linda University in Riverside (Dussek, SSB XVII), Dr. Elod J. Juhász of Radio Budapest, the late Dr. József Gát at the Budapest Academy of Music, and Professor Béla Böszörmeny-Nagy of Boston University (Hungarian sons., SSB XVII), Mr. James F. Jones at Florida State University in Tallahassee (Dohnányi, SSB XVII), Miss Carol Greene at the University of Indiana in Bloomington (Aliabiev, SSB XVIII), Mr. Vladimir Horowitz of New York City (Rachmaninoff, SSB XVIII), and Professor Delmer D. Rogers at the University of Texas in Austin (Bristow, SSB XIX).

For still other advices and/or materials I am indebted to Dr. Rudolph Kremer at The University of North Carolina at Chapel Hill (19th-c. organ sons.), Dr. Fritz Oberdoerffer and Mr. Joe W. Bratcher at the University of Texas in Austin (rare sons. in their private collections), and Mr. Harold Schonberg of the *New York Times* (spot questions on past pianists).

Much of the searching through periodicals, in several other languages as well as English, and much of the statistical work for the present volume were accomplished by able graduate assistants at The University of North Carolina at Chapel Hill. For these contributions it is a pleasure to thank the (then) Misses Katherine Ruth Boardman, Anne Chan, Marcia Judith Citron, Gloria Merle Huffman, Sophie Morgan, and Mary Vinquist. It is also a pleasure to thank certain other Chapel Hillians in and around the University, including Mr. Rudi Schnitzler for two proofreadings of the entire volume, Mrs. Hilde (Alfred T.) Brauer for providing or checking many of the German translations, Professor Alfred Engstrom for an extended French translation, Mr. John J. Bobkoff and Mrs. Angele Avizonis for Russian translations, Mrs. Helen (William E.) Jenner for "autographing" the 115 music examples that are not facsimiles, and Mrs. Jeanne D. Hudson for drawing the chart of "Regions and Production Spans" (ssb IV). (In defense of the translators, I should add that I assume full responsibility for the individual translations not otherwise credited. An average, not exceptional, sample of the translation problem is provided in the midst of the Wagner discussion, ssb X.) A particular pleasure has been the reading of many of the duo sonatas under examination with interested colleagues and students, among whom I should like especially to thank Professor Edgar Alden, Mrs. Jeanine Zenge, and Miss Ivy Geoghegan, violinists; Miss Ann Woodward, violist; and Mr. Charles Griffith and Miss Kathryn Logan, cellists.

Many of those "unconscionably urgent requests" have been directed to music librarians in numerous countries, among whom, at this point, I should like to thank especially Dr. James Pruett, Mr. Nyal Williams, and Miss Thelma Thompson of The University of North Carolina at Chapel Hill, Mr. William Lichtenwanger at the Library of Congress, Mr. Gordon Mapes at the Curtis Institute of Music in Philadelphia, Mr. Frank C. Campbell, Mr. Neil Ratliff, and Mr. Richard Jackson at the Library & Museum of the Performing Arts in New York, Mr. Neil K. Moran at the Boston Public Library, Mr. Donald W. Krummel at the Newberry Library in Chicago, Mr. A. Hyatt King at the British Museum in London, Dr. Imogen Fellinger at the Zentralstelle für Musikbibliographie des 19. Jahrhunderts in Köln, and Dr. Leopold Nowak at the Österreichische Nationalbibliothek in Vienna.

The kind permissions granted by numerous publishers or their U.S. agents to quote sentences or music examples from copyrighted publications that they control are acknowledged separately wherever the quotations occur in the present volume.

Finally, I should like to express my gratitude to the University Research Council of The University of North Carolina at Chapel Hill, the American Council of Learned Societies, and the National Endowment for the Humanities for the grants and their renewals that have provided the free time and the assistance so essential to a project of this sort. And at the same time I should like to express my gratitude to Chairman Wilton Mason and my other colleagues in the Music Department for co-operating so generously during two semesters of reduced schedules.

Some Abbreviations and Editorial Policies

All the short titles used throughout the present volume are listed in one alphabetical sequence and amplified in full in the concluding

Bibliography. A hyphenated, lowercase "-m" at the end (as in Brahms/WERKE-m) continues to indicate a source consisting primarily of music. Articles in reference works, reviews in periodicals, and prefaces in music editions are not given separate short titles, ordinarily, but the first time such an item is cited in any one discussion its author is added in parentheses (if known). Cross references to the previous two volumes in the present set, SBE and SCE, include page numbers. However, for familiar reasons of cost and accuracy, the many cross references within the present volume, SSB, give only the chapter number (or merely *supra* and *infra* within the same chapter). But knowing the chapter, the reader should then be able to locate the exact page(s) readily enough through the detailed Index. In Chapter VI only, as explained therein, each cross reference after a composer's name can be expected to lead to a music example by that composer as well as to a discussion of his music.

As in the two previous volumes, no attempt has been made here to use a parenthetical *sic* after every apparent error in a quoted source, or to apply one policy consistently to all uses of suffixes (e.g., biographic or biographical), or prefixes (La Laurencie or Laurencie), or spellings (catalog or catalogue), or transliteration (Handoshkin or Khandochkine). In each such alternative, common usage and the original or "best" available sources have had to be the prime determinants. (One is fortunate if only each alternative can be treated consistently within itself!) A main reason for supplying what must seem like excessive documentation to some readers—for example, page numbers (in fact, inclusive page numbers) for articles in reference works—has been to spare the reader the vexatious searching that can be brought on by just such alternatives, if not by an unfamiliar alphabetical order (as that of Swedish will be to some), or a variable alphabetical order (as results from the different handling of the German umlaut), or multiple divisions of a book (as in the 8 "Registers" of the *American Supplement* to GROVE, 3d ed.), or a listing under another heading (such as Calvocoressi's views on "cyclic devices" under "d'Indy" in Cobbett/CHAMBER II 3).

Quotation marks are used again around "sonata form" to distinguish the textbook concept or mold from other uses of the term form, and around "sonata" alone to indicate that a certain work is actually so called. Italics are used for a title that is quoted in full or up to a logical stopping point in its original language, wording, and spelling, whereas quotation marks are used for freer, translated, and/or partial references to a title. Abbreviated references to a particular passage in a music score—for example, Dussek's Op. 35/3/ii/1-7—follow the order of opus number (if any), other number (if any), movement (lowercase roman numeral), and measure(s). The measure numbering, which is absent, alas, from nearly all 19th-century publications, starts in ssb with the first full measure, starts anew in each movement, and includes no repeated sections except those only indicated by da capo signs. Often, when a systematic catalogue exists for a composer's works, the catalogue reference (as doubly abbreviated below) and its pertinent number replace the opus and/or other number—for example, C. 151/ii/1–7 for the Dussek passage just cited.

Major and minor keys continue to be indicated, respectively, by uppercase and lowercase letters only. And the optional accompaniments still specified in the early 19th century continue to be indicated by the plus-or-minus symbol, ±, with the plus sign reserved for obligatory (*obbligato*) accompaniments and the ampersand, &, for the simple fact of an accompaniment (as in P & Vn ± Vc). The order of P & Vn or Vn & P (etc.) depends on the earliest available source. An arrow (→) is used in the abbreviated graphs of structural designs to indicate a transition (within a movement) or *attacca* (between movements).

The abbreviations for musical terms in ssb are confined largely to the documentary apparatus. Most if not all of them should be self-evident in context. They include the following:

acc'd.	accompanied
aug.	augmented
B.	referring to a work as indexed in Brown/CHOPIN
Bn	bassoon
C.	referring to a work as indexed in Craw/DUSSEK
Cl	clarinet
D.	referring to a work indexed in Deutsch/SCHUBERT-I.
ded.	dedicated
dim.	diminished
dom.	dominant
ed.	edited, edition, editor
ex(x).	example(s)
F	fast, as the tempo of one movement in a cycle
facs.	facsimile
Fl	flute
H	harpsichord
Hn	horn
In	introduction, as the starting section of a movement in a cycle
J.	referring to a work as indexed in Jähns/WEBER

Ju.	referring to a work as indexed in Jurgenson/TSCHAÏKOWSKY
M	moderate, as the tempo of one movement in a cycle
Mi	minuet, as one movement in a cycle
mod.	modern
ms(s).	measure(s)
MS(S)	manuscript(s)
Ob	oboe
P	pianoforte
2 Ps	two pianos, four hands
P-duet	one piano, four hands
pub.	publication, published, publisher
Ro	rondo, as one movement in a cycle
S	slow, as the tempo of one movement in a cycle
Sc	scherzo
trans.	translated, translation, translator
Va	variations; viola
Vc	(violon)cello
Vn	violin
WoO	referring to a work without opus number as indexed in Kinsky & Halm/BEETHOVEN

W. S. N.

The Paperback Edition

I am indebted to W. W. Norton & Company, Inc., for permitting me to do such updating and emending as has seemed necessary in the three years that separate the original edition (1969) from this first reprinting (1972). As before, much of the information comes from new research that numerous colleagues and students, near and far, have been kind enough to call to my attention. The changes that could not be made in the text proper are keyed by marginal, numerical references to the Addenda beginning on page 776.

W. S. N., Chapel Hill, August 1971

Contents

Music Examples

Tables and Charts

Chapter I

The Scope and Gist of the Problem

The Terminal Point Reassessed

The Sonata Since Beethoven becomes the third and, contrary to earlier plans, the final volume in *A History of the Sonata Idea*. As explained at the outset (SBE 3), the over-all study had been projected originally in a single volume, then was reprojected in four volumes when the first of the sonata's four main eras alone required a full volume to cover its hypothetical minimum of detail.[1] That now only a third rather than a fourth volume completes the set needs explaining, even though the third, like the second, has grown to fully twice the length of the first volume. In other words, and as one pertinent way of getting into the scope and nature of the problem, it is necessary to explain why "The Sonata in the Romantic Era" and "The Sonata in the Modern Era" that were to complete the projected four-volume set have had to give way to this single volume with its changed title and its conclusion in late Romanticism.

Mainly, as the over-all study has come closer and closer to the Modern sonata, one realization has forced itself on me increasingly. It is that that most recent manifestation of the "sonata" cannot yet—if, indeed, it can ever—be subjected to the methods and treatment, nor adequately related to either the historical or the musical goals, that have governed the project thus far. In fact, whereas it had still seemed possible thirty years ago, in my own dissertation on "The Present Trend of the Sonata Idea" (SBE 4), to arrive at a neatly rational disposition of "Modern" trends and styles, now it no longer seems possible to arrive at any perspective whatsoever that is either clear or comprehensive. (Right away we run onto dangerous ground that is itself symptomatic of the problem!) Up to the late 1930's one could still treat "Modern" music primarily as a tonal phenomenon or departure.

---

1. The 4-vol. plan was still announced and assumed in the 2d, revised, 1966 ed. of SBE (p. 3).

And even up to the early 1950's one could still treat it rationally, in established terms, although by then less as a tonal than as a textural and syntactic problem.[2] But since the early 1950's, at least for those not to be hoodwinked here and there by the "emperor's clothes," what positive, genuinely musical tangibles have remained that are still capable of generalization?

To be sure, the term "sonata" itself continues to be applied, though less often, as a title—for example, by yesterday's avant-gardists Boulez and Henze. This fact means that we still could continue at least with our "semantic approach" (ssb 5–7) the tracing of what the word has meant and how it has been used. However, at once the crucial question follows as to whether the over-all definition that has grown out of that approach still has force. "The sonata is a solo or chamber instrumental cycle of aesthetic or diversional purpose, consisting of several contrasting movements that are based on relatively extended designs in 'absolute' music" (sbe 7). On the surface, this definition still should have some validity, even in today's newest music. But in fact it no longer makes sense at all. After some three and one-half centuries, "sonata" has come full circle back to its original use "merely as the general term for any music to be played on instruments" (sbe 6). Whatever more constructive forces may have moved in in its place, the "sonata" in our definition has been undermined at its core by the dissolution of music's very building blocks and by the abandonment, destruction, or exhaustion, whether deliberate or unwitting, of nearly everything that previously had determined the sonata's styles and forms.

Such heretical statements could bring countercharges—for example, that our once flexible definition of the sonata idea now has rigidified into a Procrustean standard; or that the era designations originally accepted here mainly as customary, convenient, man-made delimitations (sbe 3 and 7) now have graduated into historical determinants in their own right. But rather than get involved in the aesthetics and dilemma of Modern music it is more direct and pertinent here to opine that by now the intriguing yet nervously unstable, newest "music" has simply left the field of music and gone into some other field, whether it be the mathematics of chance and permutations, the acoustics and exploration of raw sound, or the science of electronics. If "extended designs in 'absolute' music" (rather than calculated disunity, discontinuity, and nihilism) are actually still a main goal in the newest medium, then, in any case, their cohesive forces are no longer those that have unified the sonata throughout its more than

2. In 1953 it was "explained" primarily as a return from "phrase grouping" to "motivic play" (Newman/UNDERSTANDING 152–54).

three centuries of changing styles and forms. They are no longer over-all tonality, nor structural rhythm, nor thematic integration through melodic recurrences, interrelationships, and development.

But then, it might well be asked, at least could not this history of the sonata idea have been extended just up to the period when these newest trends began to dominate? Thus, one might find justifications in William Austin's recent, stimulating book on *Music in the 20th Century* for stretching the concept of the "Romantic Era" so as to include much of the music composed since World War I and right up to World War II.[3] After all, not a few of the "late-Romantics" whom we do include in the present volume continued to compose through most or all of that period if not longer—for example, Strauss, d'Indy, Elgar, Nielsen, Rachmaninoff, and D. G. Mason. Indeed, every pair of music's adjacent eras has shared a substantial overlap that similarly exhibits, side by side, both the old and the new. And Austin himself devotes the first third of his book to re-evaluations of the late Roman-tics. Yet it is also Austin who argues convincingly for the firm establish-ment of "the new styles" before World War I (while, understandably for his purposes, eschewing such labels as "Romanticism" and "Mod-ernism").[4] In particular, he attributes the "remarkably sudden" con-trast and the "great dividing line" to the introduction in 1911–12 of one of the most representative works each by his three central figures of 20th-century music, Bartók, Stravinsky, and Schoenberg; and of New Orleans jazz in New York.

In the present study we have to depend less objectively on any such tangible dividing line and more subjectively on overlapping but in-creasingly divergent views that began at least a half generation earlier. Those divergent views chiefly concerned the structural functions of tonality. Thus, we retain in this study composers who continued to employ tonality as a prime agent of larger forms, even those like Reger, Nielsen, Strauss, and d'Indy, who exploited its subtleties to the point where it almost contradicted itself, and even those whose later works occasionally take us well beyond World War I. And we exclude in this study, though sometimes on scarcely more tangible grounds than personal intuition, composers who seem to have contributed principally if not deliberately to undermining the structural functions of tonality. This delimitation means excluding even those like Busoni, Joseph Haas, Debussy, Scriabin, Ives, and, for that matter, Delius (!), Janáček, Ropartz, Thirion, Bréville, and Pâque, who had all begun in the most traditional manner before World War I, and who nearly all had

3. Austin/20TH 2, 30, 179.
4. Austin/20TH 179, 24–32.

demonstrated this manner in early, traditional sonatas. Only occasionally have confirmed Romantics been rejected because they came *too* late—for example, Somervell, Boughton, F. C. Nicholls, Gretchaninov, and Harold Morris. But the sonatas of these men have seemed so outmoded in style as to be anachronistic. In any case, for all the overlapping of old and new, it is pertinent to note that this final volume generally stops with composers born before 1880.

But to continue with the question raised above, there are two other reasons besides the beginnings of the Modern Era for stopping this volume generally by World War I rather than World War II. In the first place, the newest trends are not only incompatible with past trends and indigestible as actual music; they are too close to be viewed other than myopically. Until larger views are possible, any attempts to categorize or judge those newest trends (including the attempts already made here) must remain contentious at best. Up to now, it has been hard enough to see the preceding, Romantic Era in sufficient perspective, let alone the Modern Era. Who can know yet where time will put the dividing lines, or what trends and styles will prove to be significant, or which names will plunge abruptly into obscurity and which will live on? In the second place, the 20th century still lacks many of the archival, bibliographic, biographic, and critical checks and balances that have proved so essential as starting points and controls in the previous two volumes of the present study. With such aids the approach can be historical. Without them it can only be journalistic or reportorial, however detailed.

The Starting Point

The start of the Romantic Era poses no similar problem of scope for us but is even harder to delimit than the end.[5] In fact, it is the least delimitable of any of the era divisions encountered in all three of our volumes, for it offers nothing quite so tangible as the assault on tonality and the return of motivic play that characterize that onset of the Modern Era, or the *basso continuo* practice that helps to delimit the Baroque Era (SBE 8), or the change-over from that practice to Alberti bass that marks the early phase of the Classic Era (SCE 3–5). Certain style innovations—especially the more forthright, extended melodies, the "um-pah-pah" bass, the increasingly chromatic harmony, the new, nationalistically flavored dance rhythms, the squarer phrase-and-period

5. Delimiting the start is the subject of an interesting recent article, Engel/ ROMANTISCHEN, with special reference to Mendelssohn (as also in Werner/MENDELS- SOHN 47–51). Cf., too, cols. 785–86 in F. Blume's valuable survey of the Romantic Era (MGG XI 785–845); Bücken/19. 1–2; Dannreuther/ROMANTIC 3–4.

syntax, the wider-spaced scoring, the richer and more varied textures, the more personal, subjective inscriptions, and a more formalistic or self-conscious approach to form—all these do characterize the early (and much of the later) Romantic music (ssb VI). But no one of them ever permeates or brackets the era quite so inclusively as either the *basso continuo* or the Alberti bass in its respective era. And deciding on which side of the fence to place sonata composers during the Classic-Romantic overlap has had to depend often on subjective opinion again (cf. sce 4–5)—perhaps more often than before—chiefly as to whether they have seemed to be looking backward or forward with respect to those same or related traits.

Clementi and Beethoven were still writing sonatas in the early 1820's; yet, in spite of increasing signs of those Romantic style innovations in their later music, they remained largely oriented toward Classic sonata styles (cf. sce 130, 542, 753). On the other hand, Dussek (ssb XVII), who had already died in 1812, belonged unequivocally with the future as one of the most stylistically precocious of all early Romantic sonata composers, along with Field and his obscure, short-lived companion Pinto (both ssb XIV). Even Weber completed his sonatas no later than Beethoven's. Yet who would question his just classification among the Romantics (ssb VIII)? Schubert raises more of a problem because his sonatas relate so closely to Beethoven's. Both men were great and different enough to create distinctive spurs of their own in the mountainous course of music history. But, granted that both hovered right over that Classic-Romantic fence, Schubert must still be put on the opposite side from Beethoven (as any comparative reading of their last sonatas should confirm; ssb VI and VII). Ries, Czerny, and Moscheles (ssb VII), Cramer (ssb XIV), and, to some extent Hummel (ssb VIII), might all have been put (and, indeed, kept turning up) in the preceding era, mainly for their academicisms and their epigonic imitations of the great Classic masters. But their chief service to the 19th century was as immediate transmitters of Beethoven's music throughout Europe, and in that capacity they belong with the Romantics.

Paradoxically, in the absence of a clear enough dividing line, music historians have tended to emphasize the style innovations while maintaining that the Romantic Era is only an extension, outgrowth, or exaggeration of the Classic Era.[6] Yet the name itself for the era came

---

6. Cf. Blume in mgg XI 802–6, with references to Lang/western 740, 741, and 816 (cf., also, pp. 817–25); Einstein/romantic 4; Bücken/19. (especially 17–20); Handschin (*Musikgeschichte* [Basel, 1948] 355). Cf., also, Engel/romantischen 268-69, 272.

at least loosely into use sooner, more generally, and less self-consciously than that for any other main era of music or the other arts. Of course, "Romance" (or "Romanza") as a music title (e.g., in Mozart's K. 466/ii and K. 525/ii) and as a type of novel had been employed well before the start of the 19th century.[7] Goethe's several early 19th-century mentions of "romantic," especially in reference to literature, are well known, including his preference for the objective or "classical" as against Schiller's subjective or "romantic"; and his designation of classic as healthy and romantic as sickly.[8] Jean Paul's and E. T. A. Hoffmann's interest in promoting a subjective romantic ideal as against antiquated, prosaic classicism[9] strongly influenced Schumann. Wrote Hoffmann, music "is the most romantic of all arts—one might almost say, the only purely romantic [art]." [10]

As early as 1836, Moscheles dubbed Schumann a "romantic musician" in a highly pertinent review (ssb VIII) of Schumann's Sonata in f♯, Op. 11.[11] Schumann himself wrote of musical romanticism on numerous occasions around 1840, although not altogether specifically or consistently.[12] (By the early 1840's can be found titles like "Sonate romantique," as in Op. 5 by L. Ehlert [ssb VIII], or descriptions like Schumann's own term "a big romantic sonata," for his *Faschingsschwank*, Op. 26 [ssb VIII]). Schumann got closest to our present concept when he wrote that Beethoven's "Ninth Symphony" was "the turning point from the classical to the romantic period." [13]

Main Themes (German Hegemony)

Between the early, precocious Romanticisms of Dussek, starting before 1800, and the near exhaustion of Romantic music, around World War I, the course of sonata history may be previewed by summarizing briefly its most central and frequently recurring themes. Its background is a complex of sociopolitical history that touches and even parallels music history from time to time to a surprising degree (as in the series of revolutions, monarchies, and republics that coincided almost to the year with fairly distinct episodes of sonata history in France; cf. the

7. Cf. Nagel/ROMANTISCHEN 261–62.

8. Cf. Dannreuther/ROMANTIC 3; MGG XI 791–92. In Longyear/SCHILLER "romantic" seems nowhere to be identified with Schiller and music.

9. Cf. MGG XI 792–93; Lang/WESTERN 743–44.

10. Quoted with more, in Nagel/ROMANTISCHEN 262.

11. NZM V (1836) 135–37; cf., also, RGM for June 21, 1840, p. 346 (referring to Moscheles' use of the term as the first from Leipzig and as a pedantry!).

12. His uses of the term are collected and compared in Boetticher/SCHUMANN 352–54; cf., also, pp. 394–96 (tracing other contemporary uses).

13. As quoted in Shedlock/SONATA 207.

start of ssb XII). This background begins with the convulsions of the French Revolution and continues with their aftermath in the Napoleonic empire, followed by the international revolutions of 1830 and 1848. It includes the ties, rivalries, alliances, intrigues, and eventual separation of Austria and Prussia as major powers. It includes the long-sought unification of Germany and of Italy, as well as the humiliation of France in the Franco-Prussian War, all in the early 1870's. It includes the widening and deepening relationships, intercourse, and frictions between these countries and the relatively more stable, liberal country of England as well as what are, from our viewpoint, the outlying, increasingly important countries comprehended under Scandinavia, East Europe, Russia, and the Americas. And it includes those rapid advances in industry, agriculture, communication, transportation, science, and education that benefitted society quite as much as they contributed to the causes of World War I (and II).

The course of sonata history during this same century and a quarter may be divided into three progressively shorter phases.[14] Each phase occurred much the same in time and kind throughout the regions where the sonata flourished, although without any obvious parallels to the two categories of Romantic music that clearly dominated public taste—opera and light diversional pieces. From before 1800 to about 1850 (or around the revolutions of 1848), occurred the early phase, which began in the Classic-Romantic borderland already noted (with its five Beethoven transmitters) and included the most distinguished composers of early Romantic sonatas (Dussek, Weber, Schubert, and Mendelssohn).[15] From about 1840 to 1885, an overlapping middle phase can be defined, starting with a widely alleged slump in the quantity and quality of sonata production (ssb II) that was partly belied, however, by the composition and/or publication around that time of some of the first main sonatas by Schumann, Chopin, and Liszt. Within little more than a decade this phase began to show a revival of interest, which was furthered by the first sonatas of Brahms. From the mid 1870's to World War I, a third, final, overlapping phase can be defined. It is marked at its start, concurrent with the epochal political events just noted, by a conspicuous spurt of interest almost everywhere, especially in the duo sonata (and other chamber music). Its composers include such important contributors to the sonata as the later Brahms, Richard Strauss, and Reger in Austro-Germany; Franck, Fauré, Saint-

---

14. Cf. Westerly/PIANOFORTE 183–86 for a chap. in 4 pp. that synopsizes what might be called the standard view (in 1924) of "The Sonata Since Beethoven."
15. The pat labels for Schubert and Mendelssohn, respectively, in Einstein/ROMANTIC 89–91 and 124–26 are "Romantic Classic" and "Romantic Classicist."

Saëns, and d'Indy in France; Grieg in Norway; Medtner and Rach-maninoff in (and out of) Russia; and MacDowell in the United States. But its composers also include a whole class of Romantic epigones, such as Dubois, d'Albert, Sinding, and Bortkiewicz—all men with much skill, yet too derivative and formulized in their music to survive.

Like the sonatas of Corelli in the Baroque Era (SBE 9–10) or of Haydn, Mozart, and Beethoven in the Classic Era (SCE 5–6, 454), those of four composers—Schubert, Schumann, Chopin, and Brahms—are singled out in the present volume as main cornerstones of the Romantic sonata. In particular (and as before) they comprise the reference frame-work for Chapter VI on "Styles and Forms," leaving only their back-ground, circumstances, and cultivation to be discussed in the later, pertinent composer chapters. If in turn, any one of these four com-posers is to be singled out as the one most important and central contributor to the sonata since Beethoven, the choice clearly must be Brahms. Certainly Brahms was the most sonata-minded among them, both in the proportion of his attention and the nature of his musical thinking (SSB IX). In this respect at least, Brahms deserved to be called the third "B" by Bülow.[16] If, furthermore, any one axis of composers is to be singled out as defining opposing trends of the Romantic sonata it just as clearly must be that represented by Liszt (SSB X) and Brahms, whose antipodes of style and form still contrasted sharply in the sonatas —progressive and conservative, respectively—of their second-genera-tion followers.

And, finally, if there is any one nationality or region that is to be singled out as the most germinal and central to the Romantic sonata it is no longer Italy, as it had been at least in the earlier phases of the Baroque and Classic eras (SBE 39–40 and SCE 64–65). Rather it is (Austro-)Germany from start to finish. (It would be appropriate to say Austro-Germany, without the parentheses, except that Schubert's so-natas did not gain recognition for almost a half-century after his death [SSB VII] and Brahms wrote several of his sonatas before he moved to Vienna.)

The same three phases of Romantic sonata history stand out within this German hegemony. First, following the incomparable heritage from the Classic Viennese masters, the compositions of Mendelssohn and Schumann became the loosely axial, or conservative and more progressive, reference standards, respectively, for the sonatas of a whole, mid-19th-century generation of composers.[17] Then, as was just

16. Cf. May/BRAHMS II 528–29; Cobbett/CHAMBER I 160–61 and 327 (both D. Tovey).

17. Cf. Maclean/RUBINSTEIN 139, 148, and 150 on the continuing tendency to relate all music to Mendelssohn.

observed, the music of Brahms and Liszt similarly governed the next generation. (Wagner's overpowering influence would be included here, too, except that it touched the sonata much less significantly [SSB X] apart from a few notable consequences at the end of the era, like Op. 63 by d'Indy [SSB XIII].) And finally, certain men hardly so well remembered today, especially Rheinberger in Munich and Kiel in Berlin (both SSB X), continued to maintain the German hegemony at the end of the era. But now it was not so much the surprisingly strong compositions by these men, thoroughly steeped in the previous German styles, as their high reputations as teachers that kept the German influence dominant.

Indeed, right from the start of the era, the main Austro-German centers—notably Vienna, Leipzig, and Berlin—became the international meccas for all students aspiring to the best, with the notable exception of the most important French-born composers, who trained in their own country. For example, among other outlanders of the sonata who polished their training in Germany, there were Bennett and Stanford in England, Albéniz in Spain, Grieg and Sinding in Norway, Sibelius in Finland, Rubinstein in Russia, and MacDowell (as well as most of the "Boston Classicists") in the United States. Furthermore, few of the sonata composers who did not train in Austro-German centers failed to come under the profound influence of the German masters, including even such ardent native Frenchmen as Saint-Saëns and d'Indy, as well as Franck in France, Elgar in England, Nielsen in Denmark, Martucci in Italy, and Medtner (of German descent) in Russia and elsewhere.

The Mainest Theme—Beethoven's Influence

The foregoing remarks on German hegemony in the Romantic sonata lead to what is at once the most important of these main themes and the justification for the present volume's title. That theme is the all-pervasive influence of Beethoven's sonatas throughout the era and wherever the sonata was cultivated. (Of course, their influence has extended beyond the Romantic Era, too, although it has dropped off necessarily in the same degree as have those previously mentioned forces—tonal, melodic, rhythmic—on which the Beethoven sonata thrives.) It is perhaps hard to realize now that the strongest early Romantics, including Schubert, Mendelssohn, and Weber, had to resist being swallowed up in the maelstrom of Beethovenism (the less strong did not resist) quite as Verdi and Debussy had to resist Wagnerism seventy-five years later.

The devotion to, even idolatry of, Beethoven's sonatas was extraordinary throughout the era.[18] It began as early as 1800, in his own lifetime, with the transmitters mentioned earlier, and soon spread to France, England, and other countries by way of the publishers, though not yet the public performers.[19] We see this devotion or idolatry in slavish imitations like a "Sonate pathétique" in c by L. Berger and another by Lauska published early in the century (both ssb VIII), or in such a collection, published late in the century, as John Petzler's *Twelve Sonatas for the Pianoforte, Composed in Imitation of Some of the Works of Beethoven*.[20] We see it in the articles, reviews, lectures, and whole books on Beethoven's sonatas that were published or reported frequently in every main music periodical of the era, culminating in such widely divergent studies as the multivolume sets by Rolland and Riemann.[21] We see it in the essential place given to Beethoven's solo sonatas in 19th-century piano pedagogy, as by Liszt[22] and in Wagner's proposals for an ideal music education.[23] And we see it, above all, in the public performances of Beethoven's sonatas, which occurred only sporadically before the middle of the century, then began to multiply and soon to snowball as they became general fare wherever recitals were given.[24]

To judge by contemporary reviews of those recitals and by the nature of surviving 19th-century editions of Beethoven's sonatas (such as the still ubiquitous ed. by Bülow & Lebert), the licenses taken in performance would shock present-day purists (e.g., the trills and tremolos Liszt is supposed to have added in the first mvt. when he in-

18. The cultivation of Beethoven's music has not been investigated with regard to his sons. so thoroughly or illuminatingly as it has in Mahaim/BEETHOVEN for his late quartets. But there is considerable information about this aspect of the solo sons. in Prod'homme/BEETHOVEN, and of the duo sons. in Müller-Reuter/LEXIKON II *passim*. Cf., also, SCE 542. Boyer/BEETHOVEN and Schrade/BEETHOVEN are broader studies of the developing and changing attitudes toward Beethoven in the 19th c. (the latter in France).

19. Cf. Favre/FRANÇAISE 103–4; ssb XII and XIV (opening pp.).

20. Cf. MMR XVII (1886) 39 (criticizing the composer for having to copy the masters).

21. For samples and further references, cf. SCE 503–42 *passim*. Typical of many such contributions not yet noted in the Beethoven literature are the articles in RGM for 1846 *passim;* DWIGHT's X–XVI (1856–60) *passim;* SMZ XVII (1877) 45 ff.; MT XXIV (1883) 206 (report of lectures at the London Institution). Cf., further, the reviews cited in Boyer/BEETHOVEN 202–65 *passim*.

22. Cf. BÜLOW BRIEFE I 343; Fay/GERMANY 229–30, 237–38.

23. Cf. WAGNER PROSE IV 198 and V 59–126 *passim* (especially 81–84).

24. Cf. under Cramer, Pinto, and Potter in ssb XIV and the introduction to ssb XII. A check through RGM for 1834–50 *passim* suggests that the largest number of performances before 1850 of Beethoven sons. occurred in Paris, being almost half the number of performances of sons. by all composers that occurred then and there.

troduced Op. 27/2 in Paris in 1832[25]). But we have the great pianists of the century—Liszt and Clara Schumann at first,[26] then Bülow and Rubinstein[27]—to thank for taking the lead in making Beethoven's sonatas so popular. In 1873 Rubinstein still doubted the advisability of including more than one Beethoven sonata in a recital [28] and in London five years later Bülow was censured for playing an all-Beethoven recital, for choosing the last five solo sonatas, at that, and worse still, for doing them all from memory.[29] Yet by 1861 complete cycles of the "thirty-two" were being played, soon from memory.[30]

Of course, today's favorites were yesterday's, too, and a good share of the Beethoven performances were confined to Opp. 13, 27/2, 31/2, 53, and 57, as well as the "Kreutzer Sonata," Op. 47 (played for the 48th time "at these concerts" in London, March 3, 1883 [31] and played often by Clara Schumann and Joachim,[32] among other duo teams). But by the 1870's most audiences were getting ample exposure to the other and later sonatas, too.[33] Exceptional is the awe and fascination with which Op. 106 in B♭ was regarded almost from its first publication in 1819, much as it still is today.[34] There were the deliberate imitations of it in Mendelssohn's own Op. 106 in B♭ (ssb VIII), the allusion to it in Brahms's Op. 1 in C (ssb IX), the special notices of it taken by Schumann and Wagner,[35] Marxsen's orchestration of its "Scherzo" in 1835,[36] and such amusing incidents as Potter's instruction to Bennett to ask the dealer "for the Sonata that nobody plays." [37] And there were the early performances, first in Paris by Liszt in 1836 (if what Berlioz

25. Cf. Prod'homme/BEETHOVEN 125–27; Fay/GERMANY 168 (on Bülow).

26. Cf. Hanslick/WIEN I 333–36; Litzmann/SCHUMANN III 617–24.

27. Cf. Mason/MEMORIES 226–27.

28. Mason/MEMORIES 226–27.

29. MT XIX (1878) 665. Cf., also, MT XXI (1880) 351–52 (on 3 all-Beethoven recitals by "Herr Bonawitz"). Sietz/HILLER II 80 reports all-Beethoven recitals of 4 or 5 sons. each, including one in which the audience yelled for his "Sonata in F Flat"! Cf. Pleasants/HANSLICK 185.

30. Cf. SCE 527 and the introduction to ssb XIX.

31. MT XXIV (1883) 193.

32. E.g., cf. Fay/GERMANY 162, 27.

33. E.g., a surprising representation can be found in MMR II and III (1872–73) *passim* (especially Clara Schumann) and SMZ XVI and XVII (1876–77). As early as 1833 in London Moscheles gave private performances of Opp. 109 and 111 (MO-SCHELES I 288–89).

34. On the 19th-century career of this work, cf. Newman/Op. 106 (originally read at the Annual Meeting of the American Musicological Society in 1968 [New Haven]) cf. also, SCE 530–32.

35. Cf. Schumann/SCHRIFTEN I 453; NZM XLVI (1857) 158; Prod'homme/BEETHOVEN 249.

36. Müller-Reuter/LEXIKON II 138.

37. Cf. Bennett/BENNETT 33–34 and 400; ssb XIV.

praised was actually Op. 106);[38] then in Germany, Vienna, and Russia, in 1843, 1847, and 1853, respectively, by Mortier de Fontaine;[39] in London by Moscheles (privately?) in 1845,[40] Alexandre Billet in 1850, and Arabella Goddard (from memory, in her debut) in 1853;[41] and again in Germany by Franz Wüllner in 1854 and earlier[42] and in Vienna by Clara Schumann in 1856.[43] No doubt a little of the exceptional interest in Op. 106 relates to the growing historical interest among pianists (and other musicians) throughout the century (ssb II). Thus, in 1837 Moscheles pioneered not only the idea of the solo recital but a return, that soon, to the harpsichord for the playing of Scarlatti's sonatas.[44] And by 1885–86, Anton Rubinstein brought the interest to a peak with his celebrated "seven historical concerts," ranging in content from mid-16th- to mid-19th-century music (with many sons.) and given throughout Europe.[45]

Subordinate Themes (the Great and the Small)

Along with the main themes just introduced, certain subordinate themes in the present volume may be pointed out in advance. Most of these themes, apart from the question of great and small composers that is raised below, need only to be identified here, in the interest of an introductory overview, since they all figure in the succeeding, five survey chapters of Part One. First, Beethoven's unsurpassed example and an increasing tendency to value originality for its own sake in the arts help to explain a new, elevated attitude toward the sonata as one of the loftiest and most challenging of musical forms, especially after its supposed slump around 1840 (supra) and equally in the minds of composer, performer, and perceiver (ssb II). Second, as already implied, the Romantic sonata becomes more and more of a main staple in piano solo and ensemble recitals alike (ssb III). Third, its spread comes to depend at least as much on its popularization by travelling recitalists as its propagation by publishers and its enjoyment by students or amateur groups (ssb III and IV). Fourth, its vehicle par excellence is the vehicle par excellence of Romantic instrumental music in general

38. Cf. Prod'homme/BEETHOVEN 248–49 (referring also to Liszt's later recollection of playing Op. 106 at age 10 [1821!], "very badly, undoubtedly, but with feeling").

39. Prod'homme/BEETHOVEN 247; Pleasants/HANSLICK 185 (but read B♭ for B).

40. MOSCHELES II 138 (but read B♭ for B).

41. Schonberg/PIANISTS 238; HALLÉ 26–27; MUSICAL WORLD for April, 1853, p. 243 (review of Goddard); Bache/BACHE 227, 255.

42. Kämper/WÜLLNER 8–12; BRAHMS BRIEFWECHSEL XIV 9, XV 37.

43. Litzmann/SCHUMANN III 621.

44. Cf. MOSCHELES II 22–23, 35–36 ("old masters"), 45, 224–25.

45. Cf. Rubinstein/ERINNERUNGEN 111–14, including the complete programs.

study will uncover more of his sonatas and/or more significance than has been credited to them.

Again as in our previous two volumes, the obscure composers have been brought back to light chiefly by systematic combings of the principal music encyclopedias, periodicals, catalogues, and locale or composer monographs.[49] And again (cf. SCE 8–9) the aim has been to include every composer whose sonatas reveal at least some musical or historical distinction, or have attracted at least some attention in reviews, performances, or special studies. These generally obscure composers, plus a few others included with even less apparent reason, do figure here mostly as statistical support for trends or as fillers in the over-all picture. Yet it has not seemed sufficient to bunch them into statistical, space-saving tables (except for about 60 of some 110 Americans merely tabulated in SSB XIX because too little is known about them to write more). The tables not only would sacrifice the prose continuity and condemn some to anonymity who deserve better. They would emphasize the ordinary and typical rather than whatever might distinguish any individuals. On the other hand nothing is gained by supplying more than essential orientation, sonata output, and bibliography for run-of-the-mill composers whose sonatas are remembered by nothing more than a neutral review, or even a negative one (such as the 10-page [!], partly satirical disparagement of a thoroughly unpromising Op. 1, ded. to Meyerbeer by one Maurice Levy, otherwise unknown here[50]).

The obscure composers we have been considering are not the kind implied in E. J. Dent's assertion that the history of music is written in bad music.[51] We have been thinking generally of musical conservatives who are competent but inconsequential, whereas Dent implies that it is the innovators, often rash and not necessarily conservative, who produce the historically progressive, "bad music." Even the most interesting of our more obscure composers were conservatives in the sense that they were direct disciples and not leaders—for example, Draeseke, Viole, and Reubke (all SSB X), three talented imitators of Liszt. The least interesting of our obscure composers are those who are not only conservative among their contemporaries but in relation to the whole

49. Contemporary (19th-c.) sources have been of increased value in the present vol., including especially AMZ, NZM, MW, SMW, SMZ, RGM, and MT, among periodicals, and Schilling/LEXICON, Mendel/LEXICON, Fétis/BU, BROWN & STRATTON, and GROVE Am. Suppl., among encyclopedias. The fullest recent source for names has continued to be MGG (of which only Vol. XIV was still not available at press time, mid 1968, for SSB).

50. CAECILIA XXVI (1847) 242–51. The same opinion is expressed more briefly in NZM XXVI (1847) 141–42.

51. Cf. Howes/ENGLISH 12, 27–28.

era. Thus, Sinding as an epigone arouses less historical interest here than Ries as an early-Romantic. Somewhat related is the obscure composer who has aroused no interest because he fits in no national pattern. Thus, perhaps one Otto Schweizer got in no German dictionaries because he moved to London, where Novello published his Sonata for P & Vc in 1887,[52] and in no English dictionaries because he was not native born.

Methods, Policies, and Sources

As with its two predecessors, the present volume divides into two complementary but asymmetrical parts (cf. sbe 9–10 and sce 7–8). Part One, in six chapters, provides the over-all view, surveying successively the problem, meaning, use, spread, scoring, and form of the sonata since Beethoven. Part Two, in more than twice as many chapters and nearly four times as many pages, provides the more detailed views. It takes up the individual composers and their sonatas, region by region according to early, middle, and late phases (with 1850 and 1885 being the approximate, most frequent inner dividing lines for the era). A certain minimum of overlapping and repetition is unavoidable between and within the two parts—in fact, necessary. As before, our semantic approach gives preference to works actually called "sonata," although, naturally, taking related works into consideration when they do relate (sce 6–7). And as before, each composer is identified primarily with the region where he lived, composed his sonatas, and exerted his chief influence, rather than the land of his birth when there is a difference.[53] Thus, Chopin is identified with Paris rather than Warsaw. But in that age of rapidly improving travel and more frequent changes of residence, a composer must often be located more arbitrarily, or merely returned to his birthplace, anyway. Chronologically, each composer is introduced around the time of his chief or only sonata(s), which may or may not be the time when he "flourished" in terms of any better known or more significant works by him in other categories. Thus, Mussorgsky is introduced with other composers around 1860 rather than a half generation later, when his chief operas began to appear. Also, the amount of space allocated to each composer depends first here on the artistic worth and historical significance of his sonata writing—which are largely matters of personal evaluation, in any case —and only secondarily on the over-all importance generally credited to

52. Reviewed in nzm LXXXIII/2 (1887) 466.
53. "'Made in England' was Walker's definition of English music, and it avoids difficulties raised by blood and birthplace" (Howes/ENGLISH 21).

him. Mussorgsky may be cited to illustrate that policy, too, in view of the relatively short space allocated to him here.

The literature on Romantic music is vast and mushrooming, as is suggested by the nearly 850 entries pertinent to the present study alone, in the Bibliography. But much of it still needs assimilating, consolidating, and re-organizing. A notable step in that direction has been the establishment in Köln of a Zentralstelle für Musikbibliographie des 19. Jahrhunderts.[54] Among over-all treatments of Romantic music, those by Bücken and Einstein have been utilized most here,[55] along with the first two of the three promised volumes in the Marxist-oriented survey by Knepler and the admirably planned article by Blume (MGG XI 785–845).   55a

There are no previous, over-all studies of the Romantic sonata.[56] But there are numerous studies that concentrate wholly or partly on that topic within particular regions, periods, and/or scorings. Such are the studies by Egert on the early-Romantic (mainly German) piano sonata, Favre on French piano music up to 1830, Alekseev on Russian piano music up to recent times, Asaf'ev on Russian music of all types since about 1800, Reeser similarly on Dutch music, Szabolcsi on Hungarian music history, Lissa on Romantic Polish music, Closson and Borren on Belgian music history, Temperley on early-Romantic music in England, Sloan on the American violin sonata, Wolverton on American piano music up to 1830, Shand on the violin sonata from 1851 to 1917, and still others, to be cited where they apply. Needless to say, the widened regions of the 19th-century sonata and the increasing studies from those regions, rarely translated, present the researcher with increasing problems, at times nearly insurmountable problems, in Slavic and other exotic languages.

Much richer, although still hit-or-miss, are the studies on individual composers. Schubert fares best, thanks especially to the fundamental studies by the late O. E. Deutsch, and including monographs on the sonatas by Költzsch and others (SSB VII). Brahms fares second best (SSB IX), although apart from a very few peripheral studies like

54. Warm thanks are owing to the Director, Dr. Imogen Fellinger, for several advices by correspondence. Cf., also, DMf XIX (1966) 172–76, regarding a symposium on 19th-c. "Unterhaltungs- und Gebrauchsmusik" in Coburg in 1965.

55. In this discussion of sources, when only the author's name is given, the full title of the book in question is self-evident in the Bibliography.

56. A recent one-vol. survey of all son. history, in Rumanian (Nicolescu/SONATA— recall the 2 previous over-all accounts, by Klauwell and Borrel, as cited in SBE 12, 426, 411)—includes a short chap. on the Romantic son. And there are pertinent sections in my own survey articles in MGG XII 868–910, RICORDI ENCICLOPEDIA IV 243–49, and Gatti & Basso/LA MUSICA IV 429–43 (all pub. since SCE appeared in 1963).

Mitschka's, his sonatas still offer a major, open topic for prospective and prospecting dissertationists. (So, for that matter, do the sonatas of nearly every other important Romantic composer, including Dussek, Weber, Mendelssohn, Schumann, Chopin, Liszt, Fauré, Saint-Saëns, and Grieg, there being thus far chiefly a few studies on the sonatas of minor figures like Loewe [ssb VIII] or on separate categories like Rheinberger's organ sonatas [ssb X].) Among these front-rankers of the Romantic sonata, Schumann, Chopin, and Liszt have all engendered substantial bodies of music literature, but this literature, especially on Liszt (ssb X), is in serious need of re-evaluation, revision, clarification, re-organization, and amplification. It should be added that even when a special study does exist on a Romantic composer's sonatas it is likely to be usable (with all due credit) almost exclusively for its factual information rather than its musical analysis. An initiated reader can better his understanding from another's intelligent analysis. But the writer is in a different position, still more so when confronted by the complexities of Romantic as against Baroque and Classic traits of style and form (cf. sbe 67–68 and sce 113). He must see the score for himself and go one big step further by making his own analysis, both because the most objective style-critical approach still depends heavily on subjective opinion and because each writer needs to maintain his own consistent, personal slant.[57]

The pertinent literature on Romantic music is further enriched by the many publications of memoirs, diaries, letters, travel reports, and intimate first-hand biographies by and about musicians. Among the most useful sources of this sort in the present study are those by or about Moscheles, Spohr, Mendelssohn, both Schumanns, Weber, Brahms, Joachim, Chorley, Hallé, Chopin (in Sydow & Hedley), Bülow, and both W. and D. G. Mason. Contemporary accounts of concert life have contributed much, too, especially the large number in the several collections by Hanslick in Vienna.

But more fruitful than any other of our contemporary sources for new and more detailed information have been the periodicals, the chief of which have been searched in detail here, throughout the portions of the Romantic Era (up to 1915) in which they appeared.[58] In

57. A significant dichotomy of old and new approaches, especially to "sonata form," is presented in W. J. Mitchell's thorough, enlightening review of *The Beethoven Quartets* by Joseph Kerman, in MQ LIII (1967) 421–34. Note also, with regard to Schubert, how, for example, Egert/frühromantiker 74–91 disagrees with Költzsch, and Truscott/unity with Brown.

58. These are AMZ, CAECILIA, NZM, MW, SMW, DM, DMZ, SMZ, MT, HARMONICON, QUARTERLY, RGM, and DWIGHT'S. Besides their general superiority for our purposes, these periodicals nearly all have the advantage of a full table of contents in each

order of value, these have provided many reviews of new publications, reports of concerts, announcements of publications and concerts, and larger, more general articles. In particular, the many reviews cited throughout the present volume—undoubtedly too many for some readers[59]—have provided us often with the best, if not the only, facts we have about a sonata's title, movements, keys, style traits (when the specific comments do not reduce to generalities), and "faults" in composition or scoring; about its publisher, quality of publication, and date (at least as a *terminus ad quem,* since the review might be delayed as much as several years); and even about the composer himself. Not seldom they include from one to several short or long music examples (though rarely a complete movement or complete sonata as a supplement), which may well prove to be the only actual taste we can still get of a sonata no longer locatable. In their typically discursive manner of leading from the general to the specific, the reviews frequently open with choice, quotable generalizations about the sonata's current status and function in the world of music (ssb II). The length and number of reviews (in different periodicals) give at least a statistical hint of the interest the sonata and its composer were arousing at the time of publication, especially when compared with the response to previous or subsequent sonata publications from the same man.

Moreover, the evaluations themselves in the reviews, although generally superseded by the evaluations of time (and placed last, not first, in importance here), do give at least a choice sampling of contemporary opinion and at most some eloquent, discerning critiques that still seem as valid as ever.[60] To be sure, excessive praise was likely to be lavished on the more competent but conservative, readily fathomed works, much, conversely, as undue faults and confusion were likely to be charged to the more innovative, less readily fathomed works. And the critics frequently disagreed (as on A. B. Marx's Op. 16, ssb VIII). Moreover, every significant composer from Beethoven on (sce 539) suffered at least one nemesis among his reviewers. Reger and Grieg were plagued with exceptional virulence (ssb XI and XIV). Brahms was contemptuous of his reviewers' understanding (ssb IX) and Liszt expressed hostility toward his reviewers, including the many who

vol., though not cumulative indexes except for a few runs (especially AMZ from 1798–1848). A few vols. in the runs could not be found. Numerous other periodicals, as well as a few newspapers, were of occasional help, as cited in later chaps.

59. But references to such reviews are otherwise scarce, being seldom included in any but the most detailed composer bibliographies.

60. That 19th-c. writers were alert to the problems of music criticism is suggested in repeated references to these problems, such as that in MT XXIII (1882) 337 on the misuse of critical adjectives.

hid behind initials and more cryptic signatures (e.g., numbers and Greek letters) or simply remained anonymous.[61] Yet by and large, the reviews seem about as fair in their evaluations as reviews ever do.

Certainly, Schumann left a rich legacy of reviews that have come to rank among the valued 19th-century commentaries on early 19th-century music (and the most quoted throughout much of SSB; cf. SSB VIII, including special references to Plantinga/SCHUMANN). These reviews appeared mostly during the decade after he founded the important *Neue Zeitschrift für Musik* (NZM, from 1834) and centered often around a special interest in new piano sonatas (SSB VIII). They could be ecstatic in their enthusiasms for the best (as in the encomiums of Schubert's and Mendelssohn's sons., SSB VII and VIII, or the "Hat's off!" articles that heralded both Chopin and Brahms, SSB XII and IX), although occasionally they could go overboard, too (as in the reviews that saw promise, not to be fulfilled, in D. F. E. Wilsing; SSB VIII [62]). On the other hand, over his various noms de plume, Schumann's reviews could be unqualifiedly negative, seldom miscalculating and often indulging in witty, gentle, or harsh sarcasm (as in those of sons. or related pieces by one J. Nisle,[63] by Anton Halm, SSB VII, and by Czerny, SSB VII). Whatever their direction and tone, these reviews usually start with or branch off into broader discussions that include, along with much else, significant commentaries on the history, nationalism, quality versus quantity, career values, deterioration, excessive virtuosity, surfeit of motivic play, and conservatism of the sonata.[64]

With regard to sources for dating Romantic music, it has proved possible—more so than anticipated—to arrive at the year of publication for the large majority of the sonatas under discussion and nearly that close for most of the others. Relatively few of the Romantic sonatas are dated in MGG, GROVE, or other main dictionaries, past and present, when, indeed, they are itemized and not simply lumped under "considerable piano music" or "several sonatas." Pazdírek's *Universal-Handbuch* supplies only a rough, late *terminus ad quem* (1904–10) with regard to dates, although it is invaluable as a nearly exhaustive list of all 19th-century publications. And American copyrights do not begin to help substantially until the end of the century (SSB XIX, introduction). But when a sonata cannot be found in the remarkable cumulative, annual, or even monthly volumes issued on a more or less

61. Cf. LISZT LETTERS I 328.

62. Cf. the enthusiastic review by Bülow of Viole's Op. 1 (SSB X).

63. Johann Friedrich Nisle? Cf. Schumann/SCHRIFTEN I 306–7; Schilling/LEXICON V 176–77; MGG IX 1537–38; SSB VIII.

64. Cf. Schumann/SCHRIFTEN I 59, 92–93 and 452, 123 and 306–7, 395–96, 453; II 10, 11, 118, 80–81; also, SSB II and III.

international basis since 1815 by Whistling and Hofmeister, then it is likely to turn up in a periodical announcement or review, in somebody's letters, diary, or memoirs, or in a present-day study. And if all these fail, one of the fine publishing or plate-number indexes such as those by Deutsch, Hopkinson, Weinmann, or Tyson is likely to solve the problem. The few Italian and Spanish publications that have come up here have posed the chief problems.

In any case, as before (SCE 13–14), accurate dating is essential to any discussion of influences and of which way they flowed in the tightly packed Romantic Era. Unfortunately, library catalogues that go beyond 1800, much less dated catalogues, are still few and limited. The new, 33-volume catalogue of the New York Public Library (with supplements; Cat. NYPL) is the notable exception on both counts. Cobbett's anthological *Cyclopedic Survey of Chamber Music* (including many general as well as composer articles), Altmann's *Kammermusik-Katalog,* and the Müller-Reuter *Lexikon* are indispensable tools that add some dates of published music to the majority they derive from HOFMEISTER. Although the publishers seldom dated their 19th-century editions, the composers helped as the century wore on by becoming increasingly disposed to observe a single, correct sequence of opus numbers. Modern "complete" editions, which usually cope with the dating as well as the editorial problems, exist only for the most important of the Romantics who wrote sonatas and but few others. (Otherwise, present-day reprints of Romantic sonatas are rare.)

The Pleasures of Musical Romanticism

This introductory chapter should not be concluded without at least a mention of the pleasures experienced in working on the Romantic sonata, which have been at least the equal of those experienced in working on the Baroque and on the Classic sonata. For every pianist there is, of course, the lure of the music produced by some of the foremost masters of the piano, from Dussek to Rachmaninoff, during this greatest century in the piano's development as an instrument.[65] For every devotee of good literature there is the frequent association, even through so absolute a musical genre as the sonata, with notable men of letters at every turn, not to mention the numerous composers who themselves were capable writers in this century of hybrid arts.

---

65. Although the 128 music exx. in SSB can only hint, long as many of them are, at the nature of the sons. they illustrate, they do give a broad view of advances in Romantic piano writing, including 14 facs. of autographs or first eds. (most of them not hitherto pub.).

For the historically-minded researcher there is the excitement of a century that saw precipitous advances in government, transportation, communications, industry, capital-labor relations, and science. And for the would-be humanitarian there is the idealism of noble, staunch, warm friendships, exemplified above all by the triangular interrelationships of Robert and Clara Schumann and Brahms.

Only at the end of the era does the spirit of brotherly love become distorted and sidetracked into the ominous private hates and prejudices of a Pfitzner or a d'Indy, breeding the kind of poison that eventually sickens studies such as Boetticher's immense monograph on Schumann (ssb VIII). But delving into the Romantic era before that miscarriage of brotherly love is likely to evoke much the same nostalgic feelings that are evoked today by viewing reruns of the best movies from that relative, more recent age of innocence, the decade before World War II.

Part One

The Nature of the Romantic Sonata

PART TWO

The Nature of the Romantic Spirit

Chapter II

Romantic Concepts of the Sonata

The Word Itself

This chapter concerns the views that the Romantics themselves held of the sonata, whether as a title, as a particular form, as an aesthetic problem, or as a historical phenomenon of varying significance. In all these views the single most important consideration is the transition, by mid-century, from a loose, casual concept of a free, even a fantasy, form (cf. SCE 28) to a tight, fixed concept of a highly specific form, specific enough to crystalize in the textbooks and even to become a criterion by which sonatas soon were evaluated.

Throughout the 19th century occasional uses of the word "sonata" still occurred in its generic sense, merely as an instrumental piece. Thus, in a collection published by Bacon in Philadelphia about 1815, "Twenty four sonatas for the piano forte," the two "sonatas" by Beethoven prove to be simply one piece each from his "Contretänze" and his "Ländlerische Tänze." [1] In 1860 Bülow was still asking—rhetorically, to be sure—"What is a sonata? Isn't any instrumental music a sonata?" [2]

A generic concept is also implied when "sonata" is equated with other instrumental titles. Thus, it is equated with symphony by Mendelssohn, T. Kullak, and Rheinberger; [3] with suite by Speidel (SSB X), Penfield (SSB XIX), Daneau (SSB XIII), and Kiel; [4] with the passacaglia by Moulaert (SSB XIII); with piano quintet by Brahms (SSB IX), viola concerto by Paganini (SSB XVI), and string quartet by Rode (Op. 24), [5] Paganini, and Rossini (SSB XVI); and with fantasy by many an admirer of the two sonatas "quasi una fantasia," Op. 27/1

1. Cf. LC MUSIC 206–7.
2. BÜLOW BRIEFE IV 368–69.
3. As in Rheinberger's *Symphonische Sonate*, Op. 47 (cf. MW II [1871] 389–91 and 406–7 for a discussion of this equation by A. Maczewski); also, MGG IX 62 (E. Werner) on Mendelssohn and NZM XXIV (1846) 149–50 on Kullak.
4. Cf. Egert/FRÜHROMANTIKER 157. Cf., also, MGG VI 221.
5. Cf. Bachmann/VIOLINISTES 260.

and 2, and later precedents set by Beethoven, including Schubert, Schumann, Mendelssohn, and Liszt (ssb VII, VIII, and X).[6]

Yet in far more instances there were deliberate efforts to keep "sonata" and related terms delimited and separate. Thus, "sonata" was distinguished variously, and more or less precisely, from "symphony" and "fantasy," by Schumann;[7] from (organ) "voluntary," by both Mendelssohn and his publisher;[8] from "concerto," by Moscheles, Schumann, and Liszt;[9] and from both "suite" and "programme music," by A. Spanuth.[10] Furthermore, not a few writers had sufficiently fixed concepts of what a sonata should be to rule out works called by that name when they did not conform. Thus, as late as 1906 a French audience was disturbed by Liszt's use of the title for a work in one movement,[11] and in 1929 the dissertationist Paul Egert still declared that L. Berger's Op. 18 "is no sonata" because only one and the same motive recurs throughout all three movements.[12]

"Sonatina" as the diminutive of "sonata" appears far more often in the Romantic than in the preceding eras—in fact, about as often as "sonata," though largely over short, light pedagogic sonatas in Clementi's style. Richard Strauss used the term more in the generic sense when he applied it to his two late wind ensembles (ssb XI). There are also variants or expansions of the term, like "sonatilles" (as by Raff, ssb X) or "sonatina concertante" (as by Julius Weismann, for Vc & P; ssb XI). "Grande" appears as a qualifier in sonata titles too often and variously to have any one connotation. A reviewer in 1812 (J. F. Rochlitz?) thought it should apply to a "dreadfully long" work.[13] And perhaps it was also the same reviewer who, on the basis of content as well as length, wondered both at the failure to add "grande" to the title of a large-scale sonata by Czerny and at the error of adding it to one small-scale sonata each by Kuhlau and G. Schuberth.[14] A Berlin reviewer congratulated Mendelssohn for not calling his Op. 4 "Grande Sonate" or even "Grande Sonate pathétique et mélancolique" in line with the tendency to make "everything big, big. . . ."[15] By

6. Among several references to this last equation, cf. amz XXVIII (1826) 137–40, Shedlock/sonata 195, grove IX 217 (P. Spitta).
7. Schumann/schriften I 329 and 70 (partially contradicting Vol. I, p. 395). Cf. sce 32–34.
8. Cf. Edwards/mendelssohn 2, 15–16; zimg III (1901–2) 337–38 (C. Maclean).
9. Cf. nzm VI (1837) 65; Storck/schumann 67; Wasielewski/schumann 279–80.
10. mw VIII (1877) 77–78 and 93–94.
11. mdc IV (1906) xxvi.
12. Cf. L. Berger in ssb VIII; also, sce 117 on Beethoven.
13. amz XIV (1812) 393.
14. amz XXIV (1822) 382, XXVIII (1826) 708, XXIX (1827) 99.
15. Jacob/mendelssohn 48–50.

1830 one A. Devaux's term "Grand Sonata" was regarded as a "nearly obsolete title [that] . . . conjures up in our memory all those past glories [Beethoven, Mozart, Clementi, and Steibelt] that triumphant fashion has so long covered with dust . . . [Devaux] has some formidable skips; introduced, perhaps, by the author to save himself from the danger of having a perriwig placed on his head by the ultramoderns." [16] But in 1861 Henri Herz's addition of "di bravura" to the same title was regarded as new to the "Classic tradition." [17] "Sonate brillante" had been used at least a few times (as in 1834 by Loewe; ssb VIII). Numerous other, more expressive qualifiers also occur in the Romantic sonata titles, such as "dramatique," [18] "sentimentale" (A. M. Nava; ssb XVI); "agréable," "pastorale," or "caractéristique." [19]

Explanations by Theorists

Apparently it was by or before 1837 that the industrious Carl Czerny (ssb VII) made an interesting claim by implication. In the preface to his Op. 600 he implied that he was the first to describe the sonata in any basic detail, although not until 1848 did this three-volume treatise on composition appear in print (in an English trans. of the original German, which did not appear for another year):[20]

16. HARMONICON VIII/1 (1830) 33–34.
17. DMZ II (1861) 229; but cf. HOFMEISTER 1828 (Whistling) 602.
18. MGG VIII 464 (J. Bonfils).
19. The last 3 are among a variety of titles to be found in HOFMEISTER 1828 (Whistling) 577–606.
20. Czerny/COMPOSITION I iii; cf. Newman/THEORISTS (with errors) and Newman/CZERNY (but add that, thanks to word from Mr. Neil Ratliff of the New York Public Library, the issues of the Hofmeister *Monatsbericht* in question may be found in that institution and at the University of Illinois). Warm thanks are owing to Dr. Hedwig Mitringer at the Gesellschaft der Musikfreunde in Vienna and Dr. Imogen Fellinger at the Zentralstelle für Musikbibliographie des 19. Jahrhunderts in Köln for help in dating the rare German ed. (of which Vol. I, at least, is in Vienna); also, to Mrs. Birgitte Moyer of Menlo Park, Calif., for correspondence regarding Czerny's claim and Reicha's possible priority. Mrs. Moyer is currently completing a Ph.D. diss., "Concepts of Musical Form in the 19th Century, With Special Reference to A. B. Marx and Sonata Form" (Stanford University).
While the present volume was going to press a new, thorough, and enlightening diss. on the theoretical recognition of "son. form" *ca.* 1700–1850, Ritzel/SONATENFORM (1968), was received (thanks to the kindness of Dr. Lothar Hoffmann-Erbrecht in Frankfurt/M). It has been possible here to incorporate references to the most essential points pertinent to the following discussion.
And further contributions keep coming! Still more recently, Churgin/SONATA has found another important link in a description of "son. form" (not so called) by Francesco Galeazzi in 1796 that anticipates Reicha's description of 1826 (*infra*); also in JAMS XXI/2 (summer 1968), Pierro Weiss of Columbia University is able to show (pp. 233–34) that as early as 1814 Reicha had anticipated his own description.

By the phrase *doctrine of composition,* has hitherto been understood only the instruction in thorough bass and counterpoint. These sciences are indisputably as essential to the composer, as orthography and grammar to him who desires to become a poet and author. But, even with the best-grounded knowledge of harmony and pure composition, the pupil is still ignorant of the *forms* which the different pieces must assume, and which, in music in general, and in that for single instruments in particular, are practicable and usual; and in no treatise on thorough bass which has yet appeared, has the manner of constructing a sonata, a variation, a quartett, a symphony, or even a waltz, been fundamentally described.

Then, Czerny went on to "describe" in detail, in the forty-nine pages of his sixth chapter,[21] what "must" go into each of the four movements (allegro, adagio or andante, scherzo or minuet, and finale or [i.e., especially] rondo). In connection with the first movement (and with a proscription against returning to the "original key" in the development section), he cautioned that "we must always proceed in a settled form. For, if this order were evaded or arbitrarily changed, the composition would no longer be a regular Sonata" (p. 35). He still viewed the first movement, at least nominally, as being in "two parts." Its first part (not called "exposition" by the translator) consists of the "principal subject," its extension and a modulation to "the nearest related key," a "middle subject" and its extension in the related key, and a "final melody" that closes in that key at the repeat sign. Its second part divides into two sections, a modulatory "development" (the translator's word) of any of those ideas or a new one, ending back in the original key; and a recapitulation (not so called by the translator) that restates the first part except for abridgments and adjustments needed to remain in the original key. In the further discussions of the first and succeeding movements Czerny showed how Mozart might have expanded one of his "sonata forms" (not the translator's term; Son. in D for P-duet, K. 123a/i) and he quoted other examples from successful sonatas for P solo by Haydn, Clementi, Mozart, Beethoven (as well as Beethoven's Rondo in C, Op. 51/1), and Dussek.

In terms of detail and clarity, Czerny seems to have been justified in claiming by implication that when he wrote Op. 600, sonata form was for the first time being "fundamentally described." [22] The point is

21. Czerny/COMPOSITION I 33–81.

22. But Ritzel/SONATENFORM 213–23, 228, 233, 272–73, and 274 credits significant priority to 2 articles totalling nearly 30 pp., by Heinrich Birnbach, in the 1827–28 vols. of the Berlin *Allgemeine musikalische Zeitung.* Ritzel points to Birnbach's ternary concept and his derivation of the principles from the actual literature rather than the a priori postulation of a theory, with exx. to fit, by the subsequent "pragmatists" (p. 214), Czerny, Marx, *et al.* Birnbach did not use the term "sonata form." On the inadequacy of the pragmatic approach as a source of musicological information, cf. W. F. Korte in AfMW XXI (1964) 9–10.

well worth emphasizing because to the extent that his textbook description was a fair abstraction of the still fluid Classic forms (SCE 115–17), it provided an astonishing illustration of the degree to which theory can trail practice.[23] Not until as much as sixty years after some of the masterworks of Haydn, Mozart, Beethoven, and Clementi had appeared, and not even until well after the entire sonatas of Dussek and Weber and the first of Schumann and Chopin had been composed did anyone write an explicit description of what happens in a sonata.

However, in 1845, three years before Czerny's Op. 600 finally was published, a still more explicit description appeared, nearly three times as detailed. It is a 137-page section in the first edition of the third of the four highly influential, often reprinted volumes in *Die Lehre von der musikalischen Komposition* by Adolph Bernhard Marx.[24] Marx devoted much attention to details of phrase-and-period syntax, he preferred a ternary to a binary concept of "sonata form," and he included among the other movements the overlapping types like the "sonata rondo" and the "fugal sonata." In the preface to this volume (p. v), he said that its publication was only made possible by improvements in the methods and quality of teaching over the previous few years. Actually, Marx's second volume, which had already appeared in 1838 and presumably was written about the same time as Czerny's discussion, incorporated a preliminary statement that summarizes the same basic points in five pages and even seems to assume a general knowledge of the information on the reader's part.[25] Included, at least in brief, are the distinctions between "sonata form" and the sonata cycle in several movements, "sonata form" and the rondo principle, "sonata form" as a two- and as a three-part concept, the tonal course of major and of minor "sonata forms," and variants in the thematic design of "sonata form."

The theorists' treatment of the sonata has always given the lion's share of attention to the first fast movement, sometimes to the almost total neglect of the other movements. As discussed in our previous volume (SCE 26–35), few theorists had shown more than a hazy recognition of "sonata form" during the Classic Era and up to the late 1830's. H. C. Koch was seen to come closest to such recognition in his explanation of the first movement of a symphony, with, however, an implication that the sonata was less classifiable and somewhat different (more intimate) in style (SCE 32–34). Between Koch and the clear,

---

23. D. F. Tovey comments aptly on this discrepancy in BRITANNICA XVI 11–12.
24. Marx/LEHRE III 194–330. Cf. MGG VIII 1734–38 (K. Hahn); Ritzel/SONATEN-FORM 228–36.
25. Marx/LEHRE II 497–501.

precise explanations of Czerny and Marx, a significant missing link can be found in an eight-page discussion of "fully-developed binary design" in the final volume, published in Paris in 1826,[26] of Anton Reicha's notable *Traité de haute composition musicale*. Although this discussion does not mention the word "sonata" and does not quite recognize the ternary implications of the design, it does cover the essentials (including the terms "exposition" and "development"), as the chart reproduced in Ex. 1 illustrates. It should be added that Czerny had known this chart well, since it was he who translated Reicha's work, along with two earlier treatises by Reicha, for the bilingual edition published in Vienna in 1832 (not 1834).[27]

Descriptions in Other Writings

In general, other 19th-century writers on music, even the lexicographers, were slower than these enterprising theorists to arrive at explicit statements about design in the sonata. Among representative samples of what they did have to say,[28] the description of the symphony and sonata by Friedrich Schneider (ssb VIII) in the earliest editions, 1820 and 1827, of his treatise on harmony and composition failed to disclose any structural principles.[29] F.-H.-J. Blaze wrote even less on these two genres in his dictionary of 1821, his remarks being merely paraphrased in Peter Lichtenthal's dictionary of 1826.[30] Fétis in 1830 simply likened the sonata, for one, two, or three instruments, to chamber music for more instruments, as being "a sort of symphony" in miniature, though, he said in effect, it rarely included the minuet (or scherzo) that the symphony's perfecters, from Vanhal to Beethoven, had added to the cycle of a binary quick movement ("en deux parties"), a slower movement, and a rondo.[31] Gustav Schilling, editor of the valuable, six-volume *Universal-Lexicon*, disregarded structural principles, concentrating only on the scoring and the deleterious effect of specific programmes (cf. *infra*), in his article of 1838 on the sonata.[32] The brothers Escudier dealt mainly with the cycle, values,

26. Not 1824 for Vol. II (as in MGG XI 148 and Ritzel/SONATENFORM 280); cf. GROVE VII 107 and Cat. NYPL XXV 412.

27. Reicha & Czerny/COMPOSITION, from which our Ex. 1 comes. Although Czerny did add some comments of his own, Mrs. Birgitte Moyer (*supra*) confirms that the discussion and chart in question are unaltered from the original French ed. (which is at the Library of Congress). Cf., also, Ritzel/SONATENFORM 249–57, 271–72.

28. Cf. Newman/THEORISTS for further citations; also, SCE 116 for a typical, concise summary by a theorist after Marx (Ernst Pauer, 1878).

29. Schneider/ELEMENTS 120–21.

30. CASTIL-BLAZE (1825 ed.) 287, 271–72; LICHTENTHAL 197–98, 208–9.

31. Fétis/MUSIQUE 224–30.

32. Schilling/LEXICON VI 418–20.

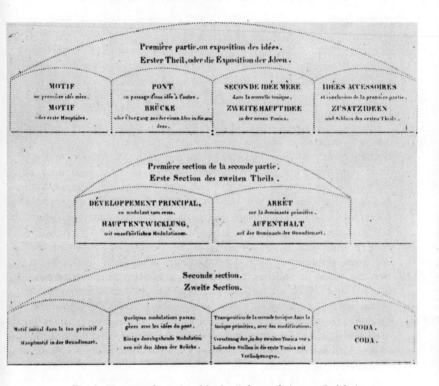

Ex. 1. "La grande coupe binaire," facs. of Anton Reicha's
chart in Reicha & Czerny/COMPOSITION IV 1165.

performance, and composers of the sonata, but not its forms, in their
music dictionary of 1844.[33] Except for names of more recent composers, F. S. Gassner did not go beyond the generalities of most 18th-
century definitions of "sonata" in his 1849 abridgment of Schilling/
LEXICON.[34] In fact, not until 1865 do we find a clear, full dictionary
summary of the principles detailed by Czerny and Marx, and then
it occurs in Arrey von Dommer's complete revision of Koch's *Musikalisches Lexikon* of 1802.[35] Even after 1865 such detailed explanations remained infrequent. Mainly, there appeared relatively brief
explanations like a pamphlet, "On the Structure of a Sonata," by
G. A. Macfarren (SSB XIV), which was published in London about

33. ESCUDIER II 87–88.
34. GASSNER 790.
35. DOMMER & KOCH 779–89 (plus pp. 789–91 on "die ältere Sonate").

1867;[36] or a paragraph in the article of 1878 in Hermann Mendel's *Musikalisches Conversations-Lexikon*;[37] or a page of explanation in an article by Ludwig Nohl, "The Father of the Symphony" (Haydn), published serially in 1880–81;[38] or about three pages in the article on "Form" by C. H. H. Parry that appeared in 1879 in the first edition (with much of it still retained through the present 5th ed.) of *Grove's Dictionary*.[39]

Interestingly enough, in spite of the lag we have noted between theory and practice, and the even greater delay in the recognition of "sonata form" by other writers on music, frequent references were made right from the start of the 19th century to "the usual form of the sonata" (or some such words), and generally with the implication that this form, however it may have been viewed, was already a matter of common knowledge. Furthermore, by the time the specific explanations did appear, the references to "sonata form" were beginning to imply that it was already passé. For example, as early as 1803 the Swiss publisher Nägeli was rejecting "the usual sonata form" (SCE 26) when he solicited sonatas from Steibelt, Liste, Hoffmann (SSB VII and VIII), and others. In a letter of 1838, Schumann wrote, "I no longer think about form [as a mold to be filled?] when I compose; [instead] I create it [intuitively?]." [40] Yet several times we shall find him calling attention to departures from what he regarded as standard sonata procedures, as in his review in 1841 of Chopin's "Funeral March Sonata," Op. 35 (SSB XII). Although in 1837 the first historian of the sonata, C. F. Becker, did not refer to any standard form,[41] six years later the second such historian did, even to summarizing the three divisions of "sonata form" in one sentence.[42] In 1849 the organ sonata was described as being less well defined (in its form) than the piano sonata.[43]

By 1862 Selmar Bagge was assuring his readers that although exact "sonata form" was not observed in Schubert's Op. 78/i, it did not have to be.[44] In 1868 a reviewer of the posthumous editions of Mendelssohn's Opp. 105 and 106 described as "obsolete" the requirement to repeat the "second part" of a "sonata form," at the same time adher-

36. Cf. the review of it in MT XV (1871) 282.
37. Mendel/LEXIKON IX 299–306 (chiefly p. 303).
38. Nohl/SYMPHONY, especially pp. 597–98.
39. GROVE 1st ed., I 548–49 and 550–51; references to this explanation suffice in Parry's article on the "Sonata," which first appeared in 1883 in Vol. III, pp. 554–84.
40. Gertler/SCHUMANN 111 fn.
41. Becker/KLAVIERSONATE. Cf. *infra*.
42. Faisst/CLAVIERSONATE 22 and 55.
43. NZM XXX (1849) 186.
44. Bagge/SCHUBERT 34.

ing to tradition by singling out the development as "that crucial test of a composer's power." [45] In 1875, a reviewer of one Gustav Wolff's "Four Sonatinas" for P solo objected to the lack of any attribute but the routine "classical mould." [46] And in 1882 a reviewer expressed disappointment in new sonatas by W. Berger (ssb XI), H. Franke (ssb XVII), F. Hummel (ssb X), and P. Rüfer (ssb XII), because they did not advance beyond traditional forms. As he put it, in scarcely one out of a hundred such works, sight unseen, would he err by starting his review, "With regard to the form, the gentlemen X, Y, and Z have in their newest works kept faithfully to the norms established by our predecessors and have strictly avoided any arbitrary deviation from the holy rules." [47]

Moreover, the same reviewer found that all but one of the composers (F. Hummel) failed to achieve what became almost a *sine qua non* of the late-Romantic Era—that is, cyclical unity, chiefly through thematic interrelationships of the movements. Elisabeth von Herzogenberg had such interrelationships in mind within a single movement when she wrote to Brahms of her delight in discovering how the coda of his Op. 108/i confirms the organism of the "sonata form." [48] We shall see in later chapters how many late-Romantics emphasized this aspect of the sonata cycle and "sonata form," among them d'Indy (ssb XIII) and MacDowell (ssb XIX), who not only exploited but wrote about it.

Meanwhile, the resistance to, and concern with, textbook "sonata form" as a musical law or standard continued to rise. In a letter of 1888 to Bülow, Richard Strauss explained his growing interest in programme music by declaring,

From the F minor symphony [1884] onwards I have found myself in a gradually ever increasing contradiction between the musical-poetic content that I want to convey a[nd] the ternary sonata form that has come down to us from the classical composers. In the case of Beethoven the musical-poetic content was for the most part completely covered by this very '*Sonata form*,' which he raised to its highest point, wholly expressing in it what he felt and wanted to say. Yet already there are to be found works of his (the last movement of the A flat major sonata, Adagio of the A minor quartet, etc.), where for a new content he had to devise a new form. Now, what was for Beethoven a 'form' absolutely in congruity with the highest, most glorious content, is now, after 60 years, used as a formula inseparable from our instrumental music (which I strongly dispute), simply to accommodate and enclose a 'pure musical' (in the strictest and narrowest meaning of the word) content, or

45. mt XIII (1868) 382 and 387. Cf. *infra*, on the question of originality.
46. mt XVII (1875) 275.
47. mw XIII (1882) 555–56.
48. brahms briefwechsel II 211.

worse, to stuff and expand a content with which it does not correspond. . . . Of course, purely formalistic, Hanslickian music-making will no longer be possible, and we cannot have any more random patterns, that mean nothing either to the composer or the listener, and no symphonies (Brahms excepted, of course) that always give me the impression of being giant's clothes, made to fit a Hercules, in which a thin tailor is trying to comport himself elegantly.[49]

But whereas Strauss sought to escape the rigidity of the form itself, others sought to escape the rigidity of form classifications. Bernard Shaw as music critic wrote in 1891 regarding a new biography of Chopin,

I am made somewhat restive by such passages as:
"In the Concerto, Chopin's subordination to, and inability to cope with, form was as conspicuous as was his superiority and independence of it in his smaller works."
This implies that form means sonata form and nothing else, an unwarranted piece of pedantry, which one remembers as common enough in the most incompetent and old-fashioned criticisms of Chopin's ballades, Liszt's symphonic poems, and Wagner's work generally, but which is now totally out of countenance.[50]

C. H. H. Parry argued about 1900 that the "sonata form" that had once served an aristocratic, conventional, complexly organized society so well was by now too formal and inflexible to be adapted to the newer poetic and spiritual content.

Others preferred to delve deeper into the meaning of "sonata form"—for instance, Otto Klauwell in 1897 (2 years before his short son. history appeared; cf. *infra*). Klauwell explained its "higher" significance, in the absence of a poetic text or any practical function, as a dramatic, dualistic conflict followed by its resolution.[51] Then there was the Russian theorist and composer S. I. Taneyev, who excelled in his imaginative, resourceful teaching of the principles of "sonata form," as reported by a former student during 1905–6.[52] And there was August Halm, who in 1913 published his study, "On Two Cultures of Music." In this study Halm saw the contrast of monistic and dualistic (sonata) principles as the essential distinction between Baroque and Classic music.[53]

49. As trans. in BÜLOW-STRAUSS 82–83. Cf., also, Ernest Newman's hope in 1908 that someone would get rid of "this system of Chinese compression" by writing a monograph "On Sonata Form, Its Cause and Cure," as quoted in Finck/GRIEG 231; and further comments in H. T. Finck's previous book on Grieg (New York: John Lane, 1906), pp. 102–3.
50. Shaw/LONDON II 209; cf., also, II 305, 306, 307.
51. Klauwell/ÄSTHETISCHE.
52. TEMPO XXXIX (1956) 14–15 (T. de Hartmann).
53. Halm/KULTUREN, especially pp. 7–143.

Pessimistic and Optimistic Views

Throughout the Romantic Era there was a steady stream of pessimistic opinions to the effect that the sonata had already or would soon come to its end, recalling similar statements encountered in both the Baroque and Classic Eras (cf. SBE 26, 31; SCE 37, 47). That there actually was something of a slump in sonata production and a turn to trivial music, especially in the 1830's (cf. SSB I), is borne out by statistics in Chapter IV. There also was a steady stream of optimistic opinions about the sonata's status and prognosis. But, true to form, the pessimists outnumbered the optimists. A sampling of these conflicting opinions, unavoidably repetitious at times, follows in one separate chronology each for the pessimists and the optimists.

To start with some negative opinions on the sonata's status, we find W. J. Tomaschek (SSB XVII) recalling in his autobiography of 1846 how even before 1810 "a strange disinterest in the sonata for piano and the symphony for orchestra had become evident. Innumerable [sets of] variations were expected to do in place of the pianist's sonatas, and overtures in place of the orchestra's symphonies." [54] The American church composer Thomas Hastings wrote briefly of the symphony and somewhat disparagingly of the extravagance and display in etudes, concertos, and variations, disregarding the sonata entirely, in his book of 1822 on musical taste.[55] With reference to three piano sonatas by Charles Ambrose (SSB XIV), an English reviewer noted in 1825 that the sonata had become unfamiliar and its style outmoded.[56] In Paris by 1830 Fétis asserted,

In the last several years the sonata has fallen into discredit. A certain futility of taste, which has contaminated music, has replaced the serious forms of this sort with kinds of lighter works that are called fantasias, *airs variés*, capriccios, etc.[57]

In 1832 a London review of Pio Cianchettini's Op. 26 began, shrewdly enough,

A *sonata* once more!—The newest fashions after all are but old ones forgotten and revived. . . . But has the sonata been defunct long enough to have slipped clean out of memory?—Hardly; and Mr. Cianchettini may have performed the operation of resuscitation rather too soon. At all events, we are quite sure that his sonata is too good, and, we must add, too difficult, to become popular just now, or to rekindle a passion for the old title.[58]

54. Trans. from the German in Kahl/LYRISCHE 61.
55. Hastings/TASTE 148–53.
56. HARMONICON III/1 (1825) 139.
57. Fétis/MUSIQUE 230.
58. HARMONICON X/1 (1832) 256.

In Germany in 1833, the lexicographer Carl Gollnick said again that sonatas had given way to potpourris and the like,[59] and in 1838 the conservative lexicographer Gustav Schilling said the sonata had become a "mere jangle." [60] Also in 1838, a reviewer (of C. Decker's Op. 10, ssb VIII) wished that the time for the sonata were more appropriate so that the considerable values it did have would not be neglected.[61] A year later, in the most extended discussion of the problem encountered here,[62] G. W. Fink attributed this neglect not to the younger composers, as was being charged by the professional pianists, but to the current taste of the public and the dilettante pianists, which was discouraging publishers from printing more than a few out of a substantial number of sonatas actually being created. It is true, he added, that the younger composer was less interested in following the past masters and was writing mainly patchwork music. But he should not be judged on his Op. 1 alone and the sonata should not be viewed as dead, merely asleep.

Schumann, though barely through composing his own three important piano sonatas, wrote similarly, in 1839 and 1841, about the decline of the sonata:

Strange [it is] that suddenly there are mostly unknowns who are writing sonatas; [and] further, that it is precisely the older composers still living amongst us—those who grew up in the sonata's heyday and from whom admittedly only Cramer and Moscheles could be named as most outstanding—who [now] cultivate the genre least. It is easy to guess what moves the former, mostly young[er] artists [i.e., the unknowns]. There is no worthier form by which they might introduce and ingratiate themselves [better] in the eyes of the finer critics. But in consequence most sonatas of this sort can be considered only as a kind of testing grounds, as studies in form. They are scarcely born out of a strong inner compulsion. . . . Occasional lovely manifestations of this sort are sure to appear here and there, and [some] already have done so. But otherwise it seems the form has run its course, and this [drop-off] is certainly in the order of things, and [what is more] we should not have to repeat the same [form] year after year and at the same time deliberate over the new. So one writes sonatas or fantasias (what matters the name!); let one not forget music and the rest will succeed through our good genius. . . .

[The sonata is] but smiled at with pity in France and scarcely more than tolerated even in Germany. . . .[63]

In 1843 a German reviewer argued that the orchestral symphony was

59. Gollnick/TERMINOLOGIE 136.
60. Schilling/LEXICON VI 418.
61. AMZ XL (1838) 160.
62. AMZ XLI (1839) 181–84.
63. Trans. from Schumann/SCHRIFTEN I 394–95, 452.

likely to retain its popularity indefinitely and unchallenged.[64] But he still felt that, with only a few exceptions, the sonata, like the fugue, was giving way to those variations, rondos, capriccios, etudes, and other types that the dilettantes, afraid of the sonata's old-fashioned name and formalism, found more suitable to the (now) favorite instrument, the pianoforte, and to helping their own popularity. It was in 1843, too, that the Leipzig publisher C. A. Klemm preferred to issue Schubert's Sonata in E, D. 459, as *Fünf Klavierstücke,* apparently because the title "sonata" had become old-fashioned.[65] Bearing out one of Schumann's remarks (*supra*), a Parisian review of 1845 began by saying the sonata had been unpopular in France for thirty years.[66] In 1852 Bülow could find nothing of value in the sonata since Beethoven except Hummel's Op. 81 in f♯ (ssb VIII) and the contributions of Schumann and Chopin.[67] In 1855 the French lexicographer Charles Soullier persisted in regarding the sonata as having "died with the 18th century that produced it so abundantly." [68] And when Rubinstein came to London in 1856, Edward Bache reported that "the publishers won't bite" on his sonatas and that in another year or so it would be "a good time [instead] for simple musical music again." [69]

Indeed, in spite of the succession of masterworks from Schubert to Reger, a decline in the sonata continued to be remarked and lamented right through the Romantic Era, and still longer. Thus, in 1871 a reviewer saw this decline in the scholasticism of the current sonata, but now he advanced its former heyday, like the symphony's, to include Schumann among its onetime masters. By 1895 Shedlock advanced the heyday another generation to include Brahms among its masters. But near the end of his pioneer sonata history he still wondered whether time would include Liszt. "Is Liszt's sonata [in b] a Phoenix rising from its ashes? Shall we be able to say 'La sonata est morte! Vive la sonate!' Time will tell. Hitherto Liszt's work has not borne fruit." [70] In 1901 in Paris the music critic Camille Bellaigue proclaimed the end of the sonata, that "admirable, vanished species." [71] In America one early writer on MacDowell said "sonata

64. amz XLV (1843) 453.
65. Cf. Brown/schubert 57. Schubert's *Grand Duo* in C, D. 812, was also originally called "Sonata" (ssb VII).
66. rgm, March 3, 1845, p. 68.
67. bülow briefe III 50; originally in nzm XXXVI (1852) 234.
68. Quoted in Shedlock/sonata 220 from Soullier/dictionnaire.
69. Bache/bache 77.
70. Shedlock/sonata 220. The answer in 1903 in Schüz/sonate was that Liszt's Son. in b does promise to be "the sonata of the future."
71. *Guide musical* (Brussels) XLVII (1901) 99–101.

form" in particular was "consigned to hopeless antiquity" and another to "perdition." [72] And in 1920 the Swiss historian Karl Nef concluded—quite unjustly, it is felt here—that the 19th century "was unable to maintain itself on the lofty plane of the sonata." [73]

Among the fewer, more optimistic views of the 19th-century sonata's trends, one might cite, from 1840, a reviewer who indicated full respect for the Classic masterworks but urged more respect for the newer, more brilliant, fuller-textured sonata styles, too.[74] Or one might cite, from 1845, another reviewer (F. Brendel?), who acknowledged a low ebb of interest, but now found sonatas stirring everywhere again, most of them better than expected. "Flügel, Chopin, Winterle, Evers, even Thalberg and Kalkbrenner have composed and published them, . . . some at their own expense and others, who had better luck or better known names, at other people's expense." [75] In the following year the same reviewer rejoiced that the quality and public interest were keeping pace with the quantity in the revival.[76] The entertaining English writer H. F. Chorley was able to acknowledge in 1860 that the thirty-year period that "has seen the return (after a season of eclipse) to the noble but grave [?] sonatas of Clementi and Dussek has also seen the establishment of the wayward, incomplete, fantastic, yet most fascinating Chopin, on a pedestal of his own." [77] The periodicals of the 1860's and 1870's do reflect a growing interest in sonatas and chamber music[78] as against the variations and potpourris of the previous generation that Schumann had opposed in his idealistic, imaginary "League of David" (ssb VIII) but that other writers and countries had accepted with much less question.[79] A German writer in 1873, exactly contradicting contemporary views by the pessimists (supra), attributed the sonata's improved status over the past thirty years to greater interest on the part of amateurs in a territory previously ruled by the aristocracy and the professionals, to increased popularity and sales of pianos, and to more frequent publications of sonatas.[80]

72. As quoted in Eagle/MACDOWELL 17.

73. Nef/HISTORY 301. Steger/CZERNY 74–77 continued in 1924 to reflect the idea that Schubert was too lyrical, Schumann too impassioned, and Chopin too confined to small forms to write fully valid (?) sons.

74. AMZ XLII (1840) 824–25.

75. NZM XXIII (1845) 177.

76. NZM XXIV (1846) 146.

77. Chorley/RECOLLECTIONS 398.

78. Cf. DMZ I–III (1860–62) passim (e.g., II [1861] 76 on music in Paris).

79. E.g., cf. RGM and HARMONICON, both passim, in the 1830's.

80. NZM LXIX/2 (1873) 493–94.

Standards and Tastes

Besides the conflicting opinions just quoted on falls and rises in the sonata's status, there were certain views or attitudes that remained more constant throughout the Romantic Era. One view was that of the sonata as an, if not *the*, ideal of both technical and musical achievement to which a composer might aspire—usually an ideal that related to Beethoven's image and one that could not be approached other than with the highest standards and greatest sincerity. Of course, especially during the sonata's slump in the second quarter of the 19th century, it is not hard to understand that almost any sonata would be likely to command high respect alongside the kinds of pieces on which the publishers were thriving. In any music catalogue or periodical of the time the sonatas appear only infrequently among long lists of pieces with titles such as those of the following piano solos: *Grand Military Divertimento*, by F. Ries (ssb VII); *A Favourite Air, from the Ballet of Nina, with Variations by Mayseder*, arranged by F. Ries; *"Cherry Ripe," composed by E. Horn, and arranged as a Rondo . . .* , by T. Valentine; *La Salle d'Apollon, a collection of German Waltzes.*[81]   81a

As a sample of respect for the sonata in that same early phase of the Romantic Era, a paragraph may be quoted from a letter of 1829 in which Karl Loewe (ssb VIII) offered four sonatas to the publisher T. Trautwein:

Don't be misled by the usual cries of unintelligent players and little informed publishers who think the sonata as such doesn't make a hit or do well; and that it would need a special title or the issuing of single movements from sonatas in order to provide a market for them, which (as one certainly sees) go as fast as they come—no; on the contrary, the sonata is for all times, and, especially for a productive composer, the most basic form, scarcely to be improved upon, [and] by [means of] which he often has the opportunity to show what he can do. And just so will the sonata always remain at the summit for unspoiled players (the Beethoven and Weber [sonatas] still demonstrate this [truth] every day). . . .[82]

In spite (or because?) of his pessimisms (*supra*), Schumann referred to the sonata as "this noble musical form" and cited a Sonata for P-duet by one G. Adler as worth mentioning only because it was cast in that "valued, distinguished form." [83] Two reviews, in 1844

---

81. These particular titles come from HARMONICON IV/1 (1826) 74–78; cf., also, the pieces pub. in Vol. IV/2.

82. Trans. from La Mara/MUSIKERBRIEFE II 131.

83. Schumann/SCHRIFTEN II 319, 320.

and 1855, of sonatas by C. Gurlitt (Opp. 3 and 16; ssb X) begin with these related statements:

> Under the pressing flood of worthless trivialities, rhapsodic ideas, pleasant nothings, [and] rehashing of foreign ideas, it is truly pleasant to find now and then the higher aspiration to, and the concentrated strength for, more important accomplishments; [and] even more pleasant to find a young aspiring artist in the beginning of his career who scorns a cheap attempt [to win] audience approval and [who] endeavors [instead] to win entrance to the temple of honor by greater and more art-worthy creations [i.e., sonatas]. . . .
>
> If a composer puts himself to the test with one of the greatest and most important art forms, which the sonata is, the highest demands will be made of him, because not only are an honorable endeavor [and] an artistic conviction required, but after such great examples [as those of the Classic masters] there must be, besides strong talent, a perfect mastery of form and, generally speaking, the technical wherewithal—in short, a superior grade of artistic maturity.[84]

Musical standards would be raised, said a reviewer in 1872, if more sonatas were still being written.[85] One M. E. Doorley was advised in 1874 to write smaller pieces rather than his Sonata in G, for P solo, under review, for the composing of sonatas presupposed "high[er] standards" of art and craft.[86] And in a typical discussion of the same question, a reviewer of a Sonata in D by J. Edwards (ssb XIV) concluded that the "higher standard of art" demanded by the sonata made it beyond the grasp of a "new" composer.[87] Two acrid reviews, in 1875 and 1879, rejected the title "sonata" for works by L. Tarnowski and A. W. Dreszer (both ssb XVII) because of low standards as well as excessive freedoms.[88]

The two reviews just mentioned bring up a special aspect of the Romantic sonata's association with high ideals, which is the constant quest for originality, almost as though originality were an aesthetic fact in itself. We saw this quest develop in the Classic Era (e.g., sce 41–42, 383–84). It was already present in the early 19th century when, for example, a reviewer wrote that a sonata cannot be a mere routine; there must be some caprice, exploration, and originality, if not excessive.[89] It reappeared endlessly in what we shall find to be the most frequent and pat expression in neutral or less favorable reviews of sonatas—"good craftsmanship, but lacking in originality." And it nettled a composer like Rubinstein who complained that "the minute

84. nzm XX (1844) 115 and XLIII (1855) 278.
85. mmr II (1872) 93.
86. mt XVI (1874) 585.
87. mt XVII (1875) 533.
88. mw VI (1875) 513 and X (1879) 366.
89. amz XIV (1812) 392.

a musician leans in his style upon Schumann, Chopin, Mendelssohn, Wagner, [or] Liszt, he is harshly reproached for it [the derivation] and it is cited as [evidence for] a lack of originality—which [inequity] leads the [musical] young to the quest for originality [for its own sake], and how often to the unbeautiful!" [90]

To be sure, originality did often lack in the many sonatas that conformed to a traditional or textbook routine. And it did lack (as too often in Rubinstein's own sons.) in the many sonatas with weak ideas—that is, without melodic distinction. But that phrase "originality, if not excessive" rightly suggests conservative limitations in the quest for originality. In most instances the reviewers' "originality" or "creative spark" could be translated as melodic distinction alone— an essential though hardly an all-inclusive trait. It will be recalled that Beethoven's originality became "bizarre" in the eyes and ears of his reviewers (e.g., SCE 512–13). As the 19th century wore on not many reviewers could greet genuine experimentation with the sympathy and understanding that Schumann's own "originality," rare musicianship, and exceptional literary background permitted. And even Schumann revealed puzzlement over a work like Chopin's Sonata in b♭, Op. 35 (SSB XII).

An incidental facet of the quest for originality is the persistent emphasis in the later 19th century (after "sonata form" had spread through the textbooks) on the development section as the main outlet for originality. Thus, we read in a review of Benjamin Dale's notable Sonata in d, ". . . we pass on to the development, in which the composer shows us of what stuff he is made of [!]." [91] Originality in that sense simply means freedom from more specific textbook stipulations. That the development section has no monopoly on originality in masterworks of the Romantic sonata hardly needs any special defense here.

Orientations, Chiefly Historical

Certain currents and conflicts within Romantic musical thought may be touched on now as they bore on the larger orientations of the Romantic sonata—that is, on its relations to other times, other music, and other art. There was, for example, the moot question as to whether the sonata was essentially an academicism in the 19th century, because of its derivation from the masterworks of musical classicism, or was actually a valid manifestation of musical Romanti-

90. Extracted from a longer statement trans. in SSB XVIII.
91. MT LIX (1918) 165.

cism. We have seen that Reicha advanced the understanding of the sonata in 1824 (*supra*). Yet his own outlook, like that of the two other main theorists in the early century, S. Sechter and M. Hauptmann, was based on the past and was anti-Romantic.[92] The writer Rochlitz was more on the fence. In a review of two sonatas by Weber, in 1818 (ssb VIII), he wondered how to treat the new phenomenon, which had expanded so greatly in size and content that all was changed but the terminology.[93] Should he measure it against past criteria and censure it accordingly, or recognize the disparity between theory and practice and view it for what it is? Schumann became an anti-Classic when he reviewed new sonatas:

> There is one group of sonatas that are most difficult to discuss. They are those correctly written, honest, well-intended ones such as the Mozart-Haydn school produced by the hundreds [and] from which examples still appear here and there. To fault them one would have to fault the sound human mind that created them. They have natural continuity, dignified bearing. . . . However, to draw attention nowadays, or merely to please, it takes more than simply being honest. And did Beethoven then live in vain? . . . In brief, the sonata style of 1790 is not that of 1840. The demands of form and content have increased in all respects.[94]

A second not quite answerable question was that of how importantly the Romantic sonata rated in the total panorama of Romantic music. Of course, its relative importance varied from country to country, as will be seen in Chapter IV, on the spread of the Romantic sonata. And that importance can be documented at least roughly by publication statistics, which also are to be found in Chapter IV. But in any case there is good reason to argue that instrumental music in general, and piano music in particular, achieved new importance in the 19th century—in fact, became the predominant "voice" of musical Romanticism.[95] To be sure, at the start of the era, much of the orientation was still toward opera or church music. Thus, Schubert was unable to get help from his teacher Salieri in the how of constructing a sonata, for "Salieri understood singing and the older operatic form but of instrumental music (sonata, quartet, symphony) he had as little idea as he had of true church music." [96]

Furthermore, some of the 18th-century suspicion of absolute, purely instrumental music still persisted in the 19th century. One reads, for

---

92. Cf. Werner/MENDELSSOHN 52.

93. AMZ XX (1818) 681–83.

94. Trans. from Schumann/SCHRIFTEN II 11; among several similar statements, cf. Vols. II 307, and I 276–77, 363.

95. Cf. Einstein/ROMANTIC 32–37, 198–200.

96. Deutsch/SCHUBERT–M 112 (L. von Sonnleithner).

example, continuing references to that celebrated quip attributed to Fontenelle at least since 1755, "Sonata, what good are you to me?" [97] But these references now turn less on the broad question of the validity of absolute music than on the specific one of the validity of a sonata tied to a programme. No student of Romanticism in the arts will be surprised at the frequency with which that specific question arises in Part Two of the present volume. But he may well be surprised at how rarely the association is more than skin deep between a sonata, even the most poetic sort, and any verbal, titular, visual, or mood-type programme. Schilling ridiculed programmatic sonata titles in 1838, suggesting, for example, that "Departure from London" could just as well be "Departure from Frankfurt." [98] But he did grant that there might be a valid analogy between poetic and musical mood in such a sonata title as that of Dussek's *Élégie harmonique*. Although Schumann ridiculed such titles, too, as well as programmatic inscriptions,[99] his numerous references in his reviews and his approaches to his own sonatas show him to have been at least ambivalent, if not on the other side, on the question of sonata programmes (as discussed, with further references and sources, in SSB VIII).

With further regard to programmatic influences, a typical discussion in 1860 centered around doubts that the listener would enjoy, say, Mendelssohn's "Calm Sea" (Overture, Op. 27) any less if he did not know the title, since "Every art work is beautiful through what it is, not through what it means." [100] Yet in the same periodical, two years later, is a statement to the effect that Schubert's Sonata in a, Op. 143 (D. 784), appeals primarily to our sense of imagery.[101] A writer in 1868 distinguished the sonata and symphony from "descriptive music," but still managed to find extramusical functions for them, the sonata being the place where "a mental problem is clearly worked out," and the symphony where a "profound system of philosophy [is] developed." [102] In 1892 Bernard Shaw as music critic wrote of a programmatic overture that it was "a predestined failure, since it is impossible to tell a story in sonata form, because the end of a story is not a recapitulation of the beginning, and the end of a move-

97. Cf. SBE 353, SCE 36–37 and 605; also, Egert/FRÜHROMANTIKER 43 (citing a reference in 1800), CASTIL-BLAZE 272 (questioning its significance, in 1821), ESCUDIER II 88 (citing, in 1844, a parody by Fétis), NZM XLVIII (1858) 103 (Bülow).

98. Schilling/LEXICON VI 419.

99. E.g., Schumann/SCHRIFTEN I 91, 92, 306.

100. DMZ I (1860) 153–56 (W. Wauer).

101. DMZ III (1862) 41.

102. MT XIII (1868) 599.

ment in sonata form is." [103] But one is then reminded of H. G. Sear's efforts to show that Strindberg called his play *Spöksonaten* (*Ghost Sonata*; 1907) because (and only because) he was actually organizing the scenes into the sections of "sonata form." [104] One is also reminded of J. Todhunter's poem called *Beethoven's* "*Sonata Appassionata*," which literally parallels the themes and sections in all three move- ments of the music, as quoted and described by Calvin S. Brown.[105] In his letter of 1888 to Bülow (quoted *supra*) Strauss, like Shaw, found "sonata form" to be an unsatisfactory vehicle for the expres- sion of an extramusical idea. But he added, on the other hand, that unity of mood and consistency of structure are "only possible through the inspiration by a poetical idea, whether or not it be introduced as a programme." [106]

Turning to another aspect of Romanticism, we find that the well- known, newly developed consciousness of history in the 19th century touched the sonata quite as much as other music and other arts. Interest in the sonatas of past eras is evidenced both by recitals and by editions of early music, and by writers, too, whose historical ac- counts range from single paragraphs to full studies. It is true that today we find faults in every aspect of those pioneer efforts. Yet without them, faulty or not, the present knowledge of sonata history could hardly have been won.

Among historical accounts, there is a vague outline made in 1808 by E. T. A. Hoffmann for a projected article, never written, on the sonata.[107] This was followed in 1837 by what might be called the first historical account, C. F. Becker's short sketch of the keyboard sonata in Germany, centering around Kuhnau's supposed priority.[108] Then in 1845 came Imanuel Faisst's enterprising doctoral dissertation (79

103. Shaw/LONDON 82.

104. Sear/SPOOK. But Dr. Harry Bergholz, Chief Bibliographer of the Wilson Library at the University of North Carolina, has kindly called to my attention Strindberg's letter of April 1, 1907, to Emil Schering, in which he relates the title specifically to Beethoven's Op. 31/2 (known as the "Specter Sonata" on the continent), probably having in mind the same passage (iii/96–107) that he had cited earlier, in the stage directions to Act II/i in *Brott och Brott*.

105. Brown/TONES 56, 63, 120–28. Brown also refers to poems that describe sons. (Chopin's Op. 35, pp. 35–36; Schumann's Op. 105, p. 76) and poems that convey their feel (p. 140). Dr. Rey Longyear at the University of Kentucky kindly has called attention, by correspondence, to what he regards as a strained effort by W. F. Mainland to find a literal "sonata form" in F. von Matthison's poem "Abend- landschaft" because Schiller said the poet "made a lovely sonata of it"; cf., also, Longyear/SCHILLER 106, 128, 173.

106. BÜLOW-STRAUSS 82–83.

107. Hoffmann/SCHRIFTEN 16; trans. in full in SSB VIII.

108. Becker/KLAVIERSONATE; revised in 1840, with exx., in Becker/HAUSMUSIK 33–39. Cf. SBE 11–12, 240.

pp. in print) on the keyboard sonata up to Emanuel Bach.[109] Along
with several more short sketches,[110] the chief further contributions up
to World War I were C. H. H. Parry's 31-page article of 1883 in
the first edition of *Grove's Dictionary* (still largely intact in the 5th
ed.); Shedlock's valued book of 1895 on the piano sonata;[111] Klauwell's
book of 1899 on the sonata over all, incorporating chiefly Shedlock's
findings and the special researches of Wasielewski;[112] and Selva's book
of 1913 on the sonata in general, largely based on d'Indy's writings.[113]

As discussed earlier,[114] two interdependent currents of thought
dominate these accounts, both founded by Faisst on a philosophy of
historical evolution.[115] One is the idea that all sonata history falls
into one continuous chain of progressive events, especially the "evolution," bit by bit, of "sonata form." The other is the related or derived
idea that in particular the keyboard sonatas of Kuhnau, Scarlatti, and
Emanuel Bach fall into one "single chronological line leading directly
to full-fledged 'sonata form' " (SBE 11). Before the end of the era these
ideas hardened into standard history-book explanations such as are
still repeated in many recent summary accounts of the sonata.[116]
Representative of the last is this statement published in 1964, with its
traditional but actually untenable explanation of Emanuel Bach's
historical significance: J. S. Bach's son "Carl Philip Emanuel, who
counts for less in artistic interest and merit, is much more important
historically, for the part he played in the evolution of sonata form,
one of the most fertile discoveries of the human brain, makes him
historically one of the most important composers who have ever
lived." [117]

The Romantic historical consciousness touched the sonata in further
ways. It showed up in archaic titles such as "Sonata da camera" (as
by A. L. Peace; SSB XIV) or "Trio Sonate" (as by A. Sandberger; SSB

109. Faisst/CLAVIERSONATE.

110. Riehl/CHARAKTERKÖPFE 222–26; a "Historical Sketch of the Sonata," from
Biber to Schubert, in MMR I (1871) 100–102; a sketch by Otto Kade, in NZM
LXXI/1 (1876) 257–59 and 265–67; Bagge/SONATE; Eitner/SONATE (on early exx.
of "son. form"); Goldschmidt/SONATENFORM; Pougin/SONATE; Schüz/SONATE; Michel/
SONATE (collected lectures); Gascue/SONATA (collected lectures). Attention to son.
history is also paid in WAGNER PROSE V 81–85 *passim*.

111. Shedlock/SONATA; cf. the evaluative Foreword, pp. v–x, in the Da Capo
reprint of 1964 (W. S. Newman).

112. Klauwell/SONATE.

113. Selva/SONATE.

114. SBE 5–6, 240; SCE 15–16, 117–18, 261.

115. E.g., cf. Faisst/CLAVIERSONATE 7, 51 fn.

116. E.g., cf. Shedlock/SONATA 11–12, 125–26; Bie/PIANOFORTE 69, 86–90, 110,
168; Pougin/SONATE; Emmanuel/FRANCK 55–63; and Emmanuel/DUKAS 71; also,
Allen/PHILOSOPHIES 156, 291, 300–301 (with further exx.).

117. Howes/ENGLISH 11. Cf. SCE 429–30.

XI). It permeated the writings of musicians not especially concerned with the historical outlook. Thus, Moscheles (SSB VII), although he found Corelli's "trio" sonatas antiquated, showed an interest in early keyboard sonatas, especially in conjunction with his pioneer historical recitals.[118] Schumann even poked fun at historical interest in the sonata —"In short, one sought to introduce historical interest (laugh not, Eusebius!)"; yet he showed a curiosity about the genesis of its movements and, of course, a strong absorption in its Classic styles as demonstrated by the past, great masters, in spite of his objections to perpetuating these styles in the mid 19th century (as quoted *supra*).[119] But near the end of the era, when MacDowell showed an interest in sonata history as it had come to him through his German training, he supplied one example of how Schumann's objections had developed into blind spots. In particular, he voiced, to an extreme degree, the late-19th-century depreciations of Mozart's piano sonatas.[120]

The increasing number of historical recitals in the 19th century (cf. SSB I and III) introduced not only the sonatas of the greatest masters but of some of the lesser ones, too—for example, sonatas by Kuhnau (SBE 239–42), Paradisi (or Paradies; SCE 686–92), D. Scarlatti (SCE 261–73), S. Arnold (SCE 765), and Porpora (SBE 258–59).[121] With the recitals came the increasing number of editions of "old masters," edited by Bülow, Ernst Pauer, Köhler, and others. We think of these as infamous editions, today, because of the undeniable violence they did to the original text and contemporary performance practices. Yet they, too, contributed essentially, albeit narrowly and one-sidedly, to the foundations of sonata history.[122]

Finally, mention should be made of the pronounced rise of nationalistic feelings in the 19th century as these touched the sonata. Such feelings comprised one more concomitant of the Romantic historical consciousness (as well as the new and changing political forces; SSB I). Even at the start of the century Rochlitz felt compelled to ask why a German, F. Ries (SSB VII), should write his sonata dedication in French to another German, Beethoven.[123] Schumann, too, showed occa-

118. E.g., cf. MOSCHELES I 261, 304–10 (regarding a Handel festival he helped to organize); II 35–36.

119. E.g., Schumann/SCHRIFTEN I 59, II 11.

120. Cf. MacDowell/ESSAYS 193, 194, 200, 239, 253; SCE 500; SSB XIX.

121. Cf. the reports of such sons. being performed, in MT XVIII (1878) 161, XX (1879) 166, XXIII (1882) 661, XXIV (1882) 20 and 229, XXV (1884) 103; MERCURE II (Jan.–June, 1906) 526–31 (an article on current performances illustrating the "evolution" of the son. since the 18th century).

122. Cf. SCE 15.

123. AMZ IX (1806–7) 365. Recall Beethoven's own preference for German as against French or Italian titles and inscriptions in his late sons. (SCE 525, 529, 531).

sional prejudices against the French and Italians when he disparaged the recollections of their styles in certain weak German sonatas.[124] In 1855 his successor (as editor of NZM), Brendel, set the pattern for claiming the priority and superiority of the German sonata,[125] a pattern that was to arouse the ire of the equally chauvinistic Italian, Torrefranca (SCE 172–74). On the other hand, a French reviewer in 1843 already lamented the infiltration of new styles and resultant deterioration after "a century of French dominance in the sonata." [126] Outlying countries, much newer to the sonata, quickly showed their own nationalistic zeal, producing sonatas "in Hungarian style," "in Russian style," and so on (SSB XVII and XVIII). Only the English and Americans seemed to welcome—in fact, sometimes prefer—foreign influences. Thus, an English reviewer, writing on a Sonata, Op. 20, by Stanford, made passing mention of those "leading German musicians, whose utterances always awaken interest and expectation" (SSB XIV).

124. E.g., cf. Schumann/SCHRIFTEN I 92 and 452.
125. E.g., Brendel/GESCHICHTE I 193, 299.
126. RGM for Dec. 10, 1843, pp. 419–20.

Chapter III

The Sonata in Romantic Society

Sources and Functions

How did the sonata figure in Romantic society? Answers to that question are no readier at hand nor easier to assemble than they were for the corresponding questions in our previous two volumes. The surprisingly few books that take a sociological view of all music history are too broad to allow appreciable space to any single instrumental genre like the sonata.[1] But the source materials that would be essential to a full account of the sonata's place in society do prove to be more abundant for the Romantic than for the Baroque or Classic Era (cf. SBE 33–34; SCE 43–44). They include all those memoirs, diaries, letters, travel reports, intimate biographies, and periodical notices or reviews that were mentioned earlier (SSB I). From such sources and from an occasional survey already done in the 19th century like Hanslick's on Vienna concert life (Hanslick/WIEN), rich studies wait to be prepared on Romantic concert life (to put the most needed topic first) and on the pursuit of music in the Romantic Era, whether as a profession, as an avocation, or in education. Clearly, any such study would be of immediate value, as in the present chapter.

In the Classic Era the three main functions of Baroque music still carried over—that is, music at court, in church, and in the theater (SBE 33–34, SCE 43–44). But the Classic sonata profited extensively only from the first of these functions, at court. Furthermore, it fulfilled two other functions increasingly, that of diversion for the middle-class amateur and that of pedagogic material for teachers and students. In

1. One does find a briefly pertinent section on the Beethoven son. in the Marxist-oriented study Knepler/XIX (Vol. II, Chap. V, *passim*), and on the instrumental soloist in Engel/GESELLSCHAFT 149. And as in both SBE and SCE, there are numerous occasions throughout SSB to cite findings on musicians, pubs., and instruments, in the excellent, more specialized study Loesser/PIANOS (cf. SCE 43–44).

the Romantic Era, all three Baroque functions ceased to concern the sonata to any important extent. No use of the sonata in the theater has turned up here. The only appreciable use in church was that of the organ sonata, mainly during the Offertory and to supply informal preludes and postludes in the Protestant service.[2] Intended for such use (according to dedications, titles, chorale themes, etc.) were numerous organ sonatas that we shall meet in later chapters, by Mendelssohn, Merkel, Reubke, Karg-Elert, Rheinberger, and several British and American composers. The sonata's use at court, especially during the earlier 19th century, was more extensive than in church—in fact, still considerable. But rarely does the court connection seem to have been the prime stimulus for any significant output of Romantic sonatas. When Schubert dedicated his Op. 42 (D. 845) to Archduke Rudolph of Austria (Beethoven's most honored dedicatee) or Weber and Loewe their Opp. 24 and 32, respectively, to Grand Duchess Maria Paulowna at Weimar, they were not serving at court but simply currying ducal favor.

In any case, of more importance to the Romantic sonata were its increasing functions as diversional and as pedagogic material, and now more than ever as solid fare in public and private recitals. Since the sonata as recital fare seems to have been a primary goal of the principal sonata composers, its function in that capacity is considered first and foremost here. After all, most Romantic sonatas are difficult to play, both artistically and athletically. Only highly trained performers could hope to project them satisfactorily. The German writer W. H. von Riehl may have been understating the abilities of not a few serious, enthusiastic, middle-class avocationalists when he wrote in 1853, "Since Beethoven the quartets and trios have become concert music, only [professional] virtuosos can still play the [music written for] piano, and the comfortable, genial, instrumental domestic music [by the Vienna Classic masters] exists not at all anymore."[3] But in the century before the widespread development of phonographs, player pianos, radio, and television, each sonata had to be performed anew and by an advanced performer every time it was to be heard. And it was the recital, public or private, that provided the chief opportunities. Our interest at the moment is in who gave these recitals and what they played.

The Recitalists

Most of the leading 19th-century recitalists who gave prominence to the sonata in their programs were cited earlier in connection with Beethoven's all-pervasive influence and with historical recitals (ssb I). Liszt, "Klara" (Schumann, née Wieck), and Moscheles were the pioneer piano recitalists in the 1830's, with Clara continuing for more than a half century. Anton Rubinstein and Bülow followed in the 1840's and 1850's, both continuing for more than forty years. And Paderewski, d'Albert, Rachmaninoff, and Hofmann were among the leaders around the end of the era.[4] Chopin was one great pianist who, in his remarkably few public recitals, played little but his own music, apart from joining in occasional duets and larger ensembles. Even among his own sonatas Chopin seems to have played only Op. 65, for Vc & P, in public (with Franchomme; ssb XII). Some of the pianists who did much for the sonata did most of their playing on their home ground rather than internationally. Such, for example, were Charles Hallé, Arabella Goddard, and Agnes Zimmerman in London; or Raoul Pugno and Blanche Selva in Paris; or Golinelli, Martucci, and Longo in Italy. Other celebrated pianists, like Field, Steibelt, Kalkbrenner, Thalberg, Henselt, Gottschalk, and Tausig, appear to have given less place to the sonata, largely because nearly all of them flourished during the sonata's slump, in the second quarter of the century (ssb I, II, IV).

Among violinists who did much for the sonata, Joachim must be named first. Certainly, his closeness to the Schumanns and Brahms and his more than sixty years of performing in all the main centers made him one of the most important of Romantic musicians. Before him Spohr deserves first mention and near the end of his career Ysaÿe and Kreisler. Paganini seems to have played only his own unorthodox sonatas at his recitals. Other important violin virtuosos, like Kreutzer, Rode, Vieuxtemps, Wieniawski, Sarasate, and Wilhelmj, seem to have made less use of sonatas, no doubt partly because the accompanied keyboard sonatas still being published in the first half-century offered no opportunities for virtuosity and the genuine duos too few. Among cellists Piatti was the nearest equivalent to Joachim.

As one description of what must have been some of the fine recital playing of the century, in typical programs that include sonatas, a review in *The Musical Times* may be quoted almost in full of four

---

4. Cf. the vivid individual accounts of these and other contemporary pianists and their almost legendary careers in Loesser/PIANOS and Schonberg/PIANISTS.

out of five recitals given within less than four weeks in 1876 by Rubinstein:[5]

The visit of Herr Rubinstein to this country, after an absence of several years, has most undoubtedly been the event of the musical season. No such excitement has been produced within our recollection by the performances of any artist in London, as by those of this great pianist. He has already given four recitals at St. James's Hall, and a fifth and last is announced to take place on May 29th, after our going to press. The programmes of the recitals are worth giving, as showing the versatility of Herr Rubinstein, and his complete command of every style of playing.

FIRST RECITAL, May 3.—Preludes and Fugues, J. S. Bach; Rondo in A minor, Mozart; Gigue in A major, Handel; Sonata in F minor, Op. 57, Beethoven; Kreisleriana, Schumann; Sonata in B flat minor, Chopin; Etudes, Chopin; Miniatures, Caprice, Barcarolle, and Valse Caprice, Rubinstein.

SECOND RECITAL, May 10.—Variations, Handel; Sonata in E, Op. 109, Beethoven; Etudes Symphoniques, Schumann; Momens Musicales, Schubert; Scherzo à Capriccio, Mendelssohn; Nocturne, Field; Polacca, Weber; Preludes, Ballades and Etudes, Chopin; Leonore, 5th Barcarolle, and Tarantelle, Rubinstein.

THIRD RECITAL, May 16.—Fantasia, Op. 15, Schubert; Sonata (Moonlight), Beethoven; Variations Sérieuses, Mendelssohn; Nocturnes and Polonaises, Chopin; Carnaval, Schumann; Suite, Romance, and Etudes, Rubinstein.

FOURTH RECITAL, May 25.—Preludes and Fugue, Rubinstein; Sonata in A flat, Weber; "Warum," "Vogel als Prophet," "Abends," and "Traumeswirren," Schumann; Sonata in C minor, Op. 111, Beethoven; Nocturne, Field; Etude, Thalberg; "Chanson d'Amour," and "Si oiseau j'étais," Henselt; Nocturne, Mazurka, Valse, and Etudes, Chopin; Barcarolle and "Erl-König," Schubert-Liszt; Rhapsodie Hongroise, Liszt.

It is almost impossible to convey in words to those who have not heard it, any idea of Rubinstein's truly astounding playing. His execution is enormous, and under his fingers the greatest difficulties seem like mere child's-play. But it is not his almost unequalled command of the keyboard which rivets the attention and enlists the sympathies of his audiences, but the wonderful depth of his expression. His touch combines the extremes of power and delicacy; his *fortissimo,* while most sonorous, is free from the least trace of thumping, while in more tender passages, his *cantabile* is most exquisite. In nothing is he so great as in the delivery of a simple melody, in this his style is so absolutely unaffected and so full of charm and feeling that it goes straight to the heart of the hearer. Such playing as that of Mozart's Rondo and the slower numbers of Schumann's "Kreisleriana" at the first recital, or of the first movement of the "Moonlight" Sonata at the third, will not soon be forgotten by those who were present. On the other hand, it must be confessed that there is one drawback to the perfect enjoyment of his performances. As will be inferred from what we have said, Rubinstein is an impulsive player, and therefore to some extent unequal. At times he appears

5. MT XVII (1876) 500–501.

to let himself be fairly carried away by his music, and to lose all self-control. Hence his Allegros are too often hurried into Prestos; and, though his execution is equal to all the demands made upon it, the music suffers in consequence.

We are inclined to think Rubinstein greatest of all in his rendering of Chopin. The dreamy and romantic music of the Polish composer finds in him a most congenial exponent, and the exquisite delicacy with which what have been called Chopin's "filagree-work passages" are given is unsurpassable.

In addition to his recitals, Herr Rubinstein has also been heard in the Concert given by M. Wieniawski at St. James's Hall on the 20th ult. The performance on that occasion by these two great artists of Beethoven's celebrated "Kreutzer" sonata was the most magnificent within our recollection, alike in the vigour and passion of the Allegros, and in the exquisite taste and delicacy with which the well-known variations were given. Herr Rubinstein was in this work heard at his best, and was most admirably seconded by M. Wieniawski, who appears to be playing more finely than ever.

Concerts, Private and Public

The sample programs just listed bring us to a further consideration of the 19th-century recitals in which sonatas figured, which is their content. Our references necessarily must be confined mostly to public recitals. Programs seem to have been printed but rarely for private recitals. Nor were there any advertisements nor more than an occasional review from which we still might get information. In letters and memoirs we do find not infrequent mentions of sonatas being played at private gatherings, but seldom with any indication of what else may have been played or sung, let alone any complete program. Most of the occasions seem to have been too informal and spontaneous for set programs, anyway. Of one thing we can be sure—that private music-making of a high order constituted a favorite, "postman's" recreation for the professionals and a main indulgence for the dilettantes. That much the records do reveal, starting from the "Schubertiaden" in early-19th-century Vienna, where Schubert himself seems to have given the only, few lifetime performances of his own sonatas.[6] Moscheles "never wearied of making music with his brother artists," as in a private concert in 1839 for the French royal family at which he played his own four-hand Sonata in E♭ with Chopin.[7] Carl Friedberg has told of the indelible impressions made on him and his excitement when he was allowed to turn pages around 1887 for Brahms in music-making

6. More information than usual is given in a diary entry of 1827 reporting a "Schubertiad" at which he participated in his own "Grand Duo," as trans. in Deutsch/SCHUBERT-D 590–92 (cf., also, pp. 568, 571, 680 on the Son. in G, D. 894).

7. Cf. MOSCHELES I 251–52 and II 57–60, SSB VII; also, Schlesinger/CRAMER 74 for the banquet concert he and Cramer gave in honor of Clementi in 1827 (including 3 Clementi sons.).

shared by Clara Schumann, Joachim, and others, music-making that included late violin sonatas by both Brahms and Beethoven.[8] Amy Fay related in 1873 how extraordinarily Liszt would play for informal gatherings of his pupils, a quarter century after he had discontinued his public concert tours, one work he played being Chopin's Sonata in b, Op. 58.[9]

Of course, sonatas were by no means the main ingredient in the private music-making, especially before 1850. And the standards and interest could hardly be expected to be so high in most instances. The same Moscheles also reported boredom and poor manners at private concerts, as in London in 1832.[10] Yet, in 1828 the discriminating English author Edward Holmes expressed agreeable surprise at the good quality of much of the music, including private and dilettante performances, that he had been hearing in his travels in Vienna, Berlin, St. Petersburg, and other centers.[11]

Up to the mid 1850's the majority of public concerts consisted not only of a variety of compositions by a variety of composers, as is still true today, but of a variety of ensembles played by a variety of performers, as had been true throughout the previous century. On such a program it was unusual to include ensemble sonatas.[12] Their lack of sufficient color or display to counterbalance their length, their continued identification with more intimate or dilettantish music (especially in the accompanied keyboard settings, earlier in the century), and their connotations of obsolescence and academicism as the century advanced (SSB II)—these were the likely reasons for excluding them. Moreover, on such a variegated program it was still more unusual to include a solo—that is, piano—sonata, especially a Romantic rather than a Classic sonata. As late as 1848, when Charles Hallé performed Beethoven's Sonata in E♭, Op. 31/3 in London, he was told by the director of the Musical Union (predecessor of the Popular Concerts) that sonatas "were not works to be played in public" and that "no solo sonatas had ever before been included in any [London] concert programme." [13] Yet within eight years the respected William Henry Holmes would be announcing piano recitals that included one sonata each by J. W. Davison, G. A. Macfarren, Brahms, and Rubinstein, and

8. Smith/FRIEDBERG 13–14, 25–26.

9. Fay/GERMANY 211–14.

10. E.g., MOSCHELES 278–79.

11. E.g., Holmes/RAMBLE 125–27, 157–58, 236–37, 265–66, 282–83.

12. For 2 typical programs, without any sons., cf. MOSCHELES I 123 and Schlesinger/CRAMER 81. The sources for specific 19th-c. programs are many but scattered. As usual, the periodicals are especially helpful, including MDC at the end of the century.

13. HALLÉ 103.

two sonatas by Schumann.[14] And actually, at least a trickle of solo sonata performances in public can be found in one center or another from the start of the century, including those of Clara Schumann from 1835 and of Moscheles from 1837 (right in London; *infra*).

If much the same near exclusion of sonatas in public concerts of the first half-century can be surmised for Germany and certainly for regions more distant from the sonata's home centers, it does not quite apply to public concerts in Paris. There the ensemble and even the solo sonata seem to have fared somewhat better. A typical program, with typically incomplete listings, was one given in La Salle Chantereine on April 1, 1838. It included a first performance in Paris of a Moscheles Septet, a *Fantaisie concertante* in which Osborne and Bériot collaborated (as composers and/or performers?), a Sonata for P & Cl (by whom?), some airs or duos by Rossini and Mercadante, a Fantaisie (played and/or composed?) by Thalberg, a Trio for P, Vn, & Vc by Franck, "played for the first time," and "still some other works." [15] But a search through the periodical *Revue et gazette musicale de Paris* from its start in 1834 to 1850, during the concert heyday of Liszt, Chopin, Kalkbrenner, Thalberg, and Herz, has hardly borne out a statement in the issue for February 8, 1835 (p. 50) that concerts in that day rarely failed to include quintets, quartets, and sonatas, as well as the names of Boccherini, Haydn, Mozart, and Bach. Mozart's and Haydn's sonatas rarely turned up. Beethoven's appeared occasionally on the programs, though not nearly so often as his symphonies nor as other composers' fantasias and opera transcriptions for piano, songs, and various instrumental chamber groups.

The first recitals performed entirely by one pianist occurred in the later 1830's. In 1837, wrote Charlotte Moscheles,

. . . there had been no recitals for pianoforte music, and these were introduced by Moscheles [in London]. Many of his colleagues called this a venturous undertaking. Moscheles, however, held to his purpose, taking the precaution to interweave a little vocal music with the instrumental, so as to relieve the monotony which people warned him against. . . . The newspapers were loud in their praises of the new scheme, but censured the introduction of vocal music, adding that it was an interruption, and the one blot in an otherwise perfect entertainment. On three occasions Moscheles played some music of Scarlatti and his contemporaries on a harpsichord, built in the year 1771. . . .[16]

Moscheles' first "soirée," on February 18, 1837, consisted of the follow-

---

14. MT VII (1856) 177. Cf. GROVE IV 330 (G. Grove).
15. Vallas/FRANCK 38–39.
16. MOSCHELES II 22–23.

ing program, interspersed with "a little vocal music," as listed in a favorable review six days later:

Part I. Grande Sonate brillante (C major, in four movements [Op. 24]) Piano-forte, Mr. Moscheles; Weber.—Cantata, Miss Birch, 'Mad Bess;' Purcell. —Three preludes and Fugues (C sharp major, C sharp minor, and D major) P[iano]. F[orte]. Mr. Moscheles; S. Bach.—German Song, Miss Masson, 'Das erste Veilchen,' (The first violet) Mendelssohn.—Sonate Dramatique (D minor, Op. 29 [31/2!], in three movements) P. F. Mr. Moscheles; Beethoven. Part II. A selection from the Suites of Lessons (including the celebrated Cat's Fugue), as originally written for the harpsichord, and, by desire, performed on that instrument by Mr. Moscheles, D. Scarlatti.—The Harmonious Black-smith, with Handel's Variations, Mr. Moscheles; Handel.—Duet, Miss Birch and Miss Masson, (Cosi fan Tutte) Mozart.—Les Adieux, l'Absence, et le Retour, sonate charactéristique [Op. 81a], P. F. Mr. Moscheles; Beethoven.— Glee, Miss Birch, Miss Masson, Messrs. Vaughan and Bradbury, 'Go, feeble tyrant;' Jackson.—A selection of new MS Studies, P. F. Mr. Moscheles; Moscheles. Conductor of the Vocal Music, Sir George Smart.[17]

In the very same month Clara Wieck began a series of eight recitals in Berlin that also consisted "purely of pieces for solo pianoforte and songs with pianoforte" (or P & Vn), including Beethoven's sonatas Opp. 47 and 57.[18] She played only the last two movements of Op. 57 on the first recital and then the whole of it, "by request," at a later one.

In early 1839 in Rome Liszt took the one further step by playing the whole program himself, although not including any sonatas. Referring to one of the recent, variegated concerts in Paris, he wrote in June of that year,

What a contrast to the tiresome *musical soliloquies* (I do not know what other name to give this invention of mine) with which I contrived to gratify the Romans, and which I am quite capable of importing to Paris, so un-bounded does my impudence become! Imagine that, wearied with warfare, not being able to compose a programme which would have common sense, I have ventured to give a series of concerts all by myself, affecting the Louis XIV style, and saying cavalierly to the public, "The concert is—myself." For the curiosity of the thing I copy one of the programmes of the soliloquies for you:—

1. Overture to William Tell, performed by M[onsieur]. L[iszt].
2. Reminiscences of the *Puritani*. Fantaisie composed and performed by the above-mentioned!
3. Etudes and fragments by the same to the same!
4. Improvisation on themes given—still by the same.

17. MUSICAL WORLD IV (1836–37) 155–56; on p. 184 the program of the 2d "soirée" (Mar. 4, 1837) is given, including Beethoven's sons. Opp. 17, 26, and 28, but none by Moscheles himself.
18. AMZ XXXIX (1837) 193, 194, 196, 257–58. Cf., also, NZM VII (1837) 87 ("Flo-restan und Eusebius"); AMZ XL (1838) 164–65 and 369 (in Vienna); Hanslick/ WIEN I 332–33.

And that was all; neither more nor less, except lively conversation during the intervals, and enthusiasm if there was room for it.[19]

The Make-Up of the Recitals

Ferdinand Hiller praised Liszt as one of the first front-rank composers to play the music of others,[20] which praise Liszt richly deserved throughout his career as a performer. His introduction of Beethoven's Op. 106 to Paris—in fact, to the musical world—in 1836, as described by Berlioz,[21] is sufficient indication of his enterprise as regards the sonata.[22] Of course, the pianists who composed less, or less successfully, had more reason to play the music of other composers. Clara Schumann's large repertoire, during the long career that saw over 2,000 recitals, included at least 51 sonatas—28 for P solo, 4 for P-duet or 2 Ps, 16 for P & Vn, and 3 for P & Vc. The composers of these sonatas, listed in the order in which she first took them up, are Czerny, Mozart (including 7 for P & Vn), Pleyel, Vanhal, Hummel, Beethoven (9 for P solo, 4 for P & Vn, one for P & Vc), Schumann (3 for P solo, 2 for P & Vn), Moscheles, Brahms (Op. 5 for P solo and all 3 Vn sons.), Mendelssohn, Scarlatti, Haydn (one), Clementi (one), and Schubert (2 for P solo and one for arpeggione).[23] It is evident that her tastes became increasingly conservative as she aged.

An exceptional set of statistics has been prepared[24] on about 285 known public performances of solo and duo sonatas in England during the first half of the 19th century and all in London except 22 in Manchester, 2 in Cambridge, and one each in Liverpool, Brighton, Reading, Norwich, and Bury St. Edmunds. The sonatas of one composer, Beethoven (especially Opp. 47, 30, 27/2, and 31/2, in that order), account for 153, or nearly 54 per cent, of the performances, with Mozart (16 performances, especially K. 497), Weber, Dussek, G. A. Macfarren, Clementi, Mendelssohn, Spohr, and perhaps a dozen others trailing far behind. Between 1801 and 1813 about 20 performances are known, 7 for P solo and the rest for H solo or for duo (P & one other instrument). Between 1814 and 1836 none are known. Between 1837 (when Moscheles began his "soirées," *supra*) and 1850, about 265 per-

19. As trans. in LISZT LETTERS I 31–32. Our present word "recital" was not introduced until Liszt played a year later in London (cf. Loesser/PIANOS 371).
20. Gertler/SCHUMANN 35 fn. 90.
21. RGM for June 12, 1836, p. 200.
22. But the samples of his programs in 1837–38 that are summarized in Romann/ LISZT I 419 and 426–27, and II/1 428 do not happen to specify sons.
23. The foregoing information, from Litzmann/SCHUMANN III 615–24, is not likely to be complete.
24. Temperley/CORRESPONDENCE.

formances are known, including 140 (53%) duos (90 for P & Vn, 37 for P & Vc, 13 other), 12 (4%) for P-duet (9 of Mozart sons.), and 113 (43%) P solos.

One begins to wonder that the pianists played as many sonatas as they did, bearing in mind not only the recurring predictions of the sonata's downfall (ssb II) but the considerable length of the Romantic sonatas in particular. Like Beethoven's Op. 106, Schubert's posthumous Sonata in A, Brahms's Op. 34b, and especially the longest sonatas of later Romantics like Raff, Rheinberger, Reger, d'Indy, Dukas, Medtner, Godowsky, and Dale, all last closer to forty than thirty minutes, and some more than an hour (cf. ssb VI). A partial answer to the length was the considerable length of the recitals themselves, as must be evident already from the programs of Rubinstein and others that have been quoted here. Clearly the audiences were less in a hurry than their present-day descendants. "A little under two hours" was given as the average length in a series of chamber music programs (including sons.) in 1880.[25] But two hours would hardly be sufficient for a solo piano recital by Oscar Beringer the following year that included Beethoven's Op. 106, Weber's Op. 39, Brahms's Op. 5, and Liszt's Sonata in b! [26] The eccentric French virtuoso Alkan (ssb XII) had the goodness to put the exact timings beside each work on the printed programs of his long piano recitals, supposedly so that his audiences would not be taken by surprise.[27]

Among related questions that the recitals raised, one was the advisability of encores. Bülow extended one of his long recitals to a considerably greater length by repeating the fugue finale of Beethoven's Op. 106.[28] Rubinstein extended one of his still more by playing the whole of Chopin's Sonata in b, Op. 58, as his "first" encore.[29] Francis Hueffer, lecturing in London in 1880, presumably would have preferred Rubinstein's way of meeting the "encore nuisance," because, he said, playing only one movement destroys the complete organism that a sonata or symphony must be.[30] Yet playing one or two movements from a sonata was common practice throughout the Romantic Era.[31] The first public exposure of Brahms's Op. 1 came when Bülow played the opening movement, only, in 1854, and of his

25. mt XXI (1880) 354.

26. mt XXII (1881) 138–39. Cf. Müller-Reuter/lexikon I 425 for an exceptionally long program, including Bülow playing the Liszt Son. in b.

27. Bloch/alkan 2.

28. Cf. bülow briefe IV 291, 292, 579, 582.

29. Friedheim/liszt 195.

30. mt XXI (1880) 344.

31. E.g., cf. the mention of this practice in Bennett/bennett 148–49.

Op. 5 when Clara Schumann played the second and third movements, only, also in 1854 (ssB IX). Not infrequently, one of the movements from a sonata has had a life of its own, anyway, like the finale, "Perpetuum mobile," from Weber's Op. 24, or the slow movement, "March funèbre," from Chopin's Op. 35.

In any case, as against that variegated type of program that had prevailed earlier, there was some effort to make a single organism of the whole recital, including not a few all-Beethoven programs (ssB I). In 1860 a reviewer even questioned the equating of different styles and the levelling effect that resulted when Bülow played Bach, Mozart, Beethoven, Wagner, Chopin, Bülow, and Liszt "all in one breath" in a solo recital.[32] Such a reviewer had little patience with the stunts and novelties that still beset many a program on which sonatas figured, usually by way of bait for the audience. For example, one George Fox, eight years old, doing an "Improvisation in Sonata Form" was the bait that was cast out to lure a full audience to a benefit recital in 1878,[33] providing but a single instance of the endless, usually vain attempts to discover prodigies in the 19th century.[34] Another method of arousing curiosity that became fashionable for a time was that of withholding the composer's name on the program, leaving the audience and reviewer to guess. This method perplexed one reviewer in 1881, as he frankly confessed, after Bülow and Wilhelmj played an anonymous, well-liked duo for P & Vn that proved to be Ferdinand Hummel's Op. 24 in c.[35]

The Sonata and the Professional

The sonata could figure in several ways in the Romantic musician's career. For one thing, as in the two previous eras (sBE 30, sCE 46–47), it seems to have made an ideal Op. 1 by which aspiring, serious-minded composers could introduce themselves in print, even though no Op. 2 might ever follow or the direction of interest might be changed entirely. Loewe stressed this advantage in a letter to his publisher quoted previously (ssB II). In 1853 the English pianist Edward Bache considered launching his career with a published sonata, although

32. DMZ I (1860) 119.

33. MT XIX (1878) 663.

34. Cf. Holmes/RAMBLE 157–58: "We have so much of child's play lately in England [1830], that it is to be hoped the fashion is on the decline; for if extremes be good, how much better it would be to employ those whose tops are bald with dry antiquity. . . ."

35. SMW XXXIX (1881) 1107.

the challenge to create so imposing a form worried him.[36] We are reminded of the ideal achievement that the sonata represented to Romantic composers and critics (ssb II). Wrote Schumann, in 1844, too involutely,

A sonata as an Op. 1 has a twofold claim on our sympathies. Since, in any case, the fullest concentration of the creative powers demands attention to compositions of larger, artistically worthier designs than fantasias [and] transcriptions (whose production today is, in a double sense [the original and its adaptation?], no longer art), then such is all the more true when an artist, instead of pouring out a few borrowed ideas in a slovenly, worn-out form flooded with passagework, introduces himself in public with a work that requires the declaration of his own ideas in a refined, noble form and hence [that requires] both capability of effort and artistic experience.[37]

Schumann seems to have taken special note of "prize sonatas" that were introductory works by neophytes, although he did not always approve of the reward.[38] Not a few other and later reviewers paid special attention to introductory sonatas, prize-winning or not, sometimes spending as much as the first half of the review repeating much the same thoughts on the significance of an Op. 1.[39]

Composing sonatas could be advantageous to the performers, too, who knew better than any other, as Biber, Tartini, Scarlatti, and other virtuosos had known in previous centuries, what to write that would show their performance skills to best advantage. The sonatas of Kalkbrenner and Thalberg were justified chiefly in that sense (ssb XII). Hanslick praised Clara Wieck (who was also a composer in her own right) for playing Beethoven's sonatas in Vienna in 1837 and for not being one of those numerous performers—including three in Vienna in 1845, Thalberg, Evers, and Willmers—who wrote sonatas as vehicles for their display "but were no Beethovens." [40] A performer had a particular chance to ingratiate himself if he introduced in his sonata some tune that was then in favor, perhaps locally. Usually he treated the tune as a subject for variations in the slow movement or for more brilliant variations in the finale. This procedure obtained especially in

36. Bache/BACHE 15–17.
37. Trans. from Schumann/SCHRIFTEN II 348. Bülow noted that a Son. as an Op. 1 permitted the composer to see his progress in perspective (NZM XLV [1856] 21–22). Cf., also, the statement of 1799 trans. in SCE 47.
38. E.g., cf. his review in 1842 of "Drei Preissonaten," in Schumann/SCHRIFTEN II 79–83.
39. For 2 later samples, cf. NZM XXV (1864) 112 (prize son.) and LXVI/2 (1870) 369–71.
40. Hanslick/WIEN I 333.

the early 19th century, as in sonatas by Wölfl (SCE 564), Moscheles (SSB VII), and Ries (SSB VII).[41]

Although composing sonatas might have the foregoing advantages for the Romantic musician, one advantage it was less likely to have was immediate financial profit. Wagner undoubtedly was recounting his own experiences when he had his imaginary pilgrim to Beethoven tell of rebuffed efforts to make money from the sale of sonatas and how the prospective publishers advised writing "galops and pot-pourris," instead.[42] Fauré found the French publishers afraid to invest in his Op. 13 and had to accept the "honor" alone of having it published by Breitkopf & Härtel in Leipzig in 1877 (SSB XIII). An article of 1889 on Algernon Ashton began,

> It is said that none but the most enthusiastic musicians in the present day devote their talents to such complicated and learned labours as are necessary to the production of sonatas and the higher forms of musical art. . . . *The answer is that they are not produced because they are not profitable.*[43]

In their way, of course, the sonata composers had to struggle with the same problems that confronted any other artist, or any other entrepreneur, for that matter. They lived ceaselessly active, hectic, exhausting lives between their composing, teaching, performing, rehearsing, hearing, and writing about music.[44] They fought to establish and preserve some scale of fair compensation for their sonatas and like products.[45] And they faced the familiar maze of charges and regulations for the rental of concert halls, use of instruments, special privileges, and so on.[46] To be sure, the few most successful composers made substantial incomes. Mendelssohn, for example, could afford the luxury of withholding his MSS from publication for considerable periods, both because he liked the prolonged opportunity to touch them up here and there and simply because in his fastidiousness he disliked

---

41. In 1824 Czerny wrote Liszt's father offering to write variations for young Liszt to play, on some tune currently popular in Paris (cf. Stegner/CZERNY 21). Cf., also, MOSCHELES I 201–2.

42. WAGNER PROSE VII 23.

43. MT XXX (1889) 616 (italics original). Ashton himself became cynical about music pub. (cf. MGG I 750 [G. Abraham]).

44. Cf. the descriptions of daily life in MOSCHELES I 211–12, 301, 314–15 and II 20–21, 168; Stanford/BENNETT 645–46.

45. For sample fees asked by representative composers (although without translation into real money), cf. Hanslick/WIEN I 279 (on Beethoven's charges); MOSCHELES I 222; MENDELSSOHN/Moscheles 273 (on Mendelssohn's charges); Jansen/SCHUMANN II 273–74 (on Schumann expecting twice what he suggested for Brahms in 1853); May/BRAHMS 134; BRAHMS BRIEFWECHSEL XII 20 and XIV no. 12; MT XV (1872) 418, 446–47, 510, 541 (only indirectly related, on church organists' salaries).

46. Cf. the list of charges and restrictions for the use of a hall, in MT XV (1872) 364.

seeing "such nice, clean manuscript pass into the dirty hands of engravers, customers and the public."[47]

Two other classes of sonata composers had less to do with these professional problems. There were the promising, short-lived composers—among them Pinto, Schunke, Reubke, and Lekeu—who barely completed their training and entered their twenties before they died or could become involved with the exigencies of a professional career. And there were the not few women who composed sonatas—among them, Emilie Meyer, Johanna Müller-Hermann, Elizabeth Kuyper, Luise Adolpha Le Beau, Cécile Chaminade, Agnes Zimmerman, Ethel Smyth, Amy Marcy Beach, Clara Anna Korn, and Clara Kathleen Rogers (not to mention the numerous other women who figure indirectly here as performers, counselors, and benefactors of some of the main champions of the sonata, including George Sand, Pauline Viardot-García, Jenny Lind, Jane Sterling, Henriette Sontag, Clara Schumann, Elisabeth von Herzogenberg, W. M. F. Neruda, Blanche Selva, and Claire Murray Newman).[48] Intentionally or not, these women were put in a class of their own by the reviewers, who were invariably well-meaning but invariably cavalier, too, and who seldom completed a review without at least implying that the sonata was "surprisingly good for a woman" and showed "fine skill if not much inspiration." This class of composer had fewer struggles with professional problems both because there were usually other sources of income and because there were generally fewer opportunities for publication and other advancements, anyway (perhaps providing one reason why Dame Ethel Smyth became such a stalwart champion of woman suffrage).

Amateurs and Students

The amateurs or dilettantes who played sonatas in the earlier 19th century were direct descendants of the later 18th-century type, who mostly preferred the lightest, frothiest examples (SCE 44–46). Living at "the time when the word 'brilliant' came into fashion" and "legions of girls had fallen in love with Czerny,"[49] they became the consumers of publications like F. W. Grund's *Trois Sonatines . . . aux amateurs,* Schubert's *Sonatas faciles* and *Grande Sonate agréable* (SSB VIII), or Steibelt's *Two Sonatas . . . Dedicated to the fair sex.*[50] After the mid-

47. Cf. his letter of June 12, 1843, to K. Klingmann, as trans. in Selden-Goth/ MENDELSSOHN 325.

48. Among special sources on women composers are Elson/WOMAN and Cobbett/ CHAMBER II 591–92 (M. Drake-Brockman) and I 185 (W. W. Cobbett).

49. Schumann/SCHRIFTEN I 162.

50. WOLFE II 842.

dle of the 19th century and the sonata's slump period, these amateurs or dilettantes seem to have branched off in three main directions. The most serious-minded and capable of them, like Brahms's surgeon friend Theodor Billroth, sought as nearly as possible to keep up with the Romantic sonata in all its structural, emotional, and athletic expansions, and with the professional masters who created and played it. The less capable amateurs, though sometimes quite as serious-minded, tended of necessity to remain or become diligent students, having to content themselves more or less with pedagogic compromises, as noted below. And the least serious-minded of the amateurs largely must have turned away to other genres for want of up-to-date sonata novelties light enough for their superficial grasp.

Closely related to these different directions taken by the amateur, is the distinct dichotomy that developed in the 19th century between sonatas designed for the concert hall and those designed for teaching. One would be tempted to oversimplify this dichotomy by calling it art versus pedagogy. But, of course, art and pedagogy should never be mutually exclusive and, for the most part, do not prove to be in the Romantic sonata. One might come closer to the dichotomy by calling it "grande sonate" versus "petite sonatine," or large-scale and difficult versus diminutive and easy, notwithstanding such exceptions, respectively, as the five sensitive, technically easy little "sonatinas," Op. 70, by Theodor Kirchner (ssb X) and the lengthy, difficult *Grande Sonate d'Étude, doigtée pour faire atteindre l'habilité supérieure du mécanisme dans plusieurs nouvelles formes de passages,* Op. 268, by Czerny (ssb VII, with exx.). But the real dichotomy is one more of kind than of degree. It is the dichotomy of new style versus old style. When Clementi wrote his delightful sonatinas (sce 751), their lightness, efficiency, naivety, and characteristic idioms were inherent in the current Classic language. When the Romantic composers continued to employ the same styles, with little or no modernization, in their teaching sonatas or sonatinas, all the way from Kuhlau to Nicolai von Wilm, they were perpetuating a language and idioms that were no longer current at all.

So well recognized was this dichotomy that it is not surprising to find one and the same composer—for example, Kuhlau (ssb XV) or Reinecke (ssb X)—using the current style for his concert sonatas and the old style for his teaching sonatas. Reviewers frequently took note of the dichotomy, as we shall discover in later chapters. Schumann generally fought the persistence of the old style in whatever sonatas came his way (". . . the sonata style of 1790 is not that of 1840," as trans. in ssb II). Yet he could recommend a thorough grounding in the old style of writing sonatas as a prerequisite to the "free [newer] style" for aspiring composers.[51] With Bülow it was not a question of a dichotomy but of the validity of any sonatas at all after Beethoven's except Chopin's, Schumann's, and Hummel's Op. 81 in f♯, and apart from his concession that "for exercise in private it [a post-Beethoven sonata] may always be accepted." [52] But he made that gloomy statement in 1852 when he was only twenty-two and before he was playing many Romantic sonatas.

In 1828 J. A. G. Heinroth began a long review of Jakob Schmitt's *Sonate à l'usage des Élèves avancés* with some specific ideas about the pedagogic values of the sonata:[53]

In each *Messkatalog* [Leipzig book fair catalog; HOFMEISTER 1828 (Whistling)?] appear music items written now for this, now for that purpose, designated to satisfy now this, now that stated need. They sprout from the fantasy of composers like mushrooms out of the ground. And although their titles tell in what category they belong, they still have this in common with the mushrooms, that one cannot distinguish the edible from the inedible or even [the] dangerous at first glance.

A lot of sonatas *à l'usage des élèves avancés* are offered to us that by no means accomplish what one rightly expects of them. Thus, when the student is tired and worn out with his *Exercices* and *Etudes* by Cramer, Müller, Clementi, etc., the teacher may give him a little [musical] relaxation. But this relaxation must always contain something whereby he [the student] is brought closer to his goal. Therefore a good teacher gives sonatas to him based on ideas that are lovely, melodious, and fluent, but not trifling, wooden, and clumsy, and whose treatment is good and intelligible; sonatas that present no mere chain of modulations and do not go astray constantly into the most outlandish keys; [and] sonatas in which natural voice-leading prevails and which are orthographically written with regard to rhythm as well as harmony. If the teacher is concerned especially with attack, fingering, and clarity in the exercises and studies, then [by contrast] he calls the student's attention in the sonatas to the theme, to the treatment of the same, [to] how it appears now in the soprano, now in the bass, etc. In this manner the student learns something useful while he relaxes.

The titles of the teaching sonatas often specify their particular values for students, thereby pleasing the reviewers. These last characteristically sought, as Spitta sought in so many of Bach's works, to find some value, whether moral, pedagogic, recreational, or concert,

---

51. Cf. Jansen/SCHUMANN II 206; also, p. 70 for further advices by him on writing sons.

52. NZM XXXVI (1852) 234.

53. CAECILIA IX (1828) 193–96.

in every work under examination.[54] Thus, we find "Easy and Pleasing Sonatas With Fingering and Interpretation Indicated" (H. Wohlfahrt, ssb IX);[55] or Sonata in F "written expressly for small hands" (E. M. Lott);[56] or, recalling Czerny's equation above, "Etudes ou Sonates" (A. Romberg, ssb VIII);[57] or "Three Sonatas in [an] Easy, Pleasing Style of Playing and [arranged in] Progressive Steps" (by the pedagogue K. R. Hennig). Series of "progressive sonatas" account for a large number of the countless teaching sonatas published in the 19th century, filling many pages of pazdírek (but represented by only a fraction of their number in the present volume).

54. Schumann emphasized such values only infrequently (as in Schumann/ schriften I 91), preferring to concentrate on aspects of the music itself. Unfortunately, conceding that a son. would serve well for teaching purposes could be as damning as calling one of the "fair sex's" sons. "well done for a woman"!
55. Cf. the typical review in nzm LXI/2 (1865) 343.
56. mt XXIV (1883) 300.
57. Cf. amz XV (1813) 839–40, reviewing only the etude aspects.

Chapter IV

The Spread of the Romantic Sonata

Trends in Space and Time

The general regions, main centers, and particular institutions where the Romantic sonata was introduced, composed, published, and enjoyed; the policies and practices by which its publication was affected; and the relative importance attached to it in the larger musical scene —these are the topics that now come up, under "The Spread of the Romantic Sonata." We come shortly to a survey of the main centers where the composers wrote their sonatas, the performers played them, the patrons heard and subsidized them, the publishers issued them, the consumers bought them, the critics reviewed them, and the teachers guided their students through them. By way of preliminary overviews, two charts of geographic spread and related time spans are offered. The first shows the distribution, by countries or larger regions, of the 629 composers who are at least touched on individually in the present volume, subdivided into early-, middle-, and late-Romantic groups (cf. SSB I). To the uncertain extent that our selection is equally representative for the several regions, it helps to confirm the hegemony in Austro-Germany and the continuing, strong sonata activities in France

The Distribution of 629 Romantic Sonata Composers by Regions and Era Phases

	Austria	Germany & Switz.	France & Low Countries	Great Britain	Scandinavia	Italy & Iberia	Eastern Europe	Russia	The Americas	Totals
Early-Rom. (1800–1850)	15	57	21	23	11	12	8	9	5	161
Mid-Rom. (1840–1885)	11	59	24	34	9		11	10	21	179
Late-Rom. (1875–1915)	17	73	45	36	21	12	31	23	31	289
TOTALS	43	189	90	93	41	24	50	42	57	629

and Great Britain during the Romantic Era. It shows the sharp increase of interest almost everywhere in the late-Romantic Era. And it also shows that the sharp drop in sonata production in Italy during the late-Classic Era continues throughout the Romantic Era, but that new interest begins to develop in regions that had been "outlying" from the standpoint of the sonata. As the standard music history books make clear enough, Italy was too preoccupied with opera throughout the era, and the "outlying" regions with national or folk interests up to the mid-century, to pay more attention than they did to the sonata.

The second geographic-time chart is more specific and more limited. Paralleling two maps and a chart of distribution in our two previous volumes (SBE 96; SCE 62–63), this chart shows the seventeen countries or regions in which, and the time spans during which, sixty-eight of the chief composers of Romantic sonatas wrote their sonatas. The countries or regions can no longer be narrowed down to cities because so often the composers moved about too much (which is why they keep reappearing in the summaries of individual city centers, *infra*). At the very least, composers had always managed to move back and forth across Europe at an astonishing rate, in spite of the most harrowing travel conditions (cf. SCE 164). But especially after the rapid development of railroads, steamships, and telegraphy, all well before the mid-century,[1] the composers seemed to become an even more peripatetic lot. And itinerant performers at the era's end, like Rachmaninoff and Kreisler, became virtual world citizens. In further regard to the second chart, the time spans must be read with latitude because publication, not composition, dates have had to suffice in most instances, and because the composer's main sonata output may have fallen within or at either end of the extremes. Like the statistics later in this chapter, this chart helps to confirm that the alleged slump in sonata output during the second quarter of the century (SSB II) was partly imagined and only partly real.

As suggested on these two geographic-time charts (and discussed in SSB I), the Austro-German hegemony with respect to the sonata constituted the main hub from which this form type fanned out during the Romantic Era, spreading as far east as Russia, as far west as the Americas, and eventually to all world centers where Western music

1. The excitement of a first train ride, in 1831, is reported in MOSCHELES I 249–50, after numerous unfortunate travel experiences (e.g., pp. 115–18 and 230–34). Schumann compared Beethoven's and Liszt's mode of travel (Boetticher/SCHUMANN 618). Chopin showed much interest, in 1844, in the telegraphic service established between Baltimore and Washington (Sydow & Hedley/CHOPIN 250).

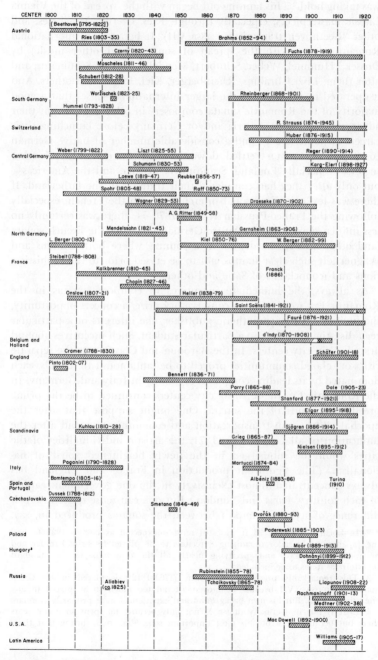

Regions and Production Spans of Some Main Romantic Sonata Composers

was taking hold.[2] This fanning out began with the spread of the Vienna Classic masterpieces, especially through Ries, Czerny, Moscheles, and other "Beethoven transmitters" (SSB VII). It became an international Romantic force with the spread of sonatas (and other music) by Dussek,[3] Hummel, Weber, Schubert, Mendelssohn, and Schumann; and after them, Liszt,[4] Brahms, Rheinberger, Kiel, Reger, and others. And it operated increasingly in the larger international senses that a good majority of the Romantic sonata composers in other regions got their advanced training in Austria and/or Germany before launching their careers at home (SSB I), and a considerable number of native German composers of sonatas settled down to their careers in those other regions—especially England, Scandinavia, Russia, and the Americas— but only *after* they had completed their training in the fatherland. If there was less of this personal interchange with the French, especially following the Franco-Prussian War of 1870–71, there was certainly no less influence exercised by Austro-German music on the French sonata (and other music)—hardly so, in a country where both Brahms and Wagner left such clear stamps, not to be erased prior to the sophistications and iconoclasms of Satie and others.

As always, the immediate incentives to compose sonatas in the Romantic Era were local—a conservatory prize, a concert opportunity, the invitation of a sympathetic publisher, the interests of a particular recitalist, the challenge to a particular student. Such incentives abound first of all in city centers. In the Baroque and Classic eras the separate cities or related communities proved to be tantamount to schools, each dominated by its leading composer, especially in Italy and Germany. In the Romantic Era the separate city centers continued to be the prime breeding grounds of the sonata. One might suppose that after the epochal advances in transportation and communication and after the unification of all Germany in 1871, the artistic individualities of the cities would be submerged in the newly heightened spirit of nationalism. (The significant production in France and England has always concentrated almost exclusively in the one government capital of each country, Paris and London.) But one can sense quite as much difference of style and import between the sonatas produced in, say,

2. In Lochner/KREISLER 93 it was still most unexpected as late as 1923 to find the Japanese ambassador organizing 8 recitals to be played by Fritz Kreisler and his pianist in Tokyo, and specifying nearly all the duo sons. in the standard repertoire as items to be included.

3. This remarkably precocious Romantic (1760–1812!) is placed in his Czech homeland in SSB XVII because he moved around too much to be placed in any one other region. But his own background and experiences were primarily German.

4. Liszt is put in Germany in SSB X not only because he spent so many years there but because he wrote his most important son., Son. in b, during that time.

Vienna, Munich, Leipzig, and Berlin, at the end of the era as at the start. It should be possible here at least to summarize the local circumstances that made these differences in the most active centers of the sonata.[5] A separate list showing the main publishers in most of these centers appears later in this chapter.

The Main City Centers

In **Vienna** the great Classic masters had brought independent instrumental music almost up to a par with opera in popular interest. From Schubert on, the cultivation of serious music became chiefly the province of the middle classes rather than the nobility. The once high-toned Augarten concerts (where Beethoven and Bridgetower had introduced the "Kreutzer Sonata" in 1803), depreciated in quality in the early 19th century below what might be called "the sonata level," [6] and sonatas virtually disappeared from public performances until the mid 1830's. But this genre was furthered in private, largely dilettante groups like the "Schubertiaden" (ssb III) or, later, the circle of performing and other friends around Brahms. The concerts of the Wiener Philharmonische orchestra and the Gesellschaft der Musikfreunde;[7] the outstanding chamber groups, including the Joachim Quartet; the presence of Schubert, Brahms, and Bruckner, among other composers; the fine teaching, from Sechter and Czerny to R. Fuchs;[8] and the residence or visits of nearly every important concert artist of the century[9]—all these contributed to an appropriate atmosphere for the sonata.

The musical life of **Munich** continued to be identified with that of the Bavarian court throughout the Romantic Era, opera being the first interest right through the association of Wagner with King Ludwig II and the opera conducting of Richard Strauss. Almost the sole institution open to public concerts was the Musikalische Akademie der Hofkapelle; but chamber music seems to have flourished only in private.[10] The main training ground was the Königliche Musikschule, founded in 1846, reorganized in 1867 by Bülow, and honored by the

5. The sources of information most utilized here are the city articles in MGG and GROVE, with further references; the articles on chamber organizations indexed country by country in Cobbett/CHAMBER; and the bibliography up to 1947 in Schaal/LOKALGESCHICHTS.

6. Cf. Hanslick/WIEN I 70–75.

7. The extensive (but inadequately cat.) collection in this society's "Archiv" is evidence of more interest in the son. than is generally realized.

8. Cf. MGG XIV 612 (A. Orel).

9. E.g., cf. Hanslick/WIEN I 328–45, II 167–71.

10. Cf. MGG IX 891, 895 (O. Kaul).

influential teaching of Rheinberger (from 1859), L. Thuille, F. Wüllner, and others.

Weimar continued to shine musically in the Romantic Era under the patronage of the Grand Dukes of Saxe-Weimar-Eisenach, as it had shone since before Bach's service there. Among leading onetime residents pertinent to the Romantic sonata were Hummel and Liszt, the latter attracting Bülow, Raff, and Joachim to his circle, each for a short time. But opera was again the reigning interest. Of chief bearing on our topic after Liszt's stay, 1848–61, was the establishment of a music school in 1872 and Richard Strauss's orchestral conductorship as Hofkapellmeister from 1889 to 1894.

Leipzig, whose musical glories also go back before Bach's service, became one of the Romantic sonata's principal centers, partly for the very reason that Leipzig had only rarely placed prime emphasis on opera. More important, it provided some of the sonata's richest if more conservative nourishments, influenced to a considerable degree by veneration of Beethoven's music. Thus, it provided numerous sympathetic publishers (*infra*), topped by Breitkopf & Härtel, which firm traces back to Bach's lifetime. It provided the celebrated Gewandhaus concerts, similarly venerable, and headed successively, between 1835 and 1895, by five important musicians of varying significance in their sonatas, Mendelssohn, F. Hiller, Gade, Rietz, and Reinecke.[11] It provided one of the most widely attended conservatories, founded by Mendelssohn in 1843 and further enhanced by the teaching of Schumann, Moscheles, Hauptmann, Ferdinand David, Reinecke, and others. And it fostered the two leading music periodicals of the time in German, the conservative *Allgemeine musikalische Zeitung* (1798–1848 under Rochlitz, G. W. Fink, and others) and the progressive *Neue Zeitschrift für Musik* (from 1834, under Schumann, Brendel, and others).

The royal court of Saxony was still the main sponsor of music in 19th-century **Dresden,** with opera—especially the German opera introduced by Weber and Wagner—and the state orchestra being the stronger, most continuous currents. But chamber music flowed strongly, too, abetted by fine instrumentalists like Karol Lipiński and Clara Schumann, by composers like Robert Schumann and Volkmann, and by the founding of the Dresden Conservatory in 1856.[12]

Like Leipzig, **Berlin** became one of the Romantic sonata's principal

---

11. Werner/MENDELSSOHN 311–23 recalls Schumann's statistics on composers performed in Leipzig in 1837–38 (quoted in part near the end of the present chap.) and discusses the content of 8 Leipzig concerts between 1837 and 1841 (not including sons.); cf. Schumann/SCHRIFTEN I 373–80 and 501–11.

12. Cf. MGG III 778–79 (H. Schnoor & K. Laux).

though more conservative centers, again with Beethoven as the catalyst, but this time in spite of the predominance of opera, song, and choral music. The factors conducive to composing and playing sonatas (and other instrumental music) in Berlin were various and the list of participants notable and long.[13] The royal patronage that had provided the 18th-century court of Frederick the Great with the services of Emanuel Bach, Quantz, the Graun brothers, and the Benda brothers (SBE 297–300, SCE 412–40) sponsored only occasional instrumental concerts in the 19th century, sometimes only single pieces as opera entr'actes. In its place, first the dilettantes became the patrons of instrumental music, in their private homes, then the middle classes, in the "garden" or other public concert series and in the halls, large and small, that began to multiply before the mid century. The concerts by a continuous parade of visiting virtuosos included at least twenty by Liszt alone in 1841. Among numerous music schools founded in 19th-century Berlin, three turn up most often in the sonata annals. A Hochschule für Musik that Friedrich Wilhelm IV had wanted Mendelssohn to establish in 1840 did not become a reality until the appointment of Joachim in 1869, with Kiel and Bargiel being two of the teachers most sought after. The Sternsche Konservatorium, founded in 1850, included A. B. Marx, Theodor Kullak, Gernsheim, and Pfitzner on its faculty. And the amalgamated Konservatorium Klindworth-Scharwenka (from 1893) had its beginnings in 1866 in the Klavier-Schule Tausig. Robert Kahn, Hugo Kaun, Wilhelm Berger, and Paul Juon were among other late Romantics in Berlin (Busoni being classified here as a Modern). Berlin also fostered important publishers (e.g., Bote & Bock) and periodicals (e.g., *Berliner Allgemeine Musikzeitung* from 1824, and its successors), though not so important as Leipzig's.

Hamburg was a merchant trading city, yet somewhat apart from the mainstream of European Romantic music.[14] A principal 19th-century dividing line in all its activities was its devastating fire of 1842. Brahms was Hamburg's most distinguished, if belatedly recognized, citizen, by birth and training, and by residence most of his years before he settled in Vienna (1863). Liszt and Joachim were among the most influential visiting performers, again. A Hamburg Konservatorium was founded in 1873, with Karl Grädener among its faculty. Before then an active series of chamber music programs had been instituted by the violinist Karl Rose. Julius Schuberth was a main publisher (from 1826).

Paris and London continued to be two of the most active and, at least in the first half of the century, most cosmopolitan centers of the

13. Cf. MGG I 1714, 1721–27, 1729–33, 1738, 1741 (D. Sasse).
14. Cf. MGG V 1401–10 (K. Stephenson).

sonata. In **Paris** the long established Concert spirituel had been a main musical casualty of the French Revolution, but there was an increasing number of public concert series to take its place in the 19th century, including that, from 1828, of the Conservatoire de Musique, which had been founded during the Revolution, in 1795.[15] Among these series and notwithstanding the major French preoccupation with opera, there were several devoted to chamber music, starting with the establishment of Baillot's quartet in 1814 but dating chiefly from about 1850 and later.[16] The Conservatoire, by virtue of its age and national control, tended to be the most conservative of the music schools. Among musicians variously associated with it who are close to our topic may be named Reicha, Fétis, Berlioz, L. Adam (SCE 655–58), Dubois, Widor, Fauré, M. Emmanuel, Dukas, and d'Indy. More liberal were the École Niedermeyer (from 1853; attended by Fauré) and the Schola cantorum (founded by d'Indy and others in 1894). Whereas the first half-century had seen the shorter or longer residences of Steibelt, Kalkbrenner, Liszt, Chopin, Thalberg, and other foreigners in Paris (much as in the later 18th century), the later 19th century saw a growing resistance to foreigners, as in the Société Nationale de Musique (which Saint-Saëns helped to found in 1871) and its offshoots (SSB XIII). This Société, which did much to promote the sonata and other chamber music, aimed first of all at "bringing to light all musical strivings, whatever their form, provided they reveal elevated and truly artistic aspirations in their authors." [17] Among 19th-century French periodicals, the *Revue et gazette musicale de Paris* (RGM) and the later, short runs of *La Musique de chambre* (MDC) and *Le Mercure musical* (MERCURE) paid considerable attention to the sonata, as did important publishers like Costallat, Hamelle, Rouart-Lerolle, and Durand.

London was the patron of patrons in 19th-century music.[18] Although no front-rank sonata composers can be cited among native Britishers, the sonata activities, like nearly all other musical activities, were at least as rich in that city as in any other. There were the dizzying successions of concert series, each with its particular hall, emphasis, and flavor, yet almost all touching the sonata in some way—the Promenade Concerts, the Popular Concerts, the Ancient Concerts, the so-called King's Concerts, and all the others, which occurred in the mornings,

---

15. Cf. the convenient lists of Parisian concert series and educational organizations in GROVE VI 550–52 (various authors); also, II 408–11 (M. L. Pereyra) on the Conservatoire.

16. Cf. GROVE VI 551 and MGG X 779 (G. Ferchault).

17. Trans. from the French quotation in MGG X 780.

18. "In Germany music is treated as an *art;* in this country [England] it is chiefly looked on as a *business*" (MMR I [1871] 39).

afternoons, or evenings, by subscriptions, for benefits, or according to some other plan, and in the Hanover Square Rooms, Argyle Rooms, St. James Hall, or some other building.[19] There were the many music societies, each with its special goals, its own concert series, and sometimes its own hall—the Society of British Musicians, the Philharmonic Society, the New Philharmonic Society, the Royal Philharmonic Society, the Queen Square Select Society, the People's Concert Society, and so on. There were the music education institutions, headed by British composers we shall be meeting later (SSB XIV), notably the Royal Academy of Music (from 1822) and the Royal College of Music (tracing back to 1873). And there were the numerous active publishers listed later in this chapter, as well as excellent periodicals that include *The Quarterly Musical Magazine and Review* (QUARTERLY), *The Harmonicon* (HARMONICON), *The Musical World* (MUSICAL WORLD), and *The Musical Times* (MT). In the early 19th century the concerts were of the older, variegated type,[20] but, as we have seen (SSB III), the newer, single-purpose type began as soon in London as elsewhere. Moreover, the tastes, originally oriented fully to Baroque and Classic music, became increasingly tolerant, even receptive, to more up-to-date music. As in Paris and Berlin, there was scarcely a major soloist or ensemble group that did not visit London.[21]

Pertinent circumstances may be noted more briefly in other important music centers that, however, contributed less to the sonata. A potential environment for this genre was created by the 19th-century activities of the Toonkunst and the Concertgebouw societies in **Amsterdam,** the Conservatoire royal de Musique and the Société philharmonique in **Brussels,** the Kammermusikforeningen and Royal Danish Conservatory in **Copenhagen,** and the government operated Academy of Music and Conservatory in **Stockholm.** In **Prague,** the Union of Musical Artists dated from 1803 and the Prague Conservatory (where Dvořák served in 1901–4) traced back to 1810. But not until the 1860's, when Germany's domination lessened and Smetana came to the fore, did the musical climate favor the eventual founding of the Czech Philharmonic Orchestra, the Chamber Music Union (from 1876; pro-German), and the Czech Chamber Music Union (from 1894). In **Warsaw** the most pertinent institutions were the Warsaw Conservatory,

---

19. Cf. the detailed articles on London in GROVE V, especially 368–69, 375–87 (K. Dale & others), and MGG VIII, especially 1158–69 (N. Temperley). As a sample, the weekly schedule, Monday through Saturday, of the Royal Albert Hall Concerts, called, respectively, for a "Ballad," "English," "Classical," "Oratorio," "Wagner," and "Popular" night (MT XVI [1874] 1).

20. For sample programs, without sons., cf. HARMONICON IV/1 (1826) 104–5, 126–30.

21. Cf. MGG VIII 1165 for a list of main visiting soloists.

opened in 1821 (at Elsner's urging) but closed during 1831–61 by the Russians, and the Chopin School, from 1861. In **Budapest** there were the Philharmonic Society, from 1853, the National Conservatory, which traces back to 1836, and the Academy of Music, from 1875 (under Liszt's aegis).

In Russia both private and public concerts go back well before the 19th century, two leading institutions being the Music Academy in **Moscow,** from 1800, and the Philharmonic Society in **Saint Petersburg,** from 1802.[22] Along with nationalistic endeavors (under five successive Czars), the German influences were strong in Russia throughout the century, especially Schumann's and Wagner's. In the United States, where German influences were all-pervasive,[23] one may recall the founding of the Handel & Haydn Society in 1815, the Harvard Musical Association in 1837, the Mendelssohn Quintette Club (for chamber music), in 1849, and a music education curriculum at Harvard University under J. K. Paine in 1861, all in **Boston;** a Euterpean orchestra dating from the 18th century and the Philharmonic Symphony Society 23a   in **New York** in 1842; and a Philadelphia Conservatory of Music in **Philadelphia** (from 1877), where numerous private chamber groups were active throughout the century.

The Publishers and Their Policies

No one circumstance helped more to spread the sonata, of course, than its publication, especially when the publisher was enterprising enough to list and advertise it adequately. In conjunction with the city centers just noted, the most active publishers of Classic and Romantic sonatas between 1800 and 1915 may be tabulated by cities, with those listed first that issued the most sonatas.[24] Publishers who moved are listed in both cities, but not their agents in other cities (such as Breitkopf & Härtel, Simrock, Schott, and Ricordi, among other agents in London).

The Most Active Publishers of Sonatas Between 1800 and 1915
Vienna: Artaria, Haslinger, Diabelli, Mechetti, Bureau des Arts et d'Industrie, Mollo, Pennauer, Traeg
Leipzig: Breitkopf & Härtel, Kistner, Peters, Schott, Zimmermann,

22. MGG XI 1154, 1160–68 (K. Laux).
23. A typical season of U.S. programs and performances is described in MT XXV (1884) 91–92.
24. Based on statistics compiled from sons. listed in Cobbett/CHAMBER and Cat. NYPL, and from work lists of the solo and ensemble sons. at the Library of Congress.

Jurgenson, Cranz, Hofmeister, Rieter-Biedermann, Siegel, Kahnt, Rahter, J. Schuberth, Senff

Berlin: Simrock, Bote & Bock, Fürstner

Paris: Durand, Richault, Costellat, Rouart-Lerolle, Schlesinger, Heugel, Eschig, Hamelle, Leduc, Mathot, Senart, Hayet, Lemoine, Durdilly

London: Novello, Augener, Cramer, Joseph Williams, Chappell, Cocks, Curwen, Forsyth, Birchall, Oxford University Press

Other of the most active sonata publishers included André in Offenbach and Frankfurt, F. W. Schuberth in Hamburg, Hansen in Copenhagen, Ricordi in Milan, Urbánek in Prague, Gebethner & Wolff in Warsaw, Rozsavolgyi in Budapest, Jurgenson in Moscow, Schmidt in Boston, G. Schirmer in New York, and Presser in Philadelphia. Although not all of these publishers were in the sonata's main centers, Leipzig, one of those centers, held a clear lead in sonata publications (especially through Breitkopf & Härtel), with Paris and London following next. Neither in Vienna nor Berlin did the publishing of sonatas keep pace with their composition.

The statistics later in this chapter indicate a healthy number of sonatas published throughout the 19th century. Yet, one gets the frequent impression, especially during that alleged slump of the second quarter-century, that publishers generally were loathe to invest in the printing of something so extended, elaborate, and precious or outmoded as a sonata (SSB II). In his letter of 1829 quoted earlier (SSB II), Loewe seemed to be arguing against this kind of resistance on his publisher's part. Most of the publishers' rejections encountered in the present study include a fear of the modern and the unfamiliar, probably explaining André's enigmatic rejection of Weber's set of accompanied sonatas Op. 10 in 1810 for no other reason than that they "are too good!" [25]

Sometimes sonatas were sold in advance on a subcription basis to eliminate the risk for the publisher.[26] Naturally, the publisher saw no risk when the composer's reputation insured success. Coventry and Hollier were only too glad to solicit the six organ sonatas Mendelssohn wrote for them in 1844–45.[27] But, like the Nürnberg publisher J. U. Haffner about a half-century earlier (SCE 71–72, 812), the Swiss pub-

25. Nohl/GLUCK & WEBER 102–3; cf. SSB VIII on Weber.
26. Cf. Vogel/SCHUBERT 493–94, explaining why so few of Schubert's sons. had been pub.; MT LIX (1918) 164 (F. Corder), on how the Society of British Composers enabled Dale's 62-p. Son. in d to be pub.
27. Cf. Edwards/MENDELSSOHN 15; SSB VIII.

lisher J. G. Nägeli followed an unusual course when he made up whole anthologies of solo sonatas by both personal and published solicitation. Advertising in August of 1803 after at least six of the seventeen volumes in his first collection (Anth. NÄGELI-m) had appeared, he explained:

It is known that the most remarkable and consequential epoch of this art form [i.e., keyboard compositions, "sonata form" being specified later] dates from Clementi. My next purpose is therefore this—to bring to light the best works of that composer and those others who align themselves with him in matters both aesthetic and historical, thereby expanding materially the arts of keyboard composition and performance. . . . I have corresponded for a long time with many excellent artists to that purpose . . . the justly important Herr von Beethoven has already sent me important tidings and Herr Abt Vogler permits me to hope of such. . . . I will add all the other keyboard composers to the list when I conquer them with the confidence of knowing the renowned composers have been won.[28]

This first of Nägeli's sonata anthologies by solicitation and commission included not only the Classic names he mentioned but several of our early-Romantics—Cramer, Dussek, Liste, and Steibelt (E. T. A. Hoffmann's several contributions being rejected; ssB VIII). His other, similar but smaller, anthology, *Die musikalische Ehrenpforte* (1827), included sonatas by Ries and Czerny (ssB VII) but not those Nägeli sought in vain from Schubert, Weber, Mendelssohn, Spohr, Hummel, Moscheles, and several others.[29]

Probably Nägeli was not publishing those sonatas simply, in modern parlance, to decorate his catalogue. Yet just that reason for publishing sonatas was given in a prolix review of 1839 by Fink (summarized in ssB II):

Only the smallest number of new sonatas find a publisher nowadays, and even those that still manage to get published owe their desired appearance in public to a certain generosity on the part of well-known music publishers who want to show to the world that they are in a position to dare to bring out publications that at best will prove not to be advantageous but to be disadvantageous financially; [in short,] they want to prove that they are willing to sacrifice for true art. [Etc.] [30]

28. Trans. from AMZ V (1802–3) Intelligenz-Blatt 97–100; cf. SCE 26 for the continuation of this extract with some curious stipulations regarding the solicited sons. Periodic progress reports also appeared throughout 1803 and 1804 in *Zeitung für die elegante Welt* and *Wiener Zeitung*.

29. Cf. Deutsch/SCHUBERT-D 541; also, MOSCHELES I 120, in which Charlotte Moscheles writes her husband in 1826: ". . . old Nägeli, of Zurich, asks you to compose a Sonata for his periodical, but you are to avoid all repeating notes, all tenths, and all the usual signs used to indicate the expression."

30. Trans. from AMZ XLI (1839) 181–84.

Fink concluded by noting how few copies were sold when a sonata did get published. It must have been a rare edition that reached the 1,150 copies made when Lamborn Cock issued W. S. Bennett's Sonata in A♭, Op. 46, *The Maid of Orleans* (reissued only 3 years later by Kistner of Leipzig).[31]

With further regard to the publication of Romantic sonatas, reviewers helped to maintain or raise the quality of the edition itself by almost always ending their longer pieces with some comment on the format, the engraving, its accuracy, the quality of paper, and perhaps the cost. Thus, Rochlitz ended with unfavorable comments on these aspects after a favorable review of two of Weber's piano sonatas, in 1818.[32] In that same letter of 1829 by Loewe to his publisher (ssb II), cited several times already, the composer said he would welcome a new cover for his sonatas, "provided I [myself] don't find it superficial or even unacceptable." But he doubted the need for "a special title or the issuing of single movements from sonatas in order to provide a market for them."

Intriguing covers and special titles, original or acquired, did indeed help to make a sonata better known and, even, more popular, sometimes distinguishing it undeservedly from its fellows. They have always helped in this way, as with Purcell's "Golden Sonata," or Tartini's "Devil's Trill," or Clementi's "Didone abbandonata." But they helped especially in the programmatically minded Romantic Era, even when there was no more of a "programme" than the title itself, as in Beethoven's "Moonlight Sonata," Moscheles' "Sonata mélancolique," or Medtner's "Sonate orageuse." [33] Of course, no programmatic title was involved, but rather a question of current taste, when, according to Schumann, Schubert (too hopefully) foresaw better publication prospects for his so-called "Grand Duo," D. 812, by entitling it "Sonata" instead of "Symphony" on the autograph.[34]

The publication of separate sonata movements came up earlier in connection with the programming of separate movements in recitals (ssb III). Such publications occurred often. For example, each of the four movements of Spohr's Op. 125 appeared separately[35] as did those

31. Cf. Bennett/BENNETT 442. In 1882, 1,000 was given as the number of copies in a choral ed. (MT XXIII [1882] 117). No study of 19th-c. son. eds. is known here comparable to the new study by K. Hortschansky for the 18th century, in AM XL (1968) 154–74.

32. AMZ XX (1818) 687–88.

33. Recall that the validity of such titles was questioned by contemporary reviewers (ssb II). Cf., also, the review in MMR III (1873) 104–5 of W. S. Bennett's, *The Maid of Orleans*, Op. 46.

34. Schumann/SCHRIFTEN I 329–30.

35. PAZDÍREK XIII 915.

of M. Labey's Sonata "en 4 parties" (ssB XIII) and S. N. Penfield's *Poem of Life,* subtitled *Four Characteristic Pieces in the Form of a Sonata* (ssB XIX). The Spohr and Labey sonatas were each published in their entirety, too. But in most instances of separate publications only one movement from a sonata was so treated, as with the favorite movements of British organ sonatas by E. Silas and W. T. Best (ssB XIV).[36] A reviewer even asked in 1875, now that a performer was no longer "mad" if he played a whole sonata at one sitting, why was it not possible to publish the whole of a "Sonata No. 1" for P solo by one E. A. Sydenham instead of merely its "Andante"? [37]

The use of opus numbers continued to be as erratic for Cramer, Dussek, and Schubert as it had been for Haydn, Mozart, and Clementi, typically with each publisher starting his own sequence, sometimes a separate sequence for each category of a composer's works (cf. scE 78–79). But after the reasonably satisfactory sequence of Beethoven's opus numbers and the apparently meticulous sequence of Czerny's 861 opus numbers (in the approximately two-thirds of his published works to which op. nos. were assigned! ssB VII), composers seem to have paid more attention to this organizational aspect of their output and taken more control of it. Ries (ssB VII) and Czerny were among those composers who assigned further, separate sequences of numbers to their sonatas,[38] thus not only confirming the chronological orders but indicating which out of a still larger number of sonatas by them they themselves regarded as important enough to go into these specially numbered lists. One effect of the composer's assigning his own opus numbers was to include MS sonatas in the sequence—an effect evident especially in the designations of many a late-Romantic's sonatas that got only partially into print (e.g., those of C. V. Stanford). The publication of sonatas in sets under single opus numbers largely disappeared in the Romantic Era except for the diminutive pedagogic types and the shorter examples of a prolific composer like Raff (ssB X) or Reger (ssB XI). Most of the serious Romantic sonatas—for instance, Schumann's or Chopin's—were too long and too individual to be levelled in this manner. Toward the end of the era some composers began to discard opus numbers entirely, as did Strauss, in his later years, and Dukas.

The accompanied sonatas of the early Romantic Era such as Dussek, Cramer, and Ries still wrote, continued to be published in separate

---

36. For an extreme example, cf. the long list of separate eds. of the finale from Weber's Op. 24 ("Perpetuum mobile"), in PAZDÍREK XV 182–83.

37. MT XVII (1875) 245.

38. Cf. Czerny's letter of 1823 to C. F. Peters as quoted in ssB VII.

parts for the keyboard and for the violin or other accompanying instrument. At most, a more soloistic passage in the "accompaniment" might be cued into the piano part (as in the finale of Ries's Op. 76/1). As this kind of ensemble became more of a true duo (ssb V), the pianist's score began to include the other part in full.

Plagiarism seems to have been much less of a problem in the Romantic than in the Baroque and Classic sonata (cf. sbe 44–45 and sce 75–76). It may have been discouraged not only by the steps taken toward better protection of creative property, including the gradually firmer and more specific U.S. provisions after the first copyright law was enacted in 1831 (ssb XIX), but by the greater emphasis on artistic individuality, originality, and self-identity that was characteristic of all Romantic art (ssb II). When the plagiarism of a sonata did occur it was less likely to be a direct steal [39] than one of the countless arrangements that were constantly being made of the most successful sonata movements, especially in the first half-century, whether for P-duet, 2 Ps, various other ensembles, large or small, or full orchestra. As but one example, Chopin's "Marche funèbre," composed in 1837 and incorporated in 1839 as the third movement of Op. 35, was arranged once or more for P & organ, harmonium, mandolin or Vn, zither, 2 Ps, harmonium & Vn-or-Vc, mandolin & P, Vn & P, Vn-or-Fl & P, P & Vc, Fl & P, 2 Vns, Fl & Vn, cornet & P, harmonium & P & Vn, and many more combinations up to full orchestra.[40]

Some Quantitative Aspects of Publication

Like the sociological approach to sonata history (ssb III) and closely related to it, the quantitative approach remains one of the most promising facets awaiting further investigation. As any trained researcher knows only too well, the statistics of quantity can be not only colorless but risky, as when they are not representative enough or are interpreted either too stiffly or too loosely. Yet, without them as one foundation, it is impossible to make safe generalizations about distributions, proportions, or trends. Thus, in our discussion earlier of the content of programs in which sonatas figured (ssb III), statistics were available for only one aspect—the sonata in England in the first

39. Brahms presumably was joking when he asked Simrock whether a theme in his "Regenlied" Sonata, Op. 78, could be regarded as a plagiarism of his song by that name, pub. by Rieter-Biedermann (BRAHMS BRIEFWECHSEL XVI 218; ssb IX).

40. PAZDÍREK III 291–92. PAZDÍREK is the most convenient and one of the most thorough listings of these arrangements, which represent a broad tangential extension of the Romantic son. that can get no more than passing mentions here except as scoring variants (ssb V).

half-century; but these provided the firmest basis we have thus far for any generalizations that could be made about the types of sonatas preferred in programs. In the present chapter statistics have already helped to illustrate the geographical spread of the Romantic sonata composers and in the remainder they will give some idea both of the quantity of published sonatas by those composers and of their quantitative relationship to other categories of Romantic music. Furthermore, quantitative statistics will be offered in Chapter V regarding the most popular settings of the Romantic sonata, and in Chapter VI regarding some of their most prevalent style and structural traits.

These statistical applications should at least suggest a few of the many further and more thorough applications that await the necessary investigations. For example, it would illuminate the topics in all four chapters (ssb III–VII on use, spread, scoring, and form) to find a better basis than chance observation for rating the sonata composers according to the contemporary popularity of their sonatas. If the proof of that popularity lies mainly in the number of sales and performances, then some sort of statistical formula would have to be worked out that might add, say, the sizes of the editions of the composer's published sonatas to the number of reprints, the number of arrangements, the number and extent (if not the consensus) of the reviews, and the number of performances, all divided by the number of the composer's published sonatas. In this way, Franck, with one sonata, would not necessarily be rated below Rheinberger, with twenty-nine sonatas. The main sources for such an investigation would be, once more, those essential bibliographic tools—the chief periodicals, plus HOFMEISTER, plus PAZDÍREK. If these tools have any main shortcoming it is their understandably strong German orientation.[41]

Unfortunately, there was nothing in the 19th century quite like our present-day *Schwann Long-Playing Record Catalog* to reflect public tastes and preferences; or, on a more systematic basis, like the periodic polls taken by the Stanford University psychologist Paul R. Farnsworth, which most recently (1964) rated Brahms, Schubert, Chopin, Schumann, R. Strauss, Mendelssohn, Tchaikovsky, and Liszt in that order of "eminence" (picking out here only Romantics who contributed consequentially to the son. out of the first 28 of 103 composers of all time rated by 853 members of the American Musicological Society).[42]

41. In MT XXIV (1883) 295–303, "The Music Publishers' Association's Catalogue" apparently was the first of its kind in England.

42. The findings of the poll were circulated by mail in 1965. Cf. Farnsworth/ TASTE 39–47, 68–80. In Fuchs/CRITIQUE, 50,000 (!) compositions and their 2,576 composers are rated as to quality (and difficulty of the music), with Schubert the only Romantic in the first class (after Bach, Beethoven, Handel, and Mozart).

At most, 19th-century writers seem to have left only brief tabulations that throw light on musical taste or popularity, and none of these found here happens to focus on the sonata. At least pertinent, however, are Schumann's counts of composers performed at the Gewandhaus and other concerts in Leipzig during the winter of 1837–38 (in the first of 2 articles on music in Leipzig during that and the next winter).[43] He found 17 performances of works by Mozart, 15 by Beethoven, 7 by Weber, 5 by Haydn, 3–5 each by Cherubini, Spohr, Mendelssohn (who was then conducting the Gewandhaus Orchestra), and Rossini, 2 each by Handel, Bach, Vogler, Cimarosa, Méhul, Onslow, and Moscheles, and one each by several others.

As to some rough idea of how many sonatas the Romantics wrote, we can start with the total of their published sonatas listed in the cumulative volumes of HOFMEISTER from 1828 (Whistling's cumulative list going back to at least 1800) to 1913, which in round numbers is about 7,475.[44] The rounding out of the numbers is necessary, at best, because it is not always possible to tell sonatas by the Romantics from those by the Classics (the latter being about twice as many in the same vols.), or reprints from first editions, or arrangements from original scorings, or one method of listing from another. Moreover, although HOFMEISTER has usually covered publications in Austro-Germany quite thoroughly, it has varied greatly in its coverage of those in other countries. Thus, probably most of at least 190 sonatas by British composers known to have been published between 1801 and 1850 [45] can be found in the early volumes of HOFMEISTER. But more and more publications outside of Germany cannot be found in the later volumes as the rising spirit of nationalism and the sheer bulk of the publications limited the coverage increasingly to Austro-Germany. An educated guess might then bring the total of published sonatas in the Romantic Era up to about 10,000, or the grand total of sonatas composed during that time to as many as 30,000, since in the experience of the present study, at least twice as many sonatas remained in MS. This conjecture of 30,000 sonatas is like the total of more than 625 composers noted in the present volume in being not less, as might be supposed on first thought, but well over a third higher than the corresponding figures for the Classic Era (SCE 68 and 8). One can only assume, again (SSB I),

43. Schumann/SCHRIFTEN I 373–80, 501–11 (less specific, but with similar conclusions). Cf. Werner/MENDELSSOHN 311–12.

44. The dates of each cumulative vol. up to 1897 and the total no. of its son. listings may be seen in our next tabulation (infra).

45. Temperley/CORRESPONDENCE. Cf. their analysis by decades and scoring types in SSB V.

that larger populations, more countries, and more participation by the middle classes largely account for the differences.

In connection with quantities, the alleged slump in sonata output during the second quarter-century gets some support from HOFMEISTER, though less than is suggested by the following breakdown for most of the 19th century:

The Number of Sonatas Listed in the Cumulative Volumes of HOFMEISTER *during the 19th Century*

Inclusive years	Number of sonatas (rounded to nearest 5)
(*ca.* 1800–)1828 (Whistling)	1,800
1829–33	130
1834–38	145
(*ca.* 1815–)43	1,885
1844–51	170
1852–59	285
1860–67	320
1868–73	310
1874–79	435
1880–85	390
1886–91	365
1892–97	260

The two large numbers actually represent much larger cumulations than the other figures, the first from at least 1800 (including HOF-MEISTER 1815 [Whistling]), the second from at least 1815 (meaning a considerable overlap). In any case, the spans of lowest output, 1829–33 and 1834–38, are hardly late enough nor the numbers of sonatas for those years small enough to bear out a statement by Kretzschmar in 1910 that in 1850 only three sonatas were published! [46] The larger figures in the second half-century represent, apart from longer cumulations, the rise of interest in the sonata especially around 1870. This rise actually lasted longer than it appears to, since allowance has to be made for that increasing tendency to exclude non-German publishers in HOFMEISTER.

Our last quantitative tabulation here gives some hint of the sonata's relative cultivation among all categories of 19th-century music, although mainly only through the critical period of the slump and, again, only insofar as this information can be culled from and is

46. Kretzschmar/AUFSÄTZE I 163.

representative in the publications listed in HOFMEISTER. This time the numbers are only systematic estimates translated into percentages of the total publications rather than exact counts rounded out. Further-more, they include all publications between about 1800 and 1851, Classic or earlier as well as Romantic, plus a late-Romantic span, 1904–8, for comparison. The heading "Other categories," by far the most numerous, covers from 20 to 25 types of settings, including miscellaneous instrumental combinations, church music, other vocal music, and arrangements. The first and fourth totals are much the largest again, for the reasons given above. Even though they are only rough estimates, these percentages give a better idea of the sonata's

Percentages of Sonatas and Other Categories in
HOFMEISTER *up to 1908*

Categories	Percentages					
	(ca. 1800–)1828	1829–33	1834–38	*(ca.* 1815–)43	1844–51	1904–8
Orchestra: symphonies, overtures, marches, fantasias	1.5	1.5	1.0	1.5	1.0	6.5
Orchestra & voice: operas & extracts, other nonchurch music	2.5	1.0	1.5	1.5	.05	4.0
Piano solo: rondos, variations, fantasias, dances	21.0	32.0	27.0	25.0	29.0	8.5
Chamber music for 3 or more instruments	10.0	8.5	5.0	7.0	8.0	8.5
Other categories (see text)	56.5	55.5	64.0	61.0	57.0	68.5
SONATAS	8.5	1.5	1.5	4.0	4.5	4.0
TOTAL LISTINGS (= 100%)	44,000	8,900	9,500	55,000	19,510	26,000

relative slump in the second quarter-century than the absolute figures in the previous tabulation. Moreover, they relate the sonata to other categories and its slump to other trends. They indicate that the slump was well on the way toward ending by the early 1840's. At the same time they show, to a lesser degree, a corresponding slump and res-toration in chamber music, and, in an approximate way, a compen-satory rise and decline in light piano music, a fact noted by nearly all those who commented on the sonata's slump during its occurrence. However, a strong word of caution is needed when this last tabulation is used to relate the sonata to categories more remote from it. The sonata has always been one of the easier genres to print because so few instruments have been involved. Naturally, the larger the ensemble the costlier is the publication, the fewer are its public sales, and the more are the compositions that remain in MS. Opera, for example, must be vastly underrated in its popularity by this tabulation. But not until there are catalogues that list the 19th-century holdings of the largest libraries, both MSS and publications, will it be possible to do any more than guess at such a rating. All that can be added here beyond the guesses is the estimate that by the 1850's the sonata returned to only about half of the relative position it had held among all music publications early in the century, during the overlap with the late-Classic Era. From the 1850's to the end of the Romantic Era, the sonata appears to have accounted for not quite a twentieth of all music publications.

Chapter V

Instruments, Settings, and
Performance Practices

The Piano as the Voice of Romanticism

The alternative of piano-or-harpsichord that prevailed in the high-Classic Era (SCE 84–89) ended with the piano's full victory around the turn of the century. From then on, as Einstein has emphasized so tellingly, the "pianoforte" became the focal instrument of musical Romanticism. It provided the most direct and universal answer to the Romantic penchant for "sheer sound" as an aesthetic fact in itself—for the mystical depths and highs of new sonorities, for a mysterious "withdrawal" from the specific "word" of a text into the greater but more occult truth of "wordless music."[1] Cortot has seen the new intimacy and techniques of the piano as opening the way to the Romantic sonata after Beethoven.[2] A eulogy on the piano credited to Liszt in 1837 amplifies its values in ways that he must have endorsed even if he was not the actual author:

My piano is to me what his boat is to the seaman, what his horse is to the Arab: nay, more, it has been till now my eye, my speech, my life. Its strings have vibrated under my passions, and its yielding keys have obeyed my every caprice. Perhaps the secret tie which holds me so closely to it is a delusion; but I hold the piano very high. In my view it takes the first place in the hierarchy of instruments; it is the oftenest used and the widest spread. . . . In the circumference of its seven octaves it embraces the whole circumference of an orchestra; and a man's ten fingers are enough to render the harmonies which in an orchestra are only brought out by the combination of hundreds of musicians. . . . We can give broken chords like the harp, long sustained tones like the wind, staccati and a thousand passages which before it seemed only possible to produce on this or that instrument. . . . The piano has on the one side the capacity of assimilation; the capacity of taking into itself the

1. Cf. Einstein/ROMANTIC 6–8, 33–35, 198–200.
2. Cortot/INTERPRÉTATION 140–41.

life of all (instruments); on the other it has its own life, its own growth, its individual development. . . . It is a microcosm, a micro-theus. . . .[3]

In less mystical terms, the piano became the most useful, the most versatile, the most characteristic of all instruments. It could sing, as Schubert rejoiced to discover,[4] and almost as the clavichord had sung for Emanuel Bach (SCE 428). It could be infinitely poetic, as Schumann reveals in his oft-quoted description in 1834 of Chopin playing his "Aeolian Harp Étude." [5] And it could be brilliant, stentorian, daemonic, overpowering, as the many descriptions of Liszt's playing make abundantly clear.[6] It became by all odds the favorite solo instrument in recitals, the indispensable instrument in most chamber music, and the standard instrument in the home. Indeed, as E.-L. F. Fétis (son of François-Joseph) observed in 1847, the piano's popularity, especially in Paris, was making the violin, flute, cello, harp, and other instruments obsolete, as well as "large amounts of music . . .—overtures and entire opera scores—arranged for two flutes, [or] two violins, [or] two guitars, [or] two flageolets." [7] There was not even a mention of the cello part when "Moscheles himself plays Beethoven's" Sonata in D, Op. 102/1, nor either the cellist or violinist when "Madame Schumann played" trios by Moscheles and Mendelssohn.[8]

The first half of the 19th century saw most of the basic improvements in pianos as we know them today.[9] The range was gradually increased to seven octaves and more; heavier, tenser strings were introduced to provide fuller tones that lasted longer and carried better; metal braces were added to resist both the greater tension of more and heavier strings and the effect of changing temperature and humidity on the strings and wood frame; and these braces were then united in a single cast-iron frame. At the same time the strings were fixed better through improved bridging; the principle of cross- or over-stringing was introduced as a means of freeing the strings from their metallic environment and improving the resonance of the sounding board, which was

3. As trans. from RGM for 1837, in Bie/PIANOFORTE 281–82. On the doubtful authorship cf. SSB X on Liszt. Cf., also, Thalberg's statement on the social value of the piano, as trans. in Rimbault/PIANOFORTE 159–61.

4. Deutsch/SCHUBERT-D 436.

5. Schumann/SCHRIFTEN I 234–35.

6. Cf. Loesser/PIANOS 365–71; Schonberg/PIANISTS 151–71.

7. As introduced and trans. in Loesser/PIANOS 413.

8. MOSCHELES II 45 and 78.

9. Cf. GROVE VI 733–44 and 606–7 (A. J. Hipkins & R. E. M. Harding), with further bibliography; also, Rimbault/PIANOFORTE 148–59 (interesting especially as a pioneer account). Further, cf. Loesser/PIANOS 301–4, 397–411, 458–65, 509–15, 518–36, 549–60, 566–74, 586–613, with much new information; Bie/PIANOFORTE 309–16.

itself improved; the hammers were covered better and more heavily, with specially prepared felt; the action was enlivened, particularly by the repetition device in the double-escapement; and both the soft or shifting pedal and the damper pedal were perfected.[10] Square and upright pianos in the home underwent similar improvements. There was also considerable experimentation, notably Paul von Janko's promising but unsuccessful redesign of the piano keyboard, in 1882–84, in favor of greater facility and stretches.[11] Broadwood, Érard, Clementi, Pleyel, Stodart, Bösendorfer, Chickering, Steinway, and Bechstein (in that approximate order) were among the leaders in the development and manufacture of pianos. The Bechstein piano was first played in recital by Bülow, in January, 1857, in Berlin, on which occasion Bülow also introduced Liszt's Sonata in b to the public.[12]

In the vanguard among proponents of these piano improvements were the composers, performers, and appreciators, themselves. Thus, right at the start of the era, Dussek, as one of his striking, prescient Romanticisms (ssb XVII), took a special interest in the piano's development. From 1793 on, he repeatedly persuaded Broadwood to extend the range of his pianos (up to 6 octaves) and in his sonata titles and scores he repeatedly specified "additional keys"; he indicated the use of the pedal for particular effects as early as 1799 and often thereafter in his sonatas; he achieved extraordinary success when he played Érard's first piano with the new repetition action in Paris in 1808; and he continued to struggle courageously with inadequate instruments up to his death in 1812.[13] In the last regard, a reviewer ended a favorable report in 1813 of a Sonata Op. 27 by Friedrich Schneider with this typical reminder:

That the work demands a well-rehearsed, solid player has already been indicated. But it also demands an effective instrument, capable of many graduations from delicate to robust, as well as expressive legato.[14]

Hummel preferred the light, clean, yet solid touch of the Streicher-Graf piano made in Vienna, for his concert playing.[15] Moscheles was another early Romantic who took a keen and continuing interest in the piano's development. In the 1820's and 1830's he preferred the lightness of touch, clarity of tone, and "more supple mechanism for my repeating notes, skips, and full chords" on the Clementi piano as

---

10. Cf. the pedal instruction under the first Schumann ex. in ssb VIII.
11. Cf. Loesser/PIANOS 566–69.
12. Raabe/LISZT II 250.
13. Cf. ssb XVII; Craw/DUSSEK 53–54, 75, 171, 175, 468–71.
14. AMZ XV (1813) 178–79 (Rochlitz).
15. Egert/FRÜHROMANTIKER 10–11. Cf. Hummel/ANWEISUNG 426–28.

against the heavier touch, yet fuller, more resonant tone of the Broadwood. The Érard's repetition also appealed to him, but not its tone at first.[16] Chopin seems to have been satisfied with the piano as he found it, regarding the still delicate, wood-frame Pleyel as "perfection," and always preferring it to the Érard (which Thalberg and Liszt used) or the Broadwood.[17]

The Organ as the Voice of the Church

In sonata history the organ has followed a rather well-defined, somewhat independent course of its own, partly because of the nature of the instrument and partly because of its primary dedication to church service (cf. SBE 36, 56–57; SCE 89–91). During the 19th century, the organ, like the piano, went through its own epochal "improvements," although not without sacrificing the ensemble of the former, "classic" organ.[18] Mainly it increased in size, power, complexity, and expressive range. Fundamental were the developments of a pneumatically assisted action, by the early 1840's, and of the application of electric power, within the next generation. Electro-pneumatic action was perfected by the turn of this century. In the words of Willi Apel,

Organists [inclined toward these "improvements"] naturally boast of, and revel in, that multiplicity of devices: couplers, swells, pistons, crescendo pedal, combination pedals, etc., which, in connection with overpowering or sentimental stops (Trumpet, Stentorphone, Tuba mirabilis, Vox angelica, Unda maris, Tremulant), enable them to pass instantly from the softest whisper to a roar far surpassing the *fff*-effects of the biggest orchestra, to imitate all conceivable colors of the orchestra, and to produce a great variety of sensational effects.[19]

The mid- to late-Romantic Era contributed more to the organ sonata than the Classic Era, with Mendelssohn's *Six Grand Sonatas for the Organ*, Op. 65 (1844–45) at the start and the peak, and further successful examples by Merkel, Reubke, A. G. Ritter, Rheinberger, Reger, Karg-Elert (who also wrote sons. for his version of the harmonium; SSB XI), Widor, Vierne, Guilmant, Lemmens, and still others.[20] The 20a organ sonata usually differed from the piano sonata, when it was not

16. MOSCHELES I 65, 106–7, 109, 111, 219, 245–47; II 15, 29, 168 (on a piano with octave coupler), 230–32.

17. Cf. Sydow & Hedley/CHOPIN 101, 305, 315, 317; CONGRESS CHOPIN 456 (J. Urbański).

18. Cf. GROVE VI 303–18 (R. Whitworth).

19. Apel/DICTIONARY 532.

20. Kremer/ORGAN includes a full bibliography of organ sonatas since 1845.

simply an arrangement of the latter (*infra*), in its greater solemnity, often being adapted to or even designated for church use (ssʙ III); in its frequent use of chorales, variations, fantasias, and fugal or related contrapuntal movements; in its somewhat more conservative idioms; and, of course, in its exploitation of the most widely divergent orchestral colors.[21] In 1849 a reviewer, though recognizing the piano sonata's greater definition since Mozart and Beethoven, found identifiable traits in the organ sonata, too. He found the extremes of its best styles in the logical, serious Sonata in d, Op. 11, by A. G. Ritter (ssʙ X), but not in the sentimental disorganized *Phantasie-Sonate*, Op. 83, by A. Hesse (ssʙ XVII).[22]

In 1871, while defending church organists' salaries as the equal of piano teachers', an English churchman derided the "average Organist of the provinces" who plays pieces "of the light, unorganlike character" and who "is fond of [appropriating] movements from the piano sonatas, and always the most unsuitable of these unsuitables." To which, one of those provincial organists rejoined, "I only get 7s. 6d. for giving a lesson on one of Beethoven's Sonatas; therefore I am amply paid if I play that same sonata to the public for 7s. 6d!" [23] Occasionally one finds piano sonatas that sound as though they should have been scored for organ and designated for church use in the first place, such as Lekeu's Sonata in g, with two fugues and three free movements (ssʙ XIII). Reger is known to have endorsed an article of 1899 by Riemann urging that the tendency toward archaic, salon lyricism and the adaptation of the "old" piano sonata in the organ sonatas from Mendelssohn to Rheinberger be abandoned for the variations, fugues, chorales, and fantasias, and a genuine return to the "Bachian spirit." [24]

Other Instruments of the Romantic Sonata

Unlike the keyboard instruments, the violin, viola, and cello had attained nearly their full developments before the Romantic Era (sʙᴇ 54, scᴇ 91–92) and underwent no such epochal changes in the 19th century. There were no advances in instrument construction beyond the perfection of the Tourte bow. And even the extreme virtuosity introduced by Paganini in his violin sonatas (and other Vn music)

---

21. Cf. Frotscher/ORGELSPIEL II 1150–51, 1164–65, 1204–11 (distinguishing between fantasy, motto [or programmatically associative], and chorale sonatas); also, the ex. by D. Buck in ssʙ XIX.

22. ɴᴢᴍ XXX (1849) 185–86, with exx. (G. Siebeck).

23. ᴍᴛ XV (1871) 283 and 315.

24. Barker/REGER 170. Cf., also, ᴢɪᴍɢ III (1901–2) 337–38 (chiefly on Mendelssohn).

did not surpass that in the Baroque Era, from Biber's to Locatelli's sonatas, as much as might be supposed (cf. sbe 146–47). There was important new literature for all three instruments, of course.[25] It includes, for example, the sonatas for Va & P by J. N. Hummel, Onslow (as alternatives to Vc & P), Rubinstein, Brahms (as alternatives to Cl & P), Bowen, and Dale; and those for Vc & P by Mendelssohn, Chopin, Brahms, Gernsheim, Kiel, Lalo, Grädener, Saint-Saëns, Hiller, Rubinstein, F. Hummel, Moór, Draeseke, Reger, Nicodé, Kahn, Rachmaninoff, Juon, Vierne, Holbrooke, and Fauré. The sonatas for Vn and P were far too numerous to summarize in any similar manner except for the observation that so few of them—chiefly those by Schumann, Brahms, Franck, Fauré, and Strauss—survive as first-class masterpieces still played today.[26] There was an occasional new stringed instrument, too—notably, H. Ritter's large, more sonorous but somewhat unmanageable "viola alta," [27] used (not in its 5-string extension) in two sonatas by Draeseke (ssb X).

The Spanish guitar and its ancestors had been the vehicle of a special branch of the sonata ever since the sonata's origins (cf. sbe 18, 65–66; sce 92–93). It still survived as such in the early, though not the later, 19th century. Sor, Giuliani, Spohr, Paganini, and Nava were among its chief exponents, both as performers and sonata composers.[28] Spohr also left harp sonatas.

The wind instruments underwent significant changes and experiments in the 19th century with respect to materials, size and range, bore, placing of holes, and perfection of the mechanical keys. Only the clarinet and flute were used to any appreciable extent in sonatas, and relatively little at that.[29] Thus, among composers of sonatas for Cl & P, chiefly in the mid- and late-Romantic Era, might be named Brahms, Draeseke, Rheinberger (as an alternative to Vn & P; ssb X, with ex.), Jenner, Reger, Stanford (ssb XIV, with ex.), and Saint-Saëns (ssb XIII, with ex. and with mentions of almost the only noteworthy examples for Ob & P and for Bn & P). Composers of sonatas for Fl & P include Kuhlau (ssb XV, with ex.), Barnett, G. A. Macfarren, Reinecke, and Widor. Both F. Hummel and Rheinberger left sonatas for Hn & P, and Nisle for P & "cor de chasse." Under wind instruments may also be

25. Cf. Cobbett/chamber II 536–53.
26. Eligible for more consideration from the later Romantic Era are sons. by R. Fuchs, Reger, Kahn, Rheinberger, Gernsheim, Saint-Saëns, and Witkowski (all discussed in ssb).
27. Cf. mgg XIII 1687–88 (A. Berner).
28. Cf. sce 663–64 and 569–70; ssb VIII and XVI, respectively.
29. Cf. Cobbett/chamber I 65, 280, 401–3, 572, and II 194; the separate listings for each instrument with P in Altmann/kammermusik; also, Tuthill/clarinet.

noted the "sonatas" for voice & P by Spohr (with text) and Medtner (on vowels only).[30]

Settings, Favorite and Less Favorite

To explore the Romantic settings of the sonata we need to start with some idea of what the settings were and which were most used. A tabulation follows that analyzes, by settings and in order of preference, the quantitative statistics derived from HOFMEISTER, in the penultimate tabulation of the previous chapter. Although exact figures, not rounded off, are given this time, they must still be regarded only as rough approximations. Those same variables, uncertainties, and possible contradictions or overlaps again stand in the way of greater precision. Recall, also, that the HOFMEISTER volumes terminating in 1828 and 1843 represent much larger, overlapping cumulations—at least a quarter-century each—than the other volumes. The headings for P-duet and 2Ps include one example each with string accompaniment. The "trios" of the earlier decades are included not only because the title "sonata" admits them in our semantic approach (SSB I) but because the genesis of the piano trio lay so clearly in the accompanied sonata. Most of these "trios" are not broken down by setting in HOFMEISTER but may be assumed, in fact, to consist largely of "sonatas" for $P\pm Vn\pm Vc$, the few others being for P with Vn & Hn, or Va & Vc, or Fl & Vn (several), or Fl & Va, or Fl & Vc (several). Also, HOFMEISTER does not distinguish between accompanied piano sonatas and true duos in the listings for P & Vn, again a problem only for the earlier decades.

The tabulation of settings happens to give us another view of the second-quarter-century slump in sonata output (SSB II and IV), once more suggesting that its significance and extent were exaggerated by contemporaries. The conspicuous absence of any 19th-century organ sonatas prior to Mendelssohn's in 1844–45 does not mean any special drop in organ publications then (preludes, fugues, chorale arrangements, etc.), but rather no inclination to adapt the sonata idea to organ use until a relative universalist like Mendelssohn set the example.[31] Above all, the tabulation brings out the strong preference for the solo piano setting in the 19th century, nearly twice (41% as against 21%) what

---

30. For further exx., cf. T. Kewitsch in SSB XI (on 3 poems for 3 mvts.) and C. Fowler in MT XXVII (1886) 109 (for voice, P, & Vn).

31. HOFMEISTER (ca. 1815–)43, p. 325 does list organ sons. by one Möller and by "Gio. Morandi," but if these men are the same that are mentioned in Frotscher/ ORGELSPIEL 1080 and 799–800, respectively, their sons. probably were too early for our tabulation.

The 19th-Century Sonata Settings, in Order of Preference, in the Cumulative Volumes of HOFMEISTER

Settings	(ca. 1800–)1828	1829–33	1834–38	(ca. 1815–)'43	1844–51	1852–59	1860–67	1868–73	1874–79	1880–85	1886–91	1892–97	Totals/%
P solo	701	83	75	777	71	138	114	167	180	151	115	62	2,634/41
P & Vn	381	16	25	333	33	53	71	58	107	79	112	108	1,376/21
P-duet	149	13	27	202	39	51	71	44	35	40	7		686/11
P & Fl	155	5	9	157	3		8		2	13	13		365/6
P & Vc	23	5	6	41	10	16	17	20	57	52	37	38	322/5
Trios	154		1	139	10	16	25	17	13	27	36	23	294/5
Organ solo	51			49		2	3		12		27	23	167/3
Duos, mixed, without P	3	2		72	3				16	3	1	1	115/2
Duos, unmixed, without P	54		1	13							7	7	113/2
Harp solo	4			4	1		1		2				75/1
2 Ps	9	1		31			1			1			42/
Guitar solo	24			17									41/
Guitar & Vn	29	1		11									41/
Harp & Vn	9			9		3	2		4	3			41/
Vn solo	4			4							3	2	40/
P & Va	11	1		10		4	1		4	3	2	7	31/
Other duos, with P	4		1	5			4		2	7	1	1	30/
P & Cl	9			9								2	25/
Guitar duos	10			3									18/
Fl solo	9												13/
Cl solo	6												9/
Vc solo										5			6/
Zither solo													5/
TOTALS	1,799	130	145	1,886	170	283	322	309	434	388	364	259	6,489/100

←-----less than one per cent-----→ (applies to the Totals/% entries from "2 Ps" through "Zither solo")

is indicated for the next most numerous setting, P & Vn. However, it is interesting to note the latter catching up near the end of the era, a trend that tallies with the output we shall be observing especially in Germany, France, and England (ssB XI, XIII, and XIV).[32] The sonata for Vc & P showed an almost equally healthy rise. It is interesting to notice, too, how much more appeal the sonata for P-duet had for composers (and performers) than that for 2 Ps, this time a trend that every present-day, two-piano team in search of original literature must have lamented. Of course, the problem of having two approximately equal pianos at hand has always been a practical deterrent. The virtual disappearance of the guitar sonata has already been mentioned.

It is possible to add one further, shorter tabulation, of some 340 19th-century sonata settings in order of preference, limited in this instance to those supposedly dating from 1801 to 1850 by composers in England from their infancy (or later if Irish).[33] Parentheses are used to indicate additional, unpublished settings. The "uncertain" settings, which cannot be ascribed to a particular decade, even include

English Sonata Settings from 1801 to 1850, in Order of Preference

Settings	1801–10	1811–20	1821–30	1831–40	1841–50	Uncertain	Totals/%
P solo	83	35	4	2	5 (3)	70	202/59
P acc'd. by 1 or more strings or winds	38 (3)	9	1			36	87/25
Duo (P + 1 other instrument)			1		8 (9)	22	40/12
Organ	3					6	9/3
P-duet	1				(2)		3/1
TOTALS	128	44	6	2	27	134	341/100

some that may not belong to the first half-century at all. They are based on indirect information and represent sonatas that may or may not have been published. Although it is not possible to relate the two tabulations any more closely and although the totals would not be proportional, anyway, since the larger tabulation includes the more chamber-music-minded, second half-century, there still is a rough concordance in the highest preferences. The chief differences are the much

32. Unperceptive is a statement in NZM LXVIII/2 (1872) 377 that nobody was writing or pub. sons. for Vn & P anymore (or trios).
33. From Temperley/CORRESPONDENCE.

greater evidence of the slump and the lesser interest in the P-duet that are shown in the English tabulation. There is actually less concordance between the latter and the summary of public sonata performances, also in England, during the same period, as given in connection with recital content in Chapter III. In the performances the settings for P & Vn slightly topped those for P solo (53% as against 49%). But this difference may well be explained by the relative infrequency of *all* solo performances during that period.

The Nature of the Settings

By virtue of its position as the most favored type, the sonata's setting for P solo deserves first attention here. Schumann summed up three main styles of piano writing with his usual astuteness (in the course of his review of a Sonata in E♭ by Loewe; ssb VIII):

The older I get, the more I realize that the piano communicates basically and idiomatically chiefly in three ways—through full texture and harmonic variety (as by Beethoven, [or] Franz Schubert), through use of the pedal (as by Field), or through volubility (as by Czerny, [or] Herz). In the first category one finds the heavy-set player, in the second the fantasying [sort], and in the third the [sort with] the pearly [touch]. Many-sided, cultivated composer-virtuosos, like Hummel, Moscheles, and, most recently, Chopin, unite all three means and therefore become most loved by the performers. . . .[34]

Further discussion of these and other treatments of the piano in the Romantic sonata would take us into problems of style that are better deferred to the next chapter. But it is worth noting here that already in 1821 the French music lexicographer F.-H.-J. Blaze had written "The sonata is most appropriate [when scored] for piano [solo, rather than the outmoded setting of Vn-or-Fl/bass], on which one can play three or four, or even more, distinct parts at once. It is also on this instrument that it [the sonata] has advanced the furthest in its astonishing progress." [35]

In 1838, Schilling also recognized that the piano rather than the violin had become the primary vehicle of the sonata. Yet he was falling behind the times in still not dissociating the piano from its traditional, often optional "accompaniment" of Vn, Fl, &/or Vc.[36] That that most characteristic Classic setting (sce 98–105) was disappearing in the early-Romantic Era is symptomized by a change of heading in

34. Schumann/SCHRIFTEN I 58.
35. CASTIL-BLAZE II 272.
36. Schilling/LEXICON VI 418.

the pertinent category in HOFMEISTER. In 1815 the heading that included accompanied-keyboard sonatas merely read "Duetten für das Pianoforte." [37] In 1828 it read "Duetten für Pianoforte und Violine etc.," already taking cognizance of the violin's rise toward equality in true duos.[38] Although many of the "accompaniments" actually continued to be subordinate under the latter heading, they were no longer qualified as optional ("ad libitum," etc.) in succeeding volumes of HOFMEISTER. On the other hand, the concept of the violin as an accompanying instrument continued to reveal itself throughout the era, long after the violin achieved full partnership. In 1844 Mendelssohn still spoke of "accompanying sonatas" when he praised the violin playing of the thirteen-year-old Joachim.[39] And ten years later Brahms still spoke of wanting "to accompany Frau Schumann" (if he could learn the flute part in Kuhlau's sonatas [SSB XV]).[40] Throughout his life, except in his Op. 120/1 and 2, Brahms was one of the large majority of composers who continued to place the piano before its partner in the titles of his duo sonatas.[41]

Of course, even in the true duos for P & Vn (or other instrument) from the Romantic Era, the piano part usually dominates, at least to the extent that it includes the bass and most of the harmonic support, it has more notes to play, and its performer can keep track of both parts in his score. Yet the custom no longer prevails of listing only the chief luminary and his part in an ensemble sonata when that luminary is the pianist (as with Moscheles and Clara Schumann, *supra*), whereas the custom does often persist when he is the violinist or other instrumentalist.[42] Certainly, piano parts that were actually subordinated to the other part, like the one by Viotti singled out in the Classic Era (SCE 676), were infrequent, apart from pedagogic examples. Gade's *Sonate Nr. 2, D moll, für Pianoforte und Violine* (1850; SSB XV) has such a part, in spite of the order of its title. Saint-Saëns' *Sonate pour clarinette, avec accompagnement*

37. In AMZ XX (1818) 632 Rochlitz reviewed Ries's Son. Op. 76 for P ± Fl with the sarcastic remark that "The flute cannot be dispensed with entirely, as the title says; it actually takes the theme alone once, in the second movement, [with] the piano [getting] nothing but mere accompaniment!" For late exx. of the acc'd. P son., cf. Ries in SSB VII and Ladurner in SSB XII.

38. HOFMEISTER 1815 (Whistling), 297–320, and 1828 (Whistling), 470–514.

39. Bennett/BENNETT 157.

40. Joachim/LETTERS 78.

41. Cf. Geiringer/BRAHMS 26. In the present vol. an effort has been made to retain the order of the original title, although contradictory listings often leave that order uncertain.

42. E.g., cf. Lochner/KREISLER 93.

de piano, Op. 167 (1921; ssʙ XIII) has one, too, in full agreement with its title.[43] Stanford was aiming at a return to Baroque styles when he used a like title (ssʙ XIV). A sonata by Paul Caro (ssʙ XVII), Op. 42 for Vc & P (in that order), was reviewed sarcastically because of its "humble" piano part:

> And the composer said: There are enough sonatas in which the cello fights a losing battle against the piano. Therefore, friends, let's do something else! I shall write you a sonata in which the pianist must humble himself and leave the Word to the cellist. And so he did.[44]

In a true duo with piano, the piano does have most of the responsibility for the harmony and all of it for the bass, unless its partner has a low enough range to share the responsibility, as the cello has. But the greater expressive and color range of the violin or other instrument may counteract this domination by the piano to a considerable degree. Apart from these considerations, in thematic, rhythmic, figural, and other textural activity the two instruments are likely to contribute about equally and in a variety of ways. For instance, each of the two instruments may accompany the other in turn. They may engage in a dialog of the same or contrasting ideas, at close or distant intervals. Or they may perform distinctly different lines simultaneously, in a counterpoint governed by rhythmic conjunction or rhythmic opposition. They may reinforce each other at the unison or one or more octaves apart, in the same note values or with either part decorating or outlining the other. Or either instrument may simply play alone for a time, with the other waiting to re-enter. At least some of these procedures are illustrated in a passage from a work (Ex. 2) by the expert, post-Brahmsian composer, Daniel Gregory Mason of Boston and New York (ssʙ XIX).

The setting for P-duet is well represented throughout much of the 19th century on our tabulation of settings (*supra*), although most of the best examples and most of the interest on the part of significant sonata composers seem to have come in the first half of the century. After substantial contributions only by Mozart and Clementi among the chief Classics, Schubert led the way in the 19th century with some of the greatest masterpieces in that category (ssʙ VII). Most of these, however, were not made known until the second half-century.[45] Weber, Ries, Moscheles, Cramer, Hummel, and Onslow were other

43. A similar title was used by F. W. Langhans in his Op. 11 (with comments to that effect in ᴍᴍʀ XIX [1889] 87).
44. Trans. from ᴅᴍ X/4 (1910–11) 189.
45. Cf. ɴᴢᴍ LXIX/2 (1873) 505–7 (A. B. Vogel).

Ex. 2. From the first movement of Daniel Gregory Mason's Sonata in g, Op. 5 (after the original ed. of 1913, by kind permission of G. Schirmer, Inc.).

substantial contributors early in the century, Hummel's Op. 92 (ssb VIII) and Onslow's Op. 22 being outstanding examples of the genre. Furthermore, Cramer and Hummel, Moscheles and Mendelssohn, Moscheles and Chopin, Cramer and Herz, Cramer and Liszt, and Chopin and Liszt were among the many pairs we find performing duets in the first half-century.[46]

A reviewer in 1847 noted—too negatively, as our tabulation suggests—that few (original) duets were being written any more, regretting the shortage as the loss of a treasured domestic pleasure.[47] His explanation was that the new virtuoso piano writing, with its octaves, arpeggios, and pedal effects, already sounded like two players, but was better left to the virtuoso soloists. It is interesting that Brahms saw fit to arrange or have arranged for P-duet much of his chamber music, chiefly so that he could try it over with Clara Schumann and other intimates.[48] An original, exceptionally attractive Sonata for P-duet from the second half-century is Op. 17 in g (composed in 1865–66) by the Swiss composer Hermann Goetz (ssb X). In Ex. 3 is quoted

46. Cf. MOSCHELES I 23, 64–65, 74, 77, 274; Schlesinger/CRAMER 71–72, 77–79.
47. NZM XXVI (1847) 41–42.
48. Cf. Altmann/KAMMERMUSIK 309–10.

Ex. 3. From the first movement of Hermann Goetz's Sonata in g, Op. 17 (after the original Kistner ed. of 1878 at the New York Public Library).

the start of the second theme in the first movement, illustrating the balance, clean texture, and melodic interchanges that the most skillful writers in this idiom could achieve.[49]

As mentioned earlier, the setting for 2 Ps fared much less well than that for P-duet. A reviewer in 1845, finding reason to praise an Op. 1 for 2 Ps by A. Bergt (ssb VIII), discussed the dearth in his opening paragraph.[50] He thought the difficulty of finding two instruments, together and sufficiently matched, had been exaggerated and that prospects for a rise in output were now good. But one still can name only two composers who left examples of some renown, these being Brahms and the prolific late Swiss Romantic, Hans Huber. And even their contributions are seldom played today. Brahms's Sonata in f, Op. 34b, is preferred, instead, in its final form as the piano Quintet in f (ssb IX) and Huber's three contributions qualify

49. Cf., also, the ex. from the start of Op. 17 in Georgii/KLAVIERMUSIK 578.
50. NZM XXIII (1845) 53.

as something short of masterpieces (ssb XI). Dussek had left several effective "Duos" or "Duos concertants," mostly still in the Classic idiom and intended for harp & P as well as 2 Ps.[51] The few further contributions, including those by Onslow (ssb XII, with ex.), H. Grädener, and Reinecke,[52] would hardly pass muster among today's performers. Rare in this general category is Smetana's one-movement Sonata in e for eight hands at 2 Ps.[53]

In the select category of sonata for unaccompanied violin,[54] inevitably under the strong influence of the styles and techniques in J. S. Bach's precedent (sbe 269–70), are late-Romantic examples of more or less distinction by Karg-Elert, J. Weismann, J. Röntgen, Ysaÿe, and, especially, Reger. Karg-Elert also left one or two sonatas each for unaccompanied Va, Fl, Cl, Bn, and saxophone (ssb XI). Earlier in the century L. Jansa had provided a "Sonate brillante" for Vn alone with an optional accompaniment by a second Vn (1828; ssb VII). And A. Romberg left three "Etudes ou sonates" for Vn alone that were reviewed as having more value in the former sense (ca. 1813; ssb VIII). Two piano sonatas in a similarly select category, [54a] for left hand alone, may be cited, by Zichy and Reinecke, but not one by Kalkbrenner usually cited as the pioneer in this setting, since it actually requires two hands (ssb XII).

Transcriptions and Arrangements

The transcribing or arranging of sonatas (and other music) in the 19th century is a major topic in itself, and one that throws considerable light on Romantic attitudes toward music. It is also a topic with its own sources, bibliography, and history. Not seldom it raises questions of stylistic and even functional propriety, such as the questions brought up earlier regarding the adaptation of piano sonatas to the organ. Indirectly and conversely, it sometimes raises the question of whether a work has been scored for its best medium in the first place—such as the solo piano sonatas of R. Fuchs, Sibelius, and Tchaikovsky (ssb XI, XV, and XVIII, with exx.), whose frequent piano writing in block chords suggests orchestration as the better mode of expression (ssb XI and XVII). Although this topic of arranging must be regarded as only tangential to the basic questions of the sonata, it comes up repeatedly, if only incidentally, throughout the present

51. Cf. Craw/dussek 406.
52. Cf. Altmann/kammermusik 285–92.
53. Cf. ssb XVII. The same setting was employed by H. Mohr in a Sonatine in G, pub. by Breitkopf & Härtel in 1894.
54. Cf. Gates/solo 179–214, with exx.

study and needs at least this separate notice here. We are interested not so much in the wide variety of settings that is involved as in the half-dozen or so ways those settings pertain to the sonata.

The simplest or least arranging was ordinarily that kind done to provide an alternative part in a duo. In the sonatas for Vn & P by Franck (ssʙ XIII) and Grieg (Op. 13, ssʙ XV) surprisingly little was done (by the composers or whom?) beyond adjustments of range to convert the Vn into Vc parts. In Brahms's two Sonatas for Cl & P, Op. 120, the composer also changed details of slurring and rests in deference to the unlike idioms when he himself made the Va (though not the Vn) parts out of the clarinet parts.[55] Such alternative parts can be found throughout the Romantic duo literature[56] for the obvious reasons that they widened the market for publication sales and permitted that many more musicians, especially the dilettantes, to have at least a go at the music. Reviewers generally reflected the public interest in such matters. For instance,

> This [Son. in B♭, Op. 2/1, by J. N. Hummel] was originally written for a violoncello accompaniment [actually H-or-P & Vn-or-Fl & Vc; ssʙ VIII], the latter now being altered for a [2d?] flute, at some expense of effect, of course, yet very pleasing in its new state. It is so arranged that it may be played without the accompaniment, which is printed in small notes over the regular piano-forte part, whenever essential.[57]

Another kind of a sonata arrangement was that that occurred during the evolution of a particular work, whether as the final setting or an earlier one. The most renowned example, among several examples that we shall be encountering in Part Two, was Brahms's Sonata in f, Op. 34b, mentioned above under settings for 2 Ps, as the forerunner of his piano Quintet in f, Op. 34. Later (ssʙ IX) the valuable lesson in scoring to be derived from this final arrangement will be discussed and illustrated. But the Sonata was not published until after the Quintet. F. W. Grund's *Grande Sonate* in g, Op. 27, for P solo, was also first published in a different version, as a *Trio de salon* for P-duet & Va-or-Vc-or-Hn, yet it won its successes, including Schumann's praise in 1839, only in the solo version (ssʙ VIII). The final published version was also the more successful one with regard to the three sonatas each, Opp. 38 and 43, for Vc & P, by B. H. Romberg (ssʙ VIII). These had been arranged, although whether by him is not clear) from three trios for 2 Vcs & Va and three "Sonatas faciles" for Vc and string bass that had been published in 1825 and 1826, respectively. Of course, no ques-

---

55. Cf. ssʙ IX; Cobbett/CHAMBER I 182 (D. F. Tovey).
56. Cf. Altmann/KAMMERMUSIK *passim.*
57. HARMONICON VI/1 (1828) 108.

tion of which version fared best is involved in the sort of P-duet mentioned earlier that Brahms made or had made from his larger ensembles
for informal trial and demonstration.

Still another kind of an arrangement was that of a favorite sonata
movement. In Chapter IV some of the incredibly many and varied
settings of the "Marche funèbre" from Chopin's Op. 35 were listed,
and nearly the same could have been done for certain other favorites,
like Weber's "Perpetuum mobile" (finale of Op. 24).[58] Highly published pianist-composers like Ries, Moscheles, and Czerny seem to
have done almost as much arranging as original composing, including
sonata movements and whole sonatas by themselves and others, among
a much larger quantity of lighter things.[59] As but one sample, Moscheles arranged his own "Sextuor" in E♭, Op. 35 (for P, Vn, Fl,
2 Hns, & Vc) as a *Grande Sonate* for P solo, for P-duet, and for 2 Ps.[60]

There was also the arranging done to popularize (or Romanticize)
favorite sonatas from the past. In some of this arranging, parts were
added without changing the original. After a Gewandhaus concert
in Leipzig in the winter of 1839–40, Schumann wrote,

. . . and Herr Concertmaster [Ferdinand] David, accompanied by Mendelssohn, [played] in an outstanding manner two movements—priceless compositions—from the sonatas for violin alone by Bach, the same of which it was
asserted formerly that "it would be unthinkable to add any other part to
them," which [assertion] Mendelssohn thereupon contradicted in the loveliest
style, enriching the original with all sorts of lines, so that it was a treat to
hear.[61]

Schumann himself added accompaniments in his last years to all six
of Bach's unaccompanied violin Partitas and Sonatas (SSB VIII). Grieg's
four volumes of "freely composed" accompaniments to be played on
a second piano with Mozart's solo piano sonatas are still used by
teachers today.[62] Among the countless other 19th-century arrangements of sonata movements by the Classic masters, and as examples
of the kind that did change the original, we might cite Elgar's arrangement of the "Allegro" from Mozart's K. 547 in F, for P & Vn, as
a choral "Gloria" (!) and the finale from Beethoven's Op. 23 in a,
for P & Vn, as a wind quintet.[63]

Finally, among categories of arranging there is the sort that makes
"sonatas" out of medleys of popular tunes and the like. Such would

58. Cf. SSB VIII; PAZDÍREK XV 182–83.
59. Cf. their long entries in PAZDÍREK.
60. PAZDÍREK X 827.
61. Schumann/SCHRIFTEN I 511.
62. Cf. their listing in PAZDÍREK VI 567.
63. Cf. Young/ELGAR 402–3.

be Czerny's fifteen *Sonatine[s] facile[s] e progressive[s] sopra i piu accredidati motive d'opere. . . .*[64] In the many potpourris of this sort "sonata" is reduced to its original meaning merely of "instrumental piece."

Some Aspects of Performance Practices

Like the topic of arrangements (*supra*), that of performance practices represents a major field in itself. It, too, must be regarded as only tangential to sonata history, yet frequently comes up in passing in the present volume and requires at least this special mention here. Oddly enough, although the Romantic Era is closest in time to our own era and should be, one would assume, that much more familiar to us, it actually has been about as little known or explored for performance practices as the Renaissance Era. Since 1963 many musicians have been shocked into an awareness of their unfamiliarity with 19th-century practices by the recordings of the Edwin Welte piano rolls that had been made about 1905.[65] They have heard how, only that recently, Carreño, Leschetizky, d'Albert, de Pachmann, and numerous other greats among both performers and composer-performers were taking liberties, especially with the tempo but also with the notes themselves, that would fail a college freshman today. (Xaver Scharwenka's playing of Beethoven's Op. 90/i is representative. Interesting is the fact that Debussy, Grieg, and the other composer-performers take decidedly fewer liberties with their own music.) Studies on 19th-century performance practices are much to be desired.[66] Bach, of course, has always drawn most of the attention, with the centuries before and after him receiving successively less attention.

It is not that the 19th-century musicians and writers themselves failed to take an interest in performance practices. A considerable interest developed early as one facet of the new interest in music history (SSB II). In the last chapters of Hummel's epochal treatise on piano playing (Hummel/ANWEISUNG), first published in 1827, the cultivated pianist made several remarks about the differing styles of past and contemporary musicians, including the ability of Mozart and Clementi to excel as performers without use of the pedal (p. 152 [452!]); the approximate metronome speeds that Beethoven, Clementi, Cramer, and numerous others intended with certain tempo markings

---

64. Cf. PAZDÍREK III 687.

65. *Legendary Masters of the Keyboard,* pub. by The Classics Record Library as album WV 6633/1–3.

66. Memoirs, letters, and periodicals are the main sources, again, along with the original MSS and eds. Cf. the interesting chap. on this topic in Schonberg/PIANISTS 119–33.

(p. 457); and the preference for uniformity of style in the music of past masters, including J. S. Bach, Handel, Scarlatti, Emanuel Bach (!), and Mozart (!), as against sharp contrasts in that of the contemporaries, especially Beethoven (p. 466). Naturally, the playing of Beethoven's sonatas became a primary topic for writers on performance practices. Pioneer landmarks were certain sections in the writings of Czerny between 1842 and 1852,[67] in which every sonata movement (among many other of Beethoven's works) is given a metronome mark and discussed briefly, too often superficially, from the standpoints of character, style, and, occasionally, specific problems.

But in the editing of past masterworks throughout the 19th century there was a remarkable difference between an avowed reverence for the authenticity of the *Urtext* and the actual policies that editors chose to follow. The typical explanation, offered time after time, can be found as recently as 1945, in the preface to editions of Schumann's sonatas Opp. 105 and 121, for Vn & P:

The present revision has been undertaken in the hope of restoring their popularity. It will be disapproved by those who are accustomed to regard an original musical text in all its details less as a guide for interpretation than as a sacred document which must never be tampered with—even if it can be irrefutably shown that this text, instead of revealing the composer's intentions, has unfortunately had the result of obscuring them.[68]

As was also typical, these editions gave no clue as to what was original and what was changed. Clara Schumann and Max Vogrich, although they came to many different conclusions, did much better in their respective editions of Robert Schumann's collected works. Otherwise, going back in time, one must report much the same of the now infamous sonata editions that Epstein did of Mozart, Bülow and Lebert of Beethoven, Bülow of Scarlatti and Emanuel Bach, and Czerny himself of Beethoven in contradictions of his own writings. According to its subtitle, Tausig's edition of five Scarlatti sonatas (Edition Peters 3014) might be exempted here as belonging in the realm of "concert transcriptions," including, for example, the unacknowledged change from d to e, articulation marks, fuller chords, double-notes, terms of expression, and tempo inflections in the much played "Pastorale." Yet there were still those astonishing, elaborate changes, not under the heading of transcriptions, that the Bach-Gesellschaft editor Wilhelm Rust made, again without acknowledgment, in and around his grandfather's sonatas, by way of fully Romanticizing or Wagnerizing them (SCE 583–89, with exx.).

67. Assembled in Badura-Skoda/CZERNY.
68. (G.) *Schirmer's Library of Musical Classics,* Vols. 1696 and 1699 (H. Bauer).

At the start of the era Dussek specified that no ornaments should be added in one of his most important sonatas, "Elégie harmonique" (C. 211). Many another musician after him showed a similar desire to adhere to the letter of the score, as did one who argued in 1877 for playing the "small notes" before the beat, as they were engraved, and not on the beat, in the subordinate theme of Beethoven's Op. 27/2/iii.[69] But the need to enrich the texture, free the rhythm, and intensify the expression was too strong for the best of the Romantics. What is most surprising is that the Romantics "improved" not only on the alleged thin scoring and strait-laced quality of "old music" (as we saw Mendelssohn and Schumann do with Bach, or Grieg with Mozart; *supra*) but on the music written by earlier Romantics. That is, we not only find, for example, defenses for editorial extensions and octave doublings in the sonatas Mozart and Beethoven had written for keyboards with only five octaves,[70] or for Bülow's alterations by way of solving technical problems in Beethoven's sonatas,[71] or for changes in the notation in order to make the rhythmic organization clearer.[72] But we also find no less a master than Liszt writing to Sigmund Lebert in 1868–70 regarding editions of Weber and Schubert,

In the *various readings* you will probably find some things not inappropriate; —I flatter myself that I have thus given performers greater licence, and have increased the effect without damaging or overloading Weber's style. . . . In the [Schubert] Sonatas you will find some various readings, which appear to me tolerably *appropriate*. Several passages, and the whole of the conclusion of the C major Fantasia, I have re-written in modern pianoforte form, and I flatter myself that Schubert would not be displeased with it. . . . My endeavor with this work is to avoid quibbling and pretentiousness, and to make the edition a practical one for teachers and players. And for this reason at the very last I added a goodly amount of fingering and pedal marks. . . . With regard to the deceptive *Tempo rubato,* I have settled the matter provisionally in a brief note (in the finale of Weber's A♭ major Sonata); other occurrences of the *rubato* may be left to the taste and momentary feeling of gifted players. A metronomical performance is certainly tiresome and nonsensical; time and rhythm must be adapted to and identified with the melody, the harmony, the accent and the poetry. . . . But how indicate all this? I shudder at the thought of it.[73]

69. MT XVIII (1877) 135 ("Allegro").
70. Cf. DMZ III (1862) 153–55, with exx.
71. Cf. MMR III (1873) 2–5 and 42–43 (E. Dannreuther), 113–16, 128–30.
72. Cf. MW XIV (1883) 397–401 (R. Westphal).
73. LISZT LETTERS II 160-61, 165, 194. Cf. the serial review in MMR III (1873) 69-70, 84-85, 99-101, 113-16, 128-30, and especially 154-57 (with exx.) ; MMR IV (1874) 133. Liszt did provide the original version, too. Cf., also, SSB XII for changes Liszt made in the finale of Chopin's Sonata in b.

Ex. 4. From Carl Maria von Weber's Sonata in A♭, Op. 39/iv/87–94 and its "modernization" by Adolph Henselt (as quoted from the Schlesinger ed. in MMR IV [1874] 149).

The Monthly Musical Record for 1874 gives an extraordinary, mostly laudatory report, complete with examples, of the changes Henselt made in an edition of Weber's Sonata in A♭, Op. 39.[74] Some of these changes add melody, harmony, and richness of sound, but most pile virtuoso difficulties on what are already virtuoso difficulties (Ex. 4).

Evidently the same sorts of changes and more were improvised, if not prepared, in public performance. Again, Liszt was one of the main exponents. Moscheles told how at a Philharmonic Concert in 1840 Liszt "played three of my 'Studies' quite admirably. Faultless in

74. MMR IV (1874) 133–34, 148–50.

the way of execution, but by his powers he has completely meta-morphosed these pieces; they have become more his Studies than mine. With all that[,] they please me and I shouldn't like to hear them played in any other way by him." [75] Thus, another free performer, Paganini, had hardly been right if he thought only Italians took liberties. In 1816, during the two-violin passages of a double-concerto by Kreutzer, "I held strictly note for note to the written text. . . . But in the solo passages I gave free rein to my imagination and played in the Italian manner—in the style that is really natural to me." [76]

With further regard to rhythm and tempo, many such advices favoring freedom have turned up in the present study, but none happened to turn up that argue for a consistent or prevailing tempo. The metronome seems to have been advocated only for setting tempos, not for maintaining them. One reviewer regretted that no metronome marks were supplied in A. G. Ritter's Op. 20 and another disagreed when he came to Op. 21, saying, as has been said so often, that a good musician will sense the right tempo.[77]

With regard to two other aspects of performance practices, the custom of playing solo music from memory was developed by Liszt among others and began to take hold by the mid century, as noted earlier.[78] The matter of taking repeats, especially in "sonata form," is brought up as part of the discussion of form in the next chapter.

75. MOSCHELES II 64. Cf. Schonberg/PIANISTS 166–67 for further instances; also, Prod'homme/BEETHOVEN 125–27 for Berlioz' anguish when Liszt added trills, tremolos, and rubato in Beethoven's Op. 27/2/i.

76. As trans. in Courcy/PAGANINI I 148.

77. NZM XXXV (1851) 258–59, XXXIX (1853) 115.

78. Cf. SSB III; Hanslick/WIEN I 421; Newman/OP. 106.

Chapter VI

Romantic Sonata Form: Process, Mold, and Unicum

The Problem

This last, yet most central, chapter in the overview that comprises Part One concentrates on the music itself—that is, on the styles and forms of the Romantic sonata since Beethoven. Its object is an ordered summary and rationale of the most representative and salient traits discovered throughout the survey that comprises Part Two, on individual composers and their sonatas. And as with the Baroque Era and Corelli, or the Classic Era and Haydn, Mozart, and Beethoven, the method of exposition in this sixth chapter has been to focus on the few masters who have exercised the greatest influences, and to draw on their contemporaries only as needed to round out the summary. Four masters serve as the focal points this time—Schubert, Chopin, Schumann, and Brahms (meaning that their sons. are examined here rather than in Part Two, where the extended, separate discussions of each master's sons. are confined to sources, background, tabulations, and circumstances [ssb VII, XII, VIII, and IX, respectively]). Except for Brahms's last works, the sonatas of these composers all fall in the early- or mid-Romantic Era as delimited here (ssb I). Furthermore, they largely fall on the more conservative side of the style dichotomy shortly to be defined, with Liszt's sonatas, in particular, requiring full recognition on the other side. Yet, next to Beethoven's it is their sonatas and not Liszt's isolated masterpieces (ssb X) that exercised the clearest, most demonstrable influences on contemporary and subsequent sonata history, which, all in all, is a conservative facet of Romantic music history, in any case.

In the examination of this music, the approach can no longer be by way of contemporary (19th-c.) concepts, as it was in Chapter II. Nor can it be by way, even, of the relatively few, pertinent, present-day studies that already have been done, fine as some of them are. These studies are acknowledged for valued insights and conclusions where they apply (*infra*),[1] and sometimes are quoted, especially for statistical findings. But as it has been necessary to emphasize more than once before (cf. ssb I), one writer cannot accept and acknowledge the music analysis of another in the way that he might accept and acknowledge another's factual discoveries. Music analysis must still depend to a considerable degree (fortunately!) on firsthand experience with the music, on subjective reactions to it, and on the particular slant being observed.

The starting point in this chapter needs to be, therefore, a restatement of the particular slant and premises that have governed, from its beginning, the present approach to styles and forms in the sonata. In revised wording that still retains the sense of previous statements (cf. sce 114–15), we may recall three essential distinctions in the meaning of the broad term "form." (1) Form may be viewed, dynamically, or in action, as a *generative process*, characterized by a certain corpus of style treatments or traits. Here the most benefit has derived from distinguishing between two processes that, in their theoretical extremes, are diametrically opposed.[2] One is "motivic play," characterized variously by imitative treatment of a significant but fragmentary idea, by relatively fast harmonic rhythm, by irregular or proselike meter, and by constant tonal flux. The other is "phrase grouping," characterized variously by pairings or larger juxtapositions of complete phrases and periods (thematically significant or not), by homophonic textures, by relatively slow harmonic rhythm, by more regular, verselike meter, and by broad tonal plateaus. (2) Form may be viewed, textbook fashion, as a *mold* or standardized design, with all the conveniences of quick reference that such classifications permit and all the dangers of Procrustean analysis and false criteria that they pose. Approaching a form as a mold puts the emphasis on everything that is typical or common practice, if not commonplace. Our best illustration, of course, is textbook "sonata form," itself. The several textbook rondo designs present almost as many conveniences and dangers. (3) Form may be viewed as a *unicum*—that is, as the one and only result of a particular corpus of generative traits and/or a particular set of variants in a mold, if, indeed, it happens to approximate *any* recognized mold. Typically, motivic play leads to a structural result that is monothematic (or monomotivic) and cursive (or open), whereas phrase grouping leads to a structural result that is polythematic and hierarchic (meaning an integration of sections within sections). But approaching a form as a

1. Most of them are cited, too, in the individual composer discussions of Part Two.
2. Cf. Newman/UNDERSTANDING 133–55; sce 113–14.

unicum puts the emphasis on everything that is *a*-typical—in other words, on whatever may distinguish it from other forms.

As an illustration of these three meanings of form within the scope of the present volume, the first movement of Chopin's Sonata in b, Op. 58, may be used. The *mold* that this movement most nearly approximates and that provides the most convenient term of reference is "sonata form," with its standardized subdivisions as convenient reference terms, too—"exposition," "development," and "recapitulation" (beginning at mss. 1, 92, and 151, respectively[3]). Of the two *generative processes* motivic play prevails only in the development section of Op. 58/i (as in most "sonata forms"), and only in its first seventeen measures, at that. Otherwise, phrase grouping prevails. Even when the phrase consists of little more than motivic reiterations, in place or in sequence (mss. 23–26), the phrase grouping prevails. Put differently, when the reiterations of a motive fall into larger rhythmic composites (as happens in one basic kind of sonata theme—e.g., Brahms's Op. 5/i/1–6), the larger composites take precedence in determining the generative process. Finally, Chopin's Op. 58/i qualifies as a *unicum* when all of its peculiarities and departures from textbook norms are brought together. To name but two of these, a peculiarity from the standpoint of its prevailing generative process, phrase grouping, is the rapid harmonic rhythm produced by the block-chords in its main theme and related phrases (e.g., mss. 1–2, 17–19, 21–22). A departure from the mold of "sonata form" is the start of its recapitulation at the second theme (ms. 151), without any return to the first theme.

It is possible and helpful to relate these three meanings of form in music to the main trends in the styles and "forms" of the Romantic sonata—in fact, to one main trend per meaning. From the standpoint of form as a generative process the most important trend was an exaggeration and, at the same time, attenuation or rarefaction of Classic sonata means.[4] Thus, the Romantic motives persisted longer and pervaded more of the structure; the phrases grew lengthier and projected more tellingly; the textures grew fuller and their activity increased; the harmonies became more dissonant, more varied, and more remotely interrelated; the tonal schemes ranged further afield and changed more abruptly. Often this exaggeration occurred at both extremes, as in the wider range, at both ends, of pitch, of tempos, of dynamics, of volume, of expressive freedom. From the standpoint of

3. The ms. nos. given in Chopin/works-m are used here, although they include separate nos. for 2d endings (contrary to the usual practice, here and elsewhere).

4. Mersmann/romantischen, on the son. principle in Romantic chamber music, stresses its attenuation after Beethoven; its loss of, or substitutes for, Classic thematic dualism; and its chief positive contribution as the advance of cyclical unity.

form as a mold the most important trend was the increasing recognition and description of an explicit "sonata form" by theorists and other writers of the 19th century, as has already been discussed in Chapter II. This trend had the levelling effect, at least among the weaker, less imaginative composers, of rigidifying the once fluid form and making it into a stereotype. And from the standpoint of form as a unicum, the most important trend was the growing dichotomy of sonatas by conservatives and absolutists as against those by progressives and programmatists. In general music this dichotomy, affecting both styles and forms, is associated chiefly with the opposition of Brahms and Wagner.[5] In sonata history it came into the open earlier, though not tangibly before the opposition of Brahms and Liszt, whose very different Op. 1 in C and Sonata in b both originated in 1853. That was the year of Brahms's awkward meeting with Liszt, his joyous meeting with the Schumanns, and Schumann's panegyric on his Op. 1, followed in the next years by the counter force of the "New German" school formed by Liszt and his disciples, then followed in turn by Brahms's "Manifesto" of 1860 against those "moderns" (all in SSB IX). The dichotomy was still much in evidence at the era's end, although often clouded by cross influences from both sides in the sonatas of the epigones.

The next three sections of this chapter consider three main, successive style phases in the Romantic sonata—early, high or middle, and late. In those sections, form is viewed as a generative process. The five remaining sections consider the Romantic sonata first for the over-all unity and relationships of its several movements, then for the nature of each of its four main types of movements (as in SCE VI). In those five sections, form is viewed now as a mold and now as a unicum. That there are only three successive style phases, not sharply defined, to distinguish in the Romantic sonata, as compared with five styles, more or less distinct, in the Classic sonata (SCE 119–33), is partly explained by the lack of a clear break between Classic and Romantic styles such as had occurred between Baroque and Classic styles (cf. SSB I). In other words, to the extent that the Romantics did exaggerate rather than alter or renounce the means of the Classics (*supra*), they did not create radically different styles. There is also the fact that the Romantic style phases, especially the second (at the time of the Brahms-Liszt opposition) presented not only one style but rather two opposed styles in that dichotomy or polarity of conservatives and progressives that was mentioned earlier. There had been no precedent for such a dichotomy in the Classic sonata, the nearest to it being either that of

5. Cf. the reappraisal of the Brahms-Wagner dichotomy and its repercussions in Waltershausen/DUALISMUS.

empfindsam versus *galant* or that of chamber versus symphonic. However, neither of these Classic dichotomies was a matter of conservative
versus progressive. The former was, rather, a matter of relative aesthetic
weight and the latter of different social functions.

The early, high, and late style phases of the Romantic sonata were,
in effect, its bubbling naive youth, its mature masterful adulthood, and
its final, more calculated flowering. They are viewed here as roughly
coterminous with the successive overlapping time spans—about 1800–
1850, 1840–85, and 1875–1915—that help to mark off our subgroups of
composers in Part Two. But the early phase did not last quite through
the first time span, its youthful bloom disappearing during the sonata
slump of the second quarter-century (SSB II and IV). Yet it lasted long
enough to take in the sonatas of some important composers, including
Dussek, Hummel, Weber, and Schubert. For our purposes Schumann is
included in that first phase, too, at least to the extent of his Op. 11.
His subsequent sonatas, like those of Chopin, Liszt, and Brahms (prior
to the late Op. 120) are put here in the second or adulthood phase.
In the last phase are included the sonatas of Reger, d'Indy, Dale, Nielsen, Medtner, and MacDowell, among other composers of distinction.

The Early-Romantic Style Phase

Although the Romantic tendency simply to exaggerate Classic means
did not favor innovational styles, certain treatments did impart more
newness than others to the "frühromantischen" or early-Romantic
sonata.[6] These are apparent first of all in that element of the generative
process requiring attention first, anyway—**melody.** However, one must
realize the impracticality of arriving at broad yet meaningful generalizations about Romantic melody, or of reducing it to useful statistics
covering its behavior. Throughout the era its variety was far too great
to permit such generalizations and statistics. Already the early-Romantic Era tended to promote this great variety, both because of the
premium it was coming to place on originality per se (SSB II) and because of the new interest it was beginning to take in past styles as part
of the growing historical consciousness (SSB II). The alternative to
arriving at generalizations and statistics concerning melodic behavior

6. Egert/FRÜHROMANTIKER and Favre/FRANÇAISE concentrate on son. styles in this
period. Cf., also, the illuminating discussions in F. Blume's article on the Romantic
Era for MGG (XI 785–845, *passim*), in Einstein/SCHUBERT 76–85 (a comparison of
Schubert's sons. with Haydn's, Beethoven's, and, especially, Hummel's and Weber's),
and in Werner/PALE (with references to textural and cyclical treatment in sons.
by composers of the Classic-Romantic borderland). Much of Chusid/SCHUBERT, on
Schubert's instrumental works for larger chamber ensembles, is relevant here, too.

is to single out the few melodic styles that have seemed most distinctive in the course of the present study. Each of these styles has tended to be associated with a particular composer. Each one may have been exhibited to best advantage in that composer's sonatas (or other music) but, in fact, every one of them can be found in the air, so to speak, as part of the musical language then current.

A primary style of melody in the early-Romantic Era was the smooth, songful, contemplative sort, couched in complete, well-defined phrases, that often is associated with Schubert, especially his lieder. As one outstanding example, the opening theme may be quoted from his posthumous Sonata in B♭ (D. 960), which theme also illustrates Schubert's particular fondness for melodies that keep centering on and turning around the initial note (Ex. 5).[7] In later chapters may be seen another such example by Schubert (in G, D. 894; ssB VII) as well as other related, if not quite so ethereal, examples by Pinto (Op. 3/2; ssB XIV), Moscheles (Op. 49; ssB VII), and Hartmann (Op. 83; ssB XV).[8]

The Moscheles' example is a simple, hymnic line that recalls Tovey's concept of "modern" (i.e., Romantic) melody as the "surface" of harmony (as well as of rhythm, form, and instrumentation).[9] In the "Andante sostenuto" from the same Schubert Sonata in B♭, D. 960/ii, the long steady line, decorated by a lilting harmonic accompaniment, supplies a most effective illustration of Tovey's concept (as does the slow movement of Schubert's string Quintet in C). Hartmann's example introduces a folklike element in its compound-metric lilt. A remarkably precocious example by Dussek (in A♭, C. 221; ssB XVII), to be cited more than once again here, points to the warming, sentimentalizing, even effeminizing effect of chromatic inflections in the melody. The same can be said for the chromaticism in the sort of theme that opens Schubert's D. 850/ii, where the gain in these effects seems to be made at the expense of the lofty nobility in Beethoven's more diatonic slow movements.

When there was a consistent rhythmic pattern and the phrase grouping became still more regular and clear, the result was likely to be an out-and-out tune. Such tunes abound in the early-Romantic sonata, especially in the faster movements. Three examples might be cited from their most fertile breeding ground, the rondo finale. These

7. Hanna/SCHUBERT 115–30 concludes, on statistical bases, that this type is third in frequency among Schubert's melodic types, preceded by scalewise and chordal melodies and followed by melodies with larger skips.

8. When specific son. passages are cited as illustrations in the present chap., they are chosen from exx. in other chaps. as often as the latter exx. apply (and as indicated, though only in this chap., by the parenthetical ssB reference).

9. BRITANNICA XV 228.

Ex. 5. The opening of Franz Schubert's Sonata in B♭, D. 960
(facs. of the autograph as reproduced in Kinsky/KOCH Facs. 13;
with the kind permission of M. A. Souchay).

are the rollicking tune in Paganini's Op. 3/6 (SSB XVI), the gay tune in
Schubert's D. 850, and the ingratiating tune in Schubert's D. 894. When
the patterns and phrase grouping became still more regular, as they
did all too often in dance and "perpetuum mobile" movements, the
risk was great that such obvious syntax would seem banal. Even the
greatest Romantics did not get by this risk altogether unscathed, as can
be heard, for example, in a waltzlike double-period by Schubert
(Ex. 6).

9a

By contrast, one can find many examples of melodic lines that are
quite as compelling in their own way, yet much more varied, supple,
and, often, subtle in their rhythmic and pitch organization. Such a
line, finely drawn by Kuhlau, is quoted later in an eight-measure phrase
with a range of a 12th, for flute (SSB XV). If this example still reveals
a late-Classic neatness of organization, one might look for more
freedom, even abandon, in the more progressive writing of the time

Ex. 6. From the "Scherzo" of Franz Schubert's Sonata in D,
D. 850/iii (after Schubert/WERKE-m X/11).

(looking toward that eventual dichotomy of styles mentioned earlier).
A bold, impassioned example is the opening of Schumann's Sonata in
f♯, Op. 11 (ssb VIII). We shall be seeing that the key of f♯ seemed to
inspire Romantic composers to write very much this sort of theme.
One would be tempted to say that it was really Schumann's precedent
that inspired them so, except that there were already earlier if more
naive precedents, as in the finale of Ries's Op. 26 (ssb VII) and the
opening of Moscheles' Op. 49.

Such anticipations of Schumann's impassioned melody can be
matched by several anticipations of Chopin's ornamental cantilena,
complete with wide expressive leaps, jagged series of chromatic appoggiaturas, and feminine endings. They already occurred in Beethoven's
Opp. 106/iii/28–36 and 109/iii/17–33, and they may be found in
Czerny's Op. 268/ii (ssb VII), Hummel's Op. 81/ii (ssb VIII), Steibelt's
Op. 64/i (ssb XII), and Kalkbrenner's Op. 56 (ssb XII).

With regard to early-Romantic **rhythm,** the exaggeration of Classic
means took the form of doggedly persistent patterns. Thus, in Schubert's D. 784 in a, the pair of somber, strong-weak half-notes repeats
relentlessly in almost every measure, always starting on the first beat
and relieved only by an occasional triplet filler, diminution, or aug-
mentation (as in mss. 219, 270, and 276–77). There is also a persistent

dotted pattern throughout much of the development section. Similar persistence can be found in the driving pattern of two 16th-notes and an 8th-note throughout the first movements of Mendelssohn's Op. 106 in B♭ and Schumann's Op. 11 in f♯. A significant difference can be found between, on the one hand, the heavy emphasis on the downbeat in such works (even in the textural background of Schumann's habitual syncopations[10]) and, on the other hand, the springier, characteristic emphasis on the offbeat in Beethoven's works of similar character and drive (e.g., Ex. 12, from Op. 81a/i, in SCE 132).[11] The Schubert "Scherzo" quoted above and the two examples quoted later from Weber's Op. 24 (SSB VIII) illustrate the downbeat emphasis, too. In his earlier sonatas Schubert, still as prodigal with his means as most other young composers, had preferred to use a variety of rhythmic patterns, although even then he saw to it that each pattern was given a thorough exposure. That treatment can be found, for example, in the first movement of his earliest Sonata in a, D. 537/i, with such typical patterns in 6/8 meter as a dotted figure, a quarter- and 8th-note, two 16th-notes leading into a quarter-note, and a pair of dotted-quarter notes, the chief rhythmic contrasts being devices like hemiola shifts (mss. 97–101) and arpeggiando septimoles (mss. 106 and 108). Fertile rhythmist that he was, Schubert often indulged his marked propensity for dotted groups and for triplets by combining the two figures throughout extended passages (as in D. 575/i/15–33).

The exaggeration of Classic **harmonic means** is evident in an increased range of dissonance, a more frequent alternation of major and minor in the same interval, a freer use of borrowed tones in either mode, a richer application of the dim.-7th, aug.-6th, and other altered chords, and a greater percentage of chord-root progressions by 2ds and 3ds. Illustrations of these harmonic tendencies may be seen, variously, in the three Dussek examples quoted later (SSB XVII), in Schubert's D. 537/i/150–82, and in the modal vacillations and other inflections, extraordinary even for Schubert, by which he brings the first movement of his "Grand Duo" in C, D. 812, to a close (Ex. 7). The dim.-7th chord —as used by Weber and Mendelssohn, for example—seems to have had a special significance for the early-Romantics and their successors, whether as a color harmony, a terrifying climax, a convenient modulatory agent (chiefly through its enharmonic re-interpretations in V_9 chords), a mainstay in passagework, a basic chord in sideslipping,

10. Honsa/SCHUMANN is a recent diss. on syncopation, hemiola, and metric changes in Schumann's instrumental music, including numerous references to, and exx. from, his sons.

11. Cf. Westphal/ROMANTISCHE 189–90.

Ex. 7. From the first movement of Franz Schubert's "Grand

Duo" in C, D. 812 (after Schubert /WERKE-m IX/12).

Ex. 8. From the first movement of Carl Maria von Weber's
Sonata in e, Op. 70 (after Augener's Ed. No. 8470).

chromatic progressions, or a means of achieving the intentionally
ambiguous and noncommittal, hence the mystical (Ex. 8).

Tonality in the sense of key organization comes up further on as a
main structural consideration in the cycle and the separate movements. But it belongs here, too, because the modulations that effect
tonal changes reveal further exaggerations of Classic means in the early-
Romantic sonata. These modulations do not increase the Classic tonal
range significantly, since at least in rare instances nearly the full range
had been explored in the Classic sonata (SCE 137–38).[12] But they do
occur more often—more often, that is, in proportion to the tonal
plateaus, so that they serve not only to attain the tonal landmarks of
the design but to decorate much of the territory in between. Furthermore, a larger proportion of the early-Romantic modulations qualify
as the moderately distant or the remote sort, based on change of mode,
chromatic harmony, and enharmony. And a larger proportion of these
sorts of modulations connect keys a major 3d apart.

We get a striking display of all three trends, by one of the greatest
masters of modulation, in the "Con moto" movement of Schubert's
Sonata in D, D. 850. In the initial 41 measures Schubert flexes his
modulatory muscles by paying effortless, transitory visits to three different keys—first going from the home key of A to the mediant, c♯, and
back, by common chord; then through the ♭VII chord to the lowered
mediant, C♮, and back by common chord and change of mode; and
then through a dim.-7th chord to the lowered supertonic, B♭, and back
through ♭II as a Neapolitan harmony. The next 44, highly syncopated

---

12. Cf. the statistical conclusions to this effect in Abbott/FORM 323–29, which also
show Schubert to have been more adventuresome than Brahms.

measures (42–85) leave the home key, starting in the subdominant, D, by assumption of key, changing to its subdominant, G, by the same method (ms. 51), then modulating to D (again; ms. 68), to F (ms. 76), and, after a cumulation of chromatic, syncopated chords progressing by roots mostly a 3d apart, back to the home key of A again (ms. 86). Comparable modulations enhance the remaining four-sevenths of this movement.

Along with the songful melody in complete phrases and periods, the most conspicuous difference in the early-Romantic sonata lies in its **textures and sonorities.**[13] This time the exaggeration extends in all directions, as though it were a photographic enlargement. First of all, as we have seen, the pitch range itself expanded both up and down, thanks especially to the expanding range of the rapidly developing piano (ssb V). Schubert and Czerny were among composers who seem to have taken special delight in the new highs and lows, as in the arpeggios reaching up to e^4 in Schubert's D. 959/iv/271–79, or the mystical trill on contra-G♭ in his D. 960/i/8 (*supra*), or the coursing over six octaves, contra-F to f^4, in the "Scherzo" of Czerny's Op. 268 (ssb VII, but the quoted mss. get down only to contra-A).

Secondly, with regard to textural changes, much of the former close-position scoring expanded into open-position scoring. In this way, the close-position Alberti bass, which had been one of the most characteristic earmarks of the Classic style (sce 122, 180–82), did not quite disappear in early-Romantic scoring. Rather, along with some continued use in close position (e.g., Steibelt's Op. 64/i; ssb XII), it expanded on occasion into its open-position equivalent. A well-known though rare instance for Beethoven occurs in his Op. 90/i/55–58, and more frequent instances occur, for example, in Dussek's sonatas (as in C. 221, ssb XVII) and Weber's (as in Op. 49/i/223–28). But much more frequent are many other wide-spaced accompaniments in a considerable variety of chordal dispositions, such as the broken chords in triplets at the start of Schumann's Op. 11 (ssb VIII), the regular arpeggio pattern in Weber's Op. 49/ii/104–12 and the irregular one in Mendelssohn's Op. 6/iv/54–75, the repeated block chords in Hummel's Op. 81/ii/21–27 and the changing ones in his Op. 106/i/217–24, and, of course, the counterpart of the Alberti bass in the Classic Era, which was the Romantic's um-pah-pah-pah or related figure. This last was the most prevalent of all Romantic accompaniments (as in Dussek's C. 221, again, ssb XVII; or Reissiger's Op. 93/i, ssb VIII). The tendency to-

13. It is significant that the 6 styles depicted in C. Potter's "Enigma" variations of 1825 differ primarily in their idiomatic piano textures, sonorities, and techniques (as discussed in ssb XIV; QUARTERLY VII [1825] 507–9).

ward open-position scoring also favored wider stretches, such as the 9ths and 10ths in Mendelssohn's Op. 106/ii/66–88, or the four-note, open-position, left-hand chords, which few pianists can reach, in Weber's Op. 39/i/58; and it favored wider skips, such as the cross-hand leaps up to three octaves and more in Schubert's D. 575/i/60–80, and four octaves in Hummel's Op. 81/i/112–26 (cf. SSB VIII).

Thirdly, with regard to textural changes, the sound is richer in the early-Romantic than in the Classic sonata, if only because there are more notes in the scoring and more use of the pedal to multiply them, as it were, by running them together and releasing their upper partials. Four- or five- rather than three-part writing becomes the norm. Sometimes the added parts come in chord doublings, or in octave doublings in either hand, or in melodic lines reinforced by 3ds and 6ths, or in the euphony of a tenor melody with its bass below and arpeggiations above (all of which may be found in Dussek's C. 221, again [SSB XVII], except the last, which is in Moscheles' Op. 49 [SSB VII]). The passagework, especially that for piano, adds to the richness of sound by being more complex, more inflected by foreign tones, and wider-ranged. Among the countless varieties there are broken octaves that outline chords (as in Hummel's Op. 81/i/63–65), chains of first-inversion chords topped by two-note appoggiatura slurs (as in Weber's Op. 24/i, SSB VIII), fleet chromatic fingerwork in close quarters (as in Spohr's Op. 125, SSB XIII, and Weber's "Perpetuum mobile," Op. 24/iv), chordal figuration divided between the hands (in anticipation of Schumann's writing, as in Cramer's Op. 23/3, SSB XIV), and rapid octaves, staccato or legato, in either or both hands (as in Weber's Op. 39/i/124–30).

It was mainly Hummel and Dussek who revealed these new athletic horizons, a fact our several citations have already indicated.[14] They left Clementi behind, to his distress, as Chopin, Thalberg, and Liszt were to leave them and Moscheles behind.[15] Along with minor innovators like Prince Louis Ferdinand (who contributed no extant sons.),[16] Weber and Schumann stood next in line in these trends, bypassing Schubert, whose genius did not happen to include a flair for innovative or especially resourceful piano techniques. But it should be remembered, in any case, that the decided trend toward increasing virtuosity could not be an entirely steady trend. For it was the product not only of the youthful early-Romanticism but of youth itself, and the trend of youth is toward maturity. In other words, within each composer's own sonatas the trend was more likely to be toward less, not greater, virtuosity, as practical experience tempered and channeled the initial animal energies until reaching for the moon became reaching for the obtainable. Like Clementi's sonatas, Weber's and Schumann's became not only more controlled in form but more reasonable to play. It is true that, like Beethoven's late sonatas, Hummel's became more difficult to play, but the new difficulties reflected not so much increased virtuosity as changing styles in a search for new expressive forces. Furthermore, however great the new athletic challenges in the early-Romantic sonata, they never quite add up to the extent and variety of challenges posed by Beethoven's last and most difficult sonatas.

A fourth kind of textural enrichment is the polyphonic activity to be found in the early-Romantic sonata. Nägeli's request for "contrapuntal movements" in 1803 (SCE 26) yielded at least two attempts at actual fugue (by Wölfl, SCE 563–64, and E. T. A. Hoffmann, SSB VIII). But if both this request and its response were unusual there still are many polyphonic passages to report, such as the close, emphatic imitations in the development section of Mendelssohn's Op. 106/i/80–95, or the nearly strict triple counterpoint in the exposition of Schubert's D. 959/i/83–91;[17] or the homage to Mozart's "Jupiter Symphony" finale in the *fugato* coda of Hummel's Op. 20/iii (SSB VIII).

The High-Romantic Style Phase

A near compendium of high-Romantic sonata styles can be found in the unabashed "editorial changes"—the programmatic titles, filled-out textures, "Meistersinger polyphony," and cyclically treated motives —that Wilhelm Rust made without acknowledgment (along with sizable additions up to whole mvts.) in the originally spare, 18th-century sonatas by his grandfather F. W. Rust (SCE 585–87, with ex.; SSB V). Yet these styles do not differ sharply from those of the early-Romantic sonata any more than the latter had from the late-Classic sonata. Rather, the high-Romantic styles reveal that the process of exaggeration was still continuing, and continuing now in relation to the early-Romantic as well as the Classic means. However, the high-Romantic styles do contrast with the early-Romantic in the greater mastery and control that they reveal and in the dichotomy of conservative and progressive that developed within them (*supra*). These several aspects call for separate discussions.

17. But Winkler/SCHUBERT 125–73 and 216–17 concludes that much of the polyphony in Schubert's sons. is of the "latent" or pseudo kind implied by different elements of the texture, cross rhythms, and contrasting sonorities.

With regard to the continuing exaggeration of previous styles, the most evident changes are again in the melody and the texture.[18] The **melody writing** continues to be too varied to permit any generalizations about types beyond describing some of the most prevalent of them again. However, one can now observe a greater breadth and plasticity in much of the melody writing. Extended phrases, especially consequent phrases, had not lacked in the early-Romantic sonata (as in Schubert's D. 960/i/24–35, *supra*, or the last 18 mss. in Mendelssohn's Son. in F/i, for P & Vn, ssʙ VIII). But now they are cultivated more frequently and knowingly, and, apparently, more deliberately, especially by that past master of artful phrase-and-period syntax, Brahms. Thus, already in the concise exposition of Brahms's Op. 5/i, the first thematic group comprises a double period of three extended phrases each, 6+5+5 and 6+8+8 measures, and the second and closing thematic groups combined comprise a double period of two extended phrases each, 8+9 and 6+10 measures. In this characteristic treatment the composer was achieving his own antidote for the curse of the square, most often four-measure, phrase.

The square phrase was a concomitant of homophonic texture.[19] It challenged, sometimes plagued, imaginative, free spirits of the sonata increasingly, from Mozart and Beethoven to the last of the Romantics. In the Brahms periods just described it shows up only in the subdivisions of the eight-measure phrases. The breadth and plasticity in the other phrases result from skillful extensions that do not simply prolong the cadence but alter the internal rhythmic organization. Schumann thought more often in regular phrases, especially in his earlier sonatas (as in the opening of Op. 11; ssʙ VIII). But he was no addict of the square phrase. His approach was flexible, as in the fantasy-like period of two phrases, 6+5 measures, that opens Op. 14 (ssʙ VIII) or the more controlled period of two antecedent phrases and a consequent, 6+6+8 measures, that opens Op. 22 (Ex. 9). In his

18. Schering/ɴᴇᴜʀᴏᴍᴀɴᴛɪᴋ compares the "new-" or high-Romantic with early-Romantic music chiefly in terms of society and other arts rather than specific musical traits, but does emphasize the increased pathos, brilliance, musico-historical consciousness, programmatic interest (in instrumental music), and fondness for characteristic means like the much used dim.-7th chord. With particular reference to 2 of our 4 focal composers in this chap., Sturke/ʙʀᴀʜᴍs explores Brahms's style traits according to early, middle, and late stages of his music (cf. Mitschka/ʙʀᴀʜᴍs 4–5) and Haase/ʙʀᴀʜᴍs with special regard to the polyphonic forms and processes in his piano writing; Meister/ᴄʜᴏᴘɪɴ, Abraham/ᴄʜᴏᴘɪɴ, Bronarski/ᴄʜᴏᴘɪɴ, Thomas/ ᴄʜᴏᴘɪɴ, and Walker/ᴄʜᴏᴘɪɴ all explore style traits in Chopin's piano writing. A new but undated study in Polish, *Studia chopinowskie* by Lew Maze, concentrates on Chopin's Fantasy in f and pieces of similar scope, with only infrequent references to the sons.

19. Cf. Newman/ᴜɴᴅᴇʀsᴛᴀɴᴅɪɴɢ 144–50.

Ex. 9. The opening thematic group in Robert Schumann's
Sonata in g, Op. 22 (after Schumann/WERKE-M VII/iv/22).

three late violin sonatas the flexibility seems to have become more deliberate (as in the opening of Son. 3 in a, ssb VIII).[20]

Chopin showed decidedly the strongest inclination among our four
focal composers to accept and live with the regular four-measure phrase.
Only his Op. 65 (ssb XII) shows an inclination, characteristic of his
last compositions,[21] to experiment with longer and more irregular
phrase lengths. Occasionally his phrases are as obviously regular as
those in Schubert's D. 850/iii quoted above—for example, in the trio
of his "Marche funèbre" (Op. 35/iii), which Bülow found "abominable" [22] but which others, playing it straight and without "interpretation," have found ideal in its simple, unsophisticated purity. Most of
the time Chopin avoided the curse of square phrases, not by defying
the regularity but by disguising it, at either or both ends and/or internally. Thus, in Ex. 10 the first phrase starts on an offbeat, the second
on a downbeat, and the third and fourth on an upbeat.[23] All four
phrases differ in their internal contours and rhythmic organization,
though only slightly between the first and second phrases. Only the
third phrase has two similar subphrases and these differ internally,
too. Only the last phrase has a masculine ending. In the four measures
of Op. 58/i/13–16 Chopin produces a cumulative effect by writing 2
groups of 4 beats, 4 of 2, and one "group" of one beat.

One of the most prevalent types of high-Romantic melody is, again,
the smooth, songful sort. Brahms's Op. 100 starts with the "Meistersinger theme" that appears actually to be based on a song (ssb IX).
Rheinberger exhibits the unusual breadth of his lyricism in the

20. Cf., also, the proselike style of Opp. 105/i/1–11 and 121/i/21–43.
21. Cf. Abraham/CHOPIN 103–4.
22. Cf. Bronarski/CHOPIN II 155.
23. Chopin's own slurs in Ex. 10 go beyond what is meant here but do not
necessarily demarcate phrases.

Ex. 10. From the first movement of Frédéric Chopin's Sonata
in b, Op. 58 (after Chopin/WORKS-m VI 82–83).

"Andante molto" of his Op. 105 (SSB X). Fauré exhibits the unusual
refinement of his lyricism in the "Andante" of his Op. 117 (SSB XIII).
Bennett reveals a gentle, contemplative outlook in the opening of his
Op. 4 (SSB XIV). A more decorative, songful melody may be seen in the
opening movement of Lalo's Sonata for P & Vc (SSB XII). And more
driving yet songful melodies may be seen in the opening movements of
A. G. Ritter's Op. 21 and Hiller's Op. 47 (both SSB X), and of Franck's
Son. in A, Fauré's Op. 13, and Saint-Saëns' Op. 75 (all SSB XIII). Not a
few of the songful melodies are folklike in their simple, reiterated
patterns and their particular scale inflections (as in Grieg's Op. 13/ii,
SSB XV).[24] Others are hymnlike in their simplicity, with one note, one
harmony, and one block chord accompaniment per beat (as in Thalberg's Op. 56/i, SSB XII, and in the trios of several Brahms scherzos—
e.g., the 3d mvts. of Opp. 1, 5, and 34b).

With regard to further aspects of high-Romantic melody, chromaticism continues to abound.[25] Often it occurs as a kind of rhythmic
filler over a relatively diatonic harmony (cf. the quotation from
Chopin's Op. 65/iv in SSB XII). And often it results from borrowed
tones and the alternation of major and minor modes (as in Brahms's Op.
99/iv/1–9). Tovey's concept of melody as the "surface" of harmony
continues to find ample illustration, too, as in the lovely diatonic
middle section in E in Chopin's Op. 58/iii (perhaps the inspiration for
the more chromatic, "Molto più lento" variation in F♯ in Franck's
"Symphonic Variations").

24. Cobbett/CHAMBER I 409–18 (W. W. Cobbett & L. Henry) offers interesting
views on folk elements in chamber music, but unfortunately (and unavoidably, in
the experience of this study) with virtually no concrete evidence nor specific
instances.
25. Cf. Hewitt/DISSERTATIONS item 776 for a study of chromaticism from Beethoven
to Brahms, in progress.

Certain types of high-Romantic melody seem also to require classification by quality, as indefinable as that term still may be in the musical laboratory. Thus, two types seem to be the province almost exclusively of the masters. One is the short, bold, trenchant, dynamic idea—that is, the type that begs for development in a "sonata form." Ideas of that type launch all three piano sonatas by Brahms, all three violin sonatas by Schumann, and Op. 58 by Chopin. The other type is the full-fledged, memorable tune, such as the admirable refrain in the rondo finale of Chopin's Op. 58, called "a sort of war song," by d'Indy, among the themes so "truly resplendent of melodic richness" in this work.[26] On the other hand, one would be tempted to make a melodic type, too, out of the many well-constructed, academically correct themes that are too flat, too naive or innocuous, and often too complete or closed in their own phrase grouping to invite any purposeful continuation in "sonata form" (as seems to be true of many of Reinecke's opening themes, for example). This type, obviously enough, would be the province especially of the second-rate composers. But it is a type that seems to be more conspicuously inadequate in high- than in early- or late-Romantic music, since flat, innocuous themes tend to prevail, anyway, in the early phase of any era (as in Loewe's sons.) and again in the late phase at least in the "creations" of the epigones (as in Sinding's sons.). All of which is tantamount to the truism that sonatas can no more succeed without significant ideas, however these may be defined and typed, than without convincing rhythmic flow, compelling tonal organization, or euphonious, idiomatic scoring. One might even argue that the significant ideas matter exceptionally in the high-Romantic sonata, where actual development of ideas is more often lacking (as in Bennett's Op. 46) than in the high-Classic sonata.

The **harmony and tonality** reveal no clear innovations in the high-Romantic sonata, although both the variety of chords and modulations and the extent of their use seem, on the average, to be proportionally greater. Chopin's fresh, resourceful harmony reveals nearly every imaginable chord type, diatonic or chromatic, and every extension, all the way to a 13th-chord; yet only a surprisingly small percentage of his total chords are altered.[27] Subsequent composers tended to make more constant use of 7th- and 9th-chords (as in Goldmark's Op. 25/ii, ssb IX). The greater co-ordination of dissonance, rhythmic drive, half-step tendencies, and bass-line direction in high-Romantic harmony all help

---

26. D'Indy/cours II/1 410 and 407.

27. According to the statistical conclusions in Thomas/chopin 639–68. The first thematic group and bridge in Op. 58/i/1–40 give as concentrated a view of Chopin's harmonic resourcefulness as any comparable section in his sons.

to make the harmonic goals more purposeful, too. A telling example is the broad cadence described in the first twenty-one measures of Brahms's Op. 100, starting and ending in the tonic and emphasizing ii, IV, and ♭II along the way, each approached through its own dominant. The dim.-7th chord continues to occupy a central place in the harmony, in the various ways mentioned earlier.[28] It is inherent right in the opening thematic complex of Liszt's Sonata in b, for example (ssʙ X), and prevalent in much of the passagework. There is more efficiency, even slickness, in the modulations, near and far. Thus, in thirteen measures Schumann moves easily from e♭ to a♭, to V-of-b = aug.-6/5 in b♭, to b♭ (Op. 14/ii/151–63). In Op. 6/ii, Draeseke simply assumes each dominant chord on an offbeat fortissimo as he slips from D♭ to D and back in three 4-measure units (ssʙ X).

Texture and sonority in the high-Romantic sonata show further increases in fullness, polyphonic interest, rhythmic diversity, and idiomatic scoring. Furthermore, the craftsmanship in matters textural is more generally of a professional level. The craftsmanship in the early-Romantic sonata had often betrayed a certain amateurishness, especially in the most progressive sonatas. Impeccable craftsmen like Hummel and Mendelssohn left no doubt of their expertise. Nor did Schubert, except for polyphonic limitations that he apparently recognized and got around artfully enough. But quite apart from an actual amateur like E. T. A. Hoffmann or an occasionally careless composer like Dussek, even such front-rankers as Weber and Schumann revealed shortcomings in their training, such as it was, and their backgrounds as littérateurs-cum-musicians (both ssʙ VIII). Thus, especially in the first sonata that each completed in his adulthood there are telltale aridities and gaucheries in the bass and filler parts taken by the left hand.[29] In the high-Romantic sonata, the professional composers (including Chopin) rarely reveal such holes in their training, no doubt reflecting the growth and spread of conservatories and the corresponding improvements in teaching (ssʙ III and IV).

The greater fullness of texture was soon taken for granted, as we gather from one reviewer, who found Gurlitt's Op. 16 for P solo archaic because of its spare texture.[30] A richly sonorous texture may be observed in the rolled chords of up to ten tones by which the piano states the chorale melody, with a poetic commentary from the cello, in Op. 58/ii by Mendelssohn (ssʙ VIII). But fullness of texture could be

28. Cf. Schering/NEUROMANTIK 58.

29. Cf. the exx. quoted in ssʙ VIII from Weber's Op. 24/i and Schumann's Op. 11/i; also, Saunders/WEBER 174, 223; Niecks/SCHUMANN 62–64.

30. NZM XLIII (1855) 278.

achieved by polyphonic enlivenment, too, as in the expressive exchanges between partners in Op. 17 for P-duet by Goetz (SSB V). Polyphonic interest of some sort, especially imitative writing, is rarely absent in the sonatas of both Schumann and Brahms.[31] And, of course, there are not a few actual fugal movements, like the finale of Brahms's Op. 38 and the "Allegro energico" of Liszt's Sonata in b. Fullness of texture could also be achieved by rhythmic enlivenment—for example, by the dexterous cross rhythms of hemiola in Brahms's Op. 78/i/11–20 or two-against-three in his Op. 100/i/51–74, or by the dotted against the even pattern in Gade's Op. 28/iii (SSB XV), or by the 16th-note syncopations in the passagework of Schumann's Op. 22/i/24–40, or by the isometric pattern, conflicting with the meter of the passagework, in Brahms's Op. 5/v/25–31.[32]

The exaggeration to be noted in high-Romantic texture occurs most conspicuously in the virtuoso piano writing, or what might now be called massive pianism. Alkan's Op. 33/ii, covering almost the whole keyboard at once, provides the extreme example to be expected of that remarkable eccentric (SSB XII). Reubke's Sonata in b♭, with its majestic sonorities and dashing runs in the Lisztian manner, is more representative (SSB X). That such writing was an exaggeration even of early-Romantic piano writing is suggested by the need Liszt and his contemporaries felt to rescore and elaborate on the compositions of Schubert, Weber, and others (as in Liszt's eds. discussed in SSB V and Henselt's version of Weber's Op. 39/iv illustrated in SSB V).[33] Not all the technically advanced writing was of the massive sort. There was, for instance, the light, extremely rapid finger work required by Chopin in Op. 58/ii and iv, or the open-position chordal passagework that often figured in more impassioned music, as in Schumann's Op. 14/i (SSB VIII) or Raff's Op. 14/ii (SSB X).

In the first section of this chapter was noted the **dichotomy of conservative and progressive styles and forms** that developed most sharply in the high-Romantic sonata between Brahms and Liszt. This dichotomy is not to be confused with the functional one of old and new, represented by the 19th-century pedagogic sonatina that never left 18th-century styles as against the full-scale 19th-century sonata that was admired in artistic circles and played in the concert halls (SSB III). Only the latter is concerned in the dichotomy now in question. The

31. Cf. Haase/BRAHMS 78 for an index of numerous polyphonic styles in Brahms's P music. A similar study, concentrating on his chamber music, is in preparation by Donald Pease at the University of North Carolina (as of 1968).

32. Cf. Kempers/ISOMETRISCHE.

33. Recall, too, Liszt's elaboration of music from his own day, including the page from Chopin's Op. 58/iv mentioned in SSB XII.

Ex. 11. From the penultimate statement of element y (cf.
ssb X) in Franz Liszt's Sonata in b (after Ed. Peters No. 3601b,
p. 315).

actual difference in this instance between conservative and progressive
might be elaborated as that between traditional law and logical order
versus experimentation and fantasy. The elements and means are
essentially the same but they are treated more freely and subjectively,
with a compensatory loss in dynamic tension.[34] Thus, the melody tends
to unfold continuously, in chain phrases or smaller units rather than
in phrase-and-period groupings. The harmony tends toward more
exploitation of third relationships, enharmony, and remoter chord
progressions (Ex. 11). The passagework depends more on sequence,
the ambiguity of the diminished 7th-chord, and continual modulations. The tempo undergoes frequent changes, graduations, and grand
pauses. And because these treatments and processes operate in all

34. This conclusion is the gist of the discussion in Mersmann/ROMANTISCHEN.
Cf., also, Lang/WESTERN 816–19.

sections of the sonata, not only in development sections, there is a sense of fantasy and improvisation throughout, however tight the logic behind it may be (as it certainly is in Liszt's Sonata in b; cf. ssb X).

One element of the progressive style we are describing was furthered in particular, and has even been called an original (German) contribution.[35] This is the full opening theme that actually proves to be a complex of several separate and separable motives, each capable of independent extension, re-formation, and development. Such a thematic complex was not really without precedent, as in Beethoven's Op. 53/i/1–4. But now it became the fund from which most if not all of the work was drawn.[36] The structural result of planting such a complex seed is a matter of over-all design rather than style (as differentiated earlier). But note may be taken here of the five thematic elements used in Liszt's Sonata in b (ssb X, with structural analysis), the first three of which comprise the initial thematic complex. As discussed in Chapter X, the double-function design that Liszt created out of this complex stands alone at its high level in the 19th-century sonata, with remarkably few imitators and these chiefly among the works of his direct disciples like Viole, Draeseke, and Reubke (all ssb X).

The Late-Romantic Style Phase

In the late-Romantic sonata the **dichotomy of styles and forms** just discussed became both more and less pronounced. It became more so in the sense that it hardened and widened, with the conservatives often becoming epigones, like, say, Dubois (ssb XIII), and the progressives often becoming radicals, like Reger (ssb XI). It became less so in the sense that there were increasing cross influences, new nationalistic influences, and men who do not really fit on either side but fall somewhere in between. Since the epigones were eclectics at bottom, they could respond equally well to influences from either side. Thus, d'Albert's Op. 10 shows some influences of Liszt as well as Brahms (ssb XI). On the other hand, composers like Tchaikovsky and Saint-Saëns, though conservative in their sonata styles, were strong and individual enough to escape the brand of epigonism (ssb XVIII and XIII). Not all the close imitators of Brahms, such as Kiel or W. Berger (ssb X and XI) are necessarily to be written off in that way, either. Nor were all the progressives as abruptly radical as Reger. Composers like Fauré and Sibelius made smoother transitions to the new, different, though

---

35. MGG XI 813–15 (F. Blume).

36. RETI/BEETHOVEN 166–75 argues, for the most part convincingly, that Op. 53, too, derives entirely from its opening material.

less debatable styles of their later sonatas or sonatinas (ssb XIII and XV).

By his very nature, the epigone offered nothing in his sonatas that could be regarded here as a stylistic change or exaggeration. Rather, he reviewed and often—again, because he was an eclectic—medlied past styles. The further marks of the epigone are high technical competence, untroubled neatness and propriety in the handling of styles and forms, sure practicalness and effectiveness, and a certain initial gloss and excitement that quickly reduce to hollow academicism. A fully representative example, among many such sonatas that still are to be rediscovered on the shelves of the larger dealers, is Op. 9 by Bortkiewicz, written under the strong influence of Chopin's Op. 58 (as described in ssb XVIII).

Without further attempts, then, to dwell on a late-Romantic dichotomy of styles, we may observe some of the relatively fewer changes and exaggerations to be found in this style phase. As before, the **melody** cannot be generalized. One can only point to certain prevalent types. There are simple, lyrical, nicely drawn melodies that could come right out of Mendelssohn except for the late-Romantic tendency to think increasingly in eight-measure phrases (as in the opening of Gernsheim's Op. 12, ssb XI). There are melodies of wider range and broader sweep, such as are in R. Strauss's Op. 6/ii (ssb XI), Sinding's Op. 91/i (ssb XV), Dohnányi's Op. 8/i (ssb XVII), and Glazunov's Op. 74/i (ssb XVIII). There are melodies that unfold in the "endless" Wagnerian manner (as in Medtner's Op. 25/1/ii, ssb XVIII). There are melodies that enter precipitately, with dramatic upward thrusts, as in R. Strauss's Op. 18/iii (ssb XI), Elgar's Op. 82/i (ssb XIV), Dale's Op. 1/i (ssb XIV), and Nicholl's Op. 21/i (ssb XIX). And there are melodies now that not only suggest but actually incorporate folk materials, including the finales of Dvořák's Op. 100 (ssb XVII), Sinding's Op. 73, and Williams' Op. 74 (ssb XIX). This last type only touched the sonata peripherally and infrequently, but does recall at least the atmosphere of nationalism in which many late-Romantic sonatas were created, especially in the "outlying" countries of the sonata.[37]

The **harmony and tonality** in the late-Romantic sonata reveal the most evident changes since the previous style phase. As discussed earlier (ssb I), the present volume stops short of Busoni, J. Haas, Scriabin, Ives, Debussy, and others who were already making frontal attacks on traditional harmony and tonality before World War I. But it still includes among their contemporaries men like Reger, Karg-Elert, Nielsen, and d'Indy who were straining so hard to find new worlds to conquer

---

37. Cf. ssb IV; Lissa/NATIONALEN.

within the logic of the old that they unintentionally, and probably unwittingly, accomplished almost equivalent attacks. Their ways of straining tradition differ with each composer, as discussed later when each is considered separately. Among others, examples are quoted from Reuss's Op. 27/i, Reger's Opp. 72/i and 89/4/i, and Karg-Elert's Op. 105 (all in ssb XI); d'Indy's Op. 63/iii (ssb XIII); and Nielsen's Op. 35/i (ssb XV). At this point the "strains" may be generalized as increased chromaticism, bigger elisions in standard harmonic progressions, diagonal relations more often and further apart, freer dissonance and voice-leading, and dominant or subdominant relationships two- or three-times removed (V-of-V-of-V, etc.). Gliding in and out of the remotest keys happens so easily and so often that modulation as a means of bridging two structural landmarks almost ceases to exist and the relatively close tonal relationships that still obtain between those landmarks scarcely stand out if at all.

Unfortunately, not all of the late-Romantic strains on harmonic and tonal tradition were quite so enterprising or worthy of respect. In the same style category, a good many other sonatas show advances, hence cannot strictly be called epigonic. But these "advances" tend to strain the good taste rather than the intelligibility of tradition, mostly by making clichés ("barber-shop" harmony) out of the standard altered-chord progressions, by overloading the active chromatic chords with half-step pulls, and by adding 2ds, 6ths, 7ths, and 9ths to diatonic as well as chromatic chords for the sake of piquancy or pungency. By way of illustrations, the three successive examples by Martucci, Longo, and Albéniz in Chapter XVI would be regarded here as stopping just short of sentimentality and triteness in their day, whereas the example by Schytte in Chapter XI would not.

The **texture and scoring** show no distinct advance in the late-Romantic beyond the high-Romantic sonata unless it be in the further exploitation of polyphonic means. An example of the latter is the extraordinary climactic coda of d'Indy's Op. 63/iii, with its culminating apotheosis, triple-forte, in the combination of the two triumphant themes (ssb XIII). Otherwise, there was little further to go in the writing for the established instruments. Karg-Elert's Op. 105 and Schäfer's Op. 9 may be more frenetic in their massive pianism and their blood-and-thunder assaults on fading Romanticism, Rachmaninoff may crowd more black notes into his Op. 36/i (ssb XVIII), but none could engulf the instrument more than had Alkan's Op. 33 a half-century earlier (ssb XII). That some would have liked to is suggested by the increased amount of overthick, unpianistic, quasi-orchestral writing for the piano, as in R. Fuchs' Op. 19/i and Tchaikovsky's Op. 37/i (ssb XI and XVIII; cf. ssb V). Sibelius wrote orchestrally and unpianistically for the piano, too (as in Op. 67/i, ssb XV), but sensitively, not thickly.

The Sonata as a Whole

Thus far, this chapter on "form" has examined the Romantic sonata for its main styles in its early, high, and late phases—that is, for the traits that have governed its behavior as a "generative process." There remains its examination for its main over-all designs—that is, for the designs that appear most often or typically in it throughout the era (form as a "mold"), and for the most noteworthy departures from those designs (form as a "unicum"). First comes the question of the sonata as an organized whole, then the separate consideration of each of its main movement types.

The sonata as a whole, meaning its unity and interrelationships as a cycle of several movements, has received remarkably little attention (cf. sce 133–43), and then chiefly with regard only to thematic interrelationships in particular sonatas by a particular composer, especially Beethoven.[38] Of course, the **one-movement sonata** raises no problems of cyclical unity, at least not when it is actually no more than a single form. But in the century before Scriabin's later piano sonatas (1907–13) the number of one-movement sonatas of any sort is remarkably small, including chiefly Moscheles' Op. 49, Liszt's "Dante Sonata," Wagner's *Album-Sonate*, Raff's Op. 129, and several examples by Medtner (both before and after Scriabin's; ssb XVIII). These are all simply single "sonata forms" or single, freer, fantasy movements. Liszt's Sonata in b is not a simple "sonata form" but a double-function form, because its several components also serve as the (unseparated) movements of the complete cycle (as discussed and diagramed in some detail in ssb X). Shedlock, Cyril Scott, and others have seen Liszt's work as the single original contribution to form in the 19th-century sonata.[39] Yet it stands alone, with only a few follow-ups, as noted earlier (*supra*), by Liszt's immediate disciples and an occasional later

38. E.g., cf. Misch/EINHEIT and Rosenberg/BEETHOVEN as listed in sce 845 and 854; Reti/BEETHOVEN. Noé/ZYKLISCHEN is a brief survey, from Beethoven on, of interlocking mvts. in a cycle. Richard Crocker has touched briefly but provocatively on whether and how a son. cycle is heard as a whole, comparing its usually substantial length with a hypothetical age-old norm of 5±4 minutes for an immediately digestible "piece" of music (*Current Musicology* V [1967] 50–56); cf., also, Newman/UNDERSTANDING 202–4.

39. Shedlock/SONATA 218–20, 235; Schüz/SONATE; Scott/SUGGESTIONS.

composer (e.g., Liapunov) and none of equivalent importance in solo or duo music.

With regard to the vast majority of **sonatas, in several movements,** only 4 out of the 47 completed, adult sonatas by our 4 focal composers offer any appreciable challenge to the most usual Classic plans of 3 and 4 movements.[40] Of those 4, one is in 2 movements and 3 are in 5 movements. Of the other 43, only 12 are in 3 movements and 31, or about 2½ times as many, are in 4 movements. This last ratio is about the same for the solo and the duo sonatas and seems to apply pretty generally throughout the era. It is no wonder that Brahms joked with his publisher Simrock about cutting his fee by one fourth because he wrote only three movements in Op. 78 (ssb IX). It will be recalled, by contrast (sce 133–34), that the 3-movement sonata had predominated in the Classic Era, with 4- and 2-movement sonatas about tied for second place. The 2-movement sonata appeared much less often in the Romantic Era, mostly only in some sonatinas.

Not a one of the 43 sonatas in 3 and 4 movements departs from what had already been standard solutions to the **order of movements** in the Classic Era (sce 135–36). The first movement is a "sonata form" in a moderate, fast, or very fast tempo and the last most often a rondo or "sonata form." In between is a slower movement, usually in A-B-A design, and, on either side of it, in 4-movement sonatas, a scherzo or dance. Among the but 4 sonatas in fewer or more movements, the one in 2 movements simply deletes the inner slow movement and the 3 in 5 movements simply add another inner movement, whether moderate or scherzo. It is obvious that, at least outwardly and in its largest outlines, the Romantic sonata showed more conformity to norms than the Classic sonata had. This conformity undoubtedly reflects the increased codification and awareness of sonata procedures in the 19th century (ssb II). But when, in 1844, a reviewer objected to the plan S/VF-Sc-Ro in Gurlitt's Op. 3 because it lacked a complete (inner) slow movement,[41] he seems to have been responding mainly to the need that has always been felt in the sonata, for contrast between adjacent movements.

In Chapter III, in connection with the long recitals that became customary during the later 19th century, the greater length of the sonatas themselves was noted. Beethoven's Op. 106, Schubert's D. 959

40. Reference may be made to the tabulations of sons. by Schubert, Schumann, Chopin, and Brahms (ssb VII, VIII, XII, and IX, respectively), which include bibliographic information plus nos., tempos, and keys of mvts., lengths in measures, and, for Schubert and Brahms, approximate performance times.

41. nzm XX (1844) 115–16.

in A, Brahms's Op. 34b in f, and further examples by Raff, Rheinberger, Reger, d'Indy, Dukas, Medtner, Godowsky, and Dale were cited as works ranging from 35 to more than 60 minutes in performance. And there are numerous occasions in the later discussions of these and other individual sonatas when the problem of length must come up again. Among sample comments, in 1822 Rochlitz was complaining about how sonatas seemed to be getting longer and more boring, partly, to be sure, because of more quantity than quality.[42] In 1839 Schumann twice made his celebrated reference to "heavenly length" in Schubert's Symphony in C.[43] In 1918 F. Corder defended Dale's huge Sonata in d against charges of excessive length, insisting that there was nothing wrong with length in itself.[44] And in 1926 Medtner answered friendly criticisms of his sonatas from Rachmaninoff with the remark that "it is *not the length* of musical compositions that creates an impression of boredom, but it is rather the *boredom* that creates the impression of length." [45]

However, there is no question that the average length of sonatas increased in the Romantic Era (if only because of longer phrases, more writing in double-periods, and more modulations to more keys) and that length per se became an increasing consideration in the over-all effect of the sonata. There is, after all, a point of diminishing returns, whether defined by the performer's musical grasp and physical endurance or by the listener's attention span. This point cannot be fixed in any absolute sense, of course, because there are too many variables— the sustaining forces of the music, the caliber of the performer(s), the comprehension and attitude of the listener, the adequacy of the instrument(s), the acoustics of the hall, and even the weather and time of day. Furthermore, the more varied the timbres and any peripheral interests, visual or programmatic, the greater is the length that can be accepted. In these regards and with other considerations being equal, the usual solo or duo settings of the sonata are at the low end of the length-tolerance scale, followed progressively, say, by larger chamber ensembles, orchestral music, oratorio, and opera (with Wagner's uncut operas, lasting five hours or more, often regarded as surpassing absolute tolerance limits).

If an absolute tolerance limit cannot be set for the length of Romantic sonatas, one might venture merely the conclusions of ex-

42. AMZ XXIV (1822) 383; cf. SSB VII.

43. Storck/SCHUMANN 222; Schumann/SCHRIFTEN I 463. Vrieslander/ORGANISCHE considers the problem of length, supporting Schumann's reference on qualitative grounds.

44. MT LIX (1918) 164.

45. Bertensson & Leyda/RACHMANINOFF 246–47; cf. pp. 180 and 276.

perience to the effect that when the Romantic sonata extends beyond about twenty-five minutes the problems of length per se begin to mount rapidly. At the other extreme, or what might be called the shortness tolerance, it is the music much more than the performer or listener that defines the limit. Regarding this limit, one might venture that any Romantic sonata lasting less than about twelve minutes scarcely has time to whip up the kinds of emotions and climaxes in which that genre ordinarily traffics. To appreciate that observation, recall the surprise that still greets the playing of the finale in Chopin's Op. 35, which averages only one minute and thirteen seconds in performance (ssb XII).

Perhaps some comparisons of lengths in the adult, completed sonatas, both solo and duo, by our four focal composers may help to put these observations regarding length on a little more solid ground, although the numbers of measures, which disregard numbers of beats and differences of tempo, can give only an approximate idea of length. The accompanying tabulation includes works on the fringe of the sonata

*The Average Number of Measures in the Adult, Completed
Sonatas of Four Masters*

	First movements/%	Final movements/%	All movements
Schubert	214/27	318/40	805
Schumann	280/36	266/34	777
Chopin	227/30	187/25	746
Brahms	244/30	257/33	806

(Schubert's "Grande Duo," D. 812; Schumann's *Fantasie,* Op. 17, though not his Op. 118/1–3, "for the young"; and Brahms's Op. 34b in f, for 2 Ps) and it makes no distinction between solo and duo. The solos actually run somewhat longer in these and most other master works of the era (except, understandably, for Brahms's Op. 34b), partly because Dussek, Weber, Brahms, Liszt, and others wrote their most monumental, grandiose sonatas for piano alone and partly because Schumann, Brahms, and others wrote their solo rather than their duo sonatas among their earlier works, before experiencing the tendency of most composers in their advancing years toward more conciseness and moderation.

Taking the sonatas of our four focal composers in the chronological order of their composition, we do not find them showing the gradual increase in length that a broader sampling, covering the whole era, would almost certainly show. But putting them all together yields a total average length of 785 measures that is 199 (or a 3d) more than

the average of 586 measures for all of Beethoven's standard 32 sonatas
for P solo. To be sure, only 34 per cent of these last are in more than
3 movements as against 72 per cent of the Romantic masterworks in
question. The average playing time for Beethoven's solo piano sonatas
is about 20 minutes, as against 27 for Schubert (about the same as for
Weber) and 26 for Brahms.[46] In our tabulation of lengths the outer
movements are averaged separately, for these are the ones most likely to
pose length problems, especially the finales. As might be expected,
Schubert's finales average substantially more measures than his first
movements. Otherwise the differences between outer movements are
not considerable, allowing for the effect on the average of the short
finale in Chopin's Op. 35. With reference only to solo piano sonatas
again, the average length of Schubert's first movements exceeds only
by a few measures that of Beethoven's, Weber's, and Dussek's.

With regard to **tonality**, the home keys selected by our four focal
composers show an even distribution of major and minor as against
a ratio of about four-to-one in favor of major in the Classic Era (SCE
137). All of Schumann's full-scale sonatas (excluding Op. 17) and all
of Chopin's are in minor keys, but Schubert's and Brahms's numerous
sonatas in major as well as minor balance the ratio. The impression
gained here has been of a continuing increase in the number of sonatas
in minor keys throughout the era, although statistics are lacking to
confirm that impression. Not a few Romantic sonatas change to the
opposite mode right from the start of the finale, most often to major.
While this change is peculiarly absent in the sonatas of our four focal
composers, it can be found early and easily in the era, in Dussek's C.
178 in e♭/E♭, Field's Op. 1/3 in c/C, and Weber's Op. 49 in d/D (as
well as Beethoven's Opp. 90 in e/E and 111 in c/C); and increasingly
often later in the era, as in three of Mendelssohn's six organ sonatas
and five of Reger's thirty-one sonatas. (Each of the 4 separate mvts.
changes from minor to major in R. Strauss's Op. 5—b/B, E/e/E,
f♯/F♯, b/B.) But it is hard to claim the "heroic" or "victorious" turn
to a major finale in the minor/major sonata as a particular Romantic
innovation[47] in the face of a fair number of major/minor examples,
too, starting with Ries's Op. 21 in A/a, Czerny's Op. 7 in A♭/a♭, and
Woržischek's Op. 5 in G/g. (R. Fuchs's Op. 19 is in G♭/f♯.)

The actual keys selected by our four composers range only up to
four sharps and three flats in major, and three sharps and five flats in
minor, with a, C, f, and A being the most frequently used keys, in that
order. Thus, in key choice, too, our four composers did not go much

46. These figures are based on averages of recordings and personal experience.
47. As in Egert/FRÜHROMANTIKER 100.

beyond the Classics (SCE 137–38). They were also somewhat on the conservative side of their times again, although the key of Pinto's Op. 3/1 in e♭ must have seemed unusual well after it appeared about 1802 (SSB XIV) and that of Woržischek's Op. 20 in b♭ still brought special mention in 1826, as well as its sections in seven sharps.[48] At first, such sections and entire movements supplied the chief instances of keys in the most sharps and flats, especially e♭ and a♭ (as in the entire middle section in a♭ in the 2d mvt., in A♭, in Loewe's Op. 41 in E♭, or a slow mvt. in e♭ in Cramer's Op. 25/1 in E♭, or the Czerny finale in a♭ noted just above).

Regarding favorite keys or key associations, f♯ was cited (*supra,* under early-Romantic melody) as a favorite key for sonatas opening with an impassioned flow. The key of A♭ was used often for opening or inner movements with a more peaceful, gentle flow, perhaps influenced by Beethoven's Op. 26/i, as in that same Op. 41/ii by Loewe, or Spohr's Op. 125/i, or Bennett's Op. 46/i (SSB XIV; cf. SCE 564). The key of f seems to have been a favorite for sonatas with a dramatic opening, like Op. 5 by Brahms. But beyond these generalizations and some key associations peculiar to individual composers,[49] no clearer case can be supported here for key associations in the Romantic sonata, especially in view of its remarkably infrequent use of specific programmes (*infra*).

The choice of key for an inner movement is more likely to be determined, of course, less by association with a mood or style than by its relation to the home key. In the adult, completed sonatas of our four focal composers, about 59 per cent have one movement in another key, 34 per cent have two movements in other keys, and the rest have only movements that change the mode of the home key. In order of frequency, the preference is strongest for the submediant major key, then the mediant major, subdominant major, dominant major, submediant minor, change of mode to major, mediant minor, change of mode to minor, subdominant minor, and raised tonic major. Including both mediant and submediant keys, major or minor, more than half of these preferences illustrate the all-important 3d relationships of Romantic tonality. (Schubert's D. 459 emphasizes the submediant major in the development of the first mvt., the trio of the second, the key of the third, and at two structural landmarks in the finale, mss. 46–47 and 61.)

The tonal organization of the sonata cycle has always been a rela-

---

48. AMZ XXVIII (1826) 204.

49. L. Aguettant argues such associations in Chopin's music, key by key, in RM/CHOPIN 79–86, though with few references to the sons.

tively passive means of achieving over-all unity, the more so in the Romantic Era, when frequent distant modulations at the local levels of form tended increasingly to obscure the tonal landmarks at the broader levels. Stylistic consistency has also been a passive means of unity, especially as it must depend chiefly on the circumscribed vocabularies and habits of any one musician. For more positive or active means one must look to four methods, all of them consciously intensified throughout the era except the third—interlocking of movements, thematic interrelationships, programmatic continuity, and an over-all curve of dynamic tension. In that order, these methods need separate comments.

Although there were interesting Classic precedents, such as those in Beethoven's Opp. 101 and 110 (sce 141–42), the **interlocking of movements** through their later repetition, partial or complete, within other movements or separate, provides some of the most evident arguments for structural innovations in the Romantic sonata.[50] The need for closer ties between the movements is suggested by the increased efforts to lead one movement into the next without a distinct break, "attacca" (as had already happened throughout Beethoven's Op. 27/i and happens before the "Scherzo" in Brahms's Op. 1 and before the finale in his Op. 5); or without more than a suspensive cadence between adjacent movements (as happens before the finale of Hummel's Op. 20); or without any more than a slowing of the rhythm (as happens before the finale of Mendelssohn's Op. 106).

Actual interlocking may be illustrated by noting a few out of numerous examples. The "Scherzo e Intermezzo" in Schumann's Op. 11 presents an A-B-A design in which the trio or "Intermezzo" contrasts so sharply in tempo, key, and style with the A or "Scherzo" section that the effect is like alternating movements. A similar procedure, in reverse tempos, occurs in Brahms's Op. 100, with the "Andante" and "Vivace" making an A-B-A-B-A-coda ("Vivace"), an example that was imitated numerous times, as we shall see in later chapters. In the finale of Brahms's Op. 78 the violin returns to the middle (slow) movement without a change in the finale tempo (ms. 83), and again in altered rhythms (mss. 93, 106, etc.), all serving to point up thematic interrelationships, too (*infra*). In Brahms's Op. 5, the fourth movement, "Intermezzo (Rückblick)," is indeed a "glance back," at the second, "Andante." In the finale of d'Indy's Op. 63 the return to the theme of the variations in the first movement is not

50. As cited earlier, Noé/ZYKLISCHEN surveys this topic briefly, starting with the statement that it has been grossly neglected by writers.

simply a recollection of an earlier idea but the incorporation of a complete section (newly scored), and with enough force to give an A-B-A sense to the whole sonata. The finale (2d mvt.) in both of Dale's sonatas is a theme-and-variations in which one or more variations each serve as a slow movement, a scherzo, and an actual finale.[51] Such interlocking through variation form seems to have encompassed the entire cycle in one Arthur O'Leary's "Theme in C Minor (with elaborate variations in form of a sonata)." [52] Of course, the most renowned and certainly one of the most successful examples of interlocking movements is Liszt's Sonata in b, cited earlier as a double-function "sonata form" and sonata cycle rather than a single-movement sonata (and described, with chart and exx., in ssb X).

By far the most prevalent and most discussed means of giving positive unity to the several movements of a Romantic sonata cycle was that of **interrelated themes.**[53] This means had ample precedents in both the Baroque and Classic sonata (sbe 78–79, sce 138–40). But in the Romantic sonata (and other music) it was elevated to a veritable credo, espoused by some of the era's finest composers and writers, including d'Indy, who credited its perfection largely to his teacher Franck and viewed the latter partly on that account as the true successor to Beethoven (ssb XIII). And in the music itself it was applied to the nth degree, until every note of the score could be related to an initial source idea. Here was the final, outermost circle in the trinity that had at its center the source or original idea, next the dualism or tension inherent in that idea, and lastly the composition that grew entirely out of it.[54] There were even those well-known varieties, not always clearly distinguishable, in both the nature and the treatment of the source idea, including Berlioz's "idée fixe," Liszt's "thematic transformation," Brahms's "basic motive," Wagner's "leitmotiv," Franck's "cyclical treatment," and Sibelius's "organic evolution of a germ idea."

Naturally, quite that much emphasis on thematic interrelationships did not go unchallenged. Time and again, later, we shall find 19th-century reviewers complaining that excess application of this means reveals lack of invention and produces dullness and cerebral writing.

---

51. In this view, the objection to the variations as topheavy in Dale's Op. 11 (mt LXIV [1923] 480) seems unjustified.

52. mt XXI (1880) 411.

53. Marx/zyklische is a brief, recent survey of this means. If a full study of it is lacking, the reason is not any lack of special studies confined to the works of single composers, especially Romantics (as noted where pertinent, in later chaps.).

54. Mersmann/romantischen.

In the 20th century the validity of the principle itself has been challenged. Thus, Calvocoressi has observed, reasonably enough, that thematic relationships in themselves are no guarantee of either vitality or beauty.[55] Others have even doubted, for example, that any "organic evolution of a germ idea" actually operates in Sibelius's music.[56] But there can be no doubt that a majority of the Romantics embraced the principle of thematic relationships as a creative way out. The masters found fresh worlds to conquer in it. The less imaginative composers welcomed the crutch it held out to them quite as our less imaginative Moderns have welcomed the tone row.

Contemporary with and soon after the many important precedents that, as always, Beethoven had supplied (sce 139–40), the principle of thematic relationships began to be taken up with a vengeance. Early examples (all discussed in ssb VIII) include L. Berger's Op. 18, based on a six-note turn without letup in all three movements; Loewe's Op. 41, based in all four movements on a motive that Schumann found increasingly tiresome in spite of his own predilection for intensive thematic relationships; and J. E. Leonhard's prize-winning Op. 5, based as relentlessly as Berger's on a weak initial motive and also deplored in that regard by Schumann.

Our four focal composers rank in the order of Schubert, Chopin, Schumann, and Brahms as regards their interest, from least to most, in exploiting thematic relationships. This order almost duplicates the chronology of their first important sonatas. Schubert, like. Mozart, Hummel, Dussek, and Weber, seems to have taken only an occasional, incidental interest in such means of unity.[57] There are always the questions of how subtle the relationships might be and how much certain tentative relationships might result merely from a uniformity of melodic style. One can only answer that Schubert was a forthright melodist and that there is no more reason to suspect unrecognizable subtleties in his music than in that of Schumann, Liszt, Brahms, or Reger, whose obviously deliberate uses of thematic relationships seem always to be recognizable, no matter how subtle. Thus, thematic relationships might be argued in Schubert's D. 459 (cf. the 4-note descents in mvt. i/2 and 33, ii/130–31, iii/1–2 and 20–22 and 24–25) or D. 568 (cf. the rising chordal incipits of the outer movements), but the ideas and their locations seem too casual for the resemblances to be more than fortui-

55. Cobbett/CHAMBER II 3 (with regard to d'Indy's music).
56. E.g., cf. Hill/SIBELIUS and Collins/GERM. In Emmanuel/DUKAS 70–71 a curious parallel in thematic relationships between Beethoven's Op. 101 and Franck's Son. in A is described simply to show how unfruitful such analysis can be.
57. Cf. the doubts raised in Einstein/SCHUBERT 130–32.

tous.[58] In the initial themes throughout his last sonata, D. 960, Schubert may seem more consciously to be establishing relationships. Yet, each of these themes grows out of one of his favorite melodic styles, turning around the first note, and in that respect all four movements of the previous sonata, D. 959, could just as well be related to those of D. 960, too.

Chopin's two most important sonatas, Opp. 35 and 58, show subtle but more positive and likely thematic relationships. Op. 35 seems to exploit 3–1–2(–3) of the minor scale, as in its opening theme (cf. mvt. i/9 and 41–44, ii/1–3 and 87–88, iii/3–4, and iv/1), although, admittedly, one could find similar figures in almost any minor piece of the times and there is the question of the "Marche funèbre" having been composed two years before the other movements. But the interrelation of the two themes in the first movement gives some support for the resemblances in the other movements. In Op. 58, Chopin seems to exploit the descending chordal anacrusis and downbeat at the start (as in mvt. i/23–24 and 41–42, ii/6 and 12–13, iii/11–12 and 29, and iv/18–20 and 257).

The thematic interrelationships in Schumann's and Brahms's sonatas are unequivocal and far too consistent to be unpremeditated. Thus, in Schumann's Op. 11, the rarely absent motive of the "Allegro vivace," starting as 1–2–3 in the minor scale, reappears clearly right from the start of each of the other movements, although it is anticipated only indirectly in the two-page "Introduction." The recurring motives in Opp. 14 and 22—5- and 4-note, stepwise descents, respectively—are similarly active as cyclic ties, but less conspicuously and more artfully so. In Schumann's late sonatas, for P & Vn, the relationships become more subtle, but the clear return in the finale of Op. 105 (at ms. 168) to that work's beginning leaves no doubt that Schumann had those relationships much in mind.

Brahms's melodic interrelationships are regarded here as being unsurpassed in the Romantic Era in the musical versatility they reveal, their functional (or structural) value, their subtlety, and their all-pervasiveness. In these respects they go beyond the related treatment in the big sonatas of Liszt (ssb X) and d'Indy (ssb XIII), and are quite the equal of (though not the same as) the leitmotiv complexes woven into Wagner's last operas. Brahms did not interrelate whole themes ordinarily, but "basic motives" or germ cells, characteristically reducible to

58. A letter from Martin Chusid argues for ties between the outer mvts. in D. 821 (not mentioned in Chusid/1824). Cf. fn. 5 in AM XL (1968) 186–95 (M. K. Whaples), with more on such ties, in Schubert's quartets.

from three to five notes.[59] Thus, in Op. 1 he bases every idea on—or, rather, generates every idea out of—the EFGAG in the opening, or its transpositions, inversions, and other recognizable alterations. Similarly, Op. 2 is based on ABC♯F♯, Op. 5 on A♭GD♭, Op. 34b on FGA♭F, Op. 38 on BCB, and so on.[60] One example, from Brahms's Op. 100, should help to illustrate some vicissitudes of a Brahms basic motive (Ex. 12). As this example also suggests, Brahms resorted to permutations of the order of the notes along with other variations of the basic motive in his later works, increasing the subtlety of the process without evident loss to its functional value. Furthermore, he tended to place the clearest references to the basic motives not necessarily in the incipits but at climaxes, principal cadences, and other strategic moments in the structure.[61] And finally, he seems to have used two similar basic motives in his final two sonatas, Op. 120/1 & 2, in order to unite them in a kind of "diptych," to use the term that already has been applied similarly to his pair of quartets Op. 51/1 & 2.[62]

Contrary to what might be expected, or to the literature of the Romantic symphony and, of course, the symphonic poem, no front-rank Romantic sonata was identified with a **programme,** even a vague one, by its composer. An over-all programme would be another means of achieving unity, at least external unity, in the Romantic sonata cycle. But the closest approaches to a programme in the masterworks are only such as the sad story of mental deterioration Weber is supposed to have had in mind when he wrote Op. 70 (SSB VIII), or the intimate thoughts of "Klara" that are supposed to be hidden in Schumann's Op. 11 (SSB VIII), or what is only possibly Liszt's own identification of his "Dante Sonata" with the *Divine Comedy* (SSB X).

A few specific programmes do appear in sonatas of minor significance, such as the descriptions in several early-19th-century "battle sonatas";[63] the gypsy dances, with explanatory inscriptions, in Loewe's *Zigeuner Sonata* (SSB VIII); the scenes before and after marriage, complete with quarrel and reunion, in Krug's *Characteristic Tone-Paintings: Three*

59. "Basic motive" is the term coined and discussed helpfully by P. Goetschius in the prefaces to his analytic eds. of Brahms's (and others') symphonies in piano reductions (pub. by Oliver Ditson in the late 1920's).

60. Fisher/BRAHMS examines Brahms's Op. 108 in detail, finding it based on 6 melodic and 2 rhythmic elements, all introduced in the opening 2 mss.

61. Cf. these same processes in his "German Requiem," as described, with exx., in MR XXIV (1963) 190–94 (W. S. Newman).

62. Hill/BRAHMS. Rubinstein's 3d Vn son. starts with quotations from his first and 2d Vn sons. (cf. Cobbett/CHAMBER II 311 [W. W. Cobbett]).

63. Cf. SCE 141, 769, 808–9; Subirá/ALBA 309 (on an ex. by one Calcina); Favre/FRANÇAISE 118 (on an ex. by V. Dourlen, SSB XII); and the finale of I. A. Ladurner, cited in SSB XII.

Ex. 12. The basic motive in Brahms's Sonata in A, Op. 100, as
it appears in (a) i/1–2, (b) i/66–68, (c) ii/1–2, (d) ii/24–25,
(e) iii/3–4, (f) iii/91–92.

Grand Sonatas . . . (ssb VIII); "the four ages" in the life of man in
Alkan's Op. 33 (ssb XII); "a life's sketch" in Kühmstedt's Op. 36;[64]
and Moorish scenes in the *Alhambra-Sonata* by Schulz-Beuthen (ssb X).

In a larger number of sonatas that have programmatic titles and/or
inscriptions, including separate movement titles, at most a mood or
style is conveyed, and sometimes nothing at all, unless it be a reminder
that sonatas with titles get published more readily and sell better than
those without (ssb III). Thus, only a mood is conveyed in Dussek's C.
211, "Élégie harmonique," and his title "Le Retour à Paris" has no
programmatic bearing on C. 221. Brahms, like MacDowell a half-
century later (ssb XIX), began with a bit of verse on occasion (Opp.
1/ii and 5/ii), but again only a mood is conveyed (ssb IX). The same
is true with regard to the titles and bits of verse over the four movements of *The Maid of Orleans* by Bennett (ssb XIV).[65] The majority
of Medtner's sonatas bear exotic titles over both the cycles and the
separate movements, as well as florid inscriptions in the musical text
(ssb XVIII), all of which have little or no direct bearing on the content
composed by this absolutist-at-heart. One can only conclude that the
absence of any significant use of programmes in Romantic sonatas is
one more confirmation of the generally conservative view that the
Romantics took of the sonata.[66]

The fourth and last means of binding the complete sonata cycle is
the creation of an over-all **curve of dynamic tension.** One almost
accepts as axiomatic the idea that in the Romantic Era a complete
sonata must describe an over-all curve of force. It must, in other

64. ssb X; described, with exx., in nzm XLVII (1857) 78–80.

65. In mw IV (1873) 51 and 68 is a long review of a Son. in a, Op. 4, for P
solo (not known here) by one Eugen Grüel, discussing its association with poetry;
cf., also, nzm LXXII/1 (1876) 124.

66. It is interesting to note the resistance to programme sons. & titles in
moscheles I 220–21, II 38, 176–77, 249. Schumann insisted more than once that his
programmes came to him only after he wrote his music (ssb VIII). Eschman/forms
141–42 calls attention to the incongruity of relating an over-all programme to a
type of cycle (the son.) in which the first mvt. is so complete within itself.

words, achieve a climax profile that takes in, and therefore unites, all of its movements. It is true that not all Romantics subscribed (or could subscribe?) to this dynamic view of the sonata. Rheinberger, Raff, Kiel, and Medtner were among those who wrote large-scale sonatas that, in spite of episodes of great power, are essentially contemplative and philosophical in their scope, especially so in the absence of orchestral or vocal color. Bennett and Balakirev were among those who made of their sonatas little more in a structural sense than successions of static tableaux. But for those very reasons, quite apart from any other "deficiencies" that might be listed, these men were neither the true representatives nor the surviving masters of the Romantic sonata.

The truly representative masters and most of the other Romantic composers who understood, did subscribe to the idea of one over-all climax profile—in fact, carried it to the broadest, most monumental applications that are known in all music history. Recognizing the special demands of a time art, these composers learned to shape the climax profile to best advantage, discovering, as in drama and literature, that the rise must be maintained almost, if not right, to the very end so that the peak will be followed by little if any anticlimax.[67] And they showed that the peak itself could be pointed, as just before the end of Wagner's *Tristan und Isolde* or of the strikingly similar ending in d'Indy's Op. 63 (ssb XIII); or it could be rounded, as in the chorale-like statements of one main theme that crown the finale of Bruckner's "Romantic Symphony" (No. 4) and the canonic episodes that similarly crown Franck's Sonata in A (all of these being gentlemanly predecessors of the orgiastic peaks in Scriabin's sonatas).

In the Classic sonata we found no clear tendency to put the climax or greatest weight in any one movement (sce 142–43). In the Romantic sonata that tendency did appear, especially after the mid-century, when conscious efforts to put the climax in the finale begin to be evident. But the question of where the profile peaks is so complex that it still has to be evaluated largely on subjective grounds. For example, is the climactic movement the movement that is the fastest, the loudest, the widest-ranged on the instrument, the harmonically most intense, the melodically most sustained, or the structurally most complex? It is hardly likely that all or even most of these extremes would obtain in the same movement. Some of them could be influenced by the performer, perhaps enough to relocate the peak.

Furthermore, there were characteristic problems with the outer

67. Muns/CLIMAX is a diss. on the aesthetic nature and history of climax in music, with considerable space devoted to 19th-c. manifestations. Cf., also, Newman/CLIMAX.

movements that could affect, and no doubt were furthered by, the problem of the over-all climax profile. The "sonata form" of the first movement posed the chief academic demands, increasingly so as its textbook definitions were elaborated and rigidified (SSB II). The finale posed the chief structural problems, one main reason apparently being a felt need to alter, intensify, and, unfortunately, overcomplicate the traditionally light, gay rondo sufficiently for it to carry more weight. Only the inner movements could be composed more freely (which undoubtedly explains why Weber and Schubert found them easier to write).[68] Finally, when all these factors are considered, one must still raise the heretical question of whether the over-all climax profile is quite the determinant of artistic worth in a sonata that the Romantics made of it. Enchanting melody, lilting or driving rhythm, euphonious scoring, idiomatic writing, and a few strokes of genius here and there —these still seem to have been the determinants at least for public success. If Brahms succeeded partly because of the climax profile, Chopin, whose battles with the larger forms no experienced musician can fail to recognize, succeeded in spite of it.

As our four focal composers are viewed here, Schubert seems to have been striving for an over-all peak in his sonata finales no more consciously than Haydn, Mozart, or Beethoven had. All three finales in his three great posthumous sonatas are still light and fast, albeit long and complex, rondos. The finale in his D. 784, in a, is one that is shorter and more intensive, but still not enough so to top the dramatic first movement or the symphonic middle movement in aesthetic weight. Chopin might be said to achieve a peak in the finale of his Op. 35 through the sheer surprise created by its shortness and under- rather than overstatement, though not in any more usual sense. The finale in his Op. 58 would be viewed here as about on a par in weight with the other movements except for the sharp edge that its distinctive, compelling refrain and rousing coda give. In each of the finales of Schumann's three main piano sonatas, there is enough added weight of sound, melodic intensity, and cumulative speed to achieve a peak. And in the coda of the finale in his Op. 105 (now after the mid century) there is that telling return to the first movement's beginning that is climactic by its very nature.

Only in Brahms's Op. 34b, the transcription of the piano Quintet in f, does any of his "sonata" finales make quite so decisive a peak, thanks to the internal climaxes and stunning "Presto, non troppo" coda, as, say, the finale of his Symphony 1, in c, with its pointed peak on a syncopated, *fortissimo* dim.-7th chord (ms. 285) and its culmi-

68. Cf. SSB VIII; Költzsch/SCHUBERT 9 and fn. 4.

nating coda. But, again, in each of the three piano sonatas (also after the mid-century), and in spite of the increased weight Brahms gives to the slow and scherzo movements, the tempo, drive, and melodic intensity of the finale are sufficient to achieve a clear peak in the over-all profile. Among other of his finale peaks, the fugue in Op. 38 and the interlocking with the previous movement in Op. 78 should be recalled.

At least two composers seem to have been striving for a steady rise in the climax profile throughout their sonata cycles. Hiller's three piano sonatas omit slow movements and generally tend to step up the speed, volume, and other means of excitement from start to finish; and A. G. Ritter does somewhat the same with the increasingly short movements of his organ sonatas (both ssb X).[69] The over-all dynamic plan, increasingly active tonal movement, and even stepped-up time signatures (from 4/4 to 3/4, and so on) become agents of the climactic rises in these sonatas. But no such agents seem to prevail in the majority of sonatas by our four focal composers.[70] As the structural charts in Chapter X should suggest, Liszt's one-movement "Dante Sonata" achieves an over-all climax profile through its tonal curve and the strong return to the tonic, but not necessarily through its dynamic contrasts, which describe, instead, several subclimaxes. His Sonata in b achieves a more compelling profile with its climactic "finale" that recapitulates the opening and its anticlimactic coda of resignation that recalls the thematic elements. His decision to reject a more brief, obvious, brilliant coda he had written earlier for this Sonata (as quoted in ssb X) bears significantly on the climax profile.

The First Fast Movement

There is less of structural consequence to write about in the separate movements of the Romantic than of the Classic sonata. In the first place, as discussed earlier, the Romantics were only expanding, not replacing the Classic structural means. In the second place, they were using fewer designs and, what is more, applying those designs more uniformly, notwithstanding structural experiments by a few of the more adventurous composers. The greater uniformity reflects, of course, the new awareness of form types (or molds), especially "sonata form," as these were now described in detail by the theorists and crystal-

---

69. Cf. nzm XXXV (1851) 258–59 on this means in Ritter's Op. 20 for P solo.
70. Fellinger/dynamik 71–77 finds dynamics used for structural unity within "sonata forms" by Brahms but not over the whole cycle.

lized in their textbooks (SSB II). The inevitable consequence was an increasingly self-conscious, academic approach to "sonata form." As Busoni wrote in 1907, the moment the composers "cross the threshold of the Principal Subject, their attitude becomes stiff and conventional, like that of a man entering some high bureau of officialdom." [71]

No better evidence of at least outer structural uniformity in Romantic sonata designs can be adduced than the fact that every first movement of every adult sonata by our four focal composers adheres more or less closely to what was to become textbook "sonata form." [72] Yet this identification of a mold does not mean that each composer with sufficient imagination could not take sufficient liberties to give a personal stamp to his handling of "sonata form." Changes, additions, and deletions within the design itself, the options of an introduction and a coda, a surprising variety in the tonal courses that could be followed, and unrestricted flexibility in the proportions throughout the design—all these, coupled with the wide choice of melodic, harmonic, rhythmic, and textural styles such as were discussed earlier in this chapter, gave ample latitude, indeed, to the composer and enabled the creation of many a structural unicum in the Romantic sonata.

Starting with the relative **proportions of the three main sections** of "sonata form," and not including any repeats, introductions, or codas, one finds the following percentages in the first movements of our four composers:

Proportions in the First Movements of the Sonatas by Four Masters

	Exposition	*Development*	*Recapitulation*
Schubert	38	25	37
Schumann	33	35	32
Chopin	47	28	25
Brahms	38	30	32

Schumann, with about equal proportions, is the only one to show even a slight preponderance in the development section. Schubert and Chopin both show their lesser interest in this section. The low percentage for Chopin's recapitulations recalls his by-passing of the opening theme in that section of all three adult sonatas (though not in his early Op. 4). The high percentage for Brahms's expositions

---

71. Busoni/SKETCH 8.

72. Among rare experiments with the scheme of "son. form" before the mid century, the chiastic (or m-n-o-n-m) principle may be noted in Op. 49/i by Weber and in several of Pocci's "son. forms" (SSB VIII).

recalls the extended bridges he customarily erects in that section.[73] Slow introductions were frequent—at least the short type Beethoven used in his Op. 78—in the sonatas of some early Romantics, like those of Ries, causing one reviewer to exclaim, "What sonatas don't have them now!" [74] But they are infrequent in the first movements now in question, there being none in Schubert's or Brahms's, one, of but 4 measures, in Chopin's (Op. 35), and 3, totalling from 7 to 17 per cent of the earlier movements, in Schumann's (Opp. 11, 121, and Son. 3 for P & Vn). On the other hand, all of the first movements but 3 early ones by Schubert (D. 459, 568, 575) and one by Schumann (Op. 11) have at least short codas, ranging from 4 to 20 per cent of the entire movements in Schubert's, 10 to 32 in Schumann's, only 3 to 5 in Chopin's, and 9 to 19 in Brahms's.

By comparison with the proportions in the sonata first movements of the Classic masters (SCE 146–47), these proportions are similar but less variable. Little reason remains in the Romantic Era for arguing a binary rather than a ternary concept of "sonata form" (cf. SCE 143–47), although we have seen that the binary concept survived a little longer in the textbooks (SSB II). The proportions in Liszt's double-function Sonata in b, when it is viewed as a single "sonata form," are 43, 26, 21, and 11 per cent (including the coda), thus already revealing the diminishing order that was to become increasingly common as a means of cumulative intensity in the late-Romantic and Modern sonata (as well as symphony).

A question vitally affecting the proportions in Romantic "sonata form" is that of taking the **repeat of the exposition** when it is called for (a question deferred in our mentions of performance practices in SSB V because of its significance here). The repeat of the second "half" (development and recapitulation) is no longer a question, because it had disappeared by 1800 with but few exceptions (e.g., Schubert's D. 537/i and 664/i). And the repeats in the other movements have never been a matter of any particular doubt. But Weber, Schubert, and Chopin called for a repeat of the exposition in all their sonata first movements, Schumann in all of his but Op. 14 and Sonata 3 for P & Vn, and Brahms in nearly half of his, not including Op. 2 or any of the sonatas for P & Vn and Cl & P. Starting with occasional examples at the outset of the era (e.g., Moscheles' Op. 49 and Loewe's Op. 41),

73. By way of cumulative statistics for first mvts. in P sons. by Haydn, Mozart, Beethoven, Brahms, and Schubert, Abbott/FORM 316–29 gives as the first 6 dispositions of the 3 sections, in descending order of frequency and descending ratios: E(xposition) D(evelopment) R(ecapitulation), ERD, DER, DRE, RED, RDE (none being equal ratios).

74. AMZ XIII (1811) 212.

the repeat was discarded more and more until, at the end of the era, it was all but gone.

H. J. Moser has concluded that the repeat (when called for) is needed on aesthetic grounds—that it contributes to a satisfying bar form, AAB (B being the development and recapitulation as one unit); and that it provides a needed re-view of the exposition material.[75] It has a psychologically different effect from the first statement, he adds, because it returns to ideas now familiar. Yet it does not have the same effect as the recapitulation because it is still leaving, not coming back home. There are also occasional facts that throw light on this repeat question. For example, only after Beethoven had several chances to hear his "*Eroica* Symphony" did he decide a repeat was needed, which he then added.[76] A review of Weber's Op. 24 expressed concern about how the first ending of the exposition might lead back to the start for the repeat.[77] The solicitation of sonatas in 1826 by the Swiss publisher Nägeli included the request that there be no repeats.[78] Instead of using repeat signs Albéniz actually wrote out the exposition a second time in his Sonata 4/i (ssb XVI), though not with the elaborations to be found some 125 years earlier in Emanuel Bach's set "mit veränderten Reprisen" (sce 424–26).   7:

All of which information merely helps to confirm that there was considerable awareness of the repeat question at the time. Weber, Schubert, and Chopin may still have been accepting the tradition of the exposition repeat without much question. Yet, all three did make careful distinctions between their first and second endings. And certainly the characteristically long recitals after the mid-century allowed ample time for sonatas to be played with all repeats (ssb III). In short, the available evidence generally suggests that the Romantics knew and meant what they were doing both when they did put the repeat sign in and when they did not.

In the Romantic "sonata form" the **tonal plan** continued to function as a main means of both cohesion and tension. However, to recall a statement made earlier about tonality in the over-all cycle, as the harmonic progressions and passing modulations grew more colorful and remote, especially near the era's end, the broader shifts in the tonality became increasingly dim and ineffectual as structural landmarks. In other words, the tonal plan retained its structural force most clearly on the conservative side of the dichotomy in style and form that

75. Moser/MUSIKÄSTHETIK 99–104.
76. Cf. NOTES XXV (1968) 41 (C. W. Hughes).
77. AMZ XV (1813) 597 (G. M. Weber).
78. Cf. MOSCHELES I 120; ssb IV.

was discussed earlier, including in this respect both Schumann and Chopin as well as Schubert and Brahms among our four focal composers. The nature of the tonal plan as organized by these four composers may be illustrated best by comparing their choice of keys at six tonally strategic landmarks in "sonata form": (1) the second theme of the exposition; (2) the end of the exposition and very start of the development; (3) the areas of the development section, typically up to three, on which the tonality settles long enough to establish a sense of key; (4) the start of the recapitulation; (5) the second theme of the recapitulation; and (6) the coda, in which one harmony other than the tonic is usually emphasized. In the following paragraph the keys in thirty-one of the sonatas by our four composers are compared, not by letter name but by function, as part of a "grand cadence" [79] in the home key. Thus, ♭II means the major key on the lowered-2d step of the home key, vi(en) means the minor key on the submediant step spelled enharmonically, and so on.

True to expectations, the key when the exposition's second theme starts is V in most major sonatas, the exceptions being vi, IV, and vii in one instance each (Brahms's Op. 1, Schubert's D. 575, and his D. 840). It is III in most minor sonatas, the exceptions being v in four instances (Schumann's Op. 14 and Brahms's Opp. 2, 38, and 120/1) and V, VI, and vi(en) in one instance each (Schubert's D. 784 and 537, and Brahms's Op. 34b). The key by which the exposition ends is the same as that of the second theme in most instances, but when it is not it is V and I in two instances each, vi and iii in one instance each. The development starts with a new key in almost two-thirds of the sonatas, the key choices being divided about equally between 14 functions, including abrupt, *sforzando* shifts from V to ♭VI and v to VI (Schubert's D. 850 and Brahms's Op. 2) and starts even on ♭vii and ♯i (Schumann's Op. 22 and Brahms's Op. 99). Schubert and Brahms are exceptional at this point in starting on the tonic in either mode in eight sonatas (Schubert's D. 575, 845, and 894, and Brahms's Opp. 1, 78, 108, and 120/1 & 2). In this way they would seem to be interrupting the arch described by the "grand cadence," and one does sense that interruption (or excess of tonic harmony) in the hearing.

The one or more keys emphasized in the development sections are too variable to generalize except for the prevalence of the third-relationship created by either mediant in either mode, often lowered. One may also note the absence of any tonal plateaus in the development of Chopin's Op. 35/i, which modulates throughout, and the pedal on the dominant that lasts right through the development of

79. Cf. d'Indy/cours II/1 45 and 286.

Brahms's Op. 108/i. On the other hand, the keys in which the recapitulations begin are almost as uniform as those at the start and end of the movement, being the tonic in the same mode except for the start on IV in three of the earlier, major sonatas by Schubert (D. 459, 537, and 575) and on ♯i (f♯) in Brahms's Op. 120/i in f. The keys used for the start of the second theme in the recapitulation occur about as uniformly in the tonic, two of the exceptions being ♯i again (Schubert's D. 960 and Brahms's Op. 34b). In the codas a good half of the sonatas place some emphasis on the subdominant in either mode, thus continuing, as in the Classic sonata (SCE 158), to counterbalance the usual movement to the dominant or mediant in either mode in the exposition and development.

Even within these relatively straightforward tonal plans in the Romantic masterworks of the sonata, the variety of procedures was far more than enough to give individual distinction in tonality alone to each composer and, in fact, each "sonata form." Only samples of this variety can be cited here. Although Schubert was the earliest of our four composers and although all of them tended toward fewer, broader, more purposeful shifts in their later tonal plans, Schubert was the freest, supplest, and most adventurous in his tonal treatment. Thus, not only could he write such an unorthodox tonal plan as that of D. 575/i in B (I-IV[2d theme]-V:‖i-remote modulations-I-IV [recapitulation]-♭VII[2d theme]-I‖). But just after the opening theme is stated in this movement he could make a startling interruption, *fortissimo,* on ♭II, followed by a 12-measure dance-like episode or aside in ♭VI and IV, prior to the second theme's entry in IV (all of which is paralleled in the keys of the recapitulation). In the wonderfully sure and effective tonal plan of D. 960/i in B♭, with its early excursion to ♭VI and second theme in ♭vi(en), the recapitulation starting in I is anticipated by its own shadow, as it were, triple *piano,* 22 measures earlier (ms. 194), and already in I. Schumann did much less modulating, but, like Chopin and Brahms, also made excursions to either mediant, as in the episode to vi(en), in place of a bridge, in Op. 11/i/107–126. Brahms is the subtlest of the four in the establishment of his key centers. Thus, already in his Op. 1, the second theme, in vi, is approached through its secondary dominant, not its dominant. His uses of borrowed tones and the resultant vacillations between modes on the same tonic frequently give a mercurial quality to the tonality (Ex. 13). The turn to major in the recapitulation of his Op. 5/i is a practice that was adopted also in Weber's Op. 49 and Liszt's Sonata in b, among other works, and increasingly in later Romantic sonatas.

Ex. 13. From the opening of Johannes Brahms's Sonata in F, Op. 99 (after Brahms/WERKE-m X 124).

Along with tonal organization, the other main cohesive force in Romantic (as in Classic) "sonata form" was **thematic organization**.[80] Any other forces that may also have been organized to implement the structure, such as the contrasting of soft and loud dynamic markings,[81] or high and low ranges, or thick and thin textures, can only be regarded as subordinate to the thematic and tonal organization. Thematic organization raises two successive, opposed problems in Romantic "sonata form." Up to the mid century there was a problem of under assimilation, and after then an increasing problem of over assimilation.

As for the problem of under assimilation, it was similar to the problem remarked above as being on the increase in later Romantic tonality—that of the trees cutting off the view of the forest. Thus, the early-Romantic thematic organization often involved closed themes, like Dussek's and Weber's complete double-periods (SSB XVII and VIII), or frank tunes, like that in Reissiger's Op. 93/i (SSB VIII), or

80. Mitschka/BRAHMS 318–30 summarizes thematic types and organization in Brahms's "son. forms," with conclusions that also bear on Romantic styles and forms in general.

81. Fellinger/DYNAMIK 71–77 charts dynamics profiles in Brahms's "son. forms." Unusual is Hiller's Op. 78/i, which describes one grand arch from *pianissimo* to *fortissimo* and back (SSB X).

melodious passagework, like that in Field's Op. 1/3/i (ssb XIV), any or all of which could be too self-sufficient, too alluring, or too intriguing in itself to be assimilable in the continuous, dynamic flow of "sonata form." [82]

In the face of such self-sufficient thematic elements how did the dualistic principle fare, the principle that figured so basically in the Classic sonata idea (sce 152–54)? The answer is that those elements favored (without insuring) the contrasts implicit in dualism itself but not the larger unity in which it had to be fostered. There was no lack of sharp contrasts in thematic style, mood, and intensity when the composers chose to make them. There are such contrasts within themes, as in the opening of Woržischek's Op. 20 (ssb VII) or Hummel's Op. 81, and between themes, as in Schubert's D. 575/i (at mss. 1 and 30) or Liszt's sonata in b, where the contrasts (as at mss. 25, 105, and 153) are inherent in the motivic complex of the initial idea (ssb X). As it happens, in the majority of their sonatas, the Romantics seem not to have been seeking such diametric, all-inclusive contrasts—no more so than the Classics had. In the Romantic "sonata form"—for example, Schubert's D. 568/i in E♭—when the contrasts do become so all-inclusive (as between mss. 1–8 and 41–48), the problem of under assimilation or of achieving over-all unity emerges in two ways. There is not only the difficulty of relating such unrelated ideas but there are those characteristic tonal digressions for the sake of color (as in mss. 60–67, to D♭) that dissipate the single dynamic trajectory into which all the musical forces ultimately must be drawn.

But, as already implied, the majority of Romantic sonatas bring up, rather, the opposite problem, the one that was to increase later in the era—over assimilation. In the Romantic as in the Classic masterworks, the dualism was achieved usually by contrasts in only one or two aspects of the theme. The second theme was more an expressive variation rather than an antipode of the first, with the sense of contrast heightened more or less by tonal polarity. Such had been true in the first movement of Mozart's K. 576, or Haydn's last Sonata in E♭, or Beethoven's Op. 57. And it was true in Schubert's D. 960 in B♭/i (starting at mss. 1 and 49), where the two ideas have much the same mood, intensity, and steady quarter-note pace but contrast in tonal mode and pitch motion (stepwise vs. chordal). Generally this degree of contrast has been just sufficient to achieve variety without destroying unity, dualism within oneness. It should be noted

82. In Westphal/romantische this argument is used to explain a loss of tension in Romantic "son. form."

that dualism rather than pluralism is ordinarily the right term. The closing idea, which not seldom had been the most distinctive idea in Baroque and Classic design (SCE 154), largely ceased to be a third new and significant idea by the start of the Romantic Era. Brahms offers some of the exceptions, as in Op. 78/i/70–77. But more often this element proves to be only a different facet of either preceding idea, as in his Op. 38/i/83–90 (deriving from the opening theme).

The problem of over assimilation, or excessive oneness, began to appear early in the era, as a concomitant of the overly persistent working of a motive. When a single motive tends to permeate all of the "sonata form's" themes, as does the strong-weak half-note pattern in Schubert's D. 784/i or the two 16th-notes and an 8th-note in Schumann's Op. 11/i, then we have in miniature a kind of cyclical interrelationship (supra). This tendency to efface the dualism through motivic oneness is not the loss of dualism that more often has been charged to Romantic "sonata form," as it still is by Hindemith:[83]

. . . despite the beauty and often even fascination of their thematic invention, [the post-Classics—i.e., early Romantics] fail to reach the heights attained by the Classic masters. They kill one beautiful theme with another, so that sharp thematic contrasts and consequent melodic tension are lacking —a lack which is brought all the more painfully to the attention of the listener by the faulty proportion between a content which is lacking in tension and a form which is of exaggerated duration.

But that charge has been overemphasized, in the sense that it subjects Romantic art to Classic standards. Moreover, it chiefly fits composers too weak to create the variety of germinal and lyrical themes that Schubert and Brahms wrote—that is, composers like Steibelt and Kalkbrenner (SSB XII), who had only one thing (if anything) to say and therefore produced nothing but "Nebenthemen."

In spite of penetrating almost every measure with his basic motive (supra), Brahms was too knowing and too terse to fall victim to over assimilation of his thematic materials. However closely his first and second themes may interrelate (as already in Op. 1/i/1–4 and 39–42), they never fail to contrast sufficiently on tonal and expressive grounds to maintain their separate identities. Schumann's Op. 105/i proves to be virtually monothematic, but it maintains a sense of dualistic tension through variety of range, texture, and rhythm. The problem becomes a more serious one in the "sonata forms" of the late-Romantics, when *the motive* tends to dominate all else and when

83. Hindemith/CRAFT 180–81. Cf., also, Carner/SCHUMANN and Parrott/SCHUMANN on the "problem" of Schumann's "son. forms."

the motivic writing becomes discursive, anyway. Once more, outstanding craftsmen like Rheinberger and Medtner come to mind, as well as Rachmaninoff, whose entire Op. 36 leaves the impression of a remarkable fantasy that never really quits its one overworked idea. In his last sonatas Fauré also reduced the dualism of "sonata forms" to different aspects of oneness. The extreme consequence of continuous motivic writing is the virtual elimination of full-fledged themes as tonal and melodic landmarks, leaving nothing but the rise and fall of portentous, modulatory passagework rich in sonority and interwoven motives. Almost that extreme is reached in the late-Romantic sonatas by Dale, Ashton, and Paderewski, at least the last two of which are melodically impoverished, for all their other worths.

One would suppose that so much motivic writing would show up especially in the working out of ideas that is identified with Classic development sections. That kind of working out, the kind one thinks of in the finale of Mozart's "Jupiter Symphony" or the first movement of Beethoven's *"Eroica* Symphony," does survive in the "sonata forms" of Brahms and his numerous late-Romantic imitators and followers— for example, in Brahms's Op. 34b/i/92–160. But the motivic writing in most other late-Romantic sonatas is less often motivic play in the sense of interwoven contrapuntal exchanges than motives reiterated, sequenced, or more freely unfolded in single continuous lines. This process brings Wagner to mind more than either Bach or the Classic masters of development (cf. the Medtner ex. in ssB XVIII). Furthermore, it goes on continuously, as much in the bridges and transitions as in the development section. In fact, in that respect it tends to lessen the significance of the development section. Typically, the latter—again, excepting Brahms's "sonata forms"—is a kaleidoscopic process of transposing the ideas, reharmonizing and recombining them, and unfolding them into further ideas (as in Schubert's D. 894/i and D. 960/i). Occasionally the development is considerably extended (as in Schumann's Op. 11/i), or concentrated on one idea (such as a closing figure, in Schubert's D. 959/i), or enlivened with new material (such as that starting at mss. 126 and 140 in Schubert's 568/i), or spun out in one long line (as in Schubert's D. 784/i), or made rhythmically cumulative (as in Schumann's Op. 14/i).

The Slowest Movement

Only a few comments are needed regarding the other movements of the Romantic sonata, chiefly on their most characteristic designs. These movements often reveal at least as much of interest as the

first movements, of course, but their other aspects have been discussed earlier under style phases and related questions of form. Of
the slowest movements in the sonatas by our four focal composers,
not a single one, surprisingly enough—not even Chopin's "March
funèbre"—calls for a tempo that would be rated "very slow" here,
or slow enough for the beat to be subdivided. A full 65 per cent
are in moderate tempos and the rest in slow tempos. Schumann and
Schubert preferred the moderate tempos in most of their sonatas,
Chopin the slow tempos. Brahms's preference was about half and half.
The movements in question do not include the kind in which Brahms
combined moderate and scherzo sections in one design (Op. 100/ii).
This design was anticipated in Schumann's Op. 11, Gade's Op. 21,
and Reinecke's Op. 167, and followed by Sjögren's Op. 35, Dohnányi's
Op. 21, and numerous others.

Two designs predominate in the slowest movements of our four
composers, A-B-A (as in Schubert's D. 959 and D. 960) and, especially,
A-B-A-B-A (as in his D. 958). Some of the longer examples of these
designs are elaborately hierarchic in their sections within sections—
for instance, Schubert's D. 850/ii, with each main section but the
last in its design, A-B-A'-B'-A/coda, subdividing into its own a-b-a
design. Schubert's D. 664/ii and D. 784/ii are monothematic A-B-A
designs in which the B section is a free variation or development
of the A section. Other sectional designs in these sonatas include A-
B-A'-B', as in Brahms's Op. 108/ii, and A-B-A-C-A, as in Schubert's D.
958. The exceptionally complex design A||:B:|||:C:||:B'-C':||:A':|||:C''-
B''-A':||:C''':||:B''':|||:C'''':||:A''-C'''':||:A'''-B'''':||coda|| in Schubert's D.
845/ii, presents highly recondite variations in an unpredictable order.
Freer variations provide the structural principle in Brahms's Opp.
1/ii and 2/ii, and more formal, regular variations in Schumann's
Op. 14/iii (on a theme by Clara Wieck).

If there is any difference in the tonal organization between the
first fast movements and these slower movements, it would be in the still
greater use of third relationships, as throughout Schubert's tonally
extraordinary "Con moto" described earlier (D. 850/ii). With regard
to thematic material, the lyrical, complete period or double-period
naturally predominates, with the demarcation of the phrases being
even more pronounced than in the first movements but not necessarily
more regular (as in Chopin's Op. 65/ii, with the first 2 periods having
2+2 and 3+5 measures).

Although the Beethovian type of lofty, serene adagio movement,
sustained by rapid harmonic rhythm, was not indigenous to the
Romantic solo or duo sonata, the latter was by no means lacking

in relatively slow movements of much expressive warmth and sincerity, with undeniable melodic depth, harmonic richness, and textural interest. Several such movements might be cited that would be ranked here among the finest of their sort in the Romantic sonata, including Schubert's "Andante sostenuto" in c♯, D. 960/ii, with its exceptionally broad melodic arch penetrating through the lilting accompaniment in slow harmonic rhythm; Schumann's "Andantino" in C, Op. 22/ii, with its tender, veiled thoughts introduced at melodic and harmonic tangents until they reach a convulsive climax; Chopin's "Largo" in B, Op. 58/iii, with its deliberately paced nocturne style in the outer sections, enclosing the still quieter, dreamlike middle section; Brahms's "Andante" in A♭/D♭, Op. 5/ii, with one of the most sustained climaxes in any of his instrumental slow movements; his "Andante, un poco Adagio" in A♭, Op. 34b/ii, with a melodic arch that is like Schubert's in its projection and accompaniment but even more drawn out, and with searching leaps in the B section, up and down, from 8ves to dim.-10ths, that must have strained the contemporary limits of melodic perception; Brahms's "Adagio" in E♭, Op. 78/ii, with its tearful chromatic line in the B section and with the return of its main theme taken by the violin in 3ds and 6ths against a new, wider accompaniment by the piano; Fauré's "Andante" in d, Op. 13/ii, with its cumulative outpourings of luscious melody and countermelody (Ex. 14); and Strauss's "Improvisation— Andante cantabile" in A♭, Op. 18/ii, with its poetically delicate, wide-ranged filigree floating through the middle section.

The Quicker of the Inner Movements

The scherzo outnumbers by a wide margin any other inner sonata movement on the quick side, throughout the Romantic Era. Furthermore, its style prevails in most such movements not actually entitled "Scherzo." In two-thirds of all the sonatas by our four composers that include quick inner movements, those movements do carry this title. Only about one-fifth of the same movements are entitled "Menuetto" (or some variant). Schubert's several minuets generally preserve the easy-going, neatly measured, Classic dance spirit in their well-defined phrases (as in D. 568/iii or D. 894/iii), although those in D. 840/iii and D. 958/iii are nearer to the fast tempo and steadier, more vigorous quarter-note drive of the scherzo that had largely replaced the minuet by then (as in Loewe's Op. 47/iii, ssʙ VIII). Schumann did not use the minuet in his sonatas, nor did Chopin in his mature sonatas. Brahms's one use in his sonatas, the "Allegretto quasi

Ex. 14. From the second movement of Fauré's Sonata in A, Op. 13 (after Wier/VIOLIN-m 263).

menuetto" in his Op. 38, serves as the middle, "slowest" movement, too, and is closer to the traditional style.

But there had been some confusion between these terms early in the century and even some equating of the two titles, as in the "Menuetto o scherzo" of Moscheles' Op. 41 or the "Minuet scherzo" in A. Schmitt's Op. 26, both of which are closer to the scherzo style. Decidedly scherzando in style are the "Minuetto" marked "allegro" in Weber's Op. 24 (SSB VIII), the "Menuetto capriciosso" marked "presto assai" in his Op. 39, and the "Menuetto" marked "presto vivace ed energico" in his Op. 70; also, the "Minuetto" marked only "allegretto" in Chopin's early Op. 4.

The sectional design of both the minuet and the scherzo in the Romantic sonata is most often the expected A-B-A or A-trio-*da capo*, each section being a binary design in itself with each "half" enclosed in repeat signs (cf. sce 162). But Schumann's Op. 22/iii and Brahms's Op. 5/iii are among frequent examples of the rondo principle in the scherzo, these having the plans A-B-A-C-A and A-B-A-C-A-B-A, respectively. The scherzo, which could still relate to the idea of a joke in Beethoven's sonatas (as in Op. 24), became exaggerated into something increasingly and variously sinister, driving, virtuosic, impassioned in a suppressed way, grotesque, or elfish during the Romantic Era (as in Chopin's Op. 35, Schumann's Op. 14, Czerny's Op. 268 [ssb VII], Brahms's Op. 99, d'Indy's Op. 63, and Fauré's Op. 13, respectively).

The scherzo in the Romantic, as in the Classic, sonata is likely to be based on a motive rather than a full-fledged theme. Motivic writing engenders some of the chief uses of imitation, most noticeably in the sonatas of some of the less polyphonically minded composers like Weber (e.g., Op. 24/iii, ssb VIII) or Schubert (e.g., D. 575/iii), and even Chopin (in the middle section of Op. 58/ii). The fugal, scherzando section, marked only "Allegro energico," in Liszt's Sonata in b, starts more polyphonically, of course, than the average. In spite of the motivic writing, phrase-and-period syntax that is both clear and regular usually obtains in the Romantic scherzo, chiefly because the motive's reiterations usually group into clear and regular phrases (as in the extreme ex. from Schubert's D. 850/iii quoted earlier).

But not all the syntax in the scherzo is of this sort. Whereas Schubert's D. 959/iii starts with a completely regular double-period of 4+4 & 4+4 measures, the A section of his D. 958/iii is quite the opposite. In fact, it seems to be deliberately problematic. In any case, it must be parsed somewhat subjectively or arbitrarily into three- , four- , five- , and six-measure phrases (if it should be parsed at all), for it presents fascinating conflicts between such usual phrase determinants as metric, weak-beat, and quantitative accents, harmonic suspense and resolution, rhythmic repetition and contrast, melodic repetition and contrast, and steady rhythmic flow interrupted by whole-measure rests! Among many other interesting though less problematic examples of Schubert's extraordinary rhythmic freshness, one might cite D. 960/iii for its use first of seven phrases of 4 measures each, then four of 6, four of 5 (if the last two are really so intended), three of 4, and a final phrase of 6 measures.

The syntax remains regular in Schumann's "Scherzo" in D♭, Op. 14/ii, but the over-all A-B-A design is made complex and hard to follow on first hearing by the many repetitions and variants of the many ideas, and by the many tonal indirections and changes, including the choice of ♯I (D) for the middle section. Besides the combined "slowest"-and-scherzo movements noted earlier, the most frequent alternative to the minuet or scherzo was the sort of tender, wistful movement to be found in Brahms's Op. 108—"Un poco presto e con sentimento," in 2/4 meter. Although not slow and not scherzando, this movement serves a little in each capacity in its central position as a foil for both, more intensive, outer movements.

The Finale

The large majority of finales in the Romantic sonata, fast or very fast, employ the rondo principle, more or less freely. Relatively few of them actually are called "Rondo," and then chiefly in the early-Romantic sonata (as in Schubert's D. 845 and Weber's Op. 24). The other finales are likely to be in "sonata form" (as in Schubert's D. 459 or D. 664), in fugal form (as in Brahms's Op. 38), or in variation form (as in several of Reger's sons. [ssb XI] but none by our 4 focal composers). In connection with the climax profile of the sonata cycle as a whole, the observation was made that the "finale posed the chief structural problem, one main reason apparently being a felt need to alter, intensify, and, unfortunately, overcomplicate the traditionally light, gay rondo sufficiently for it to carry more weight" (supra). The later discussions, in Part Two, include numerous references to this problem of the finale, with regard both to each of our four focal composers and to others as well—for example, the difficulties even Clara Wieck found with Schumann's finales (ssb VIII), or the reviewer (of Op. 17 by A. Krause) who called the finale "that Achilles' heel of modern composers of sonata form" (ssb X), or Wagner's resolve late in life to write one-movement, but not multimovement, symphonies because of the problems the finale still posed.[84]

To get some further idea of the rondo-finale problem, it is necessary to take brief note of specific solutions in representative finales by each of our four composers. In Schubert's D. 537/iii the curiously additive design is A-B-C-D-E-E||A-B-C-D-E-E||A/coda, with the tonal outline being i/I-IV-V up to the first double-bar and v/V-♭VII-I between double-bars. In his later sonatas the designs become simpler but increasingly long, with more substantial subsections, and no letup in the variety of sectional dispositions. In D. 784/iii the design is A(i)→B(VI)-A(i)→ B(III)-C(development)-A(i)-B(I)-A/coda(i). The tonal plans continue to stay close to home, requiring no further mention. In D. 845/iv, the design is A-B-A'-C-A-D-A"-B/coda; in D. 850/iv it is A-B-A'-C-A"/coda; in D. 894/iv it is A-B-A-C-A-B/coda. The outer design of

84. Newman/ARTIST 240–41.

the 717-measure finale in D. 958/iv, A-B-A'-B'-A", is so greatly stretched out, with the first, complex B section alone lasting over 300 measures, that, in spite of Schubert's remarkable genius for extension, no performer can quite hope to hold it together, even playing faster than the "allegro" that is indicated. Still further variants of the rondo principle occur in the designs of D. 959/iv, A-B-A-C-A-B-A/coda (one of Beethoven's favorite dispositions), and 960/iv, A-B-C-A-A-B-C-A/coda.

The outer designs and uncomplicated tonal organization of Schumann's earlier rondo-finales belie the tendency of these movements to sprawl and their themes and sections to run together somewhat inconclusively. The design of Op. 11/iv is A-B-A-B'-A/coda, with the most remote key being VI(en). That of Op. 14/iv falls into more sections (or 2 over-all parts) A-B-C-D-B → A-B-C-D-B/coda. If those designs (unlike Schubert's) seem to have been arrived at empirically, the design of Op. 22/iv—A-B-C-A-B-C-A/coda—seems premeditated in its organizational details and, perhaps as a consequence, somewhat formalistic in its total effect.

The extremely short, *perpetuum mobile* finale in Chopin's Op. 35 is not a rondo, if a rondo's opening idea must appear at least three times, but a balanced A-B-A design based entirely on four-measure phrases (each subdivided into 2+2 mss.) except for measures 17–19, 36–38, and 72–76 (including the final ms.). Chopin's Op. 58/iv is transparently blocked off in its nonstandard rondo design, A-A'-B-C-A-A'-B-C-A-A', but that very transparency helps to reveal the weakness in the design. One can hardly escape the monotony in performance of too many returns to the refrain in the same key (all but once) and too few alterations in its presentation.

Among our four composers, Brahms seems to have been most aware of the finale problem, right from the start (cf. ssb IX).[85] Yet, in the experience of this study, he did not quite solve it, insofar as his sonatas are concerned, until he reached Op. 78 and a more sensitive, more concise, and less pretentious sort of finale. On the other hand, each of the earlier finales discloses decided musical strengths in its separate sections and each, when read in its order of composition, discloses new gains on the problems of structural control. What is the nature of the structural deficiencies? They are not obvious. On the surface the forms look tight and clear. They do not seem to have the diffusion or imbalances that have been ventured above as handicaps in the finales of the other three composers. One can sense deficiencies in Brahms's

85. Czesla/BRAHMS is a new diss. (1968) of the finales in Brahms's "chamber" music, including the 3 P sons. (pp. 7–76, with exx.) and Op. 38 (pp. 149–69, with exx.).

earlier finales, both in performance and listening, as problems of under and over assimilation, again. But to pin them down to specific shortcomings, to second-guess a composer who was a finished craftsman right from Op. 1, would take the knowledge and appraisals of another Brahms. One can appreciate the extensive revisions Brahms himself made late in life in the finale (and other movements) of his Trio in B, Op. 8, and still not know what could or should have been done in Opp. 1, 2, and 5 if Brahms had seen fit to return to the problems of their finales, too.

In Op. 1/iv the outer plan of the sections suggests straggling and over repetition of the refrain—A-A-B-A-C-A-D-A-B-A/coda—especially in consideration of the omnipresent basic motive (*supra*). Yet the actual problem would be viewed here rather as under assimilation created by matter-of-fact breaks at the sectional joints, by square-cut rhythms still far from the later Brahmsian rhythmic subtleties, and by uncompromisingly complete presentations of every section, with as yet none of the streamlining and excisions so essential to efficient, compelling form. The same problems seem to exist, although within different and increasingly resourceful plans, in both Opp. 2/iv and 5/v. Op. 2/iv is an elastic "sonata form" enclosed by a slow prelude and postlude. Op. 5/v is a rondo, with fewer sections and more extensions than in Op. 1—A-B→A-C→A→coda.

To the extent that a structural problem does still exist in the magnificent, dramatic finale of Brahms's Op. 34b, it may lie in a certain rhythmic stiffness inherent in the squareness and repetitions of units within the themes themselves and in a type of sectional plan that is more additive than integrated—In/A → B-C → A-B'-C'-A'/coda. In Op. 38/iii the fugal movement falls into a large monothematic A-B-A design, with B being defined by the inversion of the subject and the emphasis on the mediant key. This time, if a finale problem does exist it probably lies not in the structure per se but in a subject that engenders so many single bowings, so much ungrateful "sawing" for the cello (as for all the strings in Beethoven's "Grosse Fuge" for quartet). It should be noted that along with the increasingly laconic style and Spartan excisions in his later sonatas, Brahms gave preference to the simplest rondo designs—for example, A → B → A-C-A/coda in Op. 78/iii and A-B→A-C-A(IV)-A(I)/coda in Op. 100/iii.

Part Two

The Romantic Composers and Their Sonatas

Chapter VII

Schubert and Other Viennese in
Beethoven's Sphere

Vienna as an Early 19th-Century Music Center

The early 19th-century artist in an Austro-German center had to work in a heavy environment of rapid political change. With the harsh treaties codified by the Congress of Vienna in 1814–15 and the Holy Alliance that grew out of them, Europe saw the defeat of Napoleon and the end of more than twenty years of struggle by Austria in coalitions with Prussia, Russia, and other powers against France. From then, starting under the first Austrian emperor, Francis I, and Count Metternich, to beyond the middle of the century, Austria became increasingly autocratic, aggressive, and reactionary, successfully resisting the waves of revolution and liberalism that swept France and other countries in 1830 and again in 1848. In such a continuing atmosphere of international intrigue, political oppression, even terror, it is understandable that the Viennese who were so inclined could and did find one main escape or retreat through music, music that might be at once the most noncommittal and the safest of the arts.

Yet in spite of this international political environment, in spite of the immediate past musical glories of Haydn and Mozart, in spite of the succeeding musical giants that were Beethoven and Schubert, and in spite of the continued guidance of veteran composers and pedagogues like Antonio Salieri (1750–1825) or Simon Sechter (1788–1867) and the continuing patronage of nobles like Archduke Rudolph (1788–1831; cf. sce 524), Vienna tended to fall back to relative provincialism as a music center in the first half of the 19th century.[1] This provincial-

1. Important background information on Vienna and her musical life is found in Weber/WEBER II 395–428; Thayer & Forbes/BEETHOVEN I 150–59 (early 1790's); Schindler & MacArdle/BEETHOVEN 51 and 64–66 (ca. 1800), 135 (early 1800's), 216–17 (1810's), 272 (1820's); Deutsch/SCHUBERT-D xxi–xxix (with maps; ca. 1790–1830); and, above all, except for opera, Hanslick/WIEN I 139–285 (1800–1830) and 289–363 (1830–48). Some of the poetic and musical atmosphere is conveyed in Holmes/RAMBLE 113–70 (1828) and Schumann/SCHRIFTEN I 459–63 (1839).

ism is apparent in limitations of musical taste, requirements, concert life, publishing activities, and journalism. One factor was certainly the growing suspicion of foreigners that the political reactionism fostered. Among two main nationalities under the Austrian heel, the immigrants from Italy suffered from such suspicion notwithstanding Rossini's successes during the second and third decades, but the numerous Czechs who continued to move to Vienna (cf. SCE 545–46), like Woržischek, seem to have felt it less. There were ingrown factors, too. The escape from oppression by way of music and the other arts proved to be more of a pleasurable opiate than a sublimation. If at best Viennese society could still nurture rare masterpieces like Schubert's "Great Symphony in C," if at worst it became positively debauched and dissolute, ordinarily and characteristically it took to the new Biedermeier art,[2] not to mention the *Gemütlichkeit,* of its coffee houses and taverns.

In music, such art was more conducive to the creating of early Viennese waltzes than sonatas. Sonatas did continue to appear in fair number. But the majority of them found a compromise with Biedermeier art, sometimes by introducing those waltzes or other current dances, or by adding variations on familiar tunes, or by exploiting the new preoccupation with virtuosity. Undoubtedly, if Vienna had not continued to be so provincial in her public concert life, she would have given more and earlier encouragement to the serious sort of solo or duo recital on which serious sonatas thrive. To be sure, opera in the theater did not supply the only public opportunities to pay to hear music. Public concerts did occur that included extended, serious instrumental works. But the fact remains that what were easily the most important sonatas by the composers discussed in this chapter, those of Schubert, seem never to have reached public performance. Nor can Schubert's relative obscurity be given as the sole reason. On the one hand, we saw Beethoven's sonatas similarly fail to reach public performance (SCE 528–29); and on the other, we shall see that several of Schubert's sonatas did win favor at the private evening "Schubertiads" that meant so much to him, that four of them got published before his early death (1828, only eighteen months after Beethoven's), and that two of these promptly won enthusiastic reviews as far away as Leipzig.

The underlying theme of the present chapter might be stated as the diametrically opposed influences of Beethoven and Biedermeier art on the early 19th-century sonata in Vienna. With regard to Beethoven, it applies less to his dominating influence on the sonata throughout

2. Cf. BRITANNICA III 600.

the 19th century than to his immediate sphere of personal impressions on other Viennese composers. This theme accounts for more attention here than might otherwise be warranted to three highly competent but hardly great composers—Ries, Czerny, and Moscheles. For in the practical senses of propagating and popularizing his sonatas, these three were the most direct transmitters, more so than several other men, like Wölfl (SCE 562–64), Hummel (SSB VIII), and Cramer (SSB XII), who also had at least some direct contact with Vienna and Beethoven. Of course, Schubert in his relative obscurity lived right in the shadow of Beethoven with perhaps never a chance actually to talk with him and scarcely a mention by the other followers. Yet Schubert became no mere transmitter but the most immediate and one of the few real artistic successors to Beethoven. In fact, the chief "problem" of Schubert's sonatas will be seen as that of one's never quite being able to view them independently of Beethoven's, however strong and original they are in their own right.

Peripheral but pertinent to this chapter is the publisher A. Diabelli's clever patriotic venture of 1820–24 that ultimately opposed Beethoven's lofty set of 33 "Diabelli Variations" to the set of 50 single variations by as many different composers, mostly minor Viennese, but including Hummel, Schubert, and Liszt.[3] Here in one project were the conflicting forces of genius and Biedermeier, with a waltz (the theme) at the center. Because the 50 composers provide such a full representation of the Vienna scene, including many met here earlier (SCE) or to be met soon, their names should be worth bringing together at this point:[4]

I. Assmayer, C. M. Bocklet, L. E. Czapek, *C. Czernÿ, J. Czernÿ, M. G. v. Dietrichstein, J. Drechsler, E. A. Förster, J. Fraestaedtler, J. Gänsbacher, A. Gelinek, A. Halm, *J. Hoffmann, J. Horzalka, *J. Huglmann, *J. N. Hummel, A. Hüttenbrenner, *F. Kalkbrenner, F. A. Kanne, J. Kerzkowsky, *C. Kreutzer, E. B. Lannoy, M. J. Leidesdorf, *F. Liszt, J. Mayseder, *I. Moscheles, I. F. v. Mosel, *W. A. Mozart fils, J. Panny, H. Payer, J. P. Pixis, *W. Plachy, *G. Rieger, P. J. Riotte, F. Roser, J. Schenk, *F. Schoberlechner, *F. Schubert, S. Sechter, S. R. D. [i.e., Archduke Rudolph], A. Stadler, *J. de Szalay, *W. Tomaschek, M. Umlauff, F. D. Weber, F. Weber, *C. A. v. d. Winkhler, F. Weiss, J. Wittassek, J. H. Worzischek [plus an extended "coda," also by C. Czerny].

3. Cf. Deutsch/SCHUBERT-D 348–51 and GROVE VIII 690–92 (E. Blom), both with further references; also, *Beethovenjahrbuch* I (1908) 28–50 (H. Rietsch).
4. The alphabetic order and spellings of the original Diabelli ed. are followed here. Mod. ed. of 16 of the single vars. (by the composers asterisked in this list): Newman/DIABELLI-m.

A First Direct Beethoven Transmitter: Ries

No more appropriate link connecting the previous and present volumes, and no more representative, timely opener for our individual composer discussions can be found than **Ferdinand Ries** (1784–1838),[5] best known for his close association with Beethoven (his senior by 14 years). Ries trained right in the Viennese environment and midway in that succession of the sonata's greatest Classic-Romantic masters from Haydn to Brahms. He actually studied piano with Beethoven, from late in 1801 to 1805, while studying theory and composition, on Beethoven's own recommendation, with the aging Albrechtsberger.[6] In fact, the abundant correspondence between the two men, extending from 1802 to 1825, shows Ries to have been the most lasting and one of the closest of all associates in Beethoven's day-to-day work. He was not only the successful student alone entrusted with many performances of Beethoven's music in public.[7] He was also the son in a musical family that had befriended the Beethoven family in Bonn, only to become the recipient himself of Beethoven's unsolicited contributions during early periods of near destitution in Vienna. He was at once Beethoven's confidant, secretary, copyist, and general lackey in countless professional or personal assignments and errands, even in intrigues, much as Schindler was to be all these in Beethoven's final years. He was the idolater of Beethoven's music who eventually became a near colleague as a composer (although Beethoven's request and numerous promises to exchange dedications in new works came to nought[8]). And, finally, he was Beethoven's important editorial and concert agent in London in the years from 1813 to 1824.[9]

As to being an appropriate, representative opener here, Ries was above all a musician à la mode in his day. He excelled as a pianist and

5. The chief biographic sources are Schilling/LEXICON V 747–49, Wegeler's necrologic remarks in Wegeler & Ries/BEETHOVEN v–vii, MOSCHELES I 52, and Fétis/BU VII 255–58 (all contemporary); Thayer & Forbes/BEETHOVEN I 293–96; and Ueberfeldt/RIES (on the years up to 1813, when the closest relations with Beethoven ended).

6. Cf. MacArdle/RIES 23–26; Macfarren/POTTER 45.

7. Wegeler & Ries/BEETHOVEN 115.

8. Cf. Schindler & MacArdle/BEETHOVEN 426–31, including negative appraisals of Ries undoubtedly influenced by Schindler's competitive position as another disciple and biographer of Beethoven.

9. For epistolary samples of these relationships cf. (among many similar indexed references to Ries) Anderson/BEETHOVEN I 62, 76, 87–88, 111–14; II 577; III 1033, 1064, 793–807. Cf., also, SCE 511–32, *passim;* and Ries's own valued testimonies in Wegeler & Ries/BEETHOVEN 75–77, 88–97, 101–3, 113–19, 123–26.

wrote primarily for the piano, then well on the way to its 19th-century ascendancy; and he wrote the styles of music in the kinds of settings and forms the public then most liked to play and hear (including not only the sons. in review here but much other instrumental music, from one to 8 parts, as well as songs, operas, and oratorios[10]). His talent for satisfying current tastes is the point made most often and emphatically in the numerous reviews of his sonatas, among other works, that Friedrich Rochlitz (and others?) wrote in *Allgemeine musikalische Zeitung* (AMZ) from 1807 to 1823. Especially perceptive now seems the remark that "Herr Ries is for the present time—the present state of music, the present taste, the present way of playing—what Leopold Anton Koželuch was for his time," [11] a generation earlier. That Ries was popular and successful as a composer is evident enough in the rags-to-riches story of his life. The Swiss publisher Nägeli included his piano sonata Op. 141 in the anthology *Die musikalische Ehrenpforte* (1827), which was also meant to, but did not, include works by Schubert, Weber, Mendelssohn, Spohr, Hummel, and Moscheles, among others.[12] Beethoven himself, on one occasion when he was confused as to Ries's whereabouts, addressed a letter to the "celébre compositeur a Londres." [13]

More to the point here, Ries's lifetime successes are evident in the large number of his works that got published, often in competing or successive editions by German, French, and English publishers. The following tabulation of his 54 known sonatas, of which only the first did not get published, should help not only to put them in a needed perspective but, more generally, to illustrate the fashionable titles, settings, instrumental options, programmatic and pedagogic leanings, and journalistic attention given to the sonata in the first quarter of the 19th century. The accessible facts about the earliest editions of the sonatas have been culled from yearbooks throughout the first half-century of (Whistling and) HOFMEISTER, from catalogues of an understandably large collection of Ries's works in London (Cat. ROYAL 283–88), from an early list of his works in HARMONICON II/1 (1824) 60–61 and the full list of his works still to be found in PAZDÍREK XXIV 328–31, and from the more recent information in Egert/FRÜHROMANTIKER

10. Cf. MGG XI 490–94 (R. Sietz).
11. AMZ XIII (1811) 89; cf. SCE 556–58.
12. Cf. Deutsch/SCHUBERT-D 541.
13. Anderson/BEETHOVEN II 763. Barely hinted in the conclusions of Beethoven's later letters to Ries is an envy of his success, security, and domestic joys, including frequent joshing about Beethoven's intention to go to London in order to "kiss your pretty wife" (e.g., Anderson/BEETHOVEN II 954–55, III 1006–7 and 1027).

Ferdinand Ries's Sonatas (grouped by scoring types)

Op./nos.	Keys	Scoring	Latest year (of early pub.)	Sources (of reviews) and/or remarks	Composite numbering
1/1–3	b, C, a	P	1807 (Simrock)	AMZ IX (1806–7) 362–65; Op. 1/1 not pub.	1, 2
5/1–2	B♭, F	P	1828 "	"Sonatine"	5, 6
9/1–2	D, C	P	1811 "	"Deux grandes Sonates"	10, 11
11/1–2	E♭, f	P	1815 "	"Deux grandes Sonates"	13, 14
26	f♯	P	1815 "	"Grande Sonate fantaisie intitulée L'Infortunée"	22
45	C	P	1818 "	AMZ XIX (1817) 843–44; "Sonatine"	31
49	E♭	P	1815 "	AMZ XVII (1815) 146–49; Anderson/BEETHOVEN 571; "Le Songe" or "Il Sogno"	—
114	A	P	1823 (Breitkopf)	AMZ XXV (1823) 492	47
141	A♭	P	1827 (Nägeli)		49
175	A♭	P	1835	NZM VII (1837) 127 (Schumann); "Grande Sonate"	52
6	C	P-duet	(Simrock)	"Sonatine"	7
47	B♭	P-duet	1818 (Simrock)	AMZ XIX (1817) 844	(32)
160	A	P-duet	1834	"Grande Sonate"	50
3/1–2	C, A	P + Vn	1811 (Simrock)		3, 4
8/1–2	F, c	P + Vn	1811 "	"Deux grandes Sonates"	8, 9
10	B♭	P & Vn	1811 "	"Grande Sonate"	12
16/1–3	C, B♭, D	P + Vn	1811 "	AMZ XIII (1811) 88–91	15, 16, 17
18	E♭	P + Vn	1811 "	AMZ XIII (1811) 88–91; "Grande Sonate"	18
19	f	P + Vn	1812 "	AMZ XIV (1812) 485; "Grande Sonate"	19
30/1–3	C, a, F	P & Vn	1815 "	"Sonatines doigtées"	24, 25, 26
38/1–3	e, a, g	P & Vn	1815 (Costallat)		28, 29, 30
59/1–2	D, B♭	P & Vn-or-Fl	1815 (Simrock)	AMZ XVIII (1816) 11 (no. 1, only)	34, 35
69	E♭	P & Vn	1815 (Costallat)	AMZ XIX (1817) 92	36
71	c♯	P & Vn	1815 "		37
81/1–2	E♭, d	P ± Vn	1822 (André)	AMZ XXIV (1822) 263; plate no. 4474	40, 41
83	D	P & Vn	1821 (Simrock)	AMZ XXIV (1822) 263; plate no. 1831	42
86/1–3	E♭, D, g	P & Vn-or-Fl	1828 "	"Sonates faciles" (or "non difficiles")	43, 44, 45
20	C	P + Vc	1811 (Simrock)	AMZ XIII (1811) 886; "Grande Sonate"; also pub. for P + Vn	20
21	A/a	P + Vc	1811 "	AMZ XIII (1811) 884–85; "Grande Sonate"; also pub. for P + Hn	21
34	F	P + Vc	1815 (Costallat)	"Grande Sonate"; also pub. for P + Hn	27
125	g	P & Vc-or-Vn	1828 (Kistner)	"Grande Sonate"	48
48	G	P ± Fl	1815 (Simrock)	AMZ XVII (1815) 389–91	33
76/1–2	C, B♭	P ± Fl-or-Vn	1818 "	AMZ XX (1818) 632 (no. 1, only)	38, 39
87	G	P + Fl	1819 "	"Sonatine"	46
169	E♭	P & Fl-or-Cl	1839 (Costallat)	"Sonate sentimentale"	(51)
29	g	P + Cl-or-Vn	1828 (Costallat)		23

122–24 and 159. With regard to composition dates, the 54 sonatas span
the years from 1803–6 for Op. 1 [14] to about 1835 for Op. 175, with all
but the last three or four originating by 1825. With regard to ap-

14. Egert/FRÜHROMANTIKER 122.

proximate dates of first publication, they span nearly the same years. These approximate dates, which might well be made more exact if and when more of the original publishers' plate numbers could be found, are based here mainly on the *terminus ad quem* of review dates, and only occasionally on the *terminus a quo* of a watermark.[15] In any case, our total of 54 sonatas is likely to be correct or very nearly so, since Ries himself, besides keeping his opus numbers in good order, gave a separate, composite numbering to all of his published sonatas, right from No. 1, Op. 1/2, to No. 52, Op. 175, excluding only the unpublished Op. 1/1 and "Le Songe," Op. 49, which lacks "Sonata" in the titles of some early editions. The tabulation is subdivided according to scoring.

As the tabulation shows, Ries, quite typically for that time, still left about twice as many accompanied or duo as solo and four-hand settings.[16] Yet his whole sonata output is oriented toward his own 16a favorite instrument, anyway.[17] Even the "obligé" accompaniments, which are literally obligatory only when they have lyrical ideas to state, run but poor seconds to the piano parts, whether in the allocation of thematic responsibilities or the relative virtuosity of the many connecting passages (Ex. 15). And the ad libitum parts, during this final bloom of the accompanied setting, sometimes border on the ridiculous. A near virtuoso piano concerto, with scarcely more than intermittent timid peeps from the accompaniment, is how one must describe Op. 76/1, *Sonate pour le Piano avec Accomp.ᵗ de Flute ou Violon ad Libitum dans laquelle se trouve introduit l'Air favori de H. R. Bishop, He is all the World to me.* Only when "l'Air favori" prevails, in the finale, does the piano occasionally accompany and the flute or violin take the lead. The tabulation also reveals Ries's tendency to produce fewer "grande" sonatas and "obligé" accompaniments, and more alternative settings in his later sonatas, suggesting that, unlike Beethoven, he was one more minor master who chose to court success by bowing

15. As in Cat. HIRSCH 348.

16. A brief discussion of some of Ries's earlier solo piano sons. occurs in Egert/FRÜHROMANTIKER 121–24 (superseding the little to be found in Ueberfeldt/ RIES 38–62 *passim*). A thorough, comprehensive discussion of both his solo and "accompanied" piano works would make an inviting and not unprofitable dissertation topic. Nearly all of this music is at the Library of Congress, especially in two privately bound collections of 6 and 4 vols. under M22-R56 (solo piano) and M219-R56 (piano and violin), respectively; it is chiefly in Richault editions, which, though probably not as early as those in the foregoing tabulation, included all of Ries's pub. sons. at least through Op. 76.

17. It is interesting to find a Rondo for P+Hn-or-Vc and a "Sextuor" with a variety of accompaniments (including harp, Hn, bassoon, and double-bass) both reviewed at length under the heading merely of "neuste Pianoforte-Compositionen," in CAECILIA VIII (1828) 112–18.

Ex. 15. From Sonata in D, Op. 83/i/7–17, by Ferdinand Ries (after the original Simrock ed. at The University of North Carolina at Chapel Hill).

increasingly to popular tastes. The "Sonatines doigtées" or "Sonates non difficiles" (Opp. 30 and 86) must have been designed quite as much to sell as was that sonata into which he inserted "l'Air favori." And so must the alternative settings, such as the horn and cello parts for Op. 34, which rarely differ except for essential, idiomatic adaptations of range and articulation.

From the same tabulation we see that Ries still stayed within the conservative limit of three sharps and four flats in his choice of keys, with fewer than one out of four sonatas being in minor. Only within a few movements, as in the change of mode to ab in the trio of the "Scherzo" in Op. 175, does he use signatures with more sharps or flats. In Op. 21, his change to the minor mode for the final, fourth movement is quite the opposite of the supposed later Romantic trend (SSB

VI). Moreover, the large majority of the sonatas prove to have the usual three movements in the usual order of F-S-F. An occasional "grande" sonata has four movements, such as Op. 21, just cited, or Op. 9/2 in C, in which the order M-VF-S → VF and even the styles and forms of the movements (with none in "son. form") recall Beethoven's Op. 27/1 in E♭ too closely for comfort. Conversely, some of the later sonatinas have only two moderate or faster movements (as in Op. 45).

A short slow introduction, like that to Beethoven's Op. 78, frequently leads into the fast opening and/or final movements of Ries's sonatas (as in Opp. 11/2/i and 19/i) and may even return in the course of the movement,[18] much in the way that it does in Beethoven's Op. 13/i. Most often the first movement is in "sonata form," the second is free and cursive, and the finale is a rondo, dance (especially a minuet, or a "Polacca" as in Op. 20/iii), or a set of variations on a favorite air (for instance, the set on an "Air russe" in Op. 11/1/iii). The interrelation of movements by similar melodic incipits occurs less often than in Beethoven's sonatas, and only in Ries's more serious sonatas (as in Op. 26/i and ii). The use of a binding programme occurs not at all beyond the general mood implied by "L'Infortunée" or "sentimentale" in the titles of Opp. 26 and 169, respectively. "Le Songe," Op. 49, might be taken as an exception, since it does suggest a dream in its fitful starts and stops, its kaleidoscopic changes of tempo and dynamics, and its alternations of mood. However, Rochlitz, cautiously seeking to interpret this dream section by section, seems to regret the absence of any verbal clue more specific than the "Marcia" inscribed over one section.[19] From the standpoint of our continued semantic approach, one wonders whether Ries actually regarded this piece as one of his sonatas, in spite of "Sonate" in the title of at least the early Simrock edition.[20] Not only did he depart from the usual over-all and separate designs of the sonata in this continuous piece but he gave it no number in his composite numbering of his "fifty-two" sonatas.

"Le Songe" happens to be the only work of Ries that Beethoven mentions specifically in his letters, and with the only unqualified approval he gives to Ries's music. "The Archduke Rudolph plays your works too, my dear Ries, and among these I find 'Il Sogno' particularly

18. It already does this in his first, unpublished son., according to Egert/FRÜH-ROMANTIKER 122.

19. AMZ XVII (1815) 146–49.

20. According to HOFMEISTER 1815 (Whistling), p. 374, but not in any other listing seen here.

delightful."[21] But, paradoxically, "Le Songe" also happens to be the Ries work examined here that reveals the fewest resemblances to Beethoven's music. Such resemblances, including those already noted, occur chiefly in the earlier and more serious sonatas by Ries. They are hardly surprising in view of the close association with Beethoven mentioned above, and of such further intimate contact with his music as transcribing a number of his works, probably with his blessing,[22] and even of composing the lost, final eleven measures to the "Adagio" in Beethoven's Sonata in C, WoO 51/ii.[23]

Ries dedicated Op. 1 with the words "à Louis van Beethoven par son élève," incidentally causing Rochlitz to ask why a German should dedicate a piece to a German, presumably for Germans, in the French language.[24] Rochlitz commented, as he was to do in several later reviews, on the obvious resemblances to Beethoven, without specifically mentioning how remarkably Ries's first published sonata, in C—with its fast scales, double-3rds, 6th-chords, and still other devices of brilliance —recalls Beethoven's Op. 2/3, in the same key. But the flat, inconsequential themes, excessive passagework, and empty tremolo accompaniments that often prevail represent traits that clearly separate Ries's music from Beethoven's, that bring mild yet persistent censure in those later reviews of his music, and that must explain why Rochlitz resorted in this instance to two earthy terms apparently coined for such music by Mozart, "Krabbelsonaten" and "Holzmachern" (freely, "scurry sonatas" and "claptrap players").[25] Beethoven himself was to write Ries of his objections to "mechanical" display pieces in a letter of 1823 that exempts Ries from the criticism a bit too ingenuously.[26]

To be sure, more in the subsequent reviews of Ries's sonatas is favorable than not. Besides the need Rochlitz seems to have felt for treating his successful, well-descended compatriot with respect and caution, there was genuine praise for his undeniable craftsmanship, especially the sure command of form, the advanced harmonic skill, and the fluent

21. April 3, 1816; Anderson/BEETHOVEN II 571 (and fn. 6, in which the editor is unable to identify "Il Sogno").

22. Cf. MacArdle/RIES 34.

23. Cf. G. Weber in CAECILIA XIII (1831) 285.

24. AMZ IX (1806–7) 365. The title page of Op. 16, though not dedicated to Beethoven, still capitalizes on the pupil relationship, and still in French. Only about 4 years later Beethoven himself was to object to the French inscriptions that the publishers used for his Op. 81a (SCE 525).

25. AMZ IX (1806–7) 363–64; our free translations reflect Rochlitz's own expansions of the terms. These terms may well have come from his immediate but frequently undependable recollections; they could not be traced here to previous, post-mortem accounts of Mozart, as by Niemetschek (1798) or Rochlitz himself (AMZ I and IV [1798–99 and 1801–2]).

26. Anderson/BEETHOVEN III 1064.

use of the keyboard. Only when the sameness of style became too apparent and the lighter, dilettante pieces took precedence did the reviews eventually diminish to short notices, with occasional backhanded compliments like the statement hoping Ries would continue to produce such fresh, happy, serious pieces in his second hundred *opera* as were inaugurated by the one under review, his Sonata No. 47, Op. 114, for piano.[27] Less concerned about the feelings of his compatriots, Schumann put an honest finish in 1837 to reviews of Ries's sonatas, in a paragraph about the last one, No. 52 in A♭ for piano solo, that includes this sentence: "Throughout it suffers from all too much mediocrity, and when it occasionally reaches toward the fair heights where we often met this artist earlier, it soon sinks back again as if lead weighted down its wings." [28]

From our present historical viewpoint, in addition to his close associations with Beethoven, his full representation of popular tastes in his day, and his thoroughly typical output of sonatas, Ries is worth noting for the early Romantic traits in his music. The most serious, advanced, and effective examples are found in Opp. 9, 11, and 26 for solo piano, of which the last might best be used for special mention and quotation here, since it remains the most available of all his sonatas.[29] Composed in 1808,[30] *Grande Sonate fantaisie intitulée L'Infortunée,* Op. 26, in f♯, comes nearest in its three-movement cycle, length, dynamic intensity, and keyboard treatment to the "Tempest Sonata," Op. 31/2, in d (1801–2), among Beethoven's works. It reveals a similar use of a return to a slow introduction, and even some thematic resemblances in the first movement, although its middle, slowest movement is shorter, less deliberate, and more suave, and its finale is faster and more dramatic, if somewhat longish for its content. (Ries's three movements total 255, 64, and 429 measures, or 748 in all, as against 228, 103, and 399, or 730 in all, for Beethoven.) Characteristic early Romanticisms in Ries's work are the bold projection of the lyrical ideas, the use of bass/chord or other wide-spaced accompaniments in place of the Alberti bass that still shows up in Beethoven and Schubert, the salon brilliance of passages in broken chords and octaves, and of wide stretches and leaps (all within a total range from FFF♯ to c⁴), and the vivid contrasts of dynamics, moods, tempos, and tessituras, accompanied by copious expressive markings and inscriptions, as well as articulation and accent signs.

27. AMZ XXV (1823) 492.
28. Schumann/SCHRIFTEN I 307.
29. Mod. ed.: TRÉSOR-m XIX.
30. Egert/FRÜHROMANTIKER 124.

Ex. 16. From the finale of *Grande Sonate fantaisie intitulée L'Infortunée,* Op. 26, by Ferdinand Ries (after TRÉSOR-m XIX).

The bold melodic projection of the lyrical theme, over broken chords in open position and slow harmonic rhythm, near the start of Ries's finale (Ex. 16) recalls the same style in main themes of three near successors, all likewise German sonatas in f♯—Hummel's Op. 81/iii, Moscheles' Op. 49 in one movement, and Schumann's Op. 11/i. Besides the command of form, harmony, and keyboard scoring in Op. 26, Ries displays his outstanding craftsmanship in some contrapuntal writing, especially in the middle movement, that certainly surpasses Beethoven's if not Schubert's in grace and felicity. With all these Romanticisms and skills, Ries's music survived longer than Koželuch's had. In fact, in the early 20th century, PAZDÍREK, the comprehensive catalogue of all available published music, still listed nearly all of his sonatas and related works. However, in the last half century publishers have deleted all the sonatas and virtually everything else from their catalogues by this composer once so widely patronized.

A Second Direct Beethoven Transmitter: Czerny

The association of **Carl Czerny** (1791–1857) with Beethoven was as close and durable as that of Ries, although it did not extend back to the Bonn days, nor elicit quite the same respect from Beethoven, nor exercise as much influence on the sonata writing of the younger man (Ries's junior by more than six years).[31] The two disciples must have crossed paths often. Yet they seem not to have developed any warm friendship, for the available letters and reminiscences of Ries make no mention of Czerny and those few of Czerny refer to Ries only to recall reading often at two pianos with him (including an arrangement of Beethoven's "Kreutzer Sonata," Op. 47) and reacting to his playing as being very dexterous and fluent, if not wholly to Beethoven's liking.[32]

As a piano prodigy of about ten and already a Beethoven worshipper, Czerny began his study with Beethoven in Vienna about the same year as Ries, or about 1801.[33] He was an only child, who became the main support of his parents, never married, and rarely travelled. By the time he was fifteen this gentle, kindly soul was well started on his lifetime pursuits of playing, teaching, composing, and writing, as well as studying widely in other cultural fields. He figured in Beethoven's life not only as one of his few bonafide students but as a main performer of his music (along with Ries and Dorothea von Ertmann), as a transcriber of many of his works, as a teacher of his nephew Karl, and as an occasional agent (less so than Ries) in his personal and professional affairs. He is remembered in today's view of the past as a successful Viennese pianist and pedagogue of the early 19th century; as a transmitter of Beethoven's musical ideas and intentions to Liszt, Leschetizky, T. Kullak, and other important pupils who were themselves to become transmitters; as a writer of substance on musical subjects; and, in pianists' circles, of course, as the clever manufacturer of many piano etudes still widely practiced. Much of what he transmitted on the performance of Beethoven's sonatas occurs in his own

31. Ries and Czerny are compared in Schindler & MacArdle/BEETHOVEN 426–27, with little good said about the music of either.

32. Thayer & Forbes/BEETHOVEN I 295; CZERNY 310. The arrangement of Op. 47 is not among the 3 pub. ones by Czerny noted in Kinsky & Halm/BEETHOVEN 112; cf. MacArdle/CZERNYS 132.

33. Czerny's short, valuable autobiography of 1842, trans. in full in CZERNY, is a primary source, much of it included in the chief study to date of the man and his works, which is the unpub. Ph.D. diss. Steger/CZERNY. Other primary sources are Czerny's autobiographic letter of 1824, printed in Schnapp/CZERNY (a letter intended for an unachieved new ed. of the Gerber *lexicon* and remarkable for no mention of Beethoven, especially as Schnapp's statement of a falling out between Czerny and Beethoven at that time cannot be substantiated); the contemporary account in Schilling/LEXICON II 344–46 (as of 1834); and numerous bits of information in several other sources listed in MacArdle/CZERNYS, which is itself an efficient summary of source information about Czerny (and disentanglement from the unrelated Joseph Czerny). Hanslick/TAGEBUCHE 32–40 is a general appreciation of Czerny.

edition of them (Simrock, issued separately, *ca.* 1845–55), and in the
final volume of his four-volume *Pianoforte-Schule,* Op. 500 (completed
1839–42 [?], pub. 1842–46 [?] by Diabelli in Vienna).[34] Other of his
writings include his annotated translation of Reicha's composition
treatise (1832) and his own composition treatise, Op. 600 (written by
1840?),[35] as well as his "Outline of All Music History," Op. 815 (1851).[36]

All of which leads to Czerny's extraordinary output, including
operas, masses, requiems, offertories, graduals, symphonies, overtures,
concertos, chamber works, stage music, arrangements and editions of
other composers, further treatises, essays and plays outside of music,
and many other piano pieces besides the sonatas in question! PAZDÍREK
(III 661–88) shows a total of 861 opus numbers, many being whole sets
of pieces in themselves, plus almost half as many more miscellaneous
publications, or an average of over 30 publications, large or small, each
year from 1819 to his death in 1857.[37] Such prolificity and its inevitable
compromise with low public tastes quite naturally became the target
for many a caustic remark. Mendelssohn,[38] Chopin, and Schumann
were contemptuous, while recognizing other virtues in Czerny. Chopin,
during his Vienna sojourn, 1830–31, wrote his family about "that
Viennese specialist in the manufacture of all sorts of musical sweet-
meats . . . ," following an earlier report of how Czerny was "happily
engaged in arranging some overture or other for eight pianos (sixteen

34. In MGG VII 1186 (H. Haase), "um 1830" is obviously too early for the first
Vienna ed.; but in Dale/THREE c's 142, "1839" is just possible for Vols. I–III
(only) in a pub. English trans.; John Bishop's preface to Czerny/COMPOSITION
states that Czerny sold Op. 500 to Robert Cocks while in London in 1837. The
Diabelli plate no. 8212 suggests 1846 (Deutsch/NUMMERN 11–12; cf. HOFMEISTER
1844–51, p. 209) for Vol. IV, rather than the "1842" on p. 23 of Badura-Skoda/
CZERNY (with preface and annotations), which brings together virtually everything
Czerny wrote on the performance of Beethoven's music, including portions of
the *Erinnerungen,* miscellaneous remarks, a facs. of 89 pp. from Op. 500, and a
collation of this last with the sometimes conflicting advices in the Simrock eds.
(listed in HOFMEISTER 1844–51, p. 85 [up to Op. 57] and 1852–59, p. 110 [all]).
Some of this performance advice in Op. 500 is quoted, and sometimes protested,
along with further information about Czerny and Beethoven, in Schindler &
MacArdle/BEETHOVEN 397–98, 405–26 *passim.*

35. Reicha & Czerny/COMPOSITION and Czerny/COMPOSITION, as discussed in SSB
II. The pedagogic ideas are the likely focus of a Ph.D. diss. on Czerny in progress
at Columbia Univ. (as of 1967) by Mrs. Alice Mitchell, whose advices and loan
of Steger/CZERNY for the present discussion are gratefully acknowledged.

36. Cf. E. Valentin in NZM CXVIII (1957) 356–57.

37. No one list is complete, but the relatively few gaps in PAZDÍREK can be
nearly filled in from the lists in Steger/CZERNY 110–142 (pubs. with op. nos., only),
the list of works, both pub. (up to Op. 798) and unpub., in Czerny/COMPOSITION
I vii–xiv (cf. Dale/THREE c's 146), and the summary list by categories in Prosniz/
HANDBUCH I 111–16. On Czerny's method for composing 4 pieces at a time, cf.
Loesser/PIANOS 362 and Dessauer/FIELD 75–76.

38. Cf. Werner/MENDELSSOHN 168.

hands)." [39] And Schumann reviewed Czerny's "4 brillante Phantasien," Op. 434, in 1838, with the comment, "By all means let him retire and give him a pension; truly, he deserves it and would not [have to] write any more. . . . In a word, he's gotten stale; we've gotten fed up with his things. . . ." [40] Even the more tactful editor of the *Allgemeine musikalische Zeitung* in Leipzig was already cautioning in 1827 about the danger of sacrificing quality and satiating the public by turning out so much, only to go into a much longer discussion of the problem one year later that equated Czerny and the keyboard with Rossini and the opera. [41]

In all that prolificity, Czerny's sonata writing, however commonplace much of it may seem today, stands out as a main part of his most serious composing. He himself acknowledged to Beethoven in 1825 the worthlessness of his " 'Kleinigkeiten,' since I jot them down very rapidly . . . I long to get going in earnest now with [some] larger orchestral things." [42] Particular evidence of his special regard for his sonatas turns up near the start of a letter of 1823 to the Leipzig publisher C. F. Peters:[43]

My solo piano sonatas, however many I plan to write, ought through [one separate] continuous numbering to comprise an entirety [in themselves], in which I want, little by little, to record my artistic views and experiences. Therefore I ask you to consider the 3$^{i\grave{e}me}$ *Sonate*, sent to you, as one item of an over-all series, which I hope to make more and more significant.

This statement makes clear which of his own sonatas Czerny took most seriously. Out of 64 works that could be identified here with "sonate" or "sonatine" in the title—more than Ries's, yet a mere 5 per cent of Czerny's total output as against about 22 per cent for Ries—Czerny assigned a special numbering only to the "sonatas" for solo piano, 11 in all. He did not so distinguish any of the "sonates" or "sonatines" for 4 hands at one piano (about 23 per cent of all his sonatas) or for piano and violin (about 11 per cent), nor, for that matter, any works at all called "sonatines" (about 63 per cent), including those for solo piano. [44]

The 11 solo sonatas in Czerny's special series are No. 1 in A♭, Op. 7,

39. Sydow & Hedley/CHOPIN 82 and 67.
40. Schumann/SCHRIFTEN I 364–65; cf., also, I 236–37.
41. AMZ XXIX (1827) 234 and XXX (1828) 233–38.
42. Thayer & Riemann/BEETHOVEN V 267.
43. Printed in full in La Mara/MUSIKERBRIEFE II 98–101.
44. Thus, at least for the sons., neither the proportions nor the categories can be reconciled with the translator's summary of 1848 in Czerny/COMPOSITION I vi: "Of his [Czerny's] original productions, about one third are written in the strict style, one third in the brilliant style, and the remainder for the purpose of instruction. . . ."

1820; No. 2 in a, Op. 13, 1821; No. 3 in f, Op. 57, 1824; No. 4 in G, Op. 65, 1824; No. 5 in E, Op. 76, 1824; No. 6 in d, Op. 124, 1827; No. 7 in e, Op. 143, 1827 (?); No. 8 in E♭, Op. 144, 1827 (?); No. 9 in b, Op. 145, 1827 (?); No. 10 in B♭, Op. 268, 1831 (?); and No. 11 in D♭, Op. 730, 1843 (?).[45] Czerny uses descriptive titles for his sonatas only infrequently. Each of Nos. 7–9, Opp. 143–145, carries the title "Grande Fantaisie en Forme de Sonate," but for no evident reason in the cycles or music itself; Op. 268 is rightly called "Grande Sonate d'Étude," though for little more reason than most of his sonatas might be; and the lighter sonatas or sonatinas occasionally carry terms like "faciles et brillantes," "militaire," "sentimentale," "pastorale," and even "à la Scarlatti" (a one-movement 4-hand sonatina in f♯, Op. 788) in their titles. The reviewer of Op. 7 actually asks why "grande" does not precede "Sonate" in the title, in view not only of this work's length but its design and its performance difficulties.[46] "Grande" or "grosse" does appear in the subsequent editions of Op. 7 as well as the titles of most of the other "sonatas," though not the "sonatinas."

Czerny's more serious sonatas may be seen in better perspective by comparing them with Ries's. Czerny uses over-all keys up to one more flat and sharp (D♭ and E), and puts a larger proportion, nearly half, of them in minor keys. Instead of the usual three-movement plan, F-S-F, he uses at least four movements in the standard order F-S-Sc-Ro. In Op. 7 he adds a final, fifth movement, "Capriccio fugato," putting it, as with Ries's Op. 21, in the tonic minor (a♭!) except for a Picardy 3[d] in the four ending measures. In the four-hand sonata in C minor Op. 10

45. Czerny apparently excluded from this special series his piano "Sonate" Op. 167, which is therefore relegated here to the sonatina group. "Op. 124" was assigned not only to No. 6 in this series but to some string arrangements. Czerny himself supplied pub. years for Opp. 1–85 (in his letter of 1824 printed in Schnapp/CZERNY; 1820 for Op. 7 is confirmed in Weinmann/ARTARIA item 2632, although it had been composed in 1810, according to Egert/FRÜHROMANTIKER 126). Nägeli issued Op. 124 in 1827 in *Die musikalische Ehrenpforte* (with Ries's Op. 141; cf. Deutsch/SCHUBERT-D 541). Conjectures for the years of Opp. 143–45 are based on 1827 for Op. 124, plus a review in 1828 of Op. 144 (AMZ XXX 233–39), the listing of all 3 in HOFMEISTER 1828, p. 585, and the fact of their consecutive op. nos.; for Op. 268, on 1830 for both the performance (Czerny/COMPOSITION I ix) and pub. (MacArdle/CZERNYS 133) of Op. 238; and for Op. 730, on its listing in HOFMEISTER 1843/II, p. 151, plus a review of Op. 601 in 1841 (AMZ XLIII 653).

The relatively brief discussions of Czerny's entire son. output in Steger/CZERNY 78–94 and of the solo piano sons. in Egert/FRÜHROMANTIKER 9 and 125–28 (largely derived from Steger) leave open the need for a fuller, more systematic study. Hasenöhrl/CZERNY, unaware of Steger/CZERNY and unavailable in Egert/FRÜHROMANTIKER (cf. p. 125), is a rather superficial diss. of 1927 that provides almost no bibliographic information but mainly facts about the cycles and forms of the sons. (pp. 17–39) and a survey of melodic traits (based on G. Adler and W. Fischer) by mvt. types (pp. 77–103).

46. AMZ XXIV (1822) 382–84.

(1821) he also uses five movements, and in Op. 124 he uses seven movements counting the slow introduction. But Czerny shows little of Ries's predilection for slow introductions and none for their recurrence during the movements. His only efforts to give more unity to the cycle occur with the occasional instruction "attacca" before the finale (as in Op. 65 or the duet Op. 331) and in the surprising arch effect created by the return in those last four measures of Op. 7 to the very opening of the sonata.

Where Ries is strongest, in the command of structural techniques, Czerny has here seemed weakest. One notes especially how little the ideas develop and how often the modulations lead to no clear goal in the initial, "sonata-allegro" movements. The ideas themselves show Czerny to be even less of a creative melodist than Ries. They are usually no more than slight melodic fragments reiterated sequentially or in place. For that matter, Czerny introduces and restates fewer tangible ideas, devoting even more space to passagework. But his passagework is quite as idiomatic for the keyboard as Ries's and decidedly more varied and ingenious, in spite of its exploitation of the piano's highest registers, enough to bear out Beethoven's oft-misquoted remark, "Czerny gives me too much piccolo." [47] In the scherzos and rondos, where ingenuity and charm can matter more than original ideas or development, Czerny is at his best; and even in the relatively static slow movements—to the surprise of all who know only his etudes —he can convert the passagework into remarkably Chopinesque fioriture (Ex. 17). Arthur Loesser pinpoints both the charm and pitfalls of the passagework that serves Czerny as the chief means of continuity in his sonatas as well as his etudes:[48]

Rapid, feathery, well-articulated pianistic passage-work, chiefly for the right hand, was his best product—just what the light, bouncing, leather-covered little hammer-heads of the Vienna pianos could deliver best. It was a music without depth, intensity, or wit, but always smooth and pretty and rather ear-tickling when played fast; it displayed tonal ruffles and ribbons, ruching and rickrack, in endless variety of patterns and endless monotony of import. Its low specific gravity made it easy to take, and the Viennese as well as other Europeans took it in vast quantity.

"From a spirited virtuoso and warm sensitive Romantic in his youth, Czerny developed over the years into a dry academician." [49] Although most of his "sonatas" appeared within the first quarter of his output, the same generalization might already be made within their own en-

---

47. Thayer & Riemann/BEETHOVEN V 300 fn. 2, said in reference to an arrangement of Beethoven's Op. 133 that proved not to be acceptable.
48. Loesser/PIANOS 145.
49. Georgii/WEBER 4 fn. 1.

Ex. 17. From the "Scherzo" and the slow movement of Carl Czerny's *Grande Sonate d'Étude,* Op. 268/iii and ii (after Edition Peters No. 3239).

tirety. His best sonatas—"best" not only for their spirit and warmth but their contributions to the new Romanticism—are certainly his first two, No. 1, Op. 7, in A♭ for solo piano and Op. 10 in c for four hands. Also in both these sonatas, but not in the later ones, distinct references to Beethoven turn up. Thus, in Op. 7 the restful, almost hymnlike first movement, "Andante allegro moderato ed espressivo" in C meter, suggests the opening of Beethoven's Op. 26 or even 110 in the same key. This is a monothematic movement, except for a new, rather weak line in the submediant and mediant keys (leading to uneventful sequential modulations) by way of a "development" section. A difficult "Beethoven trill" decorates the dominant retransition to the recapitulation. In the fluent, scherzando second movement, "Prestissimo agitato" in c♯ and 3/4 meter, we get hints, among others, of Beethoven's Opp. 27/1/ii and the "Trio" of the "Scherzo" in his "Sinfonia eroica," as well as some empty, repeated bass octaves that Beethoven would not have written. In the third movement, "Adagio, espressivo e cantabile" in D♭ and 3/4 meter, the start suggests the chromatic passages, with 32d-note triplets in the bass, of Beethoven's Op. 31/2/ii, but the line is vacuous again. In the "Rondo" fourth movement, "Allegretto" in A♭ and 2/4 meter, we get an introduction that recalls at least the similar function in the finale of Beethoven's first symphony, followed by a polka-like refrain typical of Czerny's freshest melodies, and soon some octaves that already sound like "too much piccolo." As observed earlier, the finale, "Tempo moderato" in 4/4 meter, is a "Capriccio fugato" in the tonic minor with an ending that brings back the sonata's opening idea. Its counterpoint is more scholastic than Ries's, but not unskillful.

Rochlitz's extended review of Op. 7 in 1822 [50] notes difficult but legitimate technical problems, sustained, impassioned, gloomy, sometimes wild content, departures from "the usual form of the sonata" leading to excessive length ("almost any two or three movements, in whatever conceivable order, could suffice well in themselves"), superiority of the first three movements, especially the "Prestissimo agitato," over the final two, and objections to certain dissonances as well as to extremes of range and dynamics. And Liszt, writing hurriedly and belatedly from Paris in 1830 to his onetime master, tells Czerny he has given special study to "your admirable Sonata" (Op. 7) and has played it for various groups of ("at least so-called") connoisseurs with overwhelmingly enthusiastic response, particularly to the "Prestissimo." [51]

But the reviews of Czerny's sonatas did not go on for long and soon began to express more cons than pros.[52] Why becomes clear enough again, if one reads through a later sonata like that in b for piano and violin, Op. 686 (1842, around the time Czerny was writing about "Sonata form"; cf. ssb II). This work is a true duo in four movements, F-S-Sc-Ro, which carefully goes through all the proper motions, modulations, and climaxes, yet advances so perfunctorily with its innocuous themes, square phrases, and empty passages, that it produces a sense only of complete sterility. Even so, as recently as the 1930's, that *Grande Sonate d'Étude,* Op. 268, was played as the required piece for the *prix du concours* by a daylong succession of graduating pianists at the

50. AMZ XXIV 382–84.

51. La Mara/MUSIKERBRIEFE II 209–10; cf. Ramann/LISZT I 488. In a letter to Dionys Pruckner 26 years later, Liszt was still speaking highly of Op. 7 (LISZT LETTERS I 266; but read Op. 7, not 6).

52. E.g., cf. AMZ XXVII (1825) 87–88 on Op. 58, or XXX (1828) 233–39 on Op. 144; also, AMA No. 20 (Nov., 1826) 153 on Op. 65.

Paris Conservatoire, undoubtedly because it exploits every standard, advanced piano technique.[53]

53a

A Third Direct Beethoven Transmitter: Moscheles

Ignaz Moscheles (1794–1870) knew Beethoven neither so well nor so long as Ries or Czerny, and received no instruction from him other than the direct and frequent advices required when he made a piano reduction of *Fidelio* in 1814.[54] On the other hand, Moscheles became at least as active and influential a champion of Beethoven's music, and for a considerably longer time, outliving Beethoven himself by 43 years, Ries by 32, and Czerny by 13. Furthermore, he won greater renown as a pianist than either of his fellow Beethoven worshipers,[55] his importance as a piano pedagogue eventually surpassed Czerny's, and two or three of his sonatas gained at least as wide and lasting acceptance as any by Ries or Czerny.

Moscheles' busy, long career is outlined by his changes of residence from Prague to Vienna in 1808, to London in 1826, and to Leipzig in 1846 (where he joined Mendelssohn at the new Conservatory). This career is recorded in exceptional detail in the perceptive and devoted (but sensitively restrained) biography that his wife published after his death, based largely on his own careful diaries and abundant correspondence.[56] As one of our best firsthand surveys of European musical life in the 19th century, this biography (covering mainly the years from 1815 to 1860) brings us close to the astonishing number of important musicians that Moscheles got to know at home and during his many recital tours or other travels. Included are not only the three masters who seem to have affected him most deeply—Beethoven,

---

53. Curiously, except for a Sam Fox ed. in 1963 of the 4-hand Son. in G, Op. 50/1, Op. 268 comes nearest of all Czerny's sons. to being a "mod. ed." Edition Peters 3239 is a reprint of it issued in 1909, though no longer in the Peters catalogue. Two other 20th-century, French appreciations of Czerny's piano writing occur in ENCYCLOPÉDIE II/3 2092–93 (Gratia & Duvernoy) and STRAVINSKY 178.

54. Cf. Thayer & Forbes/BEETHOVEN I 584–86. Regarding Schindler's scurrilous, damaging, and entirely unwarranted attempt to discredit Moscheles and his association with Beethoven (19 years after Moscheles' trans. of the first ed. of Schindler's Beethoven biography) cf. Schindler & MacArdle/BEETHOVEN 17, 29, 322, 359–60, 372–74, 391–92.

55. Cf. Hanslick/WIEN I 216–18; Schindler & MacArdle/BEETHOVEN 392 fn. 300; SSB II, III.

56. MOSCHELES (with inadequate index). Worthwhile contemporary views from the outside are added in Schilling/LEXICON V 8–11 and Mendel/LEXIKON VII 176–77. MOSCHELES and still other contemporary sources supply the choice descriptions of Moscheles in Loesser/PIANOS 145, 285–92, 302–3.

Weber, and Mendelssohn[57]—but many others like Albrechtsberger, Salieri, Ries, Czerny, Hummel, Spohr, Cramer, Liszt, Clara and Robert Schumann, Clementi, Chopin, Ferdinand David, A. B. Marx, Paganini, Field, Henriette Sontag, Jenny Lind, Thalberg, Rossini, Ferdinand Hiller, Meyerbeer, Joachim, Wagner, and Anton Rubinstein, quite apart from eminent nonmusicians like Heine and Walter Scott.   57a

The biography shows Moscheles deriving special pleasure from intimate musical sociability, from a tourist's views of the arts in general, and from everything about the piano in particular, especially its performers, music, and continuing improvements as a concert instrument. His generosity and altruism rarely permitted such mistrust as Field and Paganini aroused in him. But for all his active, often historically minded interest in Handel, (Domenico) Scarlatti, Bach "and even older composers," Clementi, and both early and late Beethoven (all furthered by his association with Mendelssohn),[58] and for all his obvious desire to understand, he could never endorse (nor compete with) the younger school of virtuosos like Thalberg and Liszt,[59] and he could only admire, never fully accept, all that he found too modern in the music of Schumann, Chopin, Berlioz, Liszt, and Wagner.[60] Hummel figured in his life somewhat as an older rival, with a similar career.[61] Among Moscheles' many piano students, Mendelssohn and Thalberg should be included for at least a few lessons each.[62]

It was his chronic, lifelong "Beethoven fever," [63] brought on by discovering and playing at *Sonata pathétique* while the little prodigy was still only seven (SCE 513), that helped decide Moscheles' move to Vienna when he was only fourteen. And it was while still in the environment of Beethoven that he wrote all of his solo and most of his duo sonatas. When increasing concert tours eventually took him away from Vienna for good, he turned to writing mostly display pieces for piano like his celebrated "Alexander Variations," Op. 32, or the Concerto in G Minor, Op. 60, and *Concerto pathétique,* Op. 93. After

57. Moscheles' long, close friendship with Mendelssohn (from 1824) is richly documented throughout both MOSCHELES and the many letters in MENDELSSOHN/ Moscheles.

58. E.g., cf. MOSCHELES II 23–24, 35–36, 45, 224–25.

59. Cf. MOSCHELES II 43, 203.

60. Cf. MOSCHELES I 295, 316, 319; II 52–53, 172, 213, 219, 228–29, 243, 260, 266, 297–98.

61. See the comparison of Moscheles, Hummel, and W. A. Mozart "the Younger" in AMZ XXII (1828) 369; but see, also, MOSCHELES I 28, 22, 241–42.

62. According to MOSCHELES I 99–100 and 131, though not mentioned in most reference works.

63. MOSCHELES I 4.

about 1840 and decreasing public performances[64] he devoted himself especially to songs and to writing more of those fine etudes, which, as with Czerny and Cramer, are mainly what keep his name alive today. The few sonatas from his later years are all duos that seem to have been written as much to satisfy his love for sociability as his later concert needs.

Out of the 173 published works or sets of pieces that his widow tabulated,[65] Moscheles left only 9 sonatas (5 per cent); besides which should be mentioned an early, three-movement piano sonatina in G, Op. 4 (or Op. 6, 1810); one early, apparently unpublished sonata each for P & Vn and P & Bn, according to the biography;[66] and a "Grande Sonate" in E♭, Op. 35, in four movements, variously arranged in 1815 for P alone, for P & Vn, Vc, Fl, & 2 Hns, and for 4 hands at one and at two pianos, from his sextet Op. 35.[67] The four solo sonatas began with Op. 22 in D (Vienna: Mechetti, between 1811 and 1813), a weak three-movement piece that evidently aroused too little interest to get special mention either in MOSCHELES or contemporary reviews.[68] The next solo sonata in numerical order, *Eine charakteristische Sonate* in B♭, Op. 27 (Vienna: Artaria, 1814), did get mentioned at least in the biography,[69] though only for the occasion its fuller German title commemorated—"Sentiments in Vienna Upon the Return of His Majesty Francis I, Emperor of Austria . . . in the Year 1814." Although the music of this equally banal, square-cut sonata is not other-

64. Cf. MOSCHELES I 221–22.

65. MOSCHELES II 302–11; the list has errors; also, dates are lacking but do appear in several instances in earlier pp. of the biography. One main source for this tabulation seems to have been VERZEICHNISS MOSCHELES, a thematic index of pub. works up to *ca.* 1860. Cf., also, the full list in PAZDÍREK XIX 826–32.

66. MOSCHELES I 13; but these may only be alternative listings, respectively, for the Son. for P & Fl, Op. 44, and the "Grand Duo concertant" for P & Vc-or-Bn, Op. 34.

67. Egert/FRÜHROMANTIKER 139–46 provides a brief discussion, with exx., of the solo sons., including Op. 35; but since Hummel's *Grand Septuor* Op. 74 did not appear until 1816, Op. 35 was not an imitation of it; only later could Moscheles have referred to Op. 35 as "a light youthful effort, not to be compared with Hummel's work" (MOSCHELES I 20). The 1963 diss. Heussner/MOSCHELES (by the authoress, née Schmidt, of the earlier article on Moscheles in MGG IX 617–20) is a more detailed historic and style study that includes unpub. letters and other new biographic information, the chamber works and concertos with piano, as well as all the solo and 4-hand P sons.; the latter are analyzed by mvt. types, with bibl., charts, and exx., on pp. 52–93.

68. Among the scarce copies today, one is listed in Cat. BRUXELLES IV 210 and one is to be found in a "complete" 8-vol. set of Moscheles' solo and chamber piano works (with all sons. through Op. 79) at the Library of Congress (M3.1/M85), pub. in Paris, *ca.* 1835? (cf. MENDELSSOHN/Moscheles 130 on Schlesinger's "complete" ed.; Hopkinson/PARISIAN 113 on Société musicale), by the Société pour la Publication de Musique Classique et Moderne.

69. MOSCHELES I 12.

wise programmatic, its two outer movements carry further inscriptions —"Expression of Inner Delight Upon the Glorious Return of His Majesty" and "Rejoicing Over Favored Austria"—and its middle movement is a set of variations on Nägeli's "Freut Euch des Lebens" ("Life Let Us Cherish"; following by about 7 years Wölfl's variations on the same theme in his technically difficult sonata "Non plus ultra"; SCE 563).[70]

The third of his four solo examples is Moscheles' *Grosse Sonate* in E, Op. 41, composed in 1816 (and pub. in Vienna by Steiner not later than 1819). Dedicated to Beethoven, it is more original, intimate, easygoing, and free of empty passagework than its predecessors.[71] There is, however, little contrast or Beethovian development of the ideas in its four movements (F-"Minuetto o Scherzo"-M-"Rondo scherzando"), the finale being the most ingratiating and convincing of the cycle. The last of these solo sonatas is the one that has come nearest to surviving today and the one "thought by [Moscheles] himself and competent judges to be among his best works"—Op. 49, *Sonate mélancolique* in f♯ (Offenbach: André, 1822?), the "subject" of which had "occurred to him [in 1814] while giving a lesson, [and] was worked out with particular pleasure."[72] This work is one of the surprisingly few one-movement sonatas of consequence from the 19th century (SSB VI). But unlike Liszt's Sonata in b, it consists not of several movements within a movement but a single movement of 247 measures that approximates "sonata form." The "sonata form" divides asymmetrically, tending to make it cumulative, with 45 per cent going to the exposition, 25 to the development, 26 to the recapitulation, and 4 to the coda.

Even though there is that distinctive "subject" (mss. 1–19), an extended bridge (mss. 20–44), a well-prepared second theme (mss. 45–79), and a chain of four differentiated closing ideas (mss. 80–109), most of the material in Op. 49 derives from or maintains the "mélancolique" lyricism of the opening, presaging Moscheles' own composition advice in 1859 "always to express some one definite thought, be it serious or gay, cheerful or anxious."[73] Only the start of the closing section, with its sudden swish of 16th-note scales, achieves enough melodic contrast

70. The Paris ed. cited in the previous fn. omits all of the programmatic inscriptions in Moscheles' Op. 27.

71. A complimentary review is cited in Heussner/MOSCHELES 54.

72. MOSCHELES I 13; cf., also, I 221, II 266 (Liszt's playing of Op. 49 in 1859) and 304 (but Weinmann/ARTARIA does not list this work). Our pub. year for Op. 49 is based on its André plate no. 4407, as in Deutsch/NUMMERN 6; Heussner/ MOSCHELES 56 cites a Cappi ed. with plate no. 1095 that also falls in 1822, also high praise of Op. 49 from F. Hiller. Mod. ed.: Newman/THIRTEEN-m 162 (with preface, pp. 25–26).

73. MOSCHELES II 267.

to contribute any appreciable structural tension. More structural tension obtains through clear tonal organization (basically f♯-A/a-C-a-dominant pedal/f♯-D-F♯), carried out in well-balanced phrases and implemented by skillful, logical harmony. There are also a few strategically located third relationships, such as the almost Wagnerian climax on an F triad (ms. 38) four measures before the cadence in A that prepares the second theme. The regularity of the phrase syntax still weighs heavy, though relief comes in an occasional unsquare phrase (e.g., mss. 17–19), or in progressive shortening of phrase elements for cumulative drives to a tonal goal. The latter procedure (as at mss. 153–62) and some contrapuntal exchanges (mss. 132–38) recall similar techniques used by Beethoven (as in Op. 57/i/110–30 and Op. 28/i/195–206), but also define the limit to which Moscheles actually developed his ideas. The style of this music is somewhat eclectic. Thus, the first theme, descending over broken chords in open position (mss. 1–8), suggests Ries's Op. 26/iii (as noted earlier). The closing section begins in the salon style of the *leggermente* close in Weber's Op. 39/i, and passes from one idea into the next much as Mozart might do in a closing section (e.g., K. 300k/iii/65–90). And the triplet figuration that embellishes the restatement of the second theme (Ex. 18) brings Beethoven to mind again, this time the corresponding passage in Op. 53/i/43–53.

Moscheles' other five sonatas, each of which enjoyed considerable success, are all duos, three with a second *concertante* instrument and two for P-duet. Of the former, the *Grande Sonate concertante* in A, Op. 44, for P & Fl was another early work, published by Artaria in 1818. The *Sonata concertante* in G, Op. 79, for P & Fl-or-Vn, published by Kistner in Leipzig in 1828, won an enthusiastic review in 1830 that preferred it "even" to Op. 44 for its consistent musical significance in all three movements, over and above its dexterous passagework.[74] And the Sonata in E, Op. 121, for P & Vc-or-Vn (or P-duet) was a late work, composed in 1850–51 (about the time Moscheles was finding "a wild overgrown forest" in Chopin's cello sonata),[75] and published within a year by Kistner. This last was dedicated to Schumann, who replied with cordial thanks for Moscheles' earlier encouragement and inspiration, in keeping with earlier praise for him (but without any detailed reference to his sons.).[76] It was arranged for violin and so played by Ferdinand David.

74. AMZ XXXII 669–70 (G. W. Fink).

75. MOSCHELES II 172, 213, 215, 218; cf. SSB XII.

76. MOSCHELES I 24–25; Schumann/SCHRIFTEN I 114–15 (1835) and 360–63 (1838) present Schumann's 2 main reviews of Moscheles.

Ex. 18. From Ignaz Moscheles' *Sonate mélancolique,* Op. 49
(after the Société . . . ed. at the Library of Congress).

The *Grande Sonate* in E♭, Op. 47, for P-duet was composed early, in
1819 (not 1816),[77] and published that same year by Artaria, with a
dedication to Archduke Rudolph (SCE 524), "who played it in musician-
like style at first sight with him." [78] Mendelssohn, Chopin, Ferdinand
Hiller, and probably Liszt were among those who also played it with
him.[79] The success with Chopin in Paris was so great and so frequent,
including a command repetition of this work in 1839 for the Royal
Family at Saint-Cloud, that it "came at last to be called and only
known by the name of 'La Sonate.' " [80] Finally, Moscheles' *Grande
Sonate symphonique* in b, Op. 112, for four hands, was composed in
Paris in 1845 (this time to be played at court with daughter Emily)
and published by Kistner, among others, in 1846, after the proofs had
been read by Mendelssohn.[81] One reviewer in 1847 welcomed this
revival of the four-hand idiom, with all its valued social intimacies,
and expressed his preference for the final two movements—a "Scherzoso
alla tedesca antica" that is "charming" and "witty," and a finale based

77. Heussner/MOSCHELES 54–55.

78. MOSCHELES I 23, 221.

79. MOSCHELES I 274; II 57–60, 88, 133, 265–66. Cf., also, Schumann/SCHRIFTEN
I 114.

80. MOSCHELES II 60; Heussner/MOSCHELES 55.

81. MOSCHELES II 149, 154; MENDELSSOHN/Moscheles 261, 269; HALLÉ 108. The
work got several passing mentions in RGM about this time.

on the chorale "Lob, Ehr' und Preis"—for they give "a glimpse into the romantic world of the newer tone poem," whereas the two first movements show more skill than youthful fire and reflect the "older period." [82]

Schubert and the Beethovian Standard

Among all who worked in the shadow of Beethoven, and among all his other contemporaries and near successors, too, it was **Franz Schubert** (1797–1828) who, though scarcely acknowledged or mentioned by these others, "understood most clearly and felt most deeply the content and force of Beethoven's music." [83] That generalization suggests that it might have been more appropriate, following our designations of Ries, Czerny, and Moscheles as "Direct Beethoven Transmitters," to head this next section "Schubert, the Prime Beethoven Transmitter." But such a heading would underplay Schubert's originality and genius in his own right, as well as his importance here, along with Brahms, as one of the two Viennese masters of the 19th-century sonata after Beethoven. Furthermore, even without guessing his own future historical eminence, Schubert himself might well have protested such a classification. For, besides being a self-avowed, although shy and distant, "Worshipper and Admirer" of Beethoven,[84] he also tended to belittle himself in those few references to Beethoven that turn up in his letters, hinting at a certain despair if not actual envy.[85]

The relationships between Beethoven and Schubert, both biographic and musical, have received considerable attention.[86] How much the two men actually met and how much notice Beethoven took of Schubert's music, if any, remain moot questions. But there can be no question that Schubert knew much of Beethoven's music well, almost certainly including each sonata about as rapidly as it appeared.[87] Nor

86a

82. NZM XXVI (1847) 41–42 (initialed "1"); echoed in brief in AMZ XLIX (1847) 691–92; cf., also, Heussner/MOSCHELES 57.

83. Frimmel/SCHUBERT 410.

84. Deutsch/SCHUBERT-D 221 and 255. Among numerous corroborations by his friends, cf. Deutsch/SCHUBERT-D 228; Deutsch/SCHUBERT-M 19, 26, 98, 121, 126, 180.

85. E.g., cf. Deutsch/SCHUBERT-D 64, 265, 339; cf., also, the observations of Josef Hüttenbrenner and Josef von Spaun in Deutsch/SCHUBERT-M 76, 77, 128.

86. Kreissle/SCHUBERT I 258–69 already summarizes most of the conflicting evidence for personal relations and meetings; cf., also, Nohl/SCHUBERT, Deutsch/ SCHUBERT-M 328. Frimmel/SCHUBERT is a pioneer study of Beethoven's musical influences; Chusid/SCHUBERT-m 98–110 illuminates especially the influences on the "Unfinished Symphony."

87. Cf. Deutsch/SCHUBERT-M 180 (A. Hüttenbrenner), 299 (K. Holz), 363 (J. v. Spaun).

can there be any question that this music clearly influenced his own. The influence is manifest in the frank imitations of the student—for example, throughout Schubert's "Tragic Symphony" in c (1816; D. 417),[88] or the opening theme of the "Allegretto" from his Sonata in e/E for piano (1817; D. 566), which so closely resembles the opening theme of the similarly paced finale in Beethoven's Op. 90, likewise in e/E.[89] And the influence is still manifest in the more confident allusions by the mature composer—for example, in the homage or less conscious respect paid throughout the Sonata in c for piano (1828; D. 958), including at the start (Ex. 19) what must have been a deliberate reference to, as well as an intensified expansion of, the theme in Beethoven's 32 Variations in c (WoO 80).

Schumann, the most important and one of the most ardent champions of Schubert, referred to him in 1838 as the feminine counterpart of Beethoven (much as Picquot had related Boccherini to Haydn, sce 256).[90] The occasion was a review of the great four-hand Sonata in C (D. 812):

To [any-]one with a measure of feeling and training, Beethoven and Schubert will be [both] related and differentiated on the[ir] very first pages. Schubert is a maidenly character [when] held up alongside the other, much more garrulous, delicate, and spacious; alongside the other, [he is] a child who sports recklessly among the giants. Thus do these symphonic movements relate to those of Beethoven, and [yet?] in their intimacy [they] certainly could not be thought of as [being] other than by Schubert. To be sure, he too introduces his vigorous passages, he too calls up large forces; nevertheless, he keeps relating as woman to man, entreating and persuading where the other commands. But all this [applies] only in contrast to Beethoven; alongside others he is still man enough—in fact, the most daring and freethinking of the newer musicians.

Especially that concluding remark on a seeming bipolarity in Schubert's musical relationships bears significantly on the familiar but not always fruitful question of his historical identification. According to typical evaluations of the later 19th century, Schubert was best, most original, and most "Romantic" in his songs and other smaller pieces; but he was more tied to the past and more circumscribed by form

---

88. Cf. Abraham/SCHUBERT 48–52 (M. Carner).

89. Cf. Vetter/SCHUBERT I 181–82, 186; but this handsome, extended, little-noted study of 1953 fails by overemphasizing the Beethoven reminiscences, too often and on too little basis (cf. DMf VII [1954] 234–35 [H. J. Moser]).

90. Schumann/SCHRIFTEN I 330. On the psychological identification of masculine and feminine traits, mostly in Romantic composers—including "Table 1" showing Schubert as more masculine than Mendelssohn or Schumann, but less so than Chopin, Brahms, or Beethoven, among others—cf. Farnsworth/PHENOMENA.

Ex. 19. From the start of Franz Schubert's Sonata in c, D. 958 (after Schubert/WERKE-m X 204).

problems, without quite being able to amalgamate his exceptional lyricism, in his symphonies, sonatas, and other larger works.[91] More recently Einstein simplified and balanced Schubert's historical identification by labelling him "the Romantic Classic" (as distinguished from Mendelssohn, "the Romantic Classicist").[92] Other recent writers have gone further to reverse the 19th-century view by preferring to consider Schubert primarily as still a Classic.[93] In any case, there can be no doubt that all of these views have so emphasized Schubert in terms of Beethoven and other contemporaries that they have stood in the way of a full view of him in his own right. Put differently, much of the criticism of Schubert that has been negative actually reduces simply to ways in which he was not like Beethoven, although escaping the fate of being too much like Beethoven must have motivated Schubert quite as much as escaping the "Wagner maelstrom" was to worry Verdi and Debussy (ssв I).

91. E.g., cf. Bie/PIANOFORTE 225–30, including "the first musical Romantic" as a designation for Schubert; or, "Schubert" in BRITANNICA XX 103–5 (W. H. Hadow).

92. Einstein/ROMANTIC 89–91, 124–26.

93. E.g., Bücken/SCHUBERT; Vetter/SCHUBERT I 60–72; GROVE VII 570 (M. J. E. Brown).

An Uphill Century for Schubert's Sonatas

Further discussion of Schubert's relation to his environment would mean delving into his music once more and returning to those problems of style and form considered in Chapter VI. In that chapter the sonatas of Schubert, Schumann, Chopin, and Brahms have already served as the main reference points for the over-all consideration of style and form in the Romantic sonata, leaving primarily a recapitulation of the facts, cultivation, and circumstances of Schubert's sonatas to be brought up in the present chapter. But we may stop on the question of historical identification enough longer here to note in particular some changing attitudes toward Schubert's sonatas since his own day. Unlike Haydn, Mozart, Beethoven, and Clementi, who saw most or all of their own sonatas published while they were still alive (SCE 464, 484, 509, 742–45), Schubert saw only about a fifth of his completed sonatas in print (as detailed shortly).[94] And to judge by extant programs, correspondence, and other pertinent documents, none of his sonatas, not even these in print, ever got performed in public while he was alive.[95] But (as also will be detailed shortly) at least five of them did get private performances before enthusiastic groups, some given by Schubert himself, and two of the sonatas published in his lifetime did win attention through substantial, largely favorable reviews.

Yet further interest in Schubert's sonatas developed remarkably little throughout the century after his death. Schumann's general evaluation, only six years after (1834), already shows the slight reservation that was to increase rather than diminish: Though few knew Schubert and then mainly his songs, and though he "may turn out to be even more original in his songs than in his instrumental works, we value these [latter] just as much for [being] thoroughly musical and original in their own right." [96] In a pioneer article of 1862, probably by Selmar Bagge,[97] Schumann's enthusiasm was the starting point. The author had noted little subsequent interest in Schubert's instrumental music, as confirmed by so little evidence of its posthumous influence. He saw

94. All of Schubert's lifetime pubs. are listed in Deutsch/SCHUBERT-D 938–46.

95. All of Schubert's works performed publicly during his lifetime are listed in Deutsch/SCHUBERT-D 934–38. These do include such related types as the String Quartet in a (D. 804), the P Trio in E♭ (D. 929), the Fantasy for Vn & P in C (D. 934), and the String Quartet in G/i (D. 887); cf. Deutsch/SCHUBERT-B 178 for the facs. of a public program in 1828 that included the trio and later quartet.

96. Schumann/SCHRIFTEN I 124, 125.

97. Bagge/SCHUBERT.

Schubert's sonatas as being somewhat interrelated with fantasias, as showing more concern for content than form (with the finales sometimes growing tedious), as imitating orchestral sonorities in their keyboard writing, and as achieving less sustained passion than Beethoven's sonatas. Seven years later (1869), Kreissle, who as yet knew the "Unfinished Symphony" only by hearsay from the "initiated," gave passing mention to a few of Schubert's solo piano sonatas, adding in one instance that it "is impossible to contemplate without emotion and wonder these precious results of quiet honest industry, which, in the majority of instances, were not to be reckoned amongst the artistic treasures of the world until long after Schubert's death." [98] In another early article, written in 1873 on Schubert's solo and duet sonatas, Adolf Bernhard Vogel still noted their neglect as against the popularity of his songs and quoted Schumann's poetic praise of them at some length.[99] Concurring in the praise, Vogel cautioned only that Schubert's inspired outpourings had been those of a youthful idealist who lacked the mature logic of thematic manipulation in which Haydn, Mozart, and Beethoven had excelled.

The well-grounded Swiss writer Arnold Niggli surveyed the available solo sonatas five years later (1878), calling them the least known of Schubert's piano works and virtually unknown in concert.[100] Although their lyricism—so effective in Schubert's smaller vocal and instrumental pieces—could not cope with the "dialectic" such as Niggli had found in Beethoven, the beauties of melody, harmony, sonority, and texture that Schumann had praised must not go unrecognized. In 1895 John Shedlock wrote what now seems like a more balanced view of the sonatas.[101] Yet as late as 1903, Alfred Mello, in a somewhat more detailed article on the piano sonatas, again lauded Schubert as a genius of melody whose incomparable songs as well as his symphonies and chamber music had become well known, but (still) not his sonatas.[102] These last Mello found to be more homophonic than Beethoven's (for Schubert was "no outstanding contrapuntist") and to be blessed with a fine sense of piano sonority, harmony, and melody, although the melody sometimes seemed obscured to him by the excessively long phrases.

98. Kreissle/SCHUBERT I 257–58, 135. It was about this time (1868) that Liszt called Schubert's sons. a "glorious treasure" but did not hesitate to make what he felt were needed changes in them (LISZT LETTERS II 164–65).

99. Vogel/SCHUBERT.

100. Niggli/SCHUBERT.

101. Shedlock/SONATA 198–206. But among Englishmen even George Grove had been markedly unreceptive to the sons. in 1882, as quoted in Brown/SCHUBERT 344–45.

102. Mello/SCHUBERT.

Meanwhile, Schubert's sonatas themselves had not been quite that inaccessible. By the mid-19th century some two-thirds of the completed ones had been made available by publishers in Austria and Germany.[103] From about that time on, nearly half of them became available in England (especially Charles Hallé's ed. for Chappell and E. Pauer's for Augener) and in France (especially in Richault's early, incomplete "Collection complète").[104] Furthermore, we read of Charles Hallé (who had played all the Beethoven sonatas in 1861; sce 527) playing all of Schubert's published sonatas "repeatedly" in public from 1863 on, in London,[105] and of Charles Alkan venturing to play the whole of Op. 78 in G, D. 894, in Paris in 1875 (only to evoke the familiar complaint of excessive length from the reviewer).[106] However, reservations about the sonatas continued to prevail, even to swell, through the first quarter of the present century. As a sample, here is what the American teacher and author Leland Hall wrote in 1915:

> The sonatas are for the most part unsatisfactory as such. In such extended forms there is need of an intellectual command of the science of music, and a sense of great proportions, both of which Schubert lacked. Hence the separate movements, the first and even more often the last, are loose and rambling in structure, and too long for the work as a whole. There is so little cohesion in the group that one may in most cases take the individual movements quite out of it and play them with perfect satisfaction.[107]

In this statement, or more general statements such as Parry had made in 1896 and d'Indy in 1909 about Schubert's lack of formal training, the use of Beethoven as the primary criterion is still implied if not mentioned.[108] Such statements tie in, too, with that other most frequent negative reaction to Schubert's sonatas (and sometimes his other larger instrumental works)—the feeling that the lyricism taken over from his songs became too much of a good thing, not wholly appropriate, especially in its tendencies toward static A-B-A designs, to the tight muscular development of pithy ideas expected in a "true" (for which read Haydn, Mozart, or Beethoven) "sonata form." [109]

103. Cf. the full lists of Schubert's sons. below; also, Brown/SCHUBERT 318–22 for a brief historical survey of Schubert eds. in these countries.
104. For scattered bits of information about these often elusive 19th-c. eds., cf. George Grove in the first ed. of GROVE III (1882) 357–58; Prod'homme/SCHUBERT 495–96, 505–6, 508–10; Brown/SCHUBERT 341–42; PAZDÍREK "S" 399; Cat. ROYAL 316; MGG XII 165, 168–70, 173–74 (K. Hortschansky).
105. GROVE (first ed.) III 358 (G. Grove). Cf., also, Shedlock/SONATA 205.
106. Prod'homme/SCHUBERT 510. Cf., also, Brown/SCHUBERT 324–26; Moser/JOACHIM I 105.
107. Hall/PIANOFORTE 195.
108. Parry/EVOLUTION 287; d'Indy/COURS II/1 402. Cf. Brown/SCHUBERT 195–96.
109. Cf. Salzer/SCHUBERT (especially pp. 98–101 and 124–25) and Adler/SCHUBERT 480.

New Interest Since the Schubertian Centenary

This summary review of a century of relatively negative attitudes and slow cultivation in the history of Schubert's sonatas is needed here not only as a partial background for their understanding but because their full acceptance—such as the question of which if any of them make consistently satisfying cycles throughout—is by no means universal even among today's writers, performers, and listeners.[110] Furthermore, so close was the proximity of time, place, and prevailing idiom that we may never be able quite to dispel that tendency to weigh Schubert in terms of Beethoven. However, a decided improvement in both the quantity and quality of interest in Schubert's sonatas did occur with the flurry of writings around 1928 that marked the centenary of his death.[111] Of major significance, equal in its way to Richard Capell's admirable book on Schubert's songs one year later, was Hans Költzsch's dissertation on Schubert's piano sonatas, published in 1927,[112] which provided both the bibliographic and style-critical foundations for further studies of the sonatas. Among the latter may be singled out the discussion of 1934 in Egert/FRÜHROMANTIKER 71–92 (with considerable exception taken to Költzsch's style-critical conclusions), the survey of 1947 in Abraham/SCHUBERT by Kathleen Dale (Dale/SCHUBERT 129–47), the dissertation of 1961 on the chamber music by Martin Chusid (Chusid/SCHUBERT), the dissertation of 1963 on text and performance problems in the sonatas by J. L. Taggart (Taggart/ SCHUBERT), the dissertation of 1965 based on style-statistical analyses by A. L. Hanna (Hanna/SCHUBERT), the chapter of 1966 in Brown/ ESSAYS 197–216 on authenticity, order and number of movements, and chronology of the solo piano sonatas, and the series of brief form analyses done in 1967 by Walter Riezler (Riezler/SCHUBERT), including most of the sonatas.[113]

110. Thus, Gillespie/KEYBOARD 204–6 continues to echo 19th-century views; Kirby/ KEYBOARD 237–44 does not. In the late 1930's Nadia Boulanger still was doing pioneer work through her lecture-recitals in this country centered around the question of why Schubert's sonatas are not played more.

111. Pertinent samples in special Schubert periodical issues of that year are Souchay/SCHUBERT in ZfMW, Salzer/SCHUBERT in SzMW, Bauer/SCHUBERT in MQ.

112. Költzsch/SCHUBERT; abstract in the reports from the international Schubert congress of 1928 (KONGRESS SCHUBERT 199–208). Cf. Kahl/SCHUBERTSCHRIFTTUMS 95; Abraham/SCHUBERT 6–7.

113. The extensive literature on Schubert is covered exhaustively and systematically for the first century after his death in Kahl/SCHUBERT (cf. Kahl/SCHUBERT- SCHRIFTTUMS) and brought up to date as late as 1963 for the more important publications, in MGG XII 174–85 (W. Pfannkuch), with further diss. listed in Schaal/ DISSERTATIONEN and Hewitt/DISSERTATIONS. A basic Schubert bibliography appears in Deutsch/SCHUBERT-D 962–65 (with additions in the 1964 German ed., pp. 615–18); cf., also, Abraham/SCHUBERT 255–62 (A. H. King).

Among other more recent studies of Schubert's styles and forms that bear tangentially on his sonatas are Maurice Brown's book of 1954 on his variations (Brown/VARIATIONS), Georg Winkler's dissertation of 1956 on the unjustly maligned or inadequately recognized polyphony in his piano writing (Winkler/SCHUBERT),[114] and Elmer Seidel's dissertation of 1963 on enharmony in his larger forms (Seidel/ENHARMONIK). And, of course, no work on Schubert can proceed today without constant recourse—as already in the present discussion—to those four voluminous, complementary mines of primary information provided over more than a half-century (1913–64) by the late Otto Erich Deutsch, including all discoverable letters and other lifetime documents, posthumous personal recollections, and iconographic matter, richly annotated throughout, plus a critical though abbreviated thematic index.[115] The complete edition of Schubert's music prepared in the late 19th century (pub. 1884–97) by Mandyczewski, Brahms, and others, furnished a largely satisfactory edition of the sonatas, with but few omissions.[116] Undoubtedly, the needed improvements will be made in the sonata volumes of the *Neue Ausgabe* that has been planned by the Internationalen Schubert-Gesellschaft and launched in 1964 with Deutsch's new German edition of the documents and letters.[117] Meanwhile, though each has yet to be completed with a third volume, two two-volume sets of Schubert's solo piano sonatas have appeared recently in excellent critical editions, one prepared in 1958 by Erwin Ratz and one in 1961 by Paul Mies.[118]

Schubert's Sonatas in Toto

The but thirty-one years of Schubert's outwardly uneventful life were brightened chiefly by those wonderful, at times almost nightly, "Schubertiaden" with his numerous artistic friends,[119] at which must have taken place most of whatever performances there were of his sonatas (as mentioned above). During the 17 years from age 15 (1812)

114. Winkler concentrates especially on "latent" polyphony in the sons.; cf. pp. 33, 52–53, 99, 124.

115. Deutsch/SCHUBERT-D, -M, -B, and -I, respectively. Cf. the prefaces to each of these vols.; also, MR XIV (1953) 257-61 (Brown) and Brown/SCHUBERT 347–48.

116. Schubert/WERKE-m VIII, IX, X, XI, and XXI. Cf. the tabulations below; also, Deutsch/COLLECTED and MGG XII 164–74 (including other eds.; [K. Hortschansky]).

117. Cf. NOTES XXII (1966) 698–99 and 1231. At about the same time a complete, unaltered reprint of Schubert/WERKE-m was well under way at low cost from Dover Publications of New York.

118. Ratz/SCHUBERT-m, with preface (cf. the detailed collation of texts in Taggart/SCHUBERT 32–55); Mies/SCHUBERT-m, with prefaces.

119. For sample accounts, cf. Deutsch/SCHUBERT-D 302–4, 571–72, 630–31.

to within 54 days of his death (Nov. 19, 1828) he left a total of 33 extant solo and duo works, complete or incomplete, that were called or have been otherwise identified as "sonatas." These 33 represent scarcely more than 2 per cent of his total known output of 1,515 pieces large and small.[120] Of the 33 sonatas, 20 are unquestionably complete as they stand, 5 may or may not be complete as we now have them, depending upon identification of missing movements as well as certain questions of tonality, and 8 are more or less clearly incomplete (including one, D. 567, that was a first draft of a complete son., D. 568). These last Schubert probably left incomplete for no more or better reason than seems to resolve out of all the theorizing about the why of the "Unfinished Symphony"[121]—nearly as much, in fact, as that about the intended recipient of Beethoven's letter to his "Eternally Beloved" (SCE 518). In short, Schubert seems to have left from 24 to as many as 39 per cent of all his sonatas (or up to 44 per cent of his solo piano sonatas) incomplete simply because he got sidetracked by some other interest. The statistics are more characteristic than not of Schubert's larger forms, including both the symphonies and the quartets.

Of course, with Schubert "incomplete" applies sometimes only in the most literal sense. As we shall see (e.g., Son. in f♯, D. 571, 570), he was satisfied simply to drop some movements at the apparent start of the recapitulation in the first drafts. Furthermore, four of the sonatas that may or may not be complete as they stand raise questions because their presumed or extant first and final movements are not in the same key (D. 48, 154/157, 279, 557, 968). Such mismatches would be rare but not unprecedented (SCE 138). An example is the solo piano Sonata in A♭/E♭, D. 557, with two manuscript sources seeming to confirm that the final "Allegro" in E♭ does constitute that work's finale.[122] But if this example is valid, why not so regard the sonatas in E/B and C/a, D. 157 and 279, each of which ends with a "Menuetto" in the then frequent manner (SCE 161–62), yet in a new key, without any other finale being known?[123]

Other of Schubert's sonatas have raised questions of completeness and identification because he wrote the movements in separate manu-

<hr>

120. Cf. the statistics in Deutsch/SCHUBERT-I xvi–xvii.

121. Cf. Abraham/SCHUBERT 63–64 (M. Carner); Brown/SCHUBERT 116–24. But Chusid/SCHUBERT-III 9–10 and 98–110 suggests that Schubert was experiencing an instrumental form crisis, perhaps under new Beethoven influences, during the period when Schubert wrote most of his truly incomplete works, 1817–23.

122. Cf. Költzsch/SCHUBERT 4–5.

123. The autographs give only contradictory hints as to whether an additional mvt. was intended in D. 157 and 279 (cf. Költzsch/SCHUBERT 4; Brown/ESSAYS 200–201).

scripts or someone after him split up the manuscripts (D. 566 and 506), or he left two versions of the work (D. 567), or the several movements were originally published as separate pieces (D. 459).[124] Perhaps some further works not yet recognized as sonatas lie scattered as separate pieces that should be united and admitted to the fold, too. Thus, Schumann insisted in 1838 that the four Impromptus Op. 142 (D. 935; 1827)—in f, A♭, B♭, and f—comprise a sonata in all but the name,[125] and Einstein has agreed enthusiastically.[126] But Brown has disagreed peremptorily,[127] arguing that the key of No. 3 is "an awkward one to square with the others" (in spite of several, more remote relationships in Schubert's unequivocal sonatas) and that "the first piece is certainly not a 'first movement' from any formal point of view" (debatable in any case and hardly tenable in view of the precedents in Beethoven's Opp. 101, 109, and 110, or Schubert's own Op. 164, D. 537). Brown is more inclined to view as the two movements of a projected, unfinished four-hand piano sonata Schubert's two extraordinary, last pieces in that scoring, the "Allegro" in a, D. 947, first published by Diabelli about 1840 as "Lebensstürme," Op. 144, and the Rondo in A, D. 951, written for Artaria and published by that firm only three weeks after Schubert's death, as "Grand Rondeau," Op. 107.[128] A work referred to in 1839 by Schubert's brother Ferdinand as a four-hand Sonata in e♭ of 1828 probably was an error for the *Drei Klavierstücke* for two hands of that year, of which No. 1 is in e♭.[129]   129a

In addition, there are works by Schubert that have suggested sonatas even where no problem of bibliography or original intentions arises. Thus, the cyclic structure and emotional range of three of his greatest "fantasias" have prompted writers, from his own day on, to ask why each is or is not like a sonata. His celebrated, four-movement "Wanderer Fantasy" in C, Op. 15, for P solo (D. 760; 1822) brought a promptly favorable review in Vienna in 1823, but one that seems to puzzle over its freedoms as though, without any specific mention, the then conventional sonata were its measuring stick.[130] Although Schu-

124. A detailed survey of these problems occurs in Taggart/SCHUBERT 225–62.

125. Schumann/SCHRIFTEN I 371–72.

126. Einstein/SCHUBERT 283–85, with trans. of most of Schumann's review.

127. Brown/SCHUBERT 269–70.

128. Brown/SCHUBERT 286–87 (but with no source for the idea of the projected sonata). Schumann's youthful wonderment over the Rondo, in a letter of Nov. 6, 1829, to Friedrich Wieck, may be read in Schumann/JUGENDBRIEFE 82–83.

129. Cf. Deutsch/SCHUBERT-D 919, 924; Brown/ESSAYS 264–66.

130. Trans. in full in Deutsch/SCHUBERT-D 272–78; still echoed in Kreissle/SCHUBERT II 210. In Hanslick/WIEN I 382, Op. 15 is actually referred to as "Sonate." Cf., also, MT XIII (1868) 318.

mann at the age of eighteen seemed only to rejoice in the freedoms of this work,[131] a century later Marc-André Souchay analyzed it in detail to show that it actually revealed the close-knit logic of the Classic masters, differing from the sonata in its emphasis more on melodic variation than development.[132] The still freer, four-movement Fantasy in C for P & Vn, Op. 159 (D. 934; 1827) brought similarly early and puzzled reactions, although mostly curt and irritated this time.[133] And though the final, great Fantasy in f for P-duet, Op. 103 (D. 940; 1828), seems not to have been reviewed after its early publication in 1829, recently it too has been considered in relation to the sonata, in a perceptive bibliographic and music analysis by Brown.[134]

The converse of all these evaluations in terms of the sonata is found in the few instances where Schubert's bona fide "sonatas" are viewed in orchestral or symphonic terms. Schumann fairly insisted in 1838 that "vierhändige Sonate" on the autograph of what the publisher called "Grand Duo" in C, Op. 140 (D. 812), was a misnomer for "symphony" and that the huge work demanded orchestration,[135] which, indeed, it got from Joachim in 1855. Joachim (and perhaps at least two later orchestraters of this work) probably got the idea from this statement by Schumann,[136] but neither Schumann nor Joachim yet identified the work with the as yet unrecognized problem of the "Gastein Symphony." [137] The possibility, however improbable, has even been raised that the sketches for this symphony may have been used for the solo piano Sonata in D, Op. 53 (D. 850), also placed in Gastein in 1825.[138]

Schubert's Solo Piano Sonatas

Although Schubert left his manuscripts in better order than many another composer, and usually dated them (to the pleasant surprise of

131. Diary entry for August 13, 1828, as reproduced in the 1964 German ed. of Deutsch/SCHUBERT-D, p. 532.

132. Souchay/SCHUBERT. Cf., also, Vetter/SCHUBERT I 289–91; Brown/SCHUBERT 124–25.

133. Trans. in Deutsch/SCHUBERT-D 715–16; cf. p. 767. Cf., also, Cobbett/CHAMBER II 360 (W. Kahl).

134. Brown/ESSAYS 85–100.

135. Schumann/SCHRIFTEN I 329–30, echoed (again) in Kreissle/SCHUBERT II 217–18, endorsed in Tovey/ANALYSIS I 215–18, but protested in Einstein/SCHUBERT 240–42.

136. Cf. Moser/JOACHIM II 82; Brown/SCHUBERT 186–88 (but with an incorrect German title for Schubert's work).

137. As is wrongly stated in Deutsch/SCHUBERT-D 364–65 (but corrected in the 1964 German ed., p. 251) and in Deutsch/SCHUBERT-I 391. The duo was composed in 1824, in any case, and the supposedly lost symphony, D. 849, not until 1825. The recent identification of this symphony with the "Great Symphony in C," D. 944, in Brown/SCHUBERT 354–61 is convincing, and is made more so in ML XL (1959) 341–49.

138. Brown/SCHUBERT 356.

Schubert scholars), he still left enough questions to engender considerable bibliographic interest and speculation. The tabulation of
the solo piano sonatas that follows, like that of the ensemble sonatas
further below, derives from nearly every item of Schubert bibliography
singled out earlier, but especially from Költzsch/SCHUBERT 1–32, Ratz/
SCHUBERT, Deutsch/SCHUBERT-I, and Brown/ESSAYS 197–216. In short,
our tabulation is hardly the first and is not likely to be the last. The
chronology followed here, in spite of uncertainties that remain in the
order of Nos. 8, 9, and 15, is the one arrived at most recently, by Brown
(1966).[139] The tabulation also shows the uncertainties that remain in
the identification and inclusion of several of the movements, as well as
the incomplete or complete status of all the sonatas. The opus numbers
and the other early series numbers have little or no numerical logic,[140]
but are included here because of the frequent reference to them.[141] The
number of measures in each movement and each cycle is included for
several reasons besides the obvious value of comparing dimensions.
Deutsch regretted not being table to include them in his *Thematic
Catalogue*,[142] they are lacking in the Schubert/WERKE-m (as is true so
often, alas, in the older complete sets), and they give at least a hint of
how incomplete the incomplete movements are. Moreover, they are
needed for consideration of that familiar problem of "heavenly
length" [143] in Schubert's larger instrumental works.[144] And as a help
toward the same problem, representative performance times to the
nearest minute are given for each of the complete and all the substantial incomplete sonatas.[145]

Some of the circumstances surrounding the individual solo sonatas
should be mentioned now (referring to these sons., only for this
immediate discussion, by the chronological order number in the leftmost column of our tabulation). What we have listed as Nos. 1 and 2
from 1815, in E/B and C/a, actually followed by some three years
several earlier student sonatas[146] (not to mention his early string
quartets and symphonies) and already show more spirit and architec-

---

139. But in the last sentence of Brown/SCHUBERT 199 read "6" for "7" and add
the question of the crossed-out "1" as an early series number for D. 566 (Költzsch/
SCHUBERT 5, 31–32).

140. Cf. Költzsch/SCHUBERT 31–32.

141. For full bibliographic listings of the first eds. cited here cf. Cat. HIRSCH IV
191–253.

142. Cf. Deutsch/SCHUBERT-I xiv.

143. To use the well-known expression in Schumann/SCHRIFTEN I 463; cf. II 432.
Cf., also, Vrieslander/ORGANISCHE.

144. Cf. Mello/SCHUBERT for an early consideration of this problem.

145. The times are those of the fine Austrian pianist Friedrich Wuehrer in his
three recorded vols. of Schubert's "complete" P sons. (Vox Box Nos. 9–11).

146. Cf. Költzsch/SCHUBERT 20; Deutsch/SCHUBERT-M 127–28 (J. v. Spaun), 369.

Schubert's Solo Piano Sonatas

Chron. order	Key	Opus no.	Deutsch no(s).	Early series no.	Composed	First edition	Schubert/ WERKE-m	Now complete or inc.	Mvts.: tempos or types / Keys: mvt.-by-mvt. / mss.: mvt.-by-mvt.	Perform-ance time in minutes	Remarks
1	E/B?		154, 157		1815	*Werke*, 1888	X/1	inc.?	3: F -M -Mi / keys: E -e -B / 563: 251-112-200	17	finale in home key lacking?
2	C/a?		279	1	1815	*Werke*, 1888	X/2	inc.?	3: F -M-Mi / keys: C -F -a / 433: 211-80-142	15	finale in home key lacking?
3	E		459		1816	Klemm, 1843	XI/14	com.	5: F -Sc -S -Sc -F / keys: E -E -C -A -E / 712: 124-231-114-137-106	27	first pub. as *Fünf Klavierstücke*
4	a	164	537	7	1817	Spina, 1852?	X/6	com.	3: F -M -VF / keys: a -E -a / 707: 196-144-367	17	
5	Ab/Eb		557	2	1817	*Werke*, 1888	X/3	com.?	3: F-M-F / keys: Ab-Eb-Eb / 328: 99-96 -133	23	finale not in home key
6	Db		567		1817	*Werke*, 1897	XXI/9	inc.	3: F -M -F / keys: Db -c# -Db / 545: 238-122-168 (1855)		last 17 (?) mss. of iii completed but lost
7	Eb	122	568	3	1817	Pennauer, 1829	X/7	com.	4: F -M -Mi-F / keys: Eb -g -Eb -Eb / 705: 258-122-102-223	24	revision of D. 567; first pub. title: "Troisième grande Sonate"
8	c		994	(3?)	1817?	Brown/SCHUBERT, 1958		inc.	1: F / key: e / 38: 38		only a fragment

No.	e/E	iv =		1? (4?)			X/4 (i) XI/5/2 (iv)	com.?		16+	
9		145/2	566, 506		1817	piecemeal, 1848–1928	X/4 (i) XI/5/2 (iv)	com.?	4: M-F -Sc -Ro keys: e -E -Ab -E 879: 97-227-266-289		first pub. as complete unit: Dale/SCHUBERT-m (1948)
10	f#		571, 570	5	1817	Werke, 1897	XXI/10 & 20	i & iii inc.	3: F -Sc -F keys: f# -D -f# 427: 141-112-174		relation of mvts. not certain
11	B	147	575		1817	Diabelli, 1846	X/5	com.	4: F -M-Sc -F keys: B -E-G -B 637: 147-82-192-216	21	order originally F-Sc-M-F; first pub. title: "Grande Sonate"
12	C		613, 612		1818	piecemeal, 1870–97	XXI/11, XI/11	i & iii inc.	3: M -S -F? keys: C -E-C 297: 121-52-124		inclusion of ii uncertain; tempo of iii missing
13	f		625, 505		1818	Werke, 1897, 1898	XXI/12 (not ii) Rev. XI/5 (ii)	i & iv inc.	4: F -S -Sc -F keys: f -Db-E -f 693: 118-22-260-293	19	nearly completed
14	c#		655		1819	Werke, 1897	XXI/13	inc.	1: F key: c# 73: 73		only an exposition
15	A	120	664		1819?	J. Czerny, 1829	X/10	com.	3: F -M-F keys: A -D-A 424: 133-75-216	22	composing formerly dated 1825
16	a	143	784		1823	Diabelli, 1839	X/8	com.	3: F -M-F keys: a -F -a 625: 290-66-269	21	first pub. title: "Grande Sonate . . ."
17	a	42	845	1	1825	Pennauer, 1826	X/9	com.	4: M -M -Sc -Ro keys: a -C -a -a 1357: 311-181-316-549	31	first pub. title: "Première grande Sonate"
18	C		840		1825	Whistling, 1862	XXI/14	iii & iv inc.	4: M -M -Mi-Ro keys: C -c -Ab -C 897: 318-121-186-272	34	first pub. title: "Reliquie . . ."
19	D	53	850	2	1825	Artaria, 1826	X/11	com.	4: F -M -Sc -Ro keys: D -A -D -D 1007: 267-197-331-212	31	first pub. title: "Seconde grande Sonate"

Schubert's Solo Piano Sonatas (Continued)

Chron. order	Key	Opus no.	Deutsch no(s).	Early series no.	Composed	First edition	Schubert/ WERKE-m	Now complete or inc.	Mvts.: tempos or types Keys: mvt.-by-mvt. mss.: mvt.-by-mvt.	Perform-ance time in minutes	Remarks
20	G	78	894	4	1826	Haslinger, 1827	X/12	com.	4: M -M -Mi-F keys: G -D -b -G 900: 174-181-134-411	29	first pub. title: "Fantasie, Andante, Menuetto und Allegretto"
21	c		958	1	1828	Diabelli, 1838	X/13	com.	4: F -S -Mi-F keys: c -Ab-Eb -c 1226: 274-115-120-717	28	D. 958, 959, 960 originally pub. as "Drei grosse Sonaten"
22	A		959	2	1828	Diabelli, 1838	X/14	com.	4: F -M -Sc -Ro keys: A -f# -A -A 1136: 360-202-192-382	35	
23	Bb		960	3	1828	Diabelli, 1838	X/15	com.	4: M -M -Sc -F keys: Bb -c# -Bb -Bb 1255: 365-138-212-540	32	

tural wisdom than would be expected from even a gifted youth of
eighteen (until one remembers that "Erlkönig" was also to be composed in that same year). Furthermore, they already show more skill in
polyphony and thematic development than would be expected from
a composer commonly taken to be deficient in these very respects.
Schubert must have been advancing by leaps and bounds then. No. 1/i,
in which he anticipates some of his "Rossini-isms" of 1816–17,[147] is
clearly in better tonal and thematic control than its incomplete sketch
of only a few days earlier (Schubert/WERKE-m XXI/8). No. 2, composed
seven months later, reveals a decidedly more dramatic idea of the
sonata. Perhaps its advance in this sense explains why Schubert chose
to label it "Sonata I" on the autograph, looking toward a specially
numbered series of sonatas, as did Czerny (supra).[148]

With regard to No. 3, the identification of the Fünf Klavierstücke as
this Sonata in E is one of several bibliographic discoveries about the
Schubert sonatas that Ludwig Scheibler made early in this century,
although the confirmation in this instance took longer.[149] Since the
second version of the duet Sonata in c, D. 48, consists of five free sections, not movements, and since Schubert wrote no other sonatas with
more than four movements, he may not have intended that both
scherzos be retained in No. 3. Formerly the year of this work was put
as 1817, partly because of the exact recurrence of the last three
measures of the first movement in Schubert's song "Elysium," D. 584
(mss. 31–33), dated September, 1817.[150] But the recurrence seems more
like a coincidence of prolificity. The advance in tonal resources, keyboard writing, and general craftmanship is again conspicuous in No.
3.

No. 4 in a is the first of nine sonatas (including Son. for P & Vn in
A, D. 574), complete or incomplete, that date from Schubert's most
prolific sonata year, 1817.[151] A concise, mature, compelling work,[152] it

147. Cf. Abraham/SCHUBERT 19–20, 38 fn., 39–40 (M. Carner).
148. But cf. Költzsch/SCHUBERT 4. Efforts to identify a finale for this work remain
in question (cf. Brown/SCHUBERT 56 and Brown/ESSAYS 201).
149. Cf. Költzsch/SCHUBERT 10–11, 169; Brown/SCHUBERT 57. However, the reviewer of the 1843 ed., in AMZ XLVI (1844) 168–69, after objecting to certain eccentricities and signs of carelessness (as in several early reviews of Schubert) already
guessed that these 5 pieces might comprise a son.
150. Cf. Költzsch/SCHUBERT 11, 90–91.
151. Cf. the excellent summary in Brown/1817. A division of Schubert's sons.
into 3 periods is frequently suggested—in fact, argued at some length in Mason/
SCHUBERT—but the short total span, the bridging of some of the divisions by more
recent dating, and certain inconsistencies all tend to make such a division less
meaningful.
152. Cf. Truscott/UNITY (arguing warmly, at length, that the organic development in No. 4 is disregarded in Brown/SCHUBERT 60–61).

is, moreover, his earliest sonata to figure rather often in the pianist's repertoire today. The year 1817 has also proved to be the most complex year for bibliographers of Schubert's sonatas. No. 5 is that Sonata in Ab/Eb mentioned earlier for appearing to have a finale not in the original key, but otherwise of lesser musical interest. No. 6 is an incomplete first version, in a different key, of No. 7 in Eb, with further complexities in the inner movements.[153] In this neat, relatively cool sonata, as in the Symphony in Bb, D. 485, one already detects a certain neo-Classicism in Schubert, referring back to Haydn and Mozart more than to Beethoven. Following the mere fragment that is No. 8 in e,[154] No. 9 in e is a bibliographic nightmare in which, besides questions of first and second versions, each movement was first published separately over a period of eighty years before all four movements were issued together—if, indeed, they all do belong together and in the order thus far preferred—twenty years later in Dale/SCHUBERT-m.[155] The music of this sonata is stirring and convincing enough to justify these efforts to put it in final order.[156]

In No. 10 in f♯, still from 1817, the choice and order of movements is even less certain,[157] with the bare possibility added that the isolated "Andante" in A, D. 604, supplies "the missing slow movement." [158] Egert believes the first movement remained unfinished because its ethereal first theme proved unsuitable for sonata treatment.[159] Certainly the exceptional lyricism of this movement's ideas illustrates what Beethoven presumably would have rejected in comparable instrumental forms. Yet Schubert did develop these ideas here in his own way, and effectively. Furthermore, he might be said to have finished this movement in his own way. For, as in several other "unfinished" sonata movements, he seems merely to have stopped for the time being where the recapitulation is expected—in this instance,

153. Cf. Költzsch/SCHUBERT 7–9, 82–94; Truscott/VERSIONS (a detailed comparison); Brown/SCHUBERT 63–64; Ratz/SCHUBERT-m I 55 (facs. of the start in the autograph).

154. First published as a facs. in 1956 (cf. Brown/ESSAYS 205) and as an "edition" in Brown/SCHUBERT 58–59.

155. As usual, the main discoveries come from Scheibler and Költzsch (Költzsch/SCHUBERT 5–7). A further, detailed summary appears in Brown/1817 36–38, with more on the finale in Brown/DISCOVERIES 307–8, and Brown/MANUSCRIPTS 182; cf., also, Taggart/SCHUBERT 239–46 (but with errors and a largely indefensible support for accepting only i and ii in No. 9, à la Op. 90 of Beethoven).

156. Schubert's slight reworking of i is taken to show his own special interest in at least that mvt., in Einstein/SCHUBERT 129–30.

157. Cf. Költzsch/SCHUBERT 9, Brown/1817 40–41, Brown/MANUSCRIPTS 182, Brown/SCHUBERT 64–66.

158. This possibility, offered in Brown/ESSAYS 207, seems more plausible than the categorical identification of D. 604 with No. 19 (Son. in D, D. 850) in Einstein/SCHUBERT 250.

159. Egert/FRÜHROMANTIKER 78–80.

evidently at one of his not untypical returns by way of the subdominant, and in the supposed, similarly incomplete finale of this
sonata, at the tonic.

No. 11 in B was the last sonata of 1817 (if the lost, final autograph
actually dates from the same year as the extant preliminary version[160]). It was only the third unequivocally complete sonata of
that year, its bibliographic problems being relatively simple ones. The
celebrated virtuoso Thalberg became the dedicatee of this highly
sensitive, tightly motivic work when Diabelli published it eighteen years
after Schubert died. But whether Thalberg ever played it on any of his
many successful recitals could not be learned here. In any case, it got
only a half-hearted nine-line review when it appeared, a review that
suggests no more than a cursory glance at it.[161]

The two, "incomplete" sonatas of 1818 lack mainly and merely
recapitulations again. For the first, No. 12 in C, Scheibler and
Költsch once more have supplied the prime conjectures.[162] Brown
adds that its supposed "Adagio" was first published alone, probably
because it was the only completed movement, and that it apparently
belongs with the other two movements not only because it is dated in
the same month but because of stylistic consistencies and the fact
that Schubert was not writing single pieces at this time.[163] Deutsch
first established the association of the "Adagio" in D♭, D. 505, with
No. 13 in f,[164] but all four movements have yet to be printed together.
Költzsch, Einstein, and Vetter all found in this work, or what Brown
dubs "Schubert's appassionata," some vivid recollections of Beethoven's Op. 57 in f that do seem justified especially for the openings,
figuration, and sustained drive of the outer movements.[165]

Following another mere fragment, No. 14 in c♯, supposedly came
one other sonata from 1819, No. 15 in A, now one of the most
played of all Schubert's sonatas. Scheibler left no doubt that "1825"
for the composition of this work was an error starting with Schindler,[166] although he provided only a likely, educated guess when

160. Cf. Költzsch/SCHUBERT 9–10, Brown/1817 41–42.
161. AMZ XLII (1848) 531–32.
162. Költzsch/SCHUBERT 11–12.
163. Brown/MANUSCRIPTS 184. The "Andante" in A, D. 604, might fit as well in
No. 12 as in No. 10, although the key relationships would be less likely if, conversely, the "Adagio" in E, D. 612, were used in No. 10 rather than No. 12.
164. Cf. Deutsch/SCHUBERT-I 277–78, Brown/RECENT 356–57. The subjective objections in Vetter/SCHUBERT II 293–94 fall before Deutsch's facts.
165. Költzsch/SCHUBERT 94–100, Vetter/SCHUBERT I 284–85, Brown/SCHUBERT 67–68.
The recapitulation of the first mvt. and other, briefer missing passages are supplied by the ed. in Ratz/SCHUBERT-m I 70, simply by drawing upon what Schubert
had already written.
166. Cf. Deutsch/SCHUBERT-M 323.

he identified it with a sonata composed, during a visit to Steyr in the summer of 1819, for "Pepi" von Koller, who, Schubert wrote his brother Ferdinand, "is very pretty, plays the pianoforte well and is going to sing several of my songs." [167] Miss von Koller's talents may very well account for both the brilliance and the ingratiating tunefulness of this work,[168] which, like No. 7 in E♭, harks back neo-Classically more to Haydn and Mozart than to Beethoven. Its publication in Vienna only a year after Schubert's death brought no printed review that could be found here.

The only gap in Schubert's yearly production of sonatas seems to have occurred in the three years, from 1820 to 1822, preceding the eight solo and two ensemble examples of his last six years, 1823–28, all of which but one (D. 840) qualify as "completed" works. The first of these mature masterpieces was the second of his three fine solo sonatas in a, No. 16. Considering the terse, dramatic thrust of No. 16, one accepts its amended title "Grande Sonate" in the first published edition[169] more readily than the similar titles for most of the other first publications of Schubert's sonatas. Was it the sinewy, lean texture, exceptional concentration on single motives, and unpianistic broken octaves in the first movement, or merely fatigue at the end of a long review, that caused Schumann to brand this highly unified work not one of Schubert's best? [170] To be sure, by then, 1839, Schumann had already spent his superlatives on some of Schubert's greatest works, including several later sonatas, adding "how much we [tend to] judge men and artists always [only] by the best each has done." [171] Schubert, too, thought enough of No. 16 to make more exacting revisions than usual in the autograph.[172]

Schumann did write in glowing terms of No. 17,[173] Schubert's final sonata in a, which was also the first of his three solo sonatas to be published and evidently the best known while he was alive; and it is one of the few sonatas by him that could be found here on public recital programs before the Schubert/WERKE-m began to

167. Költzsch/SCHUBERT 12–13; Deutsch/SCHUBERT-D 121, -M 148. Cf. Brown/SCHUBERT 68–69, Brown/ESSAYS 210–11.

168. Yet it was called uninspired, without freshness or vitality, in 1862, in Bagge/SCHUBERT 43.

169. Cf. the facs. of the first page of the autograph in MGG XII Tafel 9 with the full pub. title in HIRSCH IV 241.

170. Schumann/SCHRIFTEN I 399.

171. Schumann/SCHRIFTEN I 125.

172. Cf. Brown/SCHUBERT 128, 209–10.

173. Schumann/SCHRIFTEN I 124–25. On the dating of the first ed. of No. 17, cf. Deutsch/SCHUBERT-D 507. On Paul Badura-Skoda's discovery of errors in this (and later) eds., cf. Brown/DISCOVERIES 309–10.

appear in the 1880's.[174] Said Schumann, along with flowery metaphors and similes that include our Nos. 19 and 20 in D and G, "Most [nearly] related to it [our No. 20 in G] is the one in A minor. The first part [is] so still, so dreamlike; it could move [one] to tears; withal so lightly and simply formed out of two fragments that one must marvel at the magician who knows how to interweave and oppose them so unusually." No fewer than three reviews of No. 17 had already appeared, all favorable, in time for Schubert himself to read them. Representative passages may be quoted from the first, longest, and most knowing of these, a self-conscious, prolix, four-column piece of early 1826, probably written by G. W. Fink.[175]

. . . it moves so freely and originally within its confines, and sometimes so boldly and curiously, that it might not unjustly be called a Fantasy. In that respect it probably can be compared only with the greatest and freest of Beethoven's sonatas. . . . It is easy to see that these [original melodic and harmonic] inventions are often somewhat odd, and that their exposition is even more curious (particularly in the first movement, where for example the principal theme, which is almost dry in itself, is not only intentionally introduced in a dry manner, but often, and clearly of set purpose, repeated in the same way); also, that the composer now and again hardly knew the ins and outs of the sometimes strange harmonies that visited him (even as regards grammatical writing); and there are other things of the sort over which one can hardly refrain from shaking his head a little. But once it has been shaken . . . one cannot after all refrain from accepting it [the son.] with pleasure . . . [In the first mvt. the] predominant expression is a suppressed but sometimes violently erupting passion, alternating with melancholy seriousness. The movement is not short, which is [not?] as one would wish if one would remain in this mood without growing weary of it. . . . [The second mvt.] resembles in its invention, expression and workmanship the andantes with variations in the quartets of J. Haydn's later years; and every one knows that this [comparison] implies no small praise. . . . Restrained passion breaks out hastily and violently in the scherzo; the trio brings again some calm . . . [This mvt.] might be described as Beethovenian, without, be it understood, any attempt to dispute the composer's [Schubert's] originality. [And the finale is] long and technically very well-knit. . . . In order to perform it adequately this Sonata does not so much demand virtuoso playing (as it is commonly understood) as rather a painstaking performance, somewhat like that demanded by the largest sonatas by Beethoven or by Cramer. The instrument, too, should be good, capable of the most diverse modifications of loud and soft as well as of *legato,* sustained tone and accurate damping.

174. E.g., in MT XII (1865) 74 and 317, XV (1872) 413, and XVI (1874) 462, performances of No. 17 are reported in London as being given by Walter Macfarren, Agnes Zimmermann, Clara Schumann, and Charles Hallé, respectively.

175. AMZ XXVIII (1826) 137–40, as trans. in Deutsch/SCHUBERT-D 512–15. For the other two, shorter reviews, from Frankfurt/M in 1826 and Vienna in 1828, cf. Deutsch/SCHUBERT-D 549 and 799–800.

This first review already introduces those perennial questions in Schubert's sonatas of fantasy and strange harmony, which had so often disturbed the early reviewers of Beethoven's sonatas (SCE 511–37, *passim*); of Classic predecessors, especially Beethoven; of precarious length; and of unusual keyboard writing and requirements. The "greatest and freest of Beethoven's sonatas," especially his most recent publications, and his most favored dedicatee (cf. SCE 509, 524) may well have been in Schubert's mind when he dedicated (only) this work, our No. 17, to the same Archduke Rudolph (who, however, is not known to have taken any similar interest in Schubert).[176] Brown mentions in particular another, still more recently published work by Beethoven, the "Diabelli Variations" (1823), for the influence of its fifth variation on the powerful "Scherzo" of No. 17 [177] (which, in turn, seems to have influenced the "Scherzo" of Schubert's own string Quintet in C, D. 956). Regarding length, the problem does hinge primarily on sustaining the interest through sufficient content. But there are absolute considerations, too. As our tabulation shows, No. 17 is one of five solo sonatas by Schubert that last beyond a half-hour in performance—a long time, in any case, for a single instrument of relatively monochrome sonority. With today's streamlined recitals scarcely allowing even for "heavenly length," No. 17 is not heard often.

The performer may not be able to manage such length—whether it is he or the composer who lacks the requisite sense of architecture[178]—but it is the listener who is more likely to object to it. The performer, on the other hand, is more likely to resist playing Schubert's sonatas if and when they fail to provide him with sufficient pianistic interest—original figurations, new technical challenges, unusual sonorities, rich textures, ingenious accompaniments—as is at least hinted in the foregoing and nearly every subsequent 19th-century discussion of them.[179] In a rare reference to the content of his sonatas and to his own playing, Schubert, who also sang and played the violin well enough,[180] confirmed his own preference for the piano as a lyrical instrument:

---

176. Cf. Deutsch/SCHUBERT-D 439, 693, 873.

177. Brown/SCHUBERT 188–90. For Schubert's contribution to the "other" set of "Diabelli Variations" cf. Newman/DIABELLI-m 21.

178. The conclusion in Vrieslander/ORGANISCHE is that the "epic-lyric breadth" in Schubert's longest sonatas does sustain the interest.

179. For references to these discussions and continued resistance on the same grounds by a prominent recitalist in 1928, cf. Samaroff/SCHUBERT. Cf., also, SSB III and VI on the problem of length.

180. Cf. Deutsch/SCHUBERT-M 18, 179, 209–10, 271, 336–37; 125–26, 145.

What pleased especially were the variations in my new Sonata for two hands [our No. 17], which I performed alone and not without merit, since several people assured me that the keys became singing voices under my hands, which, if true, pleases me greatly, since I cannot endure the accursed chopping in which even distinguished pianoforte players indulge and which delights neither the ear nor the mind.[181]

Could it have been the playing of this sonata that brought forth from one well-meaning but tactless listener the remark, "Schubert, I admire your pianoforte-playing more than your compositions!"? [182] Schumann, himself one of the most resourceful composers for piano in the 19th century, made a special point of the excellence of Schubert's piano writing, yet in a way that stresses its neutral rather than its color values:[183]

Particularly as a composer for the piano has he [stood] out somewhat above others, in certain respects even above Beethoven (as remarkably acutely as the latter otherwise heard, in [spite of] his deafness, through his imagination) —namely therein, that he knows [how to] score more pianistically; that is, everything sounds out so appropriately and inherently from the [very] heart of the piano, whereas with Beethoven, for example, we first have to borrow the tone color from the horn, [or] the oboe, etc.

No. 18 in C is the longest, best known, last, and most significant of Schubert's incomplete sonatas.[184] Schumann reportedly published the "Andante" as a supplement to the *Neue Zeitschrift für Musik* of December 10, 1839,[185] presumably without discussing it. When Whistling first published all that remains of No. 18 in 1862, he mislabelled it "Letzte [last] Sonate" and romantically entitled it "Reliquie" ("Relic"), perhaps remembering that Schumann had used that title when he published posthumously some letters and poems left among Schubert's effects.[186] But the incomplete movements iii and iv do not seem to lack much, and may be further instances of Schubert's breaking off where the continuations by sectional repetition seemed obvious enough, at least to him. To those who have tried their hands

181. Letter of July 25, 1825, to his parents, as trans. in Deutsch/SCHUBERT-D 436. A short analysis of the variations may be found in Brown/VARIATIONS 72–76.

182. Kreissle/SCHUBERT I 132 fn. Franz Schober, in Schubert's circle, also may have objected to this son. (cf. Deutsch/SCHUBERT-D 588–89). For descriptions, sometimes conflicting, of Schubert's piano playing, cf. Deutsch/SCHUBERT-M 37, 146, 176, 180, 189, 194, 282–83, 330.

183. Trans. from Schumann/SCHRIFTEN I 125. The same point is developed in Mello/SCHUBERT.

184. It is analyzed in detail in Truscott/UNFINISHED.

185. Deutsch/SCHUBERT-I 408.

186. NZM X (1839) 37; cf. Schumann/SCHRIFTEN I 460. In a review of the early Whistling ed., in DMZ III (1862) 69–70, C. v. Bruyck deprecated this work and regarded its pub. as quite unnecessary.

at completing the work, including Ernst Krenek in 1921 and Walter Rehberg in 1927,[187] the continuations could not have been that obvious, since the differences are considerable.[188] In any case, No. 18 is almost never played in recital, for all its strengths and charms. Pianists do not like to play incomplete works and find it psychologically difficult to accept completions by others.[189]

No. 19 in D was composed in the but three weeks that Schubert was in Gastein in 1825, hardly leaving time, as Deutsch says, for the supposedly lost "Gastein Symphony," too.[190] It was the second of the three solo sonatas published in Schubert's lifetime (and was designated "Seconde" after his Op. 42 [191]). Curiously, though it was to win as much praise as any Schubert sonata in the 19th century, and though Joseph von Spaun described it as a "most original Sonata for the pianoforte" in his extended obituary of 1829,[192] it got no review in Schubert's two remaining years and none discovered here before Schumann's short paragraph in 1834:[193]

What a different vitality [from that in our No. 17] gushes out of the spirited D major [sonata]—pulse upon pulse, seizing and carrying [us] away! And then an Adagio [actually labelled "Con moto"], wholly in the Schubert manner, [so] compelling, [so] overflowing that he scarcely can bring it to an end. The last movement hardly fits into the whole, and is a bit comical. Who[-ever] tried to take the thing seriously, would make himself [look] very ridiculous. [The impetuous] Florestan calls it a satire on the [antiquated] Pleyel-Vanhal, nightcap style; [the gentle] Eusebius finds grimaces in the strongly contrapuntal passages such as one uses to startle children. It all adds up to humor.

Later writers have varied from moderate to warm enthusiasm for the first movement, whose exceptional brilliance may explain this sonata's dedication to the pianist Karl Maria von Bocklet.[194] They have concurred in the high worth of the second movement, with its astonishing adventures, even to present-day ears, in modulation and syncopation. But they have not concurred on the "Scherzo" (and its curiously Biedermeier waltz refrain in B♭), which Schumann did not mention, nor on the "Rondo" finale.[195]

187. Cf. Deutsch/SCHUBERT-I 407–8, -D 280. Rehberg has also completed the other sons. that are not mere fragments.

188. Cf. Truscott/UNFINISHED 129–37, with a further completion of iii.

189. But in the Wuehrer recordings cited earlier the Krenek completion is used, providing the timing used in our tabulation.

190. Deutsch/SCHUBERT-D 454–55.

191. Cf. Cat. HIRSCH IV 208 and 212.

192. Deutsch/SCHUBERT-D 873.

193. Trans. from Schumann/SCHRIFTEN I 124.

194. Cf. Költzsch/SCHUBERT 113, Einstein/SCHUBERT 249.

195. Einstein/SCHUBERT 250–51 takes particular exception to Schumann's remarks on the finale. The waltz refrain is quoted in SSB VI.

A favorite sonata of most writers on Schubert has always been No. 20 in G. This sonata used to be published with his shorter pieces rather than in collections of his sonatas because, in place of "IV. Sonate" on the title page of the autograph the title given to the original edition—"Fantasie, Andante, Menuetto und Allegretto . . ." —suggested a set of four separate pieces (Ex. 20).[196] Dedicated to his close friend Joseph von Spaun,[197] No. 20 may have been written in response to a request from the Swiss publisher Nägeli[198] and appears to have been one of the sonatas that Schubert himself played for his friends.[199] It was the last of the sonatas to be published and the only one besides our No. 17 to get reviews, three in all, while he was alive. The first review, along with commendations and a slight implication of excessive concentration on a single idea, concluded that this "Fantasy" provided more than "mere dancing-lessons for the fingers," whereas the second review, much briefer, condescended to say that the work is "quite good" and that its separate "pieces . . . are not too difficult, and are attractive; they may thus be recommended for practice"! [200] The third review was another longish, prolix, somewhat moralistic article from Leipzig, presumably by Fink again.[201] Yet it was reasonable, even prescient, in its way. The dangers of imitating so individual a genius as Beethoven were stressed at length— no doubt, to Schubert's consternation if he saw this review published midway between Beethoven's and his own death. A few excerpts here will bring us back to familiar questions in Schubert:

[In the opening "Fantasy" Schubert] uses for his basis an extremely simple, almost too insignificant melodious song, opposes it to a second, also very simple one . . . and he now develops out of both and out of their variants what is after all a closely knit whole. . . . Here and there, perhaps, he plays for playing's sake—with the instrument, too, which is asked, for example, to produce sustained notes and chords, like a string quartet; he repeats too much and becomes altogether too long for that which he intends to offer, and actually does offer. . . . The finale . . . is a fiery, curious and here and there somewhat freakish bravura movement, devised like a great, free rondo. It runs on for twelve pages, as though in a single breath, and hardly allows the player and listener to gasp. . . . But then this movement, presented as it should be, is difficult to play. . . . Not the fingerwork alone—for what daunts

196. Cf. Költzsch/SCHUBERT 18; Deutsch/SCHUBERT-D 627, -I 432–33; also, the facs. accompanying the present discussion as Ex. 20. The holograph is listed as Add. 36738 in Cat. BRITISH MS 145.

197. Cf. Spaun's own description of the circumstances as trans. in Deutsch/ SCHUBERT-M 136.

198. Cf. Deutsch/SCHUBERT-D 533–34, 536–37, 541; but Nägeli did not publish it.

199. Cf. Deutsch/SCHUBERT-D 568, 571, 680.

200. From the complete reviews as trans. in Deutsch/SCHUBERT-D 674–75, 685.

201. AMZ XXIX (1827) 877–81; trans. in Deutsch/SCHUBERT-D 693–97.

Ex. 20. The opening of Franz Schubert's Sonata in G, Op. 78 (D. 894; facs. of the autograph Add. 36738 in the British Museum).

the pianoforte players of today in that respect?—but much rather the energy, the differentiation of the parts and the bringing out of the themes or at least of the allusions to them. . . .

Schumann, though he gave only two sentences to No. 20, called it Schubert's "most perfect" sonata "in form and spirit," with everything "organic," although the finale should be avoided by those without "the imagination to solve its riddles." [202]

The final three solo sonatas, Nos. 21–23 in c, A, and B♭, were left in significant sketches, followed by one continuous, exceptionally clean autograph containing all three sonatas on ninety-four pages

202. Schumann/SCHRIFTEN I 124. Cf., also, the high praise for this work in MT XIII (1868) 318.

and raising few textual or bibliographic questions.[203] Schubert seems to have composed all three of these great swan songs of his instrumental music in the incredibly short time of less than four weeks,[204] possibly playing all three for friends on September 27, 1828, only one day (!) after completing them, then already claiming in a letter written but five days later that "I have played [them] with much success in several places. . . ." [205] In the latter, peculiarly anxious document, addressed only forty-eight days before his death to the publisher Probst, he indicated his desire to dedicate all three sonatas to Hummel. However, the almost immediate plans to publish them changed twice[206] and did not materialize for another ten years (1838), or one year after Hummel's death in 1837. By that time Diabelli very wisely sought and got permission to dedicate them to the man most qualified to appreciate them, Schumann.[207]

Yet Schumann reviewed Nos. 21–23 that same year rather briefly and somewhat halfheartedly, mainly disturbed by the sadness of the inscription "very last compositions" not quite accurately inserted by Diabelli.[208] He did write approvingly of a new preference in them for simplicity over brilliance and for continuous melodic unfolding over a succession of different phrases. Such traits seem to explain objections to No. 23 and disadvantageous comparisons when it was played in a varied London concert in 1865:[209]

The Sonata in B flat of Schubert for pianoforte alone was done ample justice to by Mr. Charles Hallé; but the want of marked character in the leading subjects was made still more apparent by its being placed between Beethoven's Quartett in C, and Mozart's Sonata in E Minor, for pianoforte and violin (most exquisitely performed by Mr. Charles Hallé and Herr Joachim), the beauties of which latter composition seemed thoroughly appreciated by the audience.

In 1895, Shedlock still sensed faults in each of the last three sonatas

203. The autograph and its circumstances are described in detail in Kinsky/ KOCH 177–79, along with Facs. 13 of the first p. of No. 23 (reproduced in SSB VI). Cf., also, Költzsch/SCHUBERT 19–20; Brown/ESSAYS 214–15. Mod. ed. of the sketches (incomplete): SCHUBERT WERKE-m *Revisionsbericht* 8–45 (not 9–34).

204. Perhaps in response to a general solicitation for compositions of Aug. 10, 1828, from the publisher Brüggemann (Deutsch/SCHUBERT-D 797; cf. pp. 783 and 785, too).

205. Deutsch/SCHUBERT-D 807–8, 810–11 (evidently the only source for Deutsch's surmise, p. 808, about Sept. 27).

206. Cf. Deutsch/SCHUBERT-D 842–44; Költzsch/SCHUBERT 19–20.

207. Diabelli's thank-you note is printed in Schumann/SCHRIFTEN II 415 fn.

208. Schumann/SCHRIFTEN I 330–31. Again, exception is taken by Einstein (Einstein/SCHUBERT 285).

209. MT XII (1865–67) 29.

that he felt counteracted their great beauties, including a weak finale
in No. 22 and excessive length in Nos. 21/iv and 23/i and iv.[210]
More recently these works have been viewed as magnificent testimo-
nials at once to Schubert's deep involvement with Beethoven, only
six to eight years after that late master's last three sonatas had appeared, and to Schubert's ultimate independence of Beethoven gained
through full control of his own idiom.[211] And at present if any
one sonata were to be rated first among Nos. 21–23—in fact, among
all Schubert's sonatas—not only most writers,[212] but most qualified
performers and initiated listeners would give the palm to the very last,
in B♭—with its almost elegiac first movement, recalling the gentle
contemplation of No. 20/i; its serene yet melancholy slow movement,
recalling that of the but recently composed Quintet in C, D. 956;
its fleet, surprisingly gay "Scherzo"; its less rapid but more brilliant
finale, starting melodically and harmonically much as in the finale of
Beethoven's then recent quartet in the same key, Op. 130;[213] and
with its truly "heavenly length" throughout.

Schubert's Ensemble Sonatas

Schubert's ten ensemble sonatas include only one work published
during his own lifetime and have always aroused much less interest
than his twenty-three complete or incomplete solo sonatas. Yet those
with violin or arpeggione seldom fail to interest musicians who do
play or hear them, and the best of those for piano duet rank by
general consent among the best in piano duet literature. A tabulation
almost like that for the solo sonatas follows (and again, as with the
solo sons., the ensemble sons. are referred to only in the subsequent
discussion by the chronological numbers in the leftmost column).
No. 1 in B♭ is a "Sonate" in one movement for piano trio that
Schubert wrote at fifteen, a precocious student piece curiously like
(but, of course, no possible source for) the solo piano sonata in the
same key Wagner was to publish at eighteen, only twenty years
later.[214] It is the earliest extant venture into the sonata by Schubert.[215] No. 2 is another early work, whose five free sections, cul-

210. Shedlock/SONATA 205–6.

211. E.g., cf. Einstein/SCHUBERT 285–88, 290.

212. As in Brown/SCHUBERT 302–4.

213. Close structural parallels between the 2 finales are also discovered in Hill/
SCHUBERT. But see further under the duet Son. in C, D. 812, in the following discussion.

214. Cf. SSB IX. Mod. ed. of our No. 1: Orel/SCHUBERT-m, with preface; cf. Orel/
SCHUBERT for further background and an analysis of the work.

215. Cf. Deutsch/SCHUBERT-M 127–28 (J. v. Spaun).

Schubert's Ensemble Sonatas

Chron. no.	Scoring	Key	Opus no.	Deutsch no.	Composed	First edition	SCHUBERT/ WERKE-m	Mvts.: tempos or types / Keys: mvt.-by-mvt. / mss.: mvt.-by-mvt.	Remarks
1	P, Vn, Vc	Bb		28	1812	Wiener Philharmonischer, 1923		1: F / key: Bb / 292: 292	
2	P-duet	c/Bb		48	1813	Gotthard, 1871 (first version)	IX/32	5: S/VF-M-F -S -F / keys: c -Bb-Bb -Db-Bb / 584: 213 -76-201-15 -79	called "Fantasie," "Sonate," and "Grande Sonnate" in early references; v lacking in first of 2 versions
3	P & Vn	D	137/1	384	1816	Diabelli, 1836	VIII/2	3: F -M-VF / keys: D -A -D / 512: 180-87-245	pub. as one of "Drei Sonatinen . . ."
4	"	a	137/2	385	"	"	VIII/3	4: F -M -Mi-F / keys: a -F -d -a / 641: 137-114-80 -310	"
5	"	g	137/3	408	"	"	VIII/4	4: F -M-Mi-F / keys: g -Eb-Bb -g / 468: 145-74-100-149	"
6	P & Vn	A	162	574	1817	Diabelli, 1851	VIII/6	4: F -Sc -M-VF / keys: A -E -C -A / 763: 177-216-92-278	pub. as "Duo . . ."
7	P-duet	Bb	30	617	1818	Sauer & Leidesdorf, 1823	IX/2	3: F -M -F / keys: Bb -d -Bb / 473: 170-112-191	pub. as "Grande Sonate"
8	P-duet	C	140	812	1824	Diabelli, 1838	IX/12	4: F -M -Sc -VF / keys: C -Ab -C -C / 1502: 384-250-401-467	pub. as "Grande Duo"
9	P & arpeggione	a/A		821	1824	Gotthard, 1871	VIII/8	3: F -S -F / keys: a -E -A / 682: 205-71-406	alternative parts for Vc or Vn pub. with first ed.
10	P-duet	C/a		968	early?	Werke, 1888	IX/29	2: F -M / keys: C -a / 193: 148-45	called "Sonatine" (Deutsch/SCHUBERT-I 478)

minating in a scholastic, four-voice fugue, make the title "Fantasia" in the second version more appropriate than "Grand Sonnate" in the first version.[216]

Nos. 3–5, in D, a, and g, get progressively more forceful in content but are still generally light enough, though hardly short enough, to explain the publisher's preference for "Sonatine" rather than the original "Sonate" as the title for each.[217] Schubert still used the phrase "with accompaniment for violin" in his title although the violin is at least a full partner here. The more versatile writing for each instrument in No. 6 in A and the richer texture, resulting mainly from the richer piano part,[218] evince the experience Schubert had gained from Nos. 3–5. This time the same publisher changed the title to "Duo" for the first edition. The only contemporary circumstance that seems to be known about Schubert's string sonatas is that No. 9 in a/A was performed for at least one private hearing late in 1824, with Vincenz Schuster playing the arpeggione or violoncello guitar.[219] This rare, six-stringed, bowed instrument, essentially a bass viola da gamba,[220] seems to have come into and gone out of being just in time for Schubert's unique but hastily written sonata,[221] and has since been replaced by the cello when the work is played.

No. 10 in C/a may actually be one of Schubert's earliest piano duets, related curiously to a lost Mass by him or one by his brother Ferdinand that utilizes the materials.[222] No. 7 in B♭ was the one ensemble sonata and the earliest of all those four sonatas (by nearly two-and-half years) that were published in Schubert's lifetime.[223] But no mention of it can be found until Schumann's, in 1834, as one of Schubert's least original works, with only occasional flashes, although a masterpiece under any other composer's name.[224] Finally,

216. The autograph of the first version is filed under ML 30 .8b .S35 D. 48 Case at the Library of Congress; this version appears in Ed. Peters 155d, pp. 14–31, lacking the fugue finale.

217. Cf. Deutsch/SCHUBERT-I 174; Cobbett/CHAMBER II 355. Performances of No. 3 (i.e., D. 384), which remains the most popular, are reported in MT XVI (1874) 417, 544.

218. Cf. Cobbett/CHAMBER II 355.

219. Cf. Deutsch/SCHUBERT-D 384 (source?) and -B 50b (not 50a; drawing).

220. Cf. GROVE I 222–23 (G. Hayes), with photograph on Plate 63/3 (VIII, after p. 146); KONGRESS SCHUBERT 136 (E. van der Straeten).

221. Cf. Einstein/SCHUBERT 245. The first ed. was reviewed as merely an "occasional piece" in MW III (1872) 493–94.

222. Cf. Brown/DISCOVERIES 300–303.

223. Cf. Deutsch/SCHUBERT-D 294, 315.

224. Schumann/SCHRIFTEN I 124–25. It got higher praise in MT XIII (1868) 318, and, recently, in Einstein/SCHUBERT 152 and Brown/SCHUBERT 88.

No. 8 in C is the so-called "Grand Duo" on which Schumann was quoted earlier, first for viewing Schubert as Beethoven's feminine counterpart, and second for viewing this work as a potential symphony. Not only its idiom but its elaborate treatment of ideas suggests symphonic thinking.[225] It is, in fact, 145 measures longer than the longest solo sonata, 52 longer than the Quintet in C, but 1,366 shorter than the "Great Symphony" in C. And both in quality and spirit, however unsatisfying may be its duet idiom, it would be placed here on a par with those latter two masterpieces in C. Perhaps, though not a quartet, No. 8 was one of the consequences of a statement Schubert wrote three months earlier. ". . . I want to write another quartet, in fact intend to pave my way towards grand symphony in that manner." [226] The finale of No. 8, by the way, is another that recalls that in Beethoven's Quartet Op. 130. Since Schubert's finale is the earlier of these two and no known biographical circumstances indicate that Beethoven could have known it, one begins to suspect that its ideas and style were then "in the air."

Some Obscure Viennese (Woržischek)

There remain to mention in this chapter, chiefly to round out the picture, a few other contemporaries or followers of Beethoven, but this time primarily men whose sonatas now rest in almost total oblivion however much those sonatas may once have prospered.[227] One such was a composer on the borderline of the Classic and Romantic eras, **Anton Franz Josef Eberl** (1765–1807). This outstanding pianist had studied with Mozart, was mistakenly credited with some of his music, and was compared favorably with Beethoven as a symphonist.[228] In all, he left 16 sonatas—6 for P solo, 2 for P-duet, and 8 accompanied by Vn or Fl—all published between 1792 and 1806.[229] In spite of many flashes of talent and significant advances in piano writing, in chromaticism, and in certain other early Romanticisms,

225. An ex. from the first mvt. is quoted in ssb VI.

226. Deutsch/schubert-d 339; cf. p. 340.

227. Most of these men are represented by one waltz each in the "other" set of "Diabelli Variations," the full contents of which was given at the start of this chapter.

228. Cf. amz VII (1804–5) 321–22; Ewens/eberl 8–9, 14–19; mgg III 1053–55 (R. Haas).

229. A thematic index, without dates or plate nos., appears in Ewens/eberl 114–22; approximate dates are given in mgg III 1054. The sons. are discussed, with exx., in Ewens/eberl 21–38 (solo; summarized in Egert/frühromantiker 52–59) and 77–83 (ensemble). Mod. ed. of a *Sonatine . . . à l'usage des Commençans* in C, Op. 5 (or 6; 1796): Giegling/solo-m no. 14.

these sonatas reveal a lack of fundamental training in composition (as Rochlitz concludes in both the first and last of several moderately favorable reviews[230]), a lack that is apparent today especially in the loose, disjointed forms. Perhaps a lack of vitality in the ideas themselves also worked against their more resourceful development.

A more obscure figure was **Philipp Jakob Riotte** (1776–1856), a successful composer for the stage who came to Vienna from Germany in 1808 and moved in the circles of Beethoven, Schubert, the Archduke Rudolph, and Weber, among others.[231] Riotte also left considerable instrumental music, including over two dozen accompanied and solo piano sonatas or sonatinas that were published from about 1805 to 1820.[232] Eleven of the solo type were still represented in PAZDÍREK XXIV 369 early in the present century. As with most composers who have bowed to public taste Riotte devoted his most extended and serious efforts to his first sonatas. The most conspicuous trait in all his sonatas is fluent, salon virtuosity. His writing is more like that of Weber than of Beethoven or Schubert, but it is less original and more square-cut.[233] His dances have a degree of piquancy and charm. His slow movements are short and inconsequential.

Another composer for the stage, as well as a church organist and pedagogue, **Joseph Drechsler** (1782–1852) also moved in the circles of Beethoven (who respected him) and Schubert.[234] Drechsler, who came to Vienna from Prague in 1807, got no sonata reviews discovered here nor did more than one of his three or four solo and accompanied piano sonatas, first published between 1809 and 1812,[235] survive in PAZDÍREK IV 408. Yet his sonatas disclose not only the virtuosity of Riotte's, ranging over the whole keyboard, but more imagination, richer textural interest, and superior craftsmanship.

Joseph Mayseder (1789–1863), a violinist who figured often in the activities of Beethoven and Schubert, among others,[236] published nearly seventy works that exploit the virtuosity of the violin. Two

230. AMZ III (1800–1801) 95–96, IV (1801–2) 592, V (1802–3) 558–60 and 763–66, VII (1804–5) 748–50, XI (1808–9) 159–60, 337–44, and 521–22.

231. Cf. MGG XI 546–49 (F. Goebels).

232. Op. 3 is reviewed in AMZ IX (1806–7) 92–4; Op. 51 is already listed in HOFMEISTER 1818 (Whistling) 38.

233. This general evaluation was already voiced in part in occasional further reviews of Riotte's sons.—e.g., AMZ X (1807–8) 109 and 256.

234. Cf. MGG III 743–44 (A. Orel); Deutsch/SCHUBERT-D 24; Thayer & Forbes/BEETHOVEN II 864–65.

235. Weinmann/ARTARIA items 1987, 2033, 2236; HOFMEISTER 1815 (Whistling) 301, 350.

236. Cf. MGG VIII 1851–53 (K. Pfannhauser), with further references but no itemized list of works.

of these, Opp. 13 in E♭ and 42 in e (*ca.* 1816 and 1826), bear the title "Grande Sonate concertante pour piano & [or "et"] Violon." [237] They reveal competence in writing, relatively moderate exploitation of both instruments, and banal ideas that are treated without creative spark.

Anton Halm (1789–1872), who established himself as pianist and teacher in Vienna from 1815, knew Beethoven well and must have crossed paths with Schubert several times.[238] He left mainly solo and "accompanied" piano music, including about a dozen sonatas first published between 1819 and 1828 except for two or three that appeared as late as 1848.[239] A teacher of Stephen Heller and Adolph von Henselt, among others, Halm excelled in his etudes and their virtuoso style, again suggestive of Weber. One of his earliest and most played sonatas, Op. 15 in c for solo piano (*ca.* 1820), deserves the "Grande" in its title for its length and technical demands, but its squareness and excessive sequences of weak ideas make it naive and unacceptable today. With its slow introduction and except for a "Scherzo" in place of a middle slow movement, it sounds like a "Warsaw Concerto" popularization of Beethoven's *Grande Sonate pathétique.* In 1837, in a review of Halm's Piano Trio Op. 57, Schumann found the highest intentions combined with utter stylistic and structural ineptness, granting at the same time that "Nature would explode if she were to give forth nothing but Beethovens." [240]

A surprisingly strong composer turns up in the short-lived **Johann Hugo Woržischek** (or Voříšek; 1791–1825), who arrived in Vienna in 1813 after study with W. J. Tomaschek in Prague, won the praise of Beethoven for his set of piano Rhapsodies, studied with Hummel, also knew Schubert and Moscheles, among others, played the piano and violin well, and conducted the Gesellschaft der Musikfreunde from 1818.[241] Although less well known, Woržischek may be ranked with those two other strong Czech-born composers of instrumental music in the early 19th century, J. L. Dussek and W. J. Tomaschek (SSB

---

237. Both are listed among many other works by Mayseder in Cat. ROYAL 216 and Altmann/KAMMERMUSIK 215 *et passim.* The approximate dates are based mainly on the dates for near op. nos. in Weinmann/ARTARIA items 2361 and 2941. MT XVIII (1877) 351 mentions a performance of Op. 42/ii and iii.

238. Cf. Thayer & Forbes/BEETHOVEN II 629, 975; Deutsch/SCHUBERT-M 280–81, -D as indexed.

239. Cf. MGG V 1375–76 (H. Federhofer); HOFMEISTER 1819 (Whistling) 27 and 35, 1828 (Whistling) 483 and 589. Three solo sons. still appear in PAZDÍREK XI 122.

240. Schumann/SCHRIFTEN I 278.

241. Cf. MAB-m No. 30, pp. vii–ix (B. Štědroň); Thayer & Riemann/BEETHOVEN III 453; GROVE IX 74 (G. Černušak); Deutsch/SCHUBERT-D 452–3, -M 344, 345; AMZ XVIII (1816) 77, 513.

XVII; cf. SCE 774–75). Only two sonatas by Woržischek have been made known thus far, both in good modern editions—Op. 5 in G/g, for P & Vn, originally published by Mechetti in Vienna about 1823, with dedication to Archduke Rudolph, and Op. 20 in b♭, for P solo, published by Pennauer in Vienna about 1825.[242] Some study has been devoted to his smaller piano forms, especially their influence on Schubert's.[243] But little seems to have been devoted to his sonatas beyond descriptive paragraphs in the modern editions, or to any other of his larger works (suggesting a significant dissertation topic).

Woržischek's Op. 5 is an extended work in four movements—S/F-Sc-S-VF—with the "Scherzo" in the submediant key, the "Andante sostenuto" in the tonic key, and the finale, exceptionally, in the tonic minor key. In spite of the length (1,114 mss. in all) the structural control remains clear and telling. The main ideas, mostly lyrical and stepwise, achieve interest through resourceful harmonic support and contrast. Their development—especially in the relatively short development section of i—attains distinction through skillful, well-spaced motivic writing. The piano and violin share in a true duo, althougl , as generally holds throughout much of the century, the piano part is technically more challenging and adventurous, including leaps and rhythmically capricious figures that anticipate Chopin's writing. Otherwise, the scale and passagework suggest Mendelssohn, occasionally Weber.

Compared with his Op. 5, Woržischek's Op. 20 is structurally tighter and more compact, more dramatic—with frequent suggestions of Beethoven[244]—and more pregnant melodically. Its plan of VF-Sc-VF includes no moderate or slow movement. Not counting the slow movement of Op. 5, Op. 20 is still 37 per cent shorter in total measures. Its technical requirements are just as interesting, though a little more practical. Unusual is the choice of C♯ for the "Scherzo," not so much for being the lowered, enharmonic mediant as simply for the number of sharps and double-sharps it presented to the pianists of the time. From the first movement, about a third of the polyphonic development section, which goes from b♭ to b and back, is illustrated in Ex. 21. The main theme with octave leaps recurs

242. Plate nos. 1221 and 168, respectively, place these works later (Deutsch/ NUMMERN 17, 18) than the *ca.* 1820 suggested for both in the 2 mod. eds.: MAB-m No. 30, p. ix and No. 4, p. [5] (L. Kundera), both with prefaces; the reference to AMZ for 1820 in Kahl/LYRISCHE 106 fn. 2 is an error, and the reference to an 1821 ed. of Op. 20/iii could not be verified here.

243. Cf. Kahl/LYRISCHE 99–110, 112–13, 117–19, 122; MAB-m No. 52, pp. xii–xvi.

244. As is emphasized in Kahl/LYRISCHE 106.

Ex. 21. From Op. 20/i by Johann Hugo Woržischek (after MAB-m No. 4, p. 12).

in ii and is hinted in iii. This theme and the staccato, rising, chordal motive that follows suggest that Woržischek knew the opening of Mozart's "Haffner Symphony" and the finale of his Symphony in g, respectively. A brief review of Op. 20 in 1826 called attention to the strength and skill of this newly encountered composer, as well as the work's technical difficulties, including keys up to seven sharps and five flats.[245] Present-day pianists would do well to consider including this fine work in a general recital.

After arriving in Vienna in 1817, the Czech violinist **Leopold Jansa** (1795–1875) studied with Woržischek and the older Czech E. A. För-ster (SCE 548–49).[246] A prolific, not unskillful composer of light duos,

245. AMZ XXVIII (1826) 204.
246. MGG VI 1716–18 (A. Wirsta).

rondos, and potpourris for his instrument,[247] he is cited here solely for the infrequent scoring of what may have been his only sonata, a "Sonate brillante" in D for unaccompanied violin with the optional accompaniment of a second violin, published by Artaria in 1828.[248]

The piano prodigy **Franz Schoberlechner** (1797–1843), a pupil of Hummel and E. A. Förster, left at least two solo piano sonatas and one for P, Vn-or-Fl.[249] Published between 1820 and 1828, these sonatas approach Hummel's in their piano writing and brilliance, but are otherwise lighter and more modish to a degree that may help explain Beethoven's refusal to endorse Schoberlechner.[250] Op. 45, "Sonate mélancolique," could well have taken at least its title from the recently published Op. 49 by Moscheles. Another violinist was **Georg Hellmesberger** ("der Ältere"; 1800–73), early classmate of Schubert, first in a long, active, family line of Viennese musicians, and teacher of Joachim and Auer, among others. He left a four-movement Sonata in A♭ for P & Vn, published about 1848, that won praise from Alfred Dörffel as a well-knit, conservative, but sensitive work of moderate difficulty.[251]

Last in this chapter may be mentioned the prolific composer **Franz Lachner** (1803–90), who wrote six of his nine solo and ensemble sonatas between 1824 and 1832 while still studying and/or living in Vienna (1822–34), the remaining three being organ sonatas (Opp. 175–77) published late in his Munich years (1876).[252] A member of an important musical family, a versatile talent acknowledged by Beethoven,[253] a close friend of Schubert,[254] a student of Sechter, and an early detractor but eventual supporter of Wagner,[255] Lachner wrote unevenly. The high spots in his later works that might justify his classification in 1922 as a significant "transitional figure between Schubert and Bruckner" [256] are only occasionally to be found amidst the skilled but often dry and insipid writing of the sonatas. In 1835 Schumann deplored at length the inconsistent quality and unsatis-

247. Cf. PAZDÍREK VIII 83–85.

248. The only listing discoverable here was that in Weinmann/ARTARIA item 2950.

249. Cf. MGG XII 1–2 (E. Badura-Skoda); HOFMEISTER 1828, 602 and 506. The sons. do not survive among the works still listed in PAZDÍREK XIII 301.

250. Cf. Thayer & Forbes/BEETHOVEN II 864.

251. NZM XXX (1849) 142–43; cf., also, MGG VI 113–14 (A. Orel).

252. Cf. MGG VIII 29–31 and 34 (A. Wurz), with further references. In the long list of his works in PAZDÍREK IX 24–29, 6 sons. still survive.

253. Cf. Thayer & Riemann/BEETHOVEN V 121; Egert/FRÜHROMANTIKER 146, with further references.

254. Cf. Deutsch/SCHUBERT-M 195–97 et passim.

255. Cf. Newman/WAGNER I 76; II 304–5, 472, 482–84.

256. As quoted in MGG VIII 32.

factory sonority of Lachner's four-hand Sonata in d, Op. 39 (1832).[257]
(In 1842, he found wholly mediocre and conservative the "Grosse
Sonate" for piano solo in F, Op. 20, by Franz's brother in Vienna,
Ignaz Lachner [1807–95].[258]) Already typical of Franz Lachner's style
is *Grande Sonate* in f♯, Op. 2 (1824?), in four movements (F-Sc-Va-F),
with its genuinely Romantic, though saccharine melodiousness, its
fluent handling of new chordal textures and wide-range passages, its
slavish observance of the four-measure phrase, and its profitless exploitation of flat ideas.[259]

257. Schumann/SCHRIFTEN I 92–94; II 382 fn. 124 (crossed out of the original
review).

258. Schumann/SCHRIFTEN II 118–19; echoed in AMZ XLV (1843) 325. Only slightly
more enthusiasm is shown for Ignaz's 4-hand "Preissonate" Op. 33, in AMZ XLVIII
(1846) 660–61. But his Vn sonatinas were liked, as in MMR XX (1890) 57 and 256.
Cf., also, Egert/FRÜHROMANTIKER 148–49.

259. The support of F. Lachner's sons. in Egert/FRÜHROMANTIKER 146–49 is hard
to justify.

Chapter VIII

Weber, Schumann, and Others in Early 19th-Century German Centers

The New Romanticism in Germany

During the first half of the 19th century the separate German states that were to confederate by 1866 still came under pronounced Austrian influence. From the standpoint of the artist much of the reactionism and oppression that beset Austria after the Congress of Vienna (ssb VII) also prevailed in these states. But there were commercial, philosophic, artistic, and other nationalistic and cultural forces that tended to pull the states away from Austria and to unify them around their strongest and largest representative, Prussia. Eight other states also gained definition and strength, especially Bavaria, Württemberg, and Saxony. The same forces help to explain why the German states soon forged ahead of Austria in military might—again, Prussia first and foremost—in scientific progress, in the industrial revolution, and in the related advances of transportation and communication; why they responded more, though not succumbed, to the international waves of revolution, especially in 1848 (as Spohr, Schumann, and Wagner knew so well); and, yes, why they took the lead in both the spirit and the content of the new Romanticism.

Of prime importance as implementers of the new Romanticism in music were several German authors who had been preceded, in part, by Schiller and the aging but still active Goethe—in particular, Wackenroder, Novalis, Tieck, E. T. A. Hoffmann, Heine, and Jean Paul.[1] Their theories, moods, and themes—night, death, indefinable longing, dreams, the world of make-believe—penetrated music even when it took so abstract a form as the sonata. All of these six authors included music among their literary topics and at least three of them played and wrote music, however amateurishly. But in that age of hybrid art

1. Pertinent here among studies of German literature and music are Longyear/ schiller, Schoolfield/german, and Siegel/germany (which gives chief attention to the above names).

and heterogeneous genius, one hardly needs to go outside of the music profession itself to find literary influences and associations. Quite apart from music theorists and writers like Gottfried Weber and A. B. Marx, nearly every one of our main composers in this chapter was active as a man of letters, too. And some of them, like Weber and Mendelssohn, were skilled in the fine arts, as well. Moreover, nearly every one of these men not only wrote for publication but faithfully maintained a prodigious personal correspondence and elaborate diaries, polished so finely and organized so systematically—how paradoxical for such artistically free spirits—that their ultimate purpose could only have been the edification of posterity.

Three music periodicals in particular provided the outlets for the reviews and other articles that our main sonata composers published, all of which already have been cited frequently in the present and even the previous volume. One was the widely respected *Allgemeine musikalische Zeitung* (AMZ), founded in 1798 and originally edited by J. F. Rochlitz, with G. W. Fink and M. Hauptmann among his successors; another was the *Neue Zeitschrift für Musik* (NZM), founded by Schumann in 1834; and the third was Caecilia (CAECILIA), founded in 1824 under the editorship of Gottfried Weber.[2] In the absence of any other survey, early or present-day, of the 19th-century sonata in Germany, we cannot help but take much interest in the opinions, attitudes, and sometimes the music analyses provided in these periodicals, especially those from so great a musical judge as Schumann. All these editors wrote with authority and carried much weight. Furthermore, the editors of AMZ and NZM made it their avowed purposes to pay as much attention as possible to the sonata, especially the piano sonata (SSB II). Their patient attention to nearly everything received from the publishers produced reviews not only of significant new sonatas but of many run-of-the-mill sonatas and of some deficient ones that could only be described as "miserable." No wonder that almost any creative spark was greeted with enthusiasm, sometimes with a degree of enthusiasm impossible to endorse today. The contrast is noteworthy between the more conservative-minded, diplomatic, and didactic reviews in AMZ and the more modern-minded, frank, even sarcastic reviews in NZM, often signed by "Florestan," "Eusebius," or "Raro" as representatives of Schumann's split personality. Undoubtedly, one reason for the collapse of AMZ in 1848 was the growing preference for the more modern views of its competitor in Leipzig, NZM, although after Schumann stopped most of his writing, in the early 1840's, F. Brendel,

2. Freystätter/ZEITSCHRIFTEN gives a summary history of each periodical. Plantinga/ SCHUMANN, as noted later, is of special value here on NZM.

A. Dörffel, and others tended to write more conservatively and diplomatically for NZM, too.

This chapter is the longest in the present volume because it not only includes four of our most influential and significant composers of 19th-century sonatas—Hummel, Weber, Schumann, and Mendelssohn—but because, in the interest of a balanced perspective (SSB I), it includes so many of those run-of-the-mill composers, or at least all of them encountered here whose sonatas were once popular or reveal some other reason for bringing them to light again. Among other recurring themes in this chapter are the remarkably wide, quick, and potent spread of Beethoven's influence; the remarkably few instances of actual programmatic sonatas, in spite of the close ties between literature and music; and the remarkably persistent output of sonatas published for piano alone or in ensemble, in spite of recurring recognition around 1840 of a low ebb in their quality (SSB II).

South Germany (Hummel)

If Ries made an ideal starter, in the previous chapter, as a direct Beethoven transmitter in Vienna, then **Johann Nepomuk Hummel** (1778–1837) makes an ideal starter here as one of the most important links between the great Classic masters in that city and the new young Romantics throughout much of the rest of Europe. Born near-by in Pressburg (Bratislava) inside the Czech border, Hummel could have been placed at least as appropriately in Vienna, where he lived from 1786 to 1787 and much of the period from 1793 (not 1795) to 1816.[3] He studied and lived with Mozart during that first stay, as a piano prodigy of but eight and nine.[4] And during that longer stay he quickly moved to the top among Viennese pianists, studied counterpoint and composition with Albrechtsberger and Salieri, taught, composed, and published extensively, studied organ with Haydn,[5] and won both Haydn's and Beethoven's friendship and respect.[6]

3. Benyovszky/HUMMEL includes many letters and other documents as well as most of the known biographic information (pp. 16–129; utilized in GROVE IV 406–9 [D. Hume] and MGG VI 927–35 [W. Kahl]). Cf., also, Hummel's autobiographic letter to J. Sonnleithner of May 22, 1826 in La Mara/MUSIKERBRIEFE II 47–51 and the necrology in NZM VII (1837) 153–54, 157–58, 165–66 (C. Montag).

4. Deutsch/MOZART 346, 569–71. Cf. Zimmerschied/HUMMEL.

5. Benyovszky/HUMMEL 49.

6. Cf. Landon & Bartha/HAYDN 451–52; Holmes/RAMBLE 19; Thayer & Forbes/ BEETHOVEN I 230 and 424, II 1044. Although he may have known Schubert's music earlier, Hummel seems not to have met Schubert until he returned to Vienna in 1827 to visit the dying Beethoven, by which time Hummel had published nearly if not all of his own sonatas and Schubert was soon to request, in vain, that his three great, final sons. of 1828 be ded. to Hummel (SSB VII; cf. Deutsch/SCHUBERT-M 28, 137, 148).

Yet it was away from Vienna that Hummel built his chief reputation and exercised his chief influence as pianist and composer, including the composition of Op. 81, his most significant sonata both musically and Romantically. He is placed here in southern Germany merely because of his first station outside of Vienna, in Stuttgart from 1816 to 1819. But between 1788 and 1793, again before 1803,[7] and during many leaves from his final station, in Weimar from 1819 to his death, he made wide concert-tours that took him variously to nearly all the main centers in Germany, England, Scotland, Bohemia, Russia, France, Holland, Belgium, and Poland. He already played for Haydn during a London concert in 1792,[8] and about the same time he studied with Clementi,[9] got to know Clementi's pupil Cramer, and probably came to know Dussek, too.[10] In later years he crossed paths often as pianist and composer with Cramer and Moscheles, being paired with each as a rival at one time or another (as he had been with Beethoven);[11] his music furnished at least early models for that of Weber, Mendelssohn, Schumann, and Chopin, all of whom he knew personally (Schumann through correspondence);[12] and he himself taught Czerny, Ferdinand Hiller, Adolph von Henselt, and probably Thalberg,[13] among others.

Hummel's range of composition was wide, including operas, church music, symphonies, concertos, chamber music, and a long list of the then fashionable variations, rondos, sonatas, studies, potpourris, dances, arrangements, and transcriptions for piano solo or duet.[14] A few of his publications achieved more than a dozen printings in his lifetime, including the still celebrated Septet in d, Op. 74, the still played "Rondo favori" in E♭, Op. 11, the most successful concertos (especially Op. 85 in a),[15] and one of the earlier solo sonatas, Op. 13 in E♭. Moreover, his

---

7. Cf. Benyovszky/HUMMEL 44; Philip H. Highfill, Jr., provides new information on Hummel in London in 1801, in JAMS IX (1956) 70–71, revealing a fine voice and ability to play the harp, a handsome face (contradicting CZERNY 308), an intellectual brilliance, a literary background, and alcoholic temperance.

8. Cf. Benyovszky/HUMMEL 42–45; Landon & Bartha/HAYDN 269–70.

9. Cf. CZERNY 309. Other evidence could not be found here.

10. Cf. Pohl/MOZART 43, 107, 127, 155.

11. Cf. Schlesinger/CRAMER 43, 47–48, 71, 77–78; MOSCHELES I 22, 241–42, 276.

12. Cf. Saunders/WEBER 79, 121, 125, 159; MENDELSSOHN/Moscheles 66; Werner/MENDELSSOHN 55; Storck/SCHUMANN 64–68; Schumann/JUGENDBRIEFE 80; Niecks/SCHUMANN 101, 141–42; Sydow & Hedley/CHOPIN 24, 70, 80.

13. Schilling/LEXICON VI 628; but further evidence for Thalberg is wanting (SSB XII).

14. Cf. the early index reprinted in Benyovszky/HUMMEL 321–28 (the 2d list, pp. 329–44, repeats PAZDÍREK), the undated list in PAZDÍREK XI 750–56, the less complete, undated list by categories in GROVE IV 408–9, and the partially but uncertainly dated list in MGG VI 929–32. In all these, different op. nos. for the same work are identified insufficiently if at all.

15. Mitchell/HUMMEL is a recent diss. on Hummel's concertos.

Ausführliche theoretische-practische Anweisung zum Piano-Forte-Spiel
of 1827, first published by Haslinger of Vienna in 1828,[16] circulated
widely during the 19th century, leaving its mark especially on the new
style of fingering and of playing trills and related ornaments.[17] Among
all those works are about 25 sonatas, representing but a small proportion numerically, yet a much larger proportion in terms of relative
attention received, both contemporary and posthumous. In the tabulation of Hummel's sonatas that follows, it has been possible to discover
more of the earliest editions and actual publication dates, also to
equate and consolidate more of the different opus numbers assigned by
different publishers to the same work, than in any previous tabulation
known here. But much still remains to be done toward a complete, accurate list of Hummel's sonatas. Not included are several transcriptions
from other settings to "sonatas," or the converse.

The 25 sonatas by Hummel that could be identified here divide into
9 (or more than a third) solos, 4 (or about a sixth) duets, and 12 (or
nearly half) other ensembles. As was so often true then, the solos provide the most serious, extended, and resourceful examples.[18] The
ensemble sonatas may have been played at least as much as the solo
sonatas during or soon after Hummel's own day,[19] and two of them
have been brought back to view by recent new editions.[20] Certainly,
for all their skill and sensitivity, these light, graceful, often brilliant

16. Hummel/ANWEISUNG. Among other contemporary eds. was that trans. and
pub. by Boosey in London as *A Complete Theoretical and Practical Course of
Instruction on the Art of Playing the Piano Forte* (cf. Cat. ROYAL 180). Cf. Bie/
PIANOFORTE 211–12.

17. Cf. Bie/PIANOFORTE 211–12, Schonberg/PIANISTS 109–10.

18. The typed, unpub., 62-page diss. on "Johann Nepomuk Hummel als Klavier-
componist," completed at Kiel in 1922 by Walter Meyer (Schaal/DISSERTATIONEN item
1614), was no longer obtainable here, but is digested in the relatively brief discussion in Egert/FRÜHROMANTIKER 108–16. Nor could a copy be found of G. Sprock,
L'Interprétation des Sonates de Johann Nepomuk Hummel (Paris, 1933; cf. RICORDI
ENCICLOPEDIA II 444). The solo sons. also figure in a recent comprehensive article
on Hummel's instrumental music, Davis/HUMMEL. But a fuller, up-to-date study of
the sons. is still much to be desired.

19. E.g., cf. the reports of Hummel P-duet sons. being played in Paris in 1846
and 1850, in RGM XIII, April 5, and XVI, March 10. Op. 81, the solo son. in f♯, was
played in public by Moscheles in Vienna for the first time in 1819 (AMZ XXI
[1819] 430); another Vienna performance of it, in 1862, is reported in Hanslick/
WIEN II 266.

20. Op. 5/3 for P & Va was published by Doblinger in 1960 (P. Doktor) and
Op. 50 for P & Fl by Peters in 1965 (Dieter Sonntag). The new diss. Zimmerschied/
KAMMERMUSIK (1966) includes descriptions of most of the acc'd sons., mvt. by mvt.,
with exx. (pp. 63–100); some information on autographs, early eds., and dates (pp.
6–19, with errors); style discussions; historical orientations; and 144 letters and
other documents (pp. 327–530).

J. N. *Hummel's Sonatas* (grouped by scoring types)

Op./no. (alternate)	Key	Scoring	Early ed., year	Reviews, sources, dedications, titles
2/3 (3/3)	C	H-or-P	André, 1793	cf. Op. 2/1–2 *infra*
13	E♭	P	Haslinger, 1803	ded. to Haydn (cf. Landon & Bartha/HAYDN 452); "1ère Sonate"
20 (29)	f	P	Bureau . . . , by 1807	AMZ IX (1806–7) 422; ded. to Magdalene von Kurzbeck; "2ème grande Sonate"
30 (38)	C	P	Artaria, 1808	AMZ XVIII (1816) 250–51; cf. Weinmann/ARTARIA item 2021; "Sonata di bravura"
81	f♯	P	Steiner, 1819	AMZ XXI (1819) 430, XXII (1820) 114–16; Schumann/JUGENDBRIEFE 80; Schumann/SCHRIFTEN I 395; "Grosse . . ."
106	D	P	Diabelli, 1824	"Grande Sonate brillante"
[no op.]/1–3	G, A♭, C	P	by 1799? Bermann, by 1828	AMZ II (1799–1800) Intelligenz-Blatt ix; HOFMEISTER 1828 (Whistling), 591, and 1834–38, 129; PAZDÍREK XI 755
1/1–2	?	P-duet	Artaria, 1798?	cf. Weinmann/ARTARIA item 731
51 (50)	E♭	P-duet	Artaria, 1815	"Sonate ou divertissement"
92	A♭	P-duet	Diabelli, *ca.* 1821	AMZ XXXIV (1832) 12–13; "Grande Sonate . . ."
2/1 (3/1)	B♭	H-or-P & Vn-or-Fl & Vc	André, 1793	HARMONICON VI/1 (1828) 108; "âgé de 14 ans"; dedicated to Queen Charlotte; "avec accompagnement de . . ."
2/2 (3/2)	G	H-or-P & Vn-or-Fl	" "	cf. Op. 2/1, *supra*; also, HARMONICON V/1 (1827) 115?
5/1–2 (3/1–2; 12/1–2?)	B♭, F	P & Vn	André, by 1798	AMZ I (1798–99) 157–58; facs. of title p.: Doktor/HUMMEL-m
5/3 (3/3; 12/3? 19)	E♭	P + Va-or-Vn	" "	AMZ I (1798–99) 157–58; AMZ XX (1818) 563–64
25		P & Vn	Richault, by 1828	
28 (30; 60)	G	P & Fl-or-Vn	Breitkopf . . . , by 1815	
37	C?	P & Vn	Richault, by 1828	
37 (54)	C	P & mandolin (or Vc?)	Diabelli, ?	cf. Bone/GUITAR 175–80
50 (61; No. 2)	D	P & Fl-or-Vn	Artaria, 1815	QUARTERLY VIII (1826) 358–59
62 (64; 126?)	A	P & Fl-or-Vn	Artaria, 1815	
104	A	P & Vc; or P & Fl	Boosey, by 1826	HARMONICON IV/1 (1826) 166–67 and V/1 (1827) 243–44; ded. to the Grand Duchess of Russia; "A Grand Sonata"; autograph in the British Museum dated 1824 (Zimmerschied/KAMMERMUSIK 16)
108	?	P & Vn	Peters, 1826	called "Amusement"; autograph dated 1825; cf. Zimmerschied/KAMMERMUSIK 16–17

works, in two or three movements, were designed primarily to win the public. But from the mid-19th to the mid-20th century—by which time virtually everything but that Rondo in E♭ had disappeared from publishers' catalogues—four of the solo sonatas were to be found among Hummel's dozen or so works that continued most generally in print. These four were Opp. 13, 20, 81, and 106.[21] If we add the two other solo sonatas that have opus numbers and at least approximate dates, Opp. 2/3 and 30, we get six very different works, yet six that give a broad view of trends and styles in all of Hummel's sonatas.

Though still an imitative, formative work, Op. 2/3 in C marks well the prodigy, "âgé de 14 ans," who had already studied with two of the greatest Classic masters. There are clear enough hints of Mozart in the feminine, sometimes chromatic cadences as well as the occasional "singing-allegro" style complete with murky and chordal, though little actual Alberti, bass. And there are clear hints of Clementi in the octave-writing and other tendencies to exploit the instrument. There are even foretastes of the brilliant sonata of the same key, opus, and number that Beethoven was to complete but two years later (1795; SCE 509). By contrast, Hummel's Op. 13 in E♭ is a fully mature work of its type—cool, elegant, skillful, straightforward, and effective both as a sonata and as piano writing. The thin texture (though now freed almost entirely of Alberti bass), the artlessly simple themes, and the feminine cadences may still be Mozartean in origin. But all these, plus the keen ear for piano resonance, the increasing technical brilliance, and the dexterous contrapuntal exploits here point even more to Clementi. There is a nod, too, to the more concentrated drive of Beethoven and to the zigzag passagework of the dedicatee, Haydn. Although, in spite of its wide circulation, the reviewers seem not to have noticed this work in Hummel's day, recent writers have found more than enough reason to hope it will be revived in performance.[22]

Published only four years later (1807), Hummel's Op. 20 in f introduces us to an even more striking change of style. It is at once warmer and more poetic in its speech, freer and more irregular in its design, and less disposed to brilliance than his Op. 13. Its improvisatory character ties in with Hummel's reputation as one of the greatest improvisers alongside Beethoven.[23] Hummel seems to be following the similar path taken by Clementi, although for the moment he has moved less in the direction of the new Romanticism than of the outdated *empfindsam* style, what with its tempo changes, frequent turns and related ornaments, deceptive cadences, and foreshortened phrases.

21. E.g., Peters, Heugel, and G. Schirmer still listed them in Hummel collections up to World War II. Nearest to complete eds. of Hummel's piano music were the 12- and 21-vol. collections pub. by Richault and Schlesinger, respectively, in Paris by 1828.

22. E.g., Egert/FRÜHROMANTIKER 110–12; Davis/HUMMEL 169–70. In Einstein/SCHUBERT 79–81, Schubert's "spontaneous" polyphony is contrasted to Hummel's "severe" or learned style, to the advantage of the former.

23. Cf. the contemporary reports in Spohr/AUTOBIOGRAPHY I 191–92 (1814), Holmes/RAMBLE 261–64, Chorley/GERMAN II 5–11, Kaiser/WEBER 90.

Perhaps it was this latter style that brought a short unfavorable review acknowledging the sonata's craftsmanship but finding too little new—in fact, too little at all—that might justify the effort to master its difficulties.[24] Objections were also raised to the scoring, which suggested an arrangement rather than original keyboard music, and to the length, especially of the slow middle movement. But one can only guess that the reviewer could not quite accept Hummel's new subtlety, sensitivity, and freedom, for none of these objections seems valid today. The sonata is the shortest of Hummel's solos described here and the least difficult athletically if not musically. Moreover, it offers more actual melodic substance than any of its fellows.

Hummel's Op. 30 in C brought a much more favorable review,[25] with only the length being deplored again, this time with more reason (802 mss. in all, including his only slow introduction in a solo son., lasting 11 mss.). Above all, this work caters to a public attracted mainly by pianistic brilliance. In this respect it recalls Beethoven's Op. 2/3 even more than Hummel's Op. 2/3 had anticipated it. Except for its greater technical exploitations it makes no advance toward Romantic styles but rather a return to Mozartean manners (including the frequently cited resemblance of Op. 30/i/44–50 to Mozart's K. 300h/i/19–26).

Certainly the most remarkable advances into the new Romanticism —whether in harmonic vocabulary, tonal range, pianistic devices, melodic arabesque, introspective fantasy, or emotional import—occur in Hummel's "biggest" though not longest sonata, Op. 81 in f$\sharp$ (601 mss. in all, as against 836 in Op. 106).[26] In retrospect, the work sounds somewhat like a style melange of its time. Passages of unmitigated salon brilliance alternate with moments of new, unabashed and unspoiled drama like those in the contemporary chefs-d'oeuvre of Ries and Moscheles (also in f$\sharp$; ssb VII), or with sections of harmonic brooding that recall the late sonatas of Beethoven and Schubert, or with ingenious melodic decoration that anticipates Chopin's delicate figuration to a surprising degree[27] (Ex. 22).

Soon after its first appearance in 1819, Op. 81 received one of Hummel's most extended and enthusiastic reviews.[28] It was recognized as bringing the "otherwise strictly defined form" of the sonata to the

26a

24. AMZ IX (1806–7) 422.

25. AMZ XVIII (1816) 250–51.

26. The first mvt. has been recorded by Robert Collett in *The History of Music in Sound* VIII/5/iv (RCA LM 6146-2 for Oxford University Press, 1958).

27. Cf. the parallels in Davis/HUMMEL *passim* as illustrated variously between sundry works by Hummel, Beethoven, and Chopin.

28. AMZ XXII (1820) 114–16.

Ex. 22. From the middle movement of Johann Nepomuk Hummel's Sonata in f♯, Op. 81 (after Edition Peters No. 275b, pp. 16–17).

world of fantasy (hardly for the first time, as over two centuries of previous sonata history should show by now), with not a little influence from Weber. The reviewer found it meaningful, noble, spirited, pathetic, skillful, logical, novel, and pianistically resourceful to an extent truly deserving the term "Grosse Sonate" and making it the finest, also the most difficult, among all sonatas to date (!). As a youth of nineteen Schumann's one performance goal was to conquer the difficulties of this "epic, Titanic work," [29] which he later referred to as the one work by Hummel that would survive.[30]

One more decided style change occurs in Hummel's last solo piano sonata, Op. 106 in D. Except for its rather dull, cut-and-dried first

29. Schumann/JUGENDBRIEFE 80.

30. Schumann/SCHRIFTEN 395. Bülow played Op. 81 along with Liszt, Schumann, and Bach, in 1860 (BÜLOW BRIEFE IV 363; cf., also, III 50).

movement, with its etudelike passages in 3ds, this work is not so much a qualitative letdown, as usually stated,[31] but a neo-Classic return to tighter motivic writing, more conservative harmony and passagework, cooler ideas, and no fantasy. The title of the second movement, in this only Hummel solo sonata with four rather than three movements, implies such a return—"Un Scherzo all'antico." Yet the "Alternativo" in particular of this scherzo has all the rhythmic subtlety and contrapuntal life of "Alla danza tedesca" in Beethoven's still later Quartet in B♭, Op. 130 (pub. in 1827 as against 1824 for Hummel's Op. 106).

As different as these six sonatas are, from Op. 2/3 to 106, they do reveal at least five traits tangible enough to set Hummel apart from his contemporaries. But first should be mentioned what are regarded here as his two chief deficiencies. First, Hummel was not a distinguished melodist; and second, he was not especially fresh or original in the subsequent treatment of his ideas. At best his melodic invention, which never extends beyond a double period in the sonatas, is routine, as in Op. 106/iii/1-17. At worst it is decidedly trite, as in Op. 13/iii/35-51. The failing seems to lie more in uncompromising, non-plastic rhythmic organization than in the pitch outlines themselves. Hummel establishes himself more comfortably, as soon as the first, relatively simple statement ends, by hiding his melody behind florid, sometimes rhapsodic variations, at the making of which he was a past master (as in Ex. 22 above). As for the unoriginal treatment, Hummel knew the possibilities and did not addict himself to standardized formulas or designs. Yet those places where one might still expect the most imagination, as in development sections, are characteristically the most meager and uneventful. Nor are there those strokes of genius such as Beethoven's abrupt turn to e in Op. 57/i/79 or Schubert's sudden *fortissimo* dotted pattern in Op. 143 (D. 784)/i/28-29. Perhaps it was a sense of shortcomings in these respects that underlay the excessive belittlement of his own talents by the reportedly sincere and modest Hummel.[32] In any case, fine and successful as his best music was—and it does stand well above the run-of-the-mill of its time in our present historical perspective—those most able to judge, even among his contemporaries, soon came to see its limitations as well as its strengths.[33]

Among the five, more positive traits in Hummel's sonatas, two have already been cited—the delicate, pre-Chopinesque figuration illustrated above and the keen ear for piano resonance (as in the use of 10ths in the bass at Op. 20/i/126-32 and iii/27-34). The latter, evident as

---

31. E.g., Egert/FRÜHROMANTIKER 116, Davis/HUMMEL 177.

32. Cf. Chorley/GERMAN II 5-6.

33. E.g., cf. Deutsch/SCHUBERT-M 68, Saunders/WEBER 79.

much in his early writing for the five-octave Viennese piano (FF-f³) as in his later, expanded writing over six octaves (FF-e⁴), reflects his contemporary reputation as a front-rank pianist.[34] Pertinent to it is a third trait, a type of wide-roaming passagework comprising rather dissonant stretched figures that anticipate Schumann's writing, and modulating sequentially in broadly spaced phrases (Ex. 23).

Ex. 23. From the opening movement of Johann Nepomuk Hummel's Sonata in f♯, Op. 81 (after Edition Peters No. 275b, pp. 8–9).

A fourth distinctive trait, related to Hummel's high polyphonic skill, is his effective, intermittent reiteration of a kind of roving *cantus firmus* or freer *ostinato*. This idea, in steady half- or quarter-notes, usually provides more melodic distinction than any of his more extended thematic periods. Near the end of Op. 13/i the fullest statement of such a reiterated idea actually bears the label "Alleluia" and does approximate though not exactly duplicate several traditional alleluias (including some now to be found in the *Liber usualis*). In the slow, middle movement of Op. 20 the simple, initial idea spanning an octave in the bass grows and changes considerably. And in the extended coda of the finale the less clear-cut idea abruptly turns into that

34a

34. Cf. CZERNY 308–9; Chorley/GERMAN II 7–8 (including a backhanded tribute from Goethe in Weimar).

ubiquitous theme of the period known best in the finale of Mozart's "Jupiter Symphony." In unmistakable imitation of Mozart, Hummel treats it as a *fugato* subject, too (Ex. 24), later converting it to a dotted pattern. In the first movement of Op. 81, the stentorian, proclamatory opening in octaves returns only as a signpost in the design. But in the finale the idea approaches the St. Anne's tune in another *fugato* treatment.

Ex. 24. From the finale of Johann Nepomuk Hummel's Sonata in f, Op. 20 (after Schirmer's Library Vol. 45, p. 39).

The fifth trait is Hummel's tendency toward additive, sectional, free variation forms in both fast and slow movements. Op. 13 demonstrates in all three movements his ability to employ closed, integrated designs when he chose to, including in the first the "sonata form" that was to become standard in 19th-century textbooks. But already in the last two movements of Op. 20 each section follows the one before more as a new variant than as a diametric contrast or unequivocal return. These variants even seem to carry over to the succeeding movements, imparting a diffuse cyclic unity, as in Op. 30. Sometimes the sectional divisions give way to continuous unfolding, whether in fugal writing or modulatory, sequential passagework, both of which govern the form of Op. 106/iii.

A few more words should be added on Hummel with regard to his lighter, but equally skillful, ensemble sonatas. The two extant duets achieved considerable popularity[35]—the "Sonate ou divertissement," Op. 51, with its "Marcia," "Andante," and "Rondo, con brio"; and the "Grande Sonate" Op. 92, with a "Grave" introduction to its three movements. The responsibilities are fairly equally divided in these duets, as they are in the other ensembles, whether the accompaniments are marked "obligato" or not. The admittedly fine Sonata in A for P & Vc, or P & Fl, Op. 104, won reviews as hyperbolic as the review cited above for Op. 81:

We say at once, and without any reservation, that this is not only one of the most masterly and beautiful compositions by Hummel that ever fell under our notice, but one of the best and most effective works of the kind, by any author, that we ever heard. The design is elegant and original; there is a definable and melodious subject running through every part of it; the modulations, unexpected and scientific as they are, seem natural and as if accomplished without any labour or research; the harmony is the handmaid of the air, and the various passages which dilate the subject, and throw it into different forms, never lose their analogy and connection, while they abound in novel and happy combinations.[36]

The Sonata for P and mandolin, Op. 37, is a reminder that **Hummel** was an expert guitarist as well as pianist.[37]

Minor Composers in South Germany and Switzerland

Other composers of sonatas in south Germany, mainly around Munich and Mannheim, call for only brief mention here. **Franz Danzi** (1763–1826) was a link between the 18th-century Mannheim School, where he was born and trained (under Vogler; SCE 573–75), and the early German Romantic opera, on which he exercised considerable influence, especially as mentor and friend to the 23-year younger Weber.[38] A pupil of Vogler (SCE 573–75), cellist, conductor, writer, and composer of opera, symphony, and chamber music, Danzi moved to Munich in 1783, Stuttgart in 1807 (9 years before Hummel), and Karlsruhe in 1812. While in these three cities he composed some fifty instrumental chamber works, including around sixteen sonatas published in Munich, Leipzig, Paris, Vienna, and Zürich between about 1797 and 1824. These

35. Cf. AMZ XXXIV (1832) 12–13 on Op. 92.

36. HARMONICON IV/1 (1826) 166–67. This review pertains to the Vc version. One year later the same work was reviewed similarly in the same periodical, in the Fl version (HARMONICON V/1 [1827] 243–44, with 2 exx.); the reviewer did not recognize the same work but recalled the earlier review and said the new work was "entitled to still higher consideration"!

37. Cf. Bone/GUITAR 173–80, with exx.

38. Cf. MGG II 1895–1900 (W. Virneisel), with further references.

last are fairly equally divided between scorings for P solo, P-duet, P & Hn-or-Vc, 2 cellos, and P & Vn, plus one unusual setting for two pianos and obligatory violin (Op. 42).[39] The three sonatas by Danzi that could be examined here, all P & Hn-or-Vc, reveal no neglected master, but they do reveal more of a true melodist than Hummel was, and a knowing composer who could write fluently, with sure purpose. The music shows less of the Romantic tendencies than are credited to his operas, and then chiefly in the breadth of his ideas and the new instrumental flare that they incorporate rather than in any special fantasy, harmonic adventure, or textural innovation.[40]

The versatile **Franz** (Graf von) **Pocci** (1807–76), a kind of E. T. A. Hoffmann in Munich, left two curious piano sonatas, published in 1832–34.[41] The first he called *Sonate fantastique* and the second *Frühlings-Sonate*. Writing as the poetic Eusebius in a review of both works (1835), Schumann railed, in part,[42]

If anyone had hidden the title [page] from me I should have guessed [it was the work of] a composeress, and perhaps have judged thus: Whatever might be your name—Adele, Zuleika—I love you right off, like all who write sonatas! If only you had ended the way you started—for example, in the Spring Sonata, where veritable sweet violets give off their scent on the first page . . . I would never frighten you with words like "tonic," "dominant," or even "counterpoint," for you would laughingly interrupt me and say, "I wrote it just so and cannot do otherwise". . . . Were I your teacher and smart [about it], I would put Bach or Beethoven in your hands often ([but] of Weber, whom you love so much, absolutely nothing), thereby to sharpen your ear and eye, so as to provide a secure foothold for your tender feelings as well as definition and form for your ideas. And then I should know nothing that even the "newest" periodical could say of you that would not rhyme with "love and beauty."

But at the end of this fanciful paragraph the rude, precipitate Florestan took over to add,

How subtly my Eusebius beats around the bush! Why not [come] right out with it: "The count has a great deal of talent but little training."

39. A partial thematic index of Danzi's chamber music, including 4 sons. (and 3 sons. Op. 1 for P & Vn by his wife Margarethe) appears in DTB-m XVI, pp. xxxi–xxxii (H. Riemann). For mod. eds. of 2 sons. for P & Hn-or-Vc, Opp. 28 and 44, cf. Richter/KAMMERMUSIK 187.

40. "Pleasing and fluent" is the burden of 6 mostly short reviews of 6 sons. by Danzi, ranging from moderate to high praise, in AMZ II (1799–1800) 456, VII (1804–5) 505–6, VIII (1805–6) 382–84 (with ex.), XI (1808–9) 192, XII (1809–10) 112, XXI (1819) 204.

41. Cf. MGG X 1363–64 (O. Kaul); Hirschberg/POCCI (mainly an annotated catalogue of his works, plus descriptive comments), especially pp. 43, 46–48, with exx.; Egert/FRÜHROMANTIKER 149–51 (with ex.).

42. Schumann/SCHRIFTEN I 92.

On the basis of this review, quite different from one the year before that dwelt mainly on the "fantastique" in the first sonata,[43] Pocci resolved to attempt no further large works.[44] Both sonatas are in minor, with the finales in relative major. *Sonate fantastique,* in a/C, has four movements, F-M-Mi-F, and *Frühlings-Sonate,* in e/G, has three, F-M-F. Several of the movements aim at arch form through the "m-n-o-n-m" mirror design of their component ideas. Along with harmonic and melodic flashes of interest, and some resourceful piano writing there are, indeed, many vapid and sophomoric pages in Pocci's sonatas.

Probably the most important violinist in south Germany, **Thomas Täglichsbeck** (1799–1867) trained and served in Munich from 1816 to 1827 and served about 125 miles west in Hechingen until 1848, apart from wide concert tours.[45] Not until 1841, while at the latter post, nor until considerable lighter music had appeared from his pen, did Täglichsbeck publish the first, Op. 16 in a,[46] of at least four sonatas for his instrument with piano. This four-movement work was reviewed from a reprint in 1846 as showing solid training but no originality; as going through the motions of the sonata without imparting life, imagination, or fantasy; as concentrating on single motives to the point of exhaustion; and as being not too difficult but not especially grateful for the two instruments.[47] A set of three further sonatas for P & Vn, Op. 30, listed as "progressive . . . preparatory studies for the Beethoven [P & Vn sons.]," appeared in 1859.[48]

In Mannheim, **Gottfried Weber** (1779–1839), remembered today chiefly as a theorist and writer (whose own occasional son. reviews are cited elsewhere in SSB), was also a conductor, composer, and, like Danzi, important mentor and friend, though no relative, of Carl Maria von Weber.[49] About 1810 Simrock published his only known sonata, a solo piano work in C, in two movements (F-In/VF), dedicated to the eight-year younger Carl Maria. In a short witty letter of June 18, 1811, Nikolaus Simrock told Gottfried his sonata "sleeps safe and sound" because "it is too lofty and, seriously, too difficult for dilettantes"; only a very favorable review could save it.[50] Such a review did follow in 1812, by Carl Maria von Weber himself, praising especially the second movement and finding the writing highly efficient in

43. AMZ XXXVI (1834) 752.
44. Hirschberg/POCCI 48.
45. Cf. MGG XIII 45–46 (F. Göthel), with further references.
46. Cf. Altmann/KAMMERMUSIK 229.
47. NZM XXV (1846) 127–28 (F. Brendel?), with exx.
48. HOFMEISTER V (1852–59) 65, Altmann/KAMMERMUSIK 229.
49. Cf. GROVE IX 224 (L. Middleton).
50. Altmann/WEBER 491.

its richness, although suggestive more of a quartet transcription, with little opportunity for the pianist to show off except through the (mainly contrapuntal?) meaning itself.[51] Perhaps both the praise and the reservation prompted Simrock to add an optional violin part (for the dilettante?) in what seems to have been only a further edition of this same work.[52] At any rate, the work does reveal the depth and skill, yet not the sterility, that might be expected of a theorist who also composed.

The brilliant pianist **Johann Peter Pixis** (1788–1874) spent his early years in Mannheim and his later years in Baden-Baden.[53] In between, he studied with Albrechtsberger and got to know both Beethoven and Schubert in Vienna,[54] before spending several years in France, England, and Italy. Both Liszt and Schumann found qualities to admire in him.[55] Yet the lexicographer Schilling, comparing his flashy performance with that of Henri Herz, considered him one step short of charlatanism.[56] Crowd-catching display is certainly a conspicuous trait of the one sonata by Pixis that could be examined here, Op. 14 in three movements (F-M-Ro), for piano with "Violon obligé." But pianistic fluency, good craftsmanship, and attractive melodies are among its traits, too.[57] Out of over 150 works by Pixis still listed in PAZDÍREK XXII 392–94, five are solo or ensemble sonatas. As many more were originally published in the same period, from about 1812 to 1832, the last of which, Op. 85 for piano solo, is dedicated to Cramer.[58]

In Switzerland, an unusual composer was the now obscure pianist, teacher, and conductor **Antoine Liste** (1772–1832), who came from Hildesheim in central Germany to study with Albrechtsberger in Vienna, eventually settling, from 1804 on, in Zürich.[59] Among a rela-

---

51. AMZ XIV (1812) 179–80, with ex.; also in Weber/WEBER III 52–53 and Kaiser/WEBER 186–88. In Kaiser/WEBER 530 is also a witty 3-voice canon, dated 1810, presumably addressed by Carl Maria to Gottfried, with the title, "When Weber wrote me that I should play his new sonata in the evening," followed by a text that begins, "I ought to play the sonata, what unspeakable terror! Ah, I tremble . like a stone!"; cf. Benedict/WEBER 163.

52. Listed in HOFMEISTER 1828 (Whistling), 512.

53. Cf. MGG X 1317–19 (R. Sietz).

54. According to MGG X 1317. Cf. Schindler & MacArdle/BEETHOVEN 441–42; Deutsch/SCHUBERT-I 302–3.

55. According to MGG X 1318. Cf. Schumann/SCHRIFTEN II 221–22.

56. Schilling/LEXICON V 477.

57. These virtues (except for specifics singled out in the part-writing), plus considerable warmth and depth, are credited to Pixis's 4-mvt. solo P Son. in E♭, Op. 3 (same as Op. 2?) in a long review in AMZ XIV (not XII; 1812) 526–30.

58. Cf. HOFMEISTER (Whistling), 1815, 372; 1828, 500; HOFMEISTER (1829–33) 132.

59. MGG VIII 961–62 (H. P. Schanzlin), with further references; also, Schilling/LEXICON IV 413–14. No confirmation of study with Mozart or solo P sons. Opp. 1 and 12 by Liste (all in Fétis/BU V 317–18) could be found here. A full study of the man and his music should be of value.

tively few works presently known by him are seven sonatas, all published between 1804 and 1815 (with six getting reviews in AMZ as
listed below):

2 Sonatas, in E♭ and G, P solo, in Anth. NÄGELI-m Suite 9, (1804). Cf.
AMZ VII (1804–5) 284–89, with exx.
"Grande Sonate" in B♭, Op. 2, P-duet, Breitkopf & Härtel, *ca.* 1810.
Cf. AMZ XIII (1811) 210–12.
"Grande Sonate" in A, P solo, in Anth. NÄGELI-m Suite 17, (1810);
ded. to Beethoven. Cf. AMZ XIII (1811) 210–13.
"Grande Sonate" in ?, Op. 3, P & Bn-or-Vc, Breitkopf & Härtel, *ca.*
1811.
"Sonate" in A, Op. 8, P solo, Breitkopf & Härtel, 1814 or 1815. Cf.
AMZ XVII (1815) 836–37.
"Sonate" in E♭, Op. 6, P solo, Breitkopf & Härtel, 1815 at latest. Cf.
AMZ XVIII (1816) 96.

Not only Nägeli's proximity in Zürich but his special tastes in the
sonata (SCE 26; SSB IV) must help to explain his publication of three
of Liste's solo sonatas. For in spite of the better foundation these
exhibit, they prove to be as uneven, unpredictable, and spotty as those
by Pocci (*supra*). Of most interest both musically and stylistically are
such newly Romantic traits as harmonic progressions and modulations
that rival Schubert's in boldness and surprise; wide-spaced scoring,
sometimes on three contrapuntal planes (which already suffer for want
of scoring on three staffs such as F. Pollini first employed, in 1820; cf.
SCE 298); naively charming melodies that achieve wide spans through
reiterations of short segments; copious dynamics and expressive inscriptions; and some inventive passagework. Our facsimile of a page
from Nägeli's enterprise, Ex. 25, illustrates several of these traits as
well as a discard of barlines, in a slow introduction by Liste; the
double-barline at the end merely precedes an immediate return to A
through its secondary dominant, followed by the second half of this
introduction. The "Minuetto molto allegro" that is the penultimate
movement (iii) in this sonata resembles Carl Maria von Weber's "Invitation to the Dance" rather than a traditional minuet.
Unfortunately, these traits in Liste's music do not offset sufficiently
the aimlessness and lack of tonal or thematic unity in the over-all structures; nor the frequent dullness of the left-hand accompaniments, with
their routine chordal figures and repeated notes. The first of several
rather long and typically wordy reviews (by Rochlitz?) of Liste's
sonatas evinces an eagerness to approve and understand the novelty,

Ex. 25. From the opening of Antoine Liste's first Sonata in A
(facs. of p. 2 in "Suite" [vol.] 17 of Anth NÄGELI-m at the Library
of Congress).

along with a desire to instruct the novice composer in the correction
of specific "errors." Some of these errors could have been made by the
engraver, for engraver's errors abound in Anth. NÄGELI (as, presumably, near the end of the foregoing example). The subsequent reviews
recall and try not to contradict the first review but show increasing
discomfort over that formlessness and rambling of the sonatas.

The notable Swiss composer and intellectual **Franz Xaver Schnyder
von Wartensee** (1786–1868) should at least be mentioned here, too,
although he left little in our field—two early piano sonatas, in C
(1814; pub. by Simrock in Bonn) and f (1814–15; not pub.), and, after
he moved to Frankfurt/M in 1817, a single sonata for P & Vn (1825;
not pub.).[60] The long "Andante" from the first of these may reflect the
formalistic influence of Schnyder von Wartensee's friend Nägeli and
the Classic influence of his stay in Vienna (1811–12, including acquaintance with Beethoven, Czerny, and Moscheles). It commands

60. Cf. MGG XI 1922–26 (P. O. Schneider), with further bibliography. Mod. ed. of
"Andante" from Son. in C for P: Frey & Schuh/SCHWEIZER-m 20.

respect for his sure control of his materials, including intricate metric relationships. The ideas lack distinction.

Weber in Central Germany

Carl Maria von Weber (1786–1826) occupies a special and important historical niche not only as the founder of Romantic German opera but, in our smaller arena, as a significant pioneer of the Romantic piano sonata. If the contributions are not quite analogous and his contribution to the sonata is not, even relatively, quite so outstanding, it is chiefly because his sonatas betray more of the shortcomings of inadequate, largely self-directed training. Furthermore, his sonatas derived more from his operatic and orchestral interests than his operas derived from his pianistic interests, and they faced more competition from contemporary works in their class, including sonatas by Schubert, Hummel, and Dussek, insofar as these sonatas also pioneered Romantic trends. Yet no less an authority than Adolf Bernhard Marx judged in 1824 that Weber's piano compositions, meaning primarily his sonatas, are "next to Beethoven's unquestionably the most important and valuable of the whole newer period, often even surpassing those in grandeur and make-up." [61] Granting that we no longer can accept that dictum, we still have to recognize the genius that could invent such fresh melodies and exploit so imaginatively the sonorities and techniques of the piano that in spite of those undeniable shortcomings at least two of his sonatas continue to attract performers.

The student looking into Weber's music will find all the precise biographic and bibliographic information he is likely to need and much more in two exhaustive, careful, fascinating labors-of-love from the third quarter of the 19th century. Only a few recent corrections or clarifications would have to be added. [62] One of these sources is the three-volume account of his father's life and cultural environment by Max Maria von Weber (1864–66), with extensive incorporation of letters, writings for publication, diaries running from 1810 to death, reviews of his own works, and other autobiographic or contemporary documents. [63] The other, leaning heavily on Max's biography and other

61. As quoted in Jähns/WEBER 8. Cf. similar praise by A. Marmontel in 1881, as quoted in Georgii/WEBER 20.

62. Dünnebeil/WEBER is a recent Weber bibliography.

63. Weber/WEBER (unindexed, but cross references occur regularly in Jähns/WEBER, q.v., pp. 9–10). Benedict/WEBER and P. Spitta's original article on Weber, cut considerably in GROVE (5th ed.) VII 195–222, summarize the essentials of Weber/WEBER efficiently, adding a few corrections and extensive independent evaluations. Kaiser/WEBER is a more complete collection of the writings. Among the many

materials made available, is—to translate the long, explicit title—"Carl Maria von Weber in his Works: Chronological-Thematic Index of His Collected Compositions Plus an Account of [Those That Are] Incomplete, Lost, Doubtful, and Spurious; With Descriptions of the Autographs, Indications of the Editions and Arrangements, Critical, Art-Historical, and Biographic Annotations, Utilizing Weber's Letters and Diaries, and a Supplement of facsimiles of His Handwriting," by the vocal pedagogue, composer, and Weber devotee Friedrich Wilhelm Jähns (1871).[64] In short, this last is an elaborate (and acknowledged) imitation of Köchel's chronological Mozart index of 1862, augmented by extended analyses and evaluations of the music.

Weber lived out his relatively short life of not quite forty years so hectically, so peripatetically, so diversely that it is not easy to find stable points of reference against which to view his sonatas.[65] His hectic existence related partly to social behavior that ranged from the giddy brink of utter moral dissolution, especially while he was enmeshed in Duke Ludwig's intrigues at Stuttgart, to the comparative peace of deeply religious convictions, especially in his last years. His peripatetic existence resulted primarily from the life in the theater, going back to earliest childhood, and from numerous concert tours as a virtuoso pianist. It included, among many, more fleeting visits, at least short residences in Salzburg from 1796 to 1798 and 1801–2 (with brief study under Michael Haydn), and in Vienna from 1803 to 1804 (with the Abbé Vogler [scE 573–75] first exercising his lasting influence on Weber). Then followed a series of increasingly important posts, all disturbed in varying degrees by professional frictions and dissatisfactions. These started with Breslau from 1804 to 1806, after which came Stuttgart from 1807 to 1810, Prague from 1813 to 1816, and finally, Dresden from 1816, or just before his marriage with Caroline Brandt, which did bring him unprecedented content and happiness, though but little abatement in the countless travels. The diversity of Weber's existence resulted largely from his own versatility. To the excellence of this appealing, debonair, resourceful artist as composer and pianist must be added his front rank as a conductor and as an opera director, also his substantial contributions as a writer on music (including re-

publications that continue to appear on Weber, Saunders/WEBER (1940) remains the most satisfactory one-vol. survey in English on his life and works. But cf. ML XLIX (1968) 233–37 (E. Croft-Murray) on Warrack/WEBER (pub. too late to be incorporated here).

64. Jähns/WEBER, in which cf. pp. 9–14.

65. His own autobiographic sketch (printed in Weber/WEBER III [a complete vol. of his writings], pp. 175–80 and Kaiser/WEBER 3–8) helps to determine the turning points up to 1818.

views of sons. by G. Weber and Lauska cited in SSB VIII). Less pertinent here were still other sides of his versatility, such as his belletristic activities outside the realm of music, or his early exploits in painting, music engraving, and singing (until the accident that damaged his voice in 1806).

Originating intermittently from his 13th to his 36th year (1799–1822), at least 14 sonatas—7 solo, one P-duet, and 6 P & Vn—were composed by Weber.[66] This total, minute and incidental as it was in terms of his over-all output, includes the four main piano solo sonatas, written in the decade from 1812 to 1822, that still figure among his comparatively few works kept alive today. It does not include the still popular *Grand duo concertant* in E♭, Op. 48, for piano and clarinet (J. 204), which Weber himself referred to as a "Sonate" in his diary references to its composition.[67] But it does include an early lost set of "Drei Sonaten für's Fortepiano" (J. Anh. 16–18 or 20–22). Apparently Weber listed the set twice, under 1799, in his own published "Werk-Verzeichniss," [68] perhaps because he submitted it for publication once in 1800 to Artaria[69] and again, in 1801 to André (both times in vain). No later record of these boyhood works exists, but they must have been written with some degree of skill, imagination, and understanding, to judge by his *Sechs Fugetten* (J. 1–6) already published as Op. 1 in 1798 (with M. Haydn's help?) or, more pertinently, by his Variations Op. 2 of 1800 (J. 7).[70] Op. 2 reveals not only the neat Classic passagework in scales and arpeggios to be expected of the young man who knew both Haydns and was a first cousin to the late Mozart. It also reveals the fast passages in octaves, wide leaps, and 10th-chords that clearly herald the virtuoso.

Weber's four-hand Sonatina in C Op. 3/1 (J. 9) is another early

66. No explanation could be found here for Weber's single mention, in a letter to J. Gänsbacher of Dec. 17, 1816 (Nohl/GLUCK & WEBER 210), of having written "up to now . . . a new sonata in D♭"; no other source discovered here mentions such a work.

67. Cf. Jähns/WEBER 217, 133; AMZ XX (1818) 442–43 (favorable review by Rochlitz); MT XX (1879) 605 (performance under the title "Sonata").

68. At least, Jähns/WEBER 427–28 seems to give 2 sets of nos. to a single set of sons. For the "Werk-Verzeichniss," cf. p. 15, item 7; also, Heyer/HISTORICAL 346.

69. Cf. Nohl/GLUCK & WEBER 86–87; Saunders/WEBER 16–17.

70. Facs. of Op. 1 engraved in open score and 4 clefs by Weber himself: Hausswald/WEBER 56–60 (but this is not a first mod. ed., as indicated on pp. 312 and 314; e.g., Op. 1 appears in condensed P score in Augener Ed. 8470, p. 184). Although H. J. Moser's abortive "Gesamtausgabe" of 1926–28 did not get to any instrumental works, the 2-vol. pub. under H. W. Stolze's editorship in 1857 had got far enough to include all the extant sons. (cf. Heyer/HISTORICAL 346–47 [with errors]). Today these are all still readily available in several eds., including Peters Ed. 188A, 191, and 717A.

work, probably composed in 1801 and first published in 1803.[71]
Dedicated to J. P. Schulthesius (SCE 302), it is a gracefully melodious,
unpretentious piece in one movement of 61 measures, the first of "Six
petites Pièces Faciles." [72] Nine years later Weber wrote a whole set of
sonatas with pedagogic intentions, this time *Six Sonates progressives
pour le pianoforte avec violon obligé,* Op. 10 (also pub. as Op. 13 and
Op. 17; J. 99–104).[73] "Dediées aux amateurs," these sonatas are also
melodious, fluent, and unpretentious. Their keys do not exceed three
sharps or flats, d being the sole minor key. With an average length of
only about 250 measures, half of the sonatas have two moderate or
quick movements and half add a middle, slow movement. The violin
is an independent though not an equal partner in the duo. Obviously
Weber knew his market. Instead of risking the sort of fantasy and
display that were to characterize the four solo sonatas, he appealed to
amateurs with light rondo finales (Sons. 1–4), with a "Tema dell' opera
Silvana," and with five movements brightened by nationalistic colors
—"Carattere espagnuolo," "Air polonais," "Air russe," "Siciliano,"
and "Polacca." As he wrote his mentor Gottfried Weber in Darmstadt,
the set "cost me more sweat than as many symphonies." [74] Yet André
rejected Op. 10 in 1810 (leaving it for Simrock to publish in 1811), on
the curious grounds that the pieces "are too good"! [75] Perhaps André's
further objections led to the revisions and enrichments made by
Moscheles, including a considerable transfer of melodic responsibility
to the violin.[76] Unfortunately, delightful as this music is, it still does
not offer the violinist enough, as it is published today, to interest him
in playing it.

Weber's Four Big Piano Sonatas

The circumstances surrounding each of Weber's four main solo
sonatas should be noted before the nature of their music is considered

71. Jähns/WEBER 45–47.

72. "Good in melody, fluent, and correct," wrote Rochlitz of the set, in AMZ
VI (1803–4) 252. Weber's Op. 60 for P-duet (1818–19) consists of 8 separate, un-
related character pieces that have been mislabeled "Sonatinas" posthumously (cf.
Jähns/WEBER 251–52).

73. Mod. ed. of Czerny's transcription of No. 6 as a P-duet: Zeitlin & Gold-
berger/DUETS-m 42. The review in AMZ XVII (1815) 609 treats Op. 10 purely as a
pedagogic collection.

74. Jähns/WEBER 121.

75. Jähns/WEBER 121–22; Nohl/GLUCK & WEBER 102–3 (with further details).

76. Jähns/WEBER 122. Cf., also, Cobbett/CHAMBER II 570 (W. Altmann and W. W.
Cobbett).

here.[77] All four sonatas were first published by Schlesinger in Berlin soon after the completion of each. Jähns could find a complete autograph only for the last one, a partial, early draft for the third, and no autograph for either the first or second. The first "Grosse Sonate" (as each was called in print), Op. 24 in C (J. 138), was composed in Berlin and first published in 1812. Weber finished the popular "Rondo" finale before the other movements, naming it "L'Infatigable," although Charles Alkan's title for it, "Perpetuum mobile," has since been preferred.[78] In some amusing letters Weber tells of practicing the "Rondo" not in C but in C♯ in order to revive "rusty" fingers, and of wanting to agree only too readily when the dedicatee despaired of ever learning this sonata, except that one hardly reacted so to the Grand Duchess Maria Paulowna of Weimar.[79] Czerny, Brahms (*Studien* No. 2), and Tchaikovsky (Ju. 92) were among those who made special arrangements of the "Rondo." [80] Gottfried Weber opened a three-column review of Op. 24 by citing its most distinctive trait as "a wealth of ideas and harmonic richness." [81] He called it a work that would delight the connoisseurs, with both aesthetic and pianistic challenges, a full melodically active texture, and a tight unity except in the second movement, which goes too long without a return of its initial idea.

Weber's second and third sonatas—Op. 39 in A♭ (J. 199), dedicated to Lauska, and Op. 49 in d/D (J. 206), without dedication—were written close together, Op. 39 alternately in Prague and Berlin in early 1814 and in 1816, and Op. 49 in Berlin in late 1816 (in but 20 days). A first performance of each by Weber followed quickly, in 1816 for Op. 39 and 1817 for Op. 49. Rochlitz, whom Weber first met in 1811 and had already known well through correspondence,[82] wrote a long and particularly glowing review covering both sonatas.[83] Before describing

77. A detailed up-to-date study of Weber's sons. is lacking. Nearest to it is still the section pp. 16–27, in the 1914 diss. Georgii/WEBER; 2 other, unpub. diss. of 1914 (Schaal/DISSERTATIONEN items 268 and 2335) include Weber's sons, but have not been available here and are not listed in Dünnebeil/WEBER nor Egert/FRÜH-ROMANTIKER 92–101. This last, as well as Selva/SONATE 172–84, Hall/PIANOFORTE 183–93, and Dale/NINETEENTH 43–53 provide 4 of the chief, more recent summaries of Weber's P sons. Saunders/WEBER 223–25 goes widest of the mark, as viewed here, in the much needed re-evaluation of these sons.

78. Jähns/WEBER 160–61.

79. Weber/WEBER I 359, 361, 372, 377, 382, 384.

80. Czerny's arrangement (cf. Egert/FRÜHROMANTIKER 101) could not be confirmed here.

81. AMZ XV (1813) 595–98. A favorable review of Op. 24 when Moscheles played it in London in 1837 appears in MUSICAL WORLD IV (1836–37) 156.

82. Weber/WEBER I 313. Regarding "modernizations" that both Liszt and Henselt made in Op. 39, cf. SSB V, with ex.

83. AMZ XX (1818) 681–88.

these very different works separately, he noted certain virtues they shared in common. Thus, he rated them among the finest sonatas of the day in their thorough and meaningful exploitation of single ideas, whether through harmonic, figural, or pianistic variants. He found the works extraordinarily difficult to play at times, but never without justification, being somewhat like Spohr's for the violin in this respect.[84] His most unqualified praise of individual movements went to the "Menuetto capriccio" ("assuredly!" he adds) of Op. 39 and the "Rondo presto" of Op. 49. The latter became known under the title "Allegro di bravura," given to it in what Jähns called "one of the most monstrous" arrangements in the pianist's world, by Czerny.[85] Overjoyed with Rochlitz's review, Weber replied with a letter to him that, understandably, emphasizes the fine perception of the reviewer and the ideal mating of review and composition.[86] In the infrequent per- [86a] formances of Weber's sonatas today Op. 39 is heard most frequently in public, although only Opp. 49 and 70 happen to be available in commercial recordings, the latter with three choices (as of 1967). In the 19th century the performances discovered here show that Op. 49 was in the lead, with Op. 39, then Op. 24, not far behind, and Op. 70 decidedly in the minority.[87] Jähns saw Op. 24 relating to Op. 39 somewhat as *Der Freischütz* to *Euryanthe,* the first opening the door to Romanticism and the second presenting it in full bloom. The last of the four sonatas, Op. 70 in e (J. 287), was composed in the three years from 1819 to 1822, mostly in Dresden and right in the same highly productive period as "Invitation to the Dance" (J. 260), *Der Freischütz* (J. 277), and *Concert-Stück* in f (J. 282). Although dedicated to Rochlitz and published promptly, it received no special reviews or other attention.

To get to the music of Weber's four big solo sonatas, we might first note their average length of 945 measures, or about nine per cent more than in Schubert's completed sonatas. But their average playing time is probably no greater than for Schubert's sonatas, because proportionately more of Weber's movements are fast or faster. Jähns observes that Weber's four "grosse" sonatas constitute his biggest in-

84. In his *Practical Pianoforte School* Charles Hallé put Op. 49/ii and iii in the "very difficult class" (MT XVI [1874] 701).

85. Jähns/WEBER 220.

86. Quoted in full in Jähns/WEBER 214.

87. E.g., cf. AMA No. 22 (Nov. 25, 1826) 169; RGM for Feb. 11, 1838; MT XII (1866) 448 (with Op. 39 called a "somewhat wild . . . composition"), XIII (1868) 446 and 580, XVI (1873) 361, XVII (1876) 500 and 708, XVIII (1877) 245, 277, and 553, XX (1879) 332 and 646, XXI (1880) 87, 173, 303, 306, and 355, XXII (1881) 138–39, XXIII (1882) 668, XXIV (1884) 135 (on neglect of Weber's sons.), etc.; Dent/BUSONI 331.

strumental works, totaling almost as many measures as all of *Euryanthe*.[88] Three of these sonatas are in four movements in typical cycles of F-S-Mi-Ro (Op. 24), F-M-Mi-Ro (Op. 39), or F-Mi-M-VF (Op. 70). Op. 49 is the exception in omitting the minuet. The sonatas are equally divided between major and minor keys. Although change of mode is frequent, including the change to the tonic major throughout the finale of Op. 49, only the moderate or slow movement is in a foreign key and then always a nearly related key. Except for the incipits of Op. 70/i, ii, and perhaps iv, Weber seems not to have tried to unify the cycles through similar thematic materials.[89]

Three of Weber's rondo finales received or acquired titles—"L'Infatigable" or "Perpetuum mobile" in Op. 24 and "Allegro bravura" in Op. 49 (as noted above), and "La Tarantella" in Op. 70—but he supplied no programmes in the four sonatas.[90] Yet, according to his biographer Julius Benedict, who had been his pupil, protégé, and close friend during the last five years, when Weber wrote Op. 70 he had in mind a sad story of gradual mental deterioration, letting up only in the third movement and leading ultimately to "exhaustion and death."[91] Jähns hears Op. 49 as being dominated much of the time by a demonic spirit, and, indeed, it has been dubbed "Demoniac." However, Weber's piano music actually belies such gloom and terror. The same genial temperament that preferred happy endings in *Der Freischütz* and *Euryanthe* also preferred not to dwell too far or long from major keys, pleasant melodies, and gay dance rhythms.

Weber's detailed diaries reveal that he wrote his final movements first, and the initial and slowest movements last.[92] In other words, he seems to have found it easiest to write the fast, light, dancelike movements—the minuets, which are scherzos in all but the name,[93] and the rondos, which all come close to being perpetual-motion finales. And right from the start of the four sonatas, these are unquestionably the most successful movements, the most resourceful in their composition techniques (Ex. 26), yet the freest from intrinsic problems of style and form. The other movements have problems not because they introduce new designs or indulge in excessive fantasy. Actually, Weber seems to have accepted traditional designs without question; when he produced

88. Jähns/WEBER 160; but his total of 4486 mss., or 64 less than in *Euryanthe*, includes all repetitions as well as da capo sections (cf. SSB Preface).

89. Contrary to the statement and exx. in Kroll/WEBER 71–73.

90. He did supply a literal romancer's sort of programme for *Concert-Stück* in f, as quoted in Weber/WEBER II 311–12.

91. Benedict/WEBER 155.

92. Jähns/WEBER 161, 214, 220, and 346; Egert/FRÜHROMANTIKER 94–96.

93. Weber actually referred to Op. 70/ii as "Scherzo" in his diary (Jähns/WEBER 346).

Ex. 26. From the "Minuetto" of Carl Maria von Weber's
Sonata in C, Op. 24 (after Augener's Ed., No. 8470, p. 14).

some tonal or thematic variant that now appears irregular for its day—
like starting the recapitulation in the lowered mediant in Op. 24/i/98,
or returning to only the first phrase and varying it three times in Op.
24/ii/65-84—this variant was as likely to be accidental as intentional.
"Sonata form" approximately like that described soon after in textbooks (SSB II) can be charted readily enough in each of the first movements, and A-B-A or a sort of variation-rondo design in each of the
slowest movements. But the problem within these designs remains that
of any musical form created in the language that was then current—
that is, how best to treat and integrate particular ideas in a particular
time span.

Thus, Op. 24/i fails, as viewed here, because it is not dynamic
enough to sustain interest throughout its 161 measures. Its charming
but naively square-cut thematic units (Ex. 27) and its apparently unpremeditated tonal course occur statically, without effective integration
or compelling direction. To be sure, the proclamatory, descending
arpeggio that opens the sonata recurs just before and during the
development section and, though not at the recapitulation, again in
the coda. But a plain arpeggio, much less one on the ambiguous dim.-
7th chord, lacks sufficient identity to unify the movement. If Beethoven
really did make that remark about *Euryanthe,* that it is "an accumula-
tion of diminished-7th chords, [all serving as] mere escapes," [94] he
could as well have been speaking of the four sonatas, especially this
first movement. The latter happens to show, of course, that back in
1812 Weber had been less touched by Beethoven's methods and struc-

94. Ascribed to Schindler by G. Kaiser, as noted, with doubts, in Kroll/
BEETHOVEN 138-39.

Ex. 27. From the first movement of Carl Maria von Weber's Sonata in C, Op. 24 (after Augener's Ed., No. 8470, p. 4).

tures in the sonata than any other important young Romantic we shall meet here. In fact, from the standpoint of Weber's style innovations, the early friction created between the two men by his juvenile, intemperate disparagement of Beethoven's third and fourth symphonies, published in 1809,[95] could be viewed as a blessing in disguise. But at the time of *Euryanthe* (1823) Weber was on the best of terms with the Viennese master.[96] It is only a pity that Beethoven, who sent both his last piano sonata, Op. 111, and his "Diabelli Variations" to Weber in Dresden in the summer of 1823, made no comments that have been preserved on Weber's later sonatas, which he may well have known. The better documented objections to a lack of melody and structural organization in *Euryanthe* that come from Schubert, who also seems to have been on fine personal terms with Weber, must be attributed at least in part to the German and Italian opera factions then competing in Vienna.[97]

Op. 24/ii fails somewhat, as viewed here, not so much because its

95. Cf. Kroll/BEETHOVEN 126–29; also, Schindler & MacArdle/BEETHOVEN 479–83.

96. Cf. Thayer & Forbes/BEETHOVEN II 863, 871–74. Benedict/WEBER 62 describes his fine spirited playing of Beethoven's sons. in 1821.

97. Cf. Jähns/WEBER 368; Deutsch/SCHUBERT-D 294–95, 301, 310, 892.

ideas again fall into square-cut, static units—such units were the norm, then, in slower movements—but because, as Gottfried Weber implied (*supra*), the form straggles. The B section in the ostensible (and intended?) A-B-A' design subdivides into two sections (12+28 mss.), each. long and distinct enough to rank on a par with the A or A' sections (24+25 mss.), so that the total effect is rather the much more additive one of A-B-C-A. Such an extended form is more likely to succeed if it has a recurring, unifying motive, as in Op. 70/iii (a variation-rondo), or if it has a text, as in Agathe's totally additive but cumulative aria "Leise, leise" (*Der Freischütz*/ii). The aria makes an interesting analogy, for Weber's melodic line in Op. 24/ii, especially in the B section, flows along for all the world like that in one of his more emotional opera arias. One almost feels the lack of a text. Unfortunately, one is helped to feel the lack of a recurring motive, too, by the routine, even stodgy bass-chord accompaniment, which certainly stands out as the most prevalent yet least attractive trait in Weber's piano scoring.

This much mention of problems in Weber's first and slowest movements needs to be countered now with the contention that his four big solo sonatas—again, as viewed here—progress steadily and conspicuously, from one to the next, in the solution of these problems and in greater skill in handling others. Whereas Op. 24 as a whole hardly passes muster in public recital today, Op. 70 is a completely satisfying masterpiece. In other words, the preference we noted in today's record catalogues is endorsed here, although pianists would be well advised and rewarded if they were to atone much more than they have for the apparent neglect of Op. 70 in the 19th century. Certain changes become especially clear when the four sonatas are read consecutively. The texture becomes thinner and more efficient (giving way to but a single line at the start of Op. 70), yet provides greatly increased interest in the left hand. The melodic unity becomes much tighter, being bound more by significant motives than full-fledged themes. The rhythm becomes more supple, as reflected in more irregular phrases in the first movements and in modifications that relieve the squareness of regular phrases in the other movements. The harmonic progressions and the tonal schemes become more purposeful and varied, and more necessary to the direction of the phrases and to the form itself. And, finally, the piano writing becomes if not less demanding then considerably more reasonable, functional, and resourceful, with most of the impractical leaps and stretches discarded (Ex. 28).

It is in all these respects that Op. 70 stands as an unalloyed masterpiece. But, of course, it is in those respects, too, that many a strong

Ex. 28. From the first movement of Carl Maria von Weber's
Sonata in e, Op. 70 (after Augener's Ed., No. 8470, p. 74).

composer has developed and matured—for example, Clementi or
Dussek, to take near contemporaries of Weber. In short, we are brought
back to the view that the striking innovations of style in Weber's Op.
24 were largely the products of inexperience, or at least of efforts to
apply structural principles and keyboard techniques that proved more
and more to be inimical to the sonata. Certainly, some of the most
characteristic writing of the first two sonatas has disappeared entirely
by the last sonata. For example, along with the early problem traits
mentioned above, one thinks of Weber's characteristic groupings by
twos, both in lines descending stepwise (e.g., Op. 39/i/20) and in
appoggiaturas on inverted triads (Ex. 26, *supra*). In 1875, W. H. Riehl
must have been thinking mainly of Opp. 24 and 39 when he cited
Weber's four "grosse . . . Virtuosensonaten, [or] Concertsonaten" as
being so called because "the instrument and its effects control the
ideas and form," whereas the difficulties in Beethoven's "grosse"
sonatas are always made to serve the form and ideas.[98] In this connection we are brought back, also, to that fantasy element so generally
—in fact, too emphatically—ascribed to Weber's sonatas, as in Spitta's
inversion of Beethoven's title (Op. 27/1 and 2) almost to read "Fantasia

98. Riehl/CHARAKTERKÖPFE II 270.

quasi una Sonata." [99] This fantasy exists in a positive sense not in the inadvertent looseness of Weber's earlier sonata forms nor in any deliberate freedoms in any of his sonatas. Rather, to the extent that the term applies at all, the fantasy must be found in the florid abandon of some of his melodic lines that suggest arias (as cited above); in orchestral effects like the chordal melody spread over a tremolo bass at the start of Op. 39 (recalling portions of the glen scene in *Der Frei-schütz*); in whimsicalities such as can be found in the delicious "Menuetto capriccio" of the same work (including perilously close anticipations of "Invitation to the Dance"); and in occasional brooding in the harmony, as during the retransition of Op. 70/i (mss. 114–132, partly quoted, for its dim.-7th harmony, in ssb VI).

Schumann in Central Germany: Littérateur and Musician

Robert Schumann (1810–56), the very epitome of musical Roman-ticism, is one of the four 19th-century composers—along with Schu-bert, Chopin, and Brahms—around whose sonatas our discussion of Romantic style and form centered in Chapter VI. Hence, at this point it is mainly the background, circumstances, and historical orientation of his sonatas that concern us. Schumann is also—along with Men-delssohn, Chopin, Liszt, and Wagner—one of five leading Romantics born close in time (1809–13) who devoted something less than their chief or most characteristic efforts to the sonata. Thus, Schumann's total of at least 15 complete or incomplete works originally or ulti-mately called sonatas (but not including his late arrangements of Bach's unaccompanied violin sons. and cello suites), constitutes scarcely 8 per cent of the cycles, sets, and other main items in his total output. Of these sonatas, the 6 completed solos called "sonata" constitute less than 10 per cent of his total keyboard output. Furthermore, as dis-cussed presently, these sonatas have commonly been regarded as falling short of his most representative and successful music.[100]

Whether from a creative, philosophic, or domestic standpoint, the main dividing line in Schumann's short, productive, emotionally tur-bulent life of forty-six years was the year 1840.[101] Prior to that year, starting with his move in 1828 from his birthplace of Zwickau to Leipzig, the main events had been his surrender to the lures of music

---

99. GROVE IX 217.

100. E.g., cf. Shedlock/SONATA 207–9; Bie/PIANOFORTE 241–42, 243, 254; Georgii/KLAVIERMUSIK 323–25; Dale/SCHUMANN 46–47; MGG XII 303 (E. A. Lippman).

101. Up-to-date, efficient summaries of his life, views, and output appear both in GROVE VII 600–640 (G. Abraham) and MGG XII 272–325 (E. A. Lippman).

and literature after a dutiful but vain try at law school;[102] his auto-didactic progress in these fields, supplemented, on and off up to 1832, by brief, rather disappointing study with Friederich Wieck, then Hein-rich Dorn;[103] his shift from a primary goal of virtuoso pianist to that of composer, especially after the permanent injury to his right hand 104a from a misguided practicing venture in mid 1832;[104] his composition of nearly all of his most important piano music (including his three main solo sonatas) and relatively few other works;[105] his founding of the *Neue Zeitschrift für Musik* in 1833 [106] and the large part of his own writing for it; and the five-year courtship of Clara Wieck, with all its frustrations and final culmination in marriage in 1840.[107]

After 1840, in a gradually slowed, less hectic existence, the main events in Schumann's life were his abrupt turn to composing songs, then orchestral, and then chamber music;[108] his fourteen years with Clara, including the growing family, the travels together on her concert tours as far off as the chief Russian centers and Vienna, and the move to Dresden in 1844, followed by the unhappy appointment as musical director at Düsseldorf in 1850;[109] his later outpouring of compositions, now in all directions including opera and other vocal works, more solo piano works (among them the three little sonatas for his daughters, Op. 118), more chamber works (among them the three violin sonatas), and the Bach transcriptions; and, after serious recurring depressions, especially in 1833 and 1844, the final two years of mental collapse starting in 1854.

The literary interests nurtured by his father and his early environ-ment—especially his almost traumatic introduction to the witty, fanciful novels of Jean Paul (Richter) in 1827—figured at least as

102. Among significant letters and other contemporary, largely autobiographic evidence, cf. Boetticher/SCHUMANN 245; Storck/SCHUMANN 50–57; Eismann/SCHUMANN I 66–68.

103. Cf. Eismann/SCHUMANN I 62–63, 74–77; Storck/SCHUMANN 64–68, 73–78.

104. Cf. Storck/SCHUMANN 78–79, 128, 195, etc. The exact cause and nature of this injury vary even in the earliest sources. Schumann's own recollection of the date as "about in Oct., 1831" (Eismann/SCHUMANN I 78) does not tally with his letter of Aug. 9, 1832. Niecks/SCHUMANN 102–6 gives a full account of the whole problem.

105. A convenient though incomplete list of other early works appears in Rehberg/SCHUMANN 727. Cf., also, Gertler/SCHUMANN 33–35; Abraham/RESEARCH 70–71; Redlich/SCHUMANN.

106. NZM, first published in 1834. Cf. Storck/SCHUMANN 86–90, 100–101, 119–22; Niecks/SCHUMANN 127–32; and, especially, Plantinga/SCHUMANN 11–34.

107. The first 2 vols. of Litzmann/SCHUMANN are still the main source. Cf., also, Eismann/SCHUMANN I 102–10, 114–24.

108. Cf. Niecks/SCHUMANN 205–9, 216–23; Gertler/SCHUMANN 33, fns. 83 and 84.

109. Chaps. XV–XXI in Niecks/SCHUMANN include essential documents from the decade 1840–50.

much in Schumann's background and youthful aspirations as his more
specifically musical interests.[110] In the present study these literary
interests matter because they contributed fundamentally to the
making of one of the most discerning critics, most representative
aestheticians,[111] and most subtle symbolists, if not programmatists, of
the Romantic Era. With regard to Schumann as a critic, his reviews
of early 19th-century sonatas are quoted and cited often here, the
more so as he made a special point of reviewing current piano music,[112]
apparently including every sonata that came his way, good or bad. With
regard to Schumann as an aesthetician, in Chapters II and III his
views were summarized in some detail as they pertained to the sonata's
historical contrasts, nationalistic differences, semantic implications,
values to the professional composer, and recent deterioration.

As for Schumann's symbolism and programmatic tendencies, these
principles prevailed chiefly before 1840. They touched the piano
sonatas much less than the collections of smaller pieces. But, as noted
especially under Opp. 11, 17, and 26 below, they did touch them somewhat. How much, is usually debatable, because the piano sonatas offer
no symbolic or programmatic associations quite so tangible as those
with Jean Paul's novel *Flegeljahre* in Schumann's *Papillons*, Op. 2,[113]
or those with the "sphinx"-motive variants of ASCH in his *Carnaval*,
Op. 9,[114] or even those with E. T. A. Hoffman's grotesque tales of
Kapellmeister Kreisler (*Fantasiestücke in Callot's Manier*) in Schumann's *Kreisleriana*, Op. 16.[115] On the other hand, anyone who recalls

110. Cf. Schumann/JUGENDBRIEFE 9-10, 16-17, 19, etc.; Storck/SCHUMANN 3-15,
20, 44, 128 (where Schumann says he learned more counterpoint from Jean Paul
than from his music teacher); Niecks/SCHUMANN 41-45; Jacobs/SCHUMANN; Lipp-
man/SCHUMANN 342-45.

111. Plantinga/SCHUMANN is a new, valuable, detailed study of Schumann's
writings in NZM, with emphasis on their critical and aesthetic significance.

112. Cf. his own explicit statement on this policy for NZM, in Storck/SCHUMANN
111; also, Plantinga/SCHUMANN 35-47.

113. Schumann's own table of derivations and parallels for Op. 2 is reproduced
in Boetticher/SCHUMANN 611-13, with further information and references. Cf.,
also, Lippman/SCHUMANN 314-20, 322, 337-38 (in a valuable article on Schumann's
application of his own aesthetic views).

114. Cf. Schumann's own mention of the motive in Storck/SCHUMANN 99 and
Niecks/SCHUMANN 175-77; also, Dale/SCHUMANN 39-41. Whether Schumann actually
developed a much more extensive and subtle "cipher" (concealing CLARA, WIECK,
ROBERT, and other related names) than is generally recognized in ASCH, ABEGG
(Op. 1), BACH (Op. 60), and GADE (Op. 68/41), is a question that has been debated
recently and hotly, especially in MT CVI (1965) 584-91 (E. Sams), 767-71 and 949
(protests, endorsements, and Sams again), CVII (1966) 1050-51 (Sams), CVIII (1967)
131-34 (Sams), and CIX (1968) 25-27 (Sams).

115. But Clara seems to have been hidden in there even more than the
Kapellmeister, according to Schumann's own letters (cf. Niecks/SCHUMANN 186-88;
also Dale/SCHUMANN 56 and Wörner/SCHUMANN 360).

Schumann's well-known, admittedly Germanic objections to the detailed, literal programme Berlioz prepared for his *Symphonie fantastique* (and to Beethoven's inscriptions in *Sinfonia pastorale*),[116] will not be surprised to discover Schumann declaring in 1838 even about his *Carnaval,*

I need hardly assure you that the putting together of the pieces and the superscriptions came about *after* the composition. . . . For is not music itself always enough and sufficiently expressive? . . . [The titles in *Carnaval* have] no artistic value whatever; the manifold states of the soul alone seem to me of interest.[117]

If Schumann was contradicting somewhat his earlier approach to *Papillons,* his statements were still no single "silly" product of "excessive diffidence," [118] for only six months later he again declared, more generally and in a different context, that the "inscriptions over my pieces always occur to me after I have finished composing the music." [119] In this latter sense there is much less question about Schumann's interest in programme music. As illustrated by numerous reviews cited in the present volume, especially when he was writing as "Eusebius," he did not hesitate to read programmes into completed works, including others', like Beethoven's or Schubert's, as well as his own.[120]

Schumann, Tools and Tabulations

The literature on Schumann is extensive and the sources are still more extensive.[121] But much of what Otto Erich Deutsch and others have done for Mozart and Schubert, or Max Weber and F. W. Jähns for Carl Maria von Weber, by way of pulling all the sources together, has yet to be done and will be a bigger task for Schumann.[122] Most of his own extraordinarily rich writings on music published in his lifetime, especially his articles for the *Neue Zeitschrift,* were first issued in collected form by Schumann himself in 1854, and more recently in

116. Schumann/SCHRIFTEN I 83–85; cf., also, Gertler/SCHUMANN 59–60. A detailed comparison of Schumann and Berlioz in their whole approach to music aesthetics and composition could be very fruitful.

117. From Schumann's letters to Moscheles of Aug. 23 and Sept. 22, 1838, as trans. in Niecks/SCHUMANN 175–76.

118. Rehberg/SCHUMANN 694.

119. Letter to Simonin de Sire of March 15, 1839, as trans. in Storck/SCHUMANN 128. Cf., also, Gertler/SCHUMANN 38–39; Lippman/SCHUMANN 318, 320, 326, 329–30, 332, 335–36.

120. Cf., also, Abraham/SCHUBERT 8–10 (W. Reich).

121. Cf. the selected bibliography in MGG XII 320–25.

122. The status of Schumann research around 1950 is variously summarized in Abraham/RESEARCH, Redlich/SCHUMANN, and Abraham/SCHUMANN v–vi.

1914 in an expanded fifth edition prepared, with excellent prefaces, notes, and indices, by Martin Kreisig.[123] Unfortunately, the two-volume translation into English of much of this material, done by Fanny Raymond Ritter in 1880,[124] and the two recent, smaller collections have proved too unreliable and/or incomplete for use here.[125] Of some 9,000 letters written by and to Schumann, most of them minutely recorded by himself, many have been lost, about 1,000 have been published in various large and small collections, and a smaller number have been translated into English.[126] Of numerous other writings not published by Schumann—diaries, travel records, reports, literary and musical notes—much still remains unpublished.[127] Important steps toward bringing this material to light were taken by Wolfgang Boetticher in his enormous dissertation of 1941 on Schumann's personality and work and his biography of 1942 told through copious letters, writings, and documents, mostly not previously published.[128] Both books are scarce, besides which the dissertation is difficult to use. It lacks an index of works, it suffers from an overrefined organization based on a pompous, rarefied theory of symbolic logic, and it stems from hateful Nazi wartime philosophies, so that every precaution Boetticher observes with each ill-starred *persona non grata* means a precaution to be observed in accepting Boetticher. In English, some of Boetticher's important findings have been digested and incorporated in Gerald Abraham's Schumann *Symposium* of 1952.[129] Recent up-to-date studies of the life and works in German include those by K. H. Wörner and Paula and Walter Rehberg, although the study regarded here as best in English still remains that by Frederick Niecks, published posthumously in 1925.[130] Studies that apply more particularly to Schumann's sonatas are noted further on, where they apply. But the fact can be stated right here that an over-all study of his sonatas is unexpectedly and conspicuously lacking.

The only "complete" edition of Schumann's music is the incom-

123. Schumann/SCHRIFTEN. Cf. Plantinga/SCHUMANN 4–5.

124. Cf. the reviews in MT XVII (1877) 334 and XXI (1880) 621.

125. Cf. JAMS XVIII (1965) 417–19, ML XLVI (1965) 267–68.

126. Cf. Boetticher/SCHUMANN 627–28; MGG XII 321. Schumann/JUGENDBRIEFE, Wasielewski/SCHUMANN, Litzmann/SCHUMANN (with about one-fifth of the letters to Clara), and Storck/SCHUMANN (with errors and omissions) contain much of the correspondence referred to here.

127. Cf. the list in Boetticher/SCHUMANN 623–29.

128. Boetticher/SCHUMANN, Boetticher/SCHRIFTEN. Cf. Abraham/RESEARCH 72–75, Redlich/SCHUMANN, Abraham/SCHUMANN v–vi, Plantinga/SCHUMANN 6–8, Werner/MENDELSSHON 265–66. Eismann/SCHUMANN (1956) is a small, selected assortment of Schumann documents.

129. Abraham/SCHUMANN, including the excellent chap. Dale/SCHUMANN.

130. Wörner/SCHUMANN; Rehberg/SCHUMANN; Niecks/SCHUMANN.

Robert Schumann's Sonatas and Related Works

Op.	Key	Scoring	Composed	First ed.	Dedicatee	Mvts.: tempos or types / Keys: mvt.-by-mvt. / mss.: mvt.-by-mvt.	SCHUMANN/ WERKE-m	Early titles; remarks
11	f#	P	1833–35	Kistner, 1836	Clara Wieck	4: S/VF-M-Sc -F / f#: f# -A-f# -f#/F# / 1145: 419 -45-219-462	VII/ii/11	Pianofortesonate, Klara zugeeignet von Florestan und Eusebius; ed. of 1840: "Grande Sonate"; Schumann preferred "1st Sonate"
14	f	P	1835–36	Haslinger, 1836	Ignaz Moscheles	4: F -Sc -Va -VF / f.: f -Db -f -f/F / 982: 249-231-143-359	VII/iii/14	Concert sans Orchestre (with no scherzo); 1853 ed. (revised, with scherzo): "Troisième grande Sonate"; dedication meant for Zuccalmaglio
22	g	P	1833–38	Breitkopf, 1839	Henriette Voigt	4: VF-M-Sc-VF / g:: g -C -g -g / 778: 317-61-64-336	VII/iv/22	"Deuxième grande Sonate" (with revised finale)
118/1	G	P	1853	Schuberth, 1854	Julie ⎫ daughters	4: F -Va-M-Ro / G: G-e -C-G / 363: 50-40 -64-209	VII/vi/35	Drei Sonaten für die Jugend; the 4 mvts. of Op. 118/1 were originally written to be 4 of Kinderszenen Op. 15
118/2	D	"	"	"	Elise ⎬ daughters	4: F -F -S -VF / D: D -b -G-D / 410: 127-62-33-188	"	
118/3	C	"	"	"	Marie ⎭ daughters	4: F -M-F -VF / C: C -F -a -C / 413: 105-29-66-213	"	
—	Ab/Db	P	1830?			F?-S / Ab-Db		only 2 mvts.; cf. Boetticher/SCHUMANN 586 (incipits; repeated in Dale/SCHUMANN 42), 640 (2d mvt.)
—	f	P	1833–37			F-?-F / f f / ca.180		"Sonate IV"? cf. Schumann/JUGENDBRIEFE 278 (Op. 14 or this work?), Boetticher/SCHUMANN 566 (with exx. that seem to be confused with this son.) and 639 (only fragmentary information)
—	Bb	P	1840			F? / Bb / 4 pp.?		"I started a little Sonatina in Bb—very pretty" (Litzmann/ SCHUMANN I 386); perhaps the same as the sketch of a son. mvt. in Bb dated around 1836 in Boetticher/SCHUMANN 639

							VII/i/8	
8	b	P	1831	Friese, 1835	Ernestine von Fricken	F b 206	VII/i/8	Allegro; from first mvt. of a projected "Sonate in H-Moll" to be ded. to Moscheles; derived from sketches for Op. 2 and projected variations on a Paganini theme; cf. Schumann/ JUGENDBRIEFE 165, Gertler/SCHUMANN 8-9, Abraham/ RESEARCH 69, Dale/SCHUMANN 34 and 42-43, HOFMEISTER 1834-38, 187
17	C	P	1836-38	Breitkopf, 1839	Franz Liszt	3: F -F -S / C: C -Eb -C / 712: 310-260-142	VII/iii/17	Fantasie; originally "Grosse Sonate," Op. 12, for proposed Beethoven monument, ded. to Clara; cf. Schumann/ JUGENDBRIEFE 278, 281, 302-3; Dale/SCHUMANN 45
26	Bb	P	1839	Mechetti, 1841	Simonin de Sire	5: VF-S -Sc -F -VF / Bb: Bb -g -Bb -eb-Bb / 1074: 555-25-128-45-321	VII/iv/26	Faschingsschwank aus Wien; originally described by Schumann as a "big romantic sonata"; iv pub. separately in 1839; cf. Dale/SCHUMANN 45
105	a	P & Vn	1851	Hofmeister, 1852		3: F -F -F / a: a -F -a / 501: 209-79-213	V/iii/10	Sonate für Pianoforte und Violine
121	d	Vn & P	1851	Breitkopf, 1853	Ferdinand David	4: S/F-VF-M -F / d: d -b -G -d/D / 813: 295-193-140-185	V/iii/11	2te Grosse Sonate für Violine und Pianoforte
—	a	P & Vn	1853	Schott, 1956	Joseph Joachim?	4: S/F-M-Sc -F / a: a -d -d -a/A / 509: 163-45-135-166		"3. Sonate"; with Schumann's own 2 mvts. added to his 2 mvts. in F-A-E SONATE-m; cf. Boetticher/SCHUMANN 638, Melkus/SCHUMANN, Melkus/VIOLINSONATE

plete, somewhat unreliable set of fourteen series in thirty-one volumes prepared by Clara Schumann and Brahms, and published in 1881–93.[131] In 1964 plans were announced for a much needed new edition of the complete works, literary as well as musical, to be published jointly by Breitkopf & Härtel and B. Schott.[132] Undoubtedly a basic aid to this edition, and presumably a part of it, will be the numerous musical sketchbooks and separate fragments left by Schumann but not investigated in detail until Wolfgang Gertler and Werner Schwarz wrote dissertations on his early keyboard music and variation treatment in 1929 and 1932, respectively.[133] Several of these sketches will be seen to throw light on derivations of the sonatas.

Out of Schumann's 15 works included here in the realm of the sonata, 3 are full-scale solo piano sonatas, 3 are diminutive solo piano sonatas, 3 are unfinished, unpublished solo piano sonatas, 3 are works that started as solo piano sonatas but came out differently, and 3 are sonatas for piano and violin. The essential facts about these 15 works are tabulated in that order (pp. 262–63), before some over-all considerations are advanced and the six main sonatas are noted individually.[134] As this tabulation recalls, Schumann's main sonatas fell into two widely separated groups, the three big piano sonatas being composed intermittently during a five-year period before 1840 (1833–38) and the three ensemble sonatas all in single, short spans during his last three years of significant composing (1851–53).[135] There is truth in the frequent generalization that Schumann—somewhat like Brahms (whose main sonatas fell into two similar groups)—began as a romantic and ended if not quite a classicist then at least a realist.[136] The late sonatas sprang forth quickly[137] because by then he had largely resolved or given up his

131. Schumann/werke-m. Cf. Heyer/historical 297. Many details of the editorial work in this set can be traced in the letters between Brahms and Clara in Litzmann/schumann III and schumann-brahms II, especially for 1877 (also, Sept. and Oct., 1892, as a sample of some of the difficulties).

132. notes XXII (1965–66) 696–97.

133. Gertler/schumann (with a preface, pp. 1–13, on the Zwickau sketchbooks) and Schwarz/schumann. A full list of sketch sources, both for pub. works with op. nos. and unpub. works, appears in Boetticher/schumann 630–640. Besides the exx. in these studies only a relatively small part of the sketches have been pub. (cf. mgg XII 321).

134. Cf. the convenient tabulation of Schumann's complete works, by categories, in grove VII 627–39 (Abraham). First eds. are listed in mgg XII 293–98 and schumann/-drucke. An up-to-date *catalogue raisonné* is much needed.

135. Nearest to the needed over-all study of Schumann's sons. is an investigation, at once more general and more specific, into his treatment of "sonata form," in the lost diss. Cohen/schumann (with the conclusions restated in Carner/form). In Abraham/schumann 307 the listing of a similar diss. by W. Schwarz is an error for Schwarz/schumann.

136. Cf. Gertler/schumann 42–45.

137. Cf. mgg XII 289, Melkus/violinsonate 190.

attempts to fuse the literary and the musical. He was now more of a pure musician, concerned primarily with refinements of structure[138] and texture (as in his polyphonic studies centered around Bach). The early sonatas had evolved somewhat erratically and insecurely in the throes of attempting that fusion. Furthermore, the three "sonatas" that came out differently and the three (or more?) that died a-borning evolved in those throes, too.

Schumann's attempts to fuse the literary and musical in his earlier works related closely to his insecurity in trying to master professional composition techniques largely on his own,[139] and to an apparent schizoid personality that manifested itself even more in his youth than in his later years, and that showed up in his art as much as in his mental state.[140] With regard to the latter, the impassioned, perturbed, harsh, precipitate "Florestan" and the gentle, deliberate, dreamy, tactful "Eusebius" constitute the diametric personifications of his schizoid temperament (cf. Ex. 29), with "Master Raro" as the arbitrating superego—the detached, temperate observer.[141]

All these traits of the young composer who struggled and vacillated so much in his sonata composing contributed in turn to the two aspects of his best known sonatas, those for piano solo, that have served most to orient them historically and musically. First, his solo piano sonatas embraced and cultivated Romantic styles more fully and consistently than any other sonatas from the first half of the 19th century that still survive in today's repertoire.[142] And second, in so doing, they posed structural problems, especially problems of extended "sonata form," that account for most of the technical reservations later writers have held about them. But the problems Schumann encountered must be distinguished from the problems many listeners find in accepting his sonatas today (to return to an observation near the start of this Schumann discussion). As noted when Schumann's styles and forms came up for earlier discussion (ssb VI), Schumann had to solve the problems of development and extent with idioms and aesthetic goals that lent themselves more to small, relatively static forms than to the previous, broader dynamic means of Beethoven and his generation.[143]

138. Cf. Boetticher/SCHUMANN 553.

139. E.g., cf. his own words in Storck/SCHUMANN 42–45, 54, 67, 70–71, 73–74.

140. For various slants, all tending to support this view, cf. Gertler/SCHUMANN 16–17, Boetticher/SCHUMANN 255, Redlich/SCHUMANN 145 and 182–83 (with indications that venereal disease was the primary cause of the final mental collapse); Lippman/SCHUMANN 328. For a summary of a century of theorizing about his illnesses cf. NZM CXXI (1960) 188–89 (D. Kerner).

141. Cf. a typical explanation by the composer himself in Schumann/SCHRIFTEN I 60 (1835); also, Lippman/SCHUMANN 340 and MGG XII 277–78.

142. Cf. Rehberg/SCHUMANN 437–38.

143. Cf. Boetticher/SCHUMANN 579–80, 586.

Ex. 29. The opening of Robert Schumann's Sonata in f♯ (facs. of the original Kistner ed. of 1836 [the only extant copy?] at the British Museum).

At best and in his own way he did solve these problems, chiefly by his personal methods of motivic extension and of sectional organization bordering on fantasy. But, almost as with Schubert, all too many listeners today cannot help evaluating even Schumann in terms of Beethovian standards. If they no longer balk at his "failure," like Beethoven's (SCE 16, 117), to comply with *a posteriori* textbook descriptions of "sonata form," they still find it difficult to hear and enjoy Schumann's sonatas on his own Romantic terms.[144]

In any case, Beethoven's music was not the first or strongest influence on Schumann's.[145] From as early as 1827, Schubert's music, in all its available categories, seems to have stood above all other music in that regard, especially during the years Schumann was composing his solo piano sonatas. "Schubert is still my 'one and only' love, the more so as he has everything in common with my one and only Jean Paul," he wrote at 21 (1830).[146] Early, too, were the single, vivid impressions made on him by the virtuosity of Moscheles (in 1819!) and Paganini (1830);[147] the special interest on his part in Hummel's Sonata in f♯, Op. 81;[148] and the highest regard on his part for Chopin and Mendelssohn among contemporaries.[149] Weber's early influence can be surmised, although the evidence is more indirect and Schumann refers to him less than might be expected in view of the common Romantic ground of the two men.[150]

---

144. The conclusion in Cohen/SCHUMANN (as restated in Carner/FORM) is that Schumann—in his sons., symphonies, concertos, etc.—loosened the tensions of Classic "son. form" and turned to poetic literary stimuli to the point of creating symphonic poems, thus providing "the earliest decisive attempts to make this classic form serve romantic ideals." Similar conclusions are reached in Gertler/SCHUMANN 110–16 and Hohenemser/SCHUMANN 49–50.

145. Boetticher/SCHUMANN 223–90 provides a detailed consideration of Schumann's derivations from, relations with, and influences or comments on 14 musicians and some "Kleinmeister," from Bach to Liszt and Wagner (to be read with the usual cautions). Cf., also, Gertler/SCHUMANN 50–55.

146. Storck/SCHUMANN 44, and cf. 122 and 222; also, Boetticher/SCHUMANN 244–47, Abraham/SCHUMANN 9, Schumann/SCHRIFTEN I 459–64 *et passim*.

147. Cf. MOSCHELES I 24–25; Eismann/SCHUMANN I 13, 58; Niecks/SCHUMANN 37; Storck/SCHUMANN 61, 45. Moscheles' Son. Op. 49 in f♯ was one of the early pieces studied by Schumann (Heussner/MOSCHELES 56).

148. Storck/SCHUMANN 42–43, 64–65.

149. Schumann's celebrated panegyric ("Hats off . . .") on Chopin's Op. 2 appeared in AMZ XXXIII (1831) 805–8, reprinted in Schumann/SCHRIFTEN 5–7. On Mendelssohn, cf. Niecks/SCHUMANN 146–56, including Schumann's statement of 1839, "I regard Mendelssohn as the foremost musician of the day, and take off my hat to him as a master."

150. Cf. Storck/SCHUMANN 65; Gertler/SCHUMANN 4 and 7; Boetticher/SCHUMANN 247.

Schumann's Sonatas for Piano

A typical view of Schumann's three completed sonatas for solo piano finds Op. 11 in f♯, which came first in order both of completion and publication,[151] to be the most satisfying to hear and play, chiefly because it is regarded as the most successful fusion of his literary and musical interests.[152] Especially in the longer, outer movements, Op. 22 is criticized as being somewhat formalistic, and Op. 14 as being both too repetitive in its motivic treatment and too discursive in its designs, in spite of some rare moments and ideas. On the other hand, the *Fantasie* Op. 17 is regarded as being superior to all three "sonatas" in musical value.[153] Schumann himself had only passing remarks to make about his own sonatas. Very early, in 1831, he had written Hummel that "the concerto form seemed to me easier [to compose] than that of the sonata . . . because of its [the concerto's] greater license." [154] Among all his major piano works, "*Kreisleriana* is my favorite," he wrote in 1839,[155] although previously he had pointed twice with some pride to both Opp. 11 and 14.[156] In any case, by 1839–40 he was finding the piano "too limited for my ideas," with the orchestra and the voice opening new horizons.[157] And even before he wrote his own symphonies he was finding both the symphony and sonata had passed their day.[158] These views and a considerable degree of emotional resolution must go far to explain Schumann's reference, already in 1843, to the "immaturity" of his earlier (that is, piano) music, with its reflection "for the most part [of] the stormy scenes of my early life." [159]

151. But "Première" did not appear in the title of the 2d ed. of 1840 (as stated in Dale/SCHUMANN 43); cf. Cat. ROYAL 320, SCHUMANN/-DRUCKE 13, HOFMEISTER 1843, 235. Boal/SCHUMANN is a recent, unpub. diss. on the extant MSS and eds. of this work.

152. E.g., cf. Shedlock/SONATA 208–9 (but with no mention of Op. 14), Georgii/KLAVIERMUSIK 325; Gillespie/KEYBOARD 215. Op. 11 "must be considered as a volume of lyric poems" (Bie/PIANOFORTE 242). Parrott/SCHUMANN, arguing that it "is more useful to appreciate what is Schumannian in Schumann, rather than flog the old sonata-form warhorse," points up positive structural and poetic values in Op. 11.

153. The only over-all discussions of Schumann's piano sons. are those included as relatively brief sections in broader surveys of his entire output for piano, as in Fuller-Maitland/SCHUMANN 23–26 and 31–32, Dale/SCHUMANN 42–48 and 83–84.

154. Storck/SCHUMANN 67.

155. Storck/SCHUMANN 128, Niecks/SCHUMANN 187–88.

156. Niecks/SCHUMANN 111 (1836), Storck/SCHUMANN 112 (1838).

157. According to letters quoted in Gertler/SCHUMANN 33, Niecks/SCHUMANN 205–6, and Storck/SCHUMANN 140.

158. Cf. Gertler/SCHUMANN 56–57; Schumann/SCHRIFTEN I 394–95; SSB II.

159. Storck/SCHUMANN 241. Cf. his reference (after 1850) to his early music as "confused stuff" (Wasielewski/SCHUMANN 121).

Although they originated variously and deviously, growing by fits and starts, three of Schumann's sonatas—presumably, Opp. 11 and 22, and the other Sonata in f, never to be finished—were all in progress at the same time in early 1834, while the Jean Paul influence still dominated and while the *Neue Zeitschrift* as well as the imaginary "Davidsbündler" were getting into full swing.[160] Schumann had wanted to make these sonatas "masterpieces" and, which did not happen, to dedicate them to his mother.[161] Actually, it was "Klara" (publicized then without her surname) who became the dedicatee of Op. 11, from "Florestan and Eusebius," [162] and it was Op. 11 that most closely related to her among Schumann's sonatas. If this was not the "gigantic work" Schumann mentioned as being started in late 1831,[163] at least it is known to have evolved tortuously by way of a reworked "Fandango, Rhapsodie . . ." of 1832 in the first movement, an early song (1828) in the second, and perhaps one of a set of rejected "Burlesken" of 1832 in the third movement, as well as considerable revision of early sketches in the last two movements.[164] As it evolved further, Clara became more and more a part of it until, as Schumann wrote to her in retrospect, it was "one entire heart's cry for you, in which your theme appears in all possible forms." [165] Naturally, Schumann was hurt when Clara did not reply (or could not because of her father) upon receipt of the published score in May, 1836.[166] But she had already played it in 1835 for Mendelssohn, Chopin, and Moscheles, among others.[167] And she played it in Leipzig in August, 1837, when this was the only way she could reveal "my inmost heart" to Schumann, hidden in the audience near the end of the eighteen months in which all correspondence and

160. Cf. GROVE VII 607; Niecks/SCHUMANN 130–32 (with Schumann's own recollections).

161. Schumann/JUGENDBRIEFE 229.

162. "Florestan und Eusebius" became the popular title of this work (Ex. 29, *supra*), which was even listed so in HOFMEISTER 1834–38, 129, prior to the 2d ed. under Schumann's own name in 1840. Cf. Jansen/NEUE 418; Wörner/SCHUMANN 143–44. The first ed. is very rare, the only complete copy known here being that at the British Museum.

163. Niecks/SCHUMANN 178 believes it was, but could Schumann's intention to dedicate it to Moscheles mean that the "gigantic work" was an early plan for Op. 14 instead? Op. 8 in its earlier stages is a possible candidate, too.

164. Cf. Gertler/SCHUMANN 9–10; Boetticher/SCHUMANN 206, 557, 562, 565–66, 630; Abraham/II & III 126, 162–63; GROVE VII 607; Dale/SCHUMANN 43–44; Boal/SCHUMANN; Lippman/SCHUMANN 314.

165. Litzmann/SCHUMANN I 109–10. On the inter-relation of the Spanish "Fandango" and Clara's own "Hexentanz" Op. 5/4 as well as the application of this material throughout Op. 11, cf. Rehberg/SCHUMANN 439–41 and 663–64.

166. Litzmann/SCHUMANN I 109. In 1838 Schumann wrote in a letter to Clara, "So your father calls me phlegmatic? Phlegmatic, and write . . . the Sonata in f♯! Phlegmatic, and your lover!" (Storck/SCHUMANN 190).

167. Litzmann/SCHUMANN I 87–89; MOSCHELES I 319; Boetticher/SCHRIFTEN 103.

personal visits had been forbidden.[168] So much special meaning did this work have for the two lovers that in most of their references they called it simply "the sonata," even after both other sonatas were completed.[169]

Moscheles left his personal reactions to Op. 11 as Clara played it, which should be qualified by his conservatism (SSB VII) and the newness of the sonata manuscript to Clara.[170] He wrote his wife that it seemed "very laboured, difficult, and somewhat intricate, although interesting music." [171] But within a year it was probably more than diplomacy and Schumann's flattering request[172] that won more favorable, though largely generalized and noncommittal, words in Moscheles' published, three-page review of Op. 11.[173] Beginning, "This work is a true sign of the awakening and sprouting Romanticism in our day," Moscheles first dwells, one at a time, on the passing of Beethoven and on the new Romanticism of Mendelssohn, Berlioz, Liszt, Hiller, and Chopin. Then, taking Florestan and Eusebius as the two sides of one mind (without divulging the pseudonym),[174] he only briefly describes each movement, finding the last strained to the point of structural incoherence. Two years later Liszt, the new lion of the piano world, gave his name to a review of Schumann's Opp. 5 (Impromptus), 11, and 14, all in one long article.[175] He called Schumann an exponent of the new school, second in individuality only to Chopin. Of Op. 11 he said that the mysterious title and its poetic associations might seem affected in Paris,[176] the treatment of his ideas in the first movement was serried and inflexible, the deep second movement was unequalled, the third movement was remarkable for its rhythms and harmonies, and the finale—again—suffered from struc-

---

168. Litzmann/SCHUMANN I 116–25 *passim*. Cf. NZM VII (1837) 87 ("Florestan und Eusebius"); also, Niecks/SCHUMANN 195, 196.

169. E.g., Schumann/JUGENDBRIEFE 271, where Clara confirms the reference; Storck/ SCHUMANN 225.

170. Litzmann/SCHUMANN 87.

171. MOSCHELES I 319.

172. Printed in Wasielewski/SCHUMANN 304–5; cf. Jansen/SCHUMANN I 95–97.

173. NZM V (1836) 135–37. Cf. MOSCHELES II 19–20; Niecks/SCHUMANN 179. Op. 11 got no review in the more conservative AMZ.

174. In a footnote the "editor" wrote that his closeness to the "composers" prompted him to get a third party to review this work. On the 2d ed. of Op. 11, under Schumann's own name, cf. Schumann/SCHRIFTEN II 374.

175. RGM No. 46 (Nov. 12, 1837) 488–90; reprinted, with postscript in Wasielewski/ SCHUMANN 274–80. If Liszt did not write this review himself (as argued convincingly in Haraszti/AUTHOR, especially pp. 492 and 501), one still assumes it had his full blessing and reflected his opinions.

176. Schumann had written in 1835 that Berlioz' programme for his *Symphonie fantastique* was appropriate in France but not in Germany (Schumann/SCHRIFTEN I 83–84)!

tural faults in spite of its great originality. Schumann wrote Clara at 176a once of the "long, very just article," [177] and early in 1840, when he and Liszt met often in Leipzig, he reported that Liszt's playing of Op. 11 "moved me strangely. Although his reading differed in many places from my [and Clara's?] own, it was always inspired, and he does not, I imagine, display such tenderness, such boldness, every day." [178] Liszt himself wrote then that he was getting to understand Schumann's music better, and though so far it had brought little applause in public it was sure eventually to take its rightful, important place. [179] Among the few important performances of Op. 11 in the years that followed were those that Hanslick reported by Brahms in 1867 [180] and Anton Rubinstein in 1884 (at which Brahms was conspicuously absent). [181]

The original manuscript of Schumann's Op. 14, completed in June, 1836, contained five movements—F-Sc-Va-Sc-VF—and bore nothing for a title but "Concert" (Ex. 30). [182] At the request of the publisher Haslinger, Schumann consented to the discard of both scherzos and the change, as Haslinger regarded it, from a passé title to one with more current appeal, "Concert sans orchestre." [183] As we shall see, Haslinger's judgment proved wrong in both respects. Moscheles, the dedicatee, wrote Schumann that Op. 14 had more the character of a "grosse Sonate" such as Beethoven or Weber composed than the brilliance one would expect in a concerto, and that the fantasy character of Op. 14 did not lend itself to brilliance, anyway. He added that its dissonances, so subtle and delayed in their resolutions, could only be appreciated by an educated ear. Schumann printed that much of Moscheles' letter, this time prefacing it by saying that the roguish Florestan and Eusebius had published Op. 14 under his

177. Niecks/SCHUMANN 179–81.
178. Storck/SCHUMANN 225.
179. Wasielewski/SCHUMANN 280–81. The immediate reference is to *Carnaval*.
180. Hanslick/WIEN II 438; but this was not the first public performance of Op. 11 (recalling Clara's in Leipzig in 1837 and Hanslick's own mention [p. 299] of a less satisfactory performance in 1863). PADEREWSKI 98 and 309–10 also describes Rubinstein's playing of Op. 11 *ca.* 1884 and Paderewski's own playing of it in 1901.
181. Pleasants/HANSLICK 228–29. On Clara's performance of Op. 11 in London in 1884, see under Op. 22 *infra*.
182. Cf. the description of this MS prepared for the publisher, Add. 37056, in Cat. BRITISH MS 147.
183. Cf. Schumann/SCHRIFTEN II 374 (Kreisig). To Moscheles Schumann tendered the dedication of "a sonata, or rather [a sonata] extended into a concerto for piano alone . . . [when you receive it] you can only wonder at the crazy brainstorms a man can have" (letter of July 30, 1836, printed in Wasielewski/SCHUMANN 304); cf., also, Jansen/SCHUMANN I 81 and 94. The sole mention of Op. 14 in AMZ (in a survey of Schumann's piano music, XLVI [1844] 1, 17, 33) puts it among works described as confused, eccentric, and difficult; on the other hand, Op. 22 is cited only for its return to sonata form.

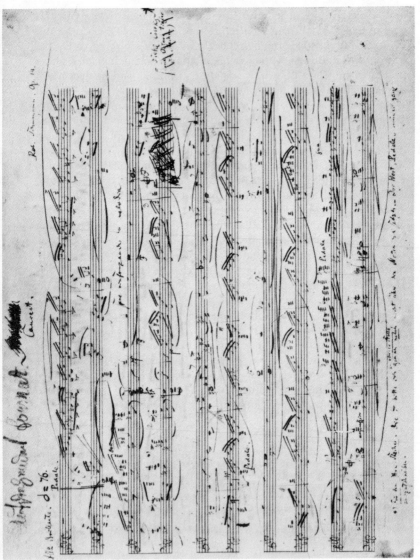

Ex. 30. The opening of Robert Schumann's Sonata in f, Op. 14 (facs. of the

(Schumann's) name.[184] Actually, one reason why musicians have not taken more to Op. 14 may well be that this unjustly neglected masterpiece—this inspired "Sonata appassionata," as it were—lets Florestan's seething, uncompromising passions dominate Eusebius almost completely, much more so than in Op. 11.[185] In his broad review of Opp. 5, 11, and 14, Liszt, the supposed author (SSB X), made even more of "Concerto" as a misnomer for "Sonata," calling attention to implications of ensemble as well as overt brilliance in the word "concerto." [186] But as a "sonata," Liszt found Op. 14 "rich and powerful," and a reminder that Schumann's works awaited introduction to the French.

These semantic objections must have played their part in the partial restoration of Op. 14's original title to *Troisième grande Sonate* in the second edition of 1853[187] ("Troisième" because in the meantime Op. 22 had appeared as "Deuxième"). There were significant changes in the music, too, notably the restoration of most of the second scherzo, now as the second movement, plus modifications in the outer movements and deletions in the resourceful "Variazioni" on an "Andantino" by Clara (the only example in Schumann's main sonatas of this important side of his writing).[188] But the new version can hardly be said to have given more voice to Eusebius, who now emerges only tentatively and briefly in the least driving moments of the first and third movements. And there is some question as to whether the restitution of the other scherzo might not have been more in keeping with the whole cycle.[189] Brahms gave the first public performance of Op. 14, in Vienna in 1862, according to Hanslick.[190]

"How little I thought when I published Op. 1 that I should ever reach Op. 22!" wrote Schumann to Clara in 1840.[191] His Op. 22 in g had gone through the longest gestation and most growing pains of his three main solo sonatas. Its first and third movements were fairly well set in 1833 except for a slower, more intense version of the opening idea that had to be rewritten.[192] The ineffably poetic

184. NZM VI (1837) 65.
185. Cf. Rehberg/SCHUMANN 452–54.
186. RGM No. 46 (Nov. 12, 1837) 488–90.
187. Cf. SCHUMANN/DRUCKE 14.
188. Cf. Schwarz/SCHUMANN 43–45, 69; Dale/SCHUMANN 27–28. The changes in Op. 14 are described in Cat. BRITISH MS 147 and both pub. versions are printed in Schumann/WERKE-m VII/iii/14.
189. Cf. Rehberg/SCHUMANN 453. This other, fine scherzo is pub. in Schumann/WERKE-m XIV 48.
190. Hanslick/WIEN II 258.
191. Storck/SCHUMANN 228.
192. Cf. Gertler/SCHUMANN 10–11.

second movement—Eusebius through and through—began as an early song in 1828 and developed into an independent "Andantino" for piano in 1830 before taking its place in the sonata.[193] The original finale, almost completed in 1835,[194] was put aside in 1838 when Clara found it "much too difficult" and Schumann fully concurred, finding it otherwise unsatisfactory, too, "except for some passionate moments." [195] Its successor he himself described as "very simple but intrinsically well suited to the first movement." [196] Gertler is in the minority in suggesting that Op. 22 is less unified than the other two piano sonatas because of its varied and protracted origins.[197] The later finale, which is less choleric or meaningful than the original one, may be a bit slight for the rest of the cycle but does match it well in style and difficulty. Furthermore, there is that same cyclically unifying motive, the stepwise descent heard at the start, that binds, or recurs in, all three piano sonatas, the Concerto in a, and many other Schumann pieces.[198]

Writing to Robert in 1838, Clara was undoubtedly sincere in expressing her pleasure with Op. 22 and the "many happy as well as painful hours" it brought back to her.[199] She reported excellent reactions to it when she introduced it in a recital in Berlin early in 1840.[200] Yet it is noteworthy that neither this nor the other two piano sonatas seem to have figured often in the approximately two thousand recitals she gave throughout much of the rest of the century.[201] It is in the first movement of Op. 22, by the way, that the

193. Cf. Gertler/SCHUMANN 10, with the title "Papillote" for one sketch; Abraham/ II & III 126–27, with ex.; Rehberg/SCHUMANN 477–79, with facs. of sketch. Boetticher/ SCHUMANN 485 finds a characteristic symbol of unsatisfied longing in mss. 8–11 of this mvt.

194. GROVE VII 608.

195. Litzmann/SCHUMANN I 186; Niecks/SCHUMANN 202. This piece is pub. in SCHUMANN/WERKE-m XIV 53.

196. Cf. Boetticher/SCHRIFTEN 139, 221, 230.

197. Gertler/SCHUMANN 70–71.

198. Cf. Rehberg/SCHUMANN 476–77.

199. Litzmann/SCHUMANN I 186, 188.

200. Litzmann/SCHUMANN I 391–93; yet cf. Boetticher/SCHUMANN 322. Schumann had asked her to play as if it were the day before their wedding, but not to "take the sonata too wildly; think of the man who wrote it for you." But previously he had advised against playing the "entire" Son. in recital (Boetticher/SCHRIFTEN 288, 303).

201. Cf. the somewhat incomplete list in Litzmann/SCHUMANN III 615–24, but note that each work is ordinarily listed only the first time it was performed. Clara still played Op. 11 in London in 1884 (MT XXV [1884] 206, with interesting remarks on Schumann's P sons. in London). Performances of Op. 22 prior to 1885 in London are reported in MMR I (1871) 37, XV (1884) 177–78; MT XVIII (1877) 553, XXIII (1882) 382, XXV (1884) 21 (by Pachmann) and 338. None of Op. 14 is reported in that period.

celebrated paradox occurs in the tempo instructions, with "as fast as possible" as the initial, reigning instruction, only to be followed by "faster" and "still faster" in the coda. Much the same occurs in the finale of Op. 14. One can be literal and decry such editorial carelessness. Or, as with the impossibly difficult coda of Op. 17/ii, one can take a transcendental approach; one can throw oneself into the laps of the gods while gambling on superhuman effort!

The three late sonatas Op. 118 that Schumann wrote for his three daughters in June of 1853 are, on the whole, too long to be called sonatinas (as our tabulation shows), too complex to make satisfactory pieces for children (in the manner of *Album for the Young*), and, save for two or three movements, too commonplace and discursive to qualify as significant music.[202] They have never aroused much interest. *Faschingsschwank aus Wien: Fantasiebilder*, Op. 26, has been linked with Schumann's sonatas mainly because he described it in 1839 as "a big romantic sonata" while working on it, but later merely as "a romantic show piece." [203] Although this work does present a tonal cycle of five movements, it scarcely relates to Schumann's main "sonatas" in drive, emotional content, or structural development, even in the finale, which is usually singled out in this connection because of its tangible "sonata form." [204] In all these respects the great *Fantasie* in C, Op. 17, deserves much more to be linked with the sonatas. Furthermore, it started as a sonata in Schumann's mind. At the outset of nearly three years of work on the music and before the original long title underwent numerous changes, this title read, "Obolen auf Beethovens Monument—Ruinen, Trophaen, Palmen—; Grosse Sonate für das Pianoforte; für Beethovens Denkmal." [205] But by early 1838, with the music now revised and completed, the dedication was changed from Clara to Liszt, the mentioned support (by Florestan and Eusebius, again) of a Beethoven monument and the imaginative movement titles were discarded, the mystic quatrain by Schlegel [206] was inscribed over the opening, and the long title including "Grosse Sonate" was replaced simply by "Fantasie." [207]

202. They are discussed briefly in Dale/SCHUMANN 69–70, 71, 73, 83–84. Op. 118/1/ii is discussed for its variations in Schwarz/SCHUMANN 45. Some details and sketches are noted in Boetticher/SCHUMANN 553–54, 571, 636.

203. Jansen/SCHUMANN I 211; cf. Niecks/SCHUMANN 203. The work is described briefly in Gertler/SCHUMANN 71–72, Dale/SCHUMANN 45, Rehberg/SCHUMANN 481–83.

204. The first mvt. is discussed in Schwarz/SCHUMANN 65–66 as a free set of variations.

205. The origins and correspondence are summarized in Niecks/SCHUMANN 188–89, Dale/SCHUMANN 45, GROVE VII 609.

206. Cf. Einstein/SCHUBERT 164–65.

207. On the importance of the fantasy to Schumann cf. Wörner/SCHUMANN 93–96.

Although Schumann did write on one occasion, ". . . sonatas or fantasias (what's in a name!) . . . ," [208] in all other references discovered here he indicated considerable concern over the best designations not only for his own works (as we have just seen) but for any works that he reviewed in which questions of terminology arose (SSB II; VII, on Schubert). And Op. 17 does stand apart clearly enough from his works actually called "sonata," both in the number, order, and types of its movements and in the freedom and sectional division, greater than usual, of its additive first movement. This is the movement that Schumann described to Clara in 1838 as "certainly the most impassioned I ever wrote—a deep lament for you." [209]

Schumann's Sonatas for Piano and Violin

Of Schumann's three late sonatas for piano and violin, the third was brought to light too recently to be widely known yet and the first two, Opp. 105 and 121, have been valued and played too little, it is felt here. Cobbett's single, redundant paragraph gives (and has undoubtedly furthered) the typical view of the latter:[210]

His mental disease was making further progress, not only affecting his musical thought and fecundity . . . but also embittering his soul. . . . Both sonatas show the disintegration of the fibre of Schumann's musical nature, the uncertainty and vagueness of his thought, the lack of firmness and definite issue and logical clarity in developing musical ideas. There is in general a depressing gloom . . . [only the] allegretto of the first one has something of the old charm.

The persistent minor key, the consistently low, ungrateful range for the violin, and a tendency to assign each instrument what suits the other better, are also usually mentioned as detractions in these works. If there is some truth in each of the charges, they all seem to go too far. The charge of mental deterioration, especially as early as 1851, has been seriously questioned, as noted earlier. In fact, no longer identified with programmatic content or the schizoid opposition of Florestan and Eusebius, these sonatas show, in some ways, more concentration and structural efficiency than the earlier sonatas. (Op. 105 is the only three-movement sonata and the shortest proportionately of all Schumann's sonatas.) And it is more plausible to hear the scoring traits of these late sonatas as premeditated aesthetic

208. Schumann/SCHRIFTEN I 395; but this view is contradicted, for example, on p. 70.

209. Schumann/JUGENDBRIEFE 278.

210. Cobbett/CHAMBER II 386. A more favorable view and brief analyses may be found in Dickinson/SCHUMANN 167–70.

effects by a now very mature, experienced composer than as inadvertent gaucheries.

It is true that Theodor Uhlig's long, contemporary review of Op. 105, in the very periodical Schumann had founded,[211] already found certain faults. But except for a mention of uncharacteristic scoring, these were of a different sort. To paraphrase and synopsize Uhlig's much padded and rarefied disquisition, Schumann is a musical mannerist who strains and stretches harmonic relationships until yesterday's dissonances become today's consonances; for the rest, all three movements reveal formal mastery and Schumann's special torrential drive, lyricism, and a certain (rhythmic?) nibbling ("Knaupeleien"), but also reveal a few commonplaces that betray prolificity and some impersonal writing. Clara first participated in a performance of Op. 105 in 1852 and Op. 121 in 1853.[212] At least Op. 121 was probably done with Joachim, for in September of 1853 he wrote a friend of his joy in playing it with her, adding, "To me it is one of the finest creations of modern times, in the wonderful unity of its feeling and the significance of its themes. It is full of a noble passion—almost harsh and bitter in its expression—and the last movement might almost remind one of a seascape, with its glorious waves of sound." [213] Other performances of these sonatas by the same and other duo teams, including Liszt and Reményi, are reported in the years that followed.[214]

Schumann's "3te Sonate," in a, for piano and violin consists of the second and fourth movements he wrote for the F[rei]-A[ber]-E[insam] Sonata in a (jointly composed with A. Dietrich and Brahms in Joachim's honor[215]) plus a first and third movement to make a complete cycle of his own, all in but two weeks' time (Ex. 31).[216] Evincing no increased mental deterioration even in late 1853, this work stands close to its two predecessors of 1851 (and to Schumann's newly discovered Violin Concerto in d of 1853) in quality as well as in

211. NZM XXXVII (1852) 117–20; cf. Boetticher/SCHUMANN 358–59.

212. Litzmann/SCHUMANN 620.

213. Joachim/LETTERS 26.

214. Joachim/LETTERS 36, 183, 217, 234, 306, 321, 364; Litzmann/SCHUMANN 95; MT XII (1866) 317, XV (1871) 306, XVIII (1877) 120, XXIII (1882) 602, XXIV (1883) 321; Hanslick/WIEN II 168–69 (in which Schumann's former warmth is missed and excessive gloom is deplored). High regard for both sons. was expressed in MMR XIII (1883) 158 and 189. Op. 121/iii is discussed for its variations in Schwarz/SCHUMANN 48.

215. Mod. ed.: F-A-E SONATE-m.

216. Mod. ed. of complete 3d Son.: Neighbor/SCHUMANN-m. The autograph is listed in Boetticher/SCHUMANN 638 (but read 1853 for 1852); the relationship to the "F-A-E" son. is also guessed in Rehberg/SCHUMANN 362. Melkus/SCHUMANN and Melkus/VIOLINSONATE include circumstances, chronology, and analyses, with exx.

Ex. 31. The opening of Robert Schumann's "3ᵗᵉ Sonate" for piano and violin (facs. of autograph [Ms. 317] at the Bibliothèque nationale).

layout and character. It differs chiefly in having more cheerful moments, more use of the violin's higher registers, and more difficult passagework.

Early Romantics in and around Dresden

We may finish our discussion of early Romantics active in central Germany by proceeding from eastern to western centers with composers of minor importance, at least to the sonata—in other words, composers who require only passing or brief mentions here, for the sake of some degree of completeness. A half dozen of these were in or near Dresden. One was the pianist and organist **August Klengel** (1783–1852), who is remembered as the composer of 24 *Canons et Fugues* (1854) that have been used widely by piano teachers and students. It was much earlier, under the strong influence of his teacher Clementi, who came to Dresden in 1803 and travelled with Klengel over a period of several years,[217] that Klengel wrote his sonatas. These include two sets of three piano sonatas each, Opp. 1 and 2, and another, three-movement sonata Op. 9, as well as fifteen *Leçons ou Sonates faciles et progressives,* Op. 15, all first published between about 1805 and 1818.[218] The lively keyboard techniques and fluency, the harmonic ingenuity, and the textural precision in Opp. 2 and 9 all suggest an overdose of Clementi (cf. SCE 749–59). But the weak ideas, dull accompaniments, and lack of any compelling sense of form do not suggest that master nor explain the respect in which he was held by his young friend Chopin.[219]

The important theorist, composer, and violinist **Moritz Hauptmann** (1792–1868) wrote his sonatas early in his career, too, and while his main center was still Dresden.[220] He left at least ten sonatas or sonatinas, all originally for P & Vn, including three sets of three each, Opp. 5, 10 ("Sonatines"), and 23, plus a single *Sonatine,* Op. 6. These were first published in the decade from about 1825 to 1836, followed by numerous further editions, especially of Op. 10.[221] In Spohr, one of Hauptmann's teachers and closest friends,[222] can be

217. Cf. Unger/CLEMENTI 132–33, 138–39, 142–43, 158–59.
218. Cf. MGG VII 1220–22 (R. Sietz), with further listing of a son. for P & Fl left in MS; AMZ VIII (1805–6) Intelligenz-Blatt for Dec.; HOFMEISTER 1819 (Whistling), 35; Cat. BRUXELLES IV 178–79.
219. Cf. Hedley/CHOPIN 24, 36.
220. Cf. MGG V 1828–35 (M. Ruhnke).
221. Cf. Altmann/KAMMERMUSIK 206. The Peters plate no. for Op. 5 was 1874 (cf. Deutsch/NUMMERN 14) and the set is announced in AMA for July 29, 1826. Among mod. eds. of Op. 10: Peters Ed. 2948.
222. Cf. Spohr/AUTOBIOGRAPHY I 169, II 241.

found the chief influence on the sonatas, rather than in Weber, whom Hauptmann knew during a Vienna stay about 1815, or in Mendelssohn or Schumann, who were close to him later. Joachim, one of Hauptmann's numerous important students, wrote Clara Schumann in 1860 that the King in Hannover had been "charmed" with Hauptmann's compositions and had requested two performances of his Sonata in g, Op. 5/1.[223] Perhaps the King was responding to some early-Romantic touches in Hauptmann's sonatas. In a more limited sense than Schumann, Hauptmann had also come under the spell of Jean Paul. But there are hints, too, of the future theorist, in the almost excessive obligations to structural law and order and to harmonic logic, obligations that later were to block acceptance of Liszt's and Wagner's music. In 1837 Schumann found, in particular, that the three sonatas Op. 23, in spite of their flow and skill, marked a dry, oversimplified retreat from their predecessors into the "primitive [ultra-]classicism of the Haydn-Mozart period."[224] Certainly the same remarks apply at least as much at the more rudimentary level of the three sonatinas Op. 10.

Karl Gottlieb Reissiger (1798–1859), successor to Weber as court opera director in Dresden, was a pianist, singer, and composer, who left well over 200 modish publications, including about 12 sonatas—6 for P & Vn, 2 for P & Vc, and 4 for P solo.[225] These appeared between about 1825 and 1850. What Schumann wrote in 1836 of Reissiger's trios applies here.[226] In essence and in a disarmingly friendly manner he depicted them as glib conversations, as smooth, ingratiating, facile products of an overly prolific composer who imitated Beethoven, Weber, and others unwittingly and betrayed his shallowness the moment he tried anything more independent. A sample of Reissiger's glibness as well as his habit of seeing every phrase right to its relentlessly pedestrian conclusion should bear Schumann out, with interest, and should be taken as a sample of all too much other Philistinism of the sort that aroused his "Davidsbündler" to do battle (Ex. 32). Allowing for differences of tempo and movement styles, this sample is a fair representative of all the sonatas by Reissiger that could be examined here. Yet other reviewers, reporting on these sonatas, must have been less discerning or less honest; for

223. Joachim/LETTERS 193.
224. Schumann/SCHRIFTEN I 276–77.
225. Cf. MGG XI 208–10 (F. Göthel); PAZDÍREK XII 186–93; Altmann/KAMMERMUSIK 222, 262; Egert/FRÜHROMANTIKER 159.
226. Schumann/SCHRIFTEN I 176–77.

Ex. 32. From the first movement of Karl Gottlieb Reissiger's *Grande Sonate* in B♭, Op. 93 (after the original Schuberth ed. at the Library of Congress).

they all played down the sterility and played up the agreeableness of the music, especially for amateur learners.[227]

Worth mentioning only because of his niche in opera history are at least ten consistently weak, unimaginative sonatas and sonatinas for P solo and P-duet (pub. between about 1815 and 1830) by a more celebrated man linked with Weber, **Heinrich August Marschner** (1795–1861).[228]

Reviewing two piano sonatas in 1835 by a Dresden pianist, one **Wilhelm Christoph Bommer** (1801–43),[229] Schumann hoped the next two might be a little less labored and structurally self-conscious. As with Hauptmann he again objected to a retrogression into the styles of Mozart and Haydn, this time in the "Adagio" of a Sonata in A♭. "Let him wear the periwig whom it fits well; but don't deprive me of the flowing locks of youth, even if they fall somewhat wildly over the brow. So, loosen up, sonata writer, and no falseness!" [230] In a similar vein, in 1838, Schumann reviewed a Sonata Op. 30 for P-duet by **Leopold Schefer** (1784–1862), a Vienna trained composer better known as poet and novelist in Muskau, northeast of Dresden.[231] He

227. Op. 45 (P) is reviewed in AMZ XXXII (1830) 509, Op. 178 (Vn & P) in NZM XXIII (1845) 70 ("E. K."), and Op. 185 (P & Vn) in NZM XXVII (1847) 254 ("E. K."); cf., also, Cobbett/CHAMBER II 287–88 (W. Altmann and W. W. Cobbett).

228. Cf. MGG VIII 1682–88 (V. Köhler); HOFMEISTER 1815 (Whistling) 596, and 1829–33, p. 131. The first mvt. of Son. 6 in A♭, Op. 39, is reprinted in DM II/2 (1903) after p. 241.

229. Cf. Mendel/LEXIKON II 128.

230. Schumann/SCHRIFTEN II 307.

231. Cf. Mendel/LEXIKON IX 88.

found it to be a strong enough example of the past century, written as though Beethoven had not yet existed. "Only in the last movement does a Romantic streak break suddenly and surprisingly into the friendly contentment, somewhat like a cloud shadow across a village sleeping in the moonlight." [232] On the other hand, in 1841 Schumann objected to a *Phantasiesonate* by **Friedrich Wilhelm Klingenberg** (1809–88), violinist and cantor in Görlitz to the east,[233] because he tried to copy Beethoven's "Sonata quasi una fantasia" and to "get free of old routine" without the requisite training or force. "And it is a misfortune when musical villagers suddenly get excited over Parisian fashions—a misfortune that, regrettably, is more common to us in Germany than elsewhere." [234] In 1843, Schumann found little but a student's scholastic efforts in a piano sonata Op. 4 by the Dresden choral director **Adolf Reichel** (1820–96),[235] which he took to be "a first venture into this difficult art form." [236] By contrast, in 1845 a reviewer already found good ideas and treatment in a two-piano sonata Op. 1 by the versatile Chemnitz musician **Adolf Bergt** (1822–62),[237] son of **Christian Gottlob Bergt** (1772–1837), whose own Op. 1 (3 sons. for P & Vn & Vc) had been announced in 1801.[238] The reviewer also mentioned the brilliance, richness, thickness, and difficulty of Adolf's work, as well as some traces of Spohr's influence.[239]

Early Romantics in and around Leipzig (Loewe)

Some of the most interesting early-Romantic sonatas among the more obscure examples now under survey came from that master of the German song ballad, **Karl Loewe** (1796–1869). Trained as a singer and as a pianist (under D. G. Türk; SCE 589–90), Loewe had already written his celebrated "Edward" and "Erlkönig" ballads the year before and in 1819 was still living in his home town of Halle, 25 miles northwest of Leipzig, when he wrote his first of five solo piano sonatas, dating from 1819 to 1847.[240] This first one, *Grande Sonate brillante* in E♭, Op. 41, in four movements (F-M-Sc-F), was

232. Schumann/SCHRIFTEN I 363.
233. Cf. Mendel/LEXIKON VI 99.
234. Schumann/SCHRIFTEN II 10–11.
235. Cf. Riemann/LEXIKON II 1483; Mendel/LEXIKON VIII 282–83.
236. Schumann/SCHRIFTEN II 118.
237. Cf. Mendel/LEXIKON I 557.
238. AMZ IV (1801–2) Intelligenz-Blatt No. 11. Cf. Schilling/LEXICON I 572–74.
239. NZM XXIII (1845) 52–53 ("E. K.").
240. Cf. GROVE V 361–62 (F. Gehring) and MGG VIII 1106–11 (H. Engel; with errors in the son. dates), both with further bibliography.

not published until 1834, when Simrock issued it.[241] Following his
move in 1820 nearly 175 miles northeast to Stettin, Loewe wrote
his second sonata in 1824, *Le Printemps* . . . "a tone poem in sonata
form," in G, Op. 47. This work, in four movements, too (S/F-M-VF-S),
was published in 1835, one year later than Op. 41, by Schlesinger
of Berlin.[242] A further edition of it in 1852 prompted a reviewer
to take note briefly of its lasting favor in spite of its "now" dated
styles of keyboard and programmatic writing.[243] Loewe wrote *Grosse
Sonate* in E, Op. 16, third in order, in 1829, with publication
following in 1830 by Wagenführ of Berlin.[244] Unusual is the optional
part for tenor and soprano in the second of the three movements
(S/F-M-Va) in this sonata, which has been viewed as the most
significant in "content, form, and originality" of all Loewe's sonatas.[245] The fourth of the sonatas, *Grande Sonate élégique* in f,
Op. 32, was another three-movement work (F-Va-VF), composed over
a period of fifteen years—in 1819, 1825, and 1834—and published
by Wagenführ in 1834. This sonata got more reviews than any of
the others—in fact, than any other work by Loewe.[246] Like Weber's Op.
24 (ssʙ VIII, *supra*), it is dedicated to the Grand Duchess Maria
Paulowna of Weimar, who told Loewe of her pleasure in the work,
rewarded him with a gold snuff-box, and relayed Hummel's praise
of it.[247] Last in order by several years was Loewe's highly programmatic cycle in five movements (VF-M-VF-S-VF), *Zigeuner*-[Gipsy-]*Sonate* in a, Op. 107, composed in 1847 and published in the same
year by Wilhelm Paul in Dresden.[248]

241. Cf. pp. 17–20 (but read Simrock plate no. 3165, not 5165) in Hirschberg/
ʟᴏᴇᴡᴇ, a useful though somewhat idolatrous monograph commemorating the 50th
anniversary of Loewe's death, with separate descriptions of 30 instrumental works,
including copious exx. and early reviews or other references to them; cf., also,
Egert/ꜰʀüʜʀᴏᴍᴀɴᴛɪᴋᴇʀ 128–39 (with exx.), 158. A systematic style-critical study of
Loewe's sons. is to be desired. An early review (1835) of Op. 41 appears in
Schumann/sᴄʜʀɪꜰᴛᴇɴ I 56–59. Mod. ed. of Op. 41: Newman/ᴛʜɪʀᴛᴇᴇɴ-m 140 (with
preface pp. 23–24 [but read 1835 for 1841]).

242. Reviewed in Schumann/sᴄʜʀɪꜰᴛᴇɴ I 91–92 (1835) and in more generalized
fashion by Rellstab in 1835 (cf. Hirschberg/ʟᴏᴇᴡᴇ 36).

243. ɴᴢᴍ XXXVII (1852) 182.

244. There is no chronological reason for Loewe's op. nos. The single review
of Op. 16, in *Berliner musikalische Zeitung* for 1833 (No. 24, p. 97), is quoted in
full in Hirschberg/ʟᴏᴇᴡᴇ 47. C. Reinecke reprinted this son. in his *Meister des
Klaviers* anth. (Breitkopf & Härtel); mod. ed. of first mvt.: Fischer/sᴏɴᴀᴛᴇ-m 33
(replaced by Schumann's Op. 118/2/i in 1957 reprint).

245. Hirschberg/ʟᴏᴇᴡᴇ 40, 47; Egert/ꜰʀüʜʀᴏᴍᴀɴᴛɪᴋᴇʀ 134, 136.

246. Hirschberg/ʟᴏᴇᴡᴇ 72. The reviews include Schumann/sᴄʜʀɪꜰᴛᴇɴ I 59–60
(1835) 338–39; G. A. Keferstein ("K. Stein") in ᴄᴀᴇᴄᴇʟɪᴀ XVII (1835) 64–65; Rellstab
in 1835 (as in Hirschberg/ʟᴏᴇᴡᴇ 73).

247. Hirschberg/ʟᴏᴇᴡᴇ 75.

248. Reviewed in ᴀᴍᴢ XLIX (1847) 310.

In a letter of June 14, 1829, to the Berlin publisher T. Trautwein (quoted further in ssb II, III, and IV), Loewe already submitted "four grand character sonatas," which he wanted to be published (as a set?) in a single volume, much, he said, as had been done for four sonatas by Dussek.[249] Although he cited these sonatas with titles not used later, presumably "Sonata melancolica" was Op. 32 in an earlier or less complete version, "Sonata pathetica" in E♭ was Op. 41, and "Sonata pastoralis" in G was Op. 47; but "Sonata capricciosa" in C must refer to a work since lost, for not a single one of all Loewe's extant instrumental works happens to be in that key and none of his solo piano works not called "sonata," including "fantasias" and "tone poems," divides into separate movements. In the same letter Loewe pointed to Beethoven's and Weber's sonatas as models of the best[250] and declared he himself was bringing "as little shame to the sonata as to the ballad."

Loewe was justified in claiming that his sonatas were both individual and unusual. Evidence can be found in their means of achieving over-all unity as well as in the details of their separate movements. Loewe put more emphasis on two means of unifying his sonata cycles than did most of his contemporaries. One was the use of a programme and the other the use of recurring motives. The programmes are not simply the moods conveyed by the published titles or the pre-publication titles cited above. Nor can they be the after-thoughts that Schumann insisted his own programmes were (ssb VIII *supra*). Especially in Loewe's *Zigeuner-Sonate* the programme dominates styles and forms, causing an early reviewer to begin by questioning its title, "This sonata (?) consists of five movements," [251] and the scholar Leopold Hirschberg to ask whether "suite," in the absence of a better term, would not at least have been a less confining title.[252] Perhaps growing out of several gypsy numbers in Loewe's oratorio of 1842, *Johann Huss*, the descriptive movements in *Zigeuner-Sonate* begin (to translate) with "Forest Scene" in a, approximately in "sonata form" except that the middle section is new material subtitled "Longing for India" (with reference to gypsy origins). The further movements are entitled "Indian March," an A-B-A design in C with the "B" section marked "Adagio,"; "Dance," in E♭, with tarantella rhythms,

---

249. La Mara/MUSIKERBRIEFE II 130–32; for the Dussek vol. cf. HOFMEISTER 1815 (Whistling), 352.

250. About the time of Op. 16 Loewe came to know Weber (MGG VIII 1106).

251. AMZ XLIX (1847) 310.

252. Hirschberg/LOEWE 96 (contested in Egert/FRÜHROMANTIKER 139). Hirschberg is surprised that Liszt failed to mention this son. in his [spurious] treatise of 1859 on "The Gypsies and Their Music in Hungary."

and with trios subtitled "Men's Dance With Firebrands" (in g♯), "The Women Dance Around the Forest Grove" (in B♭), and "Festive Dance of the Children" (in B♭); "Evening Worship," in E, when Loewe adds, "They await the moonrise, which they worship as the reflection of the Indian sun temple"; and "Breaking Up Camp in the Morning," in a, a rondo. The musical word-painting is close and frequent throughout this programmatic sonata. It is less close in Loewe's "Spring" Sonata Op. 47, written in his most productive yet saddest period (right after his wife's early death).[253] Op. 47 takes us from sunrise to sunset according to its four, more general titles and an opening six-line verse by Uhland (Ex. 33). This use of verse, the actual "Romance" sung "ad libitum" in Op. 16, and the numerous parallels with his ballads in the more pictorial and expressive sonata movements[254] remind us that Loewe was at his best when he was re-creating the ballad style. At other times his music can be trite. Among Schumann's more unfavorable remarks about Op. 47 [255] is the opinion that Beethoven was more selective in his choice of material for the "Sinfonia pastorale," that in "small ways" Loewe's compositions "are often rather pretentious, and that they require us to accept the commonplaces repeated a hundred times over along with the basically good things just because it is a distinguished composer who repeats them."

As for Loewe's use of recurring motives to unify his cycles, his first sonata already provides a clear example. In fact, in this regard Op. 41 occasioned another of Schumann's less favorable reviews, this time signed by the harsh "Florestan." [256] After growing angry with three repetitions of an empty initial motive—"Heavens, thought I while playing ahead, to tell someone four times that you have little to say seems too many to me; and then those philistine ornaments!"— Schumann finds the motive recurring as a second theme. And turning to the second movement, "what do we find?"—the same, again, not only to open the "Andantino" section but in the "Allegro agitato" and the "Adagio non troppo lento" sections that follow. In the "Scherzo," where the motive seems to recur in varied disguises (e.g., mss. 1, 345, 359–60), Schumann overlooks or prefers to disregard it, but not in the finale, where "the fearsome old familiar sounds [again,] *pianissimo* [and] *legatissimo* [mss. 460–61, then] peeps out ubiquitously in round and angular shapes [e.g., mss. 444–45, 470–72, 486–88], and

253. Cf. Hirschberg/LOEWE 31–37; Egert/FRÜHROMANTIKER 131–34.
254. Cf. Hirschberg/LOEWE 97, 99, 42–43, 31–32, *et passim.*
255. Schumann/SCHRIFTEN I 91–92.
256. Schumann/SCHRIFTEN I 56–59.

Ex. 33. From the third movement of Karl Loewe's Sonata in
G, "Le Printemps," Op. 47 (after the original Schlesinger ed. at
the Library of Congress).

now drawing to a close, in order to make me quite beside myself it
tips and taps [as in mss. 649–62]." But as viewed here, Florestan's objections seem excessively harsh. Loewe's ideas tend to be somewhat neutral, anyway. This much repetition and variation of a basic idea, which
can be found more or less in all of his sonatas (not to mention Schumann's own sons.), helps it not to pall but to gain in identity. Even
in Op. 41, whose only "programme" is its consistent "brillante" style,
sufficient variety is achieved through resourceful rhythms, passagework, and keyboard techniques. There is, by the way, considerable
affinity between Loewe's and Weber's treatment of the piano, not
excluding wide ranges and wide stretches (as in Op. 41/i/37–43).
There is also considerable affinity, and sometimes resemblance, between Loewe's themes and those of Beethoven,[257] even including the
feel of Beethoven's Op. 57 in Loewe's Op. 32, also in f.[258]

Less significant as programme sonatas were (to translate) *Characteristic Tone-Paintings: Three Grand Sonatas for Piano, Four and
Two Hands,* by the pianist **Gustav Krug** (1803–73) in Naumburg,

257. Cf. the exx. in Hirschberg/LOEWE 39 and 41, and 104; Egert/FRÜHROMANTIKER
130 (but the 3d last E probably should be ♮), 136–37.
258. But Op. 32 suggested Weber to Keferstein in CAECELIA XVII (1835) 65.

southwest of Leipzig.[259] Published in 1844 (?), these have titles and subtitles depicting three crucial aspects of marriage—No. 1, "Love Awakens": i, "First Meeting"; ii, "Serenade"; iii, "Declaration of Love"; iv, "The Betrothal." No. 2, "The Engagement": i, "The Engaged Couple"; ii, "Separation and Reunion"; iii, "Wedding Festivities." No. 3, "Wedlock": i, "The Domestic Quarrel"; ii, "The Wife's Argument"; iii, "The Husband's Retort"; iv, "Finale." Appropriately, only No. 3/ii and iii are for two rather than four hands. In a three-column review of 1845,[260] the writer jests about the wide market this music is certain to have, wonders whether quite different titles might not have fit the music just as well, and regards the musical content as too weak for the extent of these sonatas.

In Leipzig itself, the exceptional flutist (Gottlieb) Heinrich Köhler (1765–1833) left some 50 sonatas for his instrument, including a few trios (P-or-harp & Fl & Vn-or-Va), and about 30 more for P solo or P-duet.[261] These works were published in the two decades from about 1805 to 1825.[262] A representative sampling of these sonatas confirms the suspicion that such prolificity could only be identified with that long line of facile, light, pedagogically oriented, socially pleasing sonatas that continued throughout the 19th century without ever coming to firm grips with essential Romantic trends or, for that matter, with essential music (SSB III).[263] Had he continued to publish for another decade Köhler might have had the honor of being scorned by his cocitizen Florestan!

Almost as prolific in sonata writing, the learned Leipzig pianist and theorist (Johann Christian) Friedrich Schneider (1786–1853), who left well over a thousand compositions, composed some fifty sonatas nearly all in his early years, between 1803 and about 1814, with over half being published; he wrote only one sonata, in 1831 for cello, after he moved to Dessau in 1821 and made his chief niche in oratorio.[264] Most of these sonatas are for solo piano, but there are also a few each for P-duet and 2 Ps, and for piano with one other instrument (Vn, Fl,

259. Cf. Riemann/LEXIKON I 963; HOFMEISTER IV (1844–51) 70.

260. NZM XXIII (1845) 125–26.

261. Cf. MGG VII 1323–24 (R. Eller). MGG omits the better known, younger Louis Köhler (SSB XVIII), who appears not to be related to G. H. Köhler and is the only one of the two in GROVE, Riemann/LEXIKON, and BAKER.

262. Cf. the lists in HOFMEISTER 1815 and 1828 (both Whistling), passim; also, PAZDÍREK VIII 255–56.

263. Such and no more is also the uniform tenor of several short reviews in AMZ: VIII (1805–6) 192, IX (1806–7) 469–70, XVIII (1816) 448, XX (1818) 214–15.

264. Cf. Mendel/LEXIKON IX 136–38; MGG XI 1900–1904 (M. Wehnert); PAZDÍREK XIII 287–90; and the careful lists in Lomnitzer/SCHNEIDER 325–32, 339–40, 351–52, 355.

and Vc). Several, especially the earliest, were greeted with decidedly more space and interest than Köhler's sonatas in contemporary reviews, and deserved to be, although Rochlitz obviously went too far in making quite such a protégé of Schneider as a sonata composer.[265] In his last, somewhat tempered review of the sonatas Rochlitz deplored too little public interest in them, blaming it on their "unnecessary" difficulties, their "excessive," "constant" harmonic fullness that tends to obscure the melody, and a certain lack of melodic force, anyway.[266] Actually, although Schneider's later solo sonatas point toward the sort of virtuosity and pathos to be found in Hummel's and Dussek's best sonatas, they remained oriented to the two composers he himself cited as most central to his development, Mozart and, especially, Clementi.[267] In retrospect and by comparison with the sonatas of the leading early Romantics they hardly seem exceptional in their exploitation of the keyboard or their textural fullness. They do reveal considerable skill and surprising freshness in their melodic and harmonic variants, and in some original dispositions of the two-, three-, and four-movement cycles (such as Sc-Ro in Op. 37 in f). Yet their essential conservatism— something Rochlitz might have been little disposed to fault—must be the real reason why Schneider's better-than-average sonatas lost their appeal so soon. As noted earlier (ssb II), Schneider's revised harmony and composition treatise of 1827 (Schneider/ELEMENTS) showed no clear awareness of "sonata form."

The uncommonly gifted but short-lived pianist and composer (**Christian**) **Ludwig** (or **Louis**) **Schunke** (or **Schuncke**; 1810–34) left a *Grosse Sonate* in g, Op. 3, for piano solo, published by Hofmeister of Leipzig in 1834 and dedicated to the warm friend and mentor of his last year, Schumann (who dedicated his *Toccata* Op. 7 to Schunke in the same year).[268] Schunke had already studied with Reicha and met Berlioz, Kalkbrenner, Chopin, and probably Meyerbeer and the young Liszt

265. E.g., AMZ VII (1804–5) 653–57 (heralding the new talent disclosed in Op. 1), VIII (1805–6) 530–36 (enthusiastic, but with cautions about doubtful stretches and harmonies), IX (1806–7) 832–36 (confirming the promise of Op. 1; followed by the score of a "Scherzo" in e by Schneider, *Beilage* No. 2), XII (1809–10) 305–11 (by E. T. A. Hoffmann? maturing talent noted), XIII (1811) 135 (brief only because "previously discussed in such detail"), XIV (1812) 709 (same), XV (1813) 178–79, XVI (1814) 221–27 (by E. T. A. Hoffmann; mainly on P-duet Op. 29, with exx.), XVII (1815) 149–51 (still maturing), XVIII (1816) 382–84 (slight cooling).

266. AMZ XVIII (1816) 383–4. The only recent discussion of Schneider's sons. occurs on pp. 25–40 in the valuable diss. Lomnitzer/SCHNEIDER (mainly on the oratorios), which includes exx., and the autobiography of 1831 (pp. 292–301) by the extraordinarily methodical Schneider.

267. Cf. Lomnitzer/SCHNEIDER 27, 293, 295.

268. Cf. Flinsch/SCHUNKE; MGG XII 325–27 (H. Hopf); AMZ XXVII (1825) 272 and QUARTERLY VII (1825) 312 (both on his playing in Paris).

by March of 1832, when he wrote his father that he had composed "an entire grand sonata in four movements with a fugue [actually a fugal coda on the main theme] in the first [opening] allegro [movement]." [269] In 1835 Schumann wrote a poetic review of this highly Schumannesque work that also describes Schunke and how they met, and includes the sentence, "You are a master of your art and I call the sonata your best work, above all when you [yourself] play it." [270]

Another pianist and Reicha pupil, with a background in Leipzig and Dresden, **Justus Amadeus LeCerf** (1789–1868) won less enthusiasm from Schumann for a Sonata in C and a *Sonata quasi fantasia* for piano solo, published together as Op. 21 by Trautwein of Berlin in 1840 (?).[271] Much the same that the AMZ reviewer wrote in a column-and-a-half [272] Schumann said in a paragraph and we must reduce to a single, by now familiar, kind of objection: Beethoven must not have lived in vain and it was not enough simply to reproduce the successful, well-balanced styles and forms of a half century back without taking cognizance of all that had happened to composition and the instrument since then. In 1842, Schumann commended the effort but deplored at length the inevitable monotony of a prize-winning *Sonata quasi fantasia*, Op. 5 in f, composed entirely on an initial, unoriginal theme, by the pianist **Julius Emil Leonhard** (1810–83).[273] Under Mendelssohn's personal influence, Leonhard also wrote two violin sonatas (Op. 10), the second of which was reviewed as skillful but dull.[274] Still less enthusiastic, the gist of the verdict on a Sonata in D, Op. 15, for violin and piano by the once popular choral composer **Ruprecht Johannes Julius Dürrner** (1810–59) was that it was old-fashioned and pedagogic.[275] Published by Peters in 1846 (?), this work may have been composed just after Dürrner left Leipzig for Edinburgh in 1844. More promise was seen, partly because they were early works, in Sonata in a, Op. 1, and *Sonate romantique* in E♭, Op. 5, both for P solo, by the once equally popular pianist, choral director, writer, and teacher **Louis Ehlert** (1825–84), who had studied with both Schumann and Mendelssohn.[276] Published in the later 1840's, these works were praised

269. Flinsch/SCHUNKE 201.

270. Schumann/SCHRIFTEN I 62–64.

271. Schumann/SCHRIFTEN II 10, 11. Cf. Mendel/LEXIKON VI 273–74 and Suppl. 210.

272. AMZ XLII (1840) 824–25 (G. W. Fink?).

273. Schumann/SCHRIFTEN II 79, 80–82. Cf. Mendel/LEXIKON VI 301–3; Riemann/LEXIKON II 1026.

274. NZM XXIX (1848) 283 (A. Dörffel).

275. NZM XXV (1846) 128. Cf. Riemann/LEXIKON I 431; HOFMEISTER IV (1844–51) 39.

276. NZM XXV (1846) 99, and XXVIII (1849) 16–17; AMZ XLIX (1847) 291–92 (with exx.). Cf. Mendel/LEXIKON III 327; Riemann/LEXIKON I 452; HOFMEISTER IV (1844–51) 110.

mainly for their convincing flow, there being reservations about the force and originality of the ideas. Talent clearly short of genius was seen in the four-movement, motivically interrelated Sonata in a, Op. 17, for P solo, by the important successor to Mendelssohn, Hiller, and Gade as conductor of the Leipzig Gewandhaus concerts (**August Wilhelm**) **Julius Rietz** (1812–77).[277] This work, published about 1848, and one later one, Sonata in g, Op. 42, for piano and flute, published in 1876,[278] were Rietz's only ventures in the sonata among numerous instrumental compositions.

Other Central German Centers (Spohr)

In the central section of central Germany, **Johann Friedrich Nisle** (1768–at least 1837), able hornist and chamber music composer originally in Rudolstadt, may be mentioned for the novelty of two "Sonates pour le pianoforte et cor de chasse," Op. 6, dedicated to J. F. Reichardt (sce 597–601) and published in 1805 (?),[279] or five years after Beethoven's similarly scored sonata (sce 538). In Mühlhausen the organist **Ferdinand Gottfried Baake** (1800–at least 1830) won praise from two reviewers for a *Grosse Sonate* in C, Op. 6, dedicated to both Hummel and Friedrich Schneider (*supra*) and published by Breitkopf & Härtel about 1827.[280] The four movements were regarded as showing considerable individuality, skill, and motivic unity, and considerable challenge for the pianist in the manifold irregularities and variants in the note groupings. And we should not fail to take note of the one music publication by the renowned philosopher **Johann Friedrich Herbart** (1776–1841), a piano Sonata in D, originally published in 1808 and warmly praised for its skill, elevated content, and brilliant piano writing when it was reprinted (for the centennial of his birth?) in 1876.[281]

Ludwig Spohr (1784–1859), who ranked among the most esteemed and renowned Romantics in his own day, is still given considerable space by music historians,[282] especially for his high position in the history of violin playing. But among today's performers he has fallen about as hard as any once great has fallen. Even so, were the topic

277. nzm XXX (1849) 91–92 (A. G. Ritter). Cf. mgg XI 500–502 (F. Göthel).

278. Altmann/kammermusik 277. Op. 42 is reviewed briefly as unoriginal but a good exercise, in smw XXXV (1877) 531.

279. amz VIII (1805–6) Intelligenz-Blatt No. 8. Cf. mgg IX 1537–38 (E. Stiefel).

280. caecilia VIII (1828) 47–48 (G. Weber?); amz XXVIII (1826) 641–44. Cf. Schilling/lexicon I 366–67.

281. smw XXXIV (1876) 673–74; mw XI (1880) 377–78. Cf. mgg VI 183–85 (W. Kahl).

282. Cf. mgg XII 1061–77 (F. Göthel), with further bibl.

at hand his 30-odd string quartets, or his 20-odd violin concertos, or his several at least nominally programmatic works, or his numerous oratorios and operas, considerably more space could be justified here than for his 8 listed sonatas.[283] Not only were the sonatas a lesser part of his output quantitatively, but he himself spoke of them less, his contemporaries scarcely seem to have noticed them, they have no programmatic implications, and even the historians since then have rarely seen fit more than to mention them, if they do that. Yet these sonatas do have some bearing on the early-Romantic Era, beyond which Spohr did not advance stylistically. Fortunately we have rich environmental information in Spohr's autobiography.[284] This wonderfully entertaining book happens to tell only a little about the sonatas, but it tells much about his restless, transient concert life of which they were a part (and introduces us elsewhere in the present survey to almost as many sonata notables as we met in MOSCHELES).

Among pertinent landmarks in Spohr's life were his posts in Gotha from 1805 to 1812, in Vienna from 1812 to 1815 (where he knew Beethoven), and in Kassel from 1822 to his death. Six of his sonatas were written for harp and violin so that his first wife, the talented harpist Dorette Scheidler, could appear in concert with him. They date from 1805, the year before the marriage, to 1819,[285] or one year before Dorette had to stop playing harp in public (and fifteen years before her early death). The first was a Sonata in c, not published until 1917 but published again in 1954 [286] and now the only readily available sonata by Spohr. Then followed sonatas in B♭, Op. 16, composed in 1806 and published in 1809; E♭, Op. 113, 1806 and 1840 (?), respectively; A♭, Op. 115, 1809 and 1841;[287] E♭, Op. 114, 1811 and 1841; and A♭, 1819, not published. The only review found here of any of these sonatas is one of Op. 113, *Sonate concertante für Harfe oder Pianoforte und Violine oder Violoncell*.[288] The reviewer recognized this three-movement work (F-S-Ro) as an early one from its styles of melody, ornamentation, and passagework, and the freedom, as yet, from excessive fantasy or "wild Romanticism." He commented on the need to transpose the violin part, which had come about from Spohr's habit of tuning his wife's harp down a half-step (and writing the part

---

283. Cf. MGG XII 1064–68; GROVE VIII 17–19 (P. David), with a less complete but clearer view of the output.

284. Cf. our listing for Spohr/AUTOBIOGRAPHY.

285. Cf. Spohr/AUTOBIOGRAPHY I 90–96, II 59 and 93–95 (presumably referring to the 1819 Son. in A♭).

286. Zingel/SPOHR–m.

287. Cf. Spohr/AUTOBIOGRAPHY I 127 and 133.

288. NZM XV (1841) 2–3 ("O. L."). Op. 113 is called "Hamburg Sonate" in PAZDÍREK XIII 915, for no apparent reason.

a half-step higher) in order to avoid frequent string breaking and to put the harp in mechanically more convenient keys.[289]

In his later years Spohr left two other sonatas. One is his solo piano Sonata in A♭, Op. 125, in four movements (F-M-Sc-F), composed and first published in 1843, and dedicated to Mendelssohn.[290] A one-paragraph review of 1844 already arrives at an evaluation that still seems right in today's perspective.[291] The first eight measures are enough, says the reviewer, to reveal Spohr's typical chromatic suspensions and harmonic flow in triple meter; the forms are well organized, the harmony offers surprises, but the ideas lack originality; in the sense that it is written unpianistically in quartet style, it is harder to play than Chopin's or Thalberg's music. Nevertheless, nearly two pages in the autobiography referring to notices and congratulatory letters (including one from Mendelssohn, who later played the sonata for Spohr) bear witness to at least a temporary success for this one main work for piano by Spohr.[292] Spohr's final contribution of interest here was an example of his experimental bent (like his "double quartets" or his special harp tuning), a "Sonatine" for piano and voice in B♭, Op. 138, called "An Sie am Klavier," composed in 1848 and published soon after.[293] This work consists of a "Larghetto" introduction of more than one page and an "Allegro vivace" of nearly seven pages. The piano proceeds in regular phrases and characteristic piano passages through a miniature "sonata form" while the voice sings in slower notes along with it, more as an accessory than a leader.

Although the reviewer of Spohr's Op. 125 found the first eight measures typical enough, twelve later measures in the first movement (24–35), from the middle of the bridge to the middle of the second theme, will be more illustrative here (Ex. 34). They show more clearly his somewhat cloying chromaticism, some of that "quartet part-writing," the triple meter, and an undistinguished melody. They also show a hint of Weber in the figuration, in spite of some negative remarks Spohr had made about Weber's music.[294] It is true that the writing in Spohr's sonatas, as in his concertos, is always refined, never cheap and rarely faulty. As with Weber, the shortest movement—the

289. Cf. Spohr/AUTOBIOGRAPHY I 96.

290. It is discussed in Egert/FRÜHROMANTIKER 101–3. One of the more available, further eds. is in RICORDI ARTE-m X 7.

291. AMZ XLVI (1844) 151.

292. Spohr/AUTOBIOGRAPHY II 242–43. Another evidence might be seen in a pub. ed. of each separate mvt. (PAZDÍREK XIII 915).

293. Cf. PAZDÍREK XIII 915.

294. Spohr/AUTOBIOGRAPHY I 109.

Ex. 34. From the first movement of Ludwig Spohr's Sonata in
A♭, Op. 125 (after RICORDI ARTE-m X 8).

scherzo—makes the most successful form. But the forms, though well
designed outwardly—that is, in the sense of well-proportioned sections
—lack inner unity because they lack compulsion. The fault lies partly
in the melodic ideas, which are too bland and consistently lyrical to
afford the needed identity or contrast. The fault also lies in the melodic
treatment, which rarely goes as far as any organic development of the
ideas. Unfortunately, the constant chromaticism does little to create a
sense of drive. Instead, it combines with the bland melodic lyricism
to make for a somewhat effeminate style. In any case, one recalls certain
style paradoxes in Spohr's make-up—that in his early years he had
found his principal model in Mozart (Hummel being an early favorite,
too); that, like Weber, he had shown a certain resistance to Beethoven, though to late Beethoven in this instance; and that he had
been one of the first to promote Wagner's operas (producing *The
Flying Dutchman* in 1843 and *Tannhäuser* in 1853).[295] The Mozart
influence is more apparent in Spohr's fairly conservative, early sonatas,
for harp and violin. Not yet encumbered by so much chromaticism,
these are not effeminate in character. Furthermore, they do provide

295. Cf. Spohr/AUTOBIOGRAPHY I 12, 109, 188–89, 192; II 245–47, 276–78, 307–8;
Newman/WAGNER I 425–26.

some angular and rhythmically pointed ideas that contrast with the lyrical themes and give clearer definition to the forms and cycles (mostly 3-mvt., F-S-F). The violin gets the lion's share of the melodic material, the harp furnishing an accompaniment that is easy, fluent, and straightforward.

In Offenbach, where he took over his father's publishing firm and became one of the first Mozart specialists, **Johann Anton André** (1775–1842) left at least fifty solo or four-hand sonatas or sonatinas, four-hand divertimentos, and four-hand duos (preceded by several acc'd. P sons. in his youth).[296] Published by his own firm between about 1810 and 1825, these piano works are largely light, instructive pieces in two movements (M-Ro), showing decided skill and freshness in the idioms and forms of the Classic sonatina.[297] Thus, except for occasional Romanticisms in the melody, harmony, or scoring, André belongs right back with those other publishers who composed Classic sonatinas, including Clementi, Hofmeister, and Diabelli.[298] In Mainz, the violinist **Joseph Panny** (1794–1838), with a Viennese background, may be mentioned for the novelty of a *Sonate pour le Violon, sur la quatrième Corde, avec accompagnement de grand Orchestre,* published about 1830 by B. Schott's Söhnen in Mainz.[299] A reviewer (J. A. Gleichmann) welcomed this new cultivation of the long neglected G-string, obviously under Paganini's influence, and viewed it as an appropriately pathetic, three-movement work (Recitative-M-Va).[300]

The music writer and scholar **Emil Naumann** (1827–88), grandson of J. G. Naumann in Dresden (SCE 592–93) and a pupil of Schnyder von Wartensee in Frankfurt (SSB VIII, *supra*) and Mendelssohn in Leipzig, published a single Sonata in c for piano as his Op. 1, about 1846 while active in Bonn.[301] Two reviewers agreed in calling it an inept, uninspired work.[302] On the other hand, two reviewers from the same periodicals[303] agreed in finding at least some charm and talent in an early work for solo piano published about 1845—Sonata in D, Op. 4, by

296. Cf. MGG I 459–61 (H. Wirth).
297. Among mod. eds.: 6 Sonatinas, P solo, Op. 34, Augener's Ed., No. 8005; 6 Sonatinas, P-duet, Op. 45, Summy-Birchard (1959); Divertimento in a, P-duet, Ed. Peters 6059; Divertimento in F, P-duet, Townsend/DUETS-m 59.
298. Cf. SCE 751, 550–51, 566–67; SSB III. According to CAECILIA XIII (1831) 106–8, with corroboration from both men involved, André's P-duets Opp. 44 and 45 were also, but erroneously, pub. under Diabelli's name.
299. Cf. Schilling/LEXICON V 367–68; Riemann/LEXIKON II 1338.
300. CAECILIA XIII (1831) 119–20 (as part of a larger review of several of Panny's works, pp. 115–22).
301. Cf. MGG IX 1294–95 (R. Engländer); HOFMEISTER IV (1844–51) 140.
302. NZM XXVI (1847) 166–67 (A. Dörffel) and AMZ XLIX (1847) 525–26.
303. NZM XXIV (1846) 145–46; AMZ XLVIII (1846) 609 (starting, "Again a sonata!")

a violinist who had played under Hummel in Weimar and was now resident in Düsseldorf, **Carl Müller** (1818–94).[304]

Mendelssohn in Berlin and Leipzig

(**Jakob Ludwig**) **Felix Mendelssohn** (**Bartholdy**; 1809–47), the most widely celebrated and esteemed composer in the period between Beethoven and Wagner, left at least 19 sonatas (or about 4 per cent) out of a total of some 500 works, large and small, published and unpublished, that are attributed to him (not including arrangements and transcriptions).[305] Among these sonatas, as the following tabulation shows, there are 6 for piano solo, 7 for piano and one other instrument, and six for organ. Not included here are the 9 early works for string orchestra in which the titles "Sinfonia" and "Sonata" are equated.[306] Only 9 of the 19 sonatas were published—which is to say, approved by Mendelssohn for publication—in his lifetime, including the 6 for organ, 2 for piano and cello, one for piano and violin, and one for piano solo. And 4 of the others still have not been published. Furthermore, even those that he did approve for publication seem to have won relatively little interest on the part of Mendelssohn himself, and with the partial exception of the organ sonatas, still less on the part of either his contemporary or subsequent biographers.[307] Next to the ever popular *Elijah*, the violin Concerto in e, the "Scotch" and "Italian" symphonies, "A Midsummer Night's Dream Music," or the "Hebrides" Overture, the sonatas do look small. Yet it hardly would be adequate here to give only passing mention to a body of sonatas that includes, according to all evidence accumulated here,[308] two of the few most popular cello sonatas in the 19th century and what are still the most popular organ sonatas along with J. S. Bach's and "The

304. Cf. Riemann/LEXIKON II 1225; HOFMEISTER IV (1844–51) 140 (but read Op. 4 for Op. 1).

305. For this rough estimate of total works, the approximately 400 items listed in MGG IX 83–85 (E. Werner) are increased by 25 per cent to include unlisted items among some 200 works still unpub. Much needed is a full *catalogue raisonné* of Mendelssohn's works to supersede the long outdated thematic index of 1873 (VERZEICHNISS MENDELSSOHN). A convenient though not complete catalogue is that in Gatti & Basso/LA MUSICA III 310–22, with pub. dates not in GROVE V 699–706 (P. M. Young) or MGG IX 83–85. Cf. Mendelssohn/VERLEGER 353–55.

306. MGG IX 62.

307. Thus, the important recent study Werner/MENDELSSOHN (1963) takes note only of Opp. 6, 45, and 106 (pp. 64–65, 360), and the few words it gives to these 3 sons. are more derogatory than favorable.

308. Cf. the sampling in the final column of the following tabulation; but occasional guessing was necessary where the particular son. was not identified sufficiently or at all.

Mendelssohn's Sonatas

Op.	Key	Scoring	Composed	First ed.	Mendelssohn/ WERKE-m	Early titles; remarks	No. of performances reported in MT, 1860–80
105	E	P	1821	(see remarks)		"Sonatina"; facs. of first 2 pp. in Petitpierre/ MENDELSSOHNS 106–7	
	g	P	1821	Rieter-Biedermann, 1868			
4	f	P & Vn	1823	Laue, 1825	XI/iii/68	ded. to Eduard Rietz	3
	D	P	by 1824		IX/iv/43	cf. Jacob/MENDELSSOHN 54	
	c	P & Va	1824	"in preparation"		cf. MGG IX. 84	
	Eb	P & Cl	1824	Sprague-Coleman, 1941		the first ed. of 1941 is overlooked in recent lists	
	d	P & Vn	ca. 1825		XI/i/51	cf. Dahms/MENDELSSOHN 139.	
6	E	P	1826	Laue, 1826	XI/iii/69		2
106	Bb	P	1827	Rieter-Biedermann, 1868	XI/i/56		1
28	f#	P	1833	Simrock, 1834		"Phantasie"; but "Sonate *écossaise*" in the autograph MS; cf. NOTES XXI (1963–64) 92; ded. to Moscheles	
45	F	P & Vn	1838	Peters, 1953	IX/iv/45		10
58	Bb	P & Vc	1838	Breitkopf, 1839	IX/iv/46	ded. to Count Mathieu Wielhorsky	14
65/1	D	P & Vc	1841–42	Kistner, 1843	XII/84	announced as "Six Grand Sonatas"; Mendelssohn requested "Sonatas" rather than "Voluntaries" for the title; ded. to F. Schlemmer; Breitkopf & Härtel must have pub. Op. 65 in the same month (Oct, 1845; cf. Edwards/MENDELSSOHN 3–4)	12
65/2	f/F	organ	1844	Coventry and Hollier, 1845			13
65/3	c/C	"	1844	"			6
65/4	A	"	1845	"			22
65/5	Bb	"	1844	"			5
65/6	d/D	"	1845	"			8

94th Psalm" by Reubke (SBE 271–72; SSB V and X). Indeed, Mendelssohn's organ sonatas of 1845 seem to have been played more in the later 19th century than any other sonatas in any setting except Beethoven's for piano.[309]

The Mendelssohn sources and literature, both first- and secondhand, are abundant but in disarray.[310] As with Schumann, something of what Otto Erich Deutsch did for Handel, Mozart, and Schubert is needed. The letters and other documents, and the music itself all need to be corrected, completed, brought fully to light and together, and reissued in authoritative modern editions.[311] For our purposes, we can only wonder whether the unpublished documents add to the sparse information on all but the organ sonatas. And we can only hope that the edition of Mendelssohn's works newly launched in 1961 will become in fact the needed revised and completed edition, including the six sonatas (and others?) lacking in the original "complete" edition of 1874–77.[312] In any case, not only sufficient documentary details but modern studies of all but the organ sonatas are lacking.[313]

As the foregoing tabulation shows, Mendelssohn wrote about half of his sonatas, including all of those for piano, in the 6 years from age 12 to 18. His main center was still Berlin and he was still under the influence of his teachers Ludwig Berger (with his heritage of Clementi and Field) and Zelter (with his background in the sphere of J. S. Bach).[314] Thanks partly to travels, he was also under the musical influence of early acquaintances like Weber, Hummel, Moscheles, Cherubini, Paganini, Spohr, and Spontini, as well as of Haydn, Mozart,

309a

---

309. Cf. Colin Mason's bracketed comments on Mendelssohn's other chamber music in COBBETT II 135–36.

310. Brief summaries appear in MGG IX 82–83 and 95, and Werner/MENDELSSOHN 493–96.

311. In 1968 Mendelssohn/VERLEGER appeared as Vol. I of a projected complete ed.

312. Cf. Werner/MENDELSSOHN 52. Warm thanks are owing here to Professor Eric Werner, (then) at Hebrew Union School in New York, for his counsel on Mendelssohn and loan of unpub. letters and scores in microfilm. In 1961 the Deutscher Verlag für Musik in Leipzig issued 2 concertos as the initial items in the *Leipziger Ausgabe der Werke Felix Mendelssohn-Bartholdys,* sponsored by the international Felix-Mendelssohn-Gesellschaft. In 1967, Gregg Press in Farnborough (England) announced an unaltered reprint of the original Mendelssohn/WERKE-m.

313. On the organ sons. cf. Edwards/MENDELSSOHN (and further in ZIMG III [1901–2] 337–38 [C. Maclean]); Pearce/MENDELSSOHN (a 79-p. booklet of considerable interest); Mansfield/MENDELSSOHN; Werner/KIRCHENMUSIKER 119–24; Kremer/ORGAN 3–7. Dale/NINETEENTH 71–73 gives 3 pp. to a description of the P sons. (but, curiously, Egert/FRÜHROMANTIKER gives nothing); COBBETT II 134–35 gives nearly 2 cols. to Opp. 4, 45, and 58; and Horton/MENDELSSOHN 15–17 gives 3 pp. to the same works.

314. Cf. Werner/MENDELSSOHN 14–21.

and Beethoven through his studies.[315] Mendelssohn wrote nearly all of his other sonatas in the period after his move to Leipzig and the Gewandhaus orchestra conductorship, in 1835, and including his less satisfactory return to Berlin in 1841. By this period, thanks mainly to further travels, he had become acquainted with nearly every important musician of the time. But by then, too, he was much too firmly established in his own artistic directions to submit to further strong influences. Chopin and Schumann marked the limit of his conservative sympathies, while Berlioz and Liszt were generally beyond or outside the pale.[316] To revert to oft-cited tags, Mendelssohn remained in his later works more the "Romantic Classicist" than the Classicistic Romanticist.[317]

Looking back at the ripe age of eighteen in his short life, Mendelssohn took the view that only with instrumental music had he been successful thus far.[318] Although the nine or more sonatas he had already written, including even the two he had approved for publication, could not have been more than incidental to that view, their styles and forms and the few details of their circumstances that have turned up here help to explain the view. We must start with the fact that the two earliest sonatas, those preserved from his twelfth year, are surely two of history's most remarkable examples of musical precocity. Whatever their shortcomings may be in content, they not only confirm that this "wild, gay lad" [319] was already a master of his craft, but they imply an exceptional degree of confidence. Thus, surrounded by two quick, structurally secure but somewhat prim outer movements, the "Adagio" of Op. 105 in g seems to be a deliberate experiment in a more plastic, free kind of A-B-A design. This sonata was one of his own works, along with Bach fugues and pieces by Mozart and Beethoven, that Mendelssohn says he played, to the delight of Hummel and the Grand Duke at Weimar, during his remarkable visits in 1821 with the much older Goethe.[320] When the first edition of this work appeared in 1868 a London reviewer applauded it quite apart from its precocity, finding less interest only in the weaker slow movement, "as

315. Among numerous references, cf. Selden-Goth/MENDELSSOHN 22 and 31 (on Hummel), 82 (on Weber and others); MOSCHELES I 97–102; MENDELSSOHN/Moscheles 1–4; Mendelssohn/BRIEFE I 5 (on Weber); Lampadius/MENDELSSOHN 183–85 (Jules Benedict on Weber).

316. Cf. Werner/MENDELSSOHN 332, 381.

317. Cf. Einstein/ROMANTIC 124; Werner/MENDELSSOHN 515–21; Enke/MENDELSSOHN (concluding that he was a post- or "manneristic"-Classicist).

318. Letter of Sept. 24, 1827, as quoted in Werner/MENDELSSOHN 74.

319. Werner/MENDELSSOHN 19–20.

320. Selden-Goth/MENDELSSOHN 22. Cf. Werner/MENDELSSOHN 19–21.

might be expected in so juvenile a work." [321] The Sonatina in E, an eight-page piece he put into his sister Fanny's album,[322] gives clearer foretastes of his mature style. In fact, the "Lento" introduction and succeeding "Moderato" respectively anticipate by three years the lyricism and harmonic cumulation, and even the rhythmic regularity of the "Andante" as well as the light fluency of the "Presto" in the much played Rondo capriccioso in E, Op. 14. One might go further to say that here was a first germ of the second and third movements of the violin Concerto in e (1838–44).

Information is lacking on two of the next sonatas in our tabulation, those in D and c. Op. 4 in f was written for Mendelssohn's friend and violin teacher, the short-lived Eduard Rietz (older brother of the better known Julius Rietz mentioned earlier in this chapter). The Sonata in E♭ for piano and clarinet reportedly was written for the same clarinetist, Heinrich Bärmann, to whom Weber dedicated several works.[323] Besides their adjacent years of composition[324] and their similar three-movement plans (S/F-S-F; S/F-M-F), these two sonatas have in common some hints of Weber, as in the stepwise descents on two-note groups (e.g., Op. 4/i/19–20 and E♭/i/60-61) or some forthright melodic lines of folklike simplicity (e.g., Op. 4/ii/1–20; E♭/ii/1–10). For the rest, probably because of the violin, the key, and the dedicatee, Op. 4 is a more impassioned, almost rhapsodic, but not ineffective work, with a bit of the drive and purpose Mendelssohn must already have relished in Beethoven's solo piano sonatas in the same key. In 1825, a Berlin reviewer welcomed the absence of "grande," "pathétique," or "mélancholique" in the title (SSB II), remarked on young composers' predilections for F minor, and grew facetious over what he regarded as bold harmonies and other freedoms in Op. 4.[325]

Mendelssohn presumably did not consider Op. 106 to be as worthy of publication as Op. 6, though why is not clear. These two solo piano sonatas, in E and B♭, also composed in adjacent years, make a pair of about equal interest and quality, with somewhat similar four-movement cycles (totalling 703 and 528 measures, respectively). Moreover, they have in common what seems like more than chance resemblances to

323a

321. MT XIII (1867–69) 382.

322. Petitpierre/MENDELSSOHN 100.

323. GROVE V 682, I 439–40.

324. MGG IX 84 gives 1825 as the year Op. 4 was composed, but 1823 is given in all other sources known here, hence is preferred in our tabulation.

325. Trans. in part in Jacob/MENDELSSOHN 48–50 from the Berlin Allgemeine musikalische Zeitung. In AMZ XXVII (1825) 531–32 a paragraph of generalized praise is given to this work's naturalness and skill, likening it to, but not equating it with, Mozart's best sons. for P & Vn.

Beethoven's solo piano sonatas Opp. 101 and 106, respectively.[326] Mendelssohn must have had in mind a kind of "hommage à Beethoven" and his Op. 101 when he opened Op. 6 with the same meter, tempo, and mood, and on nearly the identical idea; then, after a second movement in minuet rather than march style, wrote a "Recitativo" that follows Beethoven's movement in key and tempo, and with nearly the same idea, again. Although Mendelssohn's finale is not fugal its ideas resemble those in Beethoven's finale and it, too, returns to an earlier movement (as does the finale of Mendelssohn's Op. 106). Mendelssohn's Op. 106 in B♭ is close enough to Beethoven's Op. 106 in B♭, in certain respects, to make one wonder whether Julius Rietz (editor of Mendelssohn/WERKE-m) could have assigned the nonchronological, posthumous opus number with this resemblance in mind.[327] The opening character, tempo, meter, rhythmic pattern, and melodic outline are all similar, as are the unusual modulation to the submediant through its dominant, the contrapuntally imitative development, and the *diminuendo* ending (except for Beethoven's last two strokes). Other similarities appear in the preludial passages leading to the finale, in cyclical unity through similar incipits (as also in Mendelssohn's Opp. 105 and 6), in Mendelssohn's choice of a "Scherzo" for the second movement, and in this movement's use of the same 2/4 meter and tonic-minor key that Beethoven uses for his trio section, where the elfin style seems almost to be a copy of Mendelssohn in advance! There happens to be ample evidence not only that Mendelssohn knew, played, and modeled after the late as well as the earlier music of Beethoven,[328] but that he knew Op. 106 in particular. About a year before he composed his own Sonata in B♭, he wrote an impish letter to his sister Fanny pretending he was Beethoven and assuring her that "I am sending you my Sonata in B-flat Op. 106 as a present on your birthday. . . ." [329]

In 1834, Schumann, who never ceased treating Mendelssohn as "the

326. Probably taking the cue from Schumann/SCHRIFTEN I 124, Georgii/KLAVIER-MUSIK 307 calls attention to the resemblance of Op. 6 to Beethoven's Op. 101. Bülow, unaware of these early sons., thought it was just as well that Mendelssohn had not competed with Beethoven in the field of the piano son. (BÜLOW BRIEFE III 50).

327. After Op. 72 Mendelssohn's op. nos. were assigned posthumously. They are not necessarily chronological after Op. 80. Cf. Werner/MENDELSSOHN 493–94.

328. E.g., cf. Werner/MENDELSSOHN 25, 83, 107–9, 115–16, 149, 437, *et passim;* Hiller/MENDELSSOHN 214–15.

329. As trans. from a letter of Nov. 8, 1825 in Werner/MENDELSSOHN 108–9 (with parentheses around "Op. 106" that are not in the facs. of the original letter that Dr. Werner kindly made available to this study). Op. 106 is among selected piano works by Mendelssohn scheduled (as of 1967) to appear in "Urtextausgabe" under Dr. Werner's editorship, incorporating changes Mendelssohn made in the autograph.

man to whom I look up as to a high mountain . . . a perfect God," [330] took poetic pleasure in Mendelssohn's effective treatment of the conventional in Op. 6 and already recognized a "reflective sadness" common to its first movement and that of Beethoven's Op. 101, as well as traces of Weber in its finale.[331] As for Op. 106, the same London reviewer quoted above on Op. 105 notes "a large advance, in power of thought and construction," anticipates later writers in liking the "Scherzo" best and, again, the "Andante quasi allegretto" least, and, like Schumann on Op. 6, finds traces of Weber in this finale.[332]

Mendelssohn's Op. 28 in f♯ was called "Sonate écossaise" on the autograph but its title was changed, presumably by himself, to *Phantasie* for the first edition in 1834.[333] Thus it belongs with the numerous 19th-century sonatas of Beethoven, Schubert, Schumann, Liszt, and others, that raise the question of sonata or fantasy (SSB II). In this instance the fantasy predominates over the sonata in the sense that free passagework predominates over phrase-and-period syntax, or that leading ideas tend to lose themselves in the passagework. However, the ideas do have enough identity to reveal related incipits in the three rather briefly developed movements (M-F-VF, totalling 467 mss.).

Mendelssohn's last nine sonatas, composed between 1838 and 1845, show the mature craftsman who has crystallized his style and no longer experiments so much with the form or seeks to model after his immediate predecessors. The recently published Sonata in F for piano and violin is an effective if not a greatly inspired example.[334] It is on a par with the cello sonata of the same year (1838), Op. 45 in B♭, in quality, import, and length (697 as against 773 mss.). The two works reflect Mendelssohn's new interest in chamber music in preference to solo piano music:

Pianoforte pieces are not exactly the things I write with the greatest pleasure, or even with real success; but I sometimes want a new thing to play, and then if something exactly suitable for the piano happens to come into my head,

330. Letter of April 1, 1836, as trans. in Jansen/SCHUMANN I 87.

331. Schumann/SCHRIFTEN I 123–24 and II 387, fn. 168. Moscheles' enjoyment of Op. 6 is attested in MENDELSSOHN/Moscheles 3–4. A one-col. review in AMZ XXIX (1827) 122–23 commends Mendelssohn's restraint in publishing and the worth of all he did release, especially the freshness, lyricism, expressiveness, and good piano writing in Op. 6.

332. MT XIII (1868) 382 and 387; cf. the similar views on p. 346 after a performance of Op. 106 by Arabella Goddard. An early reference to Op. 106 occurs in AMA No. 29, p. 9 (Jan. 13, 1827).

333. Cf. Dahms/MENDELSSOHN 131; Georgii/KLAVIERMUSIK 309–10. Mendelssohn's reference to a "Schottische Sonate" in his letter of May 25, 1830 (Mendelssohn/BRIEFE I 5) must refer to an early draft of Op. 28; otherwise it is unclear.

334. Mod. ed.: Peters No. 6075 (1953), with facs. from the autograph (our Ex. 35, *infra*) and a brief preface (Y. Menuhin).

even if there are no regular passages in it [i.e., characteristic opportunities for display?], why should I be afraid of writing it down? Then, a very important branch of pianoforte music which I am particularly fond of—trios, quartets, and other things with accompaniment—is quite forgotten now, and I feel greatly the want of something new in that line. I should like to do a little towards this. It was with this idea that I lately wrote the sonata for violin, and the one for cello, and I am thinking next of writing a couple of trios [the Trio in d, Op. 49, was composed in 1839].[335]

Cast in similar designs, both sonatas follow that most standard plan of two quick movements separated by a slower movement, and both still show an interest in cyclic unity through similar incipits. A description of the first movement of the violin Sonata in F should suffice for the numerous, fairly (but never rigidly) standardized uses of "sonata form" in his later sonatas and will bring to light one example of a certain rhythmic monotony or doggedness that seems to constitute the main "problem" of Mendelssohn. The opening theme (similar to systems 3 and 4 in Ex. 35, *infra*) is based on one of Mendelssohn's most characteristic rhythms, ♩ ♫ | ♩ .[336] The reiterated pattern and its continuation stretch into a 9-measure question phrase by the piano and a 10-measure answer by the violin. The same pattern and its augmentation underlie the simple modulatory bridge (mss. 19–41) to the dominant (by way of its dominant, colored by borrowed tones). The second theme (mss. 42–64) provides contrast through its steadier, quieter course and its modulation (by change of mode) to the lowered submediant, but it recalls the over-all curve of the first theme and presently returns to the pattern, augmented, in the accompaniment. Throughout the closing material (mss. 64–102), which returns to the dominant, the initial pattern and its augmentation prevail again. So do they in the development section (mss. 103–87), which passes through d, g, and E♭ before returning gradually to F by way of V of V of V. By now the pattern, which at best identifies with a rather cut-and-dried melodic figure, wears thin in spite of its elisions and imitations (but without contretemps or other rhythmic relief). Yet it returns fortissimo to initiate and dominate the recapitulation again (mss. 188–266), which remains in the home key, fortunately with a reduction of the opening thematic group by half (from 60 to 30 mss.). The coda (mss. 267–305) begins and climaxes on the initial pattern. Our Ex. 35 includes the last 22 measures, with climactic references to the second theme and to

335. From a typically chatty letter (Aug. 17, 1838, to F. Hiller), as trans. in Hiller/MENDELSSOHN 131–32. Cf., also, Selden-Goth/MENDELSSOHN 278, 281; Mendelssohn/VERLEGER 300–303.

336. E.g., this and very similar patterns predominate in 9 of the 43 nos. in *Elijah*: 11, 14, 20, 22, 34, 38, 39, 41, 43.

Ex. 35. Facs. from the autograph of Felix Mendelssohn's Sonata in F (1838) for piano and violin (after the frontispiece in Edition Peters No. 6075, by kind permission of the publisher).

the first theme played fortissimo.[337] It also includes the start of the second movement, in the submediant major key. Throughout this A-B-A design and its extended coda, our pattern, in a more gentle variant, still plays the leading role. In the finale, a deft, sparkling sonata-rondo form in nearly *perpetuum mobile* style, the pattern no longer obtrudes, although Mendelssohn may mean it to be hidden in the steady 16th-note pattern of the refrain.

Mendelssohn was probably indulging in false modesty when he wrote Hiller he was sending him the score of Op. 45 only "because of the lovely cover, and by way of a novelty—otherwise there is not much in it." [338] But there is no question as to the greater musical worth of Op. 58 in D, written about three years later. As viewed here, it ranks with Mendelssohn's finest chamber music. Compared with Op. 45,[339] it well deserves the "Grande" Mendelssohn would not let Kistner add to the title.[340] It opens on a more expansive, idiomatic cello theme, which does not wear thin for that reason even though it supplies the outline for the second theme; its initial motive recurs just as often as in Op. 45; and this motive relates to the incipits of the other three movements, too. Moreover, its harmony is richer and more subtle, with remarkable variety in the use of Mendelssohn's most favored chord, the dim.-7th (as in Op. 58/i/129–30, 191 and 193; or iii/42–44; or iv/1–4, 228–30, 249–53). The generally higher *tessitura* of the cello part and its balance with the piano part make for more telling, grateful sound. In the harmony, melodic development, and texture (as in the 3ds and 6ths of iv/149–50) are frequent anticipations of Brahms. Of special appeal are the scherzo, again (ii), and the juxtaposition in the short "Adagio" (iii) of irregular chorale phrases in the piano with quasi recitative in the cello, so that the A-B-A design consists of chorale, recitative, and a remarkable synthesis of both (as in Ex. 36).

During hectic concert and social activities in England in 1844,

337. The corrections in the neat MS illustrate "the disease" of constant alterations from which he said he suffered chronically (Edwards/MENDELSSOHN 7).

338. Hiller/MENDELSSOHN 135; he similarly disparaged his "Songs Without Words" (cf. Werner/MENDELSSOHN 220; Worbs/MENDELSSOHN 244, fn. 40). As usual, Schumann had only praise for this "latest" work by Mendelssohn, calling it "more refined, more rapturous, . . . more Mozartean than ever" (Schumann/SCHRIFTEN I 398–99; faultily trans. in Jacob/MENDELSSOHN 100–101). Mendelssohn played Opp. 45 and 58 with Julius Rietz (Lampadius/MENDELSSOHN 144; MOSCHELES II 179). Cf., also, Müller-Reuter/LEXIKON 137–38.

339. Cf., also, Dahms/MENDELSSOHN 139–40.

340. Werner/MENDELSSOHN 335. A peripheral explanation for Mendelssohn's restraint in publishing his music is the curiously fastidious argument, with reference to Op. 58 and other new works, in his letter to K. Klingemann of June 12, 1843 (Selden-Goth/MENDELSSOHN 325; SSB IV).

Ex. 36. From the third movement of Felix Mendelssohn's
Sonata in D for piano and cello, Op. 58 (after Mendelssohn/
WERKE-m IX/iv/46).

Mendelssohn's impressive playing of Bach and his improvising at the
organ brought a commission to write some organ "voluntaries." Although he agreed such a title would "suit" his pieces—"the more so as
I do not know what it means precisely," he quipped in flawless English
—he preferred to call them "sonatas," and his publisher agreed.[341]
They were, in fact, the first consequential organ pieces to bear this title
in the 19th century (SSB V). When Coventry and Hollier announced
them in 1845, now grown to six from a planned three, the high-flown
title was "Mendelssohn's School of Organ-Playing . . . Six Grand

341. Cf. Edwards/MENDELSSOHN 2–4; ZIMG III (1901–2) 337–38 (C. Maclean).

Sonatas for the Organ." But this title was soon reduced to *Six Sonatas for the Organ,* Op. 65. The early comments and reviews were just as high-flown, including Schumann's warm letter about the "intensely poetic new ideas—what a perfect picture they form in every sonata! . . . I . . . think of a St. Cecilia touching the keys; and how delightful that that should be your wife's name! Above all, Nos. 5 and 6 seem to me splendid." [342]

Mendelssohn's preference for "sonata" as the title of his organ pieces probably reflects their somewhat greater size, freedom, and exploitation of the organ as compared with the traditional English "voluntary." [343] In the present survey this majestic music must be regarded as peripheral to the mainstream of sonata history, but central to—in fact, a major landmark in—the special and equally venerable branch of the organ sonata (SBE 56 *et passim;* SCE 89–91 *et passim*). Each "sonata" is a cycle, to be sure, but the cycles, of from two to four movements nearly always in the same key, are highly irregular and foreign to the mainstream of the sonata. In fact, the separate movements seem originally to have been composed as independent organ "studies," of which three of four go back to earlier works; and only after their completion were they grouped, without any premeditated unity, into cycles.[344] More indicative are the forms of the movements, which scarcely ever approach "sonata form," [345] but nearly always are those most encountered in the organist's, especially the church organist's, literature. Among the latter are fugues, chorale fantasias, and variations, and imitative or figural preludes. The chorale, which Mendelssohn cultivated so often in his music, serves even more often and significantly here.[346] The polyphonic styles and mastery at times take us very close to the music of J. S. Bach that Mendelssohn did so much to promote. All of which is hardly conducive to the statements, dualistic opposition, and development of full-fledged themes, the transparent textures, the slow harmonic rhythm, and the broad tonal schemes that we ordinarily identify with the Classic and Romantic sonata.

342. Cf. Edwards/MENDELSSOHN 4–6. For a typical review, cf. AMZ XLVIII (1846) 97–102 (A. G. Ritter). Cf. Mendelssohn/VERLEGER 156–64, *passim,* on the Breitkopf & Härtel ed. in the same year of 1845.
343. Cf. Werner/KIRCHENMUSIKER 119–20; Pearce/MENDELSSOHN 7–9.
344. Werner/KIRCHENMUSIKER 119–20.
345. Cf. Mansfield/MENDELSSOHN 562–63.
346. Cf. Pearce/MENDELSSOHN 43–50 and MT XLII (1901) 798 (Otto Goldschmidt to John Stainer) on chorale identifications; in the latter, on p. 797, are 3 facs. of passages in the autographs of these sons. At least some of these sons. may have been intended for use in the Lutheran service (Mansfield/MENDELSSOHN 564); cf. MT XXII (1881) 589 and Pearce/MENDELSSOHN 5 for their use in English services.

Other Berlin Composers (L. Berger, E. T. A. Hoffmann)

The largest number of German sonata composers in the first half of the 19th century was in Berlin. One of Mendelssohn's principal teachers in that city was **Ludwig Berger** (1777–1839), who brought his special fondness for Mozart, Gluck, and Beethoven to the lessons, as well as his own background of associations with J. G. Naumann, Clementi, Field, Steibelt, Cramer, Klengel, and many others.[347] Although Berger made his mark chiefly as a late, somewhat Romanticized exponent of the "Berlin Liederschule," he also excelled as a pianist and teacher, and left at least eight piano sonatas, all composed relatively early, between 1800 and 1813. These last include two unpublished sonatas composed in 1800, in E♭ and G, each in three movements; a three-movement Sonata in c "über die Figur 𝅘𝅥𝅮," Op. 18, composed in 1801 but not first published until 1825;[348] a three-movement "Sonate pathétique" in c, composed by 1804, dedicated to Clementi, first published in 1813,[349] then republished by 1815 as Op. 7 in a revised ("nouvelle") edition that left only the second movement unaltered and saw "Grande" added to the title in several reprints; a Sonata in g, Op. 15, for P-duet, composed in 1805 but not published until 1825;[350] a three-movement "Grande Sonate" in F, Op. 9, arranged about 1810 from a trio for two horns and piano[351] and first published in 1818; a two-movement "Grande Sonate" in E♭, Op. 10, composed about 1810 and first published in 1818; and an unpublished, one-movement sonata in G composed in London in 1813.

Berger's Op. 18 (recalling J. E. Leonhard's "Prize Sonata," *supra*) is a highly resourceful, exhaustive, and exhausting essay on its single six-note motive. The plainness of the motive, its recurrence without letup in all three movements, the lack of a break before the second movement, and the choice of c or C for all three movements do lead to monotony in spite of the motivic resourcefulness. Yet some answers

347. The important new study Siebenkäs/BERGER, superseding and encompassing previous studies, includes a biography (pp. 9–32), a main section on the songs, a briefer discussion of the instrumental and choral works (including P sons., pp. 182–89 and 192, with exx.), letters, catalogues of the works (with sons. on pp. 250–51 and 257), and a bibliography. The sons. had previously been discussed in Egert/FRÜHROMANTIKER 104–8, with ex.

348. These first 3 sons. survive together in MSS as "Oeuvre I" (Siebenkäs/BERGER 289, fn. 444), but the pub. Op. 1 is different.

349. Peters plate no. 1112 (cf. Deutsch/NUMMERN 14); hence, probably not late 1814 or early 1815 as in Siebenkäs/BERGER 183 and 250.

350. Cf. Siebenkäs/BERGER 192.

351. Cf. Siebenkäs/BERGER 289, fn. 455.

come to mind when Paul Egert objects that Op. 18 cannot be called a "sonata" because no movement achieves "sonata form" (presumably meaning thematic dualism), or when Dieter Siebenkäs finds "no new aesthetic ideal" in Op. 18, only an artistic exploit in motivic technique.[352] A "sonata form" does exist in the first movement, although Berger's tonal and dynamic contrasts do more to outline it than his transformation of the motive by way of a "second theme." In any case, it is hardly necessary to reargue here the unjustness of disqualifying a sonata because it lacks any movement in "sonata form" (cf. SCE 16, 117–18). No question of such a lack was raised in Rellstab's unconstrained praise of Op. 18 (along with Opp. 7, 9, and 10), calling it superior "in depth of invention and meaningful beauty of form" even to Weber's and Hummel's best sonatas.[353] Also, what now seems like excessive motivic play must be recalled as one kind of "aesthetic ideal" in early, post-Beethovian Romanticism, if only because Schubert, Schumann, Mendelssohn, Weber, Hummel, and so many other early Romantics showed such a predilection for it (SSB VI).

Berger's most original and telling sonata is certainly his *Grande Sonate pathétique* in c, Op. 7, after which Opp. 9 and 10 suggest progressive retreats into the demands—mainly for facility, fluency, and regularity—of public taste. Op. 7 is original in spite of its outward imitations of Beethoven's Op. 13, imitations not only in the title and key, but in the recurrence of the slow "Introduzione" during the first movement and in some thematic resemblances (e.g., cf. Berger's Op. 7/i/28–30 with Beethoven's Op. 13/i/140–43). Op. 7 is original especially in the fresh rhythms and melodies one knows and expects in Berger's songs—for example, in its rondo, tarantella-like finale (Ex. 37). Berger's harmony and piano writing are often ingenious and effective, too. Generally less interesting are his accompaniments and his efforts to develop his ideas.

The versatile **Ernst Theodor Amadeus Hoffmann** (1776–1822) was primarily a jurist by profession, a Romantic novelist, poet, and critic by principal reputation, and a composer by preference.[354] Berlin was his chief among several centers, although he was active in the now Polish centers of Plock and Warsaw during the two or three years

352. Egert/FRÜHROMANTIKER 105–6; Siebenkäs/BERGER 182–83.

353. As quoted in Egert/FRÜHROMANTIKER 106 from *Ludwig Berger* (Berlin, 1846) by Ludwig Rellstab, pp. 20–21. Almost as much praise, of a similar nature, is given to Op. 15 in the only review of a son. by Berger found here, AMZ XXVIII (1826) 510–11. Many of the other references indexed in the first AMZ "Register" confuse this and another Ludwig Berger, in south Germany, as MGG I 1691–93 (W. Kahl) still does (cf. Siebenkäs/BERGER 246).

354. Ehinger/HOFFMANN is the main recent study of his life and works (summarized and revised in MGG VI 528–38 [H. Ehinger]).

Ex. 37. From the finale of Ludwig Berger's *Grande Sonate pathétique* in c, Op. 7 (after the Hofmeister ed. at the Library of Congress).

(1803–5) when he is thought to have written most if not all of about eight piano sonatas.[355] None of these sonatas was published in Hoffmann's lifetime, leaving little chance that they could have been known, heard, or discussed much in their day if at all. Only five have survived—in A, f, F, f, and c♯—all but the first being published in 1922 as the first volume in an abortive "complete works" (Hoffmann/WERKE-m I).[356] These sonatas interest us today primarily as coming from the 356a early-Romantic creator of the eccentric, fantastic, and fascinating tales

355. The sons. are discussed at some length in G. Becking's "Vorwort" and "Revisionsbericht" in Hoffmann/WERKE-m I, and more briefly in Kroll/HOFFMANN 536–38, in E. Kroll's review of Hoffmann/WERKE-m I (zfMW V [1922–23] 347–48), and in Ehinger/HOFFMANN 207–9 and 220 (but not in Egert/FRÜHROMANTIKER).

356. Unclear, perhaps overlapping references to other sons., some of which must pertain to one or more of the surviving sons., include a set of 3 sons. in d, f, and C, another set of 3 in similar style (according to Hoffmann's own comment in 1807, but perhaps referring only to a projected set), a Son. in b♭ mentioned in correspondence of 1809 with Nägeli, and another son. sent to Nägeli in 1809. Cf. Becking's preface to Hoffmann/WERKE-m I, Ehinger/HOFFMANN 208, zfMW V (1922–23) 348. Further mod. eds.: Son. in c♯ and Son. in F/ii, pub. by Drei Masken Verlag of Munich in 1921 (G. v. Westerman); Son. (1) in f, Newman/THIRTEEN-m 114, with preface pp. 18–20; Son. in A, Bärenreiter (BA 3420; cf. the Bärenreiter announcements for Mar., 1967, p. 10). Bücken/19. 35–36 includes exx. from Sons. 2 and 3.

that musicians first hear about by way of Schumann's *Kreisleriana*[357] or Offenbach's *Les Contes d'Hoffmann*. But if Hoffmann's opera *Undine*, representing his main forte in music, proves to be disappointingly pale and conservative beside the tales, his sonatas, without benefit of text or programme, prove to be that much more pale and conservative beside *Undine*.[358] Moreover, they have to be characterized as somewhat naive, affected, and gauche.

Probably Hoffmann wrote most or all of his sonatas in response to a general solicitation in 1803 from the Swiss publisher Nägeli. As we have noted on several earlier occasions (e.g., SCE 26; SSB IV, VIII [Liste, *supra*]), Nägeli mainly sought grand, unusual sonatas, strong especially in both counterpoint and virtuosity. However, Nägeli, who had already convinced Hoffmann in 1803 of the "Miserabilität" of a *Grosse Fantasie* he had written, never did accept for publication any of the several sonatas Hoffmann submitted up to 1809.[359] Yet Hoffmann was disposed by background and taste, if not by skill, to comply with Nägeli's requirements. Although in 1814 he criticized one of the strongest sonatas of his former teacher Reichardt as being still in Emanuel Bach's rather than Mozart's or Beethoven's style (SCE 601), his review applies even more to his own sonatas. For Hoffmann seems to have found special fascinations not simply in counterpoint but in a kind of archaic counterpoint that he must have derived in his own amateurish manner from both J. S. and Emanuel Bach by way of another former teacher, C. W. Podbielski (SCE 779). There is much else in his style that is derivative and outmoded, too. The lyrical slow introductions in all but the second of the extant sonatas show the influence of the *Fantaisie* in c, K. 475, by Mozart (after whom Hoffmann changed his third name to Amadeus). The "Scherzo" of the Sonata in c♯ may actually be modelled after Beethoven's Op. 2/1/iii or 10/2/ii. On the other hand, Hoffmann was probably furthering his own concept of the sonata when he virtually repeated the initial, fugal allegros of the first two sonatas as the finales.

In an outline of 1808 for an article "On Sonatas" that never materialized, Hoffmann gives somewhat obscure clues as to what the sonata meant to him:[360]

357. The live model for "Capellmeister Kreisler" was the gifted but eccentric Johann Ludwig Böhner (1787–1860), who himself left 2 P sons. pub. by 1815 and 1849 (cf. GROVE I 788 [G. Grove]; HOFMEISTER 1815 [Whistling] 342; NZM XXX [1849] 14; PAZDÍREK II 836–37).

358. Cf. Georgii/KLAVIERMUSIK 280–81, fn.

359. Cf. Becking's preface in Hoffmann/WERKE-m I. A premature announcement in June, 1808, that Nägeli would "soon" publish 3 of these sons. appeared in AMZ X (1807–8) 590.

360. Trans. in full from Hoffmann/SCHRIFTEN 16.

Perfection of the pianoforte.—Only beauty
of harmony, not of tone.—
Caprice must appear to prevail, and the
more the highest artistry is thus concealed, the
more perfect [the sonata will be].
Greatness of the theorist Haydn.—
Joy of the cultured man in the
artistic, etc.

Elsewhere Hoffmann is said to have acknowledged that his sonatas were composed in an old manner and made up largely of a slow introduction and a contrapuntally realized allegro.[361] Musicians today are likely to recognize the flair for the dramatic and lyrical in these sonatas but turn away from the mild, unpianistic virtuosity and from their collapse in clumsy, thick textures, with awkward, purposeless voice-leading.

Franz Lauska (1764–1825), a Czech who had studied in Vienna with Albrechtsberger, settled in Berlin in 1798 to become a successful pianist and teacher (of Meyerbeer among others). In the twenty-five years from around 1796 to 1821 about as many piano sonatas by him were published, including one each with violin and with cello "accompagnement," and one for P-duet.[362] These sonatas immediately reveal the professional, as against the neophyte in Hoffmann's sonatas. They are on a par in competence with Berger's, but lack an equivalent creative spark, or, for that matter, any such dramatic flair as Hoffmann displayed. The very number of Lauska's sonatas rightly implies facility, fluency, popularity, conservatism, and pedagogic values. And such were the traits variously emphasized, deplored, or commended in at least nine contemporary reviews of the sonatas, which do confirm that attention was once paid to them.[363] In addition, one cannot help noting a certain marchlike squareness even after Op. 21 (about 1807) and the introduction of certain Romanticisms in the rhythms, harmony, and accompaniment. Suggestions of Mozart and Clementi were remarked especially in the early reviews. But there are clear hints, too,

---

361. Cf. Becking's preface in Hoffmann/WERKE-m I and Kroll/HOFFMANN 538.

362. Cf. MGG VIII 343–44 (J. Bužga). The 25 years of pub. are suggested by the announcements of his 5th and last son. pubs. (Opp. 9 and 46, respectively) in the "Intelligenz-Blatt" for Sept., 1799, and for Jan., 1822, in AMZ II and XXIV. The sons. are discussed briefly in Egert/FRÜHROMANTIKER 43–47, with exx.

363. AMZ III (1800–1801) 120 (Op. 9; empty), V (1802–3) 562 (P + Vn), VII (1804–5) 642–45 (Op. 19; more favorable), VIII (1805–6) 799–800 (Op. 20; craft improving), XIV (1812) 517–18 (Op. 28, P + Vc; favorable) and 392–93 (Op. 30; skill but not imagination), XVII (1815) 510–11 (Op. 34; exceptional for Lauska in being of more artistic than pedagogic interest) and 631 (Op. 35; of training value), XXV (1823) 850–52 (Op. 45; pedagogically useful and pleasingly conservative, but sterile). In MW XXV (1894) 444, pedagogic values could still be found in a reprint of Op. 20 in B♭, "perhaps 100 years old by now."

of Beethoven (for whom Lauska did some proofreading of scores in 1821 [364]), as in Lauska's own *Sonate pathétique* in c, Op. 43 (about 1820). There are also eerie hints, but hardly the creative strength, of Weber in Lauska's Sonata in B♭, Op. 41 (1819), dedicated to Weber.[365] It will be recalled that in 1816 Weber had dedicated his Sonata in A♭, Op. 39, to Lauska, apparently deriving bits of themes and styles from Lauska's Sonata in the same key, Op. 24, published in 1809. And still earlier, in 1812, Weber had reviewed Lauska's *Grande Sonate* in f, Op. 30, saying little more than that it showed how Lauska worked midway between the most banal and the most lofty composers.[366]

Berlin was only one of several centers in which the concert pianist and teacher **Aloys Schmitt** (1788–1866) was active.[367] His many modish works include a substantial number of sonatas for piano alone and with violin or cello, first published over about a half century from 1813.[368] A reading of one of the most widely circulated of these, the four-movement *Sonata di bravura per il pianoforte* in C, Op. 26 (1819?), reveals a nonexploratory idiom and only moderate technical demands in spite of the title and the rapid figuration in the concluding variations on a theme of Mehul, with their coda in tarantella style.[369] After a fantasy introduction, the first movement pursues a five-note motive with considerable melodic and rhythmic variety and ingenuity. The slow second movement indulges in enharmony and ornamental passages that point toward Beethoven. Interesting is the title of the third movement, "Menuetto scherzo," during this period of transition from the minuet to the scherzo. Actually, the scherzo style prevails. A reading of a later, much simpler, more routine work by Schmitt, his *Sonata cantante* in B♭, Op. 123, for P & Vn (*ca.* 1853), suggests that he was but another composer who gradually gave in to the deadening requirements of public taste.[370]

Several other composers active for short or long periods in Berlin deserve at least a mention for forgotten sonatas that once aroused the reviewer's ire or enthusiasm, including a couple that Schumann greeted

---

364. Cf. Anderson/BEETHOVEN II 918–20.
365. Cf. Egert/FRÜHROMANTIKER 45–46.
366. Reprinted from *Zeitung für die elegante Welt* in Weber/WEBER III 71.
367. Cf. MGG XI 1868–69 (R. Sietz).
368. Cf. HOFMEISTER 1815 (Whistling)-1859, *passim*.
369. A review in AMZ XXIII (1821) 283–84 put this son. on a par with Weber's "three great bravura sonatas" (to date), finding its difficulties chiefly those of stretches and full texture and giving Schmitt the palm for systematic structure, but Weber for originality. A short duplicate review in AMZ XXXI (1829) added nothing. G. W. Fink praised Op. 26 warmly, too, in CAECILIA XV (1833) 272–73.
370. The reviewer of Schmitt's Son. in G, Op. 118, for P & Vn, in NZM XXXVII (1852) 25–26, tries to rationalize a similar conclusion.

with praise now hard to understand. One of these composers was a pupil of Berger and Zelter and a teacher of Schumann, the successful opera composer and conductor **Heinrich Dorn** (1804–92).[371] Dorn left an early three-movement Sonata in E, Op. 5, for P & Vc-or-Vn (1828?) that Gottfried Weber found genial, melodious, and skillful, though almost too effervescent,[372] and that G. W. Fink (?), citing these same qualities, found "outstanding," with that word not used loosely, he insisted.[373] In an extended review of Dorn's *Grand Sonate* in D, Op. 29, for P-duet (1838 at latest), Schumann wrote guardedly, subjectively, and discursively, mentioning mainly that its size and variety suggested a symphony and that its scherzo had special appeal.[374] Schumann found the *Grande Sonate* in A, Op. 10 (1836?) by the virtuoso pianist **Constantine Decker** (1810–78)[375] to be the typically contrived, unfeeling music of the *Kleinmeister*,[376] but Fink again—no doubt, partly because of the more conservative outlook of AMZ—saw more substance in it.[377] Schumann also found little more than lightness and charm in *Deux Duos en forme de sonates* in A and C, Op. 13, for P+Vn-or-Vc-or-Fl (1837?) by a long favorite song and opera composer, **Friedrich Wilhelm Kücken** (1810–82).[378] But he found much more interesting and original a three-movement piano Sonata in A, Op. 32 (1833 at latest), by an organist and pupil of A. Schmitt, **Heinrich Friedrich Enckhausen** (1799–1885).[379] And, cautioning only about oversimplification, he saw promise of true greatness in *Trois grandes Sonates* in f, A, and E♭, Op. 1 (1838?), by the organist **Daniel Friedrich Eduard Wilsing** (1809–93).[380] Unfortunately, no copy of Wilsing's Op. 1, dedicated to his presumed teacher, L. Berger, has turned up in the present survey, without which no up-to-date view can be added.

371. Cf. MGG III 690–93 (W. Kahl).
372. CAECILIA VIII (1828) 124.
373. AMZ XXX (1828) 598–99.
374. Schumann/SCHRIFTEN I 397–98.
375. Mendel/LEXIKON III 93.
376. Schumann/SCHRIFTEN II 321 (1837); cf., also, I 306 (1837; with similar disdain for Decker's P sonatinas Op. 11). For a later, neutral review, of Decker's Son. for P & Vn, Op. 33, cf. NZM XL (1854) 208.
377. AMZ XL (1838) 160.
378. Schumann/SCHRIFTEN I 275–76 (1837). Cf. HOFMEISTER 1834–38, 89; MGG VII 1850–51 (O. H. Mies); PAZDÍREK VIII 452–59. Four such sons. by Kücken were pub. between 1845 and 1875 (Altmann/KAMMERMUSIK 212).
379. Schumann/SCHRIFTEN II 321 (1837); cf. Plantinga/SCHUMANN 335–38, with exx. An earlier 3-mvt. son. by Enckhausen, Op. 13, was reviewed in AMA for July, 1826, No. 1, p. 4. Cf. Mendel/LEXIKON III 360; BAKER 438.
380. Schumann/SCHRIFTEN I 395–96, including Schumann's fn. added in 1853, indicating this promise had now been achieved (in a choral work). Cf. Riemann/LEXIKON II 2032; HOFMEISTER 1834–38, 131. Strong praise for this set can also be found in about a fifth of a long review by Fink (AMZ XLI [1839] 181–85), the remainder of which inquires into the low state of the son. (cf. SSB II).

Toward the middle of the century in Berlin the renowned pedagogue and pianist **Theodor Kullak** (1818–82), who studied with Czerny and taught H. Bischoff, Moszkowski, and X. Scharwenka, among others, produced two weak piano sonatas along with his large quantity of more successful salon and teaching pieces. His *Grande Sonate* in f♯, Op. 7 (1842?), was reviewed as "a veritable witch piece" with occasional depth but generally more fantasy and display than content.[381] His *Symphonie de Piano, Grande Sonate en quatres parties,* in E♭, Op. 27 (1846?), was reviewed as an unoriginal, largely tedious work with recollections of its dedicatee, Spohr, and the feel more of a symphony reduction than a symphonic creation.[382] The one sonata, Op. 27 in d for piano (1842?), by another of Kullak's teachers, the celebrated opera composer **Carl Otto Nicolai** (1810–49), had fared similarly with the reviewers.[383] So, also, fared the one sonata, Op. 40 in d, for P & Vn (1845?), by the brilliant but short-lived pianist **Alexander Ernst Fesca** (1820–49).[384] And so it was with the only sonata, Op. 16 in e/E (not A; 1846?), by the eminent theorist and writer **Adolf Bernhard Marx** (1795–1866), although the chief reviewer[385] had to ask the reader to decide between his view and a diametrically opposite one in a short (personally biased?) review that praised the work as being strong, varied, heartfelt, and rare for a theorist.[386] On the other hand, a set of *Trois Sonates pour le pianoforte* in E♭, F, and G, Op. 20 (1850 [387]) by one **Karl Lührss** (1824–82) seems to have attracted no reviewer's attention, yet will surprise the researcher looking further into this period. A Mendelssohn pupil and chamber music composer[388] (until a wealthy marriage in 1851 apparently ended the motivation[389]), Lührss struck a style midway between Schubert's and Bruckner's, with straightforward, often dancelike melodies, persistent rhythms, figuration that is essential rather than extrinsic or purely virtuosic, telling modulations, and a sure, deliberate, broad sense of form. Schubert in particular comes to mind in the piano writing (although Lührss' is more pianistic), in the use of the higher registers, in the hints of *Ländler* tunes, and in the major-minor contrasts (Ex. 38).

381. NZM XVIII (1843) 40. Another reviewer objected only to too much Beethoven influence (AMZ XLV [1843] 596–97, with ex.).

382. NZM XXIV (1846) 149–50.

383. NZM XVII (1842) 176. Cf. MGG IX 1446–50 (T.-M. Langner).

384. NZM XXII (1845) 185–86 (with exx.); AMZ XLVII (1845) 740–41. Cf. Riemann/LEXIKON I 500.

385. NZM XXV (184) 37–39, with exx.

386. AMZ XLVIII (1846) 365–66. Regarding Marx's writings on the son. cf. SSB II.

387. Announced in NZM XXXII (1850) 270.

388. A set of 3 sons. for P & Vn, Op. 21, was also announced in 1850, in NZM XXXIII (1850) 225.

389. Riemann/LEXIKON I 1072.

Our last Berliner in this chapter overlaps the Berlin group in the next chapter. The once well-known pianist **(Carl Gottfried) Wilhelm Taubert** (1811–91), a pupil of L. Berger among others, left 8 sonatas that reached publication between about 1832 and 1866—6 for P solo, and one each for P & Vn and P & Vc—along with still more that did not.[390] Florestan, Eusebius, and Raro all have a go at three of the solo sonata publications in three extended, capricious, largely neutral reviews by Schumann, including personified descriptions.[391] The first review begins with Florestan talking: "The first movement of this sonata I regard as the first, the second as the second, and the third as the last—in descending order of beauty." The third review says that

Ex. 38. From the first movement of Sonata in E♭, Op. 20/1, by Karl Lührss (after the Kistner ed. at the Library of Congress).

Taubert's Op. 35 in e resembles Weber's Op. 70 in e only in that the melancholy of the latter "seems to freeze into hypochondria" in the former. Two other reviews found two other sonatas by Taubert to be mediocre and mechanical.[392] Evidently the folklike quality that made Taubert's lieder so successful, as well as his conservative, Mendelssohnian style, did not serve his sonatas especially well.[393]

390. A detailed list of works, partly dated, follows the long article on his life (up to 1861) in Ledebur/BERLIN 583–92. Taubert also pub. 2 P sonatinas, Op. 44. Cf. PAZDÍREK XIV 41–49; also, Altmann/KAMMERMUSIK 229 and 265.

391. Schumann/SCHRIFTEN I 60–62 (1835, on Op. 20 in c), II 320–21 (1837, on Op. 21/1 & 2 in f & c♯), II 12 (1841, on Op. 35 in e).

392. NZM XLIV (1856) 268 (on Op. 104 in A for P & Vn) and XLVI (1857) 252–53 (on Op. 114 in d for P solo).

393. Cf. MGG XIII 147–49 (R. Sietz).

Other North German Centers

Born in the same year, the cousins **Andreas Jacob Romberg** (1767–1821) and **Bernhard Heinrich Romberg** (1767–1841)—violinist and cellist, respectively—were active in Paris and elsewhere, toured together (including a performance with Beethoven), and settled, on and off, in Hamburg before their sonatas were published.[394] Among his chamber works Andreas left a set of three sonatas for P & Vn in G, Bb, and c, Op. 9 (published in late 1805 or early 1806 [395]), in which the violin is more than the "accompagnement" specified in the title; and a set of three unaccompanied violin "Etudes ou Sonates" in Eb, Bb, and g, Op. 32 (published *ca.* 1813).[396] The sonatas of Op. 9, dedicated to his sister Therese, disclose professional craftsmanship, euphonious scoring, and a disposition for the tuneful that goes well with his use of "Down the burn, and thro' the mead" in the finale of Sonata II. The idiom, including neat scale passages, precise rhythms, thin texture, and Alberti bass, seldom reaches beyond the high- or late-Classic. Living longer, Bernhard got further into the Romantic idiom, but only with a strict sense of stylistic and structural propriety that now seems almost prim. He left about two dozen duos or sonatas, nearly all with or for his instrument, although their considerable popularity resulted in their publication in a variety of arrangements. Thus, the two sets of three "sonatas" each for Vc & P that International Music Company of New York City publishes today—in e, G, and Bb, Op. 38, and Bb, C, and G, Op. 43—were originally published, in 1825 and 1826, respectively,[397] as trios for 2 Vcs & Va and "sonates faciles" for Vc & bass.[398] All cast in the same three-movement plan that Andreas had used, too (F-S-F), these faultless, melodious, friendly, circumscribed "sonatas" remind us how quickly the fresh Romantic idioms could turn into stereotypes. They survive hardily today but—in a class with the "student concertos" of H. Goltermann or the "student trios" of H. Berens—only as "student sonatas."

The versatile musician **Gottlob Schuberth** (1778–1846), father of the publisher Julius, had not yet moved from Magdeburg to Hamburg

---

394. Cf. MGG XI 855–60 (K. Stephenson), with further bibliography.

395. AMZ VIII (1805–6) Intelligenz-Blatt 8 (Jan., 1806).

396. Reviewed with enthusiasm, but only as advanced "Studien," in AMZ XV (1813) 839–40. Op. 32/2 is reproduced in Gates/SOLO 315; cf., also, pp. 152–55.

397. AMZ XXVII and XXVIII (1825 and 1826) Intelligenz-Blatt 5 and 9, respectively.

398. The arrangements for Vc & P appear to go back no further than the 1870's (cf. SMZ XVII [1877] 23).

when three piano sonatas by him were published—two *Sonates faciles,* in C, Op. 1, and F, Op. 2 (both 1825?), and *Grande Sonate agréable,* Op. 3 (1826?). The first was reviewed as appealing and fluent for those not ready for anything more advanced or harmonically daring and dissonant, and the third as not worth the "grande" in its title, either in scope or content.[399] Among several piano sonatas or sonatinas left by the Hamburg cellist **Friedrich Wilhelm Grund** (1791–1874) was a *Grande Sonate* in g, Op. 27, for piano solo (1839?) that had been arranged from a *Trio de salon* for P-duet & Va-or-Vc-or-Hn.[400] A three-movement work of only fourteen pages, the piano version of Op. 27 was dedicated to Marschner. Its first, but only its first, movement won from Schumann in 1839 a "Hats off!" greeting starting like that for Chopin's Op. 2 and Brahms's Op. 1.[401] Today one can only suppose that the Romantic inscriptions and fantasy effect of changing rhythms diverted Schumann from the empty right-hand tremolo, the Alberti and murky bass, and the tawdry ideas, all conveying an emotional drive not unlike that in Suppé's "Overture" to *Poet and Peasant.* A few of the many sonatas and sonatinas for piano solo and duet by the Hamburg piano teacher **Jakob** (or **Jacques**) **Schmitt** (1803–53; brother of A. Schmitt, *supra*),[402] still hold a rightful place as skillful, graceful teaching pieces. Six of his solo sonatas, Opp. 51–56, "à l'usage des elèves avancés," were already reviewed in 1828 as models of the type (SSB III).[403]

In Bremen the talented pianist **Wilhelm Friedrich Riem** (1779–1857) won high praise from friends and reviewers for nearly a dozen sonatas and a half dozen sonatinas for piano.[404] Published between 1804 and 1815,[405] copies of most of these seem to have become very scarce.[406] Especially tantalizing are two long, strongly favorable reviews covering Opp. 1, 4, and 7/1 and 2 and enriched by several Romantically favored examples.[407] In the second review there is only

399. AMZ XXVII (1825) 755–56 and XXIX (1827) 99–101. Cf. MGG XII 186 (K. Stephenson).

400. Cf. MGG V 985–86 and 1403 (both K. Stephenson).

401. Schumann/SCHRIFTEN I 455. Cf. Plantinga/SCHUMANN 338–41, with exx.

402. Cf. MGG XII 1868–69 (D. Härtwig); PAZDÍREK XIII 271–72.

403. CAECILIA IX (1828) 193–96 and "Nachschrift" (Heinroth). Cf., also, the review of Op. 26, "aux jeunes amateurs," in AMZ XXVII (1825) 756. Re-eds. of Schmitt's sonatinas were reviewed from time to time throughout the century, as in MMR XV (1885) 160.

404. Cf. MGG XI 479–80 (F. Göthel), with incomplete list.

405. Cf. the Intelligenz-Blatt listings in AMZ VI (1803–4) for Apr., May, Aug., Nov.; VII (1804–5) for Nov.; VIII (1805–6) for June. Cf., also, HOFMEISTER 1815 (Whistling) 374.

406. Cat. BRUXELLES IV 171 lists Opp. 1, 2/1 and 2, 21, and 25.

407. AMZ VI (1803–4) 637–42; VII (1804–5) 438–41.

the significant caution about writing too much too fast. Examination of Riem's three-movement Sonata in b, Op. 25 (F-S-F; 1810?), does reveal a tendency to fall back on formulas—for example, repeated and tremolo chords in the accompanying hand, which weaken the Mendelssohnian sense of sound, flow, and form that otherwise grace this work.

Chapter IX

Brahms and Others in Austria from About 1850 to 1885

Austro-German Ties and Divergencies

In the second half of the 19th century Austro-German artists had to operate in increasingly complex political environments. Austria continued to dominate Germany until the growing rivalry and military power of Prussia forced Austria to withdraw entirely from German affairs in 1866.[1] Beginning in the following year, further lessening of her European influence saw the Dual Monarchy of Austria-Hungary, under Emperor Francis Joseph I, replace Austria's autocratic control of Hungary. The cumbersome relations that ensued between the two rival capitals, Vienna and Budapest, and the racial frictions that grew between German, Polish, Czech, Magyar, and other national groups resident in those capitals generated some of this monarchy's chief political problems right up to World War II.

Meanwhile in Germany, largely through the engineering of the ruthless, conservative Prussian statesman Count von Bismarck, the long-sought unification moved ahead with new speed and soon became a fact, first with the establishment of the North German Confederation in 1866–67 and then with the constitution of the German Empire under former King William of Prussia in 1871. It was this Empire, immediately following Prussia's victory over France, that saw the joining in of the southern German states. At once and throughout the chancellorship (until 1890) of the all-powerful Bismarck, Germany's chief problems became the control of her large, pro-Austrian Catholic population and the containment of her fast-growing, radically liberal Socialist party.

But the political separation of Austria and Germany must not be overemphasized, least of all in the arts. The two countries continued to

1. As we read in Raff/RAFF 177–78, even the composers were discommoded by the Seven Weeks' War of 1866.

be entwined in many ways. First of all, even politically, the separation was not complete. When it came to a showdown, for example, there was the protective alliance against possible Russian attacks that Bismarck set up in 1879 between Germany and Austria-Hungary, soon to be expanded into the Triple Alliance (1882) when Italy joined after concern over French threats. Second, there was always the common language, and third, there were the constant travel and intercourse between the two countries. Thus, Vienna was still the center for some of the greatest German (and other) musicians to move to rather than to be born in (Schubert excepted). Like Beethoven and Bonn, earlier, Brahms in Vienna retained lifelong ties with his home city of Hamburg in north Germany. Indeed, with regard to musical trends in Austria and Germany the ties outweighed the divergencies or bifurcations—more so, in fact, than can be said with regard to literary trends. Among literary trends, for example, Franz Grillparzer's dramas of renunciation and Adalbert Stifter's Biedermeier novels in the new Austrian literary flowering were something quite different from Friedrich Hebbel's tragic social dramas and Otto Ludwig's realistic dramas and novels in the declining literary intellectualism of post-Goethe Germany.

In this and the next chapter the sonata composers in Austria are separated from those in Germany mainly because there are too many of them to fit into a single chapter. Hence, at least this preview, serving as a preface to both chapters, is needed by way of a collective look at both the ties and the divergencies among the Austrian and German composers. The divergencies are represented above all by the polarity of Brahms, the Classic-minded conservative, and Liszt, the patron saint of the "New German" school (SSB VI and X). The ties are represented above all by each of these men and his most direct followers—by Brahms and, for example, Friedrich Kiel or Karl Grädener; by Liszt and, for example, Felix Draeseke or Julius Reubke. It would even be tempting to suggest that the polarity of Brahms and Liszt became the polarity of Vienna, still a relatively provincial center, and Weimar, Liszt's own headquarters for many years. And this suggestion does have a limited justification. But, of course, that polarity had gotten its start all in Germany, perhaps first with Brahms's somewhat unsatisfactory introduction to Liszt in 1853, then with Schumann's sensational, widely debated panegyric that same year on behalf of Brahms's "Op. 1," and with the celebrated "Manifesto" that Brahms cosigned in 1860 against the "New German" school.

In any case, in a day when virtually every important composer but Peter Cornelius wrote at least one or two sonatas, the ties and divergencies among Austrian and German sonata composers were not often so clearly defined. Naturally, there were other lines of influence, too, as well as many cross influences, especially now that more and easier travel became possible by rail. We still meet an occasional composer who had known Beethoven, Weber, or Schubert, and many more who had come under the indirect influence of any or all of these. Particularly numerous were the direct or indirect disciples of Mendelssohn and Schumann—A. G. Ritter, for example, of Mendelssohn, and Ferdinand Hiller of both. They even suggest a tripolarity of Vienna, Weimar, and Leipzig-Dresden-Berlin. Bülow is an interesting instance, not for any sonatas of his own but for his varied performances and changing allegiances, which cut across the Brahms-Liszt polarity.

Three periodicals dominated German musical journalism during the years covered in these next two chapters, although they did not define a polarity of opinion such as the *Allgemeine musikalische Zeitung* and the *Neue Zeitschrift für Musik* had done in the previous half century. One was still the *Neue Zeitschrift für Musik* (NZM), which continued to flourish under its new editors. The second was the *Signale für die Musikalische Welt* (SMW), started in 1842. And the third was the *Musikalische Wochenblatt* (MW), started in 1870. Among incidental trends to bear in mind during these same years are the continuingly high quantities of sonatas published in an increasing number of centers, even though "Op. 1" is often all we get from a particular composer; the rise in general competence of writing; the reduction in that tightly limited number of real masters, though not in near masters like Rheinberger, Raff, Ritter, and Kiel; the almost incredible output of pedagogic, progressively graded sonatinas; and the first signs of Romantic epigones and eclectics.

Brahms: Output, Resources, and Chronology

In the history of the sonata, as we have seen (SSB I), if any one composer is to be placed first in the century and a half since Beethoven it certainly must be **Johannes Brahms** (1833–97). To place Brahms in that perspective is, of course, one of the broader aims of the entire present volume. However, at least a preliminary defense of his preeminence might be made now simply by asking what other front-rank composer in this century and a half has given so much of his attention to problems bearing on the sonata idea, has found those problems so compatible with his own musical nature and methods, and has met with such universal acceptance and appreciation in his solutions to those problems. More than a third of Brahms's music with opus numbers, or nearly a fourth of the total output that he himself allowed to survive in his uncompromising self-criticism,[2] consists of thirty-eight cyclic instrumental works related to the sonata idea.[3] To be sure, with regard to our more specific area of concentration here, Brahms applied the term "sonata" to only twelve, or less than a third, of those cyclic works (or a little more than 7 per cent of the total output he approved). In other words, like most of his contemporaries, he applied "sonata" only to cyclic works in solo or duo scoring. But these alone—nearly every one an acknowledged, much played masterpiece today—suffice to confirm his pre-eminent devotion, aptitude, and success in the problems of the sonata idea.

The chart that follows tabulates the most essential facts about Brahms's twelve sonatas, including the order and lengths of the separate movements for purposes of comparison within his own works and with the sonatas of our other masters.[4] As discussed shortly, the chronological order of the first two sonatas is uncertain, but the lost sonata is included because at one point Brahms did intend that it be published. Op. 34b is included because he meant it to thrive on its own, independently of the piano Quintet in f. But not included in our tabulation are two other items. One is his fine "Scherzo" third movement in c for the four-movement *F-A-E* Sonata in a (P & Vn) that he, Schumann, and Dietrich joined to write for Joachim in 1853.[5] The other is the MS of three movements of a "Sonata" in d for two pianos. Over a period of four years (1854–57), Brahms reworked this "Sonata" with much effort, first into a symphony and then into the Concerto in d, Op. 15, except that he eventually converted the second movement into the second movement or "Funeral March" of the *German Requiem*.[6] Finally, our tabulation cannot show the several early sonatas

2. Cf. Brahms's own statement on this self-criticism, as quoted in Kalbeck/BRAHMS I/1 132–33.

3. Cf. the list of 40 items in Mitschka/BRAHMS 340–41, which includes 2 single pieces, Opp. 79/2 and 81 (Rhapsody in g and *Tragic Overture*) as well as the Piano Trio in A that E. Bücken and K. Hasse first published in 1938, but omits the lost Son. in a for Vn & P (*infra*). If that Trio in A is actually by Brahms (as argued in Mitschka/BRAHMS 355–56, fn. 11), there is still no evidence that Brahms meant it to survive (and it is not counted in our figure of 38).

4. The timings come from outstanding recordings. Tempos vary considerably, of course, from one recording to the next. But even allowing for the slow tempos Brahms is known to have preferred (e.g., cf. Kalbeck/BRAHMS III/1 66, Schauffler/BRAHMS 180–81), what accounts for the 32 minutes allowed for Op. 120/1 in Müller-Reuter/LEXIKON Suppl. 207?

5. Cf. SSB VIII, final pp. on Schumann; also, Dietrich & Widmann/BRAHMS 5; Kalbeck/BRAHMS III/1 13; Evans/BRAHMS III 336; Geiringer/BRAHMS 224. Mod. ed.: F-A-E SONATE-m 19; Brahms/WERKE-m X 88.

6. Cf. the detailed historical summary, with further references, in Müller-Reuter/LEXIKON Suppl. 168–69.

Brahms wrote and eventually destroyed because what remain are only obscure hints (as noted shortly).

The literature on Brahms is extensive and generally well organized.[7] Except for numerous, mostly minor revisions, additions, and shifts of perspective that later research and the passing years have brought, Max Kalbeck's monumental, sometimes overly thorough biography and the sixteen volumes of correspondence that he and others edited under the sponsorship early in this century of the Deutsche Brahms Gesellschaft still provide the solid foundation for all subsequent research on Brahms.[8] There is no over-all, systematic, style-critical study of Brahms's sonatas.[9] But there are numerous analytical surveys that include the sonatas, starting with Edwin Evans' academic compilation, *Historical, Descriptive and Analytical Account of the Entire Works . . . ,* in four volumes.[10] There are a few studies of individual sonatas, such as that by R. S. Fischer on "motive development" in Op. 108.[11] And there are studies of Brahms's treatment of "sonata form" in his sonatas and related form types, notably the recently completed dissertation, still oriented toward Hugo Riemann, by Arno Mitschka.[12] Brahms oversaw the editing of nearly all the works he approved for publication, including all of the sonatas but the early lost one, and an unusually high proportion of his autographs has survived, leaving comparatively few

7. For an excellent, recent, critical summary of Brahms research and bibliography cf. Grasberger/BRAHMS 445–51. Keller/BRAHMS is a bibliography up to 1912.

8. Kalbeck/BRAHMS and BRAHMS BRIEFWECHSEL. (Schauffler/BRAHMS 27 gives a little evidence that Kalbeck tampered with some of the letters.) Dietrich & Widmann/BRAHMS and May/BRAHMS continue to serve as important, nearly contemporary sources on Brahms's life. Joachim/LETTERS and SCHUMANN-BRAHMS are among significant supplements to the correspondence. Of several later studies of the man and his music that are cited here, Grasberger/BRAHMS and Gál/BRAHMS should be singled out for new information and viewpoints, and Geiringer/BRAHMS as another source of new information and as being still the most rounded, satisfactory text in English. Ehrmann/WEG, another valued source, traces the cultivation of Brahms in other countries (pp. 473–95). Warm thanks are owing to Dr. Karl Geiringer at the University of California in Santa Barbara and Mrs. Geiringer for valued correspondence bearing on the present discussion.

9. Nagel/BRAHMS, first pub. in 1913–14, is essentially a detailed, ms.-by-ms. description of the 3 P sons.

10. Evans/BRAHMS. Among representative surveys of the chamber music, including the duo sons., are Drinker/BRAHMS (chiefly historical), Mason/CHAMBER, Cobbett/CHAMBER I 158–85 (mostly by D. Tovey), and Müller-Reuter/LEXIKON Suppl. 188–208 (mainly factual and bibliographic). Kirby/BRAHMS surveys traits in the 3 solo P sons.

11. Fischer/BRAHMS.

12. Mitschka/BRAHMS comprehends and supersedes the chief previous study of this problem, Urbantschitsch/BRAHMS. A recent, similar, briefer study is Truscott/BRAHMS. Cf., also, Fellinger/DYNAMIK 71–77 and 91–92; Wetschky/KANONTECHNIK (cf. pp. 215–35).

Brahms's Sonatas

Opus	Scoring	Key	Chron. order	Brahms/ WERKE-m	Composed	First edition	Dedicatee	Mvts.: tempos or types Keys: mvt.-by-mvt. mss.: mvt.-by-mvt.	Perform- ance time in minutes	Remarks
1	P	C	3	XIII 1	1852 (ii), 1853	Breitkopf, 1853	Joachim	4: F -M-Sc -VF C: C -c -e -C 957: 270-85-310-292	23	"Andante" composed in 1852; Op. 1 originally listed by Brahms as "Op. 4" (BRAHMS BRIEFWECHSEL V 14)
2	P	f♯	2?	XIII 29	1852	Breitkopf, 1853	Clara Schumann	4: F -M -Sc -S/F f♯: f♯ -b/B-b -f♯/F♯ 674: 198-87 -109-280	23	"Nr. 2"
(5)	P & Vn	a	1?		1852?			a		lost (by Liszt?) or destroyed (by Brahms?); rejected for pub. by B. Senff of Leipzig (no Vn sons. wanted)
5	P	f	4	XIII 55	1853	B. Senff, 1854	Ida von Hohenthal	5: F -M -Sc -M-F f: f -A♭/D♭-f -b♭-f/F 1,141: 222-190 -311-53-365	33	"Nr. 3"; ii and iv composed before i, ii, and v
34b	2 Ps	f	5	XI 1	winter, 1863-64	Rieter-Biedermann, 1872	Anna von Hessen	4: F -S -Sc -S/F f: F -A♭ -c -f 1,371: 301-126-453-491	40	"Sonate für zwei Pianoforte nach dem Quintet"; the dedicatee was the same for both versions
38	P & Vc	e	6	X 96	1862, 1865 (iv)	Simrock, 1866	Josef Gänsbacher	3: F -Mi-F e: e -a -e 771: 282-191-298	23	originally in 4 mvts. (F-S-Mi-F), but Brahms discarded the "Adagio"
78	P & Vn	G	7	X 1	1878-79	Simrock, 1880		3: F -S -F G: G -E♭ -g/G 528: 243-122-163	25	sometimes called the "Regenlied" or "Frühling" son.
99	P & Vc	F	8	X 124	1886	Simrock, 1887		4: VF-S -VF-VF F: F -F♯-f -F 746: 211-71-320-144	25	"Zweite Sonate"

100	P & Vn	A	9	X 31	1886	Simrock, 1887		3: F -M/VF-F A: A -F -A 604: 279-168 -157	19	"Zweite Sonate"
108	P & Vn	d	10	X 57	1886, 1888	Simrock, 1889	Hans von Bülow	4: F -S -F -VF d: d -D-f# -d 757: 264-75-181-337	21	"Dritte Sonate"
120/1	P & Cl-or-Va	f	11	X 153	1894	Simrock, 1895		4: VF-S -M -VF f: f -Ab-Ab -F 663: 236-71-136-220	20	"Nr. 1"; Brahms arranged the alternative Va part but not the Vn part
120/2	"	Eb	12	X 179	"	"		4: F -VF-M -F Eb: Eb -eb -eb/Eb 649: 173-222-170-84	19	"Nr. 2"; as for No. 1

questions in the *Sämtliche Werke* that Breitkopf & Härtel finally published in twenty-six volumes under E. Mandyczewski's and H. Gál's
editorship, between 1926 and 1927.[13] A thematic index by the Brahms
biographer Alfred von Ehrmann followed in 1933.[14]

Brahms spaced his sonatas rather evenly throughout his outwardly
uneventful creative life. His three solo piano sonatas and the lost
sonata for piano and violin came in his "formative" period (up to
1862). They marked the start of his career (1852–53), around the time
of his epochal meetings with Joachim, Liszt, and, above all, the Schumanns, and while he was still centered in Hamburg.[15] The Sonata in
f for two pianos and the first cello sonata came in the early 1860's, at
the start of his "mature" period (1867–75). That is, they came several
years after Schumann's death (1856) and Brahms's emotional crisis with
Clara, only shortly after the ill-considered "Manifesto" (1860) that
Brahms, Joachim, and others signed against the "New German" school
headed by Liszt and Wagner,[16] and while Brahms was establishing
first ties with Vienna. And his other cello sonata, all three mature
violin sonatas, and both clarinet sonatas came during sixteen years
(1878–94) of his period of "consummation" (1876–97), well after his
decision in 1868 to make his permanent residence in Vienna.

Since Brahms was one of the four composers at the focus of our
discussion of Romantic styles and forms in Chapter VI—along with
Schubert, Schumann, and Chopin—we are concerned in the present
chapter only with the facts, circumstances, historical relationships, and
cultivation of his sonatas. Unfortunately, in spite of the extent and
relative orderliness of Brahms research, the actual amount of information available, especially on the circumstances of his compositions, is often disappointing. Not a little of the explanation lies in his
own secretiveness, his reticence whenever he had occasion to write or
speak about his own music, and even a tendency, in his little self-
effacing jokes, deliberately to laugh away the facts.[17] We know too
little, for example, about just when, where, and why Brahms composed his sonatas, or about any sonatas that he wrote in his student
days under the pseudonym "G. W. Marks" and then discarded.[18]

13. Brahms/WERKE-m. The set was reprinted in 1949 (Ann Arbor: J. W. Edwards).
14. Ehrmann/BRAHMS (cf. Ehrmann/WEG). The thematic index by J. Braunstein
(New York: Ars Musica, 1956) contains less information except for a few new
entries (not on the sons.). Cf., also, Hanslick/MUSIKALISCHES 131–41.
15. The ternary division of Brahms's creative life followed here is that advanced
in more detail in Grasberger/BRAHMS 381–83.
16. Cf. Kalbeck/BRAHMS I/2 403–6; Gál/BRAHMS 29–37.
17. Cf. Grasberger/BRAHMS 445–46.
18. Cf. MGG II 208 (R. Gerber). A little light has been thrown on Brahms's own
interpretation, teaching, and fingering of his three early piano sonatas in Kross/
BRAHMSIANA 132–36.

Brahms's Three Piano Sonatas

Like Schumann about fifteen years before him, Brahms wrote his three published piano sonatas early in his career and his three great violin sonatas, not counting the lost one, much later. The lost sonata, in a, was to have been given the opus number 5 that ultimately went to the solo piano Sonata in f.[19] Apparently Brahms wrote it in 1852 for use on his concert tour in 1853 with Reményi.[20] An exchange of several letters followed suggesting that Liszt may have borrowed or received the manuscript and lost it, possibly around the end of the year while he was in Leipzig. But perhaps only the violin part was referred to then (since Brahms could well have had the piano part in his memory for the tour) and again when Liszt wrote Klindworth that he could get no reply from Reményi. It was only the violin part that Dietrich discovered in Wasielewski's possession in 1872 in a "lengthy and beautifully written manuscript." (Where is that part, now?) Meanwhile, at Schumann's suggestion and after some final polishing, Brahms had offered what presumably was a full score of the work to Barthold Senff of Leipzig, in November, 1853, for publication. But soon he learned that "Senff prints no violin things." Did he then decide to destroy it along with at least two other early violin sonatas, and is that actually why it is lost? It would indeed be interesting to be able to hear this companion to the three solo piano sonatas, each of them so fascinating and "great in spite of its immaturity." [21]

After several letters exchanged in 1853 between himself, Schumann, Joachim, and the publisher Breitkopf & Härtel, Brahms decided to introduce himself with his Sonata in C as Op. 1. "When one first shows one's self," he wrote later to his fellow Hamburg pianist Louise Jappa, "it is to the head and not the heels that one wishes to draw attention." [22] Actually, his Sonata in f♯, finally labeled Op. 2, antedated all but the "Andante" of this work, and the Scherzo in e♭ had come even earlier (1851). In fact, on the title page of the autograph of Op. 1 is written "Vierte Sonate," indicating that at least Op. 2 and two discarded (piano) sonatas had preceded the Sonata in C.[23] Brahms dedi-

19. Scattered bits of information on this work may be found in Kalbeck/BRAHMS I/1 73, 130, and 139; Dietrich & Widmann/BRAHMS 9 and 75 (but read 1853, not 1852); BRAHMS BRIEFWECHSEL V 19 and 23, XIII 5–6; May/BRAHMS I 109, 123, 129, 136, 139, 141, and 149; SCHUMANN-BRAHMS I 2–3; Joachim/LETTERS 29 and 31; LISZT LETTERS I 196.

20. For some details of this tour cf. May/BRAHMS I 94–102, 108–14.

21. May/BRAHMS I 120.

22. As trans. in May/BRAHMS I 137, 70.

23. Ehrmann/WEG 116. Louise Jappa reported hearing Brahms at the age of 11 play a sonata he himself had composed (May/BRAHMS I 70).

cated Op. 1 to "my best friend," [24] the great violinist Joachim, who remained more or less close throughout Brahms's life. But Op. 1 identifies particularly with Robert Schumann, for it was mainly this work by which Brahms introduced himself to the Schumanns on October 1, 1853, as he had to several others in the previous four months, including Joachim, Wasielewski, and Liszt (in the embarrassing meeting at which Brahms is supposed to have fallen asleep when Liszt reciprocated with his Sonata in b).[25] And it was mainly this work that inspired Schumann to herald Brahms before the musical world as "a young blood by whose cradle graces and heroes kept watch," and as a "Minerva [springing forth] fully armed from the head of Jove"—all in the celebrated article "New Paths" that marked a last rare return for Schumann to the *Neue Zeitschrift für Musik* (Oct. 28, 1853).[26] How much that sensational "send-off" tended to antagonize musicians in other camps, especially the "Murls" or anti-Philistines in the Liszt camp, and how much it also acted as a deterrent, both psychologic and artistic, to Brahms himself, are well known and well documented.[27]

In most descriptions and discussions of Brahms's Op. 1, one of the first points to be noted is the similarity of the opening idea to that of Beethoven's Op. 106 in B♭, there being an almost exact duplication of the rhythm for five measures, and at least suggestions of the melodic outlines, as well as the phrase extensions. Usually this similarity is treated as casual or coincidental.[28] However, a fact not previously mentioned in this connection, as with the parallel relation of Mendelssohn's Op. 106 in B♭ (ssb VIII), is Brahms's special interest in Beethoven's Op. 106 around the time he wrote Op. 1. In February of 1854 he twice revealed that he had known Franz Wüllner's performance of the Op. 106,[29] and may even have heard this further lifelong friend playing the work several months earlier, before Wüllner first met Brahms officially and heard the latter play his "just

24. BRAHMS BRIEFWECHSEL V 18.

25. Cf. May/BRAHMS I 108–30; MASON MEMORIES 127–31, 141–42 (the most reliable report of the Liszt meeting; too much doubt seems to be cast on this report and the sleep incident in Ehrmann/WEG 31; cf., also, Kalbeck/BRAHMS I/1 85–86 and Gál/BRAHMS 32–33).

26. The original German is in Schumann/SCHRIFTEN II 301–2, and one of many English trans. is in May/BRAHMS I 131–32. Schumann still wrote warmly of Op. 1 in his letters of Nov. 27, 1854, and Jan. 6, 1855 (cf. Kalbeck/BRAHMS I/1 188–89).

27. Cf. BÜLOW BRIEFE II 114–15, 166; May/BRAHMS I 132–37, 142–47; Kalbeck/BRAHMS I/1 123–29, 204–8; Geiringer/BRAHMS 37–38; Gál/BRAHMS 6–8, with a further trans. of the article.

28. E.g., in Murdoch/BRAHMS 209; May/BRAHMS I 137–38. But cf. Geiringer/BRAHMS 207.

29. BRAHMS BRIEFWECHSEL XIV 9, XV 37 (a witty, sparkling document).

completed" Op. 1.[30] In any case, Brahms's clear transformation of the idea in the finale and some probable, subtle but intentional, allusions to it at least in the "Scherzo" suggest that he himself could hardly have been unaware of the similarity to Beethoven's work. Whatever his right to dub Brahms the third "B," Hans von Bülow, who was closest to Brahms in their late years, would have had as much reason to call Brahms's Op. 1 "Beethoven's thirty-third sonata" as he had when he called Brahms's first symphony "Beethoven's tenth."[31] Bülow, as it happened, was the first besides the composer himself to play Brahms's Op. 1—in fact, any Brahms work—in public, when he played the opening movement in Hamburg in 1854, though not the whole work for another thirty years.[32]

Brahms had played music by Beethoven (and Mozart) from at least his tenth year.[33] His playing of Op. 53 in C in public while he was still fifteen was favorably reviewed. And he played Op. 30/2 in c on the tour with Reményi, which included the incident of transposing the piano part up a half-step on the spot because of an out-of-tune instrument (as Beethoven had done for his own horn sonata, Op. 17).[34] Opp. 27/1 in E♭ and 111 in c, as well as the "Eroica" Variations Op. 35, were among the works of Beethoven he most liked to perform in later years.[35] There is a decided kinship with Beethoven in Brahms's use of a pregnant motive rather than a complete theme as the opening idea in Op. 1, and in his development of that motive, both intensive and extensive, which includes fughetta sections and even exceeds what Beethoven did with his motive in Op. 106. Beethovian, too, are Brahms's powerful architectonic sense and his exclusion of anything that is solely virtuosic, ornamental, or extrinsic to the structure in any other way. (Only the absence of virtuosity for its own sake and Brahms's almost phobic aversion to sham, but not any want of inherent grandeur, can explain the omission of "grosse" or "grande" from the titles of all his sonatas.) It is in this architectonic sense more than any other that Minerva sprang "fully armed from the head of Jove." Yet one must qualify the metaphor by recalling that not till later did Brahms find solutions to the problems of the finale that he wrestled with but never quite resolved in all three early

30. Cf. Kalbeck/BRAHMS I/1 104–5; Kämper/WÜLLNER 8, 12, 13. Brahms's teacher Marxsen had taken a special interest in Op. 106 as far back as 1835 (Müller-Reuter/KONZERT LITERATUR Suppl. 138; Kalbeck/BRAHMS I 28).

31. Cf. BÜLOW BRIEFE III 372, 369 (1877); May/BRAHMS II 528–29.

32. Cf. BÜLOW BRIEFE II 183, VII 197; Kalbeck/BRAHMS I/1 156–58; May/BRAHMS I 160; BRAHMS BRIEFWECHSEL IV 151.

33. Cf. May/BRAHMS I 62, 86–87, 98–99.

34. Cf. May/BRAHMS I 99–100; Thayer & Forbes/BEETHOVEN I 526.

35. Cf. Murdoch/BRAHMS 54, 55; Grasberger/BRAHMS 252–54.

sonatas,[36] and that had plagued Beethoven from time to time through-out his cyclic works (SCE 142–43, 164–66).

In most of the foregoing traits—the motivic idea, the exclusion of extrinsic matter, the problem of the finale—Brahms's Op. 1 already shows his decided kinship with Schumann, too, especially the Schumann who had written three early piano sonatas of his own. Further-more, Brahms at once reveals a lyricism, coupled with a new sense of piano sonority (as in Op. 1/i/39–62), that is more Schumannseque than Beethovian. Op. 1 was completed, of course, before Brahms met Schumann but not before he had known and studied Schumann's music. He may not have been introduced to any of this music by the relatively conservative Marxsen,[37] but the same Louise Jappa had sought to interest him in it, especially when the Schumanns appeared in public in Hamburg "several times" in 1850.[38] If Brahms's response was severely dampened after he got back, unopened, the package of compositions he had sent to Robert for comments at that time, it was greatly aroused by Joachim, Wasielewski, and others during the tour of 1853, to the point where he experienced a nearly traumatic awakening to Schumann's poetic genius and could bring himself to pay the memorable visit.[39]

Like Schumann's three piano sonatas, those of Brahms reveal scarcely any tangible programmatic influence. Nearest to such an influence, and taking us perhaps as near as Brahms's sonatas came to the "New German" school with which he was soon at odds,[40] were the three poems differently associated with the "Andante" movement of each sonata (ii in Op. 5). The only other such instances in Brahms's solo piano music are the poems cited at the head of Ballade in d, Op. 10/1, and quoted at the head of Intermezzo in E♭, Op. 117/1.[41] (In his violin sonatas we shall find Brahms making subtler poetic references through melodic quotations from his own songs.) Op. 1/ii actually presents as the theme for three free variations "an old

36. E.g., on the finale of Op. 5, cf. SCHUMANN-BRAHMS I 2 and BRAHMS BRIEF-WECHSEL V 18; cf., also, Schauffler/BRAHMS 357. In DMf XX (1967) 204 a completed diss. is announced on the finale in Brahms's chamber music, by Werner Czesla in Bonn.

37. Cf. Kalbeck/BRAHMS I 28, 30, 36.

38. May/BRAHMS I 91–92; Kalbeck/BRAHMS I/1 54–56.

39. Cf. May/BRAHMS I 116, 118, 119; Kalbeck/BRAHMS I/1 100–103, 125 (but some-thing more than "exaggeration" must have prompted Brahms to say later, "I never learned anything from Schumann but how to play chess"—Brahms, who played Schumann's Opp. 14 and 17 with such "depth" and "feeling" [according to Hanslick/WIEN II 258, in 1862]).

40. Cf. Kalbeck/BRAHMS I/1 89.

41. Cf. Evans/BRAHMS IV 29–30, 75; Ehrmann/WEG 116–17; Kalbeck/BRAHMS I/1 212, IV/1 17.

German love song," "Verstohlen geht der Mond auf," complete with words (Ex. 39).[42] Op. 2/ii neither cites nor quotes any verse, but, according to A. Dietrich, Brahms "built up the theme . . . on the words of an old German song, 'Mir is leide. . . .' " [43] Op. 5/ii quotes a stanza from the poet "Otto Sternau" (A Inkermann) beginning "Der Abend dämmert. . . ." [44]

Op. 2 in f♯ is the earliest (and shortest in number of measures) of Brahms's piano sonatas that survived but not one of the first works he wanted to publish.[45] Its dedication to the "honored Frau Schumann" was preceded by deferential, even timorous inquiries to Joachim, Robert, and Clara herself.[46] As with Opp. 1 and 5, the final page in the autograph of Op. 2 is signed "Kreisler jun." [47] This, or "Johannes Kreisler junior" in full, or even "Jean de Krösel le jeune," was Brahms's early pseudonym among his close friends.[48] Its use in 1852 for Op. 2 recalls that Brahms was already won over to E. T. A. Hoffmann (and Jean Paul) if not yet to Schumann.[49] Schumann wrote enthusiastically to Brahms about Op. 2 on March 20 (?), 1855 (in his last reference found here to any sonatas):

Your second sonata, dear friend, has brought me much closer to you again. You were quite unknown to me; I live in your music, which I can play fairly well at sight, one movement after another. Then do I feel thankful. There never was anything like the opening, the pianissimo, the whole movement. The "Andante" and these variations, and this "Scherzo" that follows, [which is] quite different from the other ["Scherzo" in Op. 1?], and the "Finale" [opened by] the "Sostenuto," the music at the start of the second part, the "Animato," and the ending—in short, [all this is] a new laurel-wreath for that other Johannes.[50]

42. The melody also serves in Brahms's *Deutsche Volkslieder* No. 49 (cf. Ehrmann/ BRAHMS 135; Kalbeck/BRAHMS I/1 52).

43. Dietrich & Widmann/BRAHMS 3–4; cf. Kalbeck/BRAHMS I/1 40, 212–13. Dietrich also said Brahms had in mind "My Heart's in the Highlands" when he wrote the purportedly Scotch-flavored finale of Op. 1.

44. Cf. Kalbeck/BRAHMS I/1 120–22; BRAHMS BRIEFWECHSEL XIV 5, XII 199–200 (on the identity of the obscure poet).

45. Cf. BRAHMS BRIEFWECHSEL V 13–15.

46. Cf. SCHUMANN-BRAHMS I 3, 5; BRAHMS BRIEFWECHSEL V 18.

47. Cf. May/BRAHMS I 95, Brahms/WERKE-m XIII iii and vi. A facs. of the first p. is in DM XII/1 (1912–13) after p. 64.

48. E.g., as in BRAHMS BRIEFWECHSEL IV 1, 2, 4; XIV 8. Cf. Kalbeck/BRAHMS I/1 102–3.

49. Cf. May/BRAHMS I 91. But this early use is not mentioned in Kalbeck/BRAHMS I/1 103, which therefore seems to be mistaken in suggesting that Brahms had Schumann in mind as "Kreisler senior."

50. Trans. from SCHUMANN-BRAHMS I 101–2; Brahms's acknowledgment of these "friendly" remarks a week later (p. 104) and Schumann's specific references leave no doubt that Op. 2 was intended, although some authors have mistaken "second sonata" to mean Op. 1 or the second sonata to be completed.

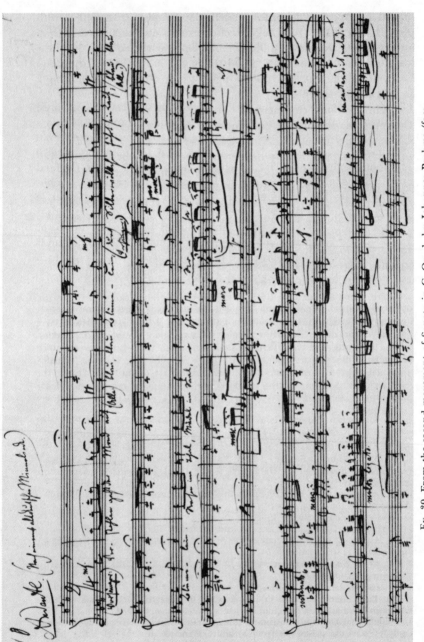

Ex. 39. From the second movement of Sonata in C, Op. 1, by Johannes Brahms (facs.

Schumann had good reason to remark how different Brahms's Op. 2 was from his Op. 1. Even though, or perhaps because, it originated earlier than most of Op. 1 it marks a more frank plunge into Romantic idioms. In fact, although it proves its worth, logic, and practicability with sufficient study, it still must be called the wildest, most bombastic, most declamatory, least playable,[51] and structurally least successful of Brahms's sonatas. Its athletic difficulties and novel harmonies provide the main reasons for believing that not all the hostility vented against Opp. 1, 2, 3, and 4 in the *Süddeutsche Musikzeitung* for 1854 and even in the *Neue Zeitschrift für Musik* for 1855 under Brendel can be charged to the anti-Brahms sentiment that Schumann's "New Paths" aroused.[52] On the other hand, the authors of these diatribes might have recognized a decidedly Lisztian quality in the second theme of Op. 2/i (mss. 10–71) and even a Chopinesque quality in the main theme of the finale.[53] That second theme brings to mind the corresponding theme in Liszt's Sonata in b, in texture, harmony, and import, and even in line. Since both works had been completed recently (except for final polishing?) when the two men first met in June of 1853, there is little likelihood of influences one way or the other, only of a common spirit in the musical air.

However, the theme of the finale, which Kalbeck relates to Liszt and the "New German" school,[54] seems here—with its particular brand of chromaticism, its rhythmic variant, and its Neapolitan approach to an abrupt cadence—to relate more to Chopin's ideas—in fact, to the theme of the finale in Chopin's own Sonata in b. At that initial meeting of Brahms and Liszt, J. J. Raff is supposed to have been the first of many to remark how much Brahms's Scherzo in e♭, Op. 4, suggests Chopin's Scherzo in b♭, Op. 31, only to have Brahms answer that (as yet) "he had never seen or heard any of Chopin's compositions." [55] But Chopin was widely published by then, Brahms was clearly sensitive to motivic relationships from the start (as between the outer movements of all three piano sonatas), he was highly impressionable in his early years—besides the influence of Beethoven's Op. 106 on his Op. 1 (*supra*), it is hard to deny the suggestions of Beethoven's Fifth Symphony in Brahms's Op. 2/iv/110–15—and not only the opening but "Trio II" (mss. 318–30, 354–79) of Op. 4

51. No public performance of Op. 2 was discovered here before Bülow's in 1882 (Ehrmann/BRAHMS 1; BÜLOW BRIEFE VII 112, 141–42).

52. Cf. Kalbeck/BRAHMS I/1 204–8 (but with no other explanation allowed); May/BRAHMS I 147–48.

53. Nagel/BRAHMS 46 finds strong suggestions of Mendelssohn and Schumann, too.

54. Kalbeck/BRAHMS I/1 85–89.

55. MASON MEMORIES 129.

suggest Chopin's Scherzo in b♭ (mss. 1–4 and 65–117, respectively). Both Dietrich and Kalbeck add further evidences that Brahms had not known Chopin's music by 1853.[56] On the other hand, Geiringer has discovered that Marxsen taught Chopin's Polonaise in A♭ to Brahms's brother Fritz in 1853,[57] leaving the question open again. As with Liszt, the thematic relationships may simply have been "in the air." Yet such relationships or derivations seem even closer in Brahms's next sonata, Op. 5 in f, as in the well-known motive of the theme that climaxes so heroically in the first "Andante" (mss. 144–78) and its recollection of the "chorale" theme in the same key of D♭, beginning similarly on a I-6/4 chord, in Chopin's Scherzo in c♯, Op. 39. (Brahms had used a similar motive in the "Trio" of Op. 2/iii.) How greatly Brahms differs from Liszt and Chopin in the disposition and development of his ideas is, of course, quite another matter (SSB VI).

With further regard to Op. 5, this second longest of all Brahms's sonatas, and the only one in five movements, has always been one of his most played sonatas and thrives today, in fact, as one of the favorites in the whole sonata repertoire since Beethoven. It was the only major work written largely during that one month of October, 1853, when Brahms was with the Schumanns (and before Robert's commitment for insanity), although Brahms himself said the two interrelated andante movements originated earlier.[58] But not until Brahms had struggled with the finale another two months did he write B. Senff that Op. 5 was ready for publication.[59] The dedication this time, to a member of the nobility in Leipzig, probably signified nothing more than thanks for hospitality.[60] At first, only the unsurpassed, celestial "Andante espressivo" and the fiery "Scherzo" (ii and iii) were performed in public, as they were initially by Clara in October of 1854 and subsequently by Brahms himself and others, at least as late as 1880.[61] Brahms played the entire sonata in public for the first time, in Vienna in 1863 (not 1862), with Hanslick reacting to the performance as more improvisatory than "clearly and sharply worked out," and to the music as deeply felt and lyrical but "form-

56. Dietrich & Widmann/BRAHMS 6; Kalbeck/BRAHMS I/1 30 and 82–84.

57. Geiringer/BRAHMS 18. Cf. the further discussion of this relationship in the article Siegmund-Schultze/CHOPIN.

58. Kalbeck/BRAHMS I/1 120; May/BRAHMS I 139.

59. Cf. BRAHMS BRIEFWECHSEL V 18 and 28, XIV 5 and 7; SCHUMANN-BRAHMS I 2. Gottschalk/MSS Plate vii is a facs. of the first p. of the autograph.

60. Kalbeck/BRAHMS I/1 139.

61. Cf. SCHUMANN-BRAHMS I 22; BRAHMS BRIEFWECHSEL IV 4; Kalbeck/BRAHMS I/1 120, 196; MT XXI (1880) 462. Brahms had played these 2 mvts. informally during his first month with the Schumanns (cf. Ehrmann/WEG 118).

less in both outer movements." [62] Bülow played the entire Op. 5 on tour in 1884.[63]

As the last of Brahms's solo piano sonatas, Op. 5 does not reveal quite the remarkable advances in craftsmanship and stylistic refinements to be found soon after in Op. 9, *Variations for Pianoforte on a Theme by Robert Schumann*—advances that both Brahms himself and Schumann recognized.[64] But Op. 5 still reveals decided advances over Opp. 1 and 2 in its more reasonable and restrained, yet effective, solutions to the sounds and techniques of the piano, in the greater substance of its ideas and the more logical, satisfying forms into which they are molded (although the finale still presents architectural instabilities to both listener and performer), and, indeed, in a new fusion of Classic ideals and Romantic styles (SSB VI). It is interesting to recall that Wagner was present when Brahms gave that first public performance of all of Op. 5 in Vienna in early 1863, and that Liszt had been among those who heard Brahms play the first "Andante" nine years earlier, at a supper party following the first performance of *Lohengrin* in Leipzig.[65] Regardless of whether either could have influenced the other, Kalbeck is able to quote two passages, one from each of the first two movements (i/39–45 and ii/144–48), that bring Brahms surprisingly close to Wagner's Elsa and Hans Sachs, respectively.[66] These passages, as well as the Chopin resemblance cited above, and some further hints of Schumann (e.g., the left-hand, long-drawn, cello-like line at i/91–117) all rightly suggest that Brahms was fitting more and more comfortably into his 19th-century musical environment. Sternau's verse may be intended to apply to the "Rückblick" as well as the first "Andante," but no over-all programme for the sonata can be guessed safely from this verse, nor any special link with the eventful but somewhat veiled circumstances of Brahms's life in 1853.[67]

Brahms's Ensemble Sonatas

As mentioned earlier, Brahms's Op. 34b, *Sonate* [in f] *für zwei Pianoforte nach dem Quintet, Op. 34*, is included here because the composer

62. Hanslick/WIEN II 258. Clara had evidently played the whole work privately as early as Sept., 1854 (Joachim/LETTERS 77, 105). In Hanslick/CONCERTE 200–201 Anton Door is mistakenly credited with the first public performance, in 1877, of Op. 5 (which is discussed as deriving from Schumann's piano music).

63. BRAHMS BRIEFWECHSEL II 23; MT XXV (1884) 338, 348.

64. SCHUMANN-BRAHMS I 36–37, 53; BRAHMS BRIEFWECHSEL XIV 14.

65. Kalbeck/BRAHMS I/1 117, II/1 34; Mason/MEMORIES 134–35.

66. Kalbeck/BRAHMS I/1 216–17.

67. Cf. Nagel/BRAHMS 76–78.

thought enough of it in its own right to have it published independ-
67a ently of the magnificent Piano Quintet in f. Thus, Brahms wrote
Rieter of Rieter-Biedermann on July 22, 1865:

> We might also keep in mind [the possibility] of publishing the work as a
> "Sonata for Two Pianos." To me and everyone who plays or hears it, it has a
> special appeal in this form and might indeed be welcomed as an interesting
> work for two pianos. In any case, I can give you a 4-hand [one-piano] arrange-
> ment (but for later publication).[68]

Mainly because the dedicatee kept the manuscript so long ("I'll never
lend any manuscript to princesses again!"),[69] publication of the two-
piano version did not occur until 1872, seven years after that of
the Quintet it had preceded. But in spite of Brahms's special interest,
Op. 34b has hardly enjoyed any independent life of its own, partly
because two pianos, even more than one piano and even in such
an outstanding work, are too monochromatic in their sound to sustain
the interest for forty minutes, and because from the start the scoring
of Op. 34b seemed to be inadequate to the task. A clue is provided
in Brahms's decision by 1871 that the (one-piano) four-hand arrangement of this work would be impractical—in fact, hardly possible—for
the work has to be played "with [too] much passion." [70] Henry S.
Drinker was alone in concluding that "there is no more glorious or
satisfactory work for two pianos." [71] Most pianists who play it are
being expedient. They love the Quintet and, having no string quartet
at hand, would rather play it on two pianos than not at all.

The genesis of Brahms's Piano Quintet in f has aroused much
interest and several investigations, a primary source being the rich
correspondence between Brahms, Clara Schumann, Joachim, publishers, and other friends during the decade from 1862.[72] For our

---

68. BRAHMS BRIEFWECHSEL XIV 114.

69. BRAHMS BRIEFWECHSEL XIV 195–6, with references to intervening letters. Princess Anna von Hessen, a good musician and friend of both Clara and Brahms,
gave Brahms the autograph of Mozart's Symphony 40 in g in return for the dedication of both Opp. 34 and 34b (Kalbeck/BRAHMS I 61–62). The autograph of Op.
34b is listed in Albrecht/CENSUS 61.

70. BRAHMS BRIEFWECHSEL XIV 196.

71. Drinker/BRAHMS 104.

72. The most thorough account is presumably that by Wilhelm Altmann in a
special issue of *Die Musikwelt* pub. in Hamburg in 1921; but it is not in any
issue of that periodical from Jan. through Nov. of 1921, and the December issue
could not be located here; a summary of the article, loosely trans., appears in the
preface to Altmann/BRAHMS-m. Cf., also, the partly complementary, partly contradictory accounts in Nagel/BRAHMS II/1 52–54, 59–62; BRAHMS BRIEFWECHSEL XIV
115–16; Müller-Reuter/LEXIKON Suppl. 191–92; Drinker/BRAHMS 100–104. The bare
possibility that Op. 34b could have succeeded rather than preceded Op. 34 (Kalbeck/
BRAHMS II/1 59) is completely ruled out by further evidence cited in these accounts (and *infra*).

purposes, it is worth noting that the three settings in the evolution of this work somewhat parallel those in the evolution of Brahms's Piano Concerto in d, Op. 15. In Op. 15, the initial Sonata in d for two pianos called for orchestral treatment, the Symphony in d that followed lacked the piano's incisiveness, and the Concerto in d provided the happy compromise. In Qp. 34 the piano again proved to be essential but not self-sufficient. Its original setting in 1862 was a string quintet, about which Clara wrote enthusiastically but Joachim much less so, objecting to a lack of sonority appropriate to the strong ideas.[73] Brahms then heard this and other lacks for himself and decided the work would sound better for two pianos.[74] In fact, he ultimately destroyed the first version,[75] which would have been interesting to see for purposes of comparison. But after completing the new version in the winter of 1863–64 and giving it its first public hearing with Carl Tausig in April, which stirred no interest,[76] Brahms had to conclude that two pianos did not provide the appropriate sonority, either. This time Clara's influence seems to have been paramount, especially when she wrote in July of 1864,

The work is so wonderfully grandiose, interesting throughout in its most ingenious combinations, masterful in every respect, but—it is not a sonata, but [rather] a work whose ideas you might—[in fact, you] must!—strew, as if from a horn of plenty, over the whole orchestra. A multitude of the most beautiful ideas get lost on the piano, [being] recognizable only to the musician [and] not enjoyable to the public. At the first playing I got the feeling of an arranged work . . . please, dear Johannes, follow [my advice] just this one time [and] rearrange the work once more.[77]

The final version that soon followed, to the all but total satisfaction and delight of everyone concerned,[78] completes an object lesson for us in the influence of content and scope on medium, and in the difference between sonata and quintet (or any other designation for a larger chamber ensemble) that was implicit by now in the word "sonata." The actual transfer of responsibilities from two pianos to piano quintet is instructive, too, to any student of scoring. Although only minute changes are made in the content,[79] the scoring changes are considerable (Ex. 40). For instance, the piano part in the Quintet

73. SCHUMANN-BRAHMS I 407–8, 418–19; BRAHMS BRIEFWECHSEL V 324–25, VI 9.

74. Joachim/LETTERS 307; SCHUMANN-BRAHMS I 442.

75. Kalbeck/BRAHMS II/1 53.

76. Cf. Kalbeck/BRAHMS II/1 59–61.

77. SCHUMANN-BRAHMS I 461 (cf. pp. 459, 460). Cf., also, Kalbeck/BRAHMS II/1 59–60 fn. and 62 fn. (indicating H. Levi's influence was strong, too).

78. E.g., cf. BRAHMS BRIEFWECHSEL VII 11–14 (H. Levi); SCHUMANN-BRAHMS I 472–73 and 475–76 (Clara).

79. E.g., Op. 34b/i/83 and 245 are deleted in Op. 34.

Ex. 40. From the first movements of Brahms's Sonata for Two Pianos in f, Op. 34b, and Piano Quintet in f, showing scoring changes and a deleted measure in Op. 34 (after Edition Peters 3662 and 3660).

comes now from "Klavier I" in the Sonata (e.g., i/1–17), now from "Klavier II" (e.g., i/17–22), with the string quartet taking what the other piano part had. At other times, the material is redistributed so that the quartet and piano in the Quintet each get something of both parts in the Sonata (e.g., i/23–32 and 35–38). There are instances where the strings are obviously more expressive (as in the 8ve and 9th leaps of ii/56–65), others where the piano's crisp articulation is more telling (e.g., i/5–11), and still others where only a complete fusion produces the needed orchestral effect (e.g., iii/23–29).

In the same year as he composed the first version of Op. 34, 1862, Brahms wrote the first three movements of what was to be a four-movement sonata for piano and cello. The finale followed in 1865. However, when Sonata in e, Op. 38, appeared in 1866 the "Adagio" that was to be the second movement had been discarded. Brahms seemed to take a whimsical delight in not letting the "Adagio" be seen by Clara or even the dedicatee, Gänsbacher, a conductor, singing teacher, and cellist who had given Brahms valuable Schubert MSS.[80] Schauffler advances tenuous arguments for a theory that this same "Adagio" reappeared as the superb second movement of Brahms's other cello sonata, Op. 99 in F.[81] One of the most solid and eloquent of Romantic cello sonatas, "which throughout is undifficult to play for both instruments," [82] Op. 38 is remarkable, among other virtues, for its powerful fugal finale. Brahms may or may not have been paying homage to J. S. Bach by recalling the subject of "Contrapunctus 13/2 (inversus)" from Die Kunst der Fuge, as Wilhelm Altmann has maintained.[83] The two subjects have in common an energetic, initial octave leap downward, with the lower note tied to the first triplet in a sequence of ascending triplets. On possible but less safe grounds, Altmann also suggests that the songful main theme of Brahms's first movement relates to the subject of Bach's "Contrapunctus 3," and that the main idea in Brahms's nostalgic middle movement derives from that main theme in the first movement. Clara was still writing to Brahms in 1890 about the pleasure it gave her to play this sonata (with the cellist Hausmann).[84] It had not been performed publicly until 1874,[85] but numerous performances as far off as London and Peabody Institute in Baltimore (1881) followed soon after.[86]

Op. 78 in G was the first of Brahms's three incomparable, surviving sonatas "für Pianoforte und Violine" (still worded, though now less justifiably, in that pre-Classic order).[87] It was composed in 1878–79 after his longest break between sonatas and near the start of his final or "consummation" period (supra). It originated, in fact, right around the time Brahms was consulting Joachim intensively about the violin

80. Kalbeck/BRAHMS I/1 190–93, 13.

81. Schauffler/BRAHMS 56, 378–80.

82. BRAHMS BRIEFWECHSEL IX 45 (to Simrock, Sept. 6, 1865).

83. Altmann/BACH-ZITATE.

84. SCHUMANN-BRAHMS II 408.

85. Ehrmann/BRAHMS 28.

86. E.g., cf. MT XXIII (1881) 99 and 215, XXVII (1886) 82; NZM LXXII/2 (1876) 466 (London) and LXXIII/1 (1877) 193 (Vienna).

87. Including the early lost or destroyed Son., in a, for P & Vn (supra) and 2 more sons. in this setting that Brahms is known to have destroyed (Kalbeck/BRAHMS III/1 191; May/BRAHMS II 545), Op. 78 was actually Brahms's 4th son. of its type.

solo writing in his Concerto in D, Op. 77.[88] His concern for the work is suggested by his careful attention to its editorial details while it was in press.[89] Both names that have been given to this sonata— "Regenlied" ("Rain-Song") and, less often, "Frühling" ("Spring")— got their sanction from Brahms himself, as in his remark to Otto Dessoff before publication took place: "You must not complain about the rain. It can be set very well to music, something I have tried to do along with [describing] spring[time] in a violin sonata." [90] Brahms referred, of course, to the first three measures of the finale and their derivation from the start of his song "Regenlied," Op. 59/3, as well as "Nachklang" ("Memories" [91]), Op. 59/4. Previously he had enquired (facetiously?) of his publisher Simrock whether plagiarism could be charged by the publisher of the songs, Rieter-Biedermann, or would the legal maximum of eight measures—that is, a musical period— still hold.[92]

Much has been written about this derivation and its effect on the poignant, exceptionally lyrical quality of the sonata, not only in the finale but throughout the first and parts of the second movements where the initial trochaic pattern of the "Regenlied" becomes a unifying cyclical motive to be reiterated, varied, or recombined almost constantly.[93] Clara could hardly write enough about how deeply this sonata and those uses of the song theme touched her, still recalling its finale in 1890 as the music she always hoped would accompany her to the world beyond.[94] Elisabeth von Herzogenberg, whose highly perceptive comments now mattered at least as much to Brahms as Clara's, wrote similarly, although she implied weariness with reviews that only dwelt on the song derivation.[95] Both women made special mention of the long pedal point near the end of the "Adagio," and both must have relished the interlocking of that movement with the finale through the return to its main theme.

88. Cf. BRAHMS BRIEFWECHSEL VI 158–72; May/BRAHMS II 542.

89. E.g., cf. BRAHMS BRIEFWECHSEL X 133; Fellinger/BRAHMS, with facs. showing changes made in the autograph. Other facs. of the autograph include the first p. of each mvt. in BRAHMS-BILDERBUCH Tafeln X and XI.

90. BRAHMS BRIEFWECHSEL XVI 218.

91. Of springtime? Cf. Kalbeck/BRAHMS III/1 189 and 191–92.

92. BRAHMS BRIEFWECHSEL X 128. In the same letter Brahms jokingly suggests his fee can be reduced by 25 per cent because the sonata is not complete, lacking a fourth mvt.

93. Cf. Kalbeck/BRAHMS II/2 377–80, III/1 189–92; Evans/BRAHMS III 60, 64 (?!); May/BRAHMS II 544; Hollander/BRAHMS.

94. SCHUMANN-BRAHMS II 177–79, 415.

95. BRAHMS BRIEFWECHSEL I 103–4, 120; cf., also, II 259, for her husband's recollection of Op. 78 just after her death in 1892.

But, as Elisabeth von Herzogenberg suggested,[96] the reviewers were not as ready to perceive such subtleties. When Brahms played Op. 78 with the violinist Hellmesberger on November 29, 1879, in Vienna, Hanslick expressed unqualified praise only for the finale. He found the treatment in the first two movements of this wonderfully plastic work less free and original and recommended transfer of the work, more contemplative than passionate, from the concert hall to more intimate, private circles.[97] When Bülow played Op. 78 in London early in 1880 with Madame Norman-Neruda, one reviewer wrote that in spite of their fine performance, the audience turned "with a feeling of relief to the harmonious lucidity and graceful, albeit passionate, melodiousness" in Mozart's Piano Quartet in g, adding:

We do not presume to have formed a definite opinion of Herr Brahms's new work after hearing it once only. We admit that some of its leading "motives" have grown upon us since the performance in question. Still, the general impression produced by the "Sonata" is that of a mind striving to depict in musical language an individual experience scarcely important enough to furnish the material for three movements. The Sonata is, in fact, a reminiscence or paraphrase of the composer's well-known "Regenlied," the contemplative character of which pervades the entire work, while it distinctly interconnects the first and third movements; thus marking a concession on the part of the composer to the "programme" principle generally repudiated by the musicians of his school. The Sonata will, no doubt, soon be repeated at these concerts.[98]

Op. 78 did get performed soon again in London, and often, with increasing favor.[99] But Brahms exhibited his typical depreciation of his own works when he sent the autograph of Op. 78 to the wife of Miller zu Aichholz, recognizing her desire for "stronger paper in which to pack birthday presents for your husband. Should the shape or anything else about this paper not be agreeable to you, I shall be glad to exchange it for other kinds—also from other manufacturers." [100]

96. BRAHMS BRIEFWECHSEL I 120.

97. Hanslick/CONCERTE 257–59; cf. Kalbeck/BRAHMS III/1 228. Müller-Reuter/LEXIKON Suppl. 203 lists three earlier performances that same month that seem to have been more intimate.

98. MT XXI (1880) 125. For other, similar reviews of the same and other concerts, cf. Evans/BRAHMS III 60–61, 64–65.

99. E.g., cf. MT XXI (1880) 192, 234, 288, 296; XXII (1881) 21, 180 (but read 5th performance, not 3d), 184 (Joachim and Hallé), 459; XXIV (1883) 135; XXV (1884) 80, 206 (Clara and Joachim); etc. Other early performances are cited in Kalbeck/BRAHMS III/1 265 and May/BRAHMS II 545.

100. As trans. in Schauffler/BRAHMS 162; cf., also, Kalbeck/BRAHMS III/1 193 fn. For a more cryptic deprecatory sentence about Op. 78 cf. Brahms's remark to

Brahms's second cello sonata, Op. 99 in F, and second violin sonata, Op. 100 in A, make a pair in that they were both written in Thun in that extraordinarily productive month of August in 1886 (along with Piano Trio in c, Op. 101, and songs).[101] Geiringer sees a contrast of "masculine defiance" and "feminine sweetness and tenderness" between them, and a youthful "ardent pathos" in Op. 99 that is exceptional in Brahms's mature writing.[102] The choice of the raised tonic for the key of the slow movement and brief melodic similarities between the main themes of Opp. 99/2 and 38/1 supplied Schauffler's main but tenuous arguments for supposing that here was the discarded slow movement of Op. 38 (supra).[103] Again, Brahms sought the reactions of Elisabeth, who replied with much enthusiasm, suggesting only that she would need to hear him play the difficult third movement and that the "quasi-lyrical theme" of the finale might contrast too greatly with the "grand style" of the other movements.[104] She had first heard about the work from the equally enthusiastic Robert Hausmann, the cellist who figured in the early history of the work and its first performances in 1886 with Brahms himself.[105]

The ever popular Sonata in A, Op. 100, for P & Vn, is called the "Thun Sonata" not only for the lovely summer retreat where it was composed but because of the eleven-stanza poem, "Thunersonate von Johannes Brahms," that it inspired Brahms's host and close friend of his last years, Joseph Viktor Widmann, to write.[106] Today it is hard for most of us to relate the sonata to Widmann's flowery, ingenuous programmatic vision in Thun of knights of old and their thrilling, apocalyptic glimpse of a fairy maiden in a passing skiff. Yet, significantly, the poem moved Brahms, who up to his last year

Joachim in BRAHMS BRIEFWECHSEL VI 175. Brahms designated no dedicatee for Op. 78, but wrote Elisabeth von Herzogenberg that he almost put her name on it (BRAHMS BRIEFWECHSEL I 105).

101. Cf. Dietrich & Widmann/BRAHMS 121 et passim; Kalbeck/BRAHMS IV/1 16–17 and 92; Schauffler/BRAHMS 8–9. The autograph is described in KRAUS/GEIRINGER/LUITHLEN 55–56.

102. Geiringer/BRAHMS 238–40, including an example of changes Brahms made in the MS of Op. 99 and evidence in the finale that Brahms "could hardly write fast enough." Cf., also, Hanslick/MUSIKALISCHES 149–51 for an earlier similar view (1889), reprinted in Hanslick/TAGEBUCHE 209–10.

103. Schauffler/BRAHMS 378–80.

104. BRAHMS BRIEFWECHSEL II 130–31, 129. Clara was hurt at this time that Brahms was not sending her such things as Op. 99, too (SCHUMANN-BRAHMS II 307–9 [but read "Op. 100, 99" in 2d fn.]; cf., BRAHMS BRIEFWECHSEL II 144).

105. Cf. BRAHMS BRIEFWECHSEL XI 129 fn. 3. A grossly negative review of Op. 99 after the first performance is quoted and trans. in Slonimsky/LEXICON 74.

106. The poem appeared mainly as an appendix to Widmann's Erinnerungen (but not in the English trans., Dietrich & Widmann/BRAHMS); it is trans. in May/BRAHMS II 593–94.

was writing for further copies of a private printing issued by Widmann.[107] Less justifiable is the better-known name of "Meistersinger
Sonate." In greater measure than the many commentators on this
name care to acknowledge,[108] the initial theme does bring Wagner's
"Prize Song" clearly to mind by its similarly forthright, downbeat
opening on the same (few) notes and by its similar rhythm and lyricism—but only for a moment, and certainly not long enough to
validate the charges of plagiarism once heard from the anti-Brahms-
ites.[109]

More plausible as the source of this theme is the opening of Brahms's
own song, "Komm bald," Op. 97/5, composed two years earlier (Ex.
41).[110] But "Komm bald" is only one of at least three probable
song derivations in Op. 100, which for this reason and its constant
songfulness might well be given still another title, the "Lieder-
sonate." [111] Thus, Op. 100/i/51–54 (the 2d theme) recalls the opening
of "Wie Melodien zieht es mir," Op. 105/1,[112] and Op. 100/iii/31–37
and 90–91 hint at measures 1–8 in the fourth song of the same set,
"Auf dem Kirchhofe." [113]

After a first reading of the sonata with Joachim at the end of
December, 1886, Elisabeth von Herzogenberg wrote Brahms ecstatically
that "the whole piece is one veritable caress." [114] Her equally enthusiastic husband raised tiny questions about the juxtaposition in the
second movement of the "lovely" andante melody in F with the
Grieg-like, "lively-melancholy," scherzando section in d;[115] also, about
a need both he and Joachim felt for a new or "second theme" instead
of the seemingly abrupt return to the main theme right after the
arrival on the dominant in measure 59 of the finale. Actually, Joachim
later reported that Brahms told him he "had cut a good deal" out

107. BRAHMS BRIEFWECHSEL VIII 146.

108. E.g., Evans/BRAHMS III 187; Drinker/BRAHMS 70; Mason/BRAHMS.

109. Cf. Kalbeck/BRAHMS IV/1 17–19.

110. The illustration of this derivation in Kalbeck/BRAHMS IV/1 19 has not
been taken up by later writers; in III/2 538 a similar theme in Symphony 4 in
e/iv/225–33 is noted.

111. Kalbeck/BRAHMS IV/1 17–22. Most of the songs concerned are settings of
poems by Brahms's elder friend, Klaus Groth.

112. As illustrated in Kalbeck/BRAHMS IV/1 20. Elisabeth von Herzogenberg
spotted this derivation at once (BRAHMS BRIEFWECHSEL II 140).

113. As noted less specifically in BRAHMS BRIEFWECHSEL II 140 fn.

114. BRAHMS BRIEFWECHSEL II 140 (on the confused date of this reading cf.
Müller-Reuter/LEXIKON Suppl. 204–5). She had been impatient to see the work
and Brahms had kept Simrock waiting while he got her reactions (BRAHMS
BRIEFWECHSEL II 131–32, XI 139). Clara recorded her fondness for Op. 100, especially
its outer mvts., only in her diary (Litzmann/SCHUMANN III 490).

115. BRAHMS BRIEFWECHSEL II 147 (with reference in fn. 1 to a possible source for
the scherzando section in Grieg's Son. in g, Op. 13/ii [1867]).

Ex. 41. The opening themes of Johannes Brahms's "Komm bald," Op. 97/5, for P & voice, and Sonata in A, Op. 100, for P & Vn (after Brahms/WERKE-m XXVI 202 and X 31).

of the finale in the interest of condensation, though apparently not at that same place but in the coda.[116] Brahms had already given a first performance of Op. 100, presumably in its final form, with Josef Hellmesberger on December 2, 1886.[117]

Brahms's Sonata in d, Op. 108, was his third and last sonata for P & Vn and the only one in four movements. It was also the only one of the last six sonatas, from his final or "consummation" period, that bore a dedication—to "his friend Hans von Bülow." Bülow had indeed become a real friend and admirer, the more so with Wagner gone. He received the dedication as if it were an "ennoblement."[118] Brahms started the sonata during that same fruitful summer of 1886 in Thun, but did not complete it until two summers later, probably because it raised weightier creative problems. Again, this late in his career, Brahms participated in the first performance, in Budapest late in 1888, his partner being the Hungarian Jenö Hubay.[119] His performance of Op. 108 in Vienna with Joachim

116. May/BRAHMS II 592.
117. Cf. Kalbeck/BRAHMS IV/1 36–37, 49, 127.
118. BÜLOW BRIEFE VIII 255; cf., also, p. 250 for his praise of the work. Less than 20 years before, Bülow had dismissed Brahms contemptuously (e.g., BÜLOW BRIEFE V 352 fn.).
119. Cf. Kalbeck/BRAHMS IV/1 120; Müller-Reuter/LEXIKON Suppl. 205 (with listings of further early performances).

soon after gave Hanslick the occasion not only to rejoice in the work but to compare all three violin sonatas in subjective terms that today's musicians might still accept.[120] He saw this one as the most brilliant, difficult, passionate, large-scale, and substantial, Op. 100 as an unassuming, easygoing, genial work, but Op. 78 as a loved and trusted friend to whom he was admittedly partial and unable to acknowledge any superior.

Kalbeck finds only one, tentative, though not implausible song derivation in Op. 108—that of the opening of the second movement from "Klage" ("Lament") Op. 105/3. He also finds traces of Schumann, as he had in Op. 100, attributable partly to Brahms's preoccupation with the new Schumann edition around this time, in conjunction with (when not in opposition to) Clara.[121] Op. 108 brought from both Elisabeth von Herzogenberg and Clara some of their most enthusiastic, extensive, and discerning reactions (more perceptive and knowing than Hanslick's).[122] So ardent was Elisabeth's first letter that Brahms replied he would rather take it as a mistake than as hypocrisy, being less suspicious of a previous, franker letter of criticism (on the songs in Opp. 104–6).[123] But Elisabeth protested and Brahms apologized,[124] and Clara repeated her own enthusiasm in her diary,[125] all tending to confirm the genuineness of both women's reactions. Brahms mailed the MS to Elisabeth first, precipitating one of several three-way rounds of caustic, injured, or admonitory remarks centering around Elisabeth's and Clara's competition to get his first attention.[126] Elisabeth expressed particular pleasure in the development section of the first movement, with its rich texture woven around the dominant pedal point; in the simpler coda; in the "Adagio" movement, thankfully free of a contrasting middle section (like that in Op. 100/ii?); in the pianistically graceful, merry, humorous content of the third movement; and in the "compelling drive" of the finale as well as its transition to the second theme through a

---

120. Hanslick/MUSIKALISCHES 151–55. As early as April 29, 1889, Op. 108 was played in New York, at a reception for Bülow (Salter/AMERICAN 89 fn.).

121. Kalbeck/BRAHMS IV/1 21 and 23. The chief estrangements between Brahms and Clara occurred in 1886–87 and 1891–92 (cf. SCHUMANN-BRAHMS II 306–12, 464–68 and 476–78).

122. BRAHMS BRIEFWECHSEL II 210–13, 215–17, 217–19, 226; SCHUMANN-BRAHMS II 366–70, 395, 541–42.

123. BRAHMS BRIEFWECHSEL II 214 (and 200–209).

124. BRAHMS BRIEFWECHSEL II 219–21.

125. Litzmann/SCHUMANN III 512.

126. BRAHMS BRIEFWECHSEL II 214, 217, 218, 220, 221, 223; SCHUMANN-BRAHMS 362–63, 364, 366.

passing D.[127] She objected (in vain) to the rhythmic difficulty and unsatisfactory violin register in measures 142 to 157 of the finale, and suggested pizzicato for the double-stops in the third movement, which suggestion Brahms did follow starting at measure 119. Although a neuralgic arm prevented her trying Op. 108 at once for herself, Clara wrote of the warmth, depth, over-all melancholy, and consistent interest of the work, singling out the pedal point (again) and the "billows of interwoven harmonies" in the first movement, the frolicking of young lovers, interrupted by "a flash of deeper passion," in the third movement, and (again) the magnificent, impassioned flow of the finale. At 74 (in 1894), after playing the work with Joachim, Clara was still writing, "I love this sonata beyond words, every movement!—who knows whether this is not the last time that I shall [be able to] play it!" [128]

Brahms's last two sonatas, Op. 120/1 in f and 120/2 in E♭, were written for clarinet and piano (the order in the title, or, as it were, "for Piano and Mühlfeld." [129] Richard Mühlfeld, as both clarinetist and person, was closely associated with all four late clarinet works of Brahms—the Trio in a, Op. 114, and the Quintet in b, Op. 115, too.[130] He joined in numerous early performances, private and public, of both sonatas with Brahms, to the latter's great delight during those remarkably peripatetic and universally applauded activities of his third and second last years.[131] Moreover, publication was delayed in 1895 so that Mühlfeld could continue to give some "first" performances abroad.[132] Joachim joined in some of the early performances with Brahms, too, and it must have been partly for these occasions that Brahms himself adapted the clarinet part to viola (chiefly shifting the octave registers).[133] Brahms presented the autographs of Op. 120 to Mühlfeld [134] and perhaps would have dedicated any or all of his late

127. Presumably mss. 37–39, although her mention of a Vn entry in the 3d measure would then have to be an error for piano entry (BRAHMS BRIEFWECHSEL II 212–13).

128. SCHUMANN-BRAHMS II 542.

129. Drinker/BRAHMS 61.

130. Hanslick/FÜNF 312–13.

131. Cf. May/BRAHMS II 643–47; Kalbeck/BRAHMS IV/2 358–66, 368; BRAHMS BRIEFWECHSEL XII 155, 156, 162.

132. Cf. Kalbeck/BRAHMS IV/2 393–94.

133. Cf. BRAHMS BRIEFWECHSEL VI 280 (but the letter is wrongly dated 1892 instead of 1894), 293, 296, 298–99, and XII 165–68, 172–75, 178; as with P-duet and other arrangements of earlier sons. (cf. XII 150–51!), Brahms asked Simrock to have an alternative part prepared for Vn, which Simrock was not to pub. until after the clarinet original had appeared (with only his Va alternative). Cf., also, Cobbett/CHAMBER I 182 (Tovey).

134. May/BRAHMS II 644. The autograph of Op. 120/1 is described in KRAUS/GEIRINGER/LUITHLEN 89.

clarinet works to him had he not come to feel increasingly that a dedication implied more satisfaction with a work than his ever severe self-criticism would allow.[135]

In several senses the two clarinet sonatas helped to round out the Indian summer of Brahms in the 1890's. He meant them to be his last compositions for the public,[136] although he did add the *Four Serious Songs* and *Eleven Chorale Preludes for Organ* in 1896. Furthermore, the sonatas provided the occasions for some of his final and most heart-warming meetings with two of his closest and most lasting friends, Clara and Joachim, both of whom he had originally met soon after completing his first surviving work (Sonata in f♯, Op. 2), more than forty-two years earlier. Elisabeth von Herzogenberg was no longer alive to record her excitement in the music,[137] but Clara was still able to provide what seems to have been one of Brahms's main incentives to composition. Although too deaf by now to hear much other than "chaos" when Brahms and Mühlfeld played both sonatas four times for her in five days, she was still able to read, play over, and express her love for them.[138]

There is also a sense of Indian summer in the music itself of Op. 120—in its sweet mellow resignation, which pervades not only such a gentle nostalgic movement as Op. 120/1/ii but the stronger allegro movements as well. It is sometimes suggested that the two sonatas reflect a late decline in Brahms's creative powers.[139] They certainly show no lessening of craftsmanship or structural control. Together, as implied by their single opus number, they make a remarkable pair. They complement each other by contrasting decidedly in their keys, moods, and aesthetic depths. Yet over all they reveal not only that pervading sense of sweet mellow resignation but some striking common melodic bonds. In fact, right from their opening themes, so idiomatically suited to the clarinet tone and cantabile style, the two sonatas might well be linked under the heading "Diptych" that William G. Hill has proposed with good and similar reason for the pair of string quartets in Brahms's Op. 51.[140] Among all Brahms's many uses of cyclical relationships and free variation techniques there are few as subtle, flexible, or rewarding as those within and between the two

135. Cf. BRAHMS BRIEFWECHSEL I 105.

136. Cf. BRAHMS BRIEFWECHSEL XII 151.

137. There is no reasonable support for calling the sons. of Op. 120 "obituary poems" for her, as in Richard Specht's *Johannes Brahms* (London: J. M. Dent, 1930, p. 327).

138. Litzmann/SCHUMANN III 589–90. Cf., also, May/BRAHMS II 649–50; SCHUMANN-BRAHMS II 563–71, 583.

139. E.g., Schauffler/BRAHMS 381–82.

140. MR XIII (1952) 110–24.

sonatas of Op. 120. Rather than any decline of creative powers in Op. 120, perhaps one might speak of increasing caution in the treatment of the ideas. Peter Latham has argued persuasively his thesis that as Brahms matured he proved not to be the prophet Schumann saw in him. Instead, partly because of the Classical orientation that had started with Marxsen and partly because of his personal background and character he learned more and more to do only what was safe and sure.[141] His unwillingness to take chances, reflected somewhat in that severe self-criticism, may explain at once the perfection of his music, the leading position he has held in the history of the sonata since Beethoven, and yet the limitation that gives pause to Bülow's claim for him as the "third B."

Other Composers in Austria

Brahms had no serious competitor in Vienna in the field of the sonata. The most likely one, the great symphonist Anton Bruckner (1824–96), came no closer than his fine String Quintet in F (1879) except for his earlier, incomplete String Quartet in c and three rather dramatic first movements to prospective piano solo sonatas in F, f, and g, all student works of 1861–63.[142] We are left, then, with scarcely more than a dozen, largely forgotten composers of sonatas in Austria, as a postscript to our discussion of Brahms. One was the pianist, organist, and singer (Friedrich) Robert Volkmann (1815–83), in whose early music both Brahms and Bülow saw much promise.[143] Volkmann actually lived in Budapest most of his life (where we shall meet him as a teacher; ssb XVII) and in Vienna only four years, from 1854.[144] But much of his music was published and made its chief mark there. Certain of his piano trios, string quartets, and symphonies won particular favor and occasionally are still played. In our more limited field of works called "sonata," he left only one substantial example, a solo piano Sonata in c, Op. 12, and three sonatinas (2 for P & Vn and one for P-duet).[145] Op. 12, published by Kistner in Leipzig in

141. Latham/BRAHMS 93–96, 168–69, 173.
142. Cf. MGG II 364 (F. Blume). The son. mvts. have yet to be pub., but are described, with exx., in Böttcher/BRUCKNER.
143. E.g., SCHUMANN-BRAHMS I 174 (1856); BÜLOW BRIEFE II 67, III 76–79.
144. Cf. MGG XIII 1921–23 (R. Sietz), with further references; also, La Mara/MUSIKERBRIEFE II 292.
145. Cf. the undated lists in PAZDÍREK XIV 290–93 and GROVE IX 68–69 (Grove). Op. 12 was reviewed in NZM LV (1861) 47 (with ex.) as a work to be more respected than loved, and not especially "new." His 2 sonatinas Opp. 60 and 61 are reviewed similarly in MW II (1870) 4.

1854 or 1855, is a three-movement sonata (M-VF-M/VF) that falls stylistically midway between the piano works of Mendelssohn and Schumann, which must already have affected Volkmann while he was still studying in Leipzig in the late 1830's. The ideas, piano writing, and rhythms all suggest these influences. But the unusual, yet convincing alternation of 6/8 and 2/8 meter in the "Prestissimo" middle movement suggest Hungarian influences while he was in Pest. The total effect is one of songful, flowing music, solidly albeit somewhat conservatively grounded, and interesting enough in content without disclosing any conspicuous originality.

The concert pianist **Carl Evers** (1819–75) studied with Karl Krebs, started to compose under Mendelssohn's influence, and met Chopin before he settled in Graz in 1841 and Vienna in 1872.[146] Between about 1842 and 1860, at least eight sonatas by him were published, mainly by Schlesinger of Berlin, and reviewed widely, including six for P solo, one for P & Vn, and one for P-duet.[147] The third solo sonata, Op. 22 in d, appeared early enough to receive one of Schumann's last and more devastating reviews, in 1844.[148] In brief, Schumann said that favorable Vienna reviews of Evers' sonatas needed to be cut down to size, for, like a talented dilettante, Evers, the professional, produced felicitous ideas here and there, but with a tasteless confusion of Classic and more recent styles and no larger sense of organization. Slightly more favorable reviews of later sonatas by Evers suggest that at least the more academic aspects of his composing may have improved,[149] but they hardly inspire any protracted search for the sonatas themselves, none of which have turned up in European or American libraries during the present study.

Only passing mention needs to be given to a well reviewed piano sonata (Op. 2, *ca.* 1854) dedicated to Schumann by one of his correspondents, **Carl Debrois van Bruyck** (1828–1902), who was active west of Vienna in Waidhofen;[150] or to the four somewhat academic solo piano sonatas, published in the 1850's, by Bruyck's teacher and

---

146. Cf. GROVE II 982 (W. Carr).

147. Cf. PAZDÍREK V 181–82.

148. Schumann/SCHRIFTEN II 346–47. An equally negative review of the same work (with revealing exx.) and a more guarded review of Evers' first son. appear in AMZ XLVI (1844) 732–33 and XLV (1843) 453–55, respectively.

149. E.g., AMZ XLVII (1845) 39–42 (on Sons. 1–3, other works, and biography) and XLVIII (1846) 598; NZM XXIII (1845) 201–2, XL (1854) 158 and 197; MW V (1874) 426–27 (A. W. Ambros). Hanslick's review of Evers' recital of his own sons. and related works in Vienna in 1855 (Hanslick/WIEN II 86–87) largely repeats the substance of the NZM reviews, without acknowledgment.

150. Cf. Riemann/LEXIKON I 242; NZM XL (1854) 209.

Brahms's occasional friend, the pianist **Johann Rufinatscha** (1812–93);[151] or to the two solo piano sonatas (Op. 6 in d, 1858, and Op. 10 in E, 1861) and the duo sonata for P & Vn (Op. 30 in e, 1871) by Brahms's longtime friend, **Franz Wüllner** (1832–1902);[152] or to two sonatas, Opp. 1 and 3 (1872 and 1874) by the Vienna-trained, widely stationed pianist and violinist **Eduard Rappoldi** (1831–1903);[153] or to two sonatas each for P & Vn and P & Vc, published between 1872 and 1881, by the Vienna pianist and teacher **Julius Zellner** (1832–1900);[154] or to the two sonatas each for P & Vc and P & Vn (plus some sonatinas) by Rheinberger's pupil in Graz, **Ferdinand Thieriot** (1838–1919), published between 1868 and 1892;[155] or to the six fairly purposeful, spare duo sonatas, three each for P & Vn and P & Vc, published between 1882 and 1897, by Brahms's close friend **Heinrich von Herzogenberg** (1843–1900).[156]

But there is more interest in the sonatas of two other men who were friends of Brahms and of each other, the pianist **Ignaz Brüll** (1846–1907) and the violinist **Karl Goldmark** (1830–1915). Among seven sonatas by Brüll published between 1871 and 1906, four are for Vn & P, one is for Vc & P,[157] one for 2 Ps, and one for solo P.[158] The last,

151. Cf. MGG XI 1080 (W. Senn); PAZDÍREK XII 681; and the mostly laudatory review of Op. 7 in C, with exx., in NZM XLV (1856) 234–35.

152. Cf. the monograph Kämper/WÜLLNER, including descriptions of the sons. (pp. 72–74) and full lists of Wüllner's works (pp. 142–59). Cf., also, GROVE IX 373–74 (M. Friedländer); BRAHMS BRIEFWECHSEL XV 192–94 (dated list of Wüllner's works); PAZDÍREK XV 572–74. Op. 6 is reviewed with qualified praise in NZM LIV (1861) 79, 80; and Op. 30 similarly in MW III (1872) 439 (G. H. Witte).

153. Cf. GROVE VII 49 (E. Blom); Altmann/KAMMERMUSIK 221; MW XI (1880) 394 (mild pros and cons in Op. 3).

154. Cf. BAKER 1841; Altmann/KAMMERMUSIK 233 and 266; PAZDÍREK XV 345 (including sonatinas for P solo and P-duet; cf. SMW XLI [1887] 643). Praise for the charm, melodic interest, and good scoring in Zellner's sons. is expressed in MW XI (1880) 589–90; Cobbett/CHAMBER II 596.

155. Cf. Riemann/LEXIKON II 1836–37; PAZDÍREK XIV 132; Altmann/KAMMERMUSIK 229 and 265; MW XI (1880) 322 (finding Op. 24 consistently interesting).

156. Cf. MGG VI 302–6 (dated but incomplete list; W. Kahl) Altmann/KAMMERMUSIK 207, 258; Cobbett/CHAMBER I 553–54 (W. Altmann & W. W. Cobbett); Shand/VIOLIN 67–72 (for exx.); MT XXV (1883) 33 and XXVII (1886) 273 (for early performances abroad, the latter by Joachim). Only 2, noncommittal references, to one son., Op. 52 for P & Vc, occur in the correspondence with Brahms (BRAHMS BRIEFWECHSEL II 128 and 151).

157. A review of this first son., Op. 9, stresses the diversity of influences it reveals (including Italian and Hungarian), hints at superficiality, and grants but faint praise (NZM LXVIII/1 [1872] 139).

158. Cf. MGG II 386–88 (H. Wirth); PAZDÍREK II 1154–57; Altmann/KAMMERMUSIK 197, 254, 286. Son. 2 for P & Vn, Op. 60 in a, is reviewed as light, fluent, and not especially attractive (SMW XLVIII [1890] 899). The Son. for 2 Ps (F-Sc-M-F) is reviewed as skillful, sonorous, and often trivial, in MW XII (1881) 411.

Op. 73 in d (1894), seems to have enjoyed the most popularity. Its first
movement suffers a bit from the hollowness and sentimentality of
Grieg's larger forms (ssb XV). In fact, the widely-spaced, chordal outline and the strategic aug.-6/5 chord of its opening theme recall some
Grieg idiosyncrasies. Though Brüll's ability to develop his ideas is
greater than Grieg's, he, too, shows up best in lighter forms, as in the
second movement, where a bright scherzando section in 2/4 meter, a
lilting "dolce cantando" section in 6/8, and an "Andante con moto"
section in 3/8 follow in an extended rondo design, A-B-A-C-A-B-A/
coda. An independent "Andante" and a toccata-like "Allegro moderato" comprise the two movements that complete this well-made but
dated and seldom distinctive work.

Goldmark left about ten instrumental chamber works along with
his much better known operas, including a Sonata in D/b, Op. 25,
for P & Vn (1875) and a Sonata in F, Op. 39, for P & Vc (1893).[159] The
two sonatas are unequal works. Instead of the smooth polish and control of Brüll's training they reveal at once the originality and rough-
nesses of the largely self-taught composer. Their ideas are frequently
fresh and unexpected, especially their rhythms and chromatic harmony
(pointing to Goldmark's love of Wagner's music; Ex. 42). But the
development of ideas so necessary to full-scale sonata forms is characteristically stiff, naive, or nonexistent. Both sonatas are in three movements (F-S-VF and M-M-F). The violin sonata, with its infrequent
tonal scheme of D-f♯-b, is somewhat larger, more serious, and more
effective than the cello sonata.[160] The finales are the weakest movements of both sonatas. It should go without saying that whatever spark
can still be heard in either Brüll's or Goldmark's sonatas will disappear entirely if they are exposed to comparison with any of Brahms's
sonatas and their incalculably greater genius and mastery. In all his
vast extant correspondence Brahms scarcely ever strained either his
kindness or integrity by attempting to comment on the music of such
good friends.

As a matter of curiosity, mention should be added of the four piano
sonatas left unfinished in MSS by **Hugo Wolf** (1860–1903).[161] They

159. Cf. mgg V 481–84 (W. Pfannkuch); Altmann/kammermusik 204 and 256.
Altmann/goldmark (with many exx.) is a survey of the chamber music (but Op.
39 is overlooked). A performance of Op. 25 is reported in nzm LXXII/2 (1876) 423.
160. A review of Op. 25 in mw X (1879) 519 rates it below Goldmark's operatic
and orchestral music, but finds it not without some attractive details; the form
is seen as the chief weakness (yet as the chief point of originality, in smw XXIII
[1875] 674). Cf., also, Hanslick/concerte 306.
161. Cf. Walker/wolf 15, 35–39, 463–64; grove IX 331, 338, 343 (F. Walker).

Ex. 42. From the middle movement of Karl Goldmark's Sonata in D/b, Op. 25, for P & Vn (after the original Schott ed. of 1875).

were composed too early to be musically significant, when he was but fifteen and sixteen (during his influential exposure to Wagner and before his unhappy meeting with Brahms). But they are worth noting as early stormy efforts of the great Viennese, late-Romantic song composer.[162]

162. A letter from Dr. Ferdinand Wernigg of the Wiener Stadtbibliothek suggests that they will be included (as of 1969) in the "Jugendwerke" to be pub. as part of the new "Hugo Wolf-Gesamtausgabe."

Chapter X

Liszt and Others in Germany from About 1850 to 1885

South Germany (Rheinberger) and Switzerland

Applicable here, too, is the preface to the previous chapter on Austro-German ties and divergencies in the second half of the 19th century. The most important sonata composer in south Germany during this period was the organist, composer, and teacher **Joseph Gabriel Rheinberger** (1839–1901). An organ prodigy, Rheinberger was thoroughly grounded in Classic music under such teachers as J. J. Maier and F. Lachner (ssB VII).[1] In Munich, where he spent his entire life from the age of twelve, he composed prolifically in nearly every category,[2] won international recognition as a teacher, especially of counterpoint (drawing students, like G. S. Chadwick and H. W. Parker, from as far off as the United States), and received many honors. A total of 29 sonatas by him was published, all in his last 33 years (1868–1901), including 20 for organ, 4 for P solo, one for P-duet, 2 for P & Vn, and one each for P & Vc and P & Hn. The organ sonatas have benefited from studies by several writers.[3] The piano and chamber sonatas deserve but have yet to receive comparable attention.[4] Those who dis-

---

1. Cf. mgg XI 377–81 (A. Würz), with further references.

2. Cf. pazdírek XII 252–63.

3. Grace/rheinberger is the chief survey. Harvey Grace also prepared a new ed. of the organ sons. for Novello (*ca.* 1934–56; Cat. nypl XXV 535) and wrote the full article on Rheinberger for the 3d and 4th eds. of grove (IV 378–82), shortened in the 5th ed. (VII 145–48). A facs. of the opening of the autograph of organ Son. 16 in g♯ appears in mgg XI 377 and all of the first mvt. of this son. is pub. in Giegling/solo-m no. 17.

4. The P sons. are briefly noted in Georgii/klaviermusik 581–82 (Op. 122, P-duet), merely cited in Kirby/keyboard 349 (with p. 350 largely devoted to the organ sons.), and disregarded (in the absence of any reference at all to Rheinberger) in Shedlock/sonata and Dale/nineteenth. The chamber sons. have fared still less well. Exceptional are the 2 short (but enthusiastic) paragraphs on the 2 Vn sons. in Cobbett/chamber II 293–94 (W. Altmann). Rheinberger gets no mention, for example, in Müller-Reuter/lexikon, which does give good space to Raff, Reinicke,

miss Rheinberger as the composer merely of teaching pieces that once enjoyed wide use, or because he has all but disappeared from publishers' catalogues are in for a surprise if they start reading into his sonatas. For nearly every one of these is a broadly conceived, serious, masterfully executed work, with many movements of decided musical interest.

In 1925 Harvey Grace ranked Rheinberger's organ music, especially the sonatas, as "second in importance only to Bach's organ music." [5] If his evaluation now seems too categorical and also somewhat confining, it should at least be acceptable to rank the sonatas on a par with the best German organ examples of the 19th century, including those of Mendelssohn, Reubke, and Merkel. Had Rheinberger lived longer he probably would have added organ sonatas in B♭, c♯, G♭, and E, since each of the twenty he did complete is in a different key and only those four keys are needed to complete the cycle. In over-all plan, these organ sonatas are more like the piano and duo sonatas of the 19th century than Mendelssohn's, although seventeen of Rheinberger's have fugues. Unlike most German organ sonatas, none of them centers around a chorale. The most frequent plan is the three-movement one, F-S-F, with or without introductions to the fast movements. Various four-movement plans occur, too. The first movement is usually a "sonata form," but a relatively free one in which the development and recapitulation tend to be shortened in favor of an extended, revelatory coda or apotheosis. The middle movement is most often a gentle foil for the outer movements, as suggested by titles like "Intermezzo," "Idyll," "Provençalisch," "Pastorale," or "Cantilene." The finale usually consists of one of the aforementioned fugues, single or double, with or without introduction; but sometimes it is the first movement in which the fugue occurs. A notable factor in the success of Rheinberger's fugues is the careful, effective design of his subjects, both melodic and rhythmic (as in Son. 13 in E♭, Op. 161/iv). Rheinberger shows relatively little interest in exploiting the traditional contrapuntal devices, although one never doubts his ability to use them.

Rheinberger's other sonatas are less free in their over-all plans and, naturally, less polyphonically disposed than his organ sonatas. But, as viewed here (contrary to Harvey Grace), they are not musically less significant. Both the excellences and shortcomings of his sonatas are

---

Draeseke, and Gernsheim. The string sons. were performed often in Rheinberger's own day (although not so often as his once ubiquitous organ sons.); e.g., cf. NZM LXXII/1 (1876) 8 and 104, LXXII/2 345, and LXXIII/1 (1877) 214 (Pittsburgh, Pa.); MT XVII (1876) 697, XVIII (1877) 553, XXV (1884) 82–83; SMZ XVI (1876) 4, 22.

5. Grace/RHEINBERGER V, 125–27. A similar evaluation was arrived at independently by A. Farmer in MT LXXVIII (1937) 538–39. Cf., also, Sandberger/AUFSÄTZE 325–26.

common, more or less, to all of them. The excellences include a seemingly inexhaustible fund of musical ideas, sometimes very distinctive
ideas; a complete command of compositional techniques, whether
melodic, rhythmic, harmonic, textural, or instrumental; an exceptional
versatility and resourcefulness in the use of these techniques; and a
broad, unfailing sense of musical architecture. The sense of architecture is most apparent in the "sonata forms," where the long-range
opposition of large sections and the steady, deliberate pursuit of a
principal motive or thematic element seem to lead gradually but surely
to that apotheosis in the coda. In this aspect, Rheinberger's sonatas
at once bring Bruckner's symphonic "sonata forms" to mind.[6] A fine
example is the first movement of Sonata in Eb, Op. 77, for P & Vn,
a telling work that duo teams overlook in their searches for worthwhile Romantic alternatives to the sonatas of Brahms, Franck, and
Fauré.

What are the shortcomings of Rheinberger's sonatas that may account for their virtual oblivion today, except for a few isolated movements in the organ sonatas? As viewed here, the problem is not one
of unoriginality, although unoriginality is blamed in most references
to Rheinberger today.[7] A movement like the "Scherzo" in Gb from
his Sonata 3 in Eb, Op. 135, for piano reveals much of the tonal color,
rhythmic ingenuity, melodic freshness, and structural purpose that
can be found in the "Scherzo" from Bruckner's Fourth Symphony. But
that analogy suggests one of the problems of Rheinberger's sonatas.
Bruckner's deliberately paced development of ideas serves well when
enhanced by the contrasts of orchestral colors, but would serve less
well, especially in the even larger forms, if the color contrasts were
limited to the piano alone or to the piano with one other instrument.
Furthermore, it is in Rheinberger's nature to be not only deliberate
but more reflective and contemplative than dynamic and agitated.
Even his fine themes tend to be serene and optimistic rather than
troubled and portentous. If we add to these traits the fact that—in

6. But Anton in Vienna seems to have been no relation of one "Herrn Franz
Bruckner, Kgl. Kammermusiker in München," to whom Rheinberger's 2d Vn
son., Op. 105, is ded. In a lengthy review of *Symphonische Sonate* for P, Op. 47,
in MW II (1871) 389–91 and 406–7, A. Maczewski discusses the differences between
the symphony and son. (cf. SSB II) and finds the long development in i explains
"Symphonische" and the "Tarantella" finale explains "Sonate" in the title. Strongly
favorable reviews of Rheinberger's *Romantische Sonate* in f♯, Op. 184, occur in
MW XXVIII (1897) 561 (L. Bödecker) and SMW LV (1897) 243.

7. E.g., cf. MGG XI 380–81. The provocative evaluation of Rheinberger in Sand-
berger/AUFSÄTZE 320–30 puts more emphasis than seems justified here on Bach,
middle Beethoven, and Mendelssohn as the main points of departure and of
Romantic limitations in Rheinberger's music.

spite of frequent titles for his sonatas like "Fantasie," "Pastoral," "Romantische," or "Sinfonische"—Rheinberger showed no special interest either in programme music or German literature, we are forced to conclude that in a Romantic sense he qualifies somewhat as an anti-sonata composer. Finally, some acknowledgment must be made of infrequent saccharinities, especially chromaticisms, in Rheinberger's melody and/or harmony that (to recall a trait not unfamiliar in Mendelssohn) can extend beyond the borderline of sentiment into sentimentality (as in that same P son., Op. 135/iii/24–30 and 43–48). On the other hand, Rheinberger can keep such moments under control and create slow movements with uncommonly long, expressive, purposeful lines, couched in harmony far more adventuresome than writers generally have credited to him—harmony, in fact, that at times seems to anticipate or parallel Fauré's. A representative illustration is the "Andante molto" from his Sonata 2 for P & Vn in e, Op. 105, from which an extract can give only a hint (Ex. 43).[8]

One of Rheinberger's few cocitizens in Munich who won any attention with their sonatas was Wagner's sometime friend **Robert von Hornstein** (1833–90), who left one published sonata each for Vn & P, P-duet, and P solo, in the 1870's.[9] The first of these, Op. 7, is reviewed as pleasingly constructed but anachronistic in its rococo figuration, and as somewhat lacking in the development or contrapuntal interest expected in a sonata.[10] Another cocitizen, at least during parts of his peregrinatory career, was the versatile conductor and composer **Bernhard Scholz** (1835–1916), who left 9 published sonatas in the 62 years from 1850 to 1912—4 each for Vn & P and Vc & P, and one, Op. 28 in B (1868 or 1869), for P solo.[11] An examination of Op. 28, "friendlily dedicated to his teacher Ernst Pauer," confirms the verdict of much skill but weak ideas on the part of this active champion of Brahms, musical conservative, and cosigner of the anti-Liszt-Wagner "Manifesto."[12] The most effective of Scholz's four movements (F-Sc-Va-F) are the last two, an "Adagio molto" theme with seven variations and a fugal finale à la Beethoven of Op. 101. And a third cocitizen for a while as well as a pupil of Rheinberger was the esteemed pianist and teacher **Luise Adolpha Le Beau** (1850–1927), one of the few women

8. In MW X (1879) 421 a review of Op. 105 offers warm praise for all mvts. apart from a slight letdown noted in the finale; cf., also, SMW XXXVII (1879) 82–83.

9. Cf. Mendel/LEXIKON V 306; Riemann/LEXIKON I 783–84; PAZDÍREK VII 672–3.

10. NZM LXVIII/2 (1872) 377; MW III (1872) 537.

11. Cf. MGG XII 36–39 (R. Sietz, with further references); Altmann/KAMMERMUSIK 225 and 263.

12. Cf. Cobbett/CHAMBER II 343 (W. Altmann); MW I (1870) 102 (on Op. 28); NZM LXXIX (1879) 185–86 and NZM IV/3/2 (Feb. 1, 1883) 2 (both on Op. 55); MW XXXIII (1902) 201 (on Op. 81); DM XI/4 (1911–12) 382 (E. Thilo on Op. 94).

Ex. 43. From the second movement of Joseph Rheinberger's Sonata in e, for P & Vn, Op. 105 (after the Kistner ed. [1893?] Op. 105a, in e♭, for Cl & P).

who find a place in the present survey.[13] Along with three sonatinas for P solo, Op. 13, this lady wrote three sonatas that were published— Op. 8 in a (*ca.* 1879) for P solo, Op. 10 in c (1882) for Vn & P, and Op. 17 in D (1883) for Vc & P.[14]

North of Munich in Lemberg the pianist and successful composer of light piano works **Joseph Christoph Kessler** (actually **Kötzler;**

13. A midway biographical account appeared in NMZ VII (1886) 53–54. Cf., also, Riemann/LEXIKON I 1010; Elson/WOMAN 164–65.

14. Cf. Altmann/KAMMERMUSIK 213 and 260, PAZDÍREK IX 230; and, on Op. 17: NMZ V (1884) 54 (commending the Vc treatment and melody), NZM LXXX/2 (1884) 498 (W. Irgang questioning some structural details and so many modulations in the finale; also, whether Vn is better for the Vc part), and MW XIV (1883) 445 (short and favorable).

1800–1872) dedicated his only sonata, Op. 47 in E♭ for piano (1852?), "to the memory of his dear friend F. Chopin." [15] Except for a few reminiscences of his Polish (and Czech?) background, especially in the middle two of its four movements (F-S-Sc-Ro), this work was reviewed at length by Bülow as competent but somewhat static and still oriented to Hummel's style, with less charm and pianistic significance than Kessler's Etudes Op. 20.[16]

Elsewhere in south Germany the sonatas of three composers in or near Stuttgart call for only the briefest mentions. The pianist and teacher **Wilhelm Speidel** (1826–99), trained and employed in Munich before moving to Stuttgart in 1857, left one published sonata each for P & Vc and P & Vn, Opp. 10 and 61, in 1855 and 1879, respectively,[17] and two published sonatas for P solo, Op. 46 (1872?).[18] The last were reviewed as generally competent, again, but lacking in depth or inspiration.[19] As the author of the first significant monograph on the sonata's history (1846; SBE 11 and SSB II), the Stuttgart organist and choral conductor **Immanuel Gottlob Friedrich Faisst** (1823–94) should at least be named here for an organ Sonata in E published posthumously.[20] And the highly esteemed organist in nearby Esslingen, **Christian Fink** (1822–1911), may be noted for at least five organ sonatas and four piano sonatas or sonatinas, published between about 1856 and 1898.[21] Several reviews acknowledge charm and skill in Fink's sonatas but sometimes find them inconsequential.[22]

The only mid-Romantic name in Switzerland to mention here is that of the gifted, versatile, short-lived musician **Hermann Goetz** (1840–76), who had been close to Bülow and Brahms before moving to Zürich in his last years.[23] To our genre Goetz contributed only two

15. Cf. Mendel/LEXIKON VI 37; Riemann/LEXIKON I 876; Sydow & Hedley/CHOPIN 35, 36, 173. Chopin ded. the original German ed. of his *24 Préludes* to Kessler.
16. NZM XXXVI (1852) 233–35, with exx. (reproduced only in part in BÜLOW BRIEFE III 49–50).
17. Cf. Altmann/KAMMERMUSIK 264 and 228 (but Op. 10 was originally for P & Vc, and in D, not d). In MW XIII (1882) 130, Op. 61 is reviewed as "a big sonata with little content"; cf., also, SMW XXXVIII (1880) 546.
18. Cf. Mendel/LEXIKON IX 350–51; Riemann/LEXIKON II 1735. Op. 111 by Speidel (1898?) is a "Suite (Quasi-Sonate)" pub. in 5 separate pieces or mvts. (cf. MW XXX [1899] 196).
19. NMZ LXVIII/2 (1872) 405–6.
20. Composed before 1876? (cf. NZM LXXII/1 [1876] 432; SMZ XVI [1876] 175). Cf., also, MGG III 1735–37 (R. Sietz).
21. Cf. Mendel/LEXIKON III 530–31; Riemann/LEXIKON I 509; PAZDÍREK V 352–53; Kremer/ORGAN 184.
22. NZM XLV (1856) 253–54, XLVII (1857) 166–67, LV (1861) 93 and 208, XL/2 286.
23. Cf. MGG V 470–73 (W. Kahl), with further bibliography.

sonatinas for P, Op. 8 (first pub. in 1869), and a Sonata in g for P-duet, Op. 17 (composed in 1865–66 and first pub. posthumously, by Kistner in 1878, plate no. 5048). But these are three fluent, fresh works of exceptional melodic and harmonic interest.[24] Some enterprising publisher seeking to enrich the piano literature at junior solo and moderately advanced levels would do well to rediscover and reprint all three, especially Op. 17. The latter, in three movements (S/VF-S-F), has a Mendelssohnian flavor and achieves depth through meaningful themes, expressive harmony, and contrapuntal exchanges between the parts.[25]   25a

Liszt in Central Germany

We reach another main landmark, in the sonatas of **Franz** (or **Ferencz**) **Liszt** (1811–86), one of the half-dozen most influential musicians of the 19th century, after Beethoven. Liszt is not known to have   25b
composed more than eight sonatas, out of a total of some 1,420 single works, large or small,[26] and only three of these have survived. Moreover, he composed all eight before the midpoint in his career (about 1855). Yet the two solo piano sonatas that won fame, especially his last sonata, in b, are so unusual as to be without significant precedent or consequent at least in solo piano music, and at the same time so generally enjoyed and esteemed by performers and listeners alike as to rank among the most successful piano sonatas of the Romantic Era.

In spite of their importance, Liszt's surviving sonatas have yet to be treated to a full study that will pull together the scattered bits of information about their background, genesis, and further circumstances, and one that will provide more detailed style-critical analyses than the numerous summary statements now to be found on the thematic elements and peculiar structure of the Sonata in b. This need only reflects in a small way the much larger need to purge, desentimentalize, correct, restore, fill out, and, at last, co-ordinate the whole

24. Cf. the enthusiastic reviews in NZM LIX/2 (1873) 400 and MMR VIII (1878) 12 and XIV (1884) 154 (all on Op. 8); MW IX (1878) 542–43 and XIII (1882) 581 (both on Op. 17); also, Georgii/KLAVIERMUSIK 577–78, with ex. (calling Op. 17 "the most beautiful four-hand sonata in the past century after Schubert"); and Ganzer & Kusche/VIERHÄNDIG 71–72.

25. Opp. 8 and 17 were most recently listed in the Augener and Kistner cats., respectively. Mod. ed. of Op. 8/2/ii and iii: Frey/SONATINA-m 42. Cf. SSB V for an ex. from Op. 17/i.

26. This total roughly combines the 1,321 works added up in Beaufort/LISZT with the 95 lost works listed in Schnapp/LISZT. The totals of 673 items in Raabe/LISZT II 242–361 and 768 items in GROVE V 264–314 (H. Searle) often include several sublistings per item.

vast but often erratic literature pertaining to Liszt.[27] The starting point
for such improvements would have to be fundamental publications
like Lina Ramann's detailed, nearly contemporary study of the man
and his works and La Mara's collections of his letters.[28] Revision and
completion of the collected edition of Liszt's works, started in 1907,
is another goal.[29] Humphrey Searle has provided a balanced, recent
overview of Liszt's music (Searle/LISZT), with new light on the remarkable significance of the late works for the 20th century.

Liszt composed six of his eight sonatas for P solo, one for P-duet,
and one for Vn & P. Of the five lost sonatas, three were little three-
movement works, apparently not unadventurous in style, yet composed
while the young prodigy was still only thirteen (1825); a fourth was
the P-duet, composed in the same year; and the fifth was only the
start of a projected Sonata in c, dating at latest from early 1835.[30]
Earliest of the three surviving sonatas is the "Duo (Sonate)" in c♯ for
Vn & P, composed in 1832–35 (presumably in Paris) but not published
until 1964, after the pianist Eugene List had called the MS to the
attention of its editor, Tibor Serly.[31] This is a full-scale work in four

27. Haraszti/LISZT summarizes the most serious needs and problems in Liszt
research and evaluates some of the contributions. A detailed, up-to-date bibliography is itself a need. The bibliography in GROVE V 262–63 stops short of special
studies; that in MGG VIII 986–88 (H. Engel) includes these, but only in limited
number. Cat. NYPL XVII 445–84 is helpful. L. Koch's exhaustive bibliography
(cf. Searle/LISZT 196) extends only to 1936.

28. Ramann/LISZT, LISZT LETTERS, "LISZT" SCHRIFTEN; on the letters, cf. ML XLVIII
(1967) 148–50. Raabe/LISZT (currently being revised by Felix Raabe) made important
advances in 1931 (but cf. Haraszti/LISZT 126–28), especially toward the co-ordination
of resources and a more accurate cat. of Liszt's works (utilized in summary form,
with revisions by H. Searle, for GROVE V 264–314). The authenticity of every writing
attributed to Liszt other than letters, including the 7 vols. in "LISZT" SCHRIFTEN, is
challenged convincingly in Haraszti/LISZT 130–35 and Haraszti/AUTHOR. The Liszt
specialist Emile Haraszti did not live to complete his long projected, over-all
study; but new advances are to be expected in the biographic study that is now
in progress (1967) by Edward Waters of the Library of Congress.

29. Liszt/WERKE-m. A "New Edition of the Complete works," projected in 7 series
totalling about 80 vols., was inaugurated in Hungary in 1970 with the *Etudes* in 2
vols., as edited by Z. Gárdonyi and I. Szelényi.

30. These 5 sons. are nos. 5, 6, 7, 10, and 19, respectively, in Schnapp/LISZT.
This study provides all known details, including the incident in which the
youngster fooled the 51-year-old French violinist Pierre Rode into thinking no. 5
(Liszt's earliest son.) was by Beethoven, and a facs. (after p. 128) of the first 14
mss. of this son. (in f) as recalled and written down by Liszt in 1881 for Miss
Ramann; also, the incipit of no. 19 (in c).

31. Serly/LISZT-m, with quadrilingual preface. Cf., also, Serly's article in *The New
York Times* for Sunday, Feb. 14, 1960, X 9, following the first performance of
this work on Feb. 5 at the Library of Congress, by List and his wife, the violinist
Carroll Glenn; Newman/LISZT (review); Searle/LISZT 34. Chopin's Mazurka in c♯,
Op. 6/2 (B. 60), on which Liszt's Vn Son. in c♯ is based, was composed in Vienna
in "late 1830," but a *terminus a quo* for Liszt's son. would be his first hearing of
Chopin on Feb. 26, 1832 (Hedley/CHOPIN 47–48), or, more likely the first pub. of

movements (totalling 628 mss.), the "one-movement" Sonata in b being 22 per cent longer (760 mss.) and the one-movement "Dante Sonata" 40 per cent shorter (376 mss.). Its 81-page score (47 pp. in print) was left in an unpolished state, requiring a little deciphering, filling in, choosing of alternatives, and even some pruning on Serly's part (and still leaving much to be desired). As it now stands, the work, composed before Liszt was 24, is still immature enough to suggest that it is not likely to win general acceptance on its musical merits alone. But it is fascinating as a major example of one of the most Romantic Romantics in the making and, especially, of the three epochal, though very different and still unassimilated, impressions made upon Liszt in Paris by his first acquaintance with the playing and/or music of Paganini in 1831, Chopin in 1832, and Berlioz in 1832.[32]

Liszt sketched "Une Fantaisie (quasi sonate [,] après une lecture de Dante" in 1837 (during his least productive years as a composer), performed it for the first time in 1839, revised it in 1849,[33] and finally saw it published by Schott in 1858 as the seventh and last piece in his second set of *Années de pèlerinage*.[34] The last part of the title is said to have been taken from Victor Hugo's 32-line poem "Après une lecture de Dante." [35] There can be no doubt that Liszt had known Hugo personally and had warmly admired his works for nearly ten years;[36] nor, for that matter, that Liszt had taken a strong, Romantically oriented interest in Dante, thanks to the Countess d'Agoult,

---

the Mazurka in c♯ in Dec., 1832 (Leipzig), or even the first Paris ed. in Nov., 1833 (Brown/CHOPIN 60–61 and 24–25). A *terminus ad quem* might well be Liszt's departure from Paris for Switzerland in 1835. Liszt's 3 surviving sons. are nos. 461, 10b7, and 21 in Raabe/LISZT II and nos. 127, 161, and 178 in Searle's cat. for GROVE. The last 2 appear in Liszt/WERKE-m II/vi/96 and II/viii/103.

32. Cf. Ramann/LISZT I 161–75, 216–33, 185–92, 205–12; Haraszti/LISZT 36–37; Hedley/CHOPIN 48–51; "Liszt" & Waters/CHOPIN 5–16. Immediate by-products were Liszt's P transcriptions of works by Paganini and Berlioz (Searle nos. 420 and 470) as well as the son. under discussion.

33. Cf. LISZT-RAFF 286.

34. Cf. Raabe/LISZT II 246; Raff/RAFF 137 (on Schott as a procrastinative pub.). The title is given here as on the facs. of the title p. in Bory/LISZT 90; it usually is cited in reverse order ("Après . . . Fantaisie . . ."). The wording "Fantaisie quasi sonate" seems to have been a deliberate reversal of Beethoven's titles in Op. 27/1 and 2, much as with Weber's sons. as Spitta described them (ssB VIII). The endless variants of the title have even included "After a Lecture by Dante"! (as cited in Sitwell/LISZT 71 fn.). The autograph, with all of at least the 2d set of *Années*, is now in the Soviet Union, according to information from Professor J. Milstein, kindly relayed by Miss Erna F. Novikova of the State Gnesin Music-Pedagogical Institute in Moscow.

35. As (first?) suggested in Sitwell/LISZT 65–66 and repeated in Searle/LISZT 32 and Dale/NINETEENTH 90–91, but not in Grew/LISZT (an article that seeks to relate Liszt's work to the *Divine Comedy* in particular).

36. E.g., cf. Ramann/LISZT I 137; LISZT LETTERS 7, 8; Haraszti/Paris 10–11.

Delacroix, and others.[37] However, the conclusion here would be that he added the last part of the title later. If not, there would be good reason to question that he derived it at all from Hugo's poem. For the poem bears the date August 6, 1837, the collection in which it appears (*Les Voix intérieures,* no. 27) could not have been published until some time after that date in 1837, and Liszt was already sketching the "Dante Sonata" in October at Lake Como in Italy, well removed from Paris with the Countess d'Agoult.[38] The question is an interesting one, because if Hugo's poem did provide the inspiration for the "Dante Sonata" then we know at least that Liszt was describing either the sharp contrasts of the *Divine Comedy* or, less likely, Hugo's analogy between the afterlife and life on earth. Otherwise we cannot even be certain, as we can unequivocally with his "Dante Symphony" completed two decades later (Searle no. 109),[39] that the *Divine Comedy* was the Dante poem Liszt had in mind in 1837.[40] An anonymous, literal prose translation of the Hugo poem follows:

When the poet paints hell, he paints his own life.
His life, a fleeing shadow pursued by spectres;
A mysterious forest where his terrified feet
Wander, stumbling astray from the well-worn paths;
A dark journey, obstructed by strange encounters;
A spiral with vague boundaries and enormous depths,
Whose hideous circles go forever onward
Into a gloom where there moves the vague and living hell!
This stair is lost in the obscure mist;
At the base of each step a wretched figure sits,
And one sees pass by with a slight sound
White teeth grinding in the dark night.
One sees visions, dreams, illusions there;
The eyes that sorrow turns to bitter tears;
Love, as a couple embracing, sad and still ardent,
Who pass in a whirlwind with a wound in their sides;
In one corner, the impious sisters, vengeance and hunger,
Crouch side by side over a skull they have gnawed;
Then pale want, with her impoverished smile;
Ambition, pride nourished upon itself,
And shameless lust, and infamous avarice,
All the leaden cloaks with which the soul can be weighed down,
Farther on, cowardice, fear, and treason

37. Cf. Haraszti/LISZT 136.
38. Ramann/LISZT I 460; LISZT LETTERS I 20–21. "LISZT" SCHRIFTEN II 173–75 describes the couple's idyllic environment and reminders of Dante and his *Divine Comedy* at that time.
39. Cf. Ramann/LISZT II/2 17–22.
40. In 1849 Liszt did refer to his "Dante Son." parenthetically as "Prologomènes zu Dantes Göttlicher Comödie" (LISZT-RAFF 287).

Offering keys for sale and tasting poison;
And then, lower still in the very depths of the gulf,
The grimacing mask of suffering hatred!
Yes, that is life, O inspired poet!
And its murky way beset with barriers.
And, so that nothing may be lacking in this narrow path,
You show us forever standing to your right
The genius with the calm brow and radiant eyes,
Vergil unperturbed saying: "Let us go on."

Liszt played the "Dante Sonata" for the first time, in its original form, in Vienna during his sensationally successful concerts there in late 1839.[41] The particular recital seems to have been one of Liszt's innovational "musical soliloquies," given entirely by himself at the piano (ssb III).[42] Although the "Dante Sonata" has become increasingly popular in recent years, no further performance of this athletically difficult work turned up in the present study (nor reviews after its publication in 1858) prior to a London (memorial?) piano recital in 1887 played by Liszt's pupil Walter Bache.[43] Busoni, one of Liszt's most important successors and champions, is reported to have played the work with "crystalline and unforgettable purity" early in this century.[44] After Bache's recital, made up almost entirely of Liszt's works, the reviewer for *The Musical Times* wrote,

The most conspicuous of Liszt's works was a so-called Fantasia *quasi* Sonate, "Après une Lecture de Dante." This is a most extraordinary composition, of which it is absolutely impossible to form any idea at first hearing. Three themes were quoted in the programme, of which the first evidently represented the "Inferno," and the last the "Paradiso," but beyond this we could not trace any definite meaning in the constant progression of discords of which the piece is made up.

Bache seems not to have studied this work formally with Liszt,[45] but some specific identifications with the *Divine Comedy* would be confirmed if we could know that two passages from "Inferno" pencilled into Bache's score (which he purchased in 1883) were actually suggested by the master.[46] These consist of (1) a few lines from near the start of Canto iii ("Here sighs . . ." to ". . . sand that in the

41. Cf. Ramann/LISZT II/1 14 and 17 (preceded by accounts of Liszt's brilliant Vienna recitals of 1838, in I 484–500); also, Loesser/PIANOS 366–74, Schonberg/PIANISTS 151–71, Pleasants/HANSLICK 107–110, for the extremes of Liszt's successes as pianist. The "Dante Sonata" is reported merely as "Fragment nach Dante" in AMZ XLII (1840) 92.

42. Cf. LISZT LETTERS I 31–33; Loesser/PIANOS 368, 371; ssb III.

43. MT XXVIII (1886) 154; cf. MT CVIII (1967) 342.

44. Cernikoff/HUMOUR 91. Cf. BUSONI-Frau 50.

45. Cf. Bache/BACHE 309 and 312.

46. Discussed at length in Grew/LISZT.

whirlwind flies," in Cary's trans. of the *Divine Comedy*), inserted plausibly enough at the start of the second theme (ms. 35; see the chart in the next section of this chap.); (2) the first and last of the opening lines of Canto xxxiv (not xxxix! from *"Vexilla regis . . ."* to "The creature eminent in beauty once"), inserted equally plausibly at the return to the initial theme (ms. 115); (3) but also the last same lines inserted, much less plausibly, at the start of the third theme (ms. 103). Eva Mary Grew views that third theme, in broad whole-notes, as Liszt's setting of the first half of the *Tonus peregrinus*[47] and rationalizes what would be an incongruous reference to the psalm of deliverance as Liszt's subtle, parodic hint of blasphemy that yet promises salvation.[48] Programmatic associations certainly abound in Liszt's instrumental music—associations of mood, that is, rather than literalities[49]—but not such subtleties as Miss Grew suggests. Moreover, it is odd that those pencilled insertions come only from "Inferno" and make no better allowance, contrary to the "Dante Symphony" (with its "Purgatorio" and "Magnificat" sections) for the "Purgatorio" and "Paradiso" of the *Divine Comedy*. If our imaginations are to have free rein, we might well relate the transformations of the "infernal" second theme (as they start at mss. 124 and 151) to "Purgatorio," and the contrasting guises of the exalted third theme (as they start at mss. 103, 136, 203, and 309) to "Paradiso." The piano is felt by Searle (but not here) to be inadequate to the expressive range of this piece, with the "far clearer and more incisive" solution being something like Constant Lambert's transcription for piano and orchestra done for a Sadler's Wells ballet called "Dante Sonata." [50]

Except for having jotted down the theme of its "Adagio" in 1849,[51] Liszt wrote his Sonata in b in 1852–53, some five years after much of his public recitaling had ended and his residence in Weimar had begun with the Princess Carolyne von Sayn-Wittgenstein.[52] This work marked the end of much of his important writing for piano. As he himself remarked just after Breitkopf & Härtel published it in 1854, "I shall have done for the present with the piano, in order to devote myself

47. Cf. the ex. in GROVE VI 955. Pirro heard the related succession of major triads near the end (mss. 364–68), over a whole-step descent in the bass, as a reference (hardly exact!) to the opening of Palestrina's much Romanticized "Stabat Mater" (Haraszti/LISZT 32).

48. Grew/LISZT 37–39.

49. Cf. Ramann/LISZT I 196–202.

50. Searle/LISZT 32.

51. According to a letter received from Mr. Arthur Hedley of London, referring to an autograph notebook in his possession.

52. Cf. Ramann/LISZT II/1 178 and II/2 28–35.

exclusively to orchestral compositions. . . ." [53] Liszt gave the sonata its first performances, for private hearings as early as May, 1853, including the somewhat unsatisfactory meeting with Brahms the next month (ssb IX).[54] As evidence of his special regard for it, he is said to have played its expressive parts "with extreme pathos" and to have written "Für die Murlbibliothek" on the autograph,[55] meaning appropriate for his clique known as "The Society of Murls" and devoted to the advancement of the "New German" school against the Philistines.

Liszt dedicated his Sonata in b to Schumann in return for the latter's dedication of his great Fantasie in C, Op. 17, to Liszt fifteen years earlier (ssb VIII).[56] The two 19th-century masterpieces, which stand almost alone in the heat and inspiration of their full-bloomed Romanticisms, might well be illuminated by a comparative study. But the dedication caused some embarrassment to Robert and Clara, who, with Brahms, represented the opposition to the Liszt school and felt a growing antagonism toward Liszt himself as well as doubts regarding his sincerity.[57] Of course, Wagner, being on the Liszt side musically as well as politically,[58] was entirely disposed to enjoy the Sonata in b when Liszt's pupil Karl Klindworth played it to him in London the following year (probably at Liszt's own behest):[59]

The sonata is beautiful beyond all belief; huge, lovable, profound, and exalted,—stately, the way you are. I have been stirred to the depths [of my soul] by it, and all the misery of London is suddenly forgotten. More I shall not [attempt to] say to you right after the hearing; but I am as filled with what I [do] tell you as any man could be. . . . Klindworth amazed me by his playing; no lesser [pianist] would dare to play your work for me the first time. Truly, truly, he is of your calibre—that's wonderful!

Good night—many thanks for this pleasure at last revealed!

53. LISZT LETTERS 186–87.
54. Cf. MASON MEMORIES 123, 125, 129–30; LISZT/Marie 68.
55. MASON MEMORIES 159. In NOTES XXI (1963–64) 83–93, the autograph was listed among important works in the "ROLF archives" to be made available in facs. under restricted conditions. Since then the MS has been withdrawn from public view. One only hopes it "surfaces" again soon and does become available for inspection.
56. Cf. LISZT LETTERS I 33 (1839, to Schumann) and 308 (1854, to Wasielewski); Ramann/LISZT II/1 72–74; ssb Frontispiece.
57. Cf. Kalbeck/BRAHMS I/1 85. Brahms referred to Liszt's Son. in b slightingly (SCHUMANN-BRAHMS I 19 [1854]).
58. Further mention of his relation to Liszt occurs in the discussion of his own sons. later in this chap.
59. Trans. from WAGNER-LISZT 69 (cf. pp. 58, 60, 63, 65); cf., also, LISZT LETTERS I 194.

The pianist, pedagogue, and writer Louis Köhler (ssʙ XVIII), to whom Liszt had sent his Sonata in b soon after publication,[60] wrote a long, early review as enthusiastic and nonspecific as Wagner's letter.[61] He started by declaring that the work would stand comparison with the best sonatas of all time, although only music lovers in tune with and equal to the spirit of the current times would appreciate it.

The idea has spread only too widely [that] even as a composer Liszt is merely a virtuoso, to the extent that he composes purely in the sense of a glorification of execution, but not [by] applying the same to the service of a higher ideal. The fact that strange themes lie at the basis of many of his works, as also that a considerable technical capability is required for their performance, appears to be at the root of a superstition that already would be contradicted simply by the original manner, by the how in the manipulation of those strange themes.[62]

Köhler accepted "sonata" as a title for this free work although its form (to be discussed shortly) was more than he could fathom, so that he had to end by saying,

I feel I probably have spoken a lot and said nothing. I confess what concerned me actually was only an unburdening of my heart, which overflows from the fresh impression of this sonata.

A very different review greeted Liszt's Sonata in b when Bülow, who had moved to Weimar to study with Liszt in 1851,[63] played it for the first time in public in Berlin in early 1857. From the public's standpoint the work immediately "took fire." [64] But Gustav Engel, reviewer for the *Spener'sche Zeitung*, noting its "very long" one-movement form and the revealing character of its opening theme, wrote among other "impersonal" observations,[65]

The structure rests on harmonic and rhythmic extravagances that no longer have anything to do with beauty; even the first theme is to be condemned as decidedly inartistic; yet, what faces us in the course of the development is surely much worse. Often it becomes impossible to speak of intelligent harmonic unity; we are expected to take pleasure in the arbitrary juxtaposition of keys; the melodies, which appear here and there, have such an affected character that all attractiveness is ruled out; [etc.]

Only the manifold transformation of piano figurations and Bülow's

60. ʟɪszᴛ ʟᴇᴛᴛᴇʀs I 186.
61. ɴzᴍ XLI (1854) 70–72.
62. In the unequalled firsthand description of Liszt as teacher and person in Fay/ɢᴇʀᴍᴀɴʏ 205–75, a similar protest and defense can be found (pp. 236–37) with regard to his prevailing reputation only as a virtuoso.
63. ʙüʟow ʙʀɪᴇғᴇ I 343.
64. ʙüʟow ʙʀɪᴇғᴇ IV 63–64. Cf. Raabe/ʟɪszᴛ II 250. Bülow became Liszt's son-in-law in the same year (1857).
65. Trans. from the complete transcript in ʙüʟow ʙʀɪᴇғᴇ IV 58, 65–66.

performance were approved by the reviewer. Bülow answered with a letter vigorously protesting the unfair judgment based on one hearing (not true, replied the reviewer) and reminiscent of the treatment Wagner got, and he kept the issue alive in letters to others.[66] In 1859 Liszt himself referred to A. H. Dietrich's playing of the "Invitation to Hissing and Stamping," "as [the critic Otto] Gumprecht designates that work of ill odour—my Sonata." [67] And it is not too surprising to find this music getting at least as hostile a reception from both Hanslick in 1881 (when Bülow played in Vienna) and *The Musical Times* critic in 1882 (in an earlier London recital by the same Walter Bache, *supra*).[68] Yet its performances multiplied steadily from the time of its publication and it became increasingly popular wherever there were performers equal to its physical and architectural difficulties and to the sufficient projection of its wide-ranging, freighted emotional content.[69]

Liszt's Styles and Forms

Liszt's three extant sonatas advance conspicuously from one to the next in their styles and forms. The violin sonata reaches toward the future boldly but naively and ineptly, with still some dependence on the traditional four-movement cycle and its individual forms. The "Dante Sonata" evinces much more control over its new resources and presents them in a free, apparently intuitive form in one movement. And the Sonata in b shows the mature master in complete and, apparently, fully conscious control of both styles and forms as he contrives a free form that is at once a one-movement "sonata form" and a four-movement sonata cycle. The three sonatas call for individual discussions in more detail.

The four movements of Liszt's "Duo (Sonate)" are all, tiresomely enough, in c♯. Furthermore, all of them begin (and iii ends) on the dominant of that key. The opening "Moderato" bows to "sonata form" only to the extent of contrasting sections, of developmental passages like the fugato starting in b♭ (mss. 65–90), and of the return to the

66. BÜLOW BRIEFE IV 66–68, 73, 74–75, 87; cf., also, pp. 366, 368–69.

67. LISZT LETTERS I 389.

68. Slonimsky/LEXICON 116 (the deleted passage may be seen in Kapp/LISZT 506); MT XXIII (1882) 663–64.

69. For a few of numerous other 19th-c. performances of Liszt's Son. in b, cf. BÜLOW BRIEFE IV 279 and 362 (Berlin, 1860); Müller-Reuter/LEXIKON 424–25 (Bülow in Leipzig, 1860); LISZT/Marie 138 (Vienna, 1869); NZM LXXII/1 18 (Rome, 1875); MT XXII (1881) 138–39 (London, 1881); MASON MEMORIES 270 (both Arthur Friedheim and Richard Burmeister, New York, about 1900); Friedheim/LISZT 5, 136, 139, 140, 141, 181, 188, 199, 213, 243, 311–12, 319; BUSONI-Frau 186, 200.

introductory idea in the tonic key, near the end (mss. 170–82). The
second movement, called "Tema con Variazioni," actually consists of
one continuous, extended, fantasy variation. The third, "Allegretto,"
has the requisite dance rhythms and harmonic caprice, if not quite
the tightly closed form, to qualify as a 19th-century scherzo movement.
And the finale, "Allegro con brio," might qualify similarly as a rondo.
The prime fact about this cycle is its derivation of all thematic material—indeed, its utter, unabashed derivation, *ad taedium*—from
Chopin's Mazurka in the same key, Op. 6/2. At best only an average,
unpretentious example of Chopin's art, this Mazurka presents an introduction that merely embellishes a dominant drone, followed by
three thematic periods, all in c♯ except for the "C" theme on the
mediant harmony. These elements are disposed as follows:

In-||:A:||:BA:||C-In-||:A:||.

If Chopin really did complain about Liszt's borrowings from his
music, as he is made to do so grossly and untypically in the fraudulent
letters to Delfina Potocka,[70] then he surely must have had in mind
more subtle derivations than those throughout this sonata. In this instance, Liszt used any and all of the Mazurka themes at random, sometimes intact and complete with Chopin's accompaniment. Thus, his
first movement opens with Chopin's introduction almost note for note
(mss. 1–10), then treats the "A" theme improvisatorily (mss. 11–40),
cadencing on a return to the introduction in the subtonic key (B) plus
another reference to "A" (mss. 41–52). The introduction and return to
"A" recur, "poco tranquillo" and altered, in D (mss. 53–64), followed
by that fugato on "A" in b♭ (mss. 69–90), next an episode freely derived from "B" (mss. 90–137), then a section based on "C" (mss. 137–
51), another derived from "B" (mss. 152–60), another from "C" (mss.
160–69), and finally the return to the introduction. The "Tema" of
the second movement is no less than the complete Mazurka minus the
introduction and last return, arranged simply for violin and piano.
The fantasy variation takes up the several themes at random again.
More of the same occurs in the other two movements, with even the
abstracted version of "C" in the finale (mss. 35–60) providing no satisfactory escape from the source themes. The monotony is compounded
by the lack of potential development in these light dance themes, at
least as they revealed themselves to the young Liszt.

The most significant musical traits in Liszt's violin sonata are its

70. E.g., cf. pp. 180–81 in *The Life and Death of Chopin* by C. Wierzynski (New
York, 1949). On those letters, cf. Sydow & Hedley/CHOPIN 377–87. Warm thanks are
owing to Mr. Arthur Hedley of London for further information by correspondence.

advanced technical figuration and its experimental harmony and tonality. Even in this early work scarcely a trace remains of Liszt's Vienna background, whether it be the formal instruction he got from Czerny and Salieri or the inspiration he found, above all, in the music of Beethoven, Schubert, and Weber.[71] One would have to observe that the new technical figurations pose unreasonable difficulties, especially for the piano that Liszt already knew so well. Unreasonable difficulties were characteristic, too, of the early writing of Weber, Schumann, Brahms, Alkan, and even Mendelssohn, before these men refined their styles (but not of Beethoven, whose trend in technical requirements was much the opposite). Also, one would have to recall that Liszt's experiments with harmony and tonality at this point, as with uncontrolled musical forms, showed him to be striking out boldly but blindly. To repeat what a critic was still to observe in 1840, ". . . the pianist has arrived, but the composer is perhaps delayed. . . ."[72] Yet, the technical figurations confirm the enormous influence of Chopin and Paganini on Liszt in the early 1830's (as in the obvious parallels with Chopin's Etudes in G♭ and E, Op. 10/5 and 3, in Ex. 44). And both the chromatic and enharmonic harmony and the wide-ranging tonality (as throughout iii) suggest the impression made by Berlioz' *Symphonie fantastique*, which Liszt was currently arranging for piano solo (Searle no. 470). Moreover, in all these traits we get remarkable previews of the Liszt to come. The piano's descending line in octaves near the start of the first movement naively anticipates the stentorian descents in both of the solo piano sonatas. The octaves and chords in the finale (as at mss. 102–8 and 147–62) point the way to many a bravura passage in these same sonatas (and in much other later piano music by Liszt). And the several areas of little or nothing but dom.- and dim.-7th harmonies (as in i/90–126) already create periods of amorphous tonality that were eventually to take Liszt to the very brink of atonality.

Liszt's "Dante Sonata" reveals major strides beyond the violin sonata toward the full control of styles and forms. The three main melodic ideas, however they might bear on Dante (*supra*), are now essentially Liszt's own and are germinant enough to lend themselves to Liszt's development and transformations of them. The piano figurations, harmony, and modulations all show considerably greater assurance and reason in their handling. And the form, if it does not show the same (conscious?) reason, *has* reason, especially in its stunning contrasts and the heights and depths of its climax structure. Liszt himself objected to standardized methods and structural formulas. In a letter to Louis

71. Cf. CZERNY 314–16; MGG VIII 965–66; LISZT LETTERS II 161, 164.
72. As trans. in "Liszt" & Waters/CHOPIN 10.

Ex. 44. From the second movement of Franz Liszt's "Duo (Sonate)" for Vn & P (after Serly/LISZT-m 29, used with the kind permission of, and copyrighted in 1957 and 1964 by, Southern Music Publishing Co.).

Köhler, written July 9, 1856, just after the "Dante Symphony" was finished, Liszt remarked,[73]

. . . [My works] are for me the necessary developments of my inner experiences, which have brought me to the conviction that *invention* and *feeling* are not so entirely *evil* in Art. Certainly you very rightly observe that the *forms* (which are too often changed by respectable people into *formulas*) "First Subject, Middle Subject, After Subject, etc., may very much grow into a habit, because they must be so thoroughly natural, primitive, and very easily intelligible." Without making the slightest objection to this opinion, I only beg for permission to be allowed to decide upon the forms by the contents, and even should this permission be withheld from me from the side of

73. As trans. in LISZT LETTERS I 273–74. Cf., also, Haraszti/LISZT 34–35.

the most commendable criticism, I shall none the less go on in my own modest way quite cheerfully. After all, in the end it comes principally to this—*what* the ideas are, and *how* they are carried out and worked up—and that leads us always back to the *feeling* and *invention,* if we would not scramble and struggle in the rut of a mere trade.

Perhaps the reviewer's failure to discover the clear landmarks of "sonata form" helps to explain the puzzled review of the "Dante Sonata" cited earlier. If the one-movement work is not only a "Fantaisie quasi sonate" but a "Sonate quasi fantaisie," it is so in the most general sense of thematic pluralism, contrast, and development, and of tonal movement and opposition (mainly between the tonic, d/D, and the raised mediant, F♯). Perhaps the audible form of this free, sectional work can be clarified by visual means—that is, by a chart scaled to the measure numbers, showing themes, keys, tempo changes, and dynamic contrasts. "I," "II," and "III" refer to the variants as well as the original versions of the main themes. The repeated "xxx" after any of these indicates its extension or development. The arrow pointing to the same or a different key center means an area of tonal flux. The symbols for increase (+) and decrease (−) of tempo and dynamic level apply to passages of at least six measures.

By comparison with the "Dante Sonata," Liszt's Sonata in b reveals its consummate mastery of composition in several tangible ways, as well as in those intangible aspects of the *Gestalt* that exercise their influence subjectively even if they still resist codification. The melodic ideas are more significant in themselves, more fruitful for development, and more susceptible to plastic transformation (or thematic "metamorphosis," to use the term usually linked with Liszt).[74] And, indeed, we do find more actual development and more frequent and subtle transformations, the latter perhaps stimulated by Liszt's transcription of Schubert's "Wanderer Fantasia" a year or so earlier (Searle no. 366).[75] Even the passagework and figural accompaniments in the Sonata in b derive from the main ideas. Moreover, this writing now exploits the piano tone and technical idiom to their every best advantage. Yet, for all the difficulties it poses, the writing still stops short of virtuosity for its own sake or physical impracticalities. The harmony and tonality continue to look forward (as at the remarkable embellishment of the

74. Liszt may have been influenced not only by the choice of key (cf. Walker/ CHOPIN 251) but by the opening theme of Chopin's Sonata in b, Op. 58, from the finale of which Liszt copied and "revised" a page in his own hand (ssb XII). In *Music and Musicians* for Feb., 1963, p. 10, Arthur Hedley ("Chopin: A False Tradition?") takes a dim view of this "revision" by Liszt.

75. In the preface to his recent ed. of the latter (Vienna: Universal, 1965), Paul Badura-Skoda sees in it perhaps unwitting discovery of the double-function form about to be described here in Liszt's Son. in b.

Franz Liszt's "Dante Sonata"

Ms. nos.	10	20	30	40	50	60	70	80	90	100	110	120	130	140	150	160	170
Themes	I XXXXXX(II)		II		II		XXXXXXXXXXXX(I)			III	I	II	III		II		X
Keys		d					→f#			F#		→F#			→F		
Tempos	M	+	−+	−VF				+		F#		M	M M	−			S+++
Dynamics	f	ff,P > P			mf		ff	+		fff	ff	[PPP]	PP	P	PPP	P	ff

Ms. nos.	180	190	200	210	220	230	240	250	260	270	280	290	300	310	320	330	340	350	360	370	376
Themes	I	XXXXX		IIXXXXXIXXXXX			XXXXXXXXX	III,III		II	(I)	III	XXIII		XX	IIXX	IIXXX	IIXXX	IIXXXXXXXX(III,I)		
Keys								→B,G		→d		D	D			→D					
Tempos	F		++	+						−[S]		M	+F			VF	+	−		M	
Dynamics	PP	P	ff		fff	fff		fff		PP P	PPP	PPP	PP	fff	ff	ff	P	−	ff	fff	

dominant harmony in F♯, mss. 415–31, a page before the fugue in b♭),
at the same time achieving a new clarity, logic, and breadth. Above
all, Liszt seems to have gained conscious control of his form, and a
highly complex, innovative form, at that, lasting nearly twice as long
as the "Dante Sonata" in performance (29 as against 16 minutes in the
fine new recordings by Alfred Brendel, Vox PL 12–150).

The idea of "conscious control" is worth stressing, if only because the
fact of such control would bolster attempts at systematic analysis of
the Sonata in b. Obviously Liszt could no more have been unconscious
of the broad sectional interrelationships than of the ingenious thematic
transformations in this work. If circumstantial evidence is needed, he
gives it by his own explanation of similar relationships in his Piano
Concerto in E♭ (Searle no. 124), revised around this same time.[76] Furthermore, in spite of his objection to structural formulas, quoted earlier, Liszt apparently was receptive to analyses of his larger forms, including an analysis of the Sonata in b left with him in 1859 by Peter
Cornelius.[77] The chief problem Liszt gives to the music analysts is to
discover quite how he could have his cake and eat it, too—that is, how
he could so unify a four-movement cycle that at the same time its
separate movements interrelate like the components of one huge
"sonata form." Although his contemporaries (as quoted above) may
not have perceived this double function, many subsequent writers on
Liszt have at least hinted at it. But, as implied earlier—and curiously
enough in view of its wide renown—writers seem generally to have
preferred to discuss the Sonata in b only briefly, sketchily, or subjectively, rather than attempt to pin down the specific divisions that define the double function.[78] Perhaps these writers have regarded it as
too free for systematic analysis. The work does seem free in the sense
of being unconstrained by squareness or artificial symmetry. But it is
not free in the sense of being loose-jointed or aimless. From its smallest
to its largest elements, it shows every sign of much stylistic refinement
and much attention to tight structural relationships.[79]

Although there is hardly space for the needed detailed analysis here,
it should be possible, after first illustrating the main thematic ele-

76. Cf. LISZT LETTERS I 330–32.

77. Cited in LISZT LETTERS I 389, but not preserved in the published writings of
Cornelius.

78. E.g., cf. Searle/LISZT 59–61, Dale/NINETEENTH 92–94, and Cortot/INTERPRÉTATION
152–57, respectively. The "hermeneutic study" Schmitz/LISZT is brief and peripheral
only. Georgii/KLAVIERMUSIK 382–85 ventures somewhat more detail, though also
without any exact delimitations. Egert/LISZT 678–82 provides the most detailed
analysis of the "Son. form" but refers to the cycle only in more general terms and
without recognition of a "scherzando movement" in the fugue.

79. For more on Liszt's concern with form cf. Kapp/LISZT 120–21.

ments in Liszt's Sonata in b, at least to chart the course of this work (scaled, again, to ms. nos.) so as to provide a concurrent view of the restatements and interplay of these elements, the principal tonal, tempo, and metric changes, and, over all, the two structural functions or interpretations, one being the complete cycle and the other the single movement. As an essential adjunct to the chart, Ex. 45 illustrates at least the start of the five thematic elements—here labeled v, w, x, y, z—at the first occurrence of each (as keyed by its ms. no.). But

Ex. 45. Five thematic elements in Franz Liszt's Sonata in b as each first occurs (at the indicated ms. no.).

it shows none of the transformations of these elements, which abound especially in the recurrences of elements w and x. The accompanying chart uses abbreviations from the list at the start of this volume; also, M., T., S., and K. for main theme, transition, second theme, and closing theme; the arrow, again, for tonal flux; and the symbols v, w, x, y, and z, for the thematic elements and their transformations (with the horizontal spaces indicating thematic extension and the symbols w/x or x/w meaning the interplay of two elements). "Sonatina form" refers to "Sonata form" in which a simple retransition ("T.") replaces the development section. But, as always, one must recall the danger of making Procrustean beds out of such classifications (SCE 114–19).

Franz Liszt's Sonata in B Minor

Ms. nos.	25	50	75	100	125	150	175	200	225	250	275	300	325	350	375	400	425	450	475	500	525	550	575	600	625	650	675	700	725	750	760
One-mvt. "sonata form"	Exposition: M. T.		S.		K.							Coda			Development (sectional):			fugue (w/x)			M. T.		Recapitulation:	S. K.			Coda (return of all themes)				
Four-mvt. cycle	i (incomplete "sonata form"): M. T.	Exposition	S.		K.				Recapitulation T. M. K.			Coda||"A" "B"	ii (A-B-A slow mvt.):		T. "A"			iii (scherzando fugue) Coda||fugue		iv (finale: incomplete "sonata form"):	M. T.			S. K.			Coda (return of all cyclic themes)				
Main tempos and meters	¢, ¢		S/F		3 ¢ / 2								S / 3 4					F / ¢			(F) / (¢)			3 3 ¢ / 2			VF	F/S / 3 3 ¢	F / 2, 4	S	
Main tonal centers	→b				D				D	(B/b)			→F#					b♭			→b			B B			B				
Main thematic elements (see Ex. 45)	vw/x	vw	v	v	y	xx	wxw		wx		vwy	x/w z	x y	z			zv	w/x	w		w/xvw&w		xy	w		vw	vw	yz		xwv	

As the lowest rank of the chart suggests, Liszt assigns much of the responsibility for thematic interest and continuity to elements x and (especially) w. The presence of these elements might be heard even in such reductions as the steady repeated notes (suggesting x) that continue over elements v and y at measures 81 to 113, or the tender leaps down and up (suggesting w) during the unfolding "slow movement" (mss. 356–59). Element w represents a Lisztian melodic type that crops up in other of his works, too.[80] The descending scale that constitutes element v has a (pre-)Wagnerian quality (as in the "Treaty Motive" from the *Ring*) and has been traced to various Central European and Near Eastern cultures.[81] It serves mainly as an initiator and terminator of sections and, indeed, of the whole sonata. Elements y and z are relatively static, tending to repeat almost intact rather than germinate significant development or transformation. They unfold into extended melodies where a "second theme" for the "sonata form" and a main theme for the slow movement are needed. (The latter and its harmonization bring us close to César Franck for a moment.) All these distinctive thematic elements, along with their various transformations and rich harmonic supports (particularly when element y occurs), must be recognized as main factors in the remarkable individuality of Liszt's Sonata in b.

The double structural function in this work results largely from three innovations and makes three modest, corollarial compromises. One innovation is the construction of the entire, continuous "cycle" primarily out of the same thematic elements. Of course, the interrelating of some or all sonata movements by the use of the same or similar themes or incipits goes back as far as the origins of the sonata (SBE 78–79; SCE 138–40). But the innovation here is the nearly total dependence in all movements on the same basic set of contrasted ideas.[82] A second innovation is the construction of the sectional development in the "sonata form" out of the slow and scherzando movements of the "cycle," the latter being a rare instance of fugue in Liszt's piano music. And the third is to make the finale of the "cycle" out of the recapitulation of the exposition in the "sonata form." One compromise, then, is the fact that the finale has nothing thematically new to say, although changes in the figuration, harmony, tonality, and succession of ideas, plus the culmination and release in the coda that follows, all seem to satisfy this need for performers and listeners. In this connection it is

80. Cf. Searle/LISZT 57, 59, 78–79 ("Faust Symphony").

81. Cf. Gárdonyi/LISZT 95; Szelényi/LISZT 313–15.

82. Extremes like L. Berger's entire Son. Op. 18 on a single 6-note motive (SSB VIII) are not considered here. The effort in Egert/LISZT 674–75 to relate *all* of the thematic elements in Liszt's Son. in b to the first of them is strained and unconvincing.

Ex. 46. Franz Liszt's original ending for his Sonata in b (as first printed in Liszt/WERKE-m II/viii/vi).

worth noting how unsatisfying is the brilliant but perfunctory ending of 25 measures that Liszt originally wrote (Ex. 46) before crossing it out and replacing it with the ending of 50 measures (from "Andante sostenuto") that we now know. A second compromise might be seen in the two relatively stationary tonal centers, F♯ and b♭, instead of the expected modulations in the development section. Again a compensation may be found, this time in the considerable tonal flux throughout the rest of the sonata. And a third compromise might be seen in certain irregularities in the form types, such as the new theme (y) that opens the development section, or the shortened recapitulation of the "sonata form," or the start of that recapitulation at a point beyond where the exposition started, or the incomplete "sonatina forms" in the outer movements of the cycle. But these instances are compromises only in that Procrustean sense, none of them being irregularities outside of textbooks in the 19th century.

At the start of this discussion of Liszt, his Sonata in b was stated to be without significant precedent or consequent in solo piano music. There were significant successors, to be sure, in his own orchestral works and in a few later orchestral and chamber works by Richard Strauss, Sibelius, Schoenberg, and others.[83] But in piano music, the relatively few one-movement sonatas that preceded Liszt's, like those of Moscheles and Dussek, or succeeded it, like those of Scriabin and his closest followers, are single "sonata forms" and nothing more. To some extent Liszt anticipated his own form in the Sonata in b (and its w thematic element) when he wrote his less important *Grosses Konzertsolo* for piano in 1849 (?; Searle no. 176), which might even be called a preparatory study.[84] And we shall be coming to occasional direct imitations, including those of more or less forgotten students (F. Draeseke, R. Viole, and J. Reubke, all later in this chap.) and those of Dale and Liapunov (ssb XIV and XVIII). Cyril Scott not only adapted the form in his sonatas but wrote about it in 1917 as the "logical" way out for the sonata.[85] But these efforts bore no special fruit and can hardly be called "significant consequents" of a work so important and widely played as Liszt's Sonata in b.

Other Central German Composers (Wagner, Raff, Draeseke, Ritter, Hiller)

The great music dramatist **Richard Wagner** (1813–83) wrote at least five sonatas, all for one piano, during his lifetime.[86] These represent but a minute, purely incidental part of his enormous output of music, poetry, and prose, and of his enormous industry as composer, writer, conductor, and controversial man of the world. Four of the sonatas, including two that are lost, were student works all completed in Leipzig by his eighteenth year, and the other is a somewhat perfunctory piece written in 1853 during his exile in Zürich. On their musical merits these sonatas would justify no more than a brief, though respectful mention here. But as historical insights into the making and

83. Cf. Hans Engel's diagram of Liszt's *Les Préludes* in MGG VIII 983–84. Cf., also, Austin/20th 136, 214; LISZT-BARTÓK 1961, pp. 279–80 (Searle).

84. Cf. Searle/LISZT 57–58; Ramann/LISZT II/2 345–46. It is in Liszt/WERKE-m II/viii/47.

85. Scott/SUGGESTIONS. The same conclusion, in more flowery words, had been reached in 1903 in Schüz/SONATE. Cf., also, Shedlock/SONATA 218–20.

86. Much of the section on Wagner that follows appeared originally under the title "Wagner's Sonatas" in Boston University's *Studies in Romanticism* VII (1968) 129–39.

aesthetic views of one of the most influential musicians of all time—and of an author whose opinions on instrumental music are cited several times in the present volume—they justify a discussion sufficient at least to graze the more general subject of Wagner and Wagnerism.

Wagner follows Liszt appropriately here because, whatever their differences, their music and tastes in the "New German" school still had many points in common; because they still were each other's best male friends throughout much of their careers, including the period when each wrote his main sonata; and because they were frequently close geographically, too, as in 1849 when the "revolutionary" fled from Dresden to Liszt's haven in Weimar, or in 1853 when Liszt visited Wagner in Zürich.[87] The practical benefits of this relationship flowed almost exclusively in Wagner's direction. The musical benefits may have flowed both ways but are less easily decided. Of course, the musical superiority of Liszt's Sonata in b over Wagner's little one-movement *Album-Sonate* in A♭ is so manifest as to make any comparison absurd except for this question of influences.

Furthermore, there cannot be any question of influences either way so far as these sonatas themselves are concerned. Wagner did not hear Liszt's Sonata in b until he wrote his warm letter to Liszt about it in 1855 (as quoted under Liszt, *supra*); and Liszt, if he knew Wagner's *Album-Sonate* at all, could not have seen or heard it until he reached Zürich in July of 1853, about five months after he had finished his own sonata (Feb. 2, 1853, is the date on the autograph), but less than a month after Wagner finished his. It is true that Liszt had conducted and/or known important music of Wagner by 1852, including *Rienzi, The Flying Dutchman, Tannhäuser,* and *Lohengrin,* and that he did much of his most serious and large-scale composing from that year on. On the other hand he had completed no less significant a work than the "Dante Sonata" by 1839, before he knew Wagner or his music at all (granted that he had yet to make substantial revisions in this work). And it is much easier to find specific antecedents of Liszt's Sonata in b in his own "Dante Sonata" and *Grosses Konzertsolo* than in anything he might yet have known by Wagner. Conversely, much the same applies to Wagner's *Album-Sonate,* which relates more specifically to his own music, both previous and concurrent, than to anything he might have got from Liszt, including Liszt's magnificent use of the piano. Yet, had the chronology permitted, it would not be hard to believe

---

87. All these aspects of their friendship are richly, if not always completely or quite accurately documented in their extensive correspondence (WAGNER-LISZT). Much further light on the ins and outs of the relationship is given in Newman/WAGNER I 277–78, 348–49, 454–55, 494–95; II 191–217, 301, 382–87 (up to 1853).

that the influences could have flowed either way between these two sonatas. As far apart as they are in size, architecture, and technical requirements, they do share the general spirit and styles of the "New German" school, and of two composers who had long found a common interest, for example, in the music of Berlioz.[88]

The critical literature on Wagner, both strong and weak, is today almost incalculable in quantity, being considerably greater than that on any other figure in music history.[89] Here there is occasion to refer only to the standard major biographies and edition of his prose writings,[90] along with a few special aids (cited where they apply) and three studies that deal especially with the sonatas. These last include a descriptive article of 1904 on Wagner's piano works by the writer, pianist, and teacher Rudolf Breithaupt;[91] a twenty-page pamphlet of 1961 by granddaughter Friedelind Wagner, accompanying Bruce Hungerford's excellent recording of the extant "Complete Piano Works";[92] and a style study of 1963 on Wagner's student works, by the veteran Wagner specialist Otto Daube.[93]

We learn all we know about the two lost, earliest sonatas by Wagner from Wagner himself. By the age of sixteen (1829?), when he already had become absorbed in Beethoven, Mozart, Weber, and E. T. A. Hoffmann, "I had composed a first Sonata[,] in D minor."[94] And around the age of seventeen (?; 1830), when he had determined on a course of "serious musical study," he wrote, but later had "no clear recollection" of, "an Overture in C major (6/8 time) and a four-hand Sonata in B-flat major, which last I practiced with my sister Ottilie, and, since it pleased us both, arranged for orchestra. . . ."[95] One assumes this early music was conspicuously untutored, both because of the amusing stories of the time Wagner told on himself and because his first successful learning did not start until his brief but productive

88. Cf. Newman/WAGNER I 322–23, II 214 and 301, etc.

89. For example, it is about double that for Beethoven, Wagner's nearest competitor, in the *British Museum General Catalogue of Printed Books*, 263 vols. (London, 1961–66). In Cat. NYPL the important special Beethoven collections account for about as many books on Beethoven as Wagner.

90. WAGNER LEBEN, WAGNER PROSE (including "Autobiographic Sketch" in I 1–19). Newman/WAGNER. The many collections of his letters have yet to be brought together in a revised, up-to-date ed.

91. Breithaupt/WAGNER, with many exx.

92. Festival Masterclasses, Inc., LO8p (2 discs). Warm thanks are owing to Miss Wagner for letters contributing to the present discussion. Vox has also issued a recording of the complete piano works (VOX-2022 and SVOX-52022).

93. Daube/WAGNER, with many exx.

94. WAGNER LEBEN 37–45, especially pp. 44–45.

95. Trans. from WAGNER LEBEN 66.

half year at the age of eighteen (1831–32) under Theodor Weinlig.[96]

Wagner's earliest extant sonata is a solo *Sonate für das Pianoforte in B♭*, composed probably late in 1831, dedicated to Weinlig, and published at Weinlig's suggestion by Breitkopf & Härtel in the spring of 1832 (Ex. 47).[97] Wagner had chafed under Weinlig's contrapuntal discipline, including the laborious writing of "the most intricate" fugues and canons, and now, as he recalled,

In order to bring me, however, fully within his friendly, calming authority, he had requested a sonata [from me] at the same time, which I, as evidence of my friendship for him, was supposed to construct according to the most insipid harmonic and thematic principles, [and as] the model for which he recommended to me one of the most childlike Pleyel sonatas. Those who knew my but recently composed overtures [including an experimental piece whose public performance was a fiasco as related in WAGNER LEBEN 66–69] surely must have been astonished that I could bring myself to write this required sonata, which is still being circulated today in a new reprinting through an indiscretion of the Breitkopf und Härtel music firm. In order to reward me for my temperance [after recent liquor sprees, as related in WAGNER LEBEN 58–60], none other than Weinlich himself took pleasure in getting my sorry work into print through that [same] publishing firm. From now on he let me do as I pleased.[98]

96. WAGNER LEBEN 66–69, 66–68; WAGNER PROSE I 6–7; Newman/WAGNER I 76–78, 84–86.

97. A facs. of the title page is in Daube/WAGNER 133 and in Panofsky/WAGNER 11. The pub. reissued the "Menuetto" separately (PAZDÍREK XV 68). The printed ed. does not differ from the autograph in "The Burrell Collection" at Curtis Institute of Music (cf. Burk/WAGNER 453). There is no basis in the first ed. itself for occasional listings of this work as Op. 1 (or Wagner's Son. in A as Op. 2).

98. WAGNER LEBEN 71; Breitkopf & Härtel's reprint in 1862 (plate no. 10433) probably was issued to capitalize on Wagner's newly won fame (Newman/WAGNER I 86). The foregoing trans. may be compared with that in the "authorized translation" of 1931 (pp. 68–69; cf. WAGNER LEBEN in SSB Bibliography) as but an average sample of all too many trans. that have proved too loose or inaccurate for use here. (The German itself is incorrectly quoted in Daube/WAGNER 132–33.) The original German (in which "zu erstaunen" seems to be an error for "zu schreiben") reads as follows: "Um mich aber vollständig in seine freundlich beruhigende Gewalt zu bekommen, hatte er zu gleicher Zeit eine Sonate verlangt, welche ich, als Beweis meiner Freundschaft für ihn, auf den nüchternsten harmonischen und thematischen Verhältnissen aufbauen sollte, zu deren Modell er mir eine der kindlichsten *Pleyel*-schen Sonaten empfahl. Wer meine noch vor kurzem verfaßten Ouvertüren kannte, mußte gewiß erstaunt sein, daß ich es über mich vermochte, diese verlangte Sonate, wie sie gegenwärtig noch durch eine Indiskretion der Breitkopf- und Härtelschen Musikhandlung zum erneuten Abdruck befördert worden ist, zu erstaunen: um mich für meine Enthaltsamkeit zu belohnen, machte sich *Weinlich* nämlich die Freude, mein dürftiges Werk durch jene Verlagshandlung zum Druck zu befördern. Von nun an erlaubte er mir alles."

The "authorized translation" reads:

"In order to keep me strictly under his calming and friendly influence, he had at the same time given me a sonata to write which, as a proof of my friendship

Ex. 47. From the opening of Richard Wagner's Sonata in B♭ (facs. of the autograph in "The Burrell Collection" at Curtis Institute of Music in Philadelphia).

Earlier, in 1842 (?), Wagner had recalled the circumstances a bit differently: "At this epoch I first acquired an intimate love and knowledge
of Mozart. I composed a Sonata, in which I freed myself from all
buckram, and strove for a natural, unforced style of composition. This
extremely simple and modest work was published by Breitkopf und
Härtel." [99] Wagner told the Londoner Edward Dannreuther in 1877
that Weinlig's teaching procedure had been to have him follow the
number, the relative length, and even the character of the themes,
modulations, and sections in some model piece, usually by Mozart.[100]
In this instance it would be interesting to discover which of the many
Pleyel sonatas then in print (SCE 551) could have been the model.[101]

Heinrich Dorn, Schumann's onetime teacher (SSB VIII), described the
Sonata in B♭ as sterile and unpromising, and said Wagner had showed
it to him at the time of its writing,[102] but probably had in mind an
earlier piece, perhaps Wagner's four-hand Sonata in B♭.[103] Stephen
Heller probably did mean the solo Sonata in B♭ when he wrote to
Charles Hallé in 1874,[104]

Wagner's sonata is idiotic. One is all the more astonished at the immense
transformation of the man. When can he have written this frippery? One
would say that he had not yet known, I won't say Beethoven, but not even
one sonata by Hummel, Dussek, nor even Kalkbrenner, who has produced
fine examples of this type. At least, this last knew his piano.

The solo Sonata in B♭ is a competent work, showing a more solid
grounding than is popularly credited to Wagner. It is carefully worked
out, surprisingly deliberate in its pace for a young man so full of
passions, ambitions, and hectic experiences, and not without some
strengths in its ideas, development, and structures. Its four movements
(F-S-Mi-VF) indicate that Wagner knew very well what was expected
in each. But this work does suggest Classic models and reveals none

for him, I had to build up on strictly harmonic and thematic lines, for which he
recommended me a very early and childlike sonata by Pleyel as a model.

"Those who had only recently heard my Overture must, indeed, have wondered
how I ever wrote this sonata, which has been published through the indiscretion
of Messrs. Breitkopf and Härtel (to reward me for my abstemiousness Weinlich
induced them to publish this poor composition). From that moment he gave me a
free hand."

99. As trans. in WAGNER PROSE I 7; cf. Daube/WAGNER 133 for the German.

100. GROVE, first ed., IV 347.

101. Dr. Rita Benton at the University of Iowa, currently (as of 1967) working
on a study of Pleyel, kindly looked for such a model throughout her large collection of Pleyel materials but found none that could have served literally and
consistently.

102. Ellis/WAGNER IV 451–53; cf., also, I 124–26. For further discussions of this
work cf. Breithaupt/WAGNER 114–17; Daube/WAGNER 132–38.

103. Cf. Newman/WAGNER I 76–77.

104. HALLÉ 300.

of the anticipations of his future styles that are to be found in the work
he himself mentions next, and with considerable pride,[105] which is
his much more interesting, multisectional "Phantasie fürs Klavier in
fis-moll" (or "Fantasie für das Pianoforte" in the autograph).[106]

Curiously, not until forty-five years later did Wagner or any of his
contemporaries leave any reference to his other early extant sonata,
"Grosse Sonate für Klavier" in A. Then he expressed interest in seeing
it again but not in having it published, after Cosima's efforts led to
the return of the autograph to him.[107] Also reported to be composed
in late 1831, this work was first described by Breithaupt, who saw it
as a "middle stage" in Wagner's piano development and "much less
interesting and attractive than the Phantasie." [108] But it was not
printed until Daube supervised its publication by Hans Gerig of Köln
in 1960.[109] Like Sonata in B♭ (totaling 848 mss.), Sonata in A (totaling
746 mss.) is a full-scale work in four movements, although its third
movement consists of an introduction and a free forty-measure fugue[110]
rather than a minuet and trio. Both works by the future master of the
leitmotiv concentrate tightly on single motives. But whereas Sonata in
B♭ exhibits a veiled relationship between (only) its two inner movements that may well have been fortuitous, Sonata in A exhibits a more
obvious relationship, marked by a repeated-note motive stated clearly
enough at or near the start of all four movements to leave no doubt
of its premeditated use. Sonata in A still makes some use of murky,
Alberti, and other more elementary bass types. Otherwise, if it also had
a model it must have been not anything by Mozart or Pleyel but one
of Beethoven's later works—or rather any of Beethoven's later works,
for with Weinlig's carte blanche to compose as he pleased, Wagner was
not likely to restrict himself to matching one model. The ideas and
styles of both the introduction and the fugue,[111] for example, recall

105. WAGNER LEBEN 71–72.

106. Cf. Breithaupt/WAGNER 120–26; Daube/WAGNER 149–68, with many exx. and
facs. of 3 pp. in the autograph.

107. As documented in some detail on pp. 2 and 3 of Friedelind Wagner's (un-
paginated) pamphlet cited earlier.

108. Breithaupt/WAGNER 113, 126–30. Breithaupt seems to have been unaware of
the fugal third movement.

109. A complete photograph of this ed., reduced in size, appears in Daube/
WAGNER 230–57, with discussion 140–48.

110. Cf. Daube/WAGNER 144–47, with extracts from Weinlig's "Anleitung zur
Fuge."

111. The fugue may or may not have been written before Weinlig's farewell
prediction that Wagner "probably never will write [any more] fugues and canons"
(WAGNER LEBEN 70). This prediction gives at least tentative circumstantial evidence
for dating Sonata in A around the end of 1831.

those in the finale of Beethoven's Op. 101 in A, whereas those of the first two movements recall passages in the first movement of the "*Eroica* Symphony" and the slow movement of Op. 106 in B♭, respectively. Only the finale, in its brilliant, more coarsely melodious manner, seems to give any foretaste of the Wagner to come—of *Rienzi,* in particular, nearly ten years later. For the rest, Sonata in A reveals new character and drive but does not have the recitative, the free sections, the sinister use of the "chalumeau" register, the clipped rhythms that open "Siegfried's Funeral March," or the abundant chromaticism that are all anticipated in the "Phantasie" in f♯.

As indicated above, Wagner wrote his *Album-Sonate* in A♭ nearly twenty-two years later, while he was a political exile in Zürich.[112] Its fuller title, "Eine Sonate für das Album von Frau M. W.[,] componirt im Jahre 1853," appears on the cover of the first edition, published with an improved coda in 1878 and after characteristic financial pressures had forced Wagner to sell the work to Schott in 1877.[113] This title reminds us that Wagner wrote the sonata and presented it to Mathilde Wesendonk as his "first composition since the completion of *Lohengrin* (6 years ago!)" and as an apparently unsolicited way of discharging one of his numerous recent debts to her generous, tolerant husband Otto.[114] In spite of the growing attachment between her and Wagner, Mathilde was able to write a warm, grateful letter to his wife Minna, rejoicing in "the glorious work" even though Mathilde was "capable of reproducing only the slightest shadow of it" by her own playing.[115] She was puzzled by the inscription on the first page of music in the autograph (only; cf. Ex. 48 below), "Wisst Ihr wie das wird?" ("Do you know what will come of it?"), which enigmatic phrase could have referred to anything from concern over his slowed down com-

112. A facs. of the title page of the autograph appears in Panofsky/WAGNER 49.
113. Plate no. 22431. Cf. Ellis/WAGNER IV 450; Newman/WAGNER IV 610. Schott pub. E. Singer's transcription for Vn & orchestra in the same year (HOFMEISTER 1878, p. 311) and K. Müller-Berghaus's orchestral transcription of the piece within 2 years (HOFMEISTER VIII [1874–79] 605). English sources often erroneously refer to this work as being in E♭ instead of A♭, as in Newman/MAN 454 and GROVE IX 123 (P. M. Young). Was the "Skizze zu einer Sonate f. Pfte." listed in 1877 (HOFMEISTER 1877, p. 280) simply a preliminary announcement by Schott of the *Album-Sonate* (cf. fn. 117, *infra*)?
114. The transmittal letter to Otto, June 20, 1853, is in WAGNER-WESENDONK 4. Nearly 25 years later he explained the debt differently (in a letter in his curious French, quoted in Friedelind Wagner's pamphlet, p. 5, cited earlier): "Don't look for too many unmentionable motivations ["choses indicibles"] in the Album Sonata. I promised it to a young woman who was very kind to me, in return for a beautiful sofa cushion that she gave as a present to me."
115. July 4, 1853; trans. in Burk/WAGNER 362–63.

116a posing to hints of impending crisis in the Wagner-Wesendonk quadrangle.[116]

The Musical Times of London ended a short, pleasantly favorable review of Wagner's *Album-Sonate,* regarded there as more of a "sonatina," with the sentence, "No person hearing this unambitious trifle would believe that Herr Wagner is its composer; but everybody must feel that it is the holiday-work of an artist." [117] Today, the stamp of Wagner, however attenuated, seems unmistakable in this work, even though it fails to appear in his two early extant sonatas. But the reminders are less of *Das Rheingold,* nearing completion in 1853, than of *Tristan und Isolde,* still a few years off, as in the anticipations of main themes from both the "Love's Death" and "Prelude," respectively, in the first eight measures of the sonata (Ex. 48).[118] The sonata's one-movement form reveals nothing of the double function in Liszt's Sonata in b. However, contrary to earlier statements,[119] this work does acknowledge "sonata form," at least a chiastic "sonata form" in which the order of the recapitulation is reversed. In the exposition the first thematic group in A♭ leads to a second thematic group in the mediant, C (from ms. 39), followed by a closing idea in that key. The development (from ms. 75), vacillating between the tonic and submediant, f, rises to a climax (on a dim.-7th chord, mss. 136–44) in a sequential manner anticipating the lovers' reunions in both the second and third acts of *Tristan und Isolde.* After a cadence in c (mss. 149–51) the recapitulation begins (ms. 158) with the second thematic group, hovering around rather than in A♭ by means of Wagner's characteristic deceptive cadences, then proceeds to the closing theme, now mainly in the dominant, E♭ (from ms. 195). Only at this point does the first theme return, in the tonic (from ms. 206), after which a coda (from ms. 230), largely on a tonic pedal-point, completes the piece.

The piano writing in this work is not especially resourceful, but it lies and sounds well, especially for a disinterested and professed non-pianist like Wagner.[120] The strongest traits are the developments of

116. Cf. Ellis/WAGNER IV 448–50; Newman/WAGNER II 508–9, 524–27, *et passim.* WAGNER LEBEN avoids saying much at all about the Wesendonks and omits all mention of the *Album-Son.*

117. MT XIX (1878) 84; on p. 33 the new pub. from Schott had been announced as "a Sketch for a Pianoforte Sonata"; a performance of the work is cited in XXI (1880) 247. It is discussed in Ellis/WAGNER IV 448–50; Breithaupt/WAGNER 130–34; Newman/MAN 284.

118. Cf. Breithaupt/WAGNER 131 for other anticipations.

119. Ellis/WAGNER IV 448–50; Breithaupt/WAGNER 130.

120. ". . . in my whole life I have never learned to play the piano properly" (WAGNER PROSE I 4). But he played at the piano, nonetheless, including Beethoven sons. for Mathilde Wesendonk. Cf. Breithaupt/WAGNER 109–12; Daube/WAGNER 17.

Ex. 48. From the opening of Richard Wagner's *Album-Sonate* in A♭ (facs. of the autograph in the Wahnfried Archive at Bayreuth, kindly provided by Miss Friedelind Wagner).

ideas, in leitmotiv fashion, the sure control of modulations and tonal directions, the effortless, slick passing from one section to the next, and, in fact, the mastery of form as a whole. The music is at its weakest in its thematic ideas, particularly the second theme with its sentimental chromaticism. All these observations recall Ernest Newman's conclusion that for all his reputation as a music dramatist Wagner was an instrumental symphonist at heart, but that his dilemma in this regard was his inability to find inspiration without a poetic programme (which his *Album-Sonate* does lack).[121]

As a matter of curiosity, mention may be made here of two weak (incomplete?) sonatas for piano, dating from not before 1862, by the philosopher **Friederich Nietzsche** (1844–1900). Still in his youth, Nietzsche had yet to become the champion and ultimate opponent of Wagner. Recently an edition of his music was projected that was to include these sonatas.[122]

The once immensely popular composer (**Joseph**) **Joachim Raff** (1822–82) also fits in here most appropriately with Liszt. In fact, in Weimar from 1850 to 1856 Raff actually dedicated all his best efforts to Liszt—as friend, copyist, orchestrator, and secretary—after which he finally had to leave to preserve his own individuality.[123] Like Liszt and Wagner, Raff, too, became identified with the "New German" school, although his continual efforts to combine the best from the past made him increasingly Classic-minded in later years and contributed to his eventual reputation as an eclectic solitary among his contemporaries and but an epigone to his successors.[124] A largely self-taught composer born in Switzerland of a Swabian family, Raff made his first mark with a series of piano pieces that Breitkopf & Härtel started to publish in 1844 on Mendelssohn's recommendation.[125] By the end of his life, spent largely in Wiesbaden after the departure from Liszt, he had composed some 250 works, in virtually all instrumental and vocal categories, and almost as many more transcriptions of other composers' works. Eleven of the original works are sonatas or "sonatilles" pub-

121. Newman/ARTIST 265–84, *passim*. Cf., also, WAGNER PROSE VI 187–91. W. Cobbett writes at some length of a sympathetic but poorly informed view of chamber music on Wagner's part (Cobbett/CHAMBER II 562–63 and I 257).

122. This information comes from an unpub. article (as of 1964) on Nietzsche's music by Andrcs Briner at the University of Pennsylvania in Philadelphia. Cf., also, Love/NIETZSCHE 27; MGG IX 1521–26 (H. G. Hoke).

123. Cf. pp. 90–113 in Raff/RAFF, the chief account of the man and his music, by his daughter. Cf., also, Mendel/LEXIKON VIII 225–29.

124. Cf. MGG X 1863 (R. Sietz); MASON MEMORIES 133–34, 161–64.

125. Cf. Raff/RAFF 32–33.

lished between about 1850 and 1873, including 5 for P solo, 5 for P & Vn, and one for P & Vc,[126] as follows:

Grande Sonate in e♭, Op. 14, P. solo; composed in Zürich late in 1845 (Raff/RAFF 34) and first pub. by Breitkopf & Härtel not later than 1851 (HOFMEISTER I [1844–51] 148).

Trois Sonatilles, in a, G, and C, Op. 99, P solo; first pub. by J. Schuberth not later than 1880 (Altmann/KAMMERMUSIK 221).

Fantasie-Sonate in d, Op. 168, P solo; pub. by C. F. W. Siegel, 1872 (HOFMEISTER 1872, p. 137).

Grosse Sonate für Pianoforte & Violine in e, Op. 73, composed in Weimar by April, 1854 (cf. Raff/RAFF 137) and first pub. by J. Schuberth in 1859 (plate no. 2444); ded. to Ferdinand Laub.

Zweite grosse Sonate für Pianoforte und Violine in A, Op. 78, composed by 1858 (Mendel/LEXIKON VIII 228) and first pub. by J. Schuberth in 1861 (Müller-Reuter/LEXIKON 425); ded. to Joseph Hellmesberger.

Dritte grosse Sonate für Pianoforte und Violine in D, Op. 128, composed between 1860 and 1865 (before the Austro-Prussian War of 1866; Raff/RAFF 177–78) and first pub. by J. Schuberth in 1867 (HOFMEISTER 1867, p. 26); ded. to Ferdinand David.

Vierte grosse Sonate (chromatische Sonate in einem Satze) für Pianoforte und Violine in g, Op. 129; composed between 1866 and 1869 (Raff/RAFF 177–78) and first pub. by J. Schuberth in 1867 (plate no. 4301); ded. to Henri Vieuxtemps.

Fünfte grosse Sonate für Pianoforte und Violine in c, Op. 145; composed in 1869 and first pub. by J. Schuberth in 1869 (Müller-Reuter/LEXIKON 427); ded. to Hubert Léonard.

Sonate für Pianoforte und Violoncello in D, Op. 183; composed in 1873 and first pub. by C. F. W. Siegel in 1873 (Müller-Reuter/LEXIKON 427; Raff/RAFF 271).

Raff's sonatas suggest a comparison with Rheinberger's (*supra*), not only because both men were masters of their craft whose music has slipped into almost total oblivion but because this music seems to have slipped thus for similar reasons. Of the two men as musical personalities, Raff is the more compelling and excitable (Ex. 49). And he could be quite as original as Rheinberger, as in the changing meters of Op. 73/ii[127] or the one-movement design, starting with a recitative, in Op. 129. Yet Raff, too—to put it bluntly—had a like problem of being long-winded and, perhaps in a more uncritical sense than with Rheinberger, of not knowing when to stop.[128] And he, too, could write senti-

126. Cf. the full list in Raff/RAFF 267–86, which is chronological (but not dated) by categories and supersedes the index by A. Schäfer made in 1888 (cf. p. 267, fn.). Cf., also, PAZDÍREK XII 15–25; Cat. NYPL XXV 205.

127. Liszt's remarkable sightreading of this scherzando mvt. is described in MASON MEMORIES 142–44; cf., also, Cobbett/CHAMBER II 267 (W. Altmann).

128. Müller-Reuter/LEXIKON 424–27 gives durations from 16 minutes (Op. 129 in one mvt.) to 38 minutes (Op. 78) among the 6 string sons.

Ex. 49. From the second movement of Joachim Raff's Sonata in e♭, Op. 14 (after the Breitkopf & Härtel re-ed. of *ca.* 1880 at the Library of Congress).

mental as well as strong themes, again more indiscriminately than Rheinberger—as sentimental, in fact, but also as well constructed (e.g., the theme of the vars. in Op. 78/ii) as the little "Cavatina" in D, Op. 85/3 for Vn & P, which alone keeps today's performers aware that Raff ever lived.[129] In a shrewd series of analytic articles published in 1875, three English writers came to much the same conclusions about six of Raff's symphonies, then enjoying much recognition.[130] They thought highly of the composer's comprehensive skills, his musical individuality, his idiomatic instrumental writing,[131] his development techniques, and the suitability of his themes to such development, but similarly found him to be the uncritical victim of his own prolificity (occasioned partly by lifelong financial needs).[132] Perhaps what we assume to have been the more leisurely pace of the 19th-century musician helps to explain how in Raff's day such lengthy, discursive sonatas as he wrote could win more favor than disfavor in reviews, as well as many performances, near and far.[133] Pertinent here are

129. Cf. Raff/RAFF 159.

130. Prout *et al.*/RAFF, with many exx. and a table (p. 33) of comparative symphony lengths, increasing from Mozart to Raff.

131. In 1846 Liszt had begged Raff "only to make your works as playable as possible, and to avoid carefully the wretched, abominable, monstrous Liszt piano style" (LISZT-RAFF 116).

132. In 1878 Raff wrote Bülow he could not answer a question about Op. 145 (1869) because he had no copy on hand and never remembered anything but what he was composing currently (La Mara/MUSIKERBRIEFE II 318–19). Liszt had warned Raff of the dangers of such prolificity (LISZT-RAFF 116).

133. The peak of their popularity seems to have been reached in the 1870's (cf. Raff/RAFF 198–99). Early performances are cited in Müller-Reuter/LEXIKON 424–27. For samples of other performances while Raff was alive, cf. NZM CXXII/1 (1876) 92, 157, 215, (2), CXXII/2 (1876) 327, CXXIII/1 107, 140, 141, 212, 240, 274; MT

excerpts from W. W. Cobbett's nostalgic recollections of Raff, following a page by Wilhelm Altmann on three of Raff's violin sonatas:[134]

. . . I am an admirer, though not a worshipper, of Raff, whose reputation has always suffered through his deplorable lack of the faculty of self-criticism. He composed at rare intervals music which alternates between extreme brilliance and sentimental tenderness, but he also poured out incessantly masses of pot-boilers with which, unfortunately, his name is only too often associated. I would not willingly be without his sonatas for piano and violin; they are not severely classical, but they are delightfully written for the violin. (After all, we fiddlers must be allowed sometimes to revel in the purely violinistic element.) [Sarasate enjoyed Raff and played his music frequently] . . . whenever he introduced into his programmes such works as the sonatas, the suite, and the *Fée d'amour,* he was rapturously applauded by the public. [Raff was] . . . a master musician, with real insight into the inner life of the violin.

Two other men in Weimar and Liszt's circle may be noted here for sonatas now forgotten but not without musical merits. One was the virtuoso organist and theorist **Johann Gottlieb Töpfer** (1791–1870), who left at least two sonatas for organ, one for P solo, and one for P & Fl, all published between about 1840 and 1865.[135] The other was the virtuoso pianist and organist, and student of Liszt, **Alexander Winterberger** (1834–1914), who left a piano sonata as Op. 1 (1857?) and at least six piano sonatinas.[136]

Many of the sonatas or sonatinas not yet mentioned from Leipzig in the mid-Romantic Era were of the light pedagogic sort (ssb III), in several instances by men now remembered only as theorists. The influential if somewhat circumscribed theorist **Salomon Jadassohn** (1831–1902), who had studied piano with Liszt and responded warmly to Wagner's *Lohengrin* before settling in Leipzig,[137] left one sonata for P & Vn in g, Op. 5 (1857), and one for P solo in A, Op. 14 (1858?),

---

XVII (1876) 461 ("The second movement [of Op. 183], marked 'Vivace,' is a perfect gem."), XX (1879) 225, XXII (1880) 43; smz XVI (1876) 45, 48, 54. Among early reviews are dmz III (1862) 46 (objecting to the exhaustive extension of weak, unoriginal motives in Op. 78, except in the "Scherzo" mvt.), Hanslick/wien II 428–29 (1867; except for a similar reservation, general praise for Op. 78), mw I (1870) 6–7 (about the same for Op. 145), mw VI (1875) 552 (on specific pros and cons in Op. 183).

134. Cobbett/chamber II 267–68.

135. Cf. mgg XIII 450–52 (R. Sietz); pazdírek XIV 227; hofmeister *passim;* Mendel/lexikon X 204–7; nzm XXXVII (1852) 90–91 (qualified review of organ Son. in d) and LXXII/1 (1876) 166 (performance of same).

136. Cf. Mendel/lexikon XI 380; Riemann/lexikon II 2036 (with further bibliography); pazdírek XV 465–69; nzm XLVIII (1858) 39–40 (reviewing Op. 1 as betraying inexperience); mw XI (1880) 608–9 (reviewing the "instructive Sonatina" Op. 46 merely as being more difficult than its title suggests) and XXIV (1893) 419 (on more sonatinas for P, Op. 93, reviewed as simple but highly musical).

137. Cf. mgg VI 1647–51 (G. Feder).

among many published works.[138] Op. 5, in four movements (F-M-M-F), is reviewed at length as skillful, light, fluent, without warmth, sometimes trite (especially the finale), and consistent with Jadassohn's training in the environment of Mendelssohn and Hauptmann.[139] A widely known father and two lesser known sons in the Leipzig area— **Heinrich Wohlfahrt** (1797–1883), **Franz Wohlfahrt** (1833–84), and **Robert Wohlfahrt** (?–?) [140]—all left instructive sonatinas for piano solo or duet, and Franz left some for Vn & P, too.[141] Dating from the late 1850's to early 1880's, these works seem to have thrived in their day.[142]

Of a more serious nature were two sonatas by the erstwhile soldier **Franz von Holstein** (1826–78), who made his mark chiefly as an opera composer, poet, and music benefactor in Leipzig.[143] One is for P solo in c, Op. 28 (1871?), and the other for P & Vn in F, Op. 40 (1899, posthumous). Op. 28, in three movements (F-M-VF), was reviewed as showing skill and vitality, but with some passages that offer only technical display and others that sound more like the reduction of an orchestral work.[144] A Czech product of the Leipzig Conservatory, the teacher **Edmund Uhl** (1853–?), left an unpublished four-movement Sonata in F for P & Vn that achieved some success through performances,[145] and a published four-movement Sonata in G, Op. 5, for P & Vc, (1889; F-S-Sc-VF) that earned approval from reviewers for its musical solidity, freshness, and sonority, though not for a certain unoriginal conservatism.[146] Even the important pioneer musicologist and sometime Leipzig resident (**Karl Wilhelm Julius**) **Hugo Riemann** (1849–1919) contributed his bit, à la mode, to sonata literature as one facet of his all-embracing industry.[147] That "bit" includes a piano Sonata in G, Op. 5 (1872), a Sonata in b, Op. 11, for Vn & P (1875), and a Sonatina in G "without octave stretches," Op. 49, for P-duet (1887), as well as several other sonatinas.[148] We may also note that the

138. Cf. PAZDÍREK VIII 60–64.

139. NZM XLVI (1857) 274–75 (A. v. Dommer). Op. 14 is similarly but only briefly reviewed in NZM LI (1859) 135.

140. Mendel/LEXIKON XI 399–400; Schuberth/LEXIKON 638; BAKER 1809.

141. Cf. PAZDÍREK XV 503–11; Altmann/KAMMERMUSIK 174, 179, 232, 307.

142. Brief, typical reviews of Heinrich's sonatinas occur in NZM LVI (1862) 59 and LXI/2 (1865) 343; DM VIII/3 (1908–9) 365–66.

143. Cf. Riemann/LEXIKON I 776; PAZDÍREK VII 643–45.

144. MW III (1872) 118, 132–33. Op. 28 was played at a memorial concert for Holstein (MT XIX [1878] 502).

145. Cf. NZM LXXII/1 (1876) 244, LXXII/2 (1876) 291, LXXIII/1 (1877) 261; SMZ XVII (1877) 120.

146. Cf. NZM LXXXV/2 (1889) 593; SMW LIX (1889) 931; MW XX (1889) 575; NMZ XI/6 (1890) p. 1 of Beilage.

147. Cf. MGG XI 480–85 (H. C. Wolff).

148. Cf. PAZDÍREK XII 323–26; Egert/FRÜHROMANTIKER 159; Altmann/KAMMERMUSIK 223 and 304. The child Reger valued the sonatinas (Stein/REGER 9). Op. 49 is reviewed favorably in SMW LIX (1887) 931.

organist and theorist, **Ernst Friedrich Eduard Richter** (1808–79), another product of the Mendelssohn environment, left four published sonatas between 1861 and 1869, including two for P solo and one each for P & Vn and P & Vc.[149]

The once renowned pianist, director, and pedagogue, **Carl (Heinrich Carsten) Reinecke** (1824–1910) won the respect of Mendelssohn, Schumann, and Liszt, toured widely, and served in several other centers besides Leipzig.[150] His enormous list of publications includes at least four sonatas that were well known in their day—Op. 42 in a (not A) for P & Vc (1855), Op. 116 in e for P & Vn (1872), Op. 167 in e ("Undine") for Fl & P (1882),[151] Op. 179 in c for P left hand alone (1884?)[152]—along with others for organ[153] and for 2 P's, and about ten sets of sonatinas for P solo.[154] As a sample, Op. 167 is a large work in three movements (F-VF-M/VF), with a slower middle section in the second movement. The music is skillful, idiomatic, up-to-date harmonically without being experimental, weak in its melodic ideas, and, as the general consensus seems to be, unable to compete with that of Schumann and Brahms, which it often approximates.[155] Regarding Op. 116, one reviewer noted how the last two movements failed to "go" in spite of all the caloric Italian inscriptions.[156] Another who won the respect of Mendelssohn, Schumann, and Liszt, among others, was the organist **Theodor Kirchner** (1823–1903), whose charming music would receive more attention here had he contributed more to our topic than his five delicate, sensitive, Schumannesque sonatinas Op. 70 (1883?).[157]

In Dresden the fine organist **Gustav Merkel** (1827–85), a protégé at one time of both Friedrich Wieck and Schumann, left nine organ sonatas that put him in the 19th-century company of Mendelssohn,

149. Cf. PAZDÍREK XII 305–8; Altmann/KAMMERMUSIK 223 and 262; MGG XI 451–52 (B. Stockmann); also, NZM LXXII/2 (1876) 510 for a performance of P Son. in E♭, Op. 33.

150. Cf. MGG XI 187–92 (R. Sietz), with further bibliography.

151. Reviewed fancifully at length as a programme son. in MUSIC IV (1893) 151–59 (E. V. Eastman).

152. Mod. ed. of Op. 179/ii ("Andante"): Ruthardt/LINKE-m 28. Cf. NMZ XVIII (1885) Beilage 2, p. 2, on Op. 179.

153. Cf. the review of Op. 284 in DM IX/1 (1909–10) 122 (E. S. v. Carolsfeld).

154. Cf. PAZDÍREK XII 135–59. A typically favorable review is in MW IX (1878) 639. Bibliographic details on 5 duo sons. are given in Müller-Reuter/LEXIKON 544–46.

155. Cf. the evaluations of Reinecke in Cobbett/CHAMBER II 286–87 (W. Altmann) and MGG XI 190–91.

156. NZM LXIX (1873), 50. Sample performances of Op. 116 are listed in NZM LXXII/1 (1875) 92, 156, and 211, all in Leipzig. Exx. from Op. 116 are included in Shand/VIOLIN 30–32. One of Reinecke's best and last sons., Op. 238 in G for P & Vc (cf. SMW LVI [1898] 321–22) seems not to have circulated widely.

157. Cf. MGG VII 943–47 (R. Sietz); DM VI/1 (1906–7) 115 (A. Göttmann). Mod. ed. of No. 3 in C: Frey/SONATINA-m 59.

Rheinberger, and Reubke, although they are rarely heard any more.[158] These sonatas (and some piano sonatinas by Merkel) were originally published between 1858 and 1886.[159] The first, Op. 30 in d, which alone is designated for "vier Händen und Doppel-Pedal," won its composer a prize when he first came to Dresden in 1858. Like most of their 19th-century companions, Merkel's organ sonatas take their starting point from J. S. Bach in their tendency toward contrapuntal forms and chorale treatment. And like these companion works, they make masterful use of the Romantic organ, yet show a decidedly more conservative harmonic style than that in the contemporary sonatas for piano alone or in duos. All nine of Merkel's sonatas are in three movements. The first movement is essentially preludial at moderate to fast tempos. It may tend to approach "sonata form," although the second theme may not provide the traditional contrast and the development is likely to be imitative, or even fugal. In Sonata 6, the first movement concentrates on the chorale melody "Aus tiefer Noth." [160] The middle movement, in slow to moderate tempos, is likely to be a spun out, free discourse, often between two ideas in aria style. And the finale, in moderate fast tempos, is an introduction and massive fugue (as in Son. 2), a contrapuntally imitative piece (as in Son. 9), or an introduction and "Passacaglia" (in Bach's sense; Son. 8).[161] Three other worthwhile organ sonatas were composed by **Karl Müller-Hartung** (1834–1908), presumably after he left Dresden in 1859 for Eisenach;[162] they were published in 1864. In a detailed, laudatory review they are described as cyclic chorale fantasias, with up-to-date harmony, brilliant use of the instrument, and a virtuoso command of imitative and fugal counterpoint.[163]

The most prominent Dresden composer at this time was the theorist and the champion of the "New German" school, **Felix Draeseke** (1835–1913).[164] Draeseke was close to Bülow as well as to Liszt and Wagner, and a pupil of Mendelssohn's friend and editor Julius Rietz (ssb VIII). Draeseke's sonatas (and their pub. years) include Op. 6 in c♯/E for P solo (1870; ded. to Bülow);[165] Op. 38 in B♭ for Cl & P (1888); Op.

158. Cf. mgg IX 126–27 (K.-E. Bergunder), with further bibliography.

159. Individual titles, keys, and dates are listed in Cat. nypl XIX 86. Novello pub. at least the first 7 in a set (mt XXI [1880] 421).

160. Mod. ed.: Edition Peters H38.

161. Cf., also, Frotscher/orgelspiel II 1173–74.

162. Cf. Mendel/lexikon VII 194; Riemann/lexikon II 1227.

163. nzm LX/2 (1864) 285–86. Cf., also, Frotscher/orgelspiel II 1209.

164. Cf. mgg III 728–34 (H. Stephani), with further bibliography and a dated list of works. The only extended study is the recent diss., Krueck/draeseke, on his symphonies (including biographical orientation).

165. hofmeister XIX (1870) 59.

51 in D for Vc & P (1892);[166] and two for Hermann Ritter's short-lived, large viola alta (ssb V) and P, of which one, (Op. 56?) in c, was composed in 1892 and first published posthumously and privately by the onetime Draeseke Gesellschaft in 1935,[167] and the other, in F, was composed in 1901–2 but remains in MS.[168]

Composed between 1862 and 1867, Op. 6, *Sonata quasi fantasia,* is the remarkable inauguration of Draeseke's five sonatas, revealing the fiery though not wholly co-ordinated impetuosity of the young musical radical.[169] In the first of its three movements, "Introduzione e Marcia funebre," the "Marcia" follows the virtuosic and rhythmic abandon of the introduction with a clear enough ternary design (A-B-A-coda). The second movement, "Intermezzo (Valse-Scherzo)," in D♭, has the swing of the waltz, the speed ("Presto"), light texture, and friskiness of the scherzo, and the frequent returns to the main idea of a rondo. And the long finale, "Allegro con brio," begins as the first movement does and never quite gets away from that movement because its other ideas relate to it, too, and because it continues throughout as a fantasy. Although the broad tonal directions, including the turn to E in the finale, border on the oversimple in this work, there is considerable harmonic and chromatic indirection, including flitting in and out of the key in a manner pointing to Richard Strauss a generation later (Ex. 50). Draeseke's sonorous, expansive, advanced piano writing and his occasional sweet lyricism (as in the B section of the "Marcia") suggest the strong influence of Liszt. But the actual content, especially the quality of the main themes, falls somewhat short of the aims and promise in this music.

Another composer of the "New German" school under Liszt's influence, and a man who had studied with Moscheles and Hauptmann, and had known Brahms, was **Heinrich Schulz-Beuthen** (1838–1915), who left a "light" sonata, Op. 5/1, for P-duet (1874); "Three Piano Pieces: Cycle in Sonata Form," Op. 23, for P solo (1876); *Alhambra-Sonate* in f♯, Op. 34, for P solo (1883?); and "Heroische oder Akropolis Sonate" in c, for P solo (composed in 1878–84 but not pub.).[170] Char-

166. Reviewed as a deeply felt, structurally convincing work, in mw XXV (1894) 162.

167. Altmann/KAMMERMUSIK 247.

168. Müller-Reuter/LEXIKON 509–11 gives bibliographic details about the duo sons. Among the few reviews (or mentions of performances) discovered here are NZM XCIX (1903) 77 (on the fiery spirit and difficulty of Op. 6), smw XLVIII (1888) 42 (on the charm and individuality of Op. 38), and smw LII (1892) 818 (on the difficulty and unequal quality of Op. 51). A full study of Draeseke's sons. should be rewarding.

169. It is compared with J. Reubke's Son. in b♭ in Georgii/KLAVIERMUSIK 422.

170. Cf. pp. 25, 67–68 and 79–80 in Zosel/SCHULZ-BEUTHEN (a short diss. on the man and his works; but on p. 67 the "Symphonic Concerto" for P & orchestra should

Ex. 50. From the second movement of Felix Draeseke's Sonata in c♯/E, Op. 6 (after the original Rózsavölgyi ed. at the Library of Congress).

acteristic of Schulz-Beuthen's music, the last two have programmatic inscriptions, although only Op. 34, regarded as one of his best works, departs from standard sonata forms to depict its programme. This "sonata" has six movements, perhaps better called scenes, in the distantly related keys of F♯, B♭, F♯, C/E♭, E, F♯, and with the subtitles "On the Way to the Alhambra," "Procession by the Church of Our Lady," "Entrance into the Alhambra," "The Abencerrages [family of Moors] (Tournament)," "In the Garden Xeneralife [summer palace] (Love Scene)," and "Retrospections." The trills and other rich ornamentation, the fantasy style, the free rhythms, and the full active texture suggest, especially in the first and fifth movements, that the composer successfully achieved the goal stated in his "preface to this 'Fantasie-Sonate' "—to capture the feel, style, and atmosphere of Arabian music without actually quoting specific themes. The music also depicts the subject matter of its titles, especially the massacre at the end of the fourth movement. Today it sounds like a more developed, refined, genuine, and ingenuous version of *In a Persian Market* by "Albert W. Ketèlbey."

Somewhat less significant though not uninteresting are the three published sonatas of Draeseke's younger but more conservative contemporary in Dresden, the highly rated pianist, teacher and director **Jean Louis Nicodé** (1853–1919).[171] One of these is Op. 19 in f for P solo (pub. in 1879) and the other two are Opp. 23 in b and 25 in G for

---

not be grouped with the solo sons.); MGG XII 254 (R. Sietz, with same error); MW XV (1884) 409–10 (detailed, enthusiastic review of Op. 34).

171. Cf. MGG IX 1445–46 (R. Sietz).

Vc & P (first pub. in 1890 and 1882, respectively).[172] All three sonatas are foretastes of the epigonic works we shall be finding often in every country throughout the last decades of the Romantic Era. The styles are derivative. The level of craftsmanship is high, including the knowing treatment of the instruments, which is always telling but reasonable; the command of harmony and counterpoint, which never advances beyond anything that might occur (more imaginatively) in Schumann; and the control of form in the standard three- and four-movement cycles, which now borders on formalism. As effective as the music sounds, and as effectively as it is put together, one finds it difficult to accept either Nicodé's lyrical melody or his impassioned development at face value.

Dresden had its share of "instructive sonatina" composers, too, among them two prolific piano teachers who held their own corner on the pedagogic market for a time. One of these last was **Fritz Spindler** (1817–1905), whose more than 400 opus numbers (about half of Czerny's output) included three sets of ten sonatinas each, a one-movement piano sonata or "sonata form" (Op. 83), and a horn sonata (Op. 347), among other such works published in the 1850's–1870's.[173] The other was **(Carl) Heinrich Döring** (1834–1916), who had trained at the Leipzig Conservatory and mainly in the 1870's left, along with much other music and some related publications, a considerable number of widely used sonatinas. These were reviewed repeatedly as pleasing, skillful, and pedagogically valuable when not too complex.[174]

Lastly among sonatas from Dresden, it would be interesting to see the three published for P solo between 1852 and 1857—Opp. 1 in E, 2 in f♯, and 5 in c (all pubs. of Breitkopf & Härtel)—by Schumann's onetime pupil **Karl Ritter** (1830–?). But these could not be found here. Indeed, nearly all we know about them, or, for that matter, about Ritter, who spent his later life in Venice, comes from Bülow's unusually long review of 1858 on these and two other publications by Ritter, the gist of which is that the young man showed real promise and would bear watching (as Schumann had written Hiller 9 years earlier, though with some misgivings as to Ritter's continued progress).[175] Bülow

---

172. Cf. Altmann/KAMMERMUSIK 261. Op. 25 is reviewed favorably in MMR XV (1875) 249.

173. Cf. Mendel/LEXIKON IX 373; Riemann/LEXIKON II 1738; PAZDÍREK XIII 892–904; NZM XLVI (1857) 253 (facetious review of Op. 83, by A. v. Dommer).

174. Cf. Mendel/LEXIKON III 195; Riemann/LEXIKON I 412; PAZDÍREK IV 302–7; MW VI (1875) 541, VII (1876) 696, VIII (1877) 465, X (1879) 300, XI (1880) 608; NZM LXXIII/1 (1877) 265–66.

175. NZM XLVIII (1858) 101–5. Cf. Wasielewski/SCHUMANN 369–70 (not 416); HOFMEISTER V (1852–59) 203; Schumann/SCHRIFTEN II 550. Ritter is not listed in any biographic dictionary used here.

emphasized the consistent force of Ritter's ideas, his inner sense of form, the nobility and depth of the music, and its origins in Beethoven's late sonatas.

In Magdeburg, well northwest of Dresden, another, better known composer with the same surname was the organist and writer on organ music **August Gottfried Ritter** (1811–85).[176] A student of J. N. Hummel and Mendelssohn's teacher Ludwig Berger, among others, this Ritter left a total of eight sonatas, including Opp. 11 in d, 19 in e, 23 in a, and 31 in A for organ, and Opp. 12 in B♭, 18 in D, 20 in D, and 21 in b for P solo, all published between about 1849 and 1858.[177] Each of these is a superior work, even Opp. 12 and 18, entitled "Instructive Sonatas in Preparation for Larger Works." And all were uniformly and warmly welcomed when they first appeared, for their sincerity, depth of content, natural flow, over-all unity, and expert writing.[178] Furthermore, all of them might be nearly as warmly welcomed if they were to be revived today. Indeed, one wonders whether it was not the mere caprice of fate quite as much as the allegedly right judgment of time and posterity that catapulted, say, Mendelssohn into one of the highest niches occupied by Romantic composers and left Ritter almost without any composer's niche. The comparison is not actually so idle, for Ritter, only two years younger and stemming from one of the same teachers, has much in common with Mendelssohn in their musical styles, including the sureness of form from the most local to the broadest levels, the frank lyrical melodies clearly projected against thin, transparent, accurate, idiomatic textures, the deft scherzando movements, the climactic uses of dim.-7th chords, and even a similar tendency toward rhythmic flatness and predictability. In some respects, especially enharmony and related harmonic resources, Ritter went beyond Mendelssohn. But in spite of their closeness in age, the precocious Mendelssohn led the way; and history focuses more on leaders than followers.

176. Cf. MGG XI 565–67 (P. Schmidt), with further bibliography (but an inadequate list of works).

177. Cf. HOFMEISTER IV (1844–51) 150 and 215, V (1852–59) 203 and 293.

178. E.g., NZM XXX (1849) 185–86 (G. Siebeck, comparing Op. 11, with exx., to the disadvantage of a *Phantasie-Sonate* for organ by Adolph Hesse), XXXII (1850) 213–14 (E. Bernsdorf discussing Op. 12 as preparation for the spirit as well as the fingerwork of the Classics), XXXII (1850) 91–92 and XXXIII (1850) 97–98 (calling Op. 19 a model of its type since Bach), XXXV (1851) 258–59 (on Op. 20, its freedom from eclecticism, its resemblance to Beethoven's Op. 28, and its increasing tonal enterprise in ii and iii), XXXIX (1853) 114–15 (E. Klitzsch on Op. 21), and XLIII (1855) 155–56 (L. Kindscher on Op. 23 as a landmark in the trend initiated by Mendelssohn).

Sample performances of Ritter's sons. are cited in NZM XXXII (1850) 91, LXXII/1 (1876) 225 and 244, LXXII/2 (1876) 475.

One sample of Ritter's writing might be quoted here from his piano Sonata in b, Op. 21 (Ex. 51), whose more driving sections recall, for example, Mendelssohn's *Capriccio brillant* for P and orchestra, Op. 22 (first pub. in 1832). In this sonata, as in Ritter's Op. 20, there are three movements—an extended "sonata-allegro" form, a scherzando ternary design marked "Träumerisch," and an expressive rondo finale. The unity of mood and style is furthered by clear cyclic links. By contrast, the organ sonatas, which include indications for Ritter's fine art of

Ex. 51. From the first movement of August Gottfried Ritter's Sonata in b, Op. 21 (after the original Breitkopf & Härtel ed. of 1853).

registration, are cast in more and shorter movements and these, in turn, are freer in all respects, often connected without breaks, more contrapuntal, and even more closely bound by related themes (but not chorale melodies).[179]

A more detailed survey of the organ sonata in this period would include the once popular examples by A. G. Ritter's organ pupil **Rudolf Palme** (1834–1909), also of Magdeburg;[180] by the organist near

179. Cf. Frotscher/ORGELSPIEL II 1164–65.

180. Cf. Riemann/LEXIKON II 1335–36; HOFMEISTER IX (1880–85) 474; NZM LXXI/1 (1876) 165–66; MT XXII (1881) 376.

Kassel **Wilhelm Valentin Volckmar** (1812–87), recently dubbed the "Czerny of the organ" for his prolificity, banality, and stereotypes;[181] by **Friedrich Kühmstedt** (1809–58) in Eisenach, who also aroused interest with his *Grosse Sonate (ein Lebensbild)* in g, Op. 36, for P solo (1857?), cited earlier for its programmatic implications (ssb VI);[182] and by his Dutch contemporary in Elberfeld (north of Köln), the organist **Jan Albert van Eyken** (or **Eijken;** 1823–68).[183]

From the pianist **Julius Otto Grimm** (1827–1903) in Münster, best known for his close friendship with Brahms, we have just one sonata, Op. 14 in A, for P & Vn, composed in 1854 and published in 1869.[184] Grimm's individual style plus the value he placed on comments from his younger friend (by 6 years) should make this scarce work interesting to see and hear.

In Köln from 1850 on lived one of the most representative and diversely active of Romantic musicians, although a man who gave but a small part of his attention to the sonata, **Ferdinand Hiller** (1811–85).[185] Trained by Hummel among others, Hiller was more disposed by nature to the Classics (he was a pioneer in his Parisian performances of Bach and Beethoven) than to the "New German" school. Yet his career brought him close to musicians of all tastes, including Moscheles and, especially, Mendelssohn, Schubert, and Beethoven while they were still alive in Vienna, Schumann, Brahms, Chopin, Liszt, Wagner (before Hiller turned against him), Berlioz, and even Verdi.

Hiller wrote at least seven sonatas, including an early one in a, for P solo, that remains in MS and another labeled Op. 2, for Vn & P;[186] three mature sonatas for P solo[187]—Op. 47 in a (pub. in 1853), Op. 59 in A♭ (composed probably in 1851–53, pub. in 1861), and Op. 78 in g

181. Cf. mgg XIII 1917 (R. Sietz); nzm LXV/2 (1869) 294 (A. W. Gottschalg); Kremer/ORGAN 228–29 (list of 44 sons., etc.).

182. Cf. Mendel/LEXIKON VI 177–78; mgg VII 1854–55 (G. Kraft); nzm XL (1854) 273 and 274, XLV (1856) 174, XLVII (1857) 78–80 (on Op. 36, with exx.); Frotscher/ORGELSPIEL II 1190; Kremer/ORGAN 198 (list of 4 sons.).

183. Cf. Mendel/LEXIKON III 445–46; Riemann/LEXIKON I 455; nzm XL (1854) 273 (somewhat negative on Son. 1, Op. 13, for organ), XLV (1856) 174 (more favorable on Son. 2, Op. 15), LV (1861) 18 (on 2 P sonatinas, Op. 3); Reeser/NEDERLANDSE 109–111; Frotscher/ORGELSPIEL II 1234, 1235; Kremer/ORGAN 181 (list of 4 sons.).

184. Cf. mgg V 930–32 (R. Sietz), with further references; Altmann/KAMMERMUSIK 205.

185. Efficient biographic summaries appear in Hering/HILLER (a diss. on his P music), pp. 7–15; mgg VI 399–409 (R. Sietz), with further bibliography; and Sietz/HILLER (an annotated collection of previously unpub. letters to and from Hiller, valuable for many insights into the era) I 1–3 (first years).

186. Hering/HILLER 17–18.

187. The 3 P solo sons. are discussed in Hering/HILLER 32–37, with exx. Cf. HOFMEISTER V (1852–59) 156 and HOFMEISTER 1861, p. 68. Hiller also left 2 sets of "easy sonatinas" for P solo (Hering/HILLER 55–56, with ex.).

(pub. probably in 1855); and two mature sonatas for P & Vc—Op. 22 in E (pub. in 1872) [188] and Op. 172 in a (pub. in 1878).[189]

Hiller's three piano sonatas all lack inner slow movements. Nearest to slow are the opening section[190] and opening movement of Opp. 47 and 59, respectively, both in moderate tempo. Starting in that tempo contributes to an apparently calculated increase of tempo and excitement from that moment right to the brilliant codas in the finales of each sonata. The same increase can be noted in Op. 78, although the plan differs markedly from that in Opp. 47 and 59. Opp. 47 and 59 employ a free "sonata form" in their first main movements and still freer, cursive forms in their finales (with no middle, scherzando movement in Op. 47). Op. 78, which dispenses with the improvisatory moments to be found in the two previous sonatas, starts with an exceptional movement that (almost like *Le Djinns* by Franck) describes a single broad dynamic curve, from *pianissimo,* "Andante agitato," to *fortissimo,* "Più vivace," and back. Then, without pauses, follow a "Scherzo" in ternary design, marked "Vivace," and a finale, "Allegro energico e con fuoco," that supplies a complete "sonata form."

At most, Hiller's compositions, even his major vocal works, achieved no conspicuous popularity. Nor have any reviews or other records turned up here that would alter this statement for the sonatas. Yet these last, especially Opp. 47 and 78, are not lacking in melodic appeal, musical conviction and freshness, rhythmic and harmonic ingenuities, or telling uses of the keyboard. Their keyboard writing is a kind of cross between the thin, precise Mendelssohnian texture we found in A. G. Ritter's sonatas and more subtle Schumannesque touches (as in Ex. 52). Perhaps the chief drawbacks in Hiller's sonatas are this sort of eclecticism and a certain tentativeness about the forms. The anticipations and build-ups promise much, but what they arrive at—in other words, the substance we have been led to expect—often disappoints. Or put still differently, Hiller had a greater gift for creating interesting crescendos and passagework than for the creation of strong ideas or for developing them. Even so, a capable pianist might revive one of the sonatas today with fair hope of a real artistic success.

The choral and orchestral director **Albert Hermann Dietrich** (1829–

188. HOFMEISTER 1872, p. 77. Actually, this is the only son. (or concerto) listed in Cobbett/CHAMBER I 555 (R. Felber); the paragraph on a "Violin Sonata in D," Op. 122, by Hiller probably refers inaccurately to his Concerto for Vn, Op. 152. A Leipzig performance of Op. 22 is listed in NZM LXXIII/1 (1877) 140. Hiller reported a performance of Op. 22 (?) in Leipzig in 1875 in which he participated (Sietz/HILLER III 179).

189. Altmann/KAMMERMUSIK 258.

190. Hering/HILLER 32–34 makes too much of this short tonally dependent section by counting it as an independent mvt.

Ex. 52. From the first movement (second theme) of Ferdinand Hiller's Sonata in a, Op. 47 (after the original J. Schuberth ed. of 1853).

1908) is mentioned in the present volume chiefly as the pupil of Schumann and longtime friend of Brahms who joined with those two men in Düsseldorf to write the *F-A-E* Sonata in a, in 1853, as a salute to Joachim.[191] Dietrich's share, the first movement, does not quite stand up with the others', partly because it pursues the "F-A-E" theme too doggedly. A Sonata in G, Op. 19, for P-duet, published in 1870,[192] after Dietrich moved to Oldenburg in northernmost Germany, was reviewed as being agreeable and unpretentious, with perhaps too much recollection of the Classic masters and some structural inadequacies.[193] Dietrich's Sonata in C, Op. 15, for P & Vc, was likewise published in that year. In Barmen, near Düsseldorf, the well-reputed piano pedagog **Anton Krause** (1834–1907) left about thirty "instructive" sonatinas or sonatas in some twelve sets published in the 1860's and 1870's.[194] They are scored for P solo, P-duet, 2 Ps, and P & Vn.[195] These received numer-

---

191. Cf. our last pp. on Schumann (ssb VIII) and the first pp. on Brahms (ssb IX).
192. Altmann/KAMMERMUSIK 298.
193. NZM LXIX/2 (1873) 418.
194. Cf. Riemann/LEXIKON I 949; HOFMEISTER VI–VIII (1860–79) *passim*.
195. Cf. PAZDÍREK VIII 354–55.

ous approving reviews, aside from occasional reservations about dryness or gaucheries, and evidently sold widely and well.[196]

North German Composers (Kiel, Reubke, Grädener)

Except for Gustav Flügel in Stettin, all our North German composers were concentrated in Berlin and Hamburg. Berlin, especially, harbored several figures of minor interest including products of Mendelssohn, Schumann, and the Leipzig Conservatory, and the opposing influences of Brahms and Liszt. The esteemed but somewhat withdrawn teacher of piano and composition **Friedrich Kiel** (1821–85) left among many other works six duo sonatas (4 for P & Vn, one for P & Va, and one for P & Vc) and two sonatinas for P-duet (Op. 6) [197] that were all published between 1850 and 1876 (chiefly in the 1860's).[198] These works disclose another master of his craft who came remarkably close to ranking with the recognized greats. But like Rheinberger versus Bruckner, or Raff versus Mendelssohn, Kiel came too close to the Brahms he admired so much, to stand independently or to withstand the competition. In the resourcefulness and conduct of his polyphony, his harmony, and his texture and scoring, and in both his tonal and his thematic unfolding and development of these techniques toward broad, serious, highly organized forms, Kiel ranked second to none. But he indicated no interest in the "New German" school or other new trends. And in the vitality of his ideas, in the imagination and flexibility of their treatment, and occasionally in that important virtue of conciseness where prolixity threatens—one of the virtues that Brahms appreciated so fully—he must be ranked below the greats. The temptation here would be to ascribe these relative weaknesses to Kiel's solitary, retiring nature, except that Brahms could be solitary and retiring in his own way, too.

Representative is Kiel's *Vierte Sonate für Pianoforte und Violine*, Op. 51 in e (1868).[199] Its movement, "Allegro maestoso," is a powerful,

196. E.g., NZM LIV (1861) 147, LXIII/1 (1867) 166-67 (on Op. 17, a more substantial, 3-mvt. Son. in E for 2 Ps), LXIX/1 (1873) 103, LXIX/2 (1873) 391, LXXIX/1 (1883) 280 (2d ed. of Op. 17); MW III (1872) 603, V (1874) 429. Cf. the biography in MW XXXV (1904) 816–17.

197. Cf. DM VIII/4 (1908–9) 242 (H. Wetzel).

198. Cf. MGG VII 880–83 (R. Sietz), with detailed, dated list of works and further bibliography. The Library of Congress also has the MS of an unpub. Son. in A for P & Vn, labeled Op. 2. In 1880 Kiel recalled writing 4 P sons. before his 21st year (La Mara/MUSIKERBRIEFE II 314).

199. Among reviews of his sons. are those in NZM LVIII (1863) 199–200 (on the skills, especially in thematic development, and on a certain unusualness in Op. 16

fully developed "sonata form" in which motivic reiteration and evolution provide the chief means of structural prolongation. In the absence of independent thematic distinction (but not lyricism) they and the Schubertian modulations in the development section also provide the chief interest. As in Brahms's duo sonatas, the range, idioms, and techniques of the piano are challenged more than those of the violin. The second movement, "Adagio con gran espressione," approaches the loftiness, sincerity, and style of a Beethoven adagio—in fact, it scarcely goes further in style, apart from some wider modulations and some chromatic figuration. The third movement, "Allegro ma non troppo," is a neatly defined scherzo, effective without any striking originality. And the finale, "Allegro agitato," is another complete "sonata form," this time in a more fluent and nearly *perpetuum mobile* style. Its most conspicuous feature is its start at a tonal tangent (Ex. 53).

Another somewhat withdrawn piano teacher in Berlin, more obscure but scarcely less interesting, was Liszt's sometime pupil **Rudolf Viole** (1825–67).[200] Viole left a total of eleven sonatas, all for piano solo. These consisted of an Op. 1 in b♭, dedicated to Bülow and published in 1855, and a series of ten more sonatas, Opp. 21–30, published between about 1866 and 1871 (posthumous), singly dedicated to Tausig, Wagner, and Liszt, among others, and perhaps originally intended to cover the keys systematically (C, a, F, d, b, d, E, f, f♯, E♭, respectively). Of first importance was Op. 1, which followed Liszt's Sonata in b by only three years and reportedly followed its style and form, too, in a naively exaggerated way. Bülow gave extravagant endorsement to it in a long review[201] that anticipates curiously the bewildered yet defensive reviews of recent years greeting each new, *avante-garde* sonata of a Pierre Boulez or a Hans Werner Henze.[202] Salient portions of Bülow's wordy, repetitive, sometimes almost incomprehensible comments may be translated here:

---

in d for P & Vn), LXI/2 (1865) 277–78 (H. Zopff on the skills, yet the conservative adherence to Beethoven and Schumann styles, in Opp. 35/1 & 2, in d and F, for P & Vn; with several exx.), LXIX/1 (1869) 197–98 (on the continuing superiority and specific delights in Opp. 51 and 52 [in a for P & Vc]), and LXXIII/1 (1877) 133 and 146–47 (A. Maczewski, similarly on Op. 67 in g for P & Va). A performance of Op. 51 is cited in MW I (1870) 459. Cobbett/CHAMBER II 51–52 (W. Altmann) gives more praise and space than usual to sons. so nearly forgotten as Kiel's. A detailed study of Kiel's sons. is clearly needed.

200. The helpful, one-column summary in MGG XIII 1691 (R. Sietz), plus the reviews noted below, and the good list of works in PAZDÍREK XIV 248, have provided all the information available here, since it has not been possible to locate any of Viole's sons. themselves in the foreign and U.S. libraries approached for this purpose.

201. NZM XLV (1856) 21–23; also in BÜLOW BRIEFE III 140–44.

202. E.g., NOTES VIII (1950–51) 135 (W. S. Newman on Boulez's 2d P Son.).

Ex. 53. From the finale of Friedrich Kiel's Sonata in e, Op. 51, for P & Vn (after the original Simrock ed.).

A surprising, unsuspected music publisher in Weimar, who dresses up the first fruits of a composer still unknown with an elegance à la Breitkopf & Härtel—what critical raven might not scent out the "future" there! And in fact, a mere try at the sonata . . . a single glance at the first page suffices to confirm this [first impression]. Here, indeed, is music-of-the-future, in the superlative, [the] music-of-the-future of [the] music-of-the-future, [the] music-of-the-future to the third power, against which perhaps musicians-of-the-future themselves would protest if they were so timid as to believe themselves compromised through certain extravagances and eccentricities and were otherwise misled, through [concern for] tangible formalities, into myopic, unreasonable disregard of the heart and soul of an individuality. For many it may well be no small sacrifice to entrust themselves but superficially with a sonata in one movement lasting thirty-one closely engraved pages, [a work] that, at least a [prima] vista, poses many riddles to solve, many obstacles to overcome, no less to the eye of the reader than to the hand of the player. . . . It is evident that the composer wants to create a new musical speech. . . . [But] in the practical realization of this recognition [of such a need] he goes, in part much too far and, in part, in a false direction. . . . The choice of such a work [Liszt's] for a model was perhaps more of a foolhardy escapade than a voyage of discovery on his own. . . . [He seems to] have wanted to get an abstract design out of Liszt's very well patterned "yet" free form. . . . The structural composition of Viole shows along with many aberrations many logical, correct principles. Where construction is concerned a considerable know-how is at his command. A lively talent for [new] combinations is undeniable in the thematic development. The exploitation of the four-measure, main motive [theme?] (which was given by Franz Liszt to the composer to work out) is seldom halting and stagnant and has also surprised us all the more agreeably by its rhythmic variety, since this last means is so frequently neglected by the German composers working in increasingly inexcusable ignorance of the Berlioz disclosures in this sphere. [Etc.]

Four reviews by other writers describe the first six in Viole's cycle of ten sonatas.[203] They tell us of a planned increase in complexity of form, treatment, harmonic richness and exploration, and technical difficulty, from one sonata to the next, all within a constant three-movement cycle but with no obligation to repeat the forms in the single movements. They also tell of an individual, subjective style that stands apart in its time and grows in freshness, subjectivity, and flexibility from one sonata to the next. Obviously, a search for this music and, if it is found, a modern study of it are warranted, perhaps to be followed by a reprinting of at least some of it.

Besides Draeseke (supra) and Viole, a third Liszt pupil who wrote under the direct influence of the Sonata in b was the extraordinarily gifted but unhappily short-lived composer **Julius Reubke** (1834–58).[204] It was just after his five years of study and teaching in Berlin and while Reubke was working with Liszt in Weimar—that is, during the winter of 1856–57 or but one year before his death at twenty-four—that he wrote his only two sonatas. One of these was the now scarce and unjustly forgotten Grosse Sonate in b♭ for piano solo, dedicated to Liszt; and the other, which became much better known and is still often played, Der 94. Psalm, grosse Sonate für Orgel in c, dedicated to the important Leipzig teacher and conductor Carl Riedel. Both of these sonatas were originally published posthumously, through the efforts of Julius's brother Otto, in 1871, by J. Schuberth of Leipzig.[205] Harmonically and melodically Reubke's piano sonata smacks strongly of Liszt's Sonata in b. In expressive range and technical exploitation of the keyboard it goes even a bit further. Structurally, including the unifying motives and the less tangible double functions of cycle and form (now 3 mvts., F-S-VF, in one), it is similar though not identical to Liszt's sonata. In all these respects, it comes still closer than Draeseke's Op. 6 to Liszt's Sonata in b; and it is on a par in quality with Draeseke's sonata.[206] Reubke's greatest talent appears in his impressively sonorous use of the piano, especially his dramatic rhapsodic

203. NZM LXII/2 (1866) 439–40 (Opp. 21 and 22), LXIII/1 (1867) 189–90 (Op. 23), LXIV/2 (1868) 237–38 (Opp. 24 and 25), LXV/2 (1869) 237–38 (Opp. 25, again, and 26).

204. Cf. MGG XI 326–28 (T.-M. Langner), with further bibliography.

205. HOFMEISTER XX (1871) 143–44. Mod. eds.: Son. in b♭ ed. by A. Stradal and pub. in 1925 and 1940 by J. Cotta in Stuttgart (along with Stradal's P transcription of the organ son.); Son. in c, cf. MGG XI 328.

206. Cf., also, Georgii/KLAVIERMUSIK 421–22.

Ex. 54. From the opening section of Julius Reubke's Sonata in b♭ (after the J. Cotta reprint of 1940).

thrusts, his ingenious runs, and his stentorian chords (Ex. 54). As with Hiller and other near greats, this talent seems somewhat less noteworthy when these anticipatory, harmonically active passages at last arrive at a tonic and a melodic moment of truth (as at ms. 53 in E). There also is an uncomfortably close resemblance, both melodic and rhythmic, between Reubke's main motive and the "w" thematic element in Liszt's Sonata in b (*supra*), although one soon discovers how much that motive was common property in the 19th century.

Reubke's popular organ sonata divides into three movements, S/F-S-F, the finale being a big, contrapuntally rich fugue. The avoidance of a complete break between these movements and their unification through thematic transformation leave no doubt, again, that

Liszt's forms were much in mind. But there is no longer a double function, the music is more personal and subjective, and it is written in an intensely chromatic idiom that now suggests Franck more than Liszt. The sonorities, challenging the resources of the largest organs, and the figuration, challenging the most advanced pedal and manual techniques, are main strengths again. The more extended themes have somewhat firmer character in this work than in Reubke's Sonata in bb. In the title reference to the 94th Psalm and in the specification of particular verses in the original edition, a programme is implied in this landmark of organ literature. But the exact association of the verses with the music has to be guessed at, as it has been by Harvey Grace.[207]

Woldemar Bargiel (1828–97), the disciple and brother-in-law of Schumann, studied under Mendelssohn and other of our notables here, then became a successful teacher himself in Berlin and elsewhere.[208] He left three sonatas among numerous other publications, one for P & Vn in f, Op. 10, first published in 1858,[209] one for P-duet in G, Op. 23, first published in 1864[210] and one for P solo in C, Op. 34, first published in 1867.[211] These standardized, three-movement works confirm Bargiel's excellent composition training and also his keen understanding of both the piano and violin idioms. At the same time, alongside the much more progressive, imaginative products of a Reubke they reveal a more limited talent and circumscribed personality. In fact, they sound not only conservative but faintly scholastic. All the nicely turned phrases, fetching rhythms, and adroit polyphonic diversions, even the fairly advanced uses of the instruments, fit too patly to leave any real artistic challenge to the performer or listener. One finds it hard to take seriously such an inscription as the "ma con passione" that follows "Allegro moderato" at the start of Op. 34. Pertinent is Riemann's observation that with Bargiel "the Romantic school took a firm foothold for the first time in the circles of the academicians." [212]

Although their style is more complex, a similar evaluation must be made of the sonatas by the brilliant pianist and respected teacher

207. GROVE VII 134–35.
208. Cf. MGG I 1267–69 (A. Adrio).
209. Altmann/KAMMERMUSIK 193. Among later eds.: Wier/VIOLIN-m 65.
210. Altmann/KAMMERMUSIK 296.
211. Breitkopf & Härtel plate no. 11357. A performance of this work (in "A Dur"!) in Pittsburgh in 1877 is listed in NZM LXXIII/1 (1877) 64.
212. MGG I 1268. A brief appreciation of Op. 10 may be read in Cobbett/CHAMBER I 58 (W. Altmann), to be weighed against a report of it in MT XVI (1874) 449 as "abounding with passages of extreme beauty . . . [yet] wearisome in length, the last movement especially not having sufficient interest to rivet the attention of the listener throughout."

Xaver Scharwenka (1850–1924). Xaver was the younger and more successful of the two well-known brothers trained in Theodor Kullak's Neue Akademie der Tonkunst in Berlin.[213] His output[214] includes four solo and duo sonatas (and two piano sonatinas, Op. 52)—Opp. 6 in c♯ and 36 in E♭ (first pub. in 1871 and 1878 [215]) for P solo, Op. 2 in d for P & Vn (1872), and Op. 46a in e for P & Vc (1879).[216] In both solo sonatas, but not in the duos,[217] a scherzando is inserted before the middle of the usual three movements (F-S-F).[218] As a more mature sample than his Op. 6, Xaver's Op. 36 differs from Bargiel's Op. 34 in its more advanced harmony, its more chromatic, active inner voices, and its rather abrupt, truncated, rhythmically precious phrases. Since the themes and underlying harmony are essentially diatonic, the chromaticism serves mainly to create the activity in those inner voices. Its effect borders on the sentimental and detracts from the genuineness of highly competent writing as well as resourceful, pleasurable pianism.[219]

Two longtime Berliners, both pianists still writing in the Mendelssohnian manner, achieved considerable recognition in their day as composers, enough to insure them of substantial space in present-day music dictionaries, although their music is now all but forgotten. **Eduard Franck** (1817–93), who actually studied with Mendelssohn and was close to Schumann, Sterndale Bennett, and Ferdinand Hiller, is credited with 2 sonatas for Vn & P, 2 for Vc & P, and 9 for P solo published between 1846 and 1882.[220] A certain lack of originality in spite of secure compositional techniques is reported in one of the violin sonatas (Op. 19) and one of the cello sonatas (Op. 42),[221] and proves to characterize Franck's six piano sonatas Op. 40 and three piano sonatas Op. 44 as well.[222] **Heinrich Karl Johann Hofmann** (1842–1902), a   222a

213. Cf. MGG XI 1602–6 (R. Sietz); H. Schonberg in *The New York Times* for Dec. 15, 1968, p. D27. Philipp Scharwenka is noted in SSB XI.

214. Cf. PAZDÍREK XIII 176–79. His prolificity is frowned upon in NZM LXXII/2 (1876) 305–6.

215. HOFMEISTER XX (1871) 155 and XXVII (1878) 267.

216. Altmann/KAMMERMUSIK 225 and 263.

217. Cf. Cobbett/CHAMBER II 332. Op. 2 was reviewed as a promising fluent, easy student work, showing a bit too much of Mendelssohn's influence, in NZM LXIX/1 (1873) 31. A performance of Op. 46a is listed in MT XXI (1880) 192.

218. Two reviews of Op. 6 offered moderate praise for both the writing skills and idiomatic keyboard treatment (MW III [1872] 470 [W. Freudenberg] and NZM LXIX/2 [1873] 361).

219. Yet it is praised for its noble themes as well as its skill in SMW XXXVI (1878) 580.

220. Cf. MGG IV 653–56 (F. Feldmann) with dated list (including 2 more Vn sons., one left in MS in 1861 and one, Op. 60, not pub. until 1910).

221. Cobbett/CHAMBER I 429 (W. Altmann) and NZM LXXIX/1 (1883), respectively.

222. Cf. NMZ V (1884) 54.

pupil of Theodor Kullak, is credited with but one full-scale sonata, Op. 67 in f, for Vn & P (1883), along with three diminutive sonatas for P-duet (Op. 86; 1887).[223] Similarly, the three movements of Op. 67 (VF-M-VF) are melodious, flowing, well-constructed applications of the standard forms, but routine in their stock accompaniments and chord progressions and in their predictably regular phrases.[224]

Further exploration of sonatas from Berlin in this period might include an Op. 1 in G for P-duet (1853?) by a teacher, director, and composer named **Ludwig Hoffmann** (1830–at least 1870), for this work was greeted by a seasoned reviewer as far above the usual Op. 1 in maturity, skill, depth, and keyboard treatment.[225] A Sonata in a, Op. 14, for P & Vn, and another in E, Op. 15, for P solo (both pub. in 1869) by the piano teacher **Constantin Bürgel** (1837–1909) won full-length, favorable reviews emphasizing his natural talent and almost unbridled passion in Op. 14.[226] A *Sonate in einem Satze* in A, Op. 2 (1863), by Bülow's pupil **Wilhelm Fritze** (1842–81), received similar praise, especially for its thematic development and harmony.[227] Several of the sonatas for Vn & P and Vc & P by "one of Germany's greatest women composers," **Emilie Meyer** (1812–83),[228] were published between 1863 and 1883. For these, prior to a more impartial estimate after her death, she received reviews that were variously chivalrous, cavalier, and facetious in their references to her high-minded goals, her dependence on Beethoven and other Classic models by way of her teacher Karl Loewe (SSB VIII), her feminine limitations not quite equal to the challenge of sonatas and symphonies, and her poetic inclinations.[229] The teacher **Leopold Amandus Leidgebel** (1816–86), a pupil of A. B. Marx, left a "third" Sonata for Vn & P, Op. 33 in E (1871) [230] that one reviewer commended highly for having the plasticity of Beethoven and

223. Cf. MGG VI 557–60 (T.-M. Langner), with full, dated list of works.

224. Like conclusions are reached in MW XVIII (1887) 434; but there is only approval in the short review in NZM LXXX/2 (1884) 343.

225. NZM XXXIX (1853) 186 (E. Klitzsch). Cf. Mendel/LEXIKON V 263–64.

226. MW I (1870) 210 (F. Stade on both sons.) and III (1872) 662–63 (C. Fuchs on Op. 15, with exx.). Cf., also, Riemann/LEXIKON I 248; Altmann/KAMMERMUSIK 198; NZM LXXII/2 (1876) 309 and 401 (on performances of, presumably, Op. 14).

227. NZM LVIII (1860) 189. Cf. NZM LXXII/1 (1876) 205, which also mentions a Son. in d, Op. 6, for Vn & P (1867); Riemann/LEXIKON I 543.

228. Cf. Ledebur/TONKÜNSTLER 357–58; Elson/WOMAN 161–62; Altmann/KAMMER-MUSIK 215 and 260.

229. NZM LXIII/1 (1867) 181–82 (H. Zopff on Opp. 17 and 18), LXV/1 (1869) 215 (on Op. 21), LXIX/2 (1873) 387 (A. Winterberger on Op. 40), LXXX/2 (1884) 544–45 (posthumously on Op. 47). Cf. SSB III.

230. Altmann/KAMMERMUSIK 213. Cf. Schuberth/LEXIKON 310–11. HOFMEISTER VIII (1874–79) 321 also lists a Son. for P solo, Op. 40.

Schubert plus the Romantic warmth and poetry of Weber and Schumann.[231] And there were six duo sonatas—4 for Vc & P, one for Vn & P, and one for harp & P—by the popular harpist **Ferdinand Hummel** (1855–1928),[232] all of which but the harp sonata (1912) were early works published between 1877 and 1885 and generally reviewed as unoriginal and in a salon style inappropriate to the sonata.[233]

The most successful composer of "instructive sonatinas" in Berlin at this time was the pianist and teacher **Albert Loeschhorn** (1819–1905), several sets by whom, all oriented largely to Classic masters, appeared in the 1870's.[234]

Also waiting to be explored in the present day are the 5 sonatas and one Sonatine for P solo and the Sonata in E, Op. 83, for organ by the organist **Gustav Flügel** (1812–1900) in Stettin (inside the Polish border north of Berlin).[235] These works were published between about 1845 and 1881. Curiosity is aroused in his now scarce piano sonatas by five lengthy, interrelated, increasingly enthusiastic reviews by at least three different reviewers.[236] For example, the fourth piano sonata, Op. 20 in c, is viewed by no less a critic than Alfred Dörffel as arriving at the universality of an imminent master. And the fifth, Op. 36 in C, with its opening inscription (from Goethe), "Oh! Who [could] bring back the beautiful days, the lovely time!" is viewed by Emanuel Klitzsch as an essay in idyllic poetry.

In Hamburg, one of the best known composers in the later 19th century was **Cornelius Gurlitt** (1820–1901), who was actually there only after 1879 and after considerable activity elsewhere that had included close associations with the Schumanns, Carl Reinecke (*supra*), and Niels Gade (ssb XIII).[237] Gurlitt is of only minor interest here because his relatively few attempts at writing serious full-size sonatas,

231. mw III (1872) 614.

232. Cf. mgg VI 921–24 (T.-M. Langner).

233. E.g., mw X (1879) 366 (on Op. 9) XI (1880) 537 (on Opp. 2 and 12), XIII (1882) 555–56 (favorable on Op. 24, ded. to Joachim, "though a Joachim is not always on hand" to play the difficult coda of its finale). smw XXXIX (1881) 1107 is also favorable on Op. 24, in a cautious way.

234. Cf. mgg VIII 1105 (K. Hahn); pazdírek IX 579; mw II (1879) 314; mmr XX (1890) 274.

235. Cf. Mendel/lexikon III 578–79; Riemann/lexikon I 521; pazdírek V 420–22. The Sonatine (Op. 54 in C) is briefly and favorably reviewed in nzm LI (1859) 209. On Flügel's fine organ music other than Op. 83 cf. Frotscher/orgelspiel II 1172–73.

236. nzm XXIII (1845) 177–79 (on Op. 7, with exx.), XXIV (1846) 145 (on Op. 4), XXV (1846) 14 (on Op. 13), XXVIII (1848) 245–46 (A. Dörffel on Op. 20), XLI (1854) 77–78 (E. Klitzsch on Op. 36). No copies of these sons. turned up in the present study.

237. Cf. mgg V 1127–28, 1131 (W. Gurlitt).

from about 1844 to 1859,[238] gave way to the production of many, much more successful, pedagogic sonatinas over the next two decades. Apparently the several reviewers discouraged him from those serious works by making only incidental mentions of their good workmanship while deploring their derivative, even archaic styles, old-fashionedly thin textures, and frequent arid sections.[239] But, ironically for the state of pedagogy, they made more of the workmanship (which does stand high) while finding only slight reasons to deplore these same shortcomings when they came to writing their seemingly endless flow of repetitive short reviews that followed the seemingly endless flow of Gurlitt's sonatinas—in sets for P solo (including even a "Fugen Sonate," Op. 99), P-duet, P & Vn, and P & Vc—that the publishers were willing to keep publishing.[240]

There is more musical interest for us in the one solo and three duo sonatas by the cellist and conductor **Karl Grädener** (1812–83), who settled in Hamburg in 1848.[241] These include Op. 11 in d (not D) for P & Vn (pub. in 1853),[242] Op. 28 in c for P solo (1862?), Op. 59 in C for P & Vc (1873), and Op. 68 in B♭ for P & Cl.[243] A strong example of these is the solo sonata in three movements (VF-S-Sc), which has the bravura dash and octave scoring of Brahms's Op. 2 in f♯, and clearly recalls Brahms, too, in its motivic development and rich textures (especially its 3ds and 6ths; Ex. 55). Grädener's writing differs from that of Brahms (who reportedly acknowledged the high quality of his music) chiefly by being a bit more discursive, somewhat more direct and simple in harmony, and a little weaker in the character of its ideas.[244]

238. Cf. Altmann/KAMMERMUSIK 205 (but Op. 3 was pub. not later than 1844); HOFMEISTER V (1852–59) 151.

239. E.g., cf. NMZ XX (1844) 115–16 and XXVII (1847) 135–36 (both on Op. 3 for P & Vn-or-Vc), XXVIII (1848) 253 (on Op. 4 for P & Vn), XLIII (1855) 278–79 (with ex.) and LIV (1861) 50 (both on Op. 16 for P solo), XLIX (1858) 49–50 (R. Viole [supra] on Op. 20 for P solo); MW I (1870) 564 (on Op. 21).

240. Cf. PAZDÍREK VI 679–87. Sample reviews: NZM LXXII/1 (1876) 106, with ex. (arguing that even in a sonatina one expects 19th-c. styles, not 18th-c.); MW VI (1875) 291, X (1879) 325; MMR XII (1882) 160–61 and 208, XIII (1883) 69, XVII (1887) 65, XX (1890) 82, etc.

241. Cf. MGG V 659–61 (K. Stephenson), with errors in the list of works.

242. Altmann/KAMMERMUSIK 205 also lists 2 sonatinas for Vn & P, Op. 41 (reviewed in NZM LVI [1856] 219 and further described by Wilhelm Altmann in Cobbett/CHAMBER I 485).

243. Op. 68 is listed only in PAZDÍREK VI 486.

244. E. Klitzsch's favorable review of this work (NZM LVI [1862] 218–19) does not mention Brahms but commends Grädener for freeing himself from an earlier influence of Schumann. Liszt, understandably, did not take much pleasure in Op. 28 when Grädener visited him in Weimar in 1855 (letter of May 7, 1855, in LISZT/ Amie 15).

Ex. 55. From the first movement of Karl Grädener's Sonata
in c, Op. 28 (after the 2d revised ed. of F. Schuberth in 1878).

This chapter may be completed with the naming of two other prolific
and, evidently, successful composers of light, educational sonatinas in
Hamburg—**Albert Biehl** (1833–at least 1892?) [245] and **Louis Bödecker**
(1845–99).[246]

245. Cf. Schuberth/LEXIKON 58; PAZDÍREK II 670–74; MW X (1879) 300 and 325, XI
(1880) 562, XIV (1883) 508.
246. Cf. Riemann/LEXIKON I 192; PAZDÍREK II 829; MW XI (1880) 608.

Chapter XI

Late Romantics in Austria, Germany, and Switzerland

Quantity and Quality

This chapter brings to an end our account of Romantic sonata composers in Austrian, German, and Swiss centers. It covers about a generation, from around 1885 to 1915 or the start of World War I (1914). As for the political environment in, for, or against which these composers operated, it was largely an extension of that summarized at the start of Chapter IX. The Austro-Hungarian Monarchy had to cope with growing nationalistic forces and to struggle against increasing ethnic frictions that embittered the Balkan and Slavic states, especially Serbia, and ultimately led to the start of World War I. In Germany the autocratic, one-man rule, from 1888, of Emperor William II, King of Prussia, favored notable growth in economic prosperity, military and naval power, and social reforms, all falsely pointing to German invincibility when war broke out.

Throughout this late-Romantic phase the quantity of sonata production continued surprisingly high. If that production takes proportionately less space here, permitting both Austrian and German activities to fit into one chapter, the reason is simply the historiographic tendency to pay less attention to epigones than pioneers. Not a few composers who once made appreciable marks with their sonatas can get only bare mentions here, and only for the sake of a more rounded view. In the same period the quality of production continued surprisingly high, too. In fact, it may have been generally and relatively higher than in our two previous phases of the Romantic Era. One explanation might be the greater sophistication, through accumulated experience, of composer, performer, and listener alike, tending either to scare off or to indoctrinate more of those rank novitiates who had previously dared to see their untutored sonatas in print. Even so, there is no abatement in the number of published sonatas listed as "Op. 1," often without a sequel. Another explanation for the continuing high quality must have been the continuing wide influence of the Brahms-Liszt polarity, with all its repercussions, and the equally pervasive influence of master teachers and craftsmen like Kiel in Berlin and, especially, Rheinberger in Munich. We meet students of these last two men throughout this chapter.

Yet, though the general quality continued at least as high, no one Austro-German great of the sonata on a par with Schumann, Brahms, or Liszt, stands out in this last Romantic phase. To be sure, one could extend that observation to cover opera, symphony, and nearly all other categories of late-Romantic music unless it be something like the waltz or the march. But even among the late-Romantic nearest-to-greats, as the world has judged them, the sonata happens to have received, for the most part, only peripheral attention. Richard Strauss stopped writing sonatas upon his early arrival at full maturity. Hans Pfitzner put his best efforts only into the earlier of his two sonatas. Reger, with his many rich sonatas, should be the chief exception. But like Pfitzner and Julius Weismann, Reger, too, remains remarkably little known outside of Germany. He has yet to achieve universal recognition as the top master of chamber music after Brahms that his staunch followers argue him to be.

The next lower level of near greats did cultivate the sonata extensively. But even in Austria and Germany, to judge from the latest publishers' catalogues and concert reports, it is astonishing how quickly most of these near-near greats have fallen into near oblivion. Men like Robert Fuchs, Karg-Elert, Friedrich Gernsheim, Robert Kahn, Conrad Ansorge, and Paul Juon—most of them centered mainly in Berlin— are only names at best to the majority of today's professional musicians. Of course, one always tends to turn away most abruptly and completely from the immediate past. If these men have not slipped from view so rapidly that they have disappeared altogether, at least some of them are likely to swing back into view a little later. But they do qualify as near-near greats, and only that, for the very reason that they are epigones and also-rans. Each is likely to be too much like Brahms or some other master to have an identity of his own, yet not quite great enough to replace his model. Only those commensurable greats able and willing to make a sufficient break with the past, during what the future writer may show to be the most difficult transition of all music history, have been able to establish more lasting identities, including Schoenberg (who left no "sonatas" as such), Joseph Haas,

and Busoni (briefly discussed with our Berlin composers, *infra*). Such
men are excluded from this chapter because they crossed the often
visible but not always definable border line into Modernism (ssb I).

Sources and scores are fewer for the epigones than the pioneers and,
naturally, the acknowledged greats. Short articles in Riemann/
LEXIKON and BAKER have to suffice for much of the biographical and
general information about forgotten turn-of-the-century composers,
Altmann/KAMMERMUSIK and HOFMEISTER for bibliographic information
and for dates where United States copyright entries were not yet made,
and Cobbett/CHAMBER for at least a brief description of numerous
sonatas that could not be found here. Of most value for reviews, new
publications, and concert notices have been the periodicals NZM and
MW (which merged briefly in the early 20th century), NMZ, and SMW.

Composers in Austria (R. Fuchs, d'Albert)

Aside from Brahms's own last five sonatas, which originated in
1886–94, just after our approximate cutoff for Chapter X, no Viennese
masterworks can be pointed to in this final phase of the Romantic
sonata. None came from Gustav Mahler (1860–1911) other than an
early duo for Vn & P (1876), now lost,[1] nor from Arnold Schoenberg
(1874–1951), whose Modern styles would exclude him from this chapter,
anyway. Nearest to qualifying as masterworks, then, are the 3 solo and
10 duo sonatas, published in the 42 years from 1878 to 1919, by the
influential composer, teacher, organist, and member of Brahms's circle
Robert Fuchs (1847–1927).[2] These include (with pub. years in parentheses) 3 sonatas for P solo: Opp. 19 in G♭/f♯ (1877), 88 in g (1910),
and 109 in D♭ (1919); 6 for P & Vn: Opp. 20 in f♯ (1877), 33 in D
(1883), 68 in d (1902), 77 in E (1905), 95 in A (1913), and 103 in g
(1919); one each for P & Va and P and contrabass: Opp. 86 in d (1909)
and 97 in g (1913); and two for P & Vc: Opp. 29 in d (1881) and 83 in
e♭ (1908).[3]

Representative samplings of this music, which Brahms admired and
warmly endorsed, confirm the sincerity, freshness, depth, outstanding
craftsmanship, and sureness of form in Fuchs's writing.[4] As with our

1. MGG VIII 1493 (H. F. Redlich).

2. Cf. MGG IV 1079–83 (A. Ott), with partially dated list of works and further
bibliography.

3. Corrections of, and additions to, the pub. years in MGG IV 1081–82 come from
HOFMEISTER, *passim*. At least 3 more sons., for P solo, are among Fuchs's unpub.
early MSS (Hagenbucher/FUCHS 108).

4. A study of his chamber music is needed; brief comments of value occur in
Cobbett/CHAMBER I 438–39 (W. Altmann and R. Felber). Hagenbucher/FUCHS is
a useful diss. on style aspects of all of Fuchs's piano music, but treating of the
small forms much more than the sons.

Ex. 56. From the development section in the first movement of Robert Fuchs's Sonata in Gb/f♯, Op. 19 (after the original Kistner ed. of 1877).

next man but one, d'Albert, it is only because Fuchs worked so close to a still greater master that his music has already lost its battle with time. It does not offer enough that is either new or different to assure it an independent life of its own. Yet it does convey a genuine musical message. And perhaps it reveals some of its chief individuality, especially its directness and expressive clarity, in the earliest published sonata, Op. 19, for P solo, a work composed before Fuchs knew Brahms well and, indeed, the work that won Brahms's first favor.[5] In this convincing four-movement sonata (M-Sc-M-VF) we also find what may be the chief deterrent to performances of Fuchs's sonatas. In keeping with the straightforward, sometimes almost austere presentation of his ideas, Fuchs's piano writing abounds in chords and octaves that actually fit the hand well enough but do not exploit the most effective and characteristic resources of either the hand or the piano. In other words, his writing frequently supplies one more example of a sonata that sounds like a symphony transcribed for P & Vn or P solo (Ex. 56).[6]

A direct disciple of Fuchs, the eminent theorist and teacher **Richard Stöhr** (1874–at least 1964), left at least twenty-three rather conservative

5. According to Hagenbucher/FUCHS 20, though without documentation.
6. A highly laudatory review of Fuchs's Op. 20 (MW IX [1878] 309–310) emphasizes its "natural flow"; a shorter, favorable review of Op. 68 (MW XXXIII [1902] 601) finds fault only with a certain monotony of scoring (cf., also, DM II/4 [1903] 380 [W. Altmann]); Op. 77 gets brief praise as a Brahmsian work in DM VI/4 240 (W. Altmann). Op. 83 is said to achieve Mendelssohnian perfection of form and fluency, in DM IX/1 (1909–10) 123 (A. Laser). Op. 86 is viewed as Brahmsian again, in DM IX/2 (1909–10) 51 (W. Altmann).

sonatas—for P & Vn, P & Vc, P & Fl, P solo, and organ—of which several were published in the 1910's and 1920's, revealing warm musicianship and a full command of resources, although the world has passed them by with little notice.[7]

Still closer to the style of Brahms—in fact, so close at times as to be almost indistinguishable from it—is the only sonata, Op. 10 in f♯ for P solo, by the Brahms acquaintance, Liszt pupil, and world-famous pianist **Eugen d'Albert** (1864–1932).[8] Published in 1893 while d'Albert was in Vienna, the Sonata in f♯ finds its point of departure in Brahms's earliest music—in fact (like K. Grädener's Op. 28; cf. Ex. 55), in Brahms's own Op. 2 in f♯ (Ex. 57). But d'Albert neatens what Brahms

Ex. 57. From the opening of Eugen d'Albert's Sonata in f♯, Op. 10 (after the original Bote & G. Bock ed. of 1893).

does, making everything more manageable and regulated, and in the process reduces the early, wilder flare of genius to the more seasoned fluency of talent. Only some brilliant octave and chord passages in the first movement and the chromatic fugue subject in the finale bring Liszt more to mind.

Otherwise one only might fault d'Albert's motivic development, which at times seems a little too persistent and uncompromising. In

7. Cf. MGG XII 1377–78 (H. Hellmann-Stojan); Altmann/KAMMERMUSIK 228, 264, 277; Cobbett/CHAMBER II 458 (R. Felber); DM XIII/4 (1913–14) 331 (C. R. Blum, with praise for Stöhr's Son. for organ, Op. 33).

8. Cf. MGG I 293–95 (H. Wirth); GROVE I 92–93 (Hipkins and Loewenberg); Schonberg/PIANISTS 292–95.

each of the fine themes of the first movement, angular or lyrical, in the noble slow theme and its free variations of the middle movement, and in both the introduction and the stirring fugue of the finale one is always aware of the cyclical motive (as announced at the start of our foregoing example). To be sure, a motive centered around four notes in stepwise succession is almost harder to avoid than to incorporate.

All in all, d'Albert's Sonata in f♯ may be regarded as an example of the epigonic trend at its best in late Romanticism. Yet just such a view was already objected to by Martin Krause in 1893 when he greeted this and two other works by d'Albert with an extended laudatory review that begins:[9]

With his three large newest works Eugen d'Albert has cast aside the very last doubts that in the realm of composition he belongs to the select few even among the select. A look into these creations—referring to the Sonata Op. 10, the Quartet Op. 11, and the Piano Concerto Op. 12—silences the complaint, often only too justified, about musical "epigonism" ["Epigonenthum"] in our day. A master in the full sense of the word, a truly great musician stands before us; and to him who does not submit willingly to admiration [of d'Albert], to him he [d'Albert] reveals himself as a powerful, irresistible conqueror of the heart. The dark, brooding tendency of earlier times has vanished [from his music] and has given way to the expression of consciously confident strength; healthy in soul and body—that is, in the idea and form—are the [afore-]mentioned works; a lovely, compelling individuality speaks out from each of its measures. Were someone to ask the amiable composer today with what trend he identifies himself, he might proudly answer, "to my own [trend]." Yes, he has found himself; a beautiful victory over foreign influences, [in fact,] over his own uncertainties, has been won, and something like jubilation sounds from the last movement of the Quartet, from the gigantic concluding fugue of the Sonata, from the fresh themes of the Concerto; or is it the joy in creating that transfigures the indicated movements so brilliantly? D'Albert has even triumphed over the form; it binds [him] no further but offers itself willingly in the service of the idea. [Etc.]

It is not possible to write quite so favorably about another lone sonata by a widely celebrated pianist, the Sonata in e by **Leopold Godowsky** (1870–1938), who was in Vienna when this work was published in 1911.[10] It is a massive work in length (1,003 mss. in 56 pp., lasting over an hour), in over-all plan (5 mvts., in the order of F-M-Sc-F-S/Fugue), emotional range, density and complexity of texture, and scope of its technical difficulties. The texture and difficulties are not surprising to anyone who knows Godowsky's transcriptions of Chopin's etudes. And the style of this music is not surprising to anyone who knows such original piano miniatures by Godowsky as *Alt Wien*

9. MW XXIV (1893) 315–16.
10. Cf. MGG V 404–5 (N. Broder); Schonberg/PIANISTS 317–23.

of 1920 (anticipated melodically and stylistically in the 4th mvt.). It is primarily because the nostalgic chromaticism of a piece like *Alt Wien* serves as the omnipresent fare of the sonata, through bold themes and gentle ones, through stormy passages and lingering ones, that the sonata topples. Large forms cannot tolerate so much preoccupation with, or distraction by, independently alluring minutiae. The broad tonal scheme, the long-range opposition of ideas, the rhythmic and tempo continuity all suffer, finally causing the form—not only "sonata form" but any form—to collapse for want of perspective. Most of Godowsky's themes, although not otherwise distinguished, do have a broad lyrical sweep. But it takes a Godowsky to keep them in view above or within the textural, often contrapuntal maze. No less difficult to play is the "Fuga" on B-A-C-H in the finale, although not quite so difficult as Godowsky's later fugue on the same subject for left hand alone (1930).

Although Godowsky himself regarded as his "best efforts" the more than two hundred short, poetic pieces of his later years, there was at least one lively champion of his Sonata in e as one of his finest works, in the person of the Australian pianist Paul Howard, a lifelong devotee of Godowsky's music, who wrote in 1937:[11]

Around 1912 I had on my piano desk the Sonata of Cyril Scott [Op. 66, pub. in 1909], and the Godowsky Sonata. I had played them through many times and was enamoured of both, the Scott for its provoking variation of time signatures and the exquisite five and seven phrases; no two measures are in the same time, but every measure is barred on the phrase. . . . I was in the Seventh Heaven over the wonders of the Godowsky Sonata, and held the Scott in one hand and the Godowsky in the other, and demanded a decision of myself as to which I would do, decided on the Godowsky at the price of the Scott, and it was a high price, too, but so worth it. I held the heavy copy of the Godowsky on my chest with both hands—I shall never forget the moment—I knew the thrills of the hot tears of ecstasy that I would one day be able to play the Godowsky Sonata. . . . And today 35 years later I am still going on and finding new light in it: although I have played it in recital many times, and to visitors hundreds of times, it is a work that is never finished, but always intrigues and offers new points of view, new aspects to be mastered. . . .

Other sonatas from Vienna at this time call for no more than passing

11. Mr. Howard's fascinating, book-length collection of correspondence and other documents pertaining to Godowsky, reproduced in 18 "instalments" for the International Godowsky Society (founded by "Apostle Paul" Howard) in the years from about 1936 to 1951, has been supplied for this study through the kindness of the pianist and Godowsky student Clarence Adler of New York. Godowsky's statement on his son. occurs in his letter of August 10, 1932 (reproduced in facs. in Instalment 16), and Howard's material on it—including equally flowery endorsements by James Huneker and E. F. McMahon—occurs in Instalment 4. Some strongly negative reactions are quoted near the end of the book, too.

mention. The violinist **Hermann Grädener** (1844–1929), son of Karl in Hamburg (ssʙ X), left a Sonata in d, Op. 18, for 2 Ps (pub. in 1882) and a Sonata in c, Op. 35, for Vn & P (pub. in 1902).[12] The pianist and song composer **Anton Rückauf** (1855–1903) left a Sonata in f, Op. 7, for Vn & P (pub. in 1888) that was reviewed as strong in the development of ideas but less so in their originality.[13] The organist **Rudolph Bibl** (1832–1902) left one published sonata each for P-duet (Op. 36 in A, 1880), P & Vn (Op. 42 in B♭, 1880), and organ (Op. 74 in d, 1895).[14] A pupil of Herzogenberg and disciple of Brahms (ssʙ IX), Prince **Heinrich XXIV von Reuss** (1855–1910) composed among numerous chamber works four duo sonatas that created moderate interest when they were published (1885–1905), including Opp. 5 and 21 in g and e for Vn & P, Op. 22 in G for Va & P, and Op. 7 in C for Vc & P.[15] **Ludwig Schytte** (1848–1909), Liszt pupil and popular composer of piano miniatures,[16] left only one full-fledged sonata, Op. 53 in B♭ for P solo, published during the first of his twenty years in Vienna (1887). A competent, fluent, pleasant, pianistic work in three movements (F-M-VF), Schytte's Sonata in B♭ does not free itself from the aroma of the piano teaching studio, including sentimental themes that explain why such a work could hardly be revived with impunity today (Ex. 58).

The blind pianist and organist **Josef Labor** (1842–1924), a pupil of Simon Sechter and a teacher of Schoenberg, left one published sonata each for Vn & P (Op. 5 in d, 1893), Vc & P (Op. 7 in A, 1896), and organ (Op. 15 in b, 1912).[17] The piano virtuoso **Max Jentsch** (1855–1918) wrote sonatas in c and A, Opp. 23 and 59, for P & Vn, pub. in 1905 and 1910, after his move to Vienna in 1894.[18] Another piano virtuoso,

12. Cf. ᴍɢɢ VI 660–61 (K. Stephenson); ᴍᴡ XIV (1883) 515 (E. Wede), ɴᴢᴍ LXXIX/1 (1883) 205, and Hanslick/ᴄᴏɴᴄᴇʀᴛᴇ 350–51, all, with reservations, on Op. 18; ɴᴢᴍ XCIX (1903) 372 (approval of Op. 35), ᴅᴍ II/4 (1903) 380 (qualified praise of Op. 35 by W. Altmann), and Cobbett/ᴄʜᴀᴍʙᴇʀ I 486 (W. Altmann, with approval of Op. 35 as a Brahmsian work).

13. ᴍᴡ XXI (1890) 140. Cf., also, Riemann/ʟᴇxɪᴋᴏɴ II 1562; ɴᴢᴍ LXXII/2 (1876) 280 (on a Son. in D, apparently not pub.); Cobbett/ᴄʜᴀᴍʙᴇʀ II 311 (W. Altmann, describing Op. 7).

14. Cf. Riemann/ʟᴇxɪᴋᴏɴ I 169; Altmann/ᴋᴀᴍᴍᴇʀᴍᴜsɪᴋ 195, 296; sᴍᴡ LIII (1895) 404 (mild approval of Op. 74); ᴍᴡ XXVIII (1897) 236 (brief and negative on Op. 74); Frotscher/ᴏʀɢᴇʟsᴘɪᴇʟ II 1207.

15. Cf. ᴍɢɢ XI 334–35 (F. Göthel); Cobbett/ᴄʜᴀᴍʙᴇʀ II 292 (W. Altmann); Altmann/ᴋᴀᴍᴍᴇʀᴍᴜsɪᴋ 207, 247, 257. Opp. 21 and 22 are reviewed as appealing, skillful, and unoriginal in ᴅᴍ V/3 (1905–6) 170.

16. Cf. ᴍɢɢ XII 421 (N. Schiørring).

17. Cf. ᴍɢɢ VIII 16 (R. Quoika); ᴍᴡ XXVIII (1897) 534 (short, unfavorable review of Op. 5); sᴍᴡ LV (1897) 628 (similar on Op. 7); but cf., also, Cobbett/ᴄʜᴀᴍʙᴇʀ II 85 (A. Mann, describing Op. 7 as a genial work superior to Op. 5).

18. Cf. ᴍɢɢ VII 6–7 (O. Wessely); ᴍᴡ XXXVII (1906) 106 (favorable references to Op. 23); ᴅᴍ VI/2 (1906–7) 255 (short, unfavorable review of Op. 23); ᴍᴡ XXXVII (1906) 106a (favorable review of Op. 23) and 143 (qualified review of the same).

as well as teacher and editor, **Emil Sauer** (1862–1942) was holding masterclasses in Vienna when his two piano sonatas appeared, in D and E♭ (1903–7).[19] The important conductor and writer **Felix Weingartner** (1863–1942) wrote two sonatas for Vn & P, Op. 41/1 and 2 in D and f♯, published together in 1907, that mark deliberate, rather ineffectual returns to Bach and Beethoven.[20] The pianist and voice instructor **Robert Gund** (**Gound**; 1865–1927) wrote two more violin sonatas (Opp. 33 in d, 1915 [?], and 44 in a [1925]), of which Op. 33 was praised as a richly Romantic, outstanding concert work.[21] The theory teacher **Johanna Müller-Hermann** (1878–1941) may be added to

Ex. 58. From the first movement of Ludwig Schytte's Sonata in B♭, Op. 53 (after the original Universal Ed. of 1887).

our small list of women composers (ssb III), for a Sonata in d, Op. 5, for P & Vn, pub. in 1907, as well as two other sonatas left in MS—Op. 8 for P solo and 17 for P & Vc.[22] The variously stationed choral director **Roderich Mojsisovics** (1877–1953), trained in Graz, left a Sonata for P & Vn in D, Op. 29 (pub. in 1911), another for P & Va in c, Op. 74 (pub. in 1927), and another for organ, in b♭, Op. 38, described as close to Reger in style (pub. *ca.* 1925).[23] And another choral director, promoted by Brahms and others, **Richard Wickenhauser** (1867–1936) contributed two sonatinas for P solo Op. 5 and one sonata each for

19. Cf. MGG XI 1431–32 (R. Sietz); DM III/3 (1903–4) 196 (negative review of "Grande Sonate" in D as being too long for its content; by J. V. da Motta); MT XLVI (1905) 261 (favorable review of the first 2 mvts. of Son. in E♭ as played by the composer, but not the last 2).

20. Cobbett/CHAMBER II 576 (W. Altmann). Cf. GROVE IX 243–45 (J. A. Fuller-Maitland and H. C. Colles); Altmann/KAMMERMUSIK 231; DM VII/2 (1907–8) 99 (W. Altmann). *Ca.* 1926 Weingartner arranged Beethoven's Op. 106 for orchestra (cf. SCE 532).

21. DM XV/2 (1915) 690. Cf. Riemann/LEXIKON I 678; Altmann/KAMMERMUSIK 204.

22. Cf. GROVE V 992 (K. Geiringer), Suppl. 314; Altmann/KAMMERMUSIK 218; Cobbett/CHAMBER II 185 (W. W. Cobbett).

23. Cf. MGG IX 429–30 (R. Federhofer-Königs); Altmann/KAMMERMUSIK 216 and 249; Frotscher/ORGELSPIEL II 1246.

Vn & P and Vc & P, Opp. 13 in e and 18 in F, all pub. between 1900 and 1902.[24]

Composers in South Germany (R. Strauss) and Switzerland (H. Huber)

Our chief late-Romantic in south Germany was the German composer in Munich "who since the death of Richard Wagner was the first to win world-wide recognition" [25] and who at the same time marks a last highpoint of the Romantic Era, **Richard Strauss** (1864–1949). Of course, that recognition has come for Strauss's best symphonic poems, operas, and songs rather than his chamber music, which includes the ten complete and incomplete sonatas or sonatinas that are extant. Yet two of these sonatas, Op. 6 for Vc & P and Op. 18 for Vn & P, have become established among the relatively few standard works in their mediums that continue to survive beyond the 19th century.[26] And like these two, three others continue in print (Op. 5 for P solo and the 2 wind "sonatinas") and two others have been available recently (1966) in recordings (Op. 5 and the first wind sonatina).

The first five of Strauss's extant sonatinas or sonatas are incomplete and complete student works in two to four movements, composed between the ages of ten and fifteen (1874–79) but never published (as of 1967).[27] Three of them are the first half of what was originally a set of six diminutive sonatas. The incipits of their movements suffice to confirm Strauss's avowedly deep roots in Mozart's music, however much his later music may conceal or abandon that interest. The fourth of the extant sonatas (in E, 1877) comes closer to the folklike solidity of Haydn. And the fifth, "Grosse Sonate" in c (1879), is another four-movement work, but twice as long (20 pp.) and now decidedly in a Beethovian style.[28] One soon realizes that Strauss was taking himself or

24. Cf. Riemann/LEXIKON II 2022–23; BAKER 1791; Altmann/KAMMERMUSIK 231 and 266; MW XXXI (1900) 146 (on Op. 5), XXXIII (1902) 601 (on Op. 13) and 600 (on Op. 18).

25. Mueller von Asow/STRAUSS I "Introduction"; cf., also, MGG XII 1474–99 (W. Pfannkuch & W. Schuh).

26. Both remain available in a choice of recordings.

27. Mueller von Asow/STRAUSS III o. Op. AV. 17 in C, 18 in F, 19 in B♭, 38 in E, and 60 in c, with generous incipits, all available bibliographic information, and further references; cf., also, Steinitzer/STRAUSS 182–84 and 185–87, with some incipits and brief descriptions, plus information on at least three student sons. that now seem to be lost. Grassberger & Hadamowsky/STRAUSS 46 lists an "Andante aus E-moll Sonate für Papa" in an undated MS (ca. 1874) not otherwise reported.

28. Strauss numbered these two sonatas consecutively, "I" and "II," and assigned op. nos., 10 and 22, that have no bearing on his later sequence of op. nos.

being taken eclectically and progressively through a century of historical styles before beginning to formulate his own.[29]

The first of Strauss's five remaining sonatas, all published soon after completion, was Op. 5 in b for P solo, composed at the incredibly early age of 16 (winter, 1880–81; first pub. in 1883).[30] The age is incredible because the craftsmanship and experience are so advanced.[31] Musically, the work flows, plays, and sounds well enough to invite an occasional performance today, but it is still derivative enough to keep it from standing on its own merits. The first movement is an obviously deliberate essay on the · · · — motive of Beethoven's Fifth Symphony, reiterated at least as often but less imaginatively. Yet except for a slightly thicker texture, both those reiterations and the harmonic idiom are more Mendelssohnian than Beethovian. Only the start of the second theme, with its leap to a dim.-7th chord (mss. 57–60), hints at Strauss's future romanticism. The remaining three movements are almost unadulterated Mendelssohn.[32] One notes especially the suggestion of the "Scherzo" from *A Midsummer Night's Dream* in the middle section in e, in 3/8 meter, of the melodious "Adagio cantabile"; or the finale of Mendelssohn's "Phantasie" Op. 28 in the "Scherzo"; or Mendelssohn's *Capriccio brillant* in b, in the figuration of Strauss's finale.[33]

Strauss wrote his cello sonata, Op. 6 in F, two years later (1882–83), with publication also following in 1883. After two early performances of the work he reported extraordinary applause from his listeners and, in particular, Joachim's pleasure in the opening idea, although by 1890 he was already noting how hard it was to play a work in which he himself no longer believed.[34] The eclectic style this time was that of his newest favorite, Brahms,[35] and with it came greater lyricism and greater freedom of phrase syntax, expanded harmonic resources, increased subjectivity, and increased authority (Ex. 59).[36] Again, the

29. Cf. Specht/STRAUSS I 105–6; Krause/STRAUSS 30 and 34–35.

30. The incipits and essential ‛circumstances and bibliography of Opp. 5, 6, and 18 are in Mueller von Asow/STRAUSS I 16–21 and 76–78; cf., also, Steinitzer/STRAUSS 203–5 and 206–7. Opp. 5, 6, and 18 are all pub. by Universal today. Dubitsky/STRAUSS 289 gives brief attention to Op. 5 in a survey of Strauss's chamber music, and Steinitzer/KLAVIER 106–7 in an article on the importance of the piano to Strauss. A detailed study of Strauss's sons. is wanting.

31. In Specht/STRAUSS I 109–10, Op. 5 is described not as a product of youth but of a child grown old too soon.

32. Del Mar/STRAUSS I 9.

33. In SMW XL (1882) 577 the reviewer found all but the first of the 4 mvts. rather empty.

34. Mueller von Asow/STRAUSS I 20; cf., also, Müller-Reuter/LEXIKON 621.

35. Cf. Krause/STRAUSS 33.

36. Brief descriptions of Op. 6 occur in Specht/STRAUSS I 111, with exx. (finding derivations from Schumann and Mendelssohn); Cobbett/CHAMBER II 461 (W.

Ex. 59. From the second movement of Richard Strauss's
Sonata in F, Op. 6 (after the Universal Ed.).

stylistic affinity is a little too close to let the work quite stand alone,
and again the motivic reiteration is a little overdone and inflexible.
Worthy of special note are the extended fughetta that completes the
development section as well as the exciting climax that tops off the
coda of the first movement; and the sensitively drawn out cantilena, so
appropriate to the cello's tenor range, in the second movement. The
rondo finale is less pretentious and less precocious, in spite of occasional
glimmerings of *Till Eulenspiegels lustige Streiche* in the humor of its
melodic twists and treatment of 6/8 meter.

The violin sonata Op. 18 in E-flat, composed and first published in
1888,[37] is Strauss's most important sonata and one of his main chamber
works. Although scarcely five years separate it from Op. 6, those few
years saw remarkable advances toward the development of his own
personality and self-expression, and toward a changed philosophy of
music (influenced by the memorable introduction the composer and
poet Alexander Ritter is credited with having given Strauss to the
music of the "New German" school in 1885–86 [38]). Right from the
heroic opening theme and its characteristic dotted-and-triplet pattern,
as well as the free, cyclical reversal of this pattern in the finale (Ex. 60),
we realize we are on the threshold of his first masterwork, *Don Juan*
(composed concurrently), and other symphonic poems to follow.[39]

Altmann, likewise); Dunhill/CHAMBER 183–85 (with exx.); Dubitsky/STRAUSS 291–92;
Steinitzer/STRAUSS 204–5; and Del Mar/STRAUSS I 15–17 (the most illuminating
discussion).

37. Cf. Mueller von Asow/STRAUSS I 76–78.

38. Cf. Krause/STRAUSS 34; Del Mar/STRAUSS 39–40.

39. For descriptions of Op. 18 cf. Specht/STRAUSS I 115–18; Cobbett/CHAMBER II
461; Del Mar/STRAUSS I 47–51 (again, the most illuminating discussion). Strauss's
sons. seem to have received almost no attention in the contemporary press. A
short paragraph on Op. 18 in MW XXI (1890) 315 found this work interesting for
its energy, lyricism, fantasy, and ideas, although not especially new.

Ex. 60.   From the openings of the two outer movements of
Richard Strauss's Sonata in E♭, Op. 18 (after the Universal Ed.).

Brahms is once more the main influence, although in its dash, wide
range, and technical difficulties Op. 18 becomes more of an exaggeration than an imitation of Brahms. Indeed, one almost senses in the
peaks of these outer movements a taste of the overconfidence, bravado,
and conceit Strauss reportedly never quite outgrew.[40] In the first
movement the "sonata form" is twisted and turned without quite being
broken, especially in the long development and shortened recapitulation sections (recalling the letter quoted in SSB II, also from 1888, in
which Strauss tells Bülow how he no longer found "sonata form"
adequate for his ideas). On the other hand, the work reaches a new
intensity of lyrical expression, as in the recapitulation of the second
theme and its climactic outcome in the first movement (mss. 221–88), or
as in the entire middle movement, rightly called "Improvisation."
Always a refreshing surprise in the latter is the middle section, whose
muted exchanges of fitful rhythms between the two instruments recall
the poetry of "Vogel als Prophet" (Op. 82/7) by Schumann. The more
lyrical sections of this movement modulate and cadence deceptively
on harmonies that recall Strauss's older contemporary Fauré.

Strauss's final two "sonatas"—actually *Sonatine für Bläser* in F and
Symphonie für Bläser in E♭ or "Second Sonatina"—were composed in

40. Cf. Del Mar/STRAUSS I xi–xii.

his last years (1943–45) and published posthumously.[41] Exceptional in the present survey, of course, is their scoring for sixteen wind instruments, including 2 Fls, 2 Obs, 5 Cls, 4 Hns, and 3 Bns. In writing these works the octogenarian was harking to earlier works in similar settings and enjoying a bit of private fun,[42] inscribing "From the workshop of an invalid" over the first (during convalescence from a prolonged illness) and "Joyful workshop" over the second. Another inscription over the "Second Sonatina," "To the divine Mozart at the end of a life of gratitude," may relate to the neo-Classic though not necessarily Mozartean style of this ebullient music. But the two works are not short, lasting 28 and 36 minutes as compared with 24 and 27 for Opp. 6 and 18, respectively. Both have the same four-movement plan (considering the combined middle mvt. of the Sonatina in F as 2 mvts. for the moment)—F-M-Mi-F or F-M-M-S/F—although Strauss originally started with only one movement in the Sonatina in E♭, and kept adding and rearranging the further movements.

Other composers in south Germany can concern us but briefly here. A pupil of, and successor to, Rheinberger in Munich, the short-lived pianist **Ludwig Thuille** (1861–1907) was also a friend of Strauss and, like Strauss, at least a partial convert to the newer Romantic styles and programme music largely through the influence of Alexander Ritter.[43] Although Thuille's operatic, choral, and chamber music, as well as his theory teaching, generally met with substantial approval, none of his four sonatas seems to have been especially successful. These include an Op. 1 in d for Vn & P (1880), reviewed as Haydnesque but promising;[44] a Sonata in a, Op. 2, for organ (1889), described as a work of substance in the lyrical Mendelssohnian vein;[45] a Sonata in d, Op. 22, for Vc & P (1902), reviewed as appealing in its first two movements though less so in its finale;[46] and a Sonata in e, Op. 30, for Vn & P (1904) that figured in the controversy over Reger's Op. 72 to be noted shortly.[47]

The brothers **Philipp Wolfrum** (1854–1919) and **Carl Wolfrum** (1857–at least 1923) were both organists, students of Rheinberger, and

41. In 1964 and 1952, respectively, by Boosey & Hawkes in London, with prefaces.

42. Cf. Del Mar/STRAUSS I 459–60.

43. Cf. MGG XIII 377–79 (O. Kaul), with further bibliography.

44. MW XII (1881) 274–75; NZM LXXIX/1 (1883) 86–87, with ex.

45. Frotscher/ORGELSPIEL II 1206.

46. MW XXXIII (1902) 600 (E. Segnitz). Cf., also, Cobbett/CHAMBER II 508–9 (R. Felber).

47. On the music of Op. 30 cf. Shand/VIOLIN 75–77, with 5 exx. Both Opp. 22 and 30 were reprinted in 1927.

composers of three sonatas each,[48] published between about 1879 and
1885, and 1892 and 1900, respectively. These somewhat conservative
works, all for organ except the middle one by Philipp (Op. 7 in e for P
& Vc), won moderate though not invariable praise for their warmth,
depth, and skill.[49] The important Munich musicologist **Adolf Sandberger** (1864–1943), another Rheinberger student,[50] left a neo-Baroque
Trio-Sonate in c, Op. 4 (1890), for Vn, Va, & P, reviewed as a skillful
exercise;[51] and a Sonata in d, Op. 10 (1892) for Vn & P, reviewed as a
Classically oriented work by a knowing and feeling musician.[52] The
landscape painter **Desiré Thomassin** (1858–at least 1929), another
Rheinberger pupil, was a reportedly superior, warm, impassioned
composer, now forgotten,[53] who left two sonatas each for P & Vn and
for P & Vc, published between 1908 and 1927.[54] Yet another Rheinberger pupil, **Anton Beer-Walbrunn** (1864–1929) left two published
sonatas—Opp. 15 in G for P & Vc (1897) and 30 in d for P & Vn
(composed by 1906, pub. in 1926)—and a "Fantasie-Sonate," Op. 58 for
P solo (in MS).[55] Op. 30, in particular, deserves renewed hearings, to
judge from the exceptional praise it received for its neo-Beethovian
spirit and outstanding skill in both form and texture.[56]

By contrast, the orientation of Thuille's versatile student **August
Reuss** (1871–1935) was decidedly toward Modernism, especially in the
sense of chord and key relationships that strain the limits of traditional
harmony and tonality (Ex. 61). But a Romantic lyrical sweep still
prevails in Reuss's four published sonatas, including Opp. 26 and 35
("Romantische Sonate"), both in D for Vn & P (1910 and 1920), and

48. Cf. Riemann/LEXIKON II 2047; PAZDÍREK XV/543.

49. On Philipp's sons., cf. MW XII (1881) 464 (Op. 1 in b); MW XVI (1885) 498,
SMW XL (1882) 978, and NZM LXXIX (1883) 118 (on Op. 7). On Carl's Op. 4 in f
and Op. 15 in F, cf. MW XXIV (1893) 257; DM III/1 (1903–4) 287 (K. Straube);
SMW L (1892) 54 and LVIII (1900) 897. On the sons. of both cf. Frotscher/ORGELSPIEL
II, 1200, 1208, 1209, 1243.

50. Cf. MGG XI 1355–58 (H. Engel); Sandberger/AUFSÄTZE 320–30.

51. MW XXI (1890) 427; but its originality is lauded in DM II/3 (1903) 46–47
(W. Altmann) and MT XXXI (1890) 426.

52. MW XXIV (1893) 594–95. Litolff pub. a 3d ed. in 1938.

53. He is listed only in Riemann/LEXIKON II 1840 among standard reference
works.

54. Cf. Altmann/KAMMERMUSIK 229 and 265; Cobbett/CHAMBER II 508 (W. W.
Cobbett); and the reviews in MW XL (1909–10) 539–40 and DM VIII/3 (1908–9) 44
(W. Altmann on Op. 72 for P & Vn); X/2 (1910–11) 362–63 (H. Schlemüller on Op.
76 for P & Vc).

55. Cf. MGG I 1508–9 (O. Kaul); Altmann/KAMMERMUSIK 194, 252.

56. Cf. DM X/4 (1910–11) 375; MERCURE II (1906) 232; and Cobbett/CHAMBER I
81 (both W. Altmann).

Opp. 27 and 55 ("Kleine Sonate"), in c and C, for P solo (1912 and 1930).[57]

The Italo-German opera composer **Ermanno Wolf-Ferrari** (1876–1948), still another Rheinberger student, left two early sonatas for Vn & P, Opp. 1 in g and 10 in a (both pub. in 1902) that deserve re-examination for their freshness of ideas and unorthodox approaches to form.[58] A composer much better known inside than outside Germany is **Julius Weismann** (1879–1950), a pupil of Rheinberger and Thuille, who left at least 15 sonatas—2 for P solo (Opp. 87 in a, 1924; 127 in B♭, 1940), one for 2 Ps (Op. 122 [Sonatine] in a, 1937), one for P-duet

Ex. 61. From the start of the development section in the first movement of August Reuss's Sonata in c, Op. 27 (after the Wunderhorn ed. of 1912).

(Op. 142 [MS?]), one for unaccompanied Vn (Op. 30 in d, 1910), one for P & Cl (Op. 72 in d, 1942), one for P & Fl (Op. 135 in g, 1942), 3 for P & Vc (Opp. 9 [MS?]; 73 in c, 1927; 137 [Sonatina concertante; MS?]), and 5 for P & Vn (Opp. 28 in F, 1911; 47 in f♯, 1913; 69 [Sonatina] in a, 1926; 72a [MS?]; and 79 [MS?]).[59] Weismann's prevailing style is disarmingly direct and simple. Combined at times with harsh, unprepared dissonances on strong beats and some rapid key

57. Cf. MGG XI 333–34 (A. Würz), with wrong pub. dates and further bibl.; HOFMEISTER, *passim;* Cobbett/CHAMBER II 291 (W. Altmann). Op. 26 is praised, with reservations, in DM X/2 (1910–11) 43 (W. Altmann).

58. Cf. GROVE IX 329–31 (F. Bonavia); MW XXXVI (1905) 464 (E. Segnitz); DM V/1 (1905–6) 416 (W. Altmann); NZM XCIX (1903) 349; Cobbett/CHAMBER II 590–91 (W. Altmann); Altmann/KAMMERMUSIK 232.

59. Cf. GROVE IX 246 (A. Loewenberg) and Suppl. 478 (with reference to a cat. of 1955); Altmann/KAMMERMUSIK, *passim;* Moser/LEXIKON II 1418–19.

shifts (as in the development section of Op. 127/i), it qualifies as 20th-century neo-Classicism. But the tonality and designs are generally clear and conservative enough, except for the variable cycles, and the warmer moments are sufficient to keep this efficient, individually flavored music safely within Romantic confines.[60]

In Swiss centers (meaning mainly Basel, Zürich, and Geneva), the most important composer not only late in the century but throughout the Romantic Era was **Hans Huber** (1852–1921), who trained in Leipzig under Richter, Reinecke, and others before eventually settling in Basel.[61] Huber's large output, which touches nearly every main category of music, includes 19 works originally composed as sonatas, all but 2 of them duos and all of them published, in the years from 1876 to 1915. Among those sonatas are 10 for Vn & P (plus one arrangement), 4 for Vc & P, 3 for 2 Ps (one of which was first scored for Vc & P), and 2 for P solo, of which one is a sonatina. There is also a Sonata in B♭, Op. 135 (1913), for 2 Vns & P, arranged from a set of pieces for Vn & P.[62] About a third of the sonatas are qualified as to mood or style by descriptive words in the titles—"Appassionata," "Graziosa," "Lirica," and "Quasi fantasia" in Sonatas 6–9 for Vn & P (and "pathétique" in the arranged son.); "Pastoralsonate" in the second cello sonata; and "Giacosa" in the third two-piano sonata.

Huber's wide popularity during his lifetime would be justification enough for the needed study of his complete sonata output.[63] From such a study we might gain a better idea of the over-all quality as well as the content and craftsmanship of this output. The craftsmanship is already confirmed, in the relatively few examples available here, by the accurate part-writing, euphonious scoring, sure command of harmony, and expert development of ideas into well conceived forms. But the quality of the ideas and their supporting harmony has proved to be disappointing here—not the equal of that, for example, from his Zürich predecessor Hermann Goetz (ssb X). The recollections of Schumann border on the sentimental, even on the banal, in spite of the charm they may have had for their day. But even in their day they

60. Cf. Cobbett/CHAMBER II 577 (H. Leichtentritt); DM XI/2 (1911–12) 169 (W. Altmann, with high praise for Op. 30 as preparation for Bach's and Reger's unaccompanied Vn sons. and in its own right).

61. Refardt/HUBER is the chief study of the man, with a full, dated, informative catalogue of his works but only brief comments on the music (and only a few sentences, pp. 117–18, on the sons.). Further documents may be found in Bundi/HUBER. Cf., also, MGG VI 810–11 (E. Refardt); SCHWEIZER LEXIKON 102–8.

62. Cf. Refardt/HUBER 151–52; DM XIII/2 (1913–14) 167 (limited approval by W. Altmann).

63. Cobbett/CHAMBER I 575–76 (W. Altmann) comments on the Vn sons. and describes 3 of them; Shand/VIOLIN 178–88 has exx.

drew reservations from the reviewers, who often give the impression of wanting to write more enthusiastically. Perhaps the reviewers hoped to spare the feelings of a man who sang forth so ingenuously, even naively. In any case, a typical comment was the following, on Huber's second sonata for 2 Ps (Op. 121 in E♭; 1905):

Nothing that I have been able to know by Huber has made an overwhelming impression on me, but almost without exception everything has touched and delighted [me].[64]

There are harsher reviews, too, as of the fourth cello sonata (Op. 130 in B♭; 1909):

Only very few artists succeed in composing good cello sonatas. But from so renowned a composer as Hans Huber one would have expected something better than the work at hand. Everything forced, nothing felt. Or should he feel thus? Motive without any charm. . . . Such literature can bring no new friends to the instrument.[65]

And there are more commendatory reviews, too, especially those by Wilhelm Altmann on the sixth and ninth violin sonatas.[66]

To some extent Huber's later music does show a tightening up of form and means, and somewhat more guarded sentiments, perhaps under the increasing influence of Brahms. But one can find this sort of writing earlier, too, especially in the slower movements. An example is the slow introduction to the first sonata for two pianos (Op. 31 in g; 1878), which, with telling sonorities, solemnly develops a single idea from a *pianissimo* opening to a *fortissimo* peak and back. Yet the main "Allegro con fuoco" that follows (in this one-mvt. work as compared with the standard 4-mvt. plan in most of Huber's sons.) depends on trite themes and chatty extensions that fail to bear out the significant opening. Sometimes one feels that Huber is writing vocal music. Thus, there are places in his single full sonata for P solo (Op. 47 in E♭; 1879) that sound curiously like anticipations of Puccini's favorite arias reduced for piano, not only in the melody and harmony but in the practical but pianistically uninviting scoring itself (e.g., Op. 47/i/20–35).

64. DM VI/3 (1906–7) 238 (R. Louis). W. Altmann's review of Op. 135, for 2 Vns & P, is similar (DM XIII/2 [1913–14] 167), as is the review of Op. 121, for P solo, in NZM CI (1905) 543.

65. DM IX/3 (1909–10) 325 (A. Laser). The 3d Vc son. (Op. 114 in c♯; 1900) is similarly reviewed in SMW LVIII (1900) 945; and the 7th Vn son. (Op. 119 in G; 1903) in DM III/2 (1903–4) 201, but more favorably in MW XXXV (1904) 608 (E. Segnitz).

66. DM II/3 (1902–3) 46 and 47 (Op. 116 in d; 1901), XIV/3 (1914–15) 183 (Op. 132 in g; 1915). These reviews are trans. in Cobbett/CHAMBER I 575–76. Cf., also, SMW XXXVI (1878) 419 (on Op. 18 in c; 1877) and LVII (1899) 833 (on Op. 112 in E, for Vn & P; 1897).

Other sonata composers resident in Switzerland in this period include the writer **Selmar Bagge** (1823–96), the author himself of an early summary of sonata history (1880; SBE 409) as well as two piano sonatas favorably reviewed in 1890 and 1891;[67] the fine pianist and teacher **Willy Rehberg** (1863–1937; father of the author and composer Walter), whose Op. 3 in g (1885?), for P solo, and especially his Op. 10 in D (1886) for P & Vn, won favor;[68] the prolific, versatile **Joseph Lauber** (1864–1952), student of Rheinberger, who left several published sonatas for P & Vn, P & Fl, and P solo;[69] the pianist **Friedrich Niggli** (1875–at least 1954; son of the musicologist Arnold), another of Rheinberger's many successful students, whose two duo sonatas—Opp. 6, in a, for P & Vc, and 7, in E, for P & Vn (both 1902)—were generally well received;[70] and the conductor **Volkmar Andreae** (1879–1962), from whom we have a three-movement Sonata in D (F-S-VF), Op. 4, for P & Vn (1903).[71] Once much played, this is a broadly arched, lyrical, driving work, with heroic passages that recall Strauss. It should remain in the all too limited repertoire of sonatas for its medium.

Composers in Central Germany (Reger, Karg-Elert, Pfitzner)

In central Germany during the late-Romantic Era, the most important composer of sonatas (and much other music) was **Max Reger** (1873–1916). Reger identified chiefly with Munich up to 1907 and with
72a   Leipzig thereafter.[72] Infused early and fully with the great masterworks from Bach to Brahms and Wagner, he got his solid training primarily from Hugo Riemann, although by the start of this century he was renouncing the more traditional influences that Riemann represented, he was finding new interest in the music of contemporaries like Busoni and Richard Strauss, and he was beginning to encounter the increasing

67. SMW XLVIII (1890) 131 and XLIX (1891) 119. Cf. GROVE I 344 (G. Grove).

68. MW XVII (1886) 54 (on Op. 3, including references to some empty and overly long sections) and XVIII (1887) 145–46 (on Op. 10 and its welcome "dolce" character in a day of so much gloomy music). Cf., also, MGG XI 143–44 (W. Schuh).

69. Cf. Riemann/LEXIKON I 1002; GROVE V 84–85 (K. v. Fischer); Altmann/KAMMERMUSIK 213, 275; SCHWEIZER LEXIKON 126–28; SMW LVIII (1900) 691 (reviewing Op. 4 in d for P & Vn and Op. 7 in f for P solo as promising and Brahmsian); NZM XCIX (1903) 247 (with praise for all aspects of Op. 7).

70. MW XXXIII (1902) 535 (E. Segnitz); DM II/4 (1902–3) 380 and 384 (W. Altmann); SMW LX (1902) 766; NZM XCIX (1903) 200. Cf. SCHWEIZER LEXIKON 157–58.

71. Cf. MGG I 461–62 (H. Ehinger); SCHWEIZER LEXIKON 12–14; BAKER Suppl. 4; Cobbett/CHAMBER I 22 (E. Evans).

72. Bagier/REGER and Stein/REGER are two main books on the man and his works. Such a book in English is lacking. A full, classified bibliography appears in Stein/VERZEICHNIS 567–604. Cf., also, GROVE VII 91–99 (K. Hasse and E. Blom); MGG XI 119–32 (H. Wirth).

hostility that greeted his "progress" as an innovative harmonist.[73] Had it not been for his expert, uncommonly sensitive piano playing and the success of his neo-Bach organ works he might not have been able to weather the opposition up to the years when his further compositions began to find more friends.[74]

Reger was one of the most prolific of the masters, with a total of several hundred published works to show for his approximately 28 years of composing.[75] Among these works are in all 33 sonatas, helping to make him both the most important composer of Romantic "absolute music after Brahms" [76] and the most prolific sonata composer among all Romantic masters of no less stature.[77] Along with 2 organ sonatas and 4 substantial "sonatinas" for P solo, there are 16 duo sonatas—9 for P & Vn, 4 for P & Vc, and 3 for P & Cl—as well as 11 that contribute significantly to that infrequent but valued setting for unaccompanied violin. A tabulation follows here of these 33 sonatas that includes, besides dates and other bibliographic essentials, the keys, tempos or types, and lengths (in mss.) of the separate movements, and lengths (in minutes) of the complete cycles,[78] all to permit comparisons with information in our Chapter VI on styles and forms. Anyone seeking such factual information will find much of it handed to him on a silver platter in the comprehensive, detailed thematic index of Reger's published music by Fritz Stein (1953).[79] This is but one product of an apparent Reger renaissance, at least in Germany, sponsored by the latest of several Reger societies and including, in addition to other aids to be cited shortly, an edition of his complete works in 35 volumes[80] begun in 1954 and almost completed as of this writing (1967).

As we have seen so many composers do, Reger made his debut in print with a sonata.[81] Op. 1 in d, dedicated to Riemann, was the first of nineteen conservative opera published by Augener in London at

73. Cf. Stein/REGER 13–21, 35–40; Bagier/REGER 256.

74. Cf. Stein/REGER 43–44, 30–32.

75. There are numerous sets of separate pieces among his 146 op. nos. and his many other pubs. without op. nos.

76. Cf. Bagier/REGER 238.

77. Schubert's 33 sons. would equal this total but for at least 8 of them being incomplete (SSB VII). Failure to complete works was not one of Reger's problems.

78. According to entries in Stein/VERZEICHNIS.

79. Stein/VERZEICHNIS.

80. Reger/WERKE-m.

81. A thorough study of Reger's sonatas is lacking and much to be desired. Useful surveys that include the sons. may be found in Bagier/REGER 238–78 and Stein/REGER 98–110, with somewhat less inclusive surveys being in Mersmann/KAMMERMUSIK 132–50 and Cobbett/CHAMBER II 277–83 (E. Wellesz). The unaccompanied Vn sons. are surveyed, with numerous exx., in Gates/SOLO 197–208. The organ sons. and Reger's concern with their special problem are discussed in Barker/REGER.

Max Reger's Sonatas (grouped by scoring types)

Scoring	Op./no.	Key	Composed	First edition	Reger/WERKE-m	Mvts.: tempos or types / Keys: mvt.-by-mvt. / mss.: mvt.-by-mvt.	Total minutes	Titles and/or dedications
P & Vn	1	d	1890	Augener, 1893	XIX 1	4: F- Sc- S-VF / d- d-Bb- d / 638: 175-126-93-244	28	ded. to H. Riemann
"	3	D	1891	Augener, 1893	" 33	4: F-Sc- S - F / D: D-f#-c#/Db- D / 415: 161-60- 70 - 124	23	ded. to T. Kirchner
"	41	A	1899	J. Aibl, 1900	" 60	4: F-VF- S- F / A: A- c#-D- A / 457: 144-112-45-156	23	ded. to J. Hösl
"	72	C	1903	Lauterbach, 1904	" 102	4: F-VF- S-VF / C: C- d-A- C / 883: 373-160-52-298	32	originally to be ded. to "the German critics," then "to many," but pub. without ded.
"	84	f#	1905	Lauterbach, 1905	" 160	3: F- F-Va/fugue / f#: f#- d- f# / 626: 205-139-282	22	ded. to Marteau
"	103B/1	d/D	1909	Bote, 1909	XX 53	3: F-VF- Va / d/D: d- a- D / 657: 198-279-180	20	"Zwei kleine Sonaten"; ded. to R. Bignell
"	103B/2	A	"	"	" 81	4: F- Sc- S- F / A: A- d-E- A / 666: 249-161-74-182	19	

"	122	e/E	1911	Bote, 1911	" 139	4: M-VF-S- F / e/E: e- d-Ab- E / 750: 218-305-58-169	37	ded. to A. Schmuller & L. Kreutzer
"	139	c/C	1914	Simrock, 1915	" 187	4: F- S-VF-Va / c/C: c-D- a- C / 877: 237-67-294-279	36	ded. to A. Sommer
P & Vc	5	f	1892	Augener, 1893	XXI 1	3: F- S- F / f: f-Db- f / 564: 232-162-170	23	ded. to T. Kirchner
"	28	g/G	1898	J. Aibl, 1899	" 34	4: F-VF- S- F / g/G: g- d-E- G / 514: 177-140-74-123	17	ded. to H. Becker
"	78	F	1904	Lauterbach, 1904	" 66	4: F-VF- Va-VF / F: F- c- A- F / 695: 140-138-118-299	26	
"	116	a/A	1910	Peters, 1911	" 121	4: F-VF-S-F / a/A: a- a-E-A / 847: 189-380-71-207	28	ded. to J. Klengel
Vn only	42/1	d	1900	J. Aibl, 1900	XXIV 2	4: F- S-VF- F / d: d- a- d- d / 294: 65-50-120-69	13	ded. to W. Burmester
"	42/2	A	"		" 10	3: F-M-VF / A: A- f#- A / 236: 96-47-93	8	
"	42/3	b	"		" 16	4: S-M- VF-VF / b: b-G- b- b / 255: 80-22- 36-117	7	
"	42/4	g	"		" 22	3: S/F- F- Va / g: g-Bb- g / 266: 79-35-152	14	

Max Reger's Sonatas (grouped by scoring types) (*continued*)

Scoring	Op./no.	Key	Composed	First edition	Reger/WERKE-m	Mvts.: tempos or types / Keys: mvt.-by-mvt. / mss.: mvt.-by-mvt.	Total minutes	Titles and/or dedications
Vn only	91/1	a	1905		XXIV 30	4: S-VF-M- F / a: a- d- F- a / 218: 56- 34-34-94	10	
"	91/2	D	"		" 39	3: F- S-VF / D: D- f#- D / 249: 68-64-117	9	
"	91/3	Bb	"		" 47	3: F- Sc- F / Bb: Bb- G- Bb / 413: 132-178-103	10	
"	91/4	b	"	Lauterbach, 1906	" 55	4: F- S- Sc- F / b: b-G- G- b / 410: 95-40-121-154	12	
"	91/5	e	"		" 64	4: F- F- S- F / e: e- b- E- e / 324: 111-83-35-95	10	
"	91/6	G	"		" 73	4: F-M-M-VF / G: G- b- e- G / 292: 99-86-28-79	12	
"	91/7	a	"		" 82	3: F- Sc- Va / a: a- d- a / 403: 98-152-153	21	

P & Cl	49/1	Ab	1900	J. Aibl, 1901	XXI 173	4: F-VF- S-VF Ab- Ab-Eb-Db-Ab 503: 145-150-52-156	ded. to K. Wagner
"	49/2	f#	"	J. Aibl, 1903	" 207	4: F-VF-S-F f#: f#- b-A-f# 447: 148-106-83-110	
"	107	Bb	1908–09	Bote, 1909	" 241	4: M-VF- S- F Bb: Bb- d-Eb- Bb 497: 106-167-48-176	ded. to (the Grand Duke) Ernst Ludwig
P solo	89/1	e	1905	Lauterbach, 1905	XI 1	3: F-Va-VF e: e- A- e 364: 128- 98-138	"Sonatine . ."; ded. to M. Czerny
"	89/2	D	"	"	" 24	4: F-M-VF- F D: D-F- A- D 472: 164-54-100-154	
"	89/3	F	1908	Lauterbach, 1908	" 45	3: M- F- F F: F- a- F 388: 164-130-94	"Sonatine . ."; ded. to R. Teichmüller
"	89/4	a	"	"	" 65	3: F-M- F a: a-C- a 375: 176-63-136	
Organ	33	f#	1899	J. Aibl, 1899	XV 119	3: F-M- Va f#: f#-c/E- f# 305: 48- 47-210	ded. to A. W. Gottschalg
"	60	d	1901	Leuckart, 1902	XVI 140	3: F- S-F/fugue d: d-E- d 286: 128-64-94	ded. to M. Krause

Riemann's behest. In a highly enthusiastic review touching on the first ten of these publications, a review that recalls Schumann's sendoff for Brahms (ssb VIII), Arthur Smolian gave first preference to Reger's duo sonatas Opp. 1, 3, and 5 and the trio Op. 2, as remarkably serious, skillful, welcome productions by an unknown in a "time of musical superficiality." [82] He saw the strong influence of Beethoven and Brahms in Reger's "heroic" Op. 1, his similarly "dramatic" Op. 5, and his more "pastoral" Op. 3, but found Reger's smaller pieces somewhat less original and the organ pieces a little overloaded with contrapuntal adornments.

Beginning with those first publications, Reger's works tend to group according to his successive locales, with Opp. 1–18 composed in Wiesbaden, 1890–96 (?); Opp. 19–57, in Weiden, 1898–1901; Opp. 58–99, in Munich, 1901–7; and Opp. 100–46, in Leipzig, Meiningen, and Jena, 1907–16. As late as his compositions of 1900, including Op. 49 among the sonatas—that is, the two clarinet sonatas, written in obvious homage to those of Brahms published five years earlier (ssb IX)[83]— Reger's works were still winning generally strong approval from the reviewers;[84] as well they might, for with all their originality they still clung to the student's solid training and deep immersion in past masterworks.[85] But from the compositions of 1901, starting with such works as his Piano Quintet in c, Op. 64, composed just after his move to Munich, his styles and the reactions they aroused changed epochally. Thus, the Quintet was viewed, whether favorably or unfavorably, as a conspicuous turn to subjective fantasy and to the true personality of Reger.[86] And with the performance and publication in 1904 of the important Sonata in C, Op. 72 for P & Vn, an admittedly long and complex work, the reactions grew until they split into sharp, sometimes virulent controversy.[87] Although he won many new supporters, Reger quickly became known as that "hypermodern, excruciating, overladen, intemperate" composer. The performance that set off this particular controversy was his own early playing of Op. 72 with the violinist Henri

82. MW XXV (1894) 518–19 and 546–49, with extended exx.

83. High praise for both appears in smw LX (1902) 766; nzm XCIX (1903) 140 and CI (1905) 866.

84. As in MW XXXVI (1905) 675–76 (E. Segnitz). But there were some reservations, as in DM II/2 (1903) 39 (W. Altmann noting both extravagances and conservatisms in Op. 41 and values less than Bach's in Op. 42/1–4); and even with regard to Opp. 1 and 3, as in MMR XXIII (1893) 34 and 165.

85. Cf. Bagier/REGER 256–58.

86. As in the multiple review just cited, in MW XXXVI, including Opp. 49, 72, and 78, among others.

87. Cf. Marteau/REGER and Hoffmann/REGER on the music and the controversy; also, Bagier/REGER 64 and 258/59, Stein/REGER 40 and 105–6, and Rösner/REGER (a new analysis and re-evaluation).

Marteau in Frankfurt/M. On the same program was Ludwig Thuille's Sonata in e, Op. 30, for P & Vn (*supra*), which proved to serve as but a weak foil to Op. 72. And sitting in front were two recognized critics from Munich who would have reacted still more venomously had they realized that behind Reger's genial performance and music were some bitter slashes aimed back at them in the music itself, perhaps inspired by the parodying of his critics that Strauss had introduced into *Ein Heldenleben* in Frankfurt/M five years earlier.

Actually, Reger, piqued by growing hostility to his "new music" and "progress," [88] had courted the controversy over Op. 72. His first idea had been to dedicate the work to "The German critics," but neither this dedication nor his inscription "To Many" in the autograph got past the publisher into print.[89] However, "many" must have recognized the musical motives that spell out "sheep" and "monkeys," which, like *B-a-c-h* in the third movement (ms. 33), are skillfully interwoven into all four, especially the outer, movements (Ex. 62; with S for *Es* or E♭ and *b* for B♭, as usual).[90] Reger himself was especially fond of this bold yet heartfelt work. After that early performance he wrote, "I am certainly not arrogant, but this much still becomes clear to me, that in Frankfurt my Op. 72 was in every respect the best work." Moreover, three weeks later he concluded, ". . . if one looks more closely, there is nothing simpler or clearer than my Op. 72; and it is a truly grievous sign of the colossal depths of the 'current' musical intelligence when one can write about the 'total perversity,' incurable sickness, [and] nerve-killing unnaturalness of my Op. 72." [91]

Today, one can certainly agree that Reger's later sonatas (and other music) continued to be logical and purposeful as regards the forms, even in their complex fantasy, and also the over-all key relationships of the cycles. Both the forms and key choices are traditional and surprisingly straightforward (a fact already surmisable from the foregoing chart of movements and keys), although his "sonata forms" become increasingly asymmetrical, elastic, dualistic, and expressively refined, with a seamless flow like that of Wagner or Bruckner.[92] But the harmony, especially the voice-leading and more local or transitory modulations, do make for a problem—in fact, *the* problem as well as the most

88. Cf. Bagier/REGER 64–65.

89. Cf. Stein/VERZEICHNIS 136.

90. The motives are not so identified in the printed ed., but a letter from Reger of Nov. 1, 1903, first pub. in Heger/REGER, leaves no doubt as to his intentions.

91. Both letters, June 16 and July 25, 1904, to K. Straube, are quoted in Stein/ REGER 105. In DM III/4 (1903–4) 463, W. Altmann wrote of the "cacophony" in Op. 72. Much more sympathetic are the reviews of Opp. 72 and 78 in NZM CI (1905) 866 and of Op. 78 in DM IV/4 (1904–5) 287 (H. Schlemüller).

92. Cf. Denecke/REGER.

Ex. 62. From the final climax of the development section in the first movement of Max Reger's Sonata in C, Op. 72 (after Reger/WERKE-m XIX 113).

conspicuous style determinant—in Reger's music. In 1920 one of Reger's students, the theorist, and composer Hermann Grabner, wrote a useful monograph on Reger's harmony, starting with the fact that Reger repeatedly insisted on the complete logic and "legality" of his harmony, then going on to expound five basic laws formulated by Reger to comprehend all (late-Romantic) harmonic behavior.[93] Briefly and in slightly modernized terms: (1) all harmonic activity, even the most remote, goes back to the three primary triads—I, V, and IV—and to nothing else. Contrary to implications in Baroque thorough bass, ii, iii, vi, and vii are not independent chords but merely substitutes (having 2 notes in common) for IV, I or V, I or IV, and V, respectively. Even alterations like B-Db-F-A (or -Ab) for V in C are included within what then becomes a very wide and flexible orbit. (2) Extending the first law, a chord (or incipient 2-note chord) functions as I, IV, or V (regardless of chromatic alterations) when it bears a third-relationship (of roots) to any of these. Thus, the progression from Ab-C-Eb to C-E-G can sound like a plagal cadence, and Reger's much cultivated Nea-

93. Grabner/REGER 1–12; written, of course, in full cognizance of Reger's own *Beiträge zur Modulationslehre* (1903 and later eds.).

politan-6th triad like iv. (3) The primary triads can be extended without modulating to encompass—parenthetically, as it were—the V-of-V and IV-of-IV. For example, a tonic triad on E will relate to the triads on B and F♯ and on A and D. One curious concomitant of this law is Reger's idea that the V-of-V may progress directly to the tonic in slow music but only after a pause in faster music. (4) Any chord may connect with any chord, except that obscure progressions may require the clarification of an intervening chord. But Reger is less likely than the listener to feel any clarification is needed, or he may supply no more than a chromatic inflection in a quick modulation attenuated to a unison passage. And finally, (5) Enharmony, including all spellings of each dim.-7th chord, may serve to bring foreign keys within the orbit of the home key.

All of which rationale seems logical and traditional enough except for oddities like that pause in faster music between V-of-V and I, or loopholes like that question of when a clarifying interpolation is needed. But one must grant that such exceptions, along with abrupt, rhythmically truncated modulations, persistent chromaticism, and angular voice-leading, can bring even a relatively short and spare piece like the piano Sonatina in a, Op. 89/4, momentarily to the edge of atonality (Ex. 63).[94] And taking a larger tonal view, one must grant a certain over-all effect, even in so rich and subjective a work as the cello Sonata in a/A, Op. 116, of monotonality, not relieved by the more specific effect of a chromatic whine in much of the cello line. But these "problems" and the fault of writing (and publishing) more than could be kept under good qualitative control, should not impede a renaissance, or at least re-evaluation, of Reger's music outside as well as inside Germany. For, sticking to the sonatas, there is much of musical wonderment, glory, and soul to be heard yet in this composer so prodigal with his talents—in the deft, muted, triple-*piano,* flawlessly formed, scherzando "Presto" of that same cello sonata, for example; or the sections of driving, soaring passion in the first movement, especially, of the ninth and last violin sonata, Op. 139; or the profoundly expressive slow movement of the third and last clarinet sonata, Op. 107;[95] or the astute recollections of Bach in the "chaconne" finale in

94. On Reger's modulations and approaches to atonality, cf. Truscott/REGER (with reply by E. Wellesz); also, Austin/20th 144–47. Even the 4 sonatinas Op. 89 got mixed reactions, favorable to nos. 1 and 2 and unfavorable to nos. 3 and 4 in DM V/3 (1905–6) 107 (H. Teibler) and VIII/3 (1908–9) 104–5 (W. Niemann), respectively. The 2 Vn sonatinas Op. 103B are similarly subtle and beyond the range of "house music" (cf. their review in DM X/3 [1910–11] 313), which is also how W. Altmann viewed Op. 122 (DM XI/2 [1911–12] 168).

95. Cf. the review in DM IX/4 (1909–10) 250 (W. Altmann).

the last of each set of unaccompanied violin sonatas,[96] and the stunning fugue that caps the second organ sonata, Op. 60 (whose first 2 mvts. are called "Improvisation" and "Invokation").[97]

Next to Reger the most important composer of sonatas (and other music) in Leipzig was one of his close friends and immediate disciples, **Sigfrid Karg-Elert** (1877–1933).[98] This harmonium virtuoso, belated organist, and generally versatile musician left some 27 sonatas and sonatinas, 20 of them published (between 1905 and 1929),[99] among a large number of varied works ranging from small piano pieces and songs to substantial solo, chamber, orchestral, and choral works. There are 2 sonatas and 3 sonatinas for "Kunstharmonium," which to Karg-Elert meant not only the special (reed) harmonium on which he ex-

Ex. 63. From the opening page of the first movement in Max Reger's Sonatina in a, Op. 89/4 (after Reger/WERKE-m XI–65).

celled but the (pipe) organ when played on the manuals only, for intimate music;[100] one free but not short "Sonatina" for the organ using pedal board, too; 5 sonatas and 3 sonatinas for P solo, "Sonata Carla Madonna" and "Sonata esaltata" in MS; 7 sonatas for 6 different, unaccompanied orchestral instruments, including Vn, Va, Cl (2), Fl ("Sonata appassionata"), saxophone, and Bn; and 7 duos, in-

96. On these sons. cf. Gates/SOLO 197–208, with exx.

97. On this son. (generally preferred to the first organ son.) cf. Brennecke/REGER 390–91; on its fugue, in particular, cf. pp. 184–85 in a diss. on Reger's fugues by one of his students, Gatscher/REGER.

98. MGG VII 682–88 (R. Sietz), with dated list of works and further references.

99. The first and last sons. left in MSS, for oboe and P and Vn & organ, respectively, are dated 1898 and 1927.

100. Cf. GROVE IV 74 (A. J. Hipkins), 703 (H. Grace), 870–71 (E. Blom); Sceats/KARG-ELERT 9.

cluding P & Vn (2), P & Vc, Fl & P, Ob & P, Cl & P ("Sonata quasi fantasia"), and Vn & organ ("Sonata quasi canzona"). Although Karg-Elert made his chief mark with his organ music, the sonatas he wrote for harmonium and organ were too early to be fully representative of his mature styles and forms, the latest being composed in 1912.[101] The published duo sonatas were similarly too early to be fully representative, only the MS duos being later.[102] All in all, as a sonata composer Karg-Elert seems to have offered most in his piano music. But only the needed full study of his sonatas, including the unpublished MSS, can confirm or correct that opinion. And such a study ought to be made before he slips entirely into the oblivion that now hides not a few other significant late Romantics.[103]

Karg-Elert's mature, boldly experimental music is said to combine the virtuosic splash of Liszt (by way of A. Reisenauer's instruction), the precise craftsmanship of Reinecke (another of his instructors), the artistic folk treatment of Grieg (a warm supporter), and the polyphonic breadth of Reger.[104] His style might best be explained further through an examination of one of his most mature, developed, phrenetic works, *Dritte Sonate (Patetica)* in c♯, Op. 105, for P solo, composed in 1920 [105] and first published in 1922. This is a big, one-movement sonata of 570 measures in 37 pages—big in length, emotional range, and pianistic demands. Its emotional and dynamic programme is indicated not only by "Patetica" in the title but by a Brahman wisdom inscribed at the start: "Death is life; life death. Out of the night the dawn. Out of the twilight the night. And the full circle is completed." Abundant advices—a few in Italian, most in German—and dynamic as well as articulation signs and footnotes add much detail, not unlike that in Scriabin's sonatas, to the emotional program: for example, "striding solemnly," "like muted horns," and triple *piano* at

101. Descriptions of these works occur in Sceats/KARG-ELERT 9, 10, 12–13, 18; Frotscher/ORGELSPIEL II 1248. A short favorable review of Sonatinas in G and a, Op. 14/1 and 3, for harmonium, occurs in DM VIII/4 (1908–9) 315. Mr. Stephen E. Young is completing a Ph.D. diss. on Karg-Elert's organ works, at the University of N.C. as of this writing (1968).

102. But even Op. 71 in A, for P & Vc, although composed as early as 1907, was already being criticized for "unprecedentedly many rhythmic and harmonic sophistries" (DM IX/4 [1909–10] 186); it is viewed more kindly in MW XLI (1910) 378 and in Cobbett/CHAMBER II 47–48 (R. Felber). Op. 88 is reviewed favorably as a demanding work, modern yet still related to Bach's unaccompanied Vn sons. (DM XI/2 [1911–12] 203 [W. Altmann]).

103. Even now (1967), whereas a few works by Reger are still available on recordings, not a single work by Karg-Elert is listed in the standard catalogues.

104. MGG VII 686.

105. According to MGG VII 684, although "[28/9. 1914]" appears beside his name in the pub. score.

the start; elsewhere, "suddenly very violent," "sinister stirring" and "secretive, spooky," "lingering and musing, still calmer, longingly"; and near the end, a quadruple-*forte* climax, followed by a quintuple-*piano* ending.

This sonata is multisectional in form, too much so to suggest any kind of standard sonata cycle, or any double function of cycle within single form such as Liszt created. Yet there is unity in the return at the end to the hushed, mystical opening, in keeping with the full circle of that Brahman wisdom; in the consistently rhapsodic style, implemented by the many contrasting sections, meter changes, and wide-ranging, idiomatic, proselike figurations (including a Schumann-esque section on one staff, mss. 450–93); and in the over-all tonal course, which touches simply and traditionally enough on c♯, E, A, A♭ (V of c♯), c♯, b♭, c♯, A♭, A, e♭, b♭, a, C♯, and c♯, among main keys. The many sections are based variously, often in contrapuntal combinations, on no fewer than fifteen identifiable motives. (Indeed, the motives have been enumerated in the printed score, presumably by the composer, not only for the first entry of each but at the resumption of each after it has been discontinued for a while.) Motive no. 14 (introduced on p. 12) is the opening of a chorale set by Bach, "Straf' mich nicht in deinem Zorn" ("Punish me not in Thy wrath"), which motive figures significantly in the return to calm and the air of sweet resignation near the end.

In spite of such structural freedom and his disregard for the traditional designs and cycles that Reger preserved so faithfully, Karg-Elert was still like Reger in making his chief advances (and arousing his main opposition) through his harmony. He, too, stretched and extended traditional principles, on occasion, to the very brink of atonality. But his method was not so much one of increasingly remote interpretations of chord relations as of increasingly oblique rather than vertical relations of both chord and foreign tones.[106] By such means and a fair amount of harmonic and melodic chromaticism he produces passages with parallel 4ths and 5ths or suggestions of linear counterpoint that seem to embrace the very styles of the three "radical leftists"—Schoenberg, Debussy, and Scriabin—with whom he decided not to join during his creative crisis of about 1915.[107] Yet, though he strained traditional harmonic limits as much as Reger had, and more than Schoenberg in *Verklärte Nacht*, the results now seem more dated, with tendencies not unlike MacDowell's toward a cloying of the appetite in

---

106. Hasse/KARG-ELERT is a helpful study of the harmonic style in the light of Karg-Elert's own notable writings on harmony.

107. Cf. MGG VII 686.

Ex. 64. From a late section (mss. 401–8) of Sigfrid Karg-Elert's *Dritte Sonate* (*Patetica*) in c♯, Op. 105 (after the original Simrock ed. of 1922, recopyrighted in 1950, and used by kind permission of the pub. and Associated Music Pubs., Inc., sole agents for the U.S.A.).

sweet melodious phrases and the abetting of bombast in those more phrenetic moments (Ex. 64).

The published sonatas of a few other composers in and near Leipzig have already disappeared from view. Another expert on the harmonium, **August Reinhard** (1831–1912) in Ballenstedt to the northwest, left three sonatinas, Op. 38, and two sonatas, Opp. 84 and 85 (both pub. in 1903–4) for his instrument. The latter were greeted as skillful, effective pieces for that instrument.[108] Another organist, at the Thomaskirche in Leipzig, was **Carl Piutti** (1846–1902), composer of three organ sonatas published between 1875 and 1896.[109] The first of these—"The Wedding: a cycle of four pieces in the form of a sonata"—proved disappointingly commonplace to one reviewer, who had hoped for a symphonic poem for organ with further inscriptions elucidating the title.[110] Still another organist was the pupil of Draeseke and Schulz-

108. DM II/3 (1903) 449 and 451 (M. Puttmann), and III/3 (1903–4) 51 (A. Göttmann).

109. Cf. Riemann/LEXIKON II 1399; Kremer/ORGAN 214.

110. MW VI (1875) 224, with exx.

Beuthen, **Paul Claussnitzer** (1867–1924), whose organ *Choral-Sonate zur Totenfeier* in c, Op. 30, was published in 1912.[111]

A theory instructor at the Leipzig Conservatory, **Gustav Ernst Schreck** (1849–1918), was hailed for his highly competent, if somewhat academic, contribution to the limited literature of sonatas for Ob & P (Op. 13, 1889?).[112] He also left a Sonata for Bn & P, Op. 9. The largely self-taught composer and protégé of Grieg, **Robert Hermann** (1869–1912), left one published sonata, Op. 13 in c♯ for P & Vn, which was reviewed as being exceptionally and consistently original and attractive, sometimes rising to unexpected expressive heights.[113]

Once successful composers of light pedagogic and diversionary sonatas or sonatinas in Leipzig still deserve a mention, including **Albert Karl Tottmann** (1837–1917);[114] **Wilhelm Moritz Vogel** (1849–1922) for several sets;[115] the better known author and pianist **Walter Niemann** (1876–1953), for some two-dozen pleasant, innocuous short sonatas or sonatinas mostly bearing titles of nature, folklore, poetry, or romance;[116] the chamber music specialist **Fritz von Bose** (1865–at least 1929) for three sets of piano sonatinas;[117] the violinist **Richard Hofmann** (1844–1918), for about two-dozen more sonatinas, scored variously for P solo, P-duet, Vn & P, Va & P, Vc & P, Ob & P, and Cl & P;[118] and the important cellist **Julius Klengel** (1859–1933), for two sets of three sonatinas each as well as a sonata for his instrument.[119]

In Dresden only minor composers of sonatas are to be found at the end of the Romantic Era. Four organ sonatas by **Friedrich Oskar Wermann** (1840–1906), pupil of Merkel and Wieck, were published in the two decades from about 1885 to 1905,[120] and at least eleven of fourteen others by the organist **Ernst Hans Fährmann** (1860–1940), pupil of J. L. Nicodé, appeared, plus a solo piano sonata, Op. 6,

111. Cf. Riemann/LEXIKON I 324–25. Op. 30 is damned with faint praise in DM XII/2 (1912–13) 364 (E. Schnorr).

112. NZM LXXXV/2 (1889) 425 and MW XXI (1890) 490. Cf. MGG XII 69–70 (G. Hempel).

113. DM V/4 (1905–6) 177 (W. Altmann). Cf. Riemann/LEXIKON I 742.

114. Cf. Riemann/LEXIKON II 1871; PAZDÍREK XIV 257; SMW XL (1882) 819 (praising Op. 32 for Vn open strings & P!).

115. Cf. Riemann/LEXIKON II 1955; PAZDÍREK XIV 269.

116. Cf. MGG IX 1517–21 (R. Sietz); DM XII/4 (1912–13) 317 (R. H. Stein on Op. 24), XV/2 (1915) 616 (on Opp. 60, 75, and 83).

117. Cf. Riemann/LEXIKON I 209; DM XII/2 (1912–13) 42 (Jenö Kerntler).

118. Cf. Riemann/LEXIKON I 770–71; PAZDÍREK VII 599–605.

119. Cf. MGG VII 1222–23, 1225 (R. Eller); Cobbett/CHAMBER II 53 (H. Leichtentritt); DM X/4 (1910–11) 374 (H. Schlemüller).

120. Cf. Riemann/LEXIKON II 2013–14; Kremer/ORGAN 230; MW XXX (1899) 642 (on Son. 3 as an improvement over 1 and 2, but still weak in ideas and development).

in the nearly three decades from 1891 to about 1918.[121] Fährmann's later organ sonatas were welcomed as resourceful, harmonically clever, eclectic pieces.[122] And there was a spate of weak to fair sonatas for cello and piano, including Op. 27 in D (1894) by Swiss-born **Albert Fuchs** (1858–1910), who also wrote a prize-winning Sonata in f, Op. 11 (1887), for P solo and three sonatinas for P & Vn, Op. 36 (1898);[123] Op. 4 in f♯ (1887) by the organist **Maximilian Heidrich** (1864–1909; father of the infamous Nazi SS officer), who had known Liszt in Weimar and also left a Sonata in g, Op. 12 (1888) for P & Vn and a big, impassioned, traditional "Phantasie-Sonate" in D, Op. 70 (1914, posthumous) for P solo;[124] Opp. 10 in D and 15 in A (1898 and 1910) by an English pianist and pupil of Draeseke among others, **Percy Sherwood** (1866–1939), who also left a Sonata in F, Op. 12, for P & Vn (1907), two sonatinas, Op. 22, for P solo (1913?), and an unpublished Sonata for 2 Ps;[125] Op. 18 in C (1908) by another Draeseke pupil, **Leland A. Cossart** (1877–?), who also left a Sonata in D, Op. 27, for P & Vn (1913);[126] and Op. 23 in b (1908) by still another Draeseke pupil, the pianist **Theodor Blumer** (1882–1964), who also left sonatas for P & Vn (Opp. 33 in d [1914] and 43 in c [1920]) and P & Fl (Op. 61 in D [1928]).[127] The violinist and choral conductor **Reinhold Becker** (1842–1924) may be added, too, for one highly commended, difficult Sonata in g for P & Vn, Op. 150 (1911).[128]

In Magdeburg to the northwest, there is only the successful choral composer and conductor **(Wenzel) Josef Krug (Krug-Waldsee; 1858– 1915)** to mention, and only one sonata by him to list—a conventional,

121. Cf. Riemann/LEXIKON I 484; Kremer/ORGAN 182–83.

122. E.g., DM III/2 (1903–4) 116 (K. Straube), VI/4 (1906–7) 308, X/1 (1910–11) 375 (E. S. v. Carolsfeld), XIII/3 (1913–14) 176 (E. Schnorr); NZM CIV (1904) 620; MW XXXVII (1906) 44a, XLI (1910) 176.

123. Cf. MGG IV 1072–74 (A. Berner); MW XXVII (1896) 178 (praising Op. 11 and, especially, Op. 27 for its fantasy-ballade style, varied rhythms, and rich harmony).

124. Cf. Riemann/LEXIKON I 728; DM III/2 (1903–4) 52 (H. Schlemüller on Op. 4 as skillful but not distinctive).

125. Cf. GROVE VII 759–60 (J. A. Fuller-Maitland); Altmann/KAMMERMUSIK 227 and 264; MW XXX (1899) 494 and SMW LVII (1899) 354 (with praise and reservations for Op. 10); MW XL (1909–10) 539 (Max Unger on Op. 15 as a large-scale, Brahmsian work); DM XIII/2 (1913–14) 165 (A. Nadel on Op. 22/1 & 2).

126. Cf. Riemann/LEXIKON I 347; Altmann/KAMMERMUSIK 199 and 254; Cobbett/ CHAMBER I 303; DM VIII/2 (1908–9) 284, with limited praise for Op. 18, and XIII/3 (1913–14) 106 (with more praise for Op. 27).

127. Cf. Riemann/LEXIKON I 289; BAKER Suppl. 15; Altmann/KAMMERMUSIK 196, 253, and 272; DM VIII/2 (1908–9) 284 (A. Laser decrying Op. 23 as alternately bombastic and trivial) and XIII/4 (1913–14) 230 (W. Altmann approving Op. 33 except for its length).

128. Cf. Riemann/LEXIKON I 132; DM XI/1 (1911–12) 236 (W. Altmann); Cobbett/ CHAMBER I 80 (W. Altmann).

trite work in c, Op. 38 (1905), in four movements (F-S-M-VF), its only distinction being good contrapuntal interest.[129] In Kassel, southwest of Magdeburg, **Richard Franck** (1858–1938), who had studied with his father Eduard in Berlin (SSB X), rose to no significant creative heights in his four well-schooled, generally light, pleasant duo sonatas, two each for P & Vn and P & Vc (1890–1903).[130] In Marburg, farther southwest, **Gustav Jenner** (1865–1920), Brahms's biographer and only composition student (during most of 1888–1895), was active after 1900. His two published sonatas—for P & Cl in G, Op. 5 (1900), and P & Vn in a, Op. 8 (1905)—are reported to be able works dominated by his teacher's influence.[131] Also in Marburg and under Brahms's strong influence (as well as Schumann's) was the violinist **Richard Barth** (1850–1923), whose three sonatas for P & Vn were published between 1899 and 1915.[132]

Among minor composers in Köln, **Ewald Strässer** (1867–1933) stands out, although his published works include only one sonata, actually a *Kleine Sonate* in f♯, Op. 54, for P solo.[133] This is a rather objective, melodious, pleasant, readily playable work in three short movements (F-S-F). It presents a stylistic melange in that it follows traditional paths and molds except for repeated, momentary digressions into harmonic progressions and relationships about as remote and abrupt as Reger's. In the middle movement the melodic and harmonic flavor is a kind of synthesis of Johann and Richard Strauss. The piano pedagog and writer **Otto Adolf Klauwell** (1851–1917) may be noted, too, in Köln, not especially for his violin sonata (Op. 6 in c, 1874)[134] and two piano sonatinas that had appeared but for his contribution of 1899 to the very few books on sonata history published in the 19th century.[135]

A U.S. expatriate to Germany, the conductor **Frank L. Limbert** (1866–1938), was studying in Frankfurt/M or Berlin when one sonata each appeared for P & Vn (Op. 4 in A, 1890) and P & Va (Op. 7

129. Cf. MGG VII 1835–36 (R. Schaal); NZM CI (1905) 543; DM V/2 (1905–6) 336 (W. Fischer).

130. Cf. Riemann/LEXIKON I 534; Altmann/KAMMERMUSIK 203 and 256; Cobbett/CHAMBER I 429 (W. Altmann); DM II/1 (1902–3) 208 and 210 (H. Schlemüller), II/2 (1902–3) 39 and 43 (W. Altmann), III/1 (1903–4) 135 (H. Schlemüller) and 287 (W. Altmann); MW XXV (1904) 324 (E. Segnitz).

131. Cf. MGG VI 1881–83 (R. Schaal); Cobbett/CHAMBER II 35 (W. W. Cobbett). Kohleick/JENNER is a study of the man and his music in relation to Brahms, including comments, with exx., on the sons. (pp. 58–61).

132. Cf. Riemann/LEXIKON I 114; Cobbett/CHAMBER I 60 (W. W. Cobbett). Op. 14 is reviewed in SMW LVIII (1900) 355 as a solid, resourceful work.

133. Cf. MGG XII 1433–34 (J. Schwermer), with further bibliography.

134. Reviewed favorably in SMW XXXIII (1875) 402.

135. Cf. Riemann/LEXIKON I 900; SBE 11–12.

in c, 1892).[136] The first was reviewed as large but empty and the second as revealing individualities (such as 5-beat meter in the finale) but as being severe, brooding, and still well short of a masterpiece.[137] Also in Frankfurt/M, a student of Raff and Liszt, **Anton Urspruch** (1850–1907), left one published sonata each for P & Vn (Op. 28 in d, 1894) and P & Vc (Op. 29 in D, 1894), following his debut in print with a *Sonata quasi fantasia* in D, Op. 1, for P-duet.[138] Op. 29 was reviewed as a convincing, effective work in which counterpoint is the essential and omnipresent means both in the presentation and development of its ideas.[139] In Wiesbaden, west of Frankfurt/M, the pianist **Nicolai von Wilm** (1834–1911) showed much composition know-how (as well any such prolific composer might) in at least a half-dozen conservative yet fresh and attractive sonatas published between about 1883 and 1899. These include two for P & Vn, one for P & Vc, and three delightful sonatinas for P solo that once were in the hands of many students.[140]

Finally, in central Germany, the important late-Romantic German **Hans Pfitzner** (1869–1949) was still a student in the Frankfurt/M Conservatory when he wrote the first of his two published sonatas, both duos.[141] This first one is Op. 1 in f♯, published in 1892. It is a long work (1,180 mss. in all), cast in the usual four movements (F-S-VF-F) and standard designs (all but ii, in binary design, being "son.-allegro" forms). Although its fluency and lyricism trace back directly to Mendelssohn, it has enough harmonic and chromatic enrichment and enough melodic and rhythmic originality to stand on its own. In fact, cellists who do not know this work (and how many musicians know Pfitzner's music outside of Germany?) are missing a remarkably expressive, potent addition to today's concert repertoire.

Pfitzner's other sonata, Op. 27 in e/E, for Vn & P, was started about 1918, during his last year in Strasbourg, and completed that year, but not published until 1922. By now Pfitzner was already becoming involved in the controversies, bitterness, disappointments,

136. Cf. Riemann/LEXIKON I 1043; Altmann/KAMMERMUSIK 214 and 248.

137. MW XXI (1890) 427, XXVIII (1897) 194; SMW XLIV (1892) 690–91.

138. Cf. MGG XIII 1180–81 (T. Kircher-Urspruch).

139. SMW LIV (1893) 850; MW XXVI (1895) 567.

140. Cf. GROVE IX 310 (J. A. Fuller-Maitland); Altmann/KAMMERMUSIK 232 and 266; MW XIV (1883) 520 (on the 3 sonatinas). The P "Sonate" in f, reported favorably in NZM LXXIII/1 (1877) 210, must be the 4-mvt. "Fantasie" in that key listed in HOFMEISTER X (1886–91) 875. Wilm's "Duo" for Vn & harp (Op. 156, 1898) is called a son. in BAKER 1802.

141. Cf. MGG X 1170–80 (W. Mohr), with full dated list and further references. The 2 sons. are analyzed in detail in the excellent recent diss. Henderson/PFITZNER (on the man and his instrumental works), pp. 154–73 and 239–56, respectively; cf., also, pp. 3, 12, 19, 65, and 66–67; and Cobbett/CHAMBER II 216–17 (R. Felber).

enmities, and tragedies that were to hang with increasing heaviness over his long career. Even though he was no conscious programmatist in his chamber music, he may have been reflecting some of his uncertainties at this point, in Op. 27—especially the conflict of the artist's need to advance and his own increasing conservatism, if not reactionism, as stated in his belated, sharp, chauvinistic reply of 1917 (*Futuristengefahr*) to Busoni's celebrated *Entwurf* . . . of 1909.[142] At any rate, Op. 27, a three-movement cycle (F-S-VF) of 654 measures, is viewed here as a curiously unequal, often ineffectual work—hardly a primary item in Pfitzner's total output. Its considerable technical demands for both instruments are on a par with those of Op. 1. But except for its finale, which is its most successful movement, anyway, it lacks the melodic strength and tonal purposefulness of the earlier work.[143] More disturbing is the harmonic idiom, which varies from conventional, occasionally banal, progressions to empirical progressions that too often seem to turn back on themselves without any expressive accomplishment or even the more abstruse paper logic of Reger's harmony. At best, this harmony reminds us of Pfitzner's strong devotion to Wagner's music (Ex. 65).

Composers of Exceptional Skill in North Germany

Among surprisingly many composers of real stature active in Berlin around the turn of this century, the most significant and influential man, the eminent pianist **Ferrucio Benvenuto Busoni** (1866–1924), can get only tangential mention here. It is not that his three early sonatas (1883–98) and six later duo sonatinas (1910–20) represent so small a part of his output, but that the latter in particular mark a conscious break with the past and striving toward the future.[144] In other words, among the borderlanders this fine, idealistic humanitarian musician belongs in spirit if not in style more with contemporary early-Moderns, like Debussy, Schoenberg, Scriabin, and Joseph Haas, than with contemporary late-Romantics, like Strauss, Reger, Pfitzner, and Karg-Elert. Even his Second Sonata for P & Vn, Op. 36a in e (composed in 1898, first pub. in 1901), has sections that anticipate his break with traditional tonality. In fact, this powerful, lyrical, deeply expressive, highly Romantic, often rhapsodic duo in four move-

142. Cf. Henderson/PFITZNER 14–17.

143. In Abendroth/PFITZNER the composer refers several times with pride to Op. 1 (e.g., pp. 187–88, 193, 210, 215) but never to Op. 27.

144. Cf. Dent/BUSONI 116, 167, 181, 211, 305–6; MGG II 520–27 (H. Wirth), especially 527; Austin/20th 110–15; BUSONI-Frau 103, 252, 260, 357.

Ex. 65. From the close of the first movement in Hans Pfitzner's Sonata in e/E, Op. 27 (after the original ed. of 1922, by kind permission of C. F. Peters Corp. in New York).

ments (S-VF-M-Va) was the earliest of his works that he continued to acknowledge in his later years.[145]

No such break with the past can be found in the highly competent sonatas of the long active pianist **Friedrich Gernsheim** (1839–1916), who taught and conducted in Berlin during most of the second half of his life.[146] Gernsheim's sonatas figure importantly in his chamber music, which figures importantly in his total choral and instrumental output. Six of them were published, over a span of 51 years, including Op. 1 in f (1863) for P solo; Opp. 4 in c (1864), 50 in C (1885), 64 in F (1899), and 85 in G (1912) for P & Vn; and Op. 12 in d (1868) for P & Vc.[147] Unpublished are another violin sonata and three more piano sonatas from his student years, and another, late cello sonata, Op. 79 in e (1906).[148]

A good clue to Gernsheim's style comes from the names of the no-

145. BUSONI-Frau 103.

146. Cf. MGG IV 1821–24 (W. Kahl), with dated list and further references.

147. For bibliographic details on Opp. 4 (dated 1864), 12, 50, and 64, cf. Mueller-Reuter/LEXIKON 593–94.

148. This last must be the same work that is (wrongly?) listed as Op. 87 in MGG IV 1823. Cf. Mueller-Reuter/LEXIKON 594.

table musicians who figured most significantly in his background and environment, whether directly or indirectly. These include Spohr by way of an early theory teacher, Ernst Pauer, Moscheles, and Ferdinand Hiller as piano teachers, the last and Hauptmann as further theory teachers, and Brahms and Max Bruch as close friends. In short, Gernsheim was a traditionalist. The sum of these influences on his sonatas is the distinct impress of Mendelssohn and Schumann, as the reviewers of the earlier sonatas usually noted, along with praise for his mastery of forms, writing techniques, and smooth flow but some hint of a lack of originality.[149] Op. 12 affords a thoroughly convincing illustration (Ex. 66). One reviewer, describing Op. 12 as a pleasant though not

Ex. 66. From the opening of Friedrich Gernsheim's Sonata in d, Op. 12 (after the original B. Schott ed. of 1868).

outstanding work, was grateful that it is, *"mirabile dictu,* not afflicted with the over-elaborations, and undue prolongation of trite themes, which too often form the leading characteristics of the school to which it belongs."[150]

But Gernsheim proved to be more than an efficient sponge and

149. E.g., cf. NZM LVIII/1 (1863) 189 on Op. 1 and LXI (1865) 117–18 on Op. 4 (viewed as more of a sonatina in its facileness and minimal development). A study of Gernsheim's sons. is in order. A paragraph on Opp. 50 and 85 appears in Cobbett/CHAMBER I 458 (W. Altmann); cf., also, DM XII/1 (1912–13) 299 (W. Altmann).

150. MT XXIV (1883) 135–36.

transmitter of past styles. To be sure, he never became a radical, thus perhaps heeding the advice on his Op. 1 that his 69-year-old teacher Moscheles had written to him in 1863:

May God keep you safely on the middle road and prevent you from getting into the labyrinth of the futurists [*Zukunfstjäger*]. You incline toward the romantic school. In the exclusiveness of that tendency lies a certain danger. The classical masters (even as far back as Bach) have their romanticism, too, but thanks to their clear motives and formally and artistically suitable developments this is always kept within the bounds of the beautiful. The romantics tend toward brooding, hypochondria, indeed despair of the world (*Weltschmerz*). Your sonata has much of that color. I wish I were able to counter such moods with a small bottle or a good sermon, or artistically speaking a little Bach ointment, Haydn salt, Beethoven steel drops and Mendelssohn heart medicine.[151]

Yet his later sonatas show increasing perfection and subtlety in overall form, rhythmic construction, idiomatic instrumental writing, and harmonic color that give them many passages and whole movements of rare distinction. For example, Op. 50, with its trenchant themes in three well-contrasted movements (F-S-VF), makes a steady, compelling, well-developed and somewhat Brahmsian chamber work (lasting about 23 minutes) that any enterprising duo team might profitably add to its recital repertoire.

Philipp Scharwenka (1847–1917), older and not quite so successful brother of Xaver (ssb X), may be credited with at least 7 published sonatas—3 for P solo, in A, f♯, and g, Op. 61/1–3 (1886), "in smaller form"; 2 for P & Vn, Opp. 110 in b (1900) and 114 in e (1904); one for P & Va, Op. 106 in g (1899); and one for P & Vc, Op. 116 in g (1910).[152] As compared with his brother in their sonatas, Philipp tended to create more extended, serious, developed forms, often somber in character, with broader themes, increased polyphonic interest, and more resourceful, piquant rhythms.[153] Even the "smaller" piano sonatas, although lighter in character, are full-scale cycles with considerable development and variety. But for all their weight and academic worth, none of Philipp's sonatas is likely to be revived in the concert hall. Their themes and outworn, unenterprising, Mendelssohnian har-

151. As trans. and kindly supplied by Professor Alexander L. Ringer at the University of Illinois from an article on correspondence between Max Bruch and Gernsheim, in the forthcoming Lloyd Hibberd Memorial Volume.

152. Cf. MGG XI 1602–3, 1606 (R. Sietz); Altmann/KAMMERMUSIK 224, 250, 263.

153. Wetzel/SCHARWENKA is a short article, with exx., on Philipp's chamber music. Cf., also, MGG XI 1603; Cobbett/CHAMBER II 332 (W. Altmann); and Shand/VIOLIN 93–95, with exx. Op. 114 is reviewed as well proportioned even though the first mvt. is as long as the combined (and interconnected) "Andante" and finale, in MW XXXVII (1906) 868a; Op. 116 is reviewed as a 3-mvt. fantasy rather than a standard form, in DM IX/4 (1909–10) 379.

monic idiom rarely sound fresh even when they do not descend into the trite.

Nor is there likely to be a revival of interest in the published sonatas by the fine pianist **Wilhelm Berger** (1861–1911), although there is more musical justification.[154] Berger was a traditionalist in his language, too, but his music rises above the trite and achieves a more compelling drive than Scharwenka's. His published sonatas include Op. 76 in B, for P solo (1899); Opp. 7 in A (1882), 29 in F (1888), and 70 in g (1898), for P & Vn; and Op. 28 in d for P & Vc (1930, posthumous).[155] The main influence on Berger is clearly that of Brahms—too clearly, in fact, because in spite of Berger's unquestioned mastery of his art and in spite of a few Wagnerisms in the harmony and of some other lesser influences, he provides another example, like Friedrich Kiel or Karl Grädener (both ssb X), of a style too close for independent distinction and not quite strong enough to compete on equal terms. His piano sonata, for instance, is a big, technically demanding, three-movement work (F-S-M) that immediately recalls the fire of Brahms's early piano sonatas (Ex. 67), but its ideas lack quite the vitality (especially in the last two movements) and its structural rhythm quite the organizational genius of the Viennese master's writing.[156]

A Sonata in d, Op. 82, for P & Vn (1908), as well as an early Sonata in A, Op. 2 (1888), and "Three Sonatinas," in c, F, and e, Op. 38 (1917) for P solo, figure at the not inconsequential fringe of the notable choral output by **Hugo Kaun** (1863–1932).[157] Kaun had studied with Friedrich Kiel (ssb X), among others, before spending fifteen valued years in Milwaukee and Chicago and settling in Berlin in 1902. Op. 82, which reportedly replaced a violin sonata withdrawn from publication about eighteen years earlier,[158] is a warmer, freer, more personal

---

154. Cf. MGG I 1693–95 (W. Kahl).

155. Cf. Altmann/KAMMERMUSIK 195, 233. The Vn sonatas are endorsed highly by Wilhelm Altmann in Cobbett/CHAMBER I 122 and greeted with increasing enthusiasm in their successive reviews—e.g., SMW IV (1882) 371 (Op. 7 regarded as unequal and harmonically disturbing but interesting and lively, anyway); MW XIII (1882) 555 and 556 (Op. 7 described as a pleasant Mendelssohnian miniature), XXI (1890) 411 (Op. 29 remarked for its contrapuntal skill and almost excessive working of themes); DM II/1 (1902–3) 359 and 361 (W. Altmann in praise of Op. 70). Cf., also, Shand/VIOLIN 82–88, with exx.

156. Yet these very traits are warmly praised in MW XXXII (1901) 54 (E. Segnitz). Less enthusiastic is SMW LVII (1899) 435.

157. Cf. MGG VII 761–65 (R. Schaal), with dated list and further references; also, Schaal/KAUN (on the man and his works), especially pp. 24–25, 29, 88–90, 102–3, with exx.

158. According to Cobbett/CHAMBER II 49 (W. Altmann); but could Altmann have been thinking of Op. 2 cited above?

work than Gernsheim's Op. 50, and hence somewhat dated. In four
movements (F-Sc-M-F), it is marked by expressive, well-defined themes,
pungent harmony, fertile rhythms, and an advanced but not frilly
use of the instruments. It deserves to be played again.

Another pupil of Kiel, as well as of Rheinberger in Munich and,
less formally, Brahms in Vienna, was the pianist **Robert Kahn** (1865–
1951).[159] Kahn's MS and published sonatas are all duos, including
Opp. 5 in g (1886), 26 in a (1897), and 50 in E (1907) for P & Vn;
and Opp. 37 in F (1903) and 56 in d (1911) for P & Vc.[160] Kahn
was another traditionalist developing along the paths started by Mendelssohn, Schumann, and Brahms. His surprisingly mature and ener-

Ex. 67. From the opening of Wilhelm Berger's Sonata in B,
Op. 76 (after the original Otto Forberg ed. of 1899).

getic Op. 5 is a three-movement work (F-S-VF) recalling the symphonic
breadth and development of Rheinberger. Op. 26 continues the promise
of Op. 5 [161] and Op. 50 becomes, according to Wilhelm Altmann in
1910, "the most valuable of the violin sonatas composed since Brahms
and one of the best works by Robert Kahn." [162] The honor might be
contested on behalf of Robert Fuchs, Strauss, Reger, and Wilhelm

159. Cf. MGG VII 427–29 (R. Schaal), with further references.

160. Cf. Altmann/KAMMERMUSIK 210 and 258. These sons. are described briefly
in Altmann/KAHN 354, 355–57. Cf., also, Shand/VIOLIN 77–82, with exx.

161. In MW XXIX (1896) 27 and SMW LVI (1898) 33–34 only the degree of inspiration in Op. 26 is questioned.

162. Altmann/KAHN 356. He had made the same statement in DM VII/2 (1907–8)
228, and made it again in Cobbett/CHAMBER II 45–46 (W. Altmann).

Berger, as well as Fauré, Saint-Saëns, and a very few other non-Germans, but remarkably few in all. Intimacy, artistic optimism, precise, resourceful writing, and intelligent scoring characterize Op. 50. The "Andante sostenuto" of the short first movement gives way twice to a "Presto" section but reappears to end both this movement and the finale. Between these outer movements is a well-developed scherzo movement. Both of Kahn's cello sonatas are significant duos, too.[163]

The fine pianist **Conrad Ansorge** (1862–1930) was one of Liszt's last students, in Weimar and Rome.[164] A Sonata in d, Op. 24 (1909), for P & Vc, and three solo piano sonatas—Opp. 1 in f (1884?), 21 in e (1905), and 23 in A (1908)—are among his few published works.[165] The Lisztian touch is evident at once in the stentorian, heroic, elegiac quality of Op. 1, in its taxing but not empty virtuosity, and in the structural freedom and variety of its three movements (F-S-F), including a brilliant fugal introduction to the finale based on the main theme of the first movement. By contrast the last of Ansorge's three piano sonatas takes a quite different turn. It exhibits all the subtle poetry remarked in his piano playing.[166] Moreover, it leaves Liszt and goes back to the Beethoven, Schubert, and Schumann he so loved to play, too—in particular, it would seem, to the Beethoven of Op. 101. But, Ansorge was no mere epigone. This work throws new light on past styles with a surprising freshness and individuality. If the harmony is traditional, the mercurial modulations and melody are not. And the structural methods make a refreshing departure from textbook sonata designs. Thus, the first movement is monothematic and freely sectional, each section starting with the governing idea and going off most often in its own, different direction, rhythmically and melodically as well as tonally. Some capable, enterprising, musicianly pianist is likely to re-discover this work and find it as rewarding and refined as late Clementi or any other composer still mainly cultivated as a cult.

The near centenarian **Ernst Eduard Taubert** (1838–1934; apparently not closely related to K. G. W. Taubert, ssb VIII) was another student of Kiel, also of Albert Dietrich.[167] To his credit among relatively few publications are only a Sonatina in A, Op. 11 (1870) for P & Vn and a *Fantasie-Sonate* in i, Op. 68 (1905), for P solo, although he also left a Sonata in d for Vn & P (1922) in MS. Op. 68 may be slightly too pat, too near to glibness, to be revivable in concert today. But it should

163. Cf. Altmann/KAHN 375; DM XI/2 (1911–12) 168 (H. Schlemüller).
164. Cf. MGG I 508–9 (Karl Laux).
165. Generally enthusiastic reviews of Op. 1 occur in NZM LXXX/2 (1884) 536–37 and LXXXIII/1 (1887) 218; also, MW XVII (1886) 102–3.
166. Cf. MGG I 507–8.
167. Cf. Riemann/LEXIKON II 1815; BAKER 1620.

make an ideal work for a student looking toward, though not quite yet ready for, the freer, bigger sonatas of Schumann, Chopin, and Brahms. Consisting of three interconnected movements (S/F-M-Va), it employs only established harmonic, structural, and keyboard techniques to move smoothly, comfortably, and surely to its clear-cut goals. If Taubert was not deliberately addressing himself to students in this work, then it brands him as the epigone Ansorge rose above being.[168]

Trained in Leipzig and related to his namesake by style though not by blood, **Georg (Alfred) Schumann** (1866–1952) was a successful director, chamber music participant, and composer who lived in Berlin after 1899.[169] Among his published works are three duo sonatas—two for P & Vn (Op. 12 in c♯, 1896; Op. 55 in d, 1912) and one for P & Vc (Op. 19 in e, 1898)—of which Op. 55 is much the most interesting.[170] This last, in three thematically related movements (F-S-VF), provides good tastes of the poetry, drama, occasional folk elements, large scope, and broad practical musical experience in Georg Schumann's writing. Of special appeal is the funeral-march coda to the finale. (Georg's brother in Eisenach, **Camillo Schumann** [1872–1946], won little success with five organ sons. and numerous duo sons., mostly unpub.[171])

A prolific, able, impassioned composer was the conductor and teacher **Waldemar von Baussnern** (1866–1931), who held posts in Mannheim, Dresden, Köln, Weimar, and Frankfurt/M between his first and last years in Berlin.[172] Out of at least nine sonatas or sonatinas composed by Baussnern, the only one to be published besides three piano sonatinas is his *Sonata eroica* in c♯ for P solo (1910). But this hot-blooded, multifaceted, sonorous, thoroughly pianistic work[173] is more than enough to arouse one's curiosity about the several ensemble sonatas still in MS, including a set of "Drei Triosonaten" for 2 Vns and P, 2 sonatas for Vn & P (one of them called "Ungarische" and one dated 1916), as well as one more for Vc & P (1896). *Sonata eroica* is a big work (41 pp.) in three movements (F-S-VF). Its rather improvisatory

168. Op. 68 is highly commended, without any such pedagogic reservation, in DM VI/4 (1906–7) 48 (A. Laser).

169. Cf. GROVE VII 602–3 (J. A. Fuller-Maitland) and MGG XII 270–71 (T.-M. Langner), with further references but no list of works.

170. Cf. Altmann/KAMMERMUSIK 226 and 264; Cobbett/CHAMBER II 367–68 (W. Altmann). Favorable reviews of each may be seen in SMW LV (1897) 114 (Op. 127); MW XXVIII (1897) 561 (Op. 12) and XXXII (1901) 603–4 (E. Segnitz, Op. 55); DM XII/2 (1912–13) 42 (W. Altmann, Op. 19); SMW LVIII (1900) 723 (Op. 19).

171. Cf. Riemann/LEXIKON II 1668; BAKER 1473. An organ son. is reviewed with no enthusiasm in MW XLI (1910) 330.

172. Cf. MGG I 1423–24 (G. F. Wehle), with full list of pub. and unpub. works.

173. The curt negative review of it in DM X/2 (1910–11) 296 (A. Leitzmann) makes no sense here.

character, furthered by frequent tempo gradations, may relate to
Baussnern's improvisational skill as a student but belies his well-or-
ganized, standard forms. Although the rich harmony and tonal third-
relationships were standard, too, by then—for Baussnern was not an
innovator—his ideas and their treatment are individual enough to
keep his music barely clear of melodic and harmonic clichés and to
make it, for the most part, ring true (Ex. 68).

Ex. 68. From the second theme in the first movement of
Waldemar von Baussnern's *Sonata eroica* in c♯ (after the original
ed. of 1910).

The renowned Berlin teacher **Paul Juon** (1872–1940) retained his
Russian background under Arensky and Taneyev, including Slavic folk
influences, even after further study with Bargiel in Berlin and after his
permanent move to that city in 1897.[174] This background contributed
to Juon's remaining more on the Romantic than the Modern side of
the border line and shows up in the sonatas—for example, in the
"Romanze" in minor introduced as variation "V" in the middle movement of Op. 7, as well as the main theme announced at once in the
finale. Brahm's marked influence seems to have contributed, too. There
are at least 8 duo sonatas and one piano sonatina by Juon, spread over
the years from 1898 to 1930 and nearly all published. The duos include 2 for Vc & P, 3 for Vn & P, one for Va & P plus another for
Cl-or-Va & P, and one for Fl & P.[175] One of the most attractive and
most played of those duos, in spite of the relative inexperience it

174. Cf. MGG VII 389–93 (T.-M. Langner), with dated list of works and further
references; GROVE IV 676–77 (E. Evans).

175. Cf. Cobbett/CHAMBER II 43 (E. Evans) and 44 (W. W. Cobbett) for 2 concurring, largely favorable paragraphs on the duo sons.

betrays in problems of tight form, is Juon's first sonata, that same Op. 7 for Vn & P (1898). All three movements (M/F-Va-VF) achieve a plasticity, sometimes even a proselike quality, in the rhythm, furthered in the first movement by the 6/4 meter, and in all movements by the frequently wide and free roaming of the melodic lines. The harmony is traditional—in fact, conspicuously diatonic (partly in keeping with the folk element). But the texture is much thicker than that economical sort, with its many open fifths, that Juon tended to cultivate in his later years.[176]

The restless, roving composer of opera and other types of music, **Paul Graener** (1872–1944), left two published duo sonatas, Opp. 56 in C, for Vn & P (1914?), and 101 in f, for Vc & P (1935).[177] These reveal Graener's decided yet unclassifiable individuality of style—the lyricism, tenderness, sadness, mysticism, and even Impressionism, expressed in late-Romantic harmony that lies somewhere between that of Strauss, Reger, and Pfitzner. Op. 56 is an improvisatory, brooding work in one extended movement of three sections.[178] The organist and conductor **Martin Grabert** (1868–1951) may be mentioned for his contribution to the sonata for Ob & P (Op. 51, 1921).[179]

Further in Berlin, organ sonatas of no lasting consequence came from the virtuoso organists **Otto Dienel** (1839–1905),[180] **Heinrich Reimann** (1850–1906),[181] **Max Gulbins** (1862–1932);[182] and **Ludwig Neuhoff** (1859–1909).[183]

Among still other, less remembered Berliners, **Theodor Kewitsch** (1834–1903) wrote an *Erste Sonate für Pianoforte und eine Singstimme*

176. A review of Op. 7, pointing to some of these same traits, appears in smw LX (1902) 765.

177. Cf. mgg V 663–66 (L. K. Mayer). The first ed. of Op. 56 did not get into hofmeister.

178. It is reviewed, somewhat confusedly, with mention of a lack of structural development, in dm XV/1 (1915) 294–95 (M. Broesike-Schoen) and noted briefly in Cobbett/chamber I 486 (H. Leichtentritt).

179. Cf. mgg V 614–15 (H. Becker) and the review in dm XV/1 (1915) 456 (describing it as well suited to the Ob but not interesting to the pianist and unexceptional as music).

180. Cf. Riemann/lexikon I 401; mt XXIII (1882) 403, XXVII (1885) 42, 358, and 364; mw XXIX (1898) 43 (reviewing the 3 mvts. of "Christmas Sonata," No. 4, as not developed enough); mt XXXIV (1893) 295–96 (more favorable on No. 4).

181. Cf. mgg XI 169–71 (T.-M. Langner); mw XXI (1890) 393 (with praise for good workmanship in the 3 mvts. of Op. 10 in d—a chorale prelude, passacaglia, and fugue); Frotscher/orgelspiel II 1216.

182. Cf. Riemann/lexikon I 677; baker 627; smw LVIII (1900) 883 (praise for the polyphony and scoring in Op. 4); dm II/2 (1903) 39, 40–41 (K. Straube, reviewing Opp. 4, 18, and 19 as trivial reversions to the Mendelssohn style); nzm CI (1905) 163 (originality of rhythm and harmony in Op. 28).

183. Cf. Riemann/lexikon II 1261; mw XXXI (1900) 121–22 (praise for "Phantasie-Sonate" in f, Op. 21); Kremer/organ 210.

(Op. 61, *ca.* 1890), with successive texts by Goethe, Tieck, and Rückert for the three movements. The work was considered interesting as an experiment but not as music.[184] The Berlin-trained conductor **Fritz Kauffmann** (1855–1934) wrote two piano sonatas, of which the second was reviewed as a worthy product of the instruction he had received from Kiel.[185] Another Kiel student and conductor, also a pupil of Liszt, **Max Puchat** (1859–1919) left at least one sonata each for P solo and for P & Vn, the latter being reviewed as a difficult but fluent and well constructed work.[186] And another Kiel student, **Eduard Behm** (1862–1946), was reported to recall Grieg in the first of his three violin sonatas.[187] The choral conductor and composer **Karl Kämpf** (1874–1950) left one published sonata each for P & Vn and P & Vc in 1904 and 1920, of which the first (Op. 23 in e) was applauded for its harmonic interest.[188] The Dutch conductor in Berlin and one of our few woman composers, **Elisabeth Kuyper** (1877 to at least 1965?), left two or more violin sonatas, one of which was published (Son. in A, 1902) and reviewed as being more interesting for its sonority than its content.[189]

Carl Bohm (1844–1920) and **Gustav Lazarus** (1861–1920) were among Berliners who wrote sonatinas.[190] **Alban Förster** (1849–1916) in Neustrelitz, north of Berlin, was another.[191] In Hamburg, to the west, the song composer **Hans Hermanns** (1879–?) [192] left an expressive, excellently scored, thoroughly convincing Sonata in b, for P solo, that is unhackneyed and was not published until 1935,[193] yet retains clear and firm ties with late-Romantic melody and harmony. In Bremen the violinist and conductor **Paul Scheinpflug** (1875–1937) left a Sonata in F, Op. 13, for Vn & P (1908) that was reviewed as a broad, substantial, appealing work, with some Brahmsian flavor but no artificialities.[194]

---

184. NZM LXXXVI/2 (1890) 538 (A. Naubert). Cf. Riemann/LEXIKON I 877.

185. MW XVI (1885) 102 (P. Mirsch). Cf. Riemann/LEXIKON I 868; BAKER 812.

186. MW XXX (1899) 522; SMW LVI (1898) 673–74. The P-solo son., Op. 3 in b♭, is reviewed as attractive, bold, and promising, in SMW XLIV (1886) 103. Cf. Riemann/LEXIKON I 140.

187. DM II/3 (1902–3) 46, 47. Cf. Riemann/LEXIKON I 140.

188. NZM C (1904) 819. Cf. Riemann/LEXIKON I 848; BAKER 804; Altmann/KAMMERMUSIK 210 and 258.

189. MW XXV (1904) 324 (E. Segnitz); cf., also, NZM XCIX (1903) 372, SMW LXI (1903) 138 and 142 (W. Altmann, with praise). Cf. Riemann/LEXIKON I 976; BAKER 889 (not in Suppl.).

190. Cf. Riemann/LEXIKON I 197 and 1009; NZM IV (1883) Beilage I, p. 4; MW XXXI (1900) 117.

191. Cf. Riemann/LEXIKON I 521; MW XI (1879) 11, XIII (1882) 390; XXVIII (1897) 99.

192. Cf. Riemann/LEXIKON I 742; but he is in no other standard dictionary.

193. Breitkopf & Härtel in Leipzig.

194. DM VIII/3 (1908–9) 173 (W. Altmann); MW XLI (1910) 378. Cf. BAKER 1431–32.

Chapter XII

Chopin and Others in France and the Low Countries up to About 1885

Revolutions, Monarchies, Republics, and Sonatas

The sociopolitical background against which the sonata flourished intermittently in 19th-century France begins with the rise and fall of the spectacular Napoleonic empire (1803–15) that had grown out of the French Revolution (1789–99). It continues with the further, familiar alternations of monarchies and republics that occurred throughout much of the century. After Napoleon Bonaparte there was the monarchic period defined by the interludial reigns (1814–30) of the brothers Louis XVIII and Charles X and the shift, with the second revolution and its wider, European repercussions (1830), to the Orléans monarchy during the reign (1830–48) of Citizen King Louis Philippe. Then, with the third revolution and its even wider repercussions (1848), came the brief Second Republic (1848–51) and from it the Second Empire (1851–70), under Napoleon III. The Franco-Prussian War of 1870–71, largely resulting from the government's suspicion and jealousy of Prussia's growing power, brought not only disastrous defeat, including the loss of Alsace and Lorraine to Germany (and some second thoughts to the more pro-German artists like Franck and d'Indy), but the establishment of the Third Republic (1870–1940), with its National Assembly, eventual constitution (1875), and more lasting control, beyond music's Romantic Era. Meanwhile, the most essential events in the Low Countries were their subjugation by the French during the French Revolution, their union in the Kingdom of the Netherlands (to Belgium's disadvantage) under terms of the Congress of Vienna in 1815, and their continuation as separate, independent kingdoms after Belgium's successful revolt during the revolutions of 1830.

Apparently more by consequence than by accident, France's musical developments, especially as viewed in this and the next chapter on the sonata in Romantic France, virtually coincided with those sociopolitical developments. Up to about 1830 and the second revolution we still are in a borderland of late-Classic and early-Romantic styles, with several composers of minor significance to sonata history, like Adam, Boieldieu, Steibelt, or Kalkbrenner, but none, to be sure, approaching their near contemporaries Clementi, Beethoven, Schubert, or Weber. Between the second and third revolutions we are in the period, almost to the year, of Chopin's active career in France (1831–48), which also comprehends the chief sonata output of other outstanding pianists in Paris, like Thalberg, Heller, and Alkan (but not Liszt, who left Paris in 1835, well before he wrote his mature sonatas; ssb X). Between the third revolution and the Franco-Prussian War (1848–71) the sonata reached its conspicuously lowest ebb in France. However, as we shall see in Chapter XIII, right from the start of the Third Republic (almost coinciding with the establishment of the Societé Nationale de Musique in 1871), it was soon to rise again, and, indeed, to attain its most important and extensive cultivation in France during the Romantic Era.

Austria and Germany are rightly thought of as the prime contributors to 19th-century instrumental music, both in quality and quantity. But the mere fact of so much going on with the sonata in France and the Low Countries will surprise those who think of these regions, especially France, as being almost as completely absorbed in opera as Italy at that time. There are over eighty composers at least to mention in these next two chapters, including thirteen who call for more or less extended discussions (though none of these in the Low Countries). It is true that, as the French author Georges Servières already noted in 1901,[1] John South Shedlock's book of 1895 on the piano sonata (Shedlock/SONATA) mentions not a single "French piano sonata" in any period. But in Shedlock's defense we should recall that (1) from Mozart's time up to about 1870 most of the more important sonata activity in France came from immigrants like Steibelt, Kalkbrenner, Chopin, and Heller in the 19th century,[2] whom Servières presumably identified rather by their nationality than (as here) by their place of chief residence; (2) even the French had not yet brought back to light their own relatively obscure contributions to the sonata in the earlier 19th century; and (3) the period after 1870 not only was too "modern" and recent for Shedlock's survey in 1895 but, like all previous periods of sonata history in France except the late-Classic and early-Romantic, the main emphasis was placed, contrary to Shedlock's, on the ensemble rather than the solo sonata.

It took the French scholar Georges Favre in the 1940's to rediscover

1. In the Brussels *Guide musical* XLVII (1901) 99–101.
2. Cf. sce 626 and 648–49 on the 18th c.

the native French contributions to the sonata in the period between the first two revolutions.[3] These contributions were furthered considerably, it should be observed, by opera composers who started as pianists, such as Méhul, Boieldieu, and Hérold. They were not furthered especially by the curriculum itself of the important Paris Conservatoire, which, in spite of its rebirth during the French Revolution (1795), was to become increasingly academic and, indeed, "conservative." [4] The ever-increasing Chopin research has helped to illuminate lesser composers active in Chopin's sphere. And now perhaps Favre or some other scholar will go on to rediscover further sonata (and other instrumental) activities during the Second Empire, when they seem to have been at such a low ebb. However, one must remember that some of the most important composers in 19th-century France took little or no interest in the sonata, including Auber, Meyerbeer, Berlioz, Bizet, and Gounod. Opera did predominate, and by a generous margin, over all other musical interests.[5]

Moreover, although Paris publishers like Leduc, Pleyel, Imbault, Lemoine, Richault, Cotelle, and Schlesinger were supplying the French public with music of the Classic masters early in the century, including their more popular sonatas,[6] actual performances of sonatas by Clementi, Haydn, and Mozart seem to have been rare, and by Beethoven almost nonexistent prior to the second revolution.[7] In other words, public performances in themselves could have provided but little incentive to the composition of sonatas in early-Romantic France. For example, although early 19th-century French treatises had already recognized the sonata's preeminence among types of piano compositions,[8] an entertaining German description of foreign and native pianists congregated in Paris and their performances in 1825 makes not one reference to sonatas.[9] And Fétis' brief but comprehensive account of the current Paris scene, published right in the year of the second

3. Favre/FRANÇAISE. Saint-Foix/PIANISTES had paved the way by rediscovering the French pianists and their contributions in the previous generation. Cf., also, Gil-Marchex/FRANÇAIS.

4. Cf. Harding/SAINT-SAËNS 34–41.

5. An excellent summary account of 19th-c. French music may be found under "Paris" (which is nearly tantamount to France in 19th-c. art) in MGG X 773–83 (G. Ferchault). Cf., also, Saint-Saëns' own description in 1900 of opera's dominance in Paris around 1860, as trans. in Cooper/FRENCH 9.

6. Cf. Favre/FRANÇAISE 80–81, 103–4.

7. Cf. Schrade/BEETHOVEN 4–38, including information on Haydn and Mozart, and further references on p. 253. To be sure, the public performance of Beethoven sons. anywhere was almost nonexistent while he was still alive (SCE 528–29; SSB XIX).

8. Cf. Favre/FRANÇAISE 127–28; also, SSB II on Reicha.

9. Trans. in QUARTERLY VIII (1825) 310–13.

revolution, makes no specific mention of sonatas either, but does say in reference to symphonies and chamber music that "nature struggled in vain to give birth to a Haydn or a Beethoven in France." [10] Beethoven's influence and both the awareness and public acceptance of the sonata certainly increased during Chopin's time, although public performances of sonatas, especially of solo as against duo sonatas or as against lighter solos (potpourris, etc.), were still infrequent. There were such performances of Thalberg's only sonata but none that could be found here of Chopin's own two main solo sonatas during his lifetime, not by himself or by close sympathizers like Liszt or Clara Schumann. Moreover, in a journal like the *Revue et gazette musicale de Paris* (RGM) we still find skepticism about the validity of absolute or purely instrumental music, as in the continued reiteration, after a full century, of the celebrated quip attributed to Fontenelle, "Sonate, que me veux-tu?" (cf. SBE 353; SCE 36–37; SSB II). And, as in the contemporary German periodicals, we still find gloom over the low state of the current sonata and premature assumptions of its early demise (SSB II). Not until the Third Republic was well under way and the finest examples of Franck, Saint-Saëns, and Fauré were published, as discussed in our next chapter, did the sonata come fully into its own in Romantic France.

Paris Residents in the Classic-Romantic Borderland (Steibelt)

Early Romantic traits began to permeate the sonata in France during the last phase of the Classic Era. They can be found in several borderland composers in our previous volume quite as Classic traits persist in several borderland composers about to be met here. Examples are the theatricalism of Johann Edelmann's and Etienne-Nicolas Méhul's sonatas (SCE 650–51 and 668–72), or the "style dramatique" and the pre-Chopinesque cantilena of Johann Ludwig Adam (SCE 655–58). On the other hand, some "Classic" composers who lived well into the Romantic Era as defined here—for example, Rodolphe Kreutzer (SCE 668) or Matthieu-Frédéric Blasius (SCE 678)—showed no ear or inclination for the newer trends.

Among further borderland composers, not mentioned in our previous volume, was one of the most successful leaders of French comic opera, **François-Adrien Boieldieu** (1775–1834). All of some seventeen sonatas identified as his, including seven now lost, were early works published in Paris between 1795, or the year that he left Rouen for Paris, and

10. Fétis/CURIOSITÉS 137–68, especially p. 145.

1803, the year he left Paris for Russia.[11] In other words, these works appeared around the time Boieldieu was teaching piano at the Conservatoire[12] and before he became completely engrossed in opera. They include 9 sonatas for P solo, 4 for P and 2 for harp with optional or obligatory Vn, and one apparently for harp solo.[13] Two were arranged from harp "duos." The sonatas are in two or three movements each, the rondo finale being the one consistent movement in the cycles.

A reading of Boieldieu's sonatas reveals little more than historical interest. We are reminded that opera composers do not necessarily make instrumental composers. The transparent, forthright melodies, which bring the light opera aria to the piano and constitute the most evident Romanticism in this music, rise above the obvious only occasionally to become charming (as in "Rondeau: Allegretto doloroso," Op. 4/2/iii). The texture grows from thin to richer between Opp. 1 and 6, even including 3ds and 6ths (as in Op. 4/2/i/109–17). But the most that can be said for the writing is that it anticipates the scoring and rhythmic mannerisms of Weber occasionally (ssb VIII) and that it is convenient for the pianist; it usually offers only the dullest, primitive, chordal accompaniments. Although the melody introduces chromatic passing tones, the harmony remains diatonic, rudimentary, and sometimes gauche in its voice-leading (Op. 4/2/ii/4–5). Least acceptable are the straggly, poorly integrated sectional forms, which are always too long for their content (with 7 of the solo sons. ranging from totals of 449 to 665 mss.). The continuous diet of square-cut, melodious phrases and periods, without benefit of significant development, are barely tolerable in the lightest movements, and not tolerable in the principal, initial allegro movements. Boieldieu's sonatas got no French reviews, but the first three of them, Op. 1 for P solo, got a German review that treated them as pleasant, good study material for the fingers, too long, lacking in consequential slow music, and unexceptional.[14]

A less remembered but more capable sonata composer among the borderlanders was the Austrian pianist and teacher **Ignaz Anton (Franz Joseph) Ladurner** (1766–1839), who trained in Munich before settling

11. Cf. Favre/BOIELDIEU (the most thorough study of the man and his music) I 79–81, 302–3 (list of sons.), but add *Grand Sonata for the Piano Forte* [in Eb], *Arranged From the Celebrated Duett* (London: Preston, *ca.* 1800; cf. Cat. ROYAL 67); also, Favre/FRANÇAISE 82–83 (which gives 1795, not 1796, for Boieldieu's arrival in Paris).

12. Cf. Favre/BOIELDIEU I 103–4.

13. Mod. ed. of 6 selected sons. for P solo: Favre/BOIELDIEU-m, with extended preface (repeated in Favre/FRANÇAISE 82–97 and 166, with generous exx.). The sons. were first explored in Saint-Foix/PIANISTES VII 102–10.

14. AMZ IV (1801–2) 226–27. It has not been possible here to concur in Favre's high opinions of Boieldieu's sons. (as in MGG I 70).

in Paris in 1788.[15] Between about 1792 and 1805 at least 31 sonatas by
Ladurner were published, singly and in sets of 3 each, including 5 sets
for P solo, 4 sets and a single for P with Vn and sometimes Vc, and
3 singles for P-duet.[16] The successive sonatas, made up of two to five
movements, display increasing virtuosity and exploitation of the instruments, starting with idioms and passages that recall Clementi and
culminating with some ideas and figurations not unlike Weber's. Moreover, Ladurner's sonatas display an increasingly imaginative variety of
styles and forms. There is even a "battle" finale—"Charge du Cavallerie
ou *la* passage du Rhin"—complete with pedal effects and other literalities. Like Boieldieu's movements, Ladurner's sometimes straggle with
too many sections and suffer from dull accompaniments, too. But
Ladurner has the requisite skill and interest in his themes, harmony,
rhythm, and texture to keep the movements alive. And there is some
depth and poetry in his slow movements and frequent slow introductions (Ex. 69), as implied by his abundant editorial advices. There is
also depth in the richly ornamented passages, in the expressive, rather
frequent cadenzas for which he pauses, and in the interplay of the
piano and the independent, essential violin parts. (The latter are sometimes cued into the upper staff of the piano score, as in the original ed.
of Ex. 69, suggesting that the indicated freedom of performance raised
ensemble problems.) Perhaps the most consistent trait of Ladurner's
sonatas other than their frequent, but no longer invariable, use of a
rondo finale is their tendency toward monothematic writing, evident in
derivations of the "contrasting" themes from the main themes, and in
the similar incipits for two or more movements in a cycle. Another
Austrian in Paris (from 1810) was the organist **Sigismund Ritter von
Neukomm** (1778–1858), who left three published sonatas, for P solo
and P ± Vn, between 1814 and 1828.[17]

In spite of his new views on the phrase and other aspects of structural
rhythm, the few solo and accompanied piano sonatas published (*ca.*
1805–15) in the name of **Jérôme-Joseph de Momigny** (1762–1842) prove
in all their skill and charm to be no later in style, no more pianistically
challenging, and no more elastically expressive than the most advanced

15. Cf. MGG VIII 51–53 (M. Briquet), with list of sons. (partly dated but not
fully reconciled); Schilling/LEXICON IV 296–98 (G. W. Fink).

16. Saint-Foix/PIANISTES VIII (1926–27) 13–20 describes Opp. 2 for P-duet, 4 for
P solo, and 5 (a set) for P + Vn. Studeny/VIOLINSONATE 12 describes Op. 7 (another
set) for P + Vn. Some of Ladurner's sons. seem to be lost.

17. Cf. MGG IX 1394–96 (H. Jancik); HOFMEISTER 1828 (Whistling), 498 and 599;
Cat. NYPL XX 626 and 627; AMZ XVIII (1816) 127 and 15 (repeated on 199), reviewing Opp. 14 and 30 as Haydnesque, with only a little that is new or original.

Ex. 69. From the opening of Ignaz Anton Ladurner's Sonata in a/A, Op. 5/2 (after the original Pleyel ed. of *ca.* 1797).

of Clementi's familiar high-Classic sonatinas.[18] The several solo, four-hand, and accompanied piano sonatas by another, younger theorist and a onetime pupil of Boieldieu, **Victor Dourlen** (1780–1864), were also published in the early 1800's and reportedly are of interest, including a "battle" sonata, *Bataille de Marengo, Sonate militaire pour le Piano-Forte,* Op. 2.[19] Several solo sonatas published between 1802 and 1819 were left by the brilliant pianist **Louis-Barthélemi Pradher** (or **Pradére;** 1781–1843), who succeeded Hyacinthe Jadin (SCE 672–73) as "Professeur de piano au Conservatoire." [20]

18. Cf. MGG IX 448 (A. Palm); HOFMEISTER 1815 (Whistling), 309 and 368. Favre/FRANÇAISE 127–28 and 131–32 quotes Momigny's high artistic opinions of the son.
19. Cf. MGG III 715–17 (G. Favre); Favre/FRANÇAISE 118–19; HOFMEISTER 1815 (Whistling), 301, 324, and 349.
20. Cf. Fétis/BU VII 110–11; Favre/FRANÇAISE 118 (with the death date [inverted to?] 1834).

We need to observe one more of those composers on the borderland between Classic and Romantic styles in France. He was the most celebrated pianist among them and the composer of the most, the best known, and the most widely published sonatas, **Daniel Gottlieb Steibelt** (1765–1823). Steibelt flourished in Paris from 1790 to 1796 and during two further, briefer stays. These stays were preceded, separated, and followed by shorter or longer stays in most of the other main centers of music in Europe during the ups and downs that beset his troubled, itinerant life.[21] Born in Berlin in a family of keyboard instrument makers, Steibelt, an eventual progressive in his styles, had received some of his chief training from the conservative theorist Kirnberger (SCE 440–43).[22] HOFMEISTER (Whistling) for 1815 lists the publication of no less than 262 sonatas by Steibelt, not including a few duplications already noted in that surprisingly careful source.[23] One supposes there were actually many more duplications in the total, not only because of Steibelt's notoriously unscrupulous dealings with publishers[24] but because pirated reprints were common, anyway, in that day of no effective copyrights, and because the same sonatas often reappeared in different settings—as solos and as duets (with "accompaniments"), for example. To arrive at a more accurate list one would have to locate all or most of the publications, which originally appeared between 1788 [25] and about 1808 (when Steibelt was last active in Paris),[26] then eliminate duplications by preparing a thematic index (a task that would justify itself chiefly in a sociological study of musical popularity). But a total of at least 150 different sonatas seems not unlikely.[27] The

21. The chief study of the man and his music (but with no list of works) is the diss. Müller/STEIBELT. Cf., also, MGG XII 1222–26 (R. Sietz), with further references (but also no detailed list of works). Some idea of Steibelt's international, lifetime popularity may be had from the big space allotted to him in Schilling/LEXICON VI 475–78, and still in Mendel/LEXIKON IX 413–16, Fétis/BU VIII 119–22, and GROVE first ed. III 699–707 (!), with detailed but undated list of works (J. H. Mee). It is also significant that Steibelt was among the "notables" represented in Anth. NÄGELI-m, with 2 sons. in "Suite" 4 (SSB IV).

22. Cf. Müller/STEIBELT 7–9, 10, 12–14.

23. Pp. 294–95, 315–17, 321, 335, and 378–82, including many references to AMZ reviews. These reviews range from moderate enthusiasm at the start (e.g., AMZ II [1799–1800] 680–82, on 2 solo and 2 4-hand sons.) to weary disparagement in several later instances (as noted, *infra*, under Op. 64). The fact that Steibelt was a German neither active nor interested in Germany did not help his reception in the German periodicals.

24. Cf. GROVE first ed. III 700 and 703; Loesser/PIANOS 178–79.

25. Cf. Müller/STEIBELT 21.

26. The highest op. no. in the sons. is 91 and Op. 84 was reviewed in 1811, probably several years late (AMZ XIII [1811] 332; cf. Müller/STEIBELT 90–92). The Library of Congress and British Museum (BUCEM II 975–76) both have many Steibelt sons.

27. Müller/STEIBELT 90 guesses "well over 100."

1828 edition of HOFMEISTER (Whistling) lists numerous further editions of Steibelt's sonatas, which can only mean more duplications. Thereafter the Steibelt entries abruptly cease. By the turn of this century even PAZDÍREK (XIII 995–98) lists no more than a few of the sonatas.

The listings of Steibelt's sonatas recall typical titles met in our previous volume. These listings stand apart from those of his many other modish pieces (mostly without op. nos.), such as "Etude," "Rondeau turc," "Fantaisie militaire," "La grande Marche de Bonaparte en Italie," "Le Retour de la Cavall. russe a Petersburg," or "Combat naval." Thus, one finds "Six grandes Sonates dédiées à la Reine de Prusse" (Op. 27), or "Trois Sonates faciles avec flutes ou violons" (Op. 42), or "Sonate périodique" (that is, a periodical pub.). About 43 per cent of Steibelt's sonatas are designated for P solo, 33 for P with Vn accompaniment, 11 for P with Fl accompaniment, 10 for P with Vn and Vc accompaniments, and 3 for P-duet or 2 Ps. The accompaniments in the duo sonatas, whether designated optional or obligatory, are generally inconsequential and dispensable.[28] Except for some later sonatas in three, and a very few in four, movements, most of his sonatas are in two movements, in the same key and with a rondo finale, probably because the needed depth in a middle, slow movement was inimical to his rather superficial artistry.[29] Primary-triad harmony and homophonic textures prevail, with the left hand relegated to empty chordal accompaniments or, at most, some doubling of and sharing with the right hand. Scales, triplets, broken octaves, 3ds and 6ths, and a few, more original figures, provide the passagework. Except for occasional dotted and march rhythms,[30] Steibelt tends to write lyrical, rather neutral themes that do not afford distinct contrasts. Mozart comes to mind when the idea is chromatic and ends in a feminine rhythm. There are considerable transposition and redisposition of the themes but almost no development of them. The forms are loosely sectional.

Yet, in spite of this summary of unpromising style traits, there are distinct pleasures in Steibelt's few best solo sonatas. If there is no significant, dynamic drive in them, nor the structural solidity commanded by his near contemporary Hummel (SSB VIII), there is still a youthful, early-Romantic bloom and a degree of elegance, grace, and

28. Müller/STEIBELT 90–102 provides the only substantial discussion of these sons. (following 17 pp. on the other main category of Steibelt's output, his etudes).

29. Cf. the remarks on his polished playing in AMZ II (1799–1800) 299; also, GROVE first ed. III 703–4.

30. Both are inherent in Steibelt's unnumbered Son. in F "In which are Introduced the favorite Airs of *If a Body Meet a Body* [ii] and *Sir David Hunter Blair* [iii]."

refinement in the nicely shaped melodies (recalling the virtues of his own refined playing). The figurations become richer and more ingenious, to the point of anticipating Chopin's in a slight way. And the music balances and sounds well on the piano. In these respects, although Steibelt himself is supposed to have preferred his *Grande Sonate martiale,* Op. 82 in D,[31] our own preference today is likely to be for the three-movement *Grande Sonate* in Eb (F-S-Ro), Op. 45 (1801?), "dédiée à Madame Bonaparte," [32] or, above all, for the more virtuosic, four-movement *Grande Sonate* in G (F-Mi-S-Ro), Op. 64 (1806? Ex. 70).[33] Even the "Adagio fantaisie" from Op. 64, in the submediant key,

Ex. 70. From the opening of Daniel Steibelt's Sonata in G, Op. 64 (after THÉSOR-m XX).

is more expressive and Beethovian than one might expect, especially when one recalls Steibelt's unhappy encounters with Beethoven in 1800.[34]

A curiosity is *A favorite Sonata for the Piano Forte or Harpsichord, called The Coquette, Composed* [in 1787] *for the late Queen Marie Antoinette of France by Hermann and Steibelt* (and pub. *ca.* 1795 by Longman and Broderip of London). **Johann David Hermann** (*ca.* 1760–1846) was a virtuoso German pianist who left some published accompanied sonatas of his own and gave lessons to Marie Antoinette

31. Müller/STEIBELT 99.

32. Reviewed in AMZ IV (1801–2) 383–84, with more than usual praise for the work and some jesting about the dedicatee's ability to play it.

33. Reviewed at length in AMZ VIII (1805–6) 305–12, with each mvt. separately deplored for its emptiness and its commonplaces; reprinted in TRÉSOR-m XX and RICORDI ARTE-m VI 19. A Son. in Eb for P solo by Steibelt is reprinted in Méreaux/CLAVECINISTES-m III no. 162.

34. Cf. Thayer & Forbes/BEETHOVEN I 257.

and King Louis XVI himself.[35] In 1787, to settle their rivalry, he and Steibelt composed the first and second movements, respectively, of this two-movement sonata, both on the same tune, "La Coquette." That Steibelt deserved his victory is evident at once from the much fresher music in his rondo finale, which seems to anticipate the 2/4 meter and rhythm of the mid-19th-century German polka.

Further Predecessors of Chopin in Paris (Kalkbrenner)

The brilliant pianist and renowned French opera composer **Louis-Joseph-Ferdinand Hérold** (1791–1833) was the musical product of several sonata composers met in our previous volume, including his Alsatian father F.-J. Hérold, J.-L. Adam, and Méhul (sce 655–59, 668–72).[36] Early in his short career, between 1810 and about 1817, he produced eight solo and two accompanied piano sonatas, some of them published then and some only posthumously. Starting with a prize-winning Op. 1 at the Conservatoire (ded. to Adam), these are described as generally tasteful but unequal works, with arid sections relieved by flashes of real talent. Precision and grace in the melody and harmony, clarity and smooth flow, and disinterest in pure display are some of their most characteristic traits. Among progressive influences to be noted are those of Boieldieu, Beethoven, and Rossini.

One of the most capable musicians among the earlier 19th-century Parisians was the pianist and organist **Alexandre-Pierre-François Boëly** (1787–1858).[37] Preferring to study with Ladurner rather than the French teachers at the Conservatoire, Boëly received an exceptionally thorough grounding that laid the foundation for his increasing devotion to past styles and made him more interesting to us for his artistic assimilations than for any pronounced Romanticisms. During the first decade of the century, although not performed publicly, Beethoven's sonatas up to Op. 30 were making rapidly growing impressions on French musical life.[38] These impressions are clearly evident, along with considerable musical perception of his own, in Boëly's two piano sonatas Op. 1 (ded. to Ladurner), both in three movements (VF-S-VF and F-Sc-Ro) and published, like Hérold's Op. 1, in 1810. Following a

35. Cf. Müller/STEIBELT 23; MGG VI 222 (J. Vigué); BUCEM I 478 and II 975; WOLFE, item 3674.

36. Cf. MGG VI 250–59 (M. Briquet), with dated list of works; Favre/FRANÇAISE 97–102 (with exx.), 166; Saint-Foix/PIANISTES IX (1927–28) 321–32.

37. Cf. MGG II 44–45 (G. Favre); GROVE I 783–84 (M. L. Pereyra); Favre/FRANÇAISE 102–12, with exx. New biographic information appears in RECHERCHES V (1965) 51–69 (N. Dufourcq).

38. Favre/FRANÇAISE 103–4 cites specific notices and descriptions in French journals.

series of additional pieces that return rather to the style of J. S. Bach, Boëly produced his only other sonata, described as an outstanding, four-movement P-duet in f (F-S-Mi-"Giga"), Op. 17,[39] showing even more depth and closer affinity with Beethoven.[40]

The next major German pianist in Paris after Steibelt was **Friedrich (Wilhelm) Kalkbrenner** (1785–1849), who was younger by twenty years. Kalkbrenner's similarly itinerant life took him to Paris from 1799 to 1803 (where his training under Adam culminated in a first prize from the Conservatoire), again from 1806 to 1814, and finally from 1824 on.[41] However, Steibelt and Kalkbrenner seem not to have been in Paris at the same time. Following the start his father had given him (SCE 579) and during his earlier travels, Kalkbrenner profited from the counsel, whether through lessons or less formal advice, of Beethoven, Haydn, Albrechtsberger, and Clementi. Later he attributed his clear, neat, dexterous, facile playing largely to the influence in London of Clementi and Cramer.[42] Although subsequently he also came to know Chopin, Liszt, and both Schumanns, their influence reportedly did not affect his somewhat older style of playing and seems not to have left any conspicuous mark in his music.

There are records of at least 18 published sonatas by Kalkbrenner, which first appeared between about 1810 and 1826 except for Op. 177 in 1845 (interrupting his last two decades of publishing nothing else but fantasias, rondos, and potpourris). Among these, 13 are for P solo, 3 for P-duet, and 2 for P with accompaniment. Because existing lists are incomplete, have conflicting opus numbers and other discrepancies, and lack dates, an attempt seems warranted to piece together the opus number(s), key, year (with "t. a. q." meaning only a *terminus ad quem*), first or early edition, and contemporary comments, insofar as any or all of these have turned up in HOFMEISTER (up to 1851), PAZDÍREK VIII 20–25, contemporary reviews, lists of plate numbers, the "Intelligenz-Blatt" entries in AMZ, and a few chance sources. The sonatas for P solo are listed first.

39. Based only on the chronology of Boëly's other works, a rough date might be 1825 for the composition, with 1855 (cf. Saint-Foix/PIANISTES IX [1927–28] 329) as the publication year of Op. 17.

40. The exx. in Favre/FRANÇAISE 109–10 are convincing.

41. Cf. MGG VII 445–53 (R. Sietz), with further references and a detailed but undated list of works.

42. Regarding this playing, cf. HALLÉ 213–15 and 221 (much of it quoted in Schonberg/PIANISTS 112–13).

Friedrich Kalkbrenner's Sonatas

Op. 1/1-3, P solo; f, C, and G; Paris: Sieber, t. a. q. 1815. A likely *terminus a quo* is Kalkbrenner's arrival in Paris in 1806. Reviewed in AMA No. 40 (Mar. 31, 1827) 373.

Op. 4/1-3, P solo; g, C, and a; Paris: Sieber, t. a. q. 1815.

Op. 13, P solo; g; Paris: Nadermann, t. a. q. 1815.

Op. 28, P solo; F; Paris: Pleyel, 1819. Ded. to Cramer. Reviewed with praise for its vitality and superior texture, including polyphonic interest, in AMZ XXI (1819) 643–44 (cf. Intelligenz-Blatt for Apr. 3); also, in AMA No. 37 (Mar. 10, 1827) 351. "Grande" in title.

Op. 35, P solo; A; Paris: Leduc (plate no. 1193), t. a. q. 1828. "Grande" in title.

Op. 42 (and 40), *Piano Forte Sonata for the left hand (obligato)*; A♭; London: Clementi, t. a. q. 1818. This son. is not for left hand *alone* (as assumed in MGG VII 452, where it is called a "unicum" for its day, as a first) but simply puts the main melodic responsibilities in that hand (as "obligato" implies in the title, or "principale" in the title of the early French and German eds., *Sonate pour la Main gauche principale*; cf. HOFMEISTER XVI [1919–23] 180). Reviewed in QUARTERLY I (1818) 534–35 as excellent training for the left hand, with almost too much neglect of the right hand and a gratifying avoidance of radical key relationships.

Op. 48, P solo; a; Paris: Pleyel, t. a. q. 1828. "Grande" in title.

Op. 56, P solo; f; Paris: Pleyel, t. a. q. 1824 (based on plate no. 67 of Probst ed. in Leipzig). Ded. "to the memory of Haydn."

Op. 177, P solo; A♭; Leipzig: Hofmeister, 1845? "Grande Sonate brillante." Reviewed in AMZ XLII (1845) 888 as a late work that still stands out for its skill, clarity and freshness; but in NZM XXIII (1845) 177 (not by Schumann) as a product of prolificity, still in the modish style now outmoded, and more appropriately called "Souvenir," "Bonbon," or "Fleur."

Op. 3, P-duet; C; Paris: Sieber, t. a. q. 1815.

Op. 76 (and 79), P-duet; F; London: Clementi, 1826? "Grande" in title. "Op. 79" assigned to the "revised" Kistner ed., t. a. q. 1833 (HOFMEISTER 1829–33, 113). Reviewed, with ex., in QUARTERLY VIII (1826) 241–42 as Kalkbrenner's best duet, tight in its form and enhanced by its contrapuntal exchanges, including double counterpoint.

Op. 80, P-duet; B♭; Leipzig: Breitkopf & Härtel, 1826 (AMZ XXVIII [1826] Intelligenz-Blatt for April 6). "Grande" in title.

Op. 22 (or 27, Sieber?), P & Vn-or-Fl; E; Paris: Carli (plate no. 568), t. a. q. 1828. "Grande" in title.

Op. 39, P & Fl-or-Vn ± Vc; B♭; Leipzig: Breitkopf & Härtel, 1826 (AMZ XXVIII [1826] Intelligenz-Blatt for April 6).

Kalkbrenner's piano music has been deplored undeservedly, if one has in mind his best sonatas and etudes. Partly responsible are those many cheap fantasias and potpourris, and partly the stories that have survived about his relationships with his contemporaries. The well-known story of Chopin turning down Kalkbrenner's proffered three years of lessons has probably been played up too much in Chopin's favor.[43] Liszt's peremptory refusal to listen to Wilhelm von Lenz's performance of Kalkbrenner's *Sonate pour la Main gauche principale* (cf. Op. 42, *supra*), presumably on the grounds that it was display purely for display's sake, seems a little unjustified, too.[44] No wonder Kalkbrenner gets such a quick, contemptuous dismissal from a late-19th-century writer like Oscar Bie.[45] But his own contemporaries knew better. After all, Chopin did dedicate his Concerto in e to Kalkbrenner and share in concerts with him, including some of those curious pieces for as many as six pianists.[46] Moscheles, who might be considered a rival, seems to have respected him highly.[47] And Schumann, ever honest, wrote that he was no "great worshipper" of Kalkbrenner but in his earlier years had enjoyed the "first, lively, truly musical sonatas" of Kalkbrenner's youth and, until genuine Romanticism passed him by, continued to enjoy the music of "one of the most skilled, masterly piano composers for finger and hand. . . ."[48]

The fact is that Kalkbrenner was a solidly grounded, resourceful musician. Although Steibelt's sonatas seem to have had still more of a following, Kalkbrenner's show him to be a much better, though only a slightly more Romanticized edition of Steibelt. In one of his best, most circulated, and most representative sonatas, Op. 56 in three movements (F-M-Ro), the melodic interest is about on a par with Steibelt's, often achieving an expressive cantilena that is a step closer to Chopin's style; the harmony is still relatively simple, although greatly intensified by

43. Cf. Schonberg/PIANISTS 113; Sydow & Hedley/CHOPIN 93–99, 115–16; Hedley/CHOPIN 44–46.

44. Cf. Ramann/LISZT I 169.

45. Bie/PIANOFORTE 192, 218. The evaluation in Georgii/KLAVIERMUSIK 271–72 has seemed more balanced here.

46. Cf. Hedley/CHOPIN 46–47.

47. MOSCHELES I 58–59, 77; II 58.

48. Schumann/SCHRIFTEN I 155–56.

Ex. 71. From the second theme in the first movement of Friedrich Kalkbrenner's Sonata in f, Op. 56 (after the Probst ed. of 1824 [?] at the Library of Congress).

the more skillfully placed appoggiaturas; the voice-leading reveals the expert craftsman, one who can summon polyphonic entries when they are needed; and the sense of good piano sound is at least as acute (Ex. 71) . The chief shortcomings are, alas, similar to Steibelt's, too. For all his solid grounding, Kalkbrenner has little sense of architecture. His forms are static, not dynamic. The cantilena themes are too similar to each other to have independent character and to serve as landmarks. Nor do they undergo any development. The passagework, including some new figurations, delights the ear but fails to relate to or derive from the themes and meanders from one irrelevant key in the total scheme to another. In short and at best, one is hypnotized mildly without being drawn, driven, or, in fact, moved.

An exceptionally strong and intriguing composer and the principal contributor to chamber music in France before Chopin's arrival was the pianist (**André**) **Georges** (**Louis**) **Onslow** (1784–1853), of noble, Anglo-French descent. An amateur in the best sense, Onslow had studied with Hüllmandel, Dussek, and Cramer before settling in his scenic home province of Auvergne, after which he studied composition with Reicha, took up the cello as a part of his special interest in chamber music, and came up to Paris only part of each year to try his new works.[49] All of the 9 known sonatas by him were composed early, before 1821 or well before his hunting accident of 1829 that he set in oft-cited programme music known as the "Bullet Quintet," and before the composition of most of those many other larger chamber ensembles that represent his chief contribution. These sonatas, which must have enjoyed wide popularity to judge by their numerous re-editions from several publishers,[50] included one (not 3) for P solo, 2 for P-duet, 3 for P & Vn, and 3 for P & Vc. Since the information has not been brought together previously,[51] there follows a list of those sonatas along with the key, the first or one early publisher, at least a *terminus ad quem* (t. a. q.), and any contemporary reviews that have turned up here. Not included are Onslow's 3 similarly constructed "Duos" for P & Vn, Opp. 15, 29, and 31 (t. a. q. 1828).

Georges Onslow's Sonatas

Op. 2, "Grande Sonate," P solo; c; Paris: Pleyel, 1807 ("13 Rue Neuve . . . Trésor public"; cf. Hopkinson/PARISIAN 99). Reviewed in AMZ XX (1818) 702–4 as the work of an unknown who must be a German (!) by virtue of the originality, skill, excellent advanced piano writing, and pathetic quality (including much use of the dim.-7th chord).

Op. 7, "Grande Sonate," P-duet; e; Paris: Pleyel, t. a. q. 1815 (HOFMEISTER 1815 [Whistling], 332).

Op. 22, P-duet; f; Leipzig: Breitkopf & Härtel, t. a. q. 1820 (AMZ XXII [1820] Intelligenz-Blatt for Jan.). Reviewed in RGM for Apr. 1, 1838, with high praise for the dramatic and pathetic character, the rich harmony with all its surprises, and the effective modulations. In a similar review in AMZ XXVII (1825) 641–44, Op. 22 is called one of the best, well-distributed 4-hand works since Mozart's 2-piano Son. in F.

Op. 11/1–3, P & Vn; D, E$\flat$, and f; Paris: Pleyel, t. a. q. 1818 (HOFMEISTER 1818 [Whistling], 28).

Op. 16, 1–3, P & Vc-or-Va; F, c, A; Leipzig: Breitkopf & Härtel, t. a. q. 1821 (AMZ XXIII [1821] Intelligenz-Blatt for Jan.). Reviewed at length in AMZ XXIII (1821) 185 as showing unusual progress (much as had been true of Haydn), surprising originality and harmonic depth (recalling Beethoven), delicate, ingenious scoring, and full partnership of the two instruments.

49. Cf. MGG IX 1937–40 (B. Schwarz), with further bibliography but no detailed list of works.

50. Fétis/CURIOSITÉS 145 attributes Onslow's exceptional success in chamber music to the social position that freed him from financial worries.

51. A study of Onslow's sonatas would make an excellent thesis topic.

Such recent evaluations of Onslow's music as there are tend to support the reviews just cited with regard to his craftsmanship (especially in creating polyphonic interest), his harmonic ingenuity, and his Beethovian pathos; but they do not agree that he was genuinely original.[52] 52a
All of which applies well enough to an early work like Op. 2 but not to the outstanding P-duet Op. 22, which proves to be another sleeper like that, Op. 17, of Hermann Goetz a generation later (ssb X).[53] The originality—particularly the harmonic diversions and unexpected modulations, the fresh ideas, and the clever, often contrapuntal distribution of parts—is apparent on every page. In Onslow's emphasis on the dim.-7th chord and its manifold treatment lies a kinship with Mendelssohn, Spohr, and sometimes Weber. Beethoven and further German orientation is suggested rather by ascending harmonic sequences driving to dramatic peaks, by the dignified pace of the slow movement, and by the witty turns in the minuet (of this 4-mvt. cycle, typical for Onslow—F-Mi-S-F). Mendelssohn comes to mind again in the scales, broken chords, and oscillating figures that supply the passagework, especially in the fluent finale in 6/8 meter. There may be a certain artificiality, self-consciousness, or posing in this music, too, which recalls Spohr more than Onslow's other contemporaries. Or one can hear those declamatory chords, the calculated pauses, and the sharp sudden contrasts as part of the unspoiled naivety that characterizes the early 19th-century Romanticism (as in Ex. 72, although the deliberate pace of Onslow's music makes it difficult to quote an example with more than two or three characteristic traits at any one time).

Such other sonatas dating before Chopin's arrival as might be mentioned here would be of no more importance, say, than the several tasteful but decidedly academic sonatas for oboe and unfigured bass to be found in the *Grande Méthode complète pour le Hautbois* (before 1828) by the then celebrated Parisian oboist, **Henri Brod** (1799–1839).[54]
In the Alsatian capital of Strasbourg there is only the violinist **Conrad Mathias Berg** (1785–1852), a product of the Paris Conservatoire, to point to, and a couple of sonatas for P solo, of which the second was described as routine but capable of pleasing the amateurs.[55]

52. E.g., Favre/FRANÇAISE 119; Cobbett/CHAMBER II 195–200 (H. Woollett and W. Cobbett); MGG IX 1939–40.

53. Georgii/KLAVIERMUSIK 565 puts Onslow's Op. 22 on a par with J. N. Hummel's Op. 92 (ssb VIII) and second in their day only to Schubert's P-duets.

54. Cf. Fétis/BU II 78–79; HOFMEISTER 1828 (Whistling), 313. There have been numerous re-eds., as by Lemoine in Paris.

55. Cf. Riemann/LEXIKON I 154; CAECILIA X (1829) 167, 172–74.

Ex. 72. From the first movement of Georges Onslow's Sonata in f, Op. 22 (after the Schlesinger re-ed. in Paris of *ca.* 1834 [plate no. 1625]).

Chopin's Niche

The great Polish-French genius of the piano, **Frédéric François** (or **Fryderyk Franciszek**) **Chopin** (1810–49) brings us to the fourth of those four main composers who figured at the center of our Chapter VI on styles and forms. As with our separate discussions of Schubert, Schumann, and Brahms (ssb VII, VIII, and IX), we limit our concern in this chapter to the circumstances, background, and effect of Chopin's sonatas. (The exception is his early Op. 4, whose music was not representative enough for Chapter VI but does have historical interest for us now.) Chopin left fewer sonatas than these other men, only four. And his sonatas have long been viewed, especially in matters of form, as being even less representative of his special genius[56] than Schubert's and Schumann's of theirs. Yet two of his solo sonatas, the mature ones, continue to retain their popularity as few other Romantic sonatas do— more so than any by Schumann, and as much as the few most successful sonatas by Schubert, Brahms, and Liszt. In fact, their popularity is consistent with that of all Chopin's music, which in its apparently greater artistic truth, more than holds its own while the piano music of every important contemporary, especially Mendelssohn, has lost ground markedly.[57] Not many pianists, even in today's world of hectic musical changes, will deny in these sonatas, as in his other music, their unsurpassed melody and poetic lyricism, drama, spontaneity, warmth, drive, resourcefulness of figurations, sonorities, and sense of good structural timing.

The information about Chopin and his music has kept pace with this devotion to it, continuing, if anything, at an increasing rate, too. One example is the compact, efficient, sympathetic little book by Arthur Hedley,[58] a leading Chopin specialist, which during the past twenty years has proven to be the best biography and general interpretation in English and a model of its sort in any language. Excellent, too, are the annotated, chronological thematic index by Maurice J. E. Brown;[59] the three chronological volumes of letters, by, to, and 59a about Chopin, edited (in French) by another leading specialist, the late Bronislas Édouard Sydow (completed by his successors);[60] Hedley's

56. E.g., Hanslick/wien II 323–24 (but read Op. 35 for Op. 4!); Bie/pianoforte 262–63; Dale/nineteenth 74–78; Jachimecki/chopin 197.

57. By comparison, the new and renewed interest in Liszt must still be recognized primarily as a cult rather than a general trend.

58. Hedley/chopin; cf. pp. v, 2, 68, and 92 regarding Niecks's standard biography.

59. Brown/chopin; cf. the review in pq XXXIII (fall 1960) 24 and 26 (W. S. Newman).

60. Sydow/chopin.

annotated English translation of these letters, revised, augmented by
a few letters not previously published, and reduced by the deletion of
many items "of little interest or importance";[61] three fascinating,
largely pictorial collections of documents;[62] and Sydow's thorough
bibliography listing 11,527 (!) items of Chopin literature (hopefully to
be brought up to date soon again).[63] The sesquicentennial in 1959–60
of Chopin's birth has stimulated further research and writing, in
special issues of periodicals[64] and in such major events as the inauguration of a *Chopin Jahrbuch* by the International Chopin Society (Warsaw, 1956) and "The First International Musicological Congress Devoted to the Works of Frederick Chopin" (Warsaw, 1960), each with its
substantial publication of more or less significant papers.[65] Unfortunately, an increasing amount of this material has appeared only in
Polish—or in Russian, Czech, or Hungarian—meaning that it is closed
to all but a very few Westerners until it is translated or paraphrased.

However, even including all of this material, the actual information
about the circumstances of Chopin's sonatas does not add up to much.
As with Schubert, it is less than it is for Schumann and Brahms. Not
only was Chopin as reticent with regard to his own sonatas as each
of these other three, but he did nothing to generate stories about them.
He inscribed no verse over a movement as Brahms was to do, he gave
no programmatic title (other than "Marche funèbre" over Op. 35/iii)[66]
as Liszt was to do, he hinted at no cryptic meanings such as Schumann
did, and he associated no colorful biographic episodes when he did
refer to his sonatas. To be sure, we are better off when we come to the
music itself. The new "Polish Complete Edition," which began to
appear in 1949, has brought us a big step closer to the ideal edition.[67]

67a

61. Sydow & Hedley/CHOPIN; cf. pp. vii–xi; also, with regard to the hotly contested "Letters to Delfina Potocka," now "officially" declared to be "spurious," cf.
pp. 377–87 (also, DMf XV [1962] 341–53 [Z. Lissa]).

62. Bory/CHOPIN; Kobylańska/CHOPIN (Polish years, through 1830, exclusively);
and Czekaj/CHOPIN (including chronological lists of works and of all main concerts
in which Chopin played).

63. Sydow/BIBLIOGRAPHIE (with Suppl.).

64. E.g., MUSICA XIV/3 (Mar., 1960).

65. CHOPIN JAHRBUCH (only 2 issues up to 1967); CONGRESS CHOPIN. Cf. the summary
of Chopin research in SMZ CIV (1964) 224–31 (W. Poźniak).

66. Cf. Hedley/CHOPIN 133–34; also, Sydow & Hedley/CHOPIN 99 (for Chopin's
ridicule of Schumann's programmatic interpretations).

67. Chopin/WORKS-m; cf. Newman/CHOPIN. The forerunners of this ed., including
the earliest "complete" ed., from England (cf., further, ML XXXIX [1958] 363–71
[M. J. E. Brown]), and the Breitkopf & Härtel "First Critically Revised Complete
Edition" (1878–80), are summarized in Brown/CHOPIN 173–77; also, in RAM XXII
(1949) 336–38 (R. Caporali) and MT XCVII (1956) 575–77 (F. Merrick).

And certain MSS have appeared in facsimiles, as noted shortly.[68] But we are not better off with respect to significant interpretative and analytic literature on the sonatas. There is no separate systematic study of them, although there are a very few, brief articles that will also be noted shortly on the individual sonatas. Most helpful are the general style studies and surveys, including primarily, those of Hugo Leichtentritt, Paul Egert, Gerald Abraham, and Ludwik Bronarski.[69]   69a

Chopin's four sonatas, three for P solo and one for P & Vc, spanned nearly the whole of his short career, from 1827 to 1846, and identify with rather clear stages in that career. They originated at shorter and shorter intervals. Op. 4 in c, for P solo (B. [for Brown/CHOPIN no.] 23), was composed in 1827 and/or 1828,[70] around the middle of his three-year course under Joseph Elsner at the Warsaw Conservatoire.[71] Chopin could have written still earlier sonatas as exercises,[72] but none have come down to us.[73] The next sonata was the one that has always been best known, Op. 35 in b♭, for P solo (B. 114 and 128). Except for its celebrated "Marche funèbre," which had been composed separately in 1837, Op. 35 was not written until 1839—that is, not until more than a decade after Op. 4 or nearly a decade after the year that saw Chopin's last concerts in Warsaw, his seven months of indecision during his second visit to Vienna, and his further travels through various centers that ended with his move to Paris in the fall of 1831. This work, Op. 35, identifies with Chopin's first happy, productive summer at Nohant with George Sand.[74] By contrast, Op. 58 in b, for P solo (B. 155) originated in 1844, five years later, during the last happy, relatively untroubled summer at Nohant with George Sand. And Op. 65 in g, for P & Vc (B. 160), originated fitfully over the next two years, 1845–46, during the crisis that was to culminate in the final break with George Sand in 1847.

68. One should not overlook, of course, the representative pp. reproduced in facs. from the best available sources in each vol. of Chopin/WORKS-m.

69. Leichtentritt/CHOPIN, especially II 210–66; Egert/CHOPIN; Abraham/CHOPIN; Bronarski/CHOPIN. Cf., also, RM/CHOPIN; Meister/CHOPIN (especially on the background); the chaps. by P. Gould and A. Walker in Walker/CHOPIN; and Jachimecki/CHOPIN 197–205.

70. Sydow/CHOPIN I xxxiv (as well as Sydow & Hedley/CHOPIN xiv) and Czekaj/CHOPIN give "1827"; Brown/CHOPIN 22–23 gives "early 1828," undoubtedly because of the "1828" on the autograph (as confirmed in Kinsky/KOCH 214), although this could be only a completion date.

71. Cf. Hedley/CHOPIN 15–16.

72. Cf. Hedley/CHOPIN 16.

73. In Czekaj/CHOPIN 66–67, several lost works are included in the listing of his earliest compositions, but no sons.

74. Cf. Hedley/CHOPIN 84.

Chopin's Sonatas

Opus	Brown/ CHOPIN	Key	Scoring	Composed	Probable first ed.	Chopin/ WORKS-m	Dedicatee	Mvts.: tempos or types; Keys: mvt.-by-mvt.; mss.: mvt.-by-mvt.	Early titles; remarks
4	23	c	P	1827–28	Haslinger, 1851	VI 15	Josef Elsner	4: F- Mi- S- VF c: c- Eb-Ab- c 818: 249-128-42-399	"Sonata" on the MS; "Grande Sonate" in the first ed. (without the ded.); original "Op. 3" changed to Op. 4 because another Op. 3 (B. 41) had appeared in the meantime
35	114, 128	bb	P	1837 (iii), 1839 (i, ii, & iv)	Breitkopf, 1840	VI 54	none	4: S/F- Sc- S-VF bb: bb- eb-bb-bb 690: 242-288-85-75	"Sonate" in the first ed.; referred to as Chopin's "first sonata" (i.e., first to be pub.), or, especially, as his "Funeral March Sonata," for iii, which originated (but was not pub.) 2 years before the other mvts.
58	155	b	P	1844	Breitkopf, 1845	VI 79	Countess E. de Perthuis	4: F- Sc- S-VF b: b/B- Eb- B-b/B 826: 204-216-120-286	"Sonate" in the autograph and the first ed.; a page copied in Liszt's own hand contains changes in the finale probably made for a student (cf. Bory/CHOPIN 166)
65	160	g	P & Vc	1845–46	Brandus (Paris), 1847	XVI 95	Auguste Franchomme	4: F- Sc- S- F g: g- d-Bb-g/G 721: 236-259-27- 199	"Sonate" in the (incomplete) autograph and the first ed.; also pub. in 1847 in Ferdinand David's arrangement for P & Vn

Most of the foregoing information is incorporated briefly in the adjoining chart, which lists the outer circumstances and facts of Chopin's sonatas and can serve for comparisons with the details in the sonata charts for our other main composers. With further regard to the circumstances, Chopin offered Op. 4 (originally as Op. "3") to Haslinger of Vienna in 1828, hoping that it would be published along with his Variations Op. 2 (which did appear early in 1830) and asking that it be dedicated to his esteemed teacher Elsner.[75] But probably fear that so difficult a work by a virtual unknown would not sell kept Haslinger from engraving Op. 4 until 1839, by which time Chopin's high reputation was international. Even then Haslinger must only have circulated some proofs to test the work's potential market, apparently without informing Chopin directly.[76] When he did send the proofs to Chopin in 1841 and indicate his desire, at last, to publish the work, Chopin refused permission, ostensibly because "it needed considerable alteration," but more accurately because he regarded the proposal as an exploitation of something that "I gave him for nothing in Vienna twelve years ago." [77] Undoubtedly this refusal caused Tobias Haslinger's son and successor Karl to defer actual publication until 1851 (without the dedication and now as Op. 4), two years after Chopin's death.

No reviews and no reports of 19th-century performances of Chopin's Op. 4, not even by Chopin himself, have turned up here. Nor is the work played today much more than as a historical curiosity. As evidence of its relative unpopularity, in the latest issue of the *Schwann Long Playing Record Catalog* (July, 1967) there is only one listing for it as against thirteen each for Opp. 35 and 58, and three for Op. 65. The discussions of Op. 4 are few, too, and then largely deprecatory. Says Gerald Abraham, ". . . the whole Sonata is so evidently a student-exercise that it is difficult to understand why Chopin should have sent it to a publisher. . . . Even the piano-writing is extraordinarily dull and conservative; perhaps because the young composer felt that any suggestion of virtuosity was incompatible with pseudo-classical sonata-composition." [78] Agreeing that the "intrinsic musical worth of the Sonata may be extremely slight," Kathleen Dale does acknowledge

75. Cf. Sydow & Hedley/CHOPIN 14, 66; Hedley/CHOPIN 22, 37. The autograph and its circumstances are described in Kinsky/KOCH 214–15 and Chopin/WORKS-m VI 125; facs. of its first p. of music are in Bory/CHOPIN 57 and Kobylańska/CHOPIN 125.

76. Cf. Sydow & Hedley/CHOPIN 182; Brown/CHOPIN 182. Haslinger's plate no.. 8147, is included incorrectly under 1840 in Deutsch/NUMMERN 25.

77. Cf. Sydow & Hedley/CHOPIN 203 and 254.

78. Abraham/CHOPIN 14–16.

its historical value for style comparisons with its two successors and, contrary to Abraham, asserts that at least the first movement "is undeniably attractive on account of the interesting part-writing and the decoratively beautiful passage-work of which it largely consists." [79]

It is true that Chopin may have been driven into a more academic stance by the very title "sonata." One still senses that stance at least in the opening movements of the three later sonatas, too. And there is already more of the eventual Chopin style in his Variations Op. 2 than in Op. 4. However, when heard in the context of its own decade and *not* that of Chopin's later, unique style development, it has seemed here to stand up well in most respects. It can hardly compete, of course, with the last, most mature sonatas by Beethoven and Schubert from that same decade. But it reveals at once a more solid craftsmanship than is generally credited to Chopin, and, like the record of his formal training, it should help, as Arthur Hedley says, to "dispose of the legend of a Chopin self-taught and ignorant of basic principles." [80] The voice-leading is precise and fluent, the counterpoint is unforced and fully adequate to the need, the motivic play is both consistent and persistent, the command of chromatic harmony is already considerable (Ex. 73), and the rhythm benefits from occasional cross accents and syncopations (as in the second section of the "Minuetto," mss. 17–32) as well as the successful introduction of 5/4 meter in the "Larghetto" movement. Moreover, it is not surprising to find the piano scoring, even in this early work, above average in sonority and resourceful figurations, in spite of somewhat fuller, more regularized part-writing than Chopin later used.

What, then, limits the interest and appeal of Op. 4? First, perhaps, is its lack of full-fledged, attractive themes. Except for one rather neutral theme in each of the last two movements, the music is taken up with recurring motives and passagework. The lack is particularly noticeable in the opening movement, where there is no real contrasting idea, hence none of the dualism or pluralism expected in "sonata form." A second limitation is the uncompromising treatment of the motives. Literal repetition, most often by twos, tends to make the motive wear thin rather soon. Third, in spite of the adroit chromatic modulations there is no simple over-all tonal scheme in the longer movements that gives purpose and direction to what otherwise can be only perfunctory designs. Too often the modulations lead nowhere, achieving no more than color contrasts in their vacillations. And fi-

79. Dale/NINETEENTH 74–78.
80. Hedley/CHOPIN 15.

Ex. 73. From the first movement of Frédéric Chopin's Sonata
in c, Op. 4 (after Chopin/WERKE-m VI 20–21).

nally, there is that academic stance, reflecting not only the early-Romantic attitude in general toward the sonata (SSB II) but Chopin's own
last concessions to formal training, already being complicated and
diffused by the medley of new influences, past and present, that were
beginning to impress him from all sides.

Those influences on the young Chopin, in Warsaw alone, were
manifold.[81] But like the young Mozart, he had a rare "talent for
appropriating what was congenial and rejecting whatever was opposed
to his nature." [82] The music of Mozart himself and J. S. Bach—always
his two favorite masters—had been inculcated from his earliest training, under Adalbert Zywny.[83] Ludwik Bronarski relates the motivic
writing of Op. 4 to Bach—specifically, the opening to the start of
Bach's Two-Part Invention in the same key,[84] which seems here like
an example of precarious melodic identification. So does Bronarski's

81. Besides the studies to be cited below, all of "Section II" in CONGRESS CHOPIN
concentrates on influences on Chopin's style.

82. SCE 498–99, as quoted from A. Einstein.

83. Cf. Hedley/CHOPIN 10; Meister/CHOPIN 25–27; CHOPIN JAHRBUCH 177–207
(F. Zagiba on Mozart's influence). In RM/CHOPIN 100–107, Wanda Landowska argues,
mostly subjectively, for the influence of the Rococo French clavecinists on Chopin's
piano writing.

84. Bronarski/CHOPIN II 48–49, with exx.

parallel between the openings of the finale and of Schubert's "Wanderer Fantasy" in C (D. 760).[85] As with the Bach instance, the rhythmic parallel is only superficial, not to mention the unlikelihood of Chopin's knowing Schubert's work so soon after its first publication in 1823. For that matter, Chopin never spoke of Schubert in his published letters, although he certainly got to know some of the songs and perhaps the impromptus after he got to Paris.[86] And Bronarski's parallel between the short chromatic rise in Chopin's Op. 4/i/9 (etc.) and Beethoven's Op. 13/i/8 (etc.) seems too tenuous to accept.[87] Chopin clearly had more exposure to Beethoven, right from the start.[88] But his sympathies for Beethoven's music remained so restricted that in his last years he could still thank Charles Hallé for the first pleasing performance of a sonata that "had always appeared to him vulgar," Beethoven's Op. 30/3.[89]

The influence of living performers and composers on the young Chopin is easier to demonstrate. It is possible that Hummel's several recitals in Warsaw in 1828, of great interest to Chopin,[90] occurred in time to leave their mark on Op. 4. In any case, we have seen that Hummel's Op. 81 in f♯, which had been circulating for nine years and which so impressed Schumann about this time, contains remarkable anticipations of Chopin's later figurations (ssb VIII)—more remarkable, in fact, than can yet be found in Chopin's own Op. 4 (though not in his Variations Op. 2 or the two concertos). Other strong impressions on Chopin while he was still in Warsaw, notably the "shock" of Paganini,[91] did occur too late to apply to Op. 4.

85. Bronarski/CHOPIN II 49–51, with exx.

86. Cf. Hedley/CHOPIN 54, 156; Sydow & Hedley/CHOPIN 177.

87. Bronarski/CHOPIN II 51–54, with exx. (including further instances of this same motive in other Beethoven and Chopin works, as also advanced, equally tenuously, in Leichtentritt/CHOPIN I 117–20, 175–76, and II 146).

88. Cf. Hedley/CHOPIN 10; also, pp. 54 and 125–26. A short article by H. Opienski relating Chopin's to Beethoven's sons. is listed under nos. 3060, 3346, and 4905 in Sydow/BIBLIOGRAPHIE.

89. HALLÉ 35. Op. 31/3 seems more likely, although Op. 30/3 (with Vn) could have been intended, still in keeping with the custom of mentioning only the pianist in a duo. But as one proof of earlier enthusiasm for Beethoven on Chopin's part, cf. Sydow & Hedley/CHOPIN 36. Wessely/CHOPIN argues (though to excess, it is felt here) that the interval of the 3d binds all 4 mvts. in Chopin's Op. 35, which trait plus the layout of the development in i and the character of the trio in iii reveal unsuspecting links with Beethoven.

90. Cf. Kobylańska/CHOPIN 153, 279, 149.

91. Cf. Kobylańska/CHOPIN 156; Hedley/CHOPIN 20.

Chopin's Mature Sonatas

By the time he completed Op. 35 in 1839, many further composers had entered into Chopin's circle of interinfluences. These included some of the most significant younger Romantics—Liszt (whose relationship was discussed in ssb X), Mendelssohn, Berlioz, Bellini (whose alleged influence contradicts chronological facts[92]), and both Schumanns (with Robert's early panegyric on Op. 2 [93] being another "Hats off!" article and a major pathbreaker for Chopin). Lesser figures, like Moscheles and John Field, passed in and out of that circle, too. But well before 1839 Chopin had arrived so completely at his own individual style that there could no longer be any question of pronounced influences from others, only more subtle, slower changes reflecting his own inner growth.

After Op. 35 appeared in 1840, it was sometimes referred to as Chopin's "first sonata," [94] since, of course, it was the first of all his sonatas to be published. More often it was referred to as the "Funeral March Sonata" or in similar wording, as by Chopin himself in 1847.[95] Although the "Marche funèbre" in b♭ had originated earlier as an independent piece and may well have been introduced as such by Chopin himself,[96] it did not come out in print before he incorporated it as the slow movement of the complete, four-movement sonata in the same key.[97] But upon the news of Chopin's death, it did come out separately, in three different editions.[98] It had already been orchestrated for Chopin's own funeral,[99] and even earlier by Franchomme, apparently along with the rest of Op. 35.[100] Moreover, it

92. Cf. Hedley/CHOPIN 58–59, 136.
93. AMZ XXXIII (1831) 805–8 and Schumann/SCHRIFTEN I 5–7.
94. E.g., "Liszt" & Waters/CHOPIN 37; Fay/GERMANY 194.
95. Sydow & Hedley/CHOPIN 290.
96. Cf. Sydow & Hedley/CHOPIN 181.
97. For facs. of the title p. of the first printed ed. and of a MS of the first p. of the "March," stated to be in Julian Fontana's handwriting, cf. Bory/CHOPIN 146. But the latter seems to be in still some other hand than Fontana's, to judge by a surer ex. of Fontana's hand (remarkably like Chopin's) as reproduced in Winternitz/AUTOGRAPHS II Plate 109 (misattributed to Chopin himself; cf. Brown/CHOPIN 73 and Hedley/AUTOGRAPH 476). The 2 facs., showing the opening p. of each outer mvt., in the front matter of Chopin/WORKS-m VI are stated in the caption to be from the autograph, but Chopin's autograph has disappeared and these seem to be in the same (unidentified) hand as the "March." On Chopin's firm price for the pub. of Op. 35 cf. Sydow & Hedley/CHOPIN 188–89.
98. Brown/CHOPIN 111.
99. Sydow/CHOPIN I liv.
100. Sydow & Hedley/CHOPIN 290.

was to continue to be arranged and played separately,[101] as *the* stand-ard funeral march, for longer than can be predicted here.[102]

But taking Op. 35 as a complete cycle, it is not the penultimate "Marche funèbre" but the short, 75-measure finale, "Presto, non tanto," that has raised the most questions. The shortness itself raises the first question, for its average duration up to the last three measures, which are usually played more freely, is only about one minute and thirteen seconds,[103] as against a total of about twenty minutes for the other three movements. Musicians expect fleet scherzos now and then that go by that quickly, but in a finale the brevity, especially right after such a relatively long movement (about 9 minutes) seems dispropor-tionate. Even so, in the more than a century-and-a-quarter since Chopin completed Op. 35 the attitude toward this "disproportion" has gen-erally changed from dismay to unqualified endorsements,[104] and from calling the finale "a sphinx with a mocking smile" [105] to calling it "one of the most remarkable movements in the entire history of the piano sonata, and at the same time, a tone-poem as compelling in effect as it is simple in the musical means it employs." [106]

Chopin himself took first note of the short finale and its unusual scoring, all in octaves, when he wrote to Julian Fontana, his compa-triot, friend, and general factotum,

At present I am writing a Sonata in B-flat minor in which will be found the march that you know. This sonata contains an allegro, a scherzo in B-flat, the march, and a short finale—three pages, perhaps, in my notation. After the march the left hand babbles in unison [at the octave] with the right.[107]

Did Chopin add "non tanto" to the "Presto" over the finale, an instruc-tion rarely believed or observed by performers,[108] because he feared he had made the movement all too short? Schumann expressed puzzle-ment when he came to this movement, near the end of full review that deserves almost complete translation here, as much for its early, contemporary view as its sympathetic perception:[109]

---

101. E.g., MT XIII (1867–69) 526, XVIII (1878) 509, and XX (1879) 327—all for organ; Habets/BORODIN 108, on Liszt's arrangement for P, Vc, and organ.

102. It was played, for example, at President Kennedy's funeral.

103. In Walker/CHOPIN 248, Alan Walker tabulates recorded performances by Horowitz, Rachmaninoff, Arthur Rubinstein, and Cortot.

104. Walker/CHOPIN 158–61 (P. Gould) and 239–50 (A. Walker).

105. Schumann/SCHRIFTEN II 14–15; cf. *infra*.

106. Dale/NINETEENTH 78.

107. Letter of Aug. 8, 1839, from Nohant, trans. from Sydow/CHOPIN II 348.

108. Walker/CHOPIN 248: "It is a mistake to take it too slowly." A half-note at a metronome speed of at least 108 is urged by Walker.

109. NZM (1841) 38–39 and Schumann/SCHRIFTEN II 12–15. An illuminating evaluation of this review, including the question of a satisfactory cycle, occurs in

To look at the first measures of the . . . sonata and still not be sure who it is by, would be unworthy of a connoisseur. Only Chopin starts so and only he ends so, with dissonances through dissonances in dissonances. And yet, how much beauty this piece contains. What he called "Sonata" might better be called a caprice, or even a wantonness [in] that he brought together four of his wildest offspring [,] perhaps in order to smuggle them under this name into a place where they otherwise might not fit. One imagines some cantor, for example, coming from the country into a music center in order to buy some good music; he is shown the newest [things]; he will have none [of them]; finally a sly fox shows him a "Sonata"; "yes," he says happily, "that is for me [,] and a piece still from the good old days"; and he buys and gets it. Arriving home he goes at the piece—but I would have to be very wrong if, before he even gets painstakingly through the first page, he will not swear by all the holy musical ghosts that this [is] no ordinary sonata style but actually godless [trash]. Yet, Chopin has still accomplished what he wanted; he finds himself in the cantor's home, and who knows whether in that very home, perhaps years later, a romantic [-ally inclined] grandson will be born and raised, will dust off and play the sonata, and will think to himself, "The man was not so wrong after all."

With all this, a half judgment has already been offered. Chopin no longer writes anything that could be found as well in [the works of] others; he remains true to himself and has reason to.

It is regrettable that most pianists, even the cultivated ones, cannot see and judge beyond anything they can master with their own fingers. Instead of first glancing over such a difficult piece, they twist and bore (their way) through it, measure by measure; and then when scarcely more than the roughest formal relationships become evident, they put it aside and call it "bizarre, confused etc." Chopin in particular (somewhat like Jean Paul) has his decorative asides and parentheses, over which one should not stop too long at the first reading in order not to lose the continuity. Such places one finds on almost every page in the sonata, and Chopin's often arbitrary and wild chord writing make the detection [of the musical goals] still more difficult. To be sure, he does not like to enharmonize, if I may call it that, and so one often gets measures and keys in ten or more sharps, which [extremes] we can tolerate only in the most exceptional cases. Often he is justified, but often he confuses without reason and, as stated, alienates a good part of the public in this way, who, that is, do not care to be fooled all the time and to be driven into a corner. Thus, the sonata has a signature of five flats, or B-flat minor, a key that certainly cannot boast any special popularity. The beginning goes thus: [The opening four measures are quoted.]

After this typically Chopinesque beginning follows one of those stormy passionate phrases such as we already know by Chopin. One has to hear it played frequently and well. But this first part of the work also brings beautiful melody; indeed, it seems as if the Polish national flavor that inhered in most of the earlier Chopin melodies vanishes more and more with time, [and]

Bronarski/CHOPIN II 101–11, along with a reference (p. 103, fn.) to a 25-page article in Polish on Chopin's four sonatas, Opieński/CHOPIN, which proves to consist of a comprehensive recapitulation of previous comments on them (from Schumann's to Leichtentritt's) plus traditional form analyses especially of Opp. 35 and 58.

as if even he sometimes turned (beyond Germany) towards Italy. One knows that Bellini and Chopin were friends, that they often told each other of their compositions, [and] probably were not without artistic influence on each other. However, as suggested, it is only a slight leaning toward the southern manner. As soon as the melody ends, the whole [barbarian tribe of] Sarmatae flashes forth again in its relentless originality and tumult. At least, Bellini never dared to write and never could write a crisscross chord pattern such as we find at the end of the first theme in the second part [undoubtedly mss. 138–53]. And similarly, the entire movement ends [but] little in Italian fashion, which reminds me of Liszt's pertinent remark. He once said, Rossini and his compatriots always ended with a "vôtre tres humble serviteur," but not so Chopin, whose finales express rather the opposite.

The second movement is only the continuation of this mood, daring, sophisticated, fantastic, [with] the trio delicate, dreamy, entirely in Chopin's manner: [that is,] a Scherzo only in name, as with many of Beethoven's [scherzos]. Still more somber, a *Marcia funebre* follows, which even has something repulsive [about it]; an adagio in its place, perhaps in Db, would have had a far more beautiful effect. What we get in the final movement under the title "Finale" seems more like a mockery than any [sort of] music. And yet, one has to admit, even from this unmelodic and joyless movement a peculiar, frightful spirit touches us, which holds down with an iron fist those who would like to revolt against it, so that we listen as if spellbound and without complaint to the very end, yet also without praise, for *music* it is not. Thus the sonata ends as it began, puzzling, like a sphinx with mocking smile.

In part, this review may have been intended alternately to counter, parody, and second a still more puzzled, rhetorical review of Op. 35 (in over 4 columns; by G. W. Fink?), in which the unity of the cycle, the harmony, and the modulations also seem to have been the main stumbling blocks.[110] Liszt is credited with writing in 1851 that Chopin shows "more determination than inspiration" in his concertos and sonatas, in the face of their Classical architectural disciplines and requirements; yet also with writing a paragraph of the highest poetic praise on the "Marche funèbre." [111] Hanslick seems to have remembered Schumann's remarks when he described a performance by Tausig in 1864 of Chopin's Op. 35 (still a novelty in Vienna).[112] He, too, questioned the binding of four such different pieces under the title "sonata" and whether Chopin was at home in this larger form. Yet he, too, found much to like in the work, including the finale, "which can hardly create any other impression than that of astonishment." Tausig himself reportedly described the "very peculiar" finale as "the ghost of the departed wandering about" after the "Marche funèbre," and subsequently, only two weeks before his own death in 1871, as

110. AMZ XLII (1840) 569–73.
111. "Liszt" & Waters/CHOPIN 35–38.
112. Hanslick/WIEN II 323–24.

"the wind blowing over my grave."[113] Later in the century, Frederick Niecks, William Henry Hadow, and Oscar Bie were still raising the same questions and doubts about Op. 35.[114] Only in recent decades have writers come to view it as a highly successful, unified cycle.[115] At any rate, long familiarity with the movements associated as they are would hardly permit us to take any other view of Op. 35 today.

The single report found here of Chopin's own performance of Op. 35 was that written when Moscheles visited him in Paris just after it was completed, in October, 1839 [116] (and just before the two men made such a hit as a duo team in "La Sonate," Op. 47, by Moscheles; ssb VII). Only after hearing Chopin, says Moscheles, "did I now for the first time understand his music, and all the raptures of the lady world become intelligible." In the decades following its publication nearly every renowned pianist, as well as many a lesser known one, seems to have included Op. 35 in his or her concert repertoire, including Bülow, Liszt, Tausig, Walter Bache, Busoni, Anton Rubinstein, and Pachmann.[117]

Chopin's known correspondence on Op. 58 merely confirms the times of its composition, sale, and publication in 1844–45,[118] without even the brief comments he left on Op. 35. But we do have an exceptionally clear facsimile of his autograph.[119] There is also a copy of a page from the finale in Liszt's own hand that includes changes presumably made by him for himself or one of his students.[120] These changes neither add nor subtract measures but enrich the right hand and reduce the left hand to 8th-notes, first in quintuplets, then in octaves and chords, producing a more incisive, stentorian, and less fluid effect.

From the start Op. 58 raised fewer questions of unity and form than Op. 35 did. Moreover, it presented nothing like the latter's march

113. Fay/GERMANY 194.

114. Niecks/CHOPIN II 246–49, with further references; Hadow/MODERN II 155–57; Bie/PIANOFORTE 262–63. The perplexity over the finale had more specific by-products, too, such as a full harmonization of it accompanying the article Stade/CHOPIN.

115. E.g., Georgii/KLAVIERMUSIK 352–53 and further pubs. as cited above.

116. MOSCHELES II 52–53. In Sydow/CHOPIN II xliii the date is pinpointed at Oct. 29.

117. For sample reports of 7 years in one Chopin center like London, alone, cf. MT XVII (1876) 500, XVIII (1877) 241 and 277, XX (1879) 262, XXI (1880) 606–7, XXII (1881) 302, XXIV (1883) 660. Also, cf. Habets/BORODIN 126 (on Liszt and the march); Pleasants/HANSLICK 228 (on Rubinstein in 1884); Dent/BUSONI 85.

118. Sydow & Hedley/CHOPIN 240, 245, 250, 254.

119. CHOPIN/facs.-m, with preface.

120. Bory/CHOPIN 166 has a facs. of Chopin's title p. and the page in Liszt's hand showing changes in mss. 207–53 of Chopin's finale. Cf. Walker/CHOPIN 251 and ssb X (Liszt) on Chopin's possible influence on Liszt's Son. in b.

or short finale to bring it special notoriety. One of its first main reviews, in 1846, called Op. 58 a distinctly superior work, citing especially its mastery of form and rich figuration.[121] Only some harmonic details of voice-leading and spelling were questioned, as they had been in the opening and other passages of Op. 35. Another early review (apparently marking a near capitulation on the part of Franz Brendel, who for long had been conspicuously hostile to Chopin)[122] asserted that no composer was entirely free of problems; that, in fact, the reviewer had been no Chopin worshipper and had repeatedly charged him with the same (harmonic?) peculiarities; but that without these peculiarities Chopin would not be Chopin and "in spite" of them Op. 58 "is and remains one of the most significant publications of the present." [123] When Pachmann played the work in London in 1883 a reviewer did find it "unequal in itself," with problems in the development section of the first movement, yet well designed to show off the performer in his "most favourable light." [124] A lack of genuine development of its ideas was Vincent d'Indy's chief reservation about Op. 58 when he preferred to analyze it alone among all four of Chopin's sonatas because of the high quality of its themes.[125] Today, as with Op. 35, several writers give unqualified endorsement to the form and content of Op. 58 as one of Chopin's finest, most mature works,[126] although most recitalists will confess to doubts about ever quite projecting a completely satisfying, purposeful form when either outer movement is played (cf. ssb VI), for all the unquestioned beauty of the themes.[127]

No report could be found here of Chopin playing Op. 58 himself. It may well have been too much for his frail body by then.[128] But there are again increasing reports, throughout the century, of performances by other pianists.[129] The work must have taken hold quickly. Scarcely six months after its publication in mid 1845 we find a deferential letter to Chopin from Kalkbrenner begging instruction for "my son Arthur [, who] makes so bold as to want to play your fine Sonata

121. AMZ XLVIII (1846) 74–75.
122. Cf. Jachimecki/CHOPIN 151, 204.
123. NZM XXIII (1845) 89–90.
124. MT XXV (1884) 21.
125. D'Indy/COURS II/1 407–10.
126. E.g., Hedley/CHOPIN 91; Jachimecki/CHOPIN 202–5.
127. Cf., also, Walker/CHOPIN 254.
128. Cf. Hedley/CHOPIN 106–7.
129. For sample reports in one 7-year period of performances as far off as Moscow and New York, cf. NZM LXXII/1 (1876) 234, LXXII/2 (1876) 498 and 510, LXIII/1 (1877) 230; MT XVIII (1878) 282, XXI (1880) 249, XXIII (1882) 662, XXIV (1882) 17, XXV (1884) 21.

in B minor. . . ." [130] It is surprising to find no record of Clara Schumann playing either this work or Op. 35, considering that she did play both of Chopin's concertos and much other music by him.[131] Among special mentions of Op. 58 is the candid description by the American pianist Amy Fay of her nervous trial of this work for Liszt in 1873 and of his masterful playing of its last three movements for her at the end of the lesson.[132] And Arthur Friedheim recalls one of Anton Rubinstein's characteristically gargantuan recitals in which all twenty-five minutes or thereabouts of Op. 58 served as the first encore![133]

There are numerous references to his last sonata, Op. 65, in Chopin's late correspondence, partly because of the involvement of its dedicatee, Auguste Franchomme, a fine cellist, a close friend in Chopin's last years, and an advisor to him in writing for the cello.[134] By mid December of 1845 Chopin was hoping to finish Op. 65—in fact, was already trying it out with Franchomme ("it goes very well") and wondering whether it could not yet be printed that year.[135] However, ten troubled months later (Oct., 1846) he still had to write, "Sometimes I am satisfied with my 'cello sonata, sometimes not. I throw it aside and then take it up again." [136] Then, in April of 1847 he reported playing it with Franchomme for Delfina Potocka ("you know how fond I am of her"); and in June he announced, besides another performance with Franchomme of Op. 65, its imminent publication (by Brandus in Paris) and its sale (the last work he himself sold) to Breitkopf & Härtel.[137]

We learn of another performance of Op. 65 by Chopin and Franchomme from Charles Hallé in which the ailing Chopin began in great pain but "warmed to his work" and improved, "the spirit having

130. Sydow & Hedley/CHOPIN 260–61.
131. Neither son. is in the repertoire listed in Litzmann/SCHUMANN III 613–24.
132. Fay/GERMANY 211–14.
133. Friedheim/LISZT 195.
134. Cf. RdM XXXVIII (1956) 168–70 (M. Debrun).
135. Sydow & Hedley/CHOPIN 258, 259.
136. Sydow & Hedley/CHOPIN 270.
137. Sydow & Hedley/CHOPIN 276, 288–89, 290, 291. Sydow/CHOPIN I xlviii reports another performance of Op. 65 by the same team. Brandus announced "immediate" pub. of Op. 65 in Oct., 1847 (Brown/CHOPIN 155), but the first advertisement of its availability does not seem to have appeared in RGM until Jan. 30, 1848 (or the same month that the Breitkopf & Härtel ed. appeared). A fragment of the autograph, dated May 23, 1846, is reported in Brown/CHOPIN Suppl. no. 160. Only such fragments of the autograph and sketches (cf. MMR LXXXV [1955] 62 [M. J. E. Brown]) seem to be extant; a facs. of the first p. of the autograph is in Bory/CHOPIN 173 (along with a facs. of the title p. of the original Brandus ed., including the ded.); the facs. of a sketch is in CONGRESS CHOPIN 336.

mastered the flesh." [138] There are reports of Walter Bache playing it with Franchomme (and others), too, in 1864;[139] and of Liszt playing it with some unidentified cellist in 1877.[140] And as with Opp. 35 and 58, the performances of Op. 65 multiplied rapidly during the last third of the century.[141]

Yet, Op. 65 has never won the general acceptance that Opp. 35 and 58 have won. Certain objections were raised from the start. Those from forerunners like Moscheles simply represented, of course, the conservative view of Chopin: "I often find passages [in Op. 65] which sound to me like some one preluding on the piano, the player knocking at the door of every key and clef to find if any melodious sounds are at home. . . . I find it a wild overgrown forest, into which only an occasional sunbeam penetrates." [142] But the objections require more notice when a contemporary reviewer writes of a deterioration in Op. 65 in the quality of Chopin's themes and a harmonic distortion of their cantabile style, in spite of the use of so songful an instrument as the cello.[143] In 1858 Hanslick criticized not only the themes but a lack of aptitude for handling the larger forms and for the polyphony expected in a duo.[144] In 1888 Niecks found nothing at all to redeem the work.[145] More recently A. Eaglefield Hull recognized "many beauties" in the work that "atone" for its structural weaknesses and an excess of ideas.[146]

As viewed here, Chopin's cello sonata has been misunderstood and wronged by these objections.[147] The reason it still is not much played lies neither in them nor in any failure, as is sometimes said, to give the cello an equal share of the musical interest. It lies rather in two kinds of difficulties that remove the work from the realm of social chamber music and restrict it to performance by advanced artists. The first difficulty is the piano part. Unless the pianist is able to put this part in suitable perspective by tossing off its many tricky passages easily and deftly, it will give, like Chopin's early Trio in g, more the effect

138. HALLÉ 36; also quoted, almost in full, in Cobbett/CHAMBER I 276 (A. E. Hull and W. W. Cobbett).

139. Bache/BACHE 173, 162.

140. Habets/BORODIN 132.

141. Sample performances over a period of 14 years may be found in MT XV (1872) 437, XX (1878–79) 146 and 621, XXI (1880) 233, XXVII (1886) 141 and 417; NZM LXXII (1876) 466.

142. MOSCHELES II 172, 213.

143. AMZ L (1848) 214–15.

144. Hanslick/WIEN II 167.

145. Niecks/CHOPIN II 250–51.

146. Cobbett/CHAMBER I 276; but one known instance does not justify the generalization that Chopin omitted the first mvt. when he played Op. 65 in public.

147. Cf. the recent and, from our standpoint, enlightened appraisals of Op. 65 in Jachimecki/CHOPIN 235–37 and Walker/CHOPIN 165–68 (P. Gould).

Ex. 74. From the finale of Frédéric Chopin's Sonata in g, Op. 65 (after Chopin/WERKE-m XVI 125).

of a weakly accompanied piano concerto. The second difficulty is the almost Schumannesque subtlety both of phrase syntax and harmony. Unless the performers fully perceive and adapt to the irregular exchanges between the instruments and the mercurial chromaticisms (Ex. 74), their playing will sound pasty and gauche. For the rest, performers able to meet the challenges will find all the thematic and polyphonic interest, all the structural unity and contrast (in this markedly cyclical work), and all the pleasure of sound needed to make Op. 65 an attractive, compelling duo. In its own way it reveals many of the traits—especially the melody, phrase syntax, rhythms, and harmony—that made Chopin one of the most influential of all 19th-century composers, whether we are thinking of his mark on Liszt (ssb X), Wagner, Brahms (ssb IX), Franck, Fauré, and lesser contemporaries, or on Rachmaninoff, Scriabin, Debussy, Ravel, and even Prokofiev, among more recent composers.[148]

Pianists in Chopin's Sphere (Thalberg, Heller, Alkan)

During and right after the hegemony of Chopinism several other fine pianists in Paris wrote almost exclusively for piano, too, although

148. Cf. the helpful discussions of Chopin's influences in RM/CHOPIN 30–34 (K. Szymanowski) and 111–15 (S. Lobaczewska); Walker/CHOPIN 258–76 (P. Badura-Skoda).

working rather independently of each other. Chopin was fully aware of one of his two most celebrated peers among pianists, **Sigismond Thalberg** (1812 [149]–71), though he liked him personally no better than the other, Liszt, and had less good to say about him as a pianist.[150] If Thalberg is hidden in the darker historical shadows of Chopin and Liszt today, he did rank on equal terms with them in the 1830's and 1840's, certainly as a pianist—contrary to some reports, his much publicized contests with Liszt did not end in any decisive defeat—and, at least within the range of his many published fantasies and other potpourris, as a composer.[151] Thalberg's justification for appearing in these pages is but one work—his only one of the sort, in fact—*Grande Sonate pour le Piano,* Op. 56 in c, published by Schlesinger of Paris in 1844 and about the same time by Breitkopf & Härtel (plate no. 7182).[152] Op. 56 is a large, technically advanced work made up of four movements in forty-five pages (F-Sc-M-VF). Although its themes, motivic concentration, handling of texture, and keyboard writing are above average,[153] and although it apparently had enjoyed real popularity for a short time,[154] the sonata is not one that could be revived successfully today. Yet it does hold interest at least to the extent that its chief traits help to confirm what we know about Thalberg's training and playing.[155]

Thus, Op. 56 reveals a neatness, objectivity, and economy of means about Thalberg's writing that tallies with his instruction by Sechter in Vienna, his reported lessons under Moscheles and Hummel,[156] his

149. MGG XIII 273–75 (R. Sietz) and most other sources still do not take cognizance of the birth certificate discovered and first reported early in this century (as noted in BAKER vii and 1635; cf., also, GROVE Suppl. 436). This certificate discredits the Romantic accounts (cf. Loesser/PIANOS 371) of Thalberg as the natural son of mixed nobility (though it does not quite clarify his Frankfurt/M parentage) and of the poetic derivations of his name.

150. Cf. Sydow & Hedley/CHOPIN 76, 135, 214, 218.

151. See the contemporary comparisons in Schumann/SCHRIFTEN I 480–81; by Chopin's pupil Joseph Filtsch in Sydow & Hedley/CHOPIN 217; and by Mendelssohn (as trans. in Schonberg/PIANISTS 174); also, the colorful accounts of Thalberg in Loesser/PIANOS 371–74 and Schonberg/PIANISTS 172–78.

152. Mühsam/THALBERG, an unpub. diss. on the piano music, includes a detailed description of Op. 56 that emphasizes "son. form" (pp. 51–65; with exx.), a short biography that does not correct long-standing errors (pp. 17–26), and an undated, unreconciled list of works by op. nos. (pp. 175–77).

153. In 1839 Schumann had described Thalberg as having "no invention except in technique" (Storck/SCHUMANN 130).

154. Passing mentions of the publication of Op. 56 and Thalberg's performances of it are numerous in issues of RGM for 1844–46 (and in 2 articles on it noted below).

155. Among contemporary descriptions of his playing, cf. Schumann/SCHRIFTEN I 233 and 410, II 19–20; Sydow & Hedley/CHOPIN 76; MOSCHELES II 12–13, 49, 61, 210.

156. More and better biographical information is needed. Schilling/LEXICON

known predilection for the Classics (on those relatively few occasions when he was not playing his own show pieces),[157] and his impassive, immobile posture at the piano. Op. 56 also reveals some of those quasi three-hand settings so widely remarked in his playing,[158] in which the theme "sings" in the middle of the texture while arpeggios, chords, or other devices accompany both below and above (as at the start and, especially, at the return in 8ves in the "Andante," though without the 3-staff scoring he sometimes used elsewhere). One might even say that Op. 56 reveals a certain elegance and dignity, in the many virtuoso passages as well as the simpler ones, that recall Thalberg's impeccable dress and polished manners.

With further regard to those passages themselves, their wide stretches (often encompassing 10ths) and the way they course up and down over the whole keyboard, bring to mind, like much else in Thalberg's sonata, his last teacher, Kalkbrenner, and both the style traits and the pros and cons of the latter's own Sonata with the same opus number (*supra*). Although they are less free and spontaneous, those passages bring Chopin to mind, too. And still more indicative of Thalberg's close relationship to Chopin[159] are certain hymnic melodies with block chord accompaniments and free tonal transpositions to the next scale degree either way. Thus, Ex. 75, the second theme of Thalberg's first movement, might be compared with the middle section of Chopin's Nocturne in g, Op. 37/1.

As with Kalkbrenner's Op. 56, the chief shortcoming of Thalberg's Op. 56, for all its fine lines and suave brilliance, is its tendency to wander on and on without a clear sense of direction at the higher architectural levels. However, contemporary criticisms did not touch on this aspect. One reviewer, acknowledging the telling sound, the objective style, the suggestions of Chopin, and the significance of "a first sonata by a first virtuoso," expressed dissatisfaction mainly with the content itself and Thalberg's failure to advance beyond the styles of

VI 628 seems to be the prime source for Hummel (SSB VIII), and MOSCHELES I 131 and II 12–13 for Moscheles. Thalberg is usually said to have studied with Hummel and Sechter in Vienna. Mrs. Moscheles twice places the lessons with Moscheles in London and says they ended in 1826 (Thalberg remained a close friend of Moscheles). Neither Moscheles nor Hummel is reported to have been in Vienna within several years of 1826. It is more possible that Thalberg could have studied with one or both in London, if at all.

157. Performances by him of Beethoven, Dussek, and Chopin are mentioned in Schumann/SCHRIFTEN I 392; of Bach, Mozart, and Moscheles in MOSCHELES II 8, 26, and 210; and of Beethoven and Mendelssohn in Schonberg/PIANISTS 177. Did he perform in public the Schubert Sonata in B (D. 575) that Diabelli pub. posthumously and ded. to him in 1846 (SSB VII)?

158. Cf. MOSCHELES II 12–13.

159. A relationship already noted in Schumann/SCHRIFTEN I 304.

Ex. 75. From the first movement of Sigismond Thalberg's
Sonata in c, Op. 56 (after the early Breitkopf & Härtel ed.).

Beethoven.[160] Neither objection seems quite justified. Another, more
verbose reviewer, in Paris, saw only good in the work—in its themes,
rhythms, modulations, nobility of style, texture (with the melody in
the middle), and figurations.[161]

Born in Hungary of Bohemian parents, trained in Vienna, **Stephen
Heller** (1813–88) moved to Paris permanently in 1838. In Vienna he
had studied with Anton Halm (ssb VII), been introduced to both Beethoven and Schubert, and made his debut as a piano prodigy.[162] Meanwhile, he had come under the influence of Schumann and Chopin,
among others, and when expected lessons with Kalkbrenner could not
follow upon his arrival in Paris, Heller apparently was glad enough to
give up the idea of a virtuoso's career in favor of composing and be-

160. nzm XXII (1845) 39–40 (C. d. Jüngste).

161. rgm for March 3, 1845, pp. 68–69 (M. Maurel); an answer to this review in
rgm for March 8, 1846, pp. 77–78 (H. Blanchard) takes exception to certain
statements but is at least as poetic and enthusiastic about Op. 56 itself.

162. Booth/HELLER is a recent diss. especially helpful for its full biography and
documents (pp. 8–61) and description of selected works (pp. 86–184); its list of
works (pp. 240–45) is partially dated. Cf., also, MGG VI 100–104 (R. Sietz) and GROVE
IV 226–29 (R. Gorer), with further references. On Heller's birth year, cf. GROVE
Suppl. 218; Booth/HELLER 8–10. Heller's autobiographic summary in HALLÉ 317–22 is
pertinent here.

coming something of a recluse.[163] As for his compositions, he wrote more than 150 that were published, nearly all for P solo and ranging from single short pieces to five cyclic sonatas and three late sonatinas (Opp. 146, 147, and 149; pub. in 1878–79).[164]

Four of Heller's five sonatas were numbered in series, beginning with Op. 9, a four-movement work (S-Sc-M-F) in d (not D) that originated between about 1835, when Schumann brought Heller into his imaginary "Davidsbündler," [165] and about 1838, before publication took place in Leipzig.[166] Schumann, strengthening Heller's confidence to continue composing, reviewed and praised Op. 9 as an imaginative, personal, unorthodox work that would shock the traditionalists and that produces some clever new resource every time it seems about to falter.[167] Sonata 2, Op. 65 in b, was published in Leipzig about 1846 (Friedrich Hofmeister, plate no. 4150). It was reviewed in 1849 as a basic, purely musical creation, full of contrast and tragic import, and quite isolated from the salon style that was making Heller a favorite of the dilettantes.[168] Sonata 3, Op. 88 in C, was first published by Breitkopf & Härtel in 1856. It is a cyclically interrelated, four-movement work (F-Sc-M-VF) suggesting some influences from Weber's piano writing and ending with a witty "Allegro umeristico e molto vivace." [169] Although no separate review of it has turned up here, it was cited in 1878 as "the greatest favourite of all his works in this fashion, because of the well sustained power in each movement, and its vigour as a whole." [170] And Sonata 4, Op. 143 in b♭, was first published by Breitkopf & Härtel in 1878, with the reviewer calling it "the most masterly of all, as well for the worth of the separate movements as for the homophonous character of the whole, so that it appears to be like the pursuit of one idea in its various phases, not so erratic, as more or less connected, with just such divergencies as would help to make

163. Cf. his description of himself in Joachim/LETTERS 355.

164. Op. 149 is favorably reviewed in MW XIV (1883) 508.

165. MGG VI 101.

166. A study of Heller's sons. is lacking. Booth/HELLER 128–38 describes Opp. 88 and 143, with exx.; cf., also, the summaries of Heller's style traits on pp. 85 and 181–83.

167. Schumann/SCHRIFTEN I 453–55. In MMR VIII (1878) 91, Op. 9 is recalled as a "well-known" work, "elaborate in form, yet lacking in melody."

168. NZM XXXI (1849) 281–82 (with ex.). In MMR VIII (1878) 91, Op. 65 is recalled as a "well-known" work of "dignified, yet somewhat uneven and sombre character."

169. Cf. Booth/HELLER 128–34.

170. MMR VIII (1878) 91; but the next sentence, on Schumann, confuses Heller's Opp. 88 and 9. Shedlock/SONATA 235–36 refers negatively to Op. 88.

the expression elegant and eloquent." [171] Charles Hallé, one of Heller's closest friends, seems to have done much to popularize this last work in England;[172] Heller's fifth sonata, not in the numbered series of four, is his *Es ist bestimmt in Gottes Rath* [*God Has Decreed It*], *Volkslied von Felix Mendelssohn-Bartholdy*,[173] *Fantasie in Form einer Sonate*, Op. 69 in D, published about 1847 by Bote et Bock. In this work the main themes of all four movements (S/F-Sc-S-F) derive freely from Mendelssohn's tune, which is stated almost literally at the start.

As surveyed today, Op. 65 represents Heller's sonatas at their best—that is, in their most enterprising and original writing. It is a serious, intense, relatively free work in four motivically interrelated movements totalling thirty pages. The first movement, in 3/4 meter, is marked "Fiery, and with potent expression" (as trans. from the German Heller preferred to use); the second, in 2/4 and in the tonic major key, is headed "Ballade," with the mark "Moderato"; the third, in 3/4 and in the submediant key, is headed "Intermezzo," "Moderately fast"; and the last, in "C" meter and in the home key of b again, is headed "Epilog" and marked "Animated to the extreme, and with appropriate expression" (Ex. 76). Those who know only Heller's etudes, preludes, or other short teaching pieces that have served so many young students so well, would scarcely recognize his much freer and, of course, more advanced writing in Op. 65. The outer movements sustain considerable intensity through successive climaxes of motives reiterated and advanced sequentially. Gentle, poetic contrasts are achieved in all movements through abrupt dynamic reductions, manifold rhythmic transformations, and a wealth of editorial detail, from articulation, pedal, and swell signs to copious inscriptions, including an initial footnote authorizing the performer to read more into Heller's tempo indications.

The more poetic aspects of Heller's sonatas have hardly borne out the prediction of Fétis that a "day will come when the influences of the clique will have passed, permitting [one] to judge the true merit of things; then one will realize, without any doubt, that Heller, even more than Chopin, is the modern poet of the piano." [174] But intimate, sensitive episodes do enhance his music, along with other original turns in the harmony and phrase syntax such as one encounters in the music of a composer who has had to fill in much of his own training. In these traits Heller's sonatas bring to mind the music of two of his

171. MMR VIII (1878) 91.
172. Cf. HALLÉ 171, 241.
173. I.e., Mendelssohn's "Volkslied," Op. 47/4 (Mendelssohn/WERKE-m XIX/145 82).
174. Fétis/BU IV 288.

EPILOG

Ex. 76. From the finale of Stephen Heller's Sonata in b, Op. 65 (after the original ed. of Friedrich Hofmeister).

Paris friends—Liszt to a small degree and Berlioz, a close friend,[175] to a greater degree. There is much less influence of Chopin than might be expected, considering Heller's devotion to Chopin and references to him in his music titles.[176] On the other hand, Heller, never really a modernist, does recall in his sonatas the sonatas of his contemporaries August Gottfried Ritter and Ferdinand Hiller (both ssb X), especially their Mendelssohnian traits,[177] including much dependence on the dim.-7th chord. In other respects Heller's sonatas are curiously lacking, or curiously ascetic, if a more positive view is preferred. In spite of their poetic episodes they reveal little lyricism—in fact, little outright melody. In spite of their harmonic color they reveal relatively little tonal movement or the tension of strong modulations—in fact, they suffer from a certain tonal monotony. In spite of their motivic reiterations and rhythmic changes, or perhaps because of these, they show little interest in polyphonic activity. And in spite of Heller's early pianistic achievements, they show little interest in exploiting the ranges

175. Cf. the high esteem for Heller expressed in BERLIOZ MEMOIRS 510.

176. Cf. GROVE IV 227–29 (including Opp. 71 and 154).

177. But in Selden-Goth/MENDELSSOHN 245, Mendelssohn pairs Heller with Berlioz in a protest against then recent music.

and diverse figurations of the keyboard. Indeed, Heller's tendency to write largely in chords and octaves is seen here as one of the main deterrents to a possible revival of sonatas that remain intriguing both despite and because of those other "lacks."

Even more of a recluse in the Chopin era, as well as an eccentric, was the native Parisian **Charles-Valentin (Morhange) Alkan** (1813–88).[178] Like Heller, Alkan began his career as a virtuoso prodigy but turned almost entirely to teaching and composing in the 1830's, with a substantial number of publications following, which are nearly all for P solo. He, too, knew Chopin[179] and Liszt, winning their respect as well as that of such other notables as Anton Rubinstein, César Franck, and Bülow.[180] His music has always seemed too difficult and experimental to win general popularity. But as often as it has been vehemently decried and dismissed it has been revived with enthusiasm, usually as a cult, winning such tributes to Alkan as Busoni's placing him on a par with Chopin, Schumann, and Brahms among "the greatest of the post-Beethoven piano composers." [181]

Three sonatas by Alkan were published—Op. 33 in b/g♯, a "Grande Sonate" for P solo sometimes called "Les quatres Âges," published by Joubert of Paris in late 1847 or early 1848;[182] Op. 47 in E (not e), a "Grande Sonate de concert" for P & Vc-or-Va, consisting of four movements (VF-VF-S-VF) that keep the piano busier than the cello, published by Costallat of Paris in 1858,[183] and described as "long and dull";[184] and Op. 61 in a, which is a thinner, lighter "Sonatine" for P solo, in four very-fast movements totalling thirty-five pages (iii being

178. Most of the known biographical information is recapitulated on pp. 1–3 of a 58-p. undergraduate study of Alkan's music done at Harvard University, Bloch/ALKAN (with bibliography, undated list of works, and many exx.). It is summarized again, more briefly (along with information about Alkan's birth certificate and the false addition of "Henri" to his name, and with mention of a book on Alkan [in progress]), in the preface (pp. v-xx, with style and performance comments) to a recent anthology of selected works for P solo by Alkan, Lewenthal/ALKAN-m. Cf., also, GROVE I 111–13 (H. Searle); MGG IX 579–80 (under "Morhange-Alkan"; R. Sietz). Warm thanks are owing to Mr. Joseph Bloch and Mr. Raymond Lewenthal for further information by correspondence.

179. Cf. Hedley/CHOPIN 54–55; Sydow & Hedley/CHOPIN 375; Bellamann/ALKAN 252.

180. Cf. BÜLOW BRIEFE III 180–85; Sietz/HILLER 121.

181. Bloch/ALKAN 3. Most recently in this country, Raymond Lewenthal's ed. (Lewenthal/ALKAN-m), recitals, and recording (Vic. LM-2815) of Alkan's music have aroused new interest.

182. It is not in HOFMEISTER but is advertised, from Feb. 13 on, in several issues of RGM for 1848. It is described and discussed, with exx., in Bloch/ALKAN 26–37 and 38, and described in Bellamann/ALKAN 255–56. The 2d mvt., "Quasi-Faust," is reprinted in Lewenthal/ALKAN-m 14 (with preface, pp. xviii–xx).

183. Cf. Altmann/KAMMERMUSIK 245 and 251.

184. Bloch/ALKAN 40.

a "Scherzo-Minuetto"), published posthumously by Costallat about
1900, and described variously as "classic" in its "purity of form" and
"as what a piano sonata by Berlioz might have been like." [185]

185a

When Alkan's music has been played at all it is his etudes that have
received most attention, including Op. 39/4–7 and 8–10, which respectively make up an enormous solo "Symphonie" and solo "Concerto"
(both played by Egon Petri in 1938).[186] Of the sonatas, the only one
that has received appreciable attention, though no performances discovered here, is Op. 33, and that chiefly because of its programme. (A
biblical quotation over the "Adagio" 3d mvt. is all the "programme" to
be found in Op. 47.) The four movements of Op. 33, approaching
Scriabin in their colorful, abundant inscriptions, bear the following
headings, starting instructions, and internal advices that are worth
quoting (excluding standard tempo and dynamic indications). Thus, we
find in i, in b/B: "20 Ans; très vite; décidément . . . gaiement . . .
ridendo [laughing] . . . palpitant . . . avec bonheur . . . bravement
avec enthousiasme . . . valeureusement"; ii, in d♯/F♯: "30 Ans, Quasi-
Faust; assez vite; sataniquement . . . Le Diable [identifying a chordal,
climactic theme] . . . avec candeur . . . passionément . . . avec dé-
sespoir . . . déchirant . . . Diabolique . . . Le Seigneur [the Lord
God; identifying another chordal, climactic theme] . . . avec délices";
iii, in G: "40 Ans, Un heureux Ménage; lentement; très lié, avec
tendreuse et quiétude . . . Les enfans [identifying a characteristic
double-note figure] . . . amoureusement . . . (10 heures [identifying
10 gonglike strokes]) . . . La prière [identifying a chordal, hymnic
theme]"; and iv, in g♯: "50 Ans, Promethée enchâiné [with 3 extracts
—lines 750–54, 1051, and 1091—from Aeschylus' *Prometheus*]; ex-
trèmement lent." The only other programmatic help comes in a
preface by Alkan that deserves translation almost in full, although it
seems to understate the importance he attached to programme music in
general:

Many things have been said and written on the limits of musical expression.
Without adopting this or that rule, without seeking to resolve any of the
far-reaching questions stirred up by this or that system, I shall tell why I
have given similar titles to these four movements and sometimes used quite
unusual terms.

It is not imitative music that is concerned here; still less music seeking its
true justification, [or] the explanation for its effect, [or] its worth in an
extramusical environment. The first movement is a Scherzo; the second an
Allegro; the third and the fourth [movements] are an Andante and a Largo;

185. Bellamann/ALKAN 261; Searle/ALKAN 277. The Library of Congress has a
copy of this scarce work, which is not listed in HOFMEISTER.
186. Cf. Bloch/ALKAN 3; Lewenthal/ALKAN-m xi–xiv, 27.

Ex. 77. From the second movement of Charles-Valentin Alkan's Sonata in b/g♯, Op. 33 (after the original Joubert ed. of 1847 or 1848).

but each one of them corresponds in my mind to a given moment of existence, to a particular kind of thought, [or] of imagination. Why shouldn't I indicate this? The musical element will always remain, and the expression can only improve in this way; the performer, without in any way giving up his individual feeling, is inspired by the same idea as the composer; such a name and [/or] such a thing seem to run aground [when] taken in a material [and literal?] sense [but] work perfectly in the realm of the intellectual. . . .

Alkan's work is long, 1,121 measures in 50 pages lasting well over a half hour, yet not too long for its musical interest, which has seemed stronger here than is usually acknowledged. If there were nothing else to further it, the interest would be sustained by the long, well-drawn, diatonic, melodic lines in each movement, with their accurate, choice, sometimes chromatic harmonic support, and the resourceful piano writing, with its excellent textural interest, variety and range of color, and euphonious scoring (except in Alkan's fullest, most bombastic chordal writing). Moreover, the technical difficulties that are always cited in Alkan's piano music, such as his characteristic full chordal climax, "The Lord God [Supreme]," late in the second movement (Ex.

77), and its equally characteristic continuation up to the edge of physical endurance, are not insurmountable. The athletic problems are certainly no greater than those in Liszt's Sonata in b, though they may be a little more uncompromising. And when the difficulties do get almost unmanageable, as in the seven-voice fughetta that leads into Ex. 77, Alkan is careful to supply a "Facilité" brace.

Op. 33 makes a satisfying cycle apart from its programme, even though the movements differ considerably in their lengths—525, 332, 192, and 72 measures—, even though the last two movements are both mostly on the slow quiet side, and even though the tonal scheme is open and unusual (b/B-d♯/F♯-G-g♯). But the tonal scheme might be said to give unity in the sense of a "grand cadence" (ssb VI). And there is the unity of thematic interrelationships in all four movements, about as much and as varied as can be found nearly twenty years earlier in Berlioz' *Symphonie fantastique; épisode de la vie d'un artiste* (a work that seems to have left its deep mark on the programme, melody, harmony, scoring, and intensity of Alkan's Op. 33).

The forms of the separate movements, if naively deliberate at times and at best not a conspicuous means of dynamic tension in themselves, are clear and balanced enough at least not to interfere with the progress of the music. The scherzo first movement is a fluent thinly scored piece in simple A-B-A design, with the B or trio section being an excellent melody for all its ingenuous simplicity. The satanic second movement, more accurately a battle with God triumphing over the Devil, is the biggest movement in design (approximately "sonata form" with coda), emotional range, and technical challenges. The climaxes are obviously meant to be both visually and aurally phrenetic and soul shattering. As an ideal foil for all this excitement, the third movement is a sweetly melodious piece in A-B-A design, not too far removed from a Mendelssohn "Song Without Words." And the short brooding finale, a kind of free rondo, could pass for one of Liszt's "Harmonies poétiques et religieuses" in advance of Liszt himself. Its treatment of Man at "50 Ans" by the approximately 33-year-old Alkan may not quite anticipate maturity to the extent that "Thanatopsis" does, by the 16-year-old William Cullen Bryant. But it provides some of the maturest moments not only of this sonata but in all of Alkan's music explored here.

Among other, more obscure composers active in Chopin's sphere should be mentioned the pianist **Louis (Trouillon-) Lacombe** (1818–84), who trained in Paris, then in Vienna under Czerny and Sechter, before returning to Paris in 1839 to give his full time to composition.[187]

187. Cf. MGG VIII 38–39 (G. Ferchault), with further references but no sons. in the partial list of works.

Lacombe's Op. 1 is a *Sonate fantastique* in f, published by Artaria in Vienna in 1839 [188] and reviewed by Schumann as promising in its best moments of virtuosity and quasi-orchestral writing.[189] To judge by a later, weak, perfunctory *Sonate de salon,* Op. 33 in e, composed about 1850, the promise did not materialize.[190] **Camille-Marie Stamaty** (1811–70) was a pianist of Italian and Greek descent who studied with Kalkbrenner and taught Gottschalk and Saint-Saëns, among others.[191] The first of two published piano sonatas by him, Opp. 8 in f and 20 in c, was reviewed flamboyantly in 1843 as a consistently outstanding example, especially in its melodies and advanced piano writing, of a new renaissance of the sonata after a century of its supremacy and decline! [192] The Czech pianist **Sigmund Goldschmidt** (1815–77), a pupil of Tomaschek (ssb XVII), was in Paris from 1845 to 1849, around the time when his two piano sonatas, Opp. 5 (or 6) in f and 8 in d, were published by Schuberth in Hamburg. These were reviewed (in 1846) as fluent, skillful, significant works in which the composer courageously renounced his virtuosic tendencies.[193]

A Low Ebb Early in the Mid Period, 1850–1885

Both qualitatively (with rare exceptions to be noted below) and quantitatively the sonata output reached a low ebb in France around the middle of the Romantic Era. Most of the composers were not native Frenchmen. Most of them can get only brief mentions, and then primarily for the usual reason of filling in the historical picture. Thus, there was the celebrated harpist from Boulogne-sur-Mer, **Dieudonné-Joseph-Guillaume-Félix Godefroid** (1818–97), who prospered in Paris and during wide concert tours abroad.[194] His *Sonate dramatique* in c, Op. 45, and a *2me Sonate* in g, Op. 53, figured among his many elegant salon and recital pieces for P solo (along with many others for harp), and were published in the mid 1850's by Heugel of Paris and Schott of Mainz. There was the Bohemian virtuoso who lived mostly in Paris, **Karl Wehle (Wehli;** 1825–83). A pupil of Moscheles and Theodor

188. Weinmann/ARTARIA item 3124.

189. Schumann/SCHRIFTEN I 452–53.

190. No lifetime ed. was found here, only an ed. pub. posthumously, about 1895, by Émile Gillet in Paris (as part of an effort to revive interest in Lacombe? cf. MGG VIII 39; Hopkinson/PARISIAN 46).

191. MGG XII 1148–49 (J. Vigué).

192. RGM for Dec. 10, 1843, pp. 419–20.

193. NZM XXV (1846) 13–14. Cf. Riemann/LEXIKON I 629.

194. Cf. MGG V 395–97 (F. Vernillat).

Kullak, Wehle left a *Grande Sonate* in four movements (F-Sc-M-VF) for P solo, Op. 38 in c, published by Schlesinger in Berlin (1856?) and reviewed as superior rather than trivial salon music, in which, however, virtuosity predominates over expressive values.[195] Another Bohemian in Paris, **Julius Schulhoff** (1825–98), was given encouragement by Chopin.[196] He left one published sonata, Op. 37 in f, for P solo (*ca.* 1855), which proves to bear the strong mark of Chopin divested of his genius. The first of its three movements clearly recalls Chopin's Etude in f, Op. 10/9, the second his Etude in c♯, Op. 25, and the third less specifically the opening movement of his Sonata in b♭, Op. 35. And there was the German cellist, **Berthold Damcke** (1812–75), who left four published sonatas after settling in Paris in 1859—Op. 43 in D, for P & Vc (1861), recommended by Heller in a letter to Joachim as "far above the *veillée* [nocturnal diversions]" that the Parisians were accepting;[197] and Opp. 44 in D (1861) and 55 in f (1876 [2d ed.?]), as well as a "Sonatine sur les cinq notes de la gamme" in C, all for P-duet. Op. 44, in four movements (F-Sc-M-F), was reviewed as a work too long for its content and idiom, and therefore not likely to succeed in spite of many good things, especially its fugal climax in the finale.[198] Damcke and Berlioz had a high regard for each other.[199]

Furthermore, there was the Norwegian born pianist **Thomas Dyke Acland Tellefsen** (1823–74), who studied with Kalkbrenner and Chopin before Richault in Paris published five sonatas by him, in the 1850's— two for P solo, one each for P & Vn and P & Vc, and one for P & Vn-or-Vc.[200] And there was the piano virtuoso of worldwide fame, **Henri Herz** (1806?–88) who, unfortunately, is remembered today for little else than Schumann's sarcastic remarks about "him and [Franz] Hünten," whom the musical world "already has long recognized as masters (and business men, too). . . ."[201] Amongst his myriad potpourris, fantasias, variations, and other salon diversions, nearly all for piano,[202] is a *Grande Sonate di bravura*, Op. 200 in E (1860?), reviewed at length and facetiously as being not appreciably different from his other works in its passages, its melodic resemblances to the music of

195. NZM XLV (1856) 279 (E. Klitzsch). Cf. Riemann/LEXIKON II 2000; Fétis/BU Suppl. II 665–66.

196. Cf. Fétis/BU VII 519; MGG XII 237–38 (R. Quoika).

197. Joachim/LETTERS 251.

198. MW IV (1873) 533–34 (G. H. Witte).

199. Cf. Berlioz/MEMOIRS 440–41, 529.

200. Cf. MGG XIII 212 (O. Gurvin), with a further reference; also, Sydow/CHOPIN III 386.

201. Schumann/SCHRIFTEN I 284 *et passim*. The amused contempt of Mendelssohn and Moscheles is suggested in MOSCHELES I 292–93.

202. Cf. PAZDÍREK VII 454–66.

Liszt and others, and its sentimental slow movement.[203] One might add, though, that the passagework is well scored and intriguing to work out, and that Herz knew his "business" as a professional should.

The two duo sonatas of a better known composer in Paris, the cellist and violinist of Spanish descent (**Victor Antoine**) **Édouard Lalo** (1823–92), have somewhat more interest.[204] The first, Op. 12 in D, for P & Vn (composed in 1854 and first pub. in 1855 [205]), is a relatively conservative work in three movements (F-Va-Ro).[206] Yet its precise, transparent texture, its frank forthright melodies, characterized throughout by frequent octave leaps, and its constant attention to rhythmic detail still make it a delight to play. The rondo is a virtual *perpetuum mobile*. Lalo's other sonata is for P & Vc, in a (not A; without op. no., composed in the 1850's; first pub. by Hartman of Paris between 1869 and 1881, then by Heugel of Paris *ca.* 1892 [207]). Although not a late work, it already reveals conspicuous advances in melodic depth and character, in harmonic range and subtlety, in structural freedom, and in the exploitation of technical resources (Ex. 78). In its three movements (M/F-M-F) are foretastes not only of Lalo's own familiar *Symphonie espagnole* (1875) but of music by Fauré, Debussy, and Ravel.

The short-lived, native French composer **Alexis de Castillon** (1838–73), bred on Bach, Beethoven, and the German Romantics and directly influenced by Franck, ranks with his friends Lalo and Saint-Saëns among the pioneers in France of absolute chamber music during the second half of the 19th century.[208] Except for some early (lost?) sonatas in which, says d'Indy, he was required by a weak teacher to make no modulations throughout,[209] Castillon wrote only one sonata, Op. 6 in C, for P & Vn (pub. by Heugel in 1872).[210] He wrote this sonata around 1870, during the much better instruction he got from Franck. Although it still betrays inexperience in the development and tonal organization of his ideas, Op. 6 is interesting especially for the structural freedoms in its four movements (In/F-Sc-M-VF). In the first movement an introduction anticipates a lovely, songful theme, followed by a weaker

203. DMZ II (1861) 229–30, with exx.

204. Cf. RM/LALO (with list of works and composition dates, pp. 123–24, by P. Lalo); Tiersot/LALO (life, works, and letters); MGG VIII 106–8 (G. Ferchault). Both sons. are described in Cobbett/CHAMBER II 88–89 (F. Schmitt).

205. Tiersot/LALO 12, 27.

206. Exx. are quoted in Shand/VIOLIN 247–48.

207. Cf. Tiersot/LALO 12, 27 (regarding another Vc son., which became an orchestral piece); Fétis/BU Suppl. II 68 and Hopkinson/PARISIAN 56; Cat. NYPL XVI 740.

208. Cf. MGG II 901–4 (A. Gauthier).

209. MGG II 902; cf. d'Indy/COURS I/1 427.

210. Op. 6 is described in some detail, with exx., in both Selva/SONATE 235–38 and Cobbett/CHAMBER I 233–34 (V. d'Indy).

Ex. 78. From the start of the development section in the first movement of Sonata in a, by Édouard Lalo (after the Heugel ed. in the New York Public Library at Lincoln Center).

second theme, a development of the first theme, a partial recapitulation in which that theme is restored to interest in a fughetta in A♭, and a coda that prepares for the scherzo. The latter, in G, reaches a melodic high point in the trio section. The third movement presents a poignant theme in a, with inspired rises and falls that anticipate similar passages in the violin sonatas of both Franck and Fauré. The finale, un extended free "sonata form," dwells too long on, and exploits too much, the vigorous, rhythmically clipped theme with which it opens. A brilliant coda closes the work. Castillon's preference for the deliberately paced, drawn out development of a single idea recalls Rheinberger's approach to form (ssʙ X).

Among other sonata composers in this period, the cosmopolitan **Louis-Théodore Gouvy** (1819–98), born in Saarbrücken of French descent, was a musician of independent means who was close to Chopin, Berlioz, and Hallé, among others.[211] His several fluent, skillful, rather routine sonatas do not show any later trends in style and form, however, than can be found in Mendelssohn's music. These sonatas include one example each for P & Vn and P & Cl, one for 2 P's, and three for

211. Cf. ᴍɢɢ V 605–7 (E. Haraszti), with inadequate list of works.

P-duet, all published between 1862 and 1880.[212] Somewhat similar, a little less dynamic, a little more square-cut and pedagogic in character, are the several sonatas by the Paris-born violinist and much published composer **Benjamin (Louis Paul) Godard** (1849–95). These include four for P & Vn, one for P & Vc, and two for P solo, all published between 1867 and 1887.[213] The fourth for violin, Op. 12 in A♭ (1880), apparently was the most played of the sonatas. It was reviewed with more praise for its skill than its content, and for its inner, lighter movements than its outer movements.[214] The second piano solo, Op. 94 in f (*ca.* 1885), is a standard sort of sonata in three movements (F-S-Sc) whereas the first solo, "Sonate fantastique" in C, Op. 63 (*ca.* 1880 [215]), is more of a four-movement suite distinguished chiefly by its programmatic titles over each movement—"The forest demons," "The goblins," "The love fairy," and "The ocean spirits" (the last with three stanzas of verse by Godard). But the facile music sounds more like a suite of four character pieces than a sonata. Its regularly paired or repeated phrases, its stock harmonies, and its run-of-the-mill themes (well short of its composer's ever favorite "Berceuse" from *Jocelyn*), preclude more serious attention.

The virtuoso, French-born pianist **Georges-Jean Pfeiffer** (1835–1908), pupil of Kalkbrenner and Damcke, among others, left one published sonata each for P & Vn (Op. 66 in e, 1879), P & Vc (Op. 28 in c, 1868), and 2 Ps (Op. 65 in ?, 1879).[216] Op. 66 was reviewed as an interesting work, more for its rhythms than its melodies or any special originality.[217] The popular German pianist and associate of Johann Baptist Cramer, **Jacob Rosenhain** (1813–94), left 3 sonatas for P & Vc (Opp. 38 in E, 53 in C, and 98 in d) and 3 more for P solo (Opp. 12 in c, 44 in f, and 74 in D), all first published between about 1847 and 1886.[218] Following Schumann's friendly, favorable reception of Rosenhain's early Piano Trio Op. 2 in 1836,[219] Rosenhain's Op. 38 (dedicated to Mendelssohn) was reviewed as a light, piquant, German-flavored "dish

---

212. Cf. Altmann/KAMMERMUSIK 204, 281, 288, 299; Cobbett/CHAMBER I 483–85 (W. Altmann), especially on Op. 61 in g, for P & Vn (1876); cf., also, the short reviews (to the same effect) of Op. 61 in SMW XXXV (1877) 708 and MW XI (1880) 250.

213. Cf. MGG V 389–91 (E. Haraszti), with inadequate list.

214. MW XII (1881) 594; NZM LXXVIII/2 (1882) 256.

215. The year is based on the approximate time the pub. J. Hamelle succeeded J. Maho (Hopkinson/PARISIAN 85 and 55).

216. Cf. Fétis/BU Suppl. II 331; MGG X 1167 (G. Ferchault), with inadequate list of works; Altmann/KAMMERMUSIK 220, 262, 289.

217. SMW XXXVIII (1880) 180.

218. Cf. GROVE VII 235–36 (G. Grove); MGG XI 912–13 (R. Sietz); Altmann/KAMMERMUSIK 263; HOFMEISTER IV (1844–51) 152, V (1852–59) 204, 1886 p. 243.

219. Schumann/SCHRIFTEN I 168–69.

for the Paris salon world," [220] and his four-movement solo Sonata Op. 44 (dedicated to Fétis) as a skillful, unoriginal work with some rhythmic ambiguity.[221]

A Few Minor Composers in Belgium and Holland

There is curiously little even to mention by way of sonatas in Belgium and Holland up to 1885. Not one Belgian example is singled out in the fine survey Closson & Borren/BELGIQUE (pp. 237–61) and only a very few, obscure Dutch examples are cited in the similarly fine survey Reeser/NEDERLANDSE (pp. 13–184). Belgium's chief name in Romantic sonata history, César Franck, is shortly to be discussed not in this section but among Parisian residents who contributed late in the era. Other, relatively important composers like Albert Grisar, Peter Benoit, François-Joseph Fétis, and François Auguste Gevaert (the last two remembered only as scholars) showed little or no interest in the sonata. Moreover, as had already been implied by Gossec and Grétry (two late-Classic Belgians who also had shown little interest in the sonata; sce 608), Belgium had hardly provided the soil for any sort of present or future artistic greatness so long as she remained "occupied" (up to 1831).[222]

The only generally recognized name among four composers in Brussels or Liège that are to be mentioned now is that of the widely travelled virtuoso **Henri Vieuxtemps** (1820–81). Vieuxtemps' leadership in French violin playing reflected the influences of Charles de Bériot (another Belgian not interested in the sonata), Paganini, and, indirectly, Viotti.[223] Two duo sonatas are among his nearly ninety publications, mostly effective display pieces. Those two are Opp. 12 in D, for P & Vn (1844), and 36 in B♭, for P & Va (1863), plus an "Allegro et Scherzo" in B♭ from an unfinished sonata (1884, posthumous).[224] The sonatas have never had the success of Vieuxtemps' violin concertos[225] and unfortunately, they lack both the substance and the imagination that might justify further discussion here.[226] In all three movements (F-M-F) of Op. 36, for example, although the treatment of the instruments is knowing, the themes are flat.

The dozen-or-so publications of another Belgian violinist and student

220. NZM XXVII (1847) 136.
221. NZM XXXIII (1850) 174.
222. Cf. Closson & Borren/BELGIQUE 237–39.
223. Cf. MGG XIII 1613–16 (B. Schwarz).
224. Cf. Altmann/KAMMERMUSIK 230 and 250; PAZDÍREK XIV 212–14.
225. Cf. Closson & Borren/BELGIQUE 243.
226. Cf., also, Cobbett/CHAMBER II 536 (W. W. Cobbett).

of Bériot, **Lambert-Joseph Meerts** (1800–63), include four "Sonatinen" for 2 Vns (*ca.* 1865, posthumous?) that were reviewed as good teaching material.[227] Among a larger number of publications the pianist **Philippe-Bartholomé Rüfer** left a Sonata in g, for P & Vn (1861), reviewed as promising for an Op. 1 in spite of certain naive, weak, or overly repetitive sections;[228] and an organ sonata, Op. 16, also in g (1875 at latest).[229] Three more organ sonatas, entitled "Pontificale" (in d), "O Filii" (in e), and "Pascale" (in a), were left by the capable Brussels organist **Jacques-Nicolas Lemmens** (1823–81), who is credited with building up the Belgian and French schools of organ music in the second half of the 19th century.[230] All first published in 1876, these sonatas were welcomed for rejecting the light French style in favor of the solid, though somewhat academic, German style, especially in the one or two fugues of each sonata.[231]

In Holland, although there was no 19th-century composer of Franck's stature, we again find little or no interest on the part of the relatively important composers. There seem to be no sonatas left by Johannes Bernardus van Bree (although a Sonata in C, for P-duet, by his scarcely known son **Herman J. van Bree** [1836–85] was pub. in 1863 [232]), or by Richard Hol, or by Johannes Verhulst. But the absence of sonatas is not surprising in a country where even Beethoven's sonatas seem to have been but rarely performed as late as the middle of the century.[233] Among works by seven composers in Holland to be mentioned here, a competent, Germanic "Fantasie-Sonate" in B♭, for organ (1849), was left in MS by the organist **Johannes Gijsbertus Bastiaans** (1812–75), a pupil of Mendelssohn among others. Consisting of four movements (F-S-Sc-VF/fugue), this work is based throughout on the Dutch national song "Wien Neêrlands bloed." [234] A "Sonate-Symphonie" in c, Op. 21, for P solo, by **Edouard de Hartog** (1829–1909), was composed before his return from Germany and France to The Hague and published by

227. nzm LXI/2 (1865) 275. Cf. Fétis/bu VI 52–54; pazdírek X 386; mgg VIII 1895 (A. Wirsta).

228. nzm LXVI/2 (1870) 369–71, with several generous exx. Cf. Fétis/bu Suppl. II 460–61; baker 1388–89.

229. Cf. Frotscher/orgelspiel II 1206.

230. Cf. Fétis/bu V 267–68 and Suppl. II 97–98; Closson & Borren/belgique 243–44; mgg VIII 606–7 (A. Van der Linden); pazdírek IX 335–36.

231. mt XVII (1876) 564 (also p. 443); but cf. Frotscher/orgelspiel II 1235, where French traits are seen.

232. Altmann/kammermusik 297. Cf. Keller & Kruseman/muzieklexicon I 77; nzm LIX (1863) 90 (reviewed as a trivial work).

233. Cf. Reeser/nederlandse 31, 34, 46, 86.

234. Cf. Reeser/nederlandse 104–8, with 2 exx.; grove I 494 (H. Antcliffe; could the reference to another Dutch national song be an error or pertain to another organ son. by Bastiaans?) and VI 21.

Meyer in Braunschweig by 1849.[235] A four-movement work (F-M-Sc-VF) with the subtitle "Poésies musicales et la Calabraise," it was reviewed as having some good and some less good, with no significance in the title's addition of the word "Symphonie." [236] No descriptive information has turned up here regarding the only sonata known by the esteemed keyboardist, conductor, and song composer **Willem Frederik Gerard Nicolai** (1829–96), Op. 4 in E, for P & Vc, first published in 1859.[237]

A Sonata in g, Op. 11, for P & Vn, by the pianist **Oskar Raif** (1847–99), was published in 1878, well after he had settled in Berlin.[238] It is a somewhat diminutive work in three movements (VF-M-VF) that might better have been called a sonatina.[239] A prize-winning Sonata in d, Op. 15, for P & Vc, by the organist **Georg Hendrik Witte** (1843–1929), appeared in 1882.[240] Two duo sonatas—Opp. 3, in D, for P & Vn, and 4, in c, for P & Vc—by the late conductor and author **Wouter Hutschenruyter** (the grandson; 1859–1943), were both published in 1883.[241] And a Sonata in f, Op. 4, by the violinist and conductor **Willem Kes** (1856–1934) was published in 1884, before he left for a series of posts in other countries.[242] Among orchestral transcriptions by Kes is that of Brahms's Sonata in C, Op. 1, for P solo.

235. Cf. Fétis/BU IV 232–33 and Suppl. 451–52; Riemann/LEXIKON I 712; Reeser/NEDERLANDSE 173–75; HOFMEISTER 1844–51 119.

236. RGM for Dec. 30, 1849, 415.

237. Cf. Riemann/LEXIKON II 1267; Reeser/NEDERLANDSE 170–73; Altmann/KAMMERMUSIK 261.

238. Cf. Riemann/LEXIKON II 1463.

239. Cf. Shand/VIOLIN 73–75, with exx.

240. Cf. BAKER 1808; Cobbett/CHAMBER II 588–89; Altmann/KAMMERMUSIK 266 (also p. 307, on a Sonatine in C, Op. 8, for P-duet).

241. Cf. Keller & Kruseman/MUZIEKLEXICON I 300; BAKER 753; MT XXIV (1883) 168 and 407. Among Hutschenruyter's books is one on Beethoven's sons. (SCE 508 and 834).

242. Cf. MGG VII 862–63 (E. Reeser); MT XXV (1884) 563.

Chapter XIII

A Peak in Late-Romantic France and the Low Countries

The Third Republic and Chamber Music

As noted early in the first of these two chapters on the Romantic sonata in France, the most important and extensive fruition came relatively late in the era (as had been true in the Baroque but not the Classic Era). It came during about the first half-century (1870–1920) of France's Third Republic (1870–1940). The Third Republic demonstrated its unprecedented durability by withstanding such strains as growing, worldwide imperialism, renewed conflicts of church and state, the rise and fall of Boulangism, the Panama Canal scandal, and "l'affaire Dreyfus." The new, positive interest in chamber music demonstrated its unexpected vitality by withstanding innumerable conflicts of art, temperament, and background, including those of national and international (meaning mainly Wagnerian) tastes, and by surviving right to the present day.[1] Now, however, although one can point to particular involvements in sociopolitical events by a Saint-Saëns or a d'Indy,[2] the relationships between those events and the broader, concurrent trends in music became less tangible.

César Franck, Camille Saint-Saëns, and Gabriel Fauré comprise the notable triumvirate who did most to elevate instrumental music in late-Romantic France, including the creation of symphonies, concertos, and larger chamber ensembles as well as duo sonatas. (Curiously, although all three excelled as pianists and organists, they did not extend their main interests to the solo sonata; nor did many of their students and other more immediate followers do so, the two chief exceptions being Dukas and d'Indy.) This triumvirate, with their contemporaries and followers, also marked the first time in about a century that most

1. Cf. the recent study based on musical criticism, Eckart-Bäcker/FRANKREICH, especially pp. 184–86.
2. E.g., cf. Harding/SAINT-SAËNS 108–9; Vallas/D'INDY I 69–77, 131, 260.

of the sonata activity was carried on by natives rather than immigrants. Moreover, all of the important native composers were trained in their own country rather than in Germany. (Even Franck, with his German and Belgian ancestry, was French trained and oriented.) And it was this whole group who made of the sonata a more developed or "symphonic" form than any earlier sonata composers in France had. Granted that along with the influences of Chopin and Berlioz those of the chief Romantic Germans—Mendelssohn, Schumann, Brahms, Liszt, and Wagner—were now paramount, the group still succeeded in disproving if not quite dispelling an age-old assumption that the French have always been too dance-minded by nature to think symphonically or in other than simple, square-cut, binary, ternary, and rondeau designs.[3] All of these considerations, plus some others less pertinent to the sonata, may help to explain the more-than-average literary attention that has been paid to fin-de-siècle music in France, by men like G. Jean-Aubry, Paul Landormy, Maurice Emmanuel, Léon Vallas, Norman Demuth, Martin Cooper, Edward Lockspeiser, and James Harding.[4]

A major aid to the advancement of French chamber music can be found in the concerts and related activities sponsored by various music societies, new and revived, of which the most important was the Société Nationale de Musique, founded in 1871 (even before the final indignities of the Franco-Prussian war had been heaped upon the French) by Saint-Saëns and Romain Bussine.[5] Frictions and dissatisfactions within this group—especially between Saint-Saëns and the followers of Franck, who were quite as devoted and numerous as those of Rheinberger in Germany—led to offshoots like the Société Musicale Indépendante, founded in 1909. The increasingly conservative Conservatoire in Paris continued to sponsor its own Société des Concerts, and there were several other outlets for chamber music, including even d'Indy's "Société Schola Cantorum" as its functions widened.[6] The composers themselves often joined in the initial performances of their works. But certain other musicians are remembered still more for first or early performances of the new sonatas. Thus, Edouard Risler and Blanche Selva each made strongly favorable impressions with what must have been outstanding performances of both the Dukas and the d'Indy piano sonatas. Above all, the Belgian violinist Eugène Ysaÿe did much to popularize the Franck, Lekeu, and several other violin sonatas that we shall find were dedicated to him.

3. On some of the background for this assumption cf. SCE 605.
4. See these names in the Bibliography.
5. Cf. Landormy/FRANÇAISE 7–13; Vallas/FRANCK 190–94.
6. Cf. Cooper/FRENCH 10; Demuth/D'INDY 14–20.

As in Chapter XI, on the late-Romantic sonata in Austro-Germany, the problem arises in this chapter of drawing some line between late-Romantic and early-Modern composers (including not a few octogenarians who lived deep into the present century). Debussy, Bréville, Ropartz and his pupil Thirion, Désiré Pâque, and Delius are among those excluded here because they seem to have looked ahead more than behind. (None of the slightly more active crop of Belgian and Dutch composers introduced in this chapter raises the problem.) But again the decisions have had to depend as much on subjective reactions as on any purely theoretical distinctions or hard-and-fast boundary. In general, those who continued to depend on tonality as a main cohesive factor in their forms (even though, like d'Indy, they may have exploited traditional harmony to a point almost beyond recognition) are retained, whereas those who tended to upset or defy tonal relationships (even though, as in Delius' lush harmony, the immediate chord progressions may still exhibit established functions) are excluded. And the same might be generalized with regard to those who still preferred complex lyrical melodies, extended or "endlessly" unfolding phrase-and-period syntax, expansive forms, and opulent textures as against those who leaned toward squarer melodies or tunes, more punctuated if not simpler syntax, concise forms, and thinner textures.

Franck, Saint-Saëns, and Fauré

Although their birth years—1822, 1835, and 1845—do not make Franck, Saint-Saëns, and Fauré exact contemporaries, these three front-rank instrumental composers in late-Romantic France were too close in their interests and milieu not to be interrelated in one section here. All three were expert pianists and organists, yet, oddly enough, left only duo sonatas that are remembered today. How they related and differed in these sonatas may be clarified in a comparison of one representative work by each to follow shortly. The important Belgian-born composer and organist **César (-Auguste) Franck** (1822–90) maintains a significant niche in sonata history for only one work, his Sonata in A for P & Vn. But that work, composed in 1886—that is, late in his career, like his other few masterpieces, including the Symphony, *Variations symphoniques,* Quintet, Quartet, and *Les Béatitudes*—continues to be one of the most popular duos of all chamber music. The lateness of his masterpieces and influence explains why Franck is grouped here with the late-Romantics in spite of his life dates. He had studied composition with Reicha, among other teachers at the Paris Conservatoire, back in the 1830's. Drawn ever closer to this interest, he had abandoned the career of a concert piano virtuoso that his opportunistic father preferred for him, made his first mark as a composer with his four piano trios Opp. 1 and 2 (attracting the attention of Liszt and others), and started teaching in Paris, all by 1844, or his 22d year.[7] Two early piano sonatas by Franck are extant in his autographs. The first, composed while he was still in Liège, "âgé de 13 Ans" (end of 1835), was dedicated to his younger brother, the violinist Joseph, and given the pre-opus number 10.[8] This "Grande Sonate pour le Piano-Forte" consists of three movements (I/F-S → Ro) in ten handsomely written pages (recalling Franck's ability at drawing, too). It is correct and talented, but juvenile, music, with a flair, already, for chromaticism and modulations in the first movement and a knowledge of keyboard technique in spite of the most banal accompaniments. Except for anticipating the opening style of the *Variations symphoniques* in the slow movement, it suggests Mozart, Hummel, and occasionally Beethoven as the chief influences on the youngster's melodies and passagework. A sense of form is not yet developed. From not much later[9] comes the autograph of a "Deuxième Sonate" for P solo, which is reported to give a foretaste of Franck's cyclical procedures.[10] Perhaps this was still the same sonata Liszt mentioned receiving from Franck in 1853, at a time when he was continuing to enjoy Franck's trios.[11] If not, then Liszt may have received and lost a third, newer sonata (in the same year he may have lost part of Brahms's early Vn son. [ssb IX]), for no further sonata by Franck is extant prior to the main one.[12]

That main one, the Sonata in A for P & Vn, seems to have been written without delay in the fall of 1886 [13] and without anyone else hearing about it until it was completed, unless this work possibly could have been the greatly belated accomplishment of a violin sonata Franck had promised to write for Bülow's wife twenty-eight years earlier (be-

7. Cf. d'Indy/FRANCK 31–36, 114–15, 110–12; Vallas/FRANCK 19–22, 24–25, 39–40, 42–43, 46–58, 87; Emmanuel/FRANCK 20–27; BÜLOW BRIEFE I 494, II 183, IV 64. Vallas/FRANCK provides one of the most up-to-date, reliable biographies of Franck. For a full bibliography cf. Borren/FRANCK 127–41 (also, pp. 13–14).

8. It is discussed, with exx., in Tiersot/FRANCK 109–11. In Vallas/FRANCK 22–23 the trans. leaves the impression that this work was "published by the composer"; the original French is less ambiguous, and no evidence could be found here of such a pub. The autograph is MS 8546 in the Bibliotèque nationale.

9. Before 1841, in any case (MGG IV 644 [W. Mohr]).

10. Tiersot/FRANCK 112.

11. Cf. Vallas/FRANCK 108–9; MASON MEMORIES 122–23.

12. D'Indy/COURS II/1 423 is not followed here in the consideration of *Grande Pièce symphonique*, in f♯ (1861), as another "Sonate" by Franck.

13. The exact dates for each mvt. are quoted from the autograph in Ysaÿe/YSAŸE 164. Further details about the early circumstances of this son. are taken here primarily from Ysaÿe/YSAŸE 163–68 and Vallas/FRANCK 195–200.

fore she left Bülow for Wagner).[14] Nor could any confirmation be found here to the effect that the Sonata in A had been intended originally for cello, as has been asserted.[15] The cello is not mentioned in the autograph[16] nor in the first edition, which Hamelle of Paris published promptly that same year of 1886.[17] On the other hand, contrary to another assertion,[18] the Sonata in A may not have been written expressly for its dedicatee, the renowned violinist and Franck's younger compatriot Eugène Ysaÿe.[19] However, Ysaÿe, who was presented with the autograph on his wedding day,[20] at once and unquestionably became the performer identified above all others with the work and the one who did most to start it on its great popularity. Thus, among reports of its early performances and growing successes (including the late afternoon when increasing darkness compelled Ysaÿe to complete its performance from memory[21]), we read how Ysaÿe and the pianist Raoul Pugno[22] "carried the Sonata round the world like a torch and gave to Franck, that misunderstood, unrecognized saint, one of the few earthly joys he knew before regaining paradise." [23] We also read that Franck welcomed and acceded to some different concepts from his own in Ysaÿe's playing, including a faster tempo at the start.[24]

Franck's Sonata in A consists of four movements (705 mss. in all;

14. Cf. Vallas/FRANCK 122–23, 195.

15. Cf. the unsigned jacket notes for the Allegro recording No. 110, with reference to unidentified information from the cellist J. A. Delsart and the harpist Carlos Salzedo. One origin for this supposition may be Franck's unrealized hope, expressed about nine weeks before he died, to write a Vc son. (cf. Vallas/230, deleting further [erroneous?] information in the original French ed., p. 289).

16. The autograph was examined for the present study when it was on display in 1963 in Seattle for the annual meeting of the American Musicological Society. Like Liszt's Son. in b (SSB X), it was to have become available under limited conditions, in facs., as part of the "ROLF archives" (cf. NOTES XXI [1963–64] 83–93, especially 91) but has since been withdrawn from public view. Early information on the autograph appears in Ysaÿe/YSAŸE 164.

17. On the title page (facs. in Ysaÿe/YSAŸE opposite p. 44) is "Sonate pour Piano et Violon" and not ". . . Violon ou Violoncelle" as in the subsequent dual-purpose ed. arranged by J. A. Delsart and pub. ca. 1906 by Hamelle (not 1886, as in Cat. NYPL XI 566; cf. Altmann/KAMMERMUSIK 256, PAZDÍREK IV 162 and V 498, Weigl/VIOLONCELL 97). Regarding Franck's unkept promise to transcribe his Son. in A for 2 Ps, cf. Vallas/FRANCK 250.

18. E.g., cf. Cobbett/CHAMBER I 424 (V. d'Indy).

19. Cf. Ysaÿe/YSAŸE 164–65 (in spite of the statement on p. 159 and Franck's immediate concern with the dedication on p. 165).

20. Cf. Vallas/FRANCK 195.

21. Ysaÿe/YSAŸE 165–66. In Cobbett/CHAMBER I 425–26, d'Indy amplifies the story.

22. The first mvt. of a "Grande Sonate" in d for P solo by Pugno (1852–1914) is noted favorably in MERCURE II/1 (1906) 531–32. This work (a copy of which is at the Boston Public Library) proves to be grandiose, stilted, and watery.

23. Ysaÿe/YSAŸE 167.

24. Ysaÿe/YSAŸE 167; Vallas/FRANCK 199–200.

M-VF-S-F, as interpreted here) lasting a total of about twenty-eight minutes—(i) "Allegretto ben moderato" in A, in 9/8 meter, which presents a miniature "sonata form"; (ii) "Allegro" in the minor sub-dominant (d), in 4/4 meter, which presents a more complete "sonata form"; (iii) "Ben moderato," primarily in f♯, in alla breve meter, a cursive, modulatory fantasy, quasi recitative at the start; and (iv) "Allegretto poco mosso," in A, in alla breve meter, a free sonata-rondo form with themes stated canonically between the two instruments and with a development section at the middle that returns to earlier movements.[25] By far the most attention to the construction of this work has focused on its cyclical organization. Taking the lead as the former, idolatrous, longtime student, Vincent d'Indy all but credits Franck with inventing the principle of evolving a complete cycle out of a few recurring, often altered motives or "cellules." [26] Indeed, this "contribution" seems to become the main support for d'Indy's equation of Franck with Beethoven, or, rather, for sanctifying him as the true successor to Beethoven, among the world's greatest composers.[27]

However, three observations need to be made on Franck's cyclical treatment, the first two recalling our broader discussion of such treatment in Chapter VI. For one thing, it would be historically absurd to call Franck the inventor of cyclical treatment. Franck was simply one of its important cultivators in a line that goes back, for example, to Palestrina and the cantus firmus Mass, or Frescobaldi and the variation ricercar, or Bach and the *Musicalisches Opfer*. Beethoven set still more of a precedent than d'Indy allows, whether in an early sonata like Op. 2/3 (SCE 139–40, with ex.) or throughout the late quartet triptych Opp. 130–32 (and Op. 133), with its recurring motive. And especially in Franck's own century, Liszt surely gave much more in his own Sonata in b than he could have received from Franck's early trios. Moreover, the main applications of Berlioz's "idée fixe," Brahms's "basic motive," Wagner's leitmotif, and Bruckner's chorale evolution all antedated or paralleled the (late) masterpieces of Franck in which

25. Among numerous analyses of this work, all relatively brief and largely centered around its cyclical treatment, those of d'Indy (d'Indy/FRANCK 169–71, d'Indy/COURS II/1 422/26, Cobbett/CHAMBER I 424–26) have been most cited, partly because of his close relation to his teacher. Selva/SONATE 227–31, as usual, follows d'Indy, *her* teacher, to the letter. Emmanuel/FRANCK 63–71 is essentially the same, too. Emmanuel/DUKAS 70–71 draws a striking parallel between Franck's 4-mvt. cycle and that of Beethoven's Op. 101 merely to argue that such tectonic analyses are purely external and fail to reveal the important (actually, more local) internal differences.

26. Franck's position as "inventor" of this principle is discussed at some length, though without sufficient historical reinforcement or significant conclusions, in Demuth/FRANCK 53–58.

27. E.g., d'Indy/COURS II/1 421–22; cf. GROVE IV 470 (L. Vallas).

cyclical treatment prevails. Certainly Franck, whose devotion to German as well as French music so embittered Saint-Saëns and the other
more nationalist minded members of the Société Nationale de Musique,[28] knew these precedents well. As a second observation, it is
doubtful that cyclical treatment makes that much difference in the
strength and conscious or even unconscious enjoyment of Franck's
music. As M. D. Calvocoressi has emphasized with regard to d'Indy's
own cyclical treatment,[29] ". . . a theme or melody must stand or fall
quite apart from the fact that its 'skeleton' is that of another heard
before or to be heard further; and the aesthetic value of a development is not determined by the origin of its materials." As our third
observation, one learns that Franck himself neither taught nor advocated the application of the cyclical principle.[30] Naturally, this is
not to suggest that he was not deliberately and consciously exploiting
the unifying and cumulative values of recalling ideas from the earlier
movements as he composed the succeeding movements of his Sonata in
A. But it may well be that he never quite thought of this work as
deriving entirely and climactically from three "cellules," as d'Indy (and,
of course, Blanche Selva) would have it, all too categorically.[31] Perhaps
d'Indy was only transferring to his teacher the highly systematized principles of generation and unity he was currently and unequivocally
evolving for his own Sonata in e (infra).

To get closer than cyclical relationships are likely to bring us to the
salient style traits, including the chief strengths and pleasures of
Franck's Sonata in A, it may help to compare this work with the most
representative violin sonata by each of his two most important near-
contemporaries in French instrumental music—that is, by Saint-Saëns
and Fauré, who come up next in this chapter, anyway. Between Saint-
Saëns' two violin sonatas, Opp. 75 in d/D (1885) and 102 in E♭ (1896),
the former is chosen for comparison, not only because it appeared
nearer in time (only one year earlier) but because it is nearer in spirit
as the more compelling and impetuous of the two[32] (although neither

28. Cf. Saint-Saëns/ESSAYS 45–49; Vallas/FRANCK 166–67, 191–95; Gatti & Basso/
LA MUSICA II 473 (Dufourcq); Harding/SAINT-SAËNS 154.

29. Cobbett/CHAMBER II 3; cf., also, the similar objections in Cortot/FRANÇAISE
II 147.

30. According to Breville, as cited in Demuth/FRANCK 55.

31. E.g., d'Indy/COURS II/1 423–26. The "x" cellule, most prevalent and most
seminal of the 3 cellules, is found in the rise and fall of a 3d, as first in the
first 3 notes of the Vn, in i/5; "y" is found in the inverted cambiata as initially
defined (sooner than d'Indy says) by the first 4 notes of the Vn in i/19; but "z"
is not found (weakening d'Indy's approach) until the middle of the 3d mvt., in
the rise and fall of both a 4th and a 5th that the Vn first plays in iii/59–60. Cf.,
also, Vallas/FRANCK 198–99.

32. It is much preferred in Servières/SAINT-SAËNS 109–11.

is played any more than any other Saint-Saëns chamber works today). Between Fauré's two violin sonatas, Opp. 13 in A (1877) and 108 in e (1917), it is the former again that is chosen, both because it appeared nearer in time and because it has been much the more successful of the two with the public (if not necessarily with the connoisseurs[33]). Like Franck's Sonata in A, both Saint-Saëns' Op. 75 and Fauré's Op. 13 fall into familiar but not identical, four-movement plans—F-S-F-VF and VF-M-VF-VF, respectively (although actually, in Saint-Saëns' Son., as in his Symphony No. 3 of the following year, 2 pairs of mvts. are indicated, with each pair separated only by a transition[34]). They last a little less long—21 minutes (948 mss.) and 26 (1,161 mss.), respectively. Neither Saint-Saëns nor Fauré happens to have showed as much interest in cyclical relationships, even though as masters, like Franck, of variation techniques both men could hardly have been unaware of the fullest possibilities. Saint-Saëns does return to the second theme of his first movement (mss. 76–83) in the coda of his finale (mss. 144–79, 210–16, plus more in the bass), and it is not hard to hear him making other, more subtle interconnections, here and there.[35]

Comparing the three violin sonatas produces no striking new conclusions but does help to confirm and sharpen familiar observations about their composers' styles. Franck's sonata reveals less of the broad symphonist in the Classic and Brahmsian architectural sense than either of the other sonatas. The differences show up especially in tonality and syntax. The tonal outlines created by Saint-Saëns and Fauré suggest premeditated organization whereas Franck's outline seems more haphazard—more like the consequence than the cause of the harmonic color that figures so prominently in Franck's style. In other words, Franck seems to modulate to new keys more for their surprise value than their larger function in any "grand cadence." Thus, to compare the tonal outlines in the most developed form of each sonata (with Roman numerals indicating the functions of the most essential key areas), Franck's finale is outlined by I-vi-V||-♭ii-♮III-I,[36] Saint-Saëns' opening movement by i-III-i||iv/IV/-iv-i, and Fauré's opening movement by I-V||-I-iii-vi/VI-I. With regard to syntax, Saint-Saëns and Fauré both achieve a dynamic structural rhythm through

33. Thus, Cobbett/CHAMBER I 390 (F. Schmitt) finds Op. 108 to be "irritating" at times because of tonal, harmonic, and motivic redundancies, whereas Koechlin/FAURÉ 43–44 prefers it as confirming "Fauré's evolution toward an ever greater purity."

34. The 4 mvts. of the 2 pairs are referred to here simply as i, ii, iii, and iv.

35. On Fauré, cf. Suckling/FAURÉ 94; also, *infra*.

36. But cf. d'Indy's defense in 1919 of this plan, in Vallas/SAINT-SAËNS 83, and Saint-Saëns' reply, pp. 86–87.

flexibility of phrase lengths. Often their phrases evolve cumulatively by growing progressively shorter, as in the succession at the start of Saint-Saëns/i: 4-4-4-2-2-2-1-1-1 (etc., with the squareness of the 4-ms. phrases relieved by meter changes); or they spin out after starting regularly, as at the start of Fauré/i: 4+4 & 4+10. Fauré gives more of a sense of spinning out, anyway, because, as in the example just cited, the consequent is more likely to contrast with the antecedent than to parallel it (in Saint-Saëns' manner). Remarkably plastic in effect are the irregular phrase lengths in the scherzo movement of each—the six-measure overlapping phrases at the start of Saint-Saëns/iii and the sharply defined three-measure phrases at the start of Fauré/iii. By contrast, Franck's phrases are most often regular in length, even in much of the recitative of iii and the canonic treatment of iv. His most frequent syntactic method is the familiar, relatively static one of two short units followed by a long unit, as in the second theme of i (e.g., 2+2+4 in mss. 32–39) or the main theme of ii (e.g., 2+2+6 in mss. 138–47). Single, long-drawn-out phrases do not occur in Franck's Sonata in A.

If Franck's is the least dynamic of the three sonatas in its tonal and syntactic organization (and in spite of its cyclical relationships), its strong appeal and success must be credited to other factors, especially its melody, harmony, and rhythmic flow.[37] Sometimes his melody barely outlines the chords (as in most of i/1–31) or traces the surface (as in i/108–17) of his luscious chromatic harmony, often toying with the minor and major 3d or 2d in the process[38] (as in iii/11–13 and 17–21); and sometimes it qualifies as an independent, songful tune (as in two main themes of iv, starting at mss. 1 and 87). At all times his melodies tend to divide into clear, relatively short units, in keeping with his regular, relatively short phrases. By contrast, the melodies of both other composers tend to give rise to, and do not rise out of, the harmony. That is, they possess sufficient intervallic and rhythmic character to be at least identifiable without harmonic qualifications and interpretations. Beyond that starting point the melodies of Saint-Saëns and Fauré differ considerably in the sonatas in question. (One must take care to delimit references to Saint-Saëns' style traits to the work or even the movement "in question," for the craft of that past master was as eclectic as it was skillful, with almost any established trait being fair game for a particular work. Witness how florid, eventually rhapsodic, the lines become during the slow movement of the same sonata "in question.") In their more developed, fast

37. Colles/FRANCK finds certain ineptitudes for "son. form" on Franck's part.
38. Cf. Colles/FRANCK 207.

movements, Saint-Saëns gives preference to narrow-ranged, technically convenient motives that violate no traditional precepts for a "good" melody yet are distinctive enough to invite development and expansion, whereas Fauré prefers wide-ranged, full-fledged, themes that are intimately bound up with their supporting harmony, yet have melodic significance in their own right. Although Fauré's themes stretch hand and ear with their frequent intervals of a 4th and larger, most of them are so essentially lyrical that they tend to flow from one to the next without sharp contrasts. In the slow movements of these particular sonatas, Fauré, as well as Saint-Saëns, prefers to deal in motives. Fauré and Franck have in common their surging, continuous, lyrical flow, which one thinks of as almost too Romantic, too heated for the more Classically oriented Saint-Saëns. That flow may be attributed not only to the compelling lines and harmony but to the rhythmic impetus of rocking, triplet, syncopated, or other motoric figures in the accompaniment. Their melodic styles and differences may at least be hinted by quoting from the first occurrence of the second theme in the first fast movement by each of our three composers (Ex. 79a, b, c).

With regard to their most characteristic harmony, all three composers indulge expertly in what might be called chromatic and enharmonic evolution, one or more voices at a time, from one chord to the next. But Saint-Saëns does this least and does it around a traditional harmonic framework—in fact, largely around a framework of primary triads. Fauré's harmony is at once more active, with a variety of resolved and unresolved 7th-chords and accented dissonances; and it is more colorful, with emphasis not only on the Neapolitan-6th chord but on the lowered mediant and submediant. And Franck's harmony, while stabilized by long bass tones, is made still more colorful and active through the introduction of frequent and varied 9th-chords treated as consonances, through an extreme use of chromatic voice-leading, through one new, unexpected, often dramatic, resolution or deceptive cadence after another, and through resourceful exploitations of the various aug.-6th chords and the dim.-7th chord. The fughetta in the development section of Saint-Saëns' first movement, Franck's canonic finale, and Fauré's nonacademic but frequent melodic duets and exchanges between piano and violin supply only part of the evidence for the polyphonic abilities and interests of all three composers.[39] But in keeping with their

---

39. Regarding Saint-Saëns' disparagement and d'Indy's defense of Franck's canonic and fugal techniques, in 1919, cf. Vallas/FRANCK 269; Vallas/SAINT-SAËNS 83 and 87; Harding/SAINT-SAËNS 218–20.

Ex. 79. From the first movements of (a) César Franck's Sonata in A, (b) Gabriel Fauré's Sonata in A, Op. 13 (after Wier/ VIOLIN-m 42 and 251, respectively), and (c) Camille Saint-Saëns' Sonata in d, Op. 75 (after the early Durand ed., p. 4).

harmonic differences, Saint-Saëns produces the thinnest, most precise, and most conveniently playable texture, not only in the very light, rapid finale, which is almost a *perpetuum mobile* (or "grand exercise de concert" [40]), but in the other movements as well. Fauré's texture is fuller and causes each player to make wider stretches and leaps, and more shifts of position about his instrument. Franck's texture is still fuller, similarly difficult in its position shifts, but much freer in its doublings and its addition and subtraction of voices, and too often unimaginative in the piano bass. One should add that the total effect of all three styles of texture, as different as they are, is almost invariably that of clear, telling sonority.

The second in our trio of important French instrumental composers, **(Charles-) Camille Saint-Saëns** (1835–1921), composed at least ten sonatas, all duos, during his long life.[41] The first of these originated 41a when he was only about six, as but one instance of his extraordinary precocity, and the last three as his last compositions, in his eighty-sixth or final year. Saint-Saëns' thorough training seems to have come as much from his own early curiosity and meticulous, self-guided

40. Selva/SONATE 235.

41. Harding/SAINT-SAËNS is a recent book (1965) on his life and artistic environment, based partly on newly explored sources and supplemented with a dated (somewhat careless) list of nearly all but the earliest works. Bonnerot/SAINT-SAËNS (1922) continues to be valuable, too. Cf., also, MGG XI 1272–84 (M. Briquet), with full bibliography and dated list of works.

study of past music (and other arts) as from Stamaty (ssʙ XII), Halévy, Boëly (ssʙ XII), and very few other teachers.[42] This training led to an increasingly successful and honored career as a prolific composer in virtually all genres; as a touring concert pianist right to his last year, expert enough to be ranked with Liszt by Liszt himself, to amaze Wagner, yet to be judged responsibly as lacking in "poetic intensity and fervour";[43] as an equally capable organist; and as an author.[44] But his life was not without the personal tragedies, loneliness, and professional frictions that should help to explain a growing, outspoken bitterness in his later years. Much of the friction related to the Société Nationale de Musique that he himself and Romain Bussine founded in 1871, and to questions of its national or international goals.[45] Saint-Saëns felt a special personal and artistic kinship with Liszt and with his own most important student, Fauré, among outstanding near contemporaries. The same cannot be said of his feelings for Franck, d'Indy, Massenet, and Debussy. Perhaps the most pertinent observation to add here is one of surprise at the extent to which all of the darker side of Saint-Saëns' life is excluded from his music.

Those ten sonatas by Saint-Saëns include five for P & Vn, two for P & Vc, and one each for P & Ob, P & Cl, and P & Bn. The first three for P & Vn remained in MS, including a very early "Sonata à Bessens" (ca. 1841), another youthful work from about 1850, and a Sonata in d placed in 1876.[46] The last was played in London in 1876 with the composer at the piano during one of his many periods of crowded touring,[47] but must have been discarded by him within a few years because in 1885 Op. 75, also in d, was published as the "1ère Sonate" for P & Vn. Op. 75 (discussed previously in connection with Franck) was composed early in 1885 for the violinist Pierre Marsick in recognition of a full, triumphal tour the two men had just completed in Switzerland.[48] The other or "2me" sonata published for P & Vn is Op. 102 in E♭, a colder, more abstract, more subtle, and

42. Cf. Harding/SAINT-SAËNS 13–16, 18–20, 23–24, 26–27, 31–39.

43. Cf. Harding/SAINT-SAËNS 223, 83–84; GROVE VII 366 (M. D. Calvocoressi).

44. Saint-Saëns/ESSAYS is the collection of his writings that applies most here.

45. Cf. Harding/SAINT-SAËNS 109–11, 113–14, 154, 173–74.

46. Cf. MGG XI 1278. Presumably "Bessens" is a misspelling of (Antoine) Bessems, the violinist who played with Saint-Saëns at the time (Bonnerot/SAINT-SAËNS 17). The second of these sons. seems to have been only an incomplete sketch done during the study with Halévy (Bonnerot/SAINT-SAËNS 25).

47. Cf. Bonnerot/SAINT-SAËNS 79–80.

48. Bonnerot/SAINT-SAËNS 118. According to Harding/SAINT-SAËNS 201, the opening theme of Op. 75 had a special appeal for Marcel Proust, in whose novel À la Recherche du temps perdu it figures as Vinteuil's celebrated "little phrase"; cf., also, A. Coeuroy in RM IV/3 (Jan., 1923) 199–201, 203–4 (but with reference to a Fauré son.), 208–12; also, Lockspeiser/FAURÉ (with Fauré suggested).

more polyphonic work. It was composed at least in part on tour in Cairo in 1896, then first played in Paris soon after, by Saint-Saëns and Sarasate, during the composer's fiftieth-anniversary recital,[49] and published there before the year was ended with a dedication "a Monsieur et Madame L. Carembat." [50]

The first of Saint-Saëns' two cello sonatas, Op. 32 in c and in only three movements (F-M-F), was composed in 1872 in the throes of grief and emptiness following the death of the great-aunt who had cared for him from infancy.[51] More specifically it is reported to have grown out of some organ improvising that actually supplied, "note-for-note, the first and last pages" of the sonata score.[52] Publication and a (first?) performance, with the composer at the piano, occurred a year later, with an extraordinary number of performances of Op. 32 following in the next few years.[53] In 1905 after retreating southeast to Biskra from a bad winter in Algiers, Saint-Saëns wrote his other, more difficult, less known "2e" cello sonata, Op. 123 in F. Published that same year and dedicated to Jules Griset, it was composed, we are told,[54] between walks to visit with "three gazelles who had become friends" with Saint-Saëns, the lifelong lover of animals. Perhaps its warmly Romantic slow movement relates to this association. The three sonatas from his last year, 1921—Opp. 166 in D for Ob & P, 167 in E♭ for Cl & P, and 168 in G for Bn & P—are all relatively short, lean, spare, muscular, economical, technically easier works reflecting great compositional maturity and wisdom, plus a fondness for and keen awareness of the instrumental idioms and a late preoccupation with Rameau and other earlier French composers. They were sketched in Algiers, completed in Paris, and published in the same year with dedications, respectively, to Louis Bas, Auguste Perrier, and Léon Letelier.[55]

The two of Saint-Saëns' seven published sonatas that seem most nearly to get past his barrier of objectivity into his emotional self are the first cello sonata (Op. 32), the one identified with his great-aunt's death, and the clarinet sonata (Op. 167), shortly preceding his own death.[56] These two works and the "first" violin sonata (Op. 75) are

49. Bonnerot/SAINT-SAËNS 161, 162.

50. A review in SMW LIV (1896) 945 calls Op. 102 a fine challenge to the enterprising, although a bit harsh in its polyphony and "baroque" (i.e., extravagant).

51. Harding/SAINT-SAËNS 124.

52. Bonnerot/SAINT-SAËNS 69.

53. As samples for but 18 months, cf. NZM LXXII/1 (1876) 224, 238, 249; LXXII/2 (1876) 300, 310, 436; LXXIII/1 (1877) 30, 52, 63, 73, 116, 249, 274.

54. Bonnerot/SAINT-SAËNS 182.

55. Bonnerot/SAINT-SAËNS 215.

56. Useful descriptions of the 7 sons. occur in Servières/SAINT-SAËNS 108–11, 115–16, and 117–18; Cobbett/CHAMBER II 322–23 (E. Baumann; string sons. only).

regarded here as the strongest of the sonatas and the ones most likely to succeed if Saint-Saëns' music is given another chance. During his lifetime, his first published sonata, Op. 32, won the most interest (as suggested above), with the interest in the later sonatas, as in his other music, tending to diminish in keeping with his changing popular image from modernist to conservative. Today (in 1967) all seven sonatas still appear in the Durand catalogues, but perhaps more indicative of public taste is the fact that only two of them are currently available in recordings—Opp. 75 and 167, as it happens.[57]

The important point is that except for two or three concertos, one symphony, and *Le Carnaval des Animaux,* Saint-Saëns is scarcely heard or played at all, anymore. He has toppled from his deserved eminence as one of the most universally skilled and talented composers. And the most tangible reason is that changing image, or, rather, the fact that Saint-Saëns stood still while the musical world passed by him. Or one might give as the reason that prevailing sense in his music of objectivity and abstract perfection, traits of which were noted in our comparison of representative violin sonatas by him, Franck, and Fauré (*supra,* including Ex. 79c). But the objectivity is only a corollary of the conservatism. Composing more than eighty of his eighty-six years, Saint-Saëns had an almost unprecedentedly long time to stand still. Far from keeping abreast of Debussy or even d'Indy, he barely kept up with Liszt, Berlioz, Wagner, and Fauré in his tastes,[58] and advanced not even that far in practice. In spite of the vast, comprehensive resources at his command and both his ability and his inclination to choose among them eclectically, the range of his "practice" might be represented realistically by his inclination in 1874 to write Variations for 2 Ps on the "Trio" in Beethoven's Sonata in E♭, Op. 31/3/iii, or in 1908 to transcribe Chopin's Sonata in b♭, Op. 35, for 2 Ps. But, of course, conservatism in itself is no more of a fault than it is a virtue in art. In the long appraisal of Saint-Saëns' sonatas one cannot deny the exceptional force and worth of his best melodies, developments, and forms, as may at least be suggested in part by one illustration from the remarkably simple yet poignant slow movement of his clarinet sonata, a movement in steady, fateful 3/2 meter that might have come right out of Bach's "St. Matthew Passion" (Ex. 80).

The third of our three outstanding instrumental composers in late-Romantic France, the organist **Gabriel-Urbain Fauré** (1845–1924), was

---

57. Cf. the laudatory review by I. Kolodin of a further recording of Op. 75, by Jascha Heifetz and Brooks Smith, in the *Saturday Review* for Oct. 28, 1967, pp. 58–59.

58. Cf. Harding/SAINT-SAËNS 148–49, 151, 53–55, 83–84, 144–46.

the least universal of the three, in several senses.[59] He touched on most   59a
branches of composition yet wrote fewer works—only about one hundred that he allowed to stand—and excelled in fewer branches, primarily chamber music and songs. By way of Saint-Saëns and other
teachers he received a thorough introduction to the great masters of
the past, up to and including Wagner and Liszt, yet underwent the
least direct influence from any of their styles, whether it be the
rhetorical drama of the last two, the "singing allegro" of Mozart, the
fugal writing of Bach, or even the Romantic mannerisms of the salon
and the virtuoso that Franck and Saint-Saëns themselves could assume

Ex. 80. From the third movement of Camille Saint-Saëns'
Sonata in E♭, Op. 167 (after the original Durand ed., with the
kind permission of Elkan-Vogel Co. in Philadelphia).

so well when they chose to. In fact, if Fauré, the teacher of Ravel,
Koechlin, Roger-Ducasse, and Florent Schmitt, may be called the most
French of our three instrumental masters,[60] he also may be called, like
Chopin, one of the most individual of stylists—precious, restrained,
refined, poetic, and subtle.

59. Suckling/FAURÉ (1946) is one of the most recent and helpful studies of the
man and his music; Vuillermoz/FAURÉ (by an important student; 1960) skirts factual
details in favor of viewpoints and philosophies (with considerable insight); cf., also,
the article by Fauré's son Philippe Fauré-Fremiet in MGG III 1867–80, digesting
his book of 1929 (Fauré-Fremiet/FAURÉ).
60. Cf. Roger-Ducasse/FAURÉ 79.

Fauré left only four sonatas, two each for Vn & P and Vc & P. Both temporally and stylistically they divide into one early work and three late works. In other words, one sonata was composed in 1876 at the end of his "first period," [61] following his service in Rennes, in the army, and at the Swiss wartime retreat of the École Niedermeyer; and the other three sonatas appeared in 1916–21 or forty and more years later, near the end of his "fourth" or "last period" and well after his advances both to the post of chief organist at the Madeleine in Paris in 1896 and to the directorship of the Paris Conservatoire in 1905.

That first sonata was the one in A, Op. 13, for Vn & P, which figures among the most successful of all his works (and was the choice, *supra,* for our comparison with one Vn son. each by Franck and Saint-Saëns). It was composed on "vacation" in the home of two longtime friends, Camille Clerc and wife, and tried over, as it grew, with the Belgian violinist Hubert Léonard.[62] Because the Paris publishers were afraid to invest in its printing, Fauré had to be content with all honor and no pay whatsoever in a contract for publication engineered by Clerc with Breitkopf & Härtel of Leipzig (1877).[63] Fauré dedicated Op. 13 to Paul Viardot, son of the influential singer and brother of the girl to whom he now became engaged after a long ardent courtship, although the breaking off of that engagement was soon to follow, leaving a wound that never quite healed. A (first?) performance in Paris on April 29, 1877,[64] followed by a more conspicuous one at the Trocadéro in 1878, got the Sonata in A off to a slow start with the public. Perhaps its progress was hindered by an early, negative review from Germany that found harmonic and modulatory eccentricities intolerable to the structure, and, notwithstanding signs of talent, predicted that only firm willpower and good nerves could get a person through the work.[65] But by the same token its progress should have been furthered by a laudatory announcement, headed simply "Une Sonate," that Saint-Saëns wrote for the *Journal de musique* of April 7 (not May 22), 1877 (p. 3), possibly in answer to the German review:[66]

It is outside the theater that one of the most interesting works of our times is revealed, a simple and modest sonata for piano and violin. . . . A

61. According to his son's division of his life into 4 periods (MGG III 1268–70).

62. Cf. Rostand/FAURÉ 54–55; Suckling/FAURÉ 15–17; Servières/FAURÉ 62.

63. Cf. Fauré-Fremiet/FAURÉ 46–47. The year of pub. is wrongly given as 1876 in most sources (and as 1878 in MGG) but should be 1877, as in HOFMEISTER 1877 66 and NZM LXXI (1877) 143.

64. This early performance, reported in NZM LXXIII/1 (1877) 214, is overlooked by all authors consulted here.

65. SMW XXXV (1877) 449.

66. Trans. from the quotation (including italics) in Servières/FAURÉ 60. Cf., also, Vuillermoz/FAURÉ 72–74.

repertoire of French instrumental music is developing [that is] capable of contesting to advantage in a closed field where, for a long time, the German school had no rival. The appearance of the sonata by Fauré has revealed to us a new champion, *perhaps the most formidable of all, for he combines with a profound musical knowledge a great melodic wealth* and a kind of unconscious naivety that is the most irresistible of forces. One finds in this sonata the most alluring delicacy, novelty of forms, resourcefulness of modulations and unusual sonorities, [and] use of the most unanticipated rhythms; above all that [allure] hovers a charm that envelops the entire work and makes the most unexpected adventures acceptable, like something entirely natural, to the crowd of ordinary listeners.

In spite of the differences noted in our comparison offered earlier, Fauré's individuality of style does bring Franck's to mind at times, especially in the realm of harmonic color displayed by both sonatas in A. As Koechlin has so aptly put it,[67]

Without knowing the facts one would say that it [Fauré's Son. in A] was inspired by the much [actually only one decade] later work of César Franck. Indeed, the vehemence of the Allegro does show some affinity at times with Franck's second movement [as may be sensed even in our Ex. 79a and b, *supra*]. But render unto Gabriel, and not unto "César," that which is Gabriel's.

Another individual stylist, Richard Strauss, took an understandable interest in Fauré's Sonata in A.[68] One suspects that d'Indy would have expressed more interest, too, and not dismissed it so politely but briefly were he not transferring to the onetime pupil some of the antagonism still felt between Saint-Saëns and himself.[69] But one looks in vain for any demonstrable affinity between this or any other sonata by Fauré and any of Saint-Saëns' sonatas.

Fauré's last three sonatas, composed during the deafness and sadly failing health of the septuagenarian's last period,[70] include Op. 108 in e/E, for Vn & P, composed in 1916, published in 1917, and dedicated to Queen Elizabeth of Belgium;[71] Op. 109 in d/D, for Vc & P, composed in 1917, published in 1918, and dedicated to the cellist Louis Hasselmans; and Op. 117 in g, for Vc & P, composed in 1921, published in 1922, and dedicated to the Alsatian-American composer Charles Martin Loeffler. All three works are available in print (Durand), but only Op.

67. Koechlin/FAURÉ 41.
68. BÜLOW-STRAUSS 20, referring to a program of chamber music planned for Jan., 1886.
69. D'Indy/COURS II/1 428, repeated, as usual, in Selva/SONATE 238-40.
70. Cf. Fauré-Fremiet/FAURÉ 110, 117; Fauré/LETTRES 229-35 and 269-70 (reporting progress on each son.).
71. The autograph was on view in 1963 (cf. NOTES XXI [1963-64] 91 and read Op. 108) but has since been withdrawn.

108 among them is available in current recordings, and none of them gets the performances that they all deserve and that are certain to be welcomed.[72] All three are three-movement cycles (F-M-VF and F-M-F), lacking the scherzo of the first sonata.[73] Furthermore, all three have in common the spareness, and preciseness, if not cerebralism, and the reduced, or at least refined, technical demands that we have found in the very late sonatas of Saint-Saëns and not a few others. They no longer reveal the opulent Romanticism of the first sonata, with its melodic expansiveness, its harmonic color for color's sake, and its communion with Mendelssohn, Schumann, and Chopin, in whom Fauré had been so thoroughly steeped. Instead we find a remarkable turn to intensive exploitation of single motives in a persistent manner that does tend at times to become cerebral and even crotchety.

Thus, in the second of the two violin sonatas, Op. 108, the motive announced at once may well have been intended to underlie the entire work, although Fauré is usually not credited with much interest in cyclical treatment.[74] There are climactic measures in the second and third movements (e.g., ii/61–63 and iii/43–45), where references to the initial motive could hardly be other than deliberate. But deliberate or not, a cyclical effect exists, and it becomes far more pervasive, sometimes to the point of irritation and/or monotony,[75] than the more obvious relationships that d'Indy so pointedly exalted in Franck's Sonata in A (*supra*). In spite of its free, plastic treatment, the initial motive is identified melodically in its reiterations by the play with the intervals of a 2d and 3d around a focal tone, and rhythmically by the syncopations in which these intervals share. Although the violin spins out long, finely drawn lines much of the time, one senses that these lines derive from or sing above the motivic reiterations.[76] If there is monotony now and then, it owes in part to the literally monotonal effect of returning so often to the focal tones of the motive (as during the curious enharmonic oscillation between the E and f triads in ii/24–33) and partly to the monothematic effect of a "sonata allegro" form in which sharp contrasts of ideas reduce to different facets of one idea.

72. Cf. the "Discographie" in Fauré-Fremiet/FAURÉ 229–31.

73. Favre/FAURÉ is a full style-critical diss. on the chamber music, though without separate or considerable mention of the sons. Koechlin/FAURÉ, Servières/FAURÉ, Cobbett/CHAMBER I 386–87 and 390–91 (F. Schmitt), Rostand/FAURÉ, and Vuillermoz/FAURÉ 166–68 and 175–78 all include brief descriptions of each son.

74. E.g., cf. Suckling/FAURÉ 94.

75. As remarked, though only in the outer mvts., by Florent Schmitt in Cobbett/CHAMBER I 390.

76. In Fauré-Fremiet/FAURÉ 157–58 it is suggested that Op. 108 will succeed if the "prudent" approach is replaced by the warm lyricism of an Ysaÿe (who never played it).

Ex. 81. From the start of the middle movement in Gabriel
Fauré's Sonata in g, Op. 117 (after the Durand ed., by kind
permission of Elkan-Vogel Co. in Philadelphia).

If there is irritation it may come from the extra emphasis given to
those focal tones by the almost jerky syncopations.

    To these traits may be added one other that probably bears on the
apparent resistance to Fauré's late sonatas in spite of all the respect
in which they are held. That is the thin, meticulous texture, in which
the dissonances—no more than those that had been cloaked in the
richer sound of his earlier music—now stand out, more bare and harsh.
In the absence of fuller sound, Fauré sometimes resorts to canonic
treatment, not, as Franck does, to provide structural extension, but as
a means of structural enrichment (e.g., Op. 108/i/8–11 and ii/20–23).
The two cello sonatas, which are similar in character and style, are
smoother in their rhythmic flow than Op. 108 is, not so dogged in their

motivic unifications (allowing for clearer contrasts), and somewhat less demanding on the pianist, relegating his part to that of simple accompaniment more of the time. Op. 109 tends to be a little more poetic, free, and troubled, and Op. 117 a little more contrived, especially in the finale. But the relative simplicity of these two works should not belie their worthwhile substance, expressive intensity, or structural tightness. The slow movements of all three late sonatas are masterpieces of affecting, simple melody, including Op. 117/ii, which starts as though recalling Fauré's own *Élégie* for Vc & P of 1883 (Ex. 81).

Followers of Franck (Dukas, d'Indy)

Although the notable composer and teacher **Paul Dukas** (1865–1935) received no formal instruction from Franck, his one sonata shows the clear influence of that master's musical language. Moreover, Dukas' sonata has much in common with the main sonata, which appeared only seven years later, by his longtime friend [77] and Franck's most illustrious and proclaimed pupil, **(Paul-Marie-Théodore-) Vincent d'Indy** (1851–1931). Hence, Dukas and d'Indy, the two chief contributors to the sonata in France at the end of the Romantic Era, are paired here as followers of Franck and by way of a sequel to our trilogic section on Franck, Saint-Saëns, and Fauré.

Dukas' Sonata in e♭, for P solo, was composed in 1899–1900 and published in 1901 by Durand in Paris.[78] It was dedicated to Saint-Saëns even though the latter seems never to have acknowledged receiving the work.[79] Its first performance, by Edouard Risler at the Salle Pleyel on May 10, 1901, was generally well received, especially in the review by Lalo's son Pierre, published two weeks later.[80] Dukas' immediate, grateful, personal reply[81] reveals chiefly the almost phobic concern for maintaining high standards and eliminating weaknesses that kept him from putting his stamp of approval on more than about a dozen works during his lifetime (including the Symphony in C, the

77. Cf. Vallas/D'INDY II 43–44.

78. Cf. pp. 23–25 in Favre/DUKAS, the chief and most recent study of the man and his works; also, MGG III 914–18 (G. Favre; but the year of pub. should read 1901, not 1906).

79. Cortot/FRANÇAISE I 234–35.

80. In the newspaper *Temps*, pub. May 23 (dated May 24); quoted almost in full in Favre/DUKAS 24–25. On Feb. 3, in the Brussels *Guide musical* XLVII (1901) 99–101, G. Servières had already reviewed the pub. work, under the heading "The Renaissance of the Piano Sonata," as skillful, with derivations from Franck and d'Indy and with more virtuosity than sentiment or melody.

81. Letter of May 24, 1901, printed in Pincherle/MUSICIENS 228–29.

P Variations on a Rameau theme, and, of course, "The Sorcerer's Apprentice," among other instrumental works). Several weeks earlier, after Dukas' Sonata in e♭ had appeared in print, his onetime classmate Debussy had written some perceptive comments on it, praising especially its tonal organization and emotional control and citing especially its last two movements.[82] But several weeks after Pierre Lalo's review appeared, Debussy added, in the guise of "Monsieur Croche the dilettante hater," that Lalo should not have gone quite so far as to sacrifice Schumann and Chopin on the altar of Dukas, or to relate Dukas to Beethoven, with which comparison Debussy says he himself would have been "only mildly flattered," since Beethoven's sonatas, especially the later ones, "are very badly scored for piano," like "orchestral transcriptions . . . lacking a third hand. . . ."[83] We can return to the music of Dukas' Sonata in e♭ after summarizing what d'Indy contributed.

Although d'Indy gave much attention to the sonata in the writings, lectures, and teaching that occupied him during a good part of his long, distinguished career, he actually composed only five sonatas among the 118 orchestral, chamber, piano, dramatic, church, and other choral works that are known by him.[84] The earliest of these was a presumably weak, inexperienced work, for P solo, composed in about his 19th year (1870) and since unexplored (and lost?).[85] The second is a *Petite Sonate dans la forme classique,* Op. 9, for P solo, composed and published (by Hamelle) in 1880—a four-movement work (F-M-Sc-VF) that is reported to be scholastic, unimaginative, and rudimentary, with some suggestions of Mendelssohn and Chopin (mainly in iv) but remarkably few evidences (mainly in ii and iii) that by now d'Indy had been with Franck seven years, become an ardent Wagnerian, and composed the trilogy of symphonic overtures known as *Wallenstein.*[86]

The third sonata we have from d'Indy is that for Vn & P, Op. 59 in C, composed in 1903–04, published in 1905, and first performed, with

---

82. DEBUSSY CROCHE 47–49, from *La Revue blanche* for Apr. 15, 1901 (cf. Lockspeiser/DEBUSSY I 63–64 and II 282).

83. DEBUSSY CROCHE 9–10.

84. Vallas/D'INDY (efficiently digested by Vallas in GROVE IV 467–77) is the chief study of the man and his works, with a full list of the compositions (II 355–66) as well as writings and lectures (II 369–76, including 3 items specifically on the son. and several others in which the son. is central). D'Indy/COURS II/1 153–433 is d'Indy's main, highly individualized, historical and stylistic discussion of the son. (to which numerous references are made in SBE, SCE, and SSB).

85. Cf. Vallas/D'INDY I 62, II 357; Cortot/FRANÇAISE II 117.

86. Cf. Cortot/FRANÇAISE II 117–20; Vallas/D'INDY I 256–57, II 165 and 357 (with a speculation that Op. 9 might be a reworking of the [lost?] son. from 1870).

much success, by d'Indy and the violinist Armand Parent on February 3, 1905.[87] Almost never heard since its debut performances, Op. 59 is a mature, lyrical, but overly intellectualized work in the standard four movements (F-Sc-S-F), cyclically bound by three "cellules," extended by skillful variation techniques, and enhanced by a folklike melody (in the trio of ii) such as had come to interest d'Indy greatly.[88] The fourth of the five sonatas, Op. 63 in e/E, for P solo (1908), is d'Indy's most important one, about to be discussed. And the last is Op. 84 in D, for Vc & P, composed in 1924–25, published in 1926, and first played in 1926, by d'Indy and the cellist Edwige Bergeron.[89] This work, one example of d'Indy's late, extraordinary, nationalistic turn to much simpler, neo-French-Baroque styles and to full themes rather than cellules, is virtually a suite, with its four movements entitled "Entrée," "Gavotte en rondeau," "Air," and "Gigue." [90]

D'Indy's *Sonate* in e/E, Op. 63, was composed in 1907, at the start of the third of his four main periods.[91] It was published in 1908, and already introduced, with much acclaim, on January 25 of that year by its dedicatee and the one pianist most identified with it, Blanche Selva.[92] The seriousness with which both the dignified master and his devoted followers approached this one piano sonata paved a broad highway for that acclaim. Yet remarkably few pianists have followed Selva in playing it. Why so few have played either it or Dukas' Sonata in e♭ brings us to a comparison and a further discussion of these two works.[93] The

87. Vallas/D'INDY II 194–95 (with further details on the circumstances of the composing). Cf., also, MERCURE II (Jan.–June, 1906) 280 and 529.

88. Cf. Vallas/D'INDY II 59, 131 (on the origins in 1896 of the [un-]"inspired" main cellule), 138, 194–97 (mentioning influences not only by Franck but by d'Indy's artistic arch rival Debussy), and 363. Op. 59 is described, with exx., in Cobbett/CHAMBER II 6–7 (M. D. Calvocoressi) and was analyzed by 2 of d'Indy's disciples at his Schola cantorum, especially for its cyclical principles—Albert Groz in 1908 (in detail; cf. Vallas/D'INDY II 196) and Blanche Selva in 1913 (Selva/SONATE 259–63).

89. Cf. Vallas/D'INDY II 201–2, 364; Cobbett/CHAMBER II 8.

90. The first mvt. of d'Indy's chamber Suite in A, Op. 91 (pub. in 1930), is called, in the manner of the early suite, "Entrée en Sonate" (cf. Vallas/D'INDY II 202–3).

91. Cf. Vallas/D'INDY II 171 and 198.

92. Vallas/D'INDY II 171.

93. Most of the rare performances of each work have occurred in France, including one of d'Indy's Op. 63 by E. Risler that is praised in Vallas/D'INDY II 175. The performances of Op. 63 by the present author, in about 3 dozen centers between 1941 and 1965, are the only ones in this country known here (not including an informal "reading" about 1935 by the fine pianist Bruce Simonds at Yale University). An Australian recording of Op. 63 (WG-A-2325, with a facs., on the jacket, of the first page of the autograph score) was made by the Australian pianist Raymond Lambert not later than 1965. Demuth/FRENCH 69 mentions performances of the Dukas Son. in e♭ by the French pianist Lélia Gousseau. A probable first

most obvious answer to that question and the most obvious trait common to both works is excessive length, that recurring problem in the larger forms of Romantic music, especially Romantic piano music (SSB VI). The three movements (Va-VF-M/F) of d'Indy's Op. 63 contain 845 measures (282+204+359) in 40 crowded pages and last nearly 38 minutes in all. The four movements (F-S-VF-S/F) of Dukas' Sonata in e♭ contain 1,502 measures (247+181+565+509) in 55 similarly crowded pages and last about 65 minutes in all! The problem exists primarily in the finales (nearly 18 and 28 minutes, respectively), each of which takes up more than 40 per cent of its cycle (as does the finale of Beethoven's Op. 106). There are arid sections in both finales and a sense, especially in d'Indy's finale, that every last detail of textbook "sonata form" must be seen through in full before the coda can begin.[94] Moreover, even if the other movements in both sonatas do not seem too long for their contents, they still help to approach both the performer's and the listener's limits of *Sitzfleisch* endurance. One never can forget that the point of diminishing returns in the length of piano pieces comes well before that of ensemble pieces enhanced by distinct contrasts of timbre.

But these chefs d'oeuvre by d'Indy and Dukas share not only their exceptional lengths and exceptional setting (since no consequential sons. for P solo were left by their chief contemporaries, Franck, Saint-Saëns, and Fauré); they also share certain more positive values by which they stand out at the end of the era.[95] First is the high and serious aesthetic

---

performance of it in this country, at Town Hall in New York on Feb. 29, 1952, brought from reviewer Harold C. Schonberg of *The New York Times* (Mar. 1, 1952, p. 8, col. 8) the opinion that "the work is as empty as can be found in the repertoire," although the possibility that a different performance might have done more for the work was acknowledged.

94. One contemporary reviewer said Op. 63 was stretched to the point of bursting the son.'s framework (Vallas/D'INDY II 176).

95. They invite a detailed comparison; they are similarly paired in Demuth/FRENCH 68 and Salazar/TRENDS 111–12 and 136 (where they are seen as "the most serious achievement[s] in this form in France and in the music of Latin countries" since Liszt's Son. in b). Dukas' Son. in e♭ is outlined, with overemphasis on cyclical relationships, in d'Indy/COURS II/1 431–33, and a little more fully, with objections only to some impractical, quasi-orchestral scoring, in Selva/SONATE 244–48; it is described more subjectively (and more illuminatingly in these instances) in Emmanuel/DUKAS 72–76 and, especially, Cortot/FRANÇAISE I 218–35 (with objections to statements by d'Indy and Selva and references to comments by others), and in Favre/DUKAS 58–69 (with further references to comments by others). D'Indy's Op. 63 is analyzed by the composer himself (with apologies) in d'Indy/COURS II/1 428–31, more briefly (but with almost religious fervor) in Selva/SONATE 263–67, and in exhaustive detail in an article by Albert Groz pub. in 1908 soon after Op. 63 appeared (cf. Selva/SONATE 254), in all instances with emphasis on the cyclical principles. It is discussed as a kind of magnificent failure, because of its intellectuality, in Cortot/FRANÇAISE II 141–48; as a potential success in spite of the

Ex. 82. From the development section in the first movement
of Paul Dukas' Sonata in e♭ (after the Durand ed., p. 8).

aim of the two works. They are lengthy because, as the polish and
perfection of every notational and editorial detail alone would suggest,
each is intended to be a monumental, all-encompassing, and indefecti-
ble experience in the loftiest reaches of the sonata idea. Neither score
gives any outward hint of a programme for that experience, yet one
guesses that nothing less than life itself must be the subject of each.[96]
Dukas was a programmatist at heart, and so was d'Indy in spite of his
avowed absolutism.[97] Second, as suggested earlier, both works show unmistakable influences of Franck, especially in their chromatic harmony,
in their use of enharmonic modulations for surprise and color values,
in certain specific melodic fragments, and in the canonic treatments of
main ideas. Ex. 82 crowds in a little of each of these traits, including a
melodic idea at the change of key that is reminiscent less of the actual
pitch outline than of a kind of idea often used by Franck (as in the
"Choral" theme of *Prélude, choral, et fugue,* or the measures just

intellectuality, given the right performers, in Vallas/D'INDY II 171–76; and as a
supreme masterwork, in which the intellectuality has been unjustly censured, in
Demuth/D'INDY 72–81.

96. Selva/SONATE 247 and 266 sees "a sort of underground cavern full of mysterious horror" in Dukas' 3d mvt., and a victory of Good over Evil in d'Indy's finale
(cf. Cortot/FRANÇAISE II 144).

97. Cf. GROVE IV 472–73.

before the development section of Symphony in d/i). D'Indy's "y" cellule (as in i/64–66) is a saccharine bit that, even without its harmony, almost exudes another melodic style of Franck (as in Son. in A/iii/11–13). (As regards their syntax and larger structural considerations, and except for d'Indy's preoccupation with cyclical principles, the two works do not show the influence of Franck.)

Third, the Dukas and d'Indy piano sonatas have in common their essential broad lyricism, including most of the textural dispositions in which the melody is set. In fact, the scores often look alike, as in sections with the melody in octaves supported by arpeggiated figures in triplets, or with the left hand crossing back and forth over a central right-hand accompaniment figure to supply both bass and soprano melody line, or with the filler being a "Beethoven trill." Fourth, and more specifically, both finales rise to unusually powerful climaxes and both begin with a slow, free introduction. Indeed, d'Indy's introduction is so much like Dukas'—in the stentorian, Lisztian octaves and chords of the first measures, in the rising arpeggiated cadenzas into which those octaves and chords dissolve, and in the unmeasured measures—that he must have taken it, at least unconsciously, as his model. (Curiously, Dukas, in turn, seems to refer deliberately to the similarly free introduction in the finale of Beethoven's Op. 106.)

But the differences between d'Indy's and Dukas' sonatas become at least as revealing as the likenesses. These differences might be explained largely by two considerations, both in d'Indy's favor. At 56, in 1907, d'Indy was more experienced than Dukas at the midpoint in his career, in 1899–1900. D'Indy had composed more and he had gotten around more in the musical world (with Liszt, Wagner, and Brahms being among those he had known).[98] Moreover, as judged here, d'Indy was the more gifted composer, with more to say and more imagination with which to say it. Hence, as a first difference, we find d'Indy's Op. 63, long as it is, to be more concentrated and intense than Dukas' Sonata in e♭. In effect, d'Indy compresses Dukas' 65 minutes into 38. As one result, we get something like the richly scored second variation or the extraordinarily expressive conclusion in d'Indy's first movement, which, as in many a page of Reger's later music, may sound almost atonal at first in the chromatic, dissonant extremes to which it extends traditional harmony. A second, related difference is the greater sense of direction in d'Indy's music, which always aims for and reaches structural goals, where Dukas', for all its broad melodic arches and its fine craftsmanship in textural details, often seems to be rambling. Contributing to the sense of rambling by Dukas is a device used so often

98. Cf. Vallas/D'INDY II 171–72.

in his outer movements that it becomes a mannerism—that is, the extension of an idea by cumulative harmonic sequence (as at the start of Ex. 82, *supra*).

As a third difference, we find d'Indy's greater imagination bearing fruit in more distinctive and more sharply contrasted themes, more resourceful, often contrapuntal dispositions of the texture, and more varied and ingenious solutions to the problems of form. Where Dukas' expanded solution to over-all design is still the standard one of the usual four movements in the usual cycle,[99] d'Indy works out a highly original three-movement cycle. His first movement includes a slow, free introduction, an extended theme and four markedly different variations, each ending with a clear, unifying return to the "y" cellule and

Ex. 83. From the climax in the finale of Vincent d'Indy's Sonata in e/E, Op. 63 (after the Durand ed., p. 39).

the fourth dissolving into some dynamic fantasying around the main ideas, then that expressive conclusion, in which the theme returns in the tonic major key. The second movement is a five-part scherzo (A-B-A-C-A-coda) cast effectively in 5/4 meter. It is difficult to play because of its maximum use of the peculiarly French device of super-imposed hands. And the greater concentration makes d'Indy's work generally more difficult to play. But contrary to some statements,[100] neither work is unreasonably difficult. Neither has quite the virtuoso problems of Liszt's Sonata in b nor the intricacies of Beethoven's Op.

99. The emphasis in Cortot/FRANÇAISE I 217 on Dukas' Son. in eb as one of France's main returns to Beethoven in piano music seems to mean no more than that Dukas followed standard Classic procedures and techniques; cf., also, p. 235.

100. Cf. Vallas/D'INDY II 172 and 175; Demuth/FRENCH 69–71.

106. D'Indy's finale opens with an introduction that returns to that of the first movement except for being freer. The exhaustive "sonata form" follows, based mainly on new themes, but with a return to the "x" cellule or main theme of the first movement, so labeled, just before the recapitulation, and finally one of the grandest climactic codas in all piano literature. This last, which more than makes up for those arid sections before it, is more telling than Dukas' climactic coda. In the first place, it reaches a clearer goal again, peaking on the biggest, most chorale-like statement of the "x" theme, with the main "sonata allegro" theme joining below its last two phrases (Ex. 83). And secondly, like a veritable "Liebestod" (the parallel, even to the line and harmony, is striking), it relaxes courageously on the last page into a quiet, gentle, sublimatory end.

Dukas showed only casual and occasional interest in cyclical relationships. But a word should be added about d'Indy's cyclical methods, his intellectuality, and his intransigent nature (including even the excessive moral principles and the hateful social prejudices), as any or all of these may have affected his masterpiece Op. 63. As noted earlier (also in SSB VI), d'Indy himself and his followers made much of his avowed creation of Op. 63 out of three germinating (contrapuntally related) "cellules," "x," "y," and "z," in that order of importance. But in this work the musician governs the theorist, the cellules never get in the way of the musical flow, and, moreover, the final climactic return to "x" achieves positive values as stunning as the complete chorale statements in the finales of Bruckner's last symphonies. If the intellectuality obstructs the musical flow at all it may be in those sections where the ultrachromatic harmony becomes most recherché and esoteric. But more likely, as an obstruction to the work, is the intransigent nature that would yield in no detail of that "sonata allegro" finale, to the point where the listener feels he cannot tolerate one more repetition of the trill bridge theme or the lyrical second theme to which it leads.

Minor Composers in Late-Romantic France

Alongside and often associated with the important composers we have been considering, most of some 30 others yet to be noted can get only passing recognition. The violinist **Paul Viardot** (1857–1941), son of the important singer Pauline Viardot-Garcia and dedicatee of Fauré's Op. 13 (*supra*), himself left three sonatas for P & Vn (pub. in 1883, ?, and 1931) and one for Vc & P (1928), the earliest of which (Op. 5 in G; 3 mvts.), was reviewed as showing little of consequence beyond too self-conscious an effort to be original.[101] A contemporary and a more facile, less imaginative version of Saint-Saëns, **Charles-Henri-René Boisdeffre** (1838–1906), left three more duo sonatas (one for P & Cl-or-Vn and 2 for P & Vn, pub. between 1875 and *ca.* 1910), among the nearly twenty chamber works that comprise his chief contribution.[102] One of the many forgotten winners of the Grand Prix de Rome from the Paris Conservatoire (in 1870), **Charles-Édouard Lefebvre** (1843–1917) left a conventional but skillful Sonata for Vc & P, Op. 98 in a (pub. in 1896) that won a good response, especially for its slow movement.[103] And the composer and conductor who presided in 1916 over the Société française de musique de chambre, **(Paul-Alexandre-) Camille Chevillard** (1859–1923), left two duo sonatas, Opp. 8 in g, for P & Vn (pub. in 1894), and 15 in B♭, for P & Vc (pub. in 1897).[104] These last are big works, superior in their originality and workmanship, and variously incisive, poetic, dramatic, and lyrical. Franck's influence is felt, though not oppressively, in their chromatic harmony, especially when there are successive unresolved 9th chords, and in both their syntax and their cyclical relationships. Each of the three-movement works derives almost entirely, and sometimes excessively, from its initial motive. Op. 8 is freer, more complex, and more changeable than Op. 15, with chromaticism that at times brings us even closer than d'Indy does to Reger's tonal amorphousness, with a fantasy slow movement, and with a "Mouv^t de Polonaise, brillant et très rhythmé" that makes a stunning finale.

Better known than Chevillard, though less deserving of renown as viewed here, was the short-lived composer **(Jean-Joseph-Nicolas-) Guillaume Lekeu** (1870–94).[105] As to the question of whether Lekeu should be grouped with (Walloon-) Belgian or French composers,[106] we resolve it here, as usual, by placing him where he was most active, in Paris. There he entered the University in 1888, started the study with his compatriot Franck in late 1889 that lasted until the latter's death a year later, then went to d'Indy for further study.[107] His late start at 19 and early death at 24 left him but few years for serious study,

---

101. mw XVIII (1887) 466–67. Cf. grove VIII 763 (F. A. Marshall); Altmann/ kammermusik 230.

102. Cf. Cobbett/chamber I 143 (A. Piriou & W. W. Cobbett); baker 175; mdc IV (1906) xxxiv.

103. mdc IV (1906) xxxviii. Cf. mgg VIII 464–65 (G. Ferchault).

104. Cf. grove II 205–6 (G. Ferrari & M. L. Pereyra); baker 284; Cobbett/chamber I 274 (W. J. Mitson).

105. Cf. mgg VIII 594–95 (A. Van der Linden), with further references; Sonneck/ lekeu (including much of the information available on the sons.).

106. Cf. Sonneck/lekeu 111–13.

107. Cf. Sonneck/lekeu 116–19, 136.

yet he managed to complete nearly 20 main works during that time and to get to various stages of completion in perhaps 40 more.[108]

Three sonatas figure in that output of Lekeu. One is the *Sonate pour piano* in g, composed in April, 1891, according to an inscription at the end of its printed score, which was published posthumously in 1900 (?) by E. Baudoux in Paris, predecessor to Rouart, Lerolle.[109] About the genesis of this work we have only two bits of unconfirmed information, supplied by Marcel Obran with the publication in the *Courrier musical* for 1910 of a few letters by Lekeu, but evidently based on letters or portions not yet published:[110]

A *Suite* for piano was published after his death under the title of Sonata. He did not consider it more than a study in composition; but it is a study of real beauty. The fugue remains a monumental example of the genre. [And quoting a reference to this work in an unpub. letter by Lekeu:] "This passage I should not to-day write again, but the fugue is *bien*."

Actually, "Suite" does seem like the more appropriate title, although no standard title applies in its textbook sense. The work is relatively short (19 pp.) and contains five movements—"Très modéré," one page, chordal and preludial; a 7-page fugue in the home key, without heading or tempo indication (probably andante); a 4-page fugue in the relative minor (b) of the major dominant key, again without initial markings (probably andante); "Dans un mouvement plus lent," 4 pages, in the home key, improvisatory, climactic, largely contrapuntal, and based on the single idea that prevails in all five movements; and a somewhat similar, 3-page conclusion, in the tonic major key, with no initial marking other than a return to the quarter-note beat "du Prélude." "Sonata" might have seemed more appropriate as a title if this work had been scored for organ and designated for church use.

Lekeu's other two sonatas are duos. One, for Vc & P in F, was composed as far as he got with it in 1888, completed by d'Indy for publication by Rouart, Lerolle in 1910, but not actually published until 1923. It is reportedly a weak and amateurish work (as well it might be at the start of Lekeu's serious study), with no acknowledgment by either Lekeu or d'Indy of its borrowing in the outer movements, note for

108. Cf. Sonneck/LEKEU 119–20, with a dated list of main works.

109. The pub. dates of all 3 sons. are given variously. The Baudoux plate no. for the P Son. is 601 and the address 37 Boulevard Haussmann (cf. Hopkinson/PARISIAN 7).

110. As trans. in Sonneck/LEKEU 130. A first collection of Lekeu's interesting letters was pub. in the *Courrier musical* for 1906, ed. by de Stoecklin; they are trans. in part in Sonneck/LEKEU, *passim*, and in Abraham/LEKEU; cf., also, Closson & Borren/BELGIQUE 274–75. Another set of Lekeu's letters, to Octave Maus, is pub. in Van der Linden/LEKEU.

note, of a main theme from the first movement of Liszt's "Faust Symphony." [111] The other duo is Lekeu's best known and most success-ful work, the Sonata for Vn & P in G, composed in 1892 and published by E. Baudoux in 1894 but posthumously.[112] The success was insured when its eventual dedicatee, Eugène Ysaÿe, undoubtedly recalling his close association and success with the violin sonata of another com-patriot, Franck (supra), suggested to Lekeu that he write such a work, in February, 1892.[113] Lekeu completed it, "at great pains" and "fa-tigued" by the effort, apparently in July, well before Ysaÿe's first of several private performances of it, in November, 1892, with Lekeu, and his first public performance of it, with a Madame Theroine, at one of Octave Maus's "Cercle des XX" concerts in Brussels, March 7, 1893.[114] Thenceforth, for a while, the work was performed widely.[115]

The most frequent evaluation of Lekeu's music might be summed up as an acknowledgment of much promise, a recognition of some gau-cheries and inexperience, and regrets that the composer did not live to fulfill the promise.[116] After a rereading of his two completed sonatas the temptation here has been to ask whether even the "much promise" does not need re-evaluation.[117] It is possible that a good part of the exceptional interest shown in Lekeu ever since his early death has grown primarily out of the patriotic Ysaÿe's masterful projections of the violin Sonata, the desire to point to a worthy Belgian successor to Franck, and the popular fascination with the tragic spectacle of such an ingenuously eager, willing composer, who could be affected almost traumatically as he discovered Beethoven, Wagner, and Franck, or when Ysaÿe played his own sonata,[118] yet had to die before he could realize his "promise"? Otherwise, even allowing for our vast changes of taste today, it is hard to understand earlier statements such as that of Sonneck in 1919, ". . . every unbiased critic will have to admit that of violin sonatas composed since Brahms and Franck, Lekeu's is in-ferior to none." [119] In the experience of this study Lekeu is not entitled

111. Cf. Weigl/VIOLONCELL 77; Sonneck/LEKEU 120, 121.
112. The date of first pub., which is lacking in HOFMEISTER and generally given incorrectly (cf. Sonneck/LEKEU 120 and 140), is correct in Altmann/KAMMERMUSIK 213 and specified as September 1894 in Selva/SONATA 240. A memorial engraving for that ed. is reproduced in Closson & Borren/BELGIQUE 283. Rouart, Lerolle re-printed the work in 1907 and 1934.
113. Cf. Sonneck/LEKEU 137; Ysaÿe/YSAŸE 184–86.
114. Ysaÿe/YSAŸE 185–86 and Van der Linden/LEKEU 158.
115. Cf. Sonneck/LEKEU 140–41. No standard recording is pub. as of 1967.
116. Cf. the sample evaluations quoted in Sonneck/LEKEU 109–11.
117. Cf. GROVE V 124 (M. Kufferath).
118. Cf. Cobbett/CHAMBER II 95 (G. Systermans); Abraham/LEKEU 62–63, 85–86, and 108–; Ysaÿe/YSAŸE 185–86.
119. Sonneck/LEKEU 140.

to compete with Strauss (at the same age!), Reger, Fauré, Saint-Saëns, and the other main composers we have been discussing. Apparently Franck was too near the end of his own years when Lekeu came to him to leave any significant comments. But it is interesting that for all of their sympathy with "the lad" and their tendency then to speak in strong terms, two of the contemporary musicians best qualified to judge, d'Indy and Dukas, wrote only in the most guarded terms of Lekeu's talent.[120] Nor, after its first performance, did the several reviewers praise the violin Sonata without distinct reservations about its skill and content.[121]

To be sure, Lekeu's violin Sonata has given many a musician real pleasure. Milhaud writes, for example, "How many times did we play together Lekeu's Sonata, which filled us with such enthusiasm in those days!" (around 1910).[122] And this work, now in the standard three-movement plan (In/F-S-F), does show improvements, as in its expressive use of the violin or several sections of melody and harmony that surge warmly; and it does show more "promise" than the piano "Sonata," which at best can be said to reveal competence in the *fugue d'école*. But further experience with the violin Sonata suggests that Lekeu's own several references to his struggles in composition and, in particular, to his dissatisfaction with that work after its completion were not simply reports of typical creative growth but included genuine and justifiable misgivings as to the actual significance of his talent.[123] Today the more curious harmonies and irregular textures (especially the voice-leading in the pedestrian piano writing) do not sound like gropings toward new styles but like the unlearned crudities of an average student who got a late start.[124] More serious is the sense one now gets that the work is based on one (not very substantial or prepossessing) idea not only in the interest of cyclical relationships but because no other ideas could be found; and that the work is free not only in the interest of Romantic abandon but because better structural solutions could not be found. The germinal idea, incidentally, happens to get uncomfortably close to that in the piano Sonata and in other works by Lekeu, too.[125]

120. Cf. Dukas/ÉCRITS 176–78; d'Indy/COURS II/2 270 and III 354; d'Indy/FRANCK 254; also, the negative evaluation in Selva/SONATE 240–42.

121. Cf. Van der Linden/LEKEU 163–64; Sonneck/LEKEU 111; also, MERCURE II (Jan.–June, 1906) 472 and 529.

122. Milhaud/NOTES 23.

123. Cf. Sonneck/LEKEU 140–41, 146, 147.

124. MacDowell was amused over the "queerness" of the Vn Son. (Gilman/MACDOWELL 75).

125. Cf. Cobbett/CHAMBER II 95.

Gabriel (Henri-Constant-) Pierné (1863–1937), a student of and successor to Franck as organist and the esteemed composer of the oratorio *La Croisade des Enfants,* left three published sonatas—Op. 36 in d, for Vn & P (pub. in 1901), the only one that has been played more than a few times; Op. 46 in f♯, for Vc & P (composed in 1922 and pub. in 1923); and Op. 48 in C, a "Sonata da camera" for Fl, Vc, and P.[126] Op. 46 is a free but well-balanced form in one movement that includes all the characteristic styles and tempos of the complete sonata cycle. Although not otherwise innovational, both of Pierné's duos achieve real musical distinction in their expressive warmth, resourceful harmony (nearer to Fauré's than Franck's), melodic grace, rhythmic variety, and light but telling sonority, all with surprising economy of means.

Four other, interassociated organists in Paris of high repute and influence made worthy if not numerous contributions to the sonata. **Charles-Marie (-Jean-Albert) Widor** (1844–1937), another successor to Franck and a productive composer in all branches, left three sonatas, two for Vn & P and one for Vc & P, that were published in the first decade of this century.[127] Although these duos have not attracted the interest of his important, variform "Symphonies" for organ, they too show, much as in Saint-Saëns, an expert craftsman, an eclectic able to draw at will on the past as far back as Bach, and a creative musician both subtle and imaginative.[128] The blind organist **Louis Vierne** (1870–1937), a pupil of both Franck and Widor, left two more duo sonatas published about the same time, one each for P & Vn (Op. 23 in g, 1908) and P & Vc (Op. 27 in b, 1911).[129] These duos are similar in style and skill to Pierné's, including the suggestions of Fauré's harmony. Ysaÿe, who introduced the four-movement violin Sonata (F-M-M-In/VF) with Pugno in 1908, won success with it, writing Vierne that this work (composed during a period of severe personal troubles for Vierne) was much the best work of its sort after Franck's.[130] The cello Sonata, a somewhat freer work in three movements (S/F-VS-F) also composed in a difficult period, has been rated similarly high in quality and idiomatic treatment among the fewer examples of its time, place, and type,[131] although one German critic, after describing the cello part as masculinely energetic and the piano part as femininely

126. Cf. mgg X 1257–61 (G. Ferchault); Cobbett/chamber II 222–23 (A. Piriou & W. W. Cobbett); mercure II (Jan.–June, 1906) 529.

127. Altmann/kammermusik 231 and 266.

128. Cf. grove IX 284–85 (H. Grace); Cobbett/chamber II 580–81 (A. Piriou).

129. Cf. mgg XIII 1612–13 (F. Raugel); Gavoty/vierne, a full study of the man and his works, with detailed list of works (pp. 298–312) and discussion of the sons. (pp. 269–71).

130. Gavoty/vierne 91, 99–101, 113.

131. Gavoty/vierne 269–70, 110–11.

delicate, found only the first movement not to be somewhat weak and dry.[132]

The prolific composer **Felix-Alexandre Guilmant** (1837–1911), a student, like Widor, of Jacques Nicolas Lemmens in Brussels and a cofounder with d'Indy of the Schola cantorum, left eight organ sonatas published between 1874 and 1907.[133] Although the harmony is more traditional and the texture heavier and simpler, these sonatas (with "Suite" as an alternate title in No. 7 and "Symphonie" in No. 8) are like Widor's "Symphonies" in their splendorous orchestral, highly idiomatic uses of the instrument, and their variform cycles. Guilmant's sonatas have three to five movements, including examples of the prelude, chorale and fugue, scherzo, march, minuet, recitative, and "sonata form." **Francois-Clement-Théodore Dubois** (1837–1924), a successor to Saint-Saëns and renowned teacher at the Paris Conservatoire, included three sonatas among his many works in all main categories of music.[134] Two are duos, Sonata in A for Vn & P (1900), a light but appealing work that Ysaÿe and Pugno enjoyed playing,[135] and Sonata in D for Vc & P (1905). The other is Sonata in a, for P solo (1908), a highly effective cycle of three movements (F-S-S/VF) that is epigonic in its conservatism, neat and convenient brilliance, and unabashed eclecticism. Typical are the dramatic opening measures (Ex. 84) that soon peter out and the clear reminders of Schubert, Wagner, Tchaikovsky, Grieg, and others as one reads from theme to theme. One is not surprised to learn that Dubois was close at one time or another to Franck, Liszt, Fauré, Ambroise Thomas, Saint-Saëns, Delibes, and numerous other contemporaries.

Albéric Magnard (1865–1914) was a pupil of d'Indy, a member of his circle early in this century, and a Wagner enthusiast though not an imitator.[136] Two of the five valued chamber works in his small (sadly interrupted) output are four-movement duo sonatas—Op. 13 in G, for Vn & P (1903; ded. to Ysaÿe) and Op. 20 in A, for Vc & P (1911). These do not lack melodic invention or emotional excitement, nor go beyond their time in free forms or styles. But they stand apart by virtue of their abstraction and aloofness from popular taste, as manifested especially in somewhat severe, harsh textures, with frequent accented, unprepared dissonances and a somewhat stark, unidiomatic

132. dm XI/2 (1911–12) 301–2.
133. Cf. mgg V 1099–1101 (F. Raugel), with further references; Dufourcq/française 172–78; Frotscher/orgelspiel II 1213–14; Kremer/organ 187–88.
134. Cf. mgg III 838–41 (F. Raugel), with dated list; Altmann/kammermusik 201 and 255.
135. Cobbett/chamber I 399 (W. W. Cobbett).
136. Cf. mgg VIII 1481–82 (G. Ferchault), with further references.

Ex. 84. From the opening of Théodore Dubois' Sonata in a (after the original Heugel ed. of 1908).

treatment of the piano.[137] A Franck pupil and another Wagnerian, the Austrian-born violinist **Sylvio Lazzari** (1857–1944) left a single sonata among numerous works, Op. 24 in E, for Vn & P (1894).[138] This three-movement work (F-S-VF), successfully introduced by Ysaÿe, is strongly reminiscent of Franck's styles and cyclical treatment. But it has enough individuality of melody, harmony, and instrumental technique to be interesting in its own right.[139] **Gustave (Marie Victor Fernand) Sama-zeuilh** (1877–?), a student of Chausson and d'Indy, a friend of Richard Strauss, and a protégé of Fauré and Dukas, left among relatively few works one sonata each for P solo (1903;?) and Vn & P (1904, in b/B).[140] The latter is described as being close to Franck in idiom, with some fine themes, but labored and often suffocatingly thick in texture.[141]

137. Cf. the slightly different reactions in Selva/SONATE 277–83 (with exx.); MERCURE I (1905) 141 and II (Jan.–June, 1906) 31 and 529; Cobbett/CHAMBER II 109–10 (M. Labey).

138. Cf. MGG VIII 403–4 (G. Ferchault).

139. It is described, with 11 generous exx., in Cobbett/CHAMBER II 91–93 (H. Woollett & W. W. Cobbett).

140. Cf. MGG XI 1331 (R. Dumesnil), but the P son. could not be confirmed in HOFMEISTER, PAZDÍREK, early Durand cats., nor other sources available here.

141. Cf. MW XXXVI (1905) 407, 408; MERCURE II (Jan.–June, 1906) 426; Cobbett/CHAMBER II 326–27 (F. Schmitt & W. W. Cobbett).

The four duo sonatas by the Languedocian composer **Paul Lacombe** (1837–1927) include three for Vn & P and one for Vc & P, all published between 1868 and 1902 in Paris.[142] These works, which show the Classical orientation to be expected of a devoted pupil of Bizet and warm admirer of Saint-Saëns, were uniformly praised for their skill and their charm when they appeared.[143] But today they seem rather flat, light, and inconsequential, probably reflecting both the prolificity of Lacombe and his continuing orientation toward Mendelssohn, Schumann, and Chopin. The Polish-born pianist **Sigismund (Denis Antoni) Stojowski** (1869 [not 1870]–1946) studied with Delibes and Massenet in Paris and with Paderewski before emigrating from Paris to the United States in 1906.[144] His three duo sonatas—two for Vn & P, one for Vc & P, published between 1894 and 1912—are melodious, transparent, and flowing enough to have immediate appeal.[145] But as heard here they suffer from rhythms and phrases that incessantly reinforce the barline and harmonic progressions that convert Fauré's idiom into clichés.

Much broader is the musical outlook in the one sonata by **Georges-Martin Witkowski** (1867–1943), a pupil of d'Indy who established his own Schola cantorum in Lyons in 1924.[146] As with d'Indy's Op. 63, Witkowski's Op. 16 in g, for Vn & P, was composed in 1907 and published a year later by Durand (ded. to the violinist Jacques Thibaud). It is a big, impassioned, soaring work, almost as long as d'Indy's, close to the latter in idiom, and even more thoroughly based on a progenitor theme and cyclical principles. The first of its but two movements is a large "sonata form" and the second a set of five variations in E, of which the last returns to g and serves as a finale. The skill and musicality of this work are impressive. Blanche Selva finds it overly complex in its cyclical derivations and too orchestrally conceived for its setting.[147] Although the writing has not seemed that orchestral as viewed here, the progenitor theme does seem to be overdone, the more so as it is lacking somewhat in inherent vitality.

142. Cf. MGG VIII 39–40 (G. Ferchault); GROVE V 8–9 (M. L. Pereyra); Cobbett/CHAMBER II 87 (L. Moulin).

143. E.g., MW XXXIV (1903) 163 (E. Segnitz) and NZM LXVI/2 (1870) 311, both on Op. 8 in a, for Vn & P; MW XI (1880) 359, on Op. 17 in f, for Vn & P; MW XXXI (1900) 619, 620 (E. Segnitz), on Op. 98 in G, for Vn & P.

144. Cf. MGG XII 1392 (J. Ekiert). BAKER 1576; Cobbett/CHAMBER II 459 (E. Evans).

145. Cf. the review of Op. 37 in E (not e), for Vn & P, in DM XII/3 (1912–13) 107.

146. Cf. Boucher/WITKOWSKI, especially pp. 198, 202, 207; GROVE IX (M. L. Pereyra) 324.

147. Selva/SONATE 252–58, with outline analysis and exx. Cf., also, Cobbett/CHAMBER II 588 (A. Piriou).

A negative review of a Sonata in f♯ (not f), for P solo, by d'Indy's pupil **Antoine Mariotte** (1875–1944) appears to reflect not on the composer but on the reviewer, who seems not to have understood either the idiom or the independent ideas and uncompromising style of Mariotte.[148] But a negative review of Sonata in b, for Vc and P (1907, not 1902) by the Belgian in Paris **Louis Delune** (1876–1940) seems justified in crediting the three-movement work (F-S-Ro) with little more than satisfactory workmanship.[149] Two duo sonatas, one each for Vn & P and Vc & P (1907 and 1910), by **Albert Bertelin** (1872–1951), pupil of Dubois, Widor, and Pugno, are described as solid in construction, cyclical in Franck's manner, and conservative.[150] Two women composers of published sonatas may be noted in late-Romantic France. The Countess **Armande de Polignac** (1876–1962), although a student of both Fauré and d'Indy, fared less well than the other, for the second of her two sonatas for Vn & P (1902 and 1911) was branded a dull and affected work.[151] But the much better known pianist and composer **Cécile (-Louise-Stéphanie) Chaminade** (1857–1944), a pupil of Godard and others, left a Sonata in c, Op. 21 for P solo (1895; ded. to Mozskowski) that, both in its ideas and their development, rises a shade above "the level of agreeable drawing-room music" usually regarded as the upper limit of her art.[152] Chaminade's Op. 21 is a concise cycle of the traditional three movements (VF-M-F), well scored in idioms no later than Mendelssohn's. Of the same ilk are at least two sonatas (especially Son. in C) and three sonatinas for P solo, and one Sonatina for P-duet, all published in the later 19th century, by the pianist, prolific composer, and longtime teacher at the Paris Conservatoire, **Theodore Lack** (1846–1921);[153] also, three duo sonatas by Dubois' pupil **Jules Mouquet** (1867–1946), one each for Vn & P, Vc & P, and Fl & P ("La Flûte de Pan"), published between 1906 and 1912.[154] A "Sonate pour piano en 4 parties" (sold together and separately; ca. 1907) by a follower of Franck and pupil of d'Indy, **Marcel Labey** (1875–?) retains the har-

148. DM VI/4 (1906–7) 306 (A. Leitzmann). Cf. MGG VIII 1660 (G. Ferchault); GROVE V 581–82 (F. Raugel).

149. DM VI/4 (1906–7) 373 (A. Laser). Cf. BAKER 369; Closson & Borren/BELGIQUE 258–59; Cobbett/CHAMBER I 323 (G. Systermans), with wrong dates and a reference, also, to a Son. in d, for Vn & P (actually 1907, too).

150. Cobbett/CHAMBER I 124 (A. Piriou). Cf. Riemann/LEXIKON I 163; LAROUSSE I 102.

151. DM X/4 (1910) 376 (W. Altmann). Cf. BAKER 1262 and Suppl. 104; Altmann/KAMMERMUSIK 221.

152. As in GROVE II 156–57 (G. Ferrari). Cf. Elson/WOMAN 174–77.

153. Cf. BAKER 894; PAZDÍREK IX 33–38; Altmann/KAMMERMUSIK 288; Westerby/PIANOFORTE 186.

154. Cf. BAKER 1122; Altmann/KAMMERMUSIK 217, 261, 277; DM XIII/3 (1912–13) 107 (W. Altmann).

monic idiom of his mentors and the standard designs but adopts a clipped, neat, chordal, and less pianistic texture and a continuously jerky alternation of triplet, duplet, and dotted rhythms that produces an almost flippant, dancelike distortion of d'Indy's style. Three duo sonatas—two for Vn & P and one for Va & P (1901–24)—resort to this style at times, but in a more folklike manner.[155]

The American-born composer **Swan Hennessy** (1866–1929) studied in England and Germany, spent most of his adult years in Paris, but paid allegiance chiefly to his Irish descent in his light, contrived "Sonata in Irish Style" for Vn & P (Op. 14 in F, 1905) and his freer, three-movement *Sonatine celtique* for Va & P (Op. 62 in E♭, 1925).[156] The Alsatian organist **Marie-Joseph Erb** (1858–1944), who studied with Saint-Saëns among others before returning to Strasbourg, left a pleasing, readily playable organ sonata in Franck's idiom and three sonatas for Vn & P, all published between 1901 and 1931, during his increasing interest in chamber music.[157]

Some Belgian and Dutch Composers in the Late-Romantic Era

The exceptionally small contribution to the sonata that we found in Belgium midway in the Romantic Era (ssb XII, near the end) was only slightly bettered by the end of the century. However, it must be remembered that here two of the best known Belgian contributors, Franck and Lekeu, have already been put where they resided, in Paris (*supra*), and another, the peripatetic Désiré Pâque (1867–1939), is put with the Moderns because, although his honeyed, Franckian chord progressions belie the fact, he deliberately cultivated his own brand of "atonalité." [158] Certain others are noted here only for the earlier works they wrote before they turned to participate in newer trends. The best known name is that of the leading Belgian violinist, **Eugène Ysaÿe** (1858–1931), who studied with Wieniawski and Vieuxtemps, and whom we have already met, sometimes with the pianist Raoul Pugno, doing yeoman's service for the violin sonatas of Franck, Lekeu, and numerous other composers.[159] Among more than two dozen published works by Ysaÿe are a set of six sonatas for unaccompanied Vn, Op. 27 (1924), and

155. Cf. Cobbett/CHAMBER II 84 (A. Piriou); MGG VIII 12–13 (F. Raugel); MERCURE I (1905) 306, on Labey's Son. for Va & P in C (1904).

156. Cf. Cobbett/CHAMBER I 550–52 (H. Woollett), with several errors and with exx. from Op. 62; MGG VI 152–53 (G. Ferchault), with dated list of works, including 2 other duo sonatinas (both 1929) but not an earlier *Sonatine*, Op. 43 (cf. DM XII/2 [1912–13] 108 [R. H. Stein]) nor Op. 14; HOFMEISTER 1905, 76.

157. Cf. MGG III 1464–65 (J. Feschotte); DM XI/2 (1911–12) 168 (E. Schnorr von Carolsfeld).

158. Cf. MGG X 739–40 (A. Van der Linden); Closson & Borren/BELGIQUE 280.

159. Cf. BAKER 1832–33.

160a   a single Sonata for unaccompanied Vc, Op. 28 in c (1924).[160] The six
sonatas of Op. 27 are dedicated respectively to Szigeti, Thibaud, Enesco,
Kreisler, Crickboom, and Quiroga. Inspired by hearing Joseph Szigeti
play one of Bach's unaccompanied "sonatas," Ysaÿe makes references
to the latter in Op. 27 (including a fugal section in Son. 1/ii and direct
quotations from the "Preludio" of Bach's Partita in E, in Son. 2/i).
For the rest, these are light, fanciful, short but multimovement works
that exploit all the standard resources of the virtuoso, ostensibly in
the national and technical styles and with movement titles appropriate
to their dedicatees. But although their dominant, chromatic harmonies
and frequent crescendo passages are often portentous, nothing significant is ever attained in these sonatas.

The best known of the few other Belgian sonata composers is the
organist and prolific composer **Joseph** (-**Marie-Alphonse-Nicolas**)
Jongen (1873–1953), who came to know Richard Strauss, d'Indy, Fauré,
and Chausson, along with other composers.[161] Among Jongen's many
chamber works (his favorite medium) are at least eight sonatas in varied
scorings, including two for Vn & P and one each for Vc & P, Fl & P,
Vn & Vc ("Sonate-duo"), P solo "Sonatine," organ, and unaccompanied
Vn (all pub. between 1903 and 1938). A sampling of Jongen's earlier,
published sonatas (before his style changed somewhat in keeping with
newer trends) reveals a knowing craftsman, sure of his form and writing
techniques, thoroughly conversant with but not overwhelmed by
Franck's idiom, and generally on the conservative side of his contemporaries. There is also sensitivity, delicate passagework, and fire in
the music. Yet it fails for the most part to achieve real creative distinction. The ideas are a little plain, the motives are worked somewhat
too hard and even mechanically, the phrase syntax tends to be too
predictable, and the piano writing is routine.[162] The composer **Victor
Vreuls** (1876–1944) left Belgium in 1901 to study with d'Indy, then
taught at the Schola cantorum, and later became director of the Luxem-
bourg Conservatory (up to 1926).[163] His chamber works include three
published duo sonatas, two for Vn & P (1901 and 1919) and one for

160. Cf. the list of works and description of Op. 27 in Ysaÿe/YSAŸE 244–45 and
222–25; also, Closson & Borren/BELGIQUE 261 (dismissing his music except for its
technical treatment of the Vn).

161. Cf. MGG VII 169–73 (A. Van der Linden); Closson & Borren/BELGIQUE 276;
Cobbett/CHAMBER II 39–40 (G. Systermans & W. W. Cobbett); Cat. BELGISCH V.

162. But except for the piano writing, these objections were not raised in contemporary reviews seen here, as in MERCURE II (Jan.–June, 1906) 168 (on Op. 27
in D, for Vn & P); DM X/3 (1910–11) 31 (W. Altmann on Op. 34 in E, for Vn & P);
DM XII/4 (1912–13) 177 (H. Schlemüller on Op. 39 in c, for Vc & P).

163. Cf. GROVE IX 78 (E. Blom); Closson & Borren/BELGIQUE 276; Cobbett/CHAMBER
II 560 (G. Systermans and W. W. Cobbett); MERCURE II (Jan.–June, 1906) 268–69.

Vc & P (1923). The first of these, dedicated to Ysaÿe and composed before Vreuls, too, became interested in newer trends, is an extended, serious, individualized, energetic, and convincing work in three movements (F-S-F) that also shows the clear influence but not the domination of Franck.

More briefly in Belgium may be mentioned a composer of "deeply lyrical, often dramatic oratorios," **Joseph Ryelandt** (1870–1965), who is credited with at least 21 sonatas—11 for P solo, 7 for Vn & P, and 3 for Vc & P, from all of which at least 4 were published, between 1897 and 1912.[164] **Raymond Moulaert** (1875–1962) left a Sonata for P solo (1917), a *Sonate en forme de passacaille* for P & Vc (1942), and a prizewinning Sonata in d for organ (1906), the last regarded as Franckian in flavor, fluent, well constructed, and conventional.[165] And **Nicolas Daneau** (1866–1944) should at least be named for his *Suite en forme de sonate* in d, for Vn & P (1912), reviewed as a concise work, accessible and likely to appeal to amateurs.[166]

The Dutch interest in the sonata was a little more. One of the better known composers was the organist **Samuel de Lange, Jr.** (1840–1911), who left at least 16 published sonatas—8 for his instrument (1870–1903), 4 for P & Vn (1875–96), 2 for P & Vc (1883 and 1899), and one each for P solo (1892) and P-duet (1881).[167] These works, several of which seem to have circulated rather widely for a time, were greeted by reviewers as skillful, derivative (mostly from Mendelssohn), and sometimes dry.[168] Only occasionally does one find in them a distinctive musical personality. Thus, in de Lange's Op. 63 in c, for P solo, the scoring is unquestionably Mendelssohnian, but there is some individuality in the bold rhythms, and in the modulations when they approach the new key with deceptive cadences and with dissonant harmonies that grow out of diagonal relationships (as in Op. 63/i/88–103). The use of "The Star-Spangled Banner" as a theme for variations in the third (final) movement of his organ Sonata 4 in D, Op. 28 (1879), may reflect its dedication to the outstanding American organist

---

164. MGG XI 1205–6 (M. Boereboom); cf. BAKER Suppl. 113.

165. DM VIII/1 298 (E. Schnorr von Carolsfeld). Cf. MGG IX 672–73 (A. Van der Linden); Cat. BELGISCH VIII; Closson & Borren/BELGIQUE 289.

166. DM XII/4 (1912–13) 318 (W. Altmann). Cf. BAKER 347.

167. Cf. Kremer/ORGAN 200–201; Altmann/KAMMERMUSIK 213, 259, 302; MGG VIII 185–86 (A. Annegarn); Reeser/NEDERLANDSE 176. **Samuel de Lange, Sr.** (1811–84), esteemed by Brahms, had also left several concert organ sons. (cf. MGG VIII 185; MW XVIII [1887] 352 [about the 4th organ son. and its marchlike fugal finale]).

168. E.g., cf. MW XII (1881) 162 (on the first Vn son., Op. 19 in G, 1875); MW XVI (1885) 218–19 (on the P-duet, Op. 33 in e, with objections to the length of the fugue, 7 pp., in the first mvt.); MW XXXIV (1903) 740 and 741 (G. Riemenschneider on the 8th organ son., finding the finale uninteresting).

Clarence Eddy.[169] Similarly numerous, conservative, and unoriginal are the at least fifteen sonatas by the conductor, editor, and prolific composer **Julius Röntgen** (1855–1933), who studied with Reinecke, Hauptmann, and Franz Lachner, met Liszt, and knew Brahms and Grieg well.[170] These sonatas, of which about eight were published (between 1873 and 1922), are scored variously for P & Vn, P & Va, P & Vc, P & Ob, unaccompanied Vn, and P solo. Numerous reviews, although more favorable in later years, largely concur on the competence, the influence of Mendelssohn, Schumann, and eventually Brahms, and the rather weak creative spark that Röntgen's sonatas reveal.[171]

The sensitive, enterprising pianist **Dirk Schäfer** (1873–1931), a pupil of Max Pauer, also turned to the past for the styles and forms in the six sonatas (1901–18) that figure among his relatively few works.[172] These include four for Vn & P, one for Vc & P, and one, *Sonate inaugurale*, Op. 9 in b♭ (pub. in 1913), for P solo. Schäfer's first two violin sonatas were well received.[173] Op. 9, which became the best known of his sonatas because of his own telling performances of it and because of its slightly programmatic title and character, was reviewed as an example of "the most modern trends," [174] although today it conveys the same sense of post Mendelssohn, Schumann, Brahms, and Wagner that the reviewers had noted in Schäfer's earlier sonatas and that dates his music to the extent of making its revival unlikely. Yet there is much skill in these well organized, smoothly flowing, richly if not too thickly scored sonatas, with their Wagnerian polyphony, their extremes of range and dynamics, and their copious editorial advices. The "inaugural" or fanfare character of Op. 9, which is also present

169. Kremer/ORGAN 74–75.

170. Cf. MGG XI 613–15 (J. H. v. d. Meer); Reeser/NEDERLANDSE 242–45; PAZDÍREK XII 439–41; Altmann/KAMMERMUSIK 223 and 263; Cobbett/CHAMBER II 301 (H. Antcliffe).

171. E.g., cf. NZM LXIX/1 (1873) 190–91 (on Opp. 1 for P & Vn and 2 for P solo); MW IV (1873) 146–47 (on Op. 2) and VI (1875) 627–28 (on Op. 1, with ex.); MMR V (1875) 173–74 (on Opp. 1 and 2); NZM LXXXI/2 (1885) 418 (E. Klitzsch on Op. 20 for P & Vn); DM VI/1 (1906–7) 231 (W. Altmann on Op. 40 for P & Vn); NZM CI (1905) 338 (on Op. 40) and XCIX (1903) 372 (on Op. 41); SMW LXI (1903) 789 (on Op. 41 for P & Vc); MW XXXV (1904) 324 (on Op. 41); DM III/1 (1903–4) 135 (H. Schlemüller on Op. 41); DM X/2 (1910–11) 43 (H. Schlemüller on Op. 56). Westerly/PIANOFORTE 169 and 186 has praise for Opp. 2 and 10 for P solo.

172. Cf. MGG XI 1530–31 (E. Reeser); Keller & Kruseman/MUZIEKLEXICON II 680; Reeser/NEDERLANDSE 253–55, with 2 exx. from Op. 9; Cobbett/CHAMBER II 330–31 (W. Landré and W. W. Cobbett, rating Schäfer's Vn sons. at the top of the Dutch output); Altmann/KAMMERMUSIK 224, 263.

173. E.g., on Op. 4, cf. MW XXXIII (1902) 599 (E. Segnitz) and DM II/1 (1902–3) 359 and 361 (W. Altmann); on Op. 6, cf. NZM C (1904) 819, MW XXXVI (1905) 367 (E. Segnitz), and DM IV/4 203–4 (W. Altmann).

174. DM XIII/2 (1913–14) 229 (C. Rorich).

to some extent in Schäfer's other sonatas examined here, gives to all of Op. 9 an atmosphere somewhere between the final entry of Wagner's "Meistersinger" and Elgar's "Pomp and Circumstance" marches. It persists not only in the outer movements—"Allegro marziale" and "Moderato, maestoso," both on the threshold of bombast (Ex. 85)—but in the middle movement, "Improvisata," with three initial instructions, "Adagio, con molto espressione," "sempre dolce e sostenuto," and "p[iano] maestosamente."

The Dutch conductor **Dirk Fock** (or **Foch**; 1886–   ) may be noted for a single, competent, relatively short sonata in four movements (F-Sc-S-Ro), Op. 1 in a, for P solo, that skirts the styles of Brahms's

Ex. 85. From the opening of Dirk Schäfer's *Sonate inaugurale,* Op. 9 (after the A. A. Noske ed. of 1913).

early piano sonatas too closely for comfort, yet without his flashes of genius. Another conductor, **Kor Kuiler** (1877–1951), left a Sonata in d, for P solo (pub. in 1899), and a Sonata in g, for Vn & P (pub. in 1902), which are conservative works of the sort we have been noting in Holland, but not without melodic character and harmonic interest.[175] Likewise conventional but not without appeal are the two duo sonatas by the organist and teacher **Jan Willem Kirsbergen** (1857–1937), Op. 4 in d, for Vn & P (pub. in 1901), and Op. 7 in F, for Vc & P (not pub. until 1928).[176] A Sonata in Eb, for P-duet (pub. in 1902), by the pianist **Louis Coenen** (son of Frans; 1856–1905) was reviewed as being skillful

175. Cf. Reeser/NEDERLANDSE 241–42 (with ex. from the Son. in d); also, GROVE IV 868 (H. Antcliffe) and Altmann/KAMMERMUSIK 212.

176. Cf. Keller & Kruseman/MUZIEKLEXICON I 334 and II 185; DM II/1 (1902–3) 359 and 361 (W. Altmann praising Op. 4); Altmann/KAMMERMUSIK 211 and 259.

enough but somewhat académic and unpianistic.[177] And the second of two duo sonatas (Op. 23 in F, Vn & P, 1905) by the pianist **Gerard H. G. von Brucken-Fock** (1859–1935) was reviewed as "spiritually barren." [178]

177. MW XXXV (1904) 902 (E. Segnitz) and DM II/2 (1902–3) 197 and 201 (R. M. Breithaupt). Cf. Keller & Kruseman/MUZIEKLEXICON I 119; Altmann/KAMMERMUSIK 297.

178. DM VIII/1 (1908–9) 367 (W. Altmann). Cf. GROVE III 177 (H. Antcliffe); Reeser/NEDERLANDSE 245–46.

Chapter XIV

Great Britain, from Cramer to Elgar

The Sonata's Changing Status

England, the almost exclusive representative of Great Britain in the present volume, enjoyed a degree of sociopolitical equilibrium throughout music's Romantic Era that seemed to provide at least outward inducements to artistic endeavor. It is true that reaction and suppression prevailed up to about 1830, relating to the fear of the Napoleonic conquests and lasting while the Tories still held sway. And there were the growing pains of the continuing industrial revolution, with its rising working classes and trends toward socialism; of an increased population and new agricultural problems; and of expanding imperial colonialism with its trade rivalries and an endless succession of relatively minor territorial wars. But from the return to power of the Whigs in 1830 and the passage of the Reform Bill in 1832, which opened the long road to universal suffrage (shared by Dame Ethel Smyth, *infra*) nearly a century later, England became the freest state in Europe. Even so, as is all too well known, that country achieved little in its own right of significance to music, least of all instrumental music,[1] throughout the short reigns, from 1820 to 1830, of George IV and, from 1830 to 1837, of William IV, and through more than half of the long, 64-year reign, from 1837 to 1901, of Queen Victoria. In spite of great and influential literary figures like Wordsworth, Coleridge, Scott, Keats, Shelley, Byron, Dickens, Thackeray, the Brontë sisters, and both Brownings, in spite of important writers and thinkers in related fields, like Darwin, Spencer, Huxley, Carlyle, Mill, and Macauley, and in spite of some distinguished painters like Blake, Constable, Turner, and Rosetti, neither the reigns immediately preceding nor the early Victorian reign produced more than two, isolated, little known figures, Pinto and Bennett, whose sonatas can even be mentioned in the same breath with those of Clementi, the notable

---

1. Cf. Walker/ENGLAND 311 *et passim*.

London resident (SCE 739–59), or Mendelssohn, the favorite London visitor (SSB VIII).

The limited contributions to the sonata before the last quarter of the 19th century should not be taken as evidence for any, more general lack of musical activities in London. Cramer, Field, and Pinto are the only early names of any consequence we shall be meeting here. (Among other notable pianist-composers resident in London at one time or another, we meet Wölfl in Vienna [SCE 562–64], Dussek in Prague [SSB XVII], and Kalkbrenner in Paris [SSB XII].) But the records of musicians active in London at the time reads more like a cross section of all Europe. In 1815, for example, Camille Pleyel (son of Ignaz; SCE 551) wrote to his family in Paris of his meetings with Cramer, Kalkbrenner, Ries, Cherubini (SCE 300–301), Clementi, Viotti (SCE 675–80), Hüllmandel (SCE 652–56), Sor (SCE 663–64), and many others.[2] In 1822, Moscheles, who met several of the same musicians and others, recorded some of the London concert life in his diaries, including the performance of considerable music by Handel, Mozart, Beethoven, and Rossini.[3] In 1825, a valuable article on the current "state of music in London" showed that the usual prominence was being given to opera, song, and other vocal music, but confirmed that instrumental music was getting its performances, too.[4] Another, like report, this time relayed to Leipzig, in 1823, includes mention of such instrumental music being played in London as a sonata for "viola" (Vn?) by Corelli, Hummel's Sonata Op. 92 for P-duet (SSB VIII), and a Mozart piano concerto.[5]

Yet even at that time the low state of composition in England was generally recognized—especially instrumental composition, as noted above. In 1830, Fétis in Paris, after describing the prevalent opera and choral music in London and the excellence of Moscheles and Cramer among "professors" of instrumental music, concluded that music was dead there because the English could not understand and appreciate it.[6] Seven years later (1837) Schumann still saw England's only musical hope as being composers like Field, Onslow, Potter, Bishop, and, above all, Bennett.[7] Fétis did not even mention the sonata

2. The letters are trans. in Benton/LONDON.

3. MOSCHELES I 64–90.

4. QUARTERLY VII (1825) 186–211, with references to instrumental music on pp. 201–3, 205–6. Henry George Farmer's article on "British Musicians a Century Ago," first pub. in ML XII (1931) 384–92 and reprinted in 1966 with slight changes as the "Introduction" to SAINSBURY I vii–xvi, provides a similarly valuable survey.

5. AMZ XXV (1823) 561 and 615. The Corelli work may have been a son. arranged for Vc & double-bass by R. Lindley and played by him with D. Dragonetti as a stunt at a Philharmonic Society program in 1823 (Temperley/CORRESPONDENCE).

6. Fétis/CURIOSITÉS 176–95, 207–21, 230–71 (especially from 260).

7. Schumann/SCHRIFTEN I 245–47.

itself in England. And to make matters worse, English reviewers anticipated Schumann's dismal outlook of 1839 (ssb II) by already calling the
sonata outmoded as much as fifteen years earlier.[8] Hence, unusual was
the piano sonata Frederick Hallé wrote for his son Charles to play at
the Concordia Society concerts in 1823.[9]

From the late 1840's on, especially after 1870, the status of the sonata
began a marked rise in England. This rise was part both of the more
general musical renaissance that Frank Howes has recently traced [10] and
of the more specific return to instrumental chamber music. Although
they were bounded by the "splendid isolation" of the later Victorian
period and their sonatas proved to be less significant, Parry, Stanford,
and Elgar comprised a trio that gave yeoman's service to the cause of
British chamber music,[11] contemporary with Franck, Saint-Saëns, and
Fauré during the similar French renaissance (ssb XIII), and with
Hartmann, Gade, and Grieg during a corresponding Scandinavian
renaissance (ssb XV). Among concomitants in this newly fired British
cause was the growing number of appropriate concerts sponsored
variously by the Royal Academy of Music, the Royal College of Music,[12]
the Philharmonic Society, and the groups behind the various series of
Promenade, Crystal Palace, and Popular Concerts.[13] There was also a
growing number of devoted chamber and solo performers, including
the pianists Charles Hallé, Walter Macfarren, Emil Pauer, and two
very active women champions, Arabella Goddard (Mrs. J. W. Davison)
and Agnes Zimmermann, as well as the violinist Wilma Maria Francisca
Neruda (later Lady Hallé) and the cellist Alfredo Carlo Piatti. Interest
in serious chamber music had begun to develop as far back as the
start of "Dando's Quartett Concerts" in 1836, as evidenced in several
daily or weekly newspapers and the important periodical *The Musical
World* (1836–91). But this interest got little attention before around
1870 in the pages of the thriving, illustrious London periodical often

8. QUARTERLY VII (1825) 104 and HARMONICON X/1 (1832) 256. In Temperley/
DOMESTIC 37–38, Nicholas Temperley (whose researches and personal advices on
early 19th-c. music in England have been utilized gratefully here, including the
information designated as Temperley/CORRESPONDENCE) describes the almost total
disappearance of the son. in England in the 1820's, 1830's, and 1840's. Cf., also,
George Hogarth's negative view in 1835, as quoted in Howes/ENGLISH 35.

9. HALLÉ 4. In 1827 a London Review of Cramer's "Last Sonata," Op. 74, begins
"A sonata is indeed a rarity! The title has remained dormant for many a long
year . . ." (HARMONICON V/1 [1827] 228 [W. Ayrton]).

10. Howes/ENGLISH; cf. p. 20, where the approximate year of 1880 is preferred as
the starting point. Cf., also, Walker/ENGLAND 316–40.

11. The three pioneers of the more general British musical renaissance are given
in Howes/ENGLISH 23–24 as Mackenzie, Parry, and Stanford.

12. Cf. Howes/ENGLISH 24, 60; O'Leary/BENNETT 124.

13. Cf. Howes/ENGLISH 44–48, *et passim*.

cited here, *The Musical Times* (MT; from 1844), which, in any case, was then becoming more sophisticated, scholarly, and cosmopolitan. (Although *The Quarterly Musical Magazine* and *The Harmonicon,* two other main predecessors of *The Musical Times,* had been surprisingly urbane, witty, and knowing in their own ways, neither periodical had evinced much interest in chamber music beyond an occasional review of a new publication, English or foreign.) In the later 19th century increasing interest of a still more serious, even scholarly sort is reflected in several papers to be cited here from the *Proceedings of the Royal Musical Association* (PMA; from 1874) and in the activities that led eventually to the important *Cyclopedic Survey of Chamber Music* (Cobbett/CHAMBER; originally pub. in 1929), edited by that inveterate avocational enthusiast and promoter Walter Willson Cobbett (1847–1937), who naturally gave extra space to his fellow countrymen.

As noted early in Chapter XIII, Frederick Delius (1862–1934), the French resident born in England of German parents, belongs tonally with the Moderns in spite of all the Romantic sentiment in his music. There were other late-Romantics—among them, Rutland Boughton (1878–   ), Frederick Charles Nicholls (1871–?), Arthur Somervell (1863–1937), and Harry Farjeon (1878–   )—who adhered thoroughly to Romantic styles yet produced their sonatas so late (after World War I) that these must be regarded rather as anachronisms of the Modern Era.

The Classic-Romantic Borderland in London *(Cramer, Field, and Pinto)*

The celebrated pianist **Johann Baptist Cramer** (1771–1858) is the most appropriate of the three main early composers with whom to begin our chapter on the Romantic sonata in England.[14] Although born in Germany, as the son of the brilliant violinist Wilhelm Cramer in Mannheim (SCE 722–23), J. B. Cramer was brought to London at about the age of three,[15] where during much of his life he became almost as influential in performance, teaching, and music publishing as the even

14. The valuable, thorough diss. Schlesinger/CRAMER remains (since 1925) the one chief study of his life, environment, piano career, and sons. (but not other works); as with Unger/CLEMENTI (cf. SCE 738), even some of the main biographic findings in this study have yet to be incorporated in present-day music dictionaries, only partially excepting MGG II 1762–66 (W. Kahl). The prolix but informative article of 1824 on Cramer in SAINSBURY I 180–85, not known to Schlesinger, was probably based on firsthand information (cf. I xvi). On Cramer as performer cf. Schonberg/PIANISTS 60–63.

15. Schlesinger/CRAMER 13 and 138.

more renowned, respected, and versatile teacher with whom he studied in 1783, Clementi (SCE 738–59). Furthermore, he became an important link with the past, not only through Clementi but as a main Beethoven transmitter, along with Hummel, Ries, Moscheles, and Czerny (SSB VII and VIII), all four of whom he knew personally though differently as friends, rivals, and fellow professionals.[16] Ries begrudgingly acknowledged that the one pianist Beethoven "praised as outstanding" was Cramer.[17] Beethoven, to whom Cramer may first have been introduced by Haydn, is also known to have had a high regard for Cramer's excellent etudes, preferring them to Czerny's (and perhaps deriving the main theme of Op. 26/iv from one of them; cf. SCE 516–17).[18] Cramer's own performances of Beethoven's sonatas (only in private circles?) undoubtedly did much to introduce them in London.[19] 18a Before his long life was ended, including prolonged visits to Vienna, Paris, and other centers, Cramer also became something of a link with the then present and future, for he got to know personally, though not keep up with, Wölfl (SCE 562–64), Dussek, Kalkbrenner, Liszt, and possibly Chopin.[20]

In the more than four decades, from Op. 1 in about 1788 [21] to "Sechs leichte Sonatinen" (without op. no.) in 1830, around 120 different sonatas or sonatinas by Cramer were published in sets or singly in London, Paris, Vienna, Leipzig, and other centers, of which about 65 per cent, especially the later sonatas, appeared originally as P solos and the rest with accompaniments (P & Vn-or-Fl, etc.).[22] A thematic index would have to be prepared, assuming that all or most of the music could still be found,[23] in order to eliminate reprints and other duplica-

16. Cf. Schlesinger/CRAMER 167, 36–37, 64, 68–69, 74, 46, 47, 77–78. Among Cramer's son. dedicatees are Clementi (Op. 7), Haydn (Op. 22), Wölfl (Op. 36), Ries (Op. 62), Hummel (Op. 63), and Moscheles (Op. 69).

17. Wegeler & Ries/BEETHOVEN 99–100; Thayer & Forbes/BEETHOVEN I 208–11; Schindler & MacArdle/BEETHOVEN 120–21. Cf. Schlesinger/CRAMER 43–49.

18. Cf. Schindler & MacArdle/BEETHOVEN 379, 394. No comment by Beethoven on Cramer's sons. is known. He could also have derived a passage like Op. 57/iii/50–57 from Cramer's Study in f, Op. 30/16 (Temperley/CORRESPONDENCE).

19. Cf. Schlesinger/CRAMER 47–48.

20. Cf. Schlesinger/CRAMER 51, 64–65, 71–72, 87, 152–53; Craw/DUSSEK 133–34, 445.

21. BUCEM I 237.

22. Schlesinger/CRAMER 93–94 gives the total that previous writers had given of 105 sons., and identifies "about 70" of these in a dated list (with some years being too late); cf. pp. 58–77 for more on dates, with mentions of numerous reviews, especially in AMZ and HARMONICON. The list in SAINSBURY I 184–85, totalling 109 sons., stops at 1823 and is the same as that in HARMONICON I/1 (1823) 181. It often does not mention the accompaniments, but if it was submitted or approved by Cramer it presumably would be free of duplications.

23. As early as 1880, S. Bagge remarked how hard it had become to obtain Cramer's sons. (Bagge/SONATE 222–23).

tions, reconcile conflicting opus numbers, and provide a reasonably accurate, consolidated catalogue of these sonatas.[24] But Cramer's sonatas are too nearly forgotten and of too little interest, except as examples of a widespread, short-lived taste in the early Romantic Era, to justify such a catalogue. In any case, a sufficient idea of the scorings, titles, and publishers may be had from similar catalogues offered here, including those of Clementi (SCE 740–45),[25] Ries (SSB VII), and Hummel (SSB VIII).

Cramer's titles include modifiers like "grande" and "easy" only infrequently and a few vaguely programmatic designations like "La Parodie," Op. 43 (or 50) in B♭ (1809?);[26] "Le Retour à Londres," Op. 62 in E (1818);[27] "L'Ultima," Op. 53 in a (1815);[28] "Les Suivantes," Op. 59/1–3 in C, B♭, and e (1817–18);[29] "Les Souvenirs," Op. 63 in d (1824 at latest);[30] and "Amicitia," arranged for P ± Vn-or-Fl from

24. Sizable collections of them can be found at the British Museum (of which a few appear in BUCEM I 237), the Royal College of Music (cf. Cat. ROYAL 95–96), and the Library of Congress; cf., also, Eitner/QL III 94–95. The list in PAZDÍREK III 589–93 is extensive but neither complete nor consolidated. Help toward a consolidated list would come from the many reviews and Intelligenz-Blatt entries in AMZ up to Vol. XXXII (1830). A thematic index of Cramer's sons. is actually projected as part of a diss. in progress by Jerald Graue at the University of Illinois (as of spring, 1968), on the English pianoforte school at the turn of the century.

25. The much needed thematic index of Clementi's sonatas has been completed (1964), by Alan Tyson, and published by Schneider of Tutzing in 1967.

26. The Johann Traeg ed. (1809? plate no. 454; one of 3 eds. of Op. 43 listed in Cat. NYPL VIII 190–91) has an inscription that reads (in French), "This piece provides a parody of a sonata composed by another celebrated author." Dussek's Op. 24 in the same key (C. 96) is stated (and seems) to be the parodied work, in a catalogue of J. B. Cramer & Co. dated 1851 (Temperley/CORRESPONDENCE). The suggestion in Schlesinger/CRAMER 164 that Haydn is that "author" has more biographic than stylistic justification. In any case, the "parody" seems not to be a caricature and does not depart from Cramer's typical sons. in style or form.

27. AMZ XX (1818) 449–51 could find no reason or musical clarification for the title. But Op. 62 appeared in time for Cramer's own return to London after continental travels (Schlesinger/CRAMER 64 and 67). Temperley/CORRESPONDENCE detects possible "street noises" in the first mvt. The title recalls Dussek's celebrated Son. in A♭ of 1807, "Le Retour à Paris" (C. 221), and Cramer's own later set of vars. Op. 85, "Le Retour à Vienne," (Weinmann/ARTARIA item 3102).

28. In AMZ XVII (1815) 473–75, the reviewer hopes Op. 53 actually will not be Cramer's last son.

29. Probably the title simply means (the first of what were to be several) additions to "L'Ultima," and not a turn to a deeper style (as guessed in Egert/FRÜH-ROMANTIKER 64).

30. AMZ XXVI (1824) 96–98 suggests that "souvenirs" means recollections of pleasant associations with Hummel, dedicatee of Op. 63; cf. Schlesinger/CRAMER 167. This outstanding work among Cramer's sons. (cf. Egert/FRÜHROMANTIKER 70) is probably the Son. in d praised by Moscheles, which would put its year of composition, if not pub., back in 1821 (MOSCHELES I 51–52).

Cramer's Quintet in E, Op. 69.[31] Not only these titles but somewhat more character and inclination toward Romantic trends account for the special popularity and more-than-average reprintings of the works just cited, among all Cramer's sonatas during his lifetime.[32] Today, however, not one of them happens to be among the few sonatas by Cramer that can be found in "old master" collections.[33]

Nearly all of Cramer's sonatas adhere to the standard plan of three movements (mainly F-S-Ro and F-M-Ro) or the plan still used in many lighter works of two movements, without the middle, slowest movement.[34] The home keys do not exceed four flats or sharps, with major keys predominating over minor by a ratio of about three to one. In the first movements, occasionally prepared by a slow introduction, "sonata form" prevails, insofar as there is any clear dualism or pluralism of main ideas. The middle movements fall chiefly into A-B-A and variation forms, and the finales into rondos. Except for the transcribed "Amicitia" (supra), the accompanied sonatas tend to be Cramer's lightest sonatas. Their accompaniments, whether indicated as optional or obligatory, are usually dispensable with regard to thematic continuity if not texture. From "L'Ultima" on,[35] most of the last few sonatas mark a conspicuous and probably a consciously motivated turn to a richer, more compelling, more emotionally involved style of writing.[36] Whereas, Haydn, Mozart, Clementi, and only the earliest Beethoven sonatas are the clear influences in Cramer's previous sonatas,[37] an awareness of the increasing pathos and agitation in the Beethoven of Opp. 13 to 31 is evident in the later sonatas. Early-Romantic traits show up in an increase of tonal tension, including a more chromatic harmonic style, a variety of more sharply defined

31. The "Amicitia" undoubtedly refers to Cramer's friendship with Moscheles, the dedicatee. Cf. MOSCHELES I 64–65.

32. Cf. Egert/FRÜHROMANTIKER 64, 69–70, 153–54; HOFMEISTER 1828 (Whistling) 582–84.

33. Op. 6/1 in D (ca. 1792) is in Méreaux/CLAVECINISTES-m III no. 164. The same plus Opp. 6/3 in F and 8/2 in G (ca. 1795) are in TRÉSOR-m XX. A few of Cramer's sons. and separate mvts. were pub. in one vol. by Steingräber in 1898 (R. Kleinmichel). Op. 23/3 in a (1799) is in "Fascicolo VIII" of B. Cesi's Biblioteca del pianista . . . autori classici (G. Ricordi). In Anth. NÄGELI II (1803) are 3 sons., in D, G, and F without op. no.; these are not mentioned in Schlesinger/CRAMER.

34. Schlesinger/CRAMER 102–33 is a style-critical discussion of the sons., with 162 exx. (up to 16 mss. each). Egert/FRÜHROMANTIKER 63–70, with exx., largely derives from the foregoing. Cf., also, Georgii/KLAVIERMUSIK 272–73.

35. Cf. Exx. 18, 20, 22, 48, 78, and 119 in the back of Schlesinger/CRAMER, all quoted from "L'Ultima."

36. Cf. Schlesinger/CRAMER 102–3; Egert/FRÜHROMANTIKER 69–70.

37. On Mozart's influence, cf. Temperley/MOZART 313.

rhythms, a more florid kind of melodic line, and some measures in the manner of recitatives.

But even with these changes in mind, one has to conclude that Cramer's sonatas are at their best in the skill at which he excelled right from the start and for which alone, as with Czerny, he is still remembered today. That skill is the writing of ingenious, cleanly scored, euphonious passagework such as is well known to pianists who play his etudes. In a sense, the passagework is more progressive than the changes noted in Cramer's last sonatas. It not only paves one way to the piano virtuosity of the 19th century but in its open-position, arpeggiando dispositions it supplants the Alberti, murky, and related basses of the Classic Era (sce 122) with fuller, more liquescent accompaniments and

Ex. 86. From near the opening of Johann Baptist Cramer's Sonata in a, Op. 23/3 (after B. Cesi's ed. for G. Ricordi, *ca.* 1900).

textures such as might grace a lyrical piece by Schumann.[38] Ex. 86 comes from a sonata in which texture and passagework rather than any distinctive melodies or tunes supply the entire and not inconsiderable interest of the outer movements.

More often Cramer does employ more tangible themes. Although his ability to construct themes, textures, and forms is always at least adequate and although his themes reveal somewhat more character and undergo a more organic sort of development in the later sonatas, at best they, their attendant harmony, and their treatment are less than inspired or original. (From the standpoint of unoriginality it is not surprising to learn that Cramer twice plagiarized his teacher's sonatas.[39]) The lack of melodic invention shows up especially in the

38. Temperley/MENDELSSOHN 226 quotes the finale of Op. 59 in G (*ca.* 1817) as an entire mvt. "that might well have been writen by Mendelssohn."
39. Cf. Schlesinger/CRAMER 66 and 157; SCE 748.

slowest movements (as in ii in the work just quoted). The themes used in the sets of variations are likely to be tuneful, sometimes folklike, enough to have melodic identities (as in Anth. NÄGELI II/2/iii). Many of the main themes in the rondos and even in the first movements in "sonata form" are likely to be of this sort, although in the latter they only occasionally seem to lend themselves to the expected extensions and developments (as in Op. 25/1/i in E♭ [1802], an ingenuous, gay mvt. of considerable charm). Actually, three of Cramer's sets of sonatas incorporate "popular airs." [40] Yet it is undoubtedly the melodic deficiencies of Cramer's sonatas that brought a quick dismissal of them from Bie, a description of Cramer as a mere "sonata-maker" (along with Steibelt and Wölfl) from Shedlock, and a frequently neutral or even negative reception from the reviewers until several of the later sonatas brought more favorable responses.[41]

Another important pupil of Clementi, also widely celebrated in his day, was the Irish-born pianist **John Field** (1782–1837).[42] In 1802 Field travelled to Russia with his teacher, remaining, after Clementi left in 1803, to spend the rest of his life in St. Petersburg and Moscow except for some less successful tours in West Europe during his last years.[43] Field's relatively small output—7 concertos, 3 piano quintets, about 60

40. Cf. HARMONICON I/1 (1823) 181.

41. Bie/PIANOFORTE 210–11; Shedlock/SONATA 192–94. Shedlock adds that no son. by Cramer was ever played at the Popular Concerts (from 1859) in London (although Cramer had played often at the earlier "professional Concerts [MGG II 1762]). Many of the German and English reviews are summarized in Schlesinger/ CRAMER 102–34 and 176, *passim*. For samples of some of these and others, cf. AMZ II (1799–1800) 67 (on the superfluity of the Vn & Vc in Op. 19), V (1802–3) 359–60 (favorable on Op. 27), V 606 (on Op. 28 as correct but sometimes dull), V 176 and 606 (on Op. 29 as uneven in quality), V 606–7 (more pros than cons in Op. 30), V 607 (on facile brilliance but melodic lacks in Op. 31), V 607–8 (on Op. 33 as best for exercises), XII (1809–10) 773–76 (on stylistic though not musical excellence in an unidentified son.), XIII (1811) 32 (neutral on Op. 41), XII (1809–10) 902–3 (mildly favorable on Op. 44), XXIII (1821) 528 (mildly negative on "La Parodie"), XXVII (1825) 596 (similar on Op. 47), XVII (1815) 473–75 (on "L'Ultima" as one of Cramer's best sons.), XX (1818) 449–51 (similar on "Le Retour à Londres"), XXVI (1824) 96–98 (similar on "Les Souvenirs"); CAECILIA V (1825) 40 (on Op. 48 as good teaching material); HARMONICON III/1 (1825) 61–62 and QUARTERLY VIII (1826) 64–66 (both with praise for "Amicitia" and 2 exx.); HARMONICON V/1 (1827) 228 (qualified praise of Op. 74, with a 16-ms. ex. from ii).

42. Cf. GROVE III 85–87 (E. Dannreuther); MGG IV 169–72 (W. Kahl, with further references). Dessauer/FIELD is a Ph.D. diss. of 1911 that contributes more on the biography than on the music. In Hopkinson/FIELD vii the supposition that Field's popularity between 1815 and 1835, which did reach surprising heights, "exceeded that of contemporaries such as Clementi, Cramer, Dussek, Hummel and Steibelt" does not tally with findings here; for example, at least as many concurrent eds. of a single pub. and considerably more reviews can be found for the more successful works of each of the others.

43. Negative reactions by both Moscheles and Chopin, in 1831 and 1832, are reported in MOSCHELES I 251 and Hedley/CHOPIN 55.

piano pieces, and a very few songs, according to Cecil Hopkinson's outstanding thematic *catalogue raisonée* (Hopkinson/FIELD)—includes 4 sonatas, all for P solo, of which 3 were published a year before the move to Russia and one later. The three early sonatas, in Eb, A, and c/C, were his only works to which Field himself assigned an opus number, Op. 1/1–3. First appearing in 1801 and dedicated to Clementi, they actually comprised his eighth publication, with no fewer than a dozen reprints or new editions of the set following during the century, and as many more of single sonatas or even single movements.[44] Field's other, fourth sonata, in B, was first published about 1813 by Dalmas in St. Petersburg, with about a dozen reprints or new editions following again, all by 1830 and mostly German.[45]

Field's four sonatas, especially the first three, have little of the musical, pianistic, or pre-Chopin interest that has rightly drawn so much attention to his nocturnes and piano concertos.[46] All four are in only two movements, mostly F-Ro, with no slow movements or key contrasts.[47] In Op. 1 the first sonata is decidedly the best. It is compact and fluent, and it is melodically fresh to an extent rarely found in Cramer. The harmony reveals some surprises, including alternations of major and minor through the use of borrowed tones and a modulation, by change of mode, to the lowered mediant (i/72–75). Of special delight is the rondo, which is based on the schottische dance (or "German polka") in 2/4 meter and might well have been in Chopin's mind when he wrote the first of his three "Écossaises" in 1826. The other two sonatas in Field's Op. 1 come closer to deserving the early review of all three that charged Field with a lack of poetry and with deriving not the seed but the chaff of his master's style, including "dry melody, [and] harsh harmonic progressions and transitions, along with many stretches of 9ths and 10ths in both hands." [48]

46a

44. Cf. Hopkinson/FIELD 13–16, with incipits of each mvt. Mod. ed. of all 3 sons. separately: Augener in London, 1939–40.

45. Cf. Hopkinson/FIELD. The correspondence following Tyson/FIELD (ML XLVIII [1967] 99) suggests that Hopkinson's "c. 1812" might be a year of two too early for the original Dalmas ed. There is no mod. ed. of this son. (as of 1967).

46. As with Cramer's sons., no son. by Field was ever performed at the London Popular Concerts (Shedlock/SONATA 229). Relatively brief discussions of the sons. occur in Dessauer/FIELD 83–89 (with exx.); Blom/FIELD 237; Egert/FRÜHROMANTIKER 116–20 (following Dessauer almost verbatim; with exx.); Georgii/KLAVIERMUSIK 261. A diss. on Field's piano music by William Perryman was reported to be in progress at Indiana University in JAMS XIX (1966) 391.

47. Hibbard/FIELD is an attempt—far-fetched and unsuccessful, as viewed here—to find intended slow mvts. and suitable key contrasts in 4 Romances (Hopkinson/FIELD 24A[r] in Eb, 25A[r] in c, 26A[n], and 46B[e] in e, respectively); both the historical and the bibliographical premises are inaccurate.

48. AMZ V (1802–3) 490–91; but the quoted ex. from Op. 1/1/ii/1–3 showing

There are moments of some local interest in Op. 1/2 and 3, such as the *fortissimo* climax marked "con fuoco" (unusual for Field at any time) in the lengthy development section of Op. 1/3/i (Ex. 87). But the ideas and textures, especially the triadic themes set in slow harmonic rhythm in Sonata 2, generally do prove to be weak and, what is more detrimental to the over-all effect, the forms straggle helplessly for want of adequate tonal organization and thematic development and because they last too long for their slight content, anyway. Field's fourth sonata is no masterpiece but shows more maturity. The first movement brings us near to his nocturnes in form and mood (evoking the title

Ex. 87. From the first movement of Sonata in c/C, Op. 1/3, by John Field (after the Augener reprint of 1940).

of "Spring Sonata" from Dessauer[49]). The second movement is an ingratiating rondo.

In the realm of the early-19th-century sonata in England, the most remarkable yet least known of our three composers was certainly the precocious, short-lived violinist and pianist **George Frederick Pinto (Sanders or Saunders; 1785–1806).**[50] Pinto was close to Field as a fellow violin student of Haydn's impresario Johann Peter Salomon, who sponsored a benefit in 1800 that included an unidentified " 'So-

---

leaps of staccato 10ths in the bass posed no unusual problem for pianists of the time.

49. Dessauer/FIELD 88–89.

50. Cf. Temperley/PINTO, with revision of the birth year and other details in MGG X 1286–87 (N. M. Temperley). A "Memoir" possibly by Pinto's mother was first pub. in 1807 and revised in HARMONICON VI/1 (1828) 215–16, with further ancestral and biographic details.

nata Concertante, Piano Forte and Violin' [played] by 'Master Field
and Master Pinto.' " [51] Although no factual evidence is at hand, it
would be hard to believe, from his music and environment, that Pinto
did not also come under at least the indirect influence of Cramer.
Credit for bringing Pinto's sonatas back to light goes to the Cambridge
scholar Nicholas Temperley and his valued studies on instrumental
music in England in the first half of the 19th century.[52]

Along with about three dozen other works—Vn-duets, smaller P
solos, and songs—by Pinto, there were at least a dozen of those sonatas,
eight for P solo and four for P & Vn, published originally (and but
once) between 1802 and 1807 except for an incomplete P solo in G
in an autograph MS of 1803 entitled "Sonata for Scotland." [53] The
solo sonatas include Op. 3/1–2, in e♭ and A (ded. to a "Miss Griffith"
and "Printed for the Author" in 1802 or 1803);[54] A Grand Sonata [in
c], "Inscribed to his Friend John Field" (and pub. in 1803 by Birchall);[55] Op. 4/1–3, in G, B♭, and C (pub. in 1804 or 1805 by Turnbull),
"in which are Introduced Marches, Quick Steps, Waltzes, and Scotch
Airs"—a set described as less serious and significant;[56] and a "Fantasia
& Sonata" in c that was published posthumously (ca. 1807) by (or
for?) Pinto's mother, "Mrs. Sanders." The last was edited by the early
champion of J. S. Bach's works, **Samuel Wesley** (1766–1837; himself
the composer of nearly 2 dozen skillful sons., more solo than accompanied and mostly pub., between 1777 and ca. 1812 [57]); it was supplied
with "an inappropriate C major conclusion" by Joseph Wölfl (then in
London; sce 562–64); and it is described as an "unequal" work, in
five (four?) interconnected movements, all in minor keys (S-F-fugue-S/F

51. As cited in Temperley/PINTO 265.

52. Besides Temperley/PINTO, cf. Temperley/ENGLISH, Temperley/MOZART, Tem-
perley/HANDEL. Warm thanks are owing to Dr. Otto Albrecht for calling attention
here to Pinto's Op. 3 and for supplying a copy from the Library of the University
of Pennsylvania; and to Dr. Temperley for further information and help by
correspondence.

53. Cf. the cat. in Temperley/PINTO 266, 269, and 270, including locations of the
rare extant copies.

54. Mod. ed. of Op. 3/1: Temperley/PINTO-m. On W. S. Bennett's reprinting and
performance of Op. 3/2 in 1841 cf. Bennett/BENNETT 110. For extracts from Op.
3/1, cf. Temperley/MOZART 312 (Op. 3/1/iii) and Temperley/PINTO 267–68 (Op.
3/2/i and ii).

55. The "Rondo" refrain of this son. (not Op. 4) is quoted in Temperley/HANDEL
171–72. Mod. eds. of this son. and Op. 3/2 have been prepared for pub. (Stainer &
Bell) by Dr. Temperley.

56. Temperley/PINTO 269. The "Rondo" of Son. 2 is quoted in Temperley/PINTO
268.

57. Cf. GROVE IX 262–65 (W. H. Hadow); BUCEM II 1069; Shedlock/SONATA 229–
30. Besides Wesley's battle son. pub. ca. 1812, "The Siege of Badajoz," there is a
"fine" 3-mvt. Son. in d, for P solo (1808), of which the middle mvt. is a "Fugue
on a Subject of Salomon's" (Temperley/CORRESPONDENCE).

[separately titled "Sonata"]).[58] Pinto's accompanied sonatas include a set of three, in g, A, and B♭, again published by his mother around the time of or soon after his early death—a set described as having essential violin parts and as being outstanding in quality except for weak slow movements in Sonatas 2 and 3; and a single Sonata in A, in the slow movement of which "is introduced the Air of 'Logie o' Buchan' " (ed. by Wesley and pub. by Pinto's mother)—a work described as undistinguished, with the accompaniment (Fl-or-Vn) incomplete in the rondo finale.[59]

Temperley regards the two sonatas of Op. 3 and the Sonata in c dedicated to Field as Pinto's "greatest achievement." [60] Among these the one that presumably came first, Op. 3/1 in e♭, is regarded here as the consistently best. But except for their standard, over-all, three-movement plans (F-S-Ro) and their general keyboard idioms in the current language of Clementi, Cramer, and Dussek, the three sonatas differ so greatly and, in their unpretentious manner, cover such a wide range of musical thinking and feeling that one finds it hard to ascribe them to a single composer, much less to a boy who could have been only sixteen or seventeen when he wrote them. Op. 3/1 is a compact work of 523 measures (179+82+262), lasting about seventeen minutes in performance. In several ways it brings to mind Beethoven's early sonatas, especially his similarly proportioned Op. 13. Beethoven's Opp. 2, 7, 10, and 13 had first appeared in Vienna between 1796 and 1799 (cf. sce 509), though not in London until much later.[61] Pinto's performances and travels are not reported to have taken him further than Paris.[62] But these works possibly could have become known to Pinto almost as soon as they appeared, through important transient or resident transmitters in London like Clementi, Cramer, and Dussek. It is not that Pinto offers any specific melodic reminders of Beethoven. Nearest to such are the similarities between the finales of Pinto's Op. 3/1 and Beethoven's Op. 10/1, as well as of Pinto's Sonata in c and Beethoven's Op. 13. Nor does he take over any specific structural devices, such as the recurrence of the introduction in Beethoven's Op. 13/i (sce 136) that Ries (ssb VII) and others expropriated. But on a somewhat lower and more naive plane of drama, intensity, melodic inspiration, and pianism, the three movements of Pinto's Op. 3/1 recall the moods, drive, frank songfulness, textural styles, cumulative syntax and dissective development, dynamic con-

58. Temperley/PINTO 269.
59. Temperley/PINTO 269.
60. Temperley/PINTO 267.
61. Cf. Tyson/BEETHOVEN 26–27.
62. HARMONICON VI/1 (1828) 216.

Ex. 88. From the retransition in the first movement of Georges Frederick Pinto's Sonata in A, Op. 3/2 (after the original ed., "Printed for the Author," at the University of Pennsylvania in Philadelphia).

trasts, harmonic surprises, syncopations and sforzandos, and even the sense of structural inevitability or "fatalism" all manifested variously and consummately in the respective movements of Beethoven's Op. 13.

By comparison, Pinto's Op. 3/2 in A is ruminative and gentle; and his Sonata in c is a turbulent "pathétique" work, with wider extremes and some brooding, at times recalling its dedicatee's (Field's) weaker Sonata in c, Op. 1/3, that had been published only recently (1801). Op. 3/2 in particular, as Temperley notes,[63] is remarkably Schubertian. It is more so, in fact, than Op. 3/1 is Beethovian, yet now, of course, with no possibility of Schubert's influence (ssb VII). Along with the tenderly expressive slow movement in D, starting at a tonal tangent (from V-of-I to V-of-IV), the outer movements contain melodies, rhythms, and parenthetical modulations, so to speak, that might well convince any trained musician he is hearing Schubert's own piano music (Ex. 88). The first movement of Pinto's accompanied Sonata in g is also Schubertian, recalling especially the style and even the main theme of Schubert's Op. 137/1/i in D.

Pinto did arouse interest and win some warm praise while he was alive,[64] and occasional editions and organ arrangements of his sonatas appeared later in the century, indicating that he and they were not entirely forgotten.[65] Although the apparent deterioration in his "later" sonatas and dissipation in his last years[66] did not augur well for a continuingly distinguished future, he belongs with Schunke, Reubke, and Lekeu (ssb VIII, X, and XIII) among the precious few in which so much promise had been seen before they were cut off in their early twenties. One is inclined to agree with Temperley that Pinto's music is indeed "a bright light in a dark hour of English music." [67]

The London pianist and composer (Philip) Cipriani (Hambly) Potter (1792–1871) was competent enough as a composer, as both Beethoven in 1818 and Wagner in 1855 found reason to observe,[68] but is more interesting here for the curiosity of his modish, empty, largely derivative piano music, and more notable for his performances and promotion during his long life in London of the continental masters from Bach to Schumann and Brahms.[69] Potter had been a student of Wölfl, Thomas Attwood (Mozart's pupil), and William Crotch (who himself had left 3 pub. sons. for P-or-H solo in London ca. 1794 [70]) before he went first to Beethoven for instruction in Vienna in 1817 and then, because Beethoven would give only informal advice, to Emanuel Alois Förster (sce 548–49).[71] Among numerous works left by Potter are at least six sonatas, all published rather early in his life, between 1817 and about 1825, plus others left in MS.[72] Of the six, Opp. 1/1–2 in C and ? (1817), 3 in D (1818?), and 4 in e (1819?) are for P solo, whereas Op. 6 is a "Grand Duo" in F for 2 Ps (1821; described in 1884 as "a noble work which has been many times played, and is very admirable for displaying the skill of the executants as much as for the interest of its ideas"),[73] and Op. 13 is a 4-movement Sonata di bravura concertante in E♭ (S-F-Va-F), for P and Hn(-or-Bn-or-Vc; 1825?), ded. to "le fameux Cor, Monsieur Puzzi." [74]

A good idea of Potter's compositional influences and tastes can be

65. E.g., cf. Temperley/PINTO 267; also, MT XV (1872) 644, XX (1879) 389, XXIV (1883) 405 and 468.

66. Cf. SAINSBURY II 294 (with wrong year of death).

67. Temperley/PINTO 265 and 270.

68. Anderson/BEETHOVEN II 759; Macfarren/POTTER 45–46; WAGNER LEBEN 606; Newman/WAGNER II 458 and 473.

69. Macfarren/POTTER (by Potter's pupil) is the main biographic account; cf., further, GROVE VI 895–96 (W. H. Hadow); MGG X 1523–24 (J. M. Allan), with further bibliography. Mr. Philip H. Peter of Mt. Prospect, Ill., is doing a diss. on Potter (as of early 1969).

70. BUCEM I 241.

71. Macfarren/POTTER 45; SAINSBURY II 304–5.

72. Cf. SAINSBURY II 305; HOFMEISTER 1828 (Whistling), 502, 517, 599.

73. Macfarren/POTTER 49.

74. Temperley/CORRESPONDENCE.

had from his piano piece, nearly 75 years in advance of Elgar's orchestral work, called *The Enigma, Variations and Fantasia on a Favorite Irish Air* (London: Boosey, 1825). With more or less confidence and some surprising pinpointing of specific traits, a contemporary reviewer identified the "Introduzione" as being in the style of Moscheles; Variations 1–5, respectively, as being in the styles of Ries, Kalkbrenner, Cramer, Rossini (even though the reviewer knew no piano music by him), and Beethoven (or Moscheles again); and the concluding "Fantasia" as being a medley of all these styles.[75] Although the identifying traits, mostly individual keyboard techniques, are tangible enough when the reviewer singles them out, today's students of the Romantic Era might find it hard to relate each of them so confidently to but one name, for they all seem to have been in the *frühromantische* air (cf. ssb VI). More conspicuous today is Potter's own approach to keyboard music, which not only provides the vehicle for introducing these traits but dominates (and constitutes nearly all that needs to be said about) most if not all of his sonatas, too. His Op. 1, reportedly deriving from Haydn and Clementi,[76] presumably reveals a more modest, established idiom. But from Op. 3 on,[77] confirming his recognized gifts as a piano virtuoso, Potter wrote little else in his piano music besides alternations of free, inconsequential thematic bits, usually highly ornamented, and still freer, emptier, but fairly difficult runs and cadenzas, all amidst copious editing and even some footnoted instructions. Whether the title is "Enigma," "Sonata di bravura," or simply "Sonata," the procedure is essentially the same, there being no use of established forms other than the variation principle.

Among a few other, more obscure composers of sonatas in early 19th-century England, mention might be added of the London organist **William Crouch** (*ca.* 1775–*ca.* 1835), for at least 23 sonatas for H-or-P, published (*ca.* 1775–*ca.* 1800) as Opp. 1, 4, 6, 7, and 9, and presumably oriented toward the past;[78] the oratorio and opera composer **Matthew Peter King** (1773–1823), for several solo and accompanied piano sonatas published between about 1785 and 1820, the latest being a programmatic, Handelian work in four movements all in D, with the title "The Coronation [of George IV?]: A Grand Sonata Sinfonia for Piano Forte";[79] the pianist and singer **Maria Hester Parke** (1775–1822), for several more solo and accompanied piano

75. QUARTERLY VII (1825) 507–9.

76. Shedlock/SONATA 230.

77. Cf. the review of Op. 3 in AMZ XXI (1819) 64 and the more general survey of Potter's earlier works, including sons., in QUARTERLY V (1823) 376–80.

78. Temperley/CORRESPONDENCE; cf. BROWN & STRATTON 109 and BUCEM I 242.

79. Temperley/CORRESPONDENCE; cf. BROWN & STRATTON 231 and BUCEM I 570.

sonatas, including "Two Grand Sonatas" for P solo, Op. 2 in C and F (*ca.* 1805), each in three movements (F-S-Ro), with distinct recollections of Mozart;[80] and the Aberdeen organist **John Ross** (1763–1837), for more than twenty solo and accompanied piano sonatas published about 1795 to 1815, including several with "favorite Scots and Irish airs" and one "with an Introductory Prelude." [81] And mention might be made, too, of the teacher **James Fisin** (1755–1847), pupil of Burney, for two sets of accompanied sonatas, Op. 10 published in 1801 and Op. 12, dedicated to "Mrs. Burney," about 1806;[82] the opera composer **Henry Rowley Bishop** (1786–1855), for a reported Sonata for P & Vn of 1807 not currently locatable;[83] the pianist **Charles Neate** (1784–1877), a piano student of Field, a cellist, and an acquaintance of Beethoven, for two sonatas for P solo (Op. 1 in c, 1808; Op. 2 in d, *ca.* 1822) and a lost sonata for P & Vc;[84] the organist **John (Freckleton) Burrowes** (1787–1852), for an accompanied sonata (P & Vc), published as Op. 7 about 1810;[85] and **George Eugene Griffin** (1781–1863) for at least five sonatas, including two for P solo (Opp. 2 in E♭ [1810?] and 7 in E [1811?]).[86]

There was also a teacher of violin and piano in Bristol, **Thomas Howell** (1783–?), who left a more elementary publication, *Six Progressive Sonatinas for the Pianoforte*, that was well received in 1818 for its musicality and training values.[87] There was the keyboardist **Charles Wesley** (1757–1834), whose one published sonata, for P solo (*ca.* 1820), is a three-movement work ("Preludio," "Aria" with one variation, "Giga") that reflects an early interest in J. S. Bach similar to his brother-and-student Samuel's (*supra*).[88] And there was one 88a **Charles Ambrose** (?–?), perhaps the ballad composer and professor in Chelmsford that Sainsbury lists without first name, whose published set of three solo piano sonatas, in E, E♭, and E, were twice reviewed in 1825 as pleasant, well-written study material in the outmoded style of Dussek or even Koželuch (SCE 556–58), with the best movement being the variations in Sonata 2 on the Irish song, "My Love's Like the Red, Red Rose." [89] Another was the precocious pianist **Pio Cian-**

80. Temperley/CORRESPONDENCE; cf. BROWN & STRATTON 308 and BUCEM II 762.
81. Temperley/CORRESPONDENCE; cf. BROWN & STRATTON 355 and BUCEM II 902.
82. Cf. GROVE III 147 (R. Gorer).
83. Temperley/CORRESPONDENCE, citing R. Northcott's biography of Bishop (London, 1920), pp. 149–58.
84. Cf. GROVE VI 40 (M. K. Ward).
85. Cf. GROVE I 1032 (W. H. Hadow).
86. Temperley/CORRESPONDENCE.
87. QUARTERLY I (1818) 382–83. Cf. SAINSBURY I 879.
88. Temperley/CORRESPONDENCE.
89. HARMONICON III/1 (1825) 139; QUARTERLY VII (1825) 104–5. Cf. SAINSBURY I 17.

chettini (1799–1851), London-born "son of F. Cianchettini, of Rome, and Veronica [sister of J. L.] Dussek"[90] (herself the composer of 3 sons. for P solo, Op. 6 [pub. *ca.* 1812] that "introduce popular tunes by Mozart and others"[91]). Pio left a published work, Op. 26 in e, called "Le Delire: Grande Sonate," for P+Vn, which a reviewer in 1832 found effective and Beethovian, but too difficult to be popular, especially with its use of the "demisemidemisemiquaver" (128th-note):

To pronounce the word, without taking breath in the midst of it, demands the lungs of a diver:—to play the note in time requires a finger as nimble as the Eclipse, or Flying Childers; and such lungs and such fingers are not so common as tubercles and chalk-stones, we can venture to assure the composer of this *Grande Sonate.*[92]

Still in the same decade, a Scottish piano pupil of Potter and eventual teacher at the Royal Academy in London, **Frederick Brown Jewson** (1823–91), left a solo Sonata in E, published in 1838 as Op. 1, that is described as a commonplace, although pianistically grandiose work in four movements.[93] In the final decade of the first half-century, mention may be made of the leading Victorian music critic, **James William Davison** (1813–85), for two missing sonatas for P solo, both in E, and published in 1842—Opp. 6, (perhaps called) "Fioretta," and 7, "Phantasmion";[94] the violinist and organist **Henry John Westrop** (1812–79), for two published duo sonatas, in B♭ (posthumous), for P & Vn, and in F, Op. 6, for P+Fl (4 mvts., F-S-Sc-F), both played for the Society of British Musicians, in 1844 and 1845, respectively;[95] the pianist and organist **Charles Edward Horsley** (1822–76), a pupil variously of his father (**William Horsley,** who himself had left 3 sons., for P solo, between about 1812–17[96]), Moscheles, Hauptmann, and Mendelssohn, for five duo sonatas—Op. 3 in A (pub. in 1843; ded. to Mendelssohn)[97] and two other, unpublished duos for P & Vc, in G and E♭ (played for the Society of British Musicians in 1847 and 1848),[98] Op. 9 in a, for P & Fl (pub. in 1846), and Op. 14 in F, for

90. SAINSBURY I 153–54. Cf. Craw/DUSSEK 15 and 102.

91. Temperley/CORRESPONDENCE.

92. HARMONICON X/1 (1832) 256. Another passage from this review is quoted in SSB II.

93. MUSICAL WORLD XI (1839) 59.

94. Cf. MUSICAL WORLD XVII (1842) 80, 216, 8. Temperley/CORRESPONDENCE refers to a limerick written a little later: "There was a J. W. D./ Who sought a composer to be;/ But his muse wouldn't budge,/ So he set up as judge/ Over better composers than he."

95. MUSICAL WORLD XIX (1844) 110 and XXI (1845) 9. Cf. BROWN & STRATTON 442, referring also to a (MS?) Son. for P & Va.

96. Mod. ed.: Son. 2 in F (1814), Smart/EIGHTEENTH-m 85.

97. Reviewed as songful, pleasant music for the home in NZM XIX (1843) 42–43.

98. MUSICAL WORLD XXII (1847) 658 and XXIII (1848) 648.

P & Vn (1848);[99] and one **John James Haite** (?–1874), for a not otherwise identified sonata played at the Society of British Musicians in 1847.[100]

The Sonata in England from about 1850 to 1885 (Bennett)

The most successful and notable sonata composer in mid-Romantic England was the pianist, violinist, and conductor **William Sterndale Bennett** (1816–75), who studied with William Crotch and Cipriani Potter, became a close friend of Mendelssohn and Schumann in the later 1830's, and devoted much of his time to the Royal Academy of Music and the London Philharmonic Society in his later years.[101] Within his rather small life's output of some 65 piano, chamber, orchestral, and choral works Bennett wrote four sonatas that were published, between 1838 and 1876, three of them for P solo and one for P & Vc.[102] Op. 13 in f, for P solo, was composed in 1836–37, mostly while Bennett was enjoying music and the frequent company of Mendelssohn and Schumann in Leipzig for several months.[103] It was, in fact, dedicated to Mendelssohn on his wedding day and published by Kistner in Leipzig in 1838. Op. 32 in A, for P & Vc, was composed for and dedicated to the then leading cellist in London, Alfredo Piatti, but not completed until the very moment of its first performance in 1852, which was successful in spite of no rehearsal; Op. 32 was also published by Kistner, in 1853.[104] Op. 46 in A♭ originally bore a bilingual title that reads in full, *Die Jungfrau von Orleans (Schiller), The Maid of Orleans, Sonata for the Pianoforte, Composed Expressly for and Dedicated to Madame Arabella Goddard*

---

99. A performance of 2 mvts. of Op. 14 in 1875 is reported in MT XVII (1875) 58. For more on Horsley cf. MGG VI 764–68 (N. M. Temperley).

100. MUSICAL WORLD XXII (1847) 658.

101. Cf. MGG I 1661–63 (W. Kahl), with partly dated list of works; GROVE I 625–28 (H. C. Colles). Among numerous first-hand accounts and memoirs, considerable background information may be found in MT XVII (1875) 7–9 (obituary by H. C. Lunn); O'Leary/BENNETT; MT XLIV (1903) 306–9, 379–81, 523–27 (F. G. Edwards); Stanford/BENNETT; MT LVII (1916) 233–35 (F. Corder), 362–63 (L. N. Parker), 456–57 (K. C. Field); also, in Bache/BACHE *passim* (in connection with Bennett's pupil F. E. Bache). Most important is his son's detailed, fascinating biography, Bennett/BENNETT, which throws much light on contemporary English musical life and gives the circumstances of (though no commentaries on) the sons. by Bennett.

102. All of these sons. are listed in Cat. ROYAL 50. The "Notturno" in B reproduced in AMZ XLII (1840) as "Beilage No. 2 [actually 3]" affords a remarkable facs. of Bennett's handwriting.

103. Cf. Bennett/BENNETT 60, 61, 456.

104. Cf. Bennett/BENNETT 194, 211–12; MT XLIV (1903) 526. The early pub. by (Benjamin or Joseph?) Williams in London that is listed in MGG I 1662 could not be confirmed here.

(celebrated pianist, and pupil and wife of Bennett's friend J. W. Davison). One of the last, if not the last, of Bennett's compositions, following several years of no works for piano,[105] Op. 46 was started in 1869 but composed mostly "at the seaside" in the summer and fall of 1872,[106] and published first in London by Lamborn Cock not later than July, 1873, then posthumously by Kistner early in 1876.[107] Bennett's charming "Sonatine" in C for P solo, also published posthumously in 1876 by Kistner, was composed in 1871 for his grandson.[108]

Bennett's Op. 13 has four movements, F-Sc-M-VF, all in the same key, with a change of mode only in one movement (from f to F in iii). The shorter, inner movements are more appealing and original than either the long, Mendelssohnian first movement or the "weak" finale.[109] Schumann never got to the review that he promised to do of this "excellent" work in 1837,[110] although he had recently lauded Bennett's poetic compositions as significant redemptions for England's disappointing contributions to music,[111] and thought enough of Bennett at that time to dedicate his *Études symphoniques*, Op. 13, to him. Bennett's Op. 32, one of the few noteworthy cello sonatas from England at the time, again puts all movements in the same key, without even a change of mode. The ingratiating first movement, framed by a slow introduction that returns as a coda, succeeds well enough, but the other two movements suffer from the tonal monotony, especially as their harmonic progressions tend to be repetitious anyway.[112] Whereas Opp. 13 and 32 are scarcely mentioned in 19th-century sources seen here,[113] Bennett's Op. 46 is mentioned often, including references to more performances than can be credited to any other English sonata discussed in the present volume.[114] Undoubtedly, as we have seen in other sonatas

105. Stanford/BENNETT 657.

106. Bennett/BENNETT 390, 418, 423, 442; O'Leary/BENNETT 135.

107. Cf. MMR III (1873) 104–5; HOFMEISTER 1876, p. 22; NZM LXXII/1 (1876) 83.

108. Bennett/BENNETT 442, 460; MT XLIV (1903) 526; NZM LXXII/2 (1876) 283.

109. This opinion is also expressed in Shedlock/SONATA 231 and Bush/BENNETT 91–92.

110. Schumann/SCHRIFTEN I 308 (cf. II 410); he must have known Op. 13 in MS, meaning to review it when it got pub. in 1838.

111. Schumann/SCHRIFTEN I 245–47. Recall the introduction to the present chap. Cf., also, Spink/BENNETT.

112. Cf. Cobbett/CHAMBER I 118 (F. Corder).

113. Two performances of Op. 32 are noted in MT XV (1871) 142, one with Walter Macfarren at the piano; another (in Berlin) is noted in NZM LXXIII/1 (1877) 172.

114. E.g., cf. MT XVI (1874) 359 (played by Franklin Taylor at Crystal Palace in Dec., 1873; first public performance?), 367, 427, 519, 544, 723; XVII (1875–76) 58 (called "Joan of Arc"), 114, 671; XVIII (1877) 20, 138; XIX (1878) 40 (played by the dedicatee), 685; XXI (1880) 91; XXII (1881) 378, 430; XXIV (1882) 21; XV (1884) 338 (played by Bülow, whom Bennett had known).

with programmatic titles (cf. ssв IV), the popularity of Op. 46 was stimulated by the attraction of such a title plus more specific programmatic associations. Moreover, although Op. 46 stands well on its purely musical merits, in this instance the content does justify the emphasis on programmatic considerations that the initial reviewers and subsequent writers have made, as is already apparent in sentences extracted from the first (?) review:[115]

A new work by Sir W. Sterndale Bennett—unquestionably the greatest of living English composers—cannot be otherwise than in the highest degree welcome. As a sonata *per se* the work before us quite comes up to any anticipations we might have formed on being told that Sir W. Sterndale Bennett was about to issue a new sonata. It is additionally welcome, because in great measure it bears out the fact, so often maintained in these columns, that since Beethoven the greatest musical composers have relied upon a "poetic basis" for their inspirations. . . . The idea that his [Bennett's] choice of subject is governed by its compressibility into some fixed form is altogether to be scouted. . . . The subject of Joan of Arc is an admirable one for musical portrayal, though it treats of one of the blackest pages of English history. One may feel some regret that England's disgrace should thus be perpetuated by music, but the beauty and interest of Bennett's work fully atone for any such regret. . . . Curiously enough . . . [Moscheles' overture on the same subject] was played under its composer's direction at a concert of the Philharmonic Society, in 1835, at which Bennett, then a youth of about seventeen, came forward with his piano concerto in E flat.[116] Can it be that it was then that he was first struck with the idea of composing a sonata on the same subject, and that so many years have gone to maturing it? . . .

Bennett's Op. 46 falls in four contrasting movements totalling 36 pages in print, each headed and influenced by its own line or two, quoted in both German and English, from *Die Jungfrau von Orleans* by Schiller. The first movement, an "Andante pastorale" in A♭ that shifts frequently and freely between 12/8, 9/8, and 6/8 meter, is a songful, tender, almost childlike piece with the title "In the Fields" and the inscription (from Act iv, Scene 1) "In innocence I led my sheep/ Adown the mountain's silent steep." The second and longest movement, "Allegro marziale" in a♭ (with enharmonically related sections in b, B, and E) and in C meter, is a dramatic yet subtle piece faintly suggestive of the "Marche au supplice" in Berlioz' *Symphonie fantastique,* with the almost identical but different title "In the Field" and the inscription (Prologue/4) "The clanging trumpets sound, the chargers rear,/ And the loud war cry thunders in mine ear." The third move-

---

115. MMR III (1873) 104–5. Cf., also, MT XVI (1874) 391 (a similar, laudatory review); Statham/BENNETT 134; Shedlock/SONATA 231–32; Bie/PIANOFORTE 279; Westerby/PIANOFORTE 127 and 130–31; Bush/BENNETT 96–97.

116. Cf. MOSCHELES I 313–14.

ment, "Adagio patetico" in E and in 3/8 meter, is a poignant but gentle prayer and lament with the title "In Prison" and the inscription (v/2) "Hear me O God in mine extremity,/ In fervent supplication up to thee;/ Up to thy heaven above, I send my Soul." And the finale, "Molto di passione" in A♭ and in ₵ meter, presents an extended, rapid, naively impetuous yet hushed piece, almost a *perpetuum mobile,* with merely "The End" as the title and "Brief is the sorrow, endless is the joy" as the inscription (v/14). No further verbal guides to the subject of the programme occur except "alla Tromba" once in the course of the martial movement and one more inscription—"When on my native hills I drove my herd/ Then was I happy as in Paradise" (iv/9)—at a "semplice," "limpido," pianissimo section of "In Prison."

Although Bennett is able to create songful, fresh, unspoiled melodies that flow freely and spontaneously (Ex. 89), the separate movements produce the over-all effects not of standard, dynamic sonata forms but of miniature tone poems for the piano, or even of musical tableaux. Their only real structural principle is that of the rondo, but even this principle is applied so loosely, if not indifferently, that it seems more aimless than organized. Similarly and pertinently, the harmonic progressions are often interesting and generally compelling enough in themselves, but the over-all tonal movement is largely without significant direction, although there is now at least the key contrast in one inner movement that lacks in Bennett's earlier sonatas. Furthermore, there is pleasure in the euphony of Bennett's piano textures but eventual monotony in the rudimentary, stereotyped nature of his accompaniments. Finally, Bennett's artistic scope is narrow. He was a conservative who, failing to keep up with his contemporaries, never got beyond *frühromantische* music. And he was at his best in his simplest, most gentle, and most delicate writing, short of letting it become sickly sweet. His occasional attempts to write with passion and drama do seem naive. In all these respects, except for his earliest works,[117] his style is less like Mendelssohn's, in spite of frequent statements to the contrary, and more like that of Spohr, whom he met and admired,[118] with some hints, too, of the styles of Mozart, Hummel, and Dussek, whose music had made deep impressions on him,[119] and of Moscheles, who took an understandable liking to Bennett's music.[120]

117. Cf. MENDELSSOHN/Moscheles 170–71.
118. Cf. Bennett/BENNETT 116–22, 213–15, 451–53; MT LVII (1916) 233–34 (a somewhat negative reappraisal of Bennett's music by F. Corder); Stanford/BENNETT 638.
119. Cf. Bennett/BENNETT 21–26, 39; Temperley/MOZART 315–17; Temperley/MENDELSSOHN 229–32.
120. Cf. MOSCHELES I 314, II 49. But one would never discover in Bennett's music

Ex. 89. From the opening of William Sterndale Bennett's Sonata in A♭, Op. 46, "The Maid of Orleans" (facs. of the J. B. Cramer reprint, *ca.* 1905).

No sonatas by Bennett's contemporaries offer as much of interest as his. The productive, respected composer and theorist **George** (**Alexander**) **Macfarren** (1813–87) [121] and his younger, less known brother, the pianist **Walter** (**Cecil**) **Macfarren** (1826–1905),[122] each left several sonatas in print or MS.[123] At least five of George's many publications are sonatas—one in C for organ (1872?);[124] three for P solo, No. 1 being a Beethovian, four-movement work in E♭ (F-S-Sc-F; 1842),[125] No. 2 being in A, with the inscription "Ma Cousine" (1843),[126] and No. 3 being a four-movement work in g (F-M-Sc-F), dedicated to Agnes Zimmermann (*infra*), played by her and others, and reported to be a skillful if not inspired work, with derivations from Weber, Schumann, and Mendelssohn;[127] and one in B♭ for P & Fl (first pub. between 1865 and 1871).[128] But performances are reported of at least four other sonatas by George, including two more for P solo, of which the first was written for Agnes Zimmermann and first played by her in 1866;[129] a Sonata in C for P & Vn, in which brother Walter played the piano part at least twice;[130] and another organ sonata, in which there is a fugue based on "Rule Britannia." [131] Walter's smaller output included three published sonatinas for P solo (in C, g, and D), two sonatas for P solo played in 1845 (in c♯ and A, the first having 4 mvts. in the order F-Sc-M-VF and in the keys of c♯-E-A♭-c♯),[132] three duo sonatas of which two are for P & Vn (in F and D) and one for P & Vc (in e),[133] and a Sonata in e for P-duet performed in 1850.[134] Subsequent reviews of the

---

that he, too, was one of the many Romantics fascinated by Beethoven's Op. 106, in this instance by way of Potter and before Bennett met Mendelssohn (SSB VIII; cf. Bennett/BENNETT 33–34 and 400).

121. Cf. GROVE V 468–69 (W. H. Hadow) and MGG VIII 1385–88 (R. A. Harman), with further bibliography. Macfarren/POTTER includes recollections of his training under Potter.

122. Cf. GROVE V 469 (W. H. Hadow).

123. The pub. sons. of each are listed in PAZDÍREK X 26 and 29.

124. MT XV (1873) 743 and XVIII (1878) 359.

125. Reviewed in MUSICAL WORLD XVIII (1843) 102 and XIX (1844) 54; played in the same years.

126. Played in 1843, as noted in MUSICAL WORLD XVIII (1843) 122 and 134.

127. Shedlock/SONATA 230–31; MT XX (1879) 185, XXI (1880) 308, XXII (1881) 105, and XIV (1884) 386; NZM LXXI (1876) 70.

128. Temperley/CORRESPONDENCE.

129. MT XII (1866) 339.

130. MT XV (1871) 108 and 340.

131. MT XXII (1881) 197. MT XVII (1876) 251 advertises George's pamphlet "On the Structure of a Sonata."

132. MUSICAL WORLD XX (1845) 86, 583.

133. The sons. in D and e were played at the Society of British Musicians in 1848 and 1846, respectively (MUSICAL WORLD XXIII [1848] 685 and XXI [1846] 533). All 3 duos were pub. in 1876. At least Sonata in e had appeared earlier, *ca.* 1860.

134. MUSICAL WORLD XXV (1850) 27, 147.

duos mention "charmingly harmonized" themes, "happy modulations," "striking" tonal schemes, effective scoring, and good audience response.[135]

The composer, writer, and teacher (Charles) Hubert (Hastings) Parry (1848–1918) is generally regarded as "the most powerful influence in English musical life" and (with C. V. Stanford, *infra*) the most effective leader of its renaissance during the late 19th and early 20th centuries.[136] He already has been cited in the present volume for his stimulating though no longer widely accepted ideas on musical evolution (Parry/EVOLUTION) and for numerous contributions to GROVE.[137] As a composer, trained primarily by Bennett, G. A. Macfarren, H. H. Piersen, and Edward Dannreuther, Parry made his chief mark in choral music. But Dannreuther had directed his early interests (about 1876–83) chiefly to chamber music.[138] Among Parry's chamber works are the six solo and duo sonatas that constitute but an inconspicuous part of his large, rounded output of published and unpublished music.[139] Three of the sonatas were not published—Op. 20 in f, for P-duet, composed in 1865, Op. 75 in b, a one-movement "Fantasie-Sonata" for P & Vn, composed in 1878, and Op. 103 in D, for P & Vn, composed by or in 1889. The three that did appear in print include two for P solo —Op. 71 in F, composed and published in 1877,[140] and Op. 79 in A, published in 1878—and one for P & Vc, Op. 85 in A, composed about 1880 and published in 1883.[141]

H. C. Colles concludes that Parry's chamber works must be regarded "rather as evidences of abilities never wholly fulfilled than achievements in themselves" and quotes Parry on his own cello sonata (Op. 85) to the effect that "it all sprawls and is too long and indefinite." [142] Except for performances sponsored by Dannreuther,[143] the sonatas seem

135. MT XV (1871) 142 (Son. in F played by the composer and M. Sainton), XVI (1874) 712 (review of Son. in e, played by the composer and "Sig. Pezze") and 657 (Son. in F pub.), XVII (1876) 379 (3 sons. pub. by Novello), 515 and 558 (Son. in D, with the composer at the P), and 696 (Son. in e pub.), XVIII (1877) 185 (Son. in D reviewed), XXI (1880) 141 (Son. in F played), XXVII (1886) 480 (Son. in D played); MMR VI (1876) 95 (Son. in D reviewed).

136. Cf. GROVE VI 561–65 (J. A. Fuller-Maitland) and WESTRUP & HARRISON 484; also, MGG X 836–39 (J. M. Allan & H. F. Redlich), with further bibliography. Graves/PARRY is a full biography (with only incidental mentions of the sons.).

137. Cf. Graves/PARRY I 224, II 237.

138. Cobbett/CHAMBER II 207–11 (H. C. Colles) discusses Parry's chamber music at length, though mostly in broad terms.

139. The fullest and most specific list is that prepared by Emily Daymond for GROVE 3d ed. (and 4th) IV 57–63.

140. Cf. Graves/PARRY I 169.

141. Cf. Graves/PARRY 207, 208. Fuller-Maitland/PARRY 31 describes Op. 85 briefly.

142. Cobbett/CHAMBER II 209–10.

143. Dannreuther played the P part in performances of Op. 85 reported in MT XXII (1881) 302 and XXVII (1885) 20.

Ex. 90. From the start of Hubert Parry's Sonata 2 in A, Op.
79 (after the Augener reprint, plate no. 10775).

not to have been played to any appreciable extent. The abiding influence of Schumann and Brahms pervades the two piano sonatas. Shedlock finds Stephen Heller's stamp in them, too.[144] Apart from a Schumannesque opening in the second one that promises better (Ex. 90),
these are competent, conservative works at best, circumscribed by flat,
occasionally sentimental ideas, couched in piano writing that is practical and convenient but colorless, and developed in a Teutonically
academic manner. Both sonatas follow usual four-movement plans
(F-Sc-M-Ro and F-S-Sc-Ro), in which their scherzos make the most successful forms.

Further exploration of the sonata in England during the period from
1850 to 1885 would lead to such obscure and forgotten composers as
the Austrian pianist and pedagogue **Ernst Pauer** (1826–1905), who had
studied with W. A. Mozart "the Younger" (sce 567–68) before living in
London from 1851 to 1896 and before composing one competent,
Mendelssohnian sonata each for P solo (Op. 22 in f, pub. *ca.* 1847), P &
Vc (Op. 45 in A, pub. in 1855), and P & Vn (Op. 46 in a, pub. in 1856),
as well as some elementary, Mozartean sonatinas for P solo.[145] From

144. Shedlock/SONATA 233. Fuller-Maitland/PARRY 25 finds Weber in Op. 79/ii
and an anticipation of the canon of Franck's Sonata in A/iv in Op. 79/iv.

145. Cf. GROVE VI 595 (A. J. Hipkins); Altmann/KAMMERMUSIK 262 and 220; MMR

the same decade around the mid century may be noted two "modest but distinguished" sonatinas for Ob & P in g/B♭ and G (No. 1 dated 1848; both pub. posthumously in 1890) by the church composer **Thomas Attwood Walmisley** (1814–56);[146] thirteen sonatas, not further identified, by the "amateur" composer trained in Rome and often resident in Germany, **John Lodge Ellerton** (1801–73);[147] two academically correct sonatas suggesting Mendelssohn and Beethoven, Opp. 1 in f and 7 in E, for P solo, by the London organist **Henry Wylde** (1822–90), who seems himself to have given performances of them in 1846 and 1850, respectively;[148] and both solo and duo sonatas by two women composers, **Caroline Orger (Reinagle**; 1818–92; possibly a niece-by-marriage of A. Reinagle in the United States, SCE 806–7) and the pianist **Kate Fanny Loder** (1825–1904).[149]

Furthermore, the German-born pupil of Hummel and Weber, **Julius Benedict** (1804–85), lived in London from 1835 on, where besides operas and other works he left two pleasant, inconsequential sonatas for P & Vn (Op. 1 in d; Op. 80 in E, pub. in 1870).[150] An otherwise unidentified (German?) composer of chamber music, **Joseph Street** (?–?) left at least 6 sonatas for P solo, 2 for P & Vn, and one for P & Vc ("Sonate quasi Fantaisie" in G) that were published in Germany during the approximately 15 years that he was in London (1860–75).[151] The outstanding German-born pianist **Agnes Zimmermann** (1847–1925), who had studied with Potter, Pauer, Stegall, and G. Macfarren, not only introduced the sonatas of many others, from Mozart to Brahms, but herself left four Mendelssohnian duo sonatas, all published between 1868 and 1879 and warmly praised for their "invention," instrumental handling, and "individuality"—Opp. 16 in d (1868; ded. to Joachim), 21 in a (1875), and 23 in g (1879) for P & Vn, and Op. 17 in g (1872) for P & Vc.[152]

XV (1885) 57 and XX (1890) 130 (short favorable reviews of the sonatinas); SCE 15 and 116 (on Pauer's eds. and textbook).

146. Temperley/CORRESPONDENCE; cf. MT XCVII (1956) 636–39 (N. Temperley).

147. Cf. BROWN & STRATTON 137.

148. MUSICAL WORLD XXI (1846) 335; Temperley/CORRESPONDENCE.

149. Temperley/CORRESPONDENCE; MUSICAL WORLD XXI (1848) 655; BROWN & STRATTON 304, 252–53.

150. GROVE I 618–19 (H. S. Edwards). Cf. Altmann/KAMMERMUSIK 195; La Mara/MUSIKERBRIEFE II 177 and 179.

151. Cf. PAZDÍREK XIII 1140; Altmann/KAMMERMUSIK 228 and 265; MT XIII (1868) 573 (generally favorable review of 2 duos); Cobbett/CHAMBER II 467 (W. W. Cobbett).

152. Cf. GROVE IX 418 (G. Grove); MT LXVII (1926) 28–29 (Arbuthnot); Elson/WOMAN 145 and 239. On Op. 16, cf. Joachim/LETTERS 377; MT XIII (1868–69) 586, 622, and 645 (favorable review); XV (1871) 95 and 613; XVII (1876) 254; XVIII (1877) 311. On Op. 21, cf. MT XVI (1874) 513 and XVII (1875) 215; XX (1879) 605;

One **Charles Gardner** (1836–?), a pupil of Pauer and Macfarren, among others, left a Sonata in A, for P solo (pub. in 1871?), that was well received when he played it.[153] The Dutch-born violinist and editor for Novello, **Berthold Tours** (1838–97), moved to London in 1861, where his single contribution to the genre pursued here—a Sonatina in G, for P solo (pub. in 1871)—was reviewed as a charming, melodious, expressive work, superior to the usual children's teaching pieces with that title.[154] The pianist **William Henry Holmes** (1812–85) contributed to the sonata indirectly as a teacher of Bennett and the Macfarren brothers, among others, but also composed at least one Sonata for P & Vn himself that was performed though not published.[155] One **Charles Henry Shepherd** (1847–86), a student at the Royal Academy of Music in London and later an organist at St. Thomas's Church, Newcastle-on-Tyne, left a Sonata for P solo that was dedicated to G. A. Macfarren, published by Augener in 1871, and reviewed with some praise for the skill and some censure of the ideas.[156] The organist, teacher, conductor, and writer **Henry Hiles** (1826–1904) won a prize in 1868 from the "College of Organists" for his Sonata in g for organ, published in that year.[157] At fourteen the pianist and "Sterndale Bennett Scholar" at the Royal Academy of Music, **Charleton (Templeman) Speer** (1859–1921), dedicated to his teacher G. A. Macfarren his only known sonata, in G for P solo, whose publication by Novello in 1875 brought strongly favorable reviews for its skill, propriety, and musical fluency, "without any allowance on the score of years." [158] The operetta composer **Julian Edwards** (1855–1910) saw his Sonata in D, for P solo, published in 1876 before he emigrated to the United States (1888).[159] One **Robert Hainworth** (?–?) left three organ sonatas that were published between 1872 and 1876 and reviewed as weak, unidiomatic, and rhythmically imprecise works in spite of prizes awarded earlier for two of them by the

---

XXIV (1883) 321 (favorable report); XXVII (1886) 141. On Op. 23, cf. MT XX (1879) 313 (favorable review) and 443; XXI (1879) 28 (favorable report from Berlin); XXIV (1883) 206. On Op. 17, cf. MT XV (1871) 115. If the reference to a Son. for P solo, Op. 22, is correct in GROVE IX 418 the work seems not have been pub.; the "Sonata" for Vn, Vc, & P was actually a "Suite." The dates of pub. in Cobbett/CHAMBER II 598 and Altmann/KAMMERMUSIK 233 are mostly incorrect.

153. MT XV (1871) 141 and XVIII (1878) 336. Cf. PAZDÍREK VI 80.

154. Cf. MGG XIII 595 (B. Ramsey); MT XV (1871) 243.

155. Cf. GROVE IV 327–28 (G. Grove); MT XV (1872) 622 and 690.

156. MT XV (1871–72) 217 and 509.

157. MT XIII (1868) 556 and XV (1871) 158. Cf. GROVE IV 277 (A. Chitty).

158. MT XVII (1875) 60, 62, 117, 282 (with excerpts from 2 other reviews). Cf. GROVE VIII 3 (G. S. K. Butterworth).

159. It is reviewed as a careful work, with poor ideas, poorly developed, in MT XVII (1875–76) 533 (cf. p. 446). Cf. BAKER 423.

"College of Organists."[160] Six more organ sonatas (1876) and three sonatas for Fl & P (1883) were left by the gifted organist, violinist, clarinetist, conductor, and much published composer (James) Hamilton (Smee) Clarke (1840–1912).[161] The theorist Henry Charles Banister (1831–97) left two unpublished sonatas for P solo, in f and f♯, that were both reported with praise after recitals of new music in 1874 and 1875.[162] The organist Charles Joseph Frost (1848–1918) left one long, favorably reviewed sonata (in A, 1876) and one sonatina for his instrument and seven sonatinas for P solo, all published, plus at least one more organ sonata (in A♭, 1877), in MS.[163] The Dutch-born organist Edouard Silas (1827–1909) left at least one sonata for P solo and twelve organ sonatas of which only the last organ sonata, Op. 82 in F, was published (1873 and later), in its entirety and in extracts.[164] Another among "all those obscure English organists,"[165] Francis Edward Gladstone (1845–1925), left a Sonata in a, for organ (pub. in 1879), that was described as being skillful and well scored but unoriginal.[166]

The German-born organist and conductor Wilhelm Meyer Lutz (1822?–1903), in England from 1848, left a Sonata for P & Vn, Op. 23 (pub. by André in Offenbach/M in 1874) that was reviewed as an essentially empty work.[167] Another born in Germany, the pianist and writer Ferdinand Christian Wilhelm Praeger (1815–91), was a protégé of both Hummel and Schumann before moving to London in 1834 and left four published sonatas—one for P & Vn and three for P solo (a, C, and E)—of which the first (1889) fared only slightly better with the reviewers.[168] The esteemed organist and theorist Frederick Arthur Gore Ouseley (1825–89) left a Sonata in C and a "Second Sonata" for organ that seemed to have enjoyed a number of performances following their respective publications in 1879 and 1883.[169] The fine organist Walter Battison Haynes (1859–1900) composed a Sonata for Vn & P (MS only?)

160. MT XII (1866) 460, XV (1872) 158 and 630 (review), XIX (1878) 301 and 453 (review); PAZDÍREK VII 97.

161. Cf. MT XVII (1876) 637; PAZDÍREK III 362–63; Altmann/KAMMERMUSIK 272; GROVE II 330 (H. G. Farmer).

162. MT XVI (1874) 583, XVII (1875) 13. Cf. GROVE I 400 (J. A. Fuller-Maitland).

163. MT XVII (1876) 685, XVIII (1877) 281 and 297; PAZDÍREK V 570–71. Cf. BAKER 516.

164. MT XV (1873) 743, XVIII (1878) 359, XX (1879) 499, XXI (1880) 645; NZM LXXII/2 (1876) 354. Cf. GROVE VII 790–91 (G. Grove).

165. Cf. GROVE I vi (E. Blom).

166. MT XX (1879) 547; XXI (1880) 137. Cf. GROVE III 655 (F. G. Rendall).

167. MW XI (1880) 203. Cf. GROVE V 449 (G. Grove).

168. SMW XLVII (1889) 737–38; MW XXI (1890) 127. Cf. GROVE VI 904 (G. Grove); PAZDÍREK XI 511.

169. MT XVIII (1877) 554, XXII (1881) 471, XXIV (1883) 638, XXV (1884) 353. Cf. GROVE VI 467–68 (H. W. Shaw); MGG X 491–93 (R. A. Harman).

and a Sonata for organ in d, Op. 11, while studying in Leipzig, Op. 11 being published in 1883 and welcomed for its free fantasy, originality, high artistry, and unusual "Scherzoso." [170] The pianist and conductor **Charles Swinnerton Heap** (1847–1900), an eventual pupil of Bennett whose "Mendelssohn scholarship" in 1865–66 had brought instruction in Leipzig from Moscheles, Hauptmann, Richter, and Reinecke, left a Sonata in Bb, for P & Cl (pub. in 1880?), and a Sonata in d, for P & Vn (pub. in 1884?), the latter being reviewed favorably for its good ideas, contrasts, and scoring.[171] Another organist and a pupil of Potter, **Charles Edward Stephens** (1821–92), composed a "Sonata piacevole," for P & Fl, that was published in 1883 and performed at least twice in public,[172] and a Sonata for P solo, Op. 8 in Ab (pub. in 1866). One **J. Conway Brown** won "ten guineas and a gold medal" in 1882 for a Sonata in E, for P & Vn, that Novello published in 1884.[173] And in Edinburgh, the respected organist and pedagogue **Herbert (Stanley) Oakeley** (1830–1903) left a four-movement Sonata in A, for P solo (presumably pub., *ca.* 1873) that was reviewed as a generally weak work, especially in its outer movements.[174]

England in the Late-Romantic Era (Stanford, Dale)

Right through World War I England continued to produce sonatas in surprising abundance, yet still without making a major contribution to that literature. Most important in this last group, although more so because of their general importance to music than the actual sonatas they left, were Stanford and Elgar. Both men were near contemporaries of Parry (*supra*) and figured similarly in the "renaissance of English music," but belong in a later grouping here because they wrote some of their sonatas much later. Born in Dublin, **Charles Villiers Stanford** (1852–1924) moved to England at the age of eighteen, studied with Reinecke and Kiel in Germany (ssb X) in the mid 1870's, came under the strong influences of Schumann's and Brahms's music, and gave his time to being a respected organist, teacher, and conductor as well as a prolific composer in all main branches of music.[175] Thirteen sonatas

170. MW XVIII (1887) 351, 352. Cf. GROVE IV 211 (F. G. Edwards).
171. MT XXI (1880) 141 and 626, XXIV (1883) 551, XXV (1884) 208 (review), XVII (1886) 283. Cf. GROVE IV 593 (W. B. Squire). The Son. for P solo cited in BAKER 681 could not be confirmed here.
172. MT XXIV (1883) 638, XXV (1884) 33, XXVII (1886) 480. Cf. GROVE VIII 79 (W. H. Hadow).
173. MT XXIII (1882) 450, XXV (1884) 596 and 670.
174. MMR III (1873) 148. Cf. GROVE VI 142 (W. H. Hadow).
175. Cf. GROVE VIII 45–55 (S. Goddard and B. D. Banner) and MGG XII 1172–84 (F. Hudson), each with a fully dated list of works (but with gaps and several errors,

by Stanford are known, dating from his student to his last years. Five of these are duos, including two each for P & Vc and P & Vn, and one for Cl-or-Va & P; two late works (Op. 165) also call for two performers but are not true duos, for they are designated, exceptionally, "for violin solo with pianoforte accompaniment" and are aimed rather at the style of the Baroque "solo" sonata;[176] and six are solos, of which one is for piano and five are late works for organ. Out of all thirteen sonatas nine have been published, including Op. 9 in A for P & Vc (1879; composed by 1877; ded. to the cellist R. Hausman)[177] and Op. 39 in D for P & Vc (1893; ded. to the cellist A. Piatti);[178] Op. 11 in D, for P & Vn (1880; ded. to the violinist L. Straus);[179] Op. 129 in F for Cl(-or-Va) & P (1918; composed in 1911; ded. to O. W. Street and C. Draper); and the five organ sonatas—Op. 149 in F, No. 1 (1917; ded. to A. Gray); Op. 151 in g/G, No. 2, "Eroica" (1919; ded. to C. M. Widor; i and iii called "Rheims" and "Verdun, 1916"); Op. 152 in d, No. 3, "Britannica" (1918; ded. to W. Parratt); Op. 153 in c/C, No. 4, "Celtica" (1920; ded. to H. Darke; iii called "St. Patrick's Breastplate"); Op. 159 in A, No. 5, "quasi una fantasia" (1921).[180]

Contemporary reviewers greeted especially Stanford's earlier sonatas with unqualified praise. Thus, with a "welcome [for] this Sonata, [simply] because it is a Sonata, and before looking at a single bar," and with "special commendation in the present instance" for a new contribution to the "strangely neglected" cello repertoire, the reviewer in the London *Musical Times* describes Op. 9 movement by movement (M/F-F-S-F), incorporating thirteen music examples, and concludes that it "is a more than creditable addition to high-class English music, and an honour to its composer." [181] In 1884, when Agnes Zimmermann introduced Stanford's "new [MS] Sonata, which is in the unusual key of D flat" (Op. 20 for P solo; unpub.), the reviewer in the same periodical had "no hesitation in characterising it as one of the most important compositions for piano solo produced within the present genera-

as also in Altmann/KAMMERMUSIK and in the cat. Hudson/STANFORD). Greene/STANFORD is the chief account of the man and his music.

176. At least one of these 2 sons., Op. 165/2, was commissioned by the British chamber music promoter W. W. Cobbett and played in London on May 7, 1919; cf. Cobbett/CHAMBER II 453 (T. F. Dunhill) and 454 (W. W. Cobbett); MT LX (1919) 306 (reporting Op. 165/2 as "characteristic of the composer in merit, while tending to an unusually simple style").

177. Cf. NZM LXXIII/1 (1877) 222 (played in London); MT XX (1879) 150, 157, 321.

178. Played by Fanny Davies and Piatti in 1886, Op. 39 is described in Fuller-Maitland/PARRY 34.

179. Cf. MT XXI (1880) 631, XXIV (1883) 147, 206, and 265.

180. These 5 sons. are described briefly in Fuller-Maitland/PARRY 102–3.

181. MT XX (1879) 150 and 157.

tion." [182] He had started by deploring the poor attendance and such "indifference on the part of the public to the claims of native art," for "We have three or four young composers whose collective ability is at least equal to that of the same number of leading German living musicians, whose utterances always awaken interest and expectation." Referring to analyses of all but the finale in the program notes, the reviewer merely summarized the three movements (S/F-F-F). Friendly but matter-of-fact approval rather than unqualified praise characterizes the short review in 1917 of the first organ sonata as a work in three movements (F-Mi-F), "of moderate length, straightforward in character, admirably suited to the instrument, and not difficult" [183] (a comment that more or less fits all of Stanford's sonatas seen here).

In a longish, ruminative article for *Cobbett's Cyclopedic Survey of Chamber Music,* T. F. Dunhill emphasizes that Stanford was a pioneer in the "revival" of English chamber music, furthered chiefly by his own students—including Vaughan Williams, Frank Bridge, Rutland Boughton, John Ireland, and Herbert Howells (as well as Dunhill himself).[184] But Dunhill concludes that Stanford in his devotion to this branch of music clung too uncompromisingly to German tradition, especially the precedent of Brahms (as might be expected of Kiel's student), and approached the composition of it almost too reverently and circumspectly to achieve the originality, sparkle, and human warmth such as have made his songs more popular. And hoping (evidently in vain) that the best of Stanford's chamber music might not drown with the weakest—"as has happened in the case of other prolific composers like Raff, or Jensen, or even Saint-Saëns"—Dunhill singled out Stanford's piano Quintet in d, the piano Trio in E♭, the cello Sonata in d (Op. 39), and the middle movement of the clarinet Sonata in F (Op. 129) as most deserving of continued or renewed attention. Others have concluded that Stanford was at his best, anyway, in shorter forms and in the more local writing techniques, and that "the vision becomes clouded" in the larger works.[185]

Here we may take Op. 129 as thoroughly representative of Stanford's published duo sonatas and as his sonata most likely to survive, if only because of its need in the relatively limited literature of both the clarinet and the viola. In this work the stamp of Brahms's two clarinet

182. MT XXV (1884) 147 (with mention of another performance 12 days later); much of the review is quoted in Shedlock/SONATA 233–34. Cf. also, Fuller-Maitland/ PARRY 24.

183. MT LVIII (1917) 549.

184. Cobbett/CHAMBER II 451–54 (with an addition by W. W. Cobbett). The substance of this article is repeated in Greene/STANFORD 224–30.

185. Cf. GROVE VIII 46.

Ex. 91. The retransition to the recapitulation in the first movement of Charles Villiers Stanford's Sonata in F, Op. 129 (after the original ed. of 1918, by kind permission of Stainer & Bell, Ltd., copyright holders).

sonatas stands clear from the start, whether in the 3ds and 6ths of the precise texture, the grouping and nature of the rhythmic incises, the arpeggiated writing for both instruments, or the chordally oriented ideas themselves. But Stanford's highly skillful writing is sparer than Brahms's (Ex. 91), sometimes almost antiseptically spare. It also poses fewer technical demands on the performer, while still presupposing an advanced command of each instrument. The closely interrelated themes in the three movements of Op. 129 (F-S-F) are well-conceived as kernels for sonata treatment, but not especially attractive or warm in their own right. The one conspicuous exception, as might be expected from the composer of the successful "Irish Rhapsodies" for orchestra, is the tender Irish lament called "Caoine," which enters at the turn to major in the middle movement in d, marked "Adagio (quasi fantasia)."

In 1898 England's most celebrated Romantic composer, **Edward (William) Elgar** (1857–1934), wrote his Novello agent August Jaeger that "you are wrong in thinking I don't like some 'forms' of music—anything 'genuine' and natural pleases me—the stuff I hate and which I know is ruining any chance for good music in England is stuff like Stanford's which is neither fish, flesh, fowl, nor good red-herring!" [186]

186. ELGAR-Nimrod 30–31.

Elgar's relations with Stanford did improve a little from time to time.[187] But there were frictions between Parry, Stanford, and Elgar, as within the similarly close trio of near contemporaries in France— Franck, Saint-Saëns, and Fauré (ssb XIII)—and, to quote Percy Young, "Considering their respective temperaments it is surprising that Elgar and Stanford did not collide more often." [188] At any rate, although he was similarly productive in all main branches of music, Elgar paid less attention to the sonata than either Parry or Stanford, and wrote only two significant examples, one for organ and one for P & Vn.[189] A so-called organ "Sonata No. 2," Op. 87a (pub. in 1933), is Ivor Atkins' arrangement of Elgar's Severn Suite for Brass Band, completed in 1930.[190] A "Sonatina, Op. 1 [!]," composed for his niece May Grafton and published by Keith Prowse in 1931 (not 1932), proves to be a purely pedagogic piece of seven pages in two movements (M-F), too elementary to be pertinent here. The MS of an early violin sonata, Op. 9, was destroyed by the composer himself.[191]

Elgar wrote his Sonata in G for organ, Op. 28, mostly in June of 1895 during a hectic year of composition, rehearsals, and perform-ances.[192] It was performed first on July 8 by Hugh Blair at the Worcester Cathedral for a congress of American organists; then published by Breitkopf & Härtel in the following year, with a dedication to Swinnerton Heap (supra). Elgar described Op. 28 as a "big" work.[193] It meets that description in the sense of four movements occupying thirty-three pages but not in greatness, for it is no more than a highly competent, routine work. Its movements (F-F-M-VF) fall into standardized though asymmetrical designs, "sonata form" in the outer and A-B-A in the inner movements. Although the texture is frequently contrapuntal, there is no preludial, fugal, or chorale movement and no titles that might suggest the frequent association of the organ sonata with the church. There is considerable chromaticism, but mostly in melodic passing tones supported by diatonic, conventional harmony. The ideas themselves are not distinguished and suffer from pedestrian rhythms in the phrases.

Elgar's Sonata in e, Op. 82, for Vn & P, was composed during a

187. Cf. ELGAR-Nimrod 10, 31, 76, 111, 197, 212; Young/ELGAR 119–20, 92–94, 126; Greene/STANFORD 149–59.

188. ELGAR-Nimrod 289.

189. The chief recent studies of the man and his music are Reed/ELGAR, Young/ELGAR, and McVeagh/ELGAR. Additional facts on the sons. may be gleaned from the letters in ELGAR-Nimrod and Elgar/LETTERS.

190. Young/ELGAR 415.

191. Cf. MT LX (1919) 162; Young/ELGAR 405.

192. Cf. Young/ELGAR 73, 406.

193. ELGAR-Nimrod 5.

burst of three master chamber works in 1918 that included the string
Quartet in e, Op. 83, and the piano Quintet in a, Op. 84. Begun while
the composer was convalescing from a minor operation in March, it
was completed in September, the background of those six months being
a delightful stay in the country, far from the continuing rages of World
War I.[194] It was dedicated to an old friend, Mrs. Marie Joshua, whose
death four days before its completion explains the turn to a gentle,
retrospective, almost elegiac section, marked "molto più lento," on the
second last page.[195] Publication by Novello followed in 1919, with the
first of two early, warmly welcomed performances occurring on March
21.[196] Among further performances of Op. 82 during Elgar's lifetime
were those by Thibaud and Cortot in 1922 and one in which the enterprising English pianist Harriet Cohen participated in 1933.[197] The
work is in three movements (F-M-F) of moderate length, comprising
asymmetrical "sonata forms" in the outer movements again, and an
A-B-A design in the middle "Romance." [198] The first movement is
direct and moderately intense as well as compelling (Ex. 92). The
second seems curiously un-Elgarian in its A section, if one has in mind
the Elgar of the violin Concerto in b, *The Dream of Gerontius,* the
ever-popular "Pomp and Circumstance" March in D, or even the
greater intimacies of the "Enigma Variations." This section is at once
gossamer in its texture, mysterious in a flippant way, and quasi-Spanish
in the vamp that supplies bits of its accompaniment. Perhaps here was
the "wood magic" that his wife reported to be coming from Elgar's
room during that summer of 1918.[199] As with the organ sonata, the
finale is the most original and convincing movement. But this whole
sonata is more alive and appealing than the organ sonata. The violin
rather than the keyboard was Elgar's own main instrument. Although
the keyboard writing is anything but resourceful in either work and
the harmony is only a little more enterprising in the later one, the
violin seems to have stimulated the bolder, more potent ideas and the
more effective idiomatic passagework that help to make this work go.
The short time span of but one generation has canceled H. C. Colles's

194. Circumstances of the composition are related in Reed/ELGAR 121–22, Young/
ELGAR 192, and Elgar/LETTERS 245–46.
195. Young/ELGAR 192.
196. Cf. MT LX (1919) 71, 179, 245; Reed/ELGAR 127 (W. H. Reed himself being
the violinist); Young/ELGAR 198.
197. Elgar/LETTERS 277 and 312.
198. Op. 82 is described briefly in MT LX (1919) 163–64 (with 5 exx.); Cobbett/
CHAMBER I 373–74 (W. H. Reed; with 8 exx.) and 377 (W. W. Cobbett); Reed/ELGAR
125 and 148–49; McVeagh/ELGAR 179–80; Young/ELGAR 349–50; Shand/VIOLIN 203–6
(with 7 exx.).
199. Young/ELGAR 192.

Ex. 92. From the opening of Edward Elgar's Sonata in e, Op. 82 (after the original ed. of 1919, by kind permission of H. W. Gray, U.S. agents for Novello & Co. in London).

remark that "in England at any rate all his [Elgar's] major works are regularly given." [200] But if there is to be a revival of Elgar's best works, Op. 82 deserves at least a chance to be tried.

Among numerous minor contemporaries of Parry, Stanford, and Elgar, **Algernon (Bennett Langton) Ashton** (1859–1937) trained under Moscheles, Reinecke, and Raff, among other Germans, and wrote music in most of the main categories.[201] After his return to England as a young man, some 160 of his many more works achieved publication, although most that did so appeared and won favor in Leipzig rather than London. These include 9 sonatas published between 1881 and 1899 (following MS duo sons. that date back to at least 1876 [202]), 4 being for P & Vn, 4 for P & Vc, and one for P & Va. Ashton's publications also include 7 of 24 sonatas for P solo that he wrote in all major and minor keys, these 7 being published between 1899 and 1925.[203] Ashton's published sonatas were generally praised for their skill, ideas, and serious purpose, although the later reviews hint at prolixity and less con-

200. GROVE 4th ed. Suppl. 196.

201. Cf. GROVE I 240–41 (F. G. Edwards); MGG I 749–50 (G. Abraham).

202. Cf. NZM LXXII/2 (1876) 475.

203. Cf. Altmann/KAMMERMUSIK 192, 245, 251. Most of the duo and all of the solo sons. are at the Library of Congress.

sequential ideas.[204] The early and late samples examined here show no pronounced changes of style.[205] They follow standard designs and plans, and adhere to traditional harmony. And they abound and excel in continuous figural writing fluent enough to be almost glib, were it not for the pointed harmony and sonorous use of the keyboard. In a somewhat flat, less imaginative manner the solo sonatas bring to mind the frequently continuous figural writing, the keyboard scoring, and the chromatic harmony of Medtner and Rachmaninoff. Ashton is at his weakest when he must stop the figural writing long enough to commit himself to a tangible idea.

A composer of exceptional craftsmanship, polish, and sensitivity was **Benjamin (James) Dale** (1885–1943), who stemmed from German training only indirectly through Frederick Corder, a pupil of F. Hiller, at the Royal Academy of Music in London.[206] Corder once claimed "that Dale had then written 'fewer and better works than any English composer of his generation'"; and Edwin Evans wrote in 1929 that Dale's first and best known publication, his Sonata in d for P solo, was "still regarded as one of the outstanding works of the English neo-romantics." [207] This publication was still a student work, composed in his late teens (1902–5), dedicated to York Bowen (*infra*) and first played by him in 1905, and published by both Charles Avison in London and Breitkopf & Härtel in Leipzig in 1906, as Op. 1.[208] Dale's only other sonata was Op. 11 in E, for P & Vn, composed in 1921–22 and first performed in 1922 after his partial recuperation from four years of war internment in Germany, then published by Augener in 1923.[209] The two sonatas follow the same unusual plan of an extended "sonata form" followed by an even more extended set of variations in which

204. E.g., cf. MT XXX (1889) 616 (on Op. 38 in E, for P & Vn; also praised in Cobbett/CHAMBER I 27 [A. Mann] as against Op. 86 in c; described, with 7 exx., in Shand/VIOLIN 206–9); MT XXXIV (1893) 613 (on Op. 75 in G, for P & Vc); SMW LIV (1896) 290 (on Op. 86 in c, for P & Vn); MW XXXII (1901) 612 (on Opp. 115 in a and 128 in B♭, for P & Vc); MW XXXII (1901) 165 and DM III/1 (1903–4) 439 (both on Op. 101 in e♭, for P solo). Cf., also, MT XXVII (1885) 33 (performance of Op. 3 D, for P & Vn).

205. W. W. Harrison describes and illustrates 2 Vn sons. in STRAD XXVII (1916–17) 135–36 (Op. 86) and 163–65 (Op. 99), and 3 Vc sons. in STRAD XXVIII (1917–18) 125–27 (Op. 75), 151–52 (Op. 115), and 181–82 (Op. 128).

206. Cf. GROVE II 578–80 (E. Evans, H. C. Colles, and W. H. Stock); MGG II 1871–73 (H. F. Redlich).

207. GROVE II 579; Cobbett/CHAMBER I 310; cf., also, MGG II 1872.

208. Cf. MT LIX (1918) 164 on the problem of getting such a big work published. No English review of either the first performance or first ed. has turned up here.

209. In MT LXV (1923) 480, Op. 11 is reviewed as charming, solid, and free of shock, but unbalanced by its overly imposing set of variations.

are embodied among other variations a slow movement, a scherzo, and a finale.[210] Whereas Dale's huge Op. 1 (totalling 1,246, or 317+929, mss. in 62 pp., and lasting nearly an hour) discloses all the exuberance and energy, plus even some of the splash, of youth, his somewhat shorter Op. 11 tends to be more refined and emotionally controlled. Yet Op. 11, with its parallel 5ths and chord strands, does not lag harmonically behind at least the less daring trends in the early 1920's. By contrast, as Corder wrote in 1918 (while revealing his own tastes), Dale's Op. 1 still manifested "not the faintest tendency to extravagance, or what is called modernism—that foolish and offensive employment of discords as concords which the younger French writers affect." [211]

But Op. 1 was not really conservative, either, for its day. Both its harmony and its unusual and flexible form were new enough to puzzle a main German reviewer.[212] In its less sentimental, obvious passages Op. 1 leaves not so much the impression of Reger (SSB XI) that H. F. Redlich finds in Dale's music[213] as of the similarly precocious Richard Strauss (SSB XI), especially in its near surfeit of continuous, bold, upward thrusts, appoggiaturas, anticipations, and passing tones (Ex. 93). There are also passages, such as the sequential crescendo in measures 85–96 of the first movement, that leave the impression of Liszt and add interest to Norman Demuth's ranking of Dale's Op. 1 on a par with Liszt's Sonata in b "for resource and design." [214] Dale's precocious chef-d'oeuvre does rank high in the late Romantic sonata and could be revived successfully by a capable pianist playing for an audience sympathetic to that period and genre. Its sustained drive during the passagework is generally convincing and exciting. Its piano writing is rich and balanced in sound, often polyphonically active, remarkably varied, decidedly idiomatic, and, though nearly as difficult as Liszt's, similarly practical to play. Its two out-and-out melodies, the second theme of the first movement and the theme of the variations, are well drawn and well drawn out. And its forms, even on such a large scale, already show a developed sense of broad organization and creative flexibility, including the asymmetrical "sonata form" and the seven-variations-and-finale, headed "Slow Movement [vars. I–IV], Scherzo [V–VII] and Finale."

210. Op. 1 was analyzed authoritatively by Corder, with frequent superlatives injected, in MT LIX (1918) 164–67 (including 14 exx.), immediately after Dale's despondent return from internment. Op. 11 is described, with 2 exx., in Cobbett/ CHAMBER I 312–13 (E. Evans).
211. MT LIX (1918) 165.
212. DM VI/4 (1906–7) 306 (A. Leitzmann).
213. MGG II 1872.
214. Demuth/TRENDS 121–22.

Ex. 93. From the first bridge in Benjamin J. Dale's Sonata in
d, Op. 1 (after the original Charles Avison ed. of 1906).

Already forgotten from late-Romantic England are three early duo
sonatas in MS and a "promising," published, four-movement Sonata in
g, for P solo (1886?), by the esteemed writer on the sonata and other
music, **William Henry Hadow** (1859–1937);[215] the two published,
Mendelssohnian sonatas, for Fl & P (1883) and P solo (Op. 45 in e;
1886), by the successful, German-trained pianist **John Francis Barnett**
(1837–1916);[216] and five early, more-or-less Brahmsian sonatas of little
musical significance, by "the most remarkable and original woman
composer in the history of music," [217] that redoubtable and, at her
best, more than competent **Ethel (Mary) Smyth** (1858–1944).[218] These

215. Cf. MGG V 1219–23 (R. A. Harman); MMR XV (1885) 233 (favorable review of
Son. in g♯). The MS duos, cited in GROVE IV 10 and BAKER II 636, seem now to be
lost.
216. Cf. MMR XVI (1886) 88 (review of Op. 45 as "melodious and elegant");
GROVE I 442–43 (E. F. Rimbault); Cobbett/CHAMBER I 59 (W. W. Cobbett). The
autograph of an unpub. 4-mvt. Son. in c (VF-Va-Mi-F), for P solo (ca. 1820), by
Barnett's father John (1802–90) is in the Boston Public Library (according to Mr.
N. K. Moran of the Rare Book Dept.).
217. In the words of George Henschel, as quoted in St. John/SMYTH 43. A similar
evaluation is made by Ernest Newman in his "Introduction," p. xi, to SMYTH MEMOIRS.
218. Cf. SMYTH MEMOIRS; St John/SMYTH (with a full list of works, pp. 305–8, and
a "critical study" of the music, by K. Dale, pp. 288–304).

last include two sonatas and most of a third for P solo, all generally unpianistic student works left in MSS dated 1877;[219] and two duos in a, both published by Peters in Leipzig in 1887, one each for P & Vc (Op. 5; first performed in London in 1926 [220]) and P & Vn (Op. 7). Op. 7 was reviewed by the same Eduard Bernsdorf who railed for so long against Grieg (ssb XV), as "corrupt and tasteless to a shocking degree scarcely believable from a woman";[221] and it was rejected by Joachim for his own performances as "unnatural, farfetched, overwrought, and not good as to sound." [222]

A London pianist of Spanish descent, **Emanuel Abraham Aguilar** (1824–1904) left among "much chamber music" three sonatas for P solo, of which one, in C, was published and two, in a and e, were played by him in 1888, bringing such noncommittal reactions as "meritorious" and "not of the most advanced school." [223] The Italian-born pianist **Carlo Albanesi** (1856–1920), a student of his father Luigi before he prospered in London (from 1882), left six sonatas for P solo. The five of these that were published (1894–1913) reveal undistinguished, sometimes trite themes, extended and developed with the typically professional know-how of the epigone, supported by traditional, chromatic harmony, spiced with added dissonances, weighted with full textures, and enhanced by varied, idiomatic uses of the keyboard.[224] Even the venerated, self-taught theorist, writer, and pedagogue **Ebenezer Prout** (1835–1909) had a try at composing sonatas, among other chamber works, his three published examples being Op. 4 for organ (ca. 1875), Op. 17 in A, for Fl & P (1882), and Op. 26 in D, for Cl-or-Va & P (1890). These were politely damned with the usual theorist's curse of much skill and little imagination.[225] On the other hand, the organist **William Henry Speer** (1863–1937), a pupil of Stanford and others (and a cousin of C. T. Speer, *supra*), won praise for the content but not the form of two Brahmsian sonatas in D, both pub-

---

219. The delectable SMYTH MEMOIRS 192, 195, 197–98, 205 describe and partly disparage these 3 sons.; cf., also, Dale/SMYTH 332–35 (with an ex. from the rondo finale of the first son., in C).

220. GROVE VII 860 (K. Dale).

221. SMW XLV (1887) 1030.

222. Joachim's letter is trans. in full in SMYTH MEMOIRS 407. Cf. this same source, pp. 396, 398–99; also, St John/SMYTH 54–55, 183 (a more favorable reaction in 1923), 292 (K. Dale's evaluation); Cobbett/CHAMBER II 433–34 (a description of Op. 7 by K. Eggar).

223. MT XXIX (1888) 356. Cf. BAKER 12; PAZDÍREK I 95.

224. Cf. GROVE I 87 (E. Blom); MT XXXV (1894) 689 (S. Lucas in a review of Son. 1 in Ab) and L (1909) 792 (review of Son. 5 in E).

225. Cf. Cobbett/CHAMBER II 244–45 (A. Mann and W. W. Cobbett); MMR XX (1890) 113–14 (on Op. 26); GROVE VI 951 (W. H. Hadow); MGG X 1661–62 (R. A. Harman).

lished by Breitkopf & Härtel in 1893 (Opp. 2 for P solo and 4 for P & Vn).[226]

The gifted but short-lived pianist **William (Yeates) Hurlstone** (1876–1906), a pupil of Stanford and Ashton, left three duo sonatas that were published, two of them posthumously in 1909. The first of these, for P & Vn in d (1897), is described as "technically interesting if not characteristic," the second, for P & Vc in D, as "a fine work," and the third, exceptionally for Bn & P, as outstanding in scoring, originality of treatment, and melodic appeal.[227] An erstwhile businessman (though no Charles Ives!), **Ernest Austin** (1874–1947) indulged his primary musical inclinations by composing "14 sonatinas on English folksongs for children" (pub. ca. 1910–30) but also left a "Lyric Sonata" for P & Vn in D, Op. 70 (pub. in 1925) and at least two sonatas for P solo, of which the second, Op. 31 in b♭ (pub. in 1907), runs on anemically, like casual dinner music, with its chief harmonic "surprise" being an occasional reference to the major triad on the lowered submediant degree.[228] The fine pianist **Oscar Beringer** (1844–1922), born and trained in Germany, also left piano sonatinas of interest to children, of which at least six appeared in full or in part in 1903, including two with programmatic title ("pastorale" and "marziale").[229]

The London violinist **Arthur Hinton** (1869–1941) probably was studying with Rheinberger in Munich before he wrote the earliest of several chamber works and his only sonata, in B♭ for P & Vn, first published by Breitkopf & Härtel in 1893 (not 1903). This is a lyrical, fluent, well-scored work in three free movements (F-M-VF) that employ traditional harmony and recall Rheinberger's deliberate treatment of single ideas (ssB X), but sacrifice broad tonal organization to a process of almost constant chromatic modulation.[230] Another violinist, the Italian-born **Alberto Randegger, Jr.** (1880–1918), introduced his own "well-written, effective," virtuosic Sonata in e, Op. 15, for Vn & P, published by Novello in 1903.[231]

226. MT XXXIV (1893) 361 and 426; Cobbett/CHAMBER II 445. Cf. GROVE VIII 3–4 (G. S. K. Butterworth).

227. Cobbett/CHAMBER I 583–85 (R. H. Walthew) and II 454. Cf. GROVE IV 417 (W. W. Cobbett), with faulty list of works (including a "Sonata" for Cl & P that is actually a Suite); MGG VI 977–78 (R. Nettel); Altmann/KAMMERMUSIK 209, 258, 283.

228. Cf. BAKER 59–60.

229. Favorable reviews of the latter 2 are found in MW XXXV (1904) 660 (M. Puttmann) and DM III/4 (1903–4) 392 (R. Kursch). Cf., also, PAZDÍREK II 562–63; GROVE I 643–44 (W. B. Squire). For an extraordinary son. recital played by Beringer in 1881 cf. ssB III.

230. Cf. MT XXXIV (1893) 426 (with praise except for the modulations); Cobbett/CHAMBER I 562 (H. W. Richards); GROVE IV 292 (J. A. Fuller-Maitland).

231. MT XLIV (1903) 802; Cobbett/CHAMBER II 268 (W. W. Cobbett); BAKER 1306.

Called "perhaps the most grievously neglected British composer of his generation," [232] the pianist, theorist, and pedagogue **John Blackwood McEwen** (1868–1948) trained first in his homeland of Scotland and then under Corder, Prout, and others after moving to London. Six of his sonatas, for P & Vn(-or Va in No. 2 in f), were published by Oxford between 1913 and 1929, and two, for P solo in e and a, in 1903 and 1918.[233] The violin sonatas disclose notable originality and variety in their styles, individual forms, and cyclic plans.[234] Thus, No. 2, which seems to have been the most successful, constitutes a single movement divided into three sections (M-In/S-VF), the last being barred according to rhythmic units rather than metric groupings. No. 4 is called "A Little Sonata" with reference mainly to the lightness of its content rather than shortness or technical ease. No. 5 is a still freer work, in two movements. The first piano sonata is a large-scale, highly charged, profusely edited work of four movements (F-S-VF[Sc]-S/VF) filling 41 pages,[235] in the general class of its contemporaries in e and d by d'Indy (ssb XIII) and Dalc (*supra*). The ideas are a little less worthy in themselves and the extensive use of both bare and filled-in octaves in the thematically interrelated, outer movements makes somewhat heavy-handed piano writing. But the rich, often subtle harmony, the imaginative rhythmic treatment, and the over-all sense of form raise this sonata well above many like-purposed works of the late-Romantic era. Thus, the one Sonata for P solo, Op. 72 in f (pub. in 1923), by the brilliant pianist **(Edwin) York Bowen** (1884–1961)[236] is a similarly large-scaled work, in three movements (M/F-M-VF), but by contrast it seems bombastic, free with a vengeance in its tempo changes, self-conscious in its rhythmic diversity, over-edited, even more heavy-handed, and more epigonic in its sentimentality and in its pseudo-Modern dissonances forced onto more conventional harmony. Another pupil of Corder, Bowen also left at least four published duo sonatas with more or less of the same traits, including two for P & Va, Opp. 18 in c[237] and 22 in F (1907 and 1912), one for P & Vc, Op. 64 in A (1923), and one for P & Vn, Op. 112 in e (1946).[238]

232. GROVE V 466–68 (E. Blom).

233. Cf. MGG VIII 1383–85 (J. M. Allan).

234. Sons. 2, 4, and 5 are described in Cobbett/CHAMBER II 107–8 (S. Dyke and W. W. Cobbett).

235. It is praised highly and described in some detail in MT XLVI (1905) 31–32.

236. Cf. GROVE I 856 (G. S. K. Butterworth).

237. A favorable review appears in MT XLVI (1905) 403, following the first performance of Op. 18 by Lionel Tertis.

238. All but Op. 112 are listed in Altmann/KAMMERMUSIK 246 and 253, and described briefly in Cobbett/CHAMBER I 157 (T. F. Dunhill).

The pianist and prolific composer of opera, orchestra, and chamber music **Josef Holbrooke** (1878–1958) left four published duo sonatas, three for Vn & P (Op. 6, "Sonatina," 1907; Op. 59 in F, 1918; Op. 83, "Oriental," 1926) and one for Vc & P (Op. 19 in g, "Fantasie-Sonate," 1914).[239] In Op. 83 the piano serves more as an accompaniment than a duo participant. In Op. 19 the "Fantasie" pertains to a chain of sections (VF-S-VF) rather than complete movements. The conventional harmony, rather thick texture, and unprepossessing themes in Holbrooke's sonatas do not account for the considerable interest other music by him has aroused from time to time.

The pianist and author on chamber music **Thomas Frederick Dunhill** (1877–1946) himself left two published sonatas for P & Vn, Opp. 27 in d (1911) and 50 in F (1920). These are described as the freest and most intimate of a group of chamber works that is notable for "melodic invention, felicity in statement, and logic in design," and for being "as companionable, healthy, and English as the South Downs on a sunny day." [240] At least five published sonatas—Opp. 4 in F, for P & Vc (1910), 16 in B♭, for P & Cl-or-Vn-or-Va (1912), 29 in C, for Vn alone ("eroica," 1913), and 30 in D for Vc alone (1914), as well as a Sonata for 2 cellos alone (1913)—may also be credited to the important writer, pianist, and teacher **Donald Francis Tovey** (1875–1940). These constitute about a fourth of a chamber music output understandably distinguished by high skill and intellectual grasp right from Op. 1, clear orientation toward the great German masters, some affinities with Reger's chamber music, and tangible individuality of its own.[241] And four published duo sonatas, including two for P & Vn (Opp. 8 in a, 1898, and 44 in E♭, 1930), and one each for P & Va (Op. 29 in C, 1912) and P & Vc (Op. 41 in f, 1928), may be credited to the esteemed music historian **Ernest Walker** (1870–1949).[242] These, too, are German oriented, skillful, and musical, though freer and more impetuous and less intellectual than Tovey's sonatas. Moreover, in Op. 41 the essentially traditional harmony is extended to some remote, chromatic relationships suggesting Reger again.

Brief mentions may be added of published organ sonatas by some

239. Cf. GROVE IV 320–21 (H. C. Colles); MGG VI 613–15 (A. J. B. Hutchings); Altmann/KAMMERMUSIK 208, 258; Cobbett/CHAMBER I 565–66 (R. W. Walthew).

240. Cobbett/CHAMBER I 345–47 (M. M. Scott), with further details on the sons. Cf. GROVE II 804–5 (G. S. K. Butterworth and H. C. Colles).

241. Cobbett/CHAMBER II 515–16 (E. Walker). Cf. GROVE VIII 524–25 (H. C. Colles); MGG XIII 598–600 (H. F. Redlich).

242. Cf. GROVE IX 141–43 (I. Keys); Cobbett/CHAMBER II 565 (H. C. Colles).

of the many once recognized organists active in late-Romantic England,[243] including **Edward Henry Thorne** (1834–1916; Son. in f, 1912),[244] **William Thomas Best** (1826–97; Sons. in G, 1862, and d, 1887),[245] **Bertram Luard Selby** (or Luard-Selby; 1853–1918; Son. in D, 1881; "Fantasia Sonata" on "Dies Irae," 1891; Son. 3, 1913; as well as Op. 21 in b, for P & Vn, 1885),[246] **William Joseph Westbrook** (1831–94; 2 sons., 1882 and *ca.* 1895),[247] **Charles Harford Lloyd** (1849–1919; Son. in d, 1886),[248] **Alan Gray** (1855–1935; 4 superior sons., 1890, as well as a Son. for P & Vn, 1900),[249] **John Ebenezer West** (1863–1929; E. Prout's nephew and pupil; 3 sons.: "Allegro maestoso," "Allegro pomposo," "Andante religioso"),[250] **Percy Carter Buck** (1871–1947; Opp. 3 in E♭, 1897, 9 in D, 1902, and 12 in B♭, 1905, as well as Op. 21 for P & Vn),[251] **Albert Lister Peace** (1844–1912; 3 "Sonate da camera" for organ, 1891–97 [?]),[252] **William Wolstenholme** (1865–1931; Son. in F, 1901, and Son. in D "in the Style of Handel," 1904, as well as Son. in G for P & Vn, 1903),[253] and one **Bernard Ramsey** (1873–?; Nos. 1 in d, 2 in b, 1906?).[254]

In Ireland almost no attention was paid to the sonata for nearly a century after Philip Cogan's last publications around 1805 (SCE 770–71).[255] The ill-fated Union established in 1800 hardly favored such an

243. Cf. Frotscher/ORGELSPIEL II 1230–33.

244. A favorable review appears in MT LIII (1912) 455. Two performances of a Son. in F, for P & Vn, in MS, are reported in MT XVII (1875) 22 and 82. Cf. GROVE VIII 435 (W. B. Squire).

245. The year 1862 comes from Temperley/CORRESPONDENCE. A strongly favorable review of Son. in d and a separate printing of its "Romanza" mvt. in D appear in MMR XVIII (1887) 16 and 227–30. Cf., also, MT XV (1871) 158; GROVE I 695–97 (W. H. Hadow & H. C. Colles).

246. Cf. MT XXII (1881) 592 and XXXIII (1891) 45 (favorable review of the 2d son.); Altmann/KAMMERMUSIK 227; GROVE V 412–13 (J. A. Fuller-Maitland); Kremer/ORGAN 222.

247. Cf. MT XXIII (1882) 423; GROVE IX 268 (G. Grove); Kremer/ORGAN 230.

248. Cf. MT XXVII (1886) 172, 438; GROVE V 347 (J. A. Fuller-Maitland & H. C. Colles); MGG VIII 1065–66 (S. Sadie).

249. Cf. MT XXXI (1890) 613 (mostly favorable review); GROVE III 765 (J. A. Fuller-Maitland); MGG V 727 (N. Fortune).

250. Cf. MT XXXVI (1895) 675–76 (Son. 1 approved "for recitals or church voluntaries"); GROVE IX 268 (H. C. Colles).

251. Favorably reviewed, respectively, in MW XLIII (1802) 538 and XLVI (1905) 401. Cf. GROVE I 993 (H. C. Colles).

252. Cf. MW XXIX (1898) 43 (unfavorable review of No. 2); GROVE VI 602 (J. Hullah); Kremer/ORGAN 212.

253. Cf. MT LXXII (1931) 799 (praise for Son. in F by F. H. Wood); Kremer/ORGAN 232; GROVE IX 352 (H. Grace), with reference to 2 worthy unpub. sons., for organ and for P solo.

254. Cf. MW XXXVII (1906) 43 and XXXVIII (1907) 1047 (high praise for No. 2); Kremer/ORGAN 215.

255. Warm thanks are owing here for information by correspondence from Pro-

interest, there being no more significant contributor than the German-born inventor of the piano-training device known as the "Chiroplast," **Johann Bernhard Logier** (1777–1846) in Dublin, who left several light, unaccompanied, solo, and four-hand piano sonatas in salon style, in the decade from about 1815 to 1825.[256] Efforts to explore the sonata in later-19th-century Dublin might start with the two examples for organ, both in d, and the Sonatina for P solo, by the English-born organist **James C. Culwick** (1845–1907);[257] and the sonatas for P & Vn (1904, 1907, 1913) as well as the prizewinning Sonata in D, Op. 43, for P & Vc (1900?) by the Italian-born pianist **Michele Esposito** (1855–1929).[258]

---

fessors Aloys Fleischmann of the Music Dept. at University College in Cork and Brian Boydell at the University of Dublin. Cf., also, Hogan/ANGLO-IRISH 145–55.

256. Cf. MGG VIII 1121–24 (G. Pugner); HOFMEISTER 1828 (Whistling), 460, 493, 542, 595.

257. Cf. BAKER 337; PAZDÍREK III 639; MMR XII (1882) 184 (negative review of the Sonatina).

258. Cf. MW XXXIII (1901) 12–13 (rather negative review of Op. 43); Altmann/KAMMERMUSIK 202 and 255; GROVE II 973 (L. M. L. Dix); MGG III 1537–38 (C. Jachino).

Chapter XV

Scandinavia, from Kuhlau to Nielsen

Relationships Musical and Political

This chapter on the sonata in Scandinavia follows that on the sonata in Great Britain not only because the two regions share geographically in lying to the north of the sonata's other main regions. They also enjoyed considerable artistic interchange throughout the Romantic Era. And especially in their instrumental music they revealed a common heritage from predominantly German training and influences. Two of the main countries of Scandinavia enjoyed good enough political relationships with England, too—Sweden, the conspicuous neutral, and Norway, her longtime recalcitrant dependency. The same can be said for Russia's autonomous little neighbor Finland. Finland is assigned her occasional classification as Scandinavian here both because of her extensive derivations from Swedish culture and because her one composer of appreciable consequence to the Romantic sonata, Sibelius, had some artistic ties with Norway through his affinity to Grieg, not to mention some of that German (and Austrian) training and some good rapport with the British musical world. The same cannot be said for the political relations between Denmark, the other main Scandinavian country, and England. Whereas Sweden had sided with England at the heart of the opposition to Napoleon's vast, terrifying conquests, Denmark had actually lent support to the Napoleonic forces, thus both answering and causing some aggressive acts by the British during the earlier 19th century.

As in France and England, the sonata in the Scandinavian countries enjoyed some cultivation early in the 19th century, still influenced largely by Classic trends (SCE 790–800), but it hardly came into its own until later in the century. Then a third triumvirate may be pointed to as roughly paralleling that of Franck, Saint-Saëns, and Fauré in France and that of Parry, Stanford, and Elgar in England (SSB XIII and XIV). This consisted of Hartmann, Gade, and Grieg.

Although there were decided ups and downs in the political relationships even between the Scandinavian countries themselves, there was no corresponding loss of sympathy or collaboration in the friendly three-way relationships between these two Danes and one Norwegian who did most to advance the cause of Scandinavian music per se. A succeeding Scandinavian triumvirate, from our viewpoint, consisted of Nielsen, Sjögren, and Sibelius, roughly concurrent with d'Indy and Dukas in France, and Dale and McEwen in England at the era's end.

Early 19th-Century Composers in Scandinavian Centers (Kuhlau)

The first composer to be met in this chapter was a Danish citizen who had been born and trained in Germany. The pianist and flutist **Friedrich Daniel Rudolph Kuhlau** (1786–1832) studied in Hamburg with a pupil of Emanuel Bach before establishing himself in Copenhagen in 1811.[1] He became an ardent champion of Beethoven, whom he met in Vienna in 1825 during a merry evening of inebriation and punnic canons.[2] Although Kuhlau made his chief contribution historically as a cofounder of national Danish opera (with his compatriot **Christoph Ernst Friedrich Weyse** [1774–1842], who also left at least 5 pub. sons., in the 1820's, for P solo and for 2 Bns [3]), he is remembered by today's performers, when he is remembered at all, for certain of his numerous sonatas and sonatinas, of which there is a total of at least 55.[4] First published in the 18 years from 1810 to 1828,[5] these last divide into 12 sonatas (mostly "grandes") and 19 sonatinas (or "sonates faciles") for P solo, 7 sonatinas for P-duet, 6 sonatas for P & Fl (not including the "Solos" Op. 57 or the "Duos" Op. 110), and 6 sonatas and 5 sonatinas for P & Vn (not including the Fl sons. that were pub. also for P & Vn).

4a

Kuhlau's sonatinas for P solo and P-duet and a few of his flute sonatas are the ones that still survive. The latter account for his somewhat extravagant, posthumous sobriquet, "The Beethoven of the

1. Cf. Schilling/LEXICON IV 252–54; GROVE IV 866 (J. Hullah); MGG VII 1874–78 (R. Seitz), with full list of works and further references.
2. Cf. Thayer & Forbes/BEETHOVEN II 958–59, 971.
3. Cf. MGG XIV 543–45 (S. Lunn), but with no mention of the sons.; GROVE IX 272 (J. Horton); HOFMEISTER 1828 (Whistling), 606; Cat. NYPL XXXIII 315; AMZ II (1799–1800) 151 (indicating that P sons. 1 and 2 [described as "very fine," especially the "brilliant" No. 1 in E] had already appeared in 1799 in a mixed collection of Weyse's songs and piano pieces).
4. Further, not wholly reconciled lists may be found in HOFMEISTER 1828 (Whistling), *passim;* PAZDÍREK VIII 487–93.
5. Based on Intelligenz-Blatt entries in AMZ XII–XXX.

Flute," [6] and put him on a par with Reicha, his contemporary (SCE 564–65). His violin and flute parts, when not marked "ad libitum," share equally with the piano parts in genuine duets. His full-scale sonatas differ from his sonatinas not only in being more advanced in their instrumental techniques, longer, larger in number of movements (mostly 3 or 4 rather than 2 or 3), more sustained and developed in their ideas, fuller in texture, and more serious in import, but also in a sense distinguished earlier (SSB III)—that is, in keeping abreast of current styles rather than exuding the atmosphere of the piano studio by what was already a neo-Classic return to the outstanding sonatinas of Clementi (SCE 751). For example, the sonatas generally employ newer, more active textures than those of the "singing-allegro" style with Alberti or similar basses (SCE 122, 126) that still prevail in many of the sonatinas. And the sonatas more often include sets of variations on popular tunes of the day (e.g., on a Danish air, in Op. 64/ii, for P & Vn-or-Fl). Exceptional are the three finales in the solo sonatinas Op. 60/1–3, each a set of variations on a different tune by Rossini.

But even the sonatas by Kuhlau were relatively conservative in their day, with few departures from established styles or forms. Already this fact was implied in a review of his Op. 8, "Grande Sonate" in a, for P solo (pub. in 1814?).[7] The reviewer emphasized in considerable detail not only the convincing melodies, the effective passage-work, and the contrapuntal interest, but the correctness and propriety of whatever Kuhlau did, qualifying his praise merely by adding that, of course, Kuhlau could only compose within his limitations. Although the fresh melodies and compelling harmony in Kuhlau's sonatas frequently take unexpected, sometimes bold turns (Ex. 94), Kuhlau was no Weber or Schumann in the advance of musical Romanticism.[8] The gist of the many, progressively brief reviews of his sonatas and sonatinas is that in spite of his prolificity he continued to put out works of noteworthy skill, variety, and interest within acceptable tastes and idioms and reasonable technical limits, there being mild objections only to excessive passagework (mostly scales) and overly prolonged endings.[9]

6. Cf. Cobbett/CHAMBER II 81–82 (H. M. Fitzgibbon).

7. AMZ XVII (1815) 179–83, with 14 mss. quoted from the start of i.

8. Brahms wrote to Joachim in 1854 that he wanted to learn flute so that he could "accompany" Clara, but that Kuhlau's (Fl?) sons. "bore her" (Joachim/LETTERS 78).

9. Other representative reviews include AMZ XV (1813) 79–80 (on Op. 5 for P solo, likening Kuhlau to Cramer) and 449–50 (on an unidentified son. "facile" for P & Vn), XXIII (1821) 410–12 (on Op. 26/1–2 for P solo, likening Kuhlau to Haydn

Ex. 94. From the finale of Friedrich Kuhlau's *Grande Sonate concertate pour piano et flûte,* Op. 85 in a (after the original Schott ed. of 1827; plate no. 2684).

The brilliant pianist **(Heinrich) Rudolf Willmers** (1821–78) was born in Copenhagen if not in Berlin,[10] studied with Hummel and others, toured widely, and settled in Vienna in 1866. His sonatas include Op. 11 for P & Vn, a Sonata in B♭ for P solo, and a "Sonate héroique," Op. 33 for P solo that was reviewed in 1846 as a distasteful example of the "contemporary fad of virtuosity." [11]

Several composers were writing sonatas in Sweden, meaning Stockholm and Uppsala almost exclusively, while Kuhlau was in Copenhagen.[12] Some of these wrote in the borderland between Classic and Romantic styles, like Olaf Åhlström (sce 800) or the important, versatile historian, poet, philosopher, and composer **Erik Gustaf Geijer** (1783–1847). Although Geijer made his musical mark primarily with

and Beethoven) and 672 (on Op. 20/1-3, the well-known Sonatinas for P solo), XXIV (1822) 215–16 (on Op. 33 for P+Vn) and 279–80 (on Op. 30 for P solo), XXV (1823) 596 (on Op. 34 for P solo) and 795 (on 3 "Grandes Sonates brillantes" for P solo), XXVIII (1826) 272 (on Op. 64 for P & Fl [Vn, originally]), XXXI (1829) 388 (on Op. 85 for P & Fl as one of Kuhlau's best sons.); caecilia XI (1829) 229–30 (I. X. Seyfried, similarly on Op. 85); ama No. 6 (Aug. 5, 1826) 42 (on Op. 69 for P & Fl).

10. Cf. Fétis/bu VIII 475; baker 1801.

11. nzm XXV (1846) 108–9. Cf. pazdírek XV 421–22.

12. It is again (cf. sce 794) a pleasure to thank Professor Ingmar Bengtsson at the University of Uppsala for specific information, counsel, and further leads on the sonata in Sweden.

songs, he also left at least eight solo and duo sonatas, including one
for P solo, in g/G (1810), and two for P-duet, in E♭/c and f (both
1819); four for P & Vn, in g/G, F/g, d/F, and A♭/E♭ (1819, 1830?,
ca. 1832, 1840 [called "Sonatina"]); and one "Sonatina" for P & Vc,
in F/a (1838–39).[13] Among these only the P-duet in f was or has
been published (Stockholm: C. Müller, 1820), the rest being MSS in
the Uppsala Universitetsbibliotek. But the melodic and harmonic
appeal of that work[14] plus the interest in Geijer's songs and in his
significant influence on Swedish cultural life in general would seem
to warrant a study of his sonatas in MSS as well. Their style recalls
that of Beethoven (up to Op. 22) and Mendelssohn. The movement
types and proportions of his sonata cycles, ranging from two to four
movements, appear to be standard enough. Furthermore, there are
subtle but unmistakable similarities between the incipits of the movements in each cycle. Yet, as the foregoing listing suggests, the cycles
are exceptional for their defiance or disregard of tonal unity. Apart
from the printed sonata and two others in which only the mode
changes, Geijer put each finale in a key other than that of the opening
movement. Most striking in this respect is the second violin sonata,
in which the successive keys of the four movements are F, B♭, b♭, and g.

Further exploration of the sonata in Sweden in the first half of the
19th century would bring us to composers some of whom are now
little remembered even in that country. The once esteemed theorist,
teacher, and folklorist **Erik Drake** (1788–1870) left an example in
MS for P & Vn (1816) in which there are four movements (S/F-S-Mi-VF)
that again defy tonal unity (E♭, B♭, g, B♭) while interrelating thematically.[15] Drake's melodic style has been likened to Spohr's and Rossini's.[16] A friend of Drake, the obscure, roving cellist and pianist **Carl
Schwencke** (1797–at least 1870) was born in a musical family in Hamburg in Emanuel Bach's sphere and spent several years in Sweden,
presumably some or all of the years from 1815 to 1819, when he wrote
at least 10 sonatas—6 for P solo, 3 for P-duet, and one for P & Vn.[17]

13. Cf. SOHLMANS II 512–15 (Törnblom); GROVE III 588–89 (K. Dale); MGG IV
1615–16 (R. Engländer). In general reference works Geijer's musical activities are
scarcely mentioned.
14. The judgment is based on incipits and related information kindly supplied
by Professor Bengtsson and his students.
15. The MS, in the Musikaliska akademiens Bibliotek (Nybrokajen, Stockholm),
lacks the Vn part. Cf. GROVE II 762–63 (K. Dale); MGG III 742–43 (M. Tegen);
SOHLMANS I 1180–81 (Å. Vretblad); Nisser/SVENSK 109.
16. GROVE II 763.
17. Cf. MGG XII 401 and 403–5 (P. Schmidt), with further references and a full,
undated list of works. Beethoven's canon on this Schwencke's name dates from
1824 (Thayer & Forbes/BEETHOVEN 923, 928).

In any case, these are all to be found in a special "Schwenckesam-longen" at the Musikaliska akademiens Bibliotek. And about half of them plus at least two others (for P & V-or-Vc and for P-duet) were published by Breitkopf & Härtel in Leipzig or Lemoine in Paris.[18] Schwencke's works are described as ranging from light, often charming diversions to pieces of considerable force and originality, with Romanticisms that point ahead to Grieg.[19] Evidently his sonatas, being early works, fall more into the former category.

The gifted but short-lived flutist **Frans Frederik Edward Brendler** (1800–31) left a three-movement "Sonatine" in C (F-S-Sc), for P-duet, that was published by Eberling in Stockholm in 1830.[20] Its melodic styles recall Kuhlau's (rather than Spohr's, as has been suggested of Brendler's more Romantically tinged works). Ranked with his friend Geijer as a song composer, **Adolf Fredrik Lindblad** (1801–78) left a Sonata in A/D, for P solo, in a MS dated 1828 that extends to 409 measures, yet may not be complete, since there are only two movements (F-M) and no return to the home key.[21] Lindblad, who worshipped Beethoven, studied with Zelter, and knew both Weber and Mendelssohn, reveals themes and harmonies much like Mendelssohn's. Variously like Clementi's and Mendelssohn's sonatas in style are two four-movement sonatas for P solo by one **Carl Ludvig Lithander** (1773–1843).[22] One of them, in C (F-M-Sc-Ro/Va), was dedicated to and published by Clementi in London (before 1832). Exceptionally, three variations on a Swedish air conclude its rondo finale whereas an "Adagio espressivo" concludes that of Lithander's other sonata, Op. 15, all in f♯/F♯ (F-S-Mi-Ro/S; composed in 1822 and pub. by Böhme in Hamburg).[23] The violinist and conductor **Johan Frederik Berwald** (1787–1861), member of an important Swedish family of musicians, left two sonatas for P & Vn, one in E♭, in three movement (F-M-Ro), composed in 1812 and published in 1816 by Breitkopf & Härtel, and the other finished only to the end of one fast movement, in f (before 1832).[24] His more important cousin, **Franz Adolf Berwald** (1796–1868), who is now ranked as Sweden's greatest 19th-century instrumental composer, left one sonata each for P & Vn (Op. 6 in E♭; 1858) and P & Vc

18. Cf. HOFMEISTER 1828 (Whistling) 506, 558, 602.
19. MGG XII 405.
20. Cf. GROVE V 926 (K. Dale).
21. Cf. MGG VIII 888–89 (A. Melander), with mention of 3 Vn sons., one of which is listed in Nisser/SVENSK 174.
22. He is not listed in any encyclopedia consulted here.
23. Op. 15 is listed in HOFMEISTER 1828 (Whistling), 595.
24. Cf. GROVE I 690–91 (M. L. Pereyra).

("Duo" Op. 7 in B♭; 1859), which do not have the importance of his forward-looking symphonies and larger chamber ensembles.[25]

Hartmann, Gade, Grieg, and Other Mid-Romantic Scandinavians

All three Scandinavians in the later-19th-century triumvirate mentioned at the start of this chapter demonstrated at least peripheral interest in the sonata.[26] The earliest of these was the organist, teacher, and best known member in a prominent family of German-Danish musicians, **Johann Peter Emil(ius) Hartmann** (1805–1900).[27] Throughout his long, outwardly uneventful life, Hartmann left many compositions, in nearly every category of music. Most of these achieved publication, over a span of more than a half-century, including at least three solo and three duo sonatas that appeared chiefly around the start and around the end of that span. There are three sonatas for P & Vn—Op. 8 ("Grande Sonate concertante") in g, composed in 1826 (?[28]), dedicated to Spohr, and published in 1837 by Kistner in Leipzig; Op. 39 in C, published in 1846 by Schuberth in Hamburg; and Op. 83 in g, published in 1888 (not 1886) by Hansen in Copenhagen. There are two sonatas for P solo—Op. 34 in F ("awarded second prize"), published not later than 1842 by Schuberth, and Op. 80 in a, published in 1885 by Hansen.[29] And there is one organ sonata, Op. 58 in g, composed in 1855 (?[30]) and published in 1888 by Hansen.

In 1837 Schumann reviewed Hartmann's Op. 8 favorably, especially for its natural flow, its cumulative interest, its craftsmanship, and its development of ideas, although he found the "Andante" too long and the first of the four movements (F-M-Sc-F) still oriented toward Hummel and Classic styles.[31] In 1842, he wrote even more favorably on Op.

25. Cf. GROVE I 691–92 (M. L. Pereyra); Cobbett/CHAMBER I 125 (G. Jeanson); Layton/BERWALD (a full survey of the man and his works), pp. 84, 181; Altmann/KAMMERMUSIK 195 and 253. A complete ed. of his works is currently (1967) being ed. by Ingmar Bengtsson and others for pub. by Bärenreiter.

26. Cf. the valuable discussion of "Grieg's relationship to N. W. Gade and J. P. E. Hartmann" in Schjelderup-Ebbe/GRIEG 149–66.

27. Cf. MGG V 1748–53 (N. Schiørring), with further references and dated list of works; also, Hammerich/HARTMANN. A Son. in F, Op. 17, by Hartmann's son Emil (1836–98; cf. MGG V 1752–53) is reviewed as a contrived work with some interesting spots, in MW XI (1880) 608.

28. MGG V 1750.

29. The Library of Congress also has a Sonatina Op. 48, for P solo, by Hartmann, pub. by Hansen. Cf. PAZDÍREK VII 181–83. Among early (unpub. student?) works cited in Hammerich/HARTMANN 459 are a Son. Op. 1, for P & Fl, and a Sonatine Op. 4, for P-duet.

30. MGG V 1750.

31. Schumann/SCHRIFTEN I 277. Praise from a contemporary Berlin review is quoted in Hammerich/HARTMANN 461.

Ex. 95. From the "Andantino" of Johann Peter Emil Hartmann's Sonata in g, Op. 83 (after the Hansen ed. of 1888).

34 as the work that should have been ranked first among "three prize
sonatas" by C. Vollweiler,[32] J. C. Leonhard, and Hartmann, declaring
the four movements (F-M-Sc-F) to be characterized by genuine artistry,
by masterly harmony and form, including interrelated themes, and by
the poetry of its inner movements as well as the strong, orchestral
coloring of its finale.[33] And in 1846 a successor to Schumann wrote
similarly on Hartmann's Op. 39.[34] A reading of Hartmann's last sonatas
suggests that his styles and forms underwent little if any change over
the near half-century, in spite of his late interest in Brahms and
Wagner. In the four interconnected movements (F-M-VF-Ro) of Op.
83, for example, the harmony still proves to be secure, uncomplicated,
and entirely traditional, the texture still proves to be precise and
rather thin, and the phrase syntax once more reveals Hartmann's own
manner of continuous unfolding through the constant but rhythmically
plastic reiteration and development of an idea (as in the extension of
the opening theme over the first two pages). Unless it be in the

32. Cf. MGG XIV 1 (R. Seitz).

33. Schumann/SCHRIFTEN II 79 and 82–83. An ex. from Op. 34/i is quoted in
Bücken/19. 291 and related to the styles of Spohr, who as one of the judges, had
also wanted Op. 34 to get first prize. Cf., further, Hammerich/HARTMANN 462, 464,
and 467; but the title of the work indicates Hartmann had won 2d, not 3d,
prize.

34. NZM XXV (1846) 176–77.

"Andantino" (Ex. 95) or the "Rondo" refrain, Op. 83, like his early sonatas, shows little of the interest in Danish folk music that Hartmann is reported to have shown in some of his other music.[35]

More renowned in his day though scarcely better remembered today than his colleague Hartmann, the violinist and composer **Niels Wilhelm Gade** (1817–90) was the strongest force in Danish music between Kuhlau and Weyse (*supra*) and Nielsen (*infra*).[36] Gade spent five years (1843–48) in Leipzig and brief Italian travels, assisting and succeeding Mendelssohn as conductor at the Gewandhaus concerts and also enjoying the warm friendship of Schumann. Otherwise he spent nearly all of his life in Copenhagen. Another prolific composer in every main branch of music, Gade left four published sonatas—Op. 28 in e (not c), for P solo (pub. by Hansen in 1840 and, with revisions, by Breitkopf & Härtel in 1854); and Opp. 6 in A, 21 in d, and 59 in B♭, for P & Vn (pub. by Breitkopf & Härtel in 1843, 1850, and 1887).[37] The piano sonata was dedicated to Liszt and the first and second violin sonatas were dedicated to Clara and Robert Schumann, respectively.

Of Gade's four sonatas, Opp. 28 for P solo and 21 for P & Vn seem to have aroused the most interest among performers.[38] But even these aroused much less interest than his symphonies or more nationalistic music and got little notice from the reviewers.[39] Yet both sonatas are convincing, well realized cycles, not suffocated by overly specific recollections of Mendelssohn's writing, as is sometimes charged,[40] but, it is true, largely confined to the range of Mendelssohn's musical language. Opp. 21 and 28 have much in common in this respect and in the general plan and emotional content of their relatively short, three-movement, thematically interrelated cycles. Op. 21 differs chiefly in having brief slow introductions in the outer movements and an alternation of S-VF in its middle movement that anticipates Op. 100/ii by Brahms. Historically Op. 28 is Gade's most noteworthy sonata, by virtue of its direct, demonstrable influence on Grieg's only piano sonata (*infra*), also in e. And Op. 28 is somewhat stronger than Op. 21, by virtue of a little

35. Hammerich/HARTMANN 466 *et passim*.

36. Cf. MGG IV 1223–28 (N. Schiørring), with further references and a (somewhat inaccurately) dated list of works.

37. In Shand/VIOLIN 122–30, 13 exx. from all 3 Vn sons. are quoted. Bücken/19. 293 gives an ex. from Op. 21/ii. The pub. years are too early in MGG IV 1226.

38. E.g., performances of Op. 21 are reported in MT XIII (1868) 446 and XVI (1874) 512; NZM LXXII/1 (1876) 79 and 146, LXXII/2 523, LXXIII/1 52, 53, and 116; and SMZ VI (1876) 29.

39. E.g., the only review of Op. 21 found here in English or German periodicals was that in MMR XIII (1883) 70–71, which greets cordially the lyricism, charm, and "adequate" development of its ideas. Neither Op. 21 nor Op. 28 is currently pub. or recorded (as of late 1967).

40. Cf. Cobbett/CHAMBER I 440–41 (W. W. Cobbett); BAKER 526.

more intensity and imagination in the former's ideas and their development. Moreover, Op. 21 is less satisfying to the pianist because it hardly qualifies as a true duo; the piano rarely takes the lead or even engages the violin antiphonally.

With further regard to Gade's Op. 28, the harmonic color and melodic lyricism reveal a more Romantic spirit than can be found in Hartmann's sonatas. The themes are not of outstanding interest in themselves, but the concentrated yet unhurried extensions and symphonic development of them, especially of the initial theme in each movement (VF-M-F), and the clear, purposeful tonal logic result in surprising structural breadth and solidity.[41] The conciseness of the

Ex. 96. From the third movement of Niels Gade's Sonata in e, Op. 28 (after the Breitkopf-Härtel reprint of about 1890 [V. A. 2299]).

forms, the superior, imaginative treatment of the main rhythms, and the fluent, eminently practical and reasonable scoring for keyboard lend further conviction to the music (Ex. 96) and compensate partially for the absence of individual master strokes and flights of inspiration such as occurred to Grieg at his best.

This mention of the Norwegian **Edvard (Hagerup) Grieg** (1843–1907) brings us to the most successful, representative, and renowned of all Scandinavian composers.[42] Trained early in piano by his talented mother in their home town of Bergen, and encouraged by the cele-

41. Similar traits already evident in Op. 6 probably account for a reviewer's observation that "harmonic masses prevail rather than melodic design" (MMR XVI [1886] 184).

42. From the considerable literature on Grieg, the studies of both the man and

brated Norwegian violinist Ole Bull, Grieg, like Gade, spent several years in Leipzig (1858–62), where he drank in the music of the late Mendelssohn, Schumann, and Chopin, along with other music as up-to-date as Wagner's *Tannhäuser,* but chafed under (and never quite forgave) the more conservative, pedantic aspects of his instruction.[43] Further influences were exercised on him by the music and counsel of both Gade and Hartmann in Copenhagen;[44] by the ardent Norwegian nationalism of Ole Bull and the short-lived composer Rikard Nordraak (1842–66);[45] by Grieg's marriage in 1867 to the fine singer (and his first cousin) Nina Hagerup;[46] and by his two memorable meetings with Liszt in Rome (1870).[47]

Grieg's output, which amounts to 74 opus numbers and a few other works, is neither so large nor so comprehensive as that of Hartmann or Gade. Along with the many sets of intimate songs and piano pieces in which he excelled, as well as the four suites for orchestra and/or piano that did much to win him fame, there are only 8 full cycles of the sonata type, including the familiar piano Concerto in a, the 2 string quartets, and 5 actual "sonatas." [48] Of the last, 3 are for P & Vn, one is for P & Vc, and one is for P solo. He wrote the solo and first two violin sonatas near the end of the formative years just summarized, and the other two sonatas about two decades later in the thick of a career defined variously by idyllic composing at "Troldhaugen" near Bergen in spite of his increasing sterile periods, by strenuous, annual, wide-ranging concert tours in spite of his chronic, increasing ill health, and by ever new honors and recognition in spite of his increasing expressions of artistic credos, broad liberalism, and political differences that created no little friction.[49]

his music that have proved to be most helpful and dependable here are Monrad-Johansen/GRIEG and Schjelderup-Ebbe/GRIEG (on the early years). Significant information and views are also to be found in Finck/GRIEG (in spite of its idolatry), Rokseth/GRIEG (with 60 intriguing photographic plates), and the "symposium" Abraham/GRIEG. Further sources are listed in the 2 chief encyclopedia articles, GROVE III 798–811 (J. Horton), with a detailed, classified "Catalogue of Works," and MGG V 896–908 (W. Kahl). *Die Sonate von Grieg* by Wera von Landesen (Nürnberg: J. L. Schrag, 1944) is an irrelevant book of fiction (cf. pp. 44, 95).

43. A main source on Grieg's background up to about 1862 is his own autobiographic article of 1903, "My First Success," which has been reprinted several times (as in Grieg/VERZEICHNIS) or drawn upon at length, as it has, with further material added, in Schjelderup-Ebbe/GRIEG 17–67, 357, *et passim.*

44. Cf. Schjelderup-Ebbe/GRIEG 149–63.

45. Cf. Monrad-Johansen/GRIEG 61–69; Schjelderup-Ebbe/GRIEG 164–66, 212–25.

46. Cf. Monrad-Johansen/GRIEG 56–60, 78, 98–99.

47. Cf. Monrad-Johansen/GRIEG 115, 122–27; Finck/GRIEG 47–57.

48. There had also been 2 student cycles—a lost string quartet in d (1861?) and a "Sinfonie" in c "never to be performed" (1863–64); cf. Schjelderup-Ebbe/GRIEG 351, 352. Grieg's 2d-P parts to 5 Mozart sons. are noted in SCE 500.

49. Cf. Monrad-Johansen/GRIEG 255–70 and 351–73.

The first sonata Grieg is known to have written, not excluding student exercises,[50] is Op. 7 in e, for P solo, composed in Rungsted, near Copenhagen, in June of 1865, dedicated to Gade, published first by Breitkopf & Härtel in June of 1866 [51] and next, with revisions, by Peters in 1887.[52] In an interview of 1893, published in English in 1904, Grieg recalled how

. . . within eleven days I had composed my sonata for the pianoforte, and very soon after my first sonata for the violin. I took them both to Gade, who was living out at Klampenborg. He glanced through them with satisfaction, nodded, tapped me on the shoulder, and said, "That's very nice indeed. Now we'll go over them carefully and look into all the seams." So we climbed a small steep staircase to Gade's studio, where he sat down at the grand pianoforte and played with absolute inspiration. I had often been told that when Gade was inspired, he drank copious draughts of water. That day the Professor emptied four large water-bottles.[53]

On November 20, 1865, during his final illness, Nordraak entered in his diary, "Grieg's letter [received] yesterday described his performance of his piano sonata and his sonata for piano and violin [Op. 8] at the evening entertainment in the Gewandhaus in Leipzig. A tremendous success. Encored. . . ." [54] In his own country less than a year later, Grieg also fared well with Opp. 7 and 8. An early review of Grieg's music up to that time found the ideas in Op. 7 to be fresher, with less of Gade's influence, but the structure of Op. 8 to be sounder; soon after, the further performances of both works aroused "great rejoicings." [55] Only a few reports of other performances of Op. 7 during the next few years have turned up in the present study.[56] Perhaps dissatisfaction with both the substance and form of the finale discouraged more performances, for Grieg's revisions of Op. 7 largely concerned that movement, especially the reduction of its length.[57] The fast tempo at which Grieg reportedly played the finale (and that of

50. These last are catalogued in careful detail, along with all his other compositions written before 1867, in Schjelderup-Ebbe/GRIEG 348–56.

51. HOFMEISTER Monatsbericht 1866, p. 93.

52. The circumstances of Op. 7 are reported in Finck/GRIEG 39; Monrad-Johansen/GRIEG 71, 81, 92–93, 281; Schjelderup-Ebbe/GRIEG 151, 234, 311–13.

53. As trans. in Finck/GRIEG 39 (cf. p. 306); cf., also, Schjelderup-Ebbe/GRIEG 244.

54. As trans. in Monrad-Johansen/GRIEG 81.

55. Monrad-Johansen/GRIEG 92–93; Schjelderup-Ebbe/GRIEG 311–13. In 2 reviews, in MMR XIII (1883) 182 and XV (1885) 137, Op. 7 is described as being less rich in "invention and constructive skill" than Op. 13, possessed of a "strong national flavour," and "a pleasing and wholesome (because healthy) work."

56. E.g., NZM LXXIII/1 (1877) 126 (Barmen, near Düsseldorf); MT XVIII (1878) 164 (London), XXI (1880) 303 (Syracuse, N.Y.), XXVII (1885) 20 (London); ML XLIX (1968) 25 (Köln, 1878, finale only).

57. Cf. MGG V 905.

Op. 8) [58] may relate to problems in it, too. But unfortunately that movement still remains an artistic obstacle to most performers. [59] Op. 7 reveals the likely influence of Gade's Op. 28 (in spite of the early review just noted), not only in the choice of over-all key, but in the number, order, and tempos of the four movements (F-M-Mi-VF in Grieg's work), and the textural styles, character, and even thematic types of the first two movements in particular. To be sure, Grieg does not develop single ideas symphonically as Gade does in Op. 28. But he creates ideas in Op. 7 that are more original, he creates more of them, he breaks up his movements into shorter sections, and he achieves his own kind of drive and drama through sharper, more imaginative contrasts. [60]

As we just learned from Grieg himself, Op. 8 in F, for P & Vn, was composed "very soon after" Op. 7 (1865), also in Rungsted. Another four-movement cycle (F-M-F-VF), it was dedicated to the Bergen violinist August Fries and published first by Peters in February, 1866. [61] This was the work that led to the two memorable meetings with Liszt in Rome. At the end of 1868 Liszt had written Grieg, out of the blue and without any direct advance on Grieg's part, [62] to congratulate him on the talent and promise revealed in Op. 8 and to encourage a visit in Weimar should Grieg be getting to Germany. [63] Actually, this unexpected support from so great a celebrity clinched the Norwegian government subsidy Grieg had been seeking for a return visit to Rome, where he called on Liszt in early February (?), 1870, and "soon after," on February 17. As related in two detailed letters to his parents (Feb. 17 and Apr. 9, 1870) and a travel report to his government, [64] Grieg played "my last violin sonata" (i.e., Op. 13 in G, pub. in 1869; *infra*) with trepidation, Liszt joining in with the violin part "higher up on the piano in octaves" and applauding it all "so copiously," including the violin's first entry on "a little baroque but national passage," that "I felt the most singular thankfulness streaming through me." Then, to hear Op. 13 a second time, Liszt

58. Cf. Schjelderup-Ebbe/GRIEG 313.

59. Cf. Schjelderup-Ebbe/GRIEG 243; Monrad-Johansen/GRIEG 73.

60. Schjelderup-Ebbe/GRIEG 240–42 also finds close parallels between Op. 7/iii and a piece by Hartmann, "Vikingefruens Dröm" ("The Viking Woman's Dream").

61. The further circumstances of Op. 8 are related in Finck/GRIEG 47–55; Monrad-Johansen/GRIEG 81, 92, 93, 286; Schjelderup-Ebbe/GRIEG 244–45, 312, 313.

62. However, contrary to Finck/GRIEG 47–49, Monrad-Johansen/GRIEG 115–16 shows that Liszt's letter was not entirely spontaneous.

63. A facs. of the original letter, in French, appears in Plates XII and XIII of Rokseth/GRIEG; it is trans. into English in LISZT LETTERS 168–69 and in Finck/GRIEG 47.

64. All three, affording fine samples of Grieg's superior literary talents, are trans. nearly in full in Monrad-Johansen/GRIEG 122–28.

played the whole affair, lock, stock and barrel, violin, piano, nay more, for he played with more fullness and breadth. The violin was given its due right in the middle of the piano part, he was literally all over the whole piano at the same time, without a note being missed. And how, then, did he play? With majesty, beauty, genius beyond compare in interpretation. I believe I laughed, like an idiot. . . . The day after the visit I have just described for you, the Italians Sgambati [pupil of Liszt] and Pinelli (pupil of Joachim) [65] played my first violin sonata [Op. 8] at a matinee where the whole fashionable world was present. Liszt came in the middle of the concert, just before my sonata, and that was well. For I do not put down the applause the sonata received to my own account. The thing is that when Liszt claps they all clap—each louder than the other.[66]

This Sgambati-Pinelli performance and the two earlier performances of Op. 8 in conjunction with Op. 7 marked only the beginning of enough performances of Op. 8 to suggest that it remained Grieg's most popular sonata, near and far, during his lifetime.[67] The undeniable worth and charm of Op. 8 supply reason enough for this popularity. But one learns with interest that its dedicatee Gade, whose influence on Op. 8 Grieg himself acknowledged, seems to have liked it partly because it was still free of the nationalistic flavors he was to object to in Op. 13.[68] On the other hand, the first Norwegian critic to review Op. 8 did find such flavors, at least in a backhanded way when, in September, 1866, he wrote, "I cannot deny that there are a few rather ugly [dissonantly experimental?] measures in the first movement (in cadential progressions [as in the start of the two 'Andante' sections?]) at the very places where he [Grieg] wants to strike the national chords." [69] And twenty-two years later a critic for the *Musical Times* of London was still writing that

Norway has no musical forms apart from simple melodies, and the Norwegian working on the higher lines of art must borrow his models. But he can fuse into his productions more or less of the national musical dialect and feeling, and this is precisely what Grieg does. The Sonata in F is a remarkable illustration of the fact.[70]

65. Cf. RICORDI ENCICLOPEDIA III 443.

66. As trans. in Monrad-Johansen/GRIEG 125.

67. Sample performances during the decade 1876–86, when Grieg's popularity was at a peak, are reported in NZM LXXII/2 (1876) 381 (Leipzig) and 498 (St. Petersburg), LXXIII/1 (1877) 72 (Leipzig), 140 (Brussels), 249 (Zwickau); MT XXI (1880) 138 (London), XXIII (1882) 83 (London), XXIV (1883) 159 (Leipzig), XXVII (1886) 147 (London) and 210 (Birmingham). Among numerous reports of performances of Grieg's Vn sons. that do not specify the key or op. no., one guesses that most also refer to Op. 8.

68. Cf. Schjelderup-Ebbe/GRIEG 244.

69. As trans. in Schjelderup-Ebbe/GRIEG 312.

70. MT XXIX (1888) 75. Cf., also, the more specific Norwegian imagery culled up by Niecks, as quoted at length in Finck/GRIEG 193–95.

The sonata Grieg showed Liszt in 1870 was his second for P & Vn. This work, Op. 13 in G, had been composed in three weeks of July, 1867, in the Norwegian capital of Christiana (Oslo) soon after the newly married couple moved there from Denmark.[71] The dedicatee was Grieg's friend, the violinist, conductor, composer, and fellow country-man Johan Svendsen, who may have joined in the first performance.[72] And the first publisher was Breitkopf & Härtel in 1869. It was after the first performance of this work that, as Grieg reported in a letter of 1905, "Gade came to the artist's room and said: 'No, Grieg, the next sonata you must not make as Norwegian.' I had at that moment tasted blood and answered: 'Yes, professor, the next one is going to be even worse.' (However, that was not the case, as you know.)"[73] We have just noted how Liszt spotted a nationalistic flavor in Op. 13, too, though more approvingly. In the years since then, several writers have described Op. 13 as Grieg's most nationalistic sonata, and some, indeed, as one of the most nationalistic of all his works.[74] Unquestionably, there are pronounced folklike elements in each of the three move-ments (S/VF-M-VF), especially rhythms in this so-called "Dance So-nata"[75] that define the oddly similar main themes of the outer move-ments[76] and characteristic scale inflections, including the lowered 7th and 2d, that also pervade the more lyrical themes (Ex. 97). But in spite of these traits and all the varied Norwegian imagery that they have inspired in writings on Op. 13,[77] the fact remains that no tangible or specific Norwegian source could be discovered here for any of the ideas in this work. Before World War I other writers already were an-ticipating more recent, ethnomusicological debates by asking whether Grieg's music was really a case of Grieg becoming more Norwegian or Norway becoming more "Griegian."[78] If such a question applies to Grieg's music in general, it certainly applies to his five sonatas in particular, which all reveal every trait in abundance that can be

71. A few circumstances of Op. 13 are reported in Monrad-Johansen/GRIEG 99. A facs. of the first page of the autograph appears as Plate X in Rokseth/GRIEG.

72. GROVE III 800; Monrad-Johansen/GRIEG 101.

73. As trans. in Schjelderup-Ebbe/GRIEG 244.

74. E.g., cf. MMR XIII (1882) 182; Cobbett/CHAMBER I 497 (M. M. Ulfrstad); Monrad-Johansen/GRIEG 99–100; Finck/GRIEG 195.

75. Cobbett/CHAMBER I 497.

76. Frank/GRIEG 35 and 39 sees the thematic similarity as a main fault of Op. 13. Although this particular similarity may confuse the hearer by falling somewhere between clear identity and subtle derivation, such an argument could not be valid per se without ruling out many cyclically interrelated works that have won almost universal approval.

77. E.g., cf. Monrad-Johansen/GRIEG 99–100; Finck/GRIEG 195.

78. Cf. Gilman/NATURE 171–74.

Ex. 97. From the middle movement of Edvard Grieg's Sonata in G, Op. 13 (after the Breitkopf & Härtel reprint of *ca.* 1887; plate no. 17877).

classified as "Griegian," but nothing more tangible that can be called "Norwegian" than their allegedly indigenous flavors.

Grieg dedicated some of his Norwegian songs to Ole Bull—Op. 17, appropriately enough[79]—but not any of his violin sonatas, not even the more nationalistic Op. 13. Nor does that colorful but circumscribed, conservatively oriented violinist seem to have participated in performances of Op. 13 (or any other Grieg sonata). For that matter, 19th-century violinists in general seem not to have chosen often to play this sonata in recital.[80] They may have felt that in spite of the nationalistic appeal, it was not feasible to appropriate folk elements to full sonata treatment, although such a view is belied by Grieg's skill in accomplishing just that.[81]

Grieg composed his Sonata in a, Op. 36 for P & Vc, in Bergen in 1883 at a time when he was reducing his activities mainly to composition and concert tours. He dedicated it to his elder brother John, a

79. Cf. Schjelderup-Ebbe/GRIEG 91–95.

80. Representative performances in a peak decade are reported in SMZ XVI (1876) 175 (Basel, with Grieg himself); NZM LXXII/2 (1876) 466 (London), LXXIII/1 (1877) 173 (Brussels); MT XXII (1881) 204 (Birmingham), XXVII (1885) 33 (London).

81. Cf. Monrad-Johansen/GRIEG 99–100.

cellist who played it and other works with Edvard, and he saw its first publication by Peters in the same year of 1883.[82] Two decades later, Grieg wrote that he himself did not rate this work "very highly, because it does not betoken any forward step in my development"; and taking his cue from this statement, the author Monrad-Johansen finds in it less of richness, charm, and contrast, and more of mannered devices aimed at routine writing and sure effect.[83] But others, seconded here, have regarded Op. 36 as one of Grieg's best sounding, most rewarding sonatas.[84] Grieg certainly did not hesitate to play Op. 36 a number of times, including its first performance, on October 22, 1883, in Dresden, with the important cellist Friedrich Grützmacher; a performance soon after with the equally recognized Julius Klengel (SSB XI) in Leipzig; and two performances with his brother two years later in Christiana.[85] Otherwise, relatively few performances of the work during Grieg's lifetime have been discovered here.[86] Perhaps some impediments to its success were created by one of the numerous, almost incomprehensible diatribes on his music that appeared in the *Signale für die musikalische Welt* of Leipzig (SMW). In this instance (Oct. 27, 1883), the reviewer (E. Bernsdorf), who had previously railed against both Opp. 8 and 13, complained of the ridiculous Scandinavianism, empty content, and unskilled development and form, yet acknowledged the enthusiastic reception given to Op. 36.[87]

Grieg composed his fifth sonata, Op. 45 in c, for P & Vn, in the winter of 1886–87, completing it on January 21 and dedicating it to the German painter Franz von Lenbach.[88] This so-called "Tragic Sonata," published by Peters in 1887, came on the heels of the third set of *Lyric Pieces* for P solo and the "Travel" songs, which had broken nearly two years of unproductivity.[89] In 1900 Grieg was to write his valued friend and cousin, the esteemed author Bjørnson, that his three violin sonatas "belong to my best works and represent [main] periods of [my] develop-

---

82. Some circumstances of Op. 36 are related in Monrad-Johansen/GRIEG 242–44, 247–48, 271. The autograph is listed in NOTES XXI (1963–64) 91 but has been withdrawn from public access.

83. Monrad-Johansen/GRIEG 242–43.

84. E.g., Finck/GRIEG 197; Cobbett/CHAMBER I 497–98; Dunhill/CHAMBER 181–82.

85. Monrad-Johansen/GRIEG 247 and 271.

86. E.g., in London 3 are reported during the first 3 years of its existence, in MT XXV (1883) 33 and 701, XXVII (1886) 336–37 (with only moderate approval of the music).

87. SMW XLI (1883) 996. Cf. SMW XXXV (1878) 1046 and XXXVI (1879) 406; also, Monrad-Johansen/GRIEG 248 and 217–19 (with the 1883 and 1878 reviews quoted in full in the original German).

88. Some circumstances of Op. 45 are related in Monrad-Johansen/GRIEG 278–81; Finck/GRIEG 112 and 196–97.

89. Monrad-Johansen/GRIEG 275–78.

ment; the first, naive, rich in models; the second, national, and the third with the wider horizons." [90] As the last and, by consensus, best of his sonata-type works, Op. 45 seems to fulfill a revealing vow uttered shortly before—"I will fight my way through the great [large?] forms, cost what it may." [91] To be sure, Bernsdorf, in still another *Signale* diatribe, attacked mainly this very question of large form after Grieg and the fine Russian violinist Adolf Brodsky played Op. 45 for the first time, with much success, in Leipzig on December 10.[92] But most other commentators, from early to recent, have agreed that Grieg met the problem successfully in Op. 45—achieving greater simplicity, development, and breadth, in fact, than in any of its four predecessors. Thus, a Parisian critic wrote in 1890, "This brilliant composition [Op. 45] seems to dispose completely of the reproach that has been levelled against Grieg, that he is not the man for works that require a long breath." [93] Tchaikovsky was understandably "enchanted" with the immediately popular work, and the critics Lawrence Gilman and Ernest Closson found grandeur, heroism, and greatness in it, to a degree Closson considered unsurpassed." [94]

In the year (1887) that Peters published Op. 45, this firm, which already controlled Opp. 8 and 36, also bought the publishing rights to Opp. 7 and 13, and by 1889, confirming Grieg's increasingly wide popularity and importance, had bought the rights to every one of his works then completed.[95] As of 1967 all five sonatas still appear in the Peters catalogues and all but Op. 7 are available in recordings.[96] However, time has scarcely borne out Henry Finck's prognostication—"In the concert halls of the future it is safe to predict that no music of this [chamber] class will be played more frequently than his superb string quartet and his no less admirable sonatas for piano and violin." [97] In spite of both the publications and this prognostication, interest in Grieg has declined conspicuously in the 20th century, especially in the last generation. What explains the decline? Or more to our specific purpose, what strengths and weaknesses stand out today in Grieg's sonatas?

90. As trans. in Schjelderup-Ebbe/GRIEG 245.

91. Monrad-Johansen/GRIEG 278.

92. SMW XLV (1887) 1127; cf. Monrad-Johansen/GRIEG 280–81, with the pertinent section quoted in the original German.

93. As trans. from *Le Matin* of Jan. 4, in Monrad-Johansen/GRIEG 279.

94. As quoted in Finck/GRIEG 112 and 196–97. Cf., also, MT XXIX (1888) 91.

95. Monrad-Johansen/GRIEG 281.

96. A notable recent release is the reissue of Op. 45 as played by Kreisler and Rachmaninoff (along with Schubert's "Duo" Sonata in A, D. 574; RCA Victor LCT 1128).

97. Finck/GRIEG 193. Although he is idolatrous and on the defensive, Finck writes significantly on "Grieg's Rank as a Composer" (pp. 225–45).

The broad answer regarding the decline would have to be simply this: Whereas Grieg's music spells the essence of Romanticism in full bloom, it is precisely his newly self-conscious, slightly mannered, yet still highly emotive phase of Romanticism that the Modern Era has rejected most uncompromisingly. But such a broad answer must not be allowed to blur either the strengths or the weaknesses of Grieg's particular style, for he did develop a particular style—too particular or "Norwegian," some have said (*infra*)—that is almost instantly recognized by seasoned musicians. First among his strengths must be put his superiority as an original, fecund melodist, a superiority, as Finck argues with some reason,[98] that can outweigh a number of more pedantic but less favorable considerations. A sample of Grieg's best melody writing is provided in the A sections of the ternary middle movement in Op. 45, marked "Allegretto espressivo alla Romanza." The piano begins alone with a homophonic double-period extended in its final phrase from a square design of 32 measures to a more plastic one of 45 measures. Thereupon, the violin overlaps by one measure to repeat the 45 measures of melody almost exactly, with the piano now supplying only the purely chordal accompaniment. Notable in this double-period is the folklike simplicity yet sustained interest of the melodic line as it unfolds intensively rather than extensively. Entirely diatonic, largely stepwise, and rather narrow-ranged (not exceeding a 12th until the final octave transplant), the line might have served in one of Grieg's most expressive songs. It achieves breadth of contour by describing only two arcs over-all and by falling into two nearly parallel periods. It achieves rhythmic plasticity by alternating feminine and masculine endings in the phrase members and by reiterating phrase members climactically to extend the cadence 13 measures in the last, 21-measure "phrase." Stamped with Grieg's name are the 8-7-5 and 6-5-3 progressions in the melody (as in mss. 6–7 and 11–12) and the dissonant, chromatic passing or neighboring tones in the harmony. It is the harmony that foretells MacDowell's style (ssb XVII) and frequently edges Grieg's warm sentiment perilously close to sentimentality. Although this harmony is rarely quite so experimental and dissonant in his sonatas (e.g., Op. 7/i/92–105 and iv/178–86) as it is in his songs and smaller piano pieces,[99] it sometimes brings to mind the harmony of Fauré, his near contemporary, admirer, and opposite

98. Finck/GRIEG 235–40.

99. Cf. Finck/GRIEG 213–18; Schjelderup-Ebbe/GRIEG *passim* (on the evolution of Grieg's early harmonic style); Fischer/GRIEG (on harmony in Grieg's songs, including anticipations of Debussy); and Dale/GRIEG 68–70.

Ex. 98. From the first movement of Edvard Grieg's Sonata in
c, Op. 45 (after the original Peters ed. of 1887).

number in France,[100] as in the turn to the lowered submediant chord
(mss. 27–28 and 71–72) in the double-period just described.

Along with his melodic strength and the concomitant strengths in
his rhythm and harmony, Grieg's scoring stands out. The sound is
almost always clear, telling, and well suited to its instrument. Occasionally a passage will fail to come off, though for reasons of technique
as much as of sonority. Thus, at the fortissimo, most climactic statement of the main theme in both the exposition and recapitulation of
Op. 45/i, the piano line fails to project as it should and as it looks, in
the score, as though it would (Ex. 98). Unfortunately, the distribution
of octaves and single notes in the right hand denies more than a weak
application of strength to the melody, and the lower, thicker chords
by which the left hand accompanies on the afterbeats interfere further,
especially if the accents on those chords are observed. More often, being
the fine pianist that he was,[101] Grieg can be counted on to write well,
if not very resourcefully, for piano. And in general, performers find his
music grateful to play and not more than moderately difficult, for, as

100. Cf. Monrad-Johansen/GRIEG 354.
101. Cf. the high praise by Hanslick and others for his "tender," "elegant,"
"flawless" playing as quoted in Finck/GRIEG 109–11.

Schjelderup-Ebbe says,[102] he addressed his music primarily to the "skilled amateur." In any case, Grieg eschewed virtuosity for its own sake, in his sonatas (and even his Concerto in a) as well as his smaller pieces. With his solid Leipzig training in harmony and counterpoint, however scholastic in retrospect, he kept as his main goal the ideal projection and treatment of the musical idea.

Finck considers at some length four "faults" attributed to Grieg by his contemporaries, especially by his German critics[103]—a lack of "logical development" in his music; an inability to "write operas, oratorios, and symphonies"; "too much of the 'Norwegian' idiom"; and more popularity than is commensurate with greatness. Only the first "fault" needs to be considered here, along with one other evaluation, pertaining to Grieg's stature. Regarding his ability to develop the musical ideas in his sonatas, there was little disagreement among earlier writers that at the outset, in Op. 7, he did too little with too much.[104] But Finck sought to rationalize the virtues of fertility[105] and later writers have regarded at least the first three movements as tighter and more logical than was previously supposed.[106] Granted that Op. 7 does offer enough interest, flow, and order to make a generally successful sonata, it is still but the first of five sonatas that show a composer's typical progress toward doing more with less, culminating in the exceptional economy and concentration of ideas in Op. 45. Grieg clearly recognized the problem of large form—that is, "sonata form"—from the start. The question is how successfully he was able to meet it. And if any "fault" does exist in his best large forms it lies, as viewed here, not in the over-all plan—these forms gratify the listener with their logic and freedom from prolixity—but at the more local level of phrase syntax. Even in Op. 45, especially in its fast, outer movements, the syntax must be described as mechanical. Thus, the first movement starts right off with phrases and shorter units of 3+3, 2+2, 1+1, 1+1, and 8 measures. Obviously, there is no failure to recognize the problem at this level, either. Grieg knew the dangers of oversquareness, but in his efforts to escape them he merely fell into another kind of pernicious symmetry. One finds the proof in his consistent need to make every consequent phrase rhyme, as it were, often by filling it out with rests or with those inevitable afterbeat patterns in his music (e.g., Op. 45/i/55–58). As with

102. Schjelderup-Ebbe/GRIEG 338.

103. Finck/GRIEG 227–45.

104. Typical views are summarized in Finck/GRIEG 229–30. Cf., also, Dale/GRIEG 57–58 and Einstein/ROMANTIC 321.

105. Finck/GRIEG 230–32.

106. Monrad-Johansen/GRIEG 71–73; Schjelderup-Ebbe/GRIEG 234–43.

his contemporary and "warm friend" [107] Tchaikovsky, or even Scriabin later, the methodologist superseded the musician in matters of phrase syntax.

Finally, Grieg's five interesting sonatas, as viewed here, fail to qualify as ideal Romantic masterpieces because his own stature as an artist was limited. To say that he was essentially a miniaturist is not quite sufficient because he fell short not only in the structural means of his larger forms (the phrase syntax just discussed) but in the expressive range. He had the fertility of ideas (when he was not in one of those sterile periods) but not the variety nor depth of imagination essential to a great composer. Thus, the comparison made with Fauré had to stop with certain harmonic traits, for—again, as viewed here—Fauré outclassed Grieg not only in the suppleness of his phrase syntax but in the variety and depth of his imagination. Nothing illustrates Grieg's limitations more graphically in the sonatas than the recurrences in each of similar, if not the same, melodic extensions, accompaniment styles, harmonic formulas, and climactic devices. Opp. 36 and 45 are remarkably similar throughout in feel and purpose. Moreover, there is an almost embarrassing similarity between the styles and even several of the ideas (not necessarily the corresponding ideas) in the three movements of the Concerto in a, Op. 16, and those of the cello sonata in the same key.[108] It should be added that once more Grieg recognized the problem. He appears to have been acknowledging his limitations honestly enough, not in false modesty, when he vowed to "fight my way through the great forms" (*supra*) or when he wrote in 1903, "I cannot understand it. So many creative spirits far more important than I do not get the sympathy I meet everywhere." [109]

Among other composers of sonatas in Scandinavian countries during the period of Hartmann, Gade, and Grieg, may be mentioned "Denmark's most important Romantic song composer," **Peter Arnold Heise** (1830–79), for five relatively early sonatas (*ca.* 1859–69)—two for P solo, two for P & Vn, and one for P & Vc.[110] Only the last, "Sonata quasi fantasia" in a (1869), was published, posthumously by Hansen, in 1902, followed by a review that dismissed it as insignificant.[111] A member of a musically active, Danish family, a longtime friend of

107. Cf. Monrad-Johansen/GRIEG 361–63.

108. Cf., also, Monrad-Johansen/GRIEG 303–4, on the similarity between Op. 8 and the String Quartet in F.

109. Monrad-Johansen/GRIEG 259–60; Grieg's own remarks on pp. 261, 293, and 301 (among others) are pertinent, too.

110. MGG VI 89–91 (N. Schiørring).

111. SMW LXI (1903) 187.

Grieg, and an organist, **Gottfred Matthison-Hansen** (1832–1909) left two duo sonatas published in 1877 by Breitkopf & Härtel that remain to be re-explored—Opp. 11 (not 10) in f, for P & Vn, and 16 in F, for P & Vc.[112] **Erik Anthon Valdemar Siboni** (1828–92), a highly regarded organist and singing coach of Italian descent whose teachers included Hartmann in Copenhagen and Moscheles and Hauptmann in Leipzig, left at least two published sonatas each for P solo and P-duet, as well as two or more each for P & Vn and P & Vc that apparently remained unpublished.[113] In Stockholm the German-born pianist (**Johan**) **Herman Berens** (1826–80) left, along with two sonatas for P-duet and six "Kunder-Sonaten" for P solo, two other published sonatas—Op. 5 for P & Vn (1847), reviewed as a promising but inconsistent work in four movements (F-M-Sc-F) with inadequate development in the first movement and meaningless brilliance in the finale, and Op. 60, for P solo (1862), a prize-winning work reviewed as a return to propriety, moderation, and tradition.[114] Another Stockholm composer and pupil of Moscheles and Hauptmann among others, the pianist (**Frederick Vilhelm**) **Ludwig Norman** (1831–85) was a protégé of Jenny Lind and Schumann, successor to the important instrumental composer F. A. Berwald (*supra*), and the composer of several sonatas and other chamber music, as well as more large-scale works. At least three duo sonatas were published—one each for P & Vn (Op. 3 in d; 1852), P & Va (Op. 32 in g; 1875), and P & Vc (Op. 28 in D; 1876)—a sample evaluation being that these are "underrated," although it is skill more than imagination or originality that makes them deserving.[115] Worth investigating, too, might be the canonic "Grand Sonata" for P solo, Op. 2 (1869), by the church music authority, influential teacher in Stockholm, and expert polyphonist **Johan Lindegren** (1842–1908).[116]

The Late-Romantic Sonata in Scandinavia (*Nielsen, Sjögren, Sibelius*)

During the *fin-de-siècle* generation after Hartmann, Gade, and Grieg had flourished, the sonata enjoyed a new rise of interest in all three main Scandinavian countries, Denmark, Norway, and Sweden. This rise paralleled the more general rise of interest in chamber and orches-

112. Cf. Altmann/KAMMERMUSIK 215, 260; MGG VIII 1816–19 (G. Hahne).

113. Cf. GROVE VII 781 (J. A. Fuller-Maitland); MGG XII 662–63 (N. Schiørring); PAZDÍREK XIII 630; Altmann/KAMMERMUSIK 306.

114. NZM XXVI (1847) 220–21 and LVI (1862) 199. Cf. GROVE I 634 (K. Dale); PAZDÍREK II 534–35; Altmann/KAMMERMUSIK 195 (but read 1847, not 1848) and 296.

115. Cobbett/CHAMBER II 191 (G. Jeanson). Cf. GROVE VI 104–5 (Sinclair & K. Dale); MGG IX 1572–74 (L. E. Sanner).

116. Cf. SOHLMANS III 642 (I. Stare); MGG VIII 890 (A. Helmer).

tral music already noted here in France, England, and other countries that had been coming increasingly under the influences of German teachers and composers (shortly before newer turns to French influences). Before taking note of Denmark's Nielsen, we may stop more briefly on two minor Danish composers, Bendix and Glass. Like several of the other Danes to be mentioned, the pianist **Victor Emanuel Bendix** (1851–1926) was a pupil of Gade.[117] His one sonata is Op. 26 in g, for P solo, published by Breitkopf & Härtel in 1901.[118] This is a long work of 46 pages in four movements (F-Sc-Va-VF), yet no typically grandiloquent product of an epigone. Instead it is marked by poeti-

Ex. 99. The start of the second movement in Victor Emanuel Bendix's Sonata in g, Op. 26 (after the original Breitkopf & Härtel ed. of 1901).

cally sensitive and nicely contrasted moods, created chiefly by Bendix's subtly variegated, chromatic harmony, with still a hint of the idiosyncratic harmonic colors and scale intervals in Grieg's writing. Exceptional harmonic ingenuity may be heard, for example, in the development of the first movement, the coda of the second, and the "Adagio" variation of the third. The sense of a broad dynamic structure is defeated somewhat in the first movement by extended, freely motivic sections that tend to unfold without clear directions. Bendix showed himself not to be weak but not to be distinctive, either, as a melodist.

117. Cf. Riemann/LEXIKON I 148; GROVE I 616–617 (E. V. d. Straeten).
118. Largely favorable reviews appear in NZM XCI (1903) 247 and MW XXXIV (1903) 40 (E. Segnitz).

He is most distinctive when he is creating a mood such as that of troubled gaiety in the "Intermezzo scherzando" of Op. 26 (Ex. 99).

The pianist **Louis Christian August Glass** (1864–1936), another sometime pupil of Gade, left four published sonatas—Opp. 7 in E♭ (1895) and 29 in C (1909) for P & Vn, and Opp. 6 in E (1892) and 25 in A♭ (1898) for P solo.[119] Except for the slighter, lighter, and more intimate Op. 29,[120] Glass's sonatas do not reveal the values found in his later works.[121] Although one reviewer of Op. 25, inverting Mattheson's remarks of 1739 (cf. SBE 26), was glad to find a sonata that could still move the heart as well as the fingers,[122] and although this work includes some chromatic and recherché harmony (as in the bridge of i), its four competently written movements (F-Sc-S-M), with their rather ordinary themes and some rather thick scoring, do bring us once more to the somewhat sterile and academic atmosphere of the epigone.

Still another pupil of Gade and a violinist, **Carl (August) Nielsen** (1865–1931) is being viewed increasingly today as one of the most significant composers among Danish Romantics and one of the most original on the threshold of Danish Modern music.[123] Nielsen's considerable, rounded output includes only two published sonatas, both duos for Vn & P,[124] among fourteen instrumental chamber works. But these two sonatas make up in outstanding quality and interest for any neglect in quantity. One is Op. 9 in A, composed in 1895, dedicated to the violinist Henri Marteau, and first performed and published in 1896 (both sonatas have been kept in print by Hansen). The other is Op. 35, in no one key (*infra*), composed in 1912,[125] first performed in 1913, and first published in 1919.

Nielsen's Opp. 9 and 35 have in common their three-movement cycles (F-M-F and F-VS-F), with about the same wide but not extreme ranges of expressive intensity and nearly the same over-all lengths (22 and 20 minutes).[126] Furthermore, they share their clear, orthodox "sonata

119. Cf. MGG V 239–40 (N. Schiørring), including the listing of a Son. in F, Op. 5, for P & Vc, in MS (1889).

120. Cf. the review by W. Altmann in DM X/2 (1910–11) 243.

121. A review of Op. 7 in SMW LIII (1895) 946 finds too much modulation and striving for effect.

122. MW XXXI (1899) 2.

123. Simpson/NIELSEN is a main account of the man (by T. Meyer) and his works (not only the symphonies). Cf., also, GROVE VI 85–88 (K. Jeppesen); MGG IX 1514–17 (N. Schiørring).

124. Items 20 and 64 in the full catalogue Fog/NIELSEN; item 3b) is an early, unpub. Son. "Nr. 1" for Vn & P, in G (1891–92; or 1892–93, as in Simpson/NIELSEN 187).

125. Cf. Simpson/NIELSEN 199; Balzer/NIELSEN 12–13 (T. Nielsen).

126. These sons. are described in Simpson/NIELSEN 149–50; in the symposium Balzer/NIELSEN 26–27 and 36–37 (P. Hamburger), 59–60 (A. Skjold-Rasmussen); and

forms" and A-B-A designs in the first and second movements, respectively; their fresh, inventive main ideas and warm, lyrical, persuasive contrasting themes (with the rising 4th being a basic interval in nearly all of Nielsen's themes known here); their clear but pliably irregular phrase syntax; their varied, frequently precious rhythms; and their well-balanced sound, with no special exploitation of instrumental display, color, or techniques, and with more understanding shown in the violin treatment than in the somewhat pedestrian, often chordal piano writing. One also notes the unfamiliar, piquant, though not programmatic inscriptions in both sonatas, such as "Allegro glorioso" and "agitato et adirato [angry]" in Op. 9/i, "Allegro piacevole e giovanile [agreeable and youthful]" in Op. 9/iii, and "Allegro con tiepidezza [with lukewarmth]" in Op. 35/i.

The parallel in the designs of Nielsen's sonatas breaks down in the finale of Op. 35, which is a decidedly freer adaptation of "sonata form" than its counterpart in Op. 9. Moreover, in Op. 35 there is the Modern tendency to develop each main idea as soon as it is introduced, leaving less reason for the traditional development section. But Nielsen's innovations pertain less to design or the other traits previously mentioned—there is actually a neo-Classic feel in the structural aspects of his music—than to harmony and tonality. In Op. 9 the broad tonal relationships are still simple and traditional, although their effect may be overshadowed somewhat by the newly bold dissonance in the harmony. This dissonance is largely explained by the diagonal harmonic relationships between the two instruments, which the listener absorbs readily enough as vertical relationships thanks to the integrity of the lines and the more conventional harmony within each part. By the time of Op. 35 Nielsen had advanced, liberated, and consolidated both his harmonic and his tonal language. The diagonal relationships sometimes border on polytonality in this sensitive thoroughbred work (Ex. 100), although at climaxes and other strategic moments they usually converge, briefly and with a clear focus, in harmonic oneness (e.g., Op. 35/i/43–47 and 74–78). In this converging, Nielsen anticipates the early polytonality of Milhaud. And when he stretches the diagonal relationships he can sound quite as recondite as Reger, with less chromaticism and less straining of traditional chord relationships, yet quite as much foundation in traditional harmony.[127]

---

in Dolleris/NIELSEN 39–42 and 183–89 (along with extracts from reviews). Op. 35 is described in Cobbett/CHAMBER II 189–90 (R. Simonsen), beginning with the assertion that it is "one of the weightiest chamber works of late years"; it is seen as the start of a compositional crisis for Nielsen in MT CVI (1965) 426–27.

127. Simpson/NIELSEN 35–36 and 145 offers further comparisons with Reger.

Ex. 100. From the start of the development section in the first movement of Carl Nielsen's Sonata Op. 35 (after the first ed. of 1919, by kind permission of Wilhelm Hansen Musik-Forlag, copyright owners in Copenhagen).

If there is a real challenge to tradition in Nielsen's Op. 35, it is at the tonal level.[128] Although key signatures still appear, the tonal center is often amorphous. In the second movement the two sharps do establish the key of b, at least at the main joints in the A-B-A design. But in the first movement the two flats can only mean the Lydian mode on E♭ when they mean anything at all. In the last movement the two flats establish B♭ at the start and the return, but in a stunning 52-measure coda the tone B♭ proves to be not a tonic but a lowered-7th step that persists until it rises to C and a triple-*piano* cadence in the Mixolydian mode on that tone. Thus, the tonality of this work is not closed but open-ended, and most of the sense of key one gets derives not from one stable, clearly established tonality but from transient tonal centers.[129]

In Denmark mention should also be given to the organist **Otto (Valdemar) Malling** (1848–1915), pupil of both Hartmann and Gade, for a charming, light-hearted, three-movement Sonata in g (F-M-F),

128. Dolleris/NIELSEN 183–89 discusses the tonal aspects in some detail.
129. Cf. Jeppesen/NIELSEN 173–74.

Op. 57, for P & Vn (pub. in 1895); [130] the organist **Johann Adam Kry-gell** (1835–1915), for a "Sonata appassionata," Op. 57 in F$\sharp$, for organ (1904); [131] the violinist **Georg Höeberg** (1872–1950), for a rhythmically interesting, cyclical, three-movement Sonata (F-Sc/M-F) in G, Op. 1, for P & Vn (pub. in 1905); [132] the fine pianist **Roger Henrichsen** (1876–1926), for a three-movement, Brahmsian Sonata in F (F-S-VF), Op. 10, for P solo (pub. in 1912), a pianistically fluent work with considerable Romantic drive and lyricism;[133] the violinist **Fini Valdemar Henriques** (1867–1940), for a once popular Sonata in g, Op. 10, for Vn & P (pub. in 1893, revised later); [134] the organist and pupil of both Hartmann and Gade, **Gustaf Helsted** (1857–1924), for two published sonatas for P & Vn, Opp. 13 in A (1908) and 20 in G (1899); [135] and **Christian Barnekow** (1837–1913), for one more Sonata for P & Vn, Op. 23 in F (pub. in 1907), whose first movement still "breathes the spirit of Schumann and Gade." [136]

Norway's most notable Romantic composer after Grieg was certainly the Leipzig-trained violinist **Christian August Sinding** (1856–1941), whose teachers included Reinecke and Jadassohn.[137] Sinding's large and rounded list of publications, in which both the piano and violin figure importantly, includes more than thirty chamber works, large and small. Among these last, excluding two early discarded MSS played in 1879,[138] are five sonatas, Op. 91 in b (not g), for P solo (1909), and Opp. 12 in C (1892, not 1894), 27 in E (1895), 73 in F (1905), and 99 in d ("im alten Stil"; 1909) for Vn & P. Although these sonatas are forgotten today, at least Op. 99 enjoyed some popularity in its day—a work that is more of a suite, with its five short, colorful (nationalistic?), relatively static movements ("Praeludium," "Andante," "Menuett," "Intermezzo" in 5/4 and 7/4 meter, and "Finale").[139] Sinding's other sonatas are all more broadly conceived works and all in the usual

130. Cf. BAKER 1018. The work gets qualified praise as pleasant amateur music in SMW LIII (1895) 930 and LXI (1903) 126; MW XXVIII (1897) 584; Cobbett/CHAMBER II 111 (W. W. Cobbett).

131. Cf. BAKER 880; MW XXXVI (1905) 143 (qualified approval).

132. Cf. BAKER 722; DM IV/4 (1904–5) 205 (W. Altmann).

133. Cf. Riemann/LEXIKON I 737.

134. Cf. MGG VI 161–62 (N. Schiørring); MW XXV (1894) 545 (approving all but an excess of motivic treatment).

135. Cf. BAKER 690; DM X/3 (1910–11) 184 (W. Altmann, praising the ideas, development, and scoring of Op. 13).

136. DM XI/3 (1911–12) 178 (W. Altmann). Cf. GROVE I 441 (H. C. Colles).

137. Cf. MGG XII 726–28 (O. Gurvin), with dated list of works.

138. MGG XII 726 (a son. for Vn & P and a son. mvt. for P solo).

139. The Vn sons. are described briefly in Cobbett/CHAMBER II 421–22 (M. M. Ulfrstad) and Shand/VIOLIN 147–50 (with exx. from Op. 27). Op. 99 is reviewed favorably in DM X/2 (1910–11) 242–43 (W. Altmann).

Ex. 101. From the opening-theme section of Christian Sinding's Sonata in b, Op. 91 (after the original Hansen ed. of 1909).

three-movement plan (F-M-F or F-M-VF). In Op. 73, the main theme of the finale is actually based on a Norwegian national dance, the "Springer."[140] Op. 73 is generally more chromatic, poetic, and sensitive than Op. 27, the style of which is as close to Richard Strauss's as to that of Wagner, of whom he was a staunch admirer. Also, at least in the first movement, there are passages that will sound familiar to anyone who knows Sinding's most popular piece, *Frühlingsrauschen*, Op. 32/3, for P solo, with its bold, sonorous dash, its cascades of arpeggio figures, and its protracted, sequential, climactic ascents to heroic peaks. The other two movements of Op. 27 are slightly thinner in texture but no less compelling (and traditional) in their harmony, nor any less songful in their attractive melodies.

Sinding's Op. 91 still recalls *Frühlingsrauschen* in its first movement, too. The almost constant modulation in that movement, chiefly through enharmonic re-interpretations of augmented and diminished chords, blurs the outlines of an entirely standardized "sonata form." Furthermore, it explains a reviewer's inability to find anything more than "swimming fantasies" in the outer movements[141] and it illustrates another product of Sinding's strong attraction to Wagner's music (Ex.

140. Cobbett/CHAMBER II 422.
141. DM IX/4 (1909–10) 50 (A. Leitzmann).

101). In the somber opening theme,[142] with its descending 5th and inner pedal, one finds a kinship with melodies by Sibelius. But here Sinding's undeniable melodic strength and originality are limited largely
and somewhat tiresomely to this type of theme and to lines that outline
scales in steady quarter- and 8th notes (as in both remaining movements). The resultant continuous, impelling flow, in conventional harmony and in textures that are idiomatic but almost too full, is, in fact,
one of the most pronounced traits in all of Sinding's sonatas.

In Sweden the most important of the late Romantics was the organist
(Johan Gustaf) Emil Sjögren (1853–1918), whose background included
composition studies under Kiel in Berlin (ssb X) in 1879–80 and opportunities to know the music of Franck and Saint-Saëns in Paris in
1885.[143] Between 1886 and 1914 eight sonatas by Sjögren were published. Two are for P solo—Opp. 35 in e (1903, not 1902) and 44 in A
(1905). Five are for Vn & P—Opp. 19 in g (1886), 24 in e (1889), 32 in
g (1901), 47 in b (1908), and 61 in a (1913). And one is for Vc & P, Op.
58 in A (1914). The first two of the violin sonatas, especially the second,
in e, were Sjögren's most successful and are now regarded as his best
chamber works in a somewhat circumscribed output otherwise noted
chiefly for its songs and shorter piano pieces.[144] These sonatas are made
distinctive mainly by their tender, fresh, songful melodies and the
choice, precise harmony that supports them rather than by any innovations in tonality and design, or, for that matter, by any conspicuous
ability to develop the ideas or control the broad outlines of the larger
designs.

The better-known of Sjögren's two piano sonatas, Op. 35, is a case
in point, too. A relatively short work of twenty pages, it approximates
his more usual four-movement plan by the not infrequent method of
alternating andante and scherzando sections in a middle movement between two fast movements.[145] Although the duple and triple meters

142. Mss. 3–6 of Ex. 101 illustrate its first half in another key.
143. Cf. GROVE VII 827 (D. Hume & K. Dale); MGG XII 742–44 (A. Helmer), with
partial, dated list of works, including a re-ed. in 1957 of the complete Vn sons. A
study of Swedish instrumental music in the 19th-c., by Bo Wallner, is reportedly
nearing completion as of this writing.
144. Cf. Cobbett/CHAMBER II 423–24 (G. Jeanson & W. W. Cobbett). But the later
Vn sons. were generally greeted with enthusiasm, too, when they first appeared.
On Op. 32, cf. DM I/1 (1901) 424 (W. Altmann); MW XXXIII (1902) 600
(E. Segnitz); SMW LXI (1903) 189 (less favorable). On Op. 47, cf. DM VIII/1 (1908–9)
367 (W. Altmann). There was also approval of the Vc son., Op. 58, in DM XII/2
(1912–13) 363 (H. Schlemüller). The 5 Vn sons. are described, with 10 exx., in Shand/
VIOLIN 152–57. Mod. ed. of the 5 Vn sons.: SJÖGREN-m. with preface.
145. In a favorable review that questions only the (already!) slightly dated
Scandinavian style, H. Teibler actually writes (erroneously) of "four concise movements" (DM III/3 [1903–4] 372). Op. 44 was reviewed as a somewhat lighter work,
of value to the amateur and student (DM V/4 [1905–6] 326).

are reversed, there is an awareness of Brahms's Op. 100/ii in this double-purpose movement, in all probability by way of Kiel. One well-pleased reviewer likened the style of Op. 35 to that in the piano works of Brahms and Reger.[146] But his reference is mainly to Sjögren's harmonic style and today this style might more accurately be likened to that of Grieg (*supra*), including even the occasional hints of Franck or Fauré (ssb XIII), as in a succession of tonics that descend by whole-steps (Ex. 102). In other respects, too, Op. 35 recalls Grieg—in fact, at least the styles and occasionally the ideas of Grieg's own piano Sonata in e, Op. 7, published 37 years earlier.[147] The melodic ideas have similar popular appeal, though a little less distinction and originality. The

Ex. 102. The subordinate theme near the start of Emil Sjögren's Sonata in e, Op. 35 (after the original Hansen ed. of 1903).

texture is similar in its moderate chordal fullness, its but moderate challenges to the pianist, its shifts of range as means of color contrasts, and its occasional uncomplicated dialog and imitations. The association of dance and other type melodies with nationalistic influences is similar (as in the subordinate theme of Op. 35/iii), but with still less possibility of pointing to specific derivations. And the aesthetic scope is similar. Like Grieg, Sjögren was a gifted musician within narrow confines. In particular, he was even less of an architectonic composer at heart (or by training), with even less inclination (or ability) to develop his ideas in the Teutonically Classic sense and still more inclination than Grieg showed to resort to fantasy, excessive sequence, and

146. MW XXXVII (1906) 205.
147. E.g., there is a certain kinship between Ex. 102 and Grieg's Op. 7/i/94 ff.

matching pairs of square-half-phrases as the structural outs in his larger forms.

Though largely self-taught in composition, the pianist **Karl Wilhelm Eugen Stenhammar** (1871–1927) did get some early training with Sjö-gren.[148] Following an early, unpublished Sonata in g, for P solo (1890), he left two published sonatas, Op. 12 in A♭, for P solo (1897), and Op. 19 in a/A (not C), for P & Vn (1904). The first movement of Op. 12 alternates a chorale-like section, "Moderato, quasi Andante," with a more agitated, dynamically cumulative section marked "Allegretto animato," somewhat in the manner of Beethoven's Op. 27/1/i (SCE 517). Then, after a light scherzando movement in the mediant key and ₵ meter, marked "Molto vivace" (and "Presto" over its "Trio" in 3/4 meter), there follows a free allegro finale in "sonata form," with a slow introduction that recalls the opening chorale idea. Op. 19, described approvingly as something of an idyll,[149] follows a simpler, more straightforward three-movement plan (F-M-F). Although Stenhammar's sonatas have been dismissed as inconsequential[150] and do tend to discourage performance with their Mendelssohnian and Brahmsian harmony and other traits that were archaic at the turn of this century, they actually reveal unexpected harmonic and melodic depths, considerable imagination in the scoring and disposition of ideas, and a broad, unconstrained command of form.

Other late-Romantic sonatas in Sweden that might repay further investigation include an Op. 1 in a, for P & Vn (pub. in 1893), by the Stockholm composer **Bror Beckman** (1866–1929); [151] Op. 19 in d, for P solo (pub. in 1899), by the organist and devotee of Franck and Widor **Gustaf Wilhelm Hägg** (1867–1925);[152] two light, charming works suggesting Grieg, in e and G, for P & Vn (composed in 1887 and 1910, and pub. in 1901 and 1916), by the pianist and prominent Swedish nationalist **Wilhelm Peterson-Berger** (1867–1942), noted mainly for his songs and operas;[153] Op. 7 in D♭, for P solo (1908?), by the Spanish-

148. Cf. GROVE VIII 75–76 (Sinclair & K. Dale) and MGG XII 1255–57 (B. Wallner), both with incomplete lists of works and further bibliography; also, SOHLMANS IV 915–22 (B. Wallner, with a more detailed survey).

149. Cobbett/CHAMBER II 455–56 (S. Broman & W. W. Cobbett). Cf., also, Shand/VIOLIN 165–67, with 5 exx.

150. MGG XII 1255. In NZM C (1904) 818, Op. 19 was reviewed with praise and as a work relatively little colored by nationalism (somewhat contrary to B. Wallner in SOHLMANS IV 918).

151. The names in this paragraph have been suggested as being of possible interest by Professor Ingmar Bengtsson of Uppsala Universitet.

152. Cf. SOHLMANS II 1210–11 (G. Percy); GROVE IV 14 (K. Dale). Op. 19 (especially its "Intermezzo") is praised in MW XXX (1899) 587.

153. Cf. MGG X 1123–24 (B. Carlberg); Shand/VIOLIN 157–62, with brief descriptions and 12 exx.; Cobbett/CHAMBER II 215 (W. W. Cobbett).

born organist and pupil of Stenhammar among others, **Olallo Juan Magnus Morales** (1874–1957);[154] and Op. 7 in e, for P & Vn (pub. in 1911), by the complex harmonist, under Wagner's and Reger's influence, **Edvin Kallstenius** (1881–   ).[155] The "Sonata à la legenda" for Vn & P, Op. 7 in C (1919), by Harold Leonard Fryklöf (1882–1919) and most of the numerous solo and duo sonatas (largely unpub.) by Ivar Henning Mankell (1868–1930) are a little late and too progressive in their harmonic and tonal styles to be grouped with the sonatas of our other late-Romantics.[156]

As suggested at the start of this chapter, the renowned Finnish master **Jean Sibelius** (1865–1957) might best be grouped with our Scandinavian, especially our Swedish composers. His early training was followed similarly by German training and by study in Austria under Fuchs and Goldmark (ssʙ XI and IX).[157] Along with his many orchestral, accompanied and unaccompanied choral, and incidental stage works, and his many smaller pieces for piano, for solo voice and piano, and for nearly every other setting he employed, he left but little in the category of chamber music.[158] Besides only one mature, large-scale work, the string Quartet "Voces intimae," there was one duo "Sonatine," Op. 80 in E, for Vn & P (composed in 1915 and pub. by Hansen in 1921). Two earlier "sonatas" in the same scoring were left unpublished (1883, 1886 in F).[159] For P solo there were also the Sonata in F (composed in 1893 and pub. by Breitkopf & Härtel in 1906) and three later "sonatines," Op. 67/1–3, in f♯ (not A, as on the printed cover!), E, and b♭ (composed and pub. in 1912). Thus, Sibelius left a total of four published sonatinas and one published sonata.

Although all five works are slight, especially in texture and expressive weight, they bear the unmistakable stamp of the master. In fact, partially excepting the less subtle and experienced Op. 12, they may be called miniature Sibelius masterpieces. Yet they have received re-

---

154. Cf. sohlmans III 987–88 (G. Percy); mgg IX 563–64 (A. Helmer), calling Op. 7 Brahmsian. Yet, Op. 7 was reviewed as another of "the many modern sonatas" that lack form and thematic development (dm IX/4 [1909–10] 109 [A. Leitzmann]).

155. Cf. mgg VII 459–61 (L. Reimers); Cobbett/chamber II 46; dm XI/1 (1911–12) 235 (W. Altmann, with praise for the poetic slow mvt. but not for harmonic excesses in the outer mvts.).

156. Cf. grove III 510–11 (K. Dale); mgg VIII 1585–87 (I. Bengtsson); stfmf XXIII (1941) 5–33 (I. Bengtsson), with full, dated cat. of Mankell's MS and pub. works.

157. For more exact biographical information than that in grove VII 772–81 (E. Blom) and mgg XII 652–62 (N.-E. Ringbom), cf. the "Persönlichkeit" section in Tanzberger/sibelius 14–69 and the additional studies singled out in the "Introduction" (especially p. ix) of the valuable bibliography Blum/sibelius.

158. Cf. the "Werkverzeichnis" of pub. works and MSS, with and without op. nos., in Tanzberger/sibelius 265–89.

159. Cf. Blum/sibelius item 42.

markably little attention by either writers or performers.[160] Even including Op. 12, when they first appeared their striking originality and independence seem to have puzzled or at least put off the reviewers.[161] And in recent studies their peripheral position in Sibelius' total output seems to have discouraged anything more than a few brief discussions of them.[162]

Sibelius' one so-called "Sonata," Op. 12, makes a publication of twenty-five pages, a fifth longer than Op. 80 and over two-and-a-half times the lengths of Op. 67/1–3. All these works divide clearly into three movements, with two quick movements enclosing a slower movement, except Op. 67/3, in which the second of the but two movements accelerates from an "Andante" to an "Allegretto" section on the same theme. The fast movements Opp. 67/3/i and 80/i and iii have brief, slower introductions. Whereas the middle movements of Opp. 12 and 80 are in contrasting keys—subdominant minor and dominant major, respectively—all movements are in the same key in each sonatina of Op. 67. Except for Op. 67/1, each of these works reveals more or less clear thematic relationships between its movements. "Sonata form" seems still to be a conscious guiding principle in the outer movements of Op. 12 in F, although the emphasis on the key of the raised 2d (g♯) in the development sections of both movements and the choice of the subdominant key (B♭) for the subordinate theme in the exposition of the first movement tend to contradict that principle. A freer "sonata form" seems to be intentional, also, in Op. 80/i, but hints of that principle seem more coincidental than intentional in Op. 67/1/i and 3/i. The rondo principle operates more or less in Opp. 12/ii and all the sonatina finales. Op. 67/2/i suggests an invention. The middle movements of the three three-movement sonatinas are all free, open forms that unfold continuously.

However, the real interest in Sibelius' forms lies not in discovering standardized designs that happen at least to be hinted in some of the movements but in the seemingly intuitive, independent process out of which all these forms grow. It was Cecil Gray, echoed by later writers,

---

160. Op. 80 was played at the first German Sibelius festival in Lübeck, in 1958 (Tanzberger/SIBELIUS 243).
161. E.g., DM VI/4 (1906–7) 305 (A. Leitzmann, reporting the originality as incompatible with "rigid sonata form" and the ideas weak except in ii); DM XII/4 (1912–13) 108 (A. Leitzmann, reviewing Op. 67/1–3 as dull and unimportant); SMW LXXXII (1924) 1942 (Op. 80 reviewed in 2 sentences as Nordic, less characteristic of Sibelius than his large, orchestral fantasias, not too difficult, and effective).
162. Cf. Abraham/SIBELIUS 96 (Op. 80, by S. Goddard), 98–100 and 101–3 (Opp. 12 and 67/1–3, by E. Blom); Tanzberger/SIBELIUS 242–43 (Op. 80) and 245 (one sentence on Opp. 12 and 67/1–3). More on the P sons. is cited in Blum/SIBELIUS item 52. Cobbett/CHAMBER II 416–19 (E. Blom) discusses only the string quartet.

who found the main generative process in Sibelius' symphonies, especially No. 4, to be the "organic evolution of a germ idea." [163] But that view, which sees the form as beginning only with thematic fragments and culminating with their ultimate synthesis in a grand theme (a process ascribed to Bruckner's symphonies, too) has rightly been challenged in Sibelius[164] and fails to apply in the sonatinas, in any case. In the latter the generative process is one of simple syntactic extensions. A main idea is likely to be toyed with and restated piecemeal through imaginative, rhythmically free, unpredictable reiterations, variations, or rondo-like recurrences of its most salient motives. Actually, this process, plus thin, precise textures sometimes attenuated to

Ex. 103. From the middle movement of Sonatina in f♯, Op. 67/1, by Jean Sibelius (after the original Breitkopf & Härtel ed. of 1912).

the point of monophony, plus persistent accompaniment figures in the manner of an *ostinato,* plus scoring that disappoints the keyboardist (especially in the unidiomatic accompaniments) but does evoke orchestral colors, plus harmonic progressions that are constantly fresh without being tonally disruptive—all these traits, which too often produce mere platitudes in Sibelius' other piano music, make his sonatinas sound not only like miniature masterpieces but like miniature Sibelius symphonies. Unfortunately, in the one example that can be allowed, only hints and only some of these traits can be illustrated (Ex. 103, including faint reminders of stentorian brass passages in Symphony 4 in a, completed about a year earlier [1910–11]).

163. As in Gray/SIBELIUS 142–43; Tovey/ANALYSIS II 121–22. The quoted expression is a composite of several similar descriptions (cf. Newman/TREND 124–35).

164. As in Hill/SIBELIUS; Collins/GERM.

Finally in this chapter, passing mention may be given to three Finnish contemporaries of Sibelius. The internationally successful, German-trained pianist **Selim Palmgren** (1878–1951), whose teachers included Busoni and whose piano works included the pedagogically popular "May Night," composed in 1900 a three-movement, pseudo-Modern, harmonically mawkish, melodically sterile, texturally thick, rhythmically free, and structurally traditional Sonata in d, Op. 11, for P solo (pub. in 1927 by Augener).[165] The theorist and conductor **Erkki Gustaf Melartin** (1875–1937), a pupil of Robert Fuchs in Vienna, left in print four sonatinas for P solo, Op. 84 (1919) and Sonata in E, Op. 10, for P & Vn (1909), described as a warm, melancholy, original concert work, although somewhat prolix.[166] And the conductor **Toivo Kuula** (1883–1918), who completed his training in Bologna, Leipzig, and Paris, left a youthful Sonata in e, Op. 1, for P & Vn (1909), which is described in similar terms.[167]

165. Cf. MGG X 714–15 (N.-E. Ringbom).
166. DM X/4 (1910–11) 247 (W. Altmann). Cf. MGG IX 7–8 (N.-E. Ringbom), with reference to two other duo sons., as well; Cobbett/CHAMBER II 127.
167. DM X/4 (1910–11) 247 (W. Altmann). Cf. MGG VII 1924–25 (N.-E. Ringbom); Cobbett/CHAMBER II 83–84 (E. Blom).

Chapter XVI

A Low Ebb in Italy, Spain, and Portugal

Circumstances and Sources

That this is the shortest of our thirteen regional chapters reflects the low ebb of the sonata not only in Spain and Portugal during the Romantic Era, but in Italy, which for so long had been a main fountainhead of independent instrumental music. After Turini in Italy and Soler in Spain (SCE 295–97 and 279–85), there are only sporadic, average products to report, at best, and scarcely more even with the instrumental renaissance of the 1870's that touched these countries as well as most of the rest of Europe. It would be tempting to blame the low ebb on the political distresses of foreign rule, civil disruptions, and scattered revolutionary movements. These distresses plagued both Spain and Portugal, with their persistently unstable monarchies, and Italy, which still remained largely a "geographical expression" until the Risorgimento. Valiantly guided by Cavour, Garibaldi, and others, the Risorgimento finally led to full unification in 1870 (the same year unification obtained in Germany) as well as emancipation, under Victor Emmanuel II, from the rival French and Austrian controls. However, the political problems did not stop important music in other categories from appearing in these countries, notably Italian opera and its Iberian counterparts. One has to assume that Bellini, Verdi, Puccini, Manuel Garcia (Sr.) and nearly all of the other most successful composers saw nothing to attract them in the sonata.[1] Men of this sort who did respond to it, including Paganini, Rossini, and Albéniz, did so only more or less incidentally within their total outputs. Furthermore, even when that instrumental renaissance occurred in Italy during the later 19th century, only two of its three main champions wrote sonatas—that is, Martucci and Bossi but not Sgambati, as against all three in the contemporary triumvirates we have already noted in France, England, and Scandinavia (early in Chaps. XIII, XIV, and XV).

1. Cf. MGG VI 1533–34, 1542, 1543, 1546 (M. Mila); XII 1006–7 (J. Subirá); X 1485 (J. d. Freitas Branco).

During travels of 1853 Moscheles found almost no evidence of creative musical distinction, pianistic or otherwise, in Italy.[2] In Venice, "I find on all sides shallowness and mediocrity. . . . The only good music . . . is that of the Austrian military band"; the music of Moscheles himself was regarded as "too serious" to play there. At the Milan Conservatory, "of Beethoven or Mendelssohn they know absolutely nothing." While in Paris in 1860 Moscheles reported Rossini's joy in the Classic masters (including Clementi and his sonatas) and in Weber, but not in the current Italian music.[3] At any rate, a curious unawareness of the "sonata" in full bloom, as it had matured in their own and other countries, becomes apparent in the reversion by Paganini, Rossini, and others to the earlier, looser meaning merely of "soundpiece." (In such a sense, even Verdi might qualify as a "sonata" composer, with his "Suona la tromba" ["Sound the trumpet"] for male chorus and P-or-orchestra, dated 1848). And we get more evidence of the little interest in the sonata in 19th-century Italy from the fact that most of the sonatas by Italians were either composed while they were residing in foreign, more receptive regions, or at least published in those regions (especially London, Paris, and Leipzig). Furthermore, during the Italian instrumental renaissance the single strongest influence was not an Italian, but a resident foreigner in Rome, Liszt.[4]

The studies are lacking that might turn up further and more significant instrumental activities in Italy, Spain, and Portugal during the Romantic Era. There is one reference work from each country that frequently contributes specific details of value—Schmidl/DIZIONARIO (by Carlo Schmidl, himself variously involved in late-19th-c. Italian music), DICCIONARIO LABOR, and DICCIONARIO PORTUGUEZES. Otherwise the sources are too often poor or nonexistent. For example, except where the publications occurred in foreign centers, precise dating of printed sonatas, such as those issued by Ricordi in Milan or Unión Musical Español in Madrid, is generally not yet possible.

Italy in the First Half-Century (Paganini and Rossini)

The two most important musicians who wrote sonatas in early 19th-century Italy were certainly the warm friends Paganini and Rossini, although those sonatas contributed only incidentally to Paganini's importance and not at all to Rossini's. The legendary master violinist **Nicolò** (or **Niccolò**) **Paganini** (1782–1840) wrote at least **51** solo and

2. MOSCHELES II 234–40.
3. MOSCHELES II 270–79.
4. Cf. De Angelis/ROMA *passim*.

ensemble "sonatas," so called, over the years from his earliest training with his father in Genoa,[5] through his rising fame in Lucca and other Italian centers, to his sensational concert triumphs (from 1828) in Austrian, German, French, and British centers, and his final years of failing health in Italy and France.[6] Of 50 "sonatas" that have been identified in the best but still somewhat unresolved lists of Paganini's compositions[7] some were written as diversional music for the amateur and some for his own electrifying, virtuosic performances, on both the violin and the guitar (which interest derived from mandolin instruction that his father had given to him).[8] No fewer than 32 of the 50 sonatas (64 per cent) are scored for violin and guitar, with the violin being the solo instrument in most, the guitar in a few, and the two instruments being partners in a few. Of these 32, 2 sets of 6 each were composed about 1802–9 and first published by G. Ricordi in 1820 (Paganini's only sons. pub. in his lifetime); 3 sets of 6 each, referred to by the collective title "Centone [medley?] di Sonate" added in another hand, were composed after 1828 and appeared only posthumously, chiefly piecemeal and in arrangements for Vn & P until W. Zimmermann of Frankfurt/M published all 3 sets in their original version in 1955–56;[9] and 2 or 3 separate sonatas for violin and guitar appeared only posthumously, including a delightful duet in A, called "Sonata concertata" (composed in 1804 [10]), and a long "Grande Suonata" in A, in which the guitar dominates entirely.[11]

5. "Even before I was eight years old, I wrote a sonata under the supervision of my father, but it is no longer in existence, having been torn up like numerous other experimental works of the same kind" (from Paganini's autobiographical sketch for J. Schottky, as trans. in Courcy/PAGANINI II 369).

6. Courcy/PAGANINI (outlined in Courcy/CHRONOLOGY) has proved to be much the fullest and most authoritative biographical and documentary source (only) since it was added in 1957 to the considerable, recently mushrooming literature on Paganini, although it still does not contain some of the information on the sons. to be found in the voluminous documentary study Codignola/PAGANINI (1935). Vyborny/PAGANINI surveys that literature up to 1964, including serious flaws that still persist from early sources, in GROVE VI 488–94 (E. Blom), and even in Courcy's article, especially in the music listings, for MGG X 627–33; cf., also, Codignola/PAGANINI 75–76. The most accurate, up-to-date encyclopedic article as of this writing (1968) is that by Pietro Berri in Gatti & Basso/LA MUSICA III 679–91, including recent bibliography.

7. Codignola/PAGANINI 653–55 (pub.) and 655–63 (unpub.), including descriptive comments by A. A. Bachmann, A. Bonaventura, and others; Courcy/PAGANINI II 373–88; Gatti & Basso/LA MUSICA III 687–91. The last 2 lists give the most recent as well as the earliest eds., but cannot be fully reconciled with PAZDÍREK XI 31–32.

8. Cf. Bone/GUITAR 262–74.

9. A recording of the first set is reviewed informatively by A. Mell in MQ XLVI (1960) 557–59.

10. Cf. Courcy/CHRONOLOGY 14; Codignola/PAGANINI 212.

11. A recording (Mace SM-9025) of these 2 sons. and another duet by Paganini,

Four more of Paganini's 50 identified "sonatas" are "Sonatines" for guitar alone.[12] Another, composed by 1834, is scored "per la grande viola," with guitar accompaniment.[13] And the remainder are scored for violin with various accompaniments, including one "a violino scordato" accompanied by 2 other violins (probably composed about 1802–6),[14] 3 with P as accompaniment (composed between 1825 and at least 1831),[15] and 9 with orchestral accompaniments.[16]

By their descriptive titles alone the separate sonatas in the category last cited—that is, for Vn with various accompaniments—would reveal that Paganini used the word sonata not with any standardized plan or designs in mind but merely in its earlier, generic sense of a relatively extended instrumental piece, often, though not always, in only one sectional movement. If his use of the word connotes any one principle it is that of variation form rather than "sonata form." Several of those titles actually specify variations in subtitles. A "Sonata a preghièra [prayer]" is subtitled (and trans.) "Introduction and Variations on the theme 'From Thy Star-Studded Throne' in Rossini's *Moïse.*" [17] A "Sonata Amorosa Galante" includes in its title, as given on a London poster of 1831, the facts of both the variation form and one of the composer's most frequent virtuoso stunts—"with Variations on a Tema by Rossini, composed expressly and performed on a SINGLE STRING, (the Fourth,) by Signor PAGANINI, with Piano-Forte Accompaniment." [18] Haydn's "Austrian National Hymn," Weigl's opera *L'Amor marinaro,* and Mozart's *Marriage of Figaro* were among other sources of themes for Paganini's variation "sonatas." [19] The sections in such

---

identified only as "Sonata Opus Posthumous," is reviewed in *The New York Times* music section for Feb. 20, 1966.

12. Cf. Courcy/PAGANINI II 385.

13. Cf. Courcy/PAGANINI II 382; Codignola/PAGANINI 379, 657.

14. Facs. of the autograph of the first and last pp. are pub. in Berri/PAGANINI 48–49. Cf. Courcy/PAGANINI I 64 and II 283.

15. Cf. Gatti & Basso/LA MUSICA III 689 and Courcy/PAGANINI II 379–80 (but "Sonata movimento perpetuo" is indicated here with chamber accompaniment; no accompaniment is shown in the facs. of the last autograph p. in Codignola/PAGANINI 142), 381, 382.

16. Cf. Gatti & Basso/LA MUSICA III 687–88.

17. Codignola/PAGANINI 265, 381; Courcy/PAGANINI II 377. The work, also known as "Moses Fantasy," was composed presumably in 1818 or 1819 after the first performance of Rossini's *Mosè in Egitto* in Naples in 1818, although the title *Moïse en Egypte* was not used until the first Paris performance in 1827.

18. Facs. of this and another Paganini poster of 1831 (including 2 more, similar sons.) appear as Plate 3 in Spivacke/PAGANINIANA. Cf., also, Gatti & Basso/LA MUSICA III 685; Courcy/PAGANINI II 381.

19. Cf. Codignola/PAGANINI 265; Courcy/PAGANINI II 380 and 382. Some of the titles were occasional, like "Sonata Napoleone," named for Paganini's performance of it on the Emperor's birthday in 1807. A facs. of the opening in the autograph

sonatas consist typically of an introduction in slow-to-moderate tempo, the theme-and-variations, and a brilliant final variation or coda. These "sonatas" do not differ tangibly from other variation works similarly scored by Paganini that happen not to include "sonata" in their titles.[20] Mainly, such variation works supplied the display pieces, including the "secret" techniques,[21] that enraptured audiences whenever and wherever he played them, at home and abroad, and inspired Schumann, Chopin, Liszt, Berlioz, and other important musicians to write verbal tributes, musical homages, and/or transcriptions adapted to their own instrumental tastes. Moscheles' lavish praise and exceptional interest were characteristic, as also, however, were certain reservations after increased exposure to Paganini's playing and compositions:

Suffice it to say, my admiration of this phenomenon, equally endowed by nature and art, was boundless. Now, however, after hearing him frequently, all this is changed; in every one of his compositions I discover *the same* effects, which betrays a poverty of invention; I also find both his style and manner of playing monotonous. His concertos are beautiful, and have even their grand moments; but they remind me of a brilliant firework on a summer's eve, one flash succeeding the other—effective, admirable—but always the same. His 'Sonata Militaire,' and other pieces, have a southern glow about them, but this hero of the violin cannot dispense with the roll of the drum; and completely as he may annihilate his less showy colleagues, I long for a little of Spohr's earnestness, Baillot's power, and even Mayseder's piquancy.[22]

Although variation forms occur in the sonatas of Paganini's Opp. 2 and 3, too, in general those sonatas and the "Centone di Sonate" for Vn & guitar come closer to the then established idea of the sonata, at least in its lighter forms and sometimes to an extent that belies Cobbett's peremptory dismissal of Paganini's compositions as "not real chamber music." [23] The most frequent plan of these duo sonatas is that of a songful slow or moderate movement followed by a simple binary, ternary, or rondo design in quick tempo. The feeling of a sonatina rather than a sonata is conveyed by the brevity of the movements, the lightness of texture, and the lack of any significant develop-

---

of the latter appears in Codignola/PAGANINI 78, and of "Suonati con variazioni," in Gatti & Basso/LA MUSICA III 686.

20. E.g., those listed in Courcy/PAGANINI II 375–76; on pp. 272 and 276 the 3 *"grandiossissime* sonatas with variations," "just composed" by Paganini, according to 2 letters he wrote in 1838, are believed to include a "Balletto Campestre" without "sonata" in the title.

21. Probably extended uses of harmonics (cf. W. Kirkendale in JAMS XVIII [1965] 394–407).

22. MOSCHELES I 251–57; cf. pp. 272 and 293. Cf., also, the contemporary reports from Vienna and Paris in praise of Paganini's wondrous effects in the same "suonata militare," as quoted in Codignola/PAGANINI 64, 66–69.

23. Cobbett/CHAMBER II 205–6 (W. W. Cobbett).

Ex. 104. From the second (final) movement of Nicolò Paganini's Sonata in e, Op. 3/6 (after the reprinting by the International Music Co., 1943).

ment of materials. As for the nature of the ideas and their treatment, Paganini's well-known violin caprices Op. 1 and his closeness to Rossini are safe clues. Clear-cut melodies and figures, organized into regular, well-defined phrases, prevail. Nor are these ideas without idiomatic refinements, some originality, and the support of appropriate well-balanced accompaniments. An illustration may be provided from the duo best known in print (Ex. 104).

Paganini undoubtedly knew another popular Italian guitarist, seven years his senior, **Antonio Maria Nava** (1775–1828), who was also the author of a guitar method (1812) as well as a vocalist.[24] Between about 1810 and 1825 Nava published numerous sonatinas and sonatas, singly and in sets, for guitar solo, as well as numerous duets for two guitars or guitar and violin that are similarly light and similarly oriented to the variation principle.[25]

Our justification for including here the major Italian opera composer **Gioacchino (Antonio) Rossini** (1792–1868) is no more than the generic title "Sonate a quattro" applied to his earliest known compositions.

---

24. Cf. Bone/GUITAR 257–58.

25. The only son. that survives in PAZDÍREK XI 45 is a "Sonatine" for guitar. But cf. HOFMEISTER 1815 (Whistling), 258, and 1828 (Whistling), 410–11. Weinmann/ARTARIA item 2194, dated 1811, is a "Sonata sentimentale" for guitar.

The set in question comprises six three-movement cycles composed in his twelfth year (1804) for a hospitable friend Agostino Triossi and scored for 2 Vns, Vc, & double-bass. In this original version, it was not made known nor published until recently, in 1954.[26] But five of the quartets (minus No. 3 [27]) appeared in other scorings, perhaps neither made nor sponsored by Rossini himself, including standard string quartets (first pub. in 1826) and, most successfully, as wind quartets (Fl, Cl, Hn, Bn; first pub. in 1828–29).[28] The original set, in other words, contained the only quartets Rossini is known to have written.[29]

Each of Rossini's six "Sonate" is in a major key of no more than three sharps or flats and contains three movements in the order F-M-F (except that Son. 1/i is "Moderato"). Three of the middle movements are in minor keys and two get as far afield tonally as the lowered submediant (Son. 1) and lowered mediant (Son. 6). The first movements fall short of anticipating textbook "sonata form" by providing no dualistic contrast beyond successions of like ideas and no development beyond mere transpositions of thematic elements.[30] Four of the middle movements return sooner or later to their openings and two do not. Four of the finales are rondos, one (Son. 3) is a naively virtuosic set of variations and one (Son. 6), marked "Tempesta," is a fantasy that anticipates distantly but significantly the "Overture," especially the storm, in *William Tell*. The Mozartean, clearly phrased tunes, the triplets and dotted patterns, the telling scoring, the prevailing gaiety, and the harmonic progressions that amount to continuous cadential formulas all anticipate later Rossini styles, too, especially the *buffa* styles of *The Barber of Seville*. In these respects Rossini was undeniably precocious (cf. SCE 289–90). As "sonatas," these early quartets, for all their brightness and Classic charm, suffer, understandably enough, from sameness of style (the compound meter in the finale of Son. 1 differs little in effect from the 4/4 meter with triplets in the first mvt.). Those successions of like ideas straggle, without thematic interrelations or development, and the lack of adequate key contrast precludes tonal tension, particularly in the first movements.

26. Rossini/SONATE-m, with a helpful preface by A. Bonaccorsi and a facs. of an autobiographical note by Rossini. Cf., also, MGG XI 948–74 (F. Lippmann), especially 957, 967, 970–71 (other versions and eds.), and 973. The original MS is in the Library of Congress.

27. No. 3 is the "ignota 'Sonata'" discovered by A. Casella in 1942 (MGG XI 973) and ed. by him for pub. in 1951 (Milan: Carisch).

28. Cf. MGG XI 970–71.

29. This fact was not realized by earlier writers, as in the primary documentary study Radiciotti/ROSSINI I 45–46 and in Cobbett/CHAMBER II 305–6 (E. Blom & W. W. Cobbett); nor in the jacket notes for the Dover recording HCR-5214 (wind version).

30. The styles and forms are not viewed here quite as they are by A. Bonaccorsi in Rossini/SONATE-m ix.

Although Vincenzo Bellini wrote no sonatas along with his "Sinfonie" and other early instrumental music, the other member besides   30a
Rossini in the illustrious trio of Italian opera composers, **Gaetano
Donizetti** (1797–1848), did do so. In fact, in Donizetti's vast and varied
output no fewer than twelve sonatas have survived.[31] All twelve survived only in MSS (all autographs but one) and, to judge from the
years 1819 or 1820 on seven of the MSS, most or all originated as
student works. Eight are P-duets and four are duos, one each for P &
Vn, P & Fl, P & Ob, and P & Vc. Very little is known about the circumstances of Donizetti's instrumental music.[32] The only information about
his sonatas consists of a few dedications and a few capricious titles or
inscriptions in the MSS, the latter including (in trans.) "The Usual
Sonata," "One of the More Freakish," and "Captain Battle." Unfortunately, the only one of these sonatas that has been made available
through a modern edition proves to be too commonplace, inconsequential, and derivative (from Mozart and his contemporaries) to stimulate exploration of the other eleven sonatas. It is a "Suonata per Oboe,
e Pianoforte di G. D. all'Amico Severino degl'Antonj . . ." in F.[33]
Two annotations in the autograph suggest orchestration of the work
was planned. The first of the two short movements is, as with Rossini,
a succession of similar, clearly phrased melodies, undeveloped, only
slightly interrelated, and accompanied by nothing but the most elementary, routine basses. The finale, an "Allegro" in 6/8 meter, is
similar in style and principle except for its rondo design.

In 1817 a set of *Dodici Sonate di stile fugato pel pianoforte,* perhaps
meant for organ as well as P solo, was published in Lucca as one of the
numerous vocal and instrumental works, mostly sacred, by the canon
of the cathedral, **Marco Santucci** (1762–1843).[34] This scarce music
awaits present-day exploration but presumably reflects Santucci's preoccupation with past styles. Scarcely less obscure are the five sonatas for
P solo, published between 1844 and 1859, by an early Chopin editor for
Ricordi and the pianist whom Ferdinand Hiller regarded as Italy's best
at the time, **Stefano Golinelli** (1818–91).[35] Golinelli's music is reported

31. Cf. Gatti & Basso/la musica II 258–83 (G. Barblan), especially pp. 277 and
288; Zavadini/donizetti 16–18; Weinstock/donizetti 385, 387.

32. Cf. Weinstock/donizetti 18, 22, 23.

33. Mod. ed.: Peters Nr. 5919 (1966), ed. and prefaced by R. Meylan.

34. The place and date are given with the listing of the MS (autograph?) in Cat.
bologna IV 64. Ricordi in Milan pub. the set, for P solo, between 1820 and 1828
(hofmeister 1828 [Whistling], 601). On Santucci, cf. mgg XI 1386–87 (A. Bonaccorsi).

35. Cf. ricordi enciclopedia II 333–34; Sietz/hiller I 51; hofmeister 1844–51,
115–16, and 1852–59, 158; pazdírek VI 369–70. Ricordi pub. all but Son. 4
(Breitkopf & Härtel), and repub. Sons. 2, 3, and 5 in the now scarce ricordi arte-m
XVII and XIX (among the 73 pieces by Golinelli that fill Vols. XVII–XX!).

to be "distinguished by elegance and grace of form, refinement of style, and originality of splendid melodies that exist in great profusion," and is regarded as unjustly forgotten today.[36] We may add that his music proves also to be worth investigating for the great breadth of its melodies, for its ingenious passagework, and for its expert piano scoring apart from some octave excesses and wide spacing that sometimes dangerously attenuate the sonorities.

Italy in the Later Romantic Era (Martucci)

The most important sonata composer in late-Romantic Italy and a pioneer in the renaissance of Italian instrumental music, **Giuseppe Martucci** (1856–1909) excelled also as a pianist, encouraged early by the support of both Liszt and Rubinstein; as an editor (like Golinelli, of Ricordi's early ed. of Chopin); and as a conductor.[37] Among a variety of instrumental (and a few vocal) works, four sonatas by Martucci were published, all in the decade 1874–84, including Op. 22 in G, for P & Vn (Ricordi, 1874); Opp. 34 in E and 41/1 ("Sonate facile"), for P solo (Ricordi, 1875 and ?); and Op. 52 in f♯, for Vc & P (Kistner in Leipzig, 1884). The last may well have been played on the recital tours in which he joined with the celebrated cellist Piatti in 1877–78. An organ sonata in D, dated 1879, was left in MS.

Opp. 34 and 52 are Martucci's most interesting, and apparently his most successful, sonatas.[38] Both sonatas are serious, substantial works in four movements, in the order F-Sc-M-F. Both are rich in texture and harmony, both show refined craftsmanship, including expert scoring and continual polyphonic interest, and both show a large, well-grounded view of the standard forms. Obviously Martucci was no descendant of Paganini or Rossini, but derived from Austro-German models. Brahms in particular comes to mind, although occasionally Mendelssohn is suggested, as in the more chromatic harmonic progressions that support the opening theme in Op. 34/i, or Chopin, as in the figural accompaniment in the middle section of Op. 34/iii. Indeed, it is the uncomfortably close resemblance to Brahms's music along with generally unprepossessing themes, sentimental chromaticism from time to time, and some moments when the textural fullness seems excessive (as in the start of Op. 34/iii) that make any appreciable revival of

36. Schmidl/DIZIONARIO I 644.

37. Cf. MGG VIII 1732–33 (D. Di Chiera); RICORDI ENCICLOPEDIA III 116–17.

38. Op. 34 was reprinted in Ricordi's 6-vol. ed. (II 112) of Martucci's *Composizioni* for P solo (plate nos. 95491–96). Op. 52 (but not Op. 22) is described, with 4 exx., at the end of an extended discussion of his main chamber works in Cobbett/ CHAMBER II 117–22 (G. Cesari).

Ex. 105. From the opening of the third movement in Giuseppe Martucci's Sonata in f♯, Op. 52 (after the original Kistner ed. of 1884).

Martucci's worthy sonatas unlikely today. Compared with Parry's similar sonatas in England, from the same decade (ssb XIV), Martucci's seem a little more fluent, expressive, and compelling. Never do they reveal quite the creative flashes of a Franck or a Fauré at his best, but they do have their special moments, as in the fresh marchlike rhythm of the opening theme in Op. 34/iv, or the exceptionally warm melody in the short "Intermezzo" of Op. 52 (Ex. 105).

Another important pioneer of the late-Romantic renaissance in Italian instrumental music, Giovanni Sgambati (1841–1914), left only larger ensembles among cyclic works, not sonatas nor their equivalents. For the rest, the few names are mostly obscure today. The concert violinist **Antonio Bazzini** (1818–97) settled in Brescia in 1864 and Milan in 1873 after wide concert tours originally encouraged by Paganini.[39] Two of his several more important instrumental publications were *Trois Morceaux en forme de Sonate,* in E♭ (Ricordi, 1866), and Sonata in e, Op. 55 (Ricordi, 1872), both for P & Vn.[40] The music writer and publisher Carlo Schmidl found Bazzini's music to be distinguished by lightness and grace of melody, nobility of style, and

39. Cf. Schmidl/DIZIONARIO I 132; RICORDI ENCICLOPEDIA I 210.
40. Altmann/KAMMERMUSIK 194.

precise, rich harmony." [41] He found somewhat similar distinction in the
music of the pianist **Carlo Rossaro** (1828–78) in Torino, whose publications include a Sonata in d, Op. 28, for P-duet (Ricordi, 1864) and a
posthumous Sonata for Vc & P (Ricordi, 1879?).[42]

Among organists, **Filippo Capocci** (1840–1911) in Rome left six full-
scale organ sonatas published between about 1878 and 1908 and both
widely and highly regarded in their day.[43] Among nearly 300 publications, mostly for piano, by the pianist **Polibio Fumagalli** in Milan
(1830–1901 [44]), there are one "sonata movement" each for organ and for
P solo, Opp. 225 and 226; a "Capriccio alla sonata," Op. 230, and three
other sonatas for organ, Opp. 269, 290, and 292; and "Giubilo, Sonata
brillante alla marcia," Op. 237, for P-duet, all published between about
1880 and 1893.[45] Somewhat stronger and more successful are the four
published sonatas within the large, rounded output by the chief organist of his day, another significant contributor to the instrumental
renaissance, and a successor to Martucci in Bologna, **Marco Enrico
Bossi** (1861–1925).[46] Two of these sonatas are for organ, Opp. 60 in D
(Ricordi, *ca.* 1890) and 71 in f (Cocks, 1894), and two are for Vn & P,
Opp. 82 in e (Breitkopf & Härtel, 1893) and 117 in C (Kistner, 1899).[47]
Cast in the standard cycles of three and four movements and aligned
less with newer trends than some of Bossi's other music, these sonatas
suggest German models again, including Brahms's music, in their ideas
and solid treatment, but are not without some melodic and harmonic
originality and strengths of their own.[48] In October of 1893 Bossi sent
what is probably his best sonata, Op. 82, to Verdi for criticism and,
hopefully, a stamp of approval, receiving a somewhat enigmatic, cautious reply, most of which follows:[49]

I have admired your work with Boïto (who was here), especially the beginning of the first movement, a most beautiful and powerful phrase; and if

41. Schmidl/DIZIONARIO I 132.

42. Schmidl/DIZIONARIO II 398; Altmann/KAMMERMUSIK 304 and 263.

43. Cf. Schmidl/DIZIONARIO I 289; Kremer/ORGAN 175–76; PAZDÍREK III 79; SMW
XLIV (1886) 371 (praise for contrapuntal skill and flow but not for the handling
of large form nor for imagination in Son. 1); MMR XVI (1886) 233 (review of Son.
3 as striking in harmony and modulations, but more of a "Suite de pièces" than a
unified son.).

44. GROVE III 524 (A. Chitty); BAKER 520 gives 1891; other sources give 1900.

45. Cf. Schmidl/DIZIONARIO I 574; PAZDÍREK V 608–12; Kremer/ORGAN 185; MMR
XVII (1887) 178 (review of Op. 269 [3 mvts., in D] as fluent and musical but not
very original). On Fumagalli's piano virtuosity, cf. MOSCHELES II 236, 239.

46. Cf. MGG II 149–51 (L. Bossi); Schmidl/DIZIONARIO I 229–30.

47. Cf. Kremer/ORGAN 173; Altmann/KAMMERMUSIK 196.

48. The Vn sons. are described, with exx., in Cobbett/CHAMBER I 153–54 (G.
Cesari) and Shand/VIOLIN 189–91.

49. As trans. in Cobbett/CHAMBER I 153. The original and a further exchange
from June, 1895, that recalls Op. 82 may be seen in Verdi/COPIALETTERE 400–401.

I said that the composition in general appears to me to be too much based on dissonance, you might answer: "Why not? dissonance and consonance are both essential elements in music; I give the preference to the former." And you would be right. On the other hand, why should I be wrong?

Was the "dissonance" the harmonic support, with 9th chords, of the second theme in the first movement? If so, it hardly seems shocking in relation to other music of its day or, for that matter, to Verdi's own late music.

Brief mention may be added of some pianists who composed duo sonatas, including the Martucci pupil and (now disfavored) Bach editor **Bruno Mugellini** (1871–1912), for a Sonata in g, for Vc & P, first published by Rieter-Biedermann of Leipzig in 1899 (not 1898 or 1908);[50] another Martucci pupil, **Guido Alberto Fano** (1875–1961), for a Sonata in d, Op. 7, that won a prize from the Società del Quartetto di Milano in 1898, appeared in Leipzig in 1905 (Breitkopf & Härtel), and brought an unfavorable review soon after in the German press;[51] and the Sgambati pupil **Giuseppe Cristiani** (1865–1933), founder of the "Quintetto romano," for a Sonata in g, for P & Vn, published by Jurgenson of Moscow in 1907 and reviewed more favorably in the German press.[52]

Among three other late-Romantics in Italy who wrote sonatas (most still awaiting investigation) was the cellist **Luigi Abbiate** (1866–1933), who spent many years in Paris, St. Petersburg, and Monaco as well as in Italian centers.[53] His sonatas include one in g, for P & Vc (year?), and at least five for P solo, composed by 1914 but, like one other—Op. 57 in B♭, for P & Vn—not published until his last years, mostly by Hayet in Paris (1925–32).[54] These are physically imposing works of three and four movements, characterized by more passagework than melody, post-Brahmsian and -Franckian harmony, almost continuous modulation and frequent metric changes (with double-bars to define numerous little sections), and thick textures. The priest **Giovanni Pagella** (1872–1944), who also spent some time in Paris, left at least five sonatas, four of them published—Op. 110 in D, for P & Vn (1914); three for organ (Nos. 2 in 1910 and 3 in 1922); and one for P solo (year?).[55] The

50. Cf. Schmidl/DIZIONARIO II 145; HOFMEISTER 1899, 118.

51. Schmidl/DIZIONARIO I 519 and MGG III 1761–62 (R. Allorto; with mentions, also, of a "Fantasia" Vn. Son. [in MS] arranged by Fano from a P son. by him, of a P Sonatina, Op. 5, pub. in 1906, and of another Son. for P solo, in E, pub. by Ricordi in 1920); DM V/2 (1905–6) 260 (A. Laser).

52. DM IX/1 (1909–10) 123 (W. Altmann). Cf. Schmidl/DIZIONARIO I 389 and Suppl. 225.

53. Cf. Schmidl/DIZIONARIO I 5 and Suppl. 2.

54. All of the last 6 sons. are in the Library of Congress.

55. Schmidl/DIZIONARIO II 212 and Suppl. 583; DICCIONARIO LABOR 1702; HOFMEISTER

Neapolitan pianist **Alessandro Longo** (1864–1945), best known for his eleven-volume edition of Domenico Scarlatti's sonatas (Ricordi, 1906; SCE 265, 266, 840), left seven sonatas for P solo—Opp. 32 in c, 36 in B, 63 in C, 66 in a, 67 in G, 70 in f, and 72 in A♭. These were all published as a one-volume set, as a "deluxe bound" one-volume set, and separately, by Kistner of Leipzig in 1912, following their individual, successive issues by various other publishers over the previous seven years or so.[56] They follow the standard three- and four-movement plans, with occasional slow introductions in the outer movements, fugal finales in Opp. 32 and 67, and cyclical relationships in every sonata. Longo's writing shows much variety, skill, and experience, although

Ex. 106. From the opening of Alessandro Longo's Sonata in C, Op. 63 (after the Kistner ed. of 1912).

his styles, this late, never go beyond the orbit described by Mendelssohn and Brahms. This limitation and his inability to be either real or urgent in his ideas and their development make him another epigone (Ex. 106).

Two Italian sonata composers of the late-Romantic Era were noted in Chapter XIV, Carlo Albanesi in London and the man to whom he dedicated his last piano sonata, Michele Esposito in Dublin. The

1910, 132, and 191; Kremer/ORGAN 211. A short, sympathetic review of Op. 110 as a melodious, sweet work, at times rhythmically piquant, appears in DM XIII/4 (1913–14) 331 (W. Dahms).

56. Cf. MGG VIII 1189–90 (A. Mondolfi); PAZDÍREK IX 621; DM XII/4 (1912–13) 251–52 (R. H. Stein), a favorable, one-column review of the set as skillful, though not very original, music throughout. Each separate Kistner ed. includes the thematic index of all mvts. of all 7 sons. The complete set is in the Library of Congress.

sonatas of three others appeared too late in the 20th century to be included here, even though their orientation to the Romantic Era remains unmistakable—the pianist Amilcare Zanella (1873–1949), the scholar Fernando Liuzzi (1884–1940), and, more important, Leone Sinigaglia (1868–1944), whose other chamber music dates back as much as a generation earlier, almost to that late-Romantic renaissance of Italian instrumental music.

Spain and Portugal (Albéniz)

Strongly influenced at first by such Italians formerly on her soil as Boccherini and Brunetti (SCE 247–58), Spain fostered several consequential instrumentalists and instrumental ensembles of her own throughout the 19th century,[57] including, among violinists, the precocious, short-lived composer Juan Crisóstomo de Arriyaga (1806–26), Jesús de Monasterio (1836–1903), and, of course, Pablo de Sarasate (1844–1908; mostly away from Spain); among cellists, Victor Mirecki and, ultimately, Pablo Casals (1876–   ); among pianists, Pedro Albéniz (1795–1855), Pedro Tintorer (1814–91), and Juan Bautista Pujol (1835–98); and, among organists, Olallo Morales (in Sweden; SSB XV). But after the heyday of the guitarists, especially Fernando Sor (1778–1839), whose sonatas appeared up to the early 1830's (SCE 663–64), almost no sonatas by Spanish composers, whether published in or out of Spain, can be found until around the end of the century. Composers like Manuel Garcia (Sr.) and his successors were too greatly preoccupied with folk, national, and theatrical music (including the *tonadilla* and revised zarzuella). At last, two of the most successful composers, Isaac Albéniz and Joaquín Turina, showed at least a side interest in our genre.

One of Spain's finest pianists and a popular idol among Spanish composers before Falla, **Isaac Albéniz** (1860–1909) spent the first half of his adventuresome career (from the age of four!) largely as a recitalist, touring as far away as South and North America; he did not start his increasing shift toward serious composition until almost his mid twenties.[58] Jadassohn and Reinecke in Leipzig (SSB X) had been among his several teachers. And the sonatas of Haydn, Mozart, and Beethoven,

57. Cf. MGG XII 1006–7 (J. Subirá); Subirá/HISTORIA 655–79; Subirá & Cherbuliez/ MUSIKGESCHICHTE 129–33; Chase/SPAIN 150–59.

58. Laplane/ALBÉNIZ is the most recent and helpful study, including the man, his music, the chief style traits, and the best critical, chronological list of his works, though incomplete, that could be assembled; it does not, however, contain much of the documentary evidence to be found in Collet/ALBÉNIZ (including pp. 50–51 and 97 on the sons.).

the concertos of the last two plus Weber, Mendelssohn, Chopin, Moscheles, Schumann, Rubinstein, Liszt, and Grieg, and pieces by Bach, Handel, Rameau, Couperin, D. Scarlatti, Schubert, Dussek, and others (including himself) had been among the experiences to which he exposed himself through recitals up to his 20th year.[59] But more influential on the new seriousness and eventual nationalism in Albéniz's composing seem to have been his few days (only) in August, 1880, and his study in Barcelona in the summer and fall of 1885 (only?) with one of the most ardent, loyal, versatile and respected champions of Spanish music, Felipe Pedrell (1841–1922).[60]

Albéniz's sonatas consist of five, all for P solo. Information about them is scant, at best, beyond the indication that he wrote them early in his shift to more serious composition, probably between 1883 and 1886 [61] and perhaps mostly during his study with Pedrell in 1885. Of Sonata 1, Op. 28, only the printed "Scherzo" can be found today (as pub. separately by Zozaya in Madrid [?], in 1883 [?]). Of Sonata 2 nothing seems to be known. Sonatas 3 (Op. 68 in A♭), 4 (Op. 72 in A), and 5 (Op. 82 in G♭) were all first published in 1887 (?) by Romero in Madrid and subsequently taken over or reprinted by Unión Musical Español.[62] Each of the last three is dedicated to a "beloved" friend—respectively, "the celebrated pianist" Manuel Guervós (3 years younger than Albéniz), "my" onetime "master [actually, sponsor]" Count Guillermo Morphy (himself the composer of a Son. for P & Vn, not accessible here), and "the eminent artist [a Catalan pianist]" Carlos Gumersindo Vidiella.[63] These three sonatas are of moderate length (20–27 pp.), in three or four movements. The outer movements are all fast and the inner movements moderate to fast, never slow. The first movements are progressively freer "sonata forms," with a rare written-out repetition of the exposition in Sonata 4 and both the most development and the widest tonal ranges in Sonata 5. With regard to inner movements, Sonata 3 has an "Andante" in the minor supertonic key, Sonata 4 has both a "Scherzino" in the dominant and a "Minuetto" in the subdominant keys, each with its trio, and Sonata 5 has both a "Minuetto del gallo" in the minor enharmonic-dominant and a "Reverie et al-

59. Laplane/ALBÉNIZ 39. Brahms is conspicuously absent, although his late pieces for P solo had yet to appear.

60. Cf. Laplane/ALBÉNIZ 35–47, 216, 217.

61. Based on the meager pub. facts in Laplane/ALBÉNIZ 140 and 192–97. No discussion of them is known here.

62. Plate nos. A. R. 6962, 7007, 7085; cf. Cat. NYPL I 186, but the pub. occurred before "189‑," to judge by near plate nos. in Albéniz's output that can be dated more accurately.

63. Cf. DICCIONARIO LABOR I 1171, II 1571 and 2225; Laplane/ALBÉNIZ 32–33 (on Morphy).

legro" in the major lowered-submediant key (with no apparent reasons for either the "cock" or the "lively" in the titles).

Extracts have been published from two reviews of Madrid recitals in 1887 at which Albéniz played at least Nos. 3 and 4 among his sonatas.[64] Besides the playing itself, the brilliance of Sonata 3/iii and the working out, second theme, and delicacy of Sonata 4/i were extolled. But finding the refrain in Sonata 4/iv unprepossessing and too often repeated, one critic saw the artist, for all his fine imagination and intuition, as still needing a structural discipline denied to him thus far by his turbulent life. The author Henri Collet concurred in the latter view, finding Albéniz's sonatas "spineless," lacking in originality and skill, and without plan in No. 5 except for its "Minuetto del gallo." [65]

But these objections have seemed too strong here, if they are deserved at all. Perhaps they partly reflect the hearer's surprise at coming on most of the familiar traits and mannerisms of Albéniz's style without so much as a hint of the popular Spanish rhythms and melodic elements that were to be introduced so profusely and effectively throughout the four-volume *Iberia* suite (1906–9). When Albéniz composed his sonatas he was not yet quite ready to put the nationalistic ideals of Liszt and Pedrell into practice. But those sonatas show his compositional skills to have been more developed by the mid 1880's and more grounded in the earlier masterworks of the 19th century than is generally acknowledged. Their craftsmanship in harmony, scoring, and voice-leading is beyond reproach. And they already exhibit some of Albéniz's favorite devices, like the chordal elaborations by two-note figures (e.g., Son. 4/ii/23–26) that contribute to several recollections of Weber's piano writing; or the accented dissonances through skips and chromatic passing-tones (e.g., Son. 5/i/85–88), with something of the piquancy of Godowsky's writing; or the allocation of songful melodies to the tenor register in the middle of the texture (e.g., Son. 3/iii/21–32); or the exploitation of advanced piano techniques (as in the finale of Son. 4, which includes all of the foregoing plus wide leaps and frequent double-note passages), although the sonatas are less hard to play in these respects than the frequently more congested, complex passages in the twelve *Iberia* "scenes." Furthermore, the best melodies in the sonatas, although never quite so compelling or characterful as those in *Iberia,* are not without their own good directional and linear qualities, as in the second theme from Sonata 5/i, with its frequent enharmonic modulations (Ex. 107).

64. Collet/ALBÉNIZ 50–51.
65. Collet/ALBÉNIZ 97.

Ex. 107. From the first movement of Sonata 5, in G♭, by Isaac Albéniz (after the ed. of Unión Musical Español, in the 1890's).

As for Albéniz's control of form, his sonatas employ the same sectional forms to be found in *Iberia,* including both simple A-B-A forms (Son. 3/ii) and more elaborate "sonata forms" (Son. 5/i). The sonatas show moderate ability to develop ideas (Son. 5/i) but more inclination toward rondo designs. The forms in *Iberia* are tighter, better planned, and more pointed toward their climaxes and returns. But even when the enharmonic changes create the widest tonal ranges, the sonata movements show at least an adequate awareness and logic of structure.

The other chief Spanish composer to present, **Joaquin Turina** (1882–1949), would be generally too late for our consideration here except that the best known of his five published sonatas (among a considerable variety and number of other works) appeared early in his career, in 1910 (not 1909).[66] This was the *Sonate romantique sur un thème espagnol,* Op. 3 (?) in c/C, for P solo, composed in 1909 "in memory of Isaac Albéniz," and published by E. Demcts (transferred to Max Eschig) in Paris. Another piano work, *Sonata fantasia,* Op. 59, did not appear until 1930, in Madrid, nor a guitar work, Sonata in d, Op. 61, until 1932, in London. And two sonatas for violin and piano, Opp. 51 in d/D and 82, freely in C ("Sonata española"), did not appear until 1930 and

66. Cf. MGG XIII 992–94 (M. Querol), with full dated list of works and further bibliography.

1934, in Paris.[67] But Turina's early and late sonatas are generally similar in styles and forms. In fact, the last of them shows little advance or contrast as compared with the first. Opp. 3 and 82 have almost identical plans in the order, type, forms, and thematic interrelationships of their movements—In/Va-VF-S/F. Both of their middle movements alternate scherzando with slower sections. And both works exhibit much the same ideas, texture, and harmony in their corresponding movements, aside from a little modernization through added dissonance and tonal freedom in the later work.

Turina's sonatas also show little qualitative or stylistic evidence of the composer's extended period of study under d'Indy in Paris (1905–14). They reveal considerable experience in composition. Their scoring is full, well balanced, and idiomatic enough. Their melodic and rhythmic ideas offer the expected allure as Spanish music, within any one group of phrases and periods. But in all these respects they hardly rise above the ordinary. And measured against the prevailing sonata idea of his time Turina's sonatas as aesthetic wholes do not offer the expected development of materials, compelling dynamism, or broad architecture. Instead one gets that more static feeling, typical in much Spanish music, of forever marking time or of always anticipating some sustained, developed section but never arriving at it.[68]

Further exploration into what little might turn up in the way of late 19th-century sonatas in Spain could start with four obscure names mentioned only in passing by the important Spanish music historian José Subíra[69]—**Marcial del Aldalid** (1827–81), for two sonatas for Vn & P; **Martín Sánchez Allú** (?–?), for another of the same; the Cuban-born **Nicolás Espadero** (?–?), for all or most of two sonatas (for P solo?); and **Vicente Zurrón** (1871–1915), for another for piano and a Sonata for P & Vc. No publication of any of these sonatas is known here.

In Portugal the one name to include here is that of the early 19th-century pianist and founder of a "Philharmonic Society" in Lisbon, **João Domingos Bomtempo** (1775–1842), who did his final training in Paris and came under Clementi's influence both there and in London.[70] Between about 1805 and 1816, at least four sonatas for P solo and seven for P ± Vn by Bomtempo were published, all where the markets for

---

67. PAZDÍREK XIV 374 also lists 3 "Sonatine ad uso dei principianti, canto."

68. In a rather more complimentary fashion Cobbett/CHAMBER II 522–24 (P. G. Morales & W. W. Cobbett) seems to come to similar conclusions about other chamber music by Turina.

69. Subíra/HISTORIA 663 and 665; cf., also, Subíra & Cherbuliez/MUSIKGESCHICHTE 127, 130, 153.

70. The detailed article in DICCIONARIO PORTUGUEZES I 108–63 includes citations from numerous contemporary documents and an undated list of works.

the solo and accompanied settings were best—that is, in Paris (Opp. 1, 5, and 9/1–2 for P solo, and 9/3 for P ± Vn) or London (Opp. 13, 15/1–2, and 18/1–3 for P ± Vn).[71] Knowing of Clementi's direct influence, one is not surprised to find Bomtempo's sonatas still firmly planted in the high-Classic style of Haydn and Clementi. But they have melodic freshness of their own, besides being skillfull, light, well formed works in two or three movements, with the fluent, sometimes brilliant passagework that would be expected of a professional pianist.

71. Cf. DICCIONARIO PORTUGUEZES I 112, 116–17, 119, 122, 123, 159; HOFMEISTER 1815 (Whistling), 342, and 1828 (Whistling), 580. In his "Introduction" of 1963 to PORTUGALIAE-m VIII (a score of Bomtempo's Sinfonia Op. 11/1 in E♭, giving a good ex. of his style), F. de Sousa mentions a full cat. of Bomtempo's works in preparation by J.-P. Sarrautte.

Chapter XVII

Composers in Czechoslovakia, Poland, and Hungary

On Fanning Out from the Austro-German Epicenter

Our remaining three chapters on the composers and their sonatas take us increasingly far, musically as well as geographically, from the prime centers of the Romantic sonata, in Austro-Germany. Brief orientations introduce each country as we fan out, first eastward, to three East European countries, then to Russia, and finally westward, to the Americas. Here it is necessary only to make a few broader generalizations about these remoter cultivations, especially those to the east.

In our previous two volumes the same outlying countries were noted chiefly for their emigrants (mostly the Czechs in Austro-Germany and London), somewhat for their immigrants (mostly Italians), and only slightly for natives or longtime residents. In this final volume it is possible to report native schools of the sonata developing more or less significantly, though slowly, in each country. The immigrants are now few. But, to be sure, the only real front-rankers of the sonata in these countries still have had to be treated here as emigrants—Chopin from Poland and Liszt from Hungary (ssb XII and X), not to mention the numerous less important emigrants from each country. Even Dussek, the important, precocious Romantic who comes first in these final chapters, can be identified with his native land, Czechoslovakia, only by virtue of his training. He, too, was an emigrant, although one who roved too much to be identified with any other one locale, either.

The historical, 19th-century pattern of the sonata continued to operate about as in the other outlying countries—that is, starting with a fair amount of late-Classic activity that carried over into the early-Romantic efforts, followed by a low ebb in the generation from about 1835, and then, around 1870, by a rather conspicuous rise, if not renaissance, of solo and duo sonatas (along with other instrumental chamber music). Furthermore, especially during that rise, Germany continued to operate as the epicenter of the sonata (and much else in music). And the conflict between German and growing nationalistic influences in each country continued to affect the course of the sonata in one direction or the other, with efforts toward a 19th-century "vermischter Geschmack" (SBE 32) being only rarely successful. Evidence both for the growing schools of the sonata in these outlying countries and for their strong German affiliations can be seen in the increasing production of their sonatas by German publishers (e.g., Dvořák's sons. pub. by Simrock in Berlin at Brahms's urging) or by publishers that established branches in German centers (e.g., numerous Russian sons. pub. by Russian firms like Jurgenson, Belaieff, and Zimmermann). Moreover, the same sonatas were duly reviewed in the German periodicals.

As in the other outlying countries, the sonata generally took a fourth place to nationalistic opera, song, and programme music. Something as specialized as the sonata could be counted on to thrive only in the largest centers and usually in the spheres of their music conservatories or chamber music societies. For our purposes, Czechoslovakia was Prague, Poland was Warsaw, Hungary was Budapest, and Russia was the somewhat interrelated pair of centers, St. Petersburg and Moscow. We shall be coming to a modest, growing literature on the activities at these centers and to a fairly solid literature on the most important composers. But much of that literature remains in the language of the country (accessible here only to the extent that translation services were practical). And in any case, all too little of it pays attention to the sonatas of the times.

Turning to Czechoslovakia as the first of our outlying countries, we find the 19th-century sonata developing as part and parcel of a growing spirit of nationalism, a new economic prosperity, and a rising educated middle class. The chief frictions that beset this proud, tradition-minded, often troubled country were still those that had long plagued and would continue to plague the effort to unite Bohemian, Moravian, and Teutonic peoples. But these frictions did little to stem the musical activities in Prague that flourished especially from the time of Mozart.[1]

Dussek and Other Early Czech Romantics

In spite of his early life dates, the notable Czech pianist and composer **Jan Ladislav Dussek (Dussik, Dusík,** etc.; 1760–1812) was

1. Helpful background summaries may be found in MGG X 1584–94 (J. Bužga); MGG IV 154–55 (P. Nettl); MGG XIII 888–96 (V. Lébl); Helfert & Steinhard, including a (somewhat careless) cat. of instrumental compositions, pp. 252–98; Newmarch/CZECHOSLOVAKIA 42, 55, *et passim;* Buchner/LISZT *passim;* Cobbett/CHAMBER I 306–9 (R. Newmarch).

deferred to the present volume (cf. SCE 5, 774) because 'of significant pre-Romanticisms in his musical style and piano writing. His sonatas actually antedate those of Schubert, Ries, Moscheles, Hummel, and Cramer, among other *Frühromantiker* who excelled at the keyboard. Moreover, as noted above, Dussek is put in his homeland here simply because he resided in too many other countries to be identified with any one of them in particular. This rather loose-living but ingratiating, well-informed, multilingual cosmopolitan left Bohemia after completing his education in Prague in 1778, apparently returning to Prague only once, in 1802. More specifically, among other places, he played, visited, or resided from 1778 to 1782 in Mechelen (Belgium), The Hague, and Hamburg (where Emanuel Bach is said to have counseled or actually taught him); from 1783 to 1784 in St. Petersburg and Lithuania; from 1784 to 1786 in cities throughout Germany; from 1786 to 1789 in Paris and Milan; from 1789 to 1799 in London (that is, until his father-in-law and he saw their publishing firm, Corri, Dussek & Co., fail); from 1800 to 1807 in Hamburg, Berlin, and numerous other European centers, serving for three of those years as *Kapellmeister* and companion to the gifted Prince Louis Ferdinand; and from 1807 to 1812 in Paris.[2] Haydn, Clementi, Cramer, Field, Spohr, and Pleyel were among the important musicians whom Dussek knew.[3]

In an order that generally decreases in both quantity and historical importance as it increases in size of ensemble, Dussek's nearly 300 works consist of many solos for piano plus a few for harp, duos for piano and another instrument, larger chamber ensembles that are mostly piano trios, concertos mainly for piano and orchestra, and a scattering of assorted vocal works.[4] Approximately 139, or nearly half of these works (not subtracting some 14 duplications or recombinations in other set-

2. The recent, valuable diss. Craw/DUSSEK brings together and augments the biographical information previously pub., reproduces all available letters by Dussek in the original language and in English trans. where needed, and provides an extended thematic catalogue that is the fullest record of Dussek's works.

3. Cf. Landon & Bartha/HAYDN 257, 278–79, 497–99, 547; Unger/CLEMENTI 23, 72, 81, 85, 88, 106–7, 143–44; Schlesinger/CRAMER 36, 53, 75; Dessauer/FIELD 5; Spohr/AUTOBIOGRAPHY 19, 79, 86–88; MMR XC (1960) 17 (S. V. Klíma).

4. The "nearly 300" is based on the tabulations in Craw/DUSSEK 207. Racek's estimate of "about 450 works," in MAB-m XLVI xxvi, appears to include a good many duplications. The thematic index in Craw/DUSSEK 210–394 lists, where possible, full titles, dates of composition and pub., first and later eds., locations of MSS, first performances, and references to early reviews; it is followed (pp. 395–426) by separate indexes of op. nos., titles, and pubs. The "C." (Craw) nos. in the index, which are meant to be chronological, are adopted here rather than the then typically inconsistent, duplicative, and conflicting op. nos. (cf. SCE 78–79; BUCEM I 300–303; PAZDÍREK IV 506–11; HOFMEISTER 1828 [Whistling], *passim* [cf. p. 1255]). A concordance of Dussek's most published sons. appears later in the present discussion.

tings) are examples of our genre, about 121 of them being called "sonatas" and 18 "sonatinas." [5] All of these were originally published over the 30 years from 1782 to 1812, rather evenly spaced and mostly in sets of 2 to 6 sonatas each, with the last, unfinished set of 2 being posthumous. And most were reprinted at least once and sometimes as many as ten times (e.g., C. 96). By scoring types, the 139 include approximately 35 sonatas and 12 sonatinas for P solo, 11 sonatas for P-duet, 2 sonatas for harp & Vn, one sonata and 6 sonatinas for harp alone, 65 sonatas for P & Vn, and 8 sonatas for P & Fl.

Dussek's scorings are often not that exact, since they may vary in different editions, with the main instrument changed (e.g., harp to P, in C. 147 and 148) or made optional (e.g., harp-or-P, C. 160–65) and the accompanying instruments, if any, added (e.g., Vn, Vc, and drums in C. 152) or deleted (e.g., the Fl in C. 88–93). The accompaniments are predominantly optional and subordinate in the earlier sonatas, and they are obligatory, making true duos, in the later ones. But not all the duos are limited to two players. Several of the earlier ones (e.g., C. 11–13, 30–32, and 141–43) mention the optional use of a "basse" in their titles, meaning a cello that largely doubles the pianist's left hand, whether or not a separate part was actually printed (cf. SCE 101). In *A Favorite Sonata for the Michrocordon, or Piano Forte, with Drum and Triangle (ad Libitum) . . . , Op. 45* (C. 182; *ca.* 1800), no additional parts were printed because the instrument intended was a small upright piano then made by Longman, Clementi and Company, with drum and triangle attachments to be introduced at will by the one performer.

Numerous other profuse titles of Dussek's sonatas add further sidelights and flavor to our knowledge of them. Thus, his alertness both as a champion of several piano construction innovations[6] and as a connoisseur of public taste is reflected in the title of his Op. 25 (C. 126–28), published by his own firm in London in 1795, *Three Sonatas for the Piano Forte, And also arranged for the Piano Forte with additional Keys, in which are introduced The Fife Hunt, A Scotch Reel, and the National Air of Rule Brittania, as Rondos, with an Accompaniment for a Violin or Flute Dedicated to the Right Honorable Lady Elizabeth Montagu.* Dussek's timely composition of programmatic *pièces d'occasion* is reflected in one of those late-18th-century battle sonatas (C. 152; cf. SCE 141), also published by Corri, Dussek & Co., *The Naval Battle*

5. These figures do not include works like "La Chasse" for P solo (C. 146), which is sometimes listed as a "sonata" (as in Craw/DUSSEK 415) but was not so called in Dussek's time; or Concerto for P and orchestra, Op. 22 (C. 97), the solo part of which was pub. as "Grande Sonate pour le Piano-Forte," Op. 40, by Artaria (Craw/DUSSEK 267). Cf., also, C. 264, 170, 98, 144, 186, 234, 243, 106–17, 214.

6. Cf. Craw/DUSSEK 53–54, 75, 171, and the listings for C. 96, 126–28, 132–34.

and Total Defeat of the Grand Dutch Fleet by Admiral Duncan on the 11th. of October 1797[,] A Characteristic Sonata for the Piano-Forte Composed and Dedicated to Viscount Duncan. His equally timely composition of more penetrating but nonliteral programme music is suggested by the title of a work commemorating a severe personal loss to him through war, *Élégie Harmonique Sur la Mort de Son Altesse Royale, le Prince Louis Ferdinand de Prusse, En forme de Sonate pour le Piano Forte, Composée et Dediée A son Altesse le Prince de Lobkovitz, Duc de Raudnitz . . . Op. 61* (C. 211; pub. by Pleyel of Paris in 1807).[7] On the other hand, Dussek's use of programmatic titles that lack similarly obvious associations or appear to be topical at most, if not merely nominal, is revealed in *L'Invocation, Grande Sonate Pour le Piano Forté . . . Op. 77* (C. 259; pub. in 1812), wherein, one writer suggests, Dussek could have been invoking thoughts of approaching death;[8] or *The Farewell[,] A New Grand Sonata, for the Piano Forte Composed and Inscribed to his Friend Muzio Clementi . . . Op. 44* (C. 178; pub. by Longman, Clementi in London in 1800), which is a generally gay work that hardly suggests the pangs of leaving London, unless in its *grave* "Introduzione" in e♭; or *Le Retour à Paris[,] Sonate Pour Le Piano Forté . . . Op. 64* (C. 221; pub. by Pleyel, presumably in late 1807). This last title is supposed merely to mark the time when Dussek returned to Paris, in 1807. It was the butt of one critic's joshing, who suggested that it could just as well have been "le départ pour Petersbourg." [9] Furthermore, this same Op. 64 (or 70, or 71, or 77, according to other eds.) was also the Op. 71 on which English publishers bestowed the title, first in 1810, "Plus ultra en opposition à celle de Joseph Wölffl intitulée Non plus ultra" (that is, Wölfl's Son. in F, Op. 41), thus archly (and rightly) claiming even greater technical difficulty for Dussek's work.[10]

Although the study has yet to appear, even in the Czech language, that will explore the styles and forms of Dussek's sonatas in sufficiently full and systematic detail,[11] at least two doctoral dissertations and a number of brief discussions and surveys have come from writers attracted to those sonatas over the last century, including Prout in 1877, Shedlock in 1895, F. L. Schiffer in 1914, Blom in 1927–28, Egert in 1929, R. Felder and Cobbett in 1929, Georgii in 1950, K. Krafka in 1950, and V. J. Sýkora in 1960.[12] The reception of Dussek's sonatas

7. Cf. Craw/DUSSEK 151–53; Shedlock/SONATA 144–45.
8. MAB-m LXIII xi (J. Racek & V. J. Sýkora).
9. AMZ XII (1809–10) 842.
10. Cf. SCE 563 and MAB-m XLVI xxvi; also, Shedlock/SONATA 149 and Craw/DUSSEK 163 and 353.
11. Cf. Craw/DUSSEK 1–6 and 477–89 (bibliographies); MAB-m XLVI xxxviii–xxxix (J. Racek).
12. Prout/DUSSEK; Shedlock/SONATA 142–52; Schiffer/DUSSEK, a pub. Ph.D. diss.

seems to have been consistently enthusiastic, right from the start, if one is to judge from fifteen or more reviews that followed original editions, the majority of them being in the Leipzig *Allgemeine musikalische Zeitung*.[13] The recurring theme in these reviews is steadily increasing praise for the originality, expressiveness, and appropriateness to the piano idiom of most of the melody, harmony, and scoring. Sometimes questioned are varying degrees of fantasy in the treatment and certain more local licenses (specific references are made in nearly every review to accented passing notes and to harmonic and tonal progressions that seemed audacious in their voice leading and remoteness). The most extended and effusive among the reviews was the nine-column discussion (by Rochlitz?) of C. 221, as Op. 70, "Le Retour à Paris," in AMZ for October 3, 1810. Along with detailed analyses of select passages (and references to 24 music exx. in the 4 extra pp. of "Beilage VIII") one finds sentences like the following:

> It is all one [grand] inspiration, one outpouring. Lofty seriousness and subjective moodiness [*sentimentale Laune*], both arising out of a profound soul, overwhelmed perhaps by extraordinary circumstances, [yet] surrounded, as it were, by a romantic twilight—[such] are the elements of this admirable sonata. It is a product of genius such as seldom occurs; [it is] one of the most characterful [of] musical poems, which will retain its value as long as music provides good pianos and accomplished pianists.

14a   Although Breitkopf & Härtel issued Dussek's so-called *Oeuvres complètes pour le pianoforte,* in twelve volumes, between 1813 and 1817,[14] actually including 19 of his sonatas for P solo, 27 for P with accompaniment, and 3 for P-duet, relatively little interest can be found in Dussek's music in the half century after his death. Some of the early publications stayed in print,[15] but almost no new editions appeared

on both the sons. and concertos that suffers chiefly from a lack of either dates of any clear chronology, permitting faulty conclusions on influences (kindly supplied in an approximate trans. by Professor H. A. Craw of Loma Linda University; cf. Craw/DUSSEK 1–2); Blom/DUSSEK (cf. Newman/K. 457); Egert/FRÜHROMANTIKER 34–42; Cobbett/CHAMBER I 351–52 (R. Felber & W. W. Cobbett, on C. 240 and 241); Georgii/KLAVIERMUSIK 262–63; Krafka/DUSÍKA, an unpub. Ph.D. diss. on Romanticisms in Dussek's sons., kindly made available by Professor Craw in a digest trans. prepared for him by S. V. Klíma of Prague (himself the author of a still unpub. "life and works" of Dussek, according to MAB-m LIX x; cf. Craw/DUSSEK ii, 2, 481, 486); MAB-m XLVI xxx–xxxii (V. J. Sýkora).

13. E.g., AMZ XII (1809–10) 540–44 (on C. 149–51), II (1799–1800) 67 and XI (1808–9) 73–75 (both on C. 166–68), XVII (1815) 156 (on C. 207), XII (1809–10) 841–49 (on C. 221) and 15–16 (on C. 230–32), XIII (1811) 555–61 (on C. 240–42) and 880–82 (on C. 247), XIV (1812) 581–82 (on C. 259), and XV (1813) 251–53 (on C. 260 and 261). For reviews in other periodicals cf. the listings in Craw/DUSSEK for C. 5–7, 71–73, 79–81, 207, 230–32.

14. Cf. AMZ XV (1813) Intelligenz-Blatt IV 21–23 (with a useful contemporary evaluation); HOFMEISTER 1828 (Whistling), 1150; Craw/DUSSEK 201 and 418 (with other, smaller collections listed on pp. 419–20); MAB-m LIX x–xi.

15. E.g., cf. HOFMEISTER 1844, pp. 22, 31, 83, 156–57.

during that time. And it is noteworthy that Dussek's name appears not at all in the available letters of Beethoven, Mendelssohn, either of the Schumanns, or Chopin, nor in the memoirs of Moscheles, and only twice, quite incidentally, in the journalism of Robert Schumann.[16] For the historical moment the music world was already making passé even the precocious Romanticisms of Dussek.[17] But starting in the 1860's a revival of interest in his sonatas was manifested by new editions, including a two-volume collection of 32 sonatas that both Breitkopf & Härtel and Litolff published in 1868–73,[18] and by numerous performances of certain favorites, especially in London.[19] Today, over and above a fair number of further editions of single sonatas by Dussek, the series *Musica antiqua bohemica* in Prague has been enriched by "the first complete Czech edition of Dusík's piano sonatas," in 4 volumes— actually, 23 of the approximately 47 solo sonatas or sonatinas plus 6 that originally had violin accompaniments.[20] Perhaps the easier availability of the sonatas will stimulate more than the few performances they have been getting, which are mainly limited to the same three or four sonatas for P solo and are mainly esoteric.[21] The following partial concordance will help to clarify references in the ensuing discussion, which for reasons both of musical interest and the reader's convenience are largely confined to the works most often published and currently available:

16. Schumann/SCHRIFTEN I 392 and II 286.

17. As early as 1825 his sons. were called "outmoded" (HARMONICON III/1 [1825] 139).

18. Cf. Craw/DUSSEK 419–20; also, the issue of separate mvts. in various arrangements—e.g., as advertised in MT XII (1865) 124 and 152, or XVIII (1877–78) 395 and 509, or XXII (1881) 97.

19. E.g., C. 259 ("L'Invocation") in MT XII (1865) 8 (which was "listened to with a breathless attention speaking volumes for the taste of a popular audience") and 339, XV (1871) 46; C. 151 (Op. 35/3 in c) in MT XIII (1867) 105, XV (1872) 420; C. 240 (Op. 69/1 in B♭) in MT XV (1871–72) 121, 436, and 500, XVI (1874) 544, XVII (1876) 443, XXI (1879) 38, XXIV (1883) 269; C. 96 (Op. 24 in B♭) in MT XVI (1874) 544. Numerous other references to performances of Dussek's sonatas do not specify the particular work sufficiently if at all, as in MT XIII (1869) 679, XV (1872) 404, XVI (1874) 582, XVIII (1878) 228, XIX (1878) 685, XXI (1880) 363, XXII (1881) 363.

20. MAB-m XLVI (cf. p. xxx), LIII, LIX, and LXIII, with prefaces by J. Racek & V. J. Sýkora (and confusions that illustrate the need for a thematic index like that in Craw/DUSSEK, as in the equating of C. 96 and C. 98 because each was pub. as Op. 23 at one time). A concordance with the C. nos. appears in Craw/DUSSEK 420, to which should be added the 8 more Dussek sons. and one duplication pub. in MAB-m, as listed in the concordance that follows here, along with 4 sons. in the recent mod. eds. Zeitlin & Goldberger/DUSSEK-m and Madden & Rees/DUSSEK-m, and 8 of the sons. reprinted in 3 of the "old masters" collections.

21. Among the few recordings of Dussek's music (cf. Craw/DUSSEK 488–89) should be noted that of 3 sons. for P solo (including C. 211, "Élégie harmonique") and one son. for P-duet, played by H. Hermanns & R. Stonebridge, SFM 1002 (reviewed by P. H. Lang in MQ XLVI [1960] 118–20).

A Concordance of 42 Selected Sonatas by J. L. Dussek

Craw/ DUSSEK no.	Op(p). no. (if any)	Key	Original scoring	Sometime name &/or dedicatee	Probable first ed.	Movement plan	MAB-m vol./no.	Other collections
43	5/3	Ab	P	Mme. de Mongeroult	1788	F-Ro	LXIII/29	
57	9/1	Bb	P & Vn		ca. 1789	F-Ro	XLVI/1	
58	9/2	C	"		"	F-S-VF	XLVI/2	
59	9/3	D	"		"	F-VF	XLVI/3	
60	10/1	A	P & Vn		ca. 1789	F-S-Ro	XLVI/4	
61	10/2	g	"		"	S-F	XLVI/5	
62	10/3	E	"		"	F-VF	XLVI/6	
80	18/2	a	P		1792	F-Ro	XLVI/7	
92	19/5; 20/5	C	P & Fl	"Sonatina"	1793	F-Ro		Tagliapietra/ANTOLOGIA-m XIV
96	24	Bb	P	Mrs. Chinnery	1793	F-F	LIII/8	
102	26	F	2 Ps	"Duetto"	1794	F-S-Ro		Madden & Rees/DUSSEK-m
127	25	D	P & Vn-or-Fl	Lady Montagu	1795	S/VF-S-Ro	LIII/9	
133	31/2	D	P & Vn-or-Fl & Vc	Misses Wheler	ca. 1795	F-S-F	LIII/10	
149	35/1	Bb	P	Clementi	1797	F-F	LIII/11	TRÉSOR-m XVIII
150	35/2	G	"	"	"	F-Ro	LIII/12	"
151	35/3	c	"	"	"	F-S-VF/VF	LIII/13	"
160		C	harp	Mme. Krumpholtz	1799	M-F	XXII/1	
161		F	"	"	"	M-F	XXII/2	
162		G	"	"	"	M-F	XXII/3	
163		Bb	"	"	"	S-F	XXII/4	
164		F	"	"	"	S-F	XXII/5	
165		Eb		"	"	S-Mi	XXII/6	
166	39/1	G	P	Mrs. Apreece	1799	F-M	LIII/14	
167	39/2	C	"	"	"	F-M-Ro	LIII/15	
168	39/3	Bb	"	"	"	F-Ro	LIII/16	

No.	Cat.	Key	Instr.	Title / Dedication	Date	Form	Ed.	Modern ed.
177	43	A	P	Mrs. Bartolozzi; "The Farewell"; Clementi	1800	F-Ro	LIX/17	
178	44	eb/Eb	P		1800	S/F-S-Mi-Ro	LIX/18	
179	45/1	Bb	P		ca. 1800	F-S-Ro	LIX/19	
180	45/2	G	"		"	S/F-Ro	LIX/20	
181	45/3	D	P		"	F-S-Ro	LIX/21	
184	47/1	D	"	Mrs. Marshall	1801	F-S-Ro	LIX/22	
185	47/2	G	P	"	"	F-Ro	LIX/23	
211	61	f#	P	"Élégie harmonique"; Prince Lobkovitz	1807	S/F-VF	LXIII/24; XX/2	RICORDI ARTE-m VI; Tagliapietra/ ANTOLOGIA-m XIV
221	64; 70; 71; 77	Ab	P	"Le Retour à Paris"; or "Plus ultra"; Princesse de Benevent	1807	F-VS-Mi-Sc	LXIII/26	TRÉSOR-m XVIII; RICORDI ARTE-m VI
230	67/1; 66/1	C	P-duet	"Sonates progressives"; Mademoiselle Talleyrand	1809	M-Ro		Zeitlin & Goldberger/ DUSSEK-m
231	67/2; 66/2	F	"		"	F-Ro		"
232	67/3; 66/3	Bb	"		"	F-Polonaise		"
240	69/1; 72/1	Bb	P+Vn	Duchess of Courlande	1811	F-S-Ro	XL/1	
241	69/2; 72/2	G	"		"	F-Ro	XL/2	
242	69/3; 72/3	D	P		"	F-S-F	LXIII/25	
247	75	Eb	P	"Grande Sonate"; Countess de Périgord	1811	F-M-Ro	LXIII/27	
259	77	f	P	"L'Invocation"; Mademoiselle Ouvrard	1812	F-Mi-S-Ro	LXIII/28	

More than half of Dussek's sonatas are in two movements, with but few of the movements being slow (e.g., S-F in C. 61 in g) and F-Ro being the most frequent plan. Nearly all of the remaining sonatas are in three movements, with F-S-Ro being the most frequent plan and F-M-Ro the next most. The three remaining sonatas, all relatively late works, have four movements with similar plans (C. 178, 221, and 259), including fast outer movements (a "sonata form" and a rondo in each) and both a slow movement and a minuet as inner movements. Major keys, up to two sharps and three flats, are in the great majority, with but a few keys having as many as four flats or three sharps, major or minor, although one of the several slow introductions, that to C. 178 in E♭, is in the tonic minor, hence in six flats. The outer movements change mode from E to e in C. 62, and, more in keeping with later Romantic predilections, from c to C in C. 151. For the inner movement in another key, in the sonatas of three and four movements, the subdominant is Dussek's choice more than half the time. More remote keys, like the lowered submediant major spelled enharmonically (e.g., B in C. 178 in e♭/E♭, or E in C. 222 in A♭), are occasional choices. All three movements remain in f♯ in "Élégie harmonique" (C. 211). In most of his sonatas, Dussek seems almost deliberately to avoid cyclical ties, for he generally contrasts both the styles and melodic directions of the main ideas in successive movements and even between slow introductions and what follows. Nearest to interrelated themes are the similarly contoured, mostly dotted, incipits in all four movements of "The Farewell" (C. 178), the syncopated figures in both the introduction and finale of "Élégie harmonique" (C. 211), and the stepwise descents that stand out in the initial themes of the first three in the four movements (F-VS-Mi-Sc) of "Le Retour à Paris" (C. 221).

Dussek's best sonatas are regarded here as close to the best of their day, including those of Clementi, Beethoven, Schubert, and Weber—a view that may well surprise all but the relative few who have had the opportunity to explore or re-explore for themselves. Moreover, in addition to their purely musical strengths, Dussek's sonatas prove to be remarkable in two other ways. One is their early exploitation of the newly popular "forte piano," an exploitation scarcely surpassed in Clementi's piano music. The other is their historical precocity. As noted earlier, their several innovational styles often go beyond Dussek's environment of high-Classicism and well into that of unequivocal, sometimes fully bloomed, Romanticism. All these traits can be found scattered throughout the sonatas (and concertos) that he produced for thirty years. But it is noteworthy that not until his later years did he write what generally (and here) are regarded as his finest sonatas—

that is, his solo sonatas that have special titles and at least slight programmatic associations, including C. 178, 211, 221, and 259.[22] In other words, although he, too, wrote timely *pièces d'occasion,* variations on favorite tunes, *tours de force,* and other pieces that show full awareness of the public pulse, he did not, as more than one contemporary reviewer noted,[23] make any of the increasing concessions to popular taste that were made so often by his less worthy contemporaries. Far from it! A fine late sonata like his "Le Retour à Paris" must have scared off not a few potential performers and purchasers with its bristling technical problems and its novel harmonic treatment.

Throughout Dussek's sonatas the respective movements tend to fall into the same few over-all designs, especially into clear previews of textbook "sonata form" in the first movements, A-B-A plans when there are slow movements, minuets with trios when there are inner dances, and the rondo principle in the finales. Some of the most convincing first movements achieve a sense of cumulative structure by being asymmetrical, with a shortened recapitulation. Thus, C. 211/i drops by almost half from an exposition of 60 measures (not including the 52 mss. of slow introduction) to a recapitulation of 31 measures, and C. 221 by over two-fifths from 103 to 64 measures. Yet at the more local levels of phrases and periods there is seldom the sense of tight organization or quite the concentrated, relentless drive one identifies with Beethoven. It is not simply the considerable length of Dussek's first movements, which averages about 206 measures as against 209 in Beethoven's solo piano sonatas and 201 in both Weber's and Schubert's. Nor, with slight reservations for C. 211/i, are Dussek's first movements discursive in the sense of Clementi's later examples, with their personalized digressions that probe a single idea fascinatingly yet gratuitously (SCE 750–51). Instead, in keeping with the first movements in the sonatas by Schubert, Weber, and other early-Romantics, Dussek's first movements reveal a preference for phrase-and-period units that are more rounded and more complete in themselves, causing the forms to seem more spacious and deliberate, and hence less dynamic and compelling.

Dussek in particular thinks most characteristically in complete, often parallel double-periods (e.g., C. 167/i/130–45: 4+4 and 4+4). When the second period parallels the first it is usually an extrinsically elaborated variation (as in the same ex. or C. 259/iv/1–16). Sometimes the

22. Fétis/BU III 96 lists only C. 178 and 221 among these 4, along with C. 57–62, 71–73, and 149–51, as the sons. Dussek himself preferred.

23. E.g., in AMZ XIII (1811) 880–82, on C. 247, noting that Dussek was no "Vielschreiber."

double-period is lengthened considerably by one or more cadence extensions—for example, by three such extensions, including prolonging of the cadential tonic-6/4 triad and of deceptive cadences on both the major and the minor subdominant triads at the end of the exposition in C. 181/i/44–80 (4+4 and 4+25 [11+6+8]; cf., also, the charming extension of the single period in mss. 31–44 [4+10]). To be sure, such procedures and other freedoms, especially in the later works, generally preclude the danger of monotony in so much use of the double-period. But one should note that phrase-and-period units of one sort or another predominate in all of Dussek's movement types and can even occur not only in every distinct theme of the "sonata-allegro" exposition but in the development section as well (as in C. 242/i). On the other hand, Dussek certainly understood the values of "chain-phrases" (to use Percy Goetschius' term), whether in sequential passage-work and modulatory bridges (e.g., C. 247/i/22–38) or actual development of ideas (e.g., C. 80/i/100–146). However, only infrequently and in his later works did Dussek achieve the same imagination and suppleness in the development of his ideas (e.g., C. 259/i/71–111) that he seems to have achieved more intuitively, from the start, in his phrase-and-period structures.

Dussek's most frequent method in the A-B-A designs of his slow movements is to put the B section in the tonic minor mode and to vary the A section when it returns (e.g., C. 181/ii in G/g). His change to the minor mode in C. 259/iii in D♭ is enharmonic. Among his rare slow movements that begin and end in the minor mode, one that mirrors the same plan is C. 58/ii in a, with the B section in the relative major. The "slow" movement in C. 166 changes not only the mode in the B section, from G to g, but the tempo, from moderate to fast. The variation of the return consists of extrinsic elaborations, as it does when a repeated period is varied (which happens about as often in Dussek's slow as in his fast mvts.). These elaborations constitute Dussek's main use of variation technique in his sonatas. Unlike his other piano music, none of his more important sonatas and but three of the less known ones contain actual sets of variations (including C. 65/ii on "God Save the King"). A larger, rondo form results, A-B-A-C-A, when Dussek inserts another contrasting, minor section in the slowest movement, namely in the subdominant minor key in C. 247/ii in B♭. C. 611 is a slow first movement in so-called "sonatina form"—that is, with only a retransition rather than a development section. C. 178/ii is a grand "sonata form" of symphonic breadth and character, with a full, intensive development section.

As with Weber, Dussek's short dances provide some of his most concentrated, structurally convincing movements. Only in his three, relatively late sonatas in four movements is a dance included as an inner movement, and in each instance this is marked "Tempo di minuetto." However, in C. 178 the qualification ". . . più tosto allegro" is added, and in C. 221 ". . . scherzo quasi allegro." In these two movements both the faster tempo and the persistent, driving quarter-notes in 3/4 meter suggest a scherzo rather than a minuet. In Dussek's two- and three-movement sonatas there are also five minuets used as finales, all more in the character of a minuet, including one with a different title, "Minuetto, Tempo di ballo" (C. 91/ii). Other finales include a "Polonaise" (C. 232/ii), a "Finale chasse, Allegro scherzo" in 6/8 meter (C. 242/iii) that groups with several other quasi tarantellas not so entitled (e.g., C. 62/ii), and a few pieces in the style of the German polka, of which C. 221/iv is a delicious masterpiece (entitled "Scherzo, Allegro con spirito"). But even in most of these finales as well as the large majority of pieces actually called "Rondo," the rondo principle prevails. And already we find the fetching refrains, the devious retransitions, the emphasis on the middle episode, the choice of the opposite mode for one episode, and other traits that distinguish Beethoven's rondos. However, Dussek usually employed the "second rondo form" (Goetschius' term, again)—for example, A-B-A-C-A-coda in C. 150/ii and 247/iii—rather than the more integrated "third rondo form," A-B-A-C-A-B'-A-coda, as in C. 211/ii and as used more often by Beethoven (e.g., Op. 13/iii).

Dussek's treatment of harmony and tonality, which aroused the most specific comments and questions on the part of his contemporary reviewers (*supra*), still stands out today, along with his piano writing, as one of his most significant contributions. The composer proved early that he knew the rules of conventional harmony (e.g., C. 57/i or 96/i) and that he could manage well enough with little more than the primary triads (e.g., C. 59/ii). But he also proved early and thereafter that he could think for himself, as in occasional parallel 5ths and 8ves that he seems to have approved between outer voices (e.g., C. 151/ii/10 and 59/ii/2) and in frequently bold, academically unauthorized dissonances. As for the latter, one might cite at random the long, chromatic, accented passing tones in the opening theme of C. 59, the cross-relation and the long appoggiatura on the minor-9th in C. 62/ii/66–68, the combined cross-relation and appoggiatura that is reiterated in C. 178/iv/101–3, the conflict of major and minor 7ths over a four-measure dominant pedal in C. 179/iii/51–54, the successive accented 7ths in C. 247/i/195–96, or the biting 7ths and 9ths that contribute to the striking sonorities in C. 181/ii/21–24 (Ex. 108). Apart from such dissonance, the harmony frequently produces new telling effects for its day through imaginative chord choices, as in the major-minor alternations in the refrain of C. 247/iii or the expressive chromaticism of C. 178/ii, with, for example, the stunning use of the Neapolitan chord at measure 12. Lowered-7ths provide unexpected modal inflections in C. 184/ii/6–7.

Telling and new for their time, too, are the numerous remote modulations or assumptions of key, which began to appear early in Dussek's sonatas. In the development section of C. 96/i, enharmony and deceptive resolutions over a bass that ascends chromatically provide the means for a wide Haydnesque excursion that proves to be no more than a long way around from the dominant to the tonic key. In C. 178/i/106–17 (cf. Ex. 109, *infra*, starting at ms. 116), after the exposition closes on the dominant, B♭, the development at once assumes the

Ex. 108. From the middle movement of Sonata in D, C. 181, by Jan Ladislav Dussek (after MAB-m LIX 102).

dominant of E, without modulation, only to return almost as abruptly to E♭ eleven measures later by letting the dim.-7th chord on C𝄪 stand for the restored dominant (-9th) harmony on B♭. Similarly, the development section of C. 149/i returns from F to B♭ after episodes in D♭, G♭, B, e♭, and b♭; the exposition of C. 221/i detours into e♭, B, and e♭ (mss. 45–61) before the subordinate theme begins in the dominant key, E♭ (as in Ex. 110, *infra*); and one 16-measure portion (mss. 87–102) of the development section in C. 259/i passes rapidly from c to f, b♭, e♭, c♯, b, a, g, and back to the home key of f. An extraordinary opening at a tonal tangent occurs when C. 221/iii, "Tempo di menuetto; scherzo quasi allegro," begins in f♯ and, by reinterpreting the dim.-7th chord on that tonic as V_9-of-ii in A♭, drives forcefully to a full cadence in the latter, home key (mss. 1–20).

Naturally, there are interinfluences between Dussek's harmonic treatment and his writing for piano. Both traits relate in turn to his own superior performance at the keyboard, whether as a virtuoso or a sensitive musician, and to his position, along with Clementi and Mozart, as a pioneer composer in the exploitation of the piano, whether as a developer of new technical idioms, sonorities, and pedal effects,[24] or as an advocate of wider ranges (cf. C. 127/iii/92–111), better action, and other construction advances.[25] Dussek's textures are predominantly homophonic, with accompaniment styles ranging from high-Classic to high-Romantic. Repeated notes or chords, murky bass, broken chords in 8th-notes and triplets, Alberti bass, and similar standard Classic devices abound, for example, throughout C. 57, whereas wider chord arpeggiations, bass-chord ("um-pah") techniques, and some less stereotyped figures characteristic of Romantic styles prevail throughout C. 221. One has to acknowledge that an excess of the stereotyped accompaniment figures representing either or both eras (as in much of C. 179 and 184) tends to weaken the textural interest all too often in Dussek's sonatas. Occasionally the harmonic rhythm is so slow—deliberately slow throughout much of C. 242?—that such solutions seem almost unavoidable.

Yet the textural solutions are generally so resourceful and happy in Dussek's finest sonatas, including C. 221, that one can only accuse him of not trying hard enough or, at least, not feeling the need for anything more enterprising in his somewhat more routine sonatas. At best his passagework and figuration anticipate some of the fine piano writing of the 19th century—for example, the exchange of appoggiatura figures, the arpeggiated chords, the broken 10ths, the double-notes, and the other figures in his C. 211/i/129–61. The technical difficulties mount conspicuously from C. 147 on, with easier sonatas occurring thereafter only infrequently, and new idiomatic problems on the increase, like trills and melodies in the same hand (C. 150/i/198–203), a dialog made by the left hand crossing high and low while the right supplies figural harmony (C. 181/i/44–46; but cf. Beethoven's similar technique 5 years earlier, in Op. 2/2/i/131–59), or tricky passages involving double-notes (C. 259/i/104–11). There also are several movements that display exceptional contrapuntal ingenuity on Dussek's part, including one that sounds at times like a two-part invention (C. 180/i), another that is a "Tempo di minuetto con moto; Canone alla seconda" (alternately "grave" and "acuta"; C. 259/ii), and a few with motivic exchanges in their development sections that also reveal exceptional rhythmic ingenuity (Ex. 109).

24. According to information kindly supplied by Professor Craw, specific pedal indications in Dussek's scores appeared at least as early as *ca.* 1799 ("Military Concerto," Op. 40); cf., also, MAB-m LIX xi; Schiffer/DUSSEK 51–52; Egert/FRÜH-ROMANTIKER 37–38).

25. Cf. Schiffer/DUSSEK 51–52; Craw/DUSSEK 53–54, 75, 175, 445–72 (*passim*).

Ex. 109. From the first movement of Jan Ladislav Dussek's Sonata in e♭/E♭, C. 178 (after MAB-m LIX 25).

Dussek is as fertile and resourceful if not quite so innovational or distinguished, in his melody writing as in his harmonic treatment and keyboard writing. Indeed, his melodic "fecundity" has been viewed as an embarrassment of riches,[26] sometimes providing more than is needed or assimilable in his "sonata forms." Only in the most intense and mature examples does a clear dualistic opposition of themes obtain (e.g., 211/i). Although a movement as nearly monothematic as C. 259/i is an exception, "sonata forms" with a pluralism of similar, not distinctly contrasted, themes are not rare (e.g., C. 127/i). The main ideas range from the concise motives of C. 96/i to the cantilena of the full-fledged themes in C. 221/i. Dotted and syncopated ideas are frequent (as in C. 149/i/1–18 and C. 211/i/53–74). Dussek implied that performers were still improvising ornamentation in slow melodic passages when he inscribed "senza ornamenti" over the start of C. 211. But he himself generally built up such lavish ornamentation and filigrees in the lines of his more serious slow movements, including the sort of rhythmic complexities introduced later in Beethoven's string quartets, that little or no opportunity remained for improvisation (as was already true in C. 60/ii and became still more so in mvts. like C. 259/iii). In his rondo finales, Dussek invented frank tunes of varying

26. As by G. A. Macfarren, quoted in Shedlock/SONATA 151–52.

originality, among the most distinctive being the pre-Chopinesque refrains in C. 222/iv and 259/iv.

One long example—in fact, the longest in this three-volume history—should help to illustrate not only some of the syntactic, variation, harmonic, textural, pianistic, melodic, and rhythmic traits observed thus far in Dussek's sonatas but also what astonishingly precocious Romanticisms these traits often produce (Ex. 110). This example comes from the sonata regarded here as Dussek's best, C. 221—more specifically, from the exposition of the first movement, beginning at measure 62 with the start of the third theme (or *the* "subordinate" theme, in that the 2d theme, starting at ms. 25, is still in the home key of A♭) and extending through its varied repetition, a closing idea, and dissolution in passagework, almost to the double-bar.

One's first impulse after reading such an excerpt from Dussek is to call him a master eclectic, almost in league with our late-Romantic epigones (cf. the start of ssb XI). However, one would have to realize that chronologically Dussek could only be an eclectic-before-the-fact, a Shakespeare who depends on "so many familiar quotations." When he does choose from the (immediate) past, he does so primarily from Haydn (as in C. 58/iii or C. 151/iii) and Mozart (as in C. 96/i). But even then he produces something new or different—namely, the exaggeration of high-Classicism that was to become one characteristic of early-Romantic music (ssb VI). In less basic ways he also derives from Clementi, as in the triplets, octaves, and broken-octaves of C. 57/i, or the mood in C. 211/i that recalls the pathos of "Didone abbandonata" (sce 749). But he shows remarkably little trace of Emanuel Bach, who, if he actually taught Dussek at one time, left none of the tangible influences that mark other of Bach's students so clearly (sce 123), unless one searches for the consequences in isolated passages and cadence extensions like those in C. 62/i/144–55 or C. 151/i/78–83.

Nor can substantial evidence be found for clear interinfluences between Dussek and his greatest contemporary, Beethoven. If anything, the influences seem to have acted on Beethoven, although the chief discussions of this possibility tread shaky ground, chronologically as well as musically, by emphasizing possible influences of Dussek's C. 151 on Beethoven's Op. 13 in the same key.[27] More plausible might be the influences of C. 62/ii on Op. 109/ii in the same key, tempo, and meter; or C. 184/i on Op. 79/i, with similar ideas, treatment, and meter. Still more plausible on internal musical grounds are Dussek's possible influences on another great, near contemporary, Schubert—for example, the sense of gentle flow, folklike simplicity, and *Gemüt-*

27. E.g., as in Blom/DUSSEK 708–9; cf. Newman/K. 457.

Ex. 110. From the first movement of Jan Ladislav Dussek's
Sonata in A♭, C. 221 (after MAB-m LXIII 45–47).

lichkeit in C. 166/ii or 179/i, which movements immediately bring certain of Schubert's impromptus and songs to mind; or the grandeur and drama of C. 178/ii in advance of the first movement of the "Unfinished Symphony"; or the peaceful, resigned, marchlike quality of C. 247/ii in advance of the "Great" Symphony in C/ii and the final "Ballet Music" from *Rosamunde*.

Returning to our Ex. 110 for anticipations of more mature Romanticisms, one can hardly help but say "Brahms" over the first eight measures, with the melody in rich 3ds and 6ths and, especially, the turn to the major key on the lowered-submediant degree (mss. 66–67). And one can hardly help saying "Weber" over the Alberti bass in open position, as it were (mss. 70–72), and the later line that descends by twos and dotted patterns above a bass-chord accompaniment (mss. 78–81); or "Hummel" and like virtuosos over the passagework that follows. Moreover, in other Dussek passages we find anticipations of Schumann (cf. C. 178/iv/90–97 with Op. 22/i/148–63, respectively), Rossini (cf. C. 59/ii/12–20 and the "Overture" to *The Barber of Seville*), Mendelssohn (cf. C. 211/ii and the Scherzo in b of 1829 or similarly deft scherzos), and Chopin (as suggested by the German-polka refrain in C. 259/iv or the *fioriture* in C. 221/ii). Anticipations of later Czech styles and composers, especially Smetana and Dvořák, also have been observed in Dussek's sonatas.[28] These include folklike themes and settings such as those in C. 127/iii/61–68 (starting with a refreshing turn to the subdominant) and C. 133/iii/1–24 (starting with a dominant harmony over a tonic drone bass).

In conclusion, Dussek's best sonatas are regarded here as being not only outstanding in quality but the most precociously Romantic sonatas, especially in harmony and keyboard writing, at the outset of the new era. If their quality does not quite match that of Beethoven's and Schubert's best sonatas, the reasons advanced here would be less, though far from little, melodic distinction in Dussek's sonatas; a less dynamic, concentrated approach to form, owing partly to the prevalence of complete double-periods; and somewhat less warmth and intimacy, except in his most expressive movements, for Dussek's variety of styles is so pronounced that it often suggests deliberate, conscious experimentation rather than subjective "inspiration."

Of considerably less significance to the sonata was Dussek's fellow countryman, onetime acquaintance, and junior by fourteen years, **Wenzel Johann Tomaschek (Václav Jan Tomášek; 1774–1850).**[29]

---

28. Cf. MAB-m XLVI xxviii and xxxi, LIII ix–x, LIX ix–x, and LXIII x–xi.

29. The order of Wenzel Johann is reversed in most sources. Thompson/ TOMASCHEK is the principal study of the man and his piano works, including a

Largely a self-taught musician, Tomaschek forwent a concert career as pianist to devote his full time to composition, creating prolifically in all categories, and to teaching, in which he stood highest among early 19th-century Czechs.[30] He idolized Mozart (but did not meet him) during that composer's last visits and operatic productions in Prague.[31] In the same city in 1798 he was greatly moved, at first even disturbed, by hearing the music and performance of Beethoven, whom he met then, as he did again in 1808 and 1814 in Vienna.[32] And in the same city he admired the music and performance of Spohr and Hummel, and met them,[33] as well as Vogler, Forkel, the Koželuch cousins, and the aging Goethe (1822).[34] He also met Clementi and Moscheles, but whether he knew Schubert in Vienna can be only a guess. His students included the gifted composer Woržischek (ssb VII) and the noted critic Eduard Hanslick. In spite of the visits to Vienna and a few lesser centers, Tomaschek was one Czech who stayed mostly at home.

Among some 110 solo piano works by Tomaschek are his only known sonatas—five in all, first published approximately in the 11 years from 1805 to 1816 (overlapping Dussek's late sonatas). These include Opp. 10 in B♭ (in Anth. NÄGELI-m XIV), 14 in C, 15 in G, 21 in F, and 48 in A (Hofmeister in Leipzig, plate no. 418), with "Grande" in the title of all but Opp. 10 and 48.[35] All are four-movement cycles with fast outer movements and, in between, the usual slow or moderate movement and the usual minuet or scherzo, or vice-versa. All but Op. 10 have slow introductions and all but Op. 15 have rondo finales.

If Dussek did exercise some of the strongest influences on Tomaschek, as has been asserted,[36] he seems to have done so, at least in the latter's sonatas, chiefly in the realm of tonal relationships and struc-

bibliography (pp. 234–42) with a brief undated list of the eds. used (pp. 239–42). Tomaschek's only opportunity to know Dussek was in Oct. and Nov. of 1802, not in 1804 as wrongly recalled by Tomaschek himself (and repeated in Thompson/ TOMASCHEK 84–86); cf. Craw/DUSSEK 124–30 and 458.

30. Cf. MGG XIII 469–72 (J. Bužga); Buchner/LISZT 42–43.

31. Cf. Thompson/TOMASCHEK 71–72.

32. Cf. Thompson/TOMASCHEK 78–79, 90; Nettl/DOCUMENTS 162–63, 178–85; TOMASCHEK (extracts from his autobiographic sketch of 1845–50) 251–61, passim (pp. 245–47 concern a visit in 1808 to Haydn in his dotage).

33. Cf. TOMASCHEK 247–48 and 261–62.

34. Cf. Thompson/TOMASCHEK 81–84, 94–95.

35. A "Sonatine" listed in MGG XIII 471 may or may not be a reprint of one of these. The 5 sons., especially Opp. 10 and 15, are described in Thompson/TOMA- SCHEK 111–49 (with copious exx.). Mod. ed.: only Op. 21/i, Giegling/SOLO-m 98 (cf. p. 18); Op. 21 is regarded here, unfortunately, as Tomaschek's weakest and least characteristic son.

36. Thompson/TOMASCHEK 84–86.

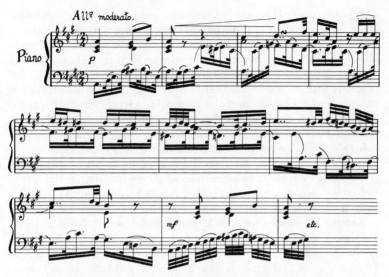

Ex. 111. From the first movement of Sonata in A, Op. 48, by
Wenzel Johann Tomaschek (after the original Hofmeister ed.
at the Library of Congress).

tural methods. His pianistic flare, which Tomaschek could have observed in person only during Dussek's one relatively brief return to
Prague in 1802 (*supra*), and his extraordinary variety of keyboard styles
did not carry over to Tomaschek's sonatas. More specifically, the influences that might be discovered on the younger Czech's sonatas can
be found primarily in such traits as a similar fondness for modulations
to moderately or distantly related keys by change of mode and enharmony, or for progressing by complete, relatively static double-
periods, especially the parallel kind in which the second period is an
elaboration of the first, or for creating driving scherzos and tuneful
rondo finales. As for keyboard treatment, Tomaschek's writing fits and
sometimes challenges the hand well enough, but it does little of what
Dussek's does to display the virtues and capabilities of piano techniques
and sounds. In fact, Tomaschek's most characteristic keyboard treatment is a close-position three- and four-part texture in the center of the
keyboard, with the hands interplaying in rather intricate dotted and
related rhythms (Ex. 111).

Tomaschek's sonatas cannot quite claim the pre-Schubertian charm
and Romanticisms that have been regarded as significant in his
"Eglogues," "Rapsodies," "Ditirambi," and other shorter piano pieces

(composed from 1807 on).[37] One must acknowledge the somewhat static form and the limits in both the texture and the piano idiom, as well as a certain predisposition toward conservatism and the high-Classic styles.[38] Also, one must acknowledge ideas that are well drawn and harmony that is appropriate without either being distinctive. There is little actual development of the ideas, most of which are too broadly and conjunctly outlined to provide kernels for development, anyway. Nor is there any of the experimenting with harmonic dissonance to be found in Dussek's music. Nor are there, for that matter, the generalized programmatic associations that seem to have given rise to Dussek's finest sonatas. All these considerations help to explain why Tomaschek's sonatas have never aroused the enthusiasm, in relation to either his own or other works, that Dussek's and even Woržischek's sonatas have.[39]

Another Czech who wrote in Mozart's shadow and had contacts with Beethoven was the dilettante pianist and professional jurist in Prague, **Johann Nepomuk Kanka** (1772–1865).[40] His two sonatas for P solo, in G and b♭, are preserved in MSS that await exploration in Prague. Tomaschek's pupil, the brilliant, widely-traveled concert pianist **Alexander Dreyschock** (1818–69) wrote at least three sonatas for P solo, presumably in the salon, virtuoso style of Kalkbrenner and Thalberg.[41] One of the sonatas by this "Hannibal of the octaves" (in Mendelssohn's words), "with two right hands" (in Cramer's words), was that in d, published as Op. 30 (Schott, *ca.* 1845); one was played in Paris in March, 1843; and the finale of one (his "third" son., in E♭) was played in Prague in 1847.[42] The Czech violinist **Johann Wenzel Kalliwoda** (1801–66) should get at least a mention here because of the interest and best moments in his symphonies, although his only two known sonatas are late works written while he was still in Donaueschingen, in southwest Germany—Opp. 135 in g, for P-duet (1845), and 176 in E♭, for P solo (1851)—and although the second of these, Op. 176, got reviewed as a formalistic, artistically worthless piece.[43] Another jurist

37. Cf. Kahl/LYRISCHE; Thompson/TOMASCHEK 89; SSB II.

38. Cf. Thompson/TOMASCHEK 222–23.

39. Cf. the early reviews in AMZ VIII (1805–6) 261–63 (praise for the ideas and treatment in Op. 10, but not the texture), XII (1809–10) 94–96 (mixed reactions to Op. 14).

40. Cf. MGG VII 511–12 (P. Nettl), with further bibl., including an unpub. Czech diss. of 1956; Thayer & Forbes/BEETHOVEN I 183–84 and 590–91; Anderson/BEETHOVEN *passim.*

41. Cf. MGG III 819–21 (W. Kahl).

42. Cf. MGG III 819–21; HOFMEISTER 1844–51, p. 108; Buchner/LISZT 43–44.

43. NZM XXXV (1851) 137–38. Cf. MGG VII 454–59 (W. Kramolisch); Altmann/KAMMERMUSIK 301.

by profession, yet also a onetime director of the Prague Conservatory, a friend of Wagner, and another pupil of Tomaschek, the pianist **Johann Friedrich Kittl** (1806–68) left a further published P-duet, Op. 27 in f (1847), that brought a similarly negative review.[44]

Smetana, Dvořák, and Other Later Czech Romantics

As compared with the obscure composers just mentioned, the major Czech composer **Friedrich Smetana** (1824–84) left two unpublished sonatas that, although not made known until recently, prove to have considerable interest and musical value.[45] Both sonatas were composed [45a] in the later 1840's, while he was still a young man, and during the least troubled years of his troubled career. One is a Sonata in g, for P solo, composed in 1846 but not published until as recently as 1949, only after a public appeal in 1944 recovered two opening pages of the MS that were missing since 1892.[46] The other is a Sonata in e, for 8 hands at 2 Ps, a rare example of this setting, composed in 1849, first published in 1906 as part of a not-quite-complete "complete" edition of Smetana's piano music, and republished in 1938.[47] These two sonatas remained unpublished because by 1879, when his successes in opera, orchestral, and chamber music would have insured publication of anything he wrote, Smetana was insisting that he had no piano works worthy of publication.[48] On the other hand, a third contribution, a Sonatina for P & Vn in d, Op. 27, did get published about a year earlier (*ca.* 1878, by F. A. Urbánek in Prague),[49] yet still remains unknown (and could not be found here).

Both of Smetana's piano sonatas reflect the circumstances of their origins. The solo sonata was composed between July and October of 1846 during his fourth and last year of study with the Romantic Czech pianist **Joseph Proksch** (1794–1864; himself the composer of at least one Sonata for P & Vn and a "Skalen-Sonate" for 4 Ps[!]).[50] In that year

---

44. NZM XXVI (1847) 41–42. Cf. MGG VII 973–74 (R. Quoika); Altmann/KAMMER-MUSIK 301.

45. Cf. GROVE VII 843–49 (G. Černušak) and MGG XII 774–87 (K. Honolka), each with further bibliography and a dated (but not quite complete) list of works; also, Newmarch/CZECHOSLOVAKIA 54–102.

46. Řepková/SMETANA-m, with valuable preface (in Czech) by M. Očadlík.

47. Kuhlmann/SMETANA-m, with "Explanatory Note." Another son. in the same setting, dated 1851, was left unfinished, according to Helfert/SMETANAS 177.

48. Kuhlmann/SMETANA-m "Explanatory Note."

49. According to Cobbett/CHAMBER II 425 (R. Newmarch & W. W. Cobbett); but no other reference to this work has turned up here.

50. Cf. MGG X 1653–54 (R. Quoika); Buchner/LISZT 47–48, 116–17; NZM LXXII/2 (1876) 318 (performance of the "Skalen-Sonate").

Smetana was deliberately experimenting with musical forms (thus, with "sonata form" in March) as part of a larger, planned exploration of the whole field of composition.[51] Whether he himself ever actually performed this work is not known. But this man, who was soon to gain distinction as a Chopin interpreter, could already derive influences, ideas, and styles from his own direct, youthful experiences and successes as a brilliant performer of Liszt, Thalberg, and Henselt.[52] And he undoubtedly derived more far-reaching and even more immediate influences on his Sonata in g (as well as his later music) from the sensational Prague visits in January, March, and April of that same year (1846) by Liszt as virtuoso and composer and Berlioz as composer and conductor (mainly of *Romeo and Juliet*).[53]

In any case, the Sonata in g, without any programmatic titles or other associations, reveals more daring, freedom, and striking originality in certain respects than *The Bartered Bride, The Moldau,* the Quartet "Aus meinem Leben," or any other of the recognized masterworks that were to be composed later, in the 1860's and 1870's, by Smetana. In its outward aspects the work offers no surprises. It is cast in the usual four movements (F-S-Sc-VF), with the opening idea—a stepwise descent and ascent within a 3d—undergoing "thematic metamorphosis" or recurring as an "idée fixe" throughout the first movement and in portions of each of the other three movements. Moreover, in these movements the over-all designs, although not conspicuous as such, are the standard ones of "sonata form," A-B-A, A-B-A, and rondo, respectively. But what does seem more conspicuous and less standard is the over-all style of progression. This style is a continuous unfolding through constant yet rhythmically plastic reiterations of a pattern. The pattern goes through frequent slight and more radical mutations, it depends on purposeful, choice, though not unusual harmonies (such as Dussek used) to move in slow harmonic rhythm toward changing tonal goals, near or far, and it lends itself well to the exploitation of varied techniques, ranges, and sonorities on the piano. In all these respects Smetana not only reflected the vivid impressions that Liszt's and Berlioz's music made on him but anticipated no other composer more than the Sibelius of the piano sonatinas noted earlier (end of ssb XV). At the same time, Smetana showed himself

51. According to M. Očadlík's preface in Řepková/SMETANA-m. Cf. pp. 64–93 (though with no special reference to the Son. in g) in the chief study of Smetana's development, Helfert/SMETANAS.

52. Cf. GROVE VII 843; BAKER 1527.

53. Cf. Ramann/LISZT II/1 270–71 and footnote 2 (giving the programs of 10 concerts just played by Liszt in Vienna); Barzun/BERLIOZ I 476 and 478; Buchner/LISZT, especially pp. 87–103 (with details on Berlioz, too).

Ex. 112. From the second movement of Sonata in g, by
Friedrich Smetana (after the original ed. of 1949, by kind permission of the publisher Melantrich in Prague).

well able to depart from or broaden his over-all style of progression
long enough to mold an expressive line such as would do honor to
his later reputation as a fine melodist. Our Ex. 112, from the slow
movement, includes a phrase with a reference to the "idée fixe" (bracketed here), approached and quitted by abrupt, remote modulations.

Whereas his Sonata in g originated as an advanced composition
exercise, Smetana's Sonata in e supposedly originated as a pedagogic
work, designed for use at the private music school that Liszt had
encouraged him to open in Prague in 1848.[54] At any rate, it is a more
regularized work, closer in phrase syntax, clarity of design, and straightforward scoring to his later comparable instrumental works or, for
example, to those of Grieg. (Indeed, there are faint melodic anticipations of Grieg's sonata in the same key, Op. 7 [ssb XV].) Its chief
structural distinction is the fact that it is in one movement, although
that movement is simply textbook "sonata form" extended to 490
measures. The work can be made to sound well and structurally con-

54. Kuhlmann/SMETANA-m "Explanatory Note."

vincing by four moderately advanced students properly coached in their ensemble and artistry.

Between the contributions of Smetana and Dvořák appeared such works as a thoroughly competent but nondistinctive Sonata in C for P & Vc, Op. 58 (pub. in 1853), by Tomaschek's onetime piano student and Liszt's friend in song, **Joseph Dessauer** (1798–1876);[55] a favorably received Sonatina and two Sonatas, Opp. 9–11 (1863–67), in A, D, and f, respectively, by Smetana's student, the important pedagogue **Josef Jiranék** (1855–1940);[56] and a Mendelssohnian "Sonatine instruktiv" in d (1884; composed *ca.* 1869), Op. 27, for P & Vn, along with a Sonata in B♭, Op. 28 (1887), for P-duet, by the successful opera composer **Zdenko Fibich** (1850–1900).[57]

A half generation younger than Smetana, the other of the two most important Czech Romantics in music, **Antonin Dvořák** (1841–1904), also left two contributions to our genre that are only on the fringe of a large output, yet have real musical interest. But unlike Smetana Dvořák made these contributions chiefly late in his life, well after he had profited from the support of Liszt, Brahms, and Bülow, and had won international recognition. Also, Dvořák, being mainly a violinist insofar as he performed and certainly not being the pianist that Smetana was, preferred to write his sonatas in duo rather than solo-piano settings.[58]

Dvořák did write two other, complete sonatas earlier in his life. One, written at the age of 32 (1873), was a three-movement duo in a, for Vn & P, actually played in 1875 but destroyed by the composer.[59] The other, written two years earlier, was a one-movement duo in f, for Vc & P (designated Op. 10), which was also destroyed by the composer, although the cello part remains.[60] Furthermore, all in 1893

55. NZM XXXIX (1853) 203–4. Cf. Mendel/LEXIKON III 121–22; Buchner/LISZT 60; LISZT LETTERS I 418 and II 502.

56. NZM LX (1864) 155; HOFMEISTER *Monatsbericht* for Dec. 1863, p. 235, Sept.–Oct. 1865, p. 158, Sept. 1867, p. 146. Cf. GROVE IV 642 (G. Černušak).

57. Cf. MGG IV 153–55 (P. Nettl); Helfert & Steinhard 254 and 269 (with further [MS?] sons., including errors); Newmarch/CZECHOSLOVAKIA 104–24.

58. Within the extensive literature on Dvořák the most recent, authoritative, and up-to-date studies that pertain here are Šourek/DVOŘÁK on the chamber music (cf., also, Šourek's remarks in Cobbett/CHAMBER I 365 and 369–70), DVOŘÁK LETTERS, Clapham/DVOŘÁK on the life (brief) and works (by categories), and Burghauser/DVOŘÁK, a trilingual thematic index, bibliography, biographic chronology, and general documentary summary. Cf., also, Newmarch/CZECHOSLOVAKIA 125–75.

59. Cf. Burghauser/DVOŘÁK 123–24 (item 33, with further [Czech] references), 67 ("DAnn"), but not the list of destroyed works on pp. 616–17; Clapham/DVOŘÁK 190 and 219.

60. Cf. Burghauser/DVOŘÁK 106 (item 20, with incipit and further [Czech] references) and 617; Clapham/DVOŘÁK 189 (cf. pp. 162–63) and 219; Šourek/DVOŘÁK 14.

Dvořák started sketches for another Sonata for Vc & P, a Sonatina for the same, and a Sonata in f for P solo.[61] But it was still two other works that comprised the only two contributions to our genre completed by him and allowed to survive, both being duos for Vn & P. One is Op. 57 in F, a three-movement, 20-minute, noncyclical sonata (F-S-VF) composed in Prague while Dvořák was working on his violin Concerto in a, tried out with success in Berlin by the composer and Joachim, first published by Simrock, and first performed publicly in Chrudim (east of Prague), all in 1880.[62] The other is a Sonatina in G, Op. 100, a four-movement but shorter work (F-S-Sc-F) that was composed in two weeks late in 1893 during his first stay in New York and soon after two larger chamber works and the "New World Symphony" had been completed.[63] Published in 1894 by Simrock, this Sonatina was "dedicated to my children . . . on the occasion of completing my hundredth work" and welcomed by 15-year-old Otilie, his eldest surviving child, as "delightful," although Dvořák wrote Simrock suggesting that adults could enjoy it, too.[64]

Both of Dvořák's contributions, if not quite the equals of his greatest masterpieces in originality, strength, or melodic and harmonic sensitivity, deserve to be kept alive in chamber music literature. Op. 57 has less of a chance because, as we have seen happen so often, it approaches too closely the musical ideas, textures, and development techniques of his staunch supporter and friend Brahms[65] to stand on its own merits. Whether during the flexible, tonally extended applications of "sonata form" in the first movement, or the expressive, broadly drawn lines of the ternary, A-B-A design in the middle movement, or the more curt, clipped themes of the sonata-rondo-form finale, almost every passage brings some idea or style from Brahms's chamber music to mind. There are even hints of contemporary or future Brahms works that Dvořák could not yet have known, such as the descending triplets in Dvořák's opening, main theme, suggesting those in the bridge to the second theme of Brahms's piano Trio in C, Op. 87/i. And in this work Dvořák shows that he, like Brahms, enjoyed a dis-

61. Cf. Burghauser/DVOŘÁK 352 and 354 (items 419, 428, and 426, respectively).

62. Cf. Burghauser/DVOŘÁK 497–98, 500, 216 (item 106), with further (Czech) bibliography; Clapham/DVOŘÁK 193–95; Šourek/DVOŘÁK 169–72 (description, with exx.); DVOŘÁK LETTERS 54, 56; MT XXVII (1885) 147, 162 (early English performances).

63. Cf. Burghauser/DVOŘÁK 563, 311–12 (item 183), with further (Czech) bibliography; Clapham/DVOŘÁK 209–10, 31–32 (sketches); Šourek/DVOŘÁK 172–78 (description); DVOŘÁK LETTERS 176, 178. Opp. 57 and 100 are reprinted in Dvořák/WERKE-m IV/1, among other mod. eds.

64. Clapham/DVOŘÁK 209, 8–9; Šourek/DVOŘÁK 172. To make this his "hundredth" work, Dvořák assigned "Op. 100" before it was quite due.

65. Cf. Clapham/DVOŘÁK 9, 13, 23.

tinct heritage from Schumann—for example, in the octave leaps (with the two instruments in contretemps) in Op. 57/i/83–95, which recall the "Scherzo" of Schumann's Symphony in d. Dvořák's piano writing is appropriate but not especially resourceful.

Dvořák's Op. 100 is in quite another style, immediately suggesting the freshness and originality, as well as some specific ideas, in the "New World Symphony" and other of his works composed in this country. To be sure, the "sonata forms" in the outer movements and A-B-A designs in the inner movements are standard again and they are exceptionally clear, as is the simpler texture, in keeping with music for children. But the freshness and originality lie less in these aspects than in the frank melodies, with their modal flavors, dancelike rhythms, and elementary yet fully appropriate harmonies. Thus, the violin and its accompaniment open on a gay theme that recalls the rising contour, dotted pattern, and single tonic major chord on which "Oh, My Darling Clementine" opens. The second theme starts in the submediant minor key with the scale pattern 8-7-5 and the lowered 7th sometimes associated with Grieg's and with American Indian music.[66] The "Larghetto" movement, in the tonic minor key, starts with a melancholy theme jotted down a few months earlier by Dvořák as he was shown the Minnehaha Falls near St. Paul, Minnesota, perhaps while longing for his family and homeland. The special appeal of this movement and this theme with its emphasis on the Indian minor 3d, 3-1, prompted Simrock to publish it separately, with such unauthorized titles as "Indian Lament," "Indian Conzonetta," and "Indian Lullaby." [67] After a bright "Scherzo" the finale announces its character with a piquant idea and syncopations that provide some of those specific recollections of the "New World Symphony" (Ex. 113). Highly characteristic of Dvořák's style, too, is the lyrical, syncopated, rising theme of the "Molto tranquillo section" in E, and the approach to it through an alternation of the tonic and mediant triads in e.

The esteemed Prague organist **Joseph Bohuslav Foerster** (1859–1951) revealed both his devotion to Dvořák and Mahler and his conservative orientation in his sonatas (as well as his other music). These include three duos for Vn & P and two for Vc & P, published over nearly a half century (1898–1943).[68] A full half-century (1891–1941) spans the composition dates of three sonatas and six sonatinas left by a similarly important but quite different conservative, the Dvořák

---

66. Chapham/DVOŘÁK 210 likens it to a "well-known Moravian folk-song."
67. Cf. Clapham/DVOŘÁK 209.
68. Cf. GROVE III 178–79 (G. Černušak), with dated cat.; MGG IV 455–57 (P. Nettl); Helfert & Steinhard 67–72; Newmarch/CZECHOSLOVAKIA 182–91.

Ex. 113. From Antonín Dvořák's Sonatina in G, Op. 100/iv
(after the original Simrock ed.).

student and further Brahms protégé **Vitězslav Novák** (1870–1949). Novák took for his models, as his style and control developed, first Mendelssohn, then Schumann, Grieg, Berlioz, Liszt, Brahms, and eventually Smetana and Dvořák in their more nationalistic guises.[69] He started at twenty-one with a Sonata in d, for P & Vn, which was not published until 1920.[70] In 1900, he followed with his single example that achieved any success, "Sonata eroica" for P solo, Op. 24 in f, first published in 1905 and again in 1951. A laudatory review greeted this work, ascribing to it some of that heroic element to be found in Bruckner's third and Beethoven's third and ninth symphonies.[71] At least the comparison with Bruckner seems appropriate today, not only in the sense of the heroic, achieved mainly by broad melodic arches moving in slow harmonic rhythm, but in the more personal and local flavors of the melody, in the dramatic tonal surprises in spite of traditional harmony, in the orchestral sonorities implicit in full piano writing that seems more like a transcription than an original, and in the persistent rhythmic patterns of both of the well-planned, freely

69. Cf. GROVE VI 130–33 (G. Černušak) and MGG IX 1723–27 (J. Bužga), both with dated cats. and further bibliography; Helfert & Steinhard 72–79; Newmarch/ CZECHOSLOVAKIA 195–201.

70. Altmann/KAMMERMUSIK 219. It is mentioned as an "acceptable" work, only as an afterthought, in Cobbett/CHAMBER II 192 (W. W. Cobbett).

71. NZM CI (1905) 543.

and emotively paced, closely edited movements (F-S/F/S). Novák's set of *Sechs Sonatinen*, Op. 54, for P solo were published originally about 1915 [72] and again in 1951. But a Sonata for Vc & P, composed by him in 1941, apparently still remains in MS.

Novák's two chief contemporaries among Czech pioneers of the 20th century, Josef Suk and Otakar Ostrčil,[73] did not happen to leave any consequential sonatas. But several other late-Romantics of less renown and success in Czechoslovakia did,[74] including, for example, a violinist and biographer of Smetana, **Karl Navrátil** (1867–1936), who left one sonata each for P & Vn (Op. 20 in d; 1894) and P & Vc (Op. 24 in d; 1903). Op. 20 was reviewed as Brahmsian, skillful for an "amateur," "but very physiognomelióse." [75] The violinist **Johann Sluníčko** (1852–1923) left five or more sonatas for P & Vn published between 1904 and 1913, at least two of which brought warm praise for fine workmanship and attractive themes still in the style of Gade and Grieg.[76] By contrast, Dvořák's last student, **Rudolf Karel** (1880–1945), left two impassioned, rhapsodic sonatas. Op. 14 in c (although the finale begins in f) is a four-movement work (M-S-Sc-F) for P solo (composed in 1910, pub. in 1921); and Op. 17 in d is a one-movement, largely polyphonic work for Vn & P (composed in 1912, pub. in 1913). Both sonatas suggest Reger in their chromatic, recherché harmony and remote tonal relationships, hence aroused the expected discomfort and puzzlement among reviewers.[77]

Composers in Poland (Paderewski)

Aside from Chopin, whose main sonatas originated in France (and are so identified in ssb XII), there is no front-rank composer to bring up in connection with the Romantic sonata in Poland. In fact, in the politically and socially unfavorable environment of the early 19th century[78] there are almost no sonata composers to mention, and even by the end of the century there are few who survive today beyond the ken of Polish specialists. As one example from the start of the era,

72. dm XV/2 (1915) 616.
73. Cf. Helfert & Steinhard 72.
74. Cf. the lists in Helfert & Steinhard, especially pp. 254–55 and 269–72, although many of the names would have to be put here with the Moderns.
75. nzm XCIX (1903) 596.
76. dm III/4 (1903–4) 463 (W. Altmann on Op. 51 in c); dm VI/4 (1906–7) 239 (W. Altmann on Op. 60 in A). Cf. Riemann/lexikon II 1715; Altmann/kammer-musik 227.
77. E.g., dm XIII/2 (1913–14) 231 (W. Dahms on Op. 14). Cf. mgg VII 680–82 (J. Bužga); Cobbett/chamber II 47 (R. Veselý); Helfert & Steinhard 97–99.
78. Cf. Lissa/polish 104–13 (part of a helpful survey of Polish music).

Chopin's versatile teacher in Warsaw, **Joseph Xaver Elsner** (1768 [BAKER]–1854), left a "Grande Sonate" for P+V+Vc, Op. 2 (1798); three "Sonaten" for P & Vn, published separately as Op. 10/1–3 (1805–7); and a "Sonate" for P-duet, Op. 16 (between 1820 and 1828).[79] Elsner's Op. 10/1 and 3 were reviewed as light if not really easy pieces good for fun and practice (including a "Polonaise" as the last variation in Op. 10/3/ii).[80] As another early example, Haydn's pupil and friend, the pianist **Franciszek Lessel** (1779–1838), left at least one set of three sonatas, Op. 2, dedicated to Haydn, and a "Grande Sonate," Op. 6, all for P solo. These sonatas were published (shortly?) before 1815 and presumably bear out the popularity of some of Lessel's music in his day as well as the present small consensus to the effect that his music is Haydnesque, includes some Polish national elements, and is above average in quality.[81] Among the few others who were successful in Poland at the era's start—for example, Karol Kurpiński and Karol Lipiński[82]—none were noted here who left sonatas.

About a half-century later, the pianist and teacher **Władysław Żeleński** (1837–1921) left three sonatas for P solo (Opp. 3, 5, and 20) and two for P & Vn (Opp. 30 and 67), all published between about 1850 and 1885.[83] Representative is Op. 20, a musicianly, fluent, well-knit work in four movements (F-Va-Sc-F) that shows Żeleński still living in the world of Schumann and Mendelssohn. The celebrated, widely travelled pianist **Joseph Wieniawski** (1837–1912) was the brother of the even more celebrated violinist Henryk, who figures here only as the joint author with Joseph of an "Allegro de sonate" in g, Op. 2, composed when they were thirteen and eleven years old, published in 1854, and reprinted in 1898. Joseph himself left three published sonatas regarded as traditional and not the equal of Henryk's music—Opp. 22 in b, for P solo (*ca.* 1865?), 24 in d, for P & Vn (1869), and 26 in E, for P & Vc (1878).[84]

Although neither the symphonist Zygmunt Noskowski (1846–1909)[85]

79. Cf. MGG III 1313–16 (W. Kahl).

80. AMZ VIII (1805–6) 144 and IX (1806–7) 660.

81. Cf. MGG VIII 667–69 (J. Morawski), with errors; Lissa/POLISH 106; HOFMEISTER 1815 (Whistling), 365–66.

82. Cf. Lissa/POLISH 105–6.

83. Cf. GROVE IX 407–8 (C. R. Halski); Lissa/POLISH 120–21; HOFMEISTER 1852–55, 231 (Op. 5); NZM LXXII (1876) 488 and LVI/1 (1880) 98 (high praise by R. Musiol of Op. 20 for its ideas, concentration, and skill; with ex.); Cat. NYPL XXXIII 688 (Op. 30).

84. Cf. DM VIII/1 (1908–9) 235 (negative review of Op. 22 by A. Leitzmann); NZM LXXXI/1 (1885) 3–4 (viewing Op. 24 more as an effective virtuoso concerto); MGG XIV 627–33 (B. Schwarz & R. Sietz); Altmann/KAMMERMUSIK 232 and 266; PAZDÍREK XV 395–96.

85. Cf. MGG IX 1595 (A. Sutkowski) and Lissa/POLISH 121.

nor the chamber composer Gustaw Roguski (1839–1921)[86] left published sonatas, the gifted, short-lived pianist **Antoni Stolpe** (1851–72), a pupil of Elsner and Kiel, left a Sonata for P & Vn and two sonatas for P solo (all *ca.* 1870?). One of the latter, in d, was played often by the pianist Joseph Wieniawski (*supra*) and has been called "remarkable for its stylistic maturity." [87] Another who also died young is the Count and onetime piano student of Liszt, **Władisław Tarnowski** (1841–78). He is credited with a "Grande Sonate" for P solo, Op. 10 (1875?), and a "Fantaisie quasi sonate" on "some themes from an unpublished opera," for P & Vn (1870), both reviewed with extreme mockery as "crass dilletantism." [88] The pianist **Anastazy Wilhelm Dreszer** (1845–1907) wrote a "Sonata appassionata" that appeared as his Op. 1 in 1865 or 1866, before he moved to Halle (in east Germany), and a "Zweite grosse Sonate" published as his Op. 13 in 1879 (?). The latter would be interesting to see, if only to evaluate the reviewer who faulted it for depending in all three movements on the "swan motive" in *Lohengrin,* for inconsistencies of texture and keyboard idiom, for poor development of ideas, and for unclear, arbitrary tonality and forms![89]

Throughout his long distinguished musical and political career, the world-renowned pianist **Ignace Jan Paderewski** (1860–1941) held composition as his foremost goal.[90] His musical training, especially in the years from 1882 to 1889, included graduation from the Warsaw Conservatory, composition study in Berlin under Kiel and with Rubinstein's encouragement,[91] and the oft-cited study in piano with Leschetizky in Vienna.[92] Among only about 35 published works or sets of pieces by Paderewski, including the opera *Manru,* the Symphony in b, and the Concerto in a, as well as solos and duos with piano, there are two sonatas. One is Op. 13 in a, for Vn & P, dedicated to Sarasate, composed and first played in Vienna in 1885, and published by Bote & G. Bock of Berlin in 1886. After hearing this work in 1885,

86. Cf. GROVE VII 207–8 (C. R. Halski).

87. Lissa/POLISH 122; a mod. ed. was pub. in Krakow in 1957. Cf. MGG XII 1396–97 (J. Ekiert), with reference to an article (in Polish) on the Son. in d, by S. Goldchowski.

88. MW VI (1875) 513; PAZDÍREK XIV 36; Altmann/KAMMERMUSIK 229. Cf. GROVE VIII 310 (C. R. Halski).

89. MW X (1879) 366. Cf. GROVE II 767 (C. R. Halski).

90. E.g., cf. pp. 36, 112, 268, and 327 in PADEREWSKI (a fascinating *fin-de-siècle* view of musical Europe and America). Cf., also, MGG X 561–64 (J. Ekiert), with list of works and further bibliography.

91. Cf. PADEREWSKI 59–60, 63–64, 95–97, 108–21.

92. Cf. PADEREWSKI 83–88.

Brahms reportedly said, "Well, Paderewski, it is very effective, very fine, but it is not chamber music; it is a concert Sonata," which criticism Paderewski says he valued.[93] Another commentator found its finale alternately "turbulent" and "tender," but too little developed, and its preceding "Intermezzo" a "charming," "skillful," "felicitous" piece that is the "best" of its three movements.[94] Paderewski's other example is his Op. 21 in e♭, for P solo, composed and first played by him in 1903 at his Châlet de Riond-Bosson on Lake Geneva, performed publicly (by him?) that winter in Boston, and issued by the same (and then his only) publisher in 1906 (?).[95]

Paderewski himself regarded Op. 21 as "one of my most important and best works. But it is extremely difficult and for that reason will never be very popular." [96] As more of a tone poet than a virtuoso he exaggerated these difficulties, which now seem quite legitimate in such good piano scoring, and only moderate in relation to those of Brahms's, Liszt's, and Chopin's solo sonatas. However, Op. 21 is as large as these sonatas in scope, for its three movements occupy 49 pages of printed score. Daniel Gregory Mason found it and the Symphony in b, from the same period, to be Wagnerian in character.[97] Chopinesque seems more appropriate to describe its prevailing style,[98] unless one thinks not so much of idiom, melody, or tonality as of continuous drive. And one cannot but feel that this drive, like that in Ashton's (SSB XIV) or other epigonic sonatas of the time, becomes essential partly to mask the late-Romantic composer's increasing inability or hesitation to commit himself to frank, clear-cut themes (SSB VI). Yet without such themes the drive sacrifices its main structural landmarks. In his opening movement Paderewski commits himself only to short ideas that scarcely interrupt the drive, for they merge both melodically and harmonically with the passagework, generally evading strong references to the tonic chord. Even in the more sectionalized, lyrical, moderate-paced middle movement in broad A-B-A design, "Andante ma non troppo," the one complete thematic period (mss. 34–49) is less a distinctive melody than a melodic and tonal climax stated and restated. In these respects, Paderewski's finale, "Allegro vivace," seems to be the most successful of the movements. Its design may be outlined

---

93. PADEREWSKI 91; cf., also, p. 97.
94. Cobbett II 205 (Adolph Mann).
95. Cf. Johns/REMINISCENCES 103.
96. PADEREWSKI 326.
97. Mason/MUSIC 168.
98. Such was the opinion, too, of H. Wetzel, reviewing its pub. in DM VII/4 (1907–8) 312, with special praise for the fluency, clarity, and structural control.

as toccata-fugue-toccata-coda. The toccata thrives on steady drive and melodic bits, and the fugue, based on a vigorous subject in two-part writing (Ex. 114), shows the devoted composer's noble command of the keyboard and his superior craftsmanship at their best.

The Warsaw conductor **Gregor Fitelberg** (1879–1953; father of Jerzy) won the Paderewski composition prize in Leipzig in 1896 for a Sonata for P & Vn, Op. 2, composed in 1894 but never published (in spite of the announcement on the jacket of Op. 12).[99] Fitelberg's Op. 12 is another Sonata for P & Vn, in F, composed in 1901, published in 1905, and described as an original, un-Germanic work in three concise movements, the middle of which is an "Intermezzo" interesting for its unusual metric organization.[100] About the same time, the

Ex. 114. From the finale of Ignace Jan Paderewski's Sonata in e♭ (after the original Bote & G. Bock ed., plate no. 15915).

German-trained organist **Mieczysław Surzyński** (1860–1924) left for his instrument a Sonata in three movements (F-M-fugue), Op. 34 in d, published in 1904 and reviewed as an original, bold, impassioned, and skillful work.[101] Three early sonatas—two for P solo, in c and f♯, and one for P & Vn, in a—were composed in 1902–3 by the important pupil of G. Fitelberg, **Ludomir Różycki** (1884–1953), before he went from Warsaw to Berlin in 1904 for further study.[102] In the latter center

---

99. Cf. MGG IV 281–82 (Z. Lissa); Altmann/KAMMERMUSIK 202.

100. DM VI/1 (1906–7) 171 (W. Altmann). GROVE III 148 (K. Geiringer) also lists a "Sonatina for 2 vns." (unpub.?).

101. NZM C (1904) 620; MW XXXVI (1905) 143 (G. Riemenschneider). Cf. MGG XII 1759–60 (H. Feicht).

102. Cf. GROVE VII 287–90 (C. R. Halski).

he also wrote a Sonata for Vc & P, Op. 10 in a (1906, pub. in 1912),[103] presumably already showing the influence of R. Strauss.

In the Lower Silesian center of Breslau (Wroclaw) as well as other sometime Polish centers under Prussian control throughout the Romantic Era (and until the end of World War II), several obscure sonata composers of German descent were active. Thus, in Breslau may be noted the organist and conductor **Adolph Hesse** (1809–63), a pupil of Hummel and Spohr among others, for a Sonata in A♭, Op. 42, for P-duet, and a *Phantasie-Sonate,* Op. 83 (1848?), for organ. The latter was reviewed as being well worked out though somewhat loose structurally and sentimental for church styles.[104] A Breslau hornist and writer, **Heinrich Gottwald** (1821–76) offered as his Op. 1 (1856?) another *Sonate fantastique,* this time for P solo, eliciting a reviewer's description of it as a three-movement, thematically interrelated cycle showing superior craftsmanship, harmonic interest, and imagination, as well as some hints of Schumann, Brahms, and Liszt.[105] After receiving Op. 1 from Gottwald, Bülow replied belatedly (Jan. 31, 1867), praising it warmly and copiously, though nonspecifically, for its "noble, pregnant, original content" and impressive structural mastery.[106] In spite of numerous performances of his chamber music, the Breslau composer **Paul Caro** (1859–1914) received only unfavorable reviews for his three published sonatas—Opp. 2 in F, for P & Vn (pub. 1883), 41 in f♯, for P solo (composed in 1886, pub. in 1911), and 42 in d, for P & Vc (pub. in 1911).[107] Two more organ sonatas, Opp. 33 in A (1902?) and 62 in D (1910), were composed by the Breslau conductor **Georg Riemenschneider** (1848–1913).[108] The first was reviewed as a highly musical, artful work in the vein of Schumann.[109]

Two other Polish centers formerly under Prussian control are represented by one obscure composer each here. In Danzig (Gdansk) the organist and pianist **Friedrich Wilhelm Markull** (1816–87) left three three-movement sonatas for P-duet, Opp. 75–77 in a, D, and E♭, that appeared in 1860–61 and brought favorable reactions for their (tradi-

103. Altmann/KAMMERMUSIK 263. The faulty listing in MGG XI 1033–34 (Z. Lissa) adds 1928 as the pub. year.

104. NZM XXX (1849) 184–86 (G. Siebeck). Cf. GROVE IV 263–64 (G. Grove); Mendel/LEXIKON V 223; PAZDÍREK VII 484.

105. NZM XLVIII (1858) 80 (R. Viole). Cf. Mendel/LEXIKON IV 310–11 and Suppl. 131.

106. BÜLOW BRIEFE IV 68–72.

107. NZM LXXXI/2 (1885) 407 (E. Klitzsch sees no hope in Op. 2); DM X/4 (1910–11) 246–47 (R. Cahn-Speyer calls Op. 41 ineffectual); DM X/4 189 (H. Schlemüller deplores the P part as inadequate). Cf. Riemann/LEXIKON I 280 and 12th ed. I 279.

108. Cf. Riemann/LEXIKON II 1517; Kremer/ORGAN 218.

109. MW XXXIV (1903) 379 (H. Schöne); DM III/2 (1903–04) 275 (K. Straube).

tional) artistic ideas and treatment, clear forms, and pedagogic values.[110] In Sorau (Żary) the cantor **Hermann Franke** (1834–1919) left two sets of sonatinas for P solo, Opp. 28 and 50, and a three-movement Sonata for P & Vc in g, Op. 69 (pub. in 1877), that was criticized negatively in 1882 not only for some lack of structural balance in the outer movements but for adhering to the traditional three-movement cycle and standard forms, by then "long since canonized" and "archaic." [111]

Composers in Hungary (Dohnányi)

Throughout music's Romantic Era the political struggle for nationalistic (Magyar) identity in Hungary and the alternate joining and clashing with Austria, even after Hungary's Revolution of 1848 and pseudo "independence" in 1867–68, are reflected in Hungary's music. There were both Germanic and nationalistic trends, sometimes clearly opposed, sometimes combined, although when they were combined, by a self-conscious process of Romantic "westernization," to produce several sonatas "in Hungarian style," the results were generally rather pale.[112] In the earlier 19th century, during the heyday of the Hungarian "Verbunkos" dance,[113] the interest in the sonata was even rarer than in Poland, with only a Liszt *in absentia*. (It was not until 1875 that Liszt figured in the founding of the Academy of Music in Budapest.) And again some of the composers whose names still stand out did not happen to write sonatas or, in their nationalistic zeal, actually resisted such Germanisms or other foreignisms—for example, the founder of Hungarian national opera, Franz Erkel, or the increasingly nationalistic Mihály Mosonyi, or the esteemed scholar, writer, and composer Gábor Mátray, or, later, the violinist Eduard Reményi and the Liszt follower Károl Aggházy. Furthermore, several composers who reportedly did write sonatas or works of a similar sort left no further traces of themselves or their sonatas that have turned up here, including Kálmán Simonffy (1832–81), Károly Huber (1828–85), and Imre Székely (1823–87).[114]

110. NZM LVI (1862) 163. Cf. GROVE V 582 (H. S. Oakeley).
111. MW XIII (1882) 555–57 (C. Kipke). Cf. Riemann/LEXIKON I 535.
112. Cf. the summaries of Romantic trends in Szabolcsi/UNGARISCHEN 75–87 and MGG XIII 1076–80 (Z. Gardonyi). Bartók/UNGHERIA and the documentary pictorial study Keresztury/MAGYAR have also proved helpful. Warm thanks for personal communications on the son. in Hungary are owing to Dr. Elod J. Juhász and the late Dr. József Gát, both at Budapest Academy of Music, and to Professor Béla Böszörmenyi-Nagy of Boston University.
113. Cf. MGG XIII 1076 and 1419–20 (B. Rajeczky). Szabolcsi/UNGARISCHEN 54–66.
114. Cf. Szabolcsi/UNGARISCHEN 69 and 82.

Although music by both Haydn and Beethoven became known as early as 1800 in Hungary,[115] no sonatas are listed among the works by two pioneers of instrumental chamber music in that country, Antal György Csérmak (1774–1822) and Márk Rózsavölgyi.[116] In fact, the first 19th-century examples known here to have been published did not appear until 1857 and 1860. These are two sonatas for P & Vn, Opp. 7 in g and 10 in d, by a capable violinist of German descent, August von Adelburg (1830–73).[117] Op. 7 was called overly simplified and repetitive, with inadequate development of its ideas and exploitation of the instruments.[118] Previously, in 1851, an unpublished Sonata for P solo had been written during the Viennese training of the Hungarian composer and engineer Julius Beliczay (1835–93), who in 1887 also wrote a "Sonata quasi fantaisie" for P solo, Op. 10 (never pub.?).[119] Two (unpublished?) sonatas dating from 1861, one for P solo, Op. 4, and the other for P & Vn, in E♭, were left by an influential pro-German composer and early Wagnerite in Hungary, Ödon von Mihalovich (1842–1929).[120] More nationalistically inclined, the pianist Henri Gobbi (1842–1920) dedicated a "first" Grande Sonate dans le style hongrois, Op. 13 in E (pub. ca. 1872), to his teacher Liszt.[121] Another of Gobbi's teachers was the distinguished German composer in Budapest, Robert Volkmann, whom we have noted earlier, during his four-year stay in Vienna (ssb IX). Further investigation into this period might also include a Sonate romantique for P & Vn, Op. 22 in D (1871), by the celebrated violinist Jenö Hubay (Eugene Huber; 1858–1937), whose music recalls his teacher Vieuxtemps (ssb XII);[122] a Sonata in E, for P solo (pub. by 1885), by the pianist Coloman Chovan (1852–?), reviewed as difficult and clumsy to play, and not worth the effort, anyway;[123] and an unpublished Sonata for P & Vn by the eminent, international conductor Arthur Nikisch (1855–1922).[124]

A prolific, able, though not outstanding sonata composer was the pianist Emánuel Moór (1863–1931), chiefly remembered for his in-

115. MGG XIII 1076.
116. Cf. GROVE II 555–56 (J. S. Weissmann); MGG XI 1030–31 (Z. Gárdonyi).
117. Cf. GROVE I 57–58 (J. S. Weissmann).
118. NZM XLVI (1857) 273–74. But cf. Cobbett/CHAMBER I 3 on his chamber style.
119. Cf. GROVE I 601–2 (J. S. Weissmann).
120. Cf. GROVE V 748–49 (J. S. Weissmann); MGG IX 284–86 (J. Ujfalussy).
121. Cf. Riemann/LEXIKON I 622; Szabolcsi/UNGARISCHEN 82; HOFMEISTER 1868–73, 154.
122. Cf. MGG VI 804–6 (H. Haase); Cobbett/CHAMBER I 575 (W. W. Cobbett); Szabolcsi/UNGARISCHEN 85.
123. MW XVI (1885) 236. Cf. PAZDÍREK III 308; Riemann/LEXIKON I 317, with mention of a Son. for P-duet, Op. 22.
124. Cf. BAKER 1162–63; MGG IX 1531–33 (M. Schuler).

vention of the rather bulky "Duplex Coupler" piano.[125] Some 25 sonatas were composed by Moór, including 12 for P & Vn, 7 for Vc & P, 3 for P solo, 2 for harp solo, and one for 4 harps, but apparently none was created especially for the 2-manual piano. Some 12 to 14 of these were published, between 1889 and about 1913, including 7 for P & Vn, 4 for Vc & P, possibly 2 for P, and possibly the one for 4 harps.[126] A sampling of the published sonatas reveals the usual standardized cycles of three and four movements, although the forms of these movements, especially in the later sonatas, prove to be either less usual, freer applications of standardized forms (as in the 3 mvts., F-S-F, of Op. 76 in a/A, for Vc & P; pub. in 1909) or so open, cursive, and free in sectional organization and tempo as not to relate readily to any standardized forms (e.g., the 4 mvts., M-F-S-VF, of Op. 60 in c♯, for P solo; pub. in 1906). Moór's themes, which tend to unfold at some length by winding around their starting notes, are not particularly compelling or original. Moreover, their reiterations and development seem somewhat perfunctory. There is more interest in the warm but traditional harmony, with its occasionally chromatic, enharmonic, and diagonal relationships (Ex. 115), and in the sonorous wide-ranging textures, although these textures, consistent with a degree of bombast in this music, soon confront the pianist with too much writing in octaves, plain or filled.

The one-armed pianist **Géza Zichy** (1849–1924), a pupil of Liszt and Volkmann, wrote a piano Sonata in G, in three movements (F-M-VF), for left hand alone, that was published by D. Rahter of Leipzig in 1887.[127] It proves to be a melodious, unoriginal work in conventional, light opera style, mildly interesting only as a keyboard scoring problem.[128] The pianist **Kornél Ábrányi** ("the Elder"; 1822–1903) was a pupil variously of Chopin, Kalkbrenner, and Mosonyi, and a devoted nationalist, who founded what was reportedly the first Hungarian music periodical in 1860, who helped to establish the Academy of Music in Budapest in 1875, and who sought to amalgamate Western European and Hungarian styles.[129] Presumed products of the amalgamation (but not seen here) are his *Sonate im ungarischen Style,* Op. 84, and *Ungarische Millenium-Sonate,* Op. 103, both for P solo and published in Budapest (*ca.* 1891 and 1896).[130] **Árpád Szendy** (1863–1922),

125. Cf. MGG IX 542–44 (P. P. Hoffer); ML III (1922) 29–48 (D. Tovey).

126. Cf. GROVE V 863–64 (J. S. Weissmann); Altmann/KAMMERMUSIK 216 and 261; PAZDÍREK X 779; Cobbett/CHAMBER II 147–48 (Adolph Mann).

127. Cf. GROVE IX 414–15 (J. S. Weissmann); HOFMEISTER 1887, 373.

128. In MW XXI (1890) 505 it is called folklike, slick, and skillful in its scoring.

129. Cf. GROVE I 15–17 (J. S. Weissmann); Szabolcsi/UNGARISCHEN 82.

130. Cf. HOFMEISTER X (1886–91) 2 and XI (1892–97) 1 (but neither is in the annual vols.).

Ex. 115. From the second theme of the first movement in
Emanuel Moór's Sonata in c♯, Op. 60 (after the C. F. W. Siegel
ed., plate no. 14482).

a pupil of Liszt, a fine pianist and teacher, and a respected editor of
musical masterpieces, left two sonatas for P solo—one in b, composed
about 1896 as his Op. 1 but apparently not published, and one in D,
composed about 1904 and published by 1908.[131]

A more successful composer at one time, the concert pianist and
conductor **Jakab Gyula Major** (1858–1925) left two sonatinas and two
sonatas for Vn & P and five sonatinas and two sonatas for P solo, all
composed and published between about 1882 and 1909.[132] The first
of Major's two solo sonatas, Op. 35 in A (1896), is another "Hungarian
Sonata." This and his later solo sonata, Op. 68 in e/E (1909; in 3
mvts., F-M-F), evince good training under Volkmann and Erkel but
still cling to the Mendelssohn idiom except for more octave writing,
and seem sterile in their trite ideas, conventional harmony, and excessive motivic reiterations. A distinguished writer and teacher at both
the Fodor Conservatory and the Academy in Budapest, **Albert Síklos**

131. HOFMEISTER 1904–8, 784 (not in the annual vols.). Cf. GROVE VIII 268–69 (J. S.
Weissmann).

132. Cf. GROVE V 524–26 (J. S. Weissmann); MGG VIII 1536–38 (J. Ujfalussy);
Altmann/KAMMERMUSIK 214 and 260 (Op. 57 in g alternatively for Vc & P).

(1878–1942) remained a traditionalist, too, in his compositions, in spite of a declared interest in some newer Hungarian idiom that would be neither German nor French in origin, and in spite of such incipient anti-Romantics within his sphere as the young Bartók and Kodály.[133] Three of Síklos's four sonatas have remained unpublished, including one each for P solo (1898; in B♭), Vn & P (1902; in A♭), and Vc & P (before 1910; in f). The fourth, for Hn & P, was composed and published in Budapest in 1920.[134]

Among further sonatas for P & Vn, one by a winner of the "Liszt prize" and friend of Liszt in the early 1880's, **János Végh** (1845–1918), was published in Budapest about 1900.[135] Another, Op. 26 in D, by the blind, pro-Hungarian pianist and teacher **Attila Horváth** (1862–1920), was published in 1902.[136] Still another, a conservative, solid, Brahmsian work in e (3 mvts., F-Sc-F), was published in 1902, being the work of **Hans Koessler** (1853–1926). Koessler was the German-born organist who, after study with Rheinberger in Munich and some choir conducting in Köln, moved to Budapest, eventually succeeding Volkmann and becoming one of the teachers of Dohnányi, Bartok, and Kodály.[137]

Probably the best known—or, rather, least forgotten—of all these sonatas from Hungary are the two full-blooded, unabashedly Romantic examples by the important, late-Romantic composer, pianist, conductor, and teacher **Ernst (Ernö) von Dohnányi** (1877–1960).[138] Dohnányi had already done much before he wrote his first duo sonata. He had written early "pianoforte sonatas" and other boyhood works (by the age of 16),[139] won Brahms's support (in 1896?) for his piano

133. Cf. GROVE VIII 788–90 (J. S. Weissmann); MGG XII 690–91 (J. Ujfalussy).

134. The only reference to its pub. known here is that in MGG XII 690.

135. Cf. Riemann/LEXIKON II 1915; Szabolcsi/UNGARISCHEN 85; Altmann/KAMMER-MUSIK 230; Keresztury/MAGYAR 238 (facs. of printed cover).

136. Cf. Riemann/LEXIKON I 784; Szabolcsi/UNGARISCHEN 82; Altmann/KAMMER-MUSIK 209.

137. Cf. GROVE IV 813 (J. S. Weissmann), with a listing, also, of a (MS?) Son. for Vc & P, by Koessler; MGG VII 1390–92 (R. Sietz); Cobbett/CHAMBER II 68 (W. Altmann); MW XXXIV (1903) 40–41 (E. Segnitz praising the force, intensity, and beauty of Son. in e).

138. Cf. GROVE II 722–23 (J. A. Fuller-Maitland & E. Blom); MGG III 624–27 (E. Haraszti). A full study of the man and his music has yet to appear. Rueth/DOHNÁNYI is a documentary M.A. thesis on his last 11 years (1949–60, at Florida State University in Tallahassee), introduced by a helpful chapter (pp. 11–24) on his life up to then; supplemented by an abbreviated cat. of works (pp. 205–12), a bibliography (almost entirely of recent articles in English), and other aids; and fortified (cf. pp. 4–7) by access to an as yet unpub. biography up to 1953 that has been prepared by his widow Ilona (Helen). Warm thanks are owing to Mr. James F. Jones, former Music Cataloger and Music Librarian at Florida State University, for further information on the Dohnányi materials.

139. GROVE II 722.

Quintet in c, Op. 1 (1895), even before graduating from the Budapest Academy (in 1897), done a little postgraduate piano study with the Brahms disciple Eugen d'Albert (in 1897; ssв XI), embarked on a brilliant wide-ranging concert career (though not reaching the United States until late 1900),[140] and composed several more large-scale works. His first duo is Op. 8 in b♭/B♭, for Vc & P, composed in 1899, originally played by the composer and Ludwig Lebell (its dedicatee) in London that same year,[141] and first published by B. Schott in Mainz in 1903. The other duo is Op. 21 in c♯, for P & Vn, composed in 1912, originally played by the composer and Karl Klingler in Berlin that same year,[142] and first published a year later by Simrock in Bonn.

Both of Dohnányi's sonatas are decidedly Brahmsian in flavor and method. Even Op. 21 still preceded by 13–14 years his more independent and most characteristic, successful works, especially the "Variations on a Nursery Song" and the *Ruralia hungarica* in several settings. Between the two sonatas, Op. 8 is preferred here as the more spontaneous, thematically significant work.[143] It is a kind of exaggeration of Brahms's duo sonatas, not in length but in scope of emotions and in range of styles, whether richness and mellowness of sonority, surprise and color of harmony, or sweep and breadth of melody (Ex. 116). In these last respects, Op. 8 brings to mind Dohnányi's *Four Rhapsodies* for P solo, Op. 11, which first appeared two years later (1905). It treats the four-movement cycle freshly, with a first movement in a surging "sonata form" that recapitulates in the tonic major; a deft, rhythmically compelling "Scherzo" and "Trio" in the minor submediant key (g); a cursive, lyrical, harmonically opulent "Adagio non troppo" in the raised subdominant key (E), leading directly, like an introduction, into the finale; and the finale itself, which is a "Tema con Variazioni" that returns in its several variations to main ideas from the previous movements (as had been done in Brahms's Quartet in the same key, Op. 67/iv). Op. 21 is also a warm, impassioned work, even more Brahmsian albeit rather more controlled, calculated, and concentrated, in its themes as well as its textures and forms. It is constructed in three thematically interrelated movements, with a first

140. Rueth/DOHNÁNYI 13–14, contrary to "1898–99" in previous reports.
141. Cf. Rueth/DOHNÁNYI 205, 242 (recording).
142. Cf. Rueth/DOHNÁNYI 205, 214, and 220 (2 late U.S. performances), 242 (recording).
143. The 2 sons. are described enthusiastically in D. F. Tovey's article in Cobbett/CHAMBER I 327–31. Op. 8 is reviewed by H. Schlemüller in DM III/3 (1903–4) 373 as "one of the most important sonatas since Brahms," and Op. 21 by W. Altmann in DM XII/4 (1912–13) 175–76 as a convincing, unlabored example of how to create a whole work out of a single idea.

Ex. 116. From the second theme in the first movement of
Ernst von Dohnányi's Sonata in bb/Bb, Op. 8 (after the original
B. Schott ed.).

movement in a tight "sonata form" that rarely loses sight of its opening
theme; a second movement, in the subdominant key, that alternates a
songful section in duple meter with a scherzando section in triple
meter, somewhat in the manner of Brahms's Op. 100/ii; and a finale,
"Vivace assai," in which a free rondo culminates in a return to the
sonata's opening and an ending of quiet, peaceful resignation.

Other sonatas for P & Vn contemporary with Dohnányi's include
Op. 3 in D (1906), reportedly an ingratiating, traditional work in three
movements, by a violin student of Hubay in Budapest, **Petar Stojanović**
(1877–1957);[144] Op. 10 in a (1908), welcomed as a colorful, brilliant,
large-scale work, and No. 2 in f♯ (1930; unpub.?), as well as a "Sonata
appassionata," Op. 13 for P solo (unpub.?), by the pianist and teacher
Ákos Buttkay (1871–1935);[145] a "Concert Sonata in Hungarian Style"
(composed in 1906 and pub. in 1909), by the cosmopolitan pianist
Theodor Szántó (1877–1934), who had studied with R. Fuchs, H. Koessler, and Busoni, among others;[146] and Opp. 9 in D (1912) and 11 in f♯

144. DM VI/4 (1906–7) 372 (W. Altmann). Cf. MGG XII 1391–92 (S. Djurić-Klajn).
145. DM VIII/2 (1908–9) 44 (W. Altmann). Cf. GROVE I 1051–52 (J. S. Weissmann).
146. Cf. MGG XIII 20–21 (F. Bónis); Altmann/KAMMERMUSIK 229.

(1918, not 1919) by the versatile pianist, teacher, and multi-prize-winning composer **Leo Weiner** (1885–1960).[147] Weiner's sonatas are both adroit, lyrical, emotionally charged works in large, thematically interrelated cycles (Op. 21/iv begins with kaleidoscopic references to the earlier mvts., as in the finale of Beethoven's Ninth Symphony). The structural methods of Brahms and, especially, the idiom of Franck are still in evidence.

Note may also be taken here of a "founder of the Rumanian instrumental school," **George Stephănescu** (1843–1925) in Bucharest, who composed two conventional (unpub.?) sonatas in 1863, one for Vc & P and one for P solo.[148]

147. Cf. mgg XIV 402–7 (F. Bónis); Szabolcsi/UNGARISCHEN 86.
148. mgg XII 1263–64 (V. Tomescu).

Chapter XVIII

Composers in Russia

From the Classic-Romantic Overlap to about 1850 (Aliabiev)

Along with the introductory remarks in the preceding chapter, a few, more specific ones are needed here. As in Poland and Hungary there was little concern with the sonata in Russia during the first half of the 19th century.[1] The relatively few examples that did originate there during the overlap of the Classic and Romantic eras were largely the contributions of visitors-in-residence—for example, J. W. Hässler (SCE 579–81),[2] Cimarosa (SCE 302–4), Sarti (SCE 229–31), Viotti (SCE 675–78), Field (SSB XIV), and a Pole who had studied with Albrechtsberger in Vienna, G. Tepper von Ferguson.[3] Of contributions by their native Russian contemporaries, mention can be made here only of some obscure sonatas, explored but little, if at all, including several for strings by I. E. Khandochkine (SCE 779);[4] five for keyboard solo (and three for keyboard + Vn, now lost) among the MSS left in the 1780's by Galuppi's pupil, the church and opera composer **Dmitri Stepanovitch**

---

1. Surveys that have provided helpful background material here are Asaf'ev/RUSSIAN 134–268 (especially 209–55); MGG XI 1156–68 (K. Laux); Cobbett/CHAMBER II 312–19 (N. Findeisen, L. Sabaneiev, & W. W. Cobbett); Seaman/RUSSIAN 114–27; and the studies of L. N. Raaben and of A. D. Alekseev (Alekseev/FORTEPIANNAIA) as partly trans., paraphrased, or summarized in Seaman/AMATEUR, Seaman/CHAMBER, and Seaman/PIANO. Warm thanks are owing to Miss Erna F. Novikova of the State Gnesin Musical Pedagogical Institute in Moscow for valued scores and information by correspondence, and for her trans. and supplementing of a valued, detailed critique of this chap. (Alekseev & Novikova) prepared by Professor A. D. Alekseev, author of Alekseev/FORTEPIANNAIA and of a new "History of Pianoforte Art" (Moscow, 1967; in Russian), among other studies.

2. Seaman/CHAMBER 329 mentions 3 Sons. by Hässler for P & Vn & Vc, pub. in 1799.

3. His *Grande Sonate* in c, Op. 8 (St. Petersburg, 1802), for P solo—a 4-mvt. work (F-M-Mi-Ro) with hints of Beethoven's Op. 13—is reprinted in Smart/EIGHTEENTH-m 106, with preface on p. 2.

4. Cf. Asaf'ev/RUSSIAN 140, 141, 306 (under "Handoshkin"); Seaman/RUSSIAN 82–83.

Bortniansky (1751–1825);[5] a Piano Sonata in d (F-S-M; [pub.?] 1794) with variations in the finale on a Russian folk theme, by the violinist **Lev Stepanovich Gurilëv** (1770–1844);[6] some sonatas for P & Vn, including one published in 1795 by Gerstenberg in St. Petersburg, by the esteemed violinist **(August) Ferdinand Titz** (**Tietz**; 1742–1810);[7] and a Sonata for Vc & P (1802) as well as some folklike sonatas for P solo, including a lost "Grand Sonata on Russian Themes" published in 1806, by **Ivan Prach** (**Johann Gottfried Pratsch**; ?–1818).[8]

Although the sonata happens not to have taken any firm hold in early 19th-century Russia, society under the successive czarist regimes, especially in St. Petersburg (now Leningrad) was becoming increasingly favorable to the cultivation of such music. Even the institution of serfdom, which bound not a few musicians and continued right through the retreat of Napoleon in 1812–13, the "Decembrist Uprising" of 1825, and the Crimean War in 1854–56, seems not to have blocked musical progress.[9] From the turn of the century at least the vocal music of Haydn, Mozart, and Beethoven, as well as nearly all their important contemporaries, began to be played.[10] Orchestral and chamber groups were formed, both professional and amateur, and concert series, both private and public, were instituted by new societies and schools.[11] At the same time, the number, proportion, and caliber of native composers increased. Their efforts as regards instrumental music were devoted at first to transcriptions of, and variations on, the popular folk, national, and opera songs and dances, then to suites, symphonies, quartets, and the infrequent sonatas.[12] As in other outlying regions of the sonata the German influence was strong, whether it was accepted or resisted in favor of nationalistic elements.

Mikhail Ivanovitch Glinka (1804–57) was one who did turn to the sonata in this period, although what he left is only the MS of an

5. Cf. Seaman/CHAMBER 330, with reference to N. F. Findeisen's study of Bortniansky; Seaman/PIANO 179, with ex. from a Son. in F purportedly showing Ukrainian folk influences; Alekseev/FORTEPIANNAIA 24–26, with further exx.; Asaf'ev/RUSSIAN 140 (naming clavichord as the intended instrument), 141; also, GROVE I 827 (A. Loewenberg).

6. Cf. Seaman/PIANO 180–82, including reference to a mod. ed.; Alekseev/FORTEPIANNAIA 33–34, with ex. from first mvt.; VODARSKY-SHIRAEFF 52; Alekseev & Novikova.

7. Cf. Seaman/CHAMBER 328–29; MGG XIII 411 (A. Weinmann).

8. Cf. Seaman/PIANO 179 fn.; Alekseev/FORTEPIANNAIA 26, with ex. from slow mvt. of Son. in C. (pub. in 1887); MGG X 1601–2 (G. Waldmann); Alekseev & Novikova.

9. Cf. Asaf'ev/RUSSIAN 137–38.

10. Cf. Asaf'ev/RUSSIAN 136–37.

11. Cf. Seaman/AMATEUR and Seaman/CHAMBER.

12. Cf. Asaf'ev/RUSSIAN 137–40.

"Allegro" and an incomplete "Larghetto ma non troppo" of a projected
Sonata in d, for P & Va.[13] In his own words,

> It was about this time [1825] that I wrote the first allegro of a D minor
> sonata for piano and viola; this composition was more tightly constructed
> than the others, and I performed it with Böhm and [with] Liglya, in the
> latter instance playing the viola myself. I wrote the adagio later [1828], but
> did not get around to the rondo (I recently used its Russian-style motif in
> a children's polka). . . . I stayed with Melgunov [in Moscow in 1828] only
> until May 9 (his name day), but in those few days I wrote the adagio (B [B♭]
> Major) for the D minor *Sonata* and I recall that I had some fairly clever
> counterpoint in this number.[14]

Glinka's Sonata is worth noting mainly because it was composed not
only by the future leader of Russian national opera but by the man
with whom truly Russian music is said to begin. However, its music is
not yet more than that of a talented student still writing in a post-
Mozartean idiom complete with feminine endings, chromatic melody,
and late-Classic accompaniments. Even so, its appropriate scoring,
which could be expected from a good pianist who could also play the
violin, its good counterpoint, as claimed by Glinka himself, and some
freshness in its themes and figures all suggest more promise for "absolute" chamber music, still five to eight years before his "serious"
training with S. W. Dehn in Berlin (1833–34), than most writers have
seen in his early instrumental works.[15]

Of more musical substance is the Sonata in e, for P & Vn, left in MS
(*ca.* 1827?), among other pioneer chamber works of significance, by the
talented Moscow composer **Alexander Alexandrovitch Aliabiev** (1787–
1851).[16] In three movements, it proves to be another post-Mozartean
work, more broadly conceived but on a par otherwise with, say,
Kuhlau's flute sonatas (ssв XV) in general idiom and style, including
quality and types of themes, textural, especially contrapuntal, interest,
equal responsibility of the two parts, conservative harmony, and pat

13. Mod. eds. appeared in 1932 (Altman/KAMMERMUSIK 247) and 1958 (Glinka/
WORKS-m IV 3; with preface, in Russian). Cf. MGG V 261–67 (G. Abraham); Seaman/
RUSSIAN 191–92.

14. Glinka/MEMOIRS 32, 41–42.

15. E.g., cf. Cobbett/CHAMBER I 472–73 (L. Sabaneiev).

16. Mod. ed.: State Music Pub. in Moscow, 1951. It is discussed, with an ex.
from the opening of each mvt., in Seaman/CHAMBER 331 and 335–36. Cf. BAKER 23
and Suppl. 3. I am indebted to Miss Carol Greene at the University of Indiana
for valued help with Aliabiev, including copies of pertinent sections from L. N.
Raaben's book on Russian instrumental ensemble music (Moscow, 1961; pp. 94–
96 as trans. by M. H. Brown) and from her own forthcoming study of Aliabiev's
chamber music, as well as a copy of Aliabiev's Son. in A♭, for P solo. Dobrokhotov/
ALIABIEV is a new book (in Russian) on the man and his music, with many exx.
(Moscow, 1966).

skill. The first movement, "Allegro con brio," is a well-balanced "sonata form." The second movement, "Adagio cantabile," is an A-B-A design based on expressive, nicely drawn lines. And the finale is a vivacious rondo design, marked "Allegretto scherzando." Aliabiev also left in MS a one-movement Sonata in A♭, for P solo.[17] This is a different sort of work, in "sonata form" but without the associated dynamism or tensions. The themes are all lyrical, without contrast, development, or integration in the passagework. But the themes are attractive, and the scoring for piano is neat and clear. The style gives support to the possibility that Aliabiev studied with Field while the latter was in Moscow.[18]

Among others who produced sonatas before 1850, the German contrabassist and pianist **Ludwig (Louis) Schuberth** (1806–50) was in Riga and Königsberg (now Kaliningrad) while his four or more published sonatas appeared (*ca.* 1835–45) and before he moved to St. Petersburg.[19] A pupil of Weber and a brief obstacle to Wagner's career,[20] Schuberth fared poorly in two reviews that Schumann wrote in 1837.[21] One review heaped recondite sarcasm and scorn on *Souvenir à Beethoven: Grande Fantaisie en forme d'une sonate,* Op. 30, for P solo, finding only desecration of the "honored" master. The other review deplored his haste and superficial talent in *Sonate* ("L'Espérance"), Op. 25 in C, for P solo. Yet Wagner did speak of Schuberth as "a very capable musician." [22] Schuberth's other published sonatas include Op. 36 in B♭, for P-duet, and some sonatinas for P & Vn, Op. 37.[23]

The pianist **Iosif Iosifovitch Genishta** (1795–1853), a pupil of both Hässler and Field and an early performer of Beethoven, left at least four sonatas, published between about 1837 and 1847—two each for P solo and for P & Vc.[24] Schumann reviewed one of each with pleasure, in 1837 and 1841,[25] finding Op. 7 in A ("Grand Sonate" for P & Vc-or-Vn) to be a transparent, lyrical "musical still life" appropriate

---

17. Mod. ed.: p. 85 in an anth. of Russian piano music ed. by A. Natanson & A. A. Nikolayev (Moscow, 1956).

18. Perhaps around 1811, according to information in B. Dobrokhotov's book on Aliabiev as supplied by Miss Greene. Aliabiev's piano Quintet in E♭, recorded on Westminster XWN 18679, is another post-Mozartean work.

19. Cf. MGG XII 186–88 (K. Stephenson); GROVE VII 593 (W. B. Squire).

20. Cf. Newman/WAGNER I 198, 201, 212–13.

21. Schumann/SCHRIFTEN I 302–3, 307. Cf. HOFMEISTER 1834–38, p. 130.

22. MGG XII 187.

23. Cf. Altmann/KAMMERMUSIK 226; HOFMEISTER 1844–51, p. 78.

24. Cf. Alekseev/FORTEPIANNAIA 74–76, with 2 exx. from Op. 9 in f; Seaman/PIANO 192, with ex.; HOFMEISTER 1834–38, p. 129, and 1844–51, pp. 115 and 49; PAZDÍREK VI 156.

25. Schumann/SCHRIFTEN I 275 and 277, II 11–12. Nikolaiev/TCHAIKOVSKY 195 emphasizes the developed pianism, lyricism, and strong finales in Genishta's sons.

for cello rather than violin, and Op. 9 in f/F (P solo) to be similarly skillful and transparent, with the first two of the three movements (F-S-VF) being "very well rounded" and the finale the best of all, suggesting the influence of Beethoven's Op. 57 (iii?). Genishta's other two sonatas are Opp. 12 in C for P solo and 13 in D for P & Vc. Uninvestigated are at least three sonatas for P solo, published between about 1844 and 1852, by the conductor and valued friend of Wagner, **Louis Alexander Balthasar Schindelmeisser** (1811–64), who moved about so much he can only be put where he was born, Königsberg.[26] Schindelmeisser's sonatas are Opp. 8 in F, entitled "Sonate héroique," 23 in g, and 40 (or 31? or both?) in D.

*From about 1850 to 1910 (A. Rubinstein, Tchaikovsky,
Rachmaninoff, Medtner, Liapunov)*

Although a number of important musicians continued to show little or no interest in composing sonatas during the later Romantic Era in Russia—including Dargomyzhsky, Borodin, Rimsky-Korsakov, Taneyev, Arensky, and Glière—the cultivation of the sonata advanced greatly during that time. The conservatories founded in St. Petersburg by Anton Rubinstein in 1862 and in Moscow by his brother Nicholas in 1866 proved to be fruitful breeding grounds. One of the pivotal Romantics in musical Russia, one of the greatest pianists of the later 19th century, and, more specifically here, one of the most notable Romantic performers of piano sonatas (especially Beethoven's), was **Anton Grigorievitch Rubinstein** (1829–94). Rubinstein was also a major force in music education, a promoter of past music, an active conductor, and a prolific, wide-ranging, once successful composer.[27] Among nearly 150 publications, chiefly in Germany, there are 11 sonatas by Rubinstein. These originally appeared between 1855 and 1878, none with special titles. For P solo there are Opp. 12 in e (1855), 20 in c (1855), 41 in F (1857), and 100 in a (1878). For Vn & P there are Opp. 13 in G (1856), 19 in a (1855), and 98 in b (1878). For Vc & P there are Opp. 18 in D (1855) and 39 in G (1857). For Va & P there is Op. 49 in f (1857), and for P-duet Op. 89 in D (1871).[28]

26. Cf. MGG XI 1726–28 (K. Rönnau); HOFMEISTER 1844–51, p. 153 and 1852–59, p. 207; PAZDÍREK XII 218.

27. Cf. GROVE VII 295–97 (author unknown according to p. 298 fn., but given as F. Corder in Maclean/RUBINSTEIN 131) and Suppl. 383, with undated list of works; MGG XI 1043–47 (G. Waldmann), with further bibl.; Rubinstein/ERINNERUNGEN, especially pp. 15–17, 21–22, 25, 27, 31, 33–34, 50–51, 66–68, 105–120 (including the itemized programs of his celebrated "seven historical concerts"); Maclean/RUBINSTEIN, with bibliographic information (pp. 143 and 146–47).

28. The foregoing dates derive from Altmann/KAMMERMUSIK and the cumulative

For a man who contributed so much to music education in Russia,[29] Rubinstein showed little interest in furthering Russian nationalism, least of all in his entirely unprogrammatic sonatas. In fact, after coming under Chopin's and Liszt's influence in Paris, after finishing his training under Dehn and others in Berlin, after speaking and writing in German much of the time, and after travelling and/or living in several other European centers and in the United States, he made clear that he saw himself as a cosmopolitan.[30] Furthermore, he recognized and defended himself as a conservative in musical styles:[31]

It is remarkable how criticism operates more strictly and harshly in music than in the other arts—for example, when Raphael leans upon Perugino, Leonardo, or Fra Bartolommeo before he arrives at his own style, or a present-day painter on Meissonier or Lenbach, then it [the derivation] is merely noted—but the minute a musician leans in his style upon Schumann, Chopin, Mendelssohn, Wagner, [or] Liszt, he is harshly reproached for it [the derivation] and it is cited as [evidence for] a lack of originality—which [inequity] leads the [musical] young to the quest for originality [for its own sake], and how often to the unbeautiful!

Together, Rubinstein's cosmopolitanism and conservatism help to explain the neutralism or what might be called excessive universalism of his style. And that style probably explains the extinction of his sonatas more than a half-century ago, beyond reasonable hope of revival. Yet the sonatas, including some duos regarded as his best chamber music,[32] have numerous pages of real musical distinction and interest (as might be expected from the composer of three works still heard on occasion, piano Concerto 4 in d, "Melody in F," and *Kammenoi Ostrow*). In any case, these sonatas must have appealed to public tastes, for during his later years at least certain of the duos were performed almost as often and widely as Brahms's, Rheinberger's, Raff's, or Grieg's most successful sonatas.[33]

---

and annual vols. of HOFMEISTER. The helpful lists of A. Rubinstein's works compiled by O. E. Albrecht in Bowen/RUBINSTEIN 375–90 are not dated.

29. Cf. Maclean/RUBINSTEIN 141–42.

30. Rubinstein/GEDANKENKORB 86. Preferring the term internationalist, Alekseev & Novikova remark that Rubinstein did exhibit national and folk interest in some (other) of his compositions.

31. Trans. from Rubinstein/GEDANKENKORB 69.

32. Cf. Cobbett/CHAMBER II 309–11 (L. Sabaneiev & W. W. Cobbett); Nikolaiev/ TCHAIKOVSKY 196 (calling Rubinstein's sons. Russia's best mid-19th-c. instrumental music). The 3 Vn sons. are described, with 11 exx., in Shand/VIOLIN 193–99.

33. Thus, for duo performances during the 15 years 1871–86 cf., on Op. 13: MT XV (1871) 319 (or Op. 19? London), NZM LXXII/2 (1876) 485 (Hildesheim and Leipzig) and LXXIII/1 (1877) 140 (Leipzig) and 193 (Prague), MT XVIII (1878) 369 (London) and XX (1879) 329 (Birmingham) and XXIV (1883) 324 (London); on Op. 18: MT XV (1871) 109 (London), NZM LXXII/1 (1876) 203 (Kiev) and LXXII/

Rubinstein's sonatas were not innovational in their day, in the sense of new language or form. Nothing more innovative happens than the quotation of themes from the first two of the three violin sonatas at the start of the last. Otherwise, they seldom depart from the three- and four-movement cycles and their respective designs as standardized by then. Yet within their own range they do reveal fairly steady advances from the more imitative and formalistic Op. 12 to the more independent and free Op. 100. In an extended, increasingly laudatory article of 1858 on all eight sonatas published by then, one "C. Petersen" emphasized this creative evolution.[34] He viewed Op. 12 as being Beethovian and somewhat scholastic, Op. 13 as "almost slavishly" Mendelssohnian, both Opp. 18 and 19 as still related to but freer of the same models and distinctive in scoring, both Opp. 20 and 49 as Schumannesque in their more imaginative, poetic ideas and treatment, and Op. 39 as a sequel to Op. 18 except for its added, spirited "Scherzo." Quoting twenty-six examples in all, Petersen singled out Op. 41 as a masterwork and its first movement, "Allegro risoluto con fuoco," as a "consummation" of "sonata form" since Beethoven, notable for its thematic architecture, transformations, and recombinations. He characterized the second movement, an "Allegretto con moto" in A-B-A design, as gloomy and more repressed; the third movement, a similarly tripartite "Andante," as filled with "grief, lamentation, and longing"; and the finale, an "Allegro vivace" in "sonata form" beginning in the tonic minor mode, as freely but firmly organized and triumphant in its ending.

Of course, from our later vantage point, later by more than a century, we can look not only for derivations but for anticipations—anticipations of works not yet born when Petersen wrote on Rubinstein's sonatas. Thus, in key, meter, texture, parts of the tonal schemes, and certain figures or ideas, the first movements of Rubinstein's Opp. 12 and 13 anticipate those of Grieg's Op. 7 and Brahms's Op. 78,

2 (1876) 475 (Leipzig) and LXXIII/1 (1877) 138 (Bremen), MT XVII (1877) 697 (London) and XX (1878–79) 23, 81, and 646 (all London) and XXII (1880–81) 40 (Birmingham) and 652 (London) and XXIII (1882) 328 (Birmingham) and XXIV (1883) 193 (London) and XXV (1884) 147 and 338 (both London); on Op. 19: NZM LXXII/1 (1876) 57–58 (Strasbourg) and 136 (Dresden) and LXXII/2 454 (Mainz) and LXXIII/1 (1877) 53 (Vienna) and 116 (Graz), SMZ XVII (1877) 39 (Geneva), MT XXI (1880) 84 (London); on Op. 39: NZM LXXII/1 (1876) 224 (Moscow) and LXXIII/1 (1877) 192 (Copenhagen), MT XXI (1880) 239 (London) and XXIV (1883) 346 (or Op. 13? Salisbury); Op. 49: MT XXI (1880) 303 (Baden-Baden); plus numerous book references, such as that in Bowen/RUBINSTEIN 221 on the playing of Op. 89 in St. Petersburg in 1870 by the 2 brothers, Anton and Nicholas, or Hanslick/WIEN II 135 (Op. 18 in 1857) and 187 (Op. 49 in 1859; negative reaction); plus numerous references in which the exact son. is not specified.
34. NZM XLIX (1858) 137–38, 143–44, 151–54, 163–66.

Ex. 117. From the opening of Anton Grigorievitch Rubinstein's Sonata in f, Op. 49 (after an ed. of 1960 by State Music
Publishers in Moscow).

respectively (pub. 10 and 24 years later). To be sure, Rubinstein's
early works lack the force and directness of Grieg's early work or
Brahms's more mature work, especially as regards melody. But some of
that force and directness did develop in the course of the style evolution just described, especially in the two works with middle opus
numbers written concurrently in 1855,[35] one being the Op. 41 for **P**
solo that was rightly singled out by Petersen and the other being Op.
49, Rubinstein's one contribution to viola literature (Ex. 117).

Unfortunately, although Rubinstein's later works continued to
evolve stylistically, they show a decline in their quality of workmanship, especially in details of texture and keyboard scoring, to the point
where most present-day performers would be likely to reject them on
that account alone. To be sure, in his previous sonatas Rubinstein had
never excelled in harmony or polyphony, and in his previous scoring
for keyboard he can merely be said at best to have scored idiomatically,
and hardly with the resourcefulness to be expected from so great a
pianist. But now, at worst and by the time of his last sonata, Op. 100

35. Cf. Rubinstein's letter of June 25, 1855, to Liszt, as trans. in the preface to
the Moscow reprint of Op. 49 in 1960. Barenboim/RUBINSTEIN 129 attributes to
Rubinstein a combination of the lyric (under Glinka's influence) and the dramatic
heroic.

for P solo, he was writing in a routine, pasty fashion that could only discourage performers. In the course of those later works critical opinion began to waver and sometimes turn against him correspondingly.[36]

Like Glinka before him, the important programmatist and contributor to Russian national opera, **Modest Petrovitch Mussorgsky** (1839–81), also tried his hand at the sonata only in his student days and without any example being published in his lifetime.[37] Exposed especially to Beethoven and Schumann and taught from his eighteenth year by the two-year-older Balakirev,[38] this second youngest of the "mighty five" actually wrote at least four sonatas in the four years from 1858 to 1862, only one of which has survived. All four were for piano and all but one (in f♯) figure among the thirty-five piano works credited to Mussorgsky in his collected works.[39] Three of them, in E♭ (1858), f♯ (1858), and D (1862), all for P solo, were lost or destroyed.[40] The remaining example is an incomplete, projected four-movement Sonata in C, for P-duet, composed in 1860 [41] and published at least twice in the present century.[42] Planned to consist of an "Allegro assai" in C, an "Andante" in D♭, a "Scherzo" in F, and an "Allegro con brio" in C, this work actually only contains the first movement and a "Scherzo" in c. It reads like the convenient reduction that its subtitle in the MS suggests, "A symphonic exercise for orchestra." [43] But it does not lack tiny hints of the freshness of melody and key contrast that were to distinguish *Boris Godunov* and *Pictures at an Exhibition*. The first movement concentrates on a single motive—too greatly for too long, in fact—suggesting a cursive prelude more than any hierarchic

36. In sмw XXXV (1877) 1041–42 Op. 98 is praised as a huge, late-Beethovian, instrumental drama, free but controlled. In sмw XXXVI (1878) 945–46 Op. 100 is praised for its youthful freshness; but in MMR VIII (1878) 27–28 it is (more justly) called an "*improvisata*" hastily done, with a finale that is a "dreary wilderness." Probably this Op. 100 was meant when a writer said in MT LXIV (1923) 480 that "the best Sonata of Rubinstein is ruined by the set of variations [3d mvt.?] which, good enough in themselves, contrive utterly to spoil the proportions of the work."

37.   MUSORGSKY READER, Riesemann/MOUSSORGSKY, and Calvocoressi/MUSSORGSKY supply the factual information used in this paragraph.

38. Cf. MUSORGSKY READER 4–6.

39. Musorgsky/WERKE-m VIII; from this vol. comes the list of piano works in MUSORGSKY READER 434–37.

40. Cf. MUSORGSKY READER 6, 9, 11 (with 3 incipits from Son. in E♭, 12, 40–41; pp. 40–41 seem to contradict the possible identification of Son. in D with the "andante" and "allegro finale" also mentioned (as suggested in Riesemann/MOUSSORGSKY 69).

41. Cf. MUSORGSKY READER 25, 30, 33, 34.

42. Musorgsky/WERKE-m VIII no. 9; Balogh/DUETS-m 104.

43. If the symphony was to be in D, the keys specified in MUSORGSKY READER 30 and 435 are not equivalents by transposition. Cf., also, Riesemann/MOUSSORGSKY 42–43; Calvocoressi/MUSSORGSKY 11, 167–70 (with exx.).

sonata design. Except for its lyrical trio section in 3/4 meter, the "Scherzo," in 2/4 meter, is a gay hopak in style.

Pleasing conservative styles and a degree of virtuosity are ascribed to four published sonatas by the German-born and -trained organist in St. Petersburg, **Heinrich Franz Daniel Stiehl** (1829–86). These include a prize-winning work, Op. 37 in a, for P & Vc (1861);[44] Op. 38 in D, for P solo (1863); a "Fantasia quasi sonata" in Bb, Op. 68, also for P solo (1876); and Op. 100 in Bb, for P & Vn (1873).[45] Talent without sufficient melodic distinction or structural control was seen in a Sonata in b, Op. 2, for P & Vc, composed (and pub. in 1863) during his Leipzig training by an eventual director of the St. Petersburg Conservatory, **Mikhail Asanchevsky** (1838–81).[46] Not explored in the present day are several sonatas for P solo, P & Vn, and P & Vc by the successful violinist and nationalist **Nikolai Jakovlevitch Afanassiev** (1821 or 1820–98), reportedly left about the same period but apparently not published.[47]

Among works produced around the same time in Königsberg should be mentioned the approximately fifteen sets or single issues of pedagogic sonatinas for P solo or P-duet by the German-born pianist, teacher, and writer on music **(Christian) Louis (Heinrich) Köhler** (1820–86). Originally published between about 1855 and 1876 (starting at Op. 33 and ending at Op. 285), these generally dry, outmoded, two-movement works appear to have won more endorsement in pedagogic than in reviewers' circles.[48] Although largely self-taught, the once esteemed pianist and composer **Adolf Jensen** (1837–79) did study briefly with Köhler, and moved variously in the circles of Gade, Hartmann, Liszt, Bülow, Wagner, Rubinstein, Clara Schumann, and Brahms![49] (Adolf was the brother of the violinist **Gustav Jensen** [1843–95] in Köln, himself the composer of a Son. in G, Op. 14, pub. in 1883, and 2 well regarded sons. for P & Vc, Op. 12 in g, a prize-winning work pub. in 1882, and Op. 26 in a, pub. in 1889.[50]) Adolf's one sonata,

44. Op. 37 is reviewed favorably in NZM LX (1864) 112. Cf. MGG XII 1297–98 (G. Karstädt).

45. The pub. dates come from the annual vols. of HOFMEISTER.

46. NZM LIX (1863) 12. Cf. GROVE I 238–39 (E. Dannreuther).

47. Alekseev & Novikova. Cf. GROVE I 65–66 (M. Montagu-Nathan).

48. E.g., cf. NZM LII (1860) 165–66 (collective negative view), LX/2 (1864) 337 (P-duet), LXVIII/1 (1872) 87 ("Sonaten-Studien"), LXIX/2 (1873) 294 (more favorable, ranking Köhler with Clementi and Kuhlau); MMR II (1872) 135 (preferring Clementi and Kuhlau). Cf., also MGG VII 1321–23 (E. Kroll).

49. Cf. MGG VII 1–5 (R. Sietz), with undated list of works and further bibliography.

50. Cf. BAKER 781; Altmann/KAMMERMUSIK 209, 258; Cobbett/CHAMBER II 35 (R. Felber, on Op. 12); MMR XX (1890) 16 (on Op. 26).

Op. 25 in f♯, for P solo (ded. to Brahms, pub. in 1864), is a four-move-ment work (F-M-Sc-VF) revealing superior craftsmanship, an adequate but not distinctive sense of melody, and strong ties with the language and idiom, though not the structural methods, of Mendelssohn. Adolf's prevailing method of writing in closed periods, typically marked off by rests and often subdivided into repeated phrases and phrase members, seems more appropriate to his sectionalized inner movements than to the "sonata forms" of his outer movements, where a more dynamic, continuous, cumulative flow is essential to the broader designs.

Like Glinka and Mussorgsky, the immensely popular Russian com-poser **Peter Ilyitch Tchaikovsky** (1840–93) cannot be met squarely here because his contribution to the sonata is so incidental to, and un-representative of, his total output.[51] That contribution consists of two works, both for P solo.[52] The Sonata in c♯ was composed in 1865, the year Tchaikovsky finished his studies at the St. Petersburg Conserva-tory, under A. Rubinstein and others. It was not published until 1901, posthumously, by his lifelong friend, benefactor, and publisher P. I. Jurgenson in Moscow.[53] The work is cast in four movements (F-M-Sc-VF) that add up to 49 pages in the original edition. Particularly in the first movement, the forthrightness of the melodic material, the shapes of certain specific ideas, the rightness of the harmony, the dependence on phrase repetition in the syntax and sequence in the de-velopment of ideas, and a very few dramatic contrasts all foretoken in a small way the Tchaikovsky of the last three symphonies. But the piano writing is unresourceful and the last three movements offer neither significance nor urgency, including the "Scherzo," which Tchaikovsky adapted to better advantage when he transposed it from c♯ to c and orchestrated it in his Symphony 1.[54] In short, his Sonata in c♯ was hardly the success that its exact contemporary was by the three-year-younger Grieg (Op. 7 in e).

51. The full documentary biography Tchaikovsky/TSCHAIKOWSKY by his younger brother Modest remains the most important source, supplemented by Peter Ilyitch's diaries and correspondence (cf. M. D. Calvocoressi's summary at the end, p. 342, of R. Newmarch's extended article in GROVE V 327–50; and BAKER 1626–27).

52. A study of these 2 sons. by S. Frolowa, pub. in Russian in 1955, is listed in Kirby/KEYBOARD 487.

53. It was later assigned the posthumous op. no. 80, as in Abraham/TCHAIKOVSKY 245 and MGG XIII 864 (D. Lloyd-Jones). It is not listed in the thematic index of 1897, Jurgenson/TSCHAÏKOWSKY, nor in Tchaikovsky/TSCHAIKOWSKY I 106 and II 825, but it is reprinted in Tchaikovsky/WORKS-m LI A no. 2. It is discussed briefly in Weinstock/TCHAIKOVSKY 41, in Stein/TSCHAIKOWSKIJ 460–61 (as containing anticipa-tions of Symphony 6, "Pathétique"), and in Abraham/TCHAIKOVSKY 40, 115, and, especially, 120–21.

54. Cf. Abraham/TCHAIKOVSKY 40.

Ex. 118. From the first movement of Peter Ilyitch Tchaikovsky's Sonata in G, Op. 37 (after a D. Rahter re-ed. of 1889,
plate no. 2534, "revised by the composer").

Tchaikovsky's other piano sonata, Op. 37 [55] in G, is only slightly better known. Composed in March and April of 1878 during stays at Lake
Geneva and in the Ukraine, it was dedicated to Karl Klindworth, first
published by Jurgenson in 1879, and already introduced to the public
that same year by one of Tchaikovsky's most valued and influential
friends, Nicholas Rubinstein.[56] Tchaikovsky had written Rubinstein
after a prehearing of Op. 37 that the performance "was one of the
finest moments of my life." [57] But Op. 37 has provided no match in
quality or popularity for the violin Concerto in D, composed in the
same year, or for the piano Concerto in b♭, completed three years
earlier.[58] Its chief problem is the elephantine, ungrateful thickness of

55. Or Op. 37a, because of *The Seasons* for P solo, Op. 37b.
56. Tchaikovsky/TSCHAIKOWSKY I 484, 504, 538. Among mod. eds.: Tchaikovsky/
WORKS-m LII no. 5; Rahter in London, 1959.
57. Tchaikovsky/TSCHAIKOWSKY II 70. Op. 37 has been recorded on Monitor MC
2034 by S. Richter. According to Alekseev & Novikova, it is performed "often" today
(1968) by Soviet pianists, notably by K. N. Igumnov. The only performances of Op.
37 in America that are known here are about a dozen in the 1940's by the present
author.
58. Op. 37 is discussed briefly in Weinstock/TCHAIKOVSKY 180–81, 184, and 218
(with some further details on its origins); Stein/TSCHAIKOWSKIJ 458–59 (negative

its piano writing. Its first movement in particular progresses almost entirely from complete handful to complete handful (Ex. 118). Otherwise, although its thematic material does not come up to Tchaikovsky's outstanding best, the work does provide enough attractive ideas, enough excitement at its peaks, and enough samples of his mature, easily recognized styles and procedures that, had he rescored it for orchestra, it would have made an acceptable Tchaikovsky symphony. In any case, it flows more convincingly and can be brought back to life more successfully than his other main sonata-type venture with piano, the Trio in a, composed four years later (1882).[59]

In the first movement of Op. 37, the phrase syntax discloses Tchaikovsky's characteristically mechanical but effective asymmetry needed for a sense of flow and goal in "sonata form" and largely lacking in his earlier piano sonata.[60] A case in point is the cumulative effect of progressively shortened phrase members in our foregoing example from the development section. This example also gives some indication of the considerable modulatory activity in the movement. The second movement, "Andante non troppo quasi moderato," is a kind of rondo-variation design in which Tchaikovsky, like Verdi, reveals some of the elemental reserve strengths upon which he can draw to enhance and "pull off" essentially obvious, even insipid themes. The third movement, a "Scherzo" in A-B-A and a *perpetuum mobile,* anticipates the third movement of the *"Pathétique* Symphony" in its busyness and quick shifts of range. By contrast, the finale, a rondo and near *perpetuum mobile* marked "Allegro vivace," anticipates the finale of the same Symphony 6 and harks back to the first movement of Symphony 4 in its more lyrical, impassioned themes and their stepwise descents. The feel of a Russian folksong lies in its first subordinate, scherzando idea, in e.

In the interest of a rounded view, mentions may be inserted here of several, more obscure works. One of these, *Fantasie in Form einer*

---

view); Asaf'ev/RUSSIAN (laudatory view, calling it "the first important Russian sonata for the piano of the concert chamber type . . ."); Abraham/TCHAIKOVSKY 121–22; Dale/NINETEENTH 69, 95 (negative view).

59. Alekseev & Novikova (citing corroborative views in Nikolaiev/TCHAIKOVSKY 201, Al'shvang/TCHAIKOVSKY 567, and A. D. Alekseev's own recent "History of Pianoforte Art" (Moscow, 1967) II 269 would have preferred a higher evaluation of Op. 37 (and the Trio), emphasizing its significance as "an important landmark in the development of the Russian sonata," its combination, essential to the sonata idea, of the brooding and introspective ("lyrico-psychological") with the popular and nationalistic (or "genre"), and the similarity, as regards this combination, to the Concerto in b♭ and the Fourth Symphony.

60. Cf. his own recognition in 1878 of limitations in his control of musical form, as quoted and trans. in Abraham/STUDIES 342–43.

Sonate for P solo, Op. 5 in b♭ (pub. by Leuckart of Leipzig in 1873),
proves to be an academic yet telling work in four movements (F-M-Sc-F)
by a German pupil of Robert Franz on military duty in Königsberg,
August Friedrich Saran (1836–1922).[61] There are *Drei Sonaten* for P
solo, Op. 9 in G, C, and C (pub. in 1872), and a Sonata in F, Op. 22,
for Vn & P (ded. to Reinecke, pub. in 1893) by the Moscow organist
Johannes Bartz (1848–1933).[62] There is a "Fantaisie-Sonate pour le
piano" in A♭, published in 1877 and highly praised for its technical
and musical worth, by one **"M. de Schoulepnikow,"** otherwise un-
identifiable here.[63] There is a Sonata in g, Op. 7 for P & Vn (pub. in
1882), reviewed as pedantic and conservative, by the violinist, organist,
and teacher in St. Petersburg, **Joseph Hunke** (or **Gunke;** 1801–83).[64]
And there is a set of two well-liked Sonatinas for P solo, Op. 46 (pub.
in 1881), by the Leipzig-trained composer **Robert Schwalm** (1845–
1912) in Königsberg.[65]

One rediscovers a fresh, short, compelling, harmonically deft Op. 1
in three movements (F-Va-Sc), for P solo (pub. in 1886), by the talented
Latvian pupil of Rimsky-Korsakov and teacher at the St. Petersburg
Conservatory, **Joseph Wihtol** (or **Vitol;** 1863–1948).[66] One comes on a
Sonata for P & Vn in A, Op. 8 (pub. in 1887), a lyrical but somewhat
cerebral work that was rescored fifteen years later as an orchestral
"Sinfonietta," by another pupil of Rimsky-Korsakov and the composer
of the popular "Caucasian Sketches," **Mikhail Mikhailovitch Ippolitov-
Ivanov** (1859–1935).[67] There is a Sonata in G for P & Vn, Op. 52 (pub.
in 1892), by the influential, Czech-trained conductor in St. Petersburg,
Eduard Nápravník (1839–1916).[68] And there can be found an epigonic,
chromatic, pedagogic, but not unskillful *Sonate en trois parties,* Op. 10
in c (ded. to Arensky and pub. in 1894), as well as a Sonata in F, Op. 27
(ded. to Rachmaninoff and pub. in 1910) by the pianist and teacher at
the Moscow Conservatory, **Heinrich Albertovitch Pachulski** (1859–
1921).[69]

---

61. Cf. Riemann/LEXIKON II 1590.
62. Cf. Riemann/LEXIKON 12th ed. I 108; MW IV (1873) 157 (viewing Op. 9 as
easy enough but too recondite for teaching purposes).
63. Cf. HOFMEISTER XXVI (1877), 236; MW XII (1881) 464.
64. MW XVI (1885) 483. Cf. Riemann/LEXIKON I 678.
65. MW XXI (1890) 214. Cf. Riemann/LEXIKON II 1674.
66. Cf. MGG XIV 638 (D. Lehmann). The listing of P sons. Opp. 30, 32, 33, and
41 in GROVE IX 291 (K. D. Hurst) seems to be in error.
67. Cf. SMW XLVI (1888) 434; Cobbett/CHAMBER II 20 (L. Sabaneiev); MGG VI
1396–99 (M. Montagu-Nathan).
68. Cf. MGG IX 1262–64 (G. Waldmann); Cobbett/CHAMBER II 187 (L. Sabaneiev
& W. W. Cobbett).
69. GROVE VI 479 (E. Blom).

Somewhat more attention has been paid to the two sonatas, both for P solo, by the versatile, highly respected musician **Aleksandr Konstantinovitch Glazunov** (1865–1936).[70] Glazunov wrote both of these sonatas, Opp. 74 in b♭/B♭ and 75 in e, in 1901 while he was still teaching composition at the St. Petersburg Conservatory. He dedicated the first of them to the wife of his most important teacher, Rimsky-Korsakov.[71] His elder friend and chief publisher, M. P. Belaiev, issued them soon after, in 1901 and 1902, and, most recently, in 1960, State Music Publishers in Moscow reprinted them. Both sonatas have three movements, fast outer movements whose main ideas interrelate, first movements that adhere to the usual "sonata form," and middle movements in A-B-A designs. Op. 74/ii is an "Andante" with a richly ornamented reprise, whereas Op. 75/ii is a "Scherzo" in 9/8 meter whose steady 16th-note patterns produce a near *perpetuum mobile.* Op. 74/iii is another near *perpetuum mobile,* in which the square phrases and change to the major mode impart a carefree, light effect, making a disappointing finale after the surging lyricism of the previous two movements.[72] Op. 75/iii makes a more impressive and original finale, consisting of an energetic preludial section, a short, equally energetic fugue on the same idea, and a restful chorale-like section in the tonic major key (E) that rises to a brilliant ending.[73]

Glazunov came under the strong influence of Liszt, Wagner, and Tchaikovsky, and, perhaps because of his technical mastery though hardly his style, he was even dubbed the "Russian Brahms." Yet the most apparent model for his Op. 74, apart from the greater polyphonic interest, is Chopin's music, especially in the first movement, where the cantilena of the subordinate theme (Ex. 119) recalls that in Chopin's Op. 58/i. And the most apparent model for Op. 75, apart from the fuller chordal writing, is Mendelssohn's music, as in that impressive finale, which recalls Mendelssohn's Fugue in e in Op. 35/1 and *its* similar choral-like ending in E.

When one first encounters Glazunov's sonatas, their technical mastery, melting lyricism, and good use of the piano make an excellent impression, explaining some enthusiastic statements about them.[74] But that impression gradually palls as one discovers no relief from the

70. Cf. MGG V 241–47 (H. Gunther).

71. During study with Rimsky-Korsakov, Glazunov had written 6 early sons. (Alekseev & Novikova).

72. But Alekseev & Novikova see it as the optimistic resolution through rejuvenation of the conflict of dramatic and lyrical in i and ii.

73. V. V. Stasov (as quoted in Yuzhak/GLAZUNOV 40) considered Op. 75, especially iii, to be Glazunov's greatest work.

74. E.g., Asaf'ev/RUSSIAN 220 and 235; Georgii/KLAVIERMUSIK 501.

chromatic double-appoggiaturas that infest nearly all of the melody and passagework, or from the lyricism that cloys to the point of seeming hollow and sentimental, or from the tonal changes and emotional climaxes that keep recurring without falling into any commanding over-all order, or, for that matter, from a style that persists without sufficient compromise and contrast, and, above all, without those bold flashes and new insights that characterize genius. It is interesting to find Gerald Abraham reaching similar conclusions about the symphonies of Glazunov, whom he rightly brands as an epigone; and it is

Ex. 119. From the recapitulation of the first movement in the Sonata in b♭/B♭, Op. 74, by Aleksandr Konstantinovitch Glazunov (after the original Belaiev ed. of 1901).

worth quoting him, because Glazunov's kind of pseudo, impassioned lyricism became all too prevalent in his day:[75]

A Glazunov symphony is just an uninterrupted flow of melodious ideas, laid out according to the classical or neo-romantic (Lisztian) forms, lusciously harmonized and beautifully orchestrated. But nothing ever happens to these ideas. The flow of music never gets anywhere. Climaxes are arranged; the current rises and falls; there are delightful touches of orchestration (such

75. Abraham/RUSSIAN 235 and 240. In an early review of both sons. (SMW LX [1902] 682), Glazunov is regarded as more able to create in smaller forms. But Alekseev & Novikova defend his handling of the large forms, citing the opinions of Ossofski/GLAZUNOV 42, Rimsky-Korsakov (in Yuzhak/GLAZUNOV 40), and Taneyev (in Glazunov/MUSICIANS 228: "I cannot help but rejoice that you implement so energetically the renaissance of the piano sonata, [which had been] supplanted temporarily by small piano forms. The greater forms have not yet outlived their times, and probably even our grandsons will not exhaust all the content that can be expressed in these forms.")

as the deliciously sugary trio of the fourth symphony) and endless—and effortless—technical skill. Melodious phrases are beautifully interwoven, ingeniously transformed. But there is no growth, not even a sense of direction.

A stylistic affinity with Glazunov's two sonatas can be heard in the three published sonatas, one for Vc & P and two for P solo, by the world-renowned pianist **Sergey Vassilievitch Rachmaninoff** (1873–1943).[76] Rachmaninoff's sonatas show similar influences of Chopin, Liszt, and Tchaikovsky,[77] over and above the solid training the younger man got from Arensky and the distinguished Taneyev. But his sonatas are regarded here as being superior to Glazunov's—mainly, as being more genuinely musical and, in spite of their equally impassioned lyricism, freer of sentimentality. They show broader, more positive approaches to form, fresher, better contrasted funds of melody and rhythm, supported by equally expressive, chromatic harmony, and still more varied, advanced treatments of the keyboard.[78]

Rachmaninoff composed the first of these three works, Op. 19 in g/G, for Vc & P, in the summer of 1901, just after completing one of the most popular of all piano concertos, his No. 2 in c. He dedicated Op. 19 to the cellist Anatoli Brandukov and gave it its first performance with him that same year, with publication following the next year (1902) by his chief publisher, Gutheil in Moscow.[79] Since then, Op. 19 has enjoyed the majority of the relatively few performances Rachmaninoff's sonatas have been given, whether in public or on recordings.[80] Like every other cyclic instrumental work by him, Op. 19 lies primarily in minor keys, but, unlike his other sonatas and his concertos, it falls into four rather than three movements, in the order S/F-Sc-M-F.[81] Its predominant mood is that of sweet, gentle, probing, melancholy, with hints, too, of the composer's characteristic self-effacement as well as the insecurity and despondency he had just

76. The chief source used here on the man and his music has been the detailed, objective study Bertensson & Leyda/RACHMANINOFF. Cf., also, MGG X 1839–44 (G. Abraham); Reither/RACHMANINOFF (on recent research and recordings).

77. On Tchaikovsky's influence, cf. MQ XXX (1944) 177 (A. & K. Swan).

78. Cf. Rachmaninoff's own, early, negative report on Glazunov's musicianship, in Bertensson & Leyda/RACHMANINOFF 73.

79. All 3 of his sons. have been pub. more recently by both Boosey & Hawkes in London and International in New York.

80. Public performances by Lamond, Casals, and Schuster are cited in Bertensson & Leyda/RACHMANINOFF 154, 219, 378; 3 recordings are cited on p. 430, as against one each (sponsored by The Rachmaninoff Society) for the 2 P sons., on pp. 431 and 432.

81. Op. 19 is described briefly (and rated among Rachmaninoff's best works) in Cobbett/CHAMBER II 264–65 (L. Sabaneiev). Yasser/RACHMANINOFF is a general discussion of Rachmaninoff's style in the light of 20th-c. trends (as of 1951).

battled.[82] If the mood seems almost too consistent throughout the work, one has to attribute it to the free recurrences of the opening theme in all movements as a cyclical tie, to that emphasis on the minor mode, and to the nature not only of the man but of the cello and its warm invitation to concentrate on songful melodies in the tenor range. Following a tenuous page of introduction, strangely reminiscent of the opening in Franck's Sonata in A, the melodies prove at once to be of a high order, with their ensuing development already confirming their composer's structural mastery. The cello gets the lion's share of the melodic material. But the piano is much the more active and technically burdened instrument, so that, in spite of Rachmaninoff's own caution that Op. 19 "is not for cello with piano accompaniment, but for two instruments in equal balance," [83] almost another Rachmaninoff is needed (as in his other sonatas) to keep the part in balance, not to mention toss it off with appropriate insouciance and *élan*.

Rachmaninoff's second sonata was his first for P solo, Op. 28 in d, a favorite key of this "d-minor composer." [84] He composed it in early 1907, partly in Moscow and partly while adjusting to the strangeness of Dresden, while he was still occupied with the Second Symphony in e.[85] In a letter of May 14 the generally secretive composer bared the creative process to the extent of revealing agonies and doubts, plus even the fact of programmatic inspirations, although these last are not identified in the score (2 years before his best known programme work, *The Isle of the Dead*):[86]

Now I'm completing a piano sonata. Yesterday I finished writing the second movement. Only the last movement is left to do, but I don't know if I can finish it before going to Paris. Probably not. This work is *not* a secret. . . . Two days ago I played the sonata for [Oskar von] Riesemann, and he *doesn't* seem to like it. Generally I've begun to notice that no matter what I write lately nobody likes it. And I myself often wonder; maybe it *is* all nonsense. The sonata is certainly wild and interminable. I think it takes about 45 [actually 40] minutes. I was lured into this length by its guiding idea. This is—three contrasting types from a literary work [Faust, Gretchen, and Mephistopheles, as in Liszt's "Faust Symphony," according to Bertensson & Leyda/ RACHMANINOFF 153]. Of course no program will be indicated, though I begin

82. Cf. Bertensson & Leyda/RACHMANINOFF 75–96 *passim*.

83. Bertensson & Leyda/RACHMANINOFF 378.

84. MGG X 1843.

85. Cf. Bertensson & Leyda/RACHMANINOFF 131–45, *passim*, and the informative notes on the jacket of M-G-M recording E3247, of Op. 28 (E. Cole). Both P sons. are discussed briefly in Asaf'ev/RUSSIAN 254 and 320 as broadly conceived works with "well-moulded" material, though somewhat hampered by diffusion, rhetoric, and massive virtuosity, and not quite the equals of Tchaikovsky's Sonata in G (contrary to the view held here).

86. As trans. in Bertensson & Leyda/RACHMANINOFF 138.

to think that the sonata would be clearer if the program were revealed. Nobody will ever play this composition, it's too difficult and long and possibly—and this is the most important—too dubious musically. At one time I wanted to make a symphony of this sonata, but this seemed impossible because of the purely pianistic style in which it is written.

Without any dedicatee, Op. 28 was published by Gutheil in June of 1908.[87] It was first played in public in an all-Rachmaninoff concert in Moscow in October, with the critic reacting to it as being overly complex and hence somewhat dry.[88] The pianist was K. N. Igumnov, who was to play it again and had advised on revisions the composer felt were needed before publication—not in vain, as Igumnov later recalled:[89]

. . . it was apparent that the most essential part of my comments had been taken into consideration by the author. A considerable part of the recapitulation in the first movement had been recomposed, shortening it by more than 50 bars; some cuts had been made in the finale, mostly in the recapitulation, about 60 bars. Changes of treatment were made only in the finale, mostly in the recapitulation. The second movement was unchanged.

Rachmaninoff himself "usually" played Op. 28 on the solo recitals during his first American tour, in 1908–9.[90]

Op. 28 has much to commend it, including the deep serenity of its middle, "Lento" movement and its numerous clear anticipations, both melodic and figural, of the Third Concerto (also in the key of d), which Rachmaninoff introduced on that same tour. But Op. 28 does seem overly complex, at least in its outer movements. The outer movements not only present problematic sonata-rondo designs[91] but their sections themselves are too subtly demarcated to define those designs. Moreover, these sections relate closely in their general style, which, unlike the consistent style in the cello sonata, grows oppressive with its heavier moods, sonorities, and technical requirements. And the sections in Op. 28 lack quite the melodic individualities and contrasts to be found in the Third Concerto. In short, the fears Rachmaninoff

87. Bertensson & Leyda/RACHMANINOFF 413.
88. Cf. Bertensson & Leyda/RACHMANINOFF 152–53.
89. As trans. in Bertensson & Leyda/RACHMANINOFF 152; cf. pp. 136–37, 141, 145.
90. Bertensson & Leyda/RACHMANINOFF 160.
91. However, Bertenssen & Leyda/RACHMANINOFF 132–33 seems to err in connecting Op. 28 with Rachmaninoff's guarded inquiry as to how rondo plans were defined in textbooks, and in Beethoven's sons. This curious inquiry, so naive for such an expert craftsman, dates from Dec. 10, 1906, before Op. 28 was begun but during the much greater troubles Rachmaninoff was having with Symphony 2 (cf. pp. 136–37, 141, 145). In any case, as they turned out, no mvts. in either work quite tally with the nonstandardized design he asked about in general terms.

expressed about Op. 28's worth and success (*supra*) cannot be dismissed entirely as mere evidences of his emotional insecurity.

Rachmaninoff's last sonata and second for P solo, Op. 36 in b♭, was composed in 1913, partly in Rome. It was played by him (in its first public performance?) in St. Petersburg in November, dedicated to Matvei Pressman (fellow pupil of N. Zverev in the 1880's), published by Gutheil in 1914, extensively revised by the composer in the summer of 1931, and published in its revised form by Gutheil (in Paris) in that year.[92] It should be instructive to compare the two versions. When Rachmaninoff played the original version, a St. Petersburg critic, who preferred the moderns (Scriabin, Debussy, Stravinsky), anyway, reported that the audience received it coolly and that he found it devoid of "interesting or profound ideas," although not without "some fresh and, for Rachmaninoff, rather unusual harmonies and counterpoint. In certain passages of the central movement the composer shows an excellent inventive capacity for variations." [93] Rachmaninoff himself is quoted as remarking in 1931, presumably still about the original version, that "so many voices [in it] are moving simultaneously, and it is too long. Chopin's Sonata [in b♭, which Rachmaninoff's Op. 36 resembles near the start] lasts nineteen minutes, and all has been said." [94] In the later version, says one commentator, "the work is much tightened and shortened and certain important simplifications of executional problems are introduced." [95] After Rachmaninoff's death Olin Downes wrote in *The New York Times* (March 26, 1944), "It can now be told that when he played Rachmaninoff's piano sonata [Op. 36] published in two versions, years apart, Mr. [Vladimir] Horowitz, after long and scrupulous study, combined the two versions in a way which earned him the very sincere thanks and musician's esteem of the composer." [96]

Certainly, Rachmaninoff's Op. 36 in its second version is structurally more compressed and concentrated and harmonically if not tonally more daring than his Op. 19 or, especially, his Op. 28. Because it never loses sight for long, in any of its three movements, of its main idea (anticipated in the initial "veloce" descent and first stated in mss. 3–4, as in Ex. 120); because there are no full breaks between movements; and because all three movements have in common a sense

92. Cf. Bertensson & Leyda/RACHMANINOFF 184, 186–87, 276–77, 415 (the mention of "Tair" as pub. could not be confirmed here for the revision; cf. Cat. NYPL XXV 225).

93. As trans. in Bertensson & Leyda/RACHMANINOFF 186–87.

94. Bertensson & Leyda/RACHMANINOFF 276–77.

95. From the unsigned jacket notes for M-G-M recording E3248.

96. According to a letter received from Mr. Horowitz, dated July 18, 1968, no score exists of the combined version, which he has played as recently as 1968.

Ex. 120. From the opening of Sergey Vassilievitch Rachmaninoff's Sonata in b♭, Op. 36 (facs. of the first autograph version of 1913, reproduced with the kind permission of Madame E. N. Alekseeva, Director of the Glinka State Central Museum in Moscow).

of fantasy, Op. 36 gives the impression on first hearing of being a free one-movement work. Its most vital structural principle is not that of sectional design nor motivic development but of variation through irregular restatements freely altered in melody, rhythm, harmony, and figuration. It is these free restatements that create the sense of fantasy. Only in the sequential ascents and descents of Rachmaninoff's artfully prolonged climactic curves is the syntax somewhat more regular. A fairly standard "sonata form" does underlie the first movement, but the middle movement, after an A-B-A treatment of two characteristically mournful themes based on stepwise descents, rises to a climax, then devotes its second half to more fantasy on the two main themes of the first movement. And the finale, introduced by nearly the same Franckian phrase that introduces the middle movement, gives us a scherzando "sonata form" that skips any trace of the recapitulation and goes right on to a brilliant coda with more references to the opening movement. Op. 36 is a rich, unusual, advanced, genuine work.[97] If reasons must be found for the rarity of its performances they may well be, first, the keyboard difficulties almost equal to those in the Third Concerto, without equally trenchant and varied ideas; and second, the degree of fantasy, which makes especially the finale hard to pull together, with its structural and motivic rhythms that are divergent enough to suggest the influence of Scriabin's later sonatas. Rachmaninoff was neither a Modern nor a modernist by nature. Such rhythms and some oblique, chromatic harmonic relationships (like those at the return in the first mvt., but never as extreme as the soloist's astonishing entry in the middle mvt. of the Third Concerto) marked the forward limits for that noniconoclastic, completely sincere musician.

A lifelong friend of Rachmaninoff, younger by seven years, **Nikolai Karlovitch Medtner** (1880–1951) likewise trained under Arensky and Taneyev, among others, excelled as a pianist, and pursued his career primarily in Moscow until he emigrated (to Berlin in 1921, Paris in 1925, and England in 1936).[98] However, unlike Rachmaninoff and notwithstanding considerable touring as a concert pianist in his own

97. Unendorsed here are the peculiarly opinionated, unprescient dismissals of Rachmaninoff (and Scriabin) by E. Blom in GROVE VII 27 and in Holt/TRIBUTE 75–76.

98. The principal, though brief, study of the man and his music is Holt/MEDTNER; followed by Holt/TRIBUTE (with an undated, careless list of works), which is a posthumous anth. of eulogistic articles, mostly short, on various aspects of Medtner's artistry and music, including emphasis on his sons. in Yasser/MEDTNER, Raybould/MEDTNER, and Ilyin/MEDTNER. Cf., also GROVE V 648–52 (E. Blom), with faulty list of works; MGG VIII 1893–94 (H. Lindlar), with inadequate list of works.

right, Medtner gave priority to composing over performing.[99] At the same time he seems to have compensated for this subordinating of the recitalist in him by writing more than half of his music for piano solo and the rest for piano and one more instrument (including about 100 songs), or piano and a group of other instruments (including a quintet and three concertos). Central in his more than 60 opus numbers, some subdivided, are 18 sonatas in one or more movements, originally published between 1904 and 1939, including 14 for P solo, 3 for Vn & P, and one for voice & P. The following chart of Medtner's 18 sonatas, in order of opus numbers and chronology, includes key, further title if any, scoring, probable or confirmed year(s) of composition, original publisher and year, volume and inclusive pages (plus total pp.) in the "Complete Works" (Medtner/WORKS-m, a set that began to appear in 1959), and number, tempo or type, and order of movement(s):[100]

In the following chart, the lengths in pages, from 9 to 85, and the number of movements, from one to 4, alone give some idea of the variety of approach and design in Medtner's sonatas.[101] Obviously Medtner was no slave to stereotypes. Even within the different movement plans there is little that can be generalized safely about his approaches or designs. The one-movement sonatas include some of the most developed and extended as well as the simplest and shortest designs (e.g., Opp. 25/2 and 11/2, respectively); and so do the multimovement sonatas (e.g., Opp. 44 and 25/1). Moreover, the line between the ten one-movement sonatas, which type Medtner seems to have followed Scriabin in preferring, and the eight multimovement sonatas is not clear. Only Opp. 30 and 53/2 are unequivocal single movements without substantial changes of mood, tempo, or style.[102] The three sonatas of Op. 11, published separately in three successive years, qualify similarly, but originally they may have been intended to comprise the three movements of one sonata, and might still be so understood, if not tonally then in order of tempos and moods (first a gentle "Allegro non troppo," then a slower "Andante molto espressivo," and last a more

101a

99. Cf. Holt/TRIBUTE 18–20 (by his wife Anna).

100. The dates of composition and pub. and the titles given in the valuable prefaces (in Russian) to the separate vols. of Medtner/WORKS-m are preferred here to those in earlier sources when the information differs.

101. There are several brief discussions and passing descriptions of one or more sons. by Medtner, as cited here when and where they apply. Ilyin/MEDTNER is of interest on Medtner's use of "sonata form" in his sons. and other works. But a thorough, comprehensive study of his sons., which is certainly warranted in any case by the interest they have aroused, seems not yet to have been done either in the Soviet Union or abroad.

102. On this subject cf. Swan/MEDTNER 51–52; Truscott/MEDTNER, which is primarily an analysis of Op. 22.

Medtner's Sonatas

Op./no.	Key	Further title	Scoring	Composed	First pub., year	Medtner/ works-m (pp.)	No. of mvts.: by types
5	f		P	1902–3; later revised	Belaiev, 1904 (1955, rev.)	I/98–142 (45)	4: F-F-S-F
11/1	Ab	["Sonaten-Triade" (no. 2 = "élégie")]	P	1904–6	Jurgenson, 1906	I/216–30 (15)	1: F
11/2	d		"	1904–6	Jurgenson, 1907	I/231–39 (9)	1: M
11/3	C		"	1907–8	Jurgenson, 1908	I/240–50 (11)	1: F
21	b		Vn & P	1909–10	Édition Russe, 1910	VII/26–68 (43)	3: M-F-M
22	g		P	1909–10?	Édition Russe, 1910	II/46–72 (27)	1: F(M)F
25/1	c	"Fairy Tale-"	P	1910–11?	Édition Russe, 1911	II/101–20 (20)	3: F-M-F
25/2	e		"	1911	Édition Russe, 1912	II/121–81 (61)	1: M/F
27	F#	"-ballade"	P	1912–14?	Édition Russe, 1913–14	II/202–43 (42)	2: F-In/F
30	a		P	1914–15?	Édition Russe, 1917	II/244–70 (27)	1: F
38/1	a	"-reminiscenza"	P	1918?	Zimmermann, 1922	III/65–85 (21)	1: F
39/5	c	"-tragica"	P	1920?	Zimmermann, 1923	III/170–89 (20)	1: F
41	C	"-vocalise"	Voice & P	1922–23?	Zimmermann, 1924	VI/97–116 (20)	1: In/F
44	G		Vn & P	1926	Zimmermann, 1928	VII/93–177 (85)	3: In/F-In-In/Va-In/Ro
53/1	bb	"Romantische-"	P	1931–32?	Zimmermann, 1933	IV/99–146 (48)	4: M-Sc-M-F
53/2	f	"-orageuse" (or "-minacciosa")	"		"	IV/147–83 (37)	1: F
56	G	"-idylle; Pastorale"	P	1937?	Novello, 1935	IV/242–61 (20)	2: F-F
57	e	"-epica"	Vn & P	1938	Novello, 1939	VII/178–260 (83)	4: In/F-Sc-M-VF

driving "Allegro moderato, con passione innocente"). Apparently, each one of these three pieces won its independence by falling into a "sonata form" of its own, almost in spite of the composer.[103]

As for Medtner's Opp. 38/1 and 39/5, these are not wholly independent, single-movement sonatas. More accurately, each is a single movement within a five-movement, thematically interrelated suite.[104] Medtner's other "one-movement" sonatas are actually something more than that. Thus, Op. 22 acquires an incipient slower movement by incorporating an "Interludium" ("Andante lugubre") into the development section of its elaborate, allegro "sonata form." Op. 25/2 (ded. to Rachmaninoff) frames a huge, complete "sonata form" with an extended "Introduzione" and an even more extended coda. On the other hand, whereas Medtner's single-movement sonatas tend to add additional, incipient movements, his multimovement sonatas tend to fuse into one long, fantasy movement. In Op. 53/1, for example, the four movements tend to fuse because they all come back to the same opening idea, they run on from one to the next, *attacca,* and much of their separate identities of tempo and mood tend to be neutralized or camouflaged by the internal contrasts of tempo and mood that each movement reveals. (In all these respects, as well as the key, year of composition, and even the very notes of the cyclical idea, Op. 53/1 is curiously like the revision of Rachmaninoff's Op. 36.)

Taneyev is supposed to have said that his important pupil "was born with sonata form." [105] Others have called Medtner "the Russian Brahms." [106] Although each of these remarks has some justification if it suggests Medtner's exceptional command of structural techniques, both of them are misleading. Medtner did show a decided predilection for "sonata form," employing other standardized designs—such as the scherzo, theme-and-variations, and rondo in the last two violin sonatas (Opp. 57/ii and 44/ii and iii)—much less often. But Medtner's "sonata forms" are as free of standardization and as variable as his sonata cycles. For instance, each of those two one-movement sonatas that belong to five-movement suites is an irregular "sonata form." Op. 38/1, which is preludial in character, repeats not its whole exposition but only its second theme. Op. 39/5, which is episodic in character, omits its second theme in its recapitulation. Other of the sonatas, in spite of the frequent instruction "sempre al rigore di tempo," give way to free sections, often labelled "cadenza," in the course or at the end of move-

103. Cf. GROVE V 650.
104. Cf. Truscott/MEDTNER 114.
105. Holt/TRIBUTE 18.
106. Cf. Holt/TRIBUTE 86 (G. Abraham); Yasser/MEDTNER 48–49.

ments (as before the indicated "Coda" of Op. 53/2 or near the ends of Opp. 21/i and 22).

Yet the point should be made that Medtner's freedoms and substantial variants of textbook form cannot be attributed to programmatic influences. One must not try to interpret literally the titles that head more than half of his sonatas (as on our tabulation, *supra*), or the titles that appear over some of the separate movements (e.g., "Meditazione" over Op. 53/1/iii), or Tutchev's desolate poem about the night wind under the title of Op. 25/2,[107] or even the interpretative instructions couched in Medtner's rich editorial vocabulary (reminiscent of, but not so wild as, Scriabin's)—for instance, "Canterellando; con fluidezza" (at the start of Op. 21), "L'istesso tempo (ma con entusiasmo)" (after an "appassionato crescendo" in Op. 53/2!), "carezzando," "sognando," "pieghevole," "sussurrando," "stentato," "sfrenetamente," "vertiginoso," "svegliando," or "fastosamente." Such titles and advices in Medtner's sonatas not only have no literal programmatic significance. They often seem not even to convey any compelling or immediate emotional message. They are more like philosophical commentaries on the designated emotions.[108] Medtner was an absolutist par excellence. Only he dared to write an extended "sonata form," the difficult, neglected *Sonate-vocalise*, Op. 41, in which, except for an introduction that sets a verse by Goethe, the voice serves purely as an instrument, singing nothing but vowels (chiefly "a," Medtner explains in a preface).[109] Even the archaic movement titles in Op. 21—"Canzona," "Danza," and "Ditirambo"—have only stylistic rather than programmatic significance.[110]

Medtner's sonatas, most of which he himself introduced to the public, did not arouse exceptional enthusiasm at the start.[111] Opp. 21 and 22 achieved a certain popularity after they appeared.[112] But not until his last years did his music win ardent champions, who, governed by special tastes, formed something of a cult (well represented by the

107. Cf. Holt/TRIBUTE 127–28 (K. S. Sorabji) and 205 (K. Klimov).

108. Medtner's sons., like Rheinberger's, might have benefited from more instrumental color, perhaps explaining why Medtner thought of orchestrating Opp. 25/2 and 57 (Raybould/MEDTNER 142).

109. Cf. Holt/TRIBUTE 38–40 (E. Newman) and 44–45 (M. Ritchie); Yasser/MEDTNER 52–53.

110. Brief, nonspecific descriptions of Medtner's first 2 Vn sons. occur in Cobbett/CHAMBER II 126–27 (L. Sabaneiev & W. W. Cobbett).

111. Op. 5 was reviewed but briefly, and with reservations about its content, in NZM CI (1905) 543 and MW XXXVII (1906) 64 (E. Segnitz). Op. 5 is described in Ilyin/MEDTNER 186–88. Cf., also, Yasser/MEDTNER 46–48. The prefaces to the pertinent vols. in Medtner/WORKS-m include information about first performances.

112. Cf. Holt/MEDTNER 141 (L. Collingwood).

contributors to Holt/TRIBUTE). Since his death, interest in Medtner's music has slipped badly and for the most part undeservedly. Today (as of 1968) his sonatas and other music rarely get performed and not a piece by him appears in the standard recording catalogues (in spite of the support The Maharajah of Mysore gave in 1950–51 to the recording of many of his works).[113] As viewed here, Medtner's sonatas have somewhat the same strengths and failings as those of another neglected master before him, Rheinberger (SSB X). The identifications of Medtner with "sonata form" and Brahms (*supra*) do have significance if they pertain to his extraordinary ability, like Rheinberger's, to evolve, transform, develop, and permute an idea (as already in Op. 5/i).[114]

Ex. 121. From the second movement of Nikolai Karlovitch Medtner's "Fairy Tale-Sonata" in c, Op. 25/1 (after the original Édition Russe).

This ability may well be his greatest, though hardly his only, strength. He is an expert, enterprising, fluent contrapuntist. Although he does not expand the traditional vocabulary or range of mid-19th-century harmony, he does apply his harmony in newly sensitive and fresh ways (as in the end of Op. 11/1 or the diagonal relationships, passing dissonances, and pungent cross relationships of Op. 25/1/19–26). He evolves similarly fresh rhythmic patterns that are both supple and subtle in their alternate support and defiance of the prevailing meter (as in Op. 30, mss. 17–29).[115] He does not exploit virtuosity for its own sake, but he does write with considerable variety, ingenuity, and, of course,

113. Cf. Holt/TRIBUTE 20–21 and 237–38 (including Opp. 22, 27, and 41).
114. Cf. the description of style traits in Yasser/MEDTNER.
115. Cf. Yasser/MEDTNER 51–52.

sympathetic understanding, for the piano in particular. And it is important to note that, when he chooses, he can create an expressive, distinctive melody, well planned and well spun out (Ex. 121).[116]

The "failings" that Medtner shares with Rheinberger are failings only while we insist that ideal "sonata form" must reflect Beethoven's example in logic, tightness, and dynamism. According to that example, Medtner's forms, especially those with almost constant developments of main ideas, are too prolix to be called "tight" (the "heavenly length" problem, again; ssB VI), too free to be called "logical," and too philosophical and homogeneous (or devoid of dramatic contrast) to be called "dynamic." [117] Although Rachmaninoff and Medtner expressed high mutual admiration for each other's music, Rachmaninoff found the development sections too long in Medtner's "sonata forms." [118] Medtner's answer on one occasion was that "it is *not the length* of musical compositions that creates an impression of boredom, but it is rather the *boredom* that creates the impression of length." [119] But this overly pat remark merely raises the chicken-or-the-egg question. We still have to account for the boredom when it does occur. As viewed here, a primary cause is found in Medtner's frequent selection of ideas—usually motives rather than themes—that are too bland to justify extensive developments. In other words, in at least some of his sonatas Medtner did not choose to write distinctive melodies, and even his most ingenious, resourceful development is not quite enough in itself to carry the music.

By way of contrast to the sonatas of Glazunov, Rachmaninoff, and Medtner, there could hardly be an example more different from the same period than the one main Sonata by **Mily Alexeyevich Balakirev** (1837 [new style]–1910). Another fine pianist, who had studied with a pupil of Field, Balakirev fed early on the inspiration and encouragement of Glinka, became thoroughly versed in all the main European masters from Mozart to Chopin and Liszt, and, among many other musical activities, organized that concert of Russian music in 1867 that brought from the writer Stasov the label "The Mighty Handful" (a term later transmuted to "The Five").[120] In addition to an unfinished Sonata in D and a weak Sonatina in G called "Esquisses"

116. Cf. Holt/TRIBUTE 155 (C. Glover) on Medtner's melody.

117. Cf. the somewhat similar appraisal of Medtner's forms in Asaf'ev/RUSSIAN 253.

118. Bertensson & Leyda/RACHMANINOFF 180 and 276.

119. Bertensson & Leyda/RACHMANINOFF 246–47.

120. Cf. the biographical section (Chaps. 1–11) in Garden/BALAKIREV, a recent study in English (1967) of the man and his music that supersedes previous studies and includes an unannotated "Catalogue of Works" (pp. 330–39) and a full "Bibliography" (pp. 321–25).

(1909), both for P solo, Balakirev completed his main work of this type, Sonata in b♭, for P solo, only after seeing it through three versions, two at the start and one almost a half century later, near the end of his career.[121] The earliest version, dating from 1855 (as Op. 3?), got to the end of four movements, with a scherzo that relates to his Octet, Op. 3, and a fugal epilogue still in the planning stage. The second version, labelled Op. 5 and probably dating from 1856–57, got as far as three completed movements, beginning with a movement in contrasting sections labelled "Andante," "Allegro assai feroce," and "Maestoso"; followed by a "Mazurka," and stopping with an "Andante" revised from the earliest version and dedicated to Cui.[122] The third version was completed in 1905, dedicated to his disciple Liapunov, published without opus number in 1906 by Zimmermann in Leipzig,[123] and already performed in public that same year as far west as Paris.[124] The second of its four movements, "Mazurka" in D, was a revision, already published separately in 1900, of the corresponding movement in the second version.

The fact that Balakirev's Sonata in b♭ is so different from other sonatas of the time may explain at least in part two reviews that deplored both its content and its treatment when it appeared.[125] The first movement is unusual for its intended synthesis of "sonata form" and fugal sections (perhaps at last realizing the "fugal epilogue" that had been planned for the earliest version). The "synthesis" does appear clearly enough on paper. But it does not produce a new, more dynamic form, since the sections simply alternate and repeat, in the same or another key, without any appreciable development. Instead, the effect is the rather static, oriental one of viewing the same material repeatedly or merely from different angles, somewhat as in "The Young Prince and the Young Princess" from Rimsky-Korsakov's *Scheherazade.* But if the music is not compelling, if it lacks the elemental, exhibitionistic drive of Balakirev's *Islamey*, or quite the forthright lyricism of "The Lark" that he transcribed so

121. Cf. Garden/BALAKIREV 35, 36, 147–48, 237–43 (including genesis and analysis), 311, 315, 317, 333–34; Liapunova & Yazovitskaya/BALAKIREV 574 (with references to further documentary information about the sons. in this new, 1967, documentary chronology); Abraham/RUSSIAN 205–15 (description and evaluation of Son. in b♭).

122. This 2d version was first pub. in Balakirev/WORKS-M I/2 in 1951, but neither the first nor the 3d version has (yet?) appeared in that set.

123. Cf. Cat. NYPL II 467.

124. Garden/BALAKIREV 153 and 156 (fn. 36).

125. DM VI/4 (1906–7) 306 (A. Leitzmann) and MERCURE II (Jan.-June, 1906) 263. Asaf'ev/RUSSIAN 231 qualifies it as a "highly interesting" but "contemplative," even "cerebral" work.

successfully from a Glinka song, it is still pleasant and intriguing music. It offers smooth counterpoint in the fugal sections, wide-spaced, euphonious, Chopinesque figurations in the more homophonic sections, and satisfying if thoroughly traditional harmony. The second movement, which is the "Mazurka" in D, in A-B-A design, could almost be mistaken for one of Chopin's, by this former devoted performer of Chopin's music. The third movement, an innocuous, cursive, tonally transitional "Intermezzo," brings more recollections of Chopin's writing and Rimsky-Korsakov's manner. And the sectional, more virtuosic "Finale," which returns to Balakirev's favorite key of b♭[126] and confirms casual cyclical relationships in this 34-page work, reminds us of his strong Russian nationalism by introducing square-cut, rhythmically clipped tunes that smack a bit of the barbaric "Polovtzian Dances" from Borodin's *Prince Igor*.

One can accept the evaluation of Balakirev's Sonata in b♭ as one of his best piano compositions, as one of his few noteworthy compositions that are not programmatic, and even as the best sonata (out of but few, incidental sons.!) to come from any of "The Five." [127] But to imply that it is a masterpiece of the Russian Romantic sonata[128] would be regarded here as too high an evaluation. Quite apart from its disregard for dynamic organization as the most inviolable principle in the tradition of the Romantic sonata,[129] it does not offer the high or fresh quality either of ideas or of treatment that might justify that evaluation.

Two Russian piano sonatas of more than average interest remain to be mentioned, both of them epigonic works evincing advanced writing skills, expert knowledge of the keyboard, and undeniable musicality if not originality. One of them, published in 1908 by Zimmermann in Leipzig, is Op. 27 in f, composed by the pianist **Sergey Mikhailovitch Liapunov** (1859–1924).[130] Liapunov had studied with Klindworth (to whom Op. 27 is ded.), Tchaikovsky, and Taneyev before becoming "of Balakirev's pupils the one who was most intimately associated with him personally and who followed most closely in his footsteps as a composer." [131] But of that last association there is

126. Cf. Davis/LYAPUNOV 187–88. Both "The Lark" and *Islamey*'s opening are also in b♭.

127. Cf. Abraham/RUSSIAN 206, 212–15; Garden/BALAKIREV 147, 237, 243, 317.

128. As in Garden/BALAKIREV 147 *et passim*.

129. Abraham/RUSSIAN 206–8 argues that this Son. sounds at first like a suite.

130. Cf. GROVE V 158–59 (E. Blom); he is overlooked in MGG. Op. 27 is described (pp. 196–98, with exx.) in a comprehensive discussion of his P music, Davis/LYAPUNOV (with dated list of P works and deds.). It is evaluated briefly and neutrally in Asaf'ev/RUSSIAN 234.

131. Abraham/RUSSIAN 206.

scarcely a trace in this highly developed and organized work beyond the most standard ingredients common to the musical language then current. Rather is there clear evidence of Liapunov's love for Liszt's, Chopin's, and a bit of Wagner's music[132] (as in the second theme, "Cantabile ed espressivo" on p. 5, which has something of all 3 masters in it; cf. *infra*).

Indeed, Liapunov's Op. 27 is one of the few consequential works modeled directly after Liszt's Sonata in b (SSB VI and X).[133] It begins, in the first 4 of its 31 pages,[134] with an exposition that moves from f to Ab as it presents virtually all of the material to be restated, developed, and transformed in the remainder of the work. There follow 3 sections in 19 pages that can be viewed, much as in Liszt's

Ex. 122. From Sergey Mikhailovitch Liapunov's Sonata in f, Op. 27 (after the original Zimmermann ed.).

double-function design, either as one huge, sectional excursion, all in foreign keys, that comprises the "development section" in a grand, complete one-movement "sonata form"; or as, respectively, the development section of a first movement (emphasizing the key centers of b, c♯, e♭, and B♭, but not followed by a return to f or a recapitulation section), a slower, second movement ("Andante sostenuto e molto espressivo," an A-B-A design in E/e/E), and a third, "scherzo" movement ("Allegro vivo" in g♯). There remain 8 pages, in f/F, that serve either as the recapitulation and coda of a one-movement design

132. Cf. Davis/LYAPUNOV 191–92 (but p. 204 unjustly contradicts p. 196).

133. It was an inability to recognize this form and its derivation that provoked the negative review of Op. 27 as a "Phantasie," not a son. (MW VIII/3 [1908–9] 365 [A. Leitzmann]).

134. Or 45 pp. in the reprint of 1951: Liapunov/PIANO-m I 88.

or the finale and coda of a 4-movement cycle. Even Liapunov's coda is modelled after Liszt's, being a similar peaceful resignation in andante tempo.

A sample of Liapunov's epigonic style may be quoted from the second theme (cited above) as it undergoes polyphonic extensions in the first development section (Ex. 122). Op. 27 is a telling work that reveals considerably more order and purpose and considerably less saccharinity than Glazunov's sonatas. Yet if it does not quite deserve to be kept alive, either, the problems lie in the same directions—excessive, insufficiently imaginative working of ideas that are not quite that important, to the point where the listener no longer can or wants to keep track of the elaborate design. Very different—in fact, sounding throughout like the Russian folk music he had formerly collected—is Liapunov's pointed, straightforward, three-movement Sonatina in Db, Op. 65, for P solo, composed in 1917 and first published in 1922 in Moscow.[135]

Our example from Liapunov's Op. 27 can serve about as well to illustrate the other epigonic piano sonata awaiting mention. This is Op. 9 in B (pub. by Rahter in Leipzig in 1909), by the pianist **Sergei Eduardovitch Bortkiewicz** (1877–1952), a pupil of Liadov and Jadassohn.[136] Again, the main influences are Chopin's and Liszt's music, as is all too clear in the parallel between the second theme of the first movement and that in Chopin's Op. 58, or the main themes in the finales of both works. Now, in the three separate, thematically unrelated movements of Op. 9, there is no question of tight, convincing forms. Nothing more irregular happens than keeping the second theme in the tonic key in the exposition of the first movement's "sonata form" and putting that much of the recapitulation in the subdominant key. But this time the epigonic style is too epigonic. One can no longer take it at face value, if it ever could be so taken.[137] Unwittingly (surely!), the composer only plays at being soldier in the stern passages and only parodies love-making in the lyrical ones. A Sonata in g, Op. 26 for Vn & P, by Bortkiewicz (pub. in 1924), has not been available here.[138]

Among further piano sonatas, passing mention can be given to Op. 10 in G (1905?), a two-movement work (F-Va) by violist **Vassily Andreyevitch Zolotarev** (1873–1964), who had been a pupil of Bala-

135. Reprinted in Liapunov/PIANO-m II 126. Cf. Davis/LYAPUNOV 202–3, 204–5, with exx.
136. Cf. GROVE I 827 (H. J. Kalcsik); BAKER 186.
137. Such was a typical reaction when the present author sought to revive Op. 9 in U.S. recitals of 1946.
138. Listed in Altmann/KAMMERMUSIK 196.

kirev, Liadov, and Rimsky-Korsakov;[139] and to Op. 4 in G♭, (1907), praised for its power, warmth, and phantasy, by another pupil of Balakirev and Rimsky-Korsakov, **Semion Alekseyevich Barmotin** (1877–?).[140]

Several composers wrote sonatas for Vn & P during the same period that also should get passing mention here, although not more, for these sonatas, like those for viola and those for cello were preceded by no Russian masterpieces such as might have stimulated stronger works.[141] Balakirev's pupil and another member of "The Five," **César Antonovitch Cui** (1835–1918) left an example published late in his life, Op. 84 in D (1911). Originally reviewed as a "pleasing" work, it now seems no better than would be expected of a generally reactionary, colorless, inadequately trained composer more recognized for his (conservative) nationalism than any special artistic heights.[142] The Moscow pianist **Alexander Fedorovitch Goedicke** (1877–1957) left a two-movement Sonata in A, Op. 10 (pub. in 1901), that is not one of his more challenging, substantial works but has been commended to amateurs for its charm.[143] The Polish-born composer **Witold Maliszewski** (1873–1939), saw his Op. 1 in G published in Leipzig (1902) after he had settled in St. Petersburg—a three-movement work (F-S-Va) welcomed at the time for its lyricism, strength, and treatment of each variation in the finale as an independent piece (as in Tchaikovsky's piano Trio).[144]

The pianist **Alexander Gustav Adolfovitch Winkler** (1865–1935) left a Sonata in c, Op. 10, for Va & P (pub. in 1902) that was reviewed as a fresh, cheerful, skillful work, although it no longer stands out today.[145] Winkler also left one sonata each for Vc & P, completed by Glazunov (Op. 19 in d, 1936), and Vn & P (Op. 20 in C, 1930).[146]

139. It is unfavorably reviewed in NZM CI (1905) 543–44 and DM V/1 (1905–6) 335 (A. Göttmann). Cf. BAKER 1852 (with reference to 2 later sons., as well) and Suppl. 143; Cobbett/CHAMBER II 598 (L. Sabaneiev & W. W. Cobbett), but not on the sons.

140. DM VIII/1 (1908–9) 116 (A. Leitzmann). Cf. VODARSKY-SHIRAEFF 18–19; Cobbett/CHAMBER I 59, for the listing of a Son. in a, Op. 14, for Vn & P.

141. Cf. Asaf'ev/RUSSIAN 229.

142. Cf. DM XI/3 (1911–12) 105 (W. Altmann); Cobbett/CHAMBER I 305 (V. N. Belaiev & W. W. Cobbett); Asaf'ev/RUSSIAN 219; MGG II 1818–22 (G. Abraham).

143. Cf. BAKER 579 and Suppl. 48; Cobbett/CHAMBER 474 (V. M. Belaiev & W. W. Cobbett); Asaf'ev/RUSSIAN 260–61 (incl. reference to a Son. in D, Op. 18, for P solo, pub. in Berlin).

144. NZM C (1904) 819; DM IV/3 (1904–5) 207 (W. Altmann). Cf. MGG VIII 1551–52 (Z. Lissa); Cobbett/CHAMBER II 110 (L. Sabaneiev & W. W. Cobbett), without evaluation of Op. 1.

145. MW XXXVI (1905) 306 (E. Segnitz); NZM C (1904) 819. Cf. Cobbett/CHAMBER II 587–88 (L. Sabaneiev & W. W. Cobbett); Asaf'ev/RUSSIAN 229; MGG XIV 711–12 (M. Goldstein).

146. MGG XIV 712.

The pianist of French descent, **Georgy Lvovitch Catoire** (1861–1926), left two published violin sonatas of some substance, depth, and skill, Opp. 15 in b (1904) and 20 ("Poème"; 1910).[147] Rimsky-Korsakov's pupil **Ivan Ivanovitch Kryzhanovsky** (1867–1924) left one published sonata each for Vc & P (Op. 2 in g [not G], 1903) and Vn & P (Op. 4 in e, 1906), the former receiving qualified praise for somewhat undisciplined spontaneity.[148] Another pupil of Balakirev and Rimsky-Korsakov, **Fyodor Stepanovitch Akimenko** (1876–1945) was the composer of four published sonatas—Opp. 32 and 38b for Vn & P, in d and G (1905 and 1911), Opp. 37 for Vc & P, in D (1908?), and 44 ("Sonate fantastique") for P solo (1910). Op. 32 was greeted as having more harmonic than melodic interest, although Cobbett later called it Akimenko's best chamber work.[149] And the pianist **Leonid Vladimirovitch Nikolayev** (1878–1942), a pupil of Taneyev and Ipolitov-Ivanov, left two sonatas, Opp. 7 in D, for P solo (pub.?), and 11 in g, for Vn & P (pub. in 1908). The latter has been described as competent but not distinctive.[150]

147. Cf. Cobbett/CHAMBER I 236–37 (V. M. Belaiev); BAKER 267–68; Cat. NYPL V 538; HOFMEISTER 1910, p. 27; DM X/1 (1910–11) 244.

148. MW XXXV (1904) 923 (E. Segnitz); DM III/4 (1903–4) 64 (H. Schlemüller). Cf. GROVE IV 861 (M. D. Calvocoressi); Asaf'ev/RUSSIAN 229.

149. DM VIII/3 (1908–9) 174 (W. Altmann); Cobbett/CHAMBER I 4 (V. M. Belaiev). Cf. VODARSKY-SHIRAEFF 11; GROVE I 80 (R. Newmarch).

150. DM IX/1 (1909–10). Cf. Cobbett/CHAMBER II 189; MGG IX 1533 (D. Lehmann); VODARSKY-SHIRAEFF 94 (including a MS Son. in g, Op. 22, for Vc & P).

Chapter XIX

The Americas Under European Guidance

U.S. Circumstances and Output

During the 19th century, in a land that still had been facing colonial struggles and reapportionments while Bach and Handel flourished, that had not attained its Constitution as an independent, unified country until the period of Haydn's and Mozart's greatest masterworks, and that was entering only its second half-century as the United States of America while Mendelssohn, Chopin, and Schumann were at their creative peaks, one could hardly expect to discover significant contributions to so specialized a genre as the sonata. Yet the familiar apology—familiar throughout the arts—that the country was still too young to do better can be both unwarranted and misleading here. It can be unwarranted because, at least after the Civil War (1861–65), the quality of the American sonata output, especially of the duo sonatas, was generally competent by anybody's standards, if not better. It can be misleading because, from before the start of the century, there was more awareness of current European trends, more interest in the sonata idea, and more actual publication of sonatas than has yet been noted or supposed. To be sure, we shall be encountering a conspicuous gap in production during slightly more than the second quarter of the century. But this gap only paralleled the low ebb of sonata production already noted at the time in the most active European countries (ssb II). And after the Civil War there was, proportionally, quite as sharp a rise of interest in the sonata (and other chamber music) as in those other countries, followed by a further spurt of interest during the wave of international good will, labor harmony, and capitalist prosperity that were enjoyed after the Spanish-American War (1898).

In any case, to temper our evaluations of the American sonata up to World War I with an apology for the country's newness would mean confusing the intended critical uniformity in the present volume by introducing a double standard. Schubert, Schumann, Chopin, and Brahms still can and should serve as our artistic points of reference. Furthermore, our composers themselves probably would have been the first to expect, even demand, comparison by European standards. In fact, if there was any one problem that beset the American sonata (and other absolute music) during the Romantic Era it was not so much the lack of a two-century tradition per se as the nearly total dependence on European traditions and practices. In particular, the dependence was on German traditions and practices, thus illustrating, at least as consistently as any other country we have visited, a recurring theme of *The Sonata Since Beethoven*. Only occasionally were there derivations from the English, especially at the start (as with A. Reinagle, J. Hewitt, and B. Carr),[1] or from the French, all toward the end of the era (as with D. G. Mason's study under d'Indy).

Some of the German influence came by way of composers born, trained, and even already established in Germany before emigrating to the United States (e.g., O. Singer). But most often—in fact, to a surprising degree—it came by way of American-born composers who followed *the* favorite course if they wanted to succeed in serious music, which was to go to Germany for their several years of advanced training. A relatively few American-born composers of some success stayed home and got their German training at second hand—for example, E. R. Kroeger in St. Louis. But most of the better known Americans went where the Germans themselves went—to Leipzig and the successors of Mendelssohn, especially Hauptmann, E. F. Richter, Jadassohn, and Reinecke; to Weimar for summer study with Liszt; to Munich and Rheinberger; to Berlin and Kiel; and to Dresden or several other German centers.[2] Generally these Americans held their own well abroad,[3] not a few making sufficient reputations before returning to get one or more sonatas published by the more receptive German firms. Our most celebrated American example was, of course, MacDowell, who was at least as Germanic as the rest of them, for all the discussions of his Americanism.

Both the German or Austro-German orientation and the U.S. alertness to foreign trends are already illustrated at the start of the era

1. On Reinagle and Hewitt cf. sce 806–9. A new, complete ed. of Reinagle's 4 Sons. for P solo was first announced by Da Capo Press in 1964 and later expected to appear in early 1969.

2. mason memories, Fay/germany, and Mannes/music are among the most entertaining and informative of numerous memoirs of such study throughout the century, though mostly pertaining to performance rather than composition.

3. In 1863 a Sandusky newspaper reported that the "best musical talent at the [Leipzig] conservatory was said to be American . . ." (dwight's XXIII–XXIV [1863–64] 255).

by the remarkable number of current European hits being published in this country, including one or more sonatas by Beethoven, Clementi, Cramer, Dussek, Edelmann, Gyrowetz, Haydn, Hook, Koczwara, Koželuch, Mozart, Nicolai, Pleyel, Steibelt, Türk, Vanhal, and Wölfl! [4] That Beethoven's sonatas may have aroused interest here earlier than hitherto supposed is suggested by a public performance of his Op. 26 in Boston by Hewitt's daughter Sophia in 1819.[5] Indeed, we have here the earliest known public performance not only of this work in this country but of any Beethoven sonata for P solo that was clearly identified, anywhere, throughout his lifetime.[6] Beethoven sonatas were played increasingly in public from the middle of the century, especially in New York and including a total of five complete series of the "thirty-two" as early as 1863 (only 2 years after the feat had first been accomplished in Europe) and 1874.[7] Corresponding interest is reflected in U.S. articles on his early and late sonatas, not excluding the usual programmes offered for the "Moonlight Sonata." [8] One New York layman asked the editor of the *Musical World and New York Musical Times* for December 25, 1852 (pp. 1–2), what it means to " 'comprehend,' 'appreciate,' 'understand,' 'feel,' and perhaps do many other things with . . . a Sonata of the great Beethoven. . . . What is the *pith* and *substance* of all this, divested of the hazy transcendentalism which surrounds it?" Replied the editor, "No un-professional person ordinarily *comprehends* . . . such music. . . . But every person may *appreciate* and keenly enjoy such music (as far as the sensuous effect goes). . . ."

That sort of interest was also found, though to a much lesser degree, in the sonatas of others—for example, Onslow, Clementi, Hauptmann, and Mendelssohn.[9] And there were further remarkably early performances of European masterworks, such as that in 1855 of Brahms's Trio in B, Op. 8, for the first time anywhere, and of his duo Op. 108 at a New York concert honoring Bülow, even before its publication took place.[10] But with all these evidences one must not lose perspec-

4. Cf. WOLFE I x, and *passim;* also, SCE 804–5 (for sons. in Thomas Jefferson's library).

5. The discovery of this information in the *Columbian Centinel* of Boston for Feb. 27, 1819, was made by H. E. Johnson in *Musical Interludes in Boston* (New York: Columbia University Press, 1943) 144.

6. Cf. SCE 528–29 (but without knowledge of the U.S. performance).

7. Cf. GROVE Am. Suppl. 407; Horton/PIANO 58–59; SCE 527.

8. E.g., DWIGHT'S X (1856) 102, 119; XI (1857) 35–36; XII (1857) 265, 274, 282, 289, 287–98; XIII (1858) 12 ("Liszt" on the "Moonlight"); XVI (1860) 346–47 (Anne Brewster on the "Moonlight").

9. As in DWIGHT'S II (1852) 2, IX (1856) 179, and XXIII–XXIV (1863–64) 6, 11, 278–79, 286–87, 376.

10. Cf. GOTTSCHALK/Notes xxxiv; Salter/AMERICAN 89; SSB IX.

tive and forget that in the total musical picture neither the sonata nor other serious independent instrumental music was any match for opera, oratorio, or light social music—certainly no more so in the United States than in Europe. A few composers of real importance, like Charles Martin Loeffler, left no sonatas at all.

Moreover, we get here the same kind of doubts expressed about the sonata's survival as we have seen in Europe (ssb II). In 1852, near the end of that conspicuous production gap, a writer for *Dwight's Journal,* noting the prevalence of capriccios, romances, sketches, and other light music for piano, asked, "Where is now the Sonata, that finished, elegant composition with its three or four varied movements, each complete in well ordered beauty? . . . This form . . . is . . . now almost extinct. . . ." [11] Within a year the same periodical took a more optimistic view, although still not quite seeing an end to the gap: "Sonatas of the old solid construction are welcome revivals at the present day, not only from Spohr, Mendelssohn, and Thalberg, but from younger pens desirous to identify themselves with music at any rate, even should the wish rather than the accomplishment be discerned. . . ." [12] Yet the Beethoven sonatas themselves, for all "their rank in history and their value in the souls of all true music-lovers," were said to be "surpassed [by the music of] a young man, an American [Gottschalk]." [13]

To the end of the century the prognosis for the sonata in the United States remained doubtful. In 1884 Willard Burr (*infra*) commented at the Cleveland meeting of the Music Teachers National Association on how important foreign publication continued to be to serious American music. Publication in America, he said, "not only gives little or no surety of success, but is it not rather in most cases a guarantee that they [the American works] do not possess any real value?" [14] In an extended article on music in this country (occasioned in 1890 by the 2d ed. of F. L. Ritter's *Music in America*), the Vienna critic Hanslick found very little at all to mention in the way of instrumental music.[15] In 1891 the American critic H. T. Finck was still advising against writing sonatas, both because "sonata form is too complicated and artificial to contain the new ideas of our time" and because it was too difficult to win acceptance of sonatas, whether by publishers, purchasers, performers, or audiences.[16] When, at last,

11. DWIGHT'S I (1852) 67.
12. DWIGHT'S II (1853) 124.
13. DWIGHT'S II (1853) 158.
14. Quoted in Salter/MTNA 19–20.
15. Hanslick/TAGEBUCHE 58–91, especially 62 and 79.
16. In "What Shall I Compose?" *Etude* IX (1891) 166.

David and Clara Mannes began their recitals of sonatas for violin and piano in the early 1900's they felt even that late that they were starting something new.[17] Spreading their repertoire from the early Italian masters to Brahms and Franck, and their touring radius from New York, Boston, and Philadelphia as far north as Bangor, as far west as Kansas City, and as far south as St. Louis they were the inspiration for several further recital pairs with the same aim.

One category of vital stimulants and standard-raisers in 19th-century American music was the succession of epochal concert series by the great performers of the age, starting with Jenny Lind's U.S. debut in 1850,[18] and followed by Gottschalk's in 1853,[19] Anton Rubinstein's in 1872,[20] Bülow's in 1875,[21] Josef Hofmann's in 1887,[22] and Paderewski's in 1891,[23] among others.[24] The incomparable Gottschalk, who left no examples of his own, occasionaly played a Mozart or Beethoven sonata or sonata movement, especially in New York, and his successors did increasingly more for our genre. Another important stimulant occurred in the prolonged visits of notable European composers, especially Dvořák's tour of duty as "artistic director" at New York's National Conservatory from 1892 to 1895 (ssb XVIII).

At first it was mainly the three big eastern centers—New York, Philadelphia, and Boston—that provided the properly hightoned environment for such music.[25] New York and Boston, with its "Boston Classicists" (including Paine, Chadwick, Foote, Parker, Beach, Hill, and D. G. Mason),[26] continued to be important. But the horizons soon spread to include Chicago, Cincinnati, St. Louis, Kansas City, Minneapolis, and many another center farther west. A significant year to note is 1867, when no fewer than five of America's leading conserv-

24a

17. Mannes/MUSIC 196–97, 282.
18. Cf. BAKER 957.
19. Cf. GOTTSCHALK/Notes xxv–xxxix (including debut program).
20. Cf. Loesser/PIANOS 515–18; Schonberg/PIANISTS 259–61.
21. Cf. Loesser/PIANOS 531–32.
22. Cf. Schonberg/PIANISTS 358–62.
23. Cf. PADEREWSKI 189–228, including programs; Schonberg/PIANISTS 289–90.
24. In addition to the pp. just cited, GOTTSCHALK/Notes 39–320 (1862–65), PADEREWSKI 247–66 (1892–93?), Mannes/MUSIC *passim*, Dent/BUSONI 97–98 (1891–94) and 190–95 (1910–11), and DAMROSCH/Life *passim* are among vivid recollections of American concert life during the Romantic Era. Cf., also, Lang/AMERICA 109–27 (N. Slonimsky); Salter/MTNA; Salter/AMERICAN; GROVE Am. Suppl. 12–16, 30–37, and 80–87.
25. For some useful surveys of American instrumental musical life by cities, cf. ART OF MUSIC IV 181–205; Howard/AMERICAN 150–58; Wolverton/KEYBOARD 171–77, 209–20, 289–92, 379–430 *passim* (all mainly on keyboard activities). Two foreign periodicals that regularly reported U.S. son. performances, city by city, were NZM and MT.
26. Cf. Chase/AMERICA 365–82.

atories were established, two in Boston and one each in Cincinnati, Oberlin, and Chicago.[27]

There follow two tabulations, one of about 160 published sonatas and the other of about 70 unpublished sonatas produced between 1801 and 1915 by residents in the United States. The published sonatas are listed in the chronological order of their (presumed) first editions, the unpublished ones only in the order of their composers' birth years, since the dates (in the rightmost column) that are known for these MSS are few. Although such tabular summaries of a country's output have been avoided earlier in the present volume (partly in the interest of maintaining a prose continuity), they can be helpful here in providing a collective view of an output that is interesting more often as one facet of 19th-century Americana than as music significant enough to merit individual discussions of more than a relatively few selected examples. Except for publications up to 1820, brought to light in WOLFE and Wolverton/KEYBOARD, our tabulations can hardly be said to approach completeness, least of all with regard to the MSS. Until Wolfe's thorough bibliography of the publications can be extended to later years and until more explorations of surviving MSS can be made, we must be content with the few, more general surveys and with the gradual improvement of information during the 19th century that results from a gradual increase of copyright entries since the first U.S. law protecting music was enacted in 1831.[28] Surely, the extraordinary gap in sonata production that now appears to exist from 1821 to 1856 will be filled in, at least in part, as our information for the period improves. For the years following, the chief help comes from the actual holdings at the Library of Congress (LC in the "References" cols.), the New York Public Library (including some not in Cat. NYPL), the Boston Public Library, and the special collection of the present author, as well as Horton/PIANO, Kremer/ORGAN and Sloan/VIOLIN (2 diss. and a thesis), and the numerous though mostly nonspecific listings in GROVE Am. Suppl.[29]

27. Cf. ART OF MUSIC IV 247–59.

28. Cf. Lang/AMERICA 285–86 (R. Burton); Sonneck/SUUM 91–93; Salter/AMERICAN 13–14. Occasionally, MS as well as pub. sons. turn up in the old U.S. copyright cats., thanks often to the naive vanity that prompted even (or especially) some of the weakest composers to copyright their frequently eccentric products. But all music listings are harder to dig out before 1891, when music began to be listed separately (and protected internationally), and 1906, when the present "Music" cat. of the U.S. Copyright Office began.

29. Our short titles for these and a few other sources are further shortened in the "Reference" cols. of the tabulation, but should be immediately identifiable in the Bibliography of SSB. The "References" merely document information about the particular work(s) to which they pertain. One should not overlook BIO.-BIBL. U.S.

In the tabulations that follow, the composer's national origin is given when known, as well as his or her first or main U.S. post and current residence at the time any sonatas were published. The tabulations include sonatas composed by U.S. residents while temporarily abroad (e.g., L. A. Coerne and H. A. Brockway), but not those composed after actual emigration, such as three by the New York-born resident in Berlin, **William Humphreys Dayas** (1863–1903),[30] nor those composed by foreigners before they became U.S. residents, such as Julian Edwards (ssb XIV), Felix Borowski (*infra*), **Hermann Spielter** (1860–1925),[31] and the world-famous pianist Josef Hofmann (1876–1957).[32] The tabulations also omit MSS that eventually achieved publication, sometime after 1915. Among those omitted sonatas are four of the five left by John Powell, which get notice in any case when his name comes up later here; a songful, flowing, orthodox four-movement Sonata in D, Op. 8 (F-VF-S-F), composed in 1891 during composition study in Berlin with Max Bruch, by the Chicago organist **Rossetter Gleason Cole** (1866–1952); [33] and eight of the nine completed sonatas left by Charles Ives,[34] which do not get notice, since they exceed the scope of the present volume by belonging with Scriabin's, Debussy's, Busoni's, and other significant innovational sonatas of the Modern Era.

To the extent that they are representative, the following tabulations provide some statistics worth noting. The approximately 110 different composers of the 230 published and unpublished sonatas represent at least 12 national origins, with 14 per cent of unknown origin and most of the rest born in 3 countries—a surprising 55 per cent in the United States and only 14 and 10 per cent in Germany and England,

---

as a valuable guide to further literature on all but the most obscure of the composers in the tabulations.

30. Cf. BAKER 356; GROVE Am. Suppl. 183; Kremer/ORGAN 178 (listing Son. 1, Op. 5 in F, for organ); SMW XLVI (1888) 501 (reviewing Son. 2 for organ, Op. 7 in c, as musically interesting but too difficult and somewhat contrived); SMW LVI (1898) 977–78 (reviewing Op. 11 in D, for Vn & P, as promising but still in Dayas' *Sturm und Drang* period and not distinguished by either originality or development of ideas).

31. Cf. BAKER 1546; Altmann/KAMMERMUSIK 264 (Op. 14 in D, for Vn & P, pub. in 1889).

32. Cf. BAKER 724–25. In SMW LI (1893) 691 a reviewer found ideas that are good but in need of more Classic discipline in the score of Hofmann's Op. 21 in F for P solo (Hainauer, 1893). And in MT XLVI (1905) 262 a reviewer found modern trends, earnest purpose, and brilliance in a performance of this work or possibly Op. 24 (unpub.) for P solo.

33. Played (first?) in 1897 (Sloan/VIOLIN 147); not pub. until 1917 (A. P. Schmidt). Cf. BAKER 4th ed. 220.

34. Kirkpatrick/IVES 70–92, 96.

respectively. The trend, of course, was toward proportionately more U.S.-born composers as the era advanced. In this country the 110 composers lived primarily in 4 out of about 30 cities, including 32 per cent in New York, 25 per cent in Boston, and 9 per cent each in Philadelphia and Chicago. Approximately 72 per cent of the published editions of the sonatas appeared in the United States and 26 per cent in Germany, with the trend this time being toward the latter as the era advanced. As for scoring, nearly 48 per cent are set for P solo, but that figure is swollen unjustly by several sets of from two to six sonatinas. Next come about 31 per cent for Vn & P, 16 for organ, 3 for Vc & P, and 2 for 3 other settings.

Immigrants Before the Gap of 1821–56

From our tabulations certain of the sonatas may be singled out, in roughly chronological order, for further discussion. The sonatas prior to the conspicuous hiatus of 1821–56 are all by foreign-born composers, all in the programmatic (mostly battle) or pedagogic categories, and all in the jargon of mid-Classic music. Ten of them figure among the totals of thirteen published sonatas each (all P solo; 1796–1815) that are known by two English-born performers, publishers, and composers. Flourishing a half generation later than Reinagle and Taylor (scE 806–8), these are the two who dominated musical life from the early 1790's on in New York and Philadelphia, respectively—that is, James Hewitt (1770–1827) [35] and **Benjamin Carr** (1768–1831) .[36] Except for less consistent, two-movement plans and more advanced technical requirements (including a right-hand, upward glissando in 6ths!), Carr's sonatas are like Hewitt's. They reveal much the same naive squareness of ideas and phrases that follow additively without any development or structural integration, and the same accompaniments, whether Alberti, chordal, or repeated-note. **Francisco Masi** (?–1853?) provided another similarly virtuosic battle sonata, complete with programmatic inscriptions, in *The Battles of Lake Champlain and Plattsburg, a Grand Sonata*.[37]

The Czech-born **Anthony Philip Heinrich** (1781–1861) wrote his only contribution, "La Buona Mattina, Sonata for the Pianoforte," as

35. scE 808–9. Cf. Wolverton/KEYBOARD 221–43, 469–73 (facs. of Op. 5/2, complete).

36. Cf. Wolverton/KEYBOARD 293–324 (including a facs. of p. 5 in "The Siege of Tripoli, an Historical Naval Sonata," p. 311, a description of Carr's sons., pp. 310 and 312–14, and a list of P works, pp. 317–24) and 474–76 (facs. of Carr's Son. 6 in B♭, pub. in 1796).

37. Cf. Wolverton/KEYBOARD 185–88, including a facs. of p. 4 and list of P works.

Some Published Sonatas by U.S. Residents, in Order of First Editions (1801–1915)

Composer	Born-died	Natl. arrived / 1st U.S. res.	post at pub.	Title, op., &/or key	Scoring	References	Publisher, year
James Hewitt	1770–1827	Eng. / 1792	New York / same	"4th of July"	P solo	WOLFE 3697; Wolverton 229–30	J. Hewitt, 1801
Benjamin Carr	1768–1831	Eng. / 1793	Philadelphia / same	"The Siege of Tripoli . . ."	P solo	WOLFE 1653–54; Wolverton 310–12	J. Carr, etc., 1804–5
J. Hewitt			New York	"to Miss M. Mount"	P solo	WOLFE 3781; Wolverton 236	J. Hewitt, 1809
B. Carr			Philadelphia	Six Progressive Sonatinas	P solo	WOLFE 1657; Wolverton 313–14	J. Carr, 1812?
J. Hewitt			Boston	"Military"	P solo	WOLFE 3743; Wolverton 240	? (U.S.), 1813–15
Francisco Masi	?–1853?	Italy / 1807	Boston / same	"Battles of Lake Champlain and Plattsburg"	P solo	WOLFE 5622; Wolverton 185–88	F. Masi, 1814
John F. W. Pchellas	?–? (U.S., 1815?–35)	1815? / ?	? / ?	"Peace of 1815"	P-or-harp solo	WOLFE 6864	J. Hewitt, 1815?
Stefano Cristiani	1768?–	Italy / 1818?	Philadelphia? / same	to the Misses Izard & Deas	P-duet	WOLFE 2215	"author," 1819?
S. Cristiani			Philadelphia	"to Miss Adele Sigoine"	harp-or-P solo	WOLFE 2214	G. E. Blake, 1820?
Peter K. Moran	?–1831	Ireland / 1817	New York / same	*Petit Sonata*	P ± Fl	WOLFE 6121; Wolverton 243–47	W. Dubois, 1820
Anthony Philip Heinrich	1781–1861	Bohemia / 1818	Philadelphia / Lexington, Ky.	"La buona Mattina"	P solo	WOLFE 3592	Bacon & Hart, 1820
J. F. W. Pchellas			Philadelphia by 1820?	3, "to Miss Mary Maden"	P & Vn	WOLFE 6863	"author," 1820
Jan Nepomucene Pychowski	1818–1900	Bohemia / 1850	New York / same	"Grande . . . ," Op. 8 in a	P & Vn	Sloan 25–32	J. Schuberth, 1857
Karl Merz	1836–90	Germ. / 1854	Philadelphia / Oxford, O.	"L'Inquiétude," Op. 50	P solo	LC; Howe 399–401	Russell, 1864
Caryl Florio (William James Robjohn)	1843–1920	Eng. / 1857	New York / touring	2, in A & B♭	P solo	Horton 195; Teal & Brown 41	C. J. Whitney, 1866

Name	Dates	Country / Year	Birthplace / Residence	Work	Medium	References	Publisher
Dudley Buck	1839–1909	U.S. / 1862	Hartford / Brooklyn	Son. 1, Op. 22 in Eb	organ	Howe 683; Kremer 174	Beer & Schirmer, 1866
Whitney Eugene Thayer	1838–89	U.S. / 1862	Boston / Berlin	Sons. 1–4, Opp. 1, 4, 5, 8, in F, d, C, d	organ	Am. Suppl. 381; Kremer 225	Bote & Bock, 1866
Stephen Albert Emery	1841–91	U.S. / 1864	Portland, Me. / Boston	"Sonatella" 1 & 2, Opp. 9 & 11	P solo	Horton 193; Am. Suppl. 198	Henry Tolman, 1866 & 1867
Louis Falk	1848–1925	Germ. / 1859	Rochester / Chicago	Op. 7	P solo	LC; Am. Suppl. 39	author, 1867
Otto Singer	1833–94	Germ. / 1867	New York / same	"Grosses Duo . . . ," Op. 3	Vn & P	Sloan 39–44; Howe 444–46	J. Schuberth, 1869
Smith Newell Penfield	1837–1920	U.S. / 1869?	Rochester? / same	"Poem of Life," Op. 10	P solo	Horton 194; Am. Suppl. 324–25	Root & Cady, 1870
G. R. Paine	?–?	? / ?	Portland, Me.?	2, in C & Bb	P solo	LC	Stockbridge, 1870 & 1871
Hugh Archibald Clarke	1839–1927	Canada / 1859	Philadelphia / same	"Three Easy . . ."	P solo	Horton 193	W. H. Boner, 1874
Richard Zeckwer	1850–1922	Germ. / 1870	Philadelphia / same	2 Sonatinas	P solo	LC; BAKER 1840	G. Andre, 1875
George Matzka	1825–83	Germ. / 1852	New York / same	Son. in D	Vn & P	Sloan 33–39	E. Schuberth (New York), 1876
D. Buck			Brooklyn	Son. 2, Op. 77 in g	organ	Kremer 174; Howe 683	G. Schirmer, 1877
Albert Rowse	?–?	? / ?	New York?	"Ariel"	P solo	LC	Pond, 1879
Walter Russell Johnston	?–?	? / ?	New York?	one Son.	P solo	LC	E. Schuberth, 1879
Henry Morton Dunham	1853–1929	U.S. / 1870	Brockton, Mass. / Boston?	Op. 10 in g	organ	Am. Suppl. 192; Kremer 180; Salter/MTNA 11	A. P. Schmidt, 1882
Minnie Koch	?–?	? / ?	Philadelphia?	one Son.	P solo	LC	J. J. Hood, 1884
Henry Maylath	1827–83	Aust. / 1867	New York / same	6 "Sonatines," Op. 301	P solo	LC; BAKER 1053	Grand Conservatory, 1884
Charles Fradel	1821–88	Aust. / 1861	New York / same	6 "Sonatines," Op. 505	P solo	Horton 66–77, 193–94, 202; LC	Grand Conservatory, 1884–1885

Some Published Sonatas by U.S. Residents, in Order of First Editions (1801–1915) (Cont.)

Composer	Born-died	Natl. / arrived	1st U.S. post / res. at pub.	Title, op., &/or key	Scoring	References	Publisher, year
Preston Ware Orem	1865–1938	U.S.	Philadelphia	Son. in f	P solo	Horton 194; Am. Suppl. 317	F. A. North, 1885
Abram Kimmell	?–?	? / 1885?	same	5 Sonatinas, Opp. 65–69	P solo	LC	author, 1885
H. Maylath		?	Kansas City, Kan.	6(?) Sonatinas, Op. 151	P solo	LC	Grand Conservatory, 1885
Carl Venth	1860–1938	Germ. / 1880	New York	2 Sonatinas, Opp. 17, 18	P solo	LC; BAKER 1696–97	J. O. von Prochazka, 1885, 1886
H. Maylath			New York / same	Sonatina	P solo	LC	Grand Conservatory, 1886
William F. Sudds	1843–1920	Eng. / "early"	Boston? / New York?	3 Sons., in F, A, c	P solo	Horton 195; BAKER 1598	F. A. Shaw, 1886
C. Fradel	1825–1902	U.S.	New York / Boston	6 Sonatinas Op. 511 & 3 Op. 523	P solo	Horton 194; LC	Grand Conservatory, 1887
Henry Stephen Cutler	1825–1902	U.S. / 1852		Son. in c	organ	Kremer 177	Oliver Ditson, 1887
William E. Ashmall	1860–1927	Eng. / ?	New York / same	2 Sonatinas, Op. 49	P solo	LC; Am. Suppl. 53	author, 1887
Frank L. Eyer	?–?	?	?	Sonatina in F, Op. 1/1	P solo	LC; Horton 193	John Church, 1887
Bruno Oscar Klein	1858–1911	Germ. / 1878	U.S. tours / New York	Op. 10 in G	P & Vn	Satter/MTNA 32; Am. Suppl. 262	Hofmeister, 1887
Horace Wadham Nicholl	1848–1922	Eng. / 1871	Pittsburgh / New York	Op. 13 in A	Vc & P	Am. Suppl. 311; Cat. NYPL XX 711	Rahter, 1888
Hugo Kaun	1863–1932	Germ. / 1887	Milwaukee / same	Op. 2 in A	P solo	SSB XI	Kaun (Berlin), 1888
George Philipp	?–?	?	?	Sonatina in C	P solo	Horton 194; LC	A. P. Schmidt, 1889
George Elbridge Whiting	1840–1923	U.S. / 1867	Hartford / Boston	"Grand" Son., Op. 25	organ	BAKER 1789–90; Kremer 230–31	A. P. Schmidt, 1890

Name	Dates	Origin	Year	Place 1	Place 2	Work	Medium	Reference	Publisher, year
Arthur Foote	1853–1937	U.S.	1874	/ Boston	/ same	Op. 20 in g	P & Vn	Sloan 79–84; Shand 220–22	A. P. Schmidt, 1890
Carl Christian Müller	1831–1914	Germ.	1854	/ New York	/ same	Op. 47/1 & 2 in f & b	organ	Kremer 209; Am. Suppl. 301	Kistner, 1890
H. M. Dunham			Boston			Op. 16 in F	organ	Kremer 181	A. P. Schmidt, 1891
Lottie H. Taft	?–?	?	?	/ ?	/ San Francisco?	"La Belle," Op. 4	P solo	LC	Broser & Schlam, 1892
Clara Kathleen Rogers	1844–1931	Eng.	1871	/ New York	/ Boston	Op. 25 in d	Vn & P	Sloan 55–58	A. P. Schmidt, 1893
Edward (Alexander) MacDowell	1861–1908	US.	1888	/ Boston	/ same	"Tragica," Op. 45 in g/G	P solo	Gilman 36–37; Sonneck/SUUM 35	Breitkopf, 1893
J. B. Schmalz	?–?	?	?	?	/ Detroit?	"Homesick," Sonatina	P solo	LC	Schwankovsky, 1894
Howard A. Brockway	1870–1951	U.S.	1895	/ New York	/ Berlin	Op. 9 in g	Vn & P	Mannes 111; Am. Suppl. 143–44; ART OF MUSIC IV 383	Schlesinger, 1894
Leo Rich Lewis	1865–1945	U.S.	1892	/ Boston	/ same	Op. 3 in A	P & Vn	Sloan 129–136	H. B. Stevens, 1894
E. (A.) MacDowell			Boston			"Eroica," Op. 50 in g	P solo		Breitkopf, 1895
Alfred Monson	?–?	?	?	/ Boston?		2 Sonatinas	P solo	LC	E. E. Truette, 1895
Frederick Newell Shackley	1868–?	?	?	/ Boston		Sonatina in C	P solo	Am. Suppl. 63; LC	Wood, 1895
Rubin Goldmark	1872–1936	U.S.	1891	/ New York	/ same	Op. 4 in G	P & Vn	Am. Suppl. 122; Cobbett I 476–77	Breitkopf, 1896
Ernst Richard Kroeger	1862–1934	U.S.	1887	/ St. Louis	/ same	Op. 32 in f♯	Vn & P	Am. Suppl. 266; Sloan 109–114	Breitkopf, 1896
C. C. Müller			New York			Op. 61 in A	P & Vn	Am. Suppl. 301	Breitkopf, 1897
Carl Adolph Preyer	1863–1947	Germ.	1881	New York / Newark	/ Lawrence, Kan.	Son. 1 in c♯, Op. 33	P solo	Gloyne 15, 25–26	Breitkopf, 1899
E. R. Kroeger			St. Louis			Op. 40 in D♭	P solo	Am. Suppl. 266	Breitkopf, 1899

Some Published Sonatas by U.S. Residents, in Order of First Editions (1801–1915) (Cont.)

Composer	Born-died	Natl. / arrived /	1st U.S. post / res. at pub.	Title, op., &/or key	Scoring	References	Publisher, year
Amy Marcy Beach	1867–1944	U.S. / 1883 /	Boston / same	Op. 34 in a	Vn & P	Shand 224–27; Cobbett I 79	A. P. Schmidt, 1899
Walter (Johannes) Damrosch	1862–1950	Germ. / 1885 /	New York / same	"At Fox Meadow," Op. 6 in G	Vn & P	Sloan 121–29	John Church, 1899
Herbert James Wrightson	1869–1949	Eng. / 1897 /	Philadelphia / Chicago?	Son. 3 in F, Op. 45	organ	BAKER 1825; Kremer 233	Clayton F. Summy, 1899
E. (A.) MacDowell			New York	"Norse," Op. 57 in d/D	P solo	Eagle passim	A. P. Schmidt, 1900
C. C. Müller			New York	Son. 3, Op. 57 in d	organ	Kremer 209	Breitkopf, 1900
Camille W. Zeckwer	1875–1924	U.S. / 1895? /	Philadelphia / same	Son. 2, Op. 7 in D	Vn & P	Am. Suppl. 410	Breitkopf, 1900
Frederick Shepherd Converse	1871–1940	U.S. / 1898 /	Boston / same	Op. 1 in A	Vn & P	Shand 222–24	Boston Music, 1900
H. W. Nicholl			abroad?	"Symphonische Sonate," Op. 42 in a	organ	Sloan 58–59; Kremer 210	Peters, 1901
E. (A.) MacDowell			New York	"Keltic," Op. 59 in e	P solo	Eagle passim	A. P. Schmidt, 1901
Ralph Layman Baldwin	1872–	U.S.? / ? /	Boston?	Op. 10 in c	organ	Kremer 168	G. Schirmer, 1901
Louis Adolphe Coerne	1870–1922	U.S. / 1894 /	Buffalo / Leipzig?	"Schwedische" Son., Op. 60 in a	Vn & P	Elson/AMERICAN 201–4	Hofmeister, 1901
William Henry Berwald	(1864–1948)	Germ. / 1892 /	Syracuse / same	Opp. 20 in Bb/ii & 21 in F	Vc & P, Vn & P	Am. Suppl. 131; Altmann 195, 253	Breitkopf, 1901
John Victor Bergquist	1877–1935	U.S. / 1895 /	Minneapolis / same	Son. in c	organ	Am. Suppl. 67; Kremer 170	Schlesinger, 1902
Henry Schoenefeld	1857–1936	U.S. / 1879 /	Chicago / same	Son. "quasi fantasia," Op. 53 in g	P & Vn	Sloan 85–92; Am. Suppl. 433–34	Simrock, 1903
Harry Newton Redman	1869–1958	U.S. / 1897 /	Boston / same	Op. 16 in c	Vn & P	Cobbett II 277; BAKER 1316	White-Smith, 1903

Name	Dates	Country	Year	City 1	City 2	Work	Medium	Reference	Publisher, year
Henry Holden Huss	1862–1953	U.S.	1885	New York	same	Op. 19 in g	Vn & P	Sloan 114–21; Shand 228–30	G. Schirmer, 1903
Felix Borowski	1872–1956	Eng.	1897	Chicago	same	Son. 1 in A	organ	Am. Suppl. 139; Kremer 172	Laudy, 1904
B. O. Klein				New York	New York	Op. 31 in b	Vn & P	Sloan 92–98	Simrock, 1904
Louis Campbell-Tipton	1877–1921	U.S.	1900	Chicago	same	Son. "Heroic" in c♯	P solo	Am. Suppl. 152; ART OF MUSIC IV 423	Wa-Wan Press, 1904
Louis Victor Saar	1868–1937	Holland	1894	New York	same	Op. 44 in G	Vn & P	Cobbett II 320; Am. Suppl. 346	Kistner, 1904
Frank Edwin Ward	1872–1953	U.S.	1902	New York	same	Son. 2, Op. 9 in G	Vn & P	Am. Suppl. 399; ART OF MUSIC IV 393	Breitkopf (New York), 1904
William Henry Pommer	1851–1937	U.S.	?	?	St. Louis	Op. 17 in a	P & Vn	Sloan 71–73	Rahter, 1905
W. H. Berwald					Syracuse	Op. 32 in c	Vn & P	Am. Suppl. 131; DM V/3 (1905–6) 171	Bosworth, 1905
H. N. Redman					Boston	Op. 17 in D	Vn & P	Cobbett II 277	White-Smith, 1905
F. Borowski	?–?				Chicago	Son. 2 in C	organ	Am. Suppl. 139; Kremer 172	Laudy, 1906
A. I. Earle	1858–1913		?	?	Lawrence, Mass.?	Sonatina, Op. 15	P solo	LC	author, 1906
Frank Lynes	1858–1913	U.S.	1885	Boston	same	Op. 49 in C	organ	BAKER 997; Kremer 203	A. P. Schmidt, 1907
Alexander Stewart Thompson	1859–?		?	?	?	Op. 21/1 in A	P solo	LC; Am. Suppl. 172, 381	Breitkopf, 1907
Mark Andrews	1875–1939	Eng.	1902	Montclair, N.J.		Op. 17 in a	organ	Kremer 166; ASCAP 16	G. Schirmer, 1908
Percy Goetschius	1853–1943	U.S.	1890	Syracuse	New York	Op. 15 in b/B	P solo	Am. Suppl. 221	G. Schirmer, 1908
H. M. Dunham				Boston	New York	Op. 22 in d	organ	Kremer 180–81	A. P. Schmidt, 1908
Horatio William Parker	1863–1919	U.S.	?	Boston	New Haven	Op. 65 in e♭/E♭	organ	BAKER 1208–9; Kremer 211–12	G. Schirmer, 1908

Some Published Sonatas by U.S. Residents, in Order of First Editions (1801–1915) (Cont.)

Composer	Born-died	Natl. / arrived / 1st U.S. post / res. at pub.	Title, op., &/or key	Scoring	References	Publisher, year
James Hotchkiss Rogers	1857–1940	U.S. / 1883 / Cleveland / same	Son. in e	organ	Kremer 219; Am. Suppl. 342–43	G. Schirmer, 1910
W. E. Thayer		/ / Boston /	"Concert" Son. 5, Op. 45 in c	organ	Kremer 225	G. Schirmer, 1911
Arthur Shepherd	1880–1958	U.S. / 1897 / Salt Lake City / Boston	Op. 4 in f	P solo	MQ XXXVI (1950) 159–79; ART OF MUSIC IV 418–19	G. Schirmer, 1911
Charles Frederick Dennée	1863–1946	U.S. / 1883 / Boston / same	4 Sonatinas, Op. 36	P solo	LC; Am. Suppl. 187–88	A. P. Schmidt, 1911
Clara Anna Korn	1866–1940	Germ. / 1893 / New York / same	"Nautical," Op. 14	P solo	Am. Suppl. 264; LC	Essex Music, 1911
Joseph Henius	ca. 1880–1912	? / ? / New York /	Op. 9	Vn & P	ART OF MUSIC IV 393	Gray, 1911
Sigismund Stojowski	1869–1946	Poland / 1906 / New York / same	Op. 37 in E	Vn & P	SSB XIII	Heugel, 1912
Mary Edwina Walker	?–?	? / ? / ? / ?	Sonatina, Op. 7	P solo	LC	Willis, 1912
Julia Mary Canfield	?–?	? / ? / ? / ?	Sonatina	P solo	LC	Willis, 1912
M. A. Andrews		? / ? / ? / ?	Son. 2, Op. 34 in c	organ	Kremer 166	H. W. Gray, 1912
Adolf Gerhard Brune	1870–1935	Germ. / 1889 / Peoria, Ill. ? / Chicago	Op. 33 in d	P & Vn	Am. Suppl. 146; DM XII/1 (1912–13) 172	Schott, 1912
James A. Bliss	?–?	? / ? / ? / Minneapolis?	Son. in C	P solo	LC	J. E. Frank, 1912
René Louis Becker	1882–1956	Alsace / 1904 / St. Louis / same?	Opp. 40 in g, 41 in F, 43 in E	organ	Am. Suppl. 128; Kremer 170	G. Schirmer, 1912, 1912, 1913
John Alden Carpenter	1876–1951	U.S. / 1897 / Chicago / same	Son. in G	Vn & P	Shand 236–37; Cobbett I 227	G. Schirmer, 1913

Heniot Lévy	1879–1946	Poland 1900	/ Chicago / same	Op. 6 in c	Vn & P	Am. Suppl. 270; DM XIII/1 (1913–14) 297	Ries & Erler, 1913
Daniel Gregory Mason	1873–1953	U.S. 1910	/ New York / same	Op. 5 in g/G	Vn & P	Mason/MUSIC 56–57, 163, 165, 170, 296–97	G. Schirmer, 1913
Harry Benjamin Jepson	1870–1952	U.S. 1895	/ New Haven / same	Son. in g	organ	Kremer 194	H. W. Gray, 1913
Frederic(k) Ayres (Johnson)	1876–1926	U.S. 1900?	/ Colorado Springs/ / same	Op. 15 in d	Vn & P	Cobbett I 49; Upton/AYRES 40, 47–48, 58	Stahl, 1914
Pauline Hospes	?–?	? ?	/ Chicago[2] / ?	Op. 2	P solo	LC	Wilcox, 1914
Mortimer Wilson	1876–1932	U.S. 1911	/ Atlanta / same	Opp. 16 in E & 14 in D	Vn & P	BAKER 1802–3	Boston Music, 1914, 1915
Charles Wakefield Cadman	1881–1946	U.S. 1908	/ Pittsburgh / Los Angeles	Op. 58 in A	P solo	Am. Suppl. 150	White-Smith, 1915

Some Unpublished Sonatas by U.S. Residents Listed in Order of Birth (1825–1882)

Composer	Born-died	Natl., main U.S. post (from)	Title, op., &/or key	Scoring	References	Year (when known)
George Frederick Bristow	1825–98	U.S., New York (1836?)	Op. 12 in G	Vn & P	at NYPL; ROGER/BRISTOW 80–81, 143–44, 159–60	before 1850
John Knowles Paine	1839–1906	U.S., Boston (1862)	"Fantasia" Son. in d	organ	DWIGHT'S XXIII (1863–64) 163	1863?
" "	" "	" "	Op. 24 in b	P & Vn	Boston Public Library; Sloan 44–50	1875
Hugh Archibald Clarke	1839–1927	Canada, Philadelphia (1859)	2 Sons.	Vn & Vn	Sloan 147; Am. Suppl. 164	
Adolph Kölling	1840–?	Germ., Poughkeepsie (1872)	Sons. in c & C	P solo	Howe 668	
" "	" "	" "	Son. in B(b?)	P & Vn	Howe 668; cf. Sloan 50–55	
Calixa Lavallée	1842–91	Canada, Boston (1822?)	?	Vn & P	Am. Suppl. 269	
Caryl Florio	1843–1920	Eng., New York (1857)	4 Sons.	Vn & P	Am. Suppl. 206	
Isaac Van Vleck Flagler	1844–1909	U.S., Auburn, N.Y. (1878?)	Son. in G	organ	MT XXI (1880) 138, 244; BAKER 486	1879?
Clara Kathleen Rogers	1844–1931	Eng., Boston (1874)	?	Vc & P	Sloan 55–58	
William Wallace Gilchrist	1846–1916	U.S., Philadelphia (1874)	?	organ	Salter/MTNA 31	by 1890
Horace Wadham Nicholl	1848–1922	Eng., Farmington, Conn. (1888)	Op. 21 in D	Vn & P	Sloan 58–64; Cat. NYPL XX–711	ca. 1890?
Richard Zeckwer	1850–1922	Germ., Philadelphia (1870)	"several" sons.	P solo	MUSIC IV (1893) 48–49	1893
" "	" "	" "	one Son.	Vn & P	" "	after 1880?
Louis Philipp Maas	1852–89	Germ., Boston (1880)	3 "important" Sons.	P solo or Vn & P	Howe 127–29; Am. Suppl. 277	after 1880?
Willard Burr	1852–1915	U.S., Boston (1880)	"Grand" Son., Op. 18 in Bb	P & Vn	Sloan 74–79; Am. Suppl. 54	
Arthur Foote	1853–1937	U.S., Boston (1878)	Op. 76	Vc & P	Am. Suppl. 207–8	ca. 1910?
Alfred Dudley Turner	1854–88	U.S., Boston (ca. 1870?)	2 Sons., in d & c	Vn & P	BAKER 1669; Sloan 153	
" "	" "	" "	one Son.	Vc & P	" "	
Marinus Van Gelder	1854–1910?	U.S., Philadelphia (by 1893)	one "fine" Son.	Vn & P	MUSIC IV (1893) 51; Keller & Kruseman I 229	1893?
Helen Hopekirk	1856–1945	Scotland, Boston (1887)	2 Sons., in e & D	Vn & P	Am. Suppl. 245	
Henry Schoenefeld	1857–1936	U.S., Los Angeles (1904)	Op. 70	Vc & P	Am. Suppl. 354	
Edgar Stillman Kelley	1857–1944	U.S., San Francisco (1880)		P solo	New York Times Jan. 26, 1969 (H. Schonberg)	ca. 1878
Carl Venth	1860–1938	Germ., New York (1880)	one Son.	P solo	Am. Suppl. 396	
" "	" "	" "	3 Sons.	Vn & P	" "	
Harrison Major Wild	1861–1929	U.S., Chicago (1876)	one Son.	organ	Howe 252–53; MT XXII (1881) 649	1881?
Arthur Battelle Whiting	1861–1936	U.S., Boston (1885)	one Son.	Vn & P	Am. Suppl. 403–4; Sloan 153	ca. 1891
Edmund Severn	1862–1942	Eng., Hartford (1890?)	one Son.	Vn & P	Am. Suppl. 359	
Henry Holden Huss	1862–1953	U.S., New York (1885)	Op. 24	Vc & P	Am. Suppl. 248–49; GROVE IV 418	ca. 1910?
Carl Adolph Preyer	1863–1947	Germ., Lawrence, Kan. (1891)	Son. 2, in f	P solo	Gloyne 34, 88	1909

Name	Dates	Place (date)	Work	Instr.	Reference	Date
Charles Frederick Dennée	1863–1946	U.S., Boston (1883)	2 Sons.	Vn & P	Howe 624, 626; Sloan 147	1885 & 1910
Winton James Baltzell	1864–1928	U.S., New York (1907)	one Son.	Vn & P	Hughes/AMERICAN 275–78; Sloan 146	before 1900
Harvey Worthington Loomis "	1865–1930 "	U.S., New York (after 1893) "	one Son. + one "Lyric Finale"	P solo / Vn & P	Am. Suppl. 274 / Hughes/AMERICAN 84–85	before 1900
Edward Benjamin Scheve "	1865–1924 "	Germ., Rochester (1888) "	Son. in c / Son. in E♭	Vn & P / organ	Am. Suppl. 352 / "	
Maurice Arnold (Strothotte) " "	1865–1937 " "	U.S., New York (by 1894) " "	one Son.	P solo	ART OF MUSIC IV 433; Hughes/AMERICAN 136	ca. 1885
Clara Anna Korn	1866–1940	Germ., New York (1893)	Son. in e	Vn & P	Hughes/AMERICAN 139; Sloan 146	before 1900
William Edwin Hoesche	1867–1929	U.S., New Haven (1877?)	one Son. / one Son.	Vn & P / Vn & P	Sloan 150; Am. Suppl. 264 / Sloan 148; Hughes/AMERICAN 500–502	
Henry Kimball Hadley	1871–1937	U.S., Garden City (1895)	one Son.	Vn & P	BAKER 635–36; Salter/AMERICAN 97	ca. 1896
Percy Lee Atherton	1871–1944	U.S., Boston (by 1915)	2 Sons.	Vn & P	Am. Suppl. 118	before 1896
Edward Burlingame Hill	1872–1960	U.S., Boston (1894)	3 Sons.: in f♯, in E ("The Light that Failed"), "Patriotica"	P solo	ART OF MUSIC IV 388–89	
Frank Edwin Ward "	1872–1953 "	U.S., New York (1902) "	Son. 1, in e / Sons. 1 (Op. 15) & 2, in f & d	Vn & P / organ	Am. Suppl. 399 / "	before 1904
Thomas Carl Whitmer	1873–1959	U.S., Columbia, Mo. (1899)	"Athenian" Son. in d	Vn & P	Am. Suppl. 404	"given many times" 1899–1908
Charles Edward Ives	1874–1954	U.S., New York (1899)	"Pre-First Violin Sonata"	Vn & P	Kirkpatrick/IVES item I.C.2	
Camille W. Zeckwer	1875–1924	U.S., Philadelphia (1895?)	(Son. 1), Op. 2	Vn & P	Am. Suppl. 410	before 1900
Frederic(k) Ayres (Johnson) "	1876–1926 "	U.S., Colorado Springs (1900?) "	Op. 16 / Op. 17	P solo / Vc & P	ART OF MUSIC IV 417	by 1915
John Victor Bergquist	1877–1935	U.S., Minneapolis (1895)	2 Sons.	organ	Am. Suppl. 67	
Mabel Wheeler Daniels	1879–	U.S., Boston (1911)	one Son.	Vn & P	Sloan 147; BAKER 347	
Heniot Lévy	1879–1946	Poland, Chicago (1900)	Op. 12 in a	Vc & P	BAKER 947	
John Powell	1882–1963	U.S., Richmond (1912)	Son. "psychologique" & "teutonica"	P solo	ART OF MUSIC IV 431–32; MGG X 1532	1912 & 1914

one among 46 miscellaneous songs and instrumental pieces that he had started to compose in 1818 and that were published in Philadelphia in 1820 with the collective title *The Dawning of Music in Kentucky, or the Pleasures of Harmony in the Solitudes of Nature, Opera Prima.*[38] Heinrich had worked his way to Kentucky after failure as a merchant in Philadelphia. Except for uncertain abilities as a pianist and violinist, his formal musical training, especially in theory and composition, his colorful, checkered career as "Father Heinrich," and some real successes at home and abroad still lay far ahead. The Sonata's dedication is a clue in itself to the musical mumbo jumbo that follows:

Especially dedicated to the Virtuosos of the United States: not as a Non plus ultra or Noli me tangere but as a "firstling" in its kind from the Backwoods and as a small Morning's Entertainment or "Buona Mattina" in addition to the Serenade or "Buona Notte," already presented to them [item 3 in the collection] by their most humble— . . .

First comes a two-page introduction in D, alla breve and "Alla maniera giusta," that consists of a separate, unexplained soprano part in coloratura operatic style, with an elaborate free accompaniment and with a dedicatory text in Italian beginning "Accettate gli Ossequi d'un povero Figlio d'Orfeo. . . ." Next comes an "Allegro di molto" in D, in 3/4 meter, that suggests a degree of musical imagination and pianistic flare in spite of being nothing but a clumsily written hodgepodge of opera and concerto impressions, mostly expressive melodic bits and cumbersome passagework treated sequentially and bombastic cadences.[39] Then follows an "Andante piu tosto Adagio" in d, 3/4 meter, that does the same more rhapsodically but still without any real melodic commitment, leading into a "Finale all Polacca" in B♭, 3/4 meter, that imparts a slight sense of theme and structure, if only because it divides into small repeated sections. The work closes with one more, perorative line of Italian text, though no separate soprano part this time: "Cari Amicivi auguro sempre felicissimi giorni Addio."

38. It is the 4th work in the collection as itemized on p. 261 of Upton/HEINRICH (a thorough, appropriately extravagant study of the man and his music); on p. 260 appears Heinrich's advertised proposal for this collection (1819), on p. 226 his recollection of it 36 years later, and on pp. 44–54 Upton's discussion of it, including (pp. 52–53) facs. of the first 2 pp. in the printed finale. Cf., also, Wolverton/KEYBOARD 420–29.

39. One wishes there were more reason to believe that the high praise of this Son. in Upton/HEINRICH 47 was written with tongue in cheek, although the concession that the "amateur is betrayed" suggests the contrary.

The Generation before MacDowell (Buck, Paine, Foote)

After the gap in sonata production, we may note first the one sonata of another Bohemian by birth and a pupil of Tomaschek, **Jan Nepomucene Pychowski** (1818–1900). His Op. 8 in a, for P & Vn, is a competent, lyrical, relatively free work in three movements (F-M-Sc), with pleasing ideas, traditional harmony, some distant modulations, and moderate exploitation as well as equal sharing of the two instruments (including some imitative exchanges).[40] The Sonata in B♭ for P solo by the English-born organist **Caryl Florio** (pseudonym for **William James Robjohn**; 1843–1920 [41]) is a rather fresh work unusual for its three-movement plan, M-Mi-Ro; its rondo finale, in which a chorale-like "Intermezzo—Larghetto, solennelle" serves both as one episode and as a coda; and for the unhackneyed rhythmic structure of its phrases and scale passages in the 6/4 meter of its first movement. Florio's forms tend to be static and additive and the idiom to be a kind of extension of Classic styles (including considerable Alberti bass and repeated-note accompaniments).

A more renowned organist and composer of church music was **Dudley Buck** (1839–1909), an American by birth who set the pattern of foreign training by studying in both Germany and France.[42] Buck's "Second Sonata" for organ, Op. 77 in g, is dedicated to another fine American organist, Clarence Eddy. It is the first U.S. work introduced here that speaks in the Romantic idiom and the first that displays professional writing skills needing no apologies. That Mendelssohn is the primary style influence is not surprising for one who studied in Leipzig with Moscheles, Hauptmann, and Rietz.[43] The first of the three movements, "Allegro moderato ma energico," is a "sonata form"; the second, "Adagio molto espressivo," is an A-B-A design with an extended, florid, retrospective coda; and the finale, "Allegro vivace non troppo," is a driving rondo that was sure to please the crowd,[44] although it includes no section quite so surefire as the fughetta on "Hail, Columbia!" in the finale of Buck's first Sonata for organ. Buck's music is fluent, harmonically resourceful, and expressive (Ex. 123), although its themes usually lack distinction and too often border on the sentimental because of chromatic subdivisions of the line.

40. Cf. Sloan/VIOLIN 25–32, with exx.
41. Cf. GROVE Am. Suppl. 206, including reference to 4 (unpub.) Vn sons.
42. Cf. Howe/AMERICA 679–84.
43. GROVE I 992–93 (R. Aldrich).
44. Op. 77 was played at the 10th annual meeting of the Music Teachers National Association, in Boston in 1886 (MT XXVII [1886] 54; Salter/MTNA 25).

Ex. 123. From the return in the middle movement of Dudley
Buck's Sonata in g, Op. 77 (after the G. Schirmer ed. of 1877).

The pianist **Stephen Albert Emery** (1841–91) reveals almost the same
German training in his ingratiating "Erste Sonatella," Op. 9 in A, and
his more driving, scherzando "Zweite Sonatella," Op. 11 in c. Each
piece is a skillful, one-movement, near *perpetuum mobile* in "sonata
form" that might have come right out of Mendelssohn's *Songs Without
Words.* Still another American-born pianist (also, organist) with the
same German training and the same professional, resourceful command of the Mendelssohnian idiom and of the instrument was **Smith
Newell Penfield** (1837–1920). Penfield's *Poem of Life, Four Characteristic Pieces in the Form of a Sonata,* adequately suggests the nature of
its four separately published movements by their effusive titles alone—
"Parnassus" ("Allegro moderato," E♭, 4/4; starting with full, rolled
chords), "The Vale of Romance" ("Adagio," c, 3/4; starting with
rising, chromatic, dotted patterns), "The Cascade of Pleasure" ("Scherzo
and Trio, Allegretto," C, 2/4), and "The Stream of Time" ("Rondo,
Allegro brillante," E♭, 6/8).

Of two German-born composers of violin sonatas in New York, **Otto
Singer** (1833–94) had studied with Moscheles, Hauptmann, and Liszt,
among others, before coming here in 1867,[45] two years before the pub-

45. Howe/AMERICA 444 mentions a Son. for P solo composed while he was still
in Leipzig.

lication of his *Grosses Duo (in Sonatenform) in einem Satze,* Op. 3 in c.[46] This last is a grandiose, somewhat repetitious and hollow movement of eighteen pages. The thick, chordal piano part, with its Lisztian arpeggios, tremolo, and sequential climaxes puts the less idiomatic, simpler violin part in the shade. The other German, **George Matzka** (1825–83), was a stringsman, as might be guessed from the more idiomatic, though not virtuosic, violin part in his Sonata in D of 1876.[47] This work, in three movements (F-Ro-VF), is more conventional, concentrated, and straightforward in form and style.

Continuing to draw from our tabulations *(supra),* we find only elementary pedagogic material, although of a generally appealing, graceful sort, in the "easy sonatas" and sonatinas for P solo by several

Ex. 124. From the start of an unpublished Sonata in D, Op. 21, by Horace Wadham Nicholl (after the autograph at the New York Public Library).

esteemed teachers, including **Hugh Archibald Clarke** (1839–1927), **Henry Maylath** (1827–83), **Charles Fradel** (1821–88), **Carl Venth** (1860–1938), and **William F. Sudds** (1843–1920). But somewhat more advanced in purpose and content is the Sonata in f, for P solo, by the Philadelphia teacher **Preston Ware Orem** (1865–1938). This work, another example of the fluent Mendelssohnian idiom, may be incomplete, for it contains only a driving first movement in f, curious for its square, clipped phrase rhythms, and a songful "Andante quasi allegretto" in B♭. The unpublished piano sonata has not been found here that **Edgar Stillman Kelley** (1857–1944) wrote during study in Stuttgart *(ca.* 1878?) and played for Liszt, never to forget how Liszt played much of it right back to him from aural memory.[48] We shall

---

46. Cf. Sloan/VIOLIN 39–44, with exx.
47. Cf. Sloan/VIOLIN 33–39, with exx.; BAKER Suppl. 85.
48. Cf. H. Schonberg's column in *The New York Times* for Jan. 26, 1969.

have to leave without further mention the "Homesick Sonatina" by one J. B. Schmalz, on our tabulation.

Several MS sonatas for Vn & P from the later 19th century deserve serious mention. The unpublished, 32-page Sonata in D, Op. 21, for Vn & P, by the English-born organist **Horace Wadham Nicholl** (1848–1922) [49] is an impassioned, energetic, virtuosic, often florid work, intriguing for its rhythmic diversity and ingenuity as well as for some rapid, remote modulations and some melodic chromaticism that occasionally challenge its tonal stability.[50] The bold rising leaps by which the first of its three movements opens (F-S-F) brings Richard Strauss's instrumental openings to mind (Ex. 124). By contrast, the unpublished, 29-page Sonata in G, Op. 12 (before 1850?), by the New York violinist and organist **George Frederick Bristow** (1825–98) is less sophisticated

Ex. 125. From the recapitulation, second theme, in the first movement of George Frederick Bristow's Sonata in G, Op. 12 (after the MS at the New York Public Library).

in its songlike charm and Weberian brilliance, yet not without freshness and originality in its figuration and in the well-contrasted styles of its three movements (M/F-M-Ro).[51] The violin often doubles one or another element in the piano part (Ex. 125).

Among further unpublished sonatas for Vn & P, Op. 24, in b, by one of the most influential American organists, composers, and music educators of the 19th century, **John Knowles Paine** (1839–1906), was composed in 1875, after his training in Berlin and in the same year that he assumed the first American professorship of music, at Harvard Uni-

49. Cf. BAKER 1157.

50. Cf. Sloan/VIOLIN 58–64, with exx. High praise for Nicholl's fugal mastery in his "Symphonische Sonate" for organ, Op. 42 in a, is voiced in MT XLII (1901) 748.

51. Cf. its description on pp. 80–81, 143–44, 159–60, and 190 (item 18), of Rogers/BRISTOW, a valuable recent diss. on the man, his environment, and his music.

Ex. 126. From the start of the finale of John Knowles Paine's Sonata in b, Op. 24 (after the autograph, dated 1875, at the Boston Public Library).

versity.[52] This duo and the earlier Fantasia Sonata in d, for organ, also unpublished,[53] were Paine's only ventures in the sonata. Op. 24 is an extended work (46 pp. of MS) in three movements, including an "Allegro con fuoco" in "sonata form," a "Larghetto" in the relative major key and in rondo design, and a canonic, cursive, monothematic finale, "Allegro vivace," back in the home key of b/B (Ex. 126). In the first movement the style is plain and direct in harmony, melody, and texture, and the main idea is amply reiterated and developed, all making for telling, sincere music when the effect is not a bit cut-and-dried. The second movement is more ornate, graceful, and melodically flowing. And the finale reveals the fluent drive of Mendelssohn as its canonic motive recurs in varied guises. Another Bostonian, the Ohio-born, German-trained composer and writer **Willard Burr** (1852–1915), left a MS duo, "Grand Sonata" in b♭, in which the three movements (F-M-F) are interrelated in all their elements by a triplet motive that prevails in the opening theme.[54] The development of materials is con-

52. Cf. BAKER 1199, with further bibliography; Sloan/VIOLIN 44–50 (with exx.); Salter/AMERICAN 22 (Op. 24, played in New York in 1885 for the Music Teachers National Association).

53. Played by Paine himself in 1863 (DWIGHT's XXIII [1863–64] 143).

54. Cf. Sloan/VIOLIN 74–79, with exx. The MS is at the Library of Congress.

siderable, the harmony is rich, the tonal range is wide (especially in the flat keys), and the melodic lines are active, although more through somewhat empty scale and chord figures than truly inventive patterns.

Among published sonatas of the later 19th century for Vn & P should be noted Op. 20 in g by still another Bostonian, **Arthur Foote** (1853–1937), one of Paine's several notable students and himself a fine pianist and organist.[55] This work is cast in four movements, VF-M-S-VF, with a light, *perpetuum mobile* B section, "Allegretto grazioso," following a songful A section, "Alla Siciliana," in the A-B-A design of the second movement. The ideas, harmony, and treatment are conservative but not dull. Also in Boston lived the English-born, German-trained soprano, teacher, pianist, and composer **Clara Kathleen Rogers** (1844–1931). She first performed her so-called "Sonata dramatico" in public in 1888 with Loeffler as the violinist.[56] It is a three-movement work, F-M-F, that is like Foote's in being conservative in all respects, apart from a few remote modulations, yet not without musical, especially melodic, appeal.

More abreast of the times in Europe is the duo, Op. 3 in A, that the American-born composer and educator **Leo Rich Lewis** (1865–1945) wrote during or just after his training under Rheinberger in Munich (1889–92). That training helps to explain the resourceful harmony and the imaginative, concentrated development of ideas, particularly their contrapuntal imitative treatment, in all three movements (F-S-VF).[57] In warmth and rhythmic urge Lewis came closer to Brahms than to his teacher. There is a Sonata in b, Op. 4, for P & Vn, by the Vienna-trained student of R. Fuchs, **Rubin Goldmark** (1872–1932; nephew of Karl), who later became identified with the Juilliard School in New York. It is described as "romantic in content and classical in form, and [it] exhibits vigorous inventiveness," yet is still "in the formative stage." [58]

The Four Sonatas by MacDowell

From the standpoints of high contemporary praise, wide international endorsement, and persistent success as publications, the four

55. Cf. Sloan/VIOLIN 79–84, with exx.; BAKER 494–95, with further bibliography; GROVE Am. Suppl. 207–8 (listing an unpub. Son. for Vc & P, Op. 76, not seen here). Op. 20 is reviewed in SMW L (1892) 23 as a delightful if not very original work that avoids "foolhardy problems."

56. Cf. Sloan/VIOLIN 55–58, with exx.; BAKER 1359.

57. Cf. Sloan/VIOLIN 129–36, with generous exx.; BAKER 948.

58. Cobbett/CHAMBER I 476–77 (A. Shepherd); but SMW LIX (1901) 948 finds it lacking in both originality and energy. Cf. BAKER 583–84.

piano sonatas by **Edward (Alexander) MacDowell** (1861–1908) easily
outrank any other U.S. sonatas produced before World War I.[59]
Furthermore, apart from the recent, mainly historical interest in
Reinagle's sonatas (*supra*) and the belated interest in Ives's sonatas (and
his other music) that has developed only in the last generation, Mac-
Dowell's sonatas are the sole examples from that whole century-and-a-
quarter that have survived, whether in print, recordings, or public
performance. In fact, they seem even to have won some new interest in
recent years.[60] To be sure, we can no longer accept the numerous extreme statements that his contemporaries made (speaking volumes for
themselves, too) about the greatness of his sonatas, of which the following is but one sample:

> If there is anything in the literature of the piano since the death of Bee-
> thoven which, for combined passion, dignity, breadth of style, weight of
> momentum, and irresistible plangency of emotion, [that] is comparable to
> the four sonatas . . . [of MacDowell], I do not know of it. And I write these
> words with a perfectly definite consciousness of all that they may be held to
> imply.[61]

Nor, for that matter, need we accept the complete reversal of the
critical pendulum, within two decades, as in the following discon-
nected remarks by Paul Rosenfeld:

> . . . as late as the Tragic and Heroic sonatas, [MacDowell continued to be]
> a mere sectary of the grandiose German romantics. . . . We cannot avoid
> hearing a reminiscence of the pompous Meistersinger march in the slow
> movement of the Celtic sonata. . . . The echoes are not only Wagnerian;
> the theme of the finale of the Celtic sonata has a strong resemblance to that
> of The Hall of the Mountain King in Grieg's Peer Gynt Suite. And to the
> end, MacDowell shared his school's narrowness of artistic vision, embracing
> little outside the confines of homophonic music. He was badly equipped in
> polyphonic technique; and where, as in a passage of the last movement of

---

59. A main source on the man and his music, in spite of what now seem like
much inflated evaluations, is Gilman/MACDOWELL. A helpful style study of the
sons., prefaced by their artistic and historical orientation, is Eagle/MACDOWELL (an
M.A. thesis of 1952). Of value as shorter surveys of MacDowell that emphasize the
sons. are the separate sections or chaps. in Hughes/AMERICAN 34–57, Howard/
AMERICAN 323–44, and, especially for their superior examinations of his aesthetic
posture and its up-to-date perspective, Chase/AMERICA 346–64 and Austin/20th
54–56.

60. For 2 recent articles intended to revive interest, cf. Kaiserman/MACDOWELL
(on Opp. 59 and 50) and Lowens/MACDOWELL (including listings of recordings of
Opp. 45, 50, and 59 in "A Selective Discography" [with M. L. Morgan]).

61. Gilman/MACDOWELL 161. ("Plangency" is a favorite word in MacDowell criti-
cism.) Cf., also, Eagle/MACDOWELL 12–14 (citing W. S. B. Matthews, H. T. Finck,
A. Seidl, J. Massenet, J. Huneker, W. Mason, and H. E. Krehbiel); Hughes/AMERI-
CAN 52.

the Norse sonata, he attempted canonic imitation, we find him essaying it clumsily, and with all the obsessive rapture of a child in possession of a new and dazzling toy. . . . He never attained real facility in moving his ideas, or in moving himself through them . . . whether we wander in the Guinevere section of the Sonata Eroica, or in the Old-Fashioned Garden of the New England Idylls, we are never far from the little old rendezvous. . . . The feelings entertained about life by him seem to have remained uncertain; and while fumbling for them he seems regularly to have succumbed to "nice" and "respectable" emotions, conventional, accepted by and welcome to, the best people. It is shocking to find how full of vague poesy he is. Where his great romantic brethren, Brahms, Wagner, and Debussy, are direct and sensitive, clearly and tellingly expressive, MacDowell minces and simpers, maidenly and ruffled. He is nothing if not a daughter of the American Revolution. . . .[62]

We must recognize such extreme judgments as the norm rather than the exception in a late-Romantic environment that found MacDowell himself giving vent, for example, to a severe deprecation of Mozart's piano sonatas. They are, he said, "entirely unworthy of . . . any composer with pretensions to anything beyond mediocrity. They are written in a style of flashy harpsichord virtuosity such as Liszt never descended to, even in those of his works at which so many persons are accustomed to sneer." [63] In short, MacDowell's four sonatas must be viewed in moderation here, as containing some of the best music by a gifted U.S. composer of limited aesthetic range.

MacDowell's four piano sonatas and two piano concertos are his only complete works of the sonata type within a modest output of about 100 works that consists mostly of solo piano pieces, solo songs, and part songs.[64] With regard to their circumstances, he composed the first two of his sonatas during his Boston years (1888–96) and the other two during his lucid New York years (1896–1905). More specifically, he composed all four during approximately the eight years from 1892 to 1900, or during approximately the last two-fifths of his over-all, 24-year creative life (1879–1903).[65] And he saw all four first published within a span also of eight years, 1893 to 1901.[66] He himself introduced "Sonata tragica," Op. 45 in g/G, to the public, first playing the third movement in Boston in 1892, the year before publication, and the whole sonata in that city in 1893. A critic wrote, "One feels genius in it

62. Rosenfeld/AMERICAN 40–46 passim.
63. MacDowell/ESSAYS 194; cf., also, pp. 193, 200, 239, and 253, as well as SCE 500.
64. Cf. Sonneck/SUUM 87 ("MacDowell Versus MacDowell: A Study in First Editions and Revisions"); Gillman/MACDOWELL 92–93.
65. The available information on MacDowell's composition dates is generally vague.
66. The complex pub. details of the first eds. and some later printings are unraveled in Sonneck/MACDOWELL 35, 38, 41, 42.

throughout. . . . The composer played it superbly, magnificently." [67]
Among others who soon performed it, too, was the American pianist
William Mason, who first played Op. 45 at a summer colony (by
1894)—in fact, played it almost daily throughout the season, completely winning over his audiences (more so than when he later played
Op. 50 in a similar experiment).[68] Most early reactions to this work
were highly favorable; but some found too conscious an obligation to
"sonata form" in MacDowell's first such effort.[69] And one early review
of the original Breitkopf & Härtel edition of "Sonata tragica" found
excesses, especially in the contrasts and chromaticism, even allowing
for the dramatic implications of the title.[70] That title has been related
to MacDowell's "memory of his grief over the death of his master
Raff," [71] although without further programme, dedication, or other
evidence and although Raff had died a full decade earlier (ssb X),
shortly after MacDowell's two years of studies with him in Frankfurt.
But, apparently some time before 1900, MacDowell's wife explained
the programme without mentioning Raff, as simply a desire

to heighten the darkness of tragedy by making it follow closely on the heels
of triumph. Therefore, he attempted to make the last movement a steadily
progressive triumph, which, at its climax, is utterly broken and shattered.
In doing this he has tried to epitomize the whole work. While in the other
movements he aimed at expressing tragic details, in the last he has tried to
generalize; thinking that the most poignant tragedy is that of catastrophe
in the hour of triumph.[72]

MacDowell's "Sonata eroica," Op. 50 [73] in g, was composed, presumably, in 1894–95 (i.e., between the pub. of Opp. 45 and 50). The composer deplored his own first performance of it in Boston (in 1895?),
although his wife and others "thought he did it wonderfully" and it
soon won new (though less) interest, as a "noble," freer, and "lovelier,"
if less "dynamic," work than Op. 45.[74] This time he did supply a dedication, a subtitle, and a programme. He dedicated Op. 50 to William

67. Cf. Gilman/MACDOWELL 36–37, 69, 147–50 (including a facs. of Op. 45/iii/1–7
in MS).

68. MASON MEMORIES 255–56; cf. [nephew Daniel Gregory] Mason/MUSIC 53; MUSIC
IX (1895–96) 429–31 (W. S. B. Mathews on the pedagogical values of Op. 45).

69. Several reactions are cited in Eagle/MACDOWELL 22–24.

70. SMW LIV (1896) 194.

71. Gilman/MACDOWELL 148. Cf. Eagle/MACDOWELL 20–22 for follow-ups of this
interpretation.

72. Quoted in Hughes/AMERICAN 53–54. An emotional 4-line poem by Philip
Becker Goetz, headed "MacDowell's Sonata Tragica," appears, isolated, in MUSIC
XI (1896–97) 503.

73. Originally it was to be Op. 49 (Sonneck/MACDOWELL 38).

74. Gilman/MACDOWELL 92, 152–53; Eagle/MACDOWELL 25; MASON MEMORIES 256;
MUSIC X (1896) 309–10 (W. S. B. Mathews on W. Mason and Op. 50).

Mason, perhaps rewarding Mason's share in popularizing Op. 45. When Op. 50 appeared (Nov., 1895), he wrote Mason that there were parts "of the sonata I am fond of and parts of it I have felt deeply, though I am afraid they—the feelings—are not fully expressed." [75] The subtitle of Op. 50 is "Flos regum Arthurus" ("The Flowering of Arthur's Princes" or more freely, "The Heyday of the Round Table") and his elaboration of it appeared not in any further inscriptions nor in the separate movement titles but in a later commentary (written for Gilman?):

> While not exactly [literal?] programme music, I had in mind the Arthurian legend when writing this work. The first movement typifies the coming of Arthur. The scherzo [an "interruption" or "aside" that might have been omitted, MacDowell confessed still later, in New York] was suggested by a picture of Doré showing [in Tennyson's *Guinevere*] a knight in the woods surrounded by elves. The third movement was suggested by my idea of Guinevere. That following represents the passing of Arthur. [76]

None of the implied programmes in this or MacDowell's other three sonatas happens to raise directly the fuzzy question of American music versus American composer,[77] analogous to the question of nationalism in Grieg's music (ssb XV). But they do raise the equally fuzzy question in MacDowell's aesthetic of sound per se versus sound as but one access to the poetic idea.[78] Whether MacDowell was or was not a programmatist at heart, it is hard to believe that the actual composition of his sonatas was not guided by considerations primarily musical.

MacDowell's "impulse to write" his "Third Sonata," Op. 57 in d, "was enhanced," according to his wife's later recollection,[79] "by the close friendship which existed between him and Edvard Grieg. They never saw each other, but they corresponded constantly." Grieg accepted MacDowell's proffered dedication in a charming letter in his own "bad English," [80] the date of which, Oct. 10, 1899, at least suggests about when the composition had been completed. The Nordic, colorful, eight-line poem at the head of Op. 57 provides another link with Grieg. Furthermore, this poem's publication in 1903, slightly extended, under the title "Norse Sonata" in a collection of *Verses by Edward MacDowell* [81] probably explains the title by which Op. 57 is generally

75. More of the letter is quoted in Mason/MUSIC 53.

76. As quoted in the course of Gilman/MACDOWELL 150–53.

77. Cf. Howard/AMERICAN 323, 326–27; Chase/AMERICA 354–56; Lowens/MACDOWELL 62, 69; Eagle/MACDOWELL 6–11 (various sources quoted); Gilman/MACDOWELL 83–85.

78. Cf. the illuminating discussion in Chase/AMERICA 356–59; also, Howard/AMERICAN 328–29; and the composer's own words in MacDowell/ESSAYS 254–73.

79. MacDowell/MACDOWELL 19.

80. A facs. of the original and a printed version are both given in Gilman/MACDOWELL 72–73.

81. Cf. Sonneck/MACDOWELL 41–42.

known. But as in his other three sonatas, nothing in the music of Op. 57, notwithstanding efforts to find a Nordic programme,[82] keeps Mac-Dowell's four sonata titles from being completely interchangeable. Yet Op. 57 seems to have posed more problems for MacDowell's contemporaries (and interested its own composer less[83]) than the other three sonatas (and is today the only one not recorded and the only one so rarely played). Although one German reviewer praised it along with Op. 59 as "tone poems in the highest sense," [84] the American organist and writer W. S. B. Mathews balked when he came to Op. 57, finding it incomprehensible and intolerable.[85] He discussed at length how MacDowell achieved his primary goal, originality, only through tonality "so vague as to leave all accidentals alike probable or improbable, according to the weird fancy of the player"; through rhythm, of which there is a "total absence" in the senses of pulsation, flow, and symmetry; through "fundamental harmonies" that are "unusual and forced"; and through "almost universal dissonances."

MacDowell composed his "Fourth Sonata (Keltic)," Op. 59 in e, presumably in 1900 (between the pubs. of Opp. 57 and 59). Originally he had sought to dedicate it to "Fiona Macleod," a pseudonym (as he did not then realize) for the Mr. and Mrs. William Sharp whose joint collection of stories and sketches, *Lyra Celtica* (1896), seems to have been the literary "inspiration" for Op. 59. Perhaps MacDowell's own Scotch-Irish ancestry had a bearing, too. At any rate, when Mr. Sharp's delighted acceptance failed to reach him[86] MacDowell decided to dedicate this work, too, to Grieg. However, this time the initial bit of verse does not relate nationalistically to the dedicatee:

> Who minds now Keltic tales of yore,
> Dark Druid rhymes that thrall,
> Deirdre's song and wizard lore
> of great Cuchullin's fall.

Following this quatrain in the 1903 collection of *Verses by Edward MacDowell* is a 22-line poem on the majestic death of Cuchillin (beginning "Cuchullin fought and fought in vain"). MacDowell wrote Gilman that the longer poem did not "entirely fit the music [only the coda of the finale, surmises Gilman]," that it might yet underlie "another musical form [a symphonic poem never started, surmises Gil-

---

82. E.g., Gilman/MACDOWELL 153–54; MUSIC XIX (1900–1901) 411 (W. S. B. Mathews). Cf. Eagle/MACDOWELL 26–27.

83. Gilman/MACDOWELL 71.

84. MW XXXIII (1902) 686 (E. Segnitz).

85. MUSIC XIX (1900–1901) 410–12.

86. Neither he nor MacDowell lived to learn that it probably got sidetracked, according to MacDowell/MACDOWELL 20.

man]," that it still could implement an "understanding of the *stimmung* of the sonata," and that in any case, "as with my 3d Sonata, the music is more a commentary [or " 'bardic' rhapsody," he said elsewhere] on the subject than an actual depiction of it [Beethoven's "more through feeling than tone painting," again; SCE 525]." [87]

The first two of MacDowell's four sonatas begin with separate, slow introductions and have four movements, with scherzando types in second place—S/F-VF-S-VF and S/F-Sc-S-VF. The last two have only three movements, both M-M-F, leaving out the scherzando types (such as had given MacDowell doubts in Op. 50). In length the sonatas are average for the time—854, 843, 478, and 579 measures, respectively. All four sonatas are in minor keys except for characteristically Roman- tic shifts to the tonic major mode in Opp. 45/iv and 57/iii. Apart from Op. 50/ii in the minor key on the mediant (b♭), the inner movements are all in nearly-related keys. Thematic ties, more or less subtle, largely interrelate the contrasting ideas within a movement (e.g., the introduc- tion and main theme in Op. 50/i or the main and subordinate themes in Op. 59/iii) and all the movements of each sonata. By these internal and over-all relationships, MacDowell was putting into practice two of his own quoted dicta, about "sonata form" and form in general:

> If the composer's ideas do not imperatively demand treatment in . . . ["sonata form"]—that is, if his first theme is not actually dependent upon his second and side themes for its poetic fulfillment—he has not composed a sonata movement, but a potpourri, which the form only aggravates.[88]
>
> Form should be a synonym for *coherence*. No idea, whether great or small, can find utterance without form, but that form will be inherent to the idea, and there will be as many forms as there are adequately expressed ideas. In the musical idea, *per se*, analysis will reveal form.[89]

Although, from one to the next, MacDowell's sonatas get somewhat freer in tempo, thicker in texture, and more smoothed over at the joints, they still adhere throughout to the standardized designs—in fact, to but two of them, "sonata form" (with only such variants as the omission of nearly all but the main theme in the recapitulation of Op. 45/iv) and the A-B-A design. Neither in form nor in style was MacDowell an experimenter or innovator in his day.

With regard to chief style traits, MacDowell reveals a severely limited but markedly individual group of solutions to specific situa- tions in his four sonatas, with mood, tempo, and major or minor

---

87. Cf. Gilman/MACDOWELL 151–61 (including a facs. of the autograph of Op. 59/i, last page).

88. As quoted in Gilman/MACDOWELL 147.

89. MacDowell/ESSAYS 264.

mode being main determinants (or main consequents, depending on one's point of view). In these senses any one sonata could do for them all, with Op. 45 being no worse for being first and slightly more restrained and Op. 59 no better for being last, slightly more bombastic, and MacDowell's own favorite.[90] Their enjoyment is limited only by the style limitations and their rapidly cloying effect, and it is only impeded, not helped, by those superimposed programmes, especially today, when musicians tend to reject both the fact and the nature of such idyllic and chimerical associations. For that matter, at least as regards styles rather than forms, the sonatas disclose little new to all who know such favorite piano pieces as "From a Wandering Iceberg" and "From Uncle Remus" (cf. the first 2 themes in Op. 59), or "Scotch Poem" and "Told at Sunset" (cf. Op. 50/i and iii).

Turning first to MacDowell's melodies, we find these typically to be wide-ranged, particularly in the slowest sections or movements and in the gayest or most energetic themes, where they may roam over more than half of the keyboard (e.g., Opp. 50/iii, throughout, and 57/i/44–66). Their range tends to be narrower, not surprisingly, in themes of "simple tenderness" like that in Op. 59/ii (recall "To a Wild Rose") or in "swift," crisp themes like that in Op. 59/iii (recall "In Autumn"). More than anything else, what seems to give MacDowell's themes their special modal or American Indian flavor, along with the inevitable lowered-7th step, is their centering around leaps or gaps in the underlying scale—for example, mostly around 3–1 in the introduction to Op. 45/i, or 5–3 in the second theme, "simply, yet with pathos," in Op. 50/i. Certain frequent rhythmic patterns add individuality to MacDowell's melodies, too, including ♩ ♪♩ in both 3/4 and 4/4 meter (e.g., the main themes of Op. 45/i and iv) or ♩.♫ and, simply, ♫♩ as a triplet or compound pulse, often an upbeat (e.g., Op. 57/iii). Frequent, too, are Scotch snaps (e.g., Op. 57/i/44–62), strategically located syncopations (e.g., Opp. 45/iii/5 or 59/ii/20), and the amplified pulse created by afterbeat accompaniments (e.g., the "Maestoso," triple forte, "grandioso" return near the end of Op. 45).

MacDowell's harmonic vocabulary, chromaticism, use of dissonance, and tonal range are all considerable, yet all more conservative, law-abiding, and metrically controlled than the early reports of them would suggest. Again, it is a few specific treatments or devices that impart the special flavor, most of which are well-known in, for example, "To a Water-lily." Those "unusual and forced" uses of "fundamental harmonies" that W. S. B. Mathews found (*supra*) might refer to such

90. He put Op. 50 second and also had a special fondness for Op. 45/iii (Gilman/ MACDOWELL 71).

harmless passages as that in Op. 57/i/19–23, where each 7th or 9th chord resolves into another 7th or 9th chord, and Op. 57/i/40–43, where, mainly, chromatic and diatonic appoggiaturas over a pedal bass disguise but do not invalidate a simple I_4^6-IV-ii-I_4^6-V-I progression. A characteristic procedure of MacDowell, and one that carries him perilously close to the brink of sentimentality, is the opposition of "fundamental harmonies" to a melodic line that descends chromatically from its peak, as in Ex. 127. Also characteristic and near to sentimentality in that example are the several major-7th dissonances, occurring both as passing notes and as untied suspensions. By such innocent means MacDowell achieved his most tender moments of poetic

Ex. 127. From the third movement of Edward MacDowell's "Sonata eroica," Op. 50 in g (after the revised Schirmer ed. of 1924).

yearning (as in Op. 50/i/121) as well as his most naughtily dissonant climaxes (as at the quadruple forte near the end of Op. 59).

MacDowell's writing for piano shows all the variety and the understanding of the instrument that can be expected of a pianist fine enough to win Liszt's own warm praise.[91] One may find writing that is heavy and chordal (Op. 59/i/16–23), thin and scherzando or fleet (Op. 50/ii), intricate in the changing figures of its passagework (Op. 59/i/84–99), purely homophonic (Op. 57/i/10–40), or moderately polyphonic and more often and successfully so than writers have generally granted [92] (e.g., the telling, concurrent lines in Opp. 45/iii/32–61 and 50/iii/57–69; or the motivic play in Op. 45/i/185–93). Yet all these traits also are typed in MacDowell's sonatas (and other piano music),

91. Cf. the reports collected in Gilman/MACDOWELL 16–19, 85–92.
92. Recall P. Rosenfeld's criticism, *supra*.

and recur often enough to become further identification tags of his style.

MacDowell's individuality is as marked, in fact, as that of the composer he most closely resembles in style, Grieg (ssb XV).[93] Though Grieg was older by eighteen years, the two men shared about the same stage of development in the language of music. Furthermore, they are often similar in more specific ways, as in their modal treatments of the scale, their problematical positions as musical nationalists, their limited range of output, and, indeed, their limited artistic scope, including the dependence of each on a few characteristic solutions to certain recurring musical situations. Most of these similarities apply to their respective sonatas, although the latter reveal no resemblances quite so close as those between the first lyrical piano themes in their respective Concertos in e and d. Coming half a generation later, MacDowell proved to be a kind of exaggeration of Grieg (and in this sense a little closer to Rachmaninoff [94]). Not necessarily did he hover still closer on that brink of sentimentality. (As always, of course, one must be both willing and able to hear each work on its own terms and in its own milieu.) But he did strive for still wider emotional extremes (including greater extremes in the dynamic indications, insofar as Mrs. MacDowell's revisions and amplifications in all 4 sons. of his somewhat careless and inadequate editorial markings are authentic[95]). But apart from the extremes, which are likely to reflect less in MacDowell's favor, MacDowell must be acknowledged as Grieg's superior in two respects. He handled the larger forms more naturally and more flexibly, mainly because he handled phrase-and-period syntax more naturally and more flexibly.[96] And he scored more interestingly and more knowingly for what was to him a "cold" yet favorite instrument, the piano.[97] Indeed, whatever his limitations, performers are likely to return to one or another of his sonatas again and again, perhaps more than to Grieg's Op. 7, for several compelling reasons. The sonatas abound in frank songful melody, in opportunities to emote with judicious abandon, and in piano writing that makes good sounds and pleasurable technical challenges (Ex. 128). Furthermore, the forms are invariably timed right and last only long enough to state their messages and achieve their goals.

93. Their styles are compared in Howard/AMERICAN 325–26.

94. But in Bertennson & Leyda/RACHMANINOFF, Rachmaninoff is quoted as disliking MacDowell's Concerto (in d?) when Carreño played it in 1906.

95. Cf. her preface to the G. Schirmer re-editions of Opp. 45 and 50 in 1922 and 1924; also, MacDowell/MACDOWELL 20–21.

96. Service/CADENCE 43–62 finds the structural landmarks clearly defined, largely owing to traditional harmony and clear phrase structure.

97. Cf. his own words to a friend as quoted in Eagle/MACDOWELL 3.

Ex. 128. From the opening of Edward MacDowell's "Sonata tragica" in g/G, Op. 45 (facs. of the autograph, with the kind permission and co-operation of the Butler Library at Columbia University).

MacDowell's Contemporaries and Successors

Among some contemporaries and successors to MacDowell in the field of the piano sonata, the active St. Louis pianist, organist, and teacher **Ernest Richard Kroeger** (1862–1934) left a three-movement example, Op. 40 in Db (F-S-VF), that shows good compositional training but utterly banal content. The same reaction greeted his Sonata for Vn & P, Op. 32 in f♯, which has a similar movement plan.[98] The equally active Kansas pianist **Carl Adolph Preyer** (1863–1947), born and trained in Germany, left three completed examples. Op. 33 in c♯ is a four-movement work (F-M-Sc-VF), well reviewed when he first played it in Cincinnati in 1899.[99] Op. 50 in f, less highly regarded by Preyer himself, has a similar cycle, of which only the third movement was published ("The Brook-Nymphs").[100] "Sonata No. 4," in Eb (without op. no. and preceded by an incomplete Son. in F), won a prize in 1939 from the National Federation of Music Clubs and was published posthumously by Carl Fischer in 1949. In spite of its outdated idiom and slightly pedagogical flavor, this three-movement, "highest fulfillment" of "Preyer's gifts" (VF-S-Sc) is still fresh in its clean pianistic scoring, its imaginative rhythm and harmony, and some genuine melody (including references to a cheer and the alma mater song of the University of Kansas).[101]

Other late piano examples include *Sonata Heroic* in c♯, by the German-trained Chicagoan **Louis Campbell-Tipton** (1877–1921). This is an effective, 22-page, one-movement "sonata form" in the epigonic grand manner, with a stentorian main theme that reportedly depicts the "Hero" and a tender, expressive subordinate theme that reportedly depicts the "Ideal." [102] The Sonata in Bb, Op. 15 for P solo, by **Percy Goetschius** (1853–1943) reveals that this long-lived, successful teacher and writer of theory texts could have done well, too, by continuing as a composer. Although not published until 1908, Op. 15 is the same sonata[103] that the young man from New Jersey showed to both Liszt

97a

98. MW XXVIII (1897) 670. Cf. Sloan/VIOLIN 109–14; GROVE Am. Suppl. 266; ART OF MUSIC IV 380.

99. Cf. pp. 25–26 in the interesting and thorough, albeit somewhat idolatrous, monograph on the man and his music, Gloyne/PREYER, including full list of works (pp. 87–91).

100. Gloyne/PREYER 34, 49–50, 88.

101. Gloyne/PREYER 47–48, 78–82 (detailed description).

102. No such identifications appear in the score, but cf. ART OF MUSIC IV 422–24. Cf., also, GROVE Am. Suppl. 152.

103. According to information kindly contributed (along with the score itself) by the late Arthur Shepherd of Cleveland. Cf., also, Shepherd/GOETSCHIUS, especially pp. 309–10; BAKER 580–81; MGG V 458 (N. Broder), listing a few compositions as well as texts.

(hence, by 1886) and Brahms while he was a student, then a teacher, in Germany. As he was to recall proudly, Liszt suggested a textural change, then kissed him on the cheek; and Brahms read it all the way through, making only one comment, "Chopin," after a particular passage. But Beethoven, Schumann, and Brahms himself are still more in evidence in this knowing, warm, rich, well scored, frankly melodious, moderately free work of three movements (F-S-VF).

The three organ sonatas by the Chicago violinist **Felix Borowski** (1872–1956) include No. 3 in d (pub. by A. P. Schmidt in 1924) and were preceded by *Grande Sonate russe* for P solo, which was reportedly liked by Grieg and had been composed and published (by Lowdy of London in 1896) before Borowski left England.[104] The Sonata in e♭/E♭, Op. 65 for organ, by the eminent composer of the oratorio *Hora Novissima,* **Horatio William Parker** (1863–1919), reveals in its concentrated motivic development the influence of his teacher Rheinberger.[105] Its four traditional, well-constructed movements include an "Allegro moderato" in "sonata form"; an "Andante" in B, in A-B-A design; an "Allegretto" in b♭, in A-B-A design; and a "Fugue."

The Richmond pianist **John Powell** (1882–1963), who studied in Vienna with Leschetizky and Karl Navrátil (ssb XVII), left three sonatas for P solo and two for Vn & P, all composed between 1908 and 1928.[106] The piano sonatas are further titled "Psychologique" (Op. 15), "Noble" (Op. 21, pub. by G. Schirmer in 1921), and "Teutonica" (Op. 24), and the first violin work is called "Sonata Virginianesque" (pub. by G. Schirmer in 1919). But the music does not bear out the interest promised in these titles and by the success of Powell's *Rapsody Nègre.* It is dull and unidiomatic in its scoring, academic in its approach to form, and indifferent in melodic and harmonic material except for its use of Negro and folk ideas.

Further late violin sonatas include Op. 34 in a (1899) by the Boston pianist Mrs. **Amy Marcy Cheney Beach** (1867–1944), a conservative, Brahmsian, four-movement work (F-Sc-S-VF) of real warmth, charm, structural skill, and imagination. This work was once widely played.[107] Op. 6 in G, "At Fox Meadow," by the German-born, New York conductor **Walter (Johannes) Damrosch** (1862–1930),[108] is a three-move-

104. Cf. BAKER 185; Cat. NYPL IV 372; Kremer/ORGAN 172.
105. Cf. BAKER 1208–9, with further bibliography.
106. Cf. MGG X 1532 (N. Broder); Mason/MUSIC 298–99; ART OF MUSIC IV 431–32.
107. Cf. BAKER 104; Goetschius/BEACH 17 (facs. of first p. of the autograph), 46, 83, 110–19 (numerous laudatory reviews); Cobbett/CHAMBER I 79 (A. Shepherd); Shand/VIOLIN 224–27 (with exx.); MUSIC XI (1896–97) 473–74 (collected, laudatory reviews of performances prior to pub.).
108. Cf. Sloan/VIOLIN 121–29, with exx.

ment work (F-M-F) that begins by pleasing with its warm melodies and good scoring and ends by glutting with its excessive, uncontrolled sweetness and passion (recalling Glazunov's sons., ssʙ XVIII). Nor is one persuaded in Damrosch's favor by such near plagiarisms as the start of the second movement, which gets uncomfortably close—hardly by accident!—to that in Brahms's Concerto in B♭. The Op. 1 in A (1900) by the esteemed Bostonian who studied with Rheinberger in Munich, **Frederick Shepherd Converse** (1871–1940), is an innocuous, four-movement work (F-M-Mi-F) still betraying the student.[109] Later a Sonata by him for Vc & P was published (1922), this time a rhapsodic, warm work in two movements (S-F). And still later a Sonata in a, for P solo, appeared (1937), a similarly convincing work in three movements (F-S-F) that differs only in coming but slightly more to grips, and somewhat uneasily, with newer directions in harmony, tonality, and independent dissonance.

109a

The prizewinning "Sonate (*quasi Fantasia*)," Op. 53 in g, for P & Vn, by the Chicago pianist **Henry Schoenefeld** (1857–1936) confirms his good German training in title, publisher, as well as writing skills. But it is his pioneer interest in Negro music that shows through the content, including lively syncopations, folklike melodies, dramatic contrasts, and colorful scoring.[110] By contrast, the two violin sonatas of the Boston teacher **Harry Newton Redman** (1869–1958) are more restrained and melodically direct.[111] The one published Sonata, Op. 19 in g, for Vn & P, by the New York pianist and pupil of Rheinberger in Munich, **Henry Holden Huss** (1862–1953), is also a transparent work, in spite of some fresh approaches to harmony and rhythm (especially in both the "Andante" and scherzando sections of ii).[112] It would be still more interesting if the writing for both instruments were not somewhat pedestrian.

The German-born, New York pianist **Bruno Oscar Klein** (1858–1911) was another Rheinberger composition student in Munich (1876–77?), just before emigrating to America.[113] Of two published sonatas by him for Vn & P, Op. 10 in G (Hofmeister in Leipzig, 1887) is a four-movement work (F-M-F-F) reviewed as skillful and knowing, though "unoriginal";[114] and Op. 31 in b (Simrock in Berlin, 1904; ded. to Ysaÿe)

109. Cf. ʙᴀᴋᴇʀ 313–14; Cobbett/ᴄʜᴀᴍʙᴇʀ 301 (A. Shepherd); Shand/ᴠɪᴏʟɪɴ 222–24 (with exx.).

110. Cf. Sloan/ᴠɪᴏʟɪɴ 85–92, with exx.; ɢʀᴏᴠᴇ Am. Suppl. 354; ᴀʀᴛ ᴏꜰ ᴍᴜѕɪᴄ IV 433–34.

111. Cf. ʙᴀᴋᴇʀ 1316; Cobbett/ᴄʜᴀᴍʙᴇʀ II 277 (A. L. Goldberg).

112. Cf. ɢʀᴏᴠᴇ IV 418 and Am. Suppl. 248–49; Sloan/ᴠɪᴏʟɪɴ 114–21, with exx.; Shand/ᴠɪᴏʟɪɴ 228–30. At least 3 later duo sons. remain in MS.

113. Cf. ʙᴀᴋᴇʀ 4th ed. 589–90.

114. ᴍᴡ XX (1889) 419.

is a somewhat more brilliant, chromatic, unidiomatic work in three well integrated movements, still reflecting Schumann and Brahms but also showing the rhythmic, melodic, and harmonic influence of Dvořák's music after his directorship at the National Conservatory in New York.[115] Like Klein, the Dutch-born composer **Louis Victor (Franz) Saar** (1868–1937) had studied with Rheinberger (as well as Brahms during a winter in Vienna) and he taught at the National Conservatory in New York. His one published Sonata, Op. 44 in G, for Vn & P (pub. by Siegel in Leipzig, 1904) was reviewed as evidence that Americans still depended on German training and as a feminine counterpart to Dirk Schäfer's Op. 6 of the same year and scoring (SSB XIII).[116] Another traditional work is the three-movement Sonata in a (F-S-VF), Op. 17 (pub. by Rahter in Hamburg, 1905), by the St. Louis organist and teacher **William Henry Pommer** (1851–1937), who had enjoyed training under Reinecke, Richter, and Bruckner, among others.[117]

The one Sonata by the important Chicago composer **John Alden Carpenter** (1876–1951) is somewhat ungrateful to play for both violinist and pianist, especially in the first of its four unorthodox, free movements (S-F-S-VF).[118] The compositional skill is considerable and both the melody and harmony are enterprising. But there is little of the distinction or character to be found in Carpenter's later, more successful works. The two mature sonatas by the equally important American composer, author, and longtime professor of music at Columbia University, **Daniel Gregory Mason** (1873–1953), are characteristic of the conservatism, exceptional craftsmanship, and scholarly reflection in his music. Op. 5 in g, for Vn & P, was composed in 1907–8 and published in 1913 by G. Schirmer. It won considerable approval—from Paderewski and John Powell, among others[119]—but gave the composer some doubts about its final worth. Broad melodic arches, plastic rhythm, concentrated motivic play, good scoring, harmonic warmth, and a strong Brahmsian flavor (with no sign of Mason's post-American study under d'Indy) are the predominant traits in all three movements (F-M-VF[Ro]). Op. 14 in c, for Cl-(or-Vn) & P, was composed in

---

115. Cf. Sloan/VIOLIN 92–98, with exx.

116. MW XXXVIII (1907) 280 and NZM C (1904) 819. Cf. GROVE Am. Suppl. 346 (with mention of a Vc son. and a Hn son., too); BAKER 1394; Cobbett/CHAMBER II 320 (A. L. Goldberg).

117. BAKER 4th ed. 856; cf. Sloan/VIOLIN 71–73, with exx.

118. Cf. BAKER 253–54; Shand/VIOLIN 236–37, with exx.; Cobbett/CHAMBER I 227 (C. Engel).

119. Cf. Mason/MUSIC 165, 170–71, 296–97; also, pp. 56–57 on Paderewski's pleasure in hearing Mason play his early Son. in B♭ for P solo. Cf., further, Shand/VIOLIN 230–32, with exx.; ART OF MUSIC IV 386; SSB V (ex. from Op. 5/i).

1912 and 1915 and was published in 1920 after it had become both an immediate occasion for founding (in 1919–20) and a first product of the Society for the Publication of American Music.[120] Dedicated to another of S.P.A.M.'s founders, the music educator, composer, and clarinetist B. C. Tuthill, Op. 14 is likewise a Brahmsian, three-movement work (M-VF-F).[121]

A student of E. S. Kelley and A. Foote, **Frederic Ayres (Johnson;** 1876–1926) left one published Sonata, Op. 15 in d, which, appearing in 1914, marks "the culmination of Ayres' earlier, more tentative period." [122] Its two movements, a slow, gentle, expressive opening and a rushing, rollicking, rondo finale, are distinguished by intensive, unsuppressed lyricism. Ayres also left one sonata each in MS for P solo (Op. 16), and for Vc & P (Op. 17, a free fantasy ded. to Pablo Casals), both by 1915, and a technically difficult "Second Violin Sonata," in b, one of his last MSS.[123] There is one published Sonata, Op. 6 in c, for Vn & P, by the Polish-born, Chicago pianist **Heniot Lévy** (1879–1946), who had studied composition with Max Bruch in Berlin. It was reviewed as a strong, concentrated, traditional work of four movements.[124] The two published violin sonatas on our tabulations (*supra*) by the American organist **Mortimer Wilson** (1876–1932) reflect his training under Reger in Leipzig, with their mercurial harmonic chromaticism, thorny technical problems, and complex rhythms.[125] Wilson's 11-page "Sonatilla" in C, Op. 52 for P solo (1919), is consistent in style with its predecessors but in a diminutive, simpler, effective projection of that style throughout its four short movements (F-Sc-M-F).

Trained in Pittsburgh, **Charles Wakefield Cadman** (1881–1946) became identified especially with American Indian music.[126] In fact, the flavor of that music, including its modal inflections and primitive rhythms, shows through even in both of his published sonatas—Op. 58 in A, for P solo (1915) and Sonata in G, for Vn & P (1932). Yet, in defiance of verses inscribed before each movement, a firm note at the start of Op. 58 insists that "No Indian or Negro themes are used in this work." Both works have the three-movement plan F-S-F. Both are somewhat rhapsodic and the second in particular stretches the tonal relationships. But this music is not innovational; nor does it come to

120. Cf. Mason/MUSIC 186–87.
121. Cf. Cobbett/CHAMBER II 123 (A. Shepherd).
122. Upton/AYRES 40, 47–48 (with exx.). Cf., also, Cobbett/CHAMBER I 49 (A. Shepherd); BAKER 62.
123. Cf. Upton/AYRES 49, 57, 59. But the P Son. is listed only in ART OF MUSIC IV 417.
124. DM XIII/1 (1913) 297 (W. Altmann). Cf. BAKER 947.
125. Cf. BAKER 1802–3; Cobbett/CHAMBER II 586 (A. L. Goldberg).
126. Cf. BAKER 239; Cobbett/CHAMBER I 224 (A. L. Goldberg).

grips with the sonata idea in any consequential manner—that is, by building the structures out of the development of basic ideas. The ideas themselves are songful bits that do not seem to invite development.

The Latin-American Sonata in the Romantic Era

No sonatas have turned up here by residents in Canada during the Romantic Era.[127] And those by residents in Latin-American countries are too few, too obscure, too often unpublished, and too inconsequential to justify much more than passing mention in one approximately chronological order (rather than chronologically by countries). Only passing mention is all that is given to these same works in the principal over-all encyclopedia of Latin-American music, Mayer-Serra/LATINOAMERICA.[128] Not until after our approximate limit here of World War I did a substantial rise begin in the Latin American cultivation of the sonata. It should be noted that even before then the primary influences and training were Italian and French rather than German.

The Cuban pianist **Nicolás Ruiz Espadero** (1832–90), influenced and praised by Gottschalk, is credited with a *Gran Sonata* for P solo in MS.[129] The Brazilian **Flavio Elisio** (actually **Alfredo d'Escragnello Taunay;** 1843–99) left a Sonata in e♭, for P solo, presumably Chopinesque and in MS.[130] The pianist and "grand old man of Argentine music" **Alberto Williams** (1862–1952) left a total of six sonatas, composed between 1905 and 1917 and published between about 1920 and 1923 by Gurina in Buenos Aires.[131] Five are duos, including Opp. 49 in a, 51 in d, and 53 in D, for Vn & P; Op. 48 in e, for Fl & P; and Op. 52 in D, for Vc & P. These fully competent examples of "musica culta" recall his study with Franck both in their harmonic style and cyclical treatment. Williams' Op. 74, *Primera Sonata Argentina* for P solo, is, as its title suggests, closer to his interest in native rhythms and melodies. In fact, an initial inscription tells us, "This Sonata is inspired by motives of Argentine dances and popular songs." Its four movements

---

127. Cf. MacMillan/CANADA 114–18; Kallmann/CANADA, especially pp. 235–55.
128. Chase/LATIN AMERICA is a valuable guide to further literature and orientation.
129. Mayer-Serra/LATINOAMERICA II 864–65.
130. Mayer-Serra/LATINOAMERICA I 342.
131. Cf. GROVE IX 302–3 (N. Fraser); Slonimsky/WILLIAMS; COMPOSITORES II 136–55 (full list of works with composition years), especially 141, 147, 154; Cat. NYPL XXXIII 421 (with pub. years approximated).

are labeled "Rumores de la Pampa," "Vidalita," "Malambo," and "Gauchos alegres" (Ex. 129).

In 1895 the Italian-, German-, and French-trained Brazilian, **Alberto Nepomuceno** (1864–1920), performed an early Sonata for P solo of his own composing.[132] Another Brazilian, trained in France and Germany, **Sylvio Deolindo Frões** (1865–?), is credited with sonatas for both P solo and Vn & P.[133] An Argentine violinist, **Ricardo Rodríguez** (1877–?), was training under d'Indy when he wrote an early Sonata in e, for P solo, followed by a later Sonatina for P solo and a still later, prize-winning Sonata for Vn & P (1943).[134] The home-trained Chilean violinist **Pédro Humberto Allende** (1885–1959) left four early, unpublished sonatas composed between 1906 and 1915, all for P solo.[135]

Ex. 129. From the opening of the finale in Alberto Williams' *Primera Sonata Argentina*, Op. 74 in c♯/D♭ (after the Gurina ed., *ca.* 1923).

The Costa Rican composer **Julio Fonseca** (1885–1950) studied in Milan before writing an unpublished Sonata in B for Vn & P.[136] And the Argentine conductor **Celestino Piaggio** (1886–1931) studied under d'Indy before writing a Sonata in c♯, for P solo (pub. in Buenos Aires not before 1913).[137] This work occasionally recalls the chromatic harmony and lyricism of d'Indy, but it more generally employs the traditional harmony, the regular phrase syntax, and the technically convenient figurations that mark the epigonic Romantic rather than the incipient Modern.

132. Mayer-Serra/LATINOAMERICA II 680–82. Cf. BAKER 1152.
133. Mayer-Serra/LATINOAMERICA I 315.
134. Mayer-Serra/LATINOAMERICA II 845.
135. Mayer-Serra/LATINOAMERICA 25–31, with dated, full list of works.
136. Mayer-Serra/LATINOAMERICA I 386–88.
137. Cf. Mayer-Serra/LATINOAMERICA II 775.

Addenda 1972

P. 19.   55a. Mention should be added of the well-balanced survey by Rey Longyear, *Nineteenth-Century Romanticism in Music* (Englewood Cliffs: Prentice-Hall, 1969; revised ed. in progress).

P. 20.   58a. Cf. Clemens C. von Gleich, *Die Bedeutung der Allgemeinen musikalische Zeitung 1798-1848 und 1863-1882* (Amsterdam: Frits Knuf, 1969).

P. 41.   81a. In Raabe/LISZT I 69-70 a review is quoted from the *Wiener Zeitschrift* of March 5, 1846, that found it to be a mixed blessing when Liszt compromised the unity of his program of transcriptions and Hungarian national airs by including a Beethoven sonata. Cf., also, the article by W. S. Newman on Liszt as cited in note 25b to p. 359.

P. 76.   23a. A surprising number of sonata performances (including about 35 of Beethoven sons.) turn up in the findings of the unpub. M.M. thesis by Andrew C. Minor, "Piano Concerts in New York City, 1849-65" (University of Michigan, 1947).

P. 90.   20a. An important new contribution is the Ph.D. diss. of Martin Weyer, *Die deutsche Orgelsonate von Mendelssohn bis Reger* (Regensburg: Gustave Bosse, 1969), including historical background, analysis, exx., and list of composers and works; cf. the review in DMf XXIII (1970) 467.

P. 101.   54a. Except for one work by Ysaÿe, no sons. for unaccompanied Vc during the period covered by SSB appear in Altmann/KAMMERMUSIK or the diss. by Kinney cited in note 45a to SBE 65.

P. 115.   9a. But in NOTES XXVII (1970) 264, R. Longyear suggests an "obvious imitation of the zither" in this passage "and the consequent rationale for its resemblance to the phrase-structure of the popular music of the time."

P. 151.   78a. In the unpub. M.A. thesis by Nellie Blanche Clarke, "Performance Practices as Revealed in A Complete Theoretical and Practical Course of Instructions on the Art of Playing the Piano by J. N. Hummel" (The University of North Carolina, 1971) 156, Clementi is credited with saying that a very long second "half" is almost never repeated (implying disregard for some conventional repeat signs), whereas Hummel, about 27 years later, is cited for his instructions on repeat signs without any mention of omitting them.

P. 173.   16a. As of Aug., 1971, Carl Teel at the University of Texas in Austin was working on a Ph.D. diss. on Reis's P sons., and Bärenreiter was scheduled to bring out a mod. ed. of Op. 169.

P. 186.   53a. A mod. ed. of Op. 7 was scheduled to appear from Bärenreiter in 1971.

P. 187.   57a. Cf. Gerald W. Spink, "Walter Scott's Musical Acquaintances," in ML LI (1970) 61-65.

P. 192.   86a. Cf. the conflicting evidences for a meeting in 1822 in Schindler & MacArdle/BEETHOVEN 375 and 392 (fn. 301).

P. 201.   129a. Another set of pieces that may have been intended to comprise a son. for P-duet are the 3 comprehended in D. 823 (cf. Deutsch/SCHUBERT-I 398-99).

P. 208.   152a. Cf. Maurice J. E. Brown, "Schubert: Discoveries of the Last Decade," in MQ LVII (1971) 351-78, including clues to the mystery of D. 557.

P. 218.   213a. Cf. Dallas Alfred Weekley, "The One-Piano, Four-Hand Compositions of Franz Schubert: An Historical and Interpretive Analysis," unpublished Mus. Ed. D. diss. (Indiana University, 1968).

P. 235.   26a. A full recording of the work was planned in 1971 by Marion Barnum at the University of Missouri, who has played it extensively since 1970 in the United States (for the first time?) and abroad, and who is doing a D.M.A. dissertation on Hummel at the University of Iowa.

P. 238.   34a. It may even have been a reference to Mozart's vocal canon in C, "Alleluja," K.V. 553, as kindly suggested to me by Marion Barnum (see note 26a to p. 235).

P. 251.   86a. Cf. Wilhelm von Lenz on Liszt's learning, teaching, and playing of Op. 39 in 1828, in MMR II (1872) 98-100.

P. 258.   104a. More specific information is provided by W. S. Newman in "The Pianist's Anatomy Re-Revisited, or What Did Happen to Schumann's Hand?" in PQ No. 76 (summer 1971) 16-17.

P. 271.   176a. Liszt expanded on this review and on Schumann in LISZT LETTERS I 305-12.

P. 297.   309a. To the literature may be added the unpub. Ph.D. diss. by John A. McDonald, "The Chamber Music of Felix Mendelssohn-Bartholdy," 2 vols. (Northwestern University, 1970), including extended exx. and thematic catalogue.

P. 299.   323a. A facs. of the "Adagio" is reproduced as Plate 31 and listed as item 150 in The Mary Flagler Cary Music Collection (New York: The Pierpont Morgan Library, 1970).

P. 309.   356a. In his preface to the Bärenreiter ed. of the Son. in A. Friedrich Schnapp reports that that work was actually pub. by Joseph Elsner in Warsaw in 1805 and believes it is superior to the 4 sons. ed. by Becking because in the writing of these Hoffmann no longer had a piano at hand (that is, in 1807-08, according to Schnapp); cf. W. S. Newman in NOTES XXVII (1970) 156-57.

P. 326. 14a. In preparation (as of 1971) for publication by G. Henle Verlag is a new thematic index.

P. 336. 67a. The autograph of Op. 34b has turned up in *The Mary Flagler Cary Music Collection* (New York: The Pierpont Morgan Library, 1970) item 85, with a facs. of the opening on Plate 13.

P. 359. 25a. Further references to Op. 17 are made by Robert Münster in "Die erst Symphonie e-moll von Hermann Goetz," DMF XXII (1969) 162-75.

P. 359. 25b. Cf. W. S. Newman, "Liszt's Interpreting of Beethoven's Piano Sonatas," scheduled (as of 1972) for pub. in MQ.

P. 360. 28a. Liszt's authorship is also doubted by L. Hübsch-Plegler, in "Liszt als Schriftsteller," in MUSICA XV (1961) 534-37, but it is at least partly supported again by R. Wangermée in AM XLII (1970) 19 (fn. 40) and by Edward Waters in NOTES XXVII (1971) 668. Haraszti's biography appeared (incomplete) in 1967 (Paris: Editions A. et J. Picard); it is reviewed along with Zsigmond László's *Franz Liszt—Sein Leben in Bildern* (Kassel: Bärenreiter, 1967) by Hans Engel in DMF XXIII (1970) 232-34.

P. 373. 78a. Scheduled for publication (as of 1971) in MR is a new structural analysis by Rey Longyear (with the fugue regarded as initiating the recapitulation rather than constituting a scherzando movement).

P. 376. 81a. But Ernest Newman, in *The Wagner Operas* (New York: Alfred A. Knopf, 1949) 414, argues that Wagner had already sketched approximately what was to be the "Treaty Motive" as early as 1850.

P. 386. 116a. Otto Albrecht has kindly called my attention to the bearing on this inscription of the Norns scene in *Götterdämmerung*.

P. 409. 222a. Cf. the pub. Ph.D. diss. by Johannes Bittner, *Die Klaviersonaten Eduard Francks und anderer Kleinmeister seiner Zeit*, 2 vols. (Universität Hamburg, 1968); Vol. II is a "Themenverzeichnis" of the sons. of all 30 composers discussed.

P. 432. 72a. Add Helmut Rösner, *Max-Reger-Bibliographie* (Bonn: Dümmler, 1968).

P. 477. 52a. In progress as of 1971 is the Ph.D. diss. by Richard Nelson Franks, "The Chamber Music of George Onslow, 1784-1853" (University of Texas).

P. 479. 59a. In preparation (as of 1971) for publication by G. Henle Verlag is a new thematic index.

P. 480. 67a. A still newer "complete works" from Poland (Polskie Wydawnictwo Muzyczne) began to appear in 1967 with the 4 Ballades (Series A, Vol. I, ed. by Jan Ekier).

P. 481. 69a. An important addition of at least peripheral bearing here is the unpub. Ph.D. diss. by Thomas Higgins, "Chopin Interpretation: A Study of Performance Directions in Selected Autographs and Other Sources" (University of Iowa, 1966), including an Appendix of exx.

P. 503. 185a. A new collection of Alkan pieces, ed., with preface, by Georges Beck (Paris: Heugel, 1969; in the series "Le Pupitre"), contains the "Sonatine," Op. 61 (described by Beck as "Alkan's best work").

P. 525.   41a. As of 1971, Elizabeth R. Larkins at New York University had started a diss. on Saint-Säens' chamber music.

P. 529.   59a. There is now an English trans. of Vuillermoz/FAURÉ (Philadelphia: Chilton, 1969).

P. 552.   160a. Op. 28 is discussed in Kinney's diss. (as cited in note 45a to SBE 65) 11 445. Cf., further, Antoine Ysaÿe. *Historique des Six Sonates pour violon seul op. 27 d'Eugène Ysaÿe* (Brussels: Les Éditions Ysaÿe, 1967).

P. 558.   1a. Cf. Alexander L. Ringer, "Beethoven and the London Pianoforte School," in MQ LVI (1970) 742-58, including Dussek, Clementi, Cramer, and Pinto.

P. 561.   18a. Cf., also, SCE note 89a to p. 517.

P. 566.   46a. The diss. cited in fn. 46 seems not to have been pursued.

P. 573.   88a. Praise for Op. 4/3 for H & Vn & Vc is voiced in NOTES XXVI (1970) 516.

P. 603.   4a. Cf. the Ph.D. diss. by Jörn Beimfohr, *Das C-dur Klavierkonzert Op. 7 und die Klaviersonaten von Friedrich Kuhlau* (Universität Hamburg, 1970).

P. 639.   4a. Cf. Bea Friedland, "Italy's Ottocento: Notes From the Musical Underground," in MQ LVI (1970) 27-53.

P. 645.   30a. But the autograph of a hitherto unreported "Sonata" in G for organ by Bellini is listed as item 77 in *The Mary Flagler Cary Music Collection* (New York: The Pierpont Morgan Library, 1970), Plate 11 being a facs. of the first page.

P. 662.   14a. *The Oeuvres complètes* have been reprinted in a facs. ed. of 12 vols. in 6 (New York: Da Capo Press, 1971).

P. 679.   45a. Add the new book on the man and his works by Brian Large, *Smetana* (London: Duckworth, 1970); cf. ML LII (1971) 177-80 (J. Clapham).

P. 722.   101a. Two studies of the sons. may be added. One is the unpub. M.A. thesis by Lorna Ruth Ginsburg, "The Piano Sonatas of Nicholas Medtner" (University of California in Los Angeles, 1961), and the other is an unpub. Ph.D. diss. by Cenieth Elmore nearing completion (as of Aug., 1971), at the University of North Carolina.

P. 738.   24a. During about 1855-65 Gottschalk played in New York on several occasions from the sons. of Chopin, Weber, Beethoven, or Mozart (according to the thesis by Minor cited in note 23a to p. 76).

P. 769.   97a. Cf. the unpub. Ph.D. diss. by Judith Ungrodt Evenson, "Macroform in American Piano Sonatas, 1901-1905, A Comparison with Piano Sonatas of Haydn, Mozart, and Beethoven" (University of Rochester and Eastman School of Music, 1969).

P. 771.   109a. Cf. the unpub. Ph.D. diss. by Robert J. Garofalo, "The Life and Works of Frederick Shepherd Converse (1871-1940)" (Catholic University, 1969).

Bibliography

Note: All the short-title references in the footnotes and main body of the present book, as well as some initials used only in this Bibliography to represent the most cited periodicals, will be found in the one alphabetical listing that follows. References with a lower-case "-m" at the end indicate sources made up primarily of music. Articles in GROVE and MGG and single volumes in the various "Denkmäler" series do not have separate entries in the Bibliography, but their authors or editors are cited where the first references occur during any one discussion in the text.

Abbott/FORM — William W. Abbott, Jr., "Certain Aspects of the Sonata-Allegro Form in Piano Sonatas of the 18th and 19th Centuries," unpublished Ph.D. diss., Indiana University, 1956.

Abendroth/PFITZNER — Walter Abendroth (ed.), *Hans Pfitzner: Reden, Schriften, Briefe*. Berlin: Hermann Luchterhand, 1955.

Abraham/CHOPIN — Gerald Abraham, *Chopin's Musical Style*, corrected ed. (first pub. in 1939). London: Oxford University Press, 1960.

Abraham/GRIEG — ——— (ed.), *Grieg: A Symposium*. Norman: University of Oklahoma Press, 1950 (first pub. in England, in 1948).

Abraham/LEKEU — Pat Abraham (trans.), "Lekeu in His Letters," MMR LXXVI (1946) 62–64, 85–89, 107–11.

Abraham/RESEARCH — Gerald Abraham, "Modern Research on Schumann," PMA LXXV (1948–49) 65–75.

Abraham/RUSSIAN — ———, *On Russian Music*. London: William Reeves, [1939].

Abraham/SCHUBERT — ——— (ed.), *The Music of Schubert*. New York: W. W. Norton, 1947.

Abraham/SCHUMANN — ———, *Schumann: A Symposium*. London: Oxford University Press, 1952.

Abraham/SIBELIUS — ———, *Sibelius: A Symposium*. London: Lindsay Drummond, 1947.

Abraham/STUDIES   Gerald Abraham, *Studies in Russian Music*. London: William Reeves, [1935].

Abraham/TCHAIKOVSKY   ——— (ed.), *The Music of Tchaikovsky*, including Chap. 6 on "The Piano Music," by A. E. F. Dickinson. New York: W. W. Norton, 1946.

Abraham/II & III   Gerald Abraham, "Schumann's Op. II and III," MMR LXXVI (1946) 123–27, 162–64, 222.

Adler/SCHUBERT   Guido Adler, "Schubert and the Viennese Classic School," MQ XIV (1928) 473–94.

AdMZ   *Allgemeine deutsche Musikzeitung* (*Allgemeine Musikzeitung* from 1883). 1874–1943.

AfMW   *Archiv für Musikwissenschaft*. 1918–27, 1952———.

Albrecht/CENSUS   Otto E. Albrecht, *A Census of Autograph Music Manuscripts of European Composers in American Libraries*. Philadelphia: University of Pennsylvania Press, 1953. A suppl. is in progress as of 1969.

Alekseev/FORTEPIANNAIA   Aleksandr Dmitrievich Alekseev, *Russkaia fortepiannaia muzyka ot istokov do vershin tvorchestva* ("Russian Piano Music from the Origins to the Peak"). Moscow: Izd-vo Akademii nauk SSSR, 1963.

Alekseev & Novikova   Unpub. critique of SSB XVIII kindly prepared in 1968 by Professor Aleksandr Dmietrivich Alekseev and trans. and suppl. by Miss Erna F. Novikova, both of Moscow.

Allen/PHILOSOPHIES   Warren Dwight Allen, *Philosophies of Music History*. New York: American Book Co., 1939.

Al'shvang/TCHAIKOVSKY   Arnold Al'shvang, *Peter Ilyitch Tchaikovsky*. Moscow, 1951. References are cited here by way of Alekseev & Novikova.

Altmann/BACH-ZITATE   Wilhelm Altmann, "Bach-Zitate in der Violoncello-Sonate Op. 38 von Brahms," DM XII/1 (1912–13) 84–85.

Altmann/BRAHMS-m   ——— (ed.), *Johannes Brahms: Quintet F moll für Pianoforte, 2 Violinen, Viola und Violoncell, Op. 34*. Leipzig: Ernst Eulenberg, [preface dated 1926].

Altmann/GOLDMARK   Wilhelm Altmann, "Karl Goldmark's Kammermusik," DM XIV/2 (1914–15) 209–21, 255–66.

Altmann/KAHN   ———, "Robert Kahn," DM IX/4 (1909–10) 532–63.

Altmann/KAMMERMUSIK   ———, *Kammermusik-Katalog*, 6th ed. (to Aug., 1944). Leipzig: Friedrich Hofmeister, 1945. Cf. Richter/KAMMERMUSIK.

Altmann/WEBER   ———, "Aus Gottfried Weber's brieflichem Nachlass," SIMG X (1908–9) 477–504.

AM   *Acta musicologica*. 1928———.

AMA   *Allgemeiner musikalischer Anzeiger* (Frankfurt/M). Nos. 1–52, 1826–27.

AMZ   *Allgemeine musikalische Zeitung.* 3 series: 1798–
               1848, 1863–65, 1866–82. The editors (and authors of
               most of the unsigned reviews) for the first series
               were J. F. Rochlitz until 1827, G. W. Fink until
               1841, C. F. Becker in 1842, M. Hauptmann until
               1846, and J. C. Lobe to the end. Cf. Mendel/
               LEXIKON XI 453, 459; Freystätter/ZEITSCHRIFTEN 32–
               34; GROVE VI 669; Hedler/TÜRK 16–17; Haupt/
               MÜLLER 13–14; MOSCHELES II 199. A reprint of the
               complete set was announced by Frits Knuf (Hilver-
               sum, Holland) in 1967.

Anderson/BEETHOVEN   Emily Anderson (ed. & trans.), *The Letters of
               Beethoven,* 3 vols. London: Macmillan, 1961.

Anth. NÄGELI-m   Johann (Hans) Georg Nägeli (ed.), *Repertoire des
               clavecinistes,* 26 sons. (and other pieces) in 17
               "Suites" (vols.). Zürich: Nägeli, 1803–10. Cf. AMZ
               V (1802–3) 579–80 and Intelligenz-Blatt 97–100;
               HIRSCH MUSIKBIBLIOTHEK IV item 1012; Heyer/
               HISTORICAL 278; MGG IX 1245–48 (Schanzlin & Wal-
               ter) and VIII 961 (H. P. Schanzlin); SCE 26; SSB IV.

Apel/DICTIONARY   Willi Apel, *Harvard Dictionary of Music.* Cam-
               bridge: Harvard University Press, 1944.

ART OF MUSIC   Daniel Gregory Mason (ed.), *The Art of Music, a
               Comprehensive Library of Information for Music
               Lovers and Musicians,* 14 vols. New York: National
               Society of Music, 1915–17.

Asaf'ev/RUSSIAN   Boris Asaf'ev (or Igor' Glebov, pseudonym), *Russian
               Music, from the Beginning of the Nineteenth Cen-
               tury,* trans. from the original Russian ed. (Moscow,
               1930) by A. J. Swan. Ann Arbor: J. W. Edwards (for
               the American Council of Learned Societies), 1953.

ASCAP   *The ASCAP Biographical Dictionary of Composers,
               Authors, and Publishers,* 3d ed. (first ed. in 1948),
               compiled and ed. by The Lynn Farnol Group. New
               York: The American Society of Composers, Authors
               and Publishers, 1966.

Austin/20th   William W. Austin, *Music in the 20th Century, from
               Debussy through Stravinsky.* New York: W. W. Nor-
               ton, 1966.

Bache/BACHE   Constance Bache, *Brother Musicians: Reminiscences
               of Edward and Walter Bache.* London: Methuen,
               1901.

Bachmann/VIOLINISTES Alberto Bachmann, *Les grands Violinistes du passé*
               (including . many thematic identifications). Paris:
               Librairie Fischbacher, 1913.

Badura-Skoda/CZERNY   Paul Badura-Skoda (ed.), *Carl Czerny: Über den
               richtigen Vortrag der sämtlichen beethoven'schen
               Klavierwerke.* Vienna: Universal, 1963.

Bagge/SCHUBERT | [Selmar Bagge?], "Franz Schubert als Claviercomponist," DMZ III (1862) 1–3, 25–28, 33–34, 41–43. The promised continuation never appeared, but the son. section seems to be complete.

Bagge/SONATA | Selmar Bagge, "Die geschichtliche Entwickelung der Sonate," in Waldersee/VORTRÄGE II 203–24.

Bagier/REGER | Guido Bagier, Max Reger. Stuttgart: Deutsche Verlags-Anstalt, 1923.

BAKER | Nicolas Slonimsky (ed.), Baker's Biographical Dictionary of Musicians, 5th ed.; plus 1965 Supplement. New York: G. Schirmer, 1958. The 5th ed. is intended except when the 4th ed. of 1940 is specified.

Balakirev/PIANO-m | Mily Alexeyevitch Balakirev, Complete Piano Works, ed. by K. S. Sorokin, 3 vols. in 5 parts. Moscow: State Music Publishers, 1949–54. Cf. Gardner/BALAKIREV 325.

Balogh/DUETS-m | Erno Balogh (ed.), Eighteen Piano Duets . . . , including Mussorgsky's Son. in C. New York: G. Schirmer (Library Vol. 1764), 1953.

Balzer/NIELSEN | Jürgen Balzer (ed.), Carl Nielsen: Centenary Essays. London: Dennis Dobson, 1966.

Barenboim/RUBINSTEIN | L. A. Barenboim, Anton Grigorievitch Rubinstein. Leningrad, 1954. References are used here by way of Alekseev & Novikova.

Barker/REGER | John Wesley Barker, "Reger's Organ Music—3," MT CIX (1968) 170–73.

Bartók/UNGHERIA | Béla Bartók, "Della Musica moderna in Ungheria," PIANOFORTE II (1921) 193–97.

Barzun/BERLIOZ | Jacques Barzun, Berlioz and the Romantic Century, 2 vols. Boston: Little, Brown, 1950.

Bauer/SCHUBERT-m | Adolf Bauer, "Scherzo aus der Klaviersonate E-moll (Juny 1817 [D. 566]) von Franz Schubert," with mod. ed. of the complete "Scherzo" and facs. of the holograph of its "Trio," in DM XXI (1928–29) 13–16 and suppls. after pp. 16 and 48.

Beaufort/LISZT | Raphaël Ledos de Beaufort, Franz Liszt: The Story of His Life, to Which Are Added Franz Liszt in Rome by Nadine Helbig. Boston: Oliver Ditson, 1887 [and 1910].

Becker/CLAVIERSONATE | Carl Ferdinand Becker, "Die Claviersonate in Deutschland," NZM VII (1837) 25–26, 29–30, 33–34. Revised, with exx. added, in Becker/HAUSMUSIK 33–39.

Becker/HAUSMUSIK | ———, Die Hausmusik in Deutschland in dem 16., 17. und 18. Jahrhundert. . . . Leipzig: Fest'sche Verlagsbuchhandlung, 1840. Cf. Becker/CLAVIERSONATE.

Bellamann/ALKAN — Henry H. Bellamann, "The Piano Works of C. V. Alkan," MQ X (1924) 251–62.

Benedict/WEBER — Julius Benedict, *Weber,* 3d ed. London: S. Low, Marston, Searle, & Rivington, 1889.

Bennett/BENNETT — James Robert Sterndale Bennett, *The Life of William Sterndale Bennett, by His Son. . . .* Cambridge [England]: University Press, 1907.

Benton/LONDON — Rita Benton, "London Music in 1815, as Seen by Camille Pleyel," ML XLVII (1966) 34–47.

Benyovszky/HUMMEL — Karl Benyovszky, *J. N. Hummel: Der Mensch und Künstler.* Bratislava: Eos-Verlag, 1934. ("English resumé" on pp. 381–84.)

BERLIOZ MEMOIRS — *Memoirs of Hector Berlioz, from 1803 to 1865, Comprising His Travels in Germany, Italy, Russia, and England* (written between 1848 and 1865 and first pub. in 1870), trans. by Rachel and Eleanor Holmes and revised, with annotations, by Ernest Newman. New York: Alfred A. Knopf, 1932.

Berri/PAGANINI — Pietro Berri, *Paganini: Documenti e testimonianze.* Genoa: Sigla Effe, 1962.

Bertensson & Leyda/RACHMANINOFF — Sergei Bertensson & Jay Leyda, *Sergei Rachmaninoff: A Lifetime in Music,* "with the assistance of [Rachmaninoff's sister-in-law] Sophia Satina." New York: New York University Press, 1956. Cf. J. Yasser's review in NOTES XIII (1956) 643–44; Reither/RACHMANINOFF 36.

Bie/PIANOFORTE — Oscar Bie, *A History of the Pianoforte and Pianoforte Players,* trans. and revised [in 1899] from the original German ed. of 1898 by E. E. Kellett and E. W. Naylor, with a Foreword to the Da Capo reprint by Aube Tzerko. New York: Da Capo Press, 1966.

BIO-BIBL. U.S. — *Bio-Bibliographical Index of Musicians in the United States of America Since Colonial Times,* prepared by the District of Columbia Historical Survey; 2d (unrevised) ed. (originally pub. in 1941). Washington, D.C.: Pan American Union, 1956.

Bloch/ALKAN — Joseph Bloch, *Charles-Valentin Alkan,* an undergraduate study done at Harvard University. (Indianapolis: privately printed for the author, 1941.)

Blom/DUSSEK — Eric Blom, "The Prophecies of Dussek," MO LI (1927–28) 271–73, 385–86, 495–96, 602, 807–8, 990–91, 1080–81; reprinted in Blom's *Classics Major and Minor* (London: J. M. Dent, 1958) 88–117. Cf. Newman/K. 457.

Blom/FIELD — ———, "John Field," CHESTERIAN XI (1930) 201–7, 233–39.

Blum/SIBELIUS — Fred Blum, *Jean Sibelius: An International Bibliog-*

raphy on the Occasion of the Centennial Celebrations, 1965. Detroit: Information Service, 1965.

Boal/SCHUMANN Dean Elmer Boal, "A Comparative Study of Existing Manuscripts and Editions of the Robert Schumann Sonata in F Sharp Minor, Op. 11 for Piano," unpub. Ph.D. diss., University of Colorado, 1959.

Böttcher/BRUCKNER Lukas Böttcher, "Unbekannte Klavierwerke von Anton Bruckner," MUSIKLEBEN II (1949) 236–37.

Boetticher/SCHRIFTEN Wolfgang Boetticher, *Robert Schumann in seinen Schriften und Briefen.* Berlin: Bernhard Hahnefeld, 1942.

Boetticher/SCHUMANN ———, *Robert Schumann: Einführung in Persönlichkeit und Werk.* Berlin: Bernhard Hahnefeld, 1941. Cf. Abraham/RESEARCH 72–75; Redlich/SCHUMANN; Abraham/SCHUMANN v–vi, 1–11 (W. Reich); Werner/MENDELSSOHN 265–66.

Bone/GUITAR Philip J. Bone, *The Guitar and Mandolin,* 2d, "enlarged" ed. (first pub. in 1914). London: Schott, 1954.

Bonnerot/SAINT-SAËNS Jean Bonnerot, *C. Saint-Saëns (1835–1921): Sa Vie et son œuvre,* 2d, revised ed. (originally pub. in 1914). Paris: A. Durand et fils, 1922.

Booth/HELLER Ronald E. Booth, Jr., "The Life and Music of Stephen Heller," unpub. Ph.D. diss., University of Iowa, 1967.

Borren/FRANCK Charles van den Borren, *César Franck.* Brussels: La Renaissance du Livre, 1950.

Bory/CHOPIN Robert Bory, *La Vie de Frédéric Chopin par l'image.* Paris: Horizons de France, [1951].

Bory/LISZT ———, *La Vie de Franz Liszt par l'image,* with a biographical introduction by Alfred Cortot. Geneva: Éditions du Journal de Genève, 1936.

Boucher/WITKOWSKI Maurice Boucher, "G.-M. Witkowski," RM VII/5 (Mar. 1, 1926) 193–223.

Bowen/RUBINSTEIN Catherine Drinker Bowen, *"Free Artist": The Story of Anton and Nicholas Rubinstein,* with lists of Anton's works on pp. 375–90, by op. nos. and types, compiled by O. E. Albrecht. New York: Random House, 1939.

Boyer/BEETHOVEN Jean Boyer. *Le "Romantisme" de Beethoven.* Paris: H. Didier, 1938.

BRAHMS-BILDERBUCH Max Kalbeck (ed.), *Ein Brahms-Bilderbuch,* issued by Viktor von Miller zu Aichholz. Vienna: R. Lechner, 1905.

BRAHMS BRIEFWECHSEL M. Kalbeck, W. Altmann, A. Moser, L. Schmidt, J. Röntgen, E. Wolff, and C. Krebs (eds.), *Johannes Brahms Briefwechsel,* first to 3d eds., 16 vols. Berlin:

Deutsche Brahms-Gesellschaft, 1908–22. Vols. I & II contain correspondence with the Herzogenbergs; III with Reinthaler, Bruch, Deiters, Heimsoeth, Reinecke, Rudorff, and the Scholzes; IV, Grimm; V and VI, Joachim; VII, Levi, Gernsheim, the Hechts, and the Fellingers; VIII, Widmann, the Detters, and Schubring; IX–XII, Simrock; XIII, Engelmann; XIV, Breitkopf, Senff, Rieter-Biedermann, Peters, Fritzsch, and Lienau; XV, Wüllner; XVI, Spitta and Dessoff. To keep the references consistent, the English trans. of Vols. I and II by Hannah Bryant (London: John Murray, 1909) is not cited in SSB. For Brahms's correspondence with the Schumanns, see SCHUMANN-BRAHMS.

Brahms/WERKE-m   Eusebius ˙Mandyczewski and Hans Gál (eds.), *Johannes Brahms sämtliche Werke*, 26 vols. Leipzig: Breitkopf & Härtel, [1926–27]. Cf. Heyer/HISTORICAL 39–40.

Breithaupt/WAGNER   Rudolf M. Breithaupt, "Richard Wagners Klaviermusik," DM III/4 (1903–4) 108–34. Cf. Daube/WAGNER vi–vii.

Brendel/GESCHICHTE   Franz Brendel, *Geschichte der Musik in Italien, Deutschland und Frankreich . . .* , 2d ed. (1st ed. in 1852), 2 vols. in one. Leipzig: Heinrich Matthes, 1855.

Brennecke/REGER   Ernest Brennecke, "The Two Reger-Legends," MQ VIII (1922) 384–96.

BRITANNICA   *Encyclopaedia Britannica,* 24 vols. Chicago: William Benton, 1963.

Bronarski/CHOPIN   Ludwik Bronarski, *Études sur Chopin,* 2 vols. (2d ed. of Vol. II, originally pub. in 1944). Lausanne: La Concorde, 1947 and 1946.

Brown/CHOPIN   Maurice J. E. Brown, *Chopin: An Index of His Works in Chronological Order.* New York: St Martin's Press, 1960. Cf. "Corrections and Additions" in MT CVI (1960) 28–30; review in PQ XXXIII (fall, 1960) 24, 26 (W. S. Newman).

Brown/DISCOVERIES   ———, "Schubert: Discoveries of the Last Decade," MQ XLVII (1961) 293–314.

Brown/ESSAYS   ———, *Essays on Schubert,* including "Towards an Edition of the Pianoforte Sonatas," pp. 197–216. New York: St Martin's Press, 1966. Cf. the reviews in ML XLVII (1966) 274–75 (M. Tilmouth); JAMS XX (1967) 505–7 (M. Chusid).

Brown/MANUSCRIPTS   ———, "Schubert's Manuscripts: Some Chronological Issues," MR XIX (1958) 180–85.

Brown/RECENT   ———, "Recent Schubert Discoveries," ML XXXII (1951) 349–61.

Brown/SCHUBERT ———, *Schubert: A Critical Biography*. New York: St Martin's Press, 1958. Cf. the reviews in JAMS XII (1959) 252–54 (D. Mintz): MQ XLVI (1960) 95–102 (K. Wolff).

Brown/TONES Calvin S. Brown, *Tones into Words, Musical Compositions as Subjects of Poetry*. Athens: University of Georgia Press, 1953.

Brown/VARIATIONS Maurice J. E. Brown, *Schubert's Variations*. New York: St Martin's Press, 1954.

Brown/1817 ———, "An Introduction to Schubert's Sonatas of 1817," MR XII (1951) 35–44.

BROWN & STRATTON James D. Brown & Stephen S. Stratton, *British Musical Biography: A Dictionary of Musical Artists, Authors and Composers Born in Britain and Its Colonies*. Birmingham: S. S. Stratton, 1897.

BUCEM Edith B. Schnapper (ed.), *The British Union Catalogue of Early Music*, printed before 1801; 2 vols. London: Butterworth, 1957.

Buchner/LISZT Alexander Buchner, *Franz Liszt in Böhmen*. Prague: Artia, 1962.

Bücken/SCHUBERT Ernst Bücken, "Schubert und die Klassik," KONGRESS SCHUBERT 47–53.

Bücken/19. ———, *Die Musik des 19. Jahrhunderts bis zur Moderne*. Potsdam: Akademische Verlagsgesellschaft Athenaion, 1932.

BÜLOW BRIEFE Marie von Bülow (ed.), *Hans von Bülow: Briefe und Schriften*, from 1841-94, 8 vols. Leipzig: Breitkopf & Härtel, 1895–1908.

BÜLOW-STRAUSS Willi Schuh and Franz Trenner (eds.), *Hans von Bülow and Richard Strauss: Correspondence*, trans. by Anthony Gishford (from the original ed. of 1953). London: Boosey & Hawkes, 1955.

Bundi/HUBER Gian Bundi, *Hans Huber: Die Persönlichkeit nach Briefen und Erinnerung*. Basel: Helbing & Lichtenhahn, 1925.

Burghauser/DVOŘÁK Jarmil Burghauser, *Antonín Dvořák: Thematic Catalogue, Bibliography, Survey of Life and Work* (in Czech, German, and English). Prague: Artia, 1960.

Burk/WAGNER John N. Burk (ed.), *Letters of Richard Wagner: The Burrell Collection*, in Eng. trans. New York: Macmillan, 1950.

Bush/BENNETT Geoffrey Bush, "Sterndale Bennett: The Solo Piano Works," PMA XCI (1964–65) 85–97.

BUSONI-Frau Ferruccio Benvenuto Busoni, *Briefe an seine Frau*. Zürich: Rotapfel, 1935.

Busoni/SKETCH ———, *Sketch of a New Esthetic of Music*, trans.

(from the original German of 1907) by T. Baker. New York: G. Schirmer, 1911.

BZMW   *Beiträge zur Musikwissenschaft.* 1959——.

CAECILIA   *Caecilia, eine Zeitschrift für die musikalische Welt.* 1824–48. Cf. Freystätter/ZEITSCHRIFTEN 41–46.

Calvocoressi/MUSSORGSKY Michael D. Calvocoressi, *Mussorgsky*, completed by G. Abraham. London: J. M. Dent, 1946.

Carner/FORM   Mosco Carner, "Some Observations on Schumann's Sonata Form," MT LXXVI (1935) 884–86. Cf. Cohen/SCHUMANN, of which this article restates and ramifies the conclusions.

CASTIL-BLAZE   François-Henri-Joseph Blaze, *Dictionnaire de musique moderne,* 2d ed. (first ed. in 1821), 2 vols. Paris: Au Magazin de Musique de la Lyre Moderne, 1825.

Cat. BELGISCH   *Catalogus van Werken van Belgische Componisten,* 20 vols. up to 1957. Brussels: Belgisch Centrum voor Muziekdocumentatie (Cebedem), 1954——.

Cat. BOLOGNA   *Catalogo della Biblioteca del Liceo musicale di Bologna,* 5 vols. Bologna: Libreria Romagnoli dall'-Acqua, 1890–1905, 1943. Reprint of vols. I–IV, with corrections by Napoleone Fanti, Oscar Mischiati, and Luigi Ferdinando Tagliavini; Bologna: Arnaldo Forni Editore, 1961.

Cat. BRITISH MS   Augustus Hughes-Hughes (ed.), *Catalogue of Manuscript Music in the British Museum, Vol. III: Instrumental Music, Treatises, etc.* London: British Museum, 1909.

Cat. BRUXELLES   Alfred Wotquenne (ed.), *Catalogue de la Bibliothèque du Conservatoire royal de musique de Bruxelles,* 4 vols. Brussels: J. J. Coosemans, 1898, 1902, 1908, 1912.

Cat. HIRSCH   A. Hyatt King and Charles Humphries (eds.), *Music in the Hirsch Library,* Part 53 of *Catalogue of Printed Music in the British Museum.* London: Trustees of the British Museum, 1951.

Cat. HIRSCH IV   Kathi Meyer and Paul Hirsch (eds.), *Katalog der Musikbibliothek Paul Hirsch,* Vol. IV. Cambridge (England): University Press, 1947.

Cat. NYPL   *The New York Public Library Reference Department: Dictionary Catalog of the Music Collection,* 33 vols. and Suppl. I. Boston: G. K. Hall, 1964–67.

Cat. ROYAL   *Catalogue of Printed Music in the Library of the Royal College of Music,* edited by W. Barclay Squire. London: Novello, 1909.

Cernikoff/HUMOUR   Vladimir Cernikoff, *Humour and Harmony.* London: Arthur Baker, 1936.

Chase/AMERICA   Gilbert Chase, *America's Music, from the Pilgrims to the Present,* revised 2d ed. (originally pub. in 1955). New York: McGraw-Hill, 1966.

Chase/LATIN AMERICA   ——, *A Guide to the Music of Latin America,* 2d ed., revised and enlarged (originally pub. in 1945). Washington: The Pan American Union and the Library of Congress, 1962.

Chase/SPAIN   ——, *The Music of Spain,* 2d ed. (first ed. pub. in 1941). New York: Dover, 1959.

CHESTERIAN   *The Chesterian.* 1915–19, 1919–40, 1947–62.

CHOPIN/facs.–m   *Fryderyk Chopin: Sonata h–moll,* facs. of autograph by way of photographs at the National Library in Warsaw (where the autograph has since been returned), with preface. Krakow: Polskie Wydawnictwo Muzyczne, 1954.

CHOPIN JAHRBUCH   Franz Zagiba (ed.), *Chopin Jahrbuch,* 2 issues to date (1967). Vienna: International Chopin Society, 1956 and 1963. Cf. DMF X (1957) 442–43 (R. Seitz) and NOTES XXI (1963–64) 379–80 (A. Loesser), respectively.

Chopin/WORKS–m   I. J. Paderewski, L. Bronarski, and J. Turczyński (eds.), *Fryderyk Chopin: Complete Works,* 27 vols. (including orchestral parts), variously 1st, 2d, or 3d ed. Warsaw: Fryderyk Chopin Institute, 1949–at least 1962. Cf. Newman/CHOPIN. The pagination of the "Critical Commentary" at the end of each vol. varies slightly depending on the language (English, in the present reference).

Chorley/GERMAN   Henry F. Chorley, *Modern German Music, Recollections and Criticisms,* 2 vols. London: Smith, Elder, 1854. Cf. Chorley/RECOLLECTIONS v-xxii (E. Newman).

Chorley/RECOLLECTIONS   ——, *Thirty Years' Musical Recollections,* ed. (from the original ed. of 1862) with an introduction by Ernest Newman. New York: Alfred Knopf, 1926.

Churgin/SONATA   Bathia Churgin, "Francesco Galeazzi's Description (1796) of Sonata Form," JAMS XXI (1968) 181–99.

Chusid/SCHUBERT   Martin Chusid, "The Chamber Music of Franz Schubert," unpub. Ph.D. diss., University of California at Berkeley, 1961.

Chusid/SCHUBERT–m   —— (ed.), *Franz Schubert: Symphony in B Minor ("Unfinished"),* with articles on "The Historical Background" (pp. 1–11) and "Beethoven and the Unfinished" (pp. 98–110), as well as studies and comments by O. E. Deutsch and others. New York: W. W. Norton, 1968.

Chusid/1824   Martin Chusid, "Schubert's Cyclic Compositions of 1824," AM XXXVI (1964) 37–45.

Clapham/DVOŘÁK   John Clapham, *Antonin Dvořák, Musician and Craftsman*. London: Faber and Faber, 1966.

Closson & Borren/ BELGIQUE   Ernest Closson and Charles van den Borren (eds.), *La Musique en Belgique du Moyen Age a nos jours*. Brussels: La Renaissance du Livre, 1950.

Cobbett/CHAMBER   Walter Willson Cobbett (ed.), *Cobbett's Cyclopedic Survey of Chamber Music*, 2 vols. reprinted from the original ed. of 1929, with suppl. prepared by Colin Mason. London: Oxford University Press, 1963. (I ix: " . . . with rare exceptions, M.S. works are ignored.")

Codignola/PAGANINI   Arturo Codignola, *Paganini intimo*. Genoa: A cura del municipio, 1935.

Cohen/SCHUMANN   Mosco Cohen [later, Mosco Carner], "Studien zur Sonatenform bei Robert Schumann," unpub. Ph.D. diss., University of Vienna, 1928. Cf. Carner/FORM. The Vienna copy was reportedly "destroyed during World War II."

Colles/FRANCK   Henry Cope Colles, "César Franck and the Sonata," MT LVI (1915) 206–9.

Collet/ALBÉNIZ   Henri Collet, *Albéniz et Granados*, 2d ed. (originally pub. in 1925). Paris: Librairie Plon, 1948.

Collins/GERM   M. Stuart Collins, "Germ Motives and Guff," MR XXIII (1962) 238–43.

COMPOSITORES   *Compositores de América, Datos biográficos y catálogos de sus obras*. Washington: Pan American Union, 1955—— (8 vols. to 1962).

CONGRESS CHOPIN   Zofia Lissa (ed.), *The Book of the First International Musicological Congress Devoted to the Works of Frederick Chopin, Warszawa, 16th-22nd February 1960*. Warsaw: Polish Scientific Publishers, 1963. Cf. ML XLV (1964) 268–70 (review by M. J. E. Brown).

Cooper/FRENCH   Martin Cooper, *French Music, from the Death of Berlioz to the Death of Fauré*. London: Oxford University Press, 1961 (first pub. in 1951).

Cortot/FRANÇAISE   Alfred Cortot, *La Musique française de piano*, 3 series (vols.), 5th ed. (originally pub. 1930–44 except for separate pubs. of I as articles in RM). Paris: Presses universitaires de France, 1948. (Also pub. in English trans. [London: Oxford, 1932], not used here.)

Cortot/INTERPRÉTATION   ——, *Cours d'Interprétation*, ed. by Jeanne Thieffry. Paris: Librarie musicale R. Legouix, 1934.

Courcy/CHRONOLOGY   Geraldine de Courcy, *Chronology of Nicolo Paganini's Life*, with parallel trans. into German by H. Dünnebeil. Wiesbaden: Rud. Erdmann, 1962 (copyright 1961).

Courcy/PAGANINI ———, *Paganini, the Genoese,* 2 vols. Norman: University of Oklahoma Press, 1957.

Craw/DUSSEK Howard Allen Craw, "A Biography and Thematic Catalog of the Works of Dussek (1760–1812)," unpub. Ph.D. diss., University of Southern California, 1964.

Czekaj/CHOPIN Kazimierz Czekaj, *Guide Chopin illustré,* trans. (from Polish mainly into French) by J. Bourilly and J. Kasińska. Warsaw: Société "Frédéric Chopin," 1960.

CZERNY Carl Czerny, "Recollections from My Life," trans. from "Erinnerungen aus meinem Leben" by Ernest Sanders, MQ XLII (1956) 302–17.

Czerny/COMPOSITION ———, *School of Practical Composition,* trans. from the original German of about 1840 (pub. by Simrock of Bonn in 1849–50 as *Die Schule der praktischen Tonsetzkunst* [cf. Newman/CZERNY]) by John Bishop (with author's "Memoir" and list of works both pub. [up to Op. 798] and unpub.), 3 vols. London: Robert Cocks, [preface dated 1848].

Czesla/BRAHMS Werner Czesla, *Studien zum Finale in der Kammermusik von Johannes Brahms* (Ph.D. diss., 1966). Bonn: Rheinische Friedrich-Wilhelms-Universität, 1968.

DA *Der Auftakt, Musikblätter für die tschechoslowakische Republik* [in Prague]. 1921–23.

Dahms/MENDELSSOHN Walter Dahms, *Mendelssohn.* Berlin: Schuster & Loeffler, [1919].

Dale/GRIEG Kathleen Dale, "The Piano Music [of Grieg]," in Abraham/GRIEG 45–70.

Dale/NINETEENTH ———, *Nineteenth-Century Piano Music.* New York: Oxford University Press, 1954.

Dale/SCHUBERT ———, "The Piano Music [of Schubert]," in Abraham/SCHUBERT 111–48.

Dale/SCHUBERT-m ——— (ed.), *Schubert: Sonata in E Minor* (D. 566 and 506, plus Adagio in D♭ and same transposed to E). London: British & Continental Music Agencies, 1948.

Dale/SCHUMANN Kathleen Dale, "The Piano Music [of Schumann]," in Abraham/SCHUMANN 12–97.

Dale/SMYTH ———, "Ethyl Smyth's Prentice Work," ML XXX (1949) 329–36.

Dale/THREE C'S ———, "The Three C's: Pioneers of Pianoforte Playing," MR VI (1945) 138–48.

DAMROSCH/Life Walter Damrosch, *My Musical Life.* New York: Charles Scribner's Sons, 1930.

Dannreuther/ROMANTIC — Edward Dannreuther, *The Romantic Period* (Vol. VI in *The Oxford History of Music*), 2d ed. (originally pub. in 1905). London: Humphrey Milford, 1931.

Daube/WAGNER — Otto Daube, *"Ich schreibe keine Symphonien mehr": Richard Wagners Lehrjahre nach den erhaltenen Dokumenten.* Köln: Hans Gerig, 1960.

Davis/HUMMEL — Richard Davis, "The Music of J. N. Hummel, Its Derivations and Development," MR XXVI (1965) 169–91.

Davis/LYAPUNOV — ———, "Sergei Lyapunov (1859–1924); the Piano Works: A Short Appreciation," MR XXI (1960) 186–206.

DDT-m — *Denkmäler deutscher Tonkunst,* erste Folge, 65 vols., 1892–1931.

De Angelis/ROMA — Alberto De Angelis, *La Musica a Roma nel secolo XIX.* Rome: Giovanni Bardi, 1935.

DEBUSSY CROCHE — Lawrence Gilman (ed.), *Monsieur Croche, the Dilettante Hater, from the French of Claude Debussy* (articles written in 1901–14, collected and abridged by the author, and first pub. in collected form in 1921; cf. Gilman's Foreword and Lockspeiser/DEBUSSY II 282–84). New York: Lear, 1948.

Del Mar/STRAUSS — Norman Del Mar, *Richard Strauss: A Critical Commentary on His Life and Works,* Vol. I of two projected vols. London: Barrie and Rockliff, 1962.

Demuth/FRANCK — Norman Demuth, *César Franck.* London: Dennis Dobson, 1949.

Demuth/FRENCH — ———, *French Piano Music.* London: Museum Press, 1959.

Demuth/D'INDY — ———, *Vincent d'Indy, 1851–1931: Champion of Classicism.* London: Rockliff, 1951.

Demuth/TRENDS — ———, *Musical Trends in the 20th Century.* London: Rockliff, 1952.

Denecke/REGER — Heinz Ludwig Denecke, "Max Regers Sonatenform in ihrer Entwicklung," in FESTSCHRIFT STEIN 26–32.

Dent/BUSONI — Edward J. Dent, *Ferruccio Busoni: A Biography.* London: Oxford University Press, 1933.

Dessauer/FIELD — Heinrich Dessauer, *John Field: sein Leben und seine Werke* (Ph.D. diss., Universität Leipzig, 1911). Langensalza: Hermann Beyer, 1912.

Deutsch/COLLECTED — Otto Erich Deutsch, "Schubert: The Collected Works," ML XXXII (1951) 226–34.

Deutsch/MOZART — ———, *Mozart: A Documentary Biography,* trans. by Eric Blom, Peter Branscombe, and Jeremy Noble. Stanford: Stanford University Press, 1965.

Deutsch/NUMMERN ———, *Musikverlags Nummern*, 2d revised and first German ed. Berlin: Merseburger, 1961. Cf. SCE 824.

Deutsch/SCHUBERT-B ——— (ed.), *Franz Schubert: Sein Leben in Bildern*. Munich: Georg Müller, 1913. Cf. Deutsch/SCHUBERT-M V.

Deutsch/SCHUBERT-D Otto Erich Deutsch, *The Schubert Reader: A Life of Franz Schubert in Letters and Documents*, trans. by Eric Blom. New York: W. W. Norton, 1947. Revised from the original German ed. of 1914. A very few new changes and additions appear in the German ed. of 1964 pub. as "Serie VIII: Supplement·Band 5" in the *Neue Ausgabe* of the Internationalen Schubert-Gesellschaft. Cf., also, Deutsch/SCHUBERT-M V.

Deutsch/SCHUBERT-I ——— (ed., with Donald R. Wakeling), *Schubert: Thematic Catalogue of All His Works in Chronological Order*. London: J. M. Dent, 1951. Cf. Deutsch/SCHUBERT-M V.

Deutsch/SCHUBERT-M ———, *Schubert: Memoirs by His Friends* (cf. p. v herein). New York: Macmillan, 1958.

DICCIONARIO LABOR Joaquín Pena and Higinio Anglés, *Diccionario de la música labor*, 2 vols. Barcelona: Editorial Labor, 1954.

DICCIONARIO PORTUGUEZES Ernesto Vieira, *Diccionario biographico de musicos portuguezes*, 2 vols. Lisbon: Mattos Moreira & Pinheiro, 1900.

Dickinson/SCHUMANN Alan Edgar Frederic Dickinson, "The Chamber Music [of Schumann]," in Abraham/SCHUMANN 138–75.

Dietrich & Widmann/ Albert Dietrich and Josef Viktor Widmann, *Recol-*
BRAHMS *lections of Johannes Brahms*, trans. by Dora A. Hecht (from two separate, complementary accounts, both originally pub. in 1898). London: Seeley, 1899.

DM *Die Musik*. 1901–41.

DMf *Die Musikforschung*. 1948———.

DMZ *Deutsche Musiz-Zeitung* (ed. by Selmar Bagge). 1860–62.

Dobrokhotov/ALIABIEV B. Dobrokhotov, *Alexander Aliabiev*. Moscow: Izdatel'stvo, 1966.

Dolleris/NIELSEN Ludvig Dolleris, *Carl Nielsen en Musikografi*, with 300 exx. Odense (Denmark): Fyns Boghandel, 1949.

DOMMER & KOCH Arrey von Dommer, *H. Ch. Koch's Musikalisches Lexikon* [originally pub. in 1802], *zweite durchaus umgearbeitete und vermehrte Auflage*. Heidelberg: J. C. B. Mohr, 1865.

Drinker/BRAHMS Henry S. Drinker, Jr., *The Chamber Music of Johannes Brahms*. Philadelphia: Elkan-Vogel, 1932.

DTB-m   *Denkmäler der Tonkunst in Bayern* (DDT-m, zweite Folge), 36 vols., 1900–31.

DTÖ-m   *Denkmäler der Tonkunst in Österreich.* 1894——.

Dubitzky/STRAUSS   Franz Dubitzky, "Richard Strauss' Kammermusik," DM XIII/3 (1913–14) 289–96.

Dünnebeil/WEBER   Hans Dünnebeil, *Schrifttum über Carl Maria von Weber,* 4th ed. Berlin: Bote & Bock, 1957.

Dufourcq/FRANÇAISE   Norbert Dufourcq, *La Musique d'orgue française de Jehan Titelouze a Jehan Alain,* 2d ed. (first pub. in 1941). Paris: Librairie Floury, 1949.

Dukas/ÉCRITS   Gustave Samazeuilh (ed.), *Les Écrits de Paul Dukas sur la musique.* Paris: Société d'Éditions françaises et internationales, 1948.

Dunhill/CHAMBER   Thomas F. Dunhill, *Chamber Music: A Treatise for Students,* 2d reprint. London: Macmillan, 1938 (originally pub. in 1913).

DVOŘÁK LETTERS   Otakar Šourek (ed.), *Antonín Dvořák: Letters and Reminiscences,* trans. (from the original Czech ed. of 1938, 9th ed. in 1951) by R. F. Samsour. Prague: Artia, 1954.

Dvořák/WERKE-m   ——, *Antonín Dvořák: Kritische Gesamtausgabe, nach Originalquellen zum Druck vorbereitet von der Kommission für die Herausgabe der Werke. . . .* Prague: Artia, 1956——. Cf. Heyer/HISTORICAL 92–93; Clapham/DVOŘÁK 319.

DWIGHT'S   *Dwight's Journal of Music, a Paper of Art and Literature.* 1852–81.

Eagle/MAC DOWELL   Nancy Eagle, "The Pianoforte Sonatas of Edward A. MacDowell, a Style-Critical Study," unpub. M.A. thesis, The University of North Carolina at Chapel Hill, 1952.

Eckart-Bäcker/ FRANKREICH   Ursula Eckart-Bäcker, *Frankreichs Musik zwischen Romantik und Moderne: Die Zeit im Spiegel der Kritik.* Regensburg: Gustav Bosse, 1965.

Edwards/MENDELSSOHN   F. G. Edwards, "Mendelssohn's Organ Sonatas," PMA XXI (1894–95) 1–16. Reprinted with deletions and additions (including facs. of three passages in the autographs) in MT XLII (1901) 794–98. Cf. ZIMG III (1901–2) 337–38 (C. Maclean).

Egert/CHOPIN   Paul Egert, *Friedrich Chopin.* Potsdam: Akademische Verlagsgesellschaft Athenaion, 1936.

Egert/FRÜHROMANTIKER   ——, *Die Klaviersonate der Frühromantiker* (Vol. I [diss., 1929] of "Die Klaviersonate im Zeitalter der Romantik," not published to date, but cf. p. 46, fn. 5). Berlin: R. Niedermayr, 1934.

Egert/LISZT   ——, "Die Klaviersonate in H-Moll von Franz Liszt," DM XXVIII/2 (1936) 673–82.

Ehrmann/BRAHMS   Alfred von Ehrmann, *Johannes Brahms: Thematisches Verzeichnis seiner Werke.* Leipzig: Breitkopf & Härtel, 1933.

Ehrmann/WEG   ———, *Johannes Brahms: Weg, Werk und Welt.* Leipzig: Breitkopf & Härtel, 1933.

Einstein/ROMANTIC   Alfred Einstein, *Music in the Romantic Era.* New York: W. W. Norton, 1947.

Einstein/SCHUBERT   ———, *Schubert: A Musical Portrait.* New York: Oxford University Press, 1951.

Eismann/SCHUMANN   Georg Eismann (ed.), *Robert Schumann: Ein Quellenwerk über sein Leben und Schaffen,* 2 vols. Leipzig: Breitkopf & Härtel, 1956. (A 2d ed. appeared in 1964.)

EITNER MISCELLANEA   Hermann Springer, Max Schneider, and Werner Wolffheim, *Miscellanea musicae bio-bibliographica* [1904–13] . . . *als Nachträge und Verbesserungen zu Eitners Quellenlexikon,* 2d ed. New York: Musurgia, 1947.

Eitner/QL   Robert Eitner, *Biographisch-bibliographisches Quellenlexikon der Musiker und Musikgelehrten* . . . , 10 vols. Leipzig: Breitkopf und Härtel, 1899–1904.

Eitner/SONATE   ———, "Die Sonate, Vorstudien zur Entstehung der Form," MfMg XX (1888) 163–70 and 179–85.

Elgar/LETTERS   *Letters of Edward Elgar and Other Writings,* selected, ed., and annotated by P. M. Young. London: Geoffrey Bles, 1956.

ELGAR-Nimrod   Percy M. Young (ed.), *Letters to Nimrod* [Elgar's trans. of Jaeger]: *Edward Elgar to August Jaeger, 1897–1908.* London: Dennis Dobson, 1965.

Ellis/WAGNER   William Ashton Ellis, *Life of Richard Wagner,* 6 vols. London: Kegan Paul, Trench, Trübner, 1900–1908. Vols. I–III are revisions of C. F. Glasenapp's *Das Leben Richard Wagner's* (Vols. I–III, 1894–99).

Elson/AMERICAN   Louis C. Elson, *The History of American Music,* 2d ed. (revision of original ed. of 1904). New York: Macmillan, 1915.

Elson/WOMAN   Arthur Elson, *Woman's Work in Music.* Boston: L. C. Page, [1913].

Emmanuel/DUKAS   Maurice Emmanuel, "La Musique de Piano de Paul Dukas," RM XVII/166 (May–June, 1936; *Paul Dukas: Numéro spécial*) 69–78.

Emmanuel/FRANCK   ———, *César Franck, Étude critique.* Paris: Henri Laurens, 1930.

ENCYCLOPÉDIE   *Encyclopédie de la musique et dictionnaire du conservatoire,* 11 vols. Paris: Delagrave, 1913–31.

Engel/GESELLSCHAFT   Hans Engel, *Musik und Gesellschaft, Bausteine zu einer Musiksoziologie.* Berlin: Max Hesse, 1960.

Engel/ROMANTISCHEN ————, "Die Grenzen der romantischen Epoche und der Fall Mendelssohn," in *Festschrift Otto Erich Deutsch* (Kassel: Bärenreiter, 1963) 259–72.

Enke/MENDELSSOHN Heinz Enke, "Mendelssohn und der Manierismus," NZM CXXV (1964) 3–5.

Eschman/FORMS Karl Eschman, *Changing Forms in Modern Music.* Boston: E. C. Schirmer, 1945.

ESCUDIER Marie & Léon Escudier, *Dictionnaire de musique,* 2 vols. in one. Paris: Bureau Central de Musique, 1844.

Evans/BRAHMS Edwin Evans, *Historical, Descriptive and Analytical Account of the Entire Works of Johannes Brahms,* 4 vols.: I, *Handbook to* [the] *Vocal Works*; II, . . . *Chamber & Orchestral Music* through Op. 67; III, . . . *Chamber & Orchestral Music* from Op. 68 to the end; IV, . . . *Pianoforte Works.* London: William Reeves, [1912, 1933, 1935, 1936].

Ewens/EBERL Franz Josef Ewens, *Anton Eberl: Ein Beitrag zur Musikgeschichte in Wien um 1800* (Ph.D. diss., Köln, 1923). Dresden: Wilhelm Limpert, 1927.

F-A-E SONATE-m Erich Valentin and Otto Kobin (eds.), *F[rei]-A[ber]-E[insam];* "in anticipation of the arrival of the revered and beloved friend Joseph Joachim, this sonata was composed by Robert Schumann [mvts. ii and iv], Albert Dietrich [i] and Johannes Brahms [iii]." Magdeburg: Heinrichshofen, 1935; reprinted by C. F. Peters in New York, 1953.

Faisst/CLAVIERSONATE Imanuel Faisst, "Beiträge zur Geschichte der Claviersonate von ihrem ersten Auftreten bis auf C. P. Emanuel Bach" (Berlin, 1845), reprinted from CAECILIA XXV (1846) 129–58 and 201–31, XXVI (1847) 1–28 and 73–83, in NBJ I (1924) 7–85.

Farnsworth/PHENOMENA Paul R. Farnsworth, "Masculinity and Femininity of Musical Phenomena," JAAC IX (1950–51) 257–62.

Farnsworth/TASTE ————, *Musical Taste: Its Measurement and Cultural Nature.* Stanford: Stanford University Press, 1950.

FASQUELLE François Michel and others (eds.), *Encyclopédie de la musique,* 3 vols. Paris: Fasquelle, 1958–61.

Fauré/LETTRES Philippe Fauré-Fremiet (ed.), *Gabriel Fauré: Lettres intimes* (extracts to his wife, 1885–1924). Paris: La Colombe, 1951.

Fauré-Fremiet/FAURÉ Philippe Fauré-Fremiet, *Gabriel Fauré* (originally pub. in 1929), plus "Réflexions sur la confiance Fauréenne" (after 1945) and "Notes sur l'interprétation des œuvres" (1950). Paris: Albin Michel, 1957.

Favre/BOIELDIEU Georges Favre, *Boieldieu: Sa Vie—son œuvre*, 2 vols. Paris: Librairie E. Droz, 1944 and 1945.

Favre/BOIELDIEU-m ——— (ed.), *Adrien Boieldieu: (6) Sonates pour le piano-forte*, 2 vols., with preface (repeated in Favre/FRANÇAISE) and facs. of title pages of Opp. 4 and 6. Paris: Librairie E. Droz, 1944, and Librairie Fischbacher, 1947.

Favre/DUKAS Georges Favre, *Paul Dukas, sa vie et son œuvre*. Paris: La Colombe, [1948].

Favre/FAURÉ Max Favre, *Gabriel Fauré's Kammermusik* (diss., prefaced in 1947). Zürich: Max Niehan, 1948.

Favre/FRANÇAISE Georges Favre, *La Musique française de piano avant 1830*. Paris: Didier, 1953. Cf. Gil-Marchex/FRANÇAIS 171–76 (evaluation and additions).

Fay/GERMANY Amy Fay, *Music-Study in Germany in the Nineteenth Century* [1869–75], with a new introduction by Frances Dillon. New York: Dover, 1965 (reprinted from the original ed. of 1880, in Chicago).

Fellinger/BRAHMS Imogen Fellinger, "Brahms' Sonate für Pianoforte und Violine Op. 78," DMf XVIII (1965) 11–24.

Fellinger/DYNAMIK ———, *Über die Dynamik in der Musik von Johannes Brahms*. Berlin: Max Hesse, 1961.

Fellinger/ MUSIKBIBLIOGRAPHIE ———, "Musikbibliographie des 19. Jahrhunderts im Forschungsunternehmen der Fritz Thyssen Stiftung," DMf XIX (1966) 172–76.

FESTSCHRIFT SANDBERGER *Festschrift zum 50. Geburtstag Adolf Sandberger, überreicht von seinen Schülern*. Munich: Hof-Musik-Verlag, 1918.

FESTSCHRIFT STEIN Hans Hoffmann and Franz Rühlmann (eds.), *Festschrift Fritz Stein zum 60. Geburtstag*. Braunschweig: Litolff, 1939.

Fétis/BU François-Joseph Fétis, *Biographie universelle des musiciens . . .* , 2d ed., 8 vols.; suppl., 2 vols. Paris: Firman-Didot, 1860–65; 1878–80.

Fétis/CURIOSITÉS ———, *Curiosités historiques de la musique, complément nécessaire de La Musique mise a la portée de tout le monde*. Paris: Janet et Cotelle, 1830.

Fétis/MUSIQUE ———, *La Musique mise a la portée de tout le monde*. Paris: Alexandre Mesnier, 1830.

Finck/GRIEG Henry T. Finck, *Grieg and His Music*, 2d. revised ed. New York: John Lane, 1909. Cf. Frank/GRIEG 36.

Fischer/BRAHMS Richard Shaw Fischer, "Brahms' Technique of Motive Development in His Sonata in D Minor, Opus 108 for Piano and Violin," unpub. D.M.A. "Paper," University of Arizona, 1964.

Fischer/GRIEG Kurt von Fischer, *Griegs Harmonik und die nordländische Folklore*. Bern: Paul Haupt, 1938.

Fischer/SONATE-m

Hans Fischer (ed.), *Die Sonate,* vol. 18 in *Musikalische Formen in historischen Reihen.* Berlin: Chr. Friedrich Vieweg (1937). References are made to this first ed. rather than the radically altered 2d ed. (Wolfenbüttel: Möseler, 1957).

Flinsch/SCHUNKE

Erich Flinsch, "Ludwig Schunke, Schumanns Freund und Mitbegründer der Neuen Zeitschrift für Musik," NZM CXXI (1960) 199–203.

Fog/NIELSEN

Dan Fog, *Carl Nielsen, Kompositioner: En Bibliografi.* Copenhagen: Nyt Nordisk, 1965.

Frank/GRIEG

Alan Frank, "The Chamber Music [of Grieg]," in Abraham/GRIEG 32–44.

Frey & Schuh/
SCHWEIZER-m

Walter Frey and Willi Schuh (eds.), *Schweizer Klaviermusik aus der Zeit der Klassik und Romantik* (including pieces by Nägeli, Schnyder von Wartensee, and Fröhlich). Zürich: Hug, 1937.

Frey/SONATINA-m

Martin Frey (ed.), *The New Sonatina Book.* London: Schott, 1936.

Freystätter/
ZEITSCHRIFTEN

Wilhelm Freystätter, *Die musikalischen Zeitschriften.* Munich: Theodor Riedel, 1884.

Friedheim/LISZT

Arthur Friedheim, *Life and Liszt: The Recollections of a Concert Pianist.* New York: Taplinger, 1961.

Frimmel/SCHUBERT

Theodor Frimmel, "Beethoven und Schubert," DM XVII/6 (1924–25) 401–16.

Frotscher/ORGELSPIEL

Gotthold Frotscher, *Geschichte des Orgelspiels und der Orgelkomposition,* 2 vols. Berlin-Schöneberg: Max Hesses Verlag, 1935–36; reprinted unaltered by Merseburger of Berlin, 1959.

Fuchs/CRITIQUE

Julius Fuchs, *A Critique of Musical Compositions;* Vol. I, *From Bach to the Present Time,* with "Preface" in French, English, and German. Leipzig: Friedrich Hofmeister, 1898.

Fuller-Maitland/PARRY

John Alexander Fuller-Maitland, *The Music of Parry and Stanford, An Essay in Comparative Criticism.* Cambridge: W. Heffer & Sons, 1934.

Fuller-Maitland/
SCHUMANN

————, *Schumann's Pianoforte Works.* London: Oxford University Press, 1927.

Gál/BRAHMS

Hans Gál, *Johannes Brahms, His Work and Personality,* trans. by Joseph Stein from the original German of 1961. New York: Alfred A. Knopf, 1963.

Ganzer & Kusche/
VIERHÄNDIG

Karl Ganzer and Ludwig Kusche, *Vierhändig.* Munich: Ernst Heimeran, 1937.

Garden/BALAKIREV

Edward Garden, *Balakirev: A Critical Study of His Life and Music.* London: Faber and Faber, 1967. Cf. the reviews by D. Brown in ML XLIX (1968) 167–69 and B. Schwarz in NOTES XXV (1968–69) 30–31.

Gárdonyi/LISZT   Zoltán Gárdonyi, *Le Style hongrois de François Liszt* (in Hungarian and French). Budapest: Magyar Nemzeti Múzeum, 1936.

Gáscue/SONATA   Francisco Gáscue, *Historia de la Sonata.* San Sebastian: Palacio de Bellas Artes, 1910.

GASSNER   Ferdinand Simon Gassner (ed.), [Schilling's] *Universal-Lexikon der Tonkunst, neue Hand-Ausgabe in einem Bande.* Stuttgart: Franz Köhler, 1849.

Gates/SOLO   Willis Cowan Gates, "The Literature for Unaccompanied Solo Violin," unpub. Ph.D. diss., The University of North Carolina at Chapel Hill, 1949.

Gatscher/REGER   Emanuel Gatscher, *Die Fugentechnik Max Regers* (Ph.D. diss., Bonn, 1924; Schaal/DISSERTATIONEN no. 663). Stuttgart: J. Engelhorn, 1925.

Gatti & Basso/   Guido M. Gatti and Alberto Basso (eds.), *La Musica:*
LA MUSICA   *Parte prima, Enciclopedia storica,* 4 vols. Torino: Unione tipografico, 1966.

Geiringer/BRAHMS   Karl Geiringer, *Brahms: His Life and Work,* 2d ed. (first ed. pub. in German in 1934). New York: Oxford, 1947; reprinted as a paperback by Doubleday in 1961.

Georgii/KLAVIERMUSIK   Walter Georgii, *Klaviermusik,* 2d ed. Zürich: Atlantis-Verlag, 1950.

Georgii/WEBER   ————, *Karl Maria von Weber als Klavierkomponist* (Ph.D. diss., Halle). Leipzig: Breitkopf & Härtel, 1914.

Gertler/SCHUMANN   Wolfgang Gertler, *Robert Schumann in seinen frühen Klavierwerken* (diss., Freiburg im Breisgau, 1929). Berlin: Georg Kallmeyer, 1931. Cf. Abraham/RESEARCH 66–69.

Giegling/SOLO-m   Franz Giegling (ed.), *The Solo Sonata* (in the *Anthology of Music* series), with extended Preface. Köln: Arno Volk, 1960. Cf. NOTES XIX (1961–62) 685–87 (review by W. S. Newman).

Gillespie/KEYBOARD   John Gillespie, *Five Centuries of Keyboard Music.* Belmont (Calif.): Wadsworth, 1965.

Gilman/MACDOWELL   Lawrence Gilman, *Edward MacDowell: A Study* (revised in 1908 from a "monograph" of 1905). New York: Dodd, Mead, 1931, and Da Capo (reprint), 1969.

Gilman/NATURE   ————, *Nature in Music, and Other Studies in the Tone-Poetry of Today.* New York: John Lane, 1914.

Gil-Marchex/FRANÇAIS   Henri Gil-Marchex, "Le Language pianistique des compositeurs français," RM No. 226 (1955) 163–87.

Glazunov/MUSICIANS   Alexandr Konstantinovitch Glazunov, *Musicians, Correspondence, Reminiscences* (in Russian). Moscow, 1958. References are cited here by way of Alekseev & Novikova.

Glinka/MEMOIRS — Mikhail Ivanovitch Glinka, *Memoirs*, written in 1854–55 and trans. from the Russian by R. B. Mudge. Norman: University of Oklahoma, 1963.

Glinka/WORKS-m — ——, *Polnoe sobranie sochinenil*, 16 vols. to date (1968). Moscow: Muzykal'nve Izdatel'stvo, 1955——.

Gloyne/PREYER — Howard F. Gloyne, *Carl A. Preyer: The Life of a Kansas Musician*. Lawrence: University of Kansas, 1949.

Goetschius/BEACH — Percy Goetschius, *Mrs. H. H. A. Beach, Analytical Sketch*. Boston: Arthur P. Schmidt, 1906.

Goldschmidt/ SONATENFORM — Hugo Goldschmidt, "Die Entwicklung der Sonatenform," *Allgemeine Musik-Zeitung* XXIX (1902) 93–95, 109–11, 129–32.

Gollmick/TERMINOLOGIE — Carl Gollmick, *Kritische Terminologie für Musiker und Musikfreunde*. Frankfurt/M: Lauten, 1833.

Gottschalk/MSS — Paul Gottschalk (ed.), *A Collection of Original Manuscripts of the World's Greatest Composers* (in facs.). Berlin: pub. by the editor, 1930.

GOTTSCHALK/Notes — Louis Moreau Gottschalk, *Notes of a Pianist*, ed. by Jeanne Behrend. New York: Alfred A. Knopf, 1964. Cf. JAMS XVIII (1965) 259–62 (H. E. Johnson).

Grabner/REGER — Hermann Grabner, *Regers Harmonik*, 2d ed. (originally pub. in 1920). Wiesbaden: Breitkopf & Härtel, 1961.

Grace/RHEINBERGER — Harvey Grace, *The Organ Works of Rheinberger*. London: Novello, [1925].

Grasberger/BRAHMS — Franz Grasberger, *Johannes Brahms: Variationen um sein Wesen*. Vienna: Paul Kaltschmid, 1952.

Grasberger & Hadamowsky/STRAUSS — Franz Grasberger and Franz Hadamowsky, *Richard-Strauss-Ausstellung zum 100. Geburtstag*. Vienna: Österreichische Nationalbibliothek, 1964.

Graves/PARRY — Charles L. Graves, *Hubert Parry: His Life and Works*, 2 vols. London: Macmillan, 1926.

Gray/SIBELIUS — Cecil Gray, *Sibelius: The Symphonies*. London: Oxford University Press, 1935.

Greene/STANFORD — Harry Plunket Greene, *Charles Villiers Stanford*. London: Edward Arnold, 1935.

Grew/LISZT — Eva Mary Grew, "Liszt's Dante Sonata," CHESTERIAN XXI (1940) 33–40.

Grieg/VERZEICHNIS — Edvard Grieg, *Verzeichnis seiner Werke mit Einleitung: Mein erster Erfolg*. Leipzig: C. F. Peters, [1910].

GROVE — Eric Blom (ed.), *Grove's Dictionary of Music and Musicians*, 5th ed., 9 vols. and Suppl. New York: St Martin's Press, 1954, 1961. References are to this ed. unless an earlier ed. is specified. Am. Suppl. refers to 1935 reprint of 2d ed. (1928) of *American*

Supplement. Cf. MMR LXXVI (1946) 99–102, 132–34 (A. H. King); PQ No. 31 (spring, 1960) 25–27 and No. 36 (summer, 1961) 28 (W. S. Newman).

Haase/BRAHMS Rudolf Haase, "Studien zum kontrapunktischen Klaviersatz von Johannes Brahms," unpub. Ph.D. diss., Universität Köln, 1951.

Habets/BORODIN Alfred Habets, *Borodin and Liszt* (through Borodin's letters), trans. (from the original French ed. of 1893) by Rosa Newmarch. London: Digby, Long, [1895].

Hadow/MODERN William Henry Hadow, *Studies in Modern Music,* Series I and II in 2 vols., 12th ed. (originally pub. in London in 1892 and 1895). New York: Macmillan, [*ca.* 1925 and later].

Hagenbucher/FUCHS Franz Hagenbucher, "Die Original-Klavierwerke zu zwei und vier Händen von Robert Fuchs," unpub. Ph.D. diss., Universität Wien, 1940.

Hall/PIANOFORTE Leland Hall, *Pianoforte and Chamber Music,* Vol. VII in *The Art of Music.* New York: The National Society of Music, 1915.

HALLÉ C. E. and Marie Hallé (eds.), *Life and Letters of Sir Charles Hallé.* London: Smith, Elder, 1896.

Halm/KULTUREN August Halm, *Von zwei Kulturen der Musik.* Munich: Georg Müller, 1913.

Hammerich/HARTMANN Angul Hammerich, "J. P. E. Hartmann," trans. from the original Danish (1900) into German by L. Freifrau von Liliencron, SIMG II (1900–1901) 455–76.

Hanna/SCHUBERT Albert Lyle Hanna, "A Statistical Analysis of Some Style Elements in the Solo Piano Sonatas of Franz Schubert," unpub. Ph.D. diss., University of Indiana, 1965.

Hanslick/CONCERTE Eduard Hanslick, *Concerte, Componisten und Virtuosen der letzten fünfzehn Jahre, 1870–1885,* 2d ed. Berlin: Allgemeiner Verein für Deutsche Litteratur, 1886.

Hanslick/FÜNF ———, *Fünf Jahre Musik* (Vol. VII of *Modernen Oper*). Berlin: Allgemeiner Verein für Deutsche Litteratur, 1896.

Hanslick/MUSIKALISCHES ———, *Musikalisches und Litterarisches* (Vol. V of *Modernen Oper*). Berlin: Allgemeiner Verein für Deutsche Litteratur, 1890.

Hanslick/TAGEBUCHE ———, *Aus dem Tagebuche eines Musikers* (Vol. VI of *Modernen Oper*). Berlin: Allgemeiner Verein für Deutsche Litteratur, 1892.

Hanslick/WIEN ———, *Geschichte des Concertwesens in Wien,* 2 vols. Vienna: Wilhelm Braumüller, 1869–70.

Haraszti/AUTHOR — Emile Haraszti, "Franz Liszt: Author Despite Himself," trans. by John A. Gutman, MQ XXXIII (1947) 490–516.

Haraszti/LISZT — ———, "Le Problème Liszt," AM IX (1937) 123–36 and X (1938) 32–46.

Haraszti/PARIS — ———, "Liszt à Paris: Quelques documents inédits," RM XVII (1936) no. 165, 240–58, and no. 167, 5–16.

Harding/SAINT-SAËNS — James Harding, Saint-Saëns and His Circle. London: Chapman & Hall, 1965.

HARMONICON — The Harmonicon. 1823–33.

Hasenöhrl/CZERNY — Franz Hasenöhrl, "Karl Czernys solistische Klavierwerke," unpub. Ph.D. diss., Universität Wien, 1927.

Hasse/KARG-ELERT — Karl Hasse, "Drei neue musiktheoretische Lehrbücher; I: Siegfried Karg-Elert, 'Polaristische Klang- und Tonalitätslehre,'" NZM C/1 (1933) 336–45.

Hastings/TASTE — Thomas Hastings, Dissertation on Musical Taste. . . . Albany: Websters and Skinners, 1822.

Haupt/MÜLLER — Günther Haupt, August Eberhard Müllers Leben und Klavierwerke. Leipzig: Breitkopf & Härtel, 1926.

Hausswald/WEBER — Günter Hausswald (ed.), Carl Maria von Weber: Eine Gedenkschrift (on the 125th anniversary of his death). Dresden: VVV Dresdner Verlag, 1951.

Hedler/TÜRK — Gretchen Emilie Hedler (Thieme), Daniel Gottlob Türk (1750–1813). Leipzig: Robert Noske, 1936.

Hedley/AUTOGRAPH — Arthur Hedley, "Some Observations on the Autograph Sources of Chopin's Works," CONGRESS CHOPIN 474–77.

Hedley/CHOPIN — ———, Chopin. London: J. M. Dent, 1947.

Heger/REGER — Erich Heger, "Max Reger: Brücke zwischen den Jahrhunderten," MUSICA VII (1953) 168–70.

Helfert/SMETANAS — Vladimír Helfert, Die schöpferische Entwicklung Friedrich Smetanas, trans. (into German from the original Czech ed. of 1924) by B. Liehm. Leipzig: Breitkopf & Härtel, 1956.

Helfert & Steinhard — Vladimír Helfert and Erich Steinhard, Histoire de la musique tschécoslovaque. Prague: Orbis, 1936.

Henderson/PFITZNER — Donald Gene Henderson, "Hans Pfitzner: The Composer and His Instrumental Works," unpub. Ph.D. diss., University of Michigan, 1963.

Hering/HILLER — Hans Hering, Die Klavierwerke F. v. Hillers (Ph.D. diss., Universität Köln). Düsseldorf: Otto Fritz, 1928.

Heussner/MOSCHELES — Ingeborg Heussner, "Ignaz Moscheles in seinen Klavier-Sonaten, -Kammermusikwerken, und -Konzerten," unpub. Ph.D. diss., Universität Marburg/Lahn, 1963.

Hewitt/DISSERTATIONS — Helen Hewitt, Doctoral Dissertations in Musicology,

4th ed. Philadelphia: American Musicological Society, 1965.

Heyer/HISTORICAL Anna Harriet Heyer, *Historical Sets, Collected Editions and Monuments of Music.* Chicago: American Library Association, 1957.

Hibbard/FIELD Trevor Davies Hibbard, "The Slow Movements of the Sonatas of John Field," MR XXII (1961) 89–93.

Hill/BRAHMS William G. Hill, "Brahms' op. 51—a Diptych," MR XIII (1952) 110–24.

Hill/SCHUBERT ———, "The Genesis of Schubert's Posthumous Sonata in B flat Major," MR XII (1951) 269–78.

Hill/SIBELIUS ———, "Some Aspects of Form in the Symphonies of Sibelius," MR X (1949) 165–82.

Hiller/MENDELSSOHN Ferdinand Hiller, *Mendelssohn: Letters and Recollections,* trans. from the German (Köln, 1874) by M. E. von Glehn, 2d ed. London: Macmillan, 1874.

Hindemith/CRAFT Paul Hindemith, *The Craft of Musical Composition;* Book I, Theoretical Part, trans. by Arthur Mendel (from the original German ed. of 1937). New York: Associated Music Publishers, 1942.

Hirschberg/LOEWE Leopold Hirschberg, *Carl Loewes Instrumentalwerke.* Hildburghausen: F. W. Gadow, 1919.

Hirschberg/POCCI ———, "Franz Pocci," zfMW I (1918–19) 40–70.

Hoffmann/REGER Hans Hoffmann, "Zu Max Regers Sonate Op. 72 für Violine und Klavier in C dur," REGER-GESELLSCHAFT X (June, 1933) 1–7.

Hoffmann/SCHRIFTEN Ernst Theodor Amadeus Hoffmann, *Schriften zur Musik,* ed. by Friedrich Schnapp. Munich: Winkler, 1963.

Hoffmann/WERKE-m Gustav Becking (ed.), *E. Th. A. Hoffmann: Musikalische Werke,* 3 vols. (inc.). Leipzig: C. F. W. Siegel in conjunction with Fr. Kistner, [1922–27]. Cf. zfMW V (1922–23) 347–48 (Kroll).

HOFMEISTER Friedrich Hofmeister (ed.; and successors), *Musikalisch-literarischer Monatsbericht, Handbuch der musikalischen Literatur, Verzeichnis* or *Jahresverzeichnis,* and related titles. Leipzig: Friedrich Hofmeister, from 1829; preceded by Carl Friedrich Whistling's *Handbuch der musikalischen Litteratur* for 1815 (with suppl. of 1818–19) and 1828 (cumulative). Cf. MGG VI 576–77 (Virneisel); Hopkinson/FIELD 173.

Hogan/ANGLO-IRISH Ita Margaret Hogan, *Anglo-Irish Music, 1780–1830.* Cork: Cork University Press, 1966.

Hohenemser/SCHUMANN Richard Hohenemser, "Formale Eigentümlichkeiten in Robert Schumanns Klaviermusik," in FESTSCHRIFT SANDBERGER 21–50.

Hollander/BRAHMS   Hans Hollander, "Der melodische Aufbau in
                    Brahms' 'Regenlied'-Sonate," NZM CXXV (1964)
                    5–7.

Holmes/RAMBLE   [Edward Holmes], A Ramble Among the Musicians
                    of Germany . . . by a Musical Professor. London:
                    Hunt and Clarke, 1828.

Holt/MEDTNER   Richard Holt, Medtner and His Music, a Tribute
                    to a Great Russian Composer, ed. by Fred Smith.
                    London: Rimington, Van Wyck, 1948.

Holt/TRIBUTE   ——— (ed.), Nicolas Medtner (1879–1951): A Trib-
                    ute to his Art and Personality. London: Dennis
                    Dobson, 1955. (A symposium of 38 items by 32
                    authors, including Medtner himself.)

Honsa/SCHUMANN   Melitta Honsa, Synkope, Hemiole und Taktwechsel
                    in den Instrumentalwerken Robert Schumanns
                    (Ph.D. diss., Leopold-Franzens-Universität zu Inns-
                    bruck). Innsbruck: pub. by the author, 1965.

Hopkinson/FIELD   Cecil Hopkinson, A Bibliographical Thematic Cata-
                    logue of the Works of John Field, 1782–1837. Lon-
                    don: Printed [by Harding & Curtis] for the author,
                    1961.

Hopkinson/PARISIAN ———, A Dictionary of Parisian Music Publishers,
                    1700–1950. London: Printed for the author, 1954.

Horton/MENDELSSOHN John Horton, The Chamber Music of Mendelssohn.
                    London: Oxford, 1946.

Horton/PIANO   Charles Allison Horton, "Serious Art and Concert
                    Music for Piano in America in the 100 Years from
                    Alexander Reinagle to Edward MacDowell," unpub.
                    Ph.D. diss., The University of North Carolina at
                    Chapel Hill, 1965.

Howard/AMERICAN   John Tasker Howard, Our American Music, a
                    Comprehensive History from 1620 to the Present,
                    4th ed. (originally pub. in 1929). New York: Thomas
                    Y. Crowell, 1965.

Howe/AMERICA   Granville L. Howe (ed.), A Hundred Years of Music
                    in America. Chicago: G. L. Howe, 1889.

Howe/PAINE   M. A. De Wolfe Howe, "John Knowles Paine," MQ
                    XXV (1939) 257–67.

Howes/ENGLISH   Frank Howes, The English Musical Renaissance.
                    New York: Stein and Day, 1966.

Hudson/STANFORD   Frederick Hudson, "A Catalogue of the Works of
                    Charles Villiers Stanford (1852–1924)," MR XXV
                    (1964) 44–57. Cf. the sequel, "C. V. Stanford: Nova
                    Bibliographica," in MT CIV (1964) 728–33.

Hughes/AMERICAN   Rupert Hughes, American Composers, 2d ed. (origi-
                    nally pub. in 1900) with new chaps. by Arthur Elson.
                    Boston: The Page Co., 1914 (11th impression, 1921).

Hughes/INSTRUMENTAL — David Hughes (ed.), *Instrumental Music: A Conference at Isham Memorial Library, May 4, 1957.* Cambridge: Harvard University Press, 1959.

Hummel/ANWEISUNG — Johann Nepomuk Hummel, *Ausführliche theoretisch-practische Anweisung zum Piano-Forte-Spiel.* Vienna: Haslinger, 1828. Pub. of the English trans. followed (London, 1828).

Humphries & Smith/PUBLISHING — Charles Humphries and William C. Smith, *Music Publishing in the British Isles.* London: Cassell, 1954.

Ilyin/MEDTNER — Ivan Ilyin, "Sonata Form in Medtner," in Holt/MEDTNER 180–88.

d'Indy/COURS — Vincent d'Indy, *Cours de composition musicale,* with collaboration of A. Sérieyx and De Lyoncourt, 3 vols. (2 parts in Vol. II). Paris: Durand, 1909–50. Cf. Demuth/D'INDY 22–41.

d'Indy/FRANCK — ———, *César Franck,* trans. from the original French of 1906 by Rosa Newmarch and reprinted from the first English ed. of 1909 (not 1910). New York: Dover, 1965.

JAAC — *Journal of Aesthetics and Art Criticism.* 1942———.

Jachimecki/CHOPIN — Zdzislaw Jachimecki, *Chopin: La Vita e le opere,* trans. and revised from the final Polish version of 1949 by Wiarosław Sandelewski, in 1959. Milan: G. Ricordi, 1962.

Jacob/MENDELSSOHN — Heinrich Eduard Jacob, *Felix Mendelssohn and His Times,* trans. from the German (Frankfurt, 1959) by Richard and Clara Winston. London: Barrie and Rockliff, 1963.

Jacobs/SCHUMANN — Robert L. Jacobs, "Schumann and Jean Paul," ML XXX (1949) 250–58.

Jähns/WEBER — Friedrich Wilhelm Jähns, *Carl Maria von Weber in seinen Werken; chronologisch-thematisches Verzeichniss seiner sämmtlichen Compositionen. . . .* Berlin: Schlesinger, 1871.

JAMS — *Journal of the American Musicological Society.* 1948———.

Jansen/NEUE — Gustav Jansen, *Robert Schumanns Briefe: Neue Folge,* 2d ed. Leipzig: Breitkopf und Härtel, 1904.

Jansen/SCHUMANN — ——— (ed.), *The Life of Robert Schumann Told in His Letters,* trans. by May Herbert (from *Briefe von Robert Schumann: Neue Folge,* 1886), 2 vols. London: R. Bentley, 1890.

Jarociński/POLISH — Stefan Jarociński (ed.), *Polish Music.* Warsaw: Polish Scientific Publishers, 1965.

Jean-Aubry/FRANÇAISE — Georges Jean-Aubry, *La Musique française d'au-*

806   BIBLIOGRAPHY

                          jourd'hui, with a preface by Gabriel Fauré. Paris:
                          Perrin, 1916.

Jeppesen/NIELSEN   Knud Jeppesen, "Carl Nielsen, a Danish Composer,"
                          MR VII (1946) 170–77.

Jiránek/LISZT   Jaroslav Jiránek, "Liszt und Smetana: ein Beitrag
                          zur Genesis und eine vergleichende Betrachtung
                          ihres Klavierstils," in LISZT-BARTÓK 1961 139–92.

JMP   *Jahrbuch der Musikbibliothek Peters.* 1894——.

Joachim/LETTERS   Nora Bickley (ed. and trans.), *Letters from and to
                          Joseph Joachim,* with a preface by J. A. Fuller-
                          Maitland. London: Macmillan, 1914.

Johns/REMINISCENCES   Clayton Johns, *Reminiscences of a Musician.* Cam-
                          bridge, [Mass.]: Washburn & Thomas, 1929.

JRME   *Journal of Research in Music Education.* 1952——.

Jurgenson/   Boris Jurgenson, *Catalogue thématique des œuvres
TSCHAÏKOWSKY   de P. Tschaïkowsky,* facs. reprint of original Mos-
                          cow ed. of 1897. New York: Am-Rus, [1941].

Kämper/WÜLLNER   Dietrich Kämper, *Franz Wüllner: Leben, Wirken
                          und kompositorisches Schaffen.* Köln: Arno Volk-
                          Verlag, 1963.

Kahl/LYRISCHE   Willi Kahl, "Das lyrische Klavierstück Schuberts und
                          seiner Vorgänger [especially W. J. Tomaschek and J.
                          H. Woržischek] seit 1810," AfMW III (1921) 54–82
                          and 99–122.

Kahl/SCHUBERT   ——, *Verzeichnis des Schrifttums über Franz
                          Schubert, 1828–1928.* Regensburg: Gustav Bosse,
                          1938.

Kahl/   ——, "Wege des Schubertschrifttums," ZMW XI
SCHUBERTSCHRIFTTUMS   (1928–29) 79–95.

Kaiser/WEBER   Georg Kaiser, *Sämtliche Schriften von Carl Maria
                          von Weber.* Berlin: Schuster & Loeffler, 1908.

Kaiserman/MACDOWELL   David Kaiserman, "Edward MacDowell—The Celtic
                          and Eroica Piano Sonatas," in *Music Journal* XXIV/
                          2 (Feb., 1966) 51 and 58.

Kalbeck/BRAHMS   Max Kalbeck, *Johannes Brahms,* first to 4th eds.,
                          4 books in 8 vols. Berlin: Deutsche Brahms-Gesell-
                          schaft, 1912–21.

Kallmann/CANADA   Helmut Kallmann, *A History of Music in Canada,
                          1534–1914.* Toronto: University of Toronto Press,
                          1960.

Kański/VIRTUOSI   Józef Kański, "Eminent [Polish] Virtuosi of the XIX
                          and XX Centuries," in Jarociński/POLISH 128–53.

Kapp/LISZT   Julius Kapp, *Franz Liszt.* Berlin: Schuster & Loeffler,
                          1909.

Keller/BRAHMS   Otto Keller, "Johannes Brahms-Literatur," DM XII/
                          1 (1912–13) 86–101.

Keller & Kruseman/ MUZIEKLEXICON
Gerard Keller and J. Philip Kruseman, *Geïllustreerd Muzieklexicon*, 2 vols. and Suppl. The Hague: J. Philip Kruseman, 1932 and 1949.

Kempers/ISOMETRISCHE
Karel Philippus Bernet Kempers, "Isometrische Begriffe und die Musik des 19. Jahrhunderts," in *Festschrift Friedrich Blume zum 70. Geburtstag* (Kassel: Bärenreiter, 1963) 34–49.

Keresztury/MAGYAR
Dezsö Keresztury, Jenö Vécsey, and Zoltán Falvy (eds.), *A Magyar zenetörténet Képeskönyve.* Budapest: Magvetö Könyvkiadó, 1960. A valuable pictorial and documentary history of Hungarian music.

Kinsky & Halm/ BEETHOVEN
Georg Kinsky, *Das Werk Beethovens, thematisch-bibliographisches Verzeichnis seiner sämtlichen vollendeten Kompositionen,* completed by Hans Halm. Munich: G. Henle Verlag, 1955.

Kinsky/KOCH
————, *Katalog der Musikautographen-Sammlung Louis Koch, . . . von Scarlatti bis Stravinsky* (completed by M. A. Souchay). Stuttgart: Hoffmannsche Buchdruckerei Felix Krais, 1953.

Kirby/BRAHMS
Frank E. Kirby, "Brahms and the Piano Sonata," in PISK ESSAYS 163–80.

Kirby/KEYBOARD
————, *A Short History of Keyboard Music.* New York: The Free Press, 1966.

Kirkpatrick/IVES
John Kirkpatrick (ed.), *A Temporary Mimeographed Catalogue of the Music Manuscripts of Charles Edward Ives, 1874–1954, given by Mrs. Ives to the Library of the Yale School of Music, September, 1955.* New Haven: Yale School of Music, 1960.

Klauwell/ÄSTHETISCHE
Otto Klauwell, "Die ästhetische Bedeutung der Sonatenform" (1897), in O. Klauwell's *Studien und Erinnerungen, gesammelte Aufsätze über Musik* (Langensalza: Hermann Beyer, 1906) 44–55.

Klauwell/SONATE
————, *Geschichte der Sonate.* Leipzig: H. vom Ende's Verlag, [1899].

Knepler/XIX.
Georg Knepler, *Musikgeschichte des 19. Jahrhunderts,* 2 vols. Berlin: Henschelverlag, 1961. A 3d vol., on Slavic countries, is in progress. Cf. Lissa in BZMW VIII (1966) 68–73; R. Longyear in JAMS XVIII (1965) 419–21.

Kobylańska/CHOPIN
Krystyna Kobylańska, *Chopin in His Own Land; Documents and Souvenirs* (with English text). Krakow: Polish Music Publications, 1955.

Koechlin/FAURÉ
Charles Koechlin, *Gabriel Fauré (1845–1924),* trans. (from the original French ed. of 1927) by Leslie Orry (with minor additions). London: Dennis Dobson, 1945.

Költzsch/SCHUBERT
Hans Költzsch, *Franz Schubert in seinen Klaviersonaten* (Ph.D. diss., Erlangen, 1926). Leipzig: Breit-

kopf & Härtel, 1927. Cf. the abstract in KONGRESS SCHUBERT 199–208 and the review in DM XXI (1928–29) 50–51 (E. Bücken).

Kohleick/JENNER   Werner Kohleick, *Gustav Jenner (1865–1920): Ein Beitrag zur Brahmsfolge*. Würzburg: K. Triltsch, 1943.

KONGRESS SCHUBERT   *Bericht über den internationalen Kongress für Schubertforschung, Wien 25. bis 29. November, 1928*. Augsburg: Benno Filser, 1929.

Krafka/DUSSEK   Karel Krafka, "Romantické Prvky v klavírních sonatách Jana Ladislava Dusíka" ("Romantic Elements in the Piano Sonatas of Jan Ladislav Dussek"), unpub. Ph.D. diss., University of Brno, 1950 (available only indirectly to the present study; cf. SSB XVII and Craw/DUSSEK 2).

KRAUS/GEIRINGER/   H. Kraus, K. Geiringer, and V. Luithlen (eds.), *J.*
LUITHLEN   *Brahms Zentenar-Ausstellung der Gesellschaft der Musikfreunde in Wien, beschreibendes Verzeichnis*. [Vienna: Gesellschaft der Musikfreunde, 1934].

Krause/STRAUSS   Ernst Krause, *Richard Strauss, the Man and His Work*, trans. by John Coombs from the 3d German ed. of 1963 (the first ed. appeared in 1955). London: Collett's, 1964.

Kreissle/SCHUBERT   Heinrich Kreissle von Hellborn, *The Life of Franz Schubert*, trans. by A. D. Coleridge, with an Appendix by George Grove, 2 vols. London: Longmans, Green, 1869. Cf. Brown/ESSAYS 170–84.

Kremer/ORGAN   Rudolph Joseph Kremer, "The Organ Sonata Since 1845," unpub. Ph.D. diss., Washington University (St. Louis), 1963.

Kretzschmar/AUFSÄTZE   Hermann Kretzschmar, *Gesammelte Aufsätze über Musik . . .*, 2 vols. Leipzig: Breitkopf & Härtel and C. F. Peters, 1910 and 1911.

Kroll/BEETHOVEN   Erwin Kroll, "Carl Maria von Weber und Beethoven," NBJ VI (1935) 124–40.

Kroll/HOFFMANN   ———, "Über den Musiker E. T. A. Hoffmann," ZfMW IV (1921–22) 530–52.

Kroll/WEBER   ———, *Carl Maria von Weber*. Potsdam: Akademische Verlagsgesellschaft Athenaion, 1934.

Kross/BRAHMSIANA   Siegfried Kross, "Brahmsiana: Der Nachlass der Schwestern Völckers," DMf XVII (1964) 110–51.

Krueck/DRAESEKE   Alan Henry Krueck, *The Symphonies of Felix Draeseke* (Ph.D. diss., University of Zürich, 1966). Roscoe, (Pa.): Roscoe Ledger, 1967.

Kuhlmann/   Georg Kuhlmann (ed.), *Friedrich Smetana: Sonata*
SMETANA-m   *in One Movement for Two Pianos (Eight Hands)*, with preface. London: Hinrichsen, 1938.

La Mara/   La Mara (Marie Lipsius; ed.), *Musikerbriefe aus*
MUSIKERBRIEFE   *fünf Jahrhunderten,* 2 vols. Leipzig: Breitkopf &
Härtel, ["Vorrede" dated 1886].

Lampadius/   Wilhelm Adolf Lampadius, *Memoirs of Felix Men-*
MENDELSSOHN   *delssohn Bartholdy,* trans. from the German (Leipzig,
1848) by W. L. Gage. Boston: Ditson, 1865.

Landon & Bartha/   H. C. Robbins Landon and Dénes Bartha, *Joseph*
HAYDN   *Haydn: Gesammelte Briefe und Aufzeichnungen.*
Kassel: Bärenreiter, 1965. Cf. K. Geiringer in JAMS
XIX (1966) 251–54.

Landormy/FRANÇAISE   Paul Landormy, *La Musique française de Franck*
à Debussy. [Paris]: Gallimard, 1943.

Lang/AMERICA   Paul Henry Lang (ed.), *One Hundred Years of*
Music in America. New York: G. Schirmer, 1961.

Lang/WESTERN   Paul Henry Lang, *Music in Western Civilization.*
New York: W. W. Norton, 1941.

Laplane/ALBENIZ   Gabriel Laplane, *Albeniz: sa vie, son œuvre.* Paris:
Milieu du Monde, [1957].

LAROUSSE   Norbert Dufourcq, Félix Raugel, and Armand Mach-
abey (eds.), *Larousse de la musique,* 2 vols. Paris:
Librairie Larousse, 1957.

Latham/BRAHMS   Peter Latham, *Brahms.* London: J. M. Dent, 1948.

Layton/BERWALD   Robert Layton, *Franz Berwald,* with a Foreword
by Gerald Abraham. London: Anthony Blond, 1959.

LC MUSIC   *The Library of Congress, Division of Music,* [report
for] *1929–30.* Washington: United States Govern-
ment Printing Office, 1931.

Ledebur/BERLIN   Carl Freiherr von Ledebur, *Tonkünstler-Lexicon*
Berlin's, von den ältesten Zeiten bis auf die Gegen-
wart. Berlin: Ludwig Rauh, 1861.

Leichtentritt/   Hugo Leichtentritt, *Analyse der Chopin'schen Kla-*
CHOPIN   *vierwerke,* 2 vols. Berlin: Max Hesse, 1921 and 1922.

Lewenthal/ALKAN-m   Raymond Lewenthal (ed.), *The Piano Music of*
Alkan, with prefaces. New York: G. Schirmer, 1964.
Cf. MT CVI (1965) 620 (F. Dawes).

Lewinski/FORM   Wolf-Eberhard von Lewinski, "Fuge und Sonate—
die Form von Morgen," MUSICA XX (1966) 201–2.

Liapunov/PIANO-m   Sergey Mikhailovitch Liapunov, *Complete Piano*
Works, 2 vols. Moscow: State Music Publishers,
1950–51.

Liapunova & Yazo-   A. S. Liapunova & E. E. Yazovitskaya, *Balakirev:*
vitskaya/BALAKIREV   *A* [documentary] *Chronology of His Life and Works*
(in Russian). Leningrad: State Music Publishers,
1967.

LICHTENTHAL   Peter Lichtenthal, *Dizionario e bibliografia della*
musica, 2 vols. Milan: Antonio Fontana, 1826.

810   **BIBLIOGRAPHY**

Lippman/SCHUMANN   Edward A. Lippman, "Theory and Practice in Schumann's Aesthetics," JAMS XVII (1964) 310–45.

Lissa/NATIONALEN   Zofia Lissa, "Über den nationalen Stil," BZMW VI (1964) 187–214.

Lissa/POLISH   ————, "Polish Romanticism and Neo-Romanticism," in Jaronciński/POLISH 104–27.

LISTENER   Felix Aprahamian (ed.), *Essays on Music: An Anthology From "The Listener."* London: Cassell, 1967.

LISZT/Amie   La Mara (Marie Lipsius, ed.), *Lettres de Franz Liszt à une Amie* (almost identical with LISZT BRIEFE III). Paris: Costallat, 1894.

LISZT-BARTÓK 1961   Zoltán Kodály (ed.), *Studia musicologica, Academiae Scientiarum Hungaricae: Liszt-Bartók,* Vol. 5, report of the Second International Musicological Conference, 1961. Budapest: Akadémiai Kiadó, 1963.

LISZT BRIEFE   La Mara (Marie Lipsius, ed.), *F. Liszt's Briefe,* 8 vols. Leipzig: Breitkopf & Härtel, 1893–1904.

LISZT LETTERS   La Mara (Marie Lipsius, ed.), *Letters of Franz Liszt,* trans. (from the early vols. of LISZT BRIEFE?), by Constance Bache, 2 vols. London: H. Grevel, 1894.

LISZT/Marie   Howard E. Hugo (trans. & ed.), *The Letters of Franz Liszt to Marie Sayn-Wittgenstein,* with "Foreword." Cambridge: Harvard University Press, 1953.

LISZT-RAFF   Helene Raff (ed.), "Franz Liszt und Joachim Raff im Spiegel ihrer Briefe," DM I/1 (1901) 36–44, 113–23, 285–93, 387–404, 499–505; I/2 (1902) 688–95, 861–71, 977–86, I/3 (1902) 1161–72, 1272–86, 1423–41.

"LISZT" SCHRIFTEN   Lina Ramann (ed. & trans. [from French to German]), *Gesammelte Schriften von Franz Liszt,* 6 books in 7 vols. Leipzig: Breitkopf und Härtel, 1880–83. Cf. Ramann/LISZT II/2 112–26; but quotation marks in our short title acknowledge the strong evidence against Liszt's authorship of all these writings (cf. Haraszti/LISZT 130–35; Haraszti/AUTHOR; also, note 28a to p. 360).

"Liszt" & Waters/CHOPIN   Franz Liszt (?), *Frederic Chopin,* trans., with an Introduction by Edward N. Waters. New York: Macmillan, 1963. Cf. NOTES XXII (1965–66) 855–61 (commentary by C. Cooke).

Liszt/WERKE-m   Peter Raabe (and others, eds.), *Franz Liszts musikalische Werke,* 34 vols. (to date). Leipzig: Breitkopf & Härtel, 1907 [1856?]–1936. Cf. Heyer/HISTORICAL 171. Reprinted in 1966 by Gregg Press (Westmead, England); cf. MT CVIII (1967) 352.

Litzmann/SCHUMANN — Berthold Litzmann, *Clara Schumann: Ein Künstlerleben nach Tagebüchern und Briefen*, 3 vols. Leipzig: Breitkopf & Härtel, 1902–8.

Lochner/KREISLER — Louis P. Lochner, *Fritz Kreisler*. New York: Macmillan, 1950. Cf. BAKER 869.

Lockspeiser/DEBUSSY — Edward Lockspeiser, *Debussy: His Life and Mind*, 2 vols. (1862–1902 and 1902–18). London: Cassell, 1962 and 1965.

Lockspeiser/FAURÉ — ———, "Gabriel Fauré and Marcel Proust," in LISTENER 111–14.

Loesser/PIANOS — Arthur Loesser, *Men, Women and Pianos*. New York: Simon and Schuster, 1954.

Lomnitzer/SCHNEIDER — Helmut Lomnitzer, *Das musikalische Werk Friedrich Schneiders (1786–1853), insbesondere die Oratorien* (Ph.D. diss.). Marburg: Universität Marburg, 1961.

Longyear/SCHILLER — Rey M. Longyear, *Schiller and Music*. ("Germanic Languages and Literatures Series," No. 54.) Chapel Hill: The University of North Carolina Press, 1966.

LOUIS FERDINAND-m — Hermann Kretzschmar (ed.), *Prinz Louis Ferdinand Werke*, with preface pp. i–ii; 8 vols. Leipzig: Breitkopf & Härtel, [1915–17 and 1926].

Love/NIETZSCHE — Frederick R. Love, *Young Nietzsche and the Wagnerian Experience*. ("Germanic Languages and Literatures Series," No. 39.) Chapel Hill: The University of North Carolina Press, 1963.

Lowens/AMERICA — Irving Lowens, *Music and Musicians in Early America*. New York: W. W. Norton, 1964.

Lowens/MACDOWELL — ———, "Edward MacDowell" (10th article in "The Great American Composers Series"), in *HiFi/Stereo Review* XIX/6 (Dec., 1967) 61–72.

MAB-m — Jan Racek (ed.), *Musica antiqua bohemica*, 67 vols. up to 1966. Prague: Artia, 1924———.

MacArdle/CZERNYS — Donald W. MacArdle, "Beethoven and the Czernys," MMR LXXXVIII (1958) 124–35.

MacArdle/RIES — ———, "Beethoven and Ferdinand Ries," ML XLVI (1965) 23–34.

MacDowell/ESSAYS — Edward MacDowell, *Critical and Historical Essays: Lectures Delivered at Columbia University*, ed. by W. J. Baltzell. Boston: Arther P. Schmidt, 1912

MacDowell/MACDOWELL — Marian MacDowell, *Random Notes on Edward MacDowell and His Music*. Boston: Arthur P. Schmidt, 1950.

Macfarren/POTTER — George Alexander Macfarren, "Cipriani Potter: His Life and Work," PMA X (1883–84) 41–55.

Maclean/RUBINSTEIN — Charles Maclean, "Rubinstein as Composer for the Pianoforte, PMA XXXIX (1912–1913) 129–51.

MacMillan/CANADA — Ernest MacMillan (ed.), *Music in Canada.* Toronto: University of Toronto Press, 1955.

McVeagh/ELGAR — Diana M. McVeagh, *Edward Elgar: His Life and Music.* London: J. M. Dent, 1955.

Madden & Rees/ DUSSEK-m — Mary Madden & Olive Rees (eds.), *J. L. Dussek: Sonata in F Major, Op. 26, for Two Pianofortes* (C. 102). London: Schott, 1957.

Mahaim/BEETHOVEN — Ivan Mahaim, *Beethoven: Naissance et Renaissance des Derniers Quatuors,* 2 vols. Paris: Desclée De Brouwer, 1964.

Mannes/MUSIC — David Mannes, *Music Is My Faith, An Autobiography.* New York: W. W. Norton, 1938.

Mansfield/ MENDELSSOHN — Orlando A. Mansfield, "Some Characteristics and Peculiarities of Mendelssohn's Organ Sonatas," MQ III (1917) 562–76.

Marteau/REGER — Henri Marteau, "Meine Erinnerungen an Max Reger," DA III/3 (1923) 69–78.

Marx/LEHRE — Adolph Bernhard Marx, *Die Lehre von der musikalischen Komposition,* 1st ed., 4 vols. Leipzig: Breitkopf & Härtel, 1837, 1838, 1845, 1847, respectively. Cf. Newman/THEORISTS; SSB II.

Marx/ZYKLISCHE — Karl Marx, "Über die zyklische Sonatenform—Zu dem Aufsatz von Gunther von Noé," NZM CXXV (1964) 142–46. Concerns thematic interrelationships; cf. Noé/ZYKLISCHEN.

Mason/BRAHMS — Colin Mason, "Brahms' Piano Sonatas," MR V (1944) 112–18.

Mason/CHAMBER — Daniel Gregory Mason, *The Chamber Music of Brahms.* New York: Macmillan, 1933.

Mason/LETTERS — Lowell Mason, *Musical Letters From Abroad* (1852–53), facs. of the original ed. of 1854, with a new introduction by Elwyn A. Wienandt. New York: Da Capo, 1967.

MASON MEMORIES — William Mason, *Memories of a Musical Life.* New York: Century, 1902.

Mason/MUSIC — Daniel Gregory Mason, *Music in My Time, and Other Reminiscences.* New York: Macmillan, 1938.

Mason/SCHUBERT — Colin Mason, "An Aspect of Schubert's Piano Sonatas," MMR LXXVI (1946) 152–57.

May/BRAHMS — Florence May, *The Life of Johannes Brahms,* 2d revised ed. (originally pub. in 1905) with Introduction by Ralph Hill, 2 vols. London: William Reeves, [1948].

Mayer-Serra/ LATINOAMERICA — Otto Mayer-Serra, *Música y músicos de Latinoamérica.* Mexico City: Editorial Atlante, 1947.

MdC — *La Musique de chambre.* (Paris: Salons Pleyel). 1893–1903 (10 vols.).

Medtner/WORKS–m — Nikolai Karlovitch Medtner, *Complete Works,* 7 vols. to date (with informative prefaces, in Russian). Moscow: State Music Publishers, 1959——.

Meister/CHOPIN — Edith Meister, *Stilelemente und die geschichtliche Grundlage der Klavierwerke Friedrich Chopins* (Ph.D. diss. at the Hansischen Universität in Hamburg, 1935). Hamburg: Carl Holler, 1936.

Melkus/SCHUMANN — Eduard Melkus, "Zur Revision unseres Schumann-Bildes" and "Schumanns letzte Werke" in ÖMZ XV (1960) 182–90 and 565–71.

Melkus/VIOLINSONATE — ——, "Eine vollständige 3. Violinsonate Schumanns," NZM CXXI (1960) 190–95.

Mello/SCHUBERT — Alfred Mello, "Franz Schuberts Klaviersonaten," NMZ XXIV (1903) 258–60, 274–75, 282–83, 294–95.

Mendel/LEXIKON — Hermann Mendel, *Musikalisches Conversations-Lexikon,* 11 vols. and "Ergänzungsband," completed from M-Z by August Reissmann. Berlin: L. Heimann, pub. from Vol. II by Robert Oppenheim, 1870–83.

Mendelssohn/BRIEFE — Paul and Carl Mendelssohn Bartholdy (eds.), *Briefe aus den Jahren 1830 bis 1847 von Felix Mendelssohn Bartholdy,* 5th ed., 2 vols. Leipzig: Hermann Mendelssohn, 1882.

MENDELSSOHN/Moscheles — Felix Moscheles (ed. and trans.), *Letters of Felix Mendelssohn to Ignaz and Charles Moscheles.* Boston: Ticknor, 1888.

Mendelssohn/VERLEGER — Felix Mendelssohn Bartholdy, *Briefe an deutsche Verleger,* compiled and ed. by R. Elvers (Vol. I of projected complete letters). Berlin: Walter de Gruyter, 1968.

Mendelssohn/WERKE-m — Julius Rietz (ed.), *Felix Mendelssohn Bartholdy's Werke; kritische durchgesehene Ausgabe,* 19 series in 37 vols. Leipzig: Breitkopf & Härtel, 1874–77.

MÉNESTREL — *Le Ménestrel.* 1833–1940.

MERCURE — *Le Mercure musical.* 1905–6.

Méreaux/CLAVECINISTES-m — Amédée Méreaux (ed.), *Les Clavecinistes de 1637 à 1790,* 4 vols. (I–III, music; IV, text). Paris: Heugel, 1867. Cf. Cat. NYPL XIX 81.

Mersmann/KAMMERMUSIK — Hans Mersmann, *Die Kammermusik,* 4 vols. (of which III is *Deutsche Romantik* and IV is *Europäische Kammermusik des XIX. und XX. Jahrhunderts*). Leipzig: Breitkopf & Härtel, 1930.

Mersmann/ROMANTISCHEN — ——, "Sonatenformen in der romantischen Kammermusik," pp. 112–17 in *Festschrift für Johannes*

Wolf zu seinen sechzigsten Geburtstage (Berlin: Breslauer, 1929).

MfMg — *Monatshefte für Musikgeschichte*. 1869–1905.

MGG — Friedrich Blume (ed.), *Die Musik in Geschichte und Gegenwart*, 13 vols. up to this writing (through "Volk-"). Kassel: Bärenreiter-Verlag, 1949——. Cf. NOTES XXIV (1967–68) 217–44 (F. Blume, trans. by J. Godwin).

Michel/SONATE — Henri Michel, *La Sonate pour clavier avant Beethoven*. Amiens: Yvert & Tellier, 1907.

Mies/SCHUBERT-m — Paul Mies (ed.), *Franz Schubert: Klaviersonaten*, 2 vols., with prefaces on texts (11 complete sons., lacking D. 459; with Vol. III, "the Fantasias and the fragments or unfinished sonatas," in progress as of 1966). Munich and Duisburg: G. Henle, 1961.

Milhaud/NOTES — Darius Milhaud, *Notes Without Music, an Aubiography*, trans. by D. Evans (from the original French ed. of 1949) and ed. by R. H. Myers. London: Dennis Dobson, 1952.

Mitchell/HUMMEL — Francis Humphries Mitchell, "The Piano Concertos of Johann Nepomuk Hummel," unpub. Ph.D. diss. Northwestern University, 1957.

Mitschka/BRAHMS — Arno Mitschka, *Der Sonatensatz in den Werken von Johannes Brahms*, (Ph.D. diss. [started in Breslau "several years" before World War II], Johannes-Gutenberg-Universität, Mainz). Gütersloh: pub. by the author, 1961.

ML — *Music and Letters*. 1920——.

MMM — *Monatschrift für moderne Musik*. 1919——.

MMR — *Monthly Musical Record*. 1871——.

MO — *Musical Opinion and Music Trade Review*. 1877——. (The title was later reduced to *Musical Opinion*.)

Monrad-Johansen/GRIEG — David Monrad-Johansen, *Edvard Grieg*, trans. from the original Norwegian of 1934 into English in 1938 by Madge Robertson. New York: Tudor, 1945. Cf. Schjelderup-Ebbe/GRIEG 333–34 *et passim*.

MOSCHELES — Charlotte Moscheles, *Life of Moscheles, With Selections From His Diaries and Correspondence*, trans. (from the original German ed., Leipzig, 1872) by A. D. Coleridge, 2 vols. London: Hurst and Blackett, 1873. (The same trans. appeared as *Recent Music and Musicians . . .* , in New York in 1874.) Cf. the review in MT XVI (1874) 862–63.

Moser/MUSIKÄSTHETIK — Hans Joachim Moser, *Musikästhetik*. Berlin: Walter de Gruyter, 1953.

Moser/JOACHIM — Andreas Moser, *Joseph Joachim: Ein Lebensbild*, 2d ed. in 2 vols. (revised from the first ed. of 1898). Berlin: Deutsche Brahms-Gesellschaft, 1908 and 1910.

Moser/LEXIKON — Hans Joachim Moser, *Musik Lexikon*, 4th ed., 2 vols. plus *Nachtrag* (1958) and *Ergänzungsband* (1963). Berlin: Max Hesse, 1955.

MOZART-JAHRBUCH — *Mozart-Jahrbuch.* Salzburg: Internationale Stiftung Mozarteum, 1950——.

MQ — *The Musical Quarterly.* 1915——.

MR — *The Music Review.* 1940——.

MT — *The Musical Times.* 1844——.

Mühsam/THALBERG — Gerd Mühsam, "Sigismund Thalberg als Klavier-komponist," unpub. Ph.D. diss., Universität Wien, 1937.

Müller/STEIBELT — Gottfried Müller, *Daniel Steibelt: sein Leben und seine Klavierwerke (Etüden und Sonaten;* Ph.D. diss., Greifswald, 1932). Leipzig: Heitz, 1933.

Müller-Reuter/LEXIKON — Theodor Müller-Reuter, *Lexikon der deutschen Konzertliteratur,* 2 vols. (Vol. II is *Nachtrag* or suppl.). Leipzig: C. F. Kahnt, 1909 and 1921.

Mueller von Asow/STRAUSS — Erich H. Mueller von Asow, *Richard Strauss: Thematisches Verzeichnis,* 2 vols. to date; 3d vol. in progress as of 1967, ed. by Alfons Ott and Franz Trenner. Vienna: L. Doblinger, 1959, 1962——.

Muns/CLIMAX — George E. Muns, Jr., "Climax in Music," unpub. Ph.D. diss., The University of North Carolina at Chapel Hill, 1955.

Murdoch/BRAHMS — William Murdoch, *Brahms, With an Analytical Study of the Complete Pianoforte Works.* London: Rich & Cowan, 1938 (first pub. 1933).

MUSIC — *Music.* (Chicago) 1891–1902.

MUSICA — *Musica.* 1947——.

MUSICAL WORLD — *The Musical World, a Weekly Record of Musical Science, Literature, and Intelligence.* 1836–91.

MUSIKLEBEN — *Das Musikleben.* 1948——.

MUSORGSKY READER — Jay Leyda & Sergei Bertensson (eds.), *The Musorgsky Reader: A Life of Modeste Petrovich Musorgsky in Letters and Documents,* largely trans. from A. Rimsky-Korsakov's Russian ed. of 1932. New York: W. W. Norton, 1947. Cf. BAKER 1141.

Musorgsky/WERKE-m — Paul Lamm (ed.), *Modest Petrovich Musorgsky Sämtliche Werke,* 8 series in 25 vols. Vienna [and Moscow]: Universal, 1928–39. Cf. MUSORGSKY READER 424–37.

MW — *Musikalisches Wochenblatt.* 1870–1910.

Nagel/BRAHMS   Willibald Nagel, *Die Klaviersonaten von Joh. Brahms; technische-äesthetische Analysen.* Stuttgart: Carl Grüninger, 1915. Originally pub. in NZM XXXIV (1913) and XXXV (1914), *passim.*

NBJ   *Neues Beethoven-Jahrbuch,* 10 vols. 1924–42.

Nef/HISTORY   Karl Nef, *An Outline of the History of Music,* trans. and enlarged from the 2d German ed. of 1930 (originally pub. in 1920) and the 2d French ed. of 1931 by Carl F. Pfatteicher. New York: Columbia University Press, 1935.

Neighbour/SCHUMANN-m Oliver Neighbour (ed.), *R. Schumann: Sonata No. 3 in A minor for Violin and Piano.* London: Schott, 1956.

Neighbour & Tyson/ENGLISH Oliver Neighbour and Alan Tyson, *English Music Publishers' Plate Numbers in the First Half of the Nineteenth Century.* London: Faber and Faber, 1965. Cf. MT CVI (1965) 521 and 683.

Nettl/DOCUMENTS   Paul Nettl, *The Book of Musical Documents.* New York: Philosophical Library, 1948.

Newman/ACCOMPANIED William S. Newman, "Concerning the Accompanied Clavier Sonata," MQ XXXIII (1947) 327–49.

Newman/ARTIST   Ernest Newman, *Wagner as Man and Artist,* 2d ed. (first pub. in 1924; first ed. pub. in 1914). New York: Random House, 1960.

Newman/CHOPIN   William S. Newman, "Fryderyk Chopin: Complete Works [Warsaw: Fryderyk Chopin Institute, 1949–at least 1962]," review in PQ No. 30 (winter 1959–60) 15, 17, and 19–21.

Newman/CLIMAX   ———, "The Climax of Music," *The University of North Carolina Extension Bulletin* XXXI/3 (Jan., 1952) 22–40; abridged in MR XIII (1952) 283–93.

Newman/CZERNY   ———, "About Carl Czerny's Op. 600 and the 'First' Description of 'Sonata Form,'" JAMS XX (1967) 513–15. Cf. Newman/THEORISTS; SSB II.

Newman/DIABELLI-m   ——— (ed.), *Diabelli Variations: 16 Contemporaries of Beethoven on a Waltz Tune* (with preface). Evanston (Ill.): Summy-Birchard, 1958.

Newman/K. 457   William S. Newman, "K. 457 and op. 13—Two Related Masterpieces in C minor," MR XXVIII (1967) 38–44; reprinted with slight changes from PQ XV (fall 1966) 11–15.

Newman/LISZT   ———, "Franz Liszt's Newly Discovered Duo (Sonate) for Violin and Piano," PQ XIII/50 (winter 1964–65) 25–26.

Newman/OP. 106   ———, "Some 19th-Century Consequences of Beethoven's 'Hammerklavier' Sonata, Op. 106," scheduled to be pub. serially in PQ nos. 67 and 68 (spring and summer, 1969).

Newman/THEORISTS ————, "The Recognition of Sonata Form by Theorists of the 18th and 19th Centuries," PAPERS AMS 1941 (printed 1946) 21–29. Cf. Newman/CZERNY; SSB II.

Newman/THIRTEEN-m ———— (ed.), *Thirteen Keyboard Sonatas of the 18th and 19th Centuries* (by Barrière, Platti, D. Alberti, G. Benda, Agrell, Neefe, Blasco de Nebra, Dittersdorf, Wölfl, E. T. A. Hoffmann, Reichardt, K. Loewe, and Moscheles). Chapel Hill: The University of North Carolina Press, 1947.

Newman/TREND William S. Newman, "The Present Trend of the Sonata Idea," unpub. Ph.D. diss., Western Reserve University, 1939.

Newman/UNDERSTANDING ————, *Understanding Music,* first pub. in 1953, 2d ed. in 1961, with revisions in Colophon paperback. New York: Harper & Row, 1967.

Newman/WAGNER Ernest Newman, *The Life of Richard Wagner,* 4 vols. New York: Alfred A. Knopf, 1933, 1937, 1941, 1946.

Newmarch/ Rosa Newmarch, *The Music of Czechoslovakia.* London: Oxford, 1942.
CZECHOSLOVAKIA

Nicolescu/SONATA Mircea Nicolescu, *Sonata: Natura, originea și evoluția ei.* [Bucharest:] Editura Muzicală, 1962.

Niecks/CHOPIN Frederick Niecks, *Friedrich Chopin als Musiker,* revised by the author and trans. from the original English ed. of 1888 by W. Langhans, 2 vols. Leipzig: F. E. C. Leuckart, 1890.

Niecks/SCHUMANN ————, *Robert Schumann.* New York: E. P. Dutton, 1925.

Niggli/SCHUBERT [Arnold Niggli], "Franz Schuberts Klaviersonaten zu 2 Händen," SMZ XVIII (1878) 21–22, 29–31, 37–38, 45–47. The authorship comes from Kahl/SCHUBERT item 374.

Nikolaiev/ Aleksandr Aleksandrovich Nikolaiev, *The Pianoforte Heritage of Tchaikovsky* (in Russian). Moscow, 1958. References are cited here by way of Alekseev & Novikova.
TCHAIKOVSKY

Nisser/SVENSK Carl Nisser, *Svensk Instrumentalkomposition 1770–1830, Nominalkatalog.* Stockholm: Gothia, 1943.

NMZ *Neue Musik-Zeitung.* 1880–1928.

Noé/ZYKLISCHEN Günther von Noé, "Der Strukturwandel der zyklischen Sonatenform," NZM CXXV (1964) 55–62. Concerns interlocking of mvts.; cf. Marx/ZYKLISCHE.

Nohl/GLUCK & WEBER Ludwig Nohl (ed.), *Lettres de Gluck et de Weber,* trans. by Guy de Charnacé. Paris: Henri Plon, 1870.

Nohl/SCHUBERT Walter Nohl, "Beethoven's and Schubert's Personal Relations," MQ XIV (1928) 553–62.

Nohl/SYMPHONY — Ludwig Nohl, "The Father of the Symphony," MT XXI (1880) 491–92, 539–40, 597–98; XXII (1881) 14–15, 72–73, 121–23.

NOTES — *Music Library Association Notes,* Second Series. 1943——.

NZM — Robert Schumann and successors (eds.), *Neue Zeitschrift für Musik.* 1834—— (with various names and affiliations after 1858; cf. Freystätter/ZEITSCHRIFTEN 57–58 [with errors] and GROVE VI 651).

ÖMZ — *Österreichische Musikzeitschrift.* 1946——.

O'Leary/BENNETT — Arthur O'Leary, "Sir William Sterndale Bennett: A Brief Review of His Life and Works," PMA VIII (1881–82) 123–45.

Opieński/CHOPIN — Henryk Opieński, "Sonaty Chopina, ich oceny i ich wartość konstrukcyjna" ("Chopin's Sonatas, Their Understanding and Their Structural Principles"), in *Kwartalnik Muzyczny* I/1 and 2 (1928–29) 59–72 and 152–62. Cf. Sydow/BIBLIOGRAPHIE item 3347; Bronarski/CHOPIN II 103.

Orel/SCHUBERT — Alfred Orel, "Franz Schuberts 'Sonate' für Klavier, Violine und Violoncell aus dem Jahre 1812," ZfMW V (1922–23) 209–18.

Orel/SCHUBERT-m — —— (ed.), *Franz Schubert: Sonate für Klavier, Violine u. Violoncell,* D. 28. Vienna: Wiener Philharmonischer Verlag, 1923.

Ossofski/GLAZUNOV — Alexandr Vyacheslavovich Ossofski, *Aleksandr Konstantinovitch Glazunov.* Leningrad (?), 1907.

PADEREWSKI — Ignace Jan Paderewski and Mary Lawton, *The Paderewski Memoirs* (up to 1914). New York: Charles Scribner, 1938.

Panofsky/WAGNER — Walter Panofsky, *Wagner: A Pictorial Biography.* New York: Viking Press, 1963.

Parrott/SCHUMANN — Ian Parrott, "A Plea for Schumann's Op. 11," ML XXXIII (1952) 55–58.

Parry/EVOLUTION — C. Hubert H. Parry, *The Evolution of the Art of Music* (originally pub. in this form in 1896). New York: D. Appleton, 1916.

Parry/STYLE — Charles Hubert Hastings Parry, *Style in Musical Art.* London: Macmillan, 1911, reprinted in 1924.

PAZDÍREK — Franz Pazdírek, *Universal-Handbuch der Musikliteratur aller Zeiten und Völker,* 34 vols. Vienna: Pazdírek, [1904–10]. Cf. MGG X 981–82 (Výborný). Limited to publications procurable at the time the set was prepared. Vol. nos. differ with the binding of this set, and occasionally conflict in the present study; but the pagination and alphabetization remain consistent. A reprint of the complete set was announced by Frits Knuf (Hilversum, Holland) in 1967.

Pearce/MENDELSSOHN — Charles William Pearce, *Mendelssohn's Organ Sonatas Technically and Critically Discussed*. London: Vincent Music, [*ca.* 1902].

Petitpierre/MENDELSSOHNS — Jacques Petitpierre, *The Romance of the Mendelssohns*, trans. from the French (Paris, 1937) by G. Micholet-Coté. London: Dennis Dobson, 1947.

PIANOFORTE — *Il Pianoforte*. 1920–27.

Pincherle/MUSICIENS — Marc Pincherle (ed.), *Musiciens peints par eux-mêmes, Lettres de compositeurs écrites en français (1771–1910)*. Paris: Pierre Cornau, 1939.

PISK ESSAYS — John Glowacki (ed.), *Paul A. Pisk: Essays in His Honor*. Austin: University of Texas Press, 1967.

Plantinga/SCHUMANN — Leon B. Plantinga, "The Musical Criticism of Robert Schumann in the *Neue Zeitschrift für Musik, 1834–44*," unpub. Ph.D. diss., Yale University, 1964. Since its use in SSB this diss. was pub. by Yale University Press (late 1967); cf. the reviews by J. A. Westrup in ML XLIX (1968) 182–83 and by P. H. Lang in MQ LIV (1968) 361–75.

Pleasants/HANSLICK — Henry Pleasants (trans. and ed.), *Eduard Hanslick: Music Criticisms, 1846–99*. Baltimore: Penguin Books, 1950.

PMA — *Proceedings of the (Royal) Musical Association*. 1874——.

Pohl/MOZART — Carl Ferdinand Pohl, *Mozart und Haydn in London*, 2 vols. Vienna: Carl Gerold's Sohn, 1867.

PORTUGALIAE-m — *Portugaliae Musica, Série A* (and B), 10 vols. up to 1967. Lisbon: Fundação Calouste Gulbenkian, 1965——.

Pougin/SONATE — Arthur Pougin, "Courte Monographie de la sonate," MÉNESTREL LXVII (1901) 275–76, 282–83, 293.

PQ — *The Piano Quarterly* (founded as *Piano Quarterly Newsletter*). 1952——.

Prod'homme/BEETHOVEN — Jacques-Gabriel Prod'homme, *Les Sonates pour Piano de Beethoven*. Paris: Delagrave, 1937.

Prod'homme/SCHUBERT — ———, "Schubert's Works in France," MQ XIV (1928) 495–514; also pub. in KONGRESS SCHUBERT 87–110 as "Les Œuvres de Schubert en France."

Prosniz/HANDBUCH — Adolf Prosniz, *Handbuch der Klavier-Literatur*, 2 vols. (1450–1830, 1830–1904). Leipzig: L. Doblinger, 1908 (2d ed.), 1907.

Prout/DUSSEK — Ebenezer Prout, "Dussek's Piano Sonatas," MT XVIII (1877) 422–24, 468–70.

Prout *et al.*/RAFF — Ebenezer Prout, John South Shedlock, and Charles Ainslee Barry, "Raff's Symphonies," MMR V (1875) 32–33, 46–49, 61–64, 77–80, 93–95, 109–11, 121–23, 133–35, 147–49, with many exx.

QUARTERLY — *The Quarterly Musical Magazine and Review.* 1818–28.

Raabe/LISZT — Peter Raabe, *Franz Liszt: Leben und Schaffen,* 2 vols. Stuttgart: J. B. Cotta, 1931. A revision by Felix Raabe (son) was in progress in 1967.

Radiciotti/ROSSINI — Giuseppe Radiciotti, *Gioacchino Rossini: Vita documentata, opere ed influenza su l'arte,* 3 vols. Tivoli: Majella di A. Chicca, 1927–29.

Raff/RAFF — Helene Raff, *Joachim Raff: Ein Lebensbild* (completed in 1922). Regensburg: Gustav Bosse, 1925.

RaM — *Rassegna musicale.* 1928–62.

Ramann/LISZT — Lina Ramann, *Franz Liszt als Künstler und Mensch,* 2 books in 3 vols. Leipzig: Breitkopf & Härtel, 1880, 1887, and 1894.

Ratz/SCHUBERT — Erwin Ratz, "Zur Chronologie der Klaviersonaten Franz Schuberts," SMZ LXXXIX (1949) 1–5; reprinted in ÖMZ V (1950) 7–14.

Ratz/SCHUBERT-m — ——— (ed.), *Franz Schubert: Klaviersonaten nach den Autographen und Erstdrucken,* with preface; 2 vols. (including 12 complete sons. plus D. 625 and D. 840; with 8 more incomplete sons. expected in a suppl. vol.). Vienna: Universal, 1958. Cf. the detailed check of the text in Taggart/SCHUBERT 32–55; also, the review by H. Ferguson in ML XLVIII (1967) 406.

Raybould/MEDTNER — Clarence Raybould, "A Monograph on Medtner," in Holt/MEDTNER 133–40.

RBdM — *Revue belge de musicologie.* 1946———.

RdM — *Revue de musicologie* (founded as *Bulletin de la Société française de musicologie*). 1917———.

RECHERCHES — *"Recherches," sur la Musique française classique.* 1960———.

Redlich/SCHUMANN — Hans Ferdinand Redlich, "Schumann Discoveries," MMR LXXX (1950) 143–47, 182–84, 261–65 ("A Postscript"); LXXXI (1951) 14–16 ("A Postscript").

Reed/ELGAR — William Henry Reed, *Elgar.* London: J. M. Dent, 1939.

Refardt/HUBER — Edgar Refardt, *Hans Huber: Leben und Werk eines schweizer Musikers.* Zürich: Atlantis, 1944.

Reeser/NEDERLANDSE — Eduard Reeser, *Een Eeuw nederlandse Musiek.* Amsterdam: N. V. Em. Querido, 1950.

REGER BRIEFE — Ottmar Schreiber (ed.), *Max Reger: Briefe zwischen der Arbeit*. Bonn: Ferdinand Dümmler, 1956.

REGER GEDENKSCHRIFT — Ottmar Schreiber & Gerd Sievers (eds.), *Max Reger, zum 50. Todestag am 11. Mai 1966: Eine Gedenkschrift*. Bonn: Ferd. Dümmler, 1966.

REGER-GEORG II — Hedwig and E. H. Mueller von Asow (eds.), *Max Reger: Briefwechsel mit Herzog Georg II von Sachsen-Meiningen*. Weimar: Hermann Böhlaus Nachfolger, 1949.

REGER-GESELLSCHAFT — *Mitteilungen der Max Reger-Gesellschaft*, 17 issues. Stuttgart: J. Engelhorn, 1921–41. Cf. Stein/VERZEICHNIS 574–76.

Reger/WERKE-m — Max Reger: *Sämtliche Werke*, in co-operation with the Max-Reger-Institut; 35 vols. projected. Wiesbaden: Breitkopf & Härtel, 1954——.

Rehberg/BRAHMS — Walter and Paula Rehberg, *Johannes Brahms: Sein Leben und Werk*. Zürich: Artemis, 1947.

Rehberg/SCHUMANN — Paula and Walter Rehberg, *Robert Schumann: Sein Leben und sein Werk*. Zürich: Artemis, 1954.

Reicha & Czerny/ COMPOSITION — Anton Reicha, *Vollständiges Lehrbuch der musikalischen Composition*, trans. (with both French and German texts) and annotated (cf. Vol. I, p. 4) by Carl Czerny; Vol. I being Reicha's *Cour de composition musicale* (Paris: Gambaro, 1816), II his *Traité de melodie* (Paris: author, 1814), and III and IV his *Traité de haute composition musicale* (Paris: Costellat, 1824–26). Vienna: Diabelli, [1832; plate no. 4170 and dated preface]. Cf. MGG XI 148 (J. Bužga); Cat. NYPL XXV 412; Newman/CZERNY.

Reither/RACHMANINOFF — Joseph Reither, "Chronicle of Exile [of Rachmaninoff]," TEMPO XXII (winter 1951–52) 29–36.

Řepková/SMETANA — Věra Řepková (ed.), *Bedřich Smetana: Sonáta pro klavir na dvě ruce*, with preface by Mirko Očadlík. Prague: Melantrich, 1949.

Reti/BEETHOVEN — Rudolph Reti, *Thematic Patterns in Sonatas of Beethoven*, ed. by Deryck Cooke. New York: Macmillan, 1967.

RGM — *Revue et gazette musicale de Paris*. 1834–80 (with changes of title). Cf. GROVE VI 647.

Richter/KAMMERMUSIK — Johannes Friedrich Richter, *Kammermusik-Katalog, Verzeichnis der von 1944 bis 1958 veröffentlichten Werke für Kammermusik und für Klavier vier- und sechshändig sowie für zwei und mehr Klaviere*. Leipzig: Friedrich Hofmeister, 1960. Cf. Altmann/KAMMERMUSIK.

RICORDI ARTE-m — *L'Arte antica e moderna, scelta di composizioni per pianoforte*, 21 vols. Milan: G. Ricordi, [ca. 1878-ca.

1910]. "Mostly derived from" TRÈSOR-m; cf. Cat. BOLOGNA IV 180.

RICORDI ENCICLOPEDIA   *Enciclopedia della musica,* 4 vols. Milano: G. Ricordi, 1963–64.

Riehl/CHARAKTERKÖPFE   Wilhelm Heinrich von Riehl, *Musikalische Charakterköpfe,* 4th ed. (first pub. in 1853–61), 2 vols. Stuttgart: J. G. Cotta, 1868 and 1875.

Riemann/LEXIKON   Alfred Einstein (ed.), *Hugo Riemann's Musik Lexikon,* 11th ed., 2 vols. Berlin: Max Hesses Verlag, 1929. This ed. is used unless the 12th ed. (Mainz: B. Schott, 1959———) is specified.

Riesemann/ MOUSSORGSKY   Oskar van Riesemann, *Moussorgsky,* trans. from the original German ed. of 1925 by P. England. New York: Alfred A. Knopf, 1929.

Riezler/SCHUBERT   Walter Riezler, *Schuberts Instrumentalmusik; Werkanalysen.* Zürich: Atlantis, 1967.

Rimbault/PIANOFORTE   Edward F. Rimbault, *The Pianoforte, Its Origin, Progress, and Construction* . . . (with music exx., pp. 237–368). London: Robert Cocks, 1860.

Ritzel/SONATENFORM   Fred Ritzel, *Die Entwicklung der "Sonatenform" im musiktheoretischen Schrifttum des 18. und 19. Jahrhunderts* (Ph.D. diss.). Wiesbaden: Breitkopf & Härtel, 1968.

RM   *La Revue musicale* (founded by H. Prunières). 1920———.

RM/CHOPIN   *Chopin: Numéro spécial* (an anthology of historical and analytical articles). RM XII/121 (Dec., 1931). Cf. Sydow/BIBLIOGRAPHIE no. 7779.

RM/FRANCK   Three articles on César Franck, by Julien Tiersot, Henri Duparc, and André Schaeffner, in RM IV/2 (Dec. 1, 1922) 97–154.

RM/LALO   Three articles on Édouard Lalo—by Paul Dukas, Adolphe Jullien, and Pierre Lalo, in RM IV/5 (March 1, 1923) 97–124.

Rösner/REGER   Helmut Rösner, "Max Regers Violinsonate Op. 72, Entwurf und endgültige Gestalt," in REGER GEDENKSCHRIFT 169–88.

Roger-Ducasse/FAURÉ   Jean-Jules Aimable Roger-Ducasse, "[Gabriel Fauré:] La Musique de chambre," RM II (Oct., 1922, *Fauré: Numéro spécial)* 60–79.

Rogers/BRISTOW   Delmar D. Rogers, "Nineteenth-Century Music in New York City as Reflected in the Career of George Frederick Bristow," unpub. Ph.D. diss., University of Michigan, 1967.

Rokseth/GRIEG   Yvonne Rokseth, *Grieg.* Paris: Rieder, 1933.

Rosenfeld/AMERICAN   Paul Rosenfeld, *An Hour with American Music.* Philadelphia: J. P. Lippincott, 1929.

Rossini/SONATE-m — Cioacchino Rossini, *Sei Sonate a quattro*, ed. by L. Liviabella, with "Prefazione" by A. Bonaccorsi; Vol. I in *Quaderni Rossiniani*. Pesaro: Fondazione Rossini, 1954.

Rostand/FAURÉ — Claude Rostand, *L'Œuvre de Fauré*, 5th ed. Paris: L. B. Janin, 1945.

Rubinstein/ERINNERUNGEN — Anton Rubinstein, *Erinnerungen aus fünfzig Jahren*, trans. into German from the original Russian ed. of 1892 by E. Kretschmann, 2d ed. Leipzig: Bartholf Senff, 1895. The English trans. by A. Delano (1903) was not used here.

Rubinstein/GEDANKENKORB — *Anton Rubinstein's Gedankenkorb*, with foreword by H. Wolff, 2d ed. Leipzig: Bartholf Senff, 1897.

Rueth/DOHNÁNYI — Marion Ursula Rueth, "The Tallahassee Years of Ernst von Dohnányi," photoduplication of typed M.A. thesis, Florida State University, 1962.

Ruthardt/LINKE-m — Adolf Ruthardt (ed.), *Album für die linke Hand für Pianoforte*. Leipzig: C. F. Peters No. 2716, [1894?].

SAINSBURY — [John S. Sainsbury], *A Dictionary of Musicians From the Earliest Times* (originally pub. in London in 1824 [not 1825] in 2 vols.), with Introduction by the late H. G. Farmer (ed. version of ML XII [1931] 384–92), 2 vols. New York: Da Capo, 1966. Cf. V. Duckles' review in NOTES XXIII (1967) 737–39.

Saint-Foix/PIANISTES — Georges de Saint-Foix, "Les premiers Pianistes parisiens," RM III (Aug., 1922) 121–36 and Suppl.: "Jean Schobert," IV (April, 1923) 193–205 and Suppl.: "Nicolas-Joseph Hüllmandel," V (June, 1924) 187–98 and Suppl.: "Edelmann (Jean-Frédéric)" and "Rigel (Henri-Joseph)," VI (June, 1925) 209–15: "Jean-Louis Adam," VI (Aug., 1925) 105–9: "Les Frères Jadin," VII (Nov., 1925) 43–46: "Les six Sonates de Méhul," VII (Feb., 1926) 102–10: "Boieldieu," VIII (Nov., 1926) 13–20: "Ignace-Antoine Ladurner," IX (Aug., 1928) 321–32: "A. P. F. Boëly."

St John/SMYTH — Christopher St John, *Ethyl Smyth, a Biography*, with additional chaps. by V. Sackville-West and K. Dale. London: Longmans, Green, 1959.

Saint-Saëns/ESSAYS — Camille Saint-Saëns, *Outspoken Essays on Music*, trans. by Fred Rothwell. London: Kegan Paul, Trench, Trubner, 1922.

Salazar/TRENDS — Adolfo Salazar, *Music in Our Time; Trends in Music Since the Romantic Era*, trans. from *Música moderna* (Buenos Aires, 1944) by Isabel Pope. New York: W. W. Norton, 1946.

Salter/AMERICAN   Sumner Salter, "Early Encouragements to American Composers," MQ XVIII (1932) 76–105.

Salter/MTNA   ———, "The Music Teachers' National Association in Its Early Relation to American Composers," *Proceedings for 1932* of the Music Teachers National Association 9–34.

Salzer/SCHUBERT   Felix Salzer, "Die Sonatenform bei Franz Schubert" (extract from unpub. Ph.D. diss., Vienna, 1926), SZMW XV (1928) 86–125.

Samaroff/SCHUBERT   Olga Samaroff (*née* Hickenlooper), "The Piano Music of Schubert," MQ XIV (1928) 596–609.

Sandberger/AUFSÄTZE   Adolf Sandberger, *Ausgewählte Aufsätze zur Musikgeschichte,* 3 vols. Munich: Drei Masken, 1921, 1924, 1934.

Saunders/WEBER   William Saunders, *Weber.* New York: E. P. Dutton, 1940.

SBE   William S. Newman, *The Sonata in the Baroque Era,* vol. I in *A History of the Sonata Idea.* Chapel Hill: The University of North Carolina Press, 1959; revised 2d ed., 1966. References in this vol. are to the 2d ed.

SCE   ———, *The Sonata in the Classic Era,* vol. II in *A History of the Sonata Idea.* Chapel Hill: The University of North Carolina Press, 1963.

Sceats/KARG-ELERT   Godfrey Sceats, *The Organ Works of Karg-Elert,* 2d ed. (originally pub. in 1940). New York: Peters, 1950.

Schaal/DISSERTATIONEN   Richard Schaal, *Verzeichnis deutschsprachiger musikwissentschaftlicher Dissertationen 1861–1960.* Kassel: Bärenreiter, 1963.

Schaal/KAUN   ———, *Hugo Kaun (1863–1932): Leben und Werk.* Regensburg: Josef Habbel, [1948].

Schaal/LOKALGESCHICHTS   ———, *Das Schrifttum zur musikalischen Lokalgeschichts-Forschung.* Kassel: Bärenreiter, 1947.

Schauffler/BRAHMS   Robert Haven Schauffler, *The Unknown Brahms: His Life, Character and Works; Based on New Material.* New York: Crown, 1940 (first pub. 1933).

Schering/NEUROMANTIK   Arnold Schering, "Aus den Jugendjahren der musikalischen Neuromantik," JMP XXIV (1917) 45–63.

Schiffer/DUSSEK   Leo Schiffer, *Johann Ladislau Dussek, seine Sonaten und seine Konzerte* (Ph.D. diss., University of Munich). Leipzig: Robert Noske, 1914 (available only indirectly to the present study; cf. SSB XVII and Craw/DUSSEK 1–2).

Schilling/LEXICON   Gustav Schilling (ed.), *Encyclopädie der gesammten musikalischen Wissenschaften oder Universal-Lexi-*

con der Tonkunst, 6 vols. Stuttgart: F. H. Köhler, 1835–38. *Supplementband,* 1842. Cf. GASSNER.

Schindler & MacArdle/ BEETHOVEN — Anton Felix Schindler, *Beethoven as I Knew Him,* trans. by Constance S. Jolly and annotated by Donald W. MacArdle from the 3d ed. of 1860, 2 vols. in one. Chapel Hill: The University of North Carolina Press, 1966. Cf. MT. CVIII (1967) 40–41 (J. Kerman).

Schjelderup-Ebbe/ GRIEG — Dag Schjelderup-Ebbe, *Edvard Grieg* [and his early works:] *1858–1867, with special reference to the evolution of his harmonic style.* Oslo: Universitetsforlaget, 1964.

Schlesinger/CRAMER — Thea Schlesinger, *Johann Baptist Cramer und seine Klaviersonaten* (Ph.D. diss. [completed in 1925], Ludwig-Maximilians-Universität in Munich). Munich: Knorr & Hirth, 1928.

Schmidl/DIZIONARIO — Carlo Schmidl, *Dizionario universale dei musicisti,* 2 vols. and "Supplemento." Milan: Sonzogno, 1926 and 1938.

Schmitz/LISZT — Eugen Schmitz, "Liszts H-moll Sonate: eine hermeneutische Studie," ADMZ XXXI (1904) 451–53, 470–71.

Schnapp/CZERNY — Friedrich Schnapp, "Ein autobiographischer Brief Carl Czernys aus dem Jahre 1824," NZM CVIII (1941) 89–96.

Schnapp/LISZT — ———, "Verschollene Kompositionen Franz Liszts," in *Festschrift zu Peter Raabes 70. Geburtstag* (Leipzig: C. F. Peters, 1942) 119–53.

Schneider/ELEMENTS — Frederick [Johann Christian Friedrich] Schneider, *The Elements of Musical Harmony and Composition,* trans. (by?) from the 2d, revised ed. of *Elementarbuch der Harmonie und Tonsetzkunst* (Leipzig: Peters, 1827; originally 1820). London: Clementi, 1828.

Schonberg/PIANISTS — Harold C. Schonberg, *The Great Pianists.* New York: Simon and Schuster, 1963.

Schoolfield/GERMAN — George C. Schoolfield, *The Figure of the Musician in German Literature.* Chapel Hill: The University of North Carolina Press, 1956.

Schrade/BEETHOVEN — Leo Schrade, *Beethoven in France, the Growth of an Idea.* New Haven: Yale University Press, 1942.

SCHUBERT WERKE-m — *Franz Schubert's Werke,* 21 Series (including suppl.) in 39 vols. (or 41 in the 1928 reprint), plus *Revisionsbericht.* Leipzig: Breitkopf & Härtel, 1884–97. Reprinted unaltered in 1964, in 19 vols., by Dover Publications, New York. Cf. Deutsch/COLLECTED.

Schuberth/LEXIKON — *Julius Schuberth's Musikalisches Conversations-*

Lexicon, 11th ed., ed. by Emil Breslauer. Leipzig: J. Schuberth, 1892.

Schüz/SONATE

Alfred Schüz, "Die Sonate der Zukunft," NMZ XXIV (1903) 4, 34–35, 58–59, 70–71.

SCHUMANN-BRAHMS

Berthold Litzmann (ed., "im Auftrage von Marie Schumann"), *Clara Schumann* [and] *Johannes Brahms: Briefe aus den Jahren 1853–1896,* 2 vols. Leipzig: Breitkopf & Härtel, 1927. Primarily because it is abridged, the trans. of this collection that appeared in the same year (New York: Longmans, Green) is not referred to in SSB.

SCHUMANN/-DRUCKE

Erst- und Frühdrucke von Robert Schumann in der Musikbibliothek Leipzig, prepared by Ferdinand Hirsch and Ellen Roeser. Leipzig: Musikbibliothek, 1960.

Schumann/
JUGENDBRIEFE

Robert Schumann, *Jugendbriefe, nach den Originalen mitgetheilt von Clara Schumann,* 2d ed. Leipzig: Breitkopf und Härtel, 1886.

Schumann/SCHRIFTEN

Martin Kreisig (ed.), *Gesammelte Schriften über Musik und Musiker von Robert Schumann,* 5th ed., 2 vols. Leipzig: Breitkopf & Härtel, 1914. (No English trans. proved adequate for reference here and none is complete; cf. SSB VIII; ML XLVI [1965] 267–68 [Westrup]; JAMS XVIII [1965] 417–19 [Plantinga].)

Schumann/WERKE-m

Clara Schumann (and Johannes Brahms; eds.), *Robert Schumann's Werke,* 14 series in 31 vols. Leipzig: Breitkopf & Härtel, 1881–93. Cf. Heyer/HISTORICAL 297; Litzmann/SCHUMANN 359–61.

Schwarz/SCHUMANN

Werner Schwarz, *Robert Schumann und die Variation, mit besonderer Berücksichtigung der Klavierwerke.* Kassel: Bärenreiter, 1932.

SCHWEIZER LEXIKON

Edgar Refardt, Willi Schuh, and Hans Ehinger (eds.), *Schweizer Musiker Lexikon.* Zürich: Atlantis, 1939.

Scott/SUGGESTIONS

Cyril Scott, "Suggestions for a More Logical Sonata Form," MR XLVII (1917) 104–5.

Seaman/AMATEUR

Gerald Seaman, "Amateur Music-Making in Russia," ML XLVII (1966) 249–59. But cf. MR XXVIII (1967) 78–82 for M. H. Brown's and C. Greene's charges of plagiarism (mere translation) from L. N. Raaben's book on Russian instrumental ensemble music (Moscow, 1961).

Seaman/CHAMBER

———, "The First Russian Chamber Music," MR XXVI (1965) 326–37. But cf. MR XXVIII (1967) 78–82 and 256 for M. H. Brown's and C. Greene's charges of plagiarism (mere translation) from L. N.

Raaben's book on Russian instrumental ensemble music (Moscow, 1961); with replies by Seaman.

Seaman/PIANO ———, "The Rise of Russian Piano Music," MR XXVII (1966) 177–93. But cf. MR XXVIII (1967) 80–82 and 256 for M. H. Brown's charges of plagiarism (mere translation) from Alekseev/FORTEPIAN-NAIA; with reply by Seaman.

Seaman/RUSSIAN ———, History of Russian Music ("an amplification of a doctoral thesis completed in 1961"), Vol. I, "From Its Origins to Dargomyzhsky." New York: Frederick A. Praeger, 1967.

Sear/SPOOK H. G. Sear, "The Spook Sonata" (by Strindberg), MMR LXXXVI (1956) 94–97.

Searle/ALKAN Humphrey Searle, "A Plea for Alkan," ML XVIII (1937) 276–79.

Searle/LISZT ———, The Music of Liszt. London: Williams & Norgate, 1954. The 2d, revised ed. (New York: Dover, 1966) was not used here.

Seidel/ENHARMONIK Elmar Seidel, Die Enharmonik in den harmonischen Grossformen Franz Schuberts (Ph.D. diss. 1962). Frankfurt am Main: Johann Wolfgang Goethe-Universität, 1963.

Selden-Goth/ MENDELSSOHN Gisella Selden-Goth (ed.), Felix Mendelssohn: Letters. London: Paul Elek, 1946.

Selva/SONATE Blanche Selva, La Sonate. Paris: Rouart, Lerolle, 1913.

Serly/LISZT-m Tibor Serly (ed.), Franz Liszt: Duo (Sonate) for Violin and Piano. New York: Southern Music, 1964.

Service/CADENCE Alfred Roy Service, "A Study of the Cadence as a Factor in Musical Intelligibility in Selected Piano Sonatas by American Composers," unpub. Ph.D. diss., State University of Iowa, 1958.

Servières/FAURÉ Georges Servières, Gabriel Fauré, étude critique. Paris: Henri Laurens, 1930.

Servières/SAINT-SAËNS ———, Saint-Saëns. Paris: Librairie Félix Alcan, 1923.

Shand/VIOLIN David Austin Shand, "The Sonata for Violin and Piano from Schumann to Debussy (1851–1917)," unpub. Ph.D. diss. (with many exx.), Boston University, 1948.

Shaw/LONDON Bernard Shaw, Music in London 1890–94, weekly criticisms contributed to The World, originally issued as an anthology in 1932; 3 vols. London: Constable, 1949.

Shedlock/SONATA John South Shedlock, The Pianoforte Sonata: Its Origin and Development (reprinted from the original ed., London, 1895), with a new Foreword by

W. S. Newman. New York: Da Capo Press, 1964. Cf. Kretzschmar/AUFSÄTZE I 61–63; NOTES XVII (1965–66) 912 (K. Speer).

Shepherd/GOETSCHIUS   Arthur Shepherd, " 'Papa' Goetschius in Retrospect," MQ XXX (1944) 307–18.

Siebenkäs/BERGER   Dieter Siebenkäs, *Ludwig Berger: Sein Leben und seine Werke unter besonderer Berücksichtigung seines Liedschaffens*. Berlin: Merseburger, 1963.

Siegel/GERMANY   Linda Siegel, "The Influence of Romantic Literature on Romantic Music in Germany During the First Half of the Nineteenth Century," unpub. Ph.D. diss., Boston University, 1964.

Siegmund-Schultze/ CHOPIN   Walther Siegmund-Schultze, "Chopin und Brahms," CONGRESS CHOPIN 388–95.

Sietz/HILLER   Reinhold Sietz, *Aus Ferdinand Hillers Briefwechsel (1826–61, 1862–69, 1870–75,* [to date]): *Beiträge zu einer Biographie Ferdinand Hillers,* 3 vols. (to date), Nos. 28, 48, and 56 in *Beiträge zur Rheinischen Musikgeschichte.* Köln: Arno Volk-Verlag, 1958, 1961, and 1964.

SIMG   *Sammelbände der Internationalen Musikgesellschaft.* 1900–1914.

Simpson/NIELSEN   Robert Simpson, *Carl Nielsen, Symphonist,* with a biographical appendix by Torben Meyer. London: J. M. Dent, 1952.

Sitwell/LISZT   Sacheverell Sitwell, *Liszt,* with "minor corrections" of the revised ed. in 1955 of the original ed. in 1934 (London). New York: Dover, 1967.

SJÖGREN-m   Emil Sjögren, *Cinq Sonates pour violon et piano,* with preface by Berta Sjögren. Stockholm: Edition Suecia, 1957 [copyright 1917 and 1945 by C. F. Peters].

Sloan/VIOLIN   Frances Sloan, "A Historical Survey of Violin Literature in America from the Colonial Period to 1880 (Composers' Birth-Date)," unpub. M.A. thesis, The University of North Carolina at Chapel Hill, 1950.

Slonimsky/LEXICON   Nicolas Slonimsky, *Lexicon of Musical Invective,* 2d ed. New York: Coleman-Ross, 1965.

Slonimsky/WILLIAMS   ———, "Alberto Williams: the Father of Argentinian Music," *Musical America* LXII/1 (Jan. 10, 1942) 11 and 37.

Smart/EIGHTEENTH-m   James R. Smart (ed.), (10) *Keyboard Sonatas of the Eighteenth* [and early 19th] *Century,* with brief prefaces. New York: G. Schirmer, 1967. Cf. NOTES XXV (1968–69) 133–34 (review by W. S. Newman).

Smith/FRIEDBERG   Julia Smith, *Master Pianist: The Career and Teaching of Carl Friedberg.* New York: Philosophical Library, 1963.

SMW   *Signale für die musikalische Welt.* 1842–1941.

SMYTH MEMOIRS   Ethel Symth, *Impressions That Remained: Memoirs* (up to 1892; first pub. in 1919), with an "Introduction" by E. Newman. New York: Alfred A. Knopf, 1946.

SMZ   *Schweizerische Musikzeitung.* 1861————.

SOHLMANS   *Sohlmans Musiklexikon,* 4 vols. Stockholm: Sohlmans Förlag, 1951–52.

Sonneck/LEKEU   Oscar George Theodore Sonneck, "Guillaume Lekeu (1870–1894)," MQ V (1919) 109–47. Reprinted in Sonneck/MISCELLANEOUS 190–240.

Sonneck/MAC DOWELL   ————, *Library of Congress Catalogue of First Editions of Edward MacDowell.* Washington: Government Printing Office, 1917.

Sonneck/MISCELLANEOUS ————, *Miscellaneous Studies in the History of Music.* New York: Macmillan, 1921.

Sonneck/SUUM   ————, *Suum Cuique: Essays in Music.* New York: G. Schirmer, 1916.

Souchay/SCHUBERT   Marc-André Souchay, "Schubert als Klassiker der Form," ZfMW XI (1928–29) 141–55.

Soullier/DICTIONNAIRE Charles Simon Pascal Soullier, *Nouveau dictionnaire de musique illustré. . . .* Paris: E. Bazault, 1855. Cf. Cat. NYPL XXIX 287.

Šourek/DVOŘÁK   Otakar Šourek, *The Chamber Music of Antonin Dvořák,* trans. (from the original Czech ed. of 1943 and its 2d ed. of 1949) by R. F. Samsour. Prague: Artia, [1956].

Specht/STRAUSS   Richard Specht, *Richard Strauss und sein Werk,* 2 vols. Zürich: E. P. Tal, 1921.

Spink/BENNETT   Gerald W. Spink, "Schumann and Sterndale Bennett," MT CV (1964) 419–21.

Spivacke/PAGANINIANA   Harold Spivacke, "Paganiniana," in *The Library of Congress Quarterly Journal of Current Acquisitions* II/2 (Feb., 1945).

Spohr/AUTOBIOGRAPHY   *Louis Spohr's Autobiography,* started by him in 1847 (cf. Vol. II, p. 285) and brought up to 1838, the remainder being completed posthumously by his family; trans. from the German in 1864, 2 vols. London: Longman, Roberts, & Green, 1865. Cf. GROVE VIII 16–17 (P. David). About a third of the original German ed. (Kassel, 1860–61), all from the journeys, has been retrans. by Henry Pleasants as *The Musical Journeys of Louis Spohr* (Norman: University of Oklahoma Press, 1961). Bärenreiter in Kassel pub. a facs. of the original German ed. in 1954. All references in SSB are to the English trans. of 1865.

SSB   William S. Newman, *The Sonata Since Beethoven* (for cross references within the present vol.).

Stade/CHOPIN   Friedrich Stade, "Die Harmonische Grundlage des letzten Satzes der B moll-Sonate von Chopin" (complete with full harmonization), MW XXXV (1904) 87–89 and "Musikbeilage."

Stanford/BENNETT   Sir Charles Villiers Stanford, "William Sterndale Bennett, 1816–1875," MQ II (1916) 628–57.

Statham/BENNETT   Henry Heathcote Statham, "Sterndale Bennett's Pianoforte Music," MT XIX (1878) 130–34, with exx.

Steger/CZERNY   Hellmuth Steger, "Beiträge zu Karl Czerny's Leben und Schaffen," unpub. Ph.D. diss., Ludwig-Maximilians-Universität, Munich, 1924.

Stein/REGER   Fritz Stein, *Max Reger*. Potsdam: Akademische Verlagsgesellschaft Athenaion, 1939.

Stein/TSCHAIKOWSKIJ   Richard H. Stein, *Tschaikowskij*. Stuttgart: Deutsche Verlags-Anstalt, 1927.

Stein/VERZEICHNIS   Fritz Stein, *Thematisches Verzeichnis der im Druck erschienenen Werke von Max Reger*. Leipzig: Breitkopf & Härtel, 1953.

Steinitzer/KLAVIER   Max Steinitzer, "Richard Strauss' Werke für Klavier," DM XXIV/1 (1931–32) 105–9.

Steinitzer/STRAUSS   ———, *Richard Strauss*. Berlin: Schuster & Loeffler, 1911.

STfMF   *Svensk Tidskrift för Musikforskning.* 1919——.

Stockmeier/ ORGELSONATE   Wolfgang Stockmeier, *Die deutsche Orgelsonate der Gegenwart* (Ph.D. diss., 1957). Köln: Universität Köln, 1958.

Storck/SCHUMANN   Karl Storck (ed.), *The Letters of Robert Schumann*, trans. by Hannah Bryant (from the original German selections and excerpts pub. in 1896). London: John Murray, 1907.

STRAD   *The Strad.* 1891——.

STRAVINSKY   Igor Stravinsky, *An Autobiography, trans. of Chroniques de ma vie,* Paris, 1935. New York: Simon and Schuster, 1936.

Studeny/ VIOLINSONATE   Bruno Studeny, *Beiträge zur Geschichte der Violinsonate im 18. Jahrhundert*. Munich: Wunderhorn-Verlag, 1911.

Sturke/BRAHMS   Auguste Sturke, *Der Stil in Johannes Brahms' Werken* (Ph.D. diss., Universität Hamburg). Würzburg: Konrad Triltsch, 1932.

Subirá/ALBA   José Subirá, *La Música en la casa de Alba*. Madrid: Sucesores de Rivadeneyra, 1927.

Subirá/HISTORIA   ———, *Historia de la música española e hispanoamericana*. Barcelona: Salvat Editores, 1953.

Subirá & Cherbuliez/   José Subirá and Antoine-E. Cherbuliez, *Musikge-*
MUSIKGESCHICHTE   *schichte von Spanien, Portugal, Lateinamerika.* Zü-
rich: Pan-Verlag, [1957]. Pp. 1–200 (up to Latin
America) are "freely translated" from Subirá/HIS-
TORIA.

Swan/MEDTNER   Alfred J. Swan, "Medtner and the Music of Our
Times," ML VIII (1927) 46–54.

Sydow/   Bronislas Édouard Sydow, *Bibliographie de F. F.*
BIBLIOGRAPHIE   *Chopin* (completed in 1947). Warsaw: Nakł. Tow.
Naukowego Warszawskiego, 1949. *Supplement.* War-
saw: Państwowe Wydawn. Naukowe, 1954.

Sydow/CHOPIN   B. E. Sydow, S. and D. Chainaye, and I. Sydow
(eds.), *Correspondence de Frédéric Chopin,* 3 vols.
(covering 1816–49). Paris: Richard-Masse, [1953–60].

Sydow & Hedley/   Bronislaw Edward Sydow and Arthur Hedley (eds.),
CHOPIN   *Selected Correspondence of Fryderyk Chopin.* New
York: McGraw-Hill, 1963.

Szabolcsi/UNGARISCHEN   Bence Szabolcsi, *Geschichte der ungarischen Musik,*
trans. (into German from the original Hungarian
ed. of 1947 [cf. Cat. NYPL XXX 401]) by I. Frommer
& G. Knepler. Budapest: Corvina, 1964.

Szelényi/LISZT   Istvan Szelényi, "Der unbekannte Liszt," in LISZT-
BARTÓK 1961, 311–31.

SZMW   *Studien zur Musikwissenschaft, Beihefte* of DTÖ-m,
1913–34, 1955——.

Taggart/SCHUBERT   James Leland Taggart, "Franz Schubert's Piano
Sonatas: A Study of Performance Problems," unpub.
Ph.D. diss., State University of Iowa, 1963.

Tagliapietra/   Gino Tagliapietra (ed.), *Antologia di musica antica*
ANTOLOGIA–m   *e moderna,* 18 vols. Milan: G. Ricordi, 1931.

Tanzberger/SIBELIUS   Ernst Tanzberger, *Jean Sibelius: Eine Monographie,*
mit einem Werkverzeichnis. Wiesbaden: Breitkopf
& Härtel, 1962.

Tchaikovsky/   Modest Tchaikovsky, *Das Leben Peter Iljitsch*
TSCHAIKOWSKY   *Tchaikowsky's,* trans. into German from the original
Russian ed. of 1900–1902 by P. Juon, 2 vols. Moscow:
P. Jurgenson, [1900?] and 1903 (not 1902). Cf.
Abraham/TCHAIKOVSKY 241; BAKER 1626.

Tchaikovsky/WORKS–m   *Peter Ilyitch Tchaikovsky: Complete Works* (transliteration), 78 vols. up to 1955. Moscow: State
Music Publishers, 1940——. Cf. Heyer/HISTORICAL
318–20.

Teal & Brown/   Mary D. Teal & Lawrence W. Brown, *The Effect*
MICHIGAN   *of the Civil War on Music in Michigan.* Lansing:
Michigan Civil War Centennial Observance Com-
mission, 1965.

Temperley/
CORRESPONDENCE

Unpub. information pertinent to ssb XIV (also III-V), kindly supplied by Professor Nicholas Temperley (at the University of Illinois as of 1968) between 1964 and 1968 and founded largely on material in his unpub. Ph.D. diss. (Cambridge, 1959), "Instrumental Music in England, 1800–1850."

Temperley/DOMESTIC

Nicholas Mark Temperley, "Domestic Music in England, 1800–1860," PMA LXXXV (1958–59) 31–47.

Temperley/HANDEL

———, "Handel's Influence on English Music," MMR XC (1960) 163–74.

Temperley/
MENDELSSOHN

———, "Mendelssohn's Influence on English Music," ML XLIII (1962) 224–33.

Temperley/ MOZART

———, "Mozart's Influence on English Music," ML XLII (1961) 307–18.

Temperley/PINTO

———, "George Frederick Pinto," MT CVI (1965) 265–70; with pertinent correspondence following on pp. 446 and 523–24.

Temperley/PINTO–m

——— (ed.), *George Frederick Pinto: Sonata in E♭ Minor* (Op. 3/1 for P solo). London: Stainer & Bell, 1963.

TEMPO

Tempo: A Quarterly Review of Modern Music. 1948———.

Thayer & Forbes/
BEETHOVEN

[Alexander Wheelock] *Thayer's Life of Beethoven,* revised and edited by Elliot Forbes, 2 vols. Princeton: Princeton University Press, 1964.

Thayer & Riemann/
BEETHOVEN

Alexander Wheelock Thayer, *Ludwig van Beethovens Leben,* revised by Hugo Riemann from the German trans. by H. Deiters, 5 vols. Leipzig: Breitkopf & Härtel, 1917–23.

Thomas/CHOPIN

Betty Jean Thomas, "Harmonic Materials and Treatment of Dissonance in the Pianoforte Music of Frederick Chopin," unpub. Ph.D. diss., University of Rochester, 1963.

Thompson/
TOMASCHEK

Verne Waldo Thompson, *Wenzel Johann Tomaschek: His Predecessors, His Life, His Piano Works* (Ph.D. diss., Eastman School of Music, 1955). Rochester: University of Rochester Press (Microcard), 1957.

Tiersot/FRANCK

Julien Tiersot, "Les Œuvres inédites de César Franck," in RM/FRANCK 97–138.

Tiersot/LALO

———, "Édouard Lalo," trans. by F. Martens, MQ XI (1925) 8–35.

TOMASCHEK

"Excerpts From the Memoirs of J. W. Tomaschek," trans. from the German original in the Prague periodical *Libussa* IV (1845–50) by Abram Loft, MQ XXXII (1946) 244–64. Cf. Craw/DUSSEK 128; Thompson/TOMASCHEK 100–104.

Tovey/ANALYSIS — Donald Francis Tovey, *Essays in Musical Analysis*, 7 vols. London: Oxford University Press, 1936–44.

Townsend/DUETS–m — Douglas Townsend (ed.), *Piano Duets of the Classical Period for One Piano, Four Hands*. Bryn Mawr: Theodore Presser, 1956

TRÉSOR–m — *Le Trésor des pianistes*, 20 vols. Paris: Aristide and Louise Farrenc, 1861–72. For contents cf. GROVE 2d ed. V 148–49; Heyer/HISTORICAL 110–11 (but with a different grouping, in 23 vols.).

Truscott/BRAHMS — Harold Truscott, "Brahms and Sonata Style," MR XXV (1964) 186–201.

Truscott/MEDTNER — ———, "Medtner's Sonata in G Minor, Op. 22," MR XXII (1961) 112–23.

Truscott/REGER — ———, "Max Reger," MR XVII (1956) 134–52; with reply by E. Wellesz, p. 272.

Truscott/UNFINISHED — ———, "Schubert's Unfinished Piano Sonata in C Major (1825)," MR XVIII (1957) 114–37.

Truscott/UNITY — ———, "Organic Unity in Schubert's Early Sonata Music," MMR LXXXIX (1959) 62–66; with follow-up by Robert L. Jacobs on p. 114.

Truscott/VERSIONS — ———, "The Two Versions of Schubert's Op. 122," MR XIV (1953) 89–106.

Tuthill/CLARINET — Burnet C. Tuthill, "The Sonatas for Clarinet and Piano," JRME XIV (1966) 197–212.

Tyson/BEETHOVEN — Alan Tyson, *The Authentic English Editions of Beethoven*. London: Faber and Faber, 1963.

Tyson/FIELD — ———, "John Field's Earliest Compositions," ML XLVII (1966) 239–48; followed by correspondence with Nicholas Temperley in ML XLVIII (1967) 97–99.

Ueberfeldt/RIES — Ludwig Ueberfeldt, *Ferdinand Ries' Jugendentwicklung* (Ph.D. diss.). Bonn: Paul Roft, 1915.

Unger/CLEMENTI — Max Unger, *Muzio Clementis Leben*. Langensalza: Hermann Beyer & Söhne, 1913.

Upton/AYRES — William Treat Upton, "Frederic Ayres (1876–1926)," MQ XVIII (1932) 39–59.

Urbantschitsch/BRAHMS — Viktor Urbantschitsch, "Die Entwicklung der Sonatenform bei Brahms," SZMW XIV (1927) 264–85.

Vallas/FRANCK — Léon Vallas, *César Franck*, trans. from the original French ed. of 1950 by Hubert Foss. New York: Oxford University Press, 1951.

Vallas/D'INDY — ———, *Vincent d' Indy*, 2 vols. (*La Jeunesse* [1851–86] and *La Maturité*[,] *La Viellesse* [*1886–1931*]). Paris: Albin Michel, 1946 and 1950.

Vallas/SAINT-SAËNS ———, "Une Discussion Saint-Saëns et d'Indy," RM XXIII/205 (1947) 79–87.

Van der Linden/ Albert Van der Linden (ed.), "Lettres de Guillaume
LEKEU Lekeu à Octave Maus (1892–93)," RBdM III (1949) 155–64.

Verdi/ Gaetano Cesari e Alessandro Luzio (eds.), *I Copia-*
COPIALETTERE *lettere di Giuseppe Verdi*. Milan: Stucchi Ceretti, 1913.

VERZEICHNISS *Thematisches Verzeichniss im Druck erschienener*
MENDELSSOHN *Compositionen von Felix Mendelssohn Bartholdy*, newly augmented (2d) ed. Leipzig: Breitkopf & Härtel, [1873]. Cf. Mendelssohn/VERLEGER 353–55.

VERZEICHNISS *Thematisches Verzeichniss im Druck erschienener*
MOSCHELES *Compositionen von Ignaz Moscheles*. Leipzig: Fr. Kistner, [1861?]; reprinted in London in 1966 (Stephen Austin for H. Baron).

Vetter/SCHUBERT Walther Vetter, *Der Klassiker Schubert*, 2 vols. Leipzig: C. F. Peters, 1953. Cf. DMf VII (1954) 234–35 (H. J. Moser).

VODARSKY-SHIRAEFF Alexandria Vodarsky-Shiraeff, *Russian Composers and Musicians: A Biographical Dictionary*. New York: H. W. Wilson, 1940.

Vogel/SCHUBERT Adolf Bernhard Vogel, "Franz Schubert's Kammer-musik-Werke: I. Sonaten für das Klavier allein; II. Vierhändige Clavierwerke," NZM LXIX/2 (1873) 493–95, 505–7.

Vrieslander/ Otto Vrieslander, "Das Organische in Schubert's
ORGANISCHE 'himmlischer Länge,'" in KONGRESS SCHUBERT 219–31.

Vuillermoz/FAURÉ Emile Vuillermoz, *Gabriel Fauré*. Paris: Flammarion, 1960.

Vyborny/PAGANINI Zdenek Vyborny, "Der 'Fall Paganini,'" DMf XVII (1964) 156–62.

WAGNER LEBEN Richard Wagner, *Mein Leben*, "first authentic pub-lication." Munich: Paul List, 1963. Written between 1865 and 1880 (cf. M. Gregor-Dellin's "Nachwort," pp. 895–912). The "authorized translation" pub. by Dodd, Mead of New York in 1931 proved not to be accurate enough for use here.

WAGNER-LISZT *Briefwechsel zwischen Wagner und Liszt*, 2 vols. (through 1861). Leipzig: Breitkopf und Härtel, 1887. All references in the present vol. are to this original ed. rather than Francis Heuffer's trans. (New York, 1889) or later, more complete eds.

WAGNER PROSE *Richard Wagner's Prose Works*, trans. by William Ashton Ellis, 8 vols. London: Kegan Paul, Trench, Trübner, 1893–99.

WAGNER-WESENDONK   Wolfgang Golther (ed.), *Richard Wagner an Mathilde Wesendonk[,] Tagebuchblätter und Briefe[,] 1853–1871*, first pub. in 1908. Leipzig: Breitkopf & Härtel, 1912.

Waldersee/VORTRÄGE   Paul Graf Waldersee (ed.), *Sammlung musikalischer Vorträge*, 5 vols. Leipzig: Breitkopf & Härtel, 1879–84.

Walker/CHOPIN   Alan Walker (ed.), *Frédéric Chopin: Profiles of the Man and the Musician*, including a chapter (pp. 144–69) by Peter Gould on the "Concertos and Sonatas" and a chapter (pp. 227–57) by Alan Walker on "Chopin and Musical Structure: An Analytical Approach." London: Barrie & Rockliff, 1966.

Walker/ENGLAND   Ernest Walker, *A History of Music in England* (first pub. in 1907), 3d ed., revised and enlarged by J. A. Westrup. Oxford: Clarendon Press, 1952.

Walker/WOLF   Frank Walker, *Hugo Wolf: A Biography*. London: J. M. Dent, 1951.

Waltershausen/DUALISMUS   Hermann Wolfgang Sartorius Freiherr von Waltershausen, "Der stilistische Dualismus in der Musik des 19. Jahrhunderts," pp. 202–6 in *Festschrift für Guido Adler zum 75. Geburtstag*. Vienna: Universal, 1930.

Warrack/WEBER   John Warrack, *Carl Maria von Weber*. London: Hamish Hamilton, 1968. Pub. too late to be incorporated in SSB; cf. ML XLIX (1968) 233–37 (E. Croft-Murray).

Wasielewski/SCHUMANN   Joseph Wilhelm von Wasielewski, *Robert Schumann*, 2d revised ed. Dresden: Rudolf Kuntze, 1869.

Weber/WEBER   Max Maria von Weber, *Carl Maria von Weber: ein Lebensbild*, 3 vols. Leipzig: Ernst Keil, 1864–66.

Wegeler & Ries/BEETHOVEN   Franz Gerhard Wegeler and Ferdinand Ries, *Biographische Notizen über Beethoven*. Koblenz: K. Bädeker, 1838.

Weigl/VIOLONCELL   Bruno Weigl, *Handbuch der Violoncell-Literatur*, 3d ed. Vienna: Universal-Edition, 1929.

Weinmann/ARTARIA   Alexander Weinmann, *Vollständiges Verlagsverzeichniss Artaria & Comp.* Vienna: Ludwig Krenn, 1952.

Weinstock/DONIZETTI   Herbert Weinstock, *Donizetti and the World of Opera in Italy, Paris, and Vienna in the First Half of the Nineteenth Century*. New York: Pantheon, 1963.

Weinstock/TCHAIKOVSKY   Herbert Weinstock, *Tchaikovsky*. New York: Alfred A. Knopf, 1943.

Werner/KIRCHENMUSIKER   Rudolf Werner, *Felix Mendelssohn Bartholdy als Kirchenmusiker*. Frankfurt: Selbstverlag des Verfassers, 1930.

Werner/MENDELSSOHN   Eric Werner, *Mendelssohn: A New Image of the Composer and His Age*, trans. from the German by Dika Newlin. New York: Macmillan, 1963.

Werner/PALE   ————, "Instrumental Music Outside the Pale of Classicism and Romanticism," in Hughes/INSTRUMENTAL 57–69 (with discussion).

Wessely/CHOPIN   Othmar Wessely, "Chopins B-moll-Sonate," ÖMZ IV (1949) 283–86.

Westerby/PIANOFORTE   Herbert Westerby, *The History of Pianoforte Music*. London: Kegan Paul, Trench, Trubner, 1924.

Westphal/MODERNEN   Kurt Westphal, "Die Sonate als Formproblem der modernen Musik," MMM XI (1929) 160–63.

Westphal/ROMANTISCHE   ————, "Die romantische Sonate als Formproblem," SMZ LXXIV (1934) 45–49, 117–22, 189–92.

WESTRUP & HARRISON   Jack A. Westrup and F. L. Harrison, *The New College Encyclopedia of Music* (first pub. in London in 1959). New York: W. W. Norton, 1960.

Westrup/SCHUBERT   Jack Allan Westrup, "The Chamber Music [of Schubert]," in Abraham/SCHUBERT 88–110.

Wetschky/KANONTECHNIK   Jürgen Wetschky, *Die Kanontechnik in der Instrumentalmusik von Johannes Brahms*. Regensburg: Gustav Bosse, 1967.

Wetzel/SCHARWENKA   Hermann Wetzel, "Philipp Scharwenka's Kammermusik," DM X/4 (1910–11) 27–35.

Wiberg/MUSIKHANDELNS   Albert Wiberg, *Den svenska Musikhandelns historia*. Stockholm: Victor Petterson, 1955.

Wier/VIOLIN–m   Albert E. Wier (ed.), [11] *Modern Sonatas for Violin* [and Piano], by Bargiel, Brahms (Opp. 78 and 100), Fauré (Op. 13), Franck, Grieg (Op. 45), Pâque, Rheinberger (Op. 77), Rubinstein (Op. 13), Schumann (Op. 121), R. Strauss. New York: Harcourt, Brace, 1935.

Winkler/SCHUBERT   Georg Winkler, "Das Problem der Polyphonie im Klavierschaffen Franz Schuberts," unpub. Ph.D. diss., Universität Wien, 1956.

Winternitz/AUTOGRAPHS   Emanuel Winternitz, *Musical Autographs from Monteverdi to Hindemith*, 2 vols. (corrected repub. of the original 1955 ed.) New York: Dover, 1965.

Wörner/SCHUMANN   Heinrich Wörner, *Robert Schumann*. Zürich: Atlantis, 1949. Cf. Redlich/SCHUMANN 146–47, 182–84.

WOLFE   Richard J. Wolfe, *Secular Music in America, 1801–1825: A Bibliography*, with an "Introduction" by C. S. Smith; 3 vols. New York: New York Public Library, 1964.

Wolverton/KEYBOARD   Byron Adams Wolverton, "Keyboard Music and Musicians in the Colonies and United States of

America Before 1830," unpub. Ph.D. diss., University of Indiana, 1966.

Worbs/MENDELSSOHN — Hans Christoph Worbs, *Felix Mendelssohn Bartholdy*. Leipzig: Koehler & Amelang, 1958.

Yasser/MEDTNER — Joseph Yasser, "The Art of Nicolas Medtner," in Holt/MEDTNER 46–65.

Yasser/RACHMANINOFF — ———, "Progressive Tendencies in Rachmaninoff's Music," TEMPO XXII (winter, 1951–52) 11–25.

Young/ELGAR — Percy M. Young, *Elgar, O. M.* [Order of Merit]: *A Study of a Musician.* London: Collins, 1955.

Ysaÿe/YSAÿE — Antoine Ysaÿe and Bertram Ratcliffe, *Ysaÿe: His Life, Work and Influence,* with a Preface by Yehudi Menuhin. London: William Heinemann, 1947. References in SSB are to this rather than the revised Fr. ed. (Brussels, 1948); cf. BAKER 1833.

Yuzhak/GLAZUNOV — K. I. Yuzhak, *Pianoforte Sonatas by A. K. Glazunov* (in Russian). Moscow, 1962.

Zavadini/DONIZETTI — Guido Zavadini, *Donizetti: Vita, musiche, epistolario.* Bergamo: Istituto Italiano d'Arti Grafiche, 1948.

Zeitlin & Goldberger/DUSSEK-m — Poldi Zeitlin & David Goldberger (eds.), *Jan Ladislaus Dussek: Sonatas for One Piano, Four Hands,* Op. 67/1–3 (C. 230–32). Philadelphia: Elkan-Vogel, 1961.

zfMW — *Zeitschrift für Musikwissenschaft.* 1918–35. Superseded by AfMF.

ZIMG — *Zeitschrift der internationalen Musikgesellschaft.* 1900–1914.

Zimmerschied/HUMMEL — Dieter Zimmerschied, "Mozartiana aus dem Nachlass von J. N. Hummel," MOZART-JAHRBUCH 1964, 142–50.

Zimmerschied/KAMMERMUSIK — ———, *Die Kammermusik Johann Nepomuk Hummels* (Ph.D. diss.). Mainz: Johannes Gutenberg-Universität, 1966.

Zingel/SPOHR — Hans Joachim Zingel (ed.), *Louis Spohr: Sonate c-moll für Violine und Harfe.* Kassel: Bärenreiter, 1954.

Zosel/SCHULZ-BEUTHEN — Alois Zosel, *Heinrich Schulz-Beuthen (1838–1915): Leben und Werke* (Ph.D. diss., Universität Leipzig, 1931). Würzburg: K. Triltsch, 1931.

Index

Note: The Index includes every name, place, or other proper noun at least when and if it gets more than passing mention. It also includes other subjects or topics when they are discussed in their own right and can be listed in terms under which the reader might be expected to look. In the longer Index entries the page numbers in italics distinguish the main discussions. The page numbers in quotation marks refer to statements quoted verbatim from the persons indexed (on the topics added in parentheses).

INDEX